dicionário bilíngue
para brasileiros

português-inglês
inglês-português

OXFORD
UNIVERSITY PRESS

OXFORD
UNIVERSITY PRESS

Great Clarendon Street, Oxford OX2 6DP

Oxford University Press is a department of the University of Oxford.
It furthers the University's objective of excellence in research, scholarship,
and education by publishing worldwide in

Oxford New York

Auckland Cape Town Dar es Salaam Hong Kong Karachi
Kuala Lumpur Madrid Melbourne Mexico City Nairobi
New Delhi Shanghai Taipei Toronto

With offices in

Argentina Austria Brazil Chile Czech Republic France Greece
Guatemala Hungary Italy Japan Poland Portugal Singapore
South Korea Switzerland Thailand Turkey Ukraine Vietnam

OXFORD and OXFORD ENGLISH are registered trade marks of
Oxford University Press in the UK and in certain other countries

ISBN-13: 978 0 19 431558 6
ISBN-10: 0 19 431558 4

Designed by Peter Burgess
Cover design by Richard Morris

Printed in Hong Kong

Índice

iv

Como utilizar o Oxford Pocket

mail /meɪl/ *s* [U] correio: ~ *order* venda por correspondência **NOTA** No inglês britânico, **post** é mais usual do que **mail**, embora **mail** seja bastante comum, sobretudo em palavras compostas como **email**, **junk mail** e **airmail**. • *vt* mandar pelo correio

notas gramaticais, culturais e de vocabulário

as palavras que se escrevem da mesma forma, mas que têm sentidos diferentes (verbetes numerados)

minute[1] /ˈmɪnɪt/ *s* **1** minuto **2** momento, instante **3** nota (*oficial*) **4** (**minutes**) [*pl*] ata (*reunião*) ► **not for a minute** nem por um segundo **the minute (that)**... assim que...

minute[2] /maˈnjuːt; *GB* - ˈnjuːt/ *adj* (**-er, -est**) **1** minúsculo **2** minucioso **minutely** *adv* minuciosamente

os diferentes significados de uma palavra (introduzidos por números)

pronúncia, acentuação tônica, e variantes britânicas

miracle /ˈmɪrəkl/ *s* milagre: *a ~ cure* uma cura milagrosa ► **do/ work miracles** (*coloq*) fazer milagres **miraculous** /mɪˈrækjələs/ *adj* milagroso

palavras utilizadas apenas en determinadas situações

adjetivos no comparativo e superlativo e formas verbais

expressões e phrasal verbs

nod /nɒd/ (**-dd-**) **1** *vt, vi* afirmar com a cabeça: *He nodded in agreement.* Ele disse sim (com a cabeça). **2** *vi* saudar com a cabeça (a alguém) **3** *vt, vi* indicar/fazer sinal com a cabeça **4** *vi* pescar (dormindo) ■ **nod off** (*coloq*) cochilar • *s* movimento da cabeça ■ **give (sb) the nod** dar permissão (a alguém) para fazer algo

as palavras derivadas diretamente relacionadas com a principal

padrões gramaticais (como se usa uma palavra dentro de uma frase)

necessário *adj* necessary: *Farei o que for ~.* I'll do whatever's necessary. ◊ *Não leve mais do que é ~.* Only take what you need. ◊ *Não é ~ que você venha.* There's no need for you to come. ► **se for ~** if necessary

exemplos

necessidade *sf* **1** (*coisa imprescindível*) necessity [*pl* -ies]: *O ar condicionado é uma ~.* Air conditioning is a necessity. **2** ~ **(de)** need (for *sth*/to do *sth*): *Não vejo ~ de ir de carro.* I don't see the need to go by car. ◊ *Não há ~ de autorização.* There's no need for authorization. ► **passar ~** suffer hardship **sem ~** needlessly

plural irregular de substantivos

A a

a¹ *art def* the: *A Maria ainda não chegou.* Maria hasn't arrived yet. → THE ▶ **a de/que...** *Ver o*¹

a² *pron pess* **1** *(ela)* her **2** *(coisa)* it **3** *(você)* you

a³ *prep*
● **direção** to: *Ela se dirigiu a mim.* She came up to me.
● **posição:** *à esquerda* on the left ◊ *ao meu lado* by my side ◊ *sentar-se à mesa* sit at the table
● **distância:** *a dez metros daqui* ten meters from here
● **tempo 1** *(horas, idade)* at: *às doze* at twelve o'clock ◊ *aos sessenta anos* at (the age of) sixty **2** *(data, parte do dia): Estamos a dois de janeiro.* It's January second. ◊ *à tarde* in the afternoon ◊ *à noite* at night ◊ *amanhã/ontem à noite* tomorrow/last night ◊ *hoje à noite* tonight
● **freqüência:** *Tenho aula às sextas.* I have lessons on Fridays.
● **modo, meio:** *ir a pé* go on foot ◊ *Faça à sua maneira.* Do it your way. ◊ *vestir-se à hippy* dress like a hippy ◊ *lavar à mão* handwash ◊ *Funciona a pilhas.* It runs on batteries.
● **objeto indireto:** *Dê a seu irmão.* Give it to your brother.
● **outras construções** *(distribuição, velocidade)* at: *Cabem três a cada um.* It works out at three each. ◊ *a 60 quilômetros por hora* at 60 kilometers an hour **2** *(tarifa, preço)*, a, per *(mais fml)*: *cinco dólares à hora* five dollars an hour **3** *(quantidade, medida)* by: *vender algo à dúzia* sell sth by the dozen **4** *(Esporte): Eles ganharam de três a zero.* They won three to nothing. ◊ *Eles empataram por dois a dois.* They tied at two.

aba *sf* *(chapéu)* brim: *um chapéu de ~ larga* a wide-brimmed hat

abacate *sm* avocado *[pl ~s]*

abacaxi *sm* pineapple

abadia *sf* abbey

abafado *adj* **1** *(tempo): Está muito ~ hoje.* It's very sultry today. ◊ *um dia muitíssimo ~ a* stiflingly hot day **2** *(aposento)* stuffy **3** *(ruído)* muffled

abafar *vt* **1** *(ruído)* muffle **2** *(notícia, escândalo)* smother **3** *(fogo)* smother ● *vi* *(fazer sucesso)* steal the show

abaixar *vt* **1** *(voz)* lower **2** *(som)* turn *sth* down: *Quer ~ o volume da televisão?* Could you turn down the TV? ● **abaixar-se** *vp* bend down

abaixo *adv* down: *rua/escadas ~* down the street/stairs ● *interj* down with... ▶ **~ de** below: *temperaturas ~ de zero* temperatures below zero *ir/vir ~* **1** *(edifício)* collapse **2** *(governo)* fall *mais ~* **1** *(mais longe)* further down **2** *(em sentido vertical)* lower down: *Ponha o quadro mais ~.* Put the picture lower down. *pôr ~* **1** *(edifício)* knock *sth* down **2** *(governo)* bring *sth* down

abajur *sm* lampshade

abalar *vt* **1** *(alterar)* shake **2** *(impressionar)* shock

abalo *sm* *(choque)* shock ▶ **~ sísmico** *(earth)* tremor

abanar *vt* **1** *(rabo)* wag **2** *(braços, bandeira)* wave ● **abanar-se** *vp* *(com leque)* fan (yourself) ▶ **~ a cabeça** *(em sinal de negação)* shake your head

abandonado *adj* *(descuidado)* derelict

abandonar *vt* **1** abandon: *~ uma criança/um projeto* abandon a child/a project **2** *(lugar)* leave **3** *(desistir)* give *sth* up: *Não abandone os seus sonhos.* Don't give up your dreams. **4** *(Esporte)* withdraw from *sth*: *~ uma corrida* withdraw from a race

abarrotado *adj* full

abarrotar *vt* fill *sth* full *(of sth)*: *Ele abarrotou a casa com livros.* He filled his house full of books.

abastecer *vt* supply *sb* *(with sth)* ● **abastecer-se** *vp* stock up on *sth*

abastecimento *sm* **1** *(ato)* supplying: *Quem se encarrega do ~ das tropas?* Who is in charge of supplying the troops? **2** *(provisão)* supply: *o ~ de água* the water supply

abater *vt* **1** *(árvore)* fell **2** *(animal)* slaughter **3** *(pessoa)* kill **4** *(debilitar)* weaken ● **abater-se** *vp* *~ sobre* fall on *sb/sth*

abatido *adj* **1** *(deprimido)* depressed **2** *(fisionomia)* haggard **3** *(debilitado)* weak

abdicar *vi* abdicate

abdome *sm* abdomen

abdominal *adj* abdominal ● **abdominais** *sm* **1** *(músculos)* abdominal muscles **2** *(exercícios): fazer ~* do sit-ups

abecedário *sm* alphabet

abelha *sf* bee

abelhudo/a *adj* **1** (*intrometido*) interfering **2** (*bisbilhoteiro*) nosy ● *sf* busybody [*pl* -ies]

abençoar *vt* bless

aberto *adj* **1** open (*to sb/sth*): *O caso continua em* ~. The case is still open. **2** (*torneira*): *deixar uma torneira aberta* leave a faucet running **3** (*fecho*) undone: *Sua braguilha está aberta*. Your fly is undone. **4** (*céu*) clear **5** (*pessoa*) (**a**) (*liberal*) open-minded (**b**) (*franco*) frank

abertura *sf* **1** opening: *a cerimônia de* ~ the opening ceremony **2** (*fenda*) crack **3** (*Mús*) overture

abeto *sm* fir (tree)

abismado *adj* astonished

abismo *sm* **1** (*Geog*) abyss **2** (*fig*) gulf

abóbada *sf* vault

abóbora *sf* pumpkin

abobrinha *sf* zucchini, courgette (*GB*)

abolição *sf* abolition

abolir *vt* abolish

abono *sm* (*gratificação*) bonus: ~ *de fim de ano* Christmas bonus

abordagem *sf* (*assunto, problema*) approach: *a* ~ *de um tema* the approach to a topic

abordar *vt* **1** (*pessoa*) approach **2** (*assunto, problema*) deal with *sth* **3** (*barco*) board

aborrecer *vt* annoy ● **aborrecer-se** *vp* get annoyed

aborrecido/a *adj* **1** (*chato*) boring **2** (*irritado*) annoyed with *sb* **3** (*que irrita*) annoying

aborrecimento *sm* annoyance

abortar *vi* **1** (*acidentalmente*) have a miscarriage **2** (*voluntariamente*) have an abortion

aborto *sm* **1** (*acidental*) miscarriage **2** (*provocado*) abortion

abotoar *vt* button (*sth*) (*up*)

abraçar *vt* hug, embrace (*fml*)

abraço *sm* hug, embrace (*fml*) ▶ **um (grande)** ~ love/lots of love: *Dê um* ~ *nos seus pais.* Give my love to your parents.

abrandar *vt* (*dor*) ease ● *vi* **1** (*chuva, dor*) ease off **2** (*vento*) drop

abrangente *adj* wide-ranging

abranger *vt* include

abrasador *adj* (*calor, sol*) scorching

abreugrafia *sf* X-ray

abreviar *vt* abbreviate

abreviatura *sf* abbreviation

abridor *sm* opener: *um* ~ *de latas* a can-opener

abrigado/a *adj* **1** (*lugar*) sheltered **2** (*pessoa*) well wrapped up

abrigar *vt* shelter *sb* (*from sth*) ● **abrigar-se** *vp* **1** (*com roupa*) wrap up **2** ~ **de** shelter from *sth*

abrigo *sm* **1** (*refúgio*) shelter: *ao* ~ *da chuva* sheltered from the rain **2** (*de ginástica*) sweatsuit

abril *sm* April (*abrev* **Apr.**)
→ **MAIO**

abrir *vt* **1** open: ~ *fogo* open fire ◇ ~ *o ferrolho* unbolt the door **2** (*torneira, gás*) turn *sth* on **3** (*túnel*) bore **4** ~ *um buraco* make a hole **5** (*cortinas*) draw *sth* back ● *vi* **1** (*abrir a porta*) open up: *Abra!* Open up! **2** (*sinal de trânsito*) turn green **3** (*flor*) open ● **abrir-se** *vp* **1** open: *A porta se abriu.* The door opened. **2** (*desabafar*) open up: *Ele acabou se abrindo e me contou tudo.* He finally opened up and told me everything. ▶ ~ **caminho** make way (*for sb/sth*) ◇ ~ **mão de forço** ~ **o apetite** whet *sb's* appetite ◇ ~ **os braços** stretch out your arms ◇ ~ **uma exceção** make an exception ◇ **não** ~ **o bico/a boca** not to say a word ◇ **num** ~ **e fechar de olhos** in the twinkling of an eye

abrupto *adj* abrupt

absolutamente *adv* **1** (*para intensificar*) absolutely: *Deixei* ~ *claro.* I made it absolutely clear. **2** (*com sentido negativo*): *—Você se importa? —Absolutamente.* "Do you mind?" "Not at all."

absoluto *adj* absolute

absolver *vt* **1** (*Relig*) absolve *sb* (*from sth*) **2** (*Jur*) acquit *sb* (*of sth*)

absolvição *sf* **1** (*Relig*) absolution **2** (*Jur*) acquittal

absorto *adj* **1** (*pensativo*) lost in thought **2** (*concentrado*) engrossed (*in sth*)

absorver *vt* absorb

abstêmio/a *sm-sf* teetotaler

abster-se *vp* abstain from (*doing*) *sth*

abstinência *sf* abstinence

abstrato *adj* abstract

absurdo *adj* absurd ● *sm* nonsense

abundância *sf* abundance

abundante *adj* abundant

abusar *vi, vt* abuse: ~ *da confiança de alguém* abuse *sb's* trust

abuso *sm* abuse: *É um ~!* That's outrageous! ▸ **~ de confiança** breach of trust

abutre *sm* vulture

acabado *adj* **1** finished **2** *uma palavra acabada em "r"* a word ending in "r" **3** (*envelhecido*) old

acabamento *sm* finish

acabar *vt*, *vi* (*terminar*) finish (*sth/doing sth*): *Acabei de lavar o carro.* I finished washing the car. ● *vi* **1** (*esgotar-se*) run out (of *sth*): *Acabou o leite.* We've run out of milk. **2 ~ (em/fazendo algo)** end up: *~ na miséria* end up broke ◇ *Acabei cedendo.* I ended up giving in. **3 ~ de fazer algo** have just done sth: *Acabo de vê-lo.* I've just seen him. **4 ~ em** end in *sth*: *Acaba em "s".* It ends in "s". **5 ~ com (a** (*pessoa*) be the death of sb: *Você vai ~ comigo.* You'll be the death of me. **(b)** (*namoro, etc.*) break up with sb **(c)** (*pôr fim*) put an end to *sth* **(d)** (*esgotar*) use *sth* up ▸ **~ mal:** *Isto vai ~ mal.* No good can come of this. ◇ *Esse menino vai ~ mal.* That boy will come to no good. **acabou-se!** that's it!

academia *sf* academy [*pl* -ies] ▸ **~ de ginástica** gym, gymnasium (*fml*)

acadêmico *adj* academic

acalmar *vt* **1** (*nervos*) calm **2** (*dor*) relieve ● *vi* (*vento, dor*) abate ● **acalmar-se** *vp* calm down: *quando se acalmarem os ânimos* once everybody has calmed down

acampamento *sm* camping

acampar *vi* camp: *ir ~* go camping

acanhado *adj* (*inibido*) shy

ação *sf* **1** action: *entrar em ~* go into action **2** (*ato*) deed: *uma boa ~* a good deed **3** (*Fin*) share **4** (*Jur*) claim (*for sth*): *mover uma ~ por algo* put in a claim for sth ▸ **~ judicial** lawsuit

acariciar *vt* **1** (*pessoa*) caress **2** (*animal*) pet

acarretar *vt* (*problemas*) cause

acasalar *vi* mate

acaso *sm* chance: *por ~* by chance ▸ **ao ~** at random

acatar *vt* (*leis, ordens*) obey

aceitar *vt* **1** accept: *Aceitam-se cartões de crédito.* We accept credit cards. **2** (*concordar*) agree to do *sth*

aceitável *adj* acceptable (*to sb*)

aceito *adj*: *As mulheres serão aceitas no exército.* Women will be admitted to the army.

aceleração *sf* acceleration

acelerador *sm* accelerator, gas pedal (*coloq*)

acelerar *vt*, *vi* accelerate: *~ o passo* quicken your pace

acenar *vi* (*saudar*) wave (*to sb*) ▸ **~ (que sim) com a cabeça** nod

acender *vt* **1** (*cigarro, vela, fogo*) light **2** (*aparelho, luz*) turn *sth* on ● *vi* **1** (*fósforo, lenha*) light: *Se estiver molhado não acende.* It won't light if it's wet. **2** (*luz*) come on ● **acender-se** *vp* (*aparelho, luz*) come on

aceno *sm* **1** (*com a mão*) wave **2** (*com a cabeça*) nod

acento *sm* accent

acentuar *vt* **1** (*palavra*) accent: *Acentuem estas palavras.* Put the accents on these words. **2** (*enfatizar, agravar*) accentuate ● **acentuar-se** *vp* (*aumentar*) increase

acepção *sf* sense

acerca *adv* ▸ **~ de** about, concerning (*fml*)

acertado *adj* **1** (*correto*) right **2** (*sensato*) smart

acertar *vt* **1** (*relógio*) set **2 ~ em (a)** (*ao disparar*) hit **(b)** (*em teste, jogo*) get *sth* right: *Só acertei em duas perguntas.* I only got two questions right. **3 ~ em/com** (*adivinhar*) guess ▸ **~ contas com alguém** even with sb ▸ **~ na mosca** hit the nail on the head **não ~ uma** be unable to do anything right: *Você não acerta uma.* You can't do anything right.

aceso *adj* lighted: *um cigarro ~* a lighted cigarette ▸ **estar ~ 1** (*com chama*) be lit: *O fogo estava ~.* The fire was lit. **2** (*aparelho*) be on: *A luz estava acesa.* The light was on.

acessível *adj* accessible

acesso *sm* **1** access **2 ~ de** fit of *sth*: *um ~ de raiva* a fit of rage

acessório *sm* accessory [*pl* -ies]

achado *sm* **1** (*descoberta*) find **2** (*pechincha*) bargain

achar *vt* **1** (*encontrar*) find: *Não acho o meu relógio.* I can't find my watch. **2** (*parecer*) *Acho-o triste.* He seems very sad to me. **3** (*pensar*) think: *Ele acha que é muito esperto.* He thinks he's very smart. ▸ **acho que sim/não** I think so/I don't think so

achatar *vt* flatten

acidentado *adj* **1** (*terreno*) rugged **2** (*estrada*) bumpy **3** (*cheio de peripécias*) ever

acidental adj accidental

acidente sm **1** accident: *sofrer um ~* have an accident **2** (Geog) (geographical) feature ▶ **~ aéreo/de automóvel** plane/car crash

ácido adj, sm acid

acima adv **1** up: *rua/escadas ~* up the street/stairs ◊ *na mesma rua, mais ~* further up the street **2 ~ de** above: *~ dos joelhos* above your knees ◊ *~ de tudo* above all

acionar vt set sth in motion

acne sf acne

aço sm steel

acocorar-se vp squat (down)

acolhedor adj welcoming

acolher vt **1** (convidado, idéia, notícia) welcome **2** (refugiado, órfão) take sb in

acolhida sf welcome

acomodar-se vp **1** (instalar-se) settle down: *~ no sofá* settle down on the couch **2 ~ a** (adaptar-se) adjust to sth

acompanhamento sm **1** (de um prato) side order **2** (Mús) accompaniment

acompanhante smf **1** (companhia) companion **2** (Mús) accompanist

acompanhar vt **1** go/come with sb/sth: *o cassete que acompanha o livro* the tape that goes with the book ◊ *Você me acompanha?* Will you come with me? **2** (Mús) accompany: *~ alguém ao piano* accompany sb on the piano

aconchegante adj (lugar) cozy

aconchegar vt **1** (em cama) tuck sb in **2** (abrigar) wrap sb/sth up (in sth): *~ o bebê na manta* wrap the baby up in the blanket ● **aconchegar-se** vp **1** (acomodar-se) curl up: *~ no sofá* curl up on the couch **2** (encostar-se) huddle (together)

aconselhar vt advise sb (to do sth): *— Compro-o? — Não lhe aconselho.* "Should I buy it?" "I wouldn't advise you to."

aconselhável adj advisable: *pouco ~* inadvisable

acontecer vi happen: *Acontece que...* So it happens that... ● **aconteça o que acontecer** come what may **caso aconteça que/não vá ~ que...** (just) in case...

acontecimento sm event

acordado adj estar ~ be awake

acordar vt, vi wake (sb) up

'corde sm (Mús) chord

acordeão sm accordion

acordo sm agreement: *chegar a um ~ em relação a algo* reach an agreement on sth ▶ **de ~** be OK: *Estamos de ~?* All right? **de ~ com** (lei, norma) in accordance with sth **estar de ~ (com)** agree (with sb/sth): *Estamos os dois de ~.* We both agree. **pôr-se de ~** reach an agreement

acostamento sm (estrada) shoulder, hard shoulder (GB)

acostumado adj estar ~ (a) be used to sth/(doing) sth

acostumar-se vp ~ (a) get used to sb/(doing) sth: *~ a madrugar* get used to getting up early

açougue sm butcher shop

açougueiro sm butcher

acreditar vt, vi believe: *Não acredite nele.* Don't believe him. ◊ *~ em Deus* believe in God

acrescentar vt add

acréscimo sm (aumento) increase

acrobacia sf acrobatics [pl]: *fazer ~s* perform acrobatics

acrobata smf acrobat

açúcar sm sugar: *~ mascavo* brown sugar

açucareiro sm sugar bowl

acudir vt ~ **a** go to sb/sth: *~ a alguém* go to sb's aid

acumular vt **1** accumulate **2** (fortuna) amass ● **acumular-se** vp accumulate

acupuntura sf acupuncture

acusação sf accusation: *fazer uma ~ contra alguém* make an accusation against sb

acusado/a sm-sf accused: *os ~s* the accused

acusar vt **1** (culpar) accuse sb (of (doing) sth) **2** (Jur) charge sb (with (doing) sth): *~ alguém de fraude* charge sb with fraud

acústica sf acoustics [pl]: *A ~ não é muito boa.* The acoustics aren't very good.

adaptador sm (Elet) adaptor

adaptar vt adapt: *~ um romance para o teatro* adapt a novel for the stage ● **adaptar-se** vp ~ (a) **1** (habituar-se) adapt (to sth): *~ às mudanças* adapt to change **2** (adequar-se) fit in (with sth)

adentro adv: *Ela entrou sala ~.* She came into the room.

adepto/a sm-sf follower

adequado adj right: *a pessoa adequada para o cargo* the right person for the post

aderir vi ~ (a) **1** (colar) stick (to

sth) **2** (*organização, partido, causa*) support **3** (*ideia*) uphold

adesão *sf* **1** (*organização*) entry (*into sth*): *a ~ do Brasil ao Mercosul* Brazil's entry into Mercosur **2** (*apoio*) support

adesivo *adj* adhesive

adeus *interj* goodbye, bye (*coloq*)

adiantado *adj* **1** (*relógio*) fast: *cinco minutos ~* five minutes fast **2** (*quase feito*): *A minha tese está bastante adiantada.* My thesis is nearly finished. **3** (*em comparações*) ahead: *Estamos muito ~s em relação à outra turma.* We're way ahead of the other class. **4** (*avançado*) advanced • *adv*: *pagar ~* pay in advance ◊ *chegar ~* arrive early

adiantamento *sm* advance

adiantar *vt* **1** (*trabalho*) get ahead with sth **2** (*dinheiro*) advance sth (*to sb*) **3** (*relógio*) put sth forward: *~ o relógio uma hora* put your watch forward one hour **4** (*conseguir*) achieve: *Não vai ~ nada discutirmos.* We won't achieve anything by arguing. • *vi* **1** (*relógio*) gain **2** (*valer a pena*): *Não adianta gritar.* There's no point in shouting. • **adiantar-se** *vp* ~ get ahead of sb/sth

adiante *adv* forward: *um passo ~* a step forward ▸ **ir ~ com algo** go ahead with sth ▸ **levar algo ~** go through with sth ▸ **mais ~ 1** (*espaço*) further on **2** (*tempo*) later

adiar *vt* **1** put sth off, postpone (*mais fml*) **2** (*pagamento*) defer

adição *sf* addition

adicionar *vt* add sth (*to sth*)

adivinhar *vt* guess ▸ **o futuro** tell fortunes

adivinho *sm* fortune teller

adjetivo *sm* adjective

administração *sf* **1** administration: *a ~ de uma empresa* running a business **2** (*Pol*) government

administrador/a *sm-sf* administrator

administrar *vt* **1** (*dirigir*) run, manage (*mais fml*): *~ uma empresa* run a business **2** (*aplicar*) administer sth (*to sb*): *~ um medicamento* administer medicine

administrativo *adj* administrative

admiração *sf* **1** (*espanto*) amazement **2** (*respeito*) admiration

admirador/a *sm-sf* admirer

admirar *vt* **1** (*contemplar*) admire: *~ a paisagem* admire the scenery **2** (*espantar*) amaze: *Muito me admira que você tenha sido aprovado.* I'm amazed you passed. • **admirar-se** *vp* ~ (**com**) be surprised (at sb/sth): *Não me admiro.* I'm not surprised.

admirável *adj* **1** (*digno de respeito*) admirable **2** (*espantoso*) amazing

admissão *sf* admission

admitir *vt* **1** (*culpa, erro*) admit: *Admito que a culpa foi minha.* I admit it was my fault. **2** (*deixar entrar*) admit sb/sth (*to sth*) **3** (*permitir*) allow: *Não admito falta de respeito.* I won't allow any insolence.

adoçante *sm* sweetener

adoção *sf* adoption

adoçar *vt* sweeten

adoecer *vi* ~ (**de**) fall ill (with sth)

adolescência *sf* adolescence

adolescente *sm-sf* adolescent

adorar *vt* **1** (*gostar de*) love: *Adoramos ir ao cinema.* We love going to the movies. **2** (*amar*) adore **3** (*Relig*) worship

adorável *adj* adorable

adormecer *vi* **1** (*cair no sono*) fall asleep **2** (*perna, etc.*) go numb • *vt* (*criança*) get sb off to sleep

adormecido *adj* **1** sleeping: *um bebê ~* a sleeping baby **2** *estar ~* be asleep/sleeping

adornar *vt* decorate

adorno *sm* **1** adornment **2** (*objeto*) ornament

adotar *vt* adopt

adotivo *adj* **1** adopted: *filho ~* adopted child **2** (*pais*) adoptive

adquirir *vt* **1** acquire **2** (*comprar*) buy

adubar *vt* (*terra*) fertilize

adubo *sm* fertilizer

adular *vt* flatter

adultério *sm* adultery

adulto/a *adj, sm-sf* adult

advérbio *sm* adverb

adversário/a *sm-sf* adversary [*pl* -ies]

advertência *sf* warning

advertir *vt* **1** (*avisar*) warn sb (*about/ of sth*): *Adverti-os do perigo.* I warned them of the danger. **2** (*dizer*) tell: *Eu adverti você!* I told you so! **3** (*repreender*) reprimand

advocacia sf legal profession ▶ **exercer/praticar ~** practice law

advogado/a sm-sf lawyer NOTA **Lawyer** é termo genérico para todos os tipos de advogados. Nos Estados Unidos usa-se **attorney** para os vários tipos de advogado: **criminal attorney, tax attorney**, etc. Na Grã-Bretanha existe uma distinção entre **barrister**, o advogado que atua em todos os tribunais, e **solicitor**, que só atua nos tribunais de instância inferior. ▶ **~ do diabo** devil's advocate

aéreo/a adj **1** air: *tráfego* ~ air traffic **2** (*vista, fotografia*) aerial **3** (*distraído*) absent-minded

aeróbica sf aerobics [*sing*]

aerodinâmico adj aerodynamic

aeródromo sm airfield

aeromoça sf flight attendant

aeronave sf aircraft

aeroporto sm airport

aerossol sm aerosol

afanar vt (*roubar*) steal

afastado/a adj **1** (*parente*) distant **2** (*distante*) remote **3** (*retirado*) isolated **4 ~ de...** (*longe de*) far from...

afastar vt **1** (*mover*) move sth (along/down/over/up): *Afaste um pouco a sua cadeira.* Move your chair over/back a bit. **2** (*retirar*) move sth away (from sb/sth): ~ *a mesa da janela* move the table away from the window **3** (*distanciar*) distance sb/sth (from sb/sth) **4** (*apartar*) separate sb/sth from sb/sth: *Os pais o afastaram dos amigos.* His parents stopped him from seeing his friends. ● **afastar-se** vp **1** (*desviar-se*) move (over): *Afaste-se, você está atrapalhando.* Move over, you're in the way. **2 ~ (de)** (*distanciar-se*) move away (from sb/sth): *Não se afastem muito.* Don't go too far away. **3** (*caminho*) leave ▶ **afastar-se do tema** wander off the subject

afável adj friendly

afeição sf (*afeto*) affection

afeiçoar-se vp become attached to sb/sth

aferrolhar vt bolt

afetado/a adj **1** affected **2** (*efeminado*) effeminate

afetar vt affect: *A morte dele me afetou muito.* I was deeply affected by his death.

afetivo/a adj (*carência, problema*) emotional

afeto sm affection

afetuoso/a adj affectionate

afiado/a adj sharp

afiar vt sharpen

aficionado/a sm-sf fan

afilhado/a sm-sf godchild [pl godchildren] [*masc* godson] [*fem* god-daughter]

afiliação sf (*partido, clube*) membership

afiliar-se vp ~ **(a)** (*organização, partido*) join (sth)

afim adj similar

afinado/a adj **1** (*motor*) tuned **2** (*instrumento, voz*) in tune

afinal adv after all

afinar vt tune

afinidade sf affinity [pl -ies] ▶ **por** ~ by marriage: *Somos primos por* ~. We're cousins by marriage.

afirmação sf statement

afirmar vt state, say (*mais coloq*)

afirmativo/a adj affirmative

afixar vt (*cartaz, etc.*) put sth up

aflição sf (*ansiedade*) anxiety

afligir(-se) vt, vp worry (*about sb/sth*): *Você não deve se* ~ *com o atraso deles.* Don't worry if they're late.

aflito/a adj upset

afobação sf fluster

afogar(-se) vt, vp drown

afônico/a adj: *estar/ficar* ~ have lost/lose your voice

afora adv ● **e por aí** ~ and so on

África sf Africa

africano/a adj, sm-sf African

afronta sf insult

afrouxar vt loosen

afta sf canker sore, ulcer (*GB*)

afugentar vt frighten sb/sth away

afundar vt ● vi sink: ~ *o barco* sink the boat ● vi **1** (*ir ao fundo*) sink **2** (*ruir*) collapse: *A ponte afundou.* The bridge collapsed. **3** (*negócio*) go under

agachar-se vp crouch (down)

agarrar vt **1** (*apanhar*) catch: ~ *uma bola* catch a ball **2** (*segurar*) hold **3** (*pegar firmemente*) grab: ~ *alguém pelo braço* grab sb by the arm ● **agarrar-se** vp hold on (to sb/sth): *Agarre-se a mim.* Hold on to me.

agasalhado/a adj (*pessoa*): *bem* ~ well wrapped up ◊ *Você está pouco* ~. You're not very warmly dressed.

agasalhar vt wrap sb up ● vi (*peça de roupa*) keep sb warm: *Esse cachecol não agasalha nada.* That scarf won't keep you warm. ● **agasalhar-se** vp wrap up: *Agasalhe-se que está frio lá fora.* Wrap up warm — it's cold outside.

agência sf 1 (*empresa*) agency [*pl* -ies]: ~ *de viagens* travel agency 2 (*repartição*) office: ~ *de correios* post office 3 (*banco, etc.*) branch ▸ ~ **funerária** funeral home, undertaker's (*GB*)

agenda sf diary [*pl* -ies]

agente smf 1 (*representante*) agent 2 (*polícia*) policeman/woman [*pl* policemen/women]

ágil adj agile

agilidade sf agility

agir vi act

agitação sf agitation

agitado adj 1 (*vida, dia*) hectic 2 (*mar*) rough 3 (*pessoa*) agitated

agitar vt 1 (*frasco*) shake 2 (*braços*) wave

agonia sf agony [*pl* -ies]: *Esperar os resultados foi pura* ~. It was agony waiting for the results.

agonizar vi be dying

agora adv now: *até* ~ up until now ◇ ~ *que você chegou podemos começar.* Now that you're here we can start. ◇ *Só* ~ *é que cheguei.* I only just arrived. ▸ ~ **mesmo** (*neste momento*) right now: *Eu lhe dou* ~ *mesmo.* I'll give it to you right away. **de** ~ **em diante** from now on **por** ~ for the time being: *Por* ~ *chega.* That's enough for the time being.

agosto sm August (*abrev* Aug.) → MAIO

agouro sm omen

agradar vi ~ a please sb [vt]: *ser difícil de* ~ be hard to please

agradável adj pleasant ▸ ~ **à vista/ao ouvido** pleasing to the eye/ear

agradecer vt thank sb (*for doing*) sth: *Agradeço a sua ajuda.* Thank you for your help. ◇ *Eu agradeceria se você pudesse vir.* I'd be grateful if you could come.

agradecido adj grateful

agradecimento sm thanks [*pl*] ▸ **os meus** ~ many thanks

agrário adj land: *reforma agrária* land reform

agravamento sm worsening

agravar vt make sth worse ● **agravar-se** vp get worse

agredir vt attack

agressão sf aggression

agressivo adj aggressive

agressor/a sm-sf aggressor

agrião sm watercress

agrícola adj agricultural

agricultor/a sm-sf farmer

agricultura sf farming, agriculture (*mais fml*)

agridoce adj (*Cozinha*) sweet and sour

agrônomo/a sm-sf agronomist

agrupar vt put sb/sth in a group ● **agrupar-se** vp 1 (*juntar-se*) gather together 2 (*formar grupos*) get into groups: ~ *quatro a quatro* get into groups of four

água sf water: ~ *corrente/potável/da torneira* running/drinking/tap water ▸ ~ **doce/salgada** fresh/salt water: *peixes de* ~ *doce* freshwater fish ~ **mineral com/sem gás** sparkling/non-carbonated mineral water ~ **oxigenada** hydrogen peroxide ~ **sanitária** (household) bleach **dar** ~ **na boca** be mouth-watering

aguaceiro sm shower

água-de-colônia sf eau de cologne

aguado adj (*café, sopa*) watery

aguardar vt, vi wait (for sb/sth)

aguardente sf liquor, spirit (*GB*)

água-viva sf jellyfish [*pl* jellyfish]

aguçado adj 1 (*sentidos*) acute 2 (*afiado*) sharp

agudo adj 1 acute: *uma dor aguda* an acute pain ◇ *ângulo/acento* ~ acute angle/accent 2 (*som, voz*) high-pitched ● sm (*Mús*) treble [*U*]

agüentar vt put up with sb/sth: ~ *a dor* put up with the pain NOTA Em frase negativa, usa-se muito **stand**: *Não agüento este calor.* I can't stand this heat. ◇ *Não os agüento.* I can't stand them. ● vi 1 (*durar*) last: *O carpete ainda agüenta mais um ano.* The carpet should last another year. 2 (*esperar*) hold on: *Agüenta um pouco que estamos quase lá.* Hold on; we're almost there. 3 (*resistir*) hold: *Esta prateleira não vai* ~. This shelf won't hold. 4 ~ **com** (*peso*) take sth [vt] ● **agüentar-se** vp 1 hold on 2 (*suportar*) put up with it: *Mesmo não gostando, você tem de se* ~. You may not like it, but you'll have to put up with it! ▸ ~ **as pontas** hold on

águia sf eagle

agulha sf 1 needle: *enfiar a linha na* ~ thread the needle ◇ ~*s de* pinheiro pine needles **2** (toca-discos) stylus

ah ah ah interj ha ha

ai interj **1** (dor) ow **2** (aflição) oh (dear)

aí adv there: Aí vão eles. There they go. ▶ lá dentro/fora: — Onde está o meu cinto? — Aí dentro do armário. "Where's my belt?" "It's in the closet." **aí embaixo/em cima** down/up there: Os meus livros estão aí embaixo? Are my books down there? **aí mesmo** right there **e aí?** (cumprimento) so how are things with you? **por aí 1** (naquela direção) that way **2** (lugar indeterminado): Andei por aí. I've been out. ◊ dar uma volta por aí go out for a walk

aidético/a sm-sf person with AIDS

AIDS sf AIDS

ainda adv **1** (orações afirmativas e interrogativas) still: ~ faltam duas horas. There are still two hours to go. ◊ Você ~ está aqui? Are you still here? **2** (orações negativas e interrogativas negativas) yet: ~ não estão maduras. They're not ripe yet. ◊ —Ainda não lhe responderam? —Ainda não. "Haven't they written back yet?" ▶ STILL **3** (orações comparativas) even: Gosto ~ mais desta. I like this one even better. ◊ Ela pinta ~ melhor. She paints even better. ▶ ~ bem que... it's just as well that...: ~ bem que já o fiz! It's just as well I've already done it! ~ por cima on top of everything

aipo sm celery

ajeitar vt (arrumar) adjust: ~ a gravata straighten your tie

ajoelhar-se vp kneel (down)

ajuda sf help [U]: Necessito de ~. I need some help. ◊ fazer algo sem ~ de ninguém do sth by yourself

ajudante adj, smf assistant

ajudar vt, vi help sb (to do sth)

ajustar vt **1** adjust **2** (apertar) take sth in: ~ uma saia take a skirt in ● **ajustar-se** vp adjust

ajuste sm ▶ ~ de contas settling of accounts

ala sf wing: a ~ esquerda do partido the left wing of the party

alagamento sm flooding [U]

alagar vt **1** widen **2** (prazo) extend **3** (peça de roupa) let sth

out ● vi stretch: Estes sapatos alargaram. These shoes have stretched.

alarmante adj alarming

alarmar vt alarm ● **alarmar-se (com)** be alarmed (at sth)

alarme sm alarm: ~ de incêndio fire alarm ◊ dar o ~ raise the alarm ◊ Soou o ~. The alarm went off.

alastrar vt, vi spread

alavanca sf lever ▶ ~ de câmbio gear shift, gearstick (GB)

albergue sm ▶ ~ da juventude youth hostel

álbum sm album

alça sf **1** (vestido, mochila, etc.) strap **2** (sacola, mala) handle

alcachofra sf artichoke

alçada sf power

alcançar vt **1** reach: Não consigo alcançá-lo. I can't reach it. **2** (conseguir) achieve: ~ os objetivos achieve your objectives **3** (apanhar) catch up to sb, catch sb up (GB): Não consigo alcançá-los. I couldn't catch up to them. **4** (triunfo) score

alcance sm **1** reach: fora do seu ~ out of your reach **2** (arma, emissora, telescópio) range: mísseis de médio ~ medium-range missiles

alcatrão sm tar

álcool sm alcohol ▶ sem ~ non-alcoholic

alcoólico/a adj, sm-sf alcoholic

alcoolismo sm alcoholism

aldeia sf small village: uma pessoa da ~ a villager

alegar vt allege: Eles alegam que não têm dinheiro. They say they have no money.

alegrar vt **1** (fazer feliz) make sb happy **2** (animar) **(a)** (pessoa) cheer sb up **(b)** (festa) liven sth up **3** (lugar) brighten sth up ● **alegrar-se** vp **1** ~ (com/por) be pleased (about sth/to do sth): ~ com a chegada de alguém be pleased to see sb **2** ~ por alguém be delighted for sb

alegre adj **1** (feliz) happy **2** (de bom humor) cheerful **3** (música, etc) lively **4** (cor, sala) bright

alegria sf joy: gritar/pular de ~ shout/jump for joy

aleijar vt (mutilar) maim

além adv over there ● o além sm the afterlife ▶ ~ de **1** (no espaço) beyond: ~ do rio beyond the river **2** (afora) besides **3** (número) (well) over **4** (assim como) as well as: ~ de feio, ele é burro. He's not only ugly, he's stupid too. ~ **disso** besides ~ **do mais** (and) what's more: ~ *do mais, não creio que eles venham.* What's more, I don't think they'll come. **mais** ~ (*mais longe*) further on

Alemanha *sf* Germany

alemão/ã *adj, sm-sf, sm* German: *os alemães* (the) Germans

alergia *sf* allergy [*pl* -ies]: *ter* ~ *a algo* to be allergic to sth

alérgico *adj* allergic

alerta *sm* alert: *em estado de* ~ on alert • *adj* alert (*to sth*)

alertar *vt* alert *sb* (*to sth*)

alfabético *adj* alphabetical

alfabetizar *vt* teach *sb* to read and write

alfabeto *sm* alphabet

alface *sf* lettuce

alfândega *sf* customs [*pl*]: *Passamos pela* ~. We went through customs.

alfazema *sf* lavender

alfinete *sm* pin ▶ ~ **de segurança** safety pin

alga *sf* **1** (*nome genérico*) algae [*pl*] **2** (*de água salgada*) seaweed [*U*]

algarismo *sm* numeral

algazarra *sf* uproar

álgebra *sf* algebra

algemar *vt* handcuff

algemas *sf* handcuffs

algo *pron* something, anything NOTA A diferença entre **something** e **anything** é a mesma que entre **some** e **any**. → SOME • *adv* rather: ~ *ingênuo* pretty naive → FAIRLY

algodão *sm* **1** (*planta, fibra*) cotton **2** (*Med*) cotton wool (*GB*): *Tapei os ouvidos com* ~. I put cotton balls in my ears. ▶ ~ **doce** cotton candy, candyfloss (*GB*)

alguém *pron* somebody, anybody: *Você acha que* ~ *vem?* Do you think anybody will come? NOTA A diferença entre **somebody** e **anybody** é a mesma que entre **some** e **any**. **Somebody** e **anybody** são acompanhados do verbo no singular, mas podem ser seguidos de um adjetivo ou pronome no plural (p. ex. "their"): *Alguém esqueceu o casaco.* Somebody's left their coat behind. → SOME

algum *adj* some, any: *Comprei alguns livros.* I bought some books. ◇ ~ *problema?* Is there a problem? → SOME **2** (*poucos*) a few: *alguns amigos* a few friends ◇ — *Quantos você*

quer? — *Alguns.* "How many would you like?" "Just a few." **3** (*com número*) several: *algumas centenas de pessoas* several hundred people **4** (*um que outro*) the occasional: *Poderão ocorrer alguns chuviscos.* There may be the occasional shower. • *pron:* Com certeza foi ~ *de vocês.* It must have been one of you. ◇ *Alguns protestaram.* Some people protested. ▶ **alguma coisa** something, anything NOTA A diferença entre **something** e **anything** é a mesma que entre **some** e **any**. → SOME **algumas vezes** sometimes **alguma vez** ever: *Você esteve lá alguma vez?* Have you ever been there? ◇ **dia** some day **em alguma coisa** in any way: *Se eu puder ajudar em alguma coisa...* If I can help in any way... **em** ~ **lugar/em alguma parte** somewhere, anywhere NOTA A diferença entre **somewhere** e **anywhere** é a mesma que entre **some** e **any**. → SOME **mais alguma coisa?** anything else?

alheio *adj* **1** (*de outro*) somebody else's: *em casa alheia* in somebody else's house **2** (*de outros*) other people's: *meter-se na vida alheia* interfere in other people's lives **3** (*distraído*) withdrawn: ~ *a algo* oblivious to something

alho *sm* garlic

alho-poró *sm* leek

ali *adv* there: *a 50 metros dali* 50 meters from there ◇ *uma moça que passava por* ~ a girl who was passing by ▶ ~ **dentro/fora** in/out there ~ **embaixo/em cima** down/up there ~ **mesmo** right there **foi** ~ **que...** that's where... **por** ~ that way

aliado *adj* allied • *sm-sf* ally [*pl* -ies]

aliança *sf* **1** (*união*) alliance **2** (*anel*) wedding ring

aliar-se *vp* form an alliance *with/against sb/sth*

aliás *adv* **1** (*a propósito*) by the way **2** (*contudo*) nevertheless **3** (*ou seja*) that is **4** (*senão*) otherwise **5** (*além disso*) what's more, furthermore (*fml*)

álibi *sm* alibi [*pl* ~s]

alicate *sm* pliers [*pl*]: *um* ~ a pair of pliers → PAIR

alicerces *sm* foundations

alimentação *sf* **1** (*ação*) feeding **2** (*comida*) food **3** (*dieta*) diet **4** (*máquina*) supply: *A* ~ *deste* *motor é a diesel.* This engine runs on diesel.

alimentar *vt* feed *sb/sth (on/with sth)* ● *vi:* **Alimenta bem.** It's very nourishing. ● **alimentar-se** *vp* **1** *(comer)* eat: *Você precisa se alimentar melhor.* You need to eat better. **2 ~ de** live on *sth*

alimentício *adj* **1** *(próprio para comer)* food: *produtos ~s* foodstuffs **2** *(nutritivo)* nutritional

alimento *sm (comida)* food

alinhar *vt (pôr em linha reta)* line *sb/sth up*

alisar *vt* smooth

alistamento *sm (Mil)* enlistment *(in sth)*

alistar-se *vp* enlist *(in sth)*

aliviar *vt* relieve: *~ a dor* relieve pain ◊ *A massagem me aliviou um pouco.* The massage made me feel a little better.

alívio *sm* relief: *Foi um ~ para todos.* It came as a relief to everybody.

alma *sf* soul: *Não se via viva ~.* There wasn't a soul to be seen. ► **ter ~ de artista, líder, etc.** be a born artist, leader, etc.

almanaque *sm* almanac

almirante *smf* admiral

almoçar *vi* have lunch: *O que a gente tem para ~?* What are we having for lunch?

almoço *sm* lunch

almofada *sf* cushion

almôndega *sf* meatball

alô *interj* hello

alojamento *sm* **1** accommodation **2** *(estudantes)* dormitory [*pl* -ies], dorm *(coloq)*, hall of residence *(GB)*

alojar *vt* **1** accommodate: *O hotel tem capacidade para ~ 200 pessoas.* The hotel can accommodate 200 people. **2** *(sem cobrar)* put *sb* up ● **alojar-se** *vp* stay: *~ num hotel* stay in a hotel

alongar *vt* extend ● **alongar-se** *vp (falando)* go on for too long

alpendre *sm* porch

alpinismo *sm* mountaineering: *fazer ~* go mountaineering

alpinista *smf* mountaineer

alta *sf* **1** *(preço, etc.)* rise **2** *(hospital)* discharge: *dar ~ a alguém/algo* ~ discharge *sb/be discharged*

altar *sm* altar

alterar *vt* alter ● **alterar-se** *vp* **1** *(mudar)* change **2** *(irritar-se)* get worked up

alternado *adj* alternate

alternar *vt, vi* **1** alternate **2 ~ (com) (para)** take turns (with *sb*) *(to do sth)*

alternativa *sf* alternative

alternativo *adj* alternative

altitude *sf* height: *a 3.000 metros de ~* at an altitude of 3,000 meters

altivo *adj* lofty

alto *adj* **1** tall, high NOTA **Tall** é usado para pessoas, árvores e edifícios que são tanto altos como estreitos: *o edifício mais ~ do mundo* the tallest building in the world ◊ *uma menina muito alta* a very tall girl. **High** é muito usado com substantivos abstratos: *níveis de poluição ~s* high levels of pollution ◊ *juros ~s* high interest rates, e para nos referirmos à altitude em relação ao nível do mar: *La Paz é a capital mais alta do mundo.* La Paz is the highest capital in the world. Os antônimos de **tall** são **short** e **small**, e o antônimo de **high** é **low**. As duas palavras têm em comum o substantivo **height**, altura. **2** *(comando, funcionário)* high-ranking **3** *(classe social, região)* upper: *o ~ Amazonas* the upper Amazon **4** *(som, voz)* loud ● *adv* **1** *(pôr, subir)* high: *Você pendurou o quadro ~ demais.* You've hung the picture too high up. **2** *(falar, tocar)* loud: *Ponha o som mais ~.* Turn the sound up. ● *sm* top: *do ~ de* from the top of ● *interj* halt ► **alta costura** haute couture **alta fidelidade** hi-fi ● **de alta categoria** first-rate **fazer algo por ~** do sth superficially **os ~s e baixos de algo** the ups and downs of sth **por ~** roughly: *Assim por ~, deviam ser umas 500 pessoas.* I think there were roughly 500 people.

alto-falante *sm* loudspeaker: *Anunciaram pelos ~s.* They announced it over the loudspeakers.

altura *sf* **1** height **2** *(época)* time [*sing*]: *nesta/por esta ~* at/around this time (of year) ◊ *a esta ~* at this point ► **~ máxima** maximum headroom **estar à ~ da situação** be equal to the task **na ~ de:** *Fica na ~ da rodoviária.* It's up near the bus terminal. **ter dois, etc. metros de ~** *(coisa)* be two, etc. meters high

alucinação *sf* hallucination: *Você está com alucinações!* You're hallucinating!

alucinante *adj* *(tremendo)* awesome

alucinar vi hallucinate

aludir vt allude to sb/sth

alugar vt

- referindo-se à pessoa que toma de aluguel NOTA Nos Estados Unidos alugar se traduz por rent: Aluguei um apartamento no Rio. I rented an apartment in Rio. Na Grã-Bretanha, usa-se hire quando se aluga algo por pouco tempo: Mais vale você ~ um carro. You'd be better off hiring a car. Rent implica períodos mais longos, por exemplo quando se aluga uma casa ou um quarto: Quanto me custaria ~ um apartamento? How much would it cost me to rent an apartment?

- referindo-se à pessoa que dá de aluguel NOTA Nos Estados Unidos diz-se rent sth out: Eles alugaram a casa de praia no verão passado. They rented out their beach house last summer. Na Grã-Bretanha, usa-se hire sth (out) ao nos referirmos a um curto espaço de tempo: ~ cavalos para turistas ber (out) horses to tourists. Rent sth (out) é empregado para períodos mais longos, tanto para objetos como para quartos ou casas: uma empresa que aluga eletrodomésticos a company that rents out household appliances. Let sth (out) é usado apenas com casas ou quartos: Há um apartamento para ~ no nosso edifício. There's an apartment to let in our building.

aluguel sm **1** (ato de alugar) rental, hire (GB): uma empresa de ~ de automóveis a car rental company **2** (preço) **(a)** rental, hire charge (GB) **(b)** (casa, quarto) rent → ALUGAR

alumínio sm aluminum

aluno/a sm-sf student

alusão sf allusion ▶ fazer ~ a allude to sb/sth

alvo sm target: tiro ao ~ target shooting

alvoroço sm **1** (barulho) racket: Por que tanto ~? What's all the racket about? **2** (distúrbio) disturbance

amabilidade sf kindness: Ela é a ~ em pessoa. She's kindness itself.

amaciar vt soften

amador/a adj, sm-sf amateur: uma companhia de teatro ~ an amateur theater company

amadurecer vi **1** (fruta) ripen **2** (pessoa) mature

amainar vi (vento) die down

amaldiçoar vt curse

amamentar vt **1** (pessoa) nurse, breastfeed (GB) **2** (animal) suckle

amanhã sm future: pensar no ~ think about the future ● adv tomorrow: ~ de manhã tomorrow morning ◊ o jornal de ~ tomorrow's paper ▶ até ~ see you tomorrow **depois de** ~ the day after tomorrow

amanhecer[1] vi dawn: Já amanhecia o dia. Day was already dawning. ● v imp: Amanheceu muito cedo. Dawn broke very early. ◊ Amanheceu chovendo. It was raining when dawn broke.

amanhecer[2] sm **1** (madrugada) dawn **2** (nascer do sol) sunrise

amante adj loving: ~ de música music-loving ● smf lover: um ~ de ópera an opera lover

amar vt love

amarelo adj, sm **1** (cor) yellow: estar/pintar algo de ~ wear/paint sth yellow **2** (semáforo) amber

amargo adj bitter

amargura sf **1** (tristeza) sorrow: um olhar de ~ a sorrowful look **2** (ressentimento) bitterness: Ela se tornou uma pessoa com muita ~. She's become very bitter.

amarrar vt **1** tie sb/sth up **2** (Náut) moor

amarrotar vt **1** (papel) crumple sth (up) **2** (roupa) crease ● **amarrotar-se** vp (roupa) crease

amassar vt **1** crumple **2** (massa de pão) knead **3** (batatas) mash **4** (cimento) mix **5** (carro) dent

amável adj kind to sb: Foi muito ~ da parte deles. It was very kind of them.

o Amazonas sm the Amazon

âmbar sm amber

ambição sf ambition

ambicionar vt (desejar) want

ambicioso adj ambitious

ambiental adj environmental

ambientalista smf environmentalist

ambiente adj background: música ~ background music ● sm **1** (natureza, meio) environment **2** (atmosfera) atmosphere: O local tem bom ~. The place has a good atmosphere.

ambíguo adj ambiguous

âmbito sm (campo de ação) scope

ambos num both (of us, you, them): Dou-me bem com ~. I get along well with both of them. ◊ ~ *gostamos de viajar.* Both of us/We both like traveling.

ambulância *sf* ambulance

ambulante *adj* traveling

ameaça *sf* threat: *sob ~* under threat

ameaçador *adj* threatening

ameaçar *vt* threaten (*to do sth*): *Eles os ameaçaram com um processo judicial.* They threatened to take them to court.

ameixa *sf* plum ▸ **~ seca** prune

ameixeira *sf* plum tree

amém *interj* amen

amêndoa *sf* almond

amendoeira *sf* almond tree

amendoim *sm* peanut

ameno *adj* 1 (*temperatura, clima*) mild 2 (*agradável*) pleasant

América *sf* America ▸ **~ Latina** Latin America **~ do Norte/Sul** North/South America

americano/a *adj, sm-sf* American

ametista *sf* amethyst

amianto *sm* asbestos

amido *sm* starch

amigável *adj* friendly

amígdala *sf* tonsil: *Fui operado das ~s.* I had my tonsils out.

amigdalite *sf* tonsillitis [U]

amigo/a *adj* 1 (*voz*) friendly 2 (*mão*) helping ▸ *sm-sf* friend: *um ~ íntimo meu* a close friend of mine ◊ *ter ~s nas altas esferas* have friends in high places ▸ **ser muito ~(s)** be good friends (*with sb*)

amistoso *sm* (*Futebol*) friendly

amizade *sf* 1 (*relação*) friendship 2 (**amizades**) friends: *meu grupo de ~s* my circle of friends ▸ **fazer ~** make friends

amnésia *sf* amnesia

amolação *sf* 1 (*incômodo*) bore, drag (*coloq*) 2 (*aborrecimento*) irritation

amolar *vt* 1 (*afiar*) sharpen 2 (*importunar*) bother, annoy

amolecer *vt, vi* soften

amoníaco *sm* ammonia

amontoar *vt* 1 (*empilhar*) pile *sth* up 2 (*acumular*) amass: *~ tralha* collect junk ● **amontoar-se** *vp* 1 pile up: *O trabalho foi amontoando-se.* The work steadily piled up. 2 (*apinhar*) cram (*with sth*)

amor *sm* love: *uma canção/ história/carta de ~* a love song/ story/letter ▸ *à primeira vista* love at first sight *fazer ~ com*

make love (*to/with sb*) *pelo ~ de Deus* for God's sake

amordaçar *vt* gag

amoroso *adj* 1 (*relativo ao amor*) love: *vida amorosa* love life 2 (*carinhoso*) loving

amor-próprio *sm* 1 (*orgulho*) pride 2 (*estima de si mesmo*) self-esteem

amostra *sf* (*Med, Estatística, mercadoria*) sample

amparar *vt* protect (and support) *sb/sth* (*against sb/sth*): *Eu preciso de alguém que me ampare.* I need someone to protect and support me. ● **amparar-se** *vp* (*apoiar-se*) seek the support of *sb/sth*

amparo *sm* support

ampère *sm* amp

ampliação *sf* enlargement

ampliar *vt* 1 (*Fot*) enlarge 2 (*aumentar*) extend: *~ o local* extend the premises 3 (*negócio, império*) expand

amplificador *sm* amplifier

amplificar *vt* (*som*) amplify

amplo *adj* 1 wide: *uma ampla variedade de produtos* a wide range of goods 2 (*lugar*) spacious: *uma casa ampla* a spacious house

amputar *vt* amputate

amuado *adj* sulky

amuar *vi* sulk

amuleto *sm* charm

analfabetismo *sm* illiteracy

analfabeto/a *adj, sm-sf* illiterate [*adj*]: *ser um ~* be illiterate

analgésico *sm* painkiller

analisar *vt* analyze

análise *sf* analysis [*pl* -yses]

anão/ã *adj, sm-sf* dwarf [*pl* ~s/ dwarves]: *uma conífera anã* a dwarf conifer

anarquia *sf* anarchy

anarquista *adj, smf* anarchist

anatomia *sf* anatomy [*pl* -ies]

anchova *sf* anchovy [*pl* -ies]

ancinho *sm* rake

âncora *sf* anchor: *lançar ~* drop anchor

andaime *sm* scaffolding [U]

andamento *sm* 1 (*progresso*) progress 2 (*rumo*) direction ▸ *dar ~ a algo* (*processo*) set sth in motion **em ~** in progress: *O projeto já está em ~.* The project is already underway.

andar¹ *vi* 1 (*caminhar*) walk: *Fomos andando até a loja.* We walked to the shop. 2 **~ de** ride: *~ de bicicleta* ride a bike 3 (*funcionar*) work 4 (*estar*) be: *~*

ocupado/deprimido be busy/
depressed ◇ ~ **à procura de um**
carro be looking for a car ► *vt* ~
por be about sth: *Ele deve ~ aí*
pelos 50 anos. He must be about
50. ► **anda** hurry up NOTA Para
outras expressões com **andar**,
ver o substantivo, adjetivo, etc.,
p. ex. **andar à deriva** em DERIVA.

andar² *sm (modo de caminhar)*
walk

andar³ *sm (edifício)* floor: *o ter-*
ceiro ~ the fourth floor ◇ *no* ~ *de*
baixo/cima on the floor below/
above → TÉRREO ► **de dois, etc.**
-es *(edifício)* two-story, etc.: *um*
prédio de cinco ~es a five-story
building

andorinha *sf* swallow

anedota *sf* joke

anel *sm* ring ► ~ **(rodo)viário**
beltway, ring road (GB)

anemia *sf* anemia

anêmico *adj* anemic

anestesia *sf* anesthetic

anestesiar *vt* anesthetize

anexo *adj (documentos)*
attached ► *sm (edifício)* annex

anfetamina *sf* amphetamine

anfíbio *adj* amphibious ● *sm*
amphibian

anfiteatro *sm* **1** *(romano)*
amphitheater **2** *(sala de aula)*
lecture hall/theater

anfitrião/ã *sm-sf* host *[fem* host-
ess]

angariar *vt (fundos)* raise

anglicano/a *adj, sm-sf* Anglican

anglo-saxão/ã *sm-sf* Anglo-
Saxon

anglo-saxônico *adj* Anglo-
Saxon

Angola *sf* Angola

angolano/a *adj, sm-sf* Angolan

ângulo *sm* angle: ~ *reto/agudo*
right/acute angle ◇ *Eu vejo as*
coisas por outro ~. I see things
from a different angle.

angústia *sf* anguish: *gritar com*
~ cry out in anguish

animação *sf* **1** *(alegria)* liveli-
ness **2** *(entusiasmo)* enthusiasm

animado *adj* **1** *(festa, cidade)*
lively **2** *(entusiasmado)* enthusiastic

animal *adj, sm* animal: ~ *domés-*
tico/selvagem domestic/wild
animal ◇ *o reino* ~ the animal
kingdom

animar *vt* **1** *(pessoa)* cheer *sb* up
2 *(conversa, jogo)* liven sth up **3**
(apoiar) cheer *sb* on ● **animar-se**
vp cheer up: *Anime-se!* Cheer
up!

ânimo *sm* spirits *[pl]*: *Faltava-*
nos ~. Our spirits were low. ●
interj cheer up

aniquilar *vt* annihilate

anis *sm* **1** *(semente)* aniseed **2**
(licor) anisette

anistia *sf* amnesty *[pl* -ies]

aniversário *sm* **1** *(pessoa)* birthday: *Feliz* ~! Happy Birthday! **2**
(instituição, evento) anniversary *[pl* -ies]: ◇ ~ *do nosso casa-*
mento our anniversary

anjo *sm* angel: ~ *da guarda*
guardian angel

ano *sm* year: *o* ~ *todo* all year
(round) ◇ *todos os* ~ *s* every year
◇ *Feliz* ~ *Novo!* Happy New
Year! ► ~ *bissexto* leap year
► ~ *sim,* ~ *não* every other year
de dois, etc. ~ *s: uma mulher de*
trinta ~ *s* a woman of thirty/a
thirty-year-old woman **fazer**
~ *s: Dentro em pouco faço* ~ *s.* It's
my birthday soon. **os** ~ *s* **50,**
60, etc. the 50s, 60s, etc. **ter**
dois, etc. ~ *s* be two, etc. (years
old): *Quantos* ~ *s você tem?* How
old are you? ◇ *Tenho dez* ~ *s.* I'm
ten (years old). → OLD

anoitecer¹ *v imp* get dark: *No*
inverno anoitece cedo. In winter
it gets dark early.

anoitecer² *sm* dusk: *ao* ~ at dusk
► **antes/depois do** ~ before/
after dark

ano-luz *sm* light year

anônimo *adj* anonymous

anorexia *sf* anorexia

anormal *adj* **1** abnormal: *um*
comportamento ~ abnormal
behavior **2** *(indivíduo)* disabled

anotar *vt* note *sth* down

ânsia *sf* **1** ~ **(de)** longing (for *sth/*
to do sth): *a* ~ *de vencer* the will
to win **2** ~ **(por)** desire (for sth):
~ *por bons resultados* a desire to
get good results ► **ter** ~ **de vômi-**
to feel like throwing up

ansiar *vi* long for sth

ansiedade *sf* anxiety *[pl* -ies]

ansioso *adj* anxious

antártico *adj* Antarctic ●
Antártico *sm (oceano)* Antarctic
Ocean

antebraço *sm* forearm

antecedência *sf* ► **com** ~ in
advance: *com um ano de* ~ a year
in advance

antecedentes *sm (criminais)*
record *[sing]*

antecipadamente *adv* in
advance

antecipar *vt* **1** *(prever)* anticipate **2** *(evento, data)* bring *sth*

forward: ~ *o exame uma semana* bring the test forward a week
antemão *adv* ► **de** ~ beforehand
antena *sf* **1** (*TV, rádio*) antenna, aerial (*GB*) **2** (*Zool*) antenna ► ~ **parabólica** satellite dish
anteontem *adv* the day before yesterday ► ~ **à noite** the night before last
antepassado/a *sm-sf* ancestor
anterior *adj* previous
antes *adv* (*previamente*) before → AGO ► ~ **de** before (*doing*) *sth*: ~ *do Natal* before Christmas ◇ ~ *de ir para a cama* before going to bed
antiaderente *adj* non-stick
antibiótico *sm* antibiotic
anticoncepcional *adj* contraceptive
anticorpo *sm* antibody [*pl* -ies]
antídoto *sm* antidote (*to sth*)
antigamente *adv* in the old days
antigo *adj* **1** old: *prédios* ~s *old buildings* ◇ *o meu* ~ *chefe* my old boss **2** (*Hist*) ancient: *a Grécia antiga* ancient Greece
antiguidade *sf* **1** (*época*) ancient times **2** (*no trabalho*) seniority **3** (*objeto*) antique: *loja de* ~s antique shop
antílope *sm* antelope
antipático *adj* (*pessoa*) unpleasant
antiquado *adj* old-fashioned
antiquário *sm* (*loja*) antique shop
anti-roubo *adj*: *dispositivo* ~ anti-theft device
anti-séptico *adj* antiseptic
antônimo *sm* opposite, antonym (*mais fml*)
antropologia *sf* anthropology
antropólogo/a *sm-sf* anthropologist
anual *adj* annual
anualmente *adv* annually
anular¹ *vt* **1** (*gol, ponto*) disallow **2** (*votação*) declare *sth* invalid **3** (*casamento*) annul
anular² *sm* (*dedo*) ring finger
anunciar *vt* **1** (*informar*) announce **2** (*fazer publicidade*) advertise: ~ *na televisão/no jornal* advertise on TV/in the paper
anúncio *sm* **1** (*imprensa, televisão*) advertisement, ad (*coloq*) **2** (*pôster*) poster **3** (*declaração*) announcement (*about sth*)
ânus *sm* anus
anzol *sm* fish hook
ao *prep* + *inf* when: *Caíram na risada ao me ver.* They burst out

laughing when they saw me. **2** (*simultaneidade*) as: *Eu o vi ao sair.* I saw him as I was leaving.
aonde *adv* where
apagado/a *adj* **1** (*pessoa*) listless **2** (*cor*) dull ● **estar** ~ **1** (*luz*) be off **2** (*fogo*) be out
apagar *vt* **1** (*com borracha*) erase **2** (*quadro*) clean **3** (*fogo*) put a fire out **4** (*vela*) blow a candle out **5** (*cigarro*) stub a cigarette out **6** (*luz*) switch *sth* off ● *vi* go out: *Meu cigarro apagou.* My cigarette went out.
apaixonado/a *adj* **1** (*enamorado*) in love **2** (*intenso*) passionate **3** ~ **por** wild about *sth* ● *sm-sf* lover: *os* ~*s por computador* computer lovers
apaixonar *vt* win *sb's* heart ● **apaixonar-se** *vp* fall in love (*with sb/sth*)
apalpar *vt* **1** touch **2** (*indecentemente*) paw **3** (*examinando, procurando*) feel: *Ele apalpou os bolsos.* He felt his pockets.
apanhado *sm* summary [*pl* -ies]: *fazer um* ~ *da situação* summarize the situation
apanhar *vt* **1** catch: ~ *uma bola/um resfriado/um trem* catch a ball/a cold/a train ◇ *ser apanhado em flagrante* be caught red-handed **2** (*objeto caído*) pick *sth* up **3** (*colher*) pick: ~ *flores/fruta* pick flowers/fruit **4** (*viajar*) take: ~ *o trem* take the train **5** (*ir buscar*) pick *sb/sth* up: ~ *as crianças na escola* pick the children up from school **6** (*encontrar*) get hold of *sb* ● *vi* get a spanking: *Olha que você vai* ~! You'll get a spanking if you're not careful! → *Para expressões com* **apanhar**, *ver o substantivo, adjetivo, etc., p. ex.* **apanhar frio** *em* FRIO.
aparafusar *vt* screw *sth* down/in/on
aparar *vt* trim
aparecer *vi* **1** appear **2** (*alguém/algo perdido*) turn up: *acabar aparecendo* turn up in the end **3** (*chegar*) show up: *Jo apareceu por volta das dez.* Jo showed up around ten. **4** (*fantasma*) appear (*to sb*)
aparecimento *sm* appearance
aparelhagem *sf* equipment
aparelho *sm* **1** (*máquina*) machine **2** (*doméstico*) appliance **3** (*TV, rádio*) set **4** (*Anat*) system: *o* ~ *digestivo* the digestive system **5** (*para os dentes*) braces, brace (*GB*): *usar* ~ wear braces **6** (*ginástica*) apparatus

[U] ► ~ **auditivo** hearing aid
~ **de som** stereo [*pl* ~**s**]

aparência *sf* appearance

aparentar *vt* (*idade*) look: *Ele aparenta ter uns 50 anos. He looks about 50.*

aparente *adj* apparent

aparição *sf* **1** (*Relig*) vision **2** (*fantasma*) apparition

apartamento *sm* apartment, flat (*GB*): *prédios de ~s apartment buildings* ► ~ **conjugado** studio apartment

apaziguar *vt* appease

apear(-se) *vp* dismount: *Ele apeou do cavalo. He dismounted.*

apegado *adj* attached (*to sth*)

apego *sm* attachment (*to sb/sth*)

apelar *vi* appeal: *Apelaram para a nossa generosidade. They appealed to our generosity.*

apelidar *vt* ~ **alguém de** nickname sb *sth*

apelido *sm* nickname

apelo *sm* appeal: *fazer um ~ a alguém appeal to sb*

apenas *adv* only: *Eu trabalho ~ aos sábados. I only work on Saturdays.*

apêndice *sm* (*Anat*, *livro*) appendix [*pl* -dices]

apendicite *sf* appendicitis

aperceber-se *vp* ~ **de** realize *sth/that...*

aperfeiçoamento *sm* improvement

aperfeiçoar *vt* (*melhorar*) improve

aperitivo *sm* **1** (*bebida*) aperitif **2** (*comida*) appetizer

apertado *adj* **1** (*roupa*, *sapatos*) tight **2** (*gente*) squashed together **3** (*curva*) sharp

apertar *vt* **1** (*botão*, *tecla*) press **2** (*campainha*) ring **3** (*parafuso*, *tampa*, *nó*) tighten **4** (*cinto de segurança*) fasten **5** (*mãos*) shake **6** (*gatilho*) pull **7** (*roupa larga*) take sth in ● *vi* **1** (*roupa*) be too tight for (*sb*) **2** (*sapatos*) pinch **3** (*dar um aperto de mão*): *Aperte aqui! Put it there!* ● **apertar-se** *vp* squeeze up (*against sth*) ► ~ **o cinto** tighten your belt

aperto *sm* **1** (*pressão*) pressure **2** (*situação difícil*) fix

apesar *adv* ► ~ **de...** **1** (+ *substantivo ou pronome*) in spite of...: *~ de tudo in spite of everything* **2** (+ *infinitivo*) although...: *~ de ser arriscado... Although it was risky...* ► ~ **que...** although...: *~ de que tivesse gostado... Although he'd*

enjoyed it... ► ~ **disso** nevertheless

apetecer *vi* **1** (*dar vontade*) be/look appetizing: *Este ensopado me apetece. This stew looks tasty.* **2** (*estar disposto*) be in the mood *to do sth*

apetite *sm* appetite: *A caminhada vai abrir o seu ~. The walk will give you an appetite.* ► **bom ~** enjoy your meal

apetrechos *sm* (*Esporte*) gear [*U*]: ~ **de pesca** fishing gear

ápice *sm* ► **no ~** at the peak of...

apinhado *adj* crowded

apitar *vi* **1** (*polícia*, *árbitro*) blow the whistle (*at sb/sth*): *O polícia apitou em nossa direção. The policeman blew his whistle at us.* **2** (*chaleira*, *trem*) whistle

apito *sm* whistle

aplacar *vt* **1** (*fome*) satisfy **2** (*sede*) quench **3** (*ânimos*) soothe

aplainar *vt* (*madeira*) plane

aplaudir *vt*, *vi* applaud: ~ **de pé** give a standing ovation

aplauso *sm* applause [*U*]: ~**s calorosos** loud applause

aplicação *sf* **1** application **2** (*da lei*) enforcement

aplicado *adj* **1** applied (*to sth*): *matemática aplicada applied mathematics* **2** (*pessoa*) hardworking

aplicar *vt* **1** apply *sth* (*to sth*): ~ *uma regra/pomada apply a rule/an ointment* **2** (*pôr em prática*) put *sth* into practice **3** (*lei*) enforce ● **aplicar-se** *vp* **1** (*leis*, *regras*) apply to sb/sth **2** (*trabalho*) apply yourself (*to sth*)

aplicável *adj* applicable

aplique *sm* **1** (*luz*) wall light **2** (*cabelo*) hairpiece

apoderar-se *vp* ~ **de** take possession of, seize: *Apoderaram-se das jóias. They seized the jewels.*

apodrecer *vt*, *vi* rot

apoiado *adj* **1** (*descansando*) resting *on/against sth* **2** (*inclinado*) leaning *against sth*: ~ *contra a parede leaning against the wall*

apoiar *vt* **1** (*inclinar*) lean *sth* against *sth* **2** (*descansar*) rest *sth* on/against *sth*: *Apóie a cabeça no meu ombro. Rest your head on my shoulder.* **3** (*defender*) support: ~ *uma greve/um companheiro support a strike/colleague* **4** (*dar apoio*) back sb/sth up: *Os meus pais me* *apoiaram tantas vezes.* My parents have backed me up so often. ● **apoiar-se** *vp* lean on/against sth

apoio *sm* support

apólice *sf* (*seguros*) policy [pl -ies]: *adquirir uma* ~ take out a policy

apologia *sf* defense (*of sb/sth*)

apontador *sm* (*lápis*) pencil sharpener

apontamento *sm* note

apontar *vt* **1** point sth out: ~ *um erro* point out a mistake ◇ ~ *algo num mapa* point sth out on a map **2** (*razões*) put sth forward ● *vt, vi* aim (*sth*) (*at sb/sth*): ~ *muito alto* aim too high

aporrinhar *vt* annoy

após *prep* **1** (*depois*) after: *dia a dia* day after day **2** (*atrás de*) behind: *A porta fechou* ~ *ela entrar.* The door closed behind her.

aposentado/a *adj* retired ● *sm-sf* senior citizen, pensioner (GB)

aposentadoria *sf* **1** (*serviço*) retirement **2** (*pensão*) pension

aposentar-se *vp* retire

aposta *sf* bet: *fazer uma* ~ make a bet

apostar *vt, vi* bet (*on sb/sth*): *Aposto o que você quiser como eles não vêm.* I bet you anything they won't come.

apostila *sf* lecture notes [pl]

apóstolo *sm* apostle

apóstrofo *sm* apostrophe

apreciação *sf* appreciation

apreciar *vt* **1** (*coisa*) appreciate **2** (*pessoa*) think highly of sb: *Eles te apreciam muito.* They think very highly of you. **3** (*avaliar*) assess **4** (*gostar*) enjoy: *Aprecio um bom vinho.* I enjoy a good wine.

apreço *sm* regard (*for sb/sth*): *ter grande* ~ *por alguém* hold sb in high regard

apreender *vt* **1** (*confiscar*) seize **2** (*compreender*) grasp

apreensão *sf* **1** (*bens, contrabando*) seizure **2** (*conhecimentos*) grasp **3** (*preocupação*) apprehension

apreensivo *adj* apprehensive

aprender *vt, vi* learn: ~ *francês/a dirigir* learn French/to drive

aprendiz/a *sm-sf* apprentice: *um* ~ *de eletricista* an apprentice electrician

aprendizagem *sf*: *a* ~ *de uma língua* learning a language

apresentação *sf* **1** presentation: *A* ~ *é importante.* Presentation is important. **2** (*apresentações*) introductions: *Você ainda não fez as apresentações.* You still haven't introduced us.

apresentador/a *sm-sf* presenter

apresentar *vt* **1** present sth with sth; present sth (*to sb*): *Ele apresentou as provas ao juiz.* He presented the judge with the evidence/the evidence to the judge. **2** (*demissão*) tender **3** ~ *uma queixa* make a complaint **4** (*pessoa*) introduce sb (*to sb*): *Apresento-lhe o meu marido.* This is my husband. NOTA Há várias formas de apresentar as pessoas, segundo o grau de formalidade. Por exemplo: "John, meet Mary." (*infml*); "Mrs. Smith, this is my daughter Jane" (*infml*); "May I introduce you, Sir Alan, this is Mr. Jones. Mr. Jones, Sir Alan." (*fml*). Ao ser apresentado a alguém, você responde "Hello" ou "Nice to meet you" se a situação é informal, ou "How do you do?" se é uma situação formal. A "How do you do?", a outra pessoa responde "How do you do?" ● **apresentar-se** *vp* **1** (*a desconhecido*) introduce yourself **2** (*compa-recer*) report (*to sb/sth*)

apressar *vt* rush: *Não me apresse.* Don't rush me. ● **apressar-se** *vp* **1** hurry up **2** ~ *a* hasten to do sth

aprimorar *vt* improve

aprofundar *vt* **1** (*conhecimentos*) go deeper into sth **2** (*escavar*) make sth deeper ● **aprofundar-se** *vp*: ~ *num assunto* deepen your knowledge of a subject

apropriado *adj* appropriate

aprovação *sf* **1** (*consentimento*) approval **2** (*em exame*) pass

aprovado *adj* (*Educ*): *ser* ~ pass

aprovar *vt* **1** (*aceitar*) approve of sb/sth **2** (*lei*) pass ● *vi* (*Educ*) pass

aproveitamento *sm* **1** (*uso*) use **2** (*Educ*) grades [pl]: *ter bom* ~ *em algo* get good grades in sth

aproveitar *vt* **1** (*utilizar*) use: ~ *bem o tempo* use your time well **2** (*recursos naturais*) make use of sth **3** (*oportunidade, tirar proveito*) take advantage of sb/sth ● **aproveitar-se** *vp* take advantage (*of sb/sth*)

aproximação *sf* **1** (*chegada*) approach **2** (*proximidade*) nearness

aproximado adj approximate

aproximar vt 1 (coisas) bring sth closer 2 (pessoas) bring sb together ● **aproximar-se** vp 1 approach, draw near 2 ~ **(de)** (acercar-se) approach (sb/sth)

aptidão sf 1 aptitude (for doing sth): teste de ~ aptitude test 2 (talento) gift

apunhalar vt stab

apuração sf 1 (averiguação) investigation 2 (aperfeiçoamento) refinement 3 (votos) counting

apurado adj 1 (paladar) refined 2 (ouvido) keen

apurar vt 1 (averiguar) investigate 2 (melhorar) refine 3 (votos) count

apuro sm 1 (situação difícil) fix [sing]: estar em ~/tirar alguém de um ~ be in a fix/get sb out of a fix 2 (apuros) trouble [U]: um alpinista em ~ a climber in trouble

aquarela sf watercolor

Aquário sm Aquarius

aquário sm aquarium

aquático adj 1 (Biol) aquatic 2 esportes ~s water sports

aquecedor sm heater: ~ elétrico/a gás/de água electric/gas/water heater

aquecer vt 1 heat sth up: Vou ~ o seu jantar. I'll heat up your dinner. 2 (pessoa, músculo) warm sb/sth up ● vi (ficar muito quente) get very hot: O motor aqueceu demais. The engine overheated. ● **aquecer-se** vp (pessoa, Esporte) warm up

aquecimento sm 1 (sistema) heating: ~ central central heating 2 (Esporte) warm-up: fazer um ~ do a warm-up

aqueduto sm aqueduct

aquele/a pron 1 (adjetivo) that [pl those] 2 (substantivo) (a) (coisa) that one [pl those (ones)]: Prefiro ~. I prefer those (ones). (b) (pessoa): Você conhece ~s ali? Do you know those people?

aqui adv 1 (lugar) here: É ~ mesmo. It's right here. 2 (agora) now: de ~ por diante from now on ◊ Até ~ tudo bem. So far so good. 3 (ao telefone): ~ é a Ana. Posso falar com o Paulo? It's Ana. May I speak to Paulo? ► **(por) perto** near here ~ **vou eu** here I come **por** ~ **(por favor)** this way (please)

aquilo pron that ► ~ **que...** what...: Lembre-se daquilo que

a sua mãe dizia. Remember what your mother used to say.

ar sm air: ar puro fresh air ► **ao ar livre** in the open air: um concerto ao ar livre an open-air concert **ar condicionado** air conditioning **dar-se ares** put on airs **estar no ar** (sendo transmitido) be on the air **ir/voar pelos ares** blow up **tomar ar** get a breath of fresh air

árabe adj, sm-sf Arab: os ~s (the) Arabs ● sm (língua) Arabic

arábico adj Arabic

arado sm plow

arame sm wire: ~ farpado barbed wire

aranha sf spider

arar vt plow

arbitragem sf 1 arbitration 2 (Esporte) refereeing

arbitrar vt 1 (Futebol, Boxe) referee 2 (Tênis) umpire

arbitrário adj arbitrary

árbitro/a sm-sf 1 (futebol, boxe) referee 2 (tênis) umpire 3 (mediador) arbitrator

arbusto sm bush

arca sf (caixa) chest

arcar vi: ~ com as conseqüências face the consequences

arcebispo sm archbishop

arco sm 1 (Arquit) arch 2 (Mat) arc 3 (Esporte, Mús) bow: um ~ e flecha a bow and arrow 4 (arcos) arcade [sing]: os ~s da praça the arcade round the square

arco-e-flecha sm archery

arco-íris sm rainbow

ardente adj 1 (que arde, queima) burning 2 (apaixonado) ardent

arder vi 1 (queimar) burn 2 (olhos) sting

ardor sm ardor

ardósia sf slate

área sf area: uma ~ de serviço a service area

areia sf sand ► ~ **movediça** quicksand

arejar vt (quarto, roupa) air ● vi get some fresh air

arena sf arena: ~ de touros bullring

arenque sm herring

arfar vi puff and pant

Argentina sf Argentina

argentino/a adj, sm-sf Argentinian

argila sf clay

argola sf 1 ring 2 (brinco) hoop earring

argumentar vt, vi argue

argumento sm 1 (razão) argument: os ~s a favor e contra the arguments for and against 2 (Cinema, livro) plot

árido adj arid

Áries sm Aries

aristocracia sf aristocracy

aristocrata smf aristocrat

aritmética sf arithmetic

arma sf 1 weapon: ~ do crime/ nuclear murder/nuclear weapon 2 (armas) arms: a indústria de ~s the arms industry ► ~ branca knife • ~ de fogo firearm

armação sf frame

armada sf navy [pl -ies]

armadilha sf trap: cair numa ~ fall into a trap

armadura sf armor [U]: uma ~ a suit of armor

armamento sm arms [pl]

armar vt 1 (fornecer armas) arm sb (with sth) 2 (montar) put sth up, assemble (mais fml): ~ uma barraca put a tent up 3 ~ confusão cause chaos

armarinho sm haberdashery

armário sm 1 cupboard (para roupa) closet, wardrobe (GB) ► ~ de remédios medicine chest

armazém sm 1 (edifício) warehouse 2 (depósito) storeroom 3 (loja) store

armazenamento sm storage

armazenar vt store

aro sm 1 (argola) ring 2 (roda) rim

aroma sm aroma

aromático adj aromatic

arpão sm harpoon

arqueologia sf archeology

arqueológico adj archeological

arqueólogo/a sm-sf archeologist

arquibancada sf bleachers, terraces (GB) [pl]

arquipélago sm archipelago [pl ~s /-es]

arquitetar vt (plano, projeto) devise

arquiteto/a sm-sf architect

arquitetura sf architecture

arquivar vt 1 (classificar) file 2 (assunto) shelve

arquivo sm 1 (polícia, Informát) file 2 (Hist) archive(s): um ~ histórico historical archives

arraigado adj deep-rooted

arrancar vt 1 (remover) take sth off, remove (mais fml): Arranque a etiqueta do preço. Take the price tag off. 2 (extrair) take sb/ sth out (of sth): O dentista arrancou-lhe um dente. The

dentist pulled his tooth out. 3 (planta, pêlo) pull sth up/out: ~ um prego pull a nail out ◊ ~ as ervas daninhas pull up the weeds 4 (página) tear a page out 5 (informação, confissão) extract • vi 1 (motor) start 2 (partir) set off • **arrancar-se** vp run off: Os ladrões se arrancaram imediatamente The thieves ran off straight away.

arranha-céu sm skyscraper

arranhão sm scratch

arranhar vt 1 scratch 2 (idioma): ~ italiano have a smattering of Italian

arranjar vt 1 (pôr em ordem) clean sth up 2 (conseguir) get: Onde é que ela arranjou o dinheiro? Where did she get the money from? 3 (resolver) sort sth out • **arranjar-se** vp 1 (dar certo) work out: No fim tudo se arranjou. It all worked out in the end. 2 (virar-se) manage, get by (coloq) ► ~ coragem pluck up courage • ~ problemas cause trouble • um jeito find a way (to do/of doing sth)

arranjo sm (disposição) arrangement

arranque sm 1 (início) start 2 (motor): ter problemas com o ~ have problems starting the car

arrasado adj (deprimido) devastated (at/by sth)

arrasar vt 1 destroy 2 (vencer) whip, thrash (GB) • vi (ganhar) win hands down

arrastar vt 1 drag: Eles não queriam ir, tive que arrastá-los. They didn't want to go, so I had to drag them away. 2 (vento, água) carry sb/sth away • **arrastar-se** vp 1 (engatinhar) crawl: ~ pelo chão crawl across the floor 2 (processo, situação) drag (on) 3 (humilhar-se) grovel (to sb)

arrebentar vt, vi burst

arrebitado adj (nariz) turned-up

arrecadar vt 1 (impostos) collect 2 (embolsar) pocket

arredondar vt round sth off

arredores sm outskirts

arregaçar vt 1 (mangas, calças) roll sth up: de mangas arregaçadas with your sleeves rolled up 2 (saia) hitch sth (up)

arregalar vt: O garotinho arregalou os olhos. The little boy's eyes almost popped out of his head.

arreganhar vt ► ~ os dentes bare your teeth

arreios *sm* harness [*sing*]

arremedar *vt* mimic

arrendar *vt* lease → ALUGAR

arrepender-se *vp* **1** (*lamentar*) regret (doing) sth: *Eu me arrependo de ter dito isso.* I regret saying it. ◊ *Você vai se arrepender!* You'll regret it! **2** (*pecado*) repent (*of sth*)

arrependido *adj* ▶ **estar ~ (de)** be sorry (for/about *sth*)

arrependimento *sm* **1** (*pesar*) regret **2** (*Relig*) repentance

arrepiado *adj* (*pele*) covered in goose bumps

arrepiar-se *vt*, *vp* shiver ▶ **de arrepiar os cabelos** horrific

arrepio *sm* shiver

arriscado *adj* **1** (*perigoso*) risky **2** (*audaz*) daring

arriscar *vt* risk ● **arriscar-se** *vp* take a risk/risks: *Se eu fosse você, não me arriscaria.* If I were you, I wouldn't risk it.

arrogância *sf* arrogance

arrogante *adj* arrogant

arrombar *vt* **1** (*porta*) force **2** (*casa*) break into sth **3** (*cofre*) crack

arrotar *vi* burp ● *vi*, *vt* (*alardear*) brag (about sth)

arroto *sm* burp

arroz *sm* rice

arroz-doce *sm* rice pudding

arruinar *vt* ruin ● **arruinar-se** *vp* (*falir*) go bankrupt

arrumadeira *sf* chambermaid

arrumado *adj* **1** neat **2** (*vestido*) dressed

arrumar *vt* **1** (*ordenar*) clear sth up: *o seu quarto* clean up your room **2** (*mala*) pack: *Você já arrumou as malas?* Have you packed yet? **3** (*mentira, desculpa*) think sth up **4** (*emprego*) find ● **arrumar-se** *vp* (*preparar-se*) get ready

arsenal *sm* arsenal

arsênico *sm* arsenic

arte *sf* **1** art: *uma obra de ~* a work of art ◊ *~s marciais* martial arts **2** (*habilidade*) skill (*at (doing) sth*) ▶ **fazer ~** get up to mischief

artéria *sf* artery [*pl* -ies]

artesanal *adj* handmade

artesanato *sm* **1** (*habilidade*) craftsmanship **2** (*produtos*) handicrafts [*pl*]

ártico *adj* Arctic ● **Ártico** *sm* (*oceano*) Arctic Ocean

articulação *sf* **1** (*Anat, Mec*) joint **2** (*pronúncia*) articulation

articular *vi* (*pronunciar bem*) speak clearly

artificial *adj* artificial

artigo *sm* article: *o ~ definido* the definite article

artilharia *sf* artillery

artista *smf* artist

artístico *adj* artistic

artrite *sf* arthritis

árvore *sf* tree: *~ frutífera/ genealógica* fruit/family tree

as *art def, pron pess* Ver **os**

ás *sm* ace → BARALHO ▶ **ser um ás** (*pessoa*) be a genius (*at (doing) sth*): *Ele é um ás do ciclismo.* He's a champion cyclist.

asa *sf* **1** wing **2** (*utensílio*) handle

asa-delta *sf* **1** (*aparelho*) hang-glider **2** (*esporte*) hang-gliding

ascensão *sf* **1** (*partido, figura pública*) rise **2** (*empregado, equipe*) promotion

asfaltar *vt* asphalt

asfalto *sm* asphalt

asfixia *sf* suffocation

asfixiar *vt* **1** (*fumaça, gás*) suffocate **2** (*almofada*) smother

Ásia *sf* Asia

asiático/a *adj, sm-sf* Asian

asilo *sm* **1** (*lar*) home **2** (*Pol*) asylum

asma *sf* asthma

asmático/a *adj, sm-sf* asthmatic

asneira *sf*: *Mas que ~!* What a dumb thing to do! ◊ *dizer ~s* talk nonsense

aspargo *sm* asparagus [*U*]

aspas *sf* quotation marks: *entre ~* in quotes

aspecto *sm* **1** (*aparência*) look: *A sua avó não está com bom ~.* Your granny doesn't look very well. **2** (*faceta*) aspect

áspero *adj* rough

aspirador *sm* vacuum cleaner: *passar o ~* vacuum

aspirar *vt* **1** (*com aspirador*) vacuum **2** (*máquina*) suck sth up **3** (*respirar*) breathe sth in **4** ~ **a** aspire to sth

aspirina *sf* aspirin: *tomar uma ~* take an aspirin

asqueroso *adj* disgusting

assado *adj* roast ▶ **~ na brasa** grilled

assalariado/a *sm-sf* salaried employee

assaltante *smf* **1** (*agressor*) assailant **2** (*banco*) robber **3** (*casa*) burglar **4** (*pessoa*) mugger → THIEF

assaltar *vt* **1** (*atacar*) attack **2** (*banco, loja, pessoa*) rob

3 (*casa*) burglarize, burgle (*GB*) **4** (*pessoa fora de casa*) mug **5** (*roubar à mão armada*) hold *sb/sth* up **6** (*saquear*) raid → ROB

assalto *sm* **1** (*agressão*) attack (*on sb*) **2** (*banco, loja, pessoa*) robbery [*pl* -ies]: *Fui vítima de um ~*. I was robbed. **3** (*casa, escritório*) burglary [*pl* -ies], break-in (*coloq*) (*pessoa fora de casa*) mugging **5** (*roubo à mão armada*) hold-up: *Fizeram um ~ a um banco.* They held up a bank. **6** (*saque*) raid (*on sth*) **7** (*Boxe*) round

assar *vt* (*carne*) roast **2** (*pão, batata*) bake ● *vi* (*passar calor*) roast

assassinar *vt* murder
NOTA O verbo **assassinate** e os substantivos **assassination** (*assassinato*) e **assassin** (*assassino*) só são usados quando se trata de uma pessoa importante: *Quem é que assassinou o senador?* Who assassinated the senator? ◇ *uma tentativa de assassinato do presidente* an assassination attempt on the President ◇ *um assassino contratado* a hired assassin.

assassinato *sm* murder: *cometer um ~* commit (a) murder → ASSASSINAR

assassino/a *sm-sf* murderer → ASSASSINAR ● *adj* (*olhar*) murderous

assédio *sm* (*perseguição*) harassment: *~ sexual* sexual harassment

assegurar *vt* **1** (*garantir*) ensure **2** (*afirmar*) assure ● **assegurar-se** *vp* (*certificar-se*) make sure (*of sth/that...*): *Assegure-se de que está tudo em ordem.* Make sure everything's OK.

asseio *sm* **1** (*limpeza*) cleanliness **2** (*apuro*) neatness

assembléia *sf* **1** (*reunião*) meeting **2** (*Pol*) assembly [*pl* -ies]

assemelhar-se *vp* look like *sb/sth*

assentar *vt* settle ● *vi* **1** (*pó, sedimento*) settle **2** (*adaptar-se*) settle down

assentir *vi, vt* **1** (*consentir*) agree (*to sth*): *Acabou assentindo.* He finally agreed to it. **2** (*com a cabeça*) nod

assento *sm* seat

assessor/a *sm-sf* advisor [*pl* -ies]

assessoria *sf* advisory body [*pl* -ies] ▶ ~ **de imprensa** press office

assim *adv, adj* **1** (*deste modo, como este*) like this **2** (*daquele modo, como aquele*) like that **3** (*portanto*) so, therefore (*mais fml*) ▶ **assim, assim** so so ~ **como** as well as ~ **de grande, gordo, etc.** this big, fat, etc. ~ **é que se fala/faz** well said/well done ~ **que** as soon as: *~ que você chegar* as soon as you arrive **como** ~? how do you mean? **e** ~ **por diante/sucessivamente** and so on (and so forth) **ou coisa** ~ or so: *uns doze ou coisa* ~ a dozen or so **por** ~ **dizer** so to speak

assimilar *vt* assimilate

assinalar *vt* **1** (*marcar*) mark **2** (*mostrar*) point *sth* out

assinar **1** *vt, vi* sign **2** *vt* (*revista*) subscribe *to sth*

assinatura *sf* **1** (*nome*) signature **2** (*ato*) signing **3** (*publicação*) subscription **4** (*Teat*) season ticket

assistência *sf* **1** (*público*) audience **2** (*doentes*) care: *~ médica/hospitalar* health care/hospital treatment **3** (*ajuda*) help, assistance (*mais fml*): *prestar ~ a alguém* give sb assistance **4** (*presença*) attendance ▶ ~ **social** social services [*pl*]

assistente *smf* assistant ▶ ~ **social** social worker

assistir *vt* **1** (*estar presente em*) attend: *~ a um espetáculo* go to a show **2** (*ver*) watch: *~ a um programa de televisão* watch a program on TV **3** (*testemunhar*) witness **4** (*ajudar*) assist

assoalho *sm* wooden floor

assoar *vt* ▶ ~ **o nariz** blow your nose

assobiar *vt, vi* whistle

assobio *sm* whistle: *os ~s do vento* the whistling of the wind

associação *sf* association

associar *vt* associate *sb/sth* (*with sb/sth*) ● **associar-se** *vp* go into partnership

assombrado *adj* (*lugar*) haunted: *uma casa assombrada* a haunted house

assombro *sm* amazement: *ser um ~* be amazing

assumir *vt* **1** (*compromissos, obrigações*) take *sth* on **2** (*responsabilidade*) accept **3** (*culpa*) admit

assunto *sm* **1** (*tema*) subject **2** (*questão*) matter: *um ~ de interesse geral* a matter of general interest **3** (*Pol*) affair ▶ ~ **encerrado** subject closed **o** ~ **do dia** the topic of the day

assustador *adj* scary, frightening (*mais fml*)

assustar *vt* scare, frighten (*mais fml*) ● **assustar-se** *vp* be scared, be frightened by/of sb/sth (*mais fml*): *Você se assusta com tudo.* You're frightened of everything.

asterisco *sm* asterisk

astro *sm* star

astrologia *sf* astrology

astrólogo/a *sm-sf* astrologer

astronauta *smf* astronaut

astronomia *sf* astronomy

astrônomo/a *sm-sf* astronomer

astuto *adj* shrewd

ata *sf* minutes [*pl*]

atacado *sm* ● **por ~** (*Com*) wholesale

atacante *smf* **1** (*Esporte*) offense, forward (*GB*): *Ele joga como ~.* He plays in offense. **2** (*agressor*) attacker

atacar *vt* attack

atadura *sf* (*bandagem*) bandage

atalho *sm* short cut: *ir por um ~* take a short cut

ataque *sm* **1** (*agressão*) attack (*on sb/sth*) **2** ~ **de** (*riso, tosse, raiva, ciúme*) fit (of sth): *um ~ de tosse/nervos* a coughing fit/a fit of hysteria **3** (*investida*) raid

atar *vt* tie sb/sth (up)

atarefado *adj* (*pessoa*) busy (*dia*) hectic

atarracado *adj* (*pessoa*) stocky

atarraxar *vt* (*parafusos*) screw sth down/in/on

até *prep*
- **tempo** until, till (*coloq*) NOTA Usa-se **till** sobretudo no inglês falado e não se deve usar no início de uma frase: *Estarei lá ~ as sete.* I'll be there until seven. ◊ *Você fica ~ quando?* How long are you staying?
- **lugar 1** (*distância*) as far as...: *Eles vieram comigo ~ Recife.* They came with me as far as Recife. **2** (*altura, quantidade*) up to...: *A água chegou ~ aqui.* The water came up to here. **3** (*para baixo*) down to...: *A saia vem ~ os tornozelos.* The skirt comes down to my ankles.
- **saudações** see you...: ~ *amanhã/segunda!* See you tomorrow/on Monday! ◊ ~ *logo!* Bye! ● *adv* even: ~ *eu fiz.* Even I did it. ◊ ~ *me deram dinheiro.* They even gave me money.

ateliê *sm* (*Arte*) studio [*pl* ~s]

atenção *sf* attention ● *interj* look out

atenciosamente *adv* (*despedida*) Sincerely yours, Yours sincerely (*GB*)

atencioso *adj* **1** (*respeitoso*) considerate **2** (*amável*) kind

atender *vt* **1** (*numa loja*) serve: *Já foram atendidos?* Are you being served? **2** (*receber*) see: *O médico tem que ~ muitas pessoas.* The doctor has to see a lot of people. **3** (*tarefa, problema, pedido*) deal with sth **4** (*à porta, ao telefone*) answer: ~ *as chamadas* answer calls

atentado *sm* **1** (*tentativa de assassinato*) attempt (*on sb's*) life **2** (*ataque*) attack (*on sb/sth*)

atento *adj* **1** (*com atenção*) attentive: *ouvir ~.* listen attentively ● **estar ~ a algo 1** (*vigiar*) watch out for sth **2** (*prestar atenção*) pay attention to sth ● **estar ~ a alguém 1** (*vigiar*) keep an eye on sb **2** (*prestar atenção*) be attentive to sb

aterrador *adj* terrifying

aterrissagem *sf* landing: *fazer uma ~ forçada* make an emergency landing

aterrissar *vi* (*pousar*) land

aterro *sm* landfill

aterrorizar *vt* **1** (*amedrontar*) terrify **2** (*com violência*) terrorize

atestado *sm* certificate: ~ *médico* sick note

ateu, atéia *sm-sf* atheist: *ser ~* be an atheist

atingir *vt* **1** (*alcançar*) reach **2** (*pessoa com arma de fogo, alvo*) hit **3** (*objetivo*) achieve **4** (*afetar*) affect **5** (*criticar*) get to sb: *Ele se sentiu atingido pelo comentário.* The remark really got to him.

atiradeira *sf* (*brinquedo*) catapult

atirar *vt* **1** throw sth (*to sb*) NOTA Quando se atira algo em alguém com a intenção de ferir, usa-se **throw sth at sb/sth**: ~ *pedras na polícia* throw stones at the police. → THROW **2** (*contra*) (*com força ou violência*) hurl sb/sth (*against sth*) **3** (*com arma*) shoot sb/sth at sb/sth ● **atirar-se** *vp* **1** (*lançar-se*): ~ *dentro d'água* throw yourself into the water **2** ~ **em cima de** (*com força ou violência*) pounce on sb/sth ▶ ~ **ao chão** knock sb over

atitude *sf* attitude (*to/towards sb/sth*)

ativar *vt* activate

atividade

A 22

atividade sf activity [pl -ies]

ativo adj active

atlântico adj Atlantic ● **Atlântico** sm Atlantic (Ocean)

atlas sm atlas

atleta smf athlete

atlético adj athletic

atletismo sm athletics [sing]

atmosfera sf atmosphere

atmosférico adj atmospheric

ato sm 1 (ação, Teat) act: um ~ violento an act of violence 2 (cerimônia) ceremony [pl -ies]: o ~ de encerramento the closing ceremony ▶ **no** ~ 1 (no momento): pagar no ~ da compra pay on the spot 2 (imediatamente) right away

atoleiro sm bog

atômico adj atomic

átomo sm atom

atônito adj: ficar ~ be speechless

ator, atriz sm-sf actor [fem actress] → ACTRESS ▶ **ator/atriz principal** male/female lead

atordoar vt 1 (golpe, notícia) stun 2 (som) deafen

atormentar vt torment

atração sf attraction: sentir ~ por alguém feel attracted to sb ◇ uma ~ turística a tourist attraction

atraente adj attractive

atrair vt 1 attract: Os homens mais velhos me atraem. I'm attracted to older men. 2 (idéia) appeal to sb

atrapalhar vt 1 (confundir) confuse 2 (incomodar) be in the way of sb/sth; be in sb's way: Avise se essas caixas estiverem atrapalhando. Tell me if those boxes are in your way. ● **atrapalhar-se** vp be confused: Eu me atrapalhei na prova oral. I got confused in the oral.

atrás adv 1 (no fundo, na parte de trás) at the back 2 (tempo) ago: anos ~ years ago ◇ **andar/estar ~ de alguém/algo** be after sb/sth ~ **de 1** behind: ~ da casa behind the house ◇ Ela não fica muito ~ de você. She's not far behind you. 2 (depois de) after: Ele fumou um cigarro ~ do outro. He smoked one cigarette after another. **ir ~ de alguém/algo** (seguir) follow sb/sth

atrasado adj 1 (país, região) backward 2 (publicação, salário) back: os números ~s de uma revista the back issues of a magazine 3 (relógio) slow 4 (pagamento, renda) late ▶ **no ~ no trabalho, etc.** behind with your

work, etc. **chegar/estar ~:** O trem chegou uma hora ~. The train was an hour late.

atrasar vt 1 (retardar) hold sb/sth up 2 (relógio) put sth back ● vi 1 (trem, ônibus) be delayed 2 (relógio) be slow: O relógio está atrasado dez minutos. The clock is ten minutes slow. ● **atrasar-se** vp (chegar tarde) be late

atraso sm 1 (demora) delay: Alguns vôos sofreram ~s. Some flights were subject to delays. 2 (subdesenvolvimento) backwardness ▶ **com ~** late: Começou com cinco minutos de ~. It began five minutes late.

atrativo adj attractive ● sm 1 (coisa que atrai) attraction: um dos ~s da cidade one of the city's attractions 2 (interesse) appeal [U] 3 (pessoa) charm

através adv ▶ ~ **de 1** through: Ele corria ~ do bosque. He was running through the woods. 2 (de um lado para o outro) across: correr ~ do parque/dos campos run across the park/fields

atravessar vt 1 cross: ~ a rua/fronteira cross the street/border ◇ ~ a rua correndo run across the street ◇ ~ o rio a nado swim across the river 2 (perfurar, experimentar) go through sth: ~ uma crise go through a crisis ◇ A bala atravessou-lhe o coração. The bullet went through his heart. ● **atravessar-se** vp 1 (no caminho) block sb's path 2 (na garganta): Uma espinha se atravessou na minha garganta. A bone was stuck in my throat.

atrelar vt hitch

atrever-se vp dare (do sth): Não me atrevo a lhe pedir dinheiro. I don't dare ask him for money. → DARE

atrevido adj 1 (audaz) daring 2 (malcriado) sassy

atrevimento sm 1 (audácia) daring 2 Que ~! What a nerve!

atribuir vt 1 (causa) attribute sth (to sb/sth) 2 (conceder) award 3 (culpa, responsabilidade) lay: ~ a culpa a outra pessoa lay the blame on someone else 4 (importância) attach 5 (cargo, função) assign

atributo sm attribute

atrito sm friction [U]

atrocidade sf atrocity [pl -ies]

atropelado adj (por um veículo): Ele morreu ~. He died after being run over by a car.

atropelar vt run sb over: *Um carro me atropelou.* I was run over by a car.

atuação sf (*desempenho*) performance

atual adj **1** (*relativo ao momento presente*) current: *o estado ~ das obras* the current state of the building work **2** (*relativo à atualidade*) present-day: *a ciência ~* present-day science

atualidade sf (*tempo presente*) present (times) ▶ **da ~** topical: *assuntos/temas da ~* topical issues

atualizar vt **1** (*informação, dados*) update **2** (*computador*) upgrade ● **atualizar-se** vp get up to date

atualmente adv currently

atuar vi **1** (*artista*) perform **2** (*agir*) act

atum sm tuna [pl tuna]

aturar vt (*agüentar*) put up with sb/sth: *Tive que ~ o filme inteiro.* I had to sit through the entire movie.

atxim interj achoo NOTA A pessoa que espirra desculpa-se com **excuse me!** Quem está perto diz **bless you!** ou não diz nada.

au-au sm, interj woof

audácia sf **1** (*ousadia*) bold **2** (*insolência*) audacity

audacioso adj bold: *uma decisão audaciosa* a bold decision

audição sf **1** (*ouvido*) hearing **2** (*teste*) audition

audiência sf audience: *o programa de maior ~* the program with the largest audience

audiovisual adj audiovisual

auditório sm **1** (*edifício*) concert hall **2** (*ouvintes*) audience

auge sm peak: *no ~ da fama* at the peak of your fame

aula sf **1** lesson: *~s de direção* driving lessons **2** (*na escola*) class ▶ **dar ~s** teach

aumentar vt **1** increase: *~ a competitividade* increase competition **2** (*volume*) turn sth up **3** (*lupa, microscópio*) magnify ● vi increase

aumento sm **1** rise, increase (*mais fml*) (*in sth*): *um ~ populacional* an increase in the population ◇ *um ~ de temperatura* a rise in temperature **2** (*salarial*) raise, rise (*GB*)

aurora sf dawn: *ao romper da ~* at daybreak

ausência sf absence

ausentar-se vp (*país, sala*) be away (*from...*): *Eu me ausentei da sala por alguns minutos.* I was out of the room for a few minutes.

ausente adj absent (*from...*) ● smf absentee

austeridade sf austerity

austero adj austere

Austrália sf Australia

australiano/a adj, sm-sf Australian

autenticado adj (*fotocópia, documento*) certified

autêntico adj genuine: *um Renoir ~* a genuine Renoir

auto-adesivo adj self-adhesive ● sm sticker

autobiografia sf autobiography [pl -ies]

autobiográfico adj autobiographical

autodefesa sf self-defense

autódromo sm racetrack

auto-escola sf driving school

auto-estrada sf highway, motorway (*GB*) → RODOVIA

autografar vt autograph

autógrafo sm autograph

automático adj automatic

automobilismo sm motor racing

automobilista smf motorist

automóvel sm automobile

autonomia sf autonomy

autônomo adj **1** (*Pol*) autonomous **2** (*trabalhador*) self-employed

autópsia sf autopsy [pl -ies]

autor/a sm-sf **1** (*escritor*) author **2** (*compositor*) composer **3** (*crime*) perpetrator

auto-retrato sm self-portrait

autoridade sf **1** authority [pl -ies] **2** (*pessoa*) expert

autorização sf authorization

autorizar vt **1** (*ação*) authorize: *Não autorizaram a greve.* The strike was unauthorized. **2** (*dar o direito*) give sb the right (*to do sth*)

auxiliar¹ adj auxiliary: *o pessoal ~* the auxiliary staff ● smf assistant

auxiliar² vt assist

auxílio sm **1** help: *prestar ~ a alguém* help sb **2** (*monetário, financeiro*) aid

avalanche sf avalanche

avaliação sf assessment

avaliar vt **1** value sth (*at sth*) **2** (*Educ*) assess **3** (*situação, riscos*) weigh sth up

avançado adj advanced

avançar vt (objeto) move sth forward ● vi advance

avanço sm advance: os ~s da medicina advances in medicine

avarento/a adj stingy ● sm-sf miser

avareza sf stinginess

ave sf bird: ~s de rapina birds of prey ▶ **rara** oddball

aveia sf oats [pl]

avelã sf hazelnut

ave-maria sf Hail Mary: rezar três ~s say three Hail Marys

avenida sf avenue (abrev **Ave.**)

avental sm **1** apron **2** (escola, trabalho) smock, overall (GB) **3** (laboratório) lab coat **4** (hospital) white coat

aventura sf **1** (peripécia) adventure **2** (caso amoroso) fling

aventureiro/a adj adventurous ● sm-sf adventurer

averiguar vt **1** (investigar) to check sth out **2** (descobrir) find sth out, discover (mais fml)

aversão sf aversion

avessas sf ▶ **às ~ 1** (ao revés) the wrong way round **2** (de cabeça para baixo) upside down

avesso sm (tecido) wrong side: O seu suéter está pelo ~. Your sweater is on inside out.

avestruz sm, sf ostrich

aviação sf aviation

avião sm plane, airplane (mais fml) ▶ ir/viajar de ~ fly

avisar vt **1** (informar) let sb know (about sth): Avise-me quando eles chegarem. Let me know when they arrive. **2** (prevenir) warn ▶ **sem ~**: Eles vieram sem ~. They turned up unexpectedly. ◇ Ele foi embora para casa sem ~. He went home without telling anyone.

aviso sm **1** notice: Fechado até novo ~. Closed until further notice. **2** (advertência) warning: sem ~ prévio without prior warning

avo sm: um doze ~ s one twelfth

avô, avó sm-sf **1** grandfather [fem grandmother], grandpa [fem grandma] (coloq) **2** (avós) grandparents

avulso adj loose

axila sf armpit

azar sm **1** (acaso) chance **2** (falta de sorte) bad luck ▶ **estar com ~** be out of luck **por ~** unfortunately

azarado adj unlucky

azedar vi (vinho, creme) go/turn sour, go off (GB)

azedo adj **1** (leite, vinho, caráter) sour **2** (comida) bad

azeite sm olive oil

azeitona sf olive: ~s recheadas/ sem caroço stuffed/pitted olives

azeviche sm jet: negro como o ~ jet black

azia sf heartburn

azul adj, sm blue

azulejo sm tile

azul-marinho adj, sm navy blue

Bb

baba sf **1** (pessoa, cachorro) dribble **2** (quiabo, lesma) slime

babá sf nanny [pl -ies]

babado sm frill

babadouro sm bib

babar-se vp **1** dribble **2** ~ (por) dote (on sb)

babysitter smf babysitter

bacalhau sm cod: ~ (seco) salt cod

bacia sf **1** (recipiente) bowl **2** (Geog) basin **3** (Anat) pelvis

baço sm spleen

bacon sm bacon

bactéria sf bacterium [pl -ria]

badalada sf (relógio) stroke: O relógio deu seis ~s. The clock struck six.

badalado adj (muito falado) much talked about

badulaques sm odds and ends

bafômetro sm breathalyzer®: fazer o teste do ~ be breathalyzed

bagageiro sm (no teto de carro) luggage rack

bagagem sf baggage, luggage: ~ de mão hand luggage ◇ preparar a ~ pack your bags

bago sm grape

baguete sf baguette

bagunça sf (desordem) mess: Mas que ~ que está o seu escritório! Your office is a real mess!

baía sf bay

bailado sm **1** (balé) ballet **2** (dança) dance

bailarino/a sm-sf dancer

baile *sm* dance ▶ ~ **de gala** ball ~ **de máscaras** costume ball, fancy dress ball (GB)

bainha *sf* hem

bairro *sm* **1** neighborhood **2** (*zona típica*) quarter **3** (*divisão administrativa*) district ▶ **do** ~: *o padeiro do* ~ the local baker

baixa *sf* **1** (*preço*) fall (*in sth*) **2** (*Mil*) casualty [*pl* -ies]

baixa-mar *sf* low tide

baixar *vt* **1** *get sth down*: *Você me ajuda a* ~ *a mala?* Could you help me get my suitcase down? **2** (*pôr mais para baixo*) bring *sth* down **3** (*olhos, voz, cabeça*) lower **4** (*som*) turn *sth* down **5** (*preço*) bring *sth* down, lower (*mais fml*) **6** (*Informát*) download L *vi* **1** (*temperatura*) fall **2** (*inchaço*) go down **3** (*maré*) go out **4** (*preços*) come down ▶ ~ **a crista de alguém** take sb down a peg or two

baixaria *sf*: *Saiu briga na festa, virou a maior* ~. A fight broke out at the party and it all turned very nasty. ◊ *Ele bebe demais e aí começa com a* ~. He drinks too much and gets really nasty.

baixela *sf* tableware

baixo¹ *sm* (*instrumento*) bass

baixo² *adv* **1** (*posição*) below: *desde* ~ from below **2** (*em edifício*) downstairs: *o vizinho de* ~ the man who lives downstairs **3** (*a pouca altura*) low **4** (*suavemente*) quietly ▶ **o de** ~ the bottom one **para** ~ downward **por** ~ **de** under(neath)

baixo³ *adj* **1** low: *uma sopa baixa em calorias* a low-calorie soup ◊ *A televisão está baixa demais.* The TV's on too low. ◊ *notas baixas* low grades **2** (*pessoa*) short **3** (*voz*) quiet: *falar em voz baixa* speak quietly **4** (*atitude*) mean

bajulação *sf* flattery [U]

bajular *vt* flatter

bala *sf* **1** (*arma*) bullet **2** (*doce*) candy [*pl* -ies], sweet (GB) ▶ **como uma** ~ like a shot

balança *sf* **1** (*instrumento*) scale, scales [*pl*] (GB) **2** (*Com*) balance ● **Balança** (*Astrol*) Libra

balançar(-se) *vt, vp* **1** swing **2** (*cadeira de balanço, barco*) rock

balanço *sm* **1** balance: ~ *positivo/negativo* a positive/negative balance **2** (*número de vítimas*) toll **3** (*balouço*) swing: *brincar no* ~ play on the swings ▶ **fazer um** ~ take stock (*of sth*): *Preciso fazer um* ~ *das minhas tarefas.* I need to take stock of what I have to do.

balão *sm* **1** balloon **2** (*história em quadrinhos*) speech bubble

balbuciar *vt, vi* **1** (*gaguejar*) stammer **2** (*dizer/falar sem clareza*) mumble

balbúrdia *sf* **1** noise **2** (*desordem*) mess: *Que* ~! What a mess!

balcão *sm* **1** (*loja*) counter **2** (*informações, recepção*) desk **3** (*bar*) bar: *Ele estava sentado ao* ~. He was sitting at the bar. **4** (*teatro*) balcony, circle (GB)

balconista *smf* salesclerk, shop assistant (GB)

balde *sm* bucket

baldeação *sf* transfer ▶ **fazer** ~ change

baldio *adj*: *terreno* ~ wasteland

balé *sm* ballet

baleia *sf* whale ▶ **uma** ~ (**de gordo**) very overweight

baliza *sf* **1** (*Esporte*) goal **2** (*Náut*) buoy **3** (*Aeronáut*) beacon

balneário *sm* spa

balsa *sf* ferry [*pl* -ies]

bambo *adj* **1** (*frouxo*) slack **2** (*vacilante*) wobbly

bambu *sm* bamboo

banana *sf* banana

bananeira *sf* banana tree

banca *sf* (*de trabalho*) bench ▶ ~ **de jornal** newsstand ▶ ~ **examinadora** examination board

bancada *sf* **1** (*estádio*) stand **2** (*de trabalho*) bench

bancar *vt* **1** (*custear*) finance **2** (*fingir*) act: ~ *o palhaço/milionário* act the fool/act like a millionaire

bancário/a *adj* bank: *conta bancária* bank account ● *sm-sf* bank clerk

bancarrota *sf* bankruptcy ▶ **ir à** ~ go bankrupt

banco *sm* **1** bank: *o* ~ *do Brasil* the Bank of Brazil ~ **de sangue** blood bank **2** (*parque, Esporte*) bench **3** (*cozinha, bar*) stool **4** (*igreja*) pew **5** (*carro*) seat ▶ ~ **de areia** sandbank ~ **de dados** database ~ **do(s) réu(s)** dock

banda *sf* **1** (*de música*) band **2** (*lado*) side

band-aid® *sm* Band-Aid®, plaster (GB)

bandeira *sf* **1** flag: ~ *branca* white flag **2** (*Mil*) colors [*pl*]

bandeirada *sf* (*táxi*) minimum fare

bandeirante *sf* Girl Scout

B

bandeja sf tray ▶ **dar de ~** hand sb sth on a plate

bandido/a sm-sf 1 (fora-da-lei) bandit 2 (pessoa marota) villain

bando sf 1 (quadrilha) gang 2 (aves) flock 3 (leões) pride

banha sf (Cozinha) lard

banhado adj: **~ em lágrimas/suor/sangue** bathed in tears/sweat/blood ▶ **~ a ouro** gold-plated

banhar vt 1 bathe, bath (GB) 2 (em metal) plate sth (with sth) ● **banhar-se** vp take a bath, have a bath (GB)

banheira sf bathtub, bath (GB)

banheiro sm 1 bathroom 2 (edifício público, restaurante) restroom, toilet (GB) → TOILET

banhista smf bather

banho sm 1 (em banheira) bath 2 (de chuveiro) shower ▶ **tomar ~** take a bath/shower **tomar ~ de sol** sunbathe **vai tomar ~** get lost

banir vt banish

banqueiro/a sm-sf banker

banqueta sf stool: **trepar numa ~** stand on a stool

banquete sm banquet (fml), dinner

banzé sm 1 (barulho) racket: **armar ~** make a racket 2 (discussão) fuss

baqueta sf (para tambor) drumstick

bar sm 1 (bebidas alcoólicas) bar 2 (lanchonete) snack bar

baralho sm deck of cards, pack of cards (GB) NOTA O baralho se divide em quatro naipes ou suits: hearts (copas), diamonds (ouros), clubs (paus) e spades (espadas). Cada um tem um ace (ás), king (rei), queen (dama), jack (valete) e nove cartas numeradas. Antes de se começar a jogar, embaralham-se (shuffle), cortam-se (cut) e dão-se (deal) as cartas.

barão/onesa sm-sf baron [fem baroness]

barata sf cockroach

barato¹ sm (curtição): **A festa foi o maior ~.** The party was awesome.

barato² adj cheap ● adv cheaply

barba sf beard: **deixar crescer a ~** grow a beard ◇ **um homem de ~** a bearded man ▶ **fazer a ~** (have a) shave

barbante sm string

barbaridade sf 1 (brutalidade) barbarity 2 (disparate) nonsense [U]

barbatana sf fin

barbeador sm razor

barbearia sf barber's

barbear(-se) vt, vp shave

barbeiragem sf careless mistake

barbeiro sm 1 (pessoa) barber 2 (local) barber's

barco sm 1 boat: **dar um passeio de ~** go for a ride in a boat ◇ **ir de ~** go by boat/ship 2 (navio) ship → BOAT ▶ **~ a motor** motorboat **~ a remo** rowboat, rowing boat (GB) **~ a vapor** steamship **~ à vela** sailboat, sailing boat (GB)

barítono sm baritone

barman sm bartender, barman

barômetro sm barometer

barra sf 1 bar: **uma ~ de ferro/chocolate** an iron/chocolate bar 2 (sinal gráfico) slash

barraca sf 1 (camping, praia) tent: **montar/desmontar uma ~** put up/take down a tent 2 (feira) stall

barraco sm shack

barragem sf (represa) dam

barranco sm ravine

barra-pesada adj 1 (pessoa) aggressive 2 (lugar) rough: **um bairro ~** a rough neighborhood 3 (situação) tough: **O exame foi ~.** The exam was really tough.

barrar vt bar

barreira sf 1 barrier: **A ~ estava levantada.** The barrier was up. 2 (Futebol) wall 3 (Esporte) hurdle: **os 400 metros com ~s** the 400 meters hurdles

barrento adj muddy

barricada sf barricade

barriga sf 1 (estômago) stomach: **Estou com dor de ~.** I have a stomach ache. 2 (ventre) belly [pl -ies] (coloq) stomach 3 (pança) paunch: **ganhar ~** get a paunch ▶ **~ da perna** calf [pl calves]

barril sm barrel

barro sm 1 (argila) clay 2 (lama) mud ▶ **de ~**: **panelas de ~** earthenware pots

barroco adj, sm baroque

barulheira sf racket

barulhento adj noisy

barulho sm noise: **O carro faz muito ~.** The car is very noisy.

base sf 1 base: **~ militar** military base 2 (fundamento) basis [pl bases] ▶ **~ espacial** space station

baseado sm joint

basear vt base sth on sth ● **basear-se** vp 1 (pessoa) have grounds (for doing) sth): **Em**

que você se baseia para afirmar isso? What grounds do you have for saying that? **2** (*teoria, filme*) be based on sth

básico *adj* basic

basquete *sm* basketball

bastante *adj* (*suficiente*) enough: *Temos dinheiro* ~. We have enough money. ● *pron* a lot: *Tenho* ~ *coisa para fazer*. I have a lot of things to do. ◊ *Faz* ~ *tempo que não a vejo*. It's been a long time since I saw her. ● *adv* **1** ~ **+ adj/adv** pretty: *Eles lêem* ~ *bem para a idade*. They read pretty well for their age. → **FAIRLY 2** (*o suficiente*) enough **3** (*muito*) a lot

bastão *sm* **1** stick **2** (*Esporte*) bat

bastar *vi* be enough: *Basta!* That's enough!

bastidores *sm* (*teatro*) wings

batalha *sf* battle

batalhão *sm* battalion ► **para um** ~: *Há comida para um* ~. There's enough food to feed an army.

batata *sf* potato [*pl* ~es] ► ~ **s fritas 1** (*pacote*) (potato) chips, crisps (*GB*) **2** (*Cozinha*) (French) fries, chips (*GB*)

batata-doce *sf* sweet potato [*pl* ~es]

bate-boca *sm* argument

batedeira *sf* **1** whisk **2** (*eletrodoméstico*) mixer

batedor/a *sm-sf* ► ~ **de carteiras** pickpocket

batente *sm* **1** (*porta*) frame **2** (*trabalho*) work

bate-papo *sm* chat: *Ficamos no* ~ *até clarear o dia*. We stayed chatting till dawn.

bater *vt* **1** beat: ~ *o adversário/o recorde mundial* beat your opponent/the world record ◊ ~ *ovos* beat eggs **2** (*creme*) whip **3** (*bola*) bounce **4** (*asas*) flap **5** (*horas*): *O relógio bateu seis horas*. The clock struck six. **6** ~ **em/com/contra** hit: *Bati com a cabeça*. I hit my head. ◊ ~ (*com*) *a porta* slam the door **7** ~ **em** (*luz, sol*) shine on sth **8** ~ **em** (*assunto*) go on about sth: *Pare de* ~ *na mesma tecla*. Stop going on about it. ● *vi* **1** beat: *O coração dela batia aceleradamente*. Her heart was beating fast. **2** (*carro, etc.*) crash ► ~ **as asas** (*fugir*) take flight ~ **as botas** (*morrer*) kick the bucket (*GB*) ~ **boca** quarrel ~ **na porta** I knock at the door **2** (*fig*): *O Natal está batendo na porta*. Christmas is just around

the corner. ~ **o pé 1** stamp **2** (*fig*) refuse to budge ~ **o queixo** shiver ~ **os dentes**: *Ele batia os dentes de frio*. His teeth were chattering. ~ **palmas** clap **não** ~ **bem** (**da bola/cabeça**) be nuts

bateria *sf* **1** (*Elet, Mil*) battery [*pl* -ies]: *A* ~ *descarregou*. The battery is flat. **2** (*Mús*) drums

baterista *smf* drummer

batida *sf* **1** (*coração*) (heart)beat **2** (*bebida*) rum cocktail **3** (*com o carro*) crash **4** (*policial*) raid

batido *adj* **1** *Isso já está muito* ~. That's old hat by now. **2** (*roupa*) worn

batismal *adj* baptismal: *pia* ~ (baptismal) font

batismo *sm* **1** (*sacramento*) baptism **2** (*ato de dar um nome*) christening

batizado *sm* baptism

batizar *vt* **1** (*Relig*) baptize **2** (*dar um nome*) **(a)** (*a uma pessoa*) christen: *Vamos batizá-la com o nome Marta*. We're going to christen her Marta. **(b)** (*a um barco, um invento*) name

batom *sm* lipstick

batuta *sf* baton

baú *sm* trunk

baunilha *sf* vanilla

bêbado/a *adj*, *sm-sf* drunk

bebê *sm* baby [*pl* -ies]

bebedeira *sf*: *tomar uma* ~ (*de uísque*) get drunk (on whiskey)

bebedor/a *sm-sf* drinker

beber *vt*, *vi* drink: *Beba tudo*. Drink it up. ► ~ **aos goles/golinhos** sip ~ **como uma esponja** drink like a fish

beberrão/ona *sm-sf* heavy drinker

bebida *sf* drink

beça *sf* ► **à** ~: *divertir-se à* ~ have a great time ◊ *Eles têm livros à* ~. They have lots of books.

beco *sm* alley ► ~ **sem saída** dead end

bedelho *sm*: *meter o* ~ *na vida de alguém* interfere in sb's life

bege *adj*, *sm* beige

beicinho *sm* ► **fazer** ~ pout

beija-flor *sm* hummingbird

beijar(-se) *vt*, *vp* kiss

beijo *sm* kiss: *Nós nos demos um* ~. We kissed each other. ◊ *atirar um* ~ *a alguém* blow sb a kiss

beira *sf* ► **à** ~ **de 1** beside: *à* ~ *d'água*, at the water's edge **2** (*fig*) on the verge of sth: *à* ~ *das lágrimas* on the verge of tears

beirada *sf* edge

beira-mar sf: à ~ by the ocean

beisebol sm baseball

belas-artes sf fine arts

beleza sf **1** (qualidade) beauty [pl -ies] **2** (coisa bela): O casamento estava uma ~. The wedding was wonderful.

beliche sm **1** (em casa) bunk bed **2** (em barco) bunk

bélico adj war: armas bélicas weapons of war

beliscão sm pinch ▶ dar um ~ pinch

beliscar vt pinch

belo adj beautiful

bem¹ adv **1** well: Não me sinto ~ hoje. I don't feel well today. ◇ falar ~ inglês speak English well **2** (de acordo, adequado) OK: Pareceu-lhes ~. They thought it was OK. **3** (qualidade, aspecto, cheiro, sabor) good: Você parece ~. You look good. ◇ Como cheira ~! It smells really good! **4** (corretamente): Respondi ~ à pergunta. I gave the right answer. **5** (muito) very: Está ~ sujo. It's very dirty. **6** (exatamente): Não foi ~ assim que aconteceu. It didn't happen quite like that. ◇ Foi ~ aqui que o deixei. I left it right here. ▶ ~ como as well as • está ~ OK: —Você me empresta? —Está ~. "Can I borrow it?" "OK." muito ~ (very) good por ~: É melhor ir você o faça por ~. It would be better if you did it willingly. por ~ ou por mal whether you like it or not, etc. NOTA Para outras expressões com bem, ver o adjetivo, verbo, etc., p. ex. bem feito em FEITO.

bem² sm **1** (o bom) good: o ~ e o mal good and evil ◇ São gente de ~. They're good-hearted people. **2** (bens) possessions ▶ bens de consumo consumer goods bens imóveis real estate para meu, seu, etc. ~ for my, your, etc. own sake para o ~ de for the good of sb/sth

bem-comportado adj well behaved → WELL BEHAVED

bem-educado adj well mannered

bem-estar sm well-being

bem-humorado adj good-tempered

bem-intencionado adj well meaning

bemol sm (Mús) flat

bem-sucedido adj successful

bem-vindo adj welcome

bem-visto adj well thought of

bênção sf blessing: dar a ~ a alguém bless sb

bendito adj blessed

beneficente adj: obras ~s charity work ◇ uma instituição ~ a charity

beneficiar(-se) vt, vp benefit (from sth)

benefício sm benefit: em seu ~ for your benefit

benéfico adj **1** beneficial **2** (salutar) healthy **3** (favorável) favorable

bengala sf **1** (bastão) walking stick **2** (pão) baguette

benigno adj benign

benzer vt bless • benzer-se vp cross yourself

berço sm crib, cot (GB)

berinjela sf eggplant, aubergine (GB)

bermuda sf Bermuda shorts, Bermudas [pl]: uma ~ a pair of Bermudas → PAIR

berrante adj **1** (cor) loud **2** (coisa) flashy

berrar vt, vi shout

berro sm shout: dar ~s shout ▶ aos ~s at the top of your voice

besouro sm beetle

besta sf beast • smf (pessoa) idiot • adj (pedante) pretentious

bexiga sf **1** (Anat) bladder **2** (marca da varíola) pockmark **3** (bexigas) (Med) smallpox [U]

bezerro/a sm-sf calf [pl calves]

Bíblia sf Bible

bíblico adj biblical

bibliografia sf bibliography [pl -ies]

biblioteca sf library [pl -ies]

bibliotecário/a sm-sf librarian

bica sf water outlet

bicada sf (pássaro) peck

bicampeão/eã sm-sf two-time champion

bicar vt, vi (pássaro) peck

bicarbonato sm bicarbonate

bíceps sm biceps [pl biceps]

bicha sf queer

bicho sm **1** (inseto) bug **2** (animal) animal ▶ ~ de pelúcia stuffed animal, soft toy (GB) que ~ mordeu você? what's eating you?

bicho-carpinteiro sm ▶ ter ~ be fidgety

bicho-da-seda sm silkworm

bicho-de-sete-cabeças sm big deal: fazer um ~ de algo make a big deal out of sth ◇ Não é nenhum ~. It's no big deal.

bicho-do-mato sm (pessoa insociável) loner

bicho-papão sm bogeyman

bicicleta sf bicycle, bike (coloq): Você sabe andar de ~? Can you ride a bike? ◊ dar um passeio de ~ go for a ride on your bicycle ◊ ~ de corrida/montanha racing/mountain bike

bico sm 1 (pássaro) beak 2 (caneta) nib 3 (gás) gas tap 4 (sapato) toe 5 (bule, chaleira) spout 6 (emprego) odd job 7 (seio) nipple 8 (mamadeira) teat 9 (boca) mouth ▶ - calado don't say a word

bicudo adj (pontiagudo) pointed

bidê sm bidet

bife sm steak

bifurcação sf fork

bifurcar-se vp fork

bigode sm 1 (pessoa) mustache: um homem de ~ a man with a mustache 2 (gato) whiskers [pl]

bijuteria sf costume jewelry

bilhão sm billion

bilhar sm (jogo) billiards [sing]

bilhete sm 1 (passagem) ticket 2 (recado) note ▶ - de ida e volta round-trip ticket, return (ticket) (GB) ~ simples/de ida one-way ticket, single (ticket) (GB)

bilheteria sf 1 (estação, Esporte) ticket office 2 (Cinema, Teat) box office

bilíngüe adj bilingual

bílis sf bile

bingo sm 1 (jogo) bingo 2 (sala) bingo hall

binóculo sm binoculars [pl]

biodegradável adj biodegradable

biografia sf biography [pl -ies]

biologia sf biology

biológico adj biological

biólogo/a sm-sf biologist

biombo sm screen

bip sm pager

biquíni sm bikini

birra sf 1 (teimosia) stubborness 2 (mau gênio) tantrum: fazer ~ throw a tantrum

birrento adj (teimoso) stubborn

biruta smf (amalucado) lunatic

bis interj encore

bisavô/ó sm-sf 1 great-grandfather [fem great-grandmother] 2 (bisavós) great-grandparents

bisbilhotar vi pry (into sth)

bisbilhoteiro/a adj nosy ● sm-sf snoop

bisbilhotice sf prying [U]

biscate sm odd job: fazer (uns) ~s do some odd jobs

biscoito sm 1 (doce) cookie, biscuit (GB) 2 (salgado) cracker

bisnaga sf 1 (recipiente) tube 2 (pão) French bread

bisneto/a sm-sf great-grandson [fem great-granddaughter] [pl great-grandchildren]

bispo sm bishop

bissexto adj: ano ~ leap year

bisturi sm scalpel

bit sm (Informát) bit

blasfemar vi blaspheme (against sb/sth)

blasfêmia sf blasphemy [U]: dizer ~s blaspheme

blazer sm blazer

blefar vi bluff

blefe sm bluff

blindado adj 1 (veículo) armored 2 (porta) reinforced ● sm armored car

bloco sm 1 block 2 (Pol) bloc ▶ ~ de apartamentos apartment building, block of flats (GB) ~ de notas/papel writing pad

bloquear vt 1 (obstruir) block: ~ o caminho block access 2 (Mil) blockade

bloqueio sm 1 (Esporte) block 2 (Mil) blockade

blusa sf blouse

blusão sm 1 jacket: um ~ de couro a leather jacket 2 (ginástica, jogging) sweatshirt

blush sm blusher

boa sf ▶ estar numa ~ be doing fine numa ~: —Você pode me dar uma mãozinha? — Claro, numa ~! "Could you give me a hand?" "Sure, no problem."

boas-festas sf: desejar ~ wish sb a merry Christmas

boas-vindas sf welcome [sing]: dar as ~ a alguém welcome sb

boate sf club

boato sm rumor ▶ correr o ~ be rumored (that...): Correu o ~ de que ele estava morto. He was rumored to be dead.

bobagem sf dumb thing: Não diga bobagens. Don't talk dumb.

bobina sf 1 (fio) reel 2 (Elet, arame) coil

bobo adj 1 (tonto) silly 2 (ingênuo) naive

boca sf 1 (Anat) mouth 2 a ~ do túnel the entrance to the tunnel ▶ apanhar alguém com a ~ na botija catch sb red-handed de boca em boca: A história foi passando de ~ em ~. The story did the rounds. de ~ para baixo/cima (virado) face down/

up de ~ suja foul-mouthed
dizer algo da ~ para fora pay lip
service to sth ficar de ~ aberta
(surpresa) be dumbfounded

bocado sm (pão, bolo) piece **2**
(relativo a tempo) while:
Chegueí há um ~. I arrived some
time ago. ▸ **maus ~s:** atravessar
maus ~s go through a bad patch

bocal sm (Mús) mouthpiece

bocejar vi yawn

bocejo sm yawn

bochecha sf cheek

bochechar vi rinse (out) your
mouth

bodas sf anniversary [sing] ▸ **~
de ouro** golden wedding [sing]

bode sm **1** (animal) billy goat **2**
(confusão) fix: Deu o maior ~
para eles. They got into a real
fix. ▸ **~ expiatório** scapegoat

bofetada sf slap (in the face):
Ela me deu uma ~. She slapped
me (in the face).

boi sm steer

bóia sf **1** (para nadar) rubber
ring **2** (pesca) float **3** (comida)
chow (coloq) ▸ **~ salva-vidas** life
preserver, lifebuoy (GB)

boiar vi float

boicotar vt boycott

boicote sm boycott

boina sf beret

bola sf **1** ball: uma ~ de tênis/de
cristal a tennis/crystal ball **2**
(sabão, chiclete) bubble: fazer
~s de sabão blow bubbles ▸ **~ de
neve** snowball **~s de naftalina**
mothballs

bolada sf: uma ~ de dinheiro a
pile of cash

boletim sm **1** (publicação) bulletin **2** (escolar) report card,
school report (GB) **3** ~ infor-
mativo/meteorológico news/
weather report

bolha sf **1** (em líquido, saliva)
bubble **2** (na pele) blister ▸ smf
(pessoa) bore

boliche sm: jogar ~ go bowling ◇
pista de ~ bowling alley

bolinha sf polka dot: uma saia de
~s a polka-dot skirt

Bolívia sf Bolivia

boliviano/a adj, sm-sf Bolivian

bolo sm cake

bolor sm mold: criar/ter ~ go/be
moldy

bolorento adj moldy

bolsa sf **1** bag **2** (de mulher)
purse, handbag (GB) **3** (concentração) pocket: uma ~ de ar an
air pocket **4** (Com) stock
exchange ▸ **~ de estudos** scholarship

bolso sm pocket: guia de ~
pocket guide ◇ ~ do casaco
coat pocket

bom, boa adj **1** good: uma boa
notícia good news **2** (amável)
nice: Eles foram muito bons
comigo. They were very nice to
me. **3** (comida) tasty **4** (correto)
right: Você não está no ~ caminho. You're on the wrong road.
5 (doente, aparelho) fine: Agora
já estou ~. I'm fine now. ▸ **está
bom** that's fine

bomba¹ sf **1** (Mil) bomb: colocar
uma ~ plant a bomb **2** (notícia)
bombshell ▸ **levar ~** fail, flunk
(coloq): Levei ~ em matemática.
I flunked math.

bomba² sf (água, ar) pump

bombardear vt **1** (com bombas)
bomb **2** (com mísseis/pergun-
tas) bombard

bomba-relógio sf time bomb

bombeiro sm **1** firefighter **2**
(encanador) plumber

bombo sm (Mús) bass drum

bombom sm chocolate

bombordo sm port: a ~ to port

bom-dia sm ▸ **dar ~** say good
morning

bondade sf goodness: Tenha a ~
de se sentar. Kindly take a seat.

bonde sm streetcar, tram (GB)

bondoso adj kind (to sb/sth)

boné sm cap

boneco/a sm-sf **1** (brinquedo)
doll **2** (ventríloquo, manequim)
dummy [pl -ies] ▸ **~ de neve**
snowman [pl -men]

bonitinho adj cute

bonito adj pretty: Ela está
bonita. She looks pretty. ◇ Que
bebê ~! What a pretty baby! **2**
(homem) good-looking **3** (coisa,
animal) beautiful

bônus sm bonus

boquiaberto adj (surpreendido)
speechless

borboleta sf **1** (Zool) butterfly
[pl -ies] **2** (portão) turnstile

borbulha sf **1** (em líquido) bubble **2** (na pele) pimple: Estou
cheio de ~s no rosto. My face has
broken out.

borbulhar vi bubble

borda sf **1** edge: na ~ da mesa on
the edge of the table **2** (objeto
circular) rim **3** (mar, etc.) shore
4 (navio) side (of the ship)

bordado sm embroidery [U]

bordar vt (Costura) embroider

bordo sm ▸ **a ~ (de)** on board:
subir a ~ do avião board the
plane

borracha sf **1** (material) rubber

B

2 (*para apagar*) eraser, rubber (GB)

borrão *sm* **1** (*mancha*) smudge **2** (*rascunho*) rough draft

borrar *vt* (*sujar*) blot

borrifar *vt* sprinkle

bosque *sm* woods [*pl*]

bota *sf* boot

botânica *sf* botany

botão *sm* **1** (*roupa*) button: *Você está com um ~ aberto.* One of your buttons is undone. **2** (*controle*) knob **3** (*flor*) bud: *um ~ de rosa* a rosebud

botar *vt* **1** (*pôr*) put: *Quer ~ esse livro na prateleira?* Could you put this book on the shelf? **2** (*vestir*) put *sth* on● *vi* (*pôr ovos*) lay eggs ► **~ defeito** find fault (*with sb/sth*) **~ para fora 1** (*expulsar*) kick *sb/sth* out **2** **~** *emoção para fora* show your feelings

bote *sm* boat ► **~ de borracha** (rubber) dinghy [*pl* -ies] **~ salva-vidas** lifeboat

botijão *sm* cylinder

boxe *sm* boxing

boxeador *sm* boxer

boxear *vi* box

braçada *sf* **1** (*Natação*) stroke **2** (*quantidade*) armful

braçadeira *sf* **1** (*tira de pano*) armband **2** (*para cano, mangueira*) bracket

bracelete *sm* bracelet

braço *sm* arm: *Quebrei o ~.* I broke my arm. **2** (*rio*) branch **3** (*mar*) inlet ► **dar o ~ a torcer** give in **de ~ dado** arm in arm **ficar de ~s cruzados**: *Não fique aí de ~s cruzados! Faça algo.* Don't just stand there! Do something. **o ~ direito** (*fig*) right-hand man **ver-se a ~s com algo** come up against *sth*

braguilha *sf* fly

branco/a *adj* white: *pão/vinho ~* white bread/wine ● *sm-sf* white man/woman [*pl* men/women]: *os ~s* (the) whites ● *sm* (*cor*) white ► **~ como a neve** as white as snow **em ~**: *um cheque/uma página em ~* a blank check/page **passar em brancas nuvens** go unnoticed **ter um ~** go blank

brando *adj* **1** gentle: *um professor ~* a gentle teacher **2** (*indulgente*) soft

branquear *vt* whiten

brasa *sf* ember

brasão *sm* coat of arms

Brasil *sm* Brazil

brasileiro/a *adj, sm-sf* Brazilian: *os ~s* (the) Brazilians

bravo *adj* **1** (*corajoso*) brave **2** (*animal*) fierce **3** (*zangado*) angry **4** (*mar*) rough ● *interj* bravo

brecha *sf* gap

brega *adj* tacky

brejo *sm* marsh ► **ir para o ~** (*coloq*) go down the drain

breu *sm* pitch

breve *adj* **1** short: *uma estada ~* a short stay **2** (*ao falar*) brief ► **até ~** see you soon **em ~** soon

briga *sf* fight: *meter-se numa ~* get into a fight

brigada *sf* **1** (*Mil*) brigade **2** (*polícia*) squad: *a ~ anti-droga* the drug squad

brigão/ona *sm-sf* troublemaker

brigar *vi, vt* **1** (*discutir*) argue (*with sb*) (*about/over sth*) **2** (*zangar-se*) get into a fight (*with sb*) (*about/over sth*) **3** (*lutar*) fight (*with sb*) (*for/against/over sb/sth*)

brilhante *adj* **1** (*luz, cor*) bright **2** (*superfície*) shiny **3** (*fenomenal, perfeito*) brilliant: *Fiz um exame ~.* I did really well on the exam. ● *sm* diamond

brilhar *vi* **1** shine: *Os olhos dela brilhavam de alegria.* Her eyes shone with joy. ◊ *Olhe como brilha!* Look how shiny it is! **2** (*lâmpada*) give off light **3** (*distinguir-se*) do really well (*in sth*)

brilho *sm* **1** brightness **2** (*cabelo, sapatos*) shine **3** (*metal, olhos*) gleam **4** (*fogo*) blaze

brincadeira *sf* **1** (*piada*) joke: *fora de ~* joking apart ◊ *levar algo na ~* treat *sth* as a joke ◊ *Deixe de ~!* Stop messing around! **2** (*jogo*) game ► **~ de criança** child's play **~ de mau gosto** practical joke **de ~** for fun **nem por ~** no way

brincalhão/ona *adj* playful ● *sm-sf* joker

brincar *vi* **1** (*criança*) play **2** (*gracejar*) joke: *dizer algo brincando* say *sth* as a joke ► **~ com alguém** (*amolar*) pull *sb's* leg

brinco *sm* earring

brincos-de-princesa *sm* fuchsia

brindar *vt* **1** drink a toast (*to sb/sth*) **2** (*presentear*) give *sth* to *sb*

brinde *sm* **1** (*saudação*) toast: *fazer um ~* drink a toast **2** (*presente*) gift

brinquedo *sm* toy: *caminhão de ~* toy truck

brisa *sf* breeze

britânico/a *adj, sm-sf* British: *os ~s* the British

broa *sf* corn bread

broca *sf* drill

broche *sm* (*jóia*) pin, brooch (GB)

brochura *sf* **1** (*folheto*) brochure **2** (*livro*) paperback

brócolis *sm* broccoli [U]

bronca *sf* reprimand, telling-off (GB) ▶ **dar ~ em alguém** scold sb

bronco/a *adj* stupid ● *sm-sf* idiot

bronquite *sf* bronchitis [U]

bronze *sm* bronze

bronzeado *adj* tanned ● *sm* (*sun*)tan

bronzeador *sm* suntan lotion

bronzear *vt* (*pele*) tan ● **bronzear-se** *vp* get a suntan

brotar *vi* **1** (*plantas*) sprout **2** (*flores*) bud **3** (*líquido*) gush (out) (*from sth*)

broto *sm* **1** (*planta*) shoot **2** (*flor*) bud

bruços *sm* ▶ **de ~** (*posição*) face down

brusco *adj* **1** (*repentino*) sudden **2** (*pessoa*) abrupt

brutal *adj* brutal

bruto/a *adj* **1** (*força*) brute **2** (*pessoa*) heavy-handed **3** (*peso, rendimento*) gross **4** (*petróleo*) crude ● *sm-sf* (*pessoa violenta*) brute ▶ **em ~** in the raw: **ter um talento ainda em ~** have raw talent

bruxa *sf* **1** (*feiticeira*) witch **2** (*mulher feia*) hag

bruxaria *sf* witchcraft

bruxo *sm* **1** (*feiticeiro*) wizard **2** (*adivinho*) psychic [*adj*]

bucha *sf* plug: *tapar um buraco com uma ~* plug a hole

budismo *sm* Buddhism

budista *adj, smf* Buddhist

bueiro *sm* storm drain

búfalo *sm* buffalo [*pl* buffalo/ ~es]

bufar *vi* snort

bufê *sm* **1** (*refeição*) buffet **2** (*móvel*) buffet, sideboard (GB) **3** (*serviço*) catering service

bujão *sm* (*gás*) (gas) cylinder

buldogue *sm* bulldog

bule *sm* **1** (*chá*) teapot **2** (*café*) coffee pot

buquê *sm* bunch

buraco *sm* **1** hole: *fazer um ~* make a hole **2** (*em estrada*) pothole ▶ **~ da fechadura** keyhole

burla *sf* fraud

burlar *vt* **1** (*enganar*) evade: *~ a justiça/os impostos* evade justice/taxes **2** (*fraudar*) swindle sb (*out of sth*) **3** (*vigilância*) get past sb/sth

burocracia *sf* **1** bureaucracy **2** (*papelada excessiva*) red tape

burocrático *adj* bureaucratic

burrada *sf* dumb thing: *Foi uma ~ o que você fez.* That was a really dumb thing to do.

burro/a *adj* **1** (*estúpido*) dumb, thick (GB): *~ como uma porta* as thick as two short planks ● *sm-sf* **1** (*animal*) donkey **2** (*pessoa*) idiot: *o ~ do meu tio* my idiot of an uncle ▶ **~ de carga** (*pessoa*) gofer

busca *sf* search (*for sb/sth*): *Realizaram uma ~ nos bosques.* They searched the woods. ▶ **em ~ de** in search of sb/sth

buscar *vt* **1** (*recolher alguém*) (a) (*de carro*) pick sb up (b) (*a pé*) meet **2** (*procurar*) look for sb/ sth ▶ **ir/vir ~ alguém/algo**: *Fui ~ o médico.* I went to get the doctor. ◇ **ir ~ pão** go and get some bread ▶ **mandar ~ alguém/algo** send for sb/sth

bússola *sf* compass

busto *sm* **1** bust **2** (*escultura*) torso [*pl* ~s]

butique *sf* boutique

buzina *sf* horn: *tocar a ~* blow your horn

buzinada *sf* honking, hooting (GB)

buzinar *vi* honk, hoot (GB) (*at sb*)

byte *sm* (*Informát*) byte

C c

cá *adv*: *Venha cá.* Come here. ◇ *Chegue-o mais para cá.* Bring it closer. ▶ **cá entre nós** between you and me

cabana *sf* shack

cabeça *sf* **1** head: *estar com a ~ girando/num turbilhão* feel dizzy/be confused ◇ *~ de alho* head of garlic **2** (*juízo*) sense ▶ **de ~ 1** (*mergulho*) headlong: *atirar-se de ~* dive headlong **2** (*mentalmente*) *Não sou capaz de fazer uma conta de ~.* I can't add in my head. **3** (*de memória*) from memory **de ~ para baixo** upside down **estar/andar com a ~ nas nuvens/na lua** have your head in the clouds ▶ **de cabeça** persuade sb *to do sth* **meter/enfiar algo na ~** take it into your head *to do sth* **não estar bom da ~** not to be right in the head **por ~** a/per head **ter ~** be very bright

cabeçada sf **1** (golpe) head butt **2** (futebol) header ▶ **dar uma ~ 1** (no teto, etc.) bang your head (on sth) **2** (na bola) head the ball

cabeça-de-casal sm head of the household

cabeça-de-vento smf scatterbrain

cabeça-dura adj, smf stubborn [adj]

cabeçalho sm **1** (jornal) masthead **2** (página, documento) heading

cabecear vi **1** (de sono) nod **2** (futebol): ~ para a rede head the ball into the net

cabeceira sf **1** head: à ~ da mesa at the head of the table **2** (cama) headboard

cabeçudo adj (teimoso) pigheaded

cabeleira sf **1** (postiça) wig **2** (verdadeira) head of hair

cabeleireiro/a sm-sf **1** (pessoa) hairstylist, hairdresser (GB) **2** (local) hairdresser's

cabelo sm hair: usar o ~ solto wear your hair loose ◊ ter o ~ encaracolado/liso have curly/straight hair ◊ Os meus ~s se arrepiaram. My hair stood on end. ▶ estar pelos ~s be fed up por um fio de ~ by the skin of your teeth: Eles se livraram de um acidente por um fio de ~. They nearly had an accident.

caber vi **1** ~ (em) fit (in/into sth): Caibo? Is there room for me? **2** (passar) go through sth: O piano não cabia na porta. The piano wouldn't go through the door. **3** ~ a be up to sb (to do sth): Cabe a você fazer o jantar. It's up to you to make dinner. **4** (vir a propósito) be appropriate (to do sth): Não cabe aqui fazer comentários. This isn't the time nor the place to comment. ▶ não ~ em si: não ~ em si de felicidade be bursting with happiness

cabide sm **1** (armário) (clothes) hanger **2** (de pé) coat stand **3** (de parede) coat hook

cabimento sm suitability ▶ ter/não ter ~ be appropriate/to be out of the question

cabine sf **1** (avião) cockpit **2** (barco) cabin **3** (caminhão) cab ▶ ~ de provas fitting room, dressing room ~ eleitoral polling booth ~ (telefônica/de telefone) telephone booth, telephone box (GB)

cabisbaixo adj (abatido) downcast

cabo sm **1** cable **2** (TV, rádio etc.) cord, lead (GB) **3** (utensílio, vassoura, esfregão, etc.) handle **4** (Náut) rope **5** (Geog) cape **6** (Mil) corporal ▶ ao ~ de after dar ~ de **1** (estragar) ruin sth **2** (acabar) finish sth (up) de ~ a rabo from beginning to end levar a ~ carry sth out

cabra sf nanny-goat

cabra-cega sf (jogo) blind man's bluff

cabrito/a sm-sf kid

caça sf poo

caça¹ sf **1** (caçada) hunting: ir à ~ go hunting **2** (com espingarda) shooting **3** (animais) game ▶ andar/ir à ~ de be after sb/sth ~ às bruxas witch-hunt

caça² sm (avião) fighter (plane)

caçada sf **1** hunt: uma ~ ao elefante an elephant hunt **2** (com espingarda) shoot

caçador/a sm-sf hunter

caça-minas sm minesweeper

caça-níqueis sm slot machine, fruit machine (GB)

caçar vt **1** hunt **2** (com espingarda) shoot **3** (capturar) catch ● vi **1** hunt **2** (com espingarda) shoot

cacarejar vi cackle

caçarola sf casserole

cacatua sf cockatoo [pl ~s]

cacau sm **1** (planta) cacao **2** (em pó) cocoa

cacetada sf whack

cacete sm stick

cachaça sf sugar cane liquor

cachecol sm scarf [pl scarves]

cachimbo sm pipe: fumar ~ smoke a pipe

cacho sm **1** (frutas) bunch **2** (cabelo) curl

cachoeira sf waterfall

cachorrinho/a sm-sf puppy [pl -ies]

cachorro/a sm-sf **1** (animal) dog → cão **2** (pessoa) scoundrel

cachorro-quente sm hot dog

caco sm **1** (louça, vidro) piece **2** (pessoa) wreck

cacto sm cactus [pl ~es/cacti]

caçula adj, smf youngest (child)

cada adj **1** each: Deram um presente a ~ criança. They gave each child a present. → EVERY **2** (expressões numéricas ou de tempo) every: ~ vez every time ◊ ~ dez dias every ten days ◊ um livro para ~ dois alunos one book between two students **3** (com valor exclamativo): Você diz ~ coisa! The things you come out with! ▶ ~ **coisa a seu tempo** all in good time ~ **doido com a sua mania** each to his own ~ **dois dias, duas semanas, etc.** every other day, week, etc. ~ **qual** everybody ~ **um** each (one): ~ *um custa dez dólares.* Each one costs ten dollars. ◇ *Deram um saco a ~ um de nós.* They gave each of us/us each a bag. ~ **vez mais** more and more: *Você está ~ vez mais bonita.* You're looking prettier and prettier. ~ **vez melhor/pior** better and better/worse and worse ~ **vez menos** less and less: *Vemo-nos ~ vez menos.* We see less and less of each other. ◇ ~ **vez há menos alunos.** There are fewer and fewer students. ~ **vez que...** whenever...

cadarço sm shoelace

cadastrar-se vp register: ~ **na Receita Federal** register with the Internal Revenue Service

cadastro sm (*bancário*) records [pl] ▶ ~ **eleitoral** electoral register

cadáver sm corpse, body [pl -ies] (*mais coloq*)

cadeado sm padlock: *fechado a* ~ padlocked

cadeia sf **1** chain **2** (*prisão*) prison **3** (*montanhas*) (mountain) range

cadeira sf **1** (*móvel*) chair: ~ **de balanço/braços/rodas** rocking chair/armchair/wheelchair **2** (*disciplina*) specialty [pl -ies], subject (*GB*)

cadela sf bitch → **CÃO**

caderneta sf **1** (*caderno*) notebook **2** (*investimento*) passbook **3** (*escolar*) report card ▶ ~ **de poupança** savings account

caderno sm notebook

caducar vi **1** (*documento, prazo*) expire **2** (*pessoa*) become senile

cafajeste sm womanizer

café sm **1** coffee: *Você quer um* ~? Would you like a cup of coffee? ◇ ~ (*preto*) **com leite/espresso** black coffee/coffee with milk/espresso [pl ~s] (*estabelecimento*) cafe ▶ ~ (**da**) **manhã**): *tomar* ~ have breakfast

cafeeiro adj coffee: *a indústria cafeeira* the coffee industry ● sm coffee plant

cafeína sf caffeine: *sem* ~ caffeine-free

cafeteira sf coffee pot ▶ ~ **elétrica** coffee maker

cafona adj tacky

cágado sm turtle

caiar vt whitewash

cãibra sf cramp: ~ **no estômago** stomach cramps

caído adj ▶ ~ **do céu**: *um presente* ~ *do céu* a real godsend

cair vi **1** fall: *Cuidado para não* ~. Careful you don't fall. **2** (*dente, cabelo*) fall out **3** (*soltar-se*) come off **4** (*responsabilidade, suspeita*) fall on sb ▶ ~ **ao** ~ **da tarde/noite** at dusk/at nightfall ~ **bem/mal 1** (*roupa*) look good/bad on sb **2** (*alimento*) agree/not agree with sb **3** (*fazer um bom efeito*) make a good/bad impression: *O discurso caiu muito bem.* The speech went down very well. **NOTA** Para outras expressões com **cair**, ver o substantivo, adjetivo, etc., p. ex. **cair na farra** em **FARRA**.

cais sm wharf [pl wharves]

caixa¹ sf **1** box: *uma* ~ **de papelão** a cardboard box ◇ *uma* ~ **de bombons** a box of chocolates **2** (*ovos*) carton **3** (*vinho*) case ▶ ~ **de descarga** cistern ~ **de ferramentas** toolbox ~ **de isopor** (*com gelo*) cooler, coolbox (*GB*) ~ **de mudanças/marchas** gearshift, gearbox (*GB*) ~ **de primeiros socorros** first-aid kit ~ **do correio** mailbox

caixa² sf **1** (*supermercado*) checkout **2** (*outras lojas*) cash desk **3** (*banco*) teller's window ● smf (*pessoa*) cashier ▶ ~ **automático** ATM, cash machine (*GB*) ~ **econômica** savings bank ~ **registradora** cash register **fazer a** ~ cash up

caixão sm casket, coffin (*GB*)

caixa-preta sf black box

caixote sm **1** (*papelão*) cardboard box **2** (*madeira*) crate

caju sm cashew

cal sf lime

calabouço sm dungeon

calado adj **1** quiet: *O seu irmão está muito* ~ *hoje.* Your brother is very quiet today. **2** (*em completo silêncio*) silent

calafrio sm shiver ▶ **dar** ~**s** send shivers down your spine **sentir/estar com** ~ shiver

calamidade sf calamity [pl -ies]

calar vt (*pessoa*) get sb to be quiet ● **calar-se** vp **1** (*não falar*) say nothing **2** (*deixar de falar ou fazer barulho*) be quiet, shut up (*coloq*): *Cale-se!* Be quiet! **3** (*não revelar*) keep quiet about sth ▶ ~ **a boca** shut up: *Faça essas crianças calarem a boca!* Tell those children to shut up!

calça sf (**calças**) pants, trousers

(GB): *a ~ do pijama* pajama pants ◇ *usar uma ~ velha* wear old pants ◇ *uma ~ preta* a pair of black pants → PAIR

calçada *sf* **1** (*de café*): *Vamos sentar na ~.* Let's sit outside. ◇ *Já puseram as mesas na ~?* Did they put the tables out yet? **2** (*para pedestres*) sidewalk, pavement (GB)

calçado *sm* footwear

calcanhar *sm* (*pé, sapato*) heel

calção *sm* shorts ▶ **~ de banho** swimming trunks [*pl*]: *um ~ de banho* a pair of swimming trunks

calcar *vt* **1** (*pisar*) stand on sb's foot **2** (*comprimir*) stick sth (to sth)

calçar *vt* **1** (*sapato*) take: *Que número você calça?* What size (shoe) do you take? **2** (*pessoa*) put sb's shoes on ● **calçar-se** *vp* put your shoes on

calcinha *sf* (**calcinhas**) panties, knickers (GB): *uma ~* a pair of panties

cálcio *sm* calcium

calço *sm* wedge

calculadora *sf* calculator

calcular *vt* **1** work sth out, calculate (*mais fml*): *Calcule quanto necessitamos.* Work out how much we need. **2** (*supor*) reckon

cálculo *sm* calculation: *fazer um ~ aproximado* make a rough estimate

calda *sf* syrup

caldeira *sf* boiler

caldo *sm* **1** (*para cozinhar*) stock **2** (*sopa*) broth

calefação *sf* heating: *~ central* central heating

calendário *sm* calendar

calha *sf* (*cano*) gutter

calhambeque *sm* (*veículo*) jalopy [*pl* -ies]

calhar *vi* (*acontecer*) happen: *Calhou eu estar em casa senão...* It's a good job I happened to be at home, otherwise... ▶ **vir a ~** come in handy

calibre *sm* caliber

cálice *sm* **1** (*copo*) wine glass **2** (*sagrado*) chalice

caligrafia *sf* **1** (*letra*) handwriting **2** (*arte*) calligraphy

calista *smf* podiatrist, chiropodist (GB)

calma *sf* calm: *manter a ~* keep calm ◇ *Leve as coisas com ~.* Take it easy. ● *interj* calm down

calmante *sm* tranquilizer

calmo *adj* calm: *uma pessoa calma* a calm person ◇ *O mar*

está ~. The sea is calm. **2** (*relaxado*) laid-back

calo *sm* **1** (*dedo do pé*) corn **2** (*mão, planta do pé*) callus

calor *sm* heat ▶ **estar com ~** (*pessoa*) be/feel hot   **estar/fazer ~** (*tempo*) be hot: *Está muito ~.* It's very hot.

caloria *sf* calorie: *uma dieta baixa em ~s* a low-calorie diet

caloroso *adj* warm

calote *sm* swindle ▶ **dar/passar (o) ~** swindle

calouro ~a *sm-sf* freshman [*pl* -men], fresher (GB)

calvo *adj* bald: *ficar ~* go bald

cama *sf* bed: *ir para a ~* go to bed ◇ *enfiar-se/meter-se na ~* get into bed ◇ *sair da ~* get out of bed ◇ *~ de casal/solteiro* double/single bed

camada *sf* **1** layer: *a ~ de ozônio* the ozone layer **2** (*tinta, verniz*) coat

camaleão *sm* chameleon

câmara *sf* **1** (*Cinema, Fot*) camera **2** chamber: *música de ~* chamber music ▶ **~ de vídeo** camcorder   **~ municipal 1** (*organismo*) council **2** (*edifício*) city hall   **em ~ lenta** in slow motion

camarada *smf* **1** (*Pol*) comrade **2** (*colega*) buddy [*pl* -ies]

camaradagem *sf* comradeship

câmara-de-ar *sf* inner tube

camarão *sm* shrimp, prawn (GB)

camarim *sm* dressing-room

camarote *sm* **1** (*navio*) cabin **2** (*teatro*) box

cambalear *vi* reel

cambalhota *sf* **1** (*pessoa*): *dar uma ~* do a somersault **2** (*veículo*): *O carro deu três ~s.* The car turned over three times.

câmbio *sm* (*Fin*) exchange rate

camélia *sf* camellia

camelo *sm* camel

camelô *sm* street peddler

caminhada *sf* **1** walk **2** (*por montanha, deserto, etc.*) trek

caminhão *sm* truck, lorry [*pl* -ies] (GB) ▶ **~ de mudanças** moving van, removal van (GB)   **~ do lixo** garbage truck, dustcart (GB)

caminhar *vi* walk ● *vt* cover: *~ 50 km* cover 50 km

caminho *sm* **1** way: *Não me lembro do ~.* I can't remember the way. ◇ *Sai do ~!* Get out of the way! ◇ *A gente decide pelo ~.* We'll decide as we go along. **2** (*estrada não asfaltada*) track **3**

(rumo) path *(to sth)*: *o ~ da fama* the path to fame ► **a ~ de…** on the/your way to… **no ~ certo/errado** on the right/wrong track **pôr-se a ~** set off

caminhoneiro/a *sm-sf* truck driver, lorry driver *(GB)*

caminhonete *sf* pickup truck

camisa *sf* shirt

camiseta *sf* **1** *(camisa)* T-shirt **2** *(roupa de baixo)* undershirt, vest *(GB)*

camisola *sf* nightgown

camomila *sf* camomile: *um chá de ~* a cup of camomile tea

campainha *sf* bell: *tocar a ~* ring the bell

campanário *sm* belfry [pl -ies]

campanha *sf* campaign

campeão/eã *sm-sf* champion: *o ~ do mundo* the world champion

campeonato *sm* championship(s): *o ~ Mundial de Atletismo* the World Athletics Championships

camping *sm* camping

campo *sm* **1** *(natureza)* country: *viver no ~* live in the country **2** *(terra de cultivo)* field: *~s de cevada* barley fields **3** *(paisagem)* countryside **4** *(âmbito, Fís, Informát)* field **5** *(Esporte)* **(a)** *(futebol, rúgbi)* field, pitch *(GB)*: *entrar em ~* come out onto the field **(b)** *(estádio)* ground **6** *(acampamento)* camp: ► *~ de concentração/prisioneiros* concentration/prison camp ► *~ de batalha* battlefield *~ de golfe* golf course *no ~ do adversário* *(Esporte)* away: *jogar no ~ do adversário* play away

camponês/esa *sm-sf* peasant

campus *sm* *(universitário)* campus

camuflagem *sf* camouflage

camuflar *vt* camouflage

camundongo *sm* mouse [pl mice]

camurça *sf* *(pele)* suede

cana *sf* cane

Canadá *sm* Canada

cana-de-açúcar *sf* sugar cane

canadense *adj, smf* Canadian

canal *sm* **1** *(estreito marítimo natural, TV)* channel **2** *(estreito marítimo artificial, irrigação)* canal **3** *(Med)* duct

canalização *sf* *(canos)* plumbing

canário *sm* *(pássaro)* canary [pl -ies]

canção *sf* song ► **~ de ninar** lullaby [pl -ies]

cancelamento *sm* cancellation

cancelar *vt* cancel

câncer *sm* **1** cancer [U] **2** **(Câncer)** *(Astrol)* Cancer

candidatar-se *vp* **1** *(em eleições)* run *(for sth)*: *~ a senador* run for the senate **2** *(emprego, bolsa)* apply *for sth*

candidato/a *sm-sf* **1** candidate *(for sth)* **2** *(emprego, bolsa, curso)* applicant *(for sth)*

candidatura *sf* **1** *(cargo)* candidacy *(for sth)*: *apresentar a ~ ao senado* run for the senate **2** *(emprego, curso)* application *(for sth)*: *uma ~ a um emprego* a job application

caneca *sf* mug

canela *sf* **1** *(especiaria)* cinnamon **2** *(perna)* shin

caneta *sf* pen ► **~ esferográfica/hidrográfica** ballpoint/felt-tip (pen) **~ marca-texto** highlighter

caneta-tinteiro *sf* fountain pen

canguru *sm* kangaroo [pl ~s]

canhão *sm* *(artilharia)* cannon

canhoto *adj* left-handed

canibal *smf* cannibal

caniço *sm* *(junco)* reed

canil *sm* **1** *(para um cão)* kennel **2** *(para muitos cães)* kennels

canino *adj* canine ● *sm* *(dente)* canine (tooth)

canivete *sm* pocket-knife, penknife *(GB)* [pl -knives]

canja *sf* **1** *(caldo)* chicken soup/broth **2** *(coisa fácil)*: *O exame foi ~.* The exam was a breeze.

cano *sm* **1** pipe: *Rebentou um ~.* A pipe burst. **2** *(espingarda)* barrel: *uma espingarda de dois ~s* a double-barrelled shotgun ► **~ de descarga** exhaust **~ de esgoto** drainpipe

canoa *sf* canoe

canoagem *sf* canoeing: *praticar ~* go canoeing

cansaço *sm* tiredness

cansado *adj* **1** *(fatigado)* tired *(from doing)* sth **2** *(farto)* sick *of sb/(doing) sth*

cansar *vt* **1** *(fatigar)* tire *sb/sth* (out) **2** *(aborrecer, fartar)*: *Cansa-me ter que repetir as coisas.* I'm sick of having to repeat things. ● *vi*: *Trabalhar com crianças cansa muito.* Working with children is very tiring. ● **cansar-se** *vp* get tired *(of sb/(doing) sth)*

cansativo *adj* **1** tiring **2** *(pessoa)* tiresome

cantada *sf* ► **dar uma ~ em alguém** make a pass at sb

cantar vt **1** (*seduzir*) sing **2** (*seduzir*) make a pass at sb • vi **1** sing **2** (*cigarra, pássaro pequeno*) chirp **3** (*galo*) crow ► **~ vitória antes do tempo** count your chickens before they're hatched

cântaro sm pitcher

cantarolar vt, vi hum

canteiro sm (*flores*) flowerbed

cântico sm chant ► **~ de Natal** Christmas carol

cantiga sf ballad

cantil sm **1** (*para água*) canteen **2** (*para bebidas alcoólicas*) (hip) flask

cantina sf (*escola, fábrica*) canteen

canto¹ sm **1** (*arte*) singing **2** (*canção, poema*) song

canto² sm corner

cantor/a sm-sf singer

canudo sm (*bebidas*) (drinking) straw

cão sm dog NOTA Falando só da fêmea, diz-se **bitch**. Os cachorrinhos são **puppies**. ► **~ de guarda** guard dog **~ que ladra não morde** his/her bark is worse than his/her bite **de ~** lousy: *um dia de ~* a lousy day **ser como ~ e gato** fight like cats and dogs

caolho adj cross-eyed

caos sm chaos: *Minha vida está um ~*. My life is in chaos.

capa sf **1** cover **2** (*disco*) sleeve **3** (*peça de vestuário*) (**a**) (*comprida*) cloak (**b**) (*curta*) cape ► **~ de chuva** raincoat

capacete sm helmet: *usar ~* wear a helmet

capacho sm (*tapete*) doormat

capacidade sf **1** capacity (*for sth*) **2** (*aptidão*) ability (*to do sth*)

capataz sm foreman [*pl* -men]

capaz adj capable (*of (doing) sth*) ► **ser ~ de 1** (*poder*) be able to do sth: *Não sou/fui ~ de fazer isso*. I just can't/couldn't do it. **2** (*talvez*) be likely to do sth: *É ~ que eu chegue hoje*. I might arrive today. ◊ *É ~ de chover*. It might rain.

capela sf chapel

capelão sm chaplain

capeta sm **1** (*diabo*) devil **2** (*criança*) brat

capital sf capital • sm (*Fin*) capital

capitalismo sm capitalism

capitalista adj, smf capitalist

capitão/ã sm-sf, sm-sf captain

capitular vi surrender

capítulo sm **1** (*livro*) chapter **2** (*TV, rádio*) episode

capô sm (*carro*) hood, bonnet (GB)

capotar vi (*carro*) overturn: *O carro capotou três vezes*. The car turned over three times.

capricho sm **1** (*desejo*) whim **2** (*esmero*) care: *fazer algo com muito ~* take great care over sth **3** (*teimosia*) obstancy ► **fazer os ~s de alguém** give in to sb's whims

caprichoso adj meticulous

Capricórnio sm Capricorn

cápsula sf capsule

captar vt **1** (*atenção*) attract **2** (*sinal, onda*) pick sth up **3** (*compreender*) grasp

captura sf **1** (*fugitivo*) capture **2** (*armas, drogas*) seizure

capturar vt **1** (*fugitivo*) capture **2** (*armas, drogas*) seize

capuz sm hood

cáqui adj, sm khaki

cara sf **1** (*rosto*) face: *~ a ~* face to face **2** (*aspecto*) look **3** (*expressão*) expression • sm (*indivíduo*) guy ► **~ cair de ~ no chão** fall flat on your face **~ ou coroa** heads or tails **dar as ~s** put in an appearance **dar de ~ com alguém/algo** come face to face with sb/sth **dar na ~ de alguém** slap sb **de ~** straight (away) **de ~ cheia** (*bêbado*) drunk **estar com uma ~ boa** (*pessoa*) look well **estar na ~** be obvious **ir com a ~ de alguém** (*gostar*) like sb: *Não vou com a ~ dele*. I can't stand him. **ser ~ de um, focinho do outro** be like two peas in a pod **ter ~ de garoto** look very young

caracol sm **1** (*animal*) snail **2** (*cabelo*) curl

característico/a adj, sf characteristic

caracterizar vt **1** (*distinguir*) characterize **2** (*Cinema, Teat*) dress sb up as sb/sth • **caracterizar-se** vp dress up as sb/sth

cara-de-pau smf (*pessoa*) wise guy ► **que ~** what a nerve

caramba interj wow ► **pra ~**: *Choveu pra ~*. It rained a lot. ◊ *divertir-se pra ~* have a terrific time ◊ *Tive de esperar pra ~*. I had to wait for hours.

caramelo sm **1** (*bala*) candy **2** (*açúcar queimado*) caramel

caranguejo sm crab

caratê sm karate: *fazer ~* do karate

caráter sm **1** character **2** (*índole*)

nature ▶ **ter bom/mau** ~ be good-natured/ill-natured **ter muito/pouco** ~ be strong-minded/weak-minded

carboidrato *sm* carbohydrate

carbonizado *adj* charred

carbono *sm* carbon

carcereiro/a *sm-sf* jailer

cardápio *sm* menu

cardeal *sm (Relig)* cardinal

cardíaco *adj: parada cardíaca* cardiac arrest

cardinal *adj* cardinal

cardume *sm (peixes)* shoal

careca *adj* bald: *ficar* ~ go bald ● *sf* bald patch

carecer *vt* **1** *(ter falta)* lack: *Carecemos de remédios.* We lack medicines. **2** *(precisar)* need

careta *sf* grimace ▶ **fazer** ~**(s)** make/pull a face *(at sb)*, grimace *(fml)*

carga *sf* **1** *(ação)* loading **2** *(peso)* load **3** *(mercadorias)* **(a)** *(avião, barco)* cargo [*pl* ~s/~es] **(b)** *(caminhão)* load **(c)** *(trem)* freight **4** *(explosivo, munição, Elet)* charge **5** *(obrigação)* burden **6** *(caneta)* refill ▶ ~ **horária** workload **por que cargas-d'água...?** why the hell...?

cargo *sm* post: *um* ~ *importante* an important post

cariar *vi (dente)* decay

caricatura *sf* **1** caricature: *fazer uma* ~ draw a caricature **2** *(em jornal)* cartoon

caricaturista *smf* **1** caricaturist **2** *(para jornal)* cartoonist

carícia *sf* caress: *fazer* ~s caress

caridade *sf* charity: *uma instituição de* ~ a charity

caridoso *adj* charitable *(to/towards sb)*

cárie *sf* **1** *(doença)* tooth decay [*U*] **2** *(buraco)* cavity [*pl* -ies]

carimbar *vt* stamp

carimbo *sm* **1** stamp **2** *(em carta)* postmark

carinho *sm* **1** *(afeto)* affection **2** *(delicadeza)* care: *tratar algo com muito* ~ take great care of sth ▶ **com** ~ *(em cartas)* with love **ter** ~ **por alguém/algo** be fond of sb/sth

carinhoso *adj* **1** affectionate *(towards sb/sth)* **2** *(abraço)* warm **3** *(pai, marido, etc.)* loving

carioca *adj, smf* (person from) Rio de Janeiro: *os* ~s the people of Rio de Janeiro

carnal *adj (sensual)* carnal

carnaval *sm* carnival

carne *sf* **1** *(Anat, Relig, fruta)*

flesh **2** *(alimento)* meat: *Gosto da* ~ *bem passada.* I like my meat well done. ◇ ~*s frias* cold cuts NOTA Existem palavras diferentes para os animais e a carne que deles se obtém: do *porco* (**pig**) obtém-se **pork**, da *vaca* (**cow**), **beef**, da *vitela* (**calf**), **veal**. Mutton é a carne de *ovelha* (**sheep**), e do *cordeiro* (**lamb**) obtém-se a carne de **lamb**. ▶ ~ **moída** ground beef, mince (GB) **de** ~ **e osso** only human **em** ~ **e osso** in the flesh **em** ~ **viva**: *Você está com o joelho em* ~ *viva.* Your knee is red and raw.

carneiro *sm* **1** *(animal)* ram **2** *(carne)* mutton

carnificina *sf* massacre

carnívoro *adj* carnivorous

caro¹ *adj* expensive ● *adv: pagar muito* ~ pay a lot for sth ▶ **custar/pagar** ~: *Eles pagarão* ~ *pelo erro.* Their mistake will cost them dearly.

caro² *adj (em cartas)* dear

caroço *sm* **1** *(Med)* lump: *um* ~ *na minha mão* a lump on my hand **2** *(fruto)* pit, stone (GB)

carona *sf* ride, lift (GB) ▶ **apanhar/pedir** ~ hitch a ride *(with sb)* **ir de** ~ hitchhike

carpa *sf* carp [*pl* carp]

carpete *sm* carpet

carpintaria *sf* carpentry

carpinteiro *sm* carpenter

carranca *sf* frown

carrapato *sm* tick

carregado *adj* **1** loaded *(with sth)*: *uma arma carregada* a loaded gun ◇ *Eles vinham* ~s *de malas.* They were loaded down with suitcases. **2** *(responsabilidades)* weighed down *with sth* **3** *(atmosfera)* stuffy

carregador *sm* **1** *(Elet)* charger: ~ *de pilhas* battery charger **2** *(profissão)* porter

carregamento *sm* **1** *(ação)* loading: *O* ~ *do navio levou vários dias.* It took several days to load the ship. **2** *(mercadorias)* **(a)** *(avião, navio)* cargo [*pl* ~s/~es] **(b)** *(caminhão)* load

carregar *vt* **1 (a)** load: ~ *uma arma/um caminhão* load a weapon/a truck **(b)** *(caneta, isqueiro)* fill **(c)** *(pilha, bateria)* charge **2 (a)** *(levar)* carry **(b)** *(responsabilidade)* shoulder

carreira *sf* **1** *(pequena corrida)* run: *dar uma* ~ go running **2** *(profissão)* career ▶ **sair às** ~s dash off

carretel *sm (bobina)* reel

carrinho sm (compras), cart, trolley (GB): ~ **de supermercado** shopping cart ▶ ~ **de bebê** baby carriage, pram (GB) ~ **de criança** stroller, pushchair (GB)

carro sm car: ~ **esporte/de corrida** sports car/racecar ◇ ~ **alugado** rental car/hire car (GB): **ir de ~** go by car ▶ ~ **alegórico** float ~ **de bombeiros** fire engine ~ **fúnebre** hearse

carro-bomba sm car bomb

carroça sf cart

carroceria sf bodywork [U]

carro-leito sm sleeping car

carro-pipa sm tanker

carrossel sm merry-go-round

carruagem sf carriage

carta sf 1 (missiva) letter: **pór uma ~ no correio** mail a letter ◇ ~ **registrada/urgente** certified/express letter ◇ **Alguma ~ para mim?** Is there any mail for me? 2 (baralho) (playing) card: **jogar ~s** play cards ▶ BARALHO 3 (navegação) chart 4 (documento) charter ▶ ~ **de apresentação** cover letter

cartão sm 1 card: ~ **de crédito/embarque/Natal** credit/boarding/Christmas card 2 (material) cardboard ▶ ~ **de crédito** credit card

cartaz sm poster: **afixar um ~** put up a poster ▶ ~ **publicitário** billboard, hoarding (GB) **em ~** (Cine, Teat) on: **O que está em ~?** What's on?

carteira sf 1 (porta-notas) wallet 2 (escrivaninha) desk 3 (de motorista) driver's license, driving licence (GB) **tirar a ~** pass your driving test

carteiro sm mailman, postman (GB) [pl -men]

cartola sf top hat

cartolina sf card

cartório sm (registro civil) registry office (GB)

cartucho sm cartridge

cartunista smf cartoonist

carvalho sm oak (tree)

carvão sm coal ▶ ~ **vegetal/de lenha** charcoal

casa sf 1 (residência) (a) house: ~ **de campo** country house (b) (apartamento) apartment, flat (GB) (c) (prédio) apartment building, block of flats (GB) 2 (lar) home: **Não há nada como a nossa ~.** There's no place like home. 3 (empresa) company [pl -ies] 4 (xadrez, damas) square 5 (botão) buttonhole ▶ ~ **da Moeda** mint ~ **de saúde** hospital ~ **lotérica** lottery agency [pl -ies] **em ~** at home NOTA No inglês americano, com os verbos **be** e **stay** costuma-se dizer **home** sem a preposição **at**: **Fiquei em ~.** I stayed home. ◇ **A sua mãe está em ~?** Is your mother home? **ir para a ~ de** go to sb's (house) **ir para ~** go home **na ~ de at** sb's (house) NOTA Assim como se omite "casa", costuma-se omitir "house" do inglês: **Eu estava na Ana.** I was at Ana's. **passar pela ~ de alguém** drop in on sb **ser de ~** be like one of the family

casaco sm 1 (sobretudo) coat 2 (de malha) cardigan

casado/a adj married to sb ● sm-sf married man/woman

casal sm 1 couple 2 (animais) pair

casamento sm 1 (instituição) marriage 2 (cerimônia) wedding: **aniversário de ~** wedding anniversary NOTA **Wedding** refere-se à cerimônia, enquanto **marriage** ao matrimônio como instituição. O casamento na igreja é um **church wedding**; no registro civil, uma **civil ceremony**. A noiva (**bride**) é acompanhada por **damas de honra** (**bridesmaids**) e o noivo (**groom**) pelo **best man** (normalmente o seu melhor amigo). Depois da cerimônia realiza-se a recepção (**reception**).

casar(-se) vi, vp 1 get married: ~ **na igreja/no civil** get married in a church/a civil ceremony 2 ~ **com** marry sb: **Nunca me casarei com você.** I'll never marry you. → CASAMENTO

casca sf 1 (ovo, noz) shell 2 (limão, laranja) peel [U] 3 (banana) skin 4 (pão) crust 5 (árvore) bark 6 (cereal) husk 7 (queijo) rind

cascalho sm (pedra britada) gravel

cascata sf waterfall

cascavel sf rattlesnake

casco sm 1 (animal) hoof [pl ~s/hooves] 2 (barco) hull 3 (garrafa vazia) empty bottle

caseiro/a adj homemade: **pão ~** homemade bread 2 (pessoa) home-loving: **ser muito ~** love being at home ● sm-sf (empregado) housekeeper

caso sm 1 case: **em qualquer ~/em todo o ~** in any case 2 (aventura amorosa) (love) affair, fling (coloq) ● conj if: ~ **ele lhe pergunte...** If he asks you...

▶ ~ **contrário** otherwise **em ~ de** in the event of sth **fazer ~ de** take notice of sth/sth **no ~ de...** if... **no melhor/pior dos ~s** at best/worst **ser um ~ à parte** be different **vir/não vir ao ~** be relevant/irrelevant

caspa sf dandruff

casquinha sf (*sorvete*) (ice cream) cone

cassar vt take sth away (*from sb/ sth*)

cassetete sm (*de polícia*) night-stick, truncheon (GB)

cassino sm casino [*pl* ~s]

casta sf caste

castanha sf (*fruto*) chestnut ▶ ~ **de caju** cashew nut

castanha-do-pará sf Brazil nut

castanho, -a sm, adj brown: **olhos** ~s brown eyes

castanholas sf castanets

castelo sm castle ▶ ~ **de areia** sandcastle

castiçal sm candlestick

castigar vt punish sb (*for sth*)

castigo sm punishment

casto adj chaste

castor sm beaver

castrar vt 1 castrate 2 (*animal doméstico*) neuter 3 (*cavalo*) geld

casual adj chance: **um encontro ~** a chance meeting

casualidade sf chance

casulo sm (*inseto*) cocoon

catalisador sm 1 (*Quím*) catalyst 2 (*carro*) catalytic converter

catálogo sm catalog

catapora sf chickenpox [U]

catarata sf 1 (*cascata*) waterfall 2 (*Med*) cataract

catarro sm catarrh

catástrofe sf catastrophe

cata-vento sm 1 (*no telhado*) weathervane 2 (*moinho*) windmill

catecismo sm catechism

catedral sf cathedral

catedrático, -a sm-sf university lecturer

categoria sf 1 (*classe*) category [*pl* -ies] 2 (*nível*) level 3 (*social, profissional*) status ▶ **de primeira, segunda, etc. ~** first-rate, second-rate, etc.

categórico adj categorical

cativante adj captivating

cativar vt (*atrair*) captivate

cativeiro sm captivity

cativo, -a adj, sm-sf captive

catolicismo sm Catholicism

católico, -a adj, sm-sf Catholic: **ser ~** be a Catholic

catorze num, sm Ver QUATORZE

caução sf (*Jur*) bail [U]

cauda sf 1 (*animal*) tail 2 (*vestido*) train

caule sm (*planta*) stalk

causa sf 1 (*origem, ideal*) cause 2 (*motivo*) reason: **sem ~ aparente** for no apparent reason 3 (*Jur, ação judicial*) case ▶ **por ~ de** because of sb/sth

causar vt 1 cause: ~ **ferimentos/ danos** cause injury/damage 2 (*sentimentos*): **Causou-me uma grande alegria.** It made me very happy.

cautela sf caution: **com ~** cautiously ◇ **ter ~** be careful ▶ **por ~** as a safeguard

cauteloso adj cautious

cavalar adj (*dose*) huge

cavalaria sf 1 (*Mil*) cavalry 2 (*Hist*) chivalry

cavalariça sf stable

cavaleiro sm 1 (*pessoa a cavalo*) rider 2 (*Hist*) knight

cavalete sm 1 (*Arte*) easel 2 (*suporte*) trestle

cavalgadura sf (*animal*) mount

cavalgar vi ride (*on sth*)

cavalheiro sm gentleman [*pl* -men]

cavalo sm 1 (*animal*) horse: ~ **de corrida** racehorse 2 (*xadrez*) knight 3 (*Mec*) horsepower (*abrev* hp): **um motor com doze ~s** a twelve horsepower engine 4 (*Ginástica*) (vaulting) horse

cavalo-marinho sm sea horse

cavalo-vapor sm horsepower

cavar vt, vi dig

caveira sf skull

caverna sf cavern

caviar sm caviar

caxias adj (*pessoa*) stickler [s]

caxumba sf mumps [*sing*]: **estar com ~** have (the) mumps

CD sm CD

cear vi have dinner, supper ● vt have sth for dinner, supper

cebola sf onion

cebolinha sf spring onion

ceder vt 1 hand sth over (*to sb*): ~ **o poder** hand over power 2 (*lugar*) give sth up 3 (*emprestar*) lend ● vi 1 (*transigir*) give in (*to sb/sth*): **saber ~** know how to give in gracefully 2 (*intensidade, força*) drop: **O vento cedeu.** The wind dropped. 3 (*não resistir*) give way: **A mesa cedeu com o peso.** The table gave way under the weight.

▶ ~ **a palavra** call upon sb to speak • ~ **a passagem** give way

cedilha sf cedilla

cedo adv early: *de manhã ~* early in the morning ▶ **mais ~ ou mais tarde** sooner or later

cedro sm cedar

cédula sf banknote ▶ ~ **eleitoral** ballot

cegar vt blind

cego/a adj **1** blind (with sth): *ficar ~* go blind ◇ *~ de raiva* blind with rage **2** (*faca*) blunt ● sm-sf blind man/woman [pl men/women]: *os ~s* the blind

cegonha sf stork

cegueira sf blindness

ceia sf dinner, supper

ceifar vt reap

cela sf cell

celebração sf celebration

celebrar vt celebrate: *~ uma missa/um aniversário* celebrate mass/a birthday

célebre adj famous

celeiro sm barn

celeste (*tb* **celestial**) adj heavenly

celofane sm cellophane

célula sf cell

celular sm (*telefone*) cellular phone, cell phone

celulite sf cellulite

cem num a hundred: *Ela faz ~ anos hoje.* She's a hundred today. ◇ *~ mil pessoas* a hundred thousand people ● sm hundred ▶ ~ **por cento** a hundred per cent

cemitério sm **1** cemetery [pl -ies] **2** (*de igreja*) graveyard

cena sf scene: *fazer uma ~* make a scene ● **em ~**: *A peça está em ~ desde o Natal.* The play's been on since Christmas. **entrar em ~ 1** (*entrar no palco*) come on **2** (*entrar em ação*) start up ▶ **pôr em ~** stage

cenário sm **1** (*filme, peça teatral*) setting **2** (*programa de televisão*) set

cenoura sf carrot

censo sm census

censor/a sm-sf censor

censura sf censorship

censurar vt **1** (*livro, filme*) censor **2** (*condenar*) censure

centavo sm cent ▶ **sem um ~** broke

centeio sm rye

centelha sf spark

centena sf **1** (*cem*) (a) hundred [pl hundred]: *unidades, dezenas e ~s* hundreds, tens and units **2**

(*cem aproximadamente*): *uma ~ de espectadores* a hundred or so spectators ◇ *~s de pessoas* hundreds of people

centenário sm centennial, centenary [pl -ies] (GB): *o sexto ~ do seu nascimento* the 600th anniversary of his birth

centésimo/a num, sm hundredth: *um ~ de segundo* a hundredth of a second

centígrado sm Celsius, centigrade (*abrev* C)

centímetro sm centimeter (*abrev* cm)

cento num, sm (a) hundred [pl hundred]: *~ e três* a hundred and three ▶ **por ~** per cent

centopéia sf centipede

central adj central ● sf **1** (*energia*): *uma ~ elétrica/nuclear* a (nuclear) power plant **2** (*repartição principal*) head office **3** ~ *telefônica* telephone exchange

centrar vt **1** (*colocar no centro*) center **2** (*atenção, olhar*) focus sth on sth ● vi (*Esporte*) center

centro sm **1** center: *o ~ das atenções* the center of attention **2** (*cidade*) downtown: *um apartamento no ~* a downtown apartment ◇ *ir ao ~* go downtown ▶ ~ **comercial** (shopping) mall • ~ **cultural** arts center • ~ **de ensino técnico-profissional** community college, technical college (GB) • ~ **de turismo** tourist information center

centroavante sm (*Futebol*) center (forward)

cera sf wax

cerâmica sf ceramics, pottery (*mais coloq*)

cerca¹ sf (*vedação*) fence ▶ ~ **viva** hedge

cerca² adv ▶ ~ **de** about: *~ de uma hora* about an hour

cercar vt **1** (*vedar*) fence sth in **2** (*rodear*) surround **3** (*sitiar*) besiege

cereal sm **1** (*planta, grão*) cereal **2** (*cereais*) cereal: *No café da manhã como cereais.* I have cereal for breakfast.

cerebral adj (Med) brain: *um tumor ~* a brain tumor

cérebro sm **1** (Anat) brain **2** (*pessoa*) brains [sing]: *o ~ da quadrilha* the brains behind the gang

cereja sf cherry [pl -ies]

cerejeira sf cherry tree

cerimônia sf ceremony [pl -ies] ▶ **de ~**: *traje ~* formal dress • **sem ~** unceremoniously

cerração sf fog

cerrado adj **1** (nevoeiro, vegetação) thick **2** (noite) dark

certamente adv definitely

certeiro adj accurate

certeza sf certainty [pl -ies] ▶ **com ~** for sure, definitely (GB) **dar ~** confirm **ter ~** be sure (of sth/that...)

certidão sf (nascimento, casamento) certificate

certificado adj (documento) certified ● sm certificate ▶ **~ escolar** high school diploma

certificar vt certify ● **certificar-se** vp (verificar) make sure (of sth)

certo adj **1** certain: a certas horas at certain times ◊ com certa ansiedade with a certain degree of anxiety **2** (correto) right ● adv (responder, agir) correctly ● interj right ▶ **ao ~** for certain **até o ~ ponto** up to a point **dar ~** work: O plano não deu ~. The plan didn't work. **o mais ~ é...:** O mais ~ é eles virem. They're bound to come. **ter por/como ~ que...** take it for granted that...

cerveja sf beer: ~ sem álcool alcohol-free beer

cessar vt, vi stop (doing sth) ▶ **sem ~** incessantly

cessar-fogo sm ceasefire

cesta sf **1** (recipiente, Esporte) basket: fazer ~ score a basket **2** (com rampa) hamper

cesto sm basket: ~ de roupa suja laundry basket ◊ um ~ de frutas a basket of fruit

cético/a adj skeptical ● sm-sf skeptic

cetim sm satin

céu sm **1** (firmamento) sky [pl skies] **2** (Relig) heaven ▶ **a ~ aberto** (ao ar livre) in the open air **~ da boca** roof of the mouth

cevada sf barley

chá sm tea: Você quer (um) ~? Would you like a cup of tea? ◊ ~ de ervas herbal tea ▶ **tomar ~ de cadeira** be a wallflower

chacal sm jackal

chácara sf smallholding

chacina sf massacre

chacota sf mockery: ser motivo de ~ be a laughing stock

chá-de-panela sm (bridal) shower

chafariz sm (fonte) fountain

chaga sf **1** (ferida aberta) sore **2** (úlcera) ulcer

chalé sm chalet

chaleira sf teakettle, kettle (GB)

chama sf flame: em ~s in flames

chamada sf **1** call: fazer uma ~ make a (phone) call **2** (exames): Fiquei para segunda ~, em junho. I'll retake the exam in June. ▶ **~ a cobrar** collect call, reverse charge call (GB) **~ interurbana** long-distance call: fazer uma ~ interurbana call long distance **fazer a ~** (na escola) call the roll

chamado adj so-called: o ~ Terceiro Mundo the so-called Third World

chamar vt call: Todos o chamam de Zé. Everyone calls him Zé. ◊ ~ a polícia call the police **chamar-se** vp be called: Eu me chamo Ana. I'm called Ana. ◊ Como você se chama? What's your name? ▶ **~ a atenção 1** (sobressair) attract attention **2** (surpreender) surprise **3** (repreender) scold **~ a cobrar** call collect, reverse the charges (GB)

chamativo adj (cor) flashy

chaminé sf **1** chimney **2** (navio) funnel

champanhe sm champagne

chamuscar vt singe

chance sf chance (to do sth): ter a ~ de fazer algo have the chance to do sth ◊ ter bastante/não ter a menor ~ de passar have a good chance/no chance of passing

chantagear vt blackmail sb (into doing sth)

chantagem sf blackmail: fazer ~ com alguém blackmail sb

chantagista smf blackmailer

chão sm ground

chapa sf **1** (lâmina, Fot) plate **2** (radiografia) X-ray **3** (placa) license plate, number plate (GB)

chapado adj (drogado) stoned

chapéu sm (cabeça) hat

charada sf riddle

charco sm stagnant pool

charlatão/ona sm-sf quack

charme sm charm ▶ **fazer ~/charminho** use your charm

charter adj, sm: um vôo ~ a charter flight

charuto sm cigar

chassi sm chassis [pl chassis]

chatear vt **1** (irritar) annoy **2** (pedir com insistência) pester ● vi (importunar) be a nuisance ● **chatear-se** vp **1** (irritar-se) get annoyed (with sb) (about sth) **2** (ficar triste) get upset: Não se chateie com isso. Don't upset yourself over it.

chatice sf **1** (incômodo) pain (in the neck): As moscas são uma ~. The flies are a real pain. **2** (tédio) drag: Esse filme é uma ~ só! This movie is a real drag!

chato adj **1** (plano) flat **2** (entediante) boring, tiresome (mais fml): Não seja ~! Don't be (so) tiresome! ◊ Que ~! What a bore! **3** (maçante) annoying: Eles são muito ~s. They're a real pain in the neck.

chauvinista adj, smf chauvinist

chave sf key (to sth): a ~ do armário the key to the closet ◊ a ~ da porta/da ignição the door/ignition key ◊ a ~ do sucesso deles the key to their success ▶ ~ fator ▶ key factor ▶ a sete ~s/debaixo de ~ under lock and key ~ de fenda screwdriver ~ inglesa wrench

chaveiro sm **1** (objeto) keyring **2** (pessoa) locksmith

check-in sm check-in: fazer o ~ check in

check-up sm (Med) checkup: fazer um ~ have a checkup

chefe smf **1** (superior) boss **2** (grupo) head: ~ de estado head of state **3** (tribo) chief ▶ ~ da quadrilha ringleader ~ de cozinha chef ~ de estação station master

chefiar vt lead

chegada sf arrival

chegado adj keen (on sth): Ele é ~ à bebidas. He really likes a drink.

chegar vt, vi arrive (at/in...): ~ ao aeroporto/ao Brasil arrive at the airport/in Brazil ◊ O trem chegou atrasado. The train was late. ◊ ~ bem arrive safely ◊ ~ em casa get home ◊ ~ cedo/tarde/a tempo be early/late/on time → ARRIVE ● vt **1** (aproximar) bring sth closer (to sb/sth) **2** ~ a reach: ~ a uma conclusão reach a conclusion ◊ A minha filha já chega no meu ombro. My daughter reaches my shoulder now. ● vi **1** (aproximar-se) get closer (to sb/sth): Chegue mais perto. Come closer. **2** (tempo) come: Chegou o momento de... The time came to... **3** (bastar) be enough: Chega! That's enough! ◊ A comida não chegou para todos. There wasn't enough food for everybody. ▶ ~ a fazer algo (conseguir) manage to do sth ~ ao fim come to an end ~ a ser become **estar chegando**: O seu pai deve estar

chegando. Your father should be here any time now.

cheia sf flood

cheio adj **1** full (of sth): O ônibus estava completamente ~. The bus was totally packed. ◊ ~ de si full of yourself **2** (coberto) covered in/with sth ▶ ~ de alguém/algo (estar farto) sick of sb/sth em ~ (precisamente): O tiro acertou em ~. The shot was right on target. ser ~ da nota (ser rico) be loaded

cheirar vt, vi smell (of sth): ~ mal smell bad ◊ ~ a queimado smell of burning → SMELL ▶ não ~ bem (fig): Esta história não me cheira bem. There's something fishy about this story.

cheiro sm smell (of sth): Esse perfume tem um ~ bom. That perfume smells good.

cheiroso adj sweet-smelling

cheque sm check: um ~ no valor de... a check for... ◊ depositar/descontar um ~ pay in/cash a check ◊ ~ em branco/sem fundos blank/bad check ▶ ~ de viagem traveler's check ~ visado authorized check

chiado sm **1** (rato, bicicleta) squeak **2** (freios, pneus) screech

chiar vi **1** (rato, bicicleta) squeak **2** (toucinho) sizzle **3** (freios, pneus) screech **4** (reclamar) complain: Não adianta ~! There's no point in complaining!

chiclete sm (chewing) gum [U]

chicotada sf **1** (golpe) lash **2** (som) crack

chicote sm whip

chifre sm horn

Chile sm Chile

chileno/a adj, sm-sf Chilean

chilique sm ▶ ter um ~ **1** (desmaiar) faint **2** (enervar-se) throw a tantrum

chimpanzé sm chimpanzee

China sf China

chinelo sm **1** (de quarto) slipper **2** (de praia) flip-flop

chinês/esa adj, sm Chinese ● sm-sf Chinese man/woman [pl men/women]: os chineses the Chinese

chip sm chip

chique adj **1** posh **2** (bem vestido) stylish

chiqueiro sm pigsty [pl -ies]

chispar vi (faiscar) flash ▶ chispando in a rush: Ele saiu chispando. He rushed off.

C

44

chocalho sm 1 bell 2 (bebê) rattle

chocante adj shocking

chocar¹ vt shock ● **chocar-se** vp (colidir) crash (into sth): ~ com outro veículo crash into another vehicle ◊ ~ contra alguém bump into sb

chocar² vt (ovo) hatch

chocolate sm chocolate

chofer sm 1 (carro particular) chauffeur 2 (caminhão, ônibus) driver

chope sm (cerveja) beer

choque sm 1 (colisão, ruído) crash 2 (confronto) clash 3 (eletricidade) (electric) shock: levar um ~ get a shock 4 (desgosto) shock

choramingas smf crybaby [pl -ies]

chorão sm (árvore) weeping willow

chorar vi cry: ~ de alegria cry with joy ▸ **a perda de alguém/algo** grieve for sb/sth ▸ **até não poder mais** cry your eyes out ▸ **rios de lágrimas** cry your eyes out ▸ **pôr-se a ~** burst into tears

choro sm crying

chover vi rain ▸ **a cântaros** pour (with rain) ~ **granizo** hail

chuchu sm chayote

chumaço sm (algodão, gaze, etc.) wad

chumbo sm 1 (metal) lead 2 (negativa) fail: Levei ~! I failed!

chupadela sf: dar ~s em algo suck sth

chupar vt 1 suck 2 (absorver) soak sth up ▸ **o dedo** 1 suck your thumb 2 (ficar sem nada) end up with nothing

chupeta sf pacifier, dummy [pl -ies] (GB)

churrasco sm barbecue: fazer um ~ have a barbecue

churrasquinho sm kebab

chutar vt 1 (dar chute) kick 2 (arriscar) guess ● vi (Esporte) shoot (at sb/sth)

chute sm kick ▸ **no ~:** acertar no ~ get sth right by guessing

chuteira sf cleat, football boot (GB)

chuva sf 1 rain: debaixo de ~ in the rain ◊ um dia de ~ a rainy day 2 (dinheiro, presentes, pó) shower of sth 3 (balas, pedras, murros, insultos) hail of sth ▸ **radioativa** radioactive fallout

chuvarada sf downpour

chuveiro sm shower: tomar banho de ~ take a shower

chuviscar vi drizzle

chuvoso adj rainy

cicatriz sf scar

cicatrizar vi heal

ciclismo sm bike riding: fazer ~ go bike riding

ciclista smf cyclist

ciclo sm cycle: um ~ de seis anos a six-year cycle ◊ um ~ de palestras a round of talks

ciclone sm cyclone

cidadania sf citizenship

cidadão/dã sm-sf citizen

cidade sf city [pl -ies] ▸ **(de) 1** ~ **geminada/natal** twin/home town ~ **universitária** (university) campus

ciência sf 1 science 2 (ciências) (Educ) science [sing]: professor de ~s science teacher

ciente adj aware of sth: não estar ~ de algo be unaware of sth

científico adj scientific

cientista smf scientist

cifra sf (número) figure

cifrão sm dollar/real sign

cigano/a adj, sm-sf gypsy [pl -ies]

cigarra sf cicada

cigarro sm cigarette

cilada sf trap

cilíndrico adj cylindrical

cilindro sm cylinder

cima adv 1 up: aquele castelo lá em ~ that castle up there ◊ da cintura para ~ from the waist up 2 (andar) upstairs: os vizinhos de ~ our upstairs neighbors ▸ **de ~ abaixo** 1 Ele me olhou de ~ abaixo. He looked me up and down. 2 (completamente) from top to bottom **em ~ (de) 1** (em) on: Deixe-o em ~ da mesa. Leave it on the table. 2 (sobre) on top (of sb/sth): Deixei-o em ~ da pilha. I put it on top of the pile. ◊ Leve o que está em ~. Take the top one. **estar/ficar em ~ de alguém** be on sb's back **para ~** upwards: mover algo para ~ move sth up a bit **para ~ de 1** (para o cimo de) onto: O gato pulou para ~ da mesa. The cat jumped onto the table. 2 (mais de) over: ~ de mil over a thousand **para ~ e para baixo** up and down **por ~ (de)** over: pôr uma coberta por ~ do sofá put a blanket over the couch

cimento sm cement

cinco num, sm 1 five 2 (data) fifth

cineasta smf movie director

cinema sm 1 (arte) the movies: um ator/diretor de ~ a movie

actor/director 2 (*sala*) movie theater, cinema (*GB*): *ir ao* ~ go to the movies

cinematográfico *adj* movie, film (*GB*): *a indústria cinematográfica* the movie industry

cínico/a *adj* cynical • *sm-sf* cynic

cinquenta *num, sm* 1 fifty 2 (*quinquagésimo*) fiftieth

cinta *sf* 1 (*cintura*) waist 2 (*peça de roupa*) girdle

cintilar *vi* 1 (*estrelas*) twinkle 2 (*luz*) glimmer 3 (*pedras, objetos, etc.*) glitter

cinto *sm* belt ► ~ **(de segurança)** seat belt

cintura *sf* waist

cinza *sf* ash • *adj* gray

cinzeiro *sm* ashtray

cinzel *sm* chisel

cinzento *adj* 1 (*cor*) gray 2 (*tempo*) dull • *sm* gray

cipreste *sm* cypress

circo *sm* circus

circuito *sm* 1 (*Esporte*) track 2 (*Elet*) circuit

circulação *sf* 1 circulation: *má ~do sangue* poor circulation 2 (*trânsito*) traffic

circular¹ *adj, sf* circular: *uma mesa* ~ a round table ◊ *enviar uma* ~ send out a circular

circular² *vt, vi* circulate • *vi* 1 (*trem, ônibus*) run 2 (*pedestre*) walk: ~ *pela esquerda* walk on the left 3 (*rumor*) go around

círculo *sm* 1 circle 2 (*associação*) society [*pl* -ies] ► ~ **polar ártico/antártico** Arctic/Antarctic Circle ~ **vicioso** vicious circle

circunferência *sf* (*perímetro*) circumference

circunflexo *adj* circumflex

circunscrição *sf* ► ~ **eleitoral** constituency [*pl* -ies]

circunstância *sf* circumstance: *nas* ~*s* under the circumstances

cirurgia *sf* surgery: ~ *plástica* plastic surgery

cirurgião/ã *sm-sf* surgeon

cirúrgico *adj* surgical: *uma intervenção cirúrgica* an operation

cisco *sm* speck: *Estou com um* ~ *no olho.* There's something in my eye.

cisma *sf* (*idéia fixa*) fixation

cismar *vt* decide to do *sth/that...* • *vi* (*refletir*) think deeply (*about sth*): *depois de muito* ~ after much thought

cisne *sm* swan

cisterna *sf* (*depósito*) tank

citação *sf* (*frase*) quotation

citar *vt* 1 (*fazer referência*) quote (*from sb/sth*) 2 (*Jur*) summons

citrinos *sm* citrus fruits

ciúme *sm* (**ciúmes**) jealousy [*U*]: *São só* ~*s.* You're just jealous. ◊ *fazer* ~ *a alguém* make sb jealous ◊ *ter* ~*s* be jealous

ciumento *adj* jealous

cívico *adj* 1 (*obrigações*) civic 2 (*relativo ao bem público*) public-spirited: *sentido* ~ public-spiritedness

civil *adj* civil • *smf* civilian

civilização *sf* civilization

civilizado *adj* civilized

civismo *sm* public spirit

clã *sm* clan

clamor *sm* shouts [*pl*]

clandestino/a *adj* clandestine: *operação clandestina* undercover operation • *sm-sf* (*passageiro*) stowaway: *viajar como* ~ stow away

claque *sf* fans [*pl*]

clara *sf* (*ovo*) egg white

claraboia *sf* skylight

clarão *sm* flash

clarear *vi, vt* 1 (*tempo, dia*) brighten up 2 (*amanhecer*) get light

clareira *sf* (*bosque*) clearing

clareza *sf* clarity: *falar com* ~ speak clearly

claridade *sf* 1 (*luz*) light 2 (*fig*) clarity

clarim *sm* bugle

clarinete *sm* clarinet

claro *adj* 1 clear: *um céu* ~/*uma mente clara* a clear sky/mind ◊ *deixar algo* ~ make sth clear 2 (*cor*) light: *verde* ~ light green 3 (*luminoso*) bright 4 (*cabelo*) fair • *adv*: *falar* ~ speak clearly • *interj* of course ► ~ **como água** crystal clear ~ **que sim/não** of course/of course not

classe *sf* class: *viajar em primeira* ~ travel first class ► ~ **alta/baixa/média** upper/lower/middle class(es)

clássico *adj* 1 (*Arte, Hist, Mús*) classical 2 (*habitual*) usual • *sm* classic

classificação *sf* 1 classification 2 (*nota escolar*) grade, mark (*GB*): *boa* ~ good grades 3 (*descrição*) description: *O comportamento dele não merece outra* ~. His behavior cannot be described in any other way. 4 (*Esporte*): *desafio para* ~ qualifying match ◊ *estar à frente*

na ~ mundial be number one in the world rankings ◊ **a ~ geral para a taça** the league table

classificados *sm* classifieds, classified ads (GB)

classificar *vt* **1** (*ordenar*) classify **2** (*descrever*) label *sb* (*as sth*): *Classificaram-na de excêntrica.* She was labelled an eccentric. ● **classificar-se** *vp* qualify (*for sth*): ~ **em segundo lugar** come second

classificatório *adj* qualifying

claustro *sm* cloister

claustrofobia *sf* claustrophobia

claustrofóbico *adj* claustrophobic

cláusula *sf* clause

clave *sf* (*Mús*): ~ **de sol/fá** treble/bass clef

clavícula *sf* collarbone

clero *sm* clergy [*pl*]

clichê *sm* (*lugar-comum*) cliché

cliente *smf* **1** (*loja, restaurante*) customer **2** (*empresa, advogado, etc.*) client

clientela *sf* customers [*pl*]

clima *sm* **1** climate **2** (*fig*) atmosphere: *um ~ de cordialidade* a friendly atmosphere

climatizado *adj* air-conditioned

clímax *sm* climax

clínica *sf* clinic

clipe *sm* **1** (*papel*) paper clip **2** (*vídeo*) video [*pl* ~s]

clone *sm* clone

clorofila *sf* chlorophyll

clube *sm* club

coadjuvante *smf*, *adj* (*Cinema, Teat*) co-star

coador *sm* (*leite, chá*) strainer

coagir *vt* coerce *sb* (*into doing sth*)

coágulo *sm* clot

coalhar *vi* (*leite*) curdle **2** (*iogurte*) set

coalizão *sf* coalition: *um governo de ~* a coalition government

coar *vt* **1** (*chá*) strain **2** (*café*) filter

coaxar *vi* croak

cobaia *sf* guinea pig

coberta *sf* **1** (*cama*) bedspread **2** (*navio*) deck

coberto *adj* **1** covered (*in/with sth*): *A mesa estava coberta de manchas/com um lençol.* The table was covered with stains/a sheet. **2** (*instalação*) indoor: *uma piscina coberta* an indoor swimming pool

cobertor *sm* blanket

cobertura *sf* **1** (*revestimento*) covering **2** (*Jornal*) coverage

cobiça *sf* **1** (*avidez*) greed **2** (*inveja*) envy **3** ~ **de** lust for *sth*: *a sua ~ de poder* their lust for power

cobiçar *vt* **1** (*ambicionar*) covet **2** (*invejar*) envy

cobra *sf* snake ▶ **dizer ~s e lagartos de alguém** call sb every name in the book

cobrador/a *sm-sf* **1** (*ônibus*) conductor **2** (*dívidas, faturas*) collector

cobrança *sf* **1** (*dívida, impostos*) collection **2** (*preço, tarifa*) charging

cobrar *vt* charge (*sb*) (*for sth*): *Cobraram-me 10 reais por um café.* They charged me 10 reals for a coffee. ● *vt* **1** (*imposto, dívida*) collect **2** (*custar*) cost: *A guerra cobrou muitas vidas.* The war cost many lives. ▶ **a ~** cash on delivery (*abrev* COD) | ~ **a/de mais/menos** overcharge/undercharge

cobre *sm* copper

cobrir *vt* **1** cover *sb/sth* (*with sth*): ~ **as despesas de viagem** cover traveling expenses ◊ ~ **uma ferida** cover a wound **2** (*Cozinha*) coat *sth* (*in/with sth*) **3** (*distância*): *Cubro 50 km de carro todo dia.* I drive 50 km every day. ▶ ~ **de beijos** smother *sb* with kisses

Coca-Cola® *sf* Coke®

cocaína *sf* cocaine

coçar *vt* scratch

cócegas *sf*: *fazer ~* tickle ◊ *Sinto muitas ~ nos pés.* My feet are very ticklish.

cochichar *vt*, *vi* whisper

cochilar *vi* **1** (*dormir*) snooze: ~ *depois do almoço* have a snooze after lunch **2** (*descuidar-se*) be distracted

cochilo *sm* **1** (*sono*) doze **2** (*descuido*) oversight

coco *sm* (*fruto*) coconut

cocô *sm* poo: *fazer ~* poo

cócoras *sf* ▶ **de ~** squatting: *pôr-se de ~* squat

codificar *vt* encode

código *sm* code ▶ ~ **da estrada** Highway Code | ~ **postal** zip code, postcode (GB)

coeficiente *sm* coefficient ▶ ~ **de inteligência** intelligence quotient (*abrev* IQ)

coelho/a *sm-sf* rabbit NOTA **Rabbit** é o substantivo genérico. **Buck** é o macho e **doe** a fêmea.

coentro *sm* cilantro, coriander (GB)

C

coerência *sf* **1** (*lógica*) coherence **2** (*congruência*) consistency

coexistência *sf* coexistence

cofre *sm* safe

cogitação *sf* ▶ **fora de ~** out of the question

cogumelo *sm* mushroom ▶ **~ venenoso** toadstool

coice *sm* **1** kick: **dar ~s** kick **2** (*arma*) recoil

coincidência *sf* coincidence: **por ~** by coincidence

coincidir *vi, vt* **1** (*acontecimentos, resultados*) coincide, clash (*mais coloq*) (*with sth*) **2** (*estar de acordo*) tally (*with sth*)

coiote *sm* coyote

coisa *sf* **1** thing: *Uma ~ ficou clara...* One thing is clear... ◇ *Alguma vez você viu tal ~?* Did you ever see anything like it? **2** (*algo*) something: *Eu queria lhe perguntar uma ~.* I wanted to ask you something. **3** (*nada*) nothing, anything: *Não há ~ melhor.* There's nothing better. **4** (*coisas*) (*assuntos*) affairs: *Ele nunca conta as ~s da sua vida particular.* He never talks about his personal life. ▶ **~ de:** *Durou ~ de uma hora.* It lasted roughly an hour. **~ s da vida** that's life **como são as ~s!** would you believe it! **uma ~ e outra** what with one thing and another **não ser grande ~** be no big deal **ou ~ parecida** or something like that **por uma ~/coisinha de nada** over the slightest thing **que ~ mais estranha** how odd **ser ~ de alguém:** *Esta brincadeira deve ser ~ da minha irmã.* This joke must be my sister's doing. **ser pouca ~** (*ferimento*) not to be serious **ter ~ (por trás de algo):** *Tem ~ por trás dessa oferta.* There's a catch to that offer.

coitado *adj* poor: **~ do menino!** Poor kid!

cola¹ *sf* **1** (*adesivo*) glue **2** (*cópia*) crib

colaboração *sf* collaboration

colaborador/a *sm-sf* collaborator

colaborar *vi* collaborate (*with sb*) (*on sth*)

colagem *sf* collage: **fazer uma ~** make a collage

colapso *sm* collapse

colar¹ *sm* necklace

colar² *vt* (*com cola*) glue *sth* (*together*): *~ uma etiqueta num pacote* glue a label on a package ● *vi* **1** (*aderir*) stick **2** (*desculpa*,

colarinho *sm* collar: **o ~ da camisa** shirt collar

colcha *sf* bedspread

colchão *sm* **1** mattress **2** (*camping, praia*) air mattress

colchete *sm* **1** (*Costura*) fastener **2** (*sinal*) square bracket

coleção *sf* collection

colecionador/a *sm-sf* collector

colecionar *vt* collect

colega *smf* **1** (*companheiro*) colleague **2** (*amigo*) friend ▶ **~ de equipe** teammate **~ de quarto/apartamento** roommate **~ de turma** classmate

colégio *sm* (*Educ*) (*private*) school: **~ interno** boarding school ◇ **~ de padres/freiras** Catholic school → SCHOOL

coleira *sf* (*cão, gato*) collar

cólera *sf* **1** (*raiva*) fury **2** (*doença*) cholera

colesterol *sm* cholesterol

coleta *sf* collection ▶ **~ de bagagem** baggage claim

colete *sm* vest, waistcoat (*GB*) ▶ **~ à prova de bala(s)** bulletproof vest **~ salva-vidas** life jacket

coletivo *adj* **1** collective **2** (*transporte*) public

colheita *sf* **1** harvest **2** (*vinho*) vintage: **a ~ de 1985** the 1985 vintage

colher¹ *sf* **1** (*objeto*) spoon: **~ de chá** teaspoon ◇ **~ de pau** wooden spoon **2** (*conteúdo*) spoonful **3** (*pedreiro*) trowel

colher² *vt* **1** (*frutos, flores, etc.*) pick **2** (*cereais*) harvest

colherada *sf* spoonful

cólica *sf* colic [*U*]

coligação *sf* coalition

colina *sf* hill

colisão *sf* collision: **uma ~ de frente** a head-on collision

colite *sf* diarrhea [*U*]

collant *sm* pantyhose, tights (*GB*)

colmeia *sf* beehive

colo *sm* (*regaço*) lap

colocar *vt* **1** (*posicionar*) put, place (*mais fml*) **2** (*bomba*) plant **3** (*emprego*) post: *Ela ficou colocada em Manaus.* She was posted to Manaus. **4** (*questões, etc.*) raise: **~ dúvidas/perguntas** raise doubts/questions

Colômbia *sf* Colombia

colombiano/a *adj, sm-sf* Colombian

cólon *sm* colon

colônia¹ *sf* colony [*pl* -ies]

colônia² *sf* (*perfume*) cologne

colonial *adj* colonial

colonização *sf* colonization

colonizador/a *adj* colonizing • *sm-sf* settler

colono/a *sm-sf* settler

coloquial *adj* colloquial

colorau *sm* paprika

colorido *adj* colorful

colorir *vt* color *sth* (*in*)

coluna *sf* **1** column: ~ *social* gossip column **2** (*Anat*) spine ► ~ **vertebral 1** (*Anat*) spinal column **2** (*fig*) backbone

com *prep* **1** with: ~ *que é que se limpa?* What do you clean it with? NOTA Às vezes se traduz por "and": *pão ~ manteiga* bread and butter ◊ *água ~ açúcar* sugar and water. Também se pode traduzir por "to": ~ *quem você estava falando?* Who were you talking to? ◊ *Ela é simpática ~ todo o mundo.* She's pleasant to everybody ◊ (*conteúdo*) of: *um balde ~ água e sabão* a bucket of soapy water **3** (*expressões com o verbo estar*): *estar ~ pressa* be in a hurry ◊ *estar ~ calor/fome/sono* be hot/hungry/sleepy

coma *smf* coma: *estar em ~* be in a coma

comandante *sm* commander

comando *sm* **1** (*direção*) **(a)** (*liderança*) leadership: *o domo do ~* leadership qualities **(b)** (*Mil*) command: *entregar/tomar o ~* hand over/take command **2** (*Mil, pessoa, divisão*) commando [*pl* -s]

combate *sm* combat [*U*] ► *de ~:* *avião/piloto de ~* fighter plane/pilot

combatente *smf* combatant

combater *vt* combat • *vi* fight

combinação *sf* **1** *a ~ de um cofre* the combination of a safe **2** (*peça de vestuário*) slip **3** (*acordo*) agreement

combinar *vt* **1** combine **2** (*roupa*) match *sth* (*with sth*): *Os sapatos não combinam com a bolsa.* The shoes don't match the purse. **3** (*planejar*) arrange *sth* (*with sb*): ~ *de sair* arrange to go out **4** (*cores*) go with *sth* • *vi* go together: *Cor-de-rosa e vermelho não combinam.* Pink and red don't go together. ► **está combinado** it's a deal

comboio *sm* convoy

combustão *sf* combustion

combustível *adj* combustible • *sm* fuel

começar *vt, vi* begin, start ((*doing*) *sth/to do sth*): *De repente ele começou a chorar.* He suddenly started to cry. ◊ *para ~* to start with ► ~ **com o pé direito** get off to a good start

começo *sm* start, beginning (*mais fml*)

comédia *sf* comedy [*pl* -ies] ► ~ **musical** musical

comemoração *sf* **1** (*recordação*) commemoration: *em ~ aos mortos de guerra* to commemorate the war dead **2** (*celebração*) celebrations [*pl*]

comemorar *vt* **1** (*lembrar*) commemorate **2** (*celebrar*) celebrate

comentar *vt* **1** (*analisar*) comment on *sth* **2** (*dizer*) say **3** (*falar mal de*) make comments about *sb/sth*

comentário *sm* **1** (*observação*) remark: *fazer um ~* make a remark **2** (*jogo de futebol*) commentary [*pl* -ies] ► ~ **de texto** textual criticism **fazer ~s** comment (*on sb/sth*) **sem ~s** no comment

comentarista *smf* commentator

comer *vt* **1** eat **2** (*palavra, etc.*) miss *sth* out **3** (*xadrez, damas*) take **4** (*insetos*): *Os mosquitos me comeram vivo.* The mosquitoes practically ate me alive. • *vi* eat: ~ *fora* eat out ► ~ **como um abade/boi/lobo** eat like a horse **dar de ~** feed *sb/sth*

comercial *adj* commercial

comerciante *smf* (*dono de loja*) storekeeper, shopkeeper (*GB*)

comerciar *vt, vi* **1** ~ (*em*) trade (*in sth*) **2** ~ (*com*) do business (*with sb*)

comércio *sm* trade: ~ *exterior* foreign trade

comestível *adj* edible • **comestíveis** *sm* foodstuffs

cometa *sm* comet

cometer *vt* **1** (*delito, infração*) commit **2** (*erro*) make

comichão *sf* **1** (*coceira*) itch: *Sinto uma ~ nas costas.* My back is itching. **2** (*desejo premente*) urge (*to do sth*)

cômico/a *adj* **1** (*engraçado*) funny **2** *ator ~* comedy actor • *sm-sf* comedian

comida *sf* **1** (*alimentos*) food **2** (*refeição*) meal: *na hora da ~* at mealtimes

comigo pron pess with me ▶ ~ **mesmo/próprio** with myself

comilão/ona adj greedy ● sm-sf glutton

cominho sm cumin

comissão sf commission: 5% de ~ 5% commission ◊ por ~ on commission

comissário/a sm-sf **1** (polícia) superintendent **2** (membro de comissão) commissioner **3** (de bordo) flight attendant

comitê sm committee

como adv **1** (modo, na qualidade de, segundo) as: Respondi ~ pude. I answered as best I could. ◊ Levei-o para casa ~ recordação. I took it home as a souvenir. ◊ ~ eu estava dizendo... As I was saying... **2** (comparação, exemplo) like: um carro ~ o nosso a car like ours ◊ chás ~ o de hortelã herbal teas like mint ◊ macio ~ seda smooth as silk **3** (interrogativas) **(a)** (de que modo) how: ~ se traduz isso? How do you translate this? ◊ Não sabemos ~ aconteceu. We don't know how it happened. **(b)** (quando não se ouviu ou entendeu algo) sorry, pardon (mais fml) **4** (exclamações): ~ você se parece com o seu pai! You're just like your father! ● conj (causa) as: ~ cheguei cedo, fiz um chá. As I was early, I made some tea. ● interj what: Como! Você ainda não se vestiu? What! Aren't you dressed yet? ▶ ~ está/estão? how much is it/are they? ~ é? (descrição) what is he/she, it, etc. like? ~ isso? how come? ~ é que...? ~ é que você não saiu? How come you didn't go out? ◊ ~ é que eu podia saber! How was I supposed to know! ~ que (aproximadamente) about: ~ que dez pessoas about ten people ~ que...?: ~ que você não sabia? What do you mean, you didn't know? ~ se as if: Ele me trata ~ se eu fosse sua filha. He treats me as if I were his daughter. NOTA Na linguagem falada usa-se muito "as if I/he/she/it was". ~ vai/vão...? how is/are...? ~ vai você? How are you? seja ~ for **1** (a qualquer preço) at all costs **2** (em qualquer dos casos) in any case

cômoda sf dresser

comodidade sf **1** (conforto) comfort **2** (conveniência) convenience

comodista smf egoist

cômodo adj **1** (confortável) comfortable **2** (conveniente) convenient ● sm room

comovente adj moving

comover vt move

compadecer-se vp feel sorry (for sb)

compaixão sf pity, compassion (mais fml): ter ~ de alguém take pity on sb

companheirismo sm comradeship

companheiro/a sm-sf **1** (amigo) companion **2** (casal) partner **3** (trabalho) colleague **4** (turma) classmate ▶ ~ **de equipe** teammate

companhia sf company [pl -ies]: ▶ ~ **aérea** airline fazer ~ a alguém keep sb company

comparação sf comparison ▶ em ~ com compared to/with sb/sth

comparar vt compare sb/sth (to/with sb/sth)

comparável adj comparable (to/with sb/sth)

comparecer vi **1** appear, turn up (coloq) **2** ~ a attend: ~ às aulas attend classes

compartilhar vt share

compartimento sm compartment

compasso sm **1** (Mat) compass **2** (Mús) **(a)** (tempo) time: o ~ de três por quatro three four time **(b)** (divisão de pentagrama) bar

compatível adj compatible

compatriota smf fellow countryman/woman [pl -men/-women]

compensação sf compensation ▶ em ~ on the other hand

compensar vt **1** make up for sth: para ~ a diferença de preços make up for the difference in price **2** (uma pessoa) repay sb (for sth) ● vi be worth (doing sth): A longo prazo compensa. It's worth it in the long run. ◊ Não compensa ir só por uma hora. It's not worth going just for an hour.

competência sf competence: falta de ~ incompetence

competente adj competent

competição sf competition

competir vt compete

complemento sm **1** (suplemento) supplement **2** (Gram) object

completar vt complete

completo adj complete: um ano ~ a whole year

complexado adj: uma pessoa muito complexada a person with a lot of hang-ups

complexo adj, sm complex: ter ~ de superioridade have a superiority complex

complicado adj 1 complicated 2 (pessoa) difficult

complicar vt complicate • **complicar-se** vp become complicated ► **complicar(-se) a vida** make life difficult for yourself

complô sm plot

componente sm component

compor vt 1 compose 2 (arrumar) clean sth up, tidy sth up (GB) • **compor-se** vp ~ **de** consist of sth

comportamento sm behavior

comportar-se vp behave

composição sf composition

compositor/a sm-sf composer

composto adj 1 compound: palavras compostas compound words 2 ~ **de/por** consisting of sth • compound

compota sf 1 (doce) preserve 2 (fruta cozida): ~ de maçã stewed apples

compra sf purchase: uma boa ~ a good buy ► **fazer (as) ~s** do the shopping **ir às ~s** go shopping

comprador/a sm-sf purchaser

comprar vt buy: ~ um presente para alguém buy sb a present

compreender vt 1 (entender) understand 2 (incluir) include

compreensão sf understanding ► **ter/mostrar** ~ be understanding (towards sb)

compreensivo adj understanding (towards sb)

comprido adj long: uma história comprida a long story ► **ao** ~ lengthwise

comprimento sm length: Quanto é que mede de ~? How long is it? ◊ Tem dez metros de ~. It's ten meters long.

comprimido sm (medicamento) tablet

comprometer vt 1 (deixar mal) compromise 2 (obrigar) commit sb to (doing) sth • **comprometer-se** vp 1 (dar a sua palavra) promise (to do sth) 2 (em casamento) get engaged (to sb)

compromisso sm 1 (obrigação) commitment: O casamento é um grande ~. Marriage is a big commitment. 2 (acordo) agreement 3 (encontro, matrimonial) engagement: Eu tenho um ~. I have a prior engagement. ► **por**

~ **out of** a sense of duty **sem** ~ no obligation

comprovação sf proof

comprovar vt prove

compulsivo adj compulsive

computador sm computer ► ~ **pessoal** personal computer (abrev PC)

computadorizar vt computerize

comum adj 1 common: ter algo em ~ have sth in common 2 (compartilhado) joint: um amigo ~ a mutual friend

comungar vi take Communion

comunhão sf communion: fazer a primeira ~ make your first Communion

comunicação sf 1 communication 2 (comunicado) statement

comunicado sm announcement

comunicar vt report sth (to sb) • **comunicar-se** vp 1 communicate (with sb/sth) 2 (pôr-se em contato) get in touch with sb 3 (quarto): O meu quarto se comunica com o seu. My room is adjoining to yours.

comunicativo adj communicative

comunidade sf community [pl -ies]

comunismo sm communism

comunista adj, smf communist

côncavo adj concave

conceber vt, vi conceive

conceder vt 1 give: ~ um empréstimo a alguém give sb a loan ◊ O senhor pode me ~ uns minutos, por favor? Could you please spare me a few minutes? 2 (prêmio, bolsa) award 3 (reconhecer) acknowledge

conceito sm 1 (idéia) concept 2 (opinião) opinion: Não sei que ~ você tem de mim. I don't know what you think of me.

concentração sf concentration

concentrado adj 1 (pessoa): Eu estava ~ na leitura. I was immersed in my book. 2 (substância) concentrated • sm concentrate: ~ de uva/tomate grape concentrate/tomato paste

concentrar vt 1 (atenção) focus (on sth) 2 (esforços) concentrate (on doing sth) • **concentrar-se** vp 1 concentrate (on sth) 2 (prestar atenção) pay attention (to sth)

concepção sf 1 (criação) conception 2 (opinião) opinion

concerto sm 1 (recital) concert 2 (composição musical) concerto [pl ~s]

concessão sf concession: *fazer uma ~* make a concession

concessionária sf dealer: *uma ~ da Sony* a Sony dealer

concha sf **1** shell **2** (*sopa*) ladle

conciliar vt combine (*with sth*)

conciso adj concise

concluir vt, vi (*terminar*) finish, conclude (*fml*) ● vt (*deduzir*) conclude *sth* (*from sth*)

conclusão sf conclusion: *chegar a/tirar uma ~* reach/draw a conclusion

concordar vi, vt agree (*with sb*) (*on/about sth/to do sth*): *Concordamos em tudo.* We agree on everything. ◇ *Concordamos em voltar ao trabalho.* We agreed to return to work.

concorrência smf competition ▶ *fazer ~ (a)* compete (with *sb/sth*)

concorrente smf **1** (*competição, concurso*) contestant **2** (*adversário*) rival

concorrer vt, vi **1** (*candidatar-se*) apply for sth: *~ a um emprego* apply for a job **2** (*competir*) compete (for *sth*) **3** (*concurso*) take part (in *sth*)

concorrido adj **1** (*cheio de gente*) crowded **2** (*popular*) popular

concreto sm concrete ● adj specific

concurso sm **1** (*Esporte, jogos de habilidade*) competition **2** (*TV, rádio*) game show **3** (*para emprego*) open competition ▶ *~ de beleza* beauty contest

conde sm count

condecoração sf medal

condenação sf **1** (*sentença*) conviction **2** (*censura*) condemnation

condenado, a sm-sf convicted prisoner

condenar vt **1** (*desaprovar*) condemn **2** (*Jur*) (a) (*pena*) sentence *sb* (to *sth*): *~ alguém à morte* sentence sb to death (b) (*por um delito*) convict *sb* (of *sth*)

condensar(-se) vt, vp condense

condescendente adj **1** (*transigente*) easygoing **2** (*com ares de superioridade*) condescending

condessa sf countess

condição sf **1** condition: *estabelecer as condições* lay down the conditions ◇ *em perfeitas condições* in perfect condition ◇ *Faço-o com a ~ de que você me ajude.* I'll do it on condition that you help me. **2** (*social*) status ▶ *estar em condições (de) (fisicamente)* be fit to do sth **2** (*ter a possibilidade*) be in a position to do sth ▶ *sem condições*: *uma rendição sem condições* an unconditional surrender ◇ *Ele aceitou sem condições.* He accepted unconditionally.

condicional adj, sm conditional

condizer vi, vt (*cores, roupa*) go with sth, go together: *As cores não condizem.* The colors don't go together.

condomínio sm **1** (*taxa*) service charge **2** (*co-propriedade*) condominium, condo [*pl* ~s] (*coloq*)

conduta sf behavior [*U*]

conduto sm (*tubo*) pipe ▶ *~ do lixo* garbage chute

conduzir vt **1** (*levar*) lead *sb* (to *sth*) **2** (*negociações, negócio*) carry *sth* out

cone sm cone

conexão sf connection (*to/with sth*); (*between...*)

confeitaria sf cake shop

conferência sf **1** (*exposição oral*) lecture **2** (*congresso*) conference

conferir vt **1** (*verificar*) check **2** (*comparar*) compare **3** (*dar*) award ● vi tally (*with sth*)

confessar vt, vi **1** confess (to *doing sth*): *~ um crime* confess to a crime ◇ *Eles confessaram ter assaltado o banco.* They confessed to robbing the bank. ◇ *~ a verdade* tell the truth **2** (*Relig*) hear (*sb's*) confession: *Não confessam aos domingos.* They don't hear confessions on Sundays. ● **confessar-se** vp (*Relig*) go to confession

confiança sf **1** confidence (*in sb/sth*): *~ em si mesmo/próprio* self-confidence **2** (*familiaridade*) familiarity: *tratar alguém com demasiada ~* be over-familiar with sb ▶ *de ~* trustworthy: *um empregado de ~* a trustworthy employee

confiar vt **1** *~ em* trust: *Confie em mim.* Trust me. **2** (*entregar em confiança*) entrust *sb/sth* with *sth*

confiável adj reliable

confidência sf confidence ▶ *em ~* in confidence

confidencial adj confidential

confirmação sf confirmation

confirmar vt confirm

confiscar vt seize

confissão sf confession

conflito sm conflict: *~ de interesses* conflict of interest

conformar-se vp **1** be happy

(with (doing) sth): *Eu me conformo com uma nota cinco.* I'll be happy with a pass. ◊ *Eles se conformam com pouco.* They're easily pleased. ◊ *(resignar-se)* put up *with sth:* Terei que me ~. I'll just have to put up with it.

conforme *prep* **1** *(de acordo com)* according to *sth* **2** *(dependendo de)* depending on *sth* • *conj* **1** *(depende)* it all depends **2** *(de acordo com o que)* according to what: ~ *ouvi dizer* from what I've heard **3** *(à medida que)* as: ~ *eles forem entrando* as they come in

conformista *adj, smf* conformist

confortar *vt* comfort

confortável *adj* comfortable

conforto *sm* comfort

confrontar *vt* **1** *(encarar)* bring *sb* face to face with *sb/sth* **2** *(comparar)* compare *sb/sth* with *sb/sth*

confronto *sm* **1** confrontation **2** *(paralelo)* comparison

confundir *vt* **1** confuse: *Não me confunda.* Don't confuse me. **2** *(misturar)* mix *sth* up: *Você confunde sempre tudo.* You always mix everything up. • **confundir-se** *vp* be confused: *Qualquer um pode se confundir.* Anyone can make a mistake.

confusão *sf* **1** *(falta de clareza)* confusion **2** *(equívoco)* mistake **3** *(desordem)* mess: *Mas que ~!* What a mess! **4** *(problema)* trouble [U]: *Não se meta em confusões.* Don't get into trouble. **5** *(tumulto)* commotion ▸ **fazer** ~ get confused

confuso *adj* **1** *(pouco claro)* confusing: *uma mensagem confusa* a garbled message **2** *(perplexo)* confused

congelador *sm* freezer

congelar *vt* freeze

congestionado *adj* **1** *(ruas)* congested **2** *(nariz)* stuffed up, blocked up *(GB)*

congestionamento *sm* *(trânsito)* congestion [U]

congestionar *vt*: *O acidente congestionou o trânsito.* The accident brought the traffic to a standstill.

congresso *sm* congress

conhaque *sm* brandy [*pl* -ies]

conhecer *vt* **1** know: *Conheço muito bem o Rio.* I know Rio very well. ◊ ~ *alguém de vista* know sb by sight **2** *(uma pessoa pela primeira vez)* meet **3** *(saber da existência)* know of

sb/sth: *Você conhece um bom hotel?* Do you know of a good hotel? **4** *(passar a ter conhecimento sobre)* get to know: ~ *novas culturas* get to know other ways of life ▸ ~ **algo como a palma da mão** know sth like the back of your hand

conhecido/a *adj (famoso)* well known • *sm-sf* acquaintance

conhecimento *sm* knowledge [U]: *É do ~ de todos.* It's common knowledge. ▸ **tomar ~ de algo** find out about sth

cônico *adj* conical

conífera *sf* conifer

conjugação *sf* conjugation

conjugar *vt* conjugate

conjunção *sf* conjunction

conjuntivite *sf* conjunctivitis

conjunto *sm* **1** *(objetos, obras)* collection **2** *(totalidade)* whole: *a indústria no* ~ industry as a whole **3** *(musical)* group **4** *(roupa)* outfit: *um* ~ *de saia e casaco* a skirt and matching jacket **5** *(Mat)* set **6** *(agrupamento de edifícios)* complex: ~ *residencial* housing development

conosco *pron pess* with us

conquista *sf* conquest

conquistador/a *adj* conquering • *sm-sf* conqueror

conquistar *vt* **1** *(Mil)* conquer **2** *(seduzir)* win *sb* over

consagrar *vt* **1** *(dedicar)* devote *sth* (*to sth*) **2** *(tornar famoso)* establish *sth* (*as sth*)

consciência *sf* **1** *(sentido moral)* conscience: *ter a* ~ *limpa* have a clear conscience **2** *(conhecimento)* consciousness: ~ *da diferença de classes* class-consciousness ▸ **ter/tomar ~ de algo** be/become aware of sth

consciente *adj* conscious

conscientizar *vt* make *sb* aware (*of sth*): ~ *a população para algo* make people aware of sth • **conscientizar-se** *vp* become aware (*of sth*)

conseguir *vt* **1** *(obter)* get: ~ *que alguém faça algo* get sb to do sth **2** *(alcançar)* achieve **3** *(ganhar)* win **4** + *inf* manage to do *sth*: *Consegui convencê-los.* I managed to persuade them.

conselheiro/a *sm-sf* advisor

conselho *sm* **1** *(recomendação)* advice [U]: *Vou lhe dar um* ~. I'll give you some advice/a piece of advice. **2** *(organismo)* council

consentimento *sm* consent

consentir *vt* *(tolerar)* allow: *Não*

consentirei que você me trate assim. I won't allow you to treat me like this.

consequência *sf* **1** (*consequence*): *arcar com as ~s* face the consequences **2** (*resultado*) result: *como/em ~ daquilo* as a result of that

consertar *vt* (*reparar*) fix

conserto *sm* repair: *fazer uns ~s do repairs* ▶ **não tem ~ 1** (*objeto, problema*) it can't be fixed **2** (*pessoa*) (s)he's a hopeless case

conserva *sf* canned food: *tomates em ~* canned tomatoes

conservação *sf* **1** (*meio ambiente*) conservation **2** (*alimentos*) preserving

conservador/a *adj, sm-sf* conservative

conservante *sm* preservative

conservar *vt* **1** (*comida*) preserve **2** (*coisas*) keep: *Ainda conservo as cartas dele.* I still have his letters. **3** (*calor*) retain

conservatório *sm* conservatory [*pl* -ies]

consideração *sf* **1** (*reflexão, cuidado*) consideration: *levar algo em ~* take sth into consideration **2** (*respeito*) respect (*for sb*) ▶ **com/sem** ~ considerately/inconsiderately **em/por** ~ **a** out of consideration for

considerar *vt* **1** (*examinar*) weigh sth up, consider (*mais fml*): ~ *os prós e os contras* weigh up the pros and cons **2** (*ver, apreciar*) regard *sb/sth* (*as sth*): *Considero-a a nossa melhor jogadora.* I consider her our best player. **3** (*pensar em*) think (*about (doing) sth*): *Não considerei essa possibilidade!* I hadn't thought of that!

considerável *adj* considerable

consigo *pron pess* **1** (*ele, ela*) with him/her **2** (*eles, elas*) with them **3** (*coisa, animal*) with it ▶ ~ **mesmo/próprio** with himself, herself, etc.

consistente *adj* **1** (*constante, firme*) consistent **2** (*refeição*) big

consistir *vt* consist *of (doing) sth*

consoante *sf* consonant

consolação *sf* consolation: *prêmio de* ~ consolation prize

consolar *vt* console

console *sm* console

consolo *sm* consolation

conspiração *sf* conspiracy [*pl* -ies]

constante *adj* constant

constar *vt* **1** (*figurar*) appear (*in*

sth): *O seu nome não consta da lista.* Your name doesn't appear on the list. **2** (*consistir*) consist *of sth* ▶ **consta que...** it is said that...

constelação *sf* constellation

constipação *sf* **1** (*prisão de ventre*) constipation **2** (*resfriado*) cold: *apanhar/pegar uma ~* catch/have a cold

constipado *adj*: *estar* ~ have a cold NOTA **Constipated** não significa "resfriado" mas *com prisão de ventre*.

constipar-se *vp* catch a cold

constitucional *adj* constitutional

constituição *sf* constitution

constituir *vt* be, constitute (*fml*)

constrangedor *adj* embarrassing

constranger *vt* embarrass

construção *sf* **1** (*edifício*) building, construction (*mais fml*) ▶ **em** ~ under construction

construir *vt, vi* build

construtor/a *sm-sf* construction worker

cônsul *smf* consul

consulado *sm* consulate

consulta *sf* consultation ▶ **de** ~: *horário de* ~ office hours ◇ *livros de* ~ reference books

consultar *vt* **1** consult *sb/sth* (*about sth*) **2** (*palavra, dado*) look sth up: *Consulte o dicionário.* Look it up in the dictionary. ▶ ~ **o travesseiro** (*sobre algo*) sleep on sth

consultor/a *sm-sf* consultant

consultório *sm* (*médico*) doctor's office, surgery (*GB*)

consumidor/a *adj*: *países ~es de petróleo* oil-consuming countries ● *sm-sf* consumer

consumir *vt* **1** consume **2** (*energia*) use **3** (*destruir*) destroy ▶ ~ **de preferência antes de...** best before...

consumo *sm* consumption

conta *sf* **1** (*Com, Fin*) account: ~ *corrente* checking account, current account (*GB*) **2** (*fatura*) (a) bill: *a ~ da luz* the electricity bill (b) (*num restaurante*) check, bill (*GB*) **3** (*operação aritmética*) sum: *fazer ~s* work sth out ▶ **afinal de/no final/no fim das ~s** after all **dar** ~ **de** cope with sth: *Não dou ~ desse trabalho todo.* I can't cope with all this work. **dar-se** ~ **de 1** (*entender*) realize (*that...*) **2** (*ver*) notice *sth/that...* **dar** ~ **de** (*fingir*) pretend: *Ele nos viu mas fez de*

~ que não. He saw us, but pretended that he hadn't. **por ~ própria**: trabalhar por ~ própria be self-employed **sem ~**: countless **ter/levar em ~ 1** (considerar) bear sth in mind **2** (fazer caso): Não leve isso em ~. Don't take it to heart. **tomar ~ de 1** (responsabilizar-se) take charge of sth **2** (cuidar de alguém) take care of sb

contabilidade sf **1** (contas) accounts [pl]: fazer a ~ do the accounts **2** (profissão) accounting, accountancy (GB)

contador/a sm-sf accountant

contagem sf counting ▸ **~ regressiva** countdown

contagiar vt infect

contagioso adj contagious

contaminação sf contamination

contaminar vt contaminate

contar vt **1** (enumerar, calcular) count **2** (explicar) tell: ~ uma história tell a story **3** ~ **com** (esperar) count on sb/sth **4** (denunciar) tell (on sb): Ele me viu copiando e foi ~ ao professor. He saw me copying and told on me to the teacher. ● vi count ▸ **~ fazer algo** expect to do sth

contatar vt ~ com contact: ~ com alguém contact sb

contato sm contact ▸ **manter-se/entrar/pôr alguém em ~ (com alguém)** keep/get/put sb in touch (with sb)

contêiner sm container

contemplar vt **1** look at sb/sth **2** (considerar) consider ● vt, vi meditate (on sth)

contemporâneo/a adj, sm-sf contemporary [pl -ies]

contentar-se vp be satisfied with sth: Ele se contenta com pouco. He's easily pleased.

contente adj **1** (feliz) happy **2** (satisfeito) pleased (with sb/sth)

conter vt **1** contain: Este texto contém alguns erros. This text contains a few mistakes. **2** (reprimir) hold sth back: ~ as lágrimas hold back the tears. **3** (inflação) control **4** (rebelião) suppress ● **conter-se** vp contain yourself

conterrâneo/a sm-sf fellow countryman/woman [pl -men/-women]

conteúdo sm contents [pl]

contexto sm context

contigo pron pess with you ▸ **~ mesmo/próprio** with yourself

continente sm continent

continuação sf continuation

continuar vt, vi **1** (atividade) carry on (with sth/doing sth), continue (with sth/to do sth) (mais fml): Continuaremos a apoiar você. We'll continue to support you. **2** (estado) be still...: Continua muito quente. It's still very hot. ▸ **~ na mesma** be just the same

contínuo¹ sm office boy

contínuo² adj **1** (sem interrupção) continuous **2** (repetido) continual → CONTINUAL

conto sm **1** story [pl -ies]: ~s de fadas fairy stories **2** (gênero literário) short story

contornar vt **1** (esquina, edifício) go around sth **2** (problema, situação) get around sth **3** (desenho) outline

contorno sm (perfil) outline

contra prep **1** against: a luta ~ o crime the fight against crime ◇ Coloque-se ~ a parede. Stand against the wall. ◇ Você é a favor ou ~? Are you for or against? **2** (com verbos como disparar, atirar) at: Eles lançaram pedras ~ as janelas. They threw stones at the windows. **3** (com verbos como chocar, arremeter) into: O meu carro chocou-se ~ a parede. My car crashed into the wall. **4** (golpe, ataque) on: dar com a cabeça ~ a porta bang your head on the door ◇ um atentado ~ a vida dele an attempt on his life **5** (resultado) to: Eles ganharam por onze votos ~ seis. They won by eleven votes to six. ▸ **ser do ~** disagree

contra-atacar vt fight back

contra-ataque sm counterattack

contrabaixo sm (instrumento) double bass

contrabandista smf smuggler

contrabando sm **1** (atividade) smuggling **2** (mercadoria) contraband

contracapa sf **1** (livro) back cover **2** (revista) back page

contracepção sf contraception

contraceptivo adj, sm contraceptive

contradição sf contradiction

contraditório adj contradictory

contradizer vt contradict

contragosto sm ▸ **a ~** reluctantly

contrair vt contract: ~ dívidas/malária contract debts/malaria

● **contrair-se** *vp* (*materiais, músculos*) contract ▸ ~ **matrimônio** get married (*to sb*)

contramão *adj*: *uma rua* ~ a one-way street ● *adv* out of my, your etc. way ● *sf*: *entrar na* ~ go the wrong way

contrariar *vt* (*aborrecer*) annoy

contrariedade *sf* (*aborrecimento*) annoyance

contrário *adj* **1** (*equipe, opinião, teoria*) opposing **2** (*direção, lado*) opposite **3** (*pessoa*) opposed (*to sth*) ● *sm* opposite ▸ **ao** ~ **1** (*mal*) wrong: *Tudo me sai ao* ~! Everything's going wrong for me! **2** (*inverso*) the other way round: *Fiz tudo ao* ~ *de você.* I did everything the other way round from you. **3** (*de cabeça para baixo*) upside down **4** (*do avesso*) inside out: *Você está com o suéter ao* ~. Your sweater's on inside out. **5** (*detrás para diante*) backward ▸ **ao** ~ **de** unlike   **do** ~ otherwise   **muito pelo** ~ on the contrary

contrastante *adj* contrasting

contrastar *vt, vi* contrast (*sth*) (*with sth*): ~ *uns resultados com os outros* contrast one set of results with another

contraste *sm* contrast

contratação *sf* **1** (*trabalhadores*) recruitment **2** (*Esporte*) signing

contratante *smf* contractor

contratar *vt* **1** (*pessoa*) recruit **2** (*esportista, artista*) sign *sb* on/ up **3** (*detetive, decorador, etc.*) employ

contratempo *sm* **1** (*problema*) setback **2** (*acidente*) mishap

contrato *sm* contract

contravenção *sf* contravention: *a* ~ *da lei* breaking the law

contribuição *sf* contribution

contribuinte *smf* taxpayer

contribuir *vi* contribute (*sth*) (*to/towards sth*): ~ *com um milhão de reais para o apelo* contribute a million reals to the appeal **2** ~ **para fazer algo** (*ajudar*) help to do sth

controlar *vt* control

controle *sm* **1** control: *perder o* ~ lose control ◇ ~ *de natalidade* birth control ◇ ~ *remoto* remote control ◇ *sob/fora de* ~ under/ out of control **2** (*de polícia*) checkpoint

controvérsia *sf* controversy [*pl* -ies]

controvertido *adj* controversial

contudo *conj* however

contundente *adj* **1** (*instrumento*) blunt **2** (*comentário*) cutting

contundir *vt* bruise

contusão *sf* bruise

convalescer *vi* convalesce

convenção *sf* convention

convencer *vt* **1** convince *sb* (*of sth/to do sth/that...*) **2** (*persuadir*) persuade *sb* (*to do sth*) ● **convencer-se** *vp* convince yourself (*that...*)

convencido *adj* (*vaidoso*) conceited

convencional *adj* conventional

conveniente *adj* convenient

convênio *sm* agreement

convento *sm* **1** (*freiras*) convent **2** (*frades*) monastery [*pl* -ies]

conversa *sf* talk: *Deixe de* ~! Stop talking! ◇ ~ *fiada* idle chatter

conversação *sf* conversation

conversão *sf* conversion

conversar *vi* talk, chat (*coloq*) (*to/with sb*) chatter

conversível *adj, sm* convertible

conversor *sm* ▸ ~ **catalítico** catalytic converter

converter *vt* **1** turn *sb/sth into sth* **2** (*Relig*) convert *sb* (*to sth*) ● **converter-se** *vp* **1** ~ **em** turn into *sth* **2** ~ **a** convert to *sth*

convés *sm* deck

convexo *adj* convex

convicção *sf* conviction

convicto *adj* convinced

convidado *adj, sm-sf* guest: *o artista* ~ the guest artist

convidar *vt* invite *sb* (*to* (*do*) *sth*)

convincente *adj* convincing

convir *vi* **1** (*ser conveniente*) suit: *o que melhor lhe convier* whatever suits you best **2** (*ser aconselhável*) convém que vc reveja tudo. You'd better go over it again. ◇ *Não convém chegar tarde.* We'd better not be late. ▸ **como me, etc. convier** however I, you etc. want: *Vou fazer como me convier.* I'll do it however I want.

convite *sm* invitation (*to* (*do*) *sth*)

conviver *vi* live together, live with *sb*: *Eles são incapazes de* ~ *um com o outro.* They're incapable of living together.

convocação *sf* **1** call: *a* ~ *de uma greve/eleições* a strike call/a call for elections **2** (*para reunião, julgamento*) summons

convocar *vt* **1** (*greve, eleições, reunião*) call **2** (*citar*) summon

convulsão *sf* convulsion

cooperar vi cooperate (with sb) (on sth)

cooperativa sf cooperative

cooperativo adj cooperative

coordenada sf coordinate

coordenar vt coordinate

copa sf 1 (*árvore*) top 2 (*aposento*) pantry 3 (*Esporte*): a ~ do Mundo the World Cup 4 (**copas**) (*naipe*) hearts → BARALHO

cópia sf copy [pl -ies]: *fazer/tirar uma* ~ make a copy ► ~ **impressa** printout

copiar vt, vi copy (sth) (from sb/sth)

co-piloto smf 1 (*avião*) co-pilot 2 (*automóvel*) co-driver

copo sm glass: *um ~ de água* a glass of water ► ~ **de plástico/papel** plastic/paper cup

coque sm (*penteado*) bun: *Ela está de* ~. She is wearing her hair in a bun.

coqueiro sm coconut palm

coqueluche sf 1 (*Med*) whooping cough [U] 2 (*modismo*) fad

coquetel sm 1 (*bebida*) cocktail 2 (*reunião*) cocktail party [pl -ies]

cor¹ sm ► **saber algo de** ~ (**e salteado**) know sth by heart

cor² sf color: *~es vivas* bright colors ◇ *uma televisão a ~es* a color TV ◇ *lápis de ~* colored pencils

coração sm heart: *no fundo do seu* ~ in his/her heart of hearts ◇ *em pleno* ~ *da cidade* in the heart of the city ► **com o** ~ **na mão** (*inquieto*) on tenterhooks **de** ~/**do fundo do meu** ~ from the heart **ter bom** ~ be kind-hearted

corado/a adj 1 (*saúde, sol*) ruddy 2 (*vergonha, embaraço*) flushed

coragem sf courage

corajoso adj courageous

coral sm 1 (*Zool*) coral 2 (*Mús*) choir

corante adj, sm coloring: *sem ~s* no artificial colorings

corar vi blush

corcunda adj hunched ● smf (*pessoa*) hunchback ● sf hump

corda sf 1 rope: *uma ~ de pular* a jump rope 2 (*Mús*) string: *instrumentos de* ~ stringed instruments 3 (*para secar roupa*) clothesline ► **com a** ~ **no pescoço** in a fix ► **bamba** tightrope **~s vocais** vocal cords **dar** ~ **a alguém** (*para conversar*) encourage sb (to talk) **dar** ~ **num relógio** wind up a clock/watch

cordão sm 1 (*barbante*) cord 2 (*sapato*) (shoe)lace 3 (*jóia*) chain 4 (*policial*) cordon ► ~ **umbilical** umbilical cord

cordeiro sm lamb

cor-de-rosa adj, sm pink

cordilheira sf mountain range: *a ~ dos Andes* the Andes

córnea sf cornea

corneta sf bugle

coro sm choir ► **em** ~ in unison

coroa sf 1 crown 2 (*flores*) wreath ● smf (*pessoa*) oldie

coroação sf coronation

coroar vt crown

coronel sm colonel

corpete sm top

corpo sm body [pl -ies] ► ~ **de bombeiros** fire department, fire brigade (GB) **de** ~ **inteiro** full-length: *um espelho de* ~ *inteiro* a full-length mirror

corporal adj body: *linguagem* ~ body language

corpulento adj burly

correção sf correction: *fazer correções num texto* make corrections to a text

corredor sm 1 corridor 2 (*igreja, avião, teatro*) aisle

corredor/a sm-sf (*atleta*) runner

correia sf 1 strap: ~ *do relógio* watch strap 2 (*máquina*) belt: ~ *transportadora/do ventilador* conveyor/fan belt

correio sm 1 mail, post (GB) ► **MAIL** 2 (*edifício*) post office ► ~ **aéreo** airmail ~ **eletrônico** email ► **EMAIL** ~ **expresso** express mail **pôr no** ~ mail, post (GB)

corrente adj 1 (*comum*) common: *de uso* ~ commonly used 2 (*atual*) current: *o ano/mês* ~ this year/month ● sf 1 (*água, eletricidade*) current 2 (*bicicleta*) chain ► ~ **de ar** draft ~ **sanguínea** bloodstream

correr vi 1 run: *As crianças corriam pelo pátio de recreio.* The children were running around in the playground. ◇ ~ *atrás de alguém* run after sb ◇ *Quando me viu, ele desatou a* ~. He ran away when he saw me. 2 (*despachar-se*) hurry 3 (*líquidos*) flow 4 (*boato, notícia*) go around: *Corria um boato.* There was a rumor going around. 5 (*resultar*): *A excursão correu muito bem.* The trip went really well. ● vt 1 (*Esporte*) compete in sth 2 (*risco*): ~ *o risco de perder* run the risk of losing ► ~ **perigo** be in danger **fazer algo correndo** do sth in a rush **sair correndo** dash off

correspondência sf 1 (*cartas*)

correspondence 2 (*relação*) relation

correspondente *adj* **1** corresponding (*to sth*): *as palavras ~s às definições* the words corresponding to the definitions **2** (*adequado*) relevant: *apresentar os documentos ~s* produce the relevant documents **3** for: *matéria ~ ao primeiro semestre* subjects for the first semester ● *smf* correspondent

corresponder *vi* correspond (*to sth*) ● **corresponder-se** *vp* write to sb: *Gostaria de me ~ com alguém inglês.* I'd like to have an English penpal.

correto *adj* correct: *a resposta correta* the correct answer ◊ *O seu avô é muito ~.* Your grandfather is very correct.

corretor,a *sm-sf* (*profissão*) broker ● *sm* (*fluido*) correction fluid ▸ ~ **de imóveis** real estate agent, estate agent (*GB*)

corrida *sf* race: ~ *automobilística/de cavalos/de revezamento* motor/horse/relay race ▸ ~ **armamentista** arms race

corrigir *vt* correct: *Corrija-me se eu estiver errada.* Correct me if I'm wrong. **2** (*Educ*) grade, mark (*GB*): ~ *provas* grade tests

corrimão *sm* (*escada*) banister(s)

corriqueiro *adj* (*habitual*) ordinary

corromper *vt* corrupt

corrosão *sf* corrosion

corrupção *sf* corruption

corrupto *adj* corrupt

cortada *sf* (*Esporte*) smash ▸ **dar uma ~ em alguém** snap at sb

cortante *adj* sharp

cortar *vt* **1** cut **2** (*água, luz, telefone, parte do corpo, ramo*) cut sth off: *Cortaram o gás.* The gas has been cut off. **3** (*com tesoura*) cut sth out: ~ *uma foto de uma revista* cut a picture out of a magazine **4** (*rasgar*) slash ● *vi* cut ▸ ~ **caminho** take a short cut ▸ ~ **o cabelo 1** (*o próprio*) cut your hair **2** (*no cabeleireiro*) have your hair cut

corte¹ *sm* cut ▸ ~ **de cabelo** haircut ▸ ~ **de energia** power outage, power cut (*GB*) ▸ ~ **e costura** dressmaking

corte² *sf* (*reino*) court

cortejo *sm* **1** (*carnaval*) parade **2** (*religioso, fúnebre*) procession

cortesia *sf* courtesy [*pl* -ies]: *por ~* out of courtesy

cortiça *sf* cork

cortina *sf* curtain: *abrir/fechar as ~s* draw the curtains

coruja *sf* owl

corvo *sm* raven

coser *vt, vi* sew: ~ *um botão* sew a button on

cosmético *adj, sm* cosmetic

cósmico *adj* cosmic

cosmos *sm* cosmos

costa *sf* **1** (*junto ao mar*) coast: *na ~ sul* on the south coast **2** (*montanha*) slope

costa-abaixo *adv* downhill

costa-acima *adv* uphill

costas *sf* **1** back [*sing*]: *Estou com dor nas ~.* My back hurts. **2** (*natação*) backstroke ▸ **às ~** on your back **de ~**: *Fique de ~ contra a parede.* Stand with your back to the wall. ◊ *ver alguém de ~* see sb from behind ▸ **de ~ um para o outro** back to back **fazer algo nas ~ de alguém** do sth behind sb's back ▸ **voltar as ~** turn your back *on sb/sth*

costela *sf* rib

costeleta *sf* **1** chop (*vitela*) cutlet **3** (**costeletas**) (*suíças*) sideburns

costumar *vi* **1** (*no presente*) usually do sth: *Não costumo tomar café da manhã.* I don't usually have breakfast. → **ALWAYS 2** (*no passado*) used to do sth: *Não costumávamos sair.* We didn't use to go out. → **USED TO**

costume *sm* **1** (*pessoa*) habit: *Temos o ~ de comer tarde.* We're in the habit of eating late. **2** (*país*) custom ▸ **como de ~** as usual **de ~** usual: *mais do que de ~* more than usual

costura *sf* **1** (*atividade*) sewing **2** (*peça de roupa*) seam: *A ~ se desfez.* The seam came undone.

costurar *vt, vi* sew: ~ *um botão* sew a button on

costureira *sf* dressmaker

cota *sf* **1** (*quantidade*) quota **2** (*de sócio, etc.*) fee: *a ~ de sócio* the membership fee

cotonete *sm* Q-tip®, cotton bud (*GB*)

cotovelada *sf* **1** (*para chamar a atenção*) nudge **2** (*violenta, para abrir caminho*): *Abri caminho às ~s.* I elbowed my way through the crowd.

cotovelo *sm* elbow

couraça *sf* **1** (*tartaruga*) shell **2** (*blindagem*) armor-plate

couraçado *sm* battleship

couro *sm* leather: *uma jaqueta de*

C

~ a leather jacket ▶ ~ **cabeludo** scalp

couve sf spring greens [pl] ▶ ~ **crespa** savoy cabbage

couve-de-bruxelas sf Brussels sprout

couve-flor sf cauliflower

cova sf 1 (*buraco*) hole 2 (*sepultura*) grave

covarde adj cowardly ● smf coward

covardia sf cowardice [U]

covil sm 1 den 2 (*ladrões*) hideout

covinha sf (*queixo, rosto*) dimple

coxa sf thigh

coxear vi (*ser coxo*) limp

coxo adj 1 (*pessoa*): ser ~ have a limp ◊ *O acidente o deixou ~.* The accident left him with a limp. 2 (*animal*) lame

cozer vi cook

cozido adj cooked

cozimento sm cooking: *tempo de* ~ cooking time

cozinha sf 1 (*lugar*) kitchen 2 (*gastronomia*) cooking

cozinhar vt, vi cook: *Não sei* ~. I can't cook. ▶ ~ **demais** overcook ~ **em fogo brando** simmer

cozinheiro/a sm-sf cook

crachá sm (*insígnia*) badge

crânio sm skull

craque smf 1 expert 2 (*Esporte*) star

crasso adj serious: *um erro* ~ a grave error

cratera sf crater

cravar vt 1 (*faca, punhal*) stick sth into sb/sth 2 (*unhas, garras, dentes*) dig sth into sth/sb

cravo sm 1 (*flor*) carnation 2 (*Cozinha*) clove 3 (*na pele*) blackhead

crawl sm crawl

creche sf nursery [pl -ies]

crédito sm credit: *a* ~ on credit

credo sm creed: *liberdade de* ~ religious freedom ● interj good heavens

credor/a sm-sf creditor

crédulo adj gullible

cremar vt cremate

crematório sm crematorium

creme sm cream: ~ *chantilly* whipped cream ◊ ~ *de cogumelos* cream of mushroom soup ◊ ~ *de limpeza/de barbear* cleanser/shaving cream ● adj (*cor*) cream

cremoso adj creamy

crença sf belief

crente smf believer

crêpe sm pancake → TERÇA (-FEIRA)

crepúsculo sm twilight

crer vt, vi 1 believe (*in sb/sth*): ~ *na justiça* believe in justice 2 (*pensar*) think: *Eles crêem ter ganhado.* They think they've won. ▶ **ver para** ~ seeing is believing

crescente adj growing

crescer vi 1 grow: *deixar* ~ *o cabelo* grow your hair 2 (*criar-se*) grow up: *Quero ser médico quando* ~. I want to be a doctor when I grow up. 3 (*bolo, pão*) rise

crescido adj 1 (*adulto*) grown-up 2 (*maduro*) old

crescimento sm growth

crespo adj (*cabelo*) curly

cria sf (*animal*) young

criação sf 1 (*criação*) creation: *a* ~ *de empregos* job creation 2 (*animais*) breeding 3 (*educação*) upbringing ▶ ~ **de gado** livestock farming

criado/a sm-sf servant

criador/a sm-sf 1 creator 2 (*animais*) breeder: ~ *de gado* livestock farmer/breeder

criança sf child [pl children], kid (*coloq*) ▶ **desde** ~: *Eu a conheço desde* ~. I've known her all my life. ◊ *amigos desde* ~ lifelong friends

criar vt 1 create: ~ *problemas* create problems ◊ ~ *inimigos* make enemies 2 (*educar*) bring sb up 3 (*empresa*) set sth up 4 (*gado*) rear 5 (*cães, cavalos*) breed ▶ **criar-se** vp (*pessoa*) grow up ▶ ~ **distúrbios** make trouble ~ **juízo** come to your senses ~ **raízes 1** (*planta*) take root 2 (*pessoa*) put down roots

criatividade sf creativity

criativo adj creative

criatura sf creature

crime sm crime: *cometer um* ~ commit a crime

criminoso/a adj, sm-sf criminal

crina sf mane

crioulo/a adj creole ● sm-sf (*pessoa*) black (person)

crise sf 1 crisis [pl crises] 2 (*histeria, nervos*) fit

crista sf 1 (*galo*) comb 2 (*outras aves, montanha, onda*) crest

cristal sm crystal

cristaleira sf glass cabinet

cristalino adj (*água*) crystal clear

cristão/ã adj, sm-sf Christian

cristianismo sm Christianity

Cristo Christus ▶ **antes/depois de** ~ B.C./A.D.

critério sm 1 (princípio) criterion [pl -ria] 2 (capacidade de julgar, Jur) judgement

crítica sf 1 criticism: Estou farta das suas ~s. I've had enough of your criticism. 2 (num jornal) review 3 (conjunto de críticos) critics [pl]

criticar vt, vi criticize

crítico/a adj critical ● sm-sf critic

crivar vt 1 (perfurar) riddle: crivado de balas riddled with bullets 2 (de perguntas) grill

crocante adj (alimento) crunchy

croché sm crochet: fazer ~ crochet

crocodilo sm crocodile

croissant sm croissant

cromo sm (metal) chromium

crônico adj chronic

cronista smf (Jornal) columnist

cronológico/a adj chronological

cronometrar vt time

cronômetro sm (Esporte) stop-watch

croquete sm croquette

crosta sf 1 (ferida) scab 2 a ~ terrestre the earth's crust

cru adj 1 (não cozido) raw 2 (realidade) harsh 3 (linguagem) crude

crucificar vt crucify

crucifixo sm crucifix

cruel adj cruel

crueldade sf cruelty [pl -ies]

crustáceo sm crustacean

cruz sf cross ● **cruzes** interj good Lord ▶ ~ **Vermelha** Red Cross **entre a** ~ **e a caldeirinha** between a rock and a hard place

cruzamento sm 1 (estradas) junction 2 (etnias) cross: um ~ de raças a crossbreed

cruzar vt cross: ~ as pernas/os braços cross your legs/fold your arms ● **cruzar-se** vp meet sb: Cruzamo-nos no caminho. We met on the way.

cruzeiro sm (viagem) cruise: fazer um ~ go on a cruise

Cuba sf Cuba

cubano/a adj, sm-sf Cuban

cúbico/a adj cubic: metro ~ cubic meter

cubículo sm cubicle

cubo sm cube: ~ de gelo ice cube

cuco sm cuckoo [pl ~s]

cueca (cuecas) sf underpants [pl]: uma ~ a pair of underpants → PAIR

cuidado sm 1 care: ter ~ com algo

be careful with sth ◇ Cuidado com muito ~ very carefully 2 ~ **com:** ~ com o cão! Beware of the dog! ◇ ~ com o degrau! Watch out for the step! ● interj look out

cuidadoso adj careful (with sth)

cuidar vt, vi take care of sb/sth: ~ das crianças take care of the children ◇ cuidar-se (bem) take (good) care of yourself

cujo pron rel whose: Aquela é a moça ~ pai me apresentaram. That's the girl whose father was introduced to me. ◇ a casa cuja porta você pintou the house whose door you painted

culatra sf (arma) breech

culinária sf cookery: um livro de ~ a cookbook

culpa sf 1 (responsabilidade) fault: A ~ não é minha. It isn't my fault. 2 (sentimento) guilt ▶ **por** ~ **de** because of sb/sth **pôr a** ~ **em alguém** blame sb **ter** ~ be to blame (for sth)

culpado/a adj guilty (of sth) ● sm-sf culprit

culpar vt blame sb (for sth)

cultivar vt 1 (terra) cultivate (plantas) grow

cultivo sm cultivation

culto adj 1 (pessoa) cultured 2 (linguagem, expressão) formal ● sm 1 (veneração) worship (of sb/sth) 2 (seita) cult 3 (missa) service

cultuar vt worship

cultura sf culture

cultural adj cultural

cume sm top: chegar ao ~ reach the top

cúmplice smf accomplice (in/to sth)

cumprimentar vt say hello (to sb), greet (mais fml): Ele não me cumprimentou. He didn't say hi.

cumprimento sm 1 (saudação) greeting 2 (elogio) compliment 3 (cumprimentos) best wishes, regards (mais fml): enviar seus ~s send your regards

cumprir vt 1 (ordem) carry sth out 2 (profecia, obrigação) fulfill 3 (promessa) keep 4 (prazo) meet 5 (pena) serve 6 ~ a alguém fazer algo be sb's responsibility to do sth ▶ ~ a sua parte do your bit

cúmulo sm ▶ **ser o** ~ be the last straw

cunha sf wedge

cunhado/a sm-sf brother-in-law [fem sister-in-law] [pl -ers-in-law]

cupim sm termite

cupom sm coupon

cúpula sf dome

cura sf cure ▸ **ter/não ter** ~ be curable/incurable

curandeiro/a sm-sf (charlatão) quack

curar vt **1** (sarar) cure (sb) (of sth): Os comprimidos me curaram do resfriado. The pills cured my cold. **2** (ferida) dress **3** (alimentos) cure ● **curar-se** vp (ficar bom) recover (from sth)

curativo sm (de uma ferida) dressing

curinga sm (baralho) joker

curiosidade sf curiosity [pl -ies]: por pura ~ out of sheer curiosity ◇ **ter** ~ **de algo** be curious about sth

curioso/a adj curious (about sth) ● sm-sf **1** (observador) onlooker **2** (indiscreto) busybody [pl -ies]

curral sm (gado) pen

currículo sm **1** (**curriculum vitae**) resumé, curriculum vitae (abrev **CV**) (GB) **2** (Educ) syllabus [pl -es] **3** (empregado, estudante) record: ter um bom ~ have a good record

curso sm **1** course: o ~ de um rio the course of a river ◇ ~s de línguas language courses (licenciatura) degree: fazer um ~ de direito do a law degree ◇ ~ universitário/superior college degree ▸ **o ano/mês em** ~ the current year/month

cursor sm cursor

curta-metragem sm (Cinema) movie short, short (film) (GB)

curtição sf **1** fun [U]: O show foi uma ~. The show was great fun. **2** (couro) tanning

curtir vt (couro) tan **2** (gostar): Curto à beça este CD. I really love this CD. ◇ ~ muito/adoidado have a great time

curto adj short: Essas calças ficam curtas em você. Those pants are too short for you. ◇ de manga curta short-sleeved

curto-circuito sm short circuit

curva sf **1** (linha, gráfico) curve **2** (estrada, rio) bend: uma ~ fechada a sharp bend

curvar(-se) vt, vp bend

curvo adj curved

cuspir vt spit sth (out) ● vi spit (at sb)

custa sf (**custas**) (Jur) costs ▸ **à** ~ **de 1** (a expensas de) at sb's expense: à nossa ~ at our expense **2** (com o auxílio de) by means of

custar vt **1** (valer) cost: O bilhete custa 30 dólares. The ticket costs 30 dollars. ◇ O acidente custou a vida de duas pessoas. The accident cost the lives of two people. **2** (achar difícil) find it hard (to do sth) ● vi (ser difícil): Custa acreditar. It's hard to believe. ▸ ~ **muito/pouco 1** (dinheiro) be expensive/cheap **2** (esforço) be hard/easy ◇ **os olhos da cara** cost an arm and a leg **custe o que** ~ at all costs

custear vt finance

custo sm cost: ~ de vida the cost of living ▸ **a** ~ **with difficulty** ◇ **a todo o** ~ at all costs

custódia sf custody

cútis sf **1** (pele) skin **2** (tez) complexion

cutucar vt **1** (com cotovelo) nudge **2** (com dedo) poke (at) sth **3** (com instrumento) prod

Dd

dado¹ sm **1** (informação) information [U]: um ~ importante an important piece of information **2** (dados) (Informát) data: processamento de ~s data processing **3** (de jogar) dice [pl dice]: lançar os ~s roll the dice ▸ ~**s pessoais** personal details

dado² adj given: em ~ momento at a given moment **2** (afável) friendly ▸ ~ **que** given that

daí adv **1** (espaço) from there: Sai ~! Get out of there! **2** (tempo): ~ em/por diante from then on ◇ ~ a um ano one year later ● e ~? so what?

dali adv **1** (espaço) from there **2** (tempo): ~ em/por diante from then on ◇ ~ a um mês one month later

daltônico adj color-blind

dama sf **1** (senhora) lady [pl -ies] **2** (baralho) queen **3** (damas) checkers, draughts (GB) ▸ ~ **de honra** bridesmaid → CASAMENTO

damasco sm apricot

danado adj **1** (zangado) angry **2** (travesso) naughty

dança sf dance

dançar vt, vi dance: tirar alguém para ~ ask sb to dance

dançarino/a sm-sf dancer

danificar vt damage

dano sm damage [U] ▸ ~**s e prejuízos** damages

daqui adv **1** (espaço) from here **2** (tempo): ~ em/por diante from now on ◇ ~ a um ano/a pouco in one year/in a little while

dar vt **1** give: ~ uma chave/a susto a alguém give sb a key/a shock **2** (quando não se quer mais algo) give sth away: Vou ~ as suas bonecas. I'm going to give your dolls away. **3** (Educ) **(a)** (professor) teach: ~ aulas teach ◇ ~ ciências teach science **(b)** (aluno) do: Agora estamos dando o passado. Now we're doing the past. **4** (Educ, trabalho para casa) set **5** (relógio): O relógio deu dez horas. The clock struck ten. ◇ Já deram cinco horas? Is it five o'clock already? **6** (fruto, flor) bear **7** (calcular): Quantos anos você dá para ela? How old do you think she is? **8** (cartas) deal **9** (ser suficiente) be enough **10** (ataque): Deu-lhe um ataque de tosse. He had a coughing fit. **11** (luz) shine: A luz dava direto nos meus olhos. The light was shining right in my eyes. **12** ~ com hit: ~ com o joelho na mesa hit your knee against the table **13** ~ para algo overlook sth: A varanda dá para a praça. The balcony overlooks the square. **14** ~ para (pessoa) be good as sth: Eu não dava para professora. I'd be no good as a teacher. ▶ (a mim) tanto se me dá I, you, etc. couldn't care less **dar-se bem/mal** get along well/ badly (with sb) ~ uma de: Não dê uma de pai para cima de mim. Don't act as if you were my father. **NOTA** Para outras expressões com dar, ver o substantivo, adjetivo, etc., p. ex. dar um passeio em PASSEIO.

dardo sm **1** (Esporte) javelin **2** (dardos) darts

data sf date: ~ de nascimento date of birth ◇ ~ de encerramento closing date ▶ ~ de validade expiration date, sell-by date (GB)

datilografar vt type

datilógrafo/a sm-sf typist

de prep

• **posse 1** (de alguém): o livro do Pedro Pedro's book ◇ o cachorro dos meus amigos my friends' dog ◇ É dela/da minha avó. It's hers/my grandmother's. **2** (de algo): uma página do livro a page of the book ◇ os cômodos da casa the rooms in the house ◇ o porto ~ Santos Santos harbor

• **origem, procedência** from: Ela é de Belém. She's from Belém. ◇ do Rio a São Paulo from Rio to São Paulo

• **meio de transporte** by: de avião/ carro by plane/car

• **descrições de pessoas 1** (qualidades físicas) **(a)** with: uma menina de cabelo louro a girl with fair hair **(b)** (roupa, cores) in: a mulher do vestido verde the woman in the green dress **2** (qualidades não físicas) of: uma pessoa de muito caráter a person of great character ◇ um homem de 30 anos a man of 30

• **descrições de coisas 1** (qualidades físicas) **(a)** (material): um vestido de linho a linen dress **(b)** (conteúdo) of: um copo de leite a glass of milk **2** (qualidades não físicas) of: um livro de grande interesse a book of great interest

• **tema, disciplina**: um livro/professor de física a physics book/ teacher ◇ uma aula de história a history class

• **números e expressões de tempo**: mais/menos de dez more/less than ten ◇ um selo de um real a one real stamp ◇ um quarto de quilo a quarter of a kilo ◇ de noite/dia at night/ during the day ◇ às dez da manhã at ten in the morning ◇ de manhã/tarde in the morning/afternoon ◇ de maio a julho from May to July ◇ de 7 até 9 from the 7th to the 9th

• **série**: de quatro em quatro metros every four meters ◇ de meia em meia hora every half hour

• **agente** by: um livro de Amado a book by Amado ◇ seguido de três jovens followed by three young people

• **causa**: morrer de fome die of hunger ◇ pular de alegria jump for joy

• **outras construções**: o melhor ator do mundo the best actor in the world ◇ de um trago in one gulp ◇ mais rápido do que o outro faster than the other one ◇ um daqueles livros one of those books

debaixo adv **1** underneath: Leve o que está ~. Take the bottom one. **2** ~ de under: ~ da mesa under the table ◇ por ~ da porta under the door ◇ ~ de chuva in the rain

debandada sf stampede

debate sm debate: ter um ~ hold a debate

debater vt (*discutir*) debate ●
debater-se vp struggle

débil adj weak

debilidade sf weakness

débito sm (Com) debit

debochar vt ~ **de** mock

deboche sm mockery [U]

debruçar-se vp (*inclinar-se*)
lean over: ~ **na janela** lean out
of the window

década sf decade: a ~ **de oitenta**
the eighties

decadência sf **1** (*declínio*)
decline **2** (*corrupção*) decadence

decadente adj decadent

decalque sm tracing: *fazer (um)*
~ *de algo* trace sth

decapitar vt behead

decente adj decent

decepar vt cut sth off

decepção sf disappointment:
ter uma ~ be disappointed

decepcionante adj disappointing

decepcionar vt **1** (*desiludir*)
disappoint: *O livro me decepcio-
nou.* The book was disappointing. **2** (*falhar*) let sb down

decidido adj (*determinado*)
determined

decidir vt, vi decide ● **decidir-se**
vp **1** make up your mind: *Deci-
da-se!* Make up your mind! **2** ~
por opt for sb/sth

decifrar vt **1** (*mensagem*) decode
2 (*escrita*) decipher **3** (*enigma*)
solve

decimal adj, sm decimal

décimo/a adj, num, sm tenth
▶ ~ **primeiro, segundo, etc.**
eleventh, twelfth, etc.

decisão sf decision: *tomar uma*
~ make a decision

decisivo adj decisive

declaração sf **1** declaration **2**
(*manifestação pública, Jur*)
statement ▶ ~ **de renda**
(income) tax return

declarar vt **1** declare: *Algo a* ~?
Anything to declare? **2** (*em
público*) state: *segundo o que
declarou o ministro* according
to the minister's statement ●
declarar-se vp **1** ~ **a favor de/
contra algo** come out in favor
of/against sth **2** (*confessar
amor*): *Ele se declarou para
mim.* He told me he loved me. **3**
(*Jur*) plead: ~ *culpado/inocente*
plead guilty/not guilty

declinar vi **1** (*sol*) sink **2** (*decair*)
decline ● vt decline: ~ *um con-
vite* decline an invitation

declínio sm decline

decodificador sm decoder

decodificar vt decode

decolagem sf (*avião*) take-off

decolar vi (*avião*) take off

decompor(-se) vt, vp (*apodrecer*) decompose

decoração sf **1** (*ação, adorno*)
decoration **2** (*estilo*) décor

decorar[1] vt (*ornamentar*)
decorate

decorar[2] vt (*memorizar*) learn
sth by heart

decorrer vi **1** (*tempo*) pass **2**
(*suceder*) take place ▶ ~ **com o ~
do tempo** in time

decotado adj low-cut

decote sm neckline: ~ **em V**
V-neck

decreto sm decree

decreto-lei sm act

dedal sm thimble

dedetizar vt spray

dedicação sf dedication

dedicar vt **1** devote sth to sb/sth:
~ *a vida a algo* devote your life
to sth **2** (*canção, poema*) dedicate sth (to sb) **3** (*exemplar*)
autograph ● **dedicar-se** vp: *A
que você se dedica no seu tempo
livre?* What do you do in your
free time? ◊ ~ *a comprar e
vender antiguidades* buy and
sell antiques for a living

dedicatória sf dedication

dedinho sm ▶ ~ **do pé** little toe

dedo sm **1** (*da mão*) finger **2** (*do
pé*) toe **3** (*medida*) half an inch
▶ ~ **anular/médio/indicador**
ring/middle/index finger
▶ **mindinho** little finger, pinkie
(*coloq*) ▶ **polegar** thumb

deduzir vt **1** (*concluir*) deduce **2**
(*descontar*) deduct sth (*from
sth*)

defeito sm **1** fault, defect (*mais
fml*): *um* ~ *na fala* a speech
defect ◊ *achar/pôr* ~ *em tudo*
find fault with everything **2**
(*veículo*) breakdown: *estar/
ficar com* ~ **break down** **3**
(*roupa*) flaw → MISTAKE

defeituoso adj faulty, defective
(*fml*)

defender vt **1** defend sb/sth
(*against sb/sth*) **2** (*gol*) save ●
defender-se vp **1** defend yourself (*against sb/sth*) **2** (*justi-
ficar-se*) stand up for yourself

defensiva sf ▶ **estar na** ~ be on
the defensive

defensivo adj defensive

defensor/a sm-sf defender

defesa sf **1** defense: *as* ~**s do
corpo** the body's defenses ◊
uma equipe com uma boa ~ **a**

team with a good defense **2** (*goleiro*) save: *fazer uma* ~ make a save **3** (*elefante, javali*) tusk ● *smf* (*Esporte*) defender

deficiência *sf* deficiency [*pl* -ies]

deficiente *adj* **1** (*carente*) deficient (*in sth*) **2** (*imperfeito*) defective (*Med*) disabled: ~ *físico/mental* physically disabled/mentally handicapped ◊ *os* ~*s* the disabled

definição *sf* definition

definido *adj* (*artigo*) definite

definir *vt* define

definitivamente *adv* **1** (*para sempre*) for good **2** (*de forma determinante*) definitively

definitivo *adj* **1** final: *o número de vítimas* the final death toll **2** (*solução*) definitive

deflagração *sf* **1** (*bomba*) explosion **2** (*guerra*) outbreak

deflagrar *vt, vi* (*bomba*) explode ● *vi* (*incêndio, epidemia*) break out

deformar *vt* **1** (*corpo*) deform **2** (*roupa*) pull *sth* out of shape **3** (*imagem, realidade*) distort ► **deformar-se** *vp* **1** (*corpo*) become deformed **2** (*roupa*) lose its shape

defrontar(-se) *vt, vp* face: *defrontar-se com dificuldades* face difficulties

defumar *vt* (*alimentos*) smoke

defunto/a *sm-sf* corpse

degenerado/a *adj, sm-sf* degenerate

degenerar *vi* degenerate

degolar *vt* cut *sb's* throat

degradante *adj* degrading

degrau *sm* step

deitado *adj* **1** (*na cama*) in bed **2** (*estendido*) lying down

deitar *vt* **1** (*pôr na cama*) put *sb* to bed **2** (*estender*) lay *sth/sb* down ● **deitar-se** *vp* **1** (*ir para a cama*) go to bed: *Está na hora de nos deitarmos.* Time for bed. **2** (*estender-se*) lie down → LIE[2] ~ **por terra** (*destruir*) ruin

deixar *vt* **1** leave: *Onde é que você deixou as chaves?* Where did you leave the keys? ◊ *Deixe-me em paz!* Leave me alone! **2** (*abandonar*) give *sth* up **3** (*permitir*) let *sb* (*do sth*) **4** ~ **de** (**a**) (*parar*) stop *doing sth* (**b**) (*abandonar*) give up *doing sth*: ~ *de fumar* give up smoking ● *v aux* + *particípio*: *A notícia nos deixou preocupados.* We were worried by the news. ► ~ **cair** drop NOTA Para outras expressões com **deixar**, ver

o substantivo, adjetivo, etc., p. ex. **deixar escapar** em ESCAPAR.

dela/a (*pessoa*) her(s): *Os pais* ~ *não a deixam sair à noite.* Her parents don't let her go out at night. ◊ *Esse colar era* ~. This necklace used to be hers. NOTA *Um amigo dela* se traduz por *a friend of hers* pois significa *um dos amigos dela.* **2** (*coisa, animal*) its

delas ther(s) → DELA

delatar *vt* inform on *sb*

delator/a *sm-sf* **1** tattletale, telltale (*GB*) **2** (*da polícia*) informer

delegação *sf* delegation

delegacia *sf* ► ~ **policial/de polícia** police station

delegado/a *sm-sf* (*Pol*) delegate ► ~ **de polícia** police chief

deles their(s): *O carro* ~ *está enguiçado.* Their car has broken down. → DELA

deliberado *adj* deliberate

delicadeza *sf* **1** delicacy **2** (*tato*) tact: *dizer algo com* ~ put *sth* tactfully ◊ *É uma falta de* ~. It's very tactless. **3** (*cortesia*) thoughtfulness **4** (*cuidado*) care

delicado *adj* **1** delicate **2** (*cortês*) thoughtful

delícia *sf* **1** (*prazer*) delight: *Que* ~*!* How delightful! **2** (*comida*) delicacy [*pl* -ies]: *ser uma* ~ be delicious

deliciar *vt* delight ● **deliciar-se** *vp* take delight *in* (*doing*) *sth*

delicioso *adj* **1** (*comida*) delicious **2** (*encantador*) delightful

delinquência *sf* crime: ~ *juvenil* juvenile delinquency

delinquente *smf* delinquent

delirante *adj* (*arrebatador*) thrilling

delirar *vi* **1** (*Med*) be delirious **2** (*dizer disparates*) talk nonsense **3** (*sentir com grande intensidade*) go wild: ~ *com a notícia* go wild at the news

delito *sm* crime: *cometer um* ~ commit a crime

delta *sm* delta

demais *adv* **1** (*modificando verbo*) too much: *beber* ~ drink too much **2** (*modificando adj ou adv*) too: *grande/depressa* ~ too big/fast **3** (+ *substantivo não contável*) too much: *Há comida*

~. There's too much food. **4** (+ *substantivo contável*) too many: *comprar coisas* ~ buy too many things • *pron* (the) others: *Os* ~ *ficaram em casa.* The others stayed at home. ◊ *ajudar os* ~ help others ► **ser** ~ (*ser muito bom*) be really great

demão *sf* coat: *uma* ~ *de tinta* a coat of paint

demasiado *adj* **1** (+ *substantivo não contável*) too much **2** (+ *substantivo contável*) too many • *adv* **1** (*modificando verbo*) too much **2** (*modificando adj ou adv*) too

demissão *sf* **1** (*voluntária*) resignation: *Ele apresentou a sua* ~. He handed in his resignation. **2** (*involuntária*) dismissal

demitir *vt* dismiss, fire (*colog*) • **demitir-se** *vp* resign (*from sth*)

democracia *sf* democracy [*pl* -ies]

democrata *smf* democrat

democrático *adj* democratic

demolição *sf* demolition

demolir *vt* demolish

demônio *sm* **1** (*diabo*) devil **2** (*espírito*) demon

demonstração *sf* **1** (*apresentação*) demonstration **2** (*manifestação*) sign: *uma* ~ *de afeto* a sign of affection

demonstrar *vt* **1** (*provar*) prove **2** (*mostrar*) show **3** (*explicar*) demonstrate

demora *sf* delay

demorar *vi* take (time) *to do sth*: *Eles demoraram muito a responder.* They took a long time to reply. ◊ *Não demore.* Don't be long.

densidade *sf* density

denso *adj* dense

dentada *sf* bite

dentadura *sf* teeth [*pl*]: ~ *postiça* false teeth

dente *sm* **1** tooth [*pl* teeth]: ~ *de leite/siso* baby/wisdom tooth **2** (*garfo, ancinho*) prong **3** (*alho*) clove

dentifrício *sm* toothpaste

dentista *smf* dentist

dentro *adv* **1** in/inside: *O gato está lá* ~. The cat is inside. ◊ *ali/aqui* ~ in there/here **2** (*edifício*) indoors: *ficar aqui* ~ stay indoors **3** ~ **de (a)** (*espaço*) in/inside **(b)** (*tempo*) in: ~ *de uma semana/seis meses* in a week/in six months' time ► **de** ~ from (the) inside ► **em breve/pouco** very soon ► **estar por** ~ **de algo** (*ter conhecimento*) be in the know about sth ► **mais para** ~

further in ► **para** ~ in: *Põe a barriga para* ~. Pull your stomach in. ► **por** ~ (on the) inside: *pintado por* ~ painted on the inside

denúncia *sf* **1** (*acidente, delito*) report **2** (*revelação*) disclosure

denunciar *vt* **1** report: ~ *alguém à polícia* report sb to the police **2** (*revelar*) denounce

deparar *vt* ~ **com** (*encontrar*) come across sth

departamento *sm* department

dependência *sf* **1** (*droga*) dependency **2** (*casa*) room

depender *vi* **1 (a)** depend *on sth/on whether…*: *Isso depende de você me trazer o dinheiro (ou não).* That depends on whether you bring me the money (or not). **(b)** (*economicamente*) ~ be dependent *on sb/sth* **2** ~ **de alguém** be up to sb (*whether…*)

depilar *vt* **1** (*sobrancelhas*) pluck **2** (*pernas, axilas*) **(a)** (*com cera*) wax: *Tenho de* ~ *as pernas.* I must have my legs waxed. **(b)** (*com lâmina*) shave

depoimento *sm* **1** (*na delegacia*) statement **2** (*no tribunal*) testimony

depois *adv* **1** (*mais tarde*) afterward, later: *pouco* ~ shortly afterward ◊ *Só muito* ~ *é que me disseram.* They didn't tell me until much later. **2** (*a seguir, em seguida*) then: *Bata os ovos e* ~ *adicione o açúcar.* Beat the eggs and then add the sugar. ◊ *Primeiro vem o hospital e* ~ *a escola.* First there's the hospital and then the school. ► ~ **de** after (*doing*) *sth*: ~ *das duas* after two o'clock ◊ *A farmácia fica* ~ *do banco.* The drugstore is after the bank. **e** ~? then what?

depor *vi* **1** (*na delegacia*) make a statement **2** (*no tribunal*) testify

deportar *vt* deport

depositar *vt* **1** (*dinheiro*) pay *sth* in: ~ *dinheiro numa conta bancária* pay money into a bank account **2** ~ **a sua confiança em alguém** place your trust in sb

depósito *sm* **1** (*reservatório*) tank: ~ *de água* water tank **2** (*dinheiro*) deposit ► ~ **de bagagem** baggage room, left luggage office (*GB*)

depredado *adj* (*zona, edifício*) run-down

depressa *adv* **1** (*em breve*) soon **2** (*rapidamente*) quickly • *interj* hurry up

depressão *sf* depression

deprimente *adj* depressing

deprimido adj depressed: estar/ficar ~ be/get depressed

deprimir vt depress

deputado/a sm-sf deputy [pl -ies] NOTA Nos Estados Unidos o equivalente do deputado federal é Representative (abrev Rep.) e na Grã-Bretanha, **Member of Parliament** (abrev **MP**).

deriva sf ▸ à ~ adrift   andar à ~ drift

derivar vt 1 (palavra) derive from sth 2 (proceder) stem from sth

derramamento sm spilling ▸ ~ **de sangue** bloodshed

derramar vt 1 (verter) spill 2 (despejar) pour 3 (sangue, lágrimas) shed

derrame sm stroke

derrapagem sf skid: ter/sofrer uma ~ skid

derrapar vi skid

derreter(-se) vt, vp 1 (manteiga, gordura) melt 2 (neve, gelo) thaw

derrota sf defeat

derrotar vt defeat

derrubar vt 1 (edifício) knock sth down, demolish (mais fml) 2 (fazer cair) knock sb/sth over 3 (porta) batter a door down 4 (governo, regime) bring sth down

desabafar vt ~ com alguém confide in sb ● **desabafar(-se)** vi, vp let off steam

desabar vi collapse

desabitado adj uninhabited

desabotoar vt unbutton

desabrigado/a adj, sm-sf homeless: os ~s the homeless

desacato sm disrespect: ~ às autoridades disrespect for the authorities

desafiar vt 1 (provocar) challenge sb (to sth) 2 (perigo) defy

desafinado adj out of tune

desafinar vi 1 (ao cantar) sing out of tune 2 (instrumento) be out of tune 3 (músico) play out of tune

desafio sm challenge

desagradar vt displease

desagradável adj unpleasant

desaguar vi (rio) flow into sth

desajeitado adj clumsy

desamparado adj helpless

desanimador adj discouraging

desanimar vt discourage ● **desanimar-se** vp lose heart

desanuviar-se vp (céu) clear up

desaparecer vi disappear ▸ ~

do mapa vanish off the face of the earth

desaparecido/a adj missing ● sm-sf missing person

desaparecimento sm disappearance

despertar vt loosen

desapontado adj disappointed: ficar ~ be disappointed

desapontamento sm disappointment

desapontar vt disappoint

desarmamento sm disarmament

desarmar vt 1 (pessoa, exército) disarm 2 (desmontar) take sth apart 3 (bomba) defuse

desarrumado adj untidy

desarrumar vt mess sth up

desastrado adj clumsy

desastre sm 1 (acidente) accident: um ~ de automóvel a car crash 2 (catástrofe) disaster

desastroso adj disastrous

desatar vt 1 (nó, corda) untie 2 ~ a (começar) start doing sth/to do sth ● **desatar-se** vp come undone ▸ ~ **a rir/chorar** burst out laughing/crying

desatento adj distracted

desativar vt 1 (bomba) defuse 2 (fábrica) shut sth down

desatualizado adj 1 (máquina, livro) outdated 2 (pessoa) out of touch

desbotar vi, vt fade

descafeinado adj decaffeinated ● sm decaf

descalçar vt (sapatos, botas) take sth off ● **descalçar-se** vp take your shoes off

descalço adj barefoot: andar ~ go around in bare feet

descampado sm open countryside

descansar vt, vi rest: ~ os olhos rest your eyes ◇ Deixe-me ~ um pouco. Let me rest for a few minutes. ● vi (fazer uma pausa) take a break: ~ cinco minutos take a five-minute break

descanso sm 1 (repouso) rest 2 (no trabalho) break: sem ~ without a break 3 (mesa) place mat

descarado adj sassy, cheeky (GB)

descaramento sm nerve

descarga sf 1 (mercadoria) unloading 2 (elétrica) discharge 3 (w.c.) flush: puxar a ~ flush the toilet

descarregado adj (pilha, bateria) flat

descarregar vt 1 unload: ~ um caminhão/um revólver unload a truck/gun 2 (raiva, frustração) vent ● vi (pilha, bateria) go flat

descarrilamento sm derailment

descarrilar vi: O trem descarrilou. The train was derailed.

descartar vt rule sb/sth out ● **descartar-se** vp ~ **de** get rid of sb/sth

descartável adj disposable

descascar vt 1 (fruta): ~ uma laranja peel an orange 2 (ervilhas, marisco, nozes) shell

descendência smf descendants [pl]

descendente smf descendant

descender vt (família) be descended from sb

descer vt 1 (levar/trazer) take/bring sth down: Você me ajuda a ~ a mala? Could you help me take my suitcase down? 2 (ir/vir para baixo) go/come down: ~ o morro go/come down the hill ● vi 1 (ir/vir para baixo) go/come down 2 ~ (de) (a) (automóvel) get out (of sth) (b) (transporte público, cavalo, bicicleta) get off (sth)

descida sf 1 (declive) descent 2 (ladeira) slope: uma ~ suave/acentuada a gentle/steep slope

descoberta sf discovery [pl -ies]: fazer uma grande ~ make a great discovery

descobridor/a sm-sf discoverer

descobrimento sm discovery [pl -ies]

descobrir vt 1 (encontrar, dar-se conta) discover: ~ uma ilha discover an island ◊ Descobri que estava sem dinheiro. I discovered I had no money. 2 (averiguar) find sth (out) 3 (destapar, desvendar) uncover

descolado adj unstuck

descolar vt 1 (tirar) pull sth off 2 (conseguir) get: ~ um emprego get a job 3 (dar) give: Dá para me ~ uns trocados? Do you have any spare change to give me? ● vi (soltar) come off

descompostura sf (repimenda) reprimand

desconcertado adj: Ele ficou ~ com a minha recusa. He was taken aback by my refusal.

desconcertar vt puzzle

desconfiado adj suspicious: ser ~ have a suspicious mind

desconfiar vt 1 (distrust): Ele desconfia até da própria sombra. He doesn't trust anyone. 2 (supor): Desconfio que vai chover. I have a feeling it's going to rain.

desconfortável adj uncomfortable

desconforto sm discomfort

descongelar vt (geladeira, alimento) defrost

desconhecer vt not know: Desconheço a razão. I don't know why.

desconhecido/a adj unknown ● sm-sf stranger

descontar vt 1 (subtrair) deduct 2 (fazer um desconto) give a discount (on sth) 3 (cheque, vale postal) cash

descontente adj dissatisfied (with sb/sth)

desconto sm discount: fazer um ~ de 10% em algo give a 10% discount on sth

descontração sf (informalidade) informality

descontrair-se vp relax

descontrolado adj 1 (máquina) out of control 2 (pessoa) hysterical

descontrolar-se vp 1 (pessoa) break down 2 (máquina) get out of control

desconversar vi change the subject

descrever vt describe

descrição sf description

descuidado adj 1 (desatento) careless 2 (desleixado) scruffy

descuidar vt neglect ● **descuidar-se** vp: Eu me descuidei da hora. I didn't notice the time.

descuido sm carelessness [U]: devido a um ~ do motorista due to the driver's carelessness ◊ Num momento de ~ dele, o cão fugiu. He wasn't paying attention and the dog ran away.

desculpa sf 1 (justificativa) excuse (for sth): Ele arranja sempre uma ~ para não vir. He always finds an excuse not to come. ◊ Isto não tem ~. There's no excuse for this. 2 (pedido de perdão) apology [pl -ies]

desculpar vt forgive ● **desculpar-se** vp apologize (to sb) (for sth) ▶ **desculpa, desculpe, etc.** 1 (para pedir desculpas) sorry: Desculpe o atraso. Sorry I'm late. ◊ Desculpe interromper. Sorry to interrupt. ◊ Desculpe, pisei em você? Sorry, did I step on your foot? 2 (para chamar a atenção) excuse me: Desculpe, o senhor tem horas, por favor? Excuse me, do you have the time, please? → EXCUSE

desde prep since: Moro aqui ~ 1986. I've lived here since 1986.

→ FOR ▶ ~ que... 1 (*depois que*) since 2 (*contanto que*) as long as

desdém *sm* scorn: *um olhar de ~* a scornful look

desdenhoso *adj* scornful

desdobrar *vt* 1 (*mapa, papel*) unfold 2 (*tropas, armamento*) deploy 3 (*esforços*) redouble ● **desdobrar-se** *vp* (*esforçar-se*) do your utmost

desejar *vt* (*querer*) want: *O que deseja?* What would you like? 2 (*ansiar*) wish for sth: *O que mais eu podia ~?* What more could I wish for? 3 (*boa sorte*) wish sb sth: *Eu lhe desejo boa sorte.* I wish you luck.

desejo *sm* 1 wish: *Faça um ~.* Make a wish. 2 (*anseio*) desire 3 (*mulher grávida*) craving: *ter ~ de algo* have a craving for sth

desemaranhar *vt* disentangle

desembaraçado *adj* 1 (*desinibido*) free and easy 2 (*engenhoso*) resourceful 3 (*expedito*) efficient

desembaraçar *vt* untangle: *~ o cabelo* get the tangles out of your hair ● **desembaraçar-se** *vp* **~ de** get rid of sb/sth

desembarcar *vt* (*mercadoria, pessoa*) land ● *vi* disembark

desembocar *vi* 1 (*rio*) flow into sth 2 (*rua, etc.*) lead to sth

desembolsar *vt* pay sth (out)

desembrulhar *vt* unwrap

desempatar *vi* 1 (*Esporte*) play off 2 (*Pol*) break the deadlock

desempate *sm* play-off

desempenhar *vt* play: *~ um papel* play a role

desempenho *sm* (*motor*) performance: *um motor de alto ~* a high-performance engine

desempregado/a *adj* unemployed ● *sm-sf* unemployed person: *os ~s* the unemployed

desemprego *sm* unemployment

desencaminhar *vt* lead sb astray ● **desencaminhar-se** *vp* go astray

desencontrar-se *vp* miss one another

desencorajar *vt* discourage

desenferrujar *vt* 1 (*metal*) remove the rust from sth 2 (*língua*) brush up (on) sth 3 (*pernas*) stretch

desenfreado *adj* (*cavalo, festa*) wild

desenhar *vi, vt* 1 draw 2 (*vestuário, mobília, produtos*) design

desenhista *smf* draftsman/woman [*pl* -men/-women]

desenho *sm* 1 (*Arte*) drawing: *estudar ~* study drawing ◊ *fazer um ~* do a drawing 2 (*Tec*) design: *~ gráfico* graphic design 3 (*padrão*) pattern ▶ ~ **animado** cartoon

desenrolar *vt* 1 (*papel*) unroll 2 (*cabo*) unwind

desenroscar *vt* unscrew

desenterrar *vt* 1 dig sth up 2 (*descobrir*) unearth

desentupir *vt* unblock

desenvoltura *sf* (*desembaraço*) self-confidence: *Ele tem muita ~.* He's full of confidence.

desenvolver(-se) *vt, vp* develop

desenvolvimento *sm* development: *países em ~* developing countries

desequilibrar-se *vp* lose your balance

deserto *adj* deserted ● *sm* desert

desertor/a *sm-sf* deserter

desesperado/a *adj* desperate

desesperar *vt* drive sb to despair ● *vi* despair

desespero *sm* despair: *para ~ meu* to my despair

desfavorável *adj* unfavorable

desfazer *vt* 1 (*nó, embrulho*) undo 2 (*cama*) unmake 3 (*dúvida, engano*) dispel 4 (*desmontar*) break sth up ● **desfazer-se** *vp* 1 (*nó, costura*) come undone 2 (*derreter-se*) melt 3 (*desmanchar-se*) fall to pieces 4 (*despedaçar*) break 5 **~ de** get rid of sb/sth

desfecho *sm* outcome

desfeita *sf* insult

desfigurar *vt* (*tornar feio*) disfigure

desfiladeiro *sm* (*Geog*) pass

desfilar *vi* 1 march 2 (*modelos*) parade

desfile *sm* parade: *~ de moda* fashion show

desforra *sf* revenge

desgastante *adj* (*cansativo*) stressful

desgastar(-se) *vt, vp* (*rochas*) wear (sth) away, erode (*fml*)

desgaste *sm* 1 (*máquina, mobília*) wear and tear 2 (*rochas*) erosion

desgosto *sm* (*tristeza*) sorrow: *A decisão dele causou-lhes um grande ~.* His decision caused them great sorrow. ▶ **dar ~ (a)** upset

desgostoso *adj* sad

desgraça *sf* misfortune

desgraçado/a *adj* 1 (*sem sorte*) unlucky 2 (*infeliz*) unhappy

• sm-sf **1** (*infeliz*) wretch **2** (*pessoa má*) swine
desgravar vt (*fita cassete*) erase
desidratação sf dehydration
design sm design
designar vt **1** (*para cargo*) appoint sb (*sth/to sth*): *Foi designado presidente/para o cargo.* He was appointed chairman/to the post. **2** (*lugar*) designate sth (*as sth*)
designer smf designer
desigual adj **1** (*tratamento*) unfair **2** (*terreno*) uneven **3** (*luta*) unequal
desigualdade sf inequality [pl -ies]
desiludir vt disappoint
desilusão sf disappointment: *sofrer uma ~ (amorosa)* be disappointed (in love)
desimpedir vt clear
desinchar vt *A pomada vai ~ o seu dedo.* This cream will make the swelling in your finger go down. • vi go down
desinfetante sm disinfectant
desinfetar vt disinfect
desinibido adj uninhibited
desintegração sf disintegration
desintegrar-se vp disintegrate
desinteressar-se vp lose interest *in sb/sth*
desinteresse sm lack of interest
desistir vt, vi give up (*doing sth*)
desleal adj disloyal
desleixado adj **1** (*pouco cuidadoso*) sloppy **2** (*desmazelado*) scruffy
desligar vt **1** (*apagar*) turn sth off **2** (*de tomada*) unplug • **desligar-se** vp **1** (*aparelho*) go off **2** (*pessoa*) turn your back on sb/sth ► **~ (o telefone)** hang up: *Não desligue, por favor.* Please hold.
deslizamento sm ► **~ de terra** landslide
deslizar vi **1** slide: *~ no gelo* slide on the ice **2** (*cobra*) slither
deslize sm (*lapso*) slip
deslocado adj: *sentir-se ~* feel out of place
deslocar vt dislocate • **deslocar-se** vp go: *~ para todo lado de táxi* go everywhere by taxi
deslumbrante adj dazzling: *uma iluminação/atuação ~* a dazzling light/performance
deslumbrar vt dazzle
desmaiado adj (*pessoa*) unconscious
desmaiar vi faint

desmaio sm fainting fit ► **ter um ~** faint
desmancha-prazeres smf spoilsport
desmantelar vt dismantle
desmatamento sm deforestation
desmazelado adj scruffy
desmentir vt deny
desmontar vt **1** take sth apart: *~ uma bicicleta* take a bicycle apart **2** (*andaime, estante, tenda*) take sth down **3** (*destruir*) smash: *~ algo por completo* smash sth to pieces
desmoralizar vt demoralize
desmoronamento sm **1** (*edifício*) collapse **2** (*terra*) landslide
desmoronar vi collapse
desnecessário adj unnecessary
desobedecer vi, vt disobey: *~ às ordens/aos seus pais* disobey orders/your parents
desobediência sf disobedience
desobediente adj disobedient
desobstruir vt unblock
desocupado adj vacant
desodorante sm deodorant
desolado adj **1** (*lugar*) desolate **2** (*pessoa*) devastated
desonesto adj dishonest
desordeiro/a sm-sf troublemaker
desordem sm mess: *A casa estava em ~.* The house was a mess.
desordenado adj messy
desordenar vt mess sth up
desorganizado adj disorganized
desorientar vt disorient • **desorientar-se** vp become disoriented
despachar vt (*mercadoria*) dispatch • **despachar-se** vp ~ de get rid of sb/sth
desparafusar vt unscrew
despedaçar(-se) vt, vp smash
despedida sf **1** farewell: *jantar de ~* farewell dinner **2** (*celebração*) farewell party ► **~ de solteiro** bachelor party, stag night (GB)
despedir vt (*empregado*) fire • **despedir-se** vp **1** (*dizer a*) say goodbye (*to sb/sth*) **2** (*demitir-se*) resign
despeitado adj spiteful
despejar vt **1** (*esvaziar*) empty: *Despeje o cesto de papéis.* Empty the wastebasket. **2** (*resíduos*) dump **3** (*para um recipiente*) pour **4** (*de casa*) evict
despencar vi plummet

despensa *sf* pantry [*pl* -ies]

despenteado *adj* disheveled: *Você está todo ~.* Your hair's messy.

despentear *vt* mess *sb's* hair up

despercebido *adj* unnoticed: *passar* ~ go unnoticed

desperdiçar *vt* waste

desperdício *sm* waste

despertador *sm* alarm (clock): *pôr o* ~ set the alarm

despertar *vt* **1** (*pessoa*) wake *sb* up **2** (*interesse, suspeitas*) arouse ● **despertar(-se)** *vi, vp* wake up

despesa *sf* expense

despido *adj* (*pessoa*) naked

despir *vt* **1** (*roupa*) take *sth* off **2** (*pessoa*) undress ● **despir-se** *vp* get undressed

despistar *vt* **1** (*desorientar*) confuse **2** (*escapar a*) throw *sb* off the scent

despontar *vi* **1** (*aurora, dia*) break **2** (*sol*) **(a)** (*amanhecer*) rise **(b)** (*por entre as nuvens*) come out

despovoado *adj* uninhabited

despovoamento *sm* depopulation

despovoar *vt* depopulate

desprender *vt* unhook ● **desprender-se** *vp* come off

desprendimento *sm* (*desapego*) detachment

despreocupado *adj* carefree

desprevenido *adj* unprepared: *apanhar/pegar alguém* ~ catch *sb* unawares

desprezar *vt* **1** (*menosprezar*) despise, look down on *sb* (*mais colog*) **2** (*rejeitar*) refuse

desprezo *sm* contempt (*for sb/sth*)

desproporcionado *adj* disproportionate (*to sth*)

desprovido *adj* lacking in *sth*

desqualificação *sf* (*Esporte*) disqualification

desqualificar *vt* (*Esporte*) disqualify

desrespeitador *adj* disrespectful (*to/towards sb/sth*)

destacar *vt* (*salientar*) point *sth* out ● **destacar-se** *vp* stand out

destampar *vt*: ~ *uma panela* take the lid off of a pot

destaque *sm* **1** (*proeminência*) prominence: *um membro de ~ da comunidade* a prominent member of the community **2** (*noticiário*) main point ► **em** ~ in focus

destemido *adj* fearless

destinatário/a *sm-sf* addressee

destino *sm* **1** (*sina*) fate **2** (*avião, navio, trem, passageiro*) destination: *o trem com* ~ *a Recife* the train for Recife

destoar *vt* clash (*with sth*)

destreza *sf* skill

destro *adj* **1** (*hábil*) skillful **2** (*ágil*) deft **3** (*que usa a mão direita*) right-handed

destroçar *vt* **1** destroy **2** (*fazer em pedaços*) smash **3** (*arruinar*) ruin: ~ *a vida de alguém* ruin *sb's* life

destroços *sm* wreckage [*sing*]

destróier *sm* destroyer

destruição *sf* destruction

destruir *vt* destroy

destrutivo *adj* destructive

desumano *adj* inhuman

desuso *sm* disuse: *cair em* ~ fall into disuse

desvalorização *sf* devaluation

desvalorizar *vt* devalue ● **desvalorizar-se** *vp* depreciate

desvantagem *sf* disadvantage: *em* ~ at a disadvantage

desviar *vt* divert: ~ *o trânsito/fundos públicos* divert the traffic/public funds ● **desviar-se** *vp* get out of the way ► ~ **o olhar** look away

desvio *sm* **1** (*trânsito*) diversion **2** (*volta*) detour: *fazer um* ~ *de cinco quilômetros* make a five-kilometer detour **3** (*irregularidade*) deviation (*from sth*) **4** (*fundos*) embezzlement

detalhadamente *adv* in detail

detalhado *adj* detailed

detalhar *vt* **1** (*contar com detalhes*) give details of *sth* **2** (*especificar*) specify

detalhe *sm* detail

detectar *vt* detect

detector *sm*: *um* ~ *de mentiras/metais* a lie/metal detector

detenção *sf* **1** (*prisão*) arrest **2** (*paralisação*) halt

deter *vt* **1** stop **2** (*prender*) arrest ● **deter-se** *vp* stop

detergente *sm* detergent ► ~ **para a louça** dishwashing liquid, washing-up liquid (*GB*)

deteriorar *vt* (*danificar*) damage ● **deteriorar-se** *vp* deteriorate

determinado *adj* **1** (*certo*) certain: *em ~s casos* in certain cases **2** (*decidido*) determined

determinar *vt* determine

detestar *vt* detest *sb/(doing) sth*, hate *sb/(doing) sth* (*mais colog*)

detetive *smf* detective: ~ *particular* private detective

detido/a adj: estar/ficar ~ be under arrest ● sm-sf detainee

deus sm god ▶ ~ me livre God forbid **meu** ~ good God **se** ~ **quiser God willing só Deus sabe/sabe Deus** God knows

deusa sf goddess

devagar adv slowly ● interj slow down ▶ ~ **e sempre** slowly but surely

dever[1] vt **1** + substantivo owe: Devo-lhe 3.000 reais/uma explicação. I owe you 3,000 reais/an explanation. **2** + inf **(a)** (no presente ou futuro, frases afirmativas) must: Você deve obedecer às regras. You must obey the rules. ◇ Ela já deve estar em casa. She must be home by now. ▶ MUST **(b)** (no presente ou futuro, frases negativas): Não deve ser fácil. It can't be easy. **(c)** (no passado ou condicional) should: Faz uma hora que você devia estar aqui. You should have been here an hour ago. ◇ Você não devia sair assim. You shouldn't go out like that. **3** be due to sth: Isto se deve à falta de fundos. This is due to a lack of funds. ▶ **como deve ser**: um escritório como deve ser a real office ● **fazer algo como deve ser** do sth right

dever[2] sm **1** (obrigação moral) duty [pl -ies]: cumprir um ~ do your duty **2** (**deveres**) (Educ) homework [U]: fazer os ~es do your homework ◇ O professor passa muitos ~es. Our teacher gives us a lot of homework.

devido adj (correto) proper ▶ ~ **a** due to sth

devolução sf **1** (artigo) return **2** (dinheiro) refund

devolver vt **1** return sth (to sb/sth) **2** (dinheiro) refund

devoto adj devout

dez num, sm **1** ten **2** (data) tenth

dezembro sm December (abrev **Dec.**) → MAIO

dezena sf **1** (Mat, número coletivo) ten **2** (aproximadamente) about ten: uma ~ de vezes about ten times

dezenove num, sm **1** nineteen **2** (data) nineteenth

dezesseis num, sm **1** sixteen **2** (data) sixteenth

dezessete num, sm **1** seventeen **2** (data) seventeenth

dezoito num, sm **1** eighteen **2** (data) eighteenth

dia sm **1** day: no ~ seguinte on the following day ◇ de ~/durante o ~ in/during the daytime ◇

todos os ~s every day **2** (em datas): no ~ de 6 de abril on the 6th of April NOTA Diz-se "April sixth" ou "the sixth of April" ▶ **ao/por** ~: três vezes ao ~ three times a day **bom** ~ (good) morning ~ **das mães/dos pais** Mother's/Father's Day ~ **de Natal** Christmas Day → NATAL ~ **de Reis** January 6 ~ **dos namorados** Valentine's Day ~ **livre/de folga 1** (não ocupado) free day **2** (sem ir trabalhar) day off **dia sim, dia não** every other day ~ **útil/de semana** working day/weekday **estar/ andar em** ~ be up to date **o** ~ **de amanhã** in the future **pôr em** ~ bring sb/sth up to date **ser (de)** ~ be light

diabetes sf ou sm diabetes

diabético/a adj, sm-sf diabetic

diabo sm devil ▶ **do(s) ~(s)**: Está um frio dos ~s. It's freezing. ◇ um problema dos ~s one hell of a problem **por que ~(s)...?** why the hell...?

diabrete sm little devil

diagnóstico sm diagnosis [pl -noses]

diagonal adj, sf diagonal

diagrama sm diagram

dialeto sm dialect

diálogo sm dialogue

diamante sm diamond

diâmetro sm diameter

diante prep ~ **de 1** (espaço) in front of sb/sth: Ela estava sentada ~ dele. She was sitting in front of him. **2** (perante) **(a)** (pessoa) in the presence of: ~ do presidente in the presence of the president **(b)** (coisa) up against: Estamos ~ de um grande problema. We're up against a major problem.

dianteira sf **1** (carro) front **2** (liderança) lead: ir na ~ be in the lead

dianteiro adj front

diário adj daily ● sm **1** (jornal) daily [pl -ies] **2** (pessoal) diary [pl -ies]

diarréia sf diarrhea [U]

dica sf tip

dicionário sm dictionary [pl -ies]: Procure no ~. Look it up in the dictionary.

didático adj educational

diesel sm diesel: motor a ~ diesel engine

dieta sf diet: estar de ~ be on a diet

difamar vt **1** (oralmente) slander **2** (por escrito) libel

diferença sf difference (bet-ween sth and sth); (in/of sth): O Rio tem duas horas de ~ em relação a Nova York. There's a two hour time difference between Rio and New York. ◇ Não há muita ~ de preço entre os dois. There's not much difference in price between the two. ◇ ~ de opinião difference of opinion

diferenciar vt differentiate sth (from sth); differentiate between sth and sth ▸ **diferenciar-se** vp: Eles não se diferenciam em nada. There's no difference between them. ◇ Como se diferenciam? What's the difference?

diferente adj different (from/than sb/sth): Pensamos de modo ~. We think differently.

difícil adj difficult

dificuldade sf difficulty [pl -ies] ▸ **ter ~ (de fazer algo)** have trouble doing sth

dificultar vt **1** (tornar difícil) make sth difficult **2** (progresso, mudança) hinder

difundido adj widespread

difundir vt **1** (TV, rádio) broadcast **2** (publicar) publish **3** (oralmente) spread ▸ **difundir-se** vp (notícia, luz) spread

difusão sf **1** (idéias) dissemination **2** (programas) broadcasting **3** (jornal, etc.) circulation

digerir vt digest

digestão sf digestion ▸ **fazer a ~** wait for your food to go down

digestivo adj digestive: o aparelho ~ the digestive system

digital adj digital

digitar vt **1** (palavra) key sth in **2** (Informát) enter

dígito sm digit

dignar-se vp deign to do sth

dignidade sf dignity

digno adj **1** decent: um trabalho ~ a decent job **2** ~ **de** worthy of sth: ~ de confiança reliable

dilatar(-se) vt, vp **1** (aumentar, distender(-se)) expand **2** (poros, pupilas) dilate

dilema sm dilemma

diluir vt **1** (sólido) dissolve **2** (líquido) dilute **3** (molho, tinta) thin

dilúvio sm **1** deluge **2** (o Dilúvio) the Flood

dimensão sf dimension

diminuição sf fall (in sth)

diminuir vt reduce: ~ a velocidade reduce your speed ● vi

drop: Os preços diminuíram. Prices have dropped.

diminutivo adj, sm diminutive

diminuto adj tiny

dinâmica sf dynamics [sing]

dinâmico adj dynamic

dinamite sf dynamite

dínamo sm dynamo [pl ~s]

dinastia sf dynasty [pl -ies]

dinheirão sm fortune: Custa um ~. It costs a fortune.

dinheiro sm money [U]: Necessito de ~. I need some money. ▸ **estar mal de ~** be short of money **~ trocado** loose change

dinossauro sm dinosaur

dióxido sm dioxide: ~ de carbono carbon dioxide

diploma sm diploma: ~ escolar high school diploma

diplomacia sf diplomacy

diplomado adj qualified

diplomata smf diplomat

diplomático adj diplomatic

dique sm dike

direção sf **1** (rumo, Cinema) direction: ir na ~ contrária go in the opposite direction ◇ sair em ~ a Osório set off for Osório ◇ ir em ~ a alguém/algo go toward sb/sth **2** (empresa) management **3** (carro) steering: ~ motorizada power steering

direito/a adj **1** (destro) right **2** (reto) straight: Sente ~ na cadeira. Sit up straight. **3** (aprumado) upright ● sm **1** (oposto de avesso) right side ● sm **1** (faculdade legal ou moral) right: Com que ~ você entra aqui? What right do you have to come in here? ◇ no seu ~ within your rights ◇ os ~s humanos human rights ◇ o ~ de voto the right to vote **3** (curso) law **4** (pé) right foot ● **direita** sf **1** right: É a segunda porta à ~. It's the second door on the right. ◇ Vire à ~. Turn right. **2** (mão) right hand: escrever com a ~ be right-handed ▸ **a direita** (Pol) the Right de direita right-wing **~s alfandegários** customs duties **~s autorais** copyright **não está** ~ it's not fair

diretamente adv straight: Regressamos ~. We went straight back.

direto/a adj direct: um vôo ~ a direct flight ◇ o caminho mais ~ the most direct route ● adv straight: Vá ~ para casa. Go straight home. ◇ ir ~ ao assunto get to the point

diretor/a sm-sf **1** director: ~ artístico/financeiro artistic/financial director ◇ um ~ de cinema a movie director **2** (escola) principal, head (teacher) (GB) **3** (jornal) editor

diretoria sf **1** (empresa) (a) (diretores) board **(b)** (sala) boardroom **2** (escola) principal

dirigente adj **1** (Pol) ruling **2** (gerente) management: *a equipe ~* the management team ● smf (Pol) leader

dirigir vt **1** (peça de teatro, filme, trânsito) direct **2** (a) (carro) drive **(b)** (moto) ride **3** (orquestra) conduct **4** (carta, mensagem) address sth to sb/sth **5** (arma, mangueira, telescópio) point sth at sb/sth **6** (debate, campanha, expedição, partido) lead **7** ~ *um negócio* run a business ● **dirigir-se** vp **1** head for ...: *~ à fronteira* head for the border **2** (a) (falar) speak to sb **(b)** (por carta) write to sb ▶ *~ a palavra* speak to sb

discar vt, vi dial: *~ errado* dial the wrong number

disciplina sf **1** discipline: *manter a ~* maintain discipline **2** (matéria) subject

discípulo/a sm-sf **1** (seguidor) disciple **2** (aluno) student

disc-jóquei smf disc jockey (abrev DJ)

disco sm **1** (Mús) record: *gravar/pôr um ~* make/play a record **2** (Informát, objeto circular) disk: *o ~ rígido* the hard disk **3** (Esporte) discus ▶ *~ voador* flying saucer

discordar vt, vi disagree (with sb) (about sth)

discoteca sf **1** (clube noturno) club **2** (loja de discos) record store ▶ **de ~** (música): *música de ~* dance music

discreto adj **1** (prudente) discreet **2** (modesto) unremarkable

discrição sf discretion

discriminação sf discrimination: *a ~ racial* racial discrimination

discriminar vt discriminate against sb

discurso sm speech: *fazer um ~* make a speech

discussão sf **1** (debate) discussion **2** (briga) argument

discutir vt **1** (debater) discuss: *~ política* discuss politics **2** (questionar) question ● vi (brigar) argue (with sb) (about sth)

disenteria sf dysentery

disfarçar vt disguise: *~ uma cicatriz* hide a scar ● vi (fingir) pretend: *Disfarce, faça como se*

você não soubesse de nada. Pretend you don't know anything.

disfarce sm disguise

disforme adj deformed

dislexia sf dyslexia

disléxico/a adj, sm-sf dyslexic

disparado adj ▶ **sair ~/em disparada** shoot out (of...): *Eles saíram ~s do banco.* They shot out of the bank.

disparar vt, vi shoot: *~ uma flecha* shoot an arrow ◇ *~ contra algo* shoot at sth ● vi **1** go off: *A pistola disparou.* The pistol went off. **2** (preços) shoot up

disparatado adj foolish

disparate sm **1** (dito) nonsense [U]: *Não diga ~s!* Don't talk nonsense! **2** (feito) stupid thing

disparo sm shot

dispensar vt **1** (passar sem) dispense with sth: *Dispensa apresentações.* Don't bother with introductions. **2** (exame, prova) let sb off sth **3** (ceder) lend sb sth: *Você pode me ~ uma folha?* Could you lend me a sheet of paper? **4** (de um cargo) relieve sb of sth

dispersar(-se) vt, vi, vp disperse

disponível adj available

dispor vt **1** arrange **2** ~ **de (a)** (ter) have sth **(b)** (utilizar) use sth: *~ das suas economias* use your savings ● **dispor-se** vp ~ **a 1** (estar pronto) get ready for sth/to do sth **2** (oferecer-se) offer to do sth

dispositivo sm device

disposto adj **1** (ordenado) arranged **2** (solicito) willing **3** (decidido) prepared to do sth

disputa sf **1** (briga) argument **2** (competição) competition

disputado adj fiercely contested

disputar vt **1** compete for sth **2** (Esporte) play

disquete sm floppy disk

dissecar vt dissect

dissertação sf paper

dissimuladamente adv surreptitiously

dissimular vt hide ● vi pretend

dissolver(-se) vt, vi, vp **1** (num líquido) dissolve **2** (manifestação) break (sth) up

dissuadir vt dissuade sb (from doing) sth

distância sf distance: *A que ~ fica a próxima cidade?* How far is it to the next town? ▶ **a/à ~** at/from a distance **a muita/pouca ~ de...** a long way/not far from...

distanciar vt **1** (no espaço, tempo) distance **2** (pessoas) drive sb apart ● **distanciar-se** vp **1** (afastar-se) move away **2** (pessoas) grow apart

distante adj distant

distinção sf distinction: fazer distinções make distinctions ◊ sem ~ de raça/sexo regardless of race/gender

distinguir vt **1** distinguish sb/sth (from sb/sth): Não consigo ~ os dois irmãos. I can't tell the brothers apart **2** (divisar) make sth out ● **distinguir-se** vp be known for sth

distinto adj **1** (diferente) different **2** (som, ruído) distinct **3** (eminente) distinguished

distorcer vt (alterar) distort: ~ uma imagem/os fatos distort an image/the facts

distração sf **1** (divertimento, esquecimento) distraction **2** (falta de atenção) absent-mindedness **3** (descuido) oversight **4** (relaxamento) relaxation

distraído adj absent-minded ▶ **estar/ir** ~ be miles away **fazer-se de** ~ pretend not to notice

distrair vt **1** (entreter) keep sb amused **2** (fazer perder a atenção) distract sb (from sth) ● **distrair-se** vp **1** ~ **com algo/ fazendo algo** (a) (passar o tempo) pass the time doing sth (b) (gostar de) enjoy doing sth **2** (descuidar-se) be distracted

distribuição sf **1** distribution **2** (correspondência) delivery **3** (casa, apartamento) layout

distribuir vt **1** (dar) distribute: Distribuirão alimentos aos refugiados. They will distribute food to the refugees. **2** (repartir) share sth out

distrito sm district

distúrbio sm **1** (perturbação) disturbance **2** (violento) riot

ditado sm **1** (para se escrito) dictation: fazer um ~ do a dictation **2** (provérbio) saying: Como diz o ~... As the saying goes...

ditador, ~a sm-sf dictator

ditadura sf dictatorship

ditar vt dictate

dito adj ~ **de outra forma/ maneira** in other words ~ **e feito** no sooner said than done

ditongo sm diphthong

divã sm divan

diversão sf **1** (distração) amusement **2** (prazer) fun: Pintar para mim é uma ~. I paint for

fun. **3** (espetáculo) entertainment

diverso adj **1** (variado, diferente) different: pessoas de diversas origens people from different backgrounds **2** (diversos) (vários) various

divertido adj **1** (engraçado) funny **2** (agradável) enjoyable ▶ **estar/ser (muito)** ~ be (great) fun

divertimento sm amusement

divertir vt amuse ● **divertir-se** vp **1** enjoy yourself: Divirta-se! Have a good time! **2** ~ **(a/com/ fazendo algo)** enjoy (doing) sth

dívida sf debt: em ~ (para) com o banco in debt to the bank

dividir vt **1** divide sth (up): ~ o trabalho/o bolo divide (up) the work/cake **2** (Mat) divide sth (by sth) **3** (partilhar) share: ~ um apartamento share an apartment ● **dividir(-se)** vt, vp **(em)** split (into sth): ~ em duas facções split into two factions

divino adj divine

divisa sf **1** (fronteira) border **2** (divisas) (dinheiro) (foreign) currency [U]: pagar em ~s pay in foreign currency

divisão sf **1** division: um time da primeira ~ a first-division team **2** (compartimento) compartment

divisória sf partition

divorciado adj divorced

divorciar-se vp get divorced (from sb)

divórcio sm divorce

divulgar(-se) vt, vp spread

dizer vt say, tell NOTA Dizer geralmente se traduz por say: — São seis horas, disse a Rosa. "It's six o'clock," said Rosa. ◊ O que é que ele disse? What did he say? Quando se especifica a pessoa com quem se está falando, é mais natural usar tell: Ele me disse que ia chegar tarde. He told me he'd be late. ◊ Quem lhe disse? Who told you? Tell também é usado para dar ordens: Ela me disse que lavasse as mãos. She told me to wash my hands. → SAY ▶ **digamos...** let's say...: Digamos às seis. Let's say six o'clock. **digo...** I mean...: Custa nove, digo dez mil reais. It costs nine, I mean ten, thousand reais. **não (me) diga** you don't say **sem ~ nada** without a word NOTA Para outras expressões com dizer, ver o substantivo, adjetivo, etc., p. ex. dizer tolices em TOLICE.

dó¹ sm ▶ **dar dó** Dá dó jogar isso

fora. It's a pity to throw it away. **sem dó nem piedade** ruthless **ter dó de alguém** take pity on sb

dó² *sm* (*Mús*) C

doação *sf* donation: *fazer uma ~* make a donation

doador/a *sm-sf* donor: *um ~ de sangue* a blood donor

doar *vt* donate

dobra *sf* 1 fold 2 (*livro, envelope*) flap

dobradiça *sf* hinge

dobradinha *sf* (*Cozinha*) tripe [U]

dobrar *vt* 1 (*sobrepor*) fold: *~ um papel em oito* fold a piece of paper into eight 2 (*curvar, flexionar*) bend: *~ o joelho/uma barra de ferro* bend your knee/ an iron bar 3 (*duplicar*) double: *Eles dobraram a oferta.* They doubled their offer. 4 (*esquina*) turn • *vi* (*sinos*) toll • **dobrar-se** *vp* (*curvar-se*) bend (over)

dobrável *adj*: *uma cama ~* a folding bed

dobro *sm* twice as much/many: *Ela ganha o ~ de mim.* She earns twice as much as me. ◊ *Havia lá o ~ das pessoas.* There were twice as many people there. ◊ *com o ~ da largura* twice as wide

doca *sf* dock

doce *adj* 1 sweet 2 (*pessoa, voz*) gentle • *sm* sweet ▶ **~ de leite** fudge

docente *adj* teaching: *corpo ~* teaching staff

dócil *adj* docile

documentação *sf* 1 (*pessoa*) ID card, identity card (*mais fml*) 2 (*carro*) documents [*pl*]

documentário *sm* documentary [*pl* -ies]

documento *sm* 1 document 2 (**documentos**) (a) (*pessoa*) identity card (*mais fml*), ID card: *Eles me pediram os ~.* They asked to see my ID. (b) (*carro*) documents

doença *sf* 1 illness: *recuperar-se de uma ~ grave* recover from a serious illness 2 (*infecciosa, contagiosa*) disease: *~ hereditária/de Parkinson* hereditary/ Parkinson's disease ▶ DISEASE

doente *adj* sick: *ficar ~* get sick • *smf* 1 sick person: *cuidar dos ~s* care for the sick 2 (*paciente*) patient ▶ **deixar alguém ~** make sb sick

doer *vi* 1 hurt: *A minha perna está doendo.* My leg hurts. 2 (*cabeça, dentes*) ache: *A minha cabeça está doendo.* I have a headache. • *vt* hurt: *Doeu-me*

eles não me terem apoiado. I was hurt by their lack of support.

doidão *adj* stoned

doidice *sf* 1 (*loucura*) madness 2 (*idéia*) crazy idea

doido/a *adj* crazy (*about sb/sth*): *ficar ~* go crazy • *sm-sf* lunatic ▶ **~ varrido** as mad as a hatter

dois, duas *num, adj* 1 two 2 (*data*) second ▶ **dois a dois** in pairs ▶ **~ pontos** colon

dólar *sm* dollar

dolorido *adj* sore: *Estou com o ombro ~.* My shoulder is sore.

doloroso *adj* painful

dom *sm* gift: *o ~ da palavra* the gift of the gab

domar *vt* 1 tame 2 (*cavalo*) break *a horse* in

domesticar *vt* domesticate

doméstica *sf* (*empregada*) maid

doméstico *adj* 1 household: *tarefas domésticas* household chores 2 (*animal*) domestic

domicílio *sm* home, residence (*fml*): *mudança de ~* change of address ◊ *entrega/serviço a ~* delivery service

dominante *adj* dominant

dominar *vt* 1 dominate 2 (*língua*) be fluent in *sth* 3 (*matéria, técnica*) be good at *sth*

domingo *sm* Sunday (*abrev* Sun.): *~ de manhã/à tarde* on Sunday morning/afternoon ◊ *Não trabalho aos ~s.* I don't work on Sundays. ◊ *~ sim, ~ não* every other Sunday ◊ *~ passada* last Sunday ◊ *Vemos-nos no ~ que vem.* We'll meet next Sunday. ◊ *no ~, 25 de julho* on Sunday, July 25 NOTA Lê-se: "Sunday, July twenty-fifth". ▶ **~ de Ramos/Páscoa** Palm/Easter Sunday

domínio *sm* 1 (*controle*) control: *~ da bola* ball control 2 (*língua*) mastery 3 (*técnica*) mastery 4 (*setor, campo*) field 5 (*território*) domain ▶ **de/do ~ público** common knowledge

dominó *sm* (*jogo*) dominoes

dona *sf*: *Dona Ana (Costa)* Mrs. (Ana) Costa ▶ **~ de casa** housewife [*pl* -wives]

donativo *sm* donation

dono/a *sm-sf* 1 owner 2 (*bar, pensão*) landlord [*fem* landlady] ▶ **ser ~ do seu nariz** know your own mind

dor *sf* 1 pain: *Ela está com ~?* Is she in pain? 2 (*mágoa*) grief ▶ **~ de barriga, cabeça, dentes**, etc. stomach ache, headache, toothache, etc.: *estar com ~ nas*

costas have a backache: ~ **de garganta** sore throat

dor-de-cotovelo sf jealousy: ter ~ **de cotovelo** be jealous

dormente adj numb: **Estou com a perna ~.** My leg's gone to sleep.

dormir vi **1** sleep: **Não consegui ~ nada.** I couldn't sleep a wink. **2** (estar adormecido) be asleep: **enquanto eu dormia** while I was asleep **3** (dormitar) doze off ▶ ~ **como uma pedra** sleep like a log **hora de ~** time for bed **não deixar ~** keep sb awake

dormitório sm bedroom

dosagem sf dosage

dose sf **1** (Med) dose **2** (bebida alcoólica) shot

dossiê sm (processo) dossier

dotado adj **1** (talentoso) gifted **2** ~ **de** (de uma qualidade) endowed with sth

dote sm **1** (de uma mulher) dowry [pl -ies] **2** (talento) gift

dourado adj **1** gold: **uma bolsa ~** a gold bag **2** (cabelo) golden

doutor/a sm-sf doctor (abrev **Dr.**)

doutoramento sm doctorate

doutrina sf doctrine

doze num, sm **1** twelve **2** (data) twelfth

dragão sm dragon

drama sm drama

dramático adj dramatic

dramatizar vt, vi dramatize: ~ **uma obra para a televisão** dramatize a book for television ◊ **Não dramatize!** Don't be over-dramatic!

dramaturgo/a sm-sf playwright

driblar vt, vi (Esporte) dribble

droga sf **1** drug: ~**s leves/pesadas** soft/hard drugs ◊ **uma campanha contra a ~** an anti-drugs campaign NOTA Usa-se o plural quando se fala de drogas ilegais. **2** (coisa de má qualidade) garbage • interj darn it

drogado/a sm-sf drug addict

drogar vt drug • **drogar-se** vp take drugs

drogaria sf drugstore, chemist's (GB)

dublar vt dub

dublê smf **1** (substituto) stand-in **2** (para cenas perigosas) stuntman/woman [pl -men/-women]

ducha sf shower: tomar uma ~ take a shower

duelo sm duel

duende sm elf [pl elves]

duna sf dune

duo sm **1** (composição) duet **2** (par) duo [pl ~s]

duodécimo/a num, sm twelfth

dupla sf pair

dúplex sm duplex (apartment)

duplicar vi double

duplo/a num double: com ~ **sentido** with a double meaning

duque/esa sm-sf duke [fem duchess] NOTA Quando se trata de um casal de duques, diz-se **the duke and duchess.**

duração sf **1** length: **Qual é a ~ do contrato?** How long is the contract for? **2** (lâmpada, pilha) life: **pilhas de longa ~** long-life batteries

durante prep during, for: ~ **o show** during the show ◊ ~ **dois anos** for two years NOTA Usa-se **during** quando o tempo ou o momento em que se inicia a ação e **for** quando se especifica a duração da ação: **Senti-me mal ~ a reunião.** I felt sick during the meeting. ◊ **Choveu ~ uma hora.** It rained for an hour.

durar vi last: ~ **muito** last a long time ◊ **Durou pouco.** It didn't last long.

duro/a adj **1** hard: **A manteiga está dura.** The butter's hard. ◊ **uma vida dura** a hard life ◊ **ser ~ com alguém** be hard on sb **2** (castigo, clima, crítica) harsh **3** (forte, resistente, carne) tough: **É preciso ser ~ para sobreviver.** You have to be tough to survive. **4** (pão) stale • adv: **trabalhar ~** work hard ▶ ~ **de ouvido** hard of hearing

dúvida sf **1** (incerteza) doubt: **estar em ~** be in some doubt ◊ **longe de ~** beyond (all) doubt **2** (problema): **Alguma ~?** Are there any questions? ◊ **O professor passou a aula toda tirando ~s.** The teacher spent the whole class answering questions. ▶ **não há ~ de que...** there is no doubt that... **sem ~** absolutely

duvidar vt, vi doubt: **Duvido!** I doubt it. ◊ ~ **da palavra de alguém** doubt sb's word ◊ **Duvido que seja fácil.** I doubt it'll be easy. • vt ~ **de alguém** mistrust sb

duvidoso/a adj **1** (suspeito) dubious: um **penalty ~** a dubious penalty **2** (incerto) doubtful: **Estou meio ~.** I'm pretty doubtful.

duzentos num, sm two hundred

dúzia sf dozen: uma ~ **de pessoas** a dozen people ◊ **às ~s** by the dozen

Ee

e *conj* **1** (*aditiva*) and **2** (*em interrogativas*) and what about?: *E você?* And what about you? **3** (*horas*) after, past (GB): *São duas e dez.* It's ten after two.

ébano *sm* ebony

ebulição *sf* boiling

echarpe *sf* scarf [*pl* scarves]

eclesiástico *adj* ecclesiastical

eclipse *sm* eclipse

eco *sm* echo [*pl* ~es]: *A gruta fazia* ~. The cave had an echo.

ecologia *sf* ecology

ecológico *adj* ecological

ecologista *adj* environmental ● *smf* environmentalist

economia *sf* economy [*pl* -ies] **2** (**economias**) (*poupança*) savings

econômico *adj* **1** (*que gasta pouco*) economical **2** (*Econ*) economic

economista *smf* economist

economizar *vt, vi* save: ~ *tempo/dinheiro* save time/money

ecossistema *sm* ecosystem

edição *sf* **1** (*publicação*) publication **2** (*tiragem, versão, TV, rádio*) edition: ~ *pirata/semanal* pirate/weekly edition

edificar *vt, vi* build

edifício *sm* building

editar *vt* **1** (*publicar*) publish **2** (*preparar texto, Informát*) edit

editor/a *sm-sf* **1** (*empresário*) publisher **2** (*textos, Jornal, TV, rádio*) editor ● **editora** *sf* (*casa editorial*) publishing house: *De que* ~ *é?* Who are the publishers?

editorial *adj* (*setor*) publishing: *o mundo* ~ the publishing world ● *sm* (*jornal*) editorial ● *sf* (*casa editorial*) publishing house

edredom *sm* **1** quilt **2** (*grosso*) comforter, duvet (GB)

educação *sf* **1** (*ensino*) education: ~ *sexual* sex education **2** (*criança*) upbringing: *Eles tiveram uma boa* ~. They were well brought up. **3** (*cortesia*) manners [*pl*]: *ter boa/má* ~ have good/bad manners ◊ *fazer algo por* ~ do sth to be polite ▶ ~ **física** physical education (*abrev* P.E.)

educado *adj* polite

educador/a *sm-sf* educator

educar *vt* **1** (*ensinar*) educate **2** (*criar*) bring *sb* up

educativo *adj* **1** educational:

brinquedos ~s educational toys **2** (*sistema*) education: *o sistema* ~ the education system

efeito *sm* **1** effect: *fazer* ~ have an effect **2** (*bola*) spin: *A bola vinha com um* ~. The ball had spin on it. ▶ ~ **com** ~ indeed ● **estufa** greenhouse effect ◊ **ficar sem** ~ (*contrato, acordo*) become invalid **para todos os** ~**s** for all intents and purposes

efeminado *adj* effeminate

efervescente *adj* effervescent

efetivo *adj* (*permanente*) permanent

efetuar *vt* carry *sth* out, effect (*fml*): ~ *um ataque/uma prova* carry out an attack/a test ◊ ~ *mudanças* effect change ● **efetuar-se** *vp* take place

eficaz *adj* **1** (*que produz efeito*) effective **2** (*eficiente*) efficient

eficiência *sf* efficiency

eficiente *adj* efficient

egocêntrico *adj* self-centered

egoísmo *sm* selfishness

egoísta *adj* selfish

égua *sf* mare

eh *interj* hey

eixo *sm* **1** (*rodas*) axle **2** (*Geom, Geog, Pol*) axis [*pl* axes] ▶ **estar/andar fora dos** ~**s** be disturbed

ela *pron* **pess 1** (*pessoa*) **(a)** (*sujeito*) she **(b)** (*complemento, comparações*) her: *É para* ~. It's for her. **2** (*coisa*) it ▶ **é ~ 1** it's her **2** (*ao telefone*) speaking ~ **mesma/própria** (she) herself

elaborar *vt* (*redigir*) draw *sth* up

elástico *adj* **1** elastic **2** (*atleta*) supple ● *sm* **1** elastic **2** (*para papéis*) rubber band

ele *pron* **pess 1** (*pessoa*) **(a)** (*sujeito*) he **(b)** (*complemento, comparações*) him: *É para* ~. It's for him. **2** (*coisa*) it ▶ **é ~ 1** it's him **2** (*ao telefone*) speaking ~ **mesmo/próprio** (he) himself

elefante *sm* elephant

elegância *sf* elegance

elegante *adj* elegant

eleger *vt* elect

eleição *sf* **1** (*escolha*) choice **2** (**eleições**) election(s): *convocar eleições* call an election ◊ *eleições legislativas/municipais* legislative/municipal

eleito *pp, adj* **1** elected **2** (*escolhido*) chosen

eleitor/a *sm-sf* voter

eleitorado *sm* electorate

eleitoral adj electoral: campa-nha/lista ~ electoral campaign/ list of candidates

elementar adj elementary

elemento sm **1** (Quím, Mat, etc.) element: no seu ~ in your element **2** (equipe) element **3** (informação) fact

elenco sm (Cinema, Teat) cast

eles, elas pron pess **1** (sujeito) they **2** (complemento, compara-ções) them: Isto é para ~. This is for them. ▶ **são** ~ it's them ♦ **mesmos/próprios** (they) them-selves: Foram ~ mesmos que me disseram. They told me them-selves.

eletricidade sf electricity

eletricista smf electrician

elétrico adj electric, electrical NOTA Usa-se **electric** para eletrodomésticos e dispositivos elétricos específicos, como elec-tric razor/car/fence; também se usa em frases feitas, como an electric shock, e em sentido figurado, em expressões como The atmosphere was electric. **Electrical** refere-se à eletricida-de num sentido mais geral, como electrical engineering ou electrical appliances. ▶ **carros/ carrinhos ~s** bumper cars

eletrodo sm electrode

eletrodoméstico sm electrical appliance

eletrônico/a adj electronic ♦ **eletrônica** sf electronics [sing]

elevado adj high: temperaturas elevadas high temperatures ▶ ~ **ao quadrado/cubo** squared/ cubed ~ **a quatro/cinco**, etc. (raised) to the power of four, etc.

elevador sm elevator, lift (GB)

elevar vt raise ♦ **elevar-se** vp rise

eliminação sf elimination

eliminar vt eliminate

eliminatória sf (Esporte) heat

elipse sf ellipse

elite sf elite

elo sm ▶ ~ **de ligação** link

elogiar vt praise sb/sth (for sth)

elogio sm praise [U]: Fizeram muitos ~s a você. They were full of praise for you. ♦ Não era uma crítica, mas um ~. It wasn't meant to be a criticism so much as a compliment.

em prep

• **lugar 1** (dentro) in/inside: As chaves estão na gaveta. The keys are in the drawer. **2** (den-tro, com movimento) into: Ele entrou no quarto. He went into the room. **3** (sobre) on: Está na

mesa. It's on the table. **4** (cidade, país, campo) in: Eles trabalham em Fortaleza/no campo. They work in Fortaleza/ in the country. **5** (ponto de refe-rência) at NOTA Ao nos refe-rirmos a um lugar não como a uma área mas como a um ponto de referência, usa-se at: Espere-me na esquina. Wait for me at the corner. ♦ Encon-tramo-nos na estação. We'll meet at the station. Também se usa at para lugares onde as pes-soas trabalham, estudam ou se divertem: Eles estão na escola. They're at school. ♦ Os meus pais estão no teatro. My parents are at the theater. ♦ Trabalho no hospital. I work at the hospital.

• **com expressões de tempo 1** (meses, anos, séculos, estações) in: no verão/no século XII in the summer/the twelfth century **2** (dia) on: na véspera de Ano Novo on New Year's Eve ♦ É numa segunda. It falls on a Monday. **3** (Natal, Páscoa, momento) at: Vou sempre para casa no Natal. I always go home at Christmas. ♦ neste momento at this moment **4** (dentro de) in: Estarei aqui numa hora. I'll be here in an hour.

• **outras construções 1** (modo) in: pagar em reais pay in reals ♦ Perguntei-lhe em inglês. I asked him in English. ♦ de porta em porta from door to door **2** (assunto): um perito em computadores an expert in/on computers **3** (+ for-mar-se em Letras graduate in Arts **3** (estado) in: em boas con-dições in good condition ♦ uma máquina em funcionamento a machine in working order **4** (+ complemento): cair em desuso fall into disuse ♦ confiar em alguém trust sb

emagrecer vi lose weight: ~ três quilos lose six pounds

emancipar-se vp become inde-pendent

emaranhar(-se) vt, vp (cabelo) get (sth) tangled (up)

embaçado adj (imagem, foto) blurred: Sem óculos vejo tudo ~. Everything looks blurred with-out my glasses.

embaçar vt **1** (vapor) cause sth to steam up **2** (olhos) cause sth to mist over ♦ **embaçar(-se)** vi, vp **1** (vapor) steam up **2** (olhos) mist over

embaixada sf embassy [pl -ies]

embaixador/a *sm-sf* ambassador

embaixo *adv* ▶ **(por)** ~ **de** under(neath)

embalado *adj*: ~ **a vácuo** vacuum-packed

embalagem *sf* packaging

embalar *vt* **1** (*produto*) pack **2** (*bebê*) rock

embaraçado *adj* embarrassed

embaraçar *vt* **1** (*desconcertar*) embarrass **2** (*cabelo*) get tangled ● **embaraçar-se** *vp* get tangled (up)

embaraçoso *adj* embarrassing

embaralhar *vt* **1** (*cartas*) shuffle **2** (*misturar*) mix sth up **3** (*confundir*) confuse ● **embaralhar-se** *vp* get confused (*about/over* sth)

embarcação *sf* boat, vessel (*fml*) → BOAT

embarcar *vt* **1** (*passageiros*) embark **2** (*mercadorias*) load ▸ *vi* board, embark (*fml*)

embarque *sm* boarding: *O avião está pronto para o* ~. The plane is ready for boarding.

emblema *sm* emblem

embolsar *vt* pocket

embora *conj* although: *eu não gostasse dele* although I didn't like him ▸ *adv* away: *ir* ~ go away ◊ *mandar alguém* ~ send sb away ◊ *levar algo* ~ take sth away

emboscada *sf* ambush: *armar uma* ~ set an ambush

embreagem *sf* clutch: *pisar na/apertar a* ~ press the clutch

embriagar *vt* get sb drunk ● **embriagar-se** *vp* get drunk (*on* sth)

embrião *sm* embryo [*pl* ~s]

embrulhar *vt* **1** (*envolver*) wrap sb/sth (up) (*in* sth) **2** (*confundir*) muddle sth up **3** (*estômago*) upset ▶ ~ **para presente** giftwrap

embrulho *sm* package

emburrado *adj* sulky: *ficar* ~ sulk

embutido *adj* built-in: *armários* ~s built-in cupboards

emenda *sf* (*Jur*) amendment

emendar *vt* **1** (*erros, defeitos*) correct **2** (*danos*) repair **3** (*lei*) amend ● **emendar-se** *vp* mend your ways

emergência *sf* emergency [*pl* -ies]

emigração *sf* emigration

emigrante *adj, smf* emigrant

emigrar *vi* emigrate

emissão *sf* emission

emissora *sf* radio/TV station

emitir *vt* **1** (*calor, luz, som*) emit **2** (*documento*) issue

emoção *sf* **1** (*comoção*) emotion **2** (*entusiasmo*) excitement: *Que* ~! How exciting!

emocionante *adj* **1** (*comovedor*) moving **2** (*estimulante*) exciting

emocionar *vt* **1** (*comover*) move **2** (*excitar*) thrill ● **emocionar-se** *vp* **1** (*comover-se*) be moved (*by* sth) **2** (*entusiasmar-se*) get excited (*about* sth)

emoldurar *vt* frame

emotivo *adj* emotional

empacotar *vt* wrap sth up

empada *sf* pasty (*GB*) [*pl* -ies]

empadão *sm* pie

empalidecer *vi* go pale

empanturrar-se *vp* stuff yourself (*with* sth)

emparelhar *vt* **1** (*pessoas*) pair sb off (*to* sb) **2** (*coisas*) match sth (*with* sth)

empatado *adj* ▶ **estar** ~: *Quando fui embora eles estavam* ~s. They were even when I left. ◊ *Estão* ~s *em dois a dois.* They're tied at two-two.

empatar *vt, vi* **1** (*Esporte*) **(a)** (*em relação ao resultado final*) tie, draw (*GB*) (*with* sb): ~ *em/por um a um* tie at one **(b)** (*no marcador*) equalize: *Temos que* ~ *antes do intervalo.* We must equalize before half-time. **2** (*votação, concurso*) tie (*with* sb)

empate *sm* tie, draw (*GB*): *um* ~ *por um a um* a one-one tie

empenhado *adj* ▶ ~ **(em fazer algo)** determined (to do sth)

empenhar *vt* pawn ● **empenhar-se** *vp* (*esmerar-se*) do your utmost (to do sth)

empenho *sm* determination (to do sth)

emperrar *vi* jam

empestear *vt* make sth stink (*of* sth)

empilhar *vt* stack

empinado *adj* **1** (*encosta*) steep **2** (*nariz*) turned-up

empinar *vt*: ~ *papagaio* fly a kite

empírico *adj* empirical

empreendedor *adj* enterprising

empregado/a *sm-sf* employee ▶ **empregada (doméstica)** maid ▶ ~ **de escritório** office worker

empregador/a *sm-sf* employer

empregar *vt* **1** (*dar trabalho*) employ **2** (*utilizar*) use **3** (*tempo, dinheiro*) spend: *Empreguei tempo demais nisto.*

I spent too long on this. ◇ ~ **mal o tempo** waste your time

emprego sm **1** (*trabalho*) job: *conseguir um bom* ~ get a good job → **WORK 2** (*Econ*) employment

empresa sf **1** (*Com*) company [*pl* -ies] **2** (*projeto*) enterprise ▶ ~ **de laticínios** dairy [*pl* -ies] ~ **estatal/pública** state-owned company ~ **privada** private company

empresarial adj business: *sentido* ~ business acumen

empresário/a sm-sf **1** businessman/woman [*pl* -men/-women] **2** (*espetáculo*) impresario [*pl* -s]

emprestado adj: *Não é meu, é* ~. It's not mine, it's borrowed. ◇ *Por que é que você não pede* ~ *a ele?* Why don't you ask him if you can borrow it?

emprestar vt lend: *Emprestei os meus livros a ela.* I lent her my books. ◇ *Você me empresta?* Can I borrow it? ◇ *Empresto se você tiver cuidado.* I'll lend it to you if you're careful. → **BORROW**

empréstimo sm loan

empunhar vt **1** (*de forma ameaçadora*) brandish **2** (*ter na mão*) hold

empurrão sm push: *dar um* ~ *em alguém* give sb a push ◇ *Eles saíram aos empurrões.* They pushed their way out.

empurrar vt push: *Não me empurre!* Don't push me! ◇ ~ *alguém para (fazer) algo* push sb into doing sth

emudecer vi **1** (*perder a fala*) go dumb **2** (*calar-se*) go quiet

encabeçar vt head

encadear vt (*idéias*) link

encadernador/a sm-sf bookbinder

encadernar vt (*livro*) bind

encaixar vt **1** (*colocar, meter*) fit sth (*into sth*) **2** (*juntar*) fit sth together: ~ *as peças do quebra-cabeça* fit the pieces of the jigsaw together ● vi fit (*into sth*) ▶ **encaixar-se** vp (*enquadrar-se*) fit in (*with sth*); (*into sth*)

encaixotar vt box sth up

encalhar vi (*embarcação*) run aground

encaminhar vt **1** (*aconselhar*) put sb on the right track **2** (*processo*) set sth in motion ● **encaminhar-se** vp head (*for...*): ~ *para casa* head for home

encanador/a sm-sf plumber

encantado adj **1** delighted (*about/at/with sb/sth*); (*to do*

sth/that...): *Estou encantada por terem vindo.* I'm delighted (that) you've come. **2** (*enfeitiçado*) enchanted (*into sth*)

encantador adj lovely

encantar vt (*enfeitiçar*) cast a spell on *sb/sth*

encanto sm (*feitiço*) spell: *quebrar um* ~ break a spell ▶ **como que por** ~ as if by magic **ser um** ~ be lovely

encapar vt cover sth (*with sth*); (*into sth*)

encaracolado adj curly

encaracolar vt curl ● vi go curly

encarar vt (*enfrentar*) face: ~ *a realidade* face (up to) reality

encarcerar vt imprison

encargo sm **1** (*responsabilidade*) responsibility [*pl* -ies] **2** (*tarefa*) errand

encarnar vt (*representar*) embody

encarregado adj in charge (*of doing sth*): *ser* ~ *de receber o dinheiro.* You're in charge of collecting the money. ● sm (*de grupo de trabalhadores*) foreman

encarregar vt (*mandar*) put sb in charge of doing sth ● **encarregar-se** vp ~ **de 1** (*ocupar-se*) take care of *sb/sth*: ~ *do bebê* look after the baby **2** (*ser responsável*) be in charge of sth **3** (*comprometer-se*) undertake *to do sth*

encenar vt **1** (*representar*) stage **2** (*adaptar*) dramatize

encerar vt wax

encerramento sm closure ▶ **de** ~ closing: *ato/discurso de* ~ closing ceremony/speech

encerrar vt, vi **1** shut (*sb/sth up*) **2** (*terminar*) end

encestar vi (*basquete*) score (a basket)

encharcado adj **1** soaked through: *ficar* ~ *até os ossos* get soaked through **2** (*terreno*) covered with puddles

encharcar vt (*molhar*) soak: *Você me encharcou a saia.* You've made my skirt soaking wet! ● **encharcar-se** vp get soaked

enchente sf flood

encher vt **1** fill *sb/sth* (*with sth*): *O garçom voltou a* ~ *o meu copo.* The waiter refilled my glass. **2** (*com ar*) blow sth up, inflate (*mais fml*) ● **encher-se** vp **1** fill (up) (*with sth*): *A casa encheu-se de convidados.* The house filled (up) with guests. **2** (*ao*

comer) stuff yourself (*with sth*)
▶ ~ a barriga (de) stuff yourself
(*with sth*) ~ a cara get drunk

enchimento *sm* (*roupa*)
padding: com ~ nos ombros with
padded shoulders

enciclopédia *sf* encyclopedia

encoberto *adj* (*céu, dia*)
overcast

encobrir *vt* **1** conceal: ~ *um
crime* conceal a crime **2** (*delinqüente*) harbor

encolher *vi* shrink ▶ ~ os
ombros shrug your shoulders

encomenda *sf* **1** (*Com*) order:
fazer/anular uma ~ place/can-
cel an order **2** (*pacote*) package:
mandar uma ~ *pelo correio* mail
a package ➤ PACKAGE

encomendar *vt* order: ~ *algo
numa loja* order sth from a store

encontrar *vt* find: *Não encontro
o meu relógio.* I can't find my
watch. ● **encontrar-se** *vp* **1** (*pessoa*) (a) (*marcar encontro*) meet
(*sb*): ~ *no café* meet at the café
(b) (*por acaso*) run into *sb*:
Encontrei-me com ela hoje. I ran
into her today. **2** (*estar*) be ▶ ~
um rumo na vida get on in life

encontro *sm* **1** (*casal*) date **2**
(*reunião*) meeting ▶ ir de ~ a
(*chocar-se*) run into *sth*: *O carro
foi de* ~ *à árvore.* The car ran
into the tree.

encorajar *vt* encourage *sb* (*to do
sth*)

encosta *sf* slope ▶ ~ acima/
abaixo uphill/downhill

encostar *vt* **1** (*apoiar*) lean *sth*
(*on sb/sth*): *Ele encostou a
cabeça no meu ombro.* He
leaned his head on my shoulder. **2** (*pôr contra*) put *sth
against sth*: ~ *a cama à janela*
put the bed against the window

encosto *sm* (*assento*) back

encrenca *sf* trouble: *meter-se
em* ~*s* get into trouble

encrenqueiro/a *sm-sf* troublemaker

encurralar *vt* (*pessoa*) corner

encurtar *vt* shorten

endereço *sm* address

endireitar(-se) *vt, vp* straighten
(up): *Endireite-se!* Stand up
straight!

endividar-se *vp* get into debt

endoidecer *vi* go crazy

endurecer *vt* **1** harden **2** (*músculos*) firm *sth* up

enegrecer *vt, vi* blacken

energia *sf* energy [*ger U*]:
~ *eólica/nuclear/solar* wind/

nuclear/solar energy ◇ *não ter*
~ not have any energy

enérgico *adj* **1** (*vigoroso*) energetic **2** (*firme*) strict

enervar *vt* **1** (*irritar*) get on *sb's*
nerves **2** (*pôr nervoso*) make *sb*
nervous ● **enervar-se** *vp* **1** (*zangar-se*) get worked up **2** (*pôr-se
nervoso*) get nervous: *Não se
enerve. Calm down!* **3** ~ (*com*)
(*por*) (*irritar-se*) get annoyed
(*with sb*) (*about sth*)

enésimo *adj* (*Mat*) nth ▶ pela
enésima vez for the umpteenth
time

enevoado *adj* (*céu*) cloudy

enfaixar *vt* bandage *sb/sth* (up)

enfarte *sm* heart attack

ênfase *sf* emphasis [*pl* -ases]

enfatizar *vt* stress

enfeitar *vt* decorate

enfeite *sm* decoration: ~*s de
Natal* Christmas decorations

enfeitiçado *adj* (*fascinado*)
bewitched

enfeitiçar *vt* cast a spell (on *sb*)

enfermagem *sf* nursing: *tirar o
curso de* ~ train as a nurse

enfermaria *sf* ward

enfermeiro/a *sm-sf* nurse

enferrujado *adj* rusty

enferrujar *vt* corrode ● *vi* go
rusty

enfiar *vt* **1** (*introduzir*) put *sth in
sth*: ~ *as mãos nos bolsos* put
your hands in your pockets **2**
(*calças, camisa*) put *sth on* **3**
(*agulha*) thread

enfim *adv* **1** (*finalmente*) at last: ~
você chegou! You're here at last!
2 (*em resumo*) in short: ~, *apa-
nharam-nos desprevenidos.* To
cut a long story short, they
caught us unawares. **3** (*bem*)
(oh) well: ~, *é a vida.* Oh well,
that's life.

enforcar(-se) *vt, vp* hang (yourself) NOTA No ~ sentido de
enforcar o verbo hang é regular,
portanto, para o passado, basta
acrescentar *-ed*.

enfraquecer *vt* weaken

enfrentar *vt* **1** face: *O país
enfrenta uma crise profunda.*
The country is facing a serious
crisis. **2** (*encarar*) face up to *sth*:
~ *a realidade* face up to reality **3**
(*Esporte*) take *sb* on

enfumaçado *adj* smoky

enfurecer *vt* infuriate ● **enfurecer-se** *vp* become furious (*with
sb*) (*at sth*)

enganado *adj* wrong: *estar* ~ be
wrong

enganar *vt* **1** (*mentir*) lie to *sb*

→ LIE² 2 (ser infiel) cheat on sb ●
enganar-se vp 1 ~ (em) (confundir-se) be wrong (about sth):
Aí é que você se engana. You're
wrong about that. 2 (errar): ~ no
número dial the wrong number
◇ ~ de estrada take the wrong
road 3 (iludir-se) fool yourself

engano sm 1 (erro) mistake:
cometer um ~ make a mistake ◇
por ~ by mistake 2 (mal-entendido) misunderstanding ▶ é ~
(ao telefone) wrong number

engarrafamento sm (trânsito)
traffic jam

engarrafar vt bottle

engasgar(-se) vt, vp 1 choke (on
sth) 2 (com palavra): Engasgo-
me sempre nesta palavra. I
always get stuck on that word.

engatar vt 1 (atrelar) hitch 2
(gancho, anzol) hook 3
(marcha): É difícil ~ a segunda
neste carro. It's hard to put this
car into second.

engatinhar vi crawl

engavetamento sm (acidente)
pile-up

engenharia sf engineering

engenheiro/a sm-sf (engineer): ~
civil/agrónomo civil engineer/
agronomist

engenho sm 1 (máquina, aparelho) device: um ~ explosivo an
explosive device 2 (fazenda)
sugar plantation

engenhoca sf contraption

engenhoso adj ingenious

engessado adj: Estou com o
braço ~. My arm's in a cast.

engessar vt (Med) put sth in a
cast

engolir vt, vi 1 (ingerir) swallow:
~ em seco swallow hard
◇ ~ o orgulho swallow your
pride ◇ Ele engoliu a história da
promoção do Zé. He swallowed
the story about Zé's promotion.
2 (comer muito rápido) gobble
sth (up/down) 3 (suportar) put
up with sth: Não sei como você
consegue ~ tanto. I don't know
how you put up with it.

engordar vt fatten sb/sth (up) ●
vi 1 (pessoa) gain weight 2 (alimento) be fattening

engordurar vt 1 (com gordura)
grease 2 (com óleo) oil

engraçadinho/a adj, sm-sf
(atrevido) sassy, cheeky (GB):
Não se meta a ~ comigo! Don't
you get smart with me!

engraçado adj funny, amusing
(fml) ▶ fazer-se de ~ play the
clown

engradado sm crate

engravidar vt, vi get (sb) pregnant

engraxar vt (sapatos) polish

engraxate smf shoeshine

engrossar vi 1 (tornar espesso)
thicken 2 (ser grosseiro) turn
nasty

enguiçar vi (motor, máquina)
break down

enigma sm enigma

enjaular vt cage

enjoado adj 1 nauseous, sick
(GB): estar ~ feel nauseous 2
(farto) sick and tired

enjoar vt 1 make sb feel nauseous, make sb feel sick (GB)
2 (fartar) get on sb's nerves ● vi
1 get nauseous, get sick (GB)
2 (em barco) get seasick

enjoativo adj nauseating

enjôo sm (náusea) nausea, sickness (GB)

enlatados sm canned foods

enlatar vt can

enlouquecedor adj maddening

enlouquecer vi go wild: ~ de
entusiasmo go wild with excitement ● vt drive sb wild

enluarado adj moonlit

enorme adj enormous: um ~
aumento nos lucros a massive
increase in profits

enquanto conj 1 while: Ele canta
~ pinta. He sings while he
paints. 2 (tanto tempo como,
sempre que) as long as:
Agüente-se ~ for possível. Put
up with it as long as you can. ▶
por ~ for the time being

enraivecido adj enraged

enredar vt (comprometer)
entangle sb (in sth) ● enredar-
se vp (disputa, assunto) get
involved (in sth)

enredo sm plot

enriquecer vt enrich ● vi become
rich

enrolado/a sm-sf, adj (pessoa)
complicated

enrolar vt 1 (fio, papel) roll sth
up: ~ um cigarro roll a cigarette
2 (cabelo) curl 3 (enganar)
deceive, con (coloq): Não se
deixe ~. Don't let yourself be
conned. ● **enrolar-se** vp (confundir-se) get mixed up

enroscar vt 1 (tampa) screw sth
on: Enrosque-a bem. Screw it on
tightly. 2 (peças, porcas) screw
sth together ● **enroscar-se** vp
1 (gato, cão) curl up 2 (cobra)
coil up

enrugar(-se) vt, vi, vp wrinkle
▶ **enrugar a testa** frown

ensaboar vt soap

ensaiar vt, vi **1** practice **2** (*Mús*, *Teat*) rehearse

ensaio sm **1** (*experiência*) test: *um tubo de* ~ a test tube **2** (*Mús*, *Teat*) rehearsal: ~ *geral* dress rehearsal **3** (*Liter*) essay

ensangüentado adj blood-stained

enseada sf cove

ensebado adj (*sujo*) greasy

ensinado adj ▶ **bem** ~ well trained

ensinar vt **1** teach sth, teach sb to do sth: *Quem ensinou você a jogar?* Who taught you how to play? **2** (*mostrar*) show

ensino sm **1** teaching **2** (*sistema educativo*) education: ~ *básico/secundário/superior* primary/secondary/higher education

ensolarado adj sunny

ensopado adj soaked: *A chuva me deixou* ~. I got soaked in the rain. ● sm stew

ensurdecedor adj deafening

ensurdecer vt deafen ● vi go deaf

entalar(-se) vt, vp jam (sth) (in sth): ~ *o dedo na porta* catch your finger in the door

entanto adv ▶ **no** ~ however, nevertheless (*fml*) ● **e no entanto...** and yet...

então adv **1** (*nesse momento*) then: *desde* ~ since then **2** (*naquela altura*) at that time **3** (*nesse caso*) so: *Eles vão vinham,* ~ *fui-me embora.* They didn't come so I left. ◇ *Quer dizer,* ~, *que vão mudar?* So you're moving, are you? ▶ **e** ~? what then?

entardecer sm dusk: *ao* ~ at dusk

enteado/a sm-sf stepchild [pl stepchildren] [masc stepson] [fem stepdaughter]

entender vt understand: *Não entendi nada do que ele disse.* I didn't understand a word he said. ◇ *fácil de* ~ easy to understand **2** ~ *de* (*saber*) know about sth ● **entender-se** vp get along (with sb) ▶ **dar a** ~ imply ~ **mal** misunderstand ~ **estou me fazendo** ~? do you see what I mean? **eu entendo que...** I think (that)...

entendido/a sm-sf expert (*at/in/on sth*) ● interj: *Entendido!* Right! ◇ *Entendido?* All right?

enterrar vt **1** bury **2** (*afundar*) sink: ~ *os pés na areia* sink your feet into the sand

enterro sm **1** funeral **2** (*sepultamento*) burial

entoar vt **1** (*cantar*) sing **2** (*dar o tom*) pitch ● vi (*Mús*) sing in tune

entonação sf intonation

entornar vt spill

entorpecente sm narcotic

entorse sf (*Med*) sprain

entortar vt (*curvar*) bend

entrada sf **1** (*ação de entrar*) **(a)** entry (*into sth*) **(b)** (*clube, hospital, instituição*) admission (*to sth*): *Os sócios não pagam* ~. Admission is free for members. ◇ ~ *grátis/livre* free admission ◇ *dar* ~ *no hospital* be admitted to hospital **2** (*bilhete*) ticket **3** (*porta*) entrance (*to sth*) **4** (*primeiro pagamento*) deposit (*on sth*): *dar 20% de* ~ pay a 20% deposit **5** (*prato*) appetizer ▶ ~ **proibida** no entry: ~ *proibida a cães.* No dogs allowed. ◇ ~ *proibida a menores de 18 anos.* No admission to persons under the age of 18.

entrar vt, vi **1** go in/inside, go into...: *Não me atrevi a* ~. I didn't dare go in. ◇ *Não entre no meu escritório.* Don't go into my office. ◇ ~ *em pormenores* go into detail **2** (*passar*) come in/inside, come into...: *Diga-lhe que entre.* Ask him to come in. ◇ *Não entre no meu quarto sem bater.* Knock before you come into my room. **3** ~ **para** (*ingressar*) **(a)** (*instituição, clube*) join **(b)** (*profissão, esfera social*) enter **4** **(a)** (*trem, ônibus*) get on, get on sth **(b)** (*automóvel*) get in, get into sth **5** (*caber*) fit: *Esta saia não me entra.* This skirt doesn't fit (me). **(b)** ~ **em** fit (*in/into sth*): *Não vai* ~ *no porta-malas.* It won't fit in the box. **6** (*participar*) take part (*in sth*) **7** ~ **com** (*contribuir*) give ▶ ~ **bem** do badly ~ **em conflito** clash ~ **em discussões** start arguing: *Não vamos* ~ *em discussões.* Let's not argue about it. ~ **em férias** start your vacation ~ **em pânico** panic ~ **em vigor** (*lei*) come into force ~ **na cabeça de alguém**: *Não me entra na cabeça.* I just don't understand. ~ **nos eixos 1** (*normalizar-se*) go back to normal **2** (*ter bom senso*) get back on the straight and narrow ~ **numa fria** get into a fix

entre prep **1** (*duas coisas, pessoas*) between: ~ *a loja e o banco* between the store and the bank

2 (*mais de duas coisas, pessoas*) among: ~ *as árvores* among the trees **3** (*no meio*): *uma cor* ~ *o verde e o azul* somewhere between green and blue ▶ ~ **si 1** (*duas pessoas*) each other: *Eles não falam* ~ *si.* They don't talk to each other. **2** (*várias pessoas*) among themselves: *Os garotos discutiam o assunto* ~ *si.* The boys were discussing it among themselves.

entreaberto *adj* (*porta*) ajar

entreabrir *vt* **1** open sth half way **2** (*porta*) leave sth ajar

entrega *sf* **1** handing over: *a* ~ *do dinheiro* handing over the money **2** (*mercadorias, correio*) delivery [*pl* -ies]: *o homem das* ~*s* the delivery man ◇ ~ *a domicílio* delivery service ▶ ~ **de medalhas/prêmios** award ceremony/prize-giving

entregador/a *sm-sf* delivery man/woman [*pl* men/women]

entregar *vt* **1** hand sb/sth over (*to sb*): ~ *as chaves* hand over the keys ◇ ~ *alguém às autoridades* hand sb over to the authorities **2** (*prêmio, medalhas*) present sth (*to sb*) **3** (*correio, mercadorias*) deliver ● **entregar-se** *vp* (*render-se*) give yourself up, surrender (*mais fml*) (*to sb*) **2** (*dedicar-se*) devote yourself to sb/sth

entretanto *conj* however

entretenimento *sm* **1** (*diversão*) entertainment **2** (*passatempo*) pastime

entreter *vt* **1** (*demorar*) keep: *Não quero* ~ *o senhor por muito tempo.* I don't want to keep you long. **2** (*divertir*) keep sb amused **3** (*distrair*) keep sb busy ● **entreter-se** *vp* (*ocupar o tempo*): *É só para me entreter.* I do it just to pass the time. ◇ *Entretenho-me com qualquer coisa.* I'm easily amused. **2** (*deter-se*) hang around (*doing sth*): *Não se entretenham por aí.* Don't hang around there.

entrevista *sf* interview ▶ ~ **coletiva** press conference

entrevistador/a *sm-sf* interviewer

entrevistar *vt* interview

entristecer *vt* make sb sad ● *vi* be sad (*because of/about sth*)

entroncamento *sm* (*ferroviário, rodoviário*) junction

entrosar-se *vp* (*relacionar-se*) get along well (*with sb*)

entupir *vt* block sth (up) ● **entupir-se** *vp* get blocked

enturmar-se *vp* make friends

entusiasmado *adj* thrilled

entusiasmo *sm* enthusiasm (*for sth*): *com* ~ enthusiastically

entusiasta *smf* enthusiast

entusiástico *adj* enthusiastic

enumerar *vt* list

enunciar *vt* enunciate

envelhecer *vi* (*pessoa*) get old ● *vt* **1** (*pessoa, vinho*) age **2** (*madeira*) season

envelope *sm* envelope

envenenar *vt* poison

envergonhado *adj* **1** (*tímido*) shy **2** (*embaraçado*) embarrassed

envergonhar *vt* **1** (*humilhar*) make sb feel ashamed **2** (*embaraçar*) embarrass ● **envergonhar-se** *vp* **1** (*arrepender-se*) be ashamed (*of doing sth*) **2** (*sentir-se incomodado*) feel embarrassed

enviado/a *sm-sf* **1** (*emissário*) envoy **2** (*Jornal*) correspondent

enviar *vt* send

enviesado *adj* (*torto*) crooked

envio *sm* **1** (*ação*) sending, dispatch **2** (*remessa*) remittance

enviuvar *vi* be widowed

envolver *vt* (*implicar*) involve sb (*in sth*) ● **envolver-se** *vp* **1** (*disputa, assunto*) get involved (*in sth*) **2** (*caso amoroso*) get involved with sb

envolvido *adj*: *estar* ~ *com alguém/algo* be involved with sb/be busy with sth

enxada *sf* hoe

enxaguar *vt* rinse

enxame *sm* swarm

enxaqueca *sf* migraine

enxergar *vt* see ▶ **não** ~ **um palmo adiante do nariz** be blind as a bat

enxofre *sm* sulfur

enxotar *vt* (*moscas*) shoo sth away

enxoval *sm* **1** (*noiva*) trousseau [*pl* ~s/~x] **2** (*bebê*) layette

enxugar *vt* **1** (*secar*) dry **2** (*suor, lágrimas*) wipe sth (away): *Ele enxugou as lágrimas.* He wiped his tears away. ● *vi* dry

enxuto *adj* **1** (*seco*) dry **2** (*corpo*): *Considerada a idade que tem, ela está bem enxuta.* She's in really good shape for her age.

epicentro *sm* epicenter

epidemia *sf* epidemic: *uma* ~ *de cólera* a cholera epidemic

epilepsia *sf* epilepsy

epiléptico/a adj, sm-sf epileptic

episódio sm **1** episode: *uma série com cinco ~s* a serial in five episodes **2** (*história curiosa*) anecdote

época sf **1** time: *naquela ~* at that time ◇ *a ~ mais fria do ano* the coldest time of the year **2** (*era*) age **3** (*temporada*) season: *a ~ das chuvas* the rainy season

equação sf equation: *~ de segundo/terceiro grau* quadratic/cubic equation

Equador sm Ecuador

equador sm equator

equatorial adj equatorial

equatoriano/a adj, sm-sf Ecuadorean

equilibrar vt balance

equilíbrio sm **1** balance: *manter/ perder o ~* keep/lose your balance ◇ *~ de forças* balance of power **2** (*Fís*) equilibrium

equilibrista smf acrobat: *~ de corda bamba* tightrope walker

equipamento sm **1** equipment [U] **2** (*Esporte*) gear [U]

equipar vt **1** equip *sb/sth (with sth)* **2** (*roupa, Náut*) supply *sb/ sth (with sth)*: *o time com chuteiras* supply the team with cleats ● **equipar-se** vp kit yourself out

equipe sf team: *uma ~ de futebol* a soccer team ◇ *uma ~ de peritos* a team of experts

equitação sf horseback riding

equivalência sf equivalence ▶ **conceder/obter** - recognize: *obter a ~ da licenciatura* have your degree recognized

equivalente adj, sm equivalent

equivaler vt be equivalent *to sth*

equivocado adj wrong

equivocar-se vp be wrong (*about sth*)

equívoco sm **1** (*erro*) mistake: *cometer um ~* make a mistake **2** (*mal-entendido*) misunderstanding

era sf **1** age: *a ~ dos computadores* the computer age **2** (*Geol*) era: *~ glacial* ice age

ereção sf erection

erguer vt **1** (*levantar*) lift *sth* up **2** (*cabeça*) hold *your head* up **3** (*monumento*) erect ● **erguer-se** vp (*levantar-se*) get up

erosão sf erosion

erótico adj erotic

erotismo sm eroticism

errado adj wrong: *tomar a decisão errada* make the wrong decision

errar vt **1** (*resposta*) get *sth*

wrong 2 (*falhar*) miss: *O caçador errou o tiro.* The hunter missed. ● vi **1** (*enganar-se*) make a mistake **2** (*vaguear*) wander **3** (*não acertar*) miss ▶ - **o caminho** lose your way

erro sm mistake: *cometer/fazer um ~* make a mistake → MISTAKE ▶ - **tipográfico** typo [*pl* ~s]

errôneo adj erroneous

erupção sf **1** eruption **2** (*Med*) rash

erva sf **1** (*Med, Cozinha*) herb **2** (*maconha*) pot ▶ - **daninha** weed

esbanjar vt (*dinheiro*) squander

esbarrão sm bump: *Ele me deu um ~.* He bumped into me.

esbarrar vt **1** (*topar, encontrar*) bump *into sb/sth*: *Esbarrei com a sua irmã hoje.* I bumped into your sister today. **2** (*problema*) come up against *sth*

esbelto adj **1** (*magro*) slender **2** (*elegante*) graceful

esboço sm **1** (*Arte*) sketch **2** (*idéia geral*) outline

esbofetear vt slap

esborrachar vt **1** (*esmagar*) squash **2** (*esmurrar*) slap ● **esborrachar-se** vp sprawl: *~ no chão* fall sprawling to the ground

esbravejar vi, vt shout

esbugalhado adj (*olhos*) bulging

escada sf **1** (*edifício*) stairs [*pl*]staircase (*mais fml*): *~ em caracol* spiral staircase ◇ *Caí pela ~ abaixo.* I fell down the stairs. **2** (*portátil*) ladder ▶ **descer/subir as ~s** go downstairs/upstairs ◇ *~ de incêndio* fire escape ● - **rolante** escalator

escala sf **1** scale: *numa ~ de um a dez* on a scale of one to ten **2** (*viagem*) stopover: *fazer ~* stop over **3** (*Mús*) scale

escalada sf **1** (*montanha*) ascent **2** (*guerra*) escalation

escalar vt (*montanha*) climb (up) *sth*

escaldar vt **1** (*legumes*) blanch **2** (*queimar*) scald ● vi (*estar muito quente*) be boiling hot

escalope sm cutlet

escama sf scale

escancarado adj (*porta*) wide open

escandalizar vt shock

escândalo sm scandal: *armar/ fazer um ~* make a fuss ◇ *dar ~* make a scene ▶ **ser um** ~ be outrageous

escandaloso adj scandalous

escangalhar-se *vp* fall apart

escaninho *sm* (*cartas, chaves*) cubby hole, pigeon-hole (GB)

escanteio *sm* (*futebol*) corner

escapada *sf* **1** (*fuga*) escape **2** (*viagem*) short break: *uma ~ de fim de semana* a weekend break

escapamento *sm* **1** (*veículo*) exhaust **2** (*gás*) leak

escapar *vi, vt* **1** (*fugir*) escape (*from sb/sth*): *O papagaio escapou da gaiola.* The parrot escaped from its cage. **2** (*evitar*) escape: *~ à justiça* escape justice **3** (*segredo, involuntariamente*) let sth slip: *Escapou-me (da boca) que ela estava grávida.* I let (it) slip that she was pregnant. **4** (*pormenores, oportunidade*) miss: *A você não escapa nada.* You don't miss a thing. **5** (*gás, líquido*) leak ▸ **deixar ~ 1** (*pessoa*) let sb get away **2** (*oportunidade*): *Você deixou ~ a oportunidade da sua vida.* You let slip the chance of a lifetime. ● **por um fio/triz** escape by the skin of your teeth

escapatória *sf* way out

escapulir *vi, vt* **1** (*escapar*) slip away **2** *~ das mãos* slip out of your hands **3** (*fugir*) run away

escarcéu *sm* (*alvoroço*) racket

escarola *sf* (*Bot*) endive

escarrado *adj*: *Ela é a cópia escarrada da mãe.* She's the spitting image of her mother.

escarrar *vt* spit

escassear *vi* be scarce

escassez *sf* shortage

escasso *adj* little: *A ajuda que eles receberam foi escassa.* They received very little help. ◇ *devido ao ~ interesse* due to lack of interest

escavação *sf* excavation

escavadora *sf* digger

escavar *vt* **1** dig **2** (*Arqueologia*) excavate

esclarecer *vt* **1** (*explicar*) clarify **2** (*crime*) clear sth up: *~ um assassinato* solve a murder

esclerosado *adj* senile

escocês/esa *adj* Scottish ● *sm-sf* Scotsman/woman [*pl* -men/-women]: *os escoceses* the Scots

Escócia *sf* Scotland

escoicear *vt* kick

escola *sf* school: *Iremos depois da ~.* We'll go after school. ◇ *Vou à ~ falar com o seu professor.* I'm going to the school to talk to your teacher. → SCHOOL ▸ *~ de belas-artes/samba* art/samba school *~ maternal* kindergarten *~ particular/pública* private/public school *~ primária/secundária* elementary/high school *~ superior (técnica)* technical college (GB) NOTA Nos Estados Unidos uma escola pública é uma **public school**. Na Grã-Bretanha, contudo, as **public schools** são colégios particulares tradicionais e com muito prestígio.

escolar *adj* **1** school: *o ano ~* the school year **2** (*sistema*) education: *o sistema ~* the education system

escolha *sf* choice

escolher *vt* choose

escolta *sf* escort

escoltar *vt* escort

escombros *sm* rubble [*U*]: *um monte de ~* a pile of rubble

esconde-esconde *sm*: *brincar de ~* play hide-and-seek

esconder *vt* hide *sb/sth* (*from sb/sth*): *ter algo para ~* have sth to hide ● **esconder-se** *vp* hide (*from sb/sth*)

esconderijo *sm* hiding place

escondido *adj* (*oculto*) hidden ▸ **às escondidas** in secret

escorpião *sm* **1** scorpion **2** (**Escorpião**) (*Astrol*) Scorpio [*pl* -s]

escorredor *sm* **1** (*verduras*) colander **2** (*louça*) dishrack

escorregadio *adj* slippery

escorregador *sm* (*parque*) slide

escorregão *sm* slip: *dar um ~* slip

escorregar *vi, vt* **1** (*pessoa*) slip (*on sth*) **2** (*superfície*) be slippery **3** *~ (de/por entre)* slip (out of/from *sth*)

escorrer *vt* (*pratos, etc.*) drain ● *vi* **1** drain: *Deixe os pratos escorrendo.* Leave the dishes to drain. **2** (*pingar*) drip **3** *~ (por)* slide (along/down *sth*)

escoteiro *sm* (Boy) Scout

escotilha *sf* hatch

escova *sf* brush ▸ **de dentes/de cabelo** toothbrush/hairbrush

escovar *vt* **1** brush: *~ os dentes* brush your teeth **2** (*cão, cavalo*) groom

escravidão *sf* slavery

escravizar *vt* enslave

escravo/a *adj, sm-sf* slave: *ser ~ do dinheiro* be a slave to money

escrever *vt* **1** write **2** (*ortografia*) spell: *Como se escreve?* How do you spell it? ● *vi* write: *Ele ainda não sabe ~.* He can't write yet. ▸ **à mão** write *sth* in longhand

escrita sf writing

escrito adj written: pôr algo por ~ put sth in writing ◇ ~ à mão/à máquina handwritten/typed ● sm 1 (documento) document 2 (mensagem) message

escritor/a sm-sf writer

escritório sm 1 (local de trabalho) office 2 (casa) study [pl -ies]

escritura sf 1 (documento legal) deed 2 (**Escritura**) Scripture(s): a Sagrada ~ the Holy Scripture(s)

escrivaninha sf desk

escrúpulo sm scruple

escrupuloso adj scrupulous

escudo sm shield

esculachado adj (desleixado) sloppy: Ele se veste de um jeito ~. He's a sloppy dresser.

esculacho sm (repreensão) lecture: levar um ~ get a lecture

esculpir vt, vi sculpt

escultor/a sm-sf sculptor

escultura sf sculpture

escurecer vt darken ● v imp get dark

escuridão sf darkness

escuro adj (cabelo, pele) dark ● sm dark: Tenho medo do ~. I'm scared of the dark. ◇ ficar no ~ be left in the dark ▶ às escuras in the dark ~ como o breu pitch-black

escutar vt, vi listen (to sb/sth): Escute! Listen to this! ◇ Você nunca me escuta. You never listen to me.

esfaquear vt stab

esfarrapado adj 1 (roto) ragged 2 (inconsistente) feeble: desculpas esfarrapadas feeble excuses

esfera sf sphere

esferográfica sf ballpoint (pen)

esfinge sf sphinx

esfolar vt (arranhar) graze

esfomeado adj starving

esforçado adj hard-working: O meu filho é muito ~ nos estudos. My son studies very hard.

esforçar-se vp try (hard) (to do sth): ~ muito try very hard

esforço sm 1 effort: fazer um ~ make an effort 2 (tentativa) attempt (at doing sth/to do sth): um ~ para evitar um desastre an attempt to avoid disaster ▶ sem ~ effortlessly

esfregão sm mop

esfregar vt 1 (limpar) scrub 2 (friccionar) rub: ~ as mãos rub your hands together 3 (panela, tacho) scour

esfriar vi 1 get cold: A sua sopa está esfriando. Your soup's getting cold. 2 cool down: De noite esfria um pouco. It cools down a little at night.

esganiçado adj (voz) shrill

esgarçar vt, vi fray

esgotado adj 1 (cansado) worn out, exhausted (mais fml) 2 (produtos, entradas) sold out 3 (edição) out of print ▶ deixar ~ (cansar) wear sb out

esgotamento sm (cansaço) exhaustion ▶ ~ nervoso nervous breakdown

esgotar vt 1 exhaust: ~ um tema exhaust a subject 2 (produtos, reservas) use up ● **esgotar-se** vp 1 run out: A minha paciência está se esgotando. My patience is running out. 2 (livro, ingressos) sell out

esgoto sm drain: rede de ~ sewage system

esgrima sf (Esporte) fencing: praticar ~ fence

esguichar vi, vt spurt (out)

esguicho sm (jato) jet

esmagar vt 1 crush: ~ alho crush garlic 2 (coisa mole, inseto) squash

esmalte sm enamel ▶ ~ de unhas nail polish

esmeralda sf emerald

esmerar-se vp try very hard (to do sth): Esmere-se um pouco mais. Try a little harder.

esmero sm (great) care: com ~ carefully

esmigalhar vt 1 break sth into small pieces 2 (pão, bolachas) crumble sth (up)

esmo sm ▶ a ~ (sem rumo) aimlessly: andar a ~ pela cidade wander aimlessly around the city

esmola sf: Nós lhe demos uma ~. We gave him some money. ◇ Uma ~, por favor. Can you spare any change, please?

esmorecer vi lose heart

esmurrar vt punch

esnobe adj snobby ● smf snob

espacial adj space: missão/vôo ~ space mission/flight

espaço sm 1 space 2 (lugar) room: Há ~ na minha mala. There's room in my suitcase. 3 (em branco) blank: Preencha os ~s. Fill in the blanks.

espaçoso adj (aposento) spacious

espada sf 1 (arma) sword 2

(espadas) *(naipe)* spades
→ BARALHO

espaguete *sm* spaghetti

espairecer *vi, vt (distrair-se)* relax

espalhado *adj* **1** *(disperso)* scattered **2** *(pelo chão)* lying on the floor ◊ *deixar tudo ~* leave everything lying around

espalhafato *sm* racket: *fazer ~* make a racket

espalhafatoso *adj* **1** *(barulhento)* loud **2** *(extravagante)* over the top: *Ela se veste de modo muito ~.* She wears very flamboyant clothes.

espalhar(-se) *vt, vi, vp* **1** *(dispersar(-se))* scatter **2** *(notícia, boato)* spread

espancamento *sm* beating

espancar *vt* beat *sb* up

Espanha *sf* Spain

espanhol ~a *adj, sm* Spanish ● *sm-sf* Spaniard: *os espanhóis* the Spanish

espantalho *sm* scarecrow

espantar(-se) *vt, vp* **1** *(surpreender)* amaze **2** *(afugentar)* drive *sb/ sth* away ● **espantar-se** *vp* **1** *(surpreender-se)* be amazed: *~ em ver alguém* be amazed to see *sb* **2** *(assustar-se)* be frightened

espanto *sm* amazement: *ter cara de ~* look amazed

espantoso *adj* amazing

esparadrapo *sm* Band-Aid®, plaster *(GB)*

esparramar *vt* **1** *(espalhar)* scatter **2** *(entornar)* spill ● **esparramar-se** *vp* *(sentar-se de qualquer jeito)* sprawl

espatifar *vt (destruir)* smash ● **espatifar-se** *vp (carro, moto)* crash

espátula *sf* spatula

especial *adj* special

especialidade *sf* speciality [*pl* -ies]

especialista *smf* specialist *(in sth)*: *um ~ em informática* an IT specialist

especializado *adj* **1** specialized *(in sth)* **2** *(trabalhador)* skilled

especializar-se *vp* specialize *(in sth)*

especialmente *adv* **1** *(sobretudo)* especially: *Adoro animais, ~ gatos.* I love animals, especially cats. **2** *(exclusivamente)* specially: *~ desenhado para deficientes* specially designed for disabled people
→ SPECIALLY

especiaria *sf* spice

espécie *sf* **1** *(Biol)* species [*pl* -ies]: *uma ~ em vias de extinção* an endangered species **2** *(tipo)* kind ▶ *pagar em ~* pay (in) cash

especificar *vt* specify

específico *adj* specific

espécime *sm* specimen

espectador/a *sm-sf* **1** *(Esporte)* spectator **2** *(TV)* viewer **3** *(Teat, Mús)* member of the audience

espectro *sm* **1** *(fantasma)* specter **2** *(Fís)* spectrum

especulação *sf* speculation

especular *vt* speculate *(on/ about sth)*

espelho *sm* mirror

espelunca *sf (lugar escuro e sujo)* dive

espera *sf* wait ▶ *estar à ~ de* be waiting for *sb/sth* → ESPERAR

esperança *sf* hope

esperar *vt* wait for *sb/sth*, expect, hope NOTA Os verbos **wait, expect** e **hope** significam *esperar*, mas não devem ser confundidos. **Wait** indica que se está à espera de que alguém chegue ou de que algo aconteça: *Espere por mim, por favor.* Wait for me, please. ◊ *~ o ônibus* wait for the bus ◊ *~ que pare de chover* wait for it to stop raining. **Expect** é usado quando o que se espera é não apenas lógico como muito provável: *Havia mais trânsito do que eu esperava.* There was more traffic than I had expected. ◊ *Estou esperando uma carta dele.* I'm expecting a letter from him. Para gravidez, também se diz **expect**: *Ela está esperando bebê.* She's expecting a baby. Com **hope** exprime-se o desejo de que algo aconteça ou tenha acontecido: *Espero voltar a vê-lo em breve.* I hope to see you again soon. ◊ *Espero que sim/ não.* I hope so/not. ● *vi* wait: *Estou farta de ~.* I'm tired of waiting. ▶ *fazer alguém ~* keep *sb* waiting *ir ~ alguém* meet *sb* *(não) saber o que ~* (not) know what to expect

espernear *vi* **1** kick (your feet) **2** *(fazer birra)* throw a tantrum

espertalhão/ona *sm-sf* sharp operator

esperto *adj* smart, bright *(GB)*: *Não se faça de ~ comigo.* Don't get smart with me.

espesso *adj* thick

espessura *sf* thickness: *Quanto tem de ~?* How thick is it?

espetacular *adj* spectacular

espetáculo sm **1** spectacle **2** (diversão) show ▸ **dar ~** make a spectacle of yourself

espetada sf prick: Dei uma ~ no dedo. I pricked my finger.

espetar vt **1** (cravar) stick **2** (com alfinete) prick ● **espetar-se** vp (picar-se) prick yourself: Espetei-me num espinho. I pricked my finger on a thorn.

espetinho sm kebab

espevitado adj **1** (vivo) lively **2** (atrevido) sassy, cheeky (GB)

espiada sf peep ▸ **dar uma ~ em algo** have/take a look at sth

espião/ã sm-sf spy [pl spies]

espiar vt, vi **1** (olhar) peek (at sb/sth) **2** (espionar) spy (on sb)

espichar vt (esticar) stretch

espiga sf (milho) ear

espinafre sm spinach

espingarda sf shotgun

espinha sf **1** (peixe) bone **2** (acne) pimple ▸ ~ **dorsal** spine

espinho sm **1** thorn **2** (de animal) spine

espionagem sf spying, espionage (mais fml)

espiral adj, sf spiral

espiritismo sm spiritualism

espírito sm spirit: ~ de equipe team spirit **2** (humor) wit ▸ ~ **Santo** Holy Spirit

espiritual adj spiritual

espirituoso adj witty

espirrar vi **1** (pessoa) sneeze → ATXIM **2** (fritura) spit

espirro sm sneeze

esplanada sf esplanade

esplêndido adj splendid

esponja sf sponge ▸ **passar uma ~ sobre o assunto** wipe the slate clean

espontâneo adj spontaneous

espora sf spur

esporádico adj sporadic

esporte sm sport: Você pratica algum ~? Do you play any sports? ● adj (roupa) casual

esportivo adj **1** sports: competição esportiva sports competition **2** (comportamento) sporting: um comportamento pouco ~ bad sportsmanship ▸ **levar as coisas na esportiva** take sth lightly

esposo/a sm-sf husband [fem wife] [pl wives]

espreguiçadeira sf sun lounger

espreguiçar-se vp stretch

espreita sf ▸ **estar à ~ 1** (vigiar) be on the lookout for sb/sth **2** (esperar escondido) lie in wait (for sb/sth)

espreitar vt, vi **1** (espiar) spy (on sb) **2** (esperar escondido) lie in wait (for sb/sth)

espremedor sm **1** (manual) (lemon-/orange-) squeezer **2** (elétrico) juicer

espremer vt (fruta) squeeze sth (out)

espresso adj espresso [pl ~s]

espuma sf **1** foam **2** (cerveja) froth **3** (sabonete, xampu) lather ▸ ~ **de um banho de ~** a bubble bath **5** (mar) surf ▸ ~ **de borracha** foam rubber **fazer** ~ **1** (ondas) foam **2** (sabão) lather

espumante adj (vinho) sparkling ● sm sparkling wine

esquadra sf **1** (Náut) fleet **2** (Mil) squad

esquadrão sm squadron

esquadro sm set square

esquartejar vt cut sth up

esquecer(-se) vt, vp **1** forget (to do) sth: ~ o passado forget the past **2** (deixar) leave sth (behind): Não se esqueça dele. Don't leave it behind.

esquecido adj (pessoa) forgetful

esquelético adj (muito magro) scrawny → MAGRO

esqueleto sm **1** (Anat) skeleton **2** (estrutura) framework

esquema sm **1** (diagrama) diagram **2** (resumo) outline **3** (plano) plan

esquentar vt, vi warm (sth) up: Como esquentou depois da chuva! It's really warmed up since the rain! ▸ ~ **a cabeça** worry about sth: Pare de ~ a cabeça. Stop worrying about it.

esquerdo/a adj left: o braço ~ my left arm ● **esquerda** sf left: Siga pela ~. Keep left. ◇ **dirigir pela ~** drive on the left ◇ a casa da ~ the house on the left ◇ A estrada vira à ~. The road bears left. ▸ **a esquerda** (Pol) the left ▸ **à esquerda** on the left **de esquerda**: grupos de esquerda left-wing groups

esqui sm **1** (objeto) ski [pl skis] **2** (Esporte) skiing ▸ ~ **aquático** waterskiing: fazer ~ aquático go waterskiing

esquiar vi ski: Eles esquiam todo ano. They go skiing every year.

esquilo sm squirrel

esquina sf corner: Espere-me na ~. Wait for me on the corner. ◇ É a casa que faz ~ com a Rua da Moeda. It's the house on the corner of Rua da Moeda. ▸ **virando a ~** (just) around the corner

esquisito adj (estranho) strange: Que ~! How strange!

esquivar-se vp 1 dodge 2 (pessoa) avoid

esquizofrenia sf schizophrenia

esquizofrênico/a adj, sm-sf schizophrenic

esse/a pron 1 (adjetivo) that/this [pl these]: ~s livros these books 2 (substantivo) **(a)** (coisa) that/this one [pl those/these (ones)]: Não quero ~/~s. I don't want this one/these. **(b)** (pessoa): Foi essa aí! It was her! ◊ Não vou com ~s aí. I'm not going with those people.

essência sf essence

essencial adj essential (to/for sth)

estabelecer vt 1 (determinar, ordenar) establish 2 (criar) set sth up: ~ uma sociedade set up a company 3 (recorde) set ► **estabelecer-se** vp 1 (fixar-se) settle 2 (num negócio) set up: ~ por conta própria set up your own business

estabelecimento sm establishment

estabilidade sf stability

estabilizar(-se) vt, vp stabilize

estábulo sm cowshed

estaca sf 1 stake 2 (tenda) peg

estação sf 1 station 2 (do ano) season ► ~ **de águas** spa

estacar vi (pessoa) freeze

estacionamento sm 1 (ato) parking 2 (vaga) parking space 3 (local) parking lot, car park (GB): um ~ subterrâneo an underground parking lot

estacionar vt, vi park: ~ em fila dupla double-park

estada (tb **estadia**) sf 1 stay 2 (gastos) living expenses [pl]: os custos de ~ living expenses

estádio sm (Esporte) stadium [pl ~s/stadia]

estadista smf statesman [fem stateswoman]

estado sm 1 state: a segurança do ~ state security 2 (condição médica) condition ► **em bom/mau** ~ 1 in good/bad condition 2 (estrada) in a good/bad state of repair ► **civil** marital status ► **de espírito** state of mind

Estados Unidos sm (the) United States (abrev **USA**)

estadual adj state: lei ~ state law

estafa sf 1 (cansaço) fatigue 2 (esgotamento nervoso) nervous breakdown

estafado/a adj (cansado) exhausted

estagiário/a sm-sf trainee

estagnado adj (água) stagnant

estagnar vi 1 (água) stagnate 2 (negociações) come to a standstill

estalactite sf stalactite

estalagmite sf stalagmite

estalar vt 1 crack 2 (língua) click 3 (dedos) snap ► vi 1 crack 2 (lenha) crackle

estaleiro sm shipyard

estalido sm 1 crack 2 (fogueira) crackle

estalo sm 1 (som) crack 2 (língua) click: dar um ~ com a língua click your tongue 3 (dedos) snap ► **de** ~ suddenly ter/dar um ~: De repente me deu um ~. Suddenly it clicked. ◊ Eu tive um ~ e encontrei a solução. The solution suddenly occurred to me.

estampa sf (ilustração) plate

estampar vt (imprimir) print

estampilha sf (selo fiscal) official stamp

estandarte sm banner

estanho sm tin

estante sf bookcase

estar vi be: A Ana está em casa? Is Ana home? ► v lig 1 (achar-se) be: ~ doente/cansado be sick/tired 2 (aspecto) look: Você está muito bonito. You look very nice. ► vt ~ **em** (consistir) lie in sth: O êxito do grupo está na sua originalidade. The group's success lies in their originality. ► v aux be doing sth: Eles estavam jogando. They were playing. ► v imp (clima): Está frio/calor/ventando. It's cold/hot/windy. ► **está bem** 1 (de acordo) OK 2 (chega) that's enough ► ~ **a** (data): Estamos a três de maio. It's the third of May. 2 (preço) cost: A quanto estão as bananas? How much are the bananas? ~ **aí** (mesmo) (estar chegando): O verão está aí. Summer's just around the corner. ~ **com** (apoiar): Ânimo, que nós estamos contigo! Go for it, we're rooting for you! ~/ficar bom be/get well ► **que...**: Estou que nem me agüento em pé. I'm dead on my feet. **estar que estar** be in seventh heaven **não** ~ **para**: Não estou para brincadeiras. I'm not in the mood for jokes. NOTA Para outras expressões com estar, ver o substantivo, adjetivo, etc., p. ex. **estar numa boa** em BOA.

estardalhaço sm (ruído) racket: fazer ~ make a racket

estatal adj state: empresa ~ state-owned company

estático adj static

estatística sf 1 (ciência) statistics [sing] 2 (cifra) statistic

estátua sf statue

estatura sf height: de ~ mediana of average height ◊ Ele é de baixa ~. He's short.

estatuto sm statute

estável adj stable

este/a pron 1 (adjetivo) this [pl these] 2 (substantivo) this one [pl these (ones)]: Prefiro aquele terno a ~. I prefer that suit to this one.

esteira sf 1 (tapete) rug 2 (rastro) wake ► **rolante** conveyor belt

estender vt 1 (esticar, braço, mão) stretch sth out 2 (alargar) extend: ~ uma mesa/o prazo das matrículas extend a table/the registration period 3 (desdobrar, espalhar) spread sth (out): ~ um mapa sobre a mesa spread a map out on the table 4 (roupa no varal) hang sth out: ~ a roupa hang the laundry out ● **estender-se** vp 1 (deitar-se) lie down → LIE² 2 (no espaço) stretch: O jardim se estende até o lago. The garden stretches down to the lake. 3 (no tempo) last 4 (propagar-se) spread: A epidemia se estendeu país afora. The epidemic spread throughout the country. 5 ~ **sobre** (alongar-se) speak at length about sth

estendido adj 1 (pessoa) lying: Ele estava ~ no chão. He was lying on the floor. 2 (roupa): A roupa está estendida. The laundry is out on the line. 3 (braços, pernas) outstretched

estepe sm (pneu) spare tire

esterco sm manure

estereofônico adj stereo

estereótipo sm stereotype

estéril adj sterile

esterilizar vt sterilize

esterlina adj sterling: libras ~s pounds sterling

estética sf aesthetics [sing]

esteticista smf beautician

estético adj aesthetic

estetoscópio sm stethoscope

estibordo sm starboard

esticada sf ► **dar uma** ~: Depois da festa, demos uma ~ numa boate. After the party we went on to a club.

esticado adj (estendido) tight

esticar vt 1 stretch: ~ uma corda stretch a rope tight 2 (braço, perna) stretch sth out 3 ~ o dinheiro spin your money out 4 (alisar) smooth ● **esticar-se** vp (espreguiçar-se) stretch ► **as canelas** kick the bucket

estilhaçar(-se) vt, vp shatter

estilista smf (moda) fashion designer

estilo sm style: com muito ~ stylish ► **de** ~: móveis de ~ period furniture   ~ **de vida** lifestyle

estima sf esteem ► **ter alguém em alta/grande** ~ think highly of sb

estimação sf esteem ► **de** ~ favorite: um animal de ~ a pet (animal) ◊ objetos de ~ objects of sentimental value

estimativa sf estimate

estimulante adj stimulating ● sm stimulant

estimular vt 1 (incitar) stimulate 2 (animar) encourage

estímulo sm stimulus [pl -li] (to do) sth

estirada sf (distância) way: É uma boa ~ até a minha casa. It's quite a way to the house.

estivador sm longshoreman, docker (GB)

estofamento sm (carro, móvel) upholstery [U]

estofar vt (móvel, carro) upholster

estojo sm 1 (lápis, instrumento musical) case 2 (maquiagem, jóias) box ► ~ **de primeiros socorros** first aid kit

estômago sm stomach

estoque sm stock(s): controle de ~ stock control

estorvar vt 1 (incomodar) annoy 2 (dificultar) block: ~ as saídas block the exits

estourar vi 1 (balão, pneu) burst 2 (guerra) break out 3 (escândalo) break

estouro sm (explosão) explosion

estrábico adj cross-eyed

estrabismo sm squint

estrada sf road: ~ de terra dirt road ► ~ **de ferro** railroad, railway (GB)   ~ **de rodagem** highway, motorway (GB) → RODOVIA

estrado sm platform

estragado adj 1 (alimento) spoiled, off (GB) 2 (máquina) out of order

estragar vt 1 ruin 2 (aparelho) break 3 (desperdiçar) waste ● **estragar-se** vp 1 (não funcionar) break down 2 (comida) go bad

estrago sm (dano) damage [U]: causar/sofrer ~s cause/suffer damage

estrangeiro/a adj foreign ● sm-sf foreigner ▶ no/para o ~ abroad

estrangular vt strangle

estranhar vt find sth strange: No princípio você vai ~. At first you'll find it strange.

estranho/a adj strange ● sm-sf stranger

estratagema sf scheme

estratégia sf strategy [pl -ies]

estratégico adj strategic

estrato sm (Geol, social) stratum [pl strata]

estrear vt 1 Estou estreando estes sapatos. I am wearing new shoes. 2 (filme, peça de teatro) première

estréia sf 1 (filme, peça de teatro) première 2 (ator) debut

estreitar vt narrow

estreito/a adj narrow ● sm strait(s): o ~ de Bering the Bering Strait(s)

estrela sf star: ~ cadente/polar shooting/pole star ◇ um hotel de três ~s a three-star hotel ◇ uma ~ de cinema a movie star ▶ ver ~s see stars

estrelado adj 1 (noite, céu) starry 2 (figura) star-shaped 3 (ovo) fried

estrelar vt 1 (filme) star in sth 2 (ovos) fry

estrelato sm stardom: chegar ao ~ become a star

estremecer vt, vi (tremer) shake: ~ de dor/de medo tremble with pain/tremble with fear

estresse sm Ver STRESS

estria sf 1 groove 2 (pele) stretch mark

estribeira sf ▶ perder as ~s lose your temper

estribilho sm chorus

estribo sm stirrup

estridente adj (som) shrill

estrito adj strict

estrofe sf verse

estrondo sm bang: A porta se fechou com um grande ~. The door slammed shut. ◇ o ~ do trovão the rumble of thunder

estrondoso adj 1 aplausos ~s thunderous applause 2 (sucesso) resounding

estrutura sf structure

estuário sm estuary [pl -ies]

estudante smf student: ~ de medicina medical student

estudar vt, vi study: Ela estuda num colégio particular. She's at a private school.

estúdio sm (Cinema, Fot, TV) studio [pl ~s]

estudioso adj studious

estudo sm 1 study [pl -ies]: realizar ~s sobre algo carry out a study of sth 2 (estudos) education [sing]: Ele não tem ~s. He hasn't had a formal education. ▶ em ~ under consideration

estufa sf (de plantas) greenhouse

estupendo adj fantastic

estupidez sf 1 (grosseria) rudeness 2 (burrice) stupidity

estúpido/a adj 1 (grosseiro) rude 2 (burro) stupid ● sm-sf idiot

esturricado adj burned

esvair-se vp vanish

esvaziar vt 1 empty sth (out) 2 (tirar o ar) let the air out of sth ● **esvaziar-se** vp (perder o ar) go down

etapa sf stage: por ~s in stages

etc. sm et cetera (abrev **etc.**)

eternidade sf 1 eternity 2 (uma eternidade) forever: Ele demorou uma ~. He took forever.

eterno adj eternal

ético/a adj ethical ● **ética** sf ethics [sing]

etimologia sf etymology [pl -ies]

etiqueta sf 1 label 2 (preço) price tag 3 (social) etiquette

etiquetar vt label

etnia sf ethnic group

étnico adj ethnic

eu pron pess 1 (sujeito) I 2 (comparações, com preposição) me: como eu like me ▶ eu? me?: Quem? Eu? Who do you mean? Me? **eu mesmo/próprio** I myself: Eu mesmo o farei. I'll do it myself. ◇ Fui eu mesma quem lhe disse. I was the one who told you. **se eu fosse você** if I were you **sou eu** it's me

eucalipto sm eucalyptus

eucaristia sf Eucharist

euforia sf euphoria

eufórico adj euphoric

euro sm euro [pl ~s]

Europa sf Europe

europeu/éia adj, sm-sf European

eutanásia sf euthanasia

evacuar vt evacuate: Evacuem a sala, por favor. Please clear the hall.

evadir-se vp escape (from sth)

evangelho sm gospel:

o ~ segundo São João the Gospel according to Saint John

evaporar(-se) *vt, vp* evaporate

evasão *sf* **1** (*fuga*) escape **2** (*subterfúgio*) evasion: ~ *de impostos* tax evasion

evasiva *sf* excuse: *Não me venha com ~s.* Don't give me excuses.

evento *sm* **1** (*acontecimento*) event **2** (*incidente*) incident

eventual *adj* (*fortuito*) accidental

evidência *sf* evidence

evidente *adj* obvious

evitar *vt* **1** (*prevenir*) avert: ~ *uma catástrofe* avert a disaster **2** (*esquivar-se*) avoid *sb/* (*doing*) *sth*: *Ele faz de tudo para me ~.* He does everything he can to avoid me. **3** (*pessoa*) give *sb* the slip **4** (*golpe, obstáculo*) dodge ▶ **não consigo ~/não posso ~** I, you, etc. can't help it *se você pudesse ~* if you could help it

evolução *sf* **1** (*Biol*) evolution **2** (*desenvolvimento*) development

evoluir *vi* **1** (*Biol*) evolve **2** (*desenvolver-se*) develop

exagerado *adj* **1** exaggerated: *Não seja ~.* Don't exaggerate. **2** (*excessivo*) excessive

exagerar *vt, vi* exaggerate: ~ *a importância de algo* exaggerate the importance of sth

exalar *vt* (*gás, odor*) give *sth* off ● *vi* breathe out, exhale (*fml*)

exaltado *adj* **1** (*excitado*) in a state of excitement: *Os ânimos estão ~s.* Feelings are running high. **2** (*irritado*) angry (*about sth*)

exaltar *vt* (*elogiar*) praise ● **exaltar-se** *vp* **1** (*irritar-se*) get annoyed **2** (*excitar-se*) get excited

exame *sm* (*Educ*) exam, examination (*fml*): *prestar/repetir um ~* take/retake an exam ▶ **~ de sangue/motorista** blood/driving test **~ médico/de aptidão física** physical, medical (*GB*)

examinador/a *sm-sf* examiner

examinar *vt* examine

exatamente *interj* exactly

exato *adj* **1** (*correto*) exact: *as medidas exatas* the exact measurements ◇ *Dois quilos ~s.* Exactly two kilos. **2** (*descrição, relógio*) accurate

exaustivo *adj* thorough

exausto *adj* exhausted

exaustor *sm* (*de ar*) extractor (fan)

exceção *sf* exception ▶ **com ~ de** except (for) *sb/sth*

exceder *vt* exceed ● **exceder-se** *vp* overdo *sth*: *Acho que você se excedeu no sal.* I think you put in too much salt.

excelência *sf* ▶ **por ~** par excellence **Sua/Vossa E~** His/Her/Your Excellency

excelente *adj* **1** (*resultado, referência, tempo*) excellent **2** (*qualidade, nível*) top **3** (*preço, recorde*) unbeatable **4** (*atuação*) outstanding

excepcional *adj* exceptional

excessivo *adj* excessive

excesso *sm* excess (*of sth*) ▶ **em ~** too much ~ **de bagagem** excess baggage ~ **de velocidade** speeding

exceto *prep* except (for) *sb/sth*: *todos ~ o último* all of them except (for) the last one

excitado *adj* **1** (*entusiasmado*) enthusiastic **2** ~ **com** excited about (*doing*) *sth*

excitar *vt* excite ● **excitar-se** *vp* get excited (*about/over sth*)

exclamação *sf* exclamation

exclamar *vi, vt* exclaim

excluir *vt* **1** exclude *sb/sth* (*from sth*) **2** (*Informát*) delete

exclusiva *sf* (*reportagem*) exclusive

exclusivo *adj* exclusive

excomungar *vt* excommunicate

excursão *sf* excursion, trip (*mais coloq*): *fazer uma ~* go on an excursion/a trip

excursionista *smf* tourist

executar *vt* **1** (*realizar*) carry *sth* out **2** (*pena de morte, Jur, Informát*) execute

executivo/a *adj, sm-sf* executive: *órgão ~* executive body ◇ *um ~ importante* an important executive

exemplar *adj* exemplary ● *sm* copy [*pl* -ies]

exemplo *sm* example: *dar o ~* set an example ◇ *Espero que isto lhe sirva de ~.* Let this be an example to you. ▶ **por ~** for example (*abrev* e. g.)

exercer *vt* **1** (*profissão*) practice: ~ *a advocacia* practice law **2** (*autoridade, poder, direitos*) exercise **3** (*função*) fulfill **4** ~ *um cargo* hold a position

exercício *sm* **1** exercise: *Você deveria fazer mais ~.* You should exercise more. **2** (*Educ*) problem: *fazer um ~ de matemática* do a math problem **3** (*profissão*) practice

exército *sm* army [*pl* -ies]

exibição *sf* exhibition ▶ **em ~** *(filme, peça)* showing

exibicionista *smf* exhibitionist

exibido/a *sm-sf* showoff

exibir *vt* **1** *(expor)* exhibit **2** *(filme)* show ● **exibir-se** *vp* show off

exigência *sf* **1** *(requisito)* requirement **2** *(imposição)* demand *(for sth/that...)*

exigente *adj* **1** *(que pede muito)* demanding **2** *(rigoroso)* strict

exigir *vt* **1** *(pedir)* demand *sth (from sb)* **2** *(requerer)* require

exilado/a *adj* exiled ● *sm-sf* exile

exilar *vt* exile *sb (from...)* ● **exilar-se** *vp* go into exile *(in...)*

exílio *sm* exile

existência *sf* existence

existente *adj* existing

existir *vi* **1** exist **2** *(haver)*: *Não existe espírito de luta.* There is no fighting spirit.

êxito *sm* success ▶ **ter ~ be** successful

exótico/a *adj* exotic

expandir(-se) *vt, vp* expand

expansão *sf* expansion

expectativa *sf* expectation: *Foi além das minhas ~s.* It exceeded my expectations. ◊ *A ~ está aumentando.* Expectation is growing. ▶ **estar/ficar na ~** be on the lookout *(for sth)* **~ de vida** life expectancy

expedição *sf (viagem)* expedition

expediente *sm (horário de trabalho)* working hours *[pl]*: *O ~ está encerrado por hoje.* We've finished working for the day.

expedir *vt* **1** *(carta, encomenda)* send **2** *(visto, passaporte)* issue

experiência *sf* **1** experience: *Foi uma grande ~.* It was a great experience. ◊ *sem ~* inexperienced **2** *(teste)* experiment: *fazer uma ~* carry out an experiment ◊ *Fui contratado em caráter de ~.* I was taken on for a trial period.

experiente *adj* experienced

experimental *adj* experimental: *em caráter ~* on an experimental basis

experimentar *vt* **1** *(testar)* try *sth* out: *~ uma nova marca de batom* try out a new brand of lipstick **2** *(tentar)* try *(doing sth)*: *Você experimentou abrir a janela?* Did you try opening the window? **3** *(roupa)* try *sth* on **4** *(mudança)* experience ● *vi* experiment *(with sth)*

experimento *sm* (*tb* **experimen-**

tação *sf)* experiment: *fazer um ~* conduct an experiment

expirar *vt, vi* breathe *(sth)* out ● *vi (morrer)* expire

explicação *sf* explanation

explicar *vt* explain *sth (to sb)*

explodir *vt, vi (destruir)* blow *(sth)* up, explode *(mais fml)*

explorador/~a *sm-sf* **1** *(pesquisador)* explorer **2** *(oportunista)* exploiter

explorar *vt* **1** *(investigar)* explore **2** *(abusar)* exploit

explosão *sf* explosion: *uma ~ nuclear/demográfica* a nuclear/population explosion

explosivo *adj, sm* explosive

expor *vt* **1** *(pintura, escultura)* exhibit **2** *(ideias)* present **3** *(produtos)* display **4** *(submeter)* subject *sb/sth* to sth ● **expor-se** *vp* expose yourself to sth: *Não se exponha demais ao sol.* Don't stay out in the sun too long.

exportação *sf* export

exportador/~a *adj, sm-sf* exporter: *os países ~es de petróleo* the oil-exporting countries

exportar *vt* export

exposição *sf* **1** *(arte)* exhibition: *montar uma ~* put on an exhibition **2** *(de um tema)* presentation

exposto *adj (pintura, escultura, produtos)* on show

expressão *sf* expression

expressar *(tb* **exprimir)** *vt* express

expressivo *adj* **1** expressive **2** *(olhar)* meaningful

expresso *adj* express: *correio ~* express mail

expulsão *sf* expulsion

expulsar *vt* **1** expel *sb (from...)* **2** *(Esporte)* send *sb* off

êxtase *sm* ecstasy *[pl* -ies*]*

extensão *sf* **1** *(superfície)* area: *uma grande ~ de terra* a large area of land **2** *(duração)*: *uma grande ~ de tempo* a long period of time **3** *(prazo, acordo, telefone)* extension

extenso *adj* **1** *(grande)* extensive **2** *(comprido)* long ▶ **por ~** in full

exterior *adj* **1** outside: *as paredes ~es* the outside walls **2** *(superfície)* outer: *a camada ~ da Terra* the outer layer of the Earth **3** *(comércio, política)* foreign ● *sm* **1** outside: *o ~ da casa* the outside of the house ◊ *do ~ do teatro* from outside the theater **2** *(o estrangeiro)* abroad: *morar no ~* live abroad

exterminar *vt* exterminate

externo *adj* external

extinção *sf* extinction: *em vias de ~* on the verge of extinction

extinguir *vt* **1** *(fogo)* put sth out **2** *(espécie)* wipe sth out ● **extinguir-se** *vp* **1** *(fogo)* go out **2** *(espécie)* become extinct

extinto *adj* extinct

extintor *sm* (fire) extinguisher

extorsão *sf* extortion

extra *adj* **1** *(adicional)* extra **2** *(superior)* top quality ● *smf (Cinema, Teat)* extra

extracurricular *adj*: *atividades ~es* extracurricular activities

extrair *vt* extract sth *(from sb/sth)*: *~ ouro/informaçoes* extract gold/information

extraordinário *adj* **1** *(excepcional)* extraordinary **2** *(excelente)* excellent: *A comida estava extraordinária.* The food was excellent. **3** *(especial)* special: *edição/missão extraordinária* special edition/mission **4** *(reunião)* extraordinary

extraterrestre *adj* extraterrestrial ● *smf* alien

extrato *sm* **1** extract **2** *(de conta)* statement

extravagante *adj* extravagant

extraviar *vt* lose ● **extraviar-se** *vp* go astray

extremidade *sf (ponta)* end

extremo *adj, sm* extreme: *um caso ~* an extreme case ◇ *ir de um ~ ao outro* go from one extreme to another

extrovertido *adj* extrovert [s]: *Ele é ~.* He's an extrovert.

F f

fá *sm (Mús)* F

fã *smf* fan

fábrica *sf* **1** factory [pl -ies]: *uma ~ de conservas* a canning factory **2** *(cimento, tijolos)* works ▶ *~ de cerveja* brewery [pl -ies] *~ de papel* paper mill

fabricação *sf* manufacture: *de ~ brasileira* made in Brazil

fabricante *smf* manufacturer

fabricar *vt* manufacture, make *(mais coloq)* ▶ *~ em série* mass-produce

fabuloso *adj* fabulous

faca *sf* knife [pl knives]

facada *sf* stab: *matar alguém a ~s* stab sb to death ▶ *dar uma ~ em alguém (pedir dinheiro)* get money out of sb

façanha *sf* exploit

facção *sf (Mil, Pol)* faction

face *sf* **1** face **2** *(Geom)* side ▶ *em ~ de* in view of **face a face** face to face

fachada *sf* façade *(fml)*, front

facho *sm* beam: *um ~ de luz* a beam of light

fácil *adj* easy: *É mais ~ do que parece.* It's easier than it looks.

facilidade *sf* **1** ease **2** *(talento)* gift: *ter ~ para línguas* have a gift for languages

faculdade *sf* **1** *(capacidade)* faculty [pl -ies] **2** *(Educ)* ◇ *(universidade)* college: *um colega de ~* a college friend **(b)** *(Faculdade)* Faculty [pl -ies]: *~ de Letras* Arts Faculty

facultativo *adj* optional

fada *sf* fairy [pl -ies]: *um conto de ~s* a fairytale

fadiga *sf* fatigue

faisão *sm* pheasant

faísca *sf* spark: *soltar ~s* send out sparks

faixa *sf* **1** *(estrada)* lane: *~ de ônibus/bicicletas* bus/bicycle lane **2** *(tira de pano)* sash **3** *(caratê)* belt: *ser ~ preta* be a black belt ▶ *~ etária* age group *~ para pedestres* crosswalk, pedestrian crossing *(GB)*

fala *sf (faculdade)* speech

falado *adj* spoken

falador/a *adj* talkative ● *sm-sf* chatterbox

falar *vt, vi* **1** speak, talk *(to sb) (about sb/sth)* NOTA **Speak** e **talk** têm o mesmo significado, mas **speak** é um termo mais geral: *Fale mais alto.* Speak louder. ◇ *~ em público* speak in public ◇ *Posso ~ com o José?* Can I speak to José? **Talk** é mais usado ao nos referirmos a vários falantes: *~ de política* talk about politics ◇ *Eles estão falando de se mudar.* They're talking about moving. ◇ *Falamos a noite inteira.* We talked all night. **2** *(língua)* speak: *Você fala russo?* Do you speak Russian? ▶ *~ pelos cotovelos* talk a blue streak, talk nineteen to the dozen *(GB)* *~ sério: Você está falando sério?* Are you serious? *não ~ com alguém* not be on speaking terms with sb *~ a verdade* to tell the truth *por ~ nisso* by the way *quem fala? (ao telefone)* who's calling? *sem ~ em alguém/algo* not to mention sb/sth

falatório sm (ruído de vozes) talking

falcão sm falcon

falecer vi pass away

falecido/a adj late: o ~ presidente the late president • sm-sf deceased: os familiares do ~ the family of the deceased

falecimento sm death

falência sf bankruptcy [pl -ies]
▶ **ir à ~** go bankrupt **levar à ~** make sb bankrupt

falha sf 1 (erro) mistake, error (mais fml): devido a uma ~ humana due to human error 2 (problema) fault: uma ~ nos freios a fault in the brakes 3 (imperfeição) flaw 4 (omissão) omission ➤ MISTAKE

falhar vi fail: O motor está falhando. The engine's misfiring.

falido adj (Fin) bankrupt

falir vi go bankrupt

falsificação sf forgery [pl -ies]

falsificar vt forge

falso adj 1 false: um alarme ~ a false alarm 2 (de imitação) fake: diamantes ~s fake diamonds 3 (documento) forged 4 (dinheiro) counterfeit 5 (pessoa) two-faced

falta sf 1 (carência) lack 2 (erro) mistake (futebol) foul: cometer uma ~ commit a foul 3 (ausência): Você já teve duas ~s este mês. You've already missed school twice this month. ◇ A professora me deu ~. I was marked absent.▶ **~ de educação** rudeness: Que ~ de educação! How rude! **~ de jeito** clumsiness **fazer ~1** (sendo preciso) need sb/sth [vt]: Um carro me faz ~. I need a car. ◇ Esse lápis não vai te fazer ~? Won't you need that pencil? 2 (provocando saudade) miss sb/sth [vt]: Os meus pais me fazem muita ~. I really miss my parents. **sem ~** without fail **sentir ~ de alguém/algo** miss sb/sth: Sinto ~ da minha cama. I miss my own bed.

faltar vi 1 (necessitar) need sb/sth [vt]: Falta-lhes carinho. They need affection. ◇ Falta um gerente aqui. This place needs a manager. ◇ Faltam duas fichas para eu poder telefonar. I need two tokens to make a phone call. ◇ Faltam medicamentos em muitos hospitais. Many hospitals lack medicines. 2 (não estar) be missing: Cinco alunos faltaram. Five students were absent. 3 (restar tempo): Faltam

dez (minutos) para as nove. It's ten to nine. ◇ Faltam dez minutos (para que termine a aula). There are ten minutes to go (till the end of the class). ◇ Falta muito para o almoço? Is it long till lunch? ◇ Faltam três dias para as férias. It's only three days until our vacation. 4 (enfraquecer) flag: Começam a me ~ as forças. My strength is flagging. • vt ~ a 1 (escola, trabalho) (a) (intencionalmente) skip: ~ às aulas cut/skip class (b) (não intencional) miss: ~ a uma aula miss a class 2 (prometido) break 3 (respeito): ~ ao respeito de be disrespectful ▶ **era só o que faltava** that's all I/we need **~ um parafuso em alguém** have a screw loose

fama sf 1 (celebridade) fame 2 (reputação) reputation (for doing sth): ter boa/má ~ have a good/bad reputation ◇ Ele tem ~ de ser duro. He has a reputation for being strict.

famigerado adj 1 (malfeitor) notorious 2 (célebre) famous

família sf family [pl -ies]: uma ~ numerosa a large family **NOTA** Há duas formas de dizer o nome de família: com **family** ("the Robertson family") ou com o sobrenome no plural ("the Robertsons"). ▶ **mãe/pai de ~** mother/father **ser de ~** run in the family: Esse mau gênio dele é de ~. That bad temper of his runs in the family.

familiar adj 1 (da família) family: laços ~es family ties 2 (conhecido) familiar • smf relative

faminto adj starving

famoso adj 1 (célebre) famous (for sth): tornar-se ~ become famous 2 (com má fama) notorious (for sth): Ele é ~ pelo mau gênio. He's notoriously bad-tempered.

fanático/a sm-sf fanatic

fanatismo sm fanaticism

fanhoso adj (voz) nasal

faniquito sm ▶ **ter/dar (um) ~** get flustered

fantasia sf 1 fantasy [pl -ies] 2 (máscara) costume, fancy dress (GB)

fantasiar-se vp (para uma festa) dress up (as sb/sth)

fantasma sm ghost: uma história de ~s a ghost story

fantástico adj fantastic

fantoche sm puppet

faqueiro *sm* set of silverware, cutlery set (*GB*)

farda *sf* uniform: *estar de* ~ be in uniform

fardado *adj* uniformed

farejar *vi* **1** (*cheirar*) sniff around **2** (*pesquisar*) snoop around: *A polícia andou farejando por aqui*. The police were snooping around here. • *vt* **1** (*cheirar*) sniff **2** (*seguir o rastro*) follow the scent of *sb/sth*

farinha *sf* flour

farmacêutico/a *sm-sf* pharmacist

farmácia *sf* pharmacy [*pl* -ies]: ~ *de plantão* all-night pharmacy ➤ PHARMACY

faro *sm* (*cão*) smell ► **ter** ~ have a nose for *sth*

faroeste *sm* (*filme*) western

farol *sm* **1** (*torre*) lighthouse **2** (*carro, moto*) headlight **3** (*bicicleta*) (bicycle) lamp ► ~ **alto** brights, full beam (*GB*) ► ~ **baixo** low beam, dipped headlight (*GB*)

farolete *sm* parking light, sidelight (*GB*)

farpa *sf* **1** (*lasca de madeira*) splinter **2** (*arame*) barb

farra *sf* partying: *cair na* ~ go out partying ◊ *Fizemos uma tremenda* ~. We had a big party. ► *por* ~ as a joke

farrapo *sm* rag

farsa *sf* (*fingimento*) sham

fartar-se *vp* **1** (*cansar-se*) get sick (*of sb/doing sth*) **2** (*empanturrar-se*) (**a**) be stuffed: *Comi até me fartar*. I ate till I was stuffed. (**b**) ~ *de stuff yourself* (*with sth*)

farto *adj* **1** (*cheio*) full (*of sth*) **2** (*cansado*) sick (*of sb/sth*)

fartura *sf* (*abundância*) abundance

fascículo *sm* installment

fascinante *adj* fascinating

fascinar *vt* fascinate

fascismo *sm* fascism

fascista *adj, smf* fascist

fase *sf* phase: *a* ~ *inicial/classificatória* the preliminary/qualifying stage ► *em* ~ *de* in the process of *doing sth*: *em* ~ *de atualização* in the process of updating

fatal *adj* fatal: *um acidente* ~ a fatal accident

fatalidade *sf* misfortune

fatia *sf* slice: *uma* ~ *de pão* a slice of bread ► *em* ~**s** sliced

fatigado *adj* tired

fatigante *adj* tiring

fato *sm* **1** fact **2** (*acontecimento*) event ► *de* ~ in fact **pelo** ~ **de** because: *Pelo* ~ *de ser rico, ele acha que tem direito a privilégios*. Because he's rich, he thinks he's entitled to special treatment. ◊ *pelo simples* ~ *de eu ter dito a verdade* just because I spoke the truth ► *um* ~ *consumado* a fait accompli

fator *sm* factor: *um fator-chave* a key factor

fatura *sf* invoice

fauna *sf* fauna

fava *sf* broad bean

favela *sf* shantytown

favelado/a *sm-sf* shantytown dweller

favo *sm* ► ~ (**de mel**) honeycomb

favor *sm* favor: *fazer/pedir um* ~ *a alguém* do/ask sb a favor ◊ *Faça o* ~ *de entrar*. Do come in. ► *a* ~ *de* in favor of *sb/(doing) sth* ► *por* ~ **1** (*para pedir algo*) please **2** (*para chamar a atenção*) excuse me

favorável *adj* favorable

favorecer *vt* **1** favor **2** (*roupa, penteado*) suit: *O vermelho te favorece*. Red suits you.

favoritismo *sm* favoritism

favorito/a *adj, sm-sf* favorite

fax *sm* fax: *Mandaram por* ~. They faxed it.

faxina *sf* clean: *O seu quarto está precisando de uma boa* ~. Your room needs a good clean.

faxineiro/a *sm-sf* cleaner

fazenda *sf* **1** (*tecido*) cloth **2** (*sítio*) farm

fazer *vt*
● traduz-se por **make** nos seguintes casos: **1** (*fabricar*): ~ *bicicletas/uma blusa* make bicycles/a blouse **2** (*dinheiro, barulho, cama*): ~ *a cama* make your bed **3** (*comentário, promessa, esforço*): ~ *um esforço* make an effort **4** (*amor*): *Faça amor, não faça guerra*. Make love, not war. **5** (*tornar*): *O sofrimento nos faz mais fortes*. Suffering makes us stronger.
● traduz-se por **do** nos seguintes casos: **1** ao falar de uma atividade sem dizer do que se trata: *O que vamos* ~ *esta tarde*? What should we do this afternoon? ◊ *Faço o que posso*. I do what I can. **2** (*estudos*): ~ *contas/os deveres* do arithmetic/your homework **3** (*favor*): *Você me faz um favor*? Can you do me a favor?
● outros usos: **1** get *sb* to do *sth*: *Eles nos fazem vir todos os*

sábados. They're getting us to come in every Saturday. ◊ *Eu os fiz mudarem o pneu*. I got them to change the tire. **2** *(quando outra pessoa realiza a ação)* have sth done: *Estão fazendo obra na casa.* They're having the house done up. **3** *(anos)* be: *Ela faz 16 anos em maio.* She'll be 16 in May. **4** *(escrever)* write: *~ uma redação* write an essay **5** *(pintar, desenhar)* paint, draw: *~ um desenho* draw a picture **6** *(nó)* tie: *~ um laço* tie a bow **7** *(pergunta)* ask: *~ ask questions* **8** *(papel)* play: *Fiz o papel de Romeo.* I played the part of Romeo. **9** *(Esporte)*: *~ judô/aeróbica* do judo/aerobics ◊ *~ ciclismo/alpinismo* go bike riding/climbing ● *vi imp* **1** *(tempo cronológico)*: *Faz dez anos que me casei.* I got married ten years ago. → AGO **2** *(tempo meteorológico)*: *Faz frio.* It's cold. ◊ *Fez um tempo ótimo no verão passado.* The weather was beautiful last summer. **3** *(temperatura)*: *Está fazendo 30°C no Rio.* It's 86°F in Rio. ● **fazer-se** *vp* **~ de** pretend to be sth: *Não se faça de surdo.* Don't pretend you didn't hear me. ◊ *Não se faça de esperta comigo.* Don't get smart with me. ▶ **~ bem/mal 1** *(agir com)* be right/wrong *(to do sth)*: *Fiz bem em ir?* Was I right to go? **2** *(para a saúde)* be good/bad for sb/sth: *Fumar faz mal.* Smoking is bad for you. **~ de** *(agir como)* act as sth **~ pouco (de)** make fun of sb/sth **~ que...** pretend: *Ele fez que não me viu.* He pretended not to see me. **fazer-se passar por...** pass yourself off as sb/sth **~ uma das suas** ◊ *O Antônio voltou a ~ uma das suas.* Antônio's been up to his old tricks again. **não faz mal** *(não importa)* it doesn't matter **o que (é que) você faz?** **1** *(profissão)* what do you do? **2** *(neste momento)* what are you doing? NOTA Para outras expressões com **fazer**, ver entrada adjetivo, etc., p. ex. **fazer contas** em CONTA.

fé *sf* faith *(in sb/sth)*

febre *sf* **1** *(temperatura alta)* temperature: *ter ~* have a temperature ◊ *Ele tem 38° de ~.* He has a temperature of 38°C. **2** *(doença)* fever: *~ amarela* yellow fever

fechado/a *adj* **1** closed, shut *(mais coloq)* **2** *(à chave)* locked **3**

(espaço) enclosed **4** *(torneira)* turned off **5** *(cara)* stern **6** *(pessoa)* reserved **7** *(tempo)* overcast

fechadura *sf* lock

fechamento *sm* *(ato de encerrar)* closure

fechar *vt* **1** close, shut *(mais coloq)*: *~ os olhos* close your eyes ◊ *~ a porta na cara de alguém* shut the door in sb's face **2** *(permanentemente)* close sth down: *Fecharam a fábrica.* They closed down the factory. **3** *(gás, torneira)* turn sth off **4** *(envelope)* seal **5** *~ um negócio* close a business deal ● *vi* **1** *(encerrar expediente)* close, shut *(mais coloq)*: *~ para o almoço* close for lunch **2** *(sinal de trânsito)*: *O sinal fechou.* The traffic light turned red. **3** *(tempo)* cloud over ● **fechar-se** *vp* **1** close, shut *(mais coloq)* **2** *(a si próprio)* **(a)** shut yourself in **(b)** *(com chave)* lock yourself in ▶ **fechar a cara** frown **fechar à chave/com tranca** lock/bolt

fecho *sm* **1** *(peça de roupa)* zipper, zip *(GB)*: *Não consigo subir o ~.* I can't do my zipper up. ◊ *Abra o ~ (do meu vestido).* Unzip my dress for me. **2** *(colar, pulseira)* clasp ▶ **~ de segurança** safety catch

fecundar *vt* fertilize

federação *sf* federation

federal *adj* federal

fedor *sm* stink

feijão *sm* beans [pl]

feijoada *sf* bean stew

feio *adj* **1** *(aspecto)* ugly: *uma casa/pessoa feia* an ugly house/person **2** *(desagradável)* nasty: *Que costume mais ~!* What a nasty habit! ▶ **~ de doer/como o diabo** as ugly as sin

feira *sf* **1** fair: *~ do livro/industrial* book/trade fair **2** *(mercado)* market

feiticeiro/a *sm-sf* **1** wizard *[fem* witch*]* **2** *(em tribos primitivas)* witch doctor

feitiço *sm* spell

feito *adj* **1** *(manufaturado)* made: *~ à mão* handmade ◊ *É ~ de quê?* What's it made of? **2** *um homem ~* a grown man ● **bem ~** *it* serves you right **que é ~ de...?**: *Que é ~ da sua irmã?* What became of your sister?

feiúra *sf* ugliness

feixe *sm* bundle

felicidade *sf* **1** happiness: *cara*

de ~ a happy face **2 (felicidades)** best wishes *(on sth)*

felicitar *vt* congratulate *sb (on sth)*

feliz *adj* happy ▶ ~ **aniversário** Happy Birthday ~ **Natal** Merry Christmas

felizmente *adv* fortunately

feltro *sm* felt

fêmea *sf* female: *um leopardo* ~ *a female leopard* → FEMALE

feminino *adj* **1** female: *o sexo* ~ *the female sex* **2** *(Esporte, moda)* women's: *a equipe* ~ *the women's team* **3** *(característico da mulher, Gram)* feminine: *Ela veste roupas muito femininas. She wears very feminine clothes.* → FEMALE

feminismo *sm* feminism

feminista *adj, smf* feminist

fenda *sf* **1** crack **2** *(ranhura)* slot

feno *sm* hay

fenomenal *adj* fantastic

fenômeno *sm* phenomenon [*pl* -mena] ▶ **ser um** ~: *Este ator é um* ~. *This actor is fantastic.*

fera *sf* wild animal ▶ **estar/ficar uma** ~ **be** be furious　**ser** ~ **em algo** be a whiz at sth

feriado *sm* holiday: *Amanhã é* ~ *(nacional). Tomorrow's a holiday.*

férias *sf* vacation [*sing*]holiday (GB): *estar/sair de* ~ *be/go on vacation* ◇ ~ *escolares* summer vacation, school holidays (GB)

ferida *sf* ulcer

ferido/a *sm-sf* casualty [*pl* -ies]

ferimento *sm, sf* **1** injury [*pl* -ies] **2** *(bala, navalha)* wound **NOTA** É difícil saber quando usar **wound** ou **injury/injure.** **Wound** é utilizado para ferimentos causados por feridas (p. ex. uma navalha, pistola, etc.) de forma deliberada: *~s de bala gunshot wounds* ◇ *O* ~ *não tardará a cicatrizar.* The wound will soon heal. ◇ *Ele foi ferido durante a guerra.* He was wounded in the war. Se o ferimento é resultado de acidente, usa-se **injury** ou **injure,** que às vezes também se pode traduzir por *lesão* ou *lesionar: sofrer* ~ *leves suffer minor injuries* ◇ *lesões cerebrais brain injuries* ◇ *Os estilhaços de vidro feriram várias pessoas.* Several people were injured by flying glass.

ferir *vt* **1** injure: *gravemente ferido* badly injured **2** *(bala, navalha)* wound **3** *(ofender)* hurt → FERIMENTO

fermentar *vt, vi* ferment

fermento *sm* yeast

feroz *adj* fierce

ferrado *adj* ▶ **estar** ~ be in a fix **estar** ~ **no sono** be fast asleep

ferradura *sf* horseshoe

ferragem *sf (objetos)* hardware

ferramenta *sf* tool

ferrão *sm (inseto)* sting: *cravar o* ~ *em alguém* sting sb

ferrar *vt (cavalo)* shoe ● **ferrar-se** *vp* fail

ferreiro *sm (pessoa)* blacksmith

ferro *sm (material, eletrodomésti-co)* iron: ~ *batido/fundido* wrought/cast iron

ferroada *sf (abelha, vespa)* sting

ferrolho *sm* bolt

ferro-velho *sm (local)* scrapyard

ferrovia *sm* railroad, railway (GB)

ferroviário/a *adj* railroad, railway (GB): *estação ferroviária* train station ● *sm-sf* railroad worker

ferrugem *sf (metal)* rust

fértil *adj* fertile

fertilizante *sm* fertilizer

ferver *vt, vi* boil: *Sinto o sangue* ~ *só de lembrar.* Just thinking about it makes my blood boil. ● *vi (estar muito quente)* be boiling hot

festa *sf* **1** *(celebração)* party [*pl* -ies]: *dar uma* ~ *de aniversário* hold a birthday party **2** *(festas) (festividades):* as ~s *locais* the local festival ▶ **Boas** ~s Merry Christmas **fazer** ~**(s) (a) 1** *(animal)* pet **2** *(pessoa)* caress

festejar *vt, vi* celebrate

festival *sm* festival

festividade *sf: as* ~s *natalinas/ locais* the Christmas festivities/the local festival

fétido *adj* foul

feto *sm* fetus

fevereiro *sm* February *(abrev* **Feb.)** → MAIO

fiança *sf (Jur)* bail [*U*]

fiapo *sm* thread

fiar *vt: O padeiro me fiou o pão.* The baker let me have the bread on credit. ● *vi* give credit ● **fiar-se** *vp* ~ **em** trust *sb/sth*

fiasco *sm* fiasco [*pl* ~s/~es]

fibra *sf* fiber

ficar *vi* **1** *(estar situado, alcançar)* be: *Onde fica a casa deles? Where's their house?* ◇ *Ficamos em terceiro lugar no concurso.* We came third in the competition. **2** *(permanecer)* stay: ~ *na cama/em casa* stay in bed/at home **3** *(restar)* be left (over): *Se tiramos três de cinco, ficam dois.* If you take three from five, you get two. **4** (*roupa*) look: *Que tal fica?* How does it look? ◊ *Este vestido fica muito mal em mim.* This dress doesn't look good on me. ◊ *Você fica bem de cabelo curto.* You look good with short hair. ◊ *A saia fica muito grande em mim.* The skirt's very big for me. ● vt **1** ~ **com** (*guardar*) keep: *~ com o troco* keep the change **2** ~ **de** (*concordar*) agree to do sth **3** ~ **em** (*custar*) cost **4** ~ **sem** (**a**) (*perder*) lose: *~ sem emprego* lose your job (**b**) (*esgotar-se*): *~ sem dinheiro trocado* run out of change ● v lig **1** (*estar*) be: *~ doente/velho* get sick/old **2** (*tornar-se*) go: *~ cego/louco* go blind/crazy ► ~ **na sua** *Não se meta, você fique na sua.* Stay out of it and get on with your own life. NOTA Para outras expressões com *ficar*, ver o substantivo, adjetivo, etc., p. ex. **ficar para trás** em TRÁS.

ficção *sf* fiction ► ~ **científica** science fiction, sci-fi (*coloq*)

ficha *sf* **1** (*fichário*) (index) card **2** ~ **médica/na polícia** medical/police record **3** (*formulário*) form: *preencher uma* ~ fill in a form **4** (*telefone*) token **5** (*peça de jogo*) (playing) piece

fichar vt (*polícia*) open a file on sb

fichário *sm* **1** file **2** (*caixa*) card catalog, card index (GB) **3** (*móvel*) filing cabinet

fidelidade *sf* faithfulness

fiel *adj* **1** (*leal*) faithful (*to sb/sth*) **2** (*princípios, etc.*) true to sth

fígado *sm* liver

figo *sm* fig

figueira *sf* fig tree

figura *sf* figure: *uma* ~ *política* a political figure ► **estar uma** ~: *Ele estava uma* ~ *com aquele blusão!* He looked ridiculous in that jacket! **ser uma** ~ (*fig*) be a (real) character

figurante *smf* (*Cinema, Teatro*) extra

figurão *sm* big shot

figurar vi (*encontrar-se*) be: *O seu nome não figura na lista.* Your name isn't on the list.

figurinha *sf* (*coleção*) picture card

figurinista *smf* designer

fila *sf* **1** (*um ao lado do outro*) row: *na primeira/última* ~ in the front/back row **2** (*um atrás do outro*) line, queue (GB):

Formem uma ~. Get in line. ► **(em)** ~ **indiana** (in) single file **fazer** ~ line up, queue (up) (GB)

filar vt (*dinheiro, cigarros*) bum sth (*off sb*)

filarmônica *sf* philharmonic (orchestra)

filé *sm* steak

fileira *sf* **1** (*um ao lado do outro*) row **2** (*um atrás do outro*) line

filhinho/a *sm-sf* ► ~ **de papai** rich kid

filho/a *sm-sf* son [*fem* daughter] [*pl* children]: *Eles têm três* ~*s, duas meninas e um menino.* They have two daughters and a son. ◊ *Não temos* ~*s.* We don't have any children. ► **único** ~ only child

filhote *sm* **1** cub: *um* ~ *de leão* a lion cub **2** (*cachorro*) puppy [*pl* -ies]

filial *sf* (*empresa*) branch

filiar-se *vp* join: *filiar-se ao partido* join the party

filmagem *sf* filming

filmar vt film

filme *sm* **1** (*Cinema*) movie, film (GB): *passar um* ~ show a movie ◊ ~ *mudo/de terror* silent/horror movie **2** (*Fot*) film ► ~ **de cowboy/bangue-bangue** western

filologia *sf* philology

filosofia *sf* philosophy [*pl* -ies]

filósofo/a *sm-sf* philosopher

filtrar vt filter

filtro *sm* filter

fim *sm* **1** end: *no* ~ *do mês/corredor* at the end of the month/corridor ◊ *Não é o* ~ *do mundo.* It's not the end of the world. **2** (*finalidade*) purpose ► **a** ~ **de** in order to do sth ◊ **é o** ~ **da picada** it's the last straw **estar a** ~ (*fazer algo*) feel like doing sth: *Não estou a* ~ *de discutir.* I'm not in the mood to argue. ~ **de semana** weekend: *no* ~ *de semana* on the weekend **no** ~ **das contas** after all **no** ~ **de** (*tarde*) late: *terça* ~ *no* ~ *da* late last Tuesday **por** ~ at last **sem** ~ endless **ter por** ~ aim to do sth **ter um** ~ **em mente** have an end in mind

final *adj* final ● *sm* **1** end: *a dois minutos do* ~ two minutes from the end (*filme, etc.*) ending: *um* ~ *feliz* a happy ending ● *sf* final: *a* ~ *da Copa* the Cup Final

finalidade *sf* (*objetivo*) purpose

finalista *adj, smf* finalist [s]: *as equipes* ~s the finalists ◊ *ser um dos* ~ *do torneio* reach the final

finanças *sf* **1** (*economia*) finances **2** (*departamento*) finance department

financiar *vt* finance

fincar *vt* **1** (*apoiar*) plant sth on sth **2** (*olhos*) fix your eyes on sb/sth **3** (*estaca*) drive sth into sth

fingimento *sm* pretense

fingir *vt, vi* pretend: *Eles fingiram não nos ver.* They pretended they hadn't seen us.

fino *adj* **1** (*delgado*) fine: *um lápis ~* a fine pencil **2** (*dedos, cintura*) slender **3** (*elegante*) classy **4** (*educado*) polite ▶ **a fina flor** the crème de la crème

fio *sm* **1** thread: *Perdi o ~ da meada.* I lost the thread of the argument. **2** (*de metal, eletricidade*) wire: *~ de aço/elétrico* (steel) wire **3** (*líquido*) trickle: *um ~ de água/óleo* a trickle of water/oil **4** (*faca, navalha*) blade ▶ **estar por um ~:** *A vida dele está por um ~.* His life's hanging by a thread. **sem ~:** *um telefone sem ~* a cordless phone

firma *sf* company [*pl* -ies]

firme *adj* firm

fiscal *adj* tax: *encargos fiscais* taxes ● *smf* inspector

fiscalizar *vt* **1** (*exame*) invigilate **2** (*inspecionar*) inspect

física *sf* physics [*sing*]

físico *adj* **1** physical **2** (*necessidades, funções, contato*) bodily ● *sm-sf* (*cientista*) physicist ● *sm* (*pessoa*) physique

fisionomia *sf* (*expressão*): *Você está com uma ~ cansada.* You look tired.

fisioterapeuta *smf* physical therapist, physiotherapist (*GB*)

fisioterapia *sf* physical therapy, physiotherapy (*GB*)

fita *sf* **1** tape: *~ isolante* insulating tape **2** (*cabelo*) band: *uma ~ para o cabelo* a hair band **3** (*tira, máquina de escrever*) ribbon ▶ **~ cassete** tape NOTA *Rewind* é rebobinar e *fast forward* é avançar. **~ Durex®** Scotch tape®, Sellotape® (*GB*) **~ métrica** tape measure

fitar *vt* stare at sb/sth

fivela *sf* buckle

fixar *vt* **1** fix: *~ um preço/uma data* set a price/date **2** (*memorizar*) memorize

fixo *adj* **1** fixed: *um preço ~* a fixed price **2** *um posto/contrato ~* a permanent post/contract

flácido *adj* flabby

flagrante *sm* ▶ **em ~** red-handed: *apanhar alguém em ~* catch sb red-handed

flamingo *sm* flamingo [*pl* ~s/~es]

flâmula *sf* pennant

flanco *sm* flank

flanela *sf* flannel

flash *sm* flash

flauta *sf* flute ▶ **~ doce** recorder

flautista *smf* flutist

flecha *sf* arrow

flertar *vi* flirt

flexão *sf* push-up, press-up (*GB*)

flexionar *vt* flex

flexível *adj* flexible

fliperama *sm* pinball

floco *sm* flake: *~s de neve* snowflakes

flor *sf* **1** flower: *~es secas* dried flowers **2** (*árvore, arbusto*) blossom [*ger U*]: *~ da laranjeira* orange blossom ▶ **em ~** in bloom **na ~ da idade** in the prime of life **não ser ~ que se cheire** be a nasty piece of work

flora *sf* flora

florescer *vi* **1** (*planta*) flower **2** (*árvore frutífera, arbusto*) blossom **3** (*fig*) flourish

floresta *sf* forest: *~ tropical* tropical rainforest

florestal *adj* forest: *um incêndio ~* a forest fire

florista *sf* florist

fluência *sf* fluency: *Ela fala francês com ~.* She speaks fluent French.

fluido *adj* **1** (*circulação, diálogo*) free-flowing **2** (*linguagem, estilo*) fluent ● *sm* fluid

fluir *vi* flow

fluminense *adj, smf* (person from) Rio de Janeiro State: *os ~s* the people of Rio de Janeiro State

flúor *sm* **1** (*gás*) fluorine **2** (*dentifrício*) fluoride

fluorescente *adj* fluorescent

flutuar *vi* float

fluvial *adj* river: *o transporte ~* river transportation

fluxo *sm* flow

foca *sf* seal

focalizar *vt* **1** (*focar*) focus sth (on sb/sth) **2** (*assunto, problema*) approach

focinheira *sf* muzzle

focinho *sm* **1** muzzle **2** (*porco*) snout

foco *sm* **1** (*luz*) focus **2** (*ponto de vista*) angle: *abordar um assunto sob um ~ diferente* approach an issue from a different angle

fofo *adj* (*macio*) soft

fofoca sf gossip [U]

fofoqueiro/a sm-sf gossip

fogão sm (Cozinha) stove, cooker (GB)

fogo sm fire: pôr ~ em algo set fire to sth ▶ em ~ brando/alto over a low/high heat ◇ **~s de artifício** fireworks

fogueira sf bonfire → BONFIRE NIGHT

foguete sm rocket

foice sf 1 (pequena) sickle 2 (grande) scythe

folclore sm folklore

fôlego sm breath: tomar ~ get your breath back ▶ **sem** ~ out of breath

folga sf 1 (dia livre) day off: ter/ tirar (um dia de) ~ have a day off 2 (espaço livre) gap

folgado adj 1 (roupa) baggy 2 (pessoa) cheeky

folha sf 1 leaf [pl leaves] 2 (livro, jornal) page: virar a ~ turn over (the page) 3 (papel) sheet of paper: uma ~ em branco a clean sheet of paper 4 (metal, faca) blade ▶ ~ **de pagamento** payroll

folhagem sf foliage

folhear vt leaf through sth: ~ uma revista leaf through a magazine

folhetim sm (romance) serial → SERIES

folheto sm 1 (publicidade) brochure: um ~ de viagens a travel brochure 2 (informação) leaflet

fome sf hunger, starvation, famine NOTA Não se devem confundir **hunger, starvation** e **famine**. **Hunger** é o termo geral e usa-se em casos como: fazer greve de ~ go on (a) hunger strike, ou para exprimir um desejo: ~ de conhecimento/ poder hunger for knowledge/ power. **Starvation** refere-se à fome sofrida durante um período prolongado: morrer de ~ die of starvation, e o verbo **starve** significa morrer de fome e também é usado na expressão: Estou morto de ~. I'm starving. **Famine** é a fome que afeta um grande número de pessoas, normalmente depois de uma catástrofe natural: A seca prolongada foi seguida de longos meses de ~. The long drought was followed by months of famine. ▶ **estar com** ~ be hungry **passar/sentir** ~ go/feel hungry **ter uma** ~ **de lobo** be starving

fone sm (telefone) receiver ▶ ~**s de ouvido** headphones

fonte sf 1 (nascente) spring 2 (praça, jardim) fountain 3 (origem) source: ~s próximas do governo sources close to the government 4 (cabeça) temple

fora adv 1 outside: Está rachado por ~. It's cracked on the outside. ◇ ~ do Brasil outside Brazil 2 (ausente de casa) out: jantar ~ eat out ◇ Passam o dia todo ~. They're out all day. 3 (em viagem) away: ~ a negócios away on business 4 ~ **de** (fig) out of sth: ~ de controle/perigo out of control/danger ◇ ~ do normal out of the ordinary ◇ Manter ~ do alcance das crianças. Keep out of reach of children. ● sm (gafe) blunder: Que ~ que eu dei! I really goofed! ● interj get out ▶ **dá** o ~ get lost **deixar alguém** ~ **de si** drive sb crazy ~ **de si** beside yourself

forasteiro/a sm-sf stranger

forca sf 1 (cadafalso) gallows [sing] 2 (jogo) hangman

força sf 1 (potência, Fís, Mil, Pol) force: as ~s armadas the armed forces 2 (energia física) strength [U]: recobrar as ~s get your strength back ▶ **à** ~ (violentamente) by force **com** ~ 1 hard: puxar uma corda com ~ pull a rope hard 2 (firmemente) tight: Segure com ~! Hold on tight! ~ **aérea** air force ~ **de vontade** willpower

forçar vt force: ~ a barra force the issue

forjar vt forge

forma sf 1 (contorno) shape: em ~ de cruz in the shape of a cross 2 (modo) way: Desta ~ é mais fácil. It's easier if you do it this way. ▶ **de** ~ **espontânea, indefinida, etc.** spontaneously, indefinitely, etc. **estar/ficar em** ~ be/ get in (good) shape

fôrma sf 1 mold 2 (Cozinha) baking tin

formação sf 1 formation 2 (educação) education ▶ ~ **profissional** vocational training

formal adj formal

formar vt 1 (criar) form 2 (educar) educate ◇ vi (Mil) fall in ● **formar-se** vp 1 (tomar forma) form 2 (Educ) graduate: Ela se formou pela Universidade de Oxford. She graduated from Oxford University.

formato sm format

formiga sf ant

formigueiro sm 1 (buraco) ants' nest 2 (montículo) anthill 3 (comichão) sentir um ~ have pins and needles

formoso adj beautiful

fórmula sf formula [pl ~s/-lae]

formulário sm form: preencher um ~ fill in a form

fornecedor/a sm-sf supplier

fornecer vt supply (sb) (with sth)

fornecimento sm supply

forno sm 1 oven: acender o ~ turn the oven on ◊ Esta sala é um ~. It's like an oven in here. 2 (Tec) furnace 3 (cerâmica, etc.) kiln

forquilha sf fork

forra sf ▸ ir à ~ get your own back

forrar vt line sth (with sth)

forro sm 1 (interior) lining 2 (exterior) cover

fortalecer vt strengthen

fortaleza sf fortress

forte adj 1 strong 2 (chuva, neve) heavy 3 (dor, crise) severe 4 (abraço) big ● sm fort

fortuna sf fortune: fazer uma ~ make a fortune

fosforescente adj phosphorescent

fósforo sm 1 match: acender um ~ light a match 2 (Quím) phosphorus

fossa sf pit ▸ estar na ~ (triste) be down in the dumps

fóssil sm fossil

foto sf photo [pl ~s]

fotocópia sf photocopy [pl -ies]

fotocopiar vt photocopy

fotogênico adj photogenic

fotografar vt photograph

fotografia sf 1 (atividade) photography 2 (imagem) photo [pl ~s], photograph (mais fml): Ele tirou uma ~ minha. He took a photo of me.

fotográfico adj photographic

fotógrafo/a sm-sf photographer

foz sf mouth

fração sf fraction

fracassar vi 1 fail 2 (planos) fall through

fracasso sm failure

fraco adj 1 weak: um café ~ a weak coffee ◊ estar ~ em algo be weak at/in sth 2 (sem qualidade) poor 3 (som) faint 4 (luz) dim

frade sm friar

frágil adj fragile

fragmento sm fragment

fralda sf diaper, nappy [pl -ies] (GB)

framboesa sf raspberry [pl -ies]

França sf France

francamente adv frankly ● interj honestly

francês/esa adj, sm French ● sm-sf Frenchman/woman [pl -men/-women]: os franceses the French

franco adj 1 (sincero) frank 2 (claro) marked: um ~ declínio a marked decline ● sm (moeda) franc ▸ para ser ~... to be quite honest...

frango sm chicken: ~ assado/na brasa roast/barbecued chicken

franja sf 1 (cabelo) bangs [pl] fringe (GB) 2 (franjas) (adorno) fringe [sing]: um casaco de couro com ~s a fringed leather jacket

franquear vt (carta, encomenda) pay postage on sth

franqueza sf frankness: Falemos com ~. Let's be frank.

franquia sf postage

franzir vt 1 (Costura) gather 2 (enrugar) crease ▸ ~ a testa/as sobrancelhas frown ○ ~ o nariz wrinkle your nose

fraqueza sf weakness

frasco sm 1 (perfume, medicamento) bottle 2 (conservas, compota) jar

frase sf 1 (oração) sentence 2 (locução) phrase ▸ ~ feita set phrase

fraternal adj brotherly, fraternal (fml): o amor ~ brotherly love

fraternidade sf brotherhood

fratura sf fracture

fraturar vt fracture

fraudar vt defraud

fraude sf fraud ▸ ~ fiscal tax evasion

fraudulento adj fraudulent

freada sf: Ouviu-se uma ~. There was a screech of brakes. ▸ dar uma ~ slam on the brakes

frear vi brake: Freei de repente. I slammed on the brakes.

freguês/esa sm-sf (cliente) customer

freguesia sf (clientela) customers [pl]

freio sm brake: pisar no/soltar o ~ put on/release the brake(s) ▸ ~ de mão emergency brake, handbrake (GB)

freira sf nun

frenético adj hectic

frente sf front: uma ~ fria a cold front ▸ à ~ de (encarregado de) in charge of sth ○ da ~ front: os assentos da ~ the front seats em/à ~ forward: dar um passo à ~ take a step forward ○ Siga sempre em ~ até o fim da rua. Go straight on to the end of the road. ◊ o motorista à ~ the driver in front **em ~ (de)** across from *sb/sth*, opposite (GB) *o homem sentado em ~* the man sitting across from me ◊ **em ~** do estádio across from the stadium ◊ *O hospital fica em ~.* The hospital is just across the road. **estar na ~ (em competição)** be in the lead **fazer ~ a alguém/algo** stand up to sb/sth **frente a frente** face to face **na ~ (de)** in front (of *sb/sth*): *Sente na ~, se não conseguir ver o quadro.* Sit at the front if you can't see the board. ◊ *Ela me contou na ~ de outras pessoas.* She told me in front of other people. **para a ~** forward **pela ~** ahead: *ter uma longa viagem pela ~* have a long journey ahead of you

frequência *sf* frequency [*pl* -ies] ▸ **com ~** often **com que ~?** how often?

frequentar *vt* **1** (*lugar*) frequent **2** (*curso*) attend

frequente *adj* frequent

frequentemente *adv* often

frescão *sm* air-conditioned bus

fresco *adj* **1** (*temperatura, roupa*) cool: *O dia está um pouco ~.* It's fairly cool today. → FRIO **2** (*comida, ar*) fresh: *apanhar/ tomar ar ~* get some fresh air **3** (*notícia*) latest: *notícias frescas* the latest news **4** (*efeminado*) camp **5** (*cheio de manias*) fussy

frescobol *sm* beach tennis

frescura *sf* ▸ **ter ~** be fussy

fresta *sf* crack

friccionar *vt* rub

frigideira *sf* frying pan: *~ anti-aderente* non-stick frying pan

frigorífico *sm* freezer

frio *adj, sm* cold: *ser ~ com alguém* be cold towards sb ◊ *Feche a porta, senão entra ~.* Shut the door, or you'll let the cold in. NOTA Não confundir **cold** e **cool** ou **hot** e **warm**. Cold indica uma temperatura mais baixa do que **cool** e muitas vezes desagradável: *Este inverno foi ~.* It was a cold winter. Cool significa mais *fresco* do que frio: *Lá fora está calor, mas aqui está fresco.* It's hot outside but it's nice and cool in here. Hot descreve uma temperatura bem mais quente do que **warm**, que corresponde a *morno* ou *ameno* e quase sempre tem conotações agradáveis. Compare os exemplos: *uma brisa quente* a warm breeze ◊ *Não posso bebê-lo, está muito*

quente. I can't drink it; it's too hot. ◊ *Que calor que está aqui!* It's so hot in here! ▸ **apanhar ~** catch (a) cold **estar com ~** be cold: *Estou com ~.* I'm cold. **estar ~** be cold: *Está muito ~ na rua.* It's very cold outside. **estar um ~ de rachar** be freezing (cold) **passar/sentir/ter ~** feel cold: *Tenho ~ nas mãos.* My hands are cold.

friorento *adj*: *Sou muito ~.* I feel the cold a lot.

frisar *vt* **1** (*cabelo*) crimp **2** (*enfatizar*) stress

fritar *vt, vi* fry

frito *adj* fried ▸ **estar ~** be done for

fronha *sf* pillowcase

fronteira *sf* border, frontier (*mais fml*): *atravessar a ~* cross the border ◊ *A Argentina faz ~ com o Brasil.* Argentina borders on Brazil. → BORDER

frota *sf* fleet

frouxo *adj* (*elástico, corda*) slack

frustração *sf* frustration

frustrado/a *adj* frustrated ● *sm-sf: Ele é um ~.* He feels like a failure.

frustrante *adj* frustrating

fruta *sf* fruit [*ger U*]: *Você quer (uma) ~?* Do you want some fruit? ◊ *~s secas* dried fruit

fruteiro/a *sm-sf* (*loja*) greengrocer's ● **fruteira** *sf* (*prato*) fruit bowl

frutífero *adj* **1** fruit: *uma árvore frutífera* a fruit tree **2** (*proveitoso*) fruitful

fruto *sm* **1** fruit **2** (*resultado*) result: *Isto é ~ de muito trabalho.* This is the result of a lot of hard work. ▸ **dar ~** bear fruit

fuga *sf* escape

fugaz *adj* fleeting

fugir *vi* **1** (*país*) flee: *~ do país* flee the country **2** (*prisão*) escape (*from sb/sth*) **3** (*casa, colégio*) run away (*from sth*) ▸ **em debandada** scatter in all directions

fugitivo/a *adj, sm-sf* fugitive

fulano/a *sm-sf* so-and-so [*pl* so-and-so's]: *Imagine que vem ~…* Just imagine so-and-so comes…

fuligem *sf* soot

fulminante *adj* (*olhar*) withering

fulo *adj* furious: *estar ~ (de raiva/da vida)* be furious

fumaça *sf* **1** smoke **2** (*carro*) fumes [*pl*]: *a ~ do cano de descarga* exhaust fumes

fumante *smf* smoker ▶ **ou não-fumante?** smoking or non-smoking?

fumar *vt, vi* smoke: ~ *cachimbo* smoke a pipe ◊ *deixar de* ~ give up smoking ◊ *Proibido* ~. No smoking.

fumo *sm* (*tabaco*) tobacco

função *sf* function

funcionamento *sm* operation: *pôr algo em* ~ put sth into operation

funcionar *vi* work: *Como é que funciona?* How does it work?

funcionário/a *sm-sf* **1** employee: ~ *público* public employee **2** (*representante de organização*) official: *um* ~ *do governo* a government official

fundação *sf* foundation

fundador/~a *adj, sm-sf* founder: *os membros* ~*es* the founding members

fundamental *adj* fundamental

fundamento *sm* **1** (*motivo*) grounds [*pl*] **2** (*princípio*) fundamental ▶ **sem** ~ unfounded: *uma acusação sem* ~ an unfounded accusation

fundar *vt* found

fundir(-se) *vt, vp* melt

fundo *adj, sm* ● *sm* **1** bottom: *ir ao* ~ *da questão* get to the bottom of the matter **2** (*mar, rio*) bed **3** (*quarto, cenário*) back: *no* ~ *do restaurante* at the back of the restaurant ◊ *o quarto dos* ~*s* the back room **4** (*quadro*) background **5** (**fundos**) (*financiamento*) funds: *arranjar* ~*s* raise funds ▶ **a** ~ thorough: *uma revisão a* ~ a thorough review **de** ~ cross-country: *esqui de* ~ cross-country skiing **no** ~ **1** (*apesar das aparências*) deep down: *Você diz que não, mas no* ~ *você se importa.* You say you don't like it, but deep down you do. **2** (*na realidade*) basically: *No* ~ *eu penso o mesmo.* I basically think the same. ~ **musical** soundtrack ▶ **sem** ~ bottomless

fúnebre *adj* **1** (*para um funeral*) funeral: *a marcha* ~ the funeral march **2** (*triste*) gloomy

funeral *sm* funeral

funerária *sf* funeral home, undertaker's (*GB*)

fungo *sm* fungus [*pl* -gi/-guses]

funil *sm* funnel

furacão *sm* hurricane

furado *adj* **1** (*dente*) bad **2** (*cano*) leaky **3** (*calçado*): *O seu sapato está* ~. You have a hole in your shoe. **4** (*orelha*) pierced **5** (*pneu*) flat: *É o segundo pneu* ~ *esta semana.* That's the second flat I've had this week.

furar *vt* **1** make a hole in *sth* **2** (*com máquina de furar*) drill a hole in *sth* **3** (*folha com furador*) punch holes in *sth* **4** (*orelha*) pierce **5** (*bola, pneu*) puncture **6** (*fila*) jump: ~ *o sinal* jump the lights

furgão *sm* van

fúria *sf* fury ▶ **com** ~ furiously

furioso *adj* furious ▶ **ficar** ~ fly into a rage

furo *sm* **1** (*pneu*) flat (tire), puncture (*GB*): *remendar um* ~ fix a flat tire **2** (*buraco*) hole **3** (*jornalístico*) scoop

furtar *vt* steal

furtivo *adj* furtive

furto *sm* theft

fusão *sf* **1** (*Fís*) fusion **2** (*gelo, metais*) melting **3** (*empresas, partidos políticos*) merger

fusível *sm* fuse: *Queimaram os fusíveis.* The fuses blew.

futebol *sm* soccer, football (*GB*) NOTA Nos Estados Unidos usa-se apenas soccer, para não haver confusão com o futebol americano. ▶ ~ **toto/de salão** table/five-a-side football (*GB*)

fútil *adj* **1** (*frívolo*) frivolous **2** (*insignificante*) trivial

futuro *adj, sm* future

fuzil *sm* rifle

Gg

gabar-se *vt* boast (*about of sth*)

gabinete *sm* **1** (*escritório*) office **2** (*Pol*) Cabinet

gado *sm* livestock ▶ ~ **bovino/equino/ovino/suíno** cattle/horses/sheep/pigs [*pl*]

gafanhoto *sm* **1** grasshopper **2** (*praga*) locust

gafe *sf* blunder: *cometer uma* ~ make a blunder

gago/a *adj, sm-sf*: *ser* ~ have a stutter ◊ *os* ~*s* people who stutter

gaguejar *vt, vi* stutter

gaiola *sf* cage

gaita *sf* (*instrumento musical*) harmonica ▶ ~ **de foles** bagpipes [*pl*]

gaivota *sf* seagull

gala *sf* gala: *um jantar de* ~ gala dinner

galáctico adj galactic

galão¹ sm (uniforme) stripe

galão² sm (medida) gallon

galáxia sf galaxy [pl -ies]

galeria sf (Arte, Teat) gallery [pl -ies]: uma ~ de arte an art gallery → MUSEUM

galês/esa adj, sm Welsh ● sm-sf Welshman/woman [pl -men/ -women]: os galeses the Welsh

galgo sm greyhound

galinha sf hen: ~ choca broody hen

galinheiro sm hen house

galo sm 1 (ave) rooster 2 (inchaço) bump

galopar vi gallop: ir ~ go for a gallop

galope sm gallop: partir a ~ gallop off

gama sf range: uma grande ~ de cores a wide range of colors

gamar vi fall in love (with sb)

ganância sf greed

ganancioso adj greedy

gancho sm hook

gandula smf ballboy [fem ballgirl]

gangrena sf gangrene

gângster sm gangster

gangue sf gang

ganhador/a adj winning ● sm-sf winner

ganhar vt 1 (dinheiro, respeito) earn: ~ a vida/o pão de cada dia earn your living 2 (prêmio, jogo, guerra) win: ~ a loteria win the lottery 3 (conseguir) gain (by/ from (doing) sth): O que é que eu ganho em lhe dizer? What do I gain by telling you? ● vi 1 (vencer) win 2 ~ de (derrotar) beat sb/sth [vt] ▶ ~ tempo save time **sair ganhando** do well out of sth

ganho sm gain

ganir vi whine

ganso sm goose [pl geese] NOTA Falando só do macho, diz-se **gander**.

garagem sf garage

garantia sf guarantee

garantir vt guarantee: Eu lhe garanto que eles virão. I can guarantee they'll come.

garçom sm waiter

garçonete sf waitress

garfo sm fork

gargalhada sf roar of laughter

gargalo sm neck ▶ beber pelo ~ drink straight out of the bottle

garganta sf 1 (Anat) throat: Estou com dor de ~. I have a sore throat. 2 (Geog) gorge

gargantilha sf choker

gargarejar vi gargle

garimpar vi prospect

garoto/a sm-sf boy [fem girl]

garra¹ sf 1 (animal) claw 2 (ave de rapina) talon

garra² sf (entusiasmo) drive

garrafa sf bottle ▶ de/em ~ bottled ~ **térmica** Thermos® bottle, Thermos® flask [GB]

garrafão sm (recipiente) flagon

gás sm 1 gas: Cheira a ~. It smells of gas. 2 (**gases**) (Med) gas, wind (GB) [U]: O bebê está com gases. The baby has gas. 3 (pessoa): uma pessoa de pouco ~ a person with very little get-up-and-go ▶ com/sem ~ (bebida) sparkling/non-carbonated ~ **lacrimogêneo** tear gas

gasolina sf gas, petrol (GB): ~ sem chumbo unleaded gas

gasoso adj 1 (Quím) gaseous 2 (bebida) sparkling

gastador/-a adj, sm-sf spendthrift [s]

gastar vt 1 (dinheiro) spend sth (on sb/sth) 2 (consumir) use: ~ menos gasolina use less gas 3 (desperdiçar) waste: ~ tempo e dinheiro waste time and money ● **gastar(-se)** vt, vp (calçado) wear (sth) out

gasto adj 1 (dinheiro) spent: calcular o dinheiro ~ work out what you've spent 2 (água, eletricidade) (a) (usado) used (b) (desperdiçado) wasted 3 (roupa, sapatos) worn out ● sm 1 (dinheiro) expense 2 (água, energia, gasolina) consumption

gatilho sm trigger: apertar o ~ pull the trigger

gatinhas sf ▶ de ~: ficar de ~ get down on all fours ◇ andar de ~ crawl

gato/a sm-sf cat: ~ siamês Siamese NOTA **Tom-cat** ou **tom** é um gato macho, **kittens** são os gatinhos. Os gatos ronronam (**purr**) e miam (**meow**). ▶ **Gata Borralheira** Cinderella ~ **de Botas** Puss in Boots

gaúcho/a adj, sm-sf (person from) Rio Grande do Sul: os ~s the people of Rio Grande do Sul

gaveta sf drawer

gavião sm hawk

gay adj, sm gay

gaze sf 1 (tecido) gauze 2 (curativo) bandage

gazela sf gazelle

geada sf frost

gel sm gel: ~ de banho shower gel

geladeira sf refrigerator

gelado a adj **1** (congelado) frozen **2** (pessoa, quarto) freezing

gelatina sf **1** (substância) gelatin **2** (Cozinha) Jell-O®, jelly (GB)

geléia 1 jam **2** (de laranja) marmalade ▸ ~ **real** royal jelly

geleira sf glacier

gelo sm ice [U]: ~ **picado** crushed ice ▸ **dar o** ~ give sb the cold shoulder

gema sf (ovo) (egg) yolk

gêmeo a adj, sm-sf twin ● **Gêmeos** sm (Astrol) Gemini

gemer vi **1** (pessoa) groan **2** (animal) whine

gemido sm **1** (pessoa) groan: Ouviam-se os ~s do doente. You could hear the sick man groaning. **2** (animal) whine: os ~s do cão the whining of the dog

gene sm gene

genealógico adj genealogical

general sm (Mil) general

generalizado adj widespread

generalizar vt, vi generalize

genérico a adj generic

gênero sm **1** (tipo) kind **2** (Arte) genre **3** (Gram) gender **4** (gêneros) (mercadoria) goods ▸ **algo do** ~ something like that ▸ ~ **policial** crime writing   ~**s alimentícios** foodstuffs

generosidade sf generosity

generoso adj generous: Ele é ~ com os amigos. He is generous to his friends.

genético a adj genetic ● **genética** sf genetics [sing]

gengiva sf gum

genial adj brilliant: uma idéia/ um pianista ~ a brilliant idea/ pianist

gênio sm genius (at (doing) sth) ▸ **ter (mau)** ~ have a (bad) temper

genital adj genital

genro sm son-in-law [pl sons-in-law]

gente sf people [pl]: Havia muita ~. There were a lot of people. ▸ ~ **comum** ordinary folk ▸ ~ **grande** grown-ups [pl] **ser boa** ~/~ **fina** be a nice person

gentil adj kind

gentileza sf kindness: Foi muita ~ da sua parte. That was very kind of you. ▸ **que** ~ how thoughtful **ter a** ~ **de** be so kind as to do sth

geografia sf geography

geográfico adj geographical

geógrafo a sm-sf geographer

geologia sf geology

geológico adj geological

geólogo a sm-sf geologist

geometria sf geometry

geométrico adj geometric(al)

geração sf generation

gerador sm generator

geral adj general ▸ **em** ~/**de um modo** ~ as a general rule   **no** ~ in general

gerânio sm geranium

gerar vt **1** (causar) generate: ~ **energia** generate energy **2** (conceber) conceive

gerente smf manager

gerir vt run: ~ **um negócio** run a business

germe sm germ

germinar vi germinate

gesso sm **1** plaster **2** (Med) plaster cast

gestão sf management

gesticular vi gesticulate

gesto sm gesture: um ~ **simbólico** a symbolic gesture ◊ **comunicar por** ~s communicate by gestures

gigante adj **1** gigantic **2** (Bot) giant: um olmo ~ a giant elm ● sm giant

gigantesco adj enormous

gilete sf razor blade

gim sm gin

gim-tônica sm gin and tonic

ginástica sf **1** gymnastics [sing] **2** (educação física) physical education (abrev PE) ▸ **fazer** ~ exercise, work out (mais coloq)

ginecologia sf gynaecology

ginecologista smf gynaecologist

girafa sf giraffe

girar vt, vi **1** turn **2** (pião) spin ▸ ~ **em torno de alguém/algo** revolve around sb/sth

girassol sm sunflower

gíria sf **1** (linguagem coloquial) slang **2** (profissional) jargon

girino sm tadpole

giro sm turn

giz sm chalk [ger U]: um (pedaço de) ~ a piece of chalk

glacial adj **1** (vento) icy **2** (temperatura) freezing **3** (época, zona) glacial **4** (olhar, atmosfera) frosty

glândula sf gland

glicose sf glucose

global adj (mundial) global: o **aquecimento** ~ global warming

globalização sf globalization

globo sm: o ~ (terrestre) the globe ▸ ~ **ocular** eyeball

glória sf glory [pl -ies]

glossário sm glossary [pl -ies]

glutão/ona adj greedy ● sm-sf glutton

gol sm goal: *marcar um ~* score a goal ◊ *o ~ do empate* the equalizer ◊ *um empate sem ~* a scoreless tie

gola sf collar ► **rulê** turtleneck, polo neck (GB)

gole sm sip: *tomar um ~ de algo* have a sip of sth ► **aos ~s** in sips

golear vt, vi: *O Brasil goleou o Peru por cinco a zero.* Brazil beat Peru five to nothing.

goleiro/a sm-sf goalkeeper

golfe sm golf

golfinho sm dolphin

golfo sm gulf: *o ~ Pérsico* the Persian Gulf

golpe sm blow ► **~ baixo**: *dar um ~ baixo em alguém* play a dirty trick on sb ► **~ de estado** coup ► **~ de mestre** master stroke

gomo sm (*fruta*) segment

gorar vi (*fracassar*) founder

gordo/a adj **1** (*pessoa, animal*) fat **2** (*alimento*) fatty ● sm-sf fat man/woman [pl men/women]

gordura sf **1** fat **2** (*sujeira*) grease

gorduroso (*tb* **gordurento**) adj greasy

gorila sm gorilla

gorjeta sf tip: *três dólares de ~* a three-dollar tip

gostar vi **1** like *(doing) sth* [vt]: *Não gosto.* I don't like it. ◊ *Eles gostam de passear.* They like walking. ◊ *Não gosto nem um pouco de me levantar cedo.* I hate having to get up early. **2** (*sentimentalmente*) have a crush on *sb* [vt] ► **~ mais de** prefer *(doing) sth* ► **~ muito de** thoroughly enjoy *(doing) sth*

gosto sm **1** taste: *de mau ~* in bad taste ◊ *para todos os ~s* to suit all tastes **2** (*prazer*) pleasure: *ter o ~ de fazer algo* have the pleasure of doing sth ► **não se discute** there's no accounting for taste ► **ter ~ (de algo)** taste (of sth): *Tem um ~ delicioso!* It tastes delicious! ◊ *Tem ~ de queimado.* It tastes burned.

gota sf drop ► **a última gota/a gota d'água** the last straw

goteira sf (*fenda*) leak: *Sempre que chove, temos ~s.* The roof leaks every time it rains.

gotejar vi drip

gótico adj, sm Gothic

governador/a sm-sf governor

governamental adj governamento: *fontes governamentais* government sources

governanta sf housekeeper

governante adj governing ● smf leader

governar vt **1** (*país*) govern **2** (*barco*) steer

governo sm government

gozar vt, vi **1** (*fazer troça*) make fun of *sb/sth* **2** (*desfrutar*) enjoy *(doing) sth*: *~ de boa saúde* enjoy good health

Grã-Bretanha sf Great Britain (*abrev* GB)

graça sf **1** (*elegância, Relig*) grace **2** (*piada*) witty remark ► **dar ~s a Deus**: *Dou-lhe cinco reais, e dê ~s a Deus!* I'll give you five reals, and you can count yourself lucky. ► **de ~** free: *entrar/viajar de ~* get in for free/travel free **graças a...** thanks to *sb/sth* ► **sem ~** dull ► **ser uma ~** be lovely ► **ter ~** be funny: *Isso não tem ~ nenhuma.* It isn't the least bit funny.

grade sf **1** (*janela, carro*) grille **2** (*grades*) **(a)** (*varanda, vedação*) railings **(b)** (*prisão*) bars: *atrás das ~s* behind bars

gradeado sm bars [pl]

gradual adj gradual

graduar vt (*regular*) adjust ● **graduar-se** vp graduate

gráfica sf (*local*) printer's

gráfico adj graphic ● sm graph

grafite sm graffiti [U]

gralha sf rook

grama[1] sf grass: *Proibido pisar na ~.* Keep off the grass.

grama[2] sm gram(me) (*abrev* **g**) → Ver pág. 224

gramado sm **1** (*em jardim*) lawn **2** (*em campo de futebol, etc.*) turf

gramática sf grammar

grampear vt **1** (*papéis*) staple **2** (*telefone*) tap

grampo sm **1** (*para cabelo*) hair clip **2** (*para papéis*) staple **3** (*telefone*) telephone tapping

grande adj **1** (*tamanho*) large, big (*mais coloq*): *uma casa/cidade ~* a big house/city ◊ *~ ou pequeno?* Large or small? → BIG **2** (*fig*) big: *um ~ problema* a big problem **3** (*número, quantidade*) large: *um ~ número de pessoas* a large number of people **4** (*importante, notável*) great: *um ~ músico* a great musician ► **(a/uma) ~ parte de** most of

granel sm ► **a ~ 1** in bulk **2** (*vinho*) from the cask

granito sm granite

granizo sm hail: *tempestade de ~* hailstorm

granja sf small farm

grão sm 1 grain: *um ~ de areia* a grain of sand 2 (*semente*) seed 3 (*café*) bean 4 (*poeira*) speck

grão-de-bico sm garbanzo, chickpea (*GB*)

grasnar vi 1 (*pessoa*) shriek 2 (*pato*) quack

gratidão sf gratitude: *Que falta de ~!* How ungrateful!

grátis adj free

grato adj grateful

gratuitamente adv 1 (*de graça*) for free: *distribuir ingressos ~* hand out free tickets 2 (*sem motivo*) gratuitously

gratuito adj 1 (*de graça*) free 2 (*sem motivo*) gratuitous

grau sm degree: *queimaduras de terceiro ~* third-degree burns ◊ *Está fazendo dois ~s abaixo de zero.* It's two below (zero).

gravação sf recording

gravador sm tape recorder

gravadora sf record company [pl -ies]

gravar vt 1 (*som, imagem*) record 2 (*metal, pedra*) engrave

gravata sf tie: *usar ~* wear a tie

grave adj 1 serious: *um problema/uma doença ~* a serious problem/illness ◊ *sofrer ferimentos ~s* be seriously injured 2 (*solene*) solemn 3 (*som, nota*) low 4 (*voz*) deep 5 (*acento*) grave

gravemente adv seriously

grávida adj pregnant: *Ela está ~ de cinco meses.* She's five months pregnant.

gravidade sf 1 (*Fís*) gravity 2 (*importância*) seriousness

gravidez sf pregnancy [pl -ies]

gravura sf 1 engraving 2 (*em livro*) illustration

graxa sf (*calçado*) (shoe) polish: *Passe ~ nos sapatos.* Polish your shoes.

Grécia sf Greece

grego/a adj, sm Greek ● sm-sf Greek man/woman [pl men/women]: *os ~s* the Greeks

grelha sf grill: *bife na ~* grilled steak

grelhar vt grill

grêmio sm (*estudantes*) student union

greve sf strike: *estar em/fazer ~* be/go on strike ◊ *de fome* go on hunger strike

grevista smf striker

grid sm ▶ **~ de largada** (*Automobilismo*) starting grid

grilo sm cricket

gripe sf (the) flu [U]: *Estou com ~.* I've got (the) flu.

grisalho adj gray: *ser ~* have gray hair

gritar vi shout (*at sb*) ▶ **~ de dor** cry out in pain

grito sm 1 shout: *dar um ~* shout 2 (*auxílio, dor, alegria*) cry [pl cries] ▶ **aos ~s** at the top of your voice: *O professor pediu aos ~s que nos calássemos.* The teacher shouted at us to be quiet.

groselha sf red currant

grosseiro adj 1 (*pessoa, tecido, linguagem*) coarse 2 (*piada*) rude

grosseria sf obscenity [pl -ies]: *dizer ~s* make obscene remarks

grosso/a adj 1 thick 2 (*voz*) deep ● adj, sm-sf (*mal-educado*) rude: *Você é um ~.* You're very rude.

grossura sf 1 (*espessura*) thickness: *Esta tábua tem dois centímetros de ~.* This piece of wood is two centimeters thick. 2 (*grosseria*) rudeness

grua sf crane

grunhir vi 1 (*pessoa, porco*) grunt 2 (*resmungar*) grumble

grupo sm 1 group: *formar ~s de seis* get into groups of six ◊ *trabalho em ~* group work ◊ *~ sanguíneo* blood group 2 (*musical*) band

gruta sf 1 (*natural*) cave 2 (*artificial*) grotto [pl ~s/~es]

guarda smf 1 (*polícia*) policeman/woman [pl -men/-women] 2 **~ de segurança** security guard ● sf guard: *montar ~* mount guard

guarda-chuva sm umbrella: *abrir/fechar um ~* put up/take down an umbrella

guarda-costas smf bodyguard

guarda-florestal smf forest ranger

guarda-louça sm (*armário*) sideboard

guardanapo sm napkin

guarda-noturno sm nightwatchman [pl -men]

guardar vt 1 keep: *~ um bilhete/um segredo* keep a ticket/a secret 2 (*recolher*) put sth away: *Já guardei a roupa de inverno.* I've put away my winter clothes. 3 (*vigiar*) guard ▶ **~ rancor a / contra alguém** bear a grudge against sb

guarda-roupa sm wardrobe

guarda-sol sm (*sombrinha*) sunshade

guardião/ã sm-sf guardian

guarita *sf* **1** (*sentinela*) sentry box **2** (*portaria*) janitor's quarters, porter's lodge (*GB*)

guarnição *sf* **1** (*Cozinha*) garnish **2** (*Mil*) garrison

gude *sm* marbles [*sing*]: *jogar bola de* ~ play marbles

guerra *sf* war: *em* ~ at war ◊ *declarar* ~ *a alguém* declare war on sb ◊ *filmes de* ~ war films

guerreiro/a *adj* (*bélico*) warlike ● *sm-sf* warrior

guerrilha *sf* **1** (*grupo*) guerrillas [*pl*] **2** (*tipo de guerra*) guerrilla warfare

gueto *sm* ghetto [*pl* ~s/~es]

guia *smf* (*pessoa*) guide ● *sm* **1** (*guide*(book)): ~ *turístico/de hotéis* tourist/hotel guide **2** (*estudos*) prospectus

guiar *vt* (*indicar o caminho*) guide ● *vt, vi* drive ● **guiar-se por algo**: *guiar-se pelas estrelas* be guided by the stars ◊ *Você não deve se* ~ *pelas aparências.* You can't go by appearances.

guichê *sm* **1** (*banco, correios*) counter **2** (*cinema, teatro, estádio*) window

guidão *sm* (*bicicleta*) handlebars [*pl*]

guinada *sf* **1** (*Náut*) lurch **2** (*carro*) swerve: *dar uma* ~ swerve

guinar *vi* **1** (*Náut*) lurch **2** (*carro*) swerve: ~ *para a direita* swerve to the right

guinchar¹ *vi* **1** (*pessoa*) shriek **2** (*ave*) screech

guinchar² *vt* (*carro*) tow *sth* (*away*)

guincho *sm* **1** (*pessoa*) shriek **2** (*ave*) screech **3** (*veículo*) tow truck **4** (*máquina*) winch

guindaste *sm* crane

guisado *sm* stew

guisar *vt, vi* braise

guitarra *sf* (*electric*) guitar

guitarrista *smf* guitarist

guizo *sm* bell

gula *sf* gluttony

guloseima *sf* titbit

guloso/a *adj* greedy ● *sm-sf* glutton

gume *sm* cutting edge

H h

hábil *adj* **1** skillful **2** (*astuto*) clever: *uma manobra* ~ a clever move

habilidade *sf* skill

habilidoso *adj* handy

habilitações *sf* qualifications

habitação *sf* housing [U]

habitante *smf* inhabitant

habitar *vt* live in: ~ *no campo* live in the country

habitat *sm* habitat

hábito *sm* habit: *adquirir o* ~ *de fazer algo* get into the habit of doing sth ● **como (é) de** ~ as usual **por** ~ out of habit

habitual *adj* **1** (*normal*) usual **2** (*cliente, leitor, visitante*) regular

habituar *vt* (*acostumar*) get *sb/sth* used to (*doing*) *sth* ● **habituar-se** *vp* **1** (*acostumar-se*) get used to (*doing*) sth: *Você vai acabar se habituando.* You'll get used to it eventually. **2** (*prazer, vício*) acquire a taste for *sth*

hálito *sm* breath: *ter mau* ~ have bad breath

hall *sm* (*entrance*) hall

halterofilismo *sm* **1** bodybuilding **2** (*Esporte*) weightlifting

hambúrguer *sm* (ham)burger

hamster *sm* hamster

handebol *sm* handball

harmonia *sf* harmony [*pl* -ies]

harmônica *sf* concertina

harpa *sf* harp

haste *sf* **1** (*bandeira*) flagpole **2** (*óculos*) arm

haver *v aux* **1** (*tempos compostos*) have: *Haviam me dito que viriam.* They had told me they would come. **2** ~ **que**: *Há que ser valente.* You must be brave. **3** ~ **de**: *Hei de chegar lá.* I'll get there. ● *v imp* **1** (*existir*) there is/are **NOTA There is** é usado com substantivos no singular e substantivos não contáveis: *Há uma garrafa de vinho aqui.* There's a bottle of wine here. ◊ *Não há pão.* There isn't any bread. ◊ *Não havia ninguém.* There wasn't anybody. Utiliza-se **there are** com substantivos no plural: *Quantas cervejas há?* How many beers are there? **2** (*tempo cronológico*): *Há anos que me casei.* I got married ten years ago. ◊ *Eles tinham se conhecido havia um mês.* They had met a month earlier. ◊ *Você mora aqui há muito tempo?* Have you been living here long? ◊ *Há anos que nos conhecemos.* We've known each other for years. ◊ *Eles estão esperando há uma hora.* They've been waiting for an hour. ◊ *Há quanto tempo você está no Rio?* How long have you

haxixe

H

110

been in Rio? → AGO ▶ **haja o que houver** whatever happens **haver-se com alguém** answer to sb: *Se bater no meu irmão, você vai ter de se ~ comigo!* If you hit my brother you'll have me to deal with! **o que é que há?** what's up?

haxixe *sm* hashish

hectare *sm* hectare (*abrev* **ha**)

hélice *sf* propeller

helicóptero *sm* helicopter

hélio *sm* helium

hematoma *sm* bruise

hemisfério *sm* hemisphere

hemofílico/a *sm-sf* hemophiliac

hemorragia *sf* hemorrhage

hepatite *sf* hepatitis [*U*]

hera *sf* ivy [*pl* ivies]

herança *sf* inheritance

herbívoro *adj* herbivorous

herdar *vt* inherit *sth* (*from sb*)

herdeiro/a *sm-sf* heir (*to sth*): *o ~/a herdeira do trono* the heir to the throne

hereditário *adj* hereditary

hermético/a *adj* airtight

hérnia *sf* hernia

herói, heroína *sm-sf* hero [*pl* ~es] [*fem* heroine]

heróico *adj* heroic

heroína *sf* (*droga*) heroin

hesitar *vt, vi* hesitate (*to do sth*)

heterossexual *adj, smf* heterosexual

hexágono *sm* hexagon

hibernação *sf* hibernation

hibernar *vi* hibernate

hidratante *adj* moisturizing: *creme/loção* ~ moisturizer

hidráulico *adj* hydraulic

hidroavião *sm* seaplane

hidroelétrico *adj* hydroelectric

hidrogênio *sm* hydrogen

hierarquia *sf* hierarchy [*pl* -ies]

hieróglifo *sm* hieroglyphic

hífen *sm* hyphen

higiene *sf* hygiene

higiênico *adj* hygienic

hindu *adj, smf* (*Relig*) Hindu

hino *sm* hymn ▶ **~ nacional** national anthem

hipermercado *sm* superstore

hipermetropia *sf* far-sightedness, long-sightedness (*GB*): *ter* ~ be far-sighted

hípico *adj* horseback riding: *clube ~/corrida hípica* horseback riding club/competition

hipismo *sm* horseback riding

hipnose *sf* hypnosis

hipnotizar *vt* hypnotize

hipocondríaco/a *adj, sm-sf* hypochondriac

hipocrisia *sf* hypocrisy: *Deixe de* ~! Don't be such a hypocrite!

hipócrita *adj* hypocritical ● *smf* hypocrite

hipódromo *sm* racetrack, racecourse (*GB*)

hipopótamo *sm* hippo [*pl* ~s]

hipótese *sf* **1** (*possibilidade*) possibility [*pl* -ies] **2** (*suposição*) hypothesis [*p* -eses] ▶ **em ~ alguma** under no circumstances **na ~ de** in the event of **na melhor/pior das ~s** at best/worst

histeria *sf* hysteria: *ter um ataque de* ~ become hysterical

histérico *adj* hysterical: *ficar* ~ have hysterics

história *sf* **1** history: *~ natural* natural history **2** (*relato*) story [*pl* -ies]: *contar uma* ~ tell a story **3** (*mentira*) lie: *Não me venha com* ~s. Don't tell lies. ▶ **deixar de ~(s)** get to the point **~s da carochinha** fairy tales

historiador/a *sm-sf* historian

histórico *adj* **1** historical: *personagens* ~s historical figures **2** (*importante*) historic: *uma vitória histórica* an historic victory ● *sm* record: *~ médico* medical record

hoje *adv* today: *a música de* ~ the music of today ◊ *o jornal de* ~ today's paper ▶ **de ~ em diante** from now on **~ em dia** nowadays

Holanda *sf* Holland

holandês/esa *adj, sm* Dutch ● *sm-sf* Dutchman/woman [*pl* -men/-women]: *os holandeses* the Dutch

holocausto *sm* holocaust

holofote *sm* **1** (*estádio*) floodlight **2** (*teatro*) spotlight

homem *sm* **1** man [*pl* men]: *o ~ moderno* modern man ◊ *uma conversa de ~ para ~* a man-to-man talk **2** (*humanidade*) mankind → MAN ▶ **de/para ~** for men: *roupa de* ~ menswear **tornar-se ~** grow up

homem-rã *sm* frogman [*pl* -men]

homenagear *vt* pay tribute to *sb/sth*

homenagem *sf* tribute [*U*]: *fazer uma* ~ *a alguém* pay tribute to sb ▶ **em ~ a** in honor of *sb/sth*

homeopatia *sf* homeopathy

homicida *smf* murderer

homicídio *sm* homicide

homogêneo *adj* homogeneous

homônimo sm **1** homonym **2** (xará) namesake

homossexual adj, smf homossexual

honestidade sf honesty

honesto adj honest

honorários sm fees

honra sf honor: o convidado de ~ the guest of honor ▶ **com muita ~ and proud of it** **ter a ~ de** have the honor of doing sth

honrado adj honest

honrar vt honor sb (with sth)

hóquei sm field hockey, hockey (GB) ▶ **~ sobre o gelo** hockey, ice hockey (GB)

hora sf **1** hour: 90 km por ~ 90 km an hour **2** (relógio, momento, horário) time: Que ~s são? What time is it? ◊ a qualquer ~ do dia at any time of the day ◊ na ~ do almoço/jantar at lunchtime/dinner time **3** (encontro) appointment: ter ~ marcada no dentista have a dental appointment ▶ **bem na/em cima da ~** in the nick of time **estar na ~ de** be time to do sth: Está na ~ de ir para a cama. It's time to go to bed. **fazer ~** kill time **ficar/passar ~s** spend ages (doing sth): Ele passa ~s no banheiro. He spends ages in the bathroom. ◊ passar-se a fio/~s/e ~s fazendo algo do sth for hours on end ▶ **do hora** rush hour **~s extras/vagas** overtime/spare time [sing] **já era ~** about time too **na ~ on time na ~ H** when it comes to the crunch

horário sm **1** (aulas, trem) schedule, timetable (GB) **2** (consulta, trabalho, visita) hours [pl]: o ~ de trabalho office hours

horizontal adj horizontal

horizonte sm horizon: no ~ on the horizon

hormônio sm hormone

horóscopo sm horoscope

horrível adj awful

horror sm horror: um grito de ~ a cry of horror ◊ os ~es da guerra the horrors of war ◊ dizer ~es de alguém say horrible things about sb ▶ **que ~** how awful **ter ~ a** hate (doing) sth

horroroso adj **1** (aterrador) horrific **2** (muito feio) hideous **3** (mau) awful: O tempo está ~. The weather's awful. ◊ Faz um calor ~. It's awfully hot.

horta sf vegetable garden

hortaliça sf vegetables [pl]

hortelã sf mint

hospedar vt put sb up: Vamos ~ uns amigos no verão. We have some friends coming to stay with us in the summer. ● **hospedar-se** vp stay: ~ num hotel stay at a hotel

hóspede smf guest

hospital sm hospital → SCHOOL

hospitaleiro adj hospitable

hospitalidade sf hospitality

hospitalizar vt hospitalize

hostil adj hostile

hotel sm hotel

humanidade sf humanity [pl -ies]

humanitário adj humanitarian

humano adj **1** human: direitos ~s human rights **2** (compreensivo, justo) humane ● sm human being

humildade sf humility

humilde adj humble

humilhante adj humiliating

humilhar vt humiliate

humor sm humor: ter senso de ~ have a sense of humor ◊ ~ negro black humor ▶ **de bom/mau ~** in a good/bad mood

humorista smf **1** (de palco) comedian **2** (escritor) humorist

humorístico adj: um seriado ~ a comedy series

I i

iate sm yacht

içar vt hoist

ICMS sm VAT (GB)

ícone sm icon

ida sf outward journey: durante a ~ on the way there ▶ **~ e volta:** ~ e volta são três horas. It's three hours there and back.

idade sf age: com a/na sua ~ at your age ◊ Não havia ninguém da minha ~. There wasn't anybody my age. ◊ Que ~ eles têm? How old are they? ▶ **a ~ Média** the Middle Ages [pl] ▶ **~ adulta** adulthood **não ter ~ (para)** be too young/too old (for sth/to do sth) **ter ~ (para)** be old enough (for sth/to do sth)

ideal adj, sm ideal: Isso seria o ~. That would be ideal. ◊ um homem sem ideais a man without ideals

idealista adj idealistic ● smf idealist

idealizar vt idealize

idéia *sf* **1** idea: *ter ~s malucas* have strange ideas **2** *(conceito)* concept: *a ~ de igualdade* the concept of equality **3** *(idéias)* *(ideologia)* beliefs: *~s políticas* political beliefs ▶ **não faço a menor ~** I don't have a clue *que ~* you must be joking

idem *pron* **1** *(numa lista)* ditto → DITTO **2** *(igualmente)*: *Ele é um mentiroso e o filho ~.* He's a liar and the same for his son.

idêntico *adj* identical *(to sb/ sth)*: *gêmeos ~s* identical twins

identidade *sf* identity [*pl* -ies] ▶ **carteira/cédula de ~** ID, identity card *(mais fml)*

identificação *sf* identification

identificar *vt* identify ● **identificar-se** *vp* **1** *(mostrar identificação)* identify yourself **2 ~ com** identify with *sb/sth*

ideologia *sf* ideology [*pl* -ies]

idioma *sm* language

idiota *adj* dumb ● *smf* idiot: *Que ~ que ele é!* What an idiot he is!

idiotice *sf* stupidity ▶ **dizer ~s** talk nonsense

ídolo *sm* idol

idoso/a *adj* elderly ● *sm-sf* elderly man/woman [*pl* men/ women]: *os ~* the elderly

ignorância *sf* ignorance

ignorante *adj* ignorant ● *smf* ignoramus

ignorar *vt* **1** *(desconhecer)* not to know: *Ignoro se já saíram.* I don't know if they've already left. **2** *(não querer saber)* ignore

igreja *sf* church: *a ~ Católica* the Catholic Church → SCHOOL

igual *adj* **1** equal: *Todos os cidadãos são iguais.* All citizens are equal. ◇ *A é ~ a B.* A is equal to B. **2** *(idêntico)* the same *(as sb/sth)* ● *smf* equal ▶ **sem ~** unrivaled

igualar *vt* **1** *(ser igual)* equal **2** *(fazer igual)* make *sb/sth* equal **3** *(nivelar)* level ● *vi* **1** be the equal *(of sb/sth)* **2** *(ficar no mesmo nível)* be level *(with sth)*

igualdade *sf* equality

igualmente *adv* equally: *São ~ culpados.* They are equally to blame. ● *interj* the same to you

ilegal *adj* illegal

ilegível *adj* illegible

ileso *adj* unharmed: *escapar/ sair ~* escape unharmed

ilha *sf* island: *~ deserta* desert island ▶ **as ~s Britânicas** the British Isles

ilhéu/oa *sm-sf* islander

ilimitado *adj* unlimited

ilógico *adj* illogical

iluminação *sf* lighting

iluminado *adj* lit (up) *(with sth)*

iluminar *vt* **1** light *sth* up: *~ uma igreja* light a church up **2** *(apontar uma luz)* shine a light on *sth*: *Ilumine a caixa dos fusíveis.* Shine a light on the fuse box. ● **iluminar-se** *vp* light up: *O rosto dele se iluminou.* His face lit up.

ilusão *sf* illusion ▶ **perder as ilusões** become disillusioned *ter ilusões* cherish fond hopes

ilustração *sf* illustration

ilustrar *vt* illustrate

ilustre *adj* illustrious

ímã *sm* magnet

imagem *sf* **1** image: *mudar de ~* change your image **2** *(TV)* picture

imaginação *sf* imagination

imaginar *vt* imagine: *Imagino que sim.* I imagine so. ◇ *Imagine!* Just imagine!

imaginário *adj* imaginary

imaturo *adj* immature

imbecil *adj* dumb ● *smf* idiot

imediato *adj* immediate

imenso *adj* **1** immense **2** *(sentimentos)* great: *uma alegria/ dor imensa* great happiness/ sorrow

imigração *sf* immigration

imigrante *smf* immigrant

imigrar *vi* immigrate

imitação *sf* imitation ▶ **de ~** fake

imitar *vt* **1** *(copiar)* imitate **2** *(reproduzir)* mimic: *Ele te imita muito bem.* He's really good at mimicking you.

imobiliária *sf* *(agência)* real estate agency, estate agent's *(GB)*

imoral *adj* immoral

imortal *adj, smf* immortal

imóvel *adj* still: *permanecer ~* stand still

impaciência *sf* impatience

impacientar *vt* exasperate ● **impacientar-se** *vp* lose your patience *(with sb/sth)*

impaciente *adj* impatient

impacto *sm* impact

ímpar *adj* **1** *(Mat)* odd: *números ~es* odd numbers **2** *(único)* unique

imparcial *adj* unbiased

impedido *adj* **1** blocked **2** *(futebol)* offside

impedimento *sm* **1** *(obstáculo)* obstacle **2** *(Jur)* impediment **3** *(futebol)* offside

impedir *vt* **1** *(passagem)* block

sth (up) 2 (*impossibilitar*) stop sb/sth (*from doing sth*)

impenetrável *adj* impenetrable

impensável *adj* unthinkable

imperador/triz *sm-sf* emperor [*fem* empress]

imperativo *adj, sm* imperative

imperdoável *adj* unforgivable

imperfeição *sf* imperfection

imperial *adj* imperial

imperialismo *sm* imperialism

império *sm* empire

impermeável *adj* waterproof ● *sm* raincoat, mac (*GB*)

impertinente *adj* impertinent

impessoal *adj* impersonal

implacável *adj* (*impiedoso*) ruthless

implantar *vt* introduce

implicar *vt* 1 (*comprometer*) implicate: *Implicaram-no no assassinato*. He was implicated in the murder. 2 (*significar*) imply 3 (*acarretar*) involve ● ~ **com** pick on sb

implorar *vt* beg sb for sth; beg sb to do sth: ~ *ajuda aos amigos* beg your friends for help

impor *vt* 1 (*ordem, silêncio*) impose: ~ *condições/uma multa* impose conditions/a fine 2 (*respeito*) command ● **impor-se** *vp* (*fazer-se respeitar*) command respect

importação *sf* import: *um negócio de* ~ *e exportação* an import-export business

importador/a *sm-sf* importer

importância *sf* 1 importance: *adquirir/ganhar* ~ become important ◊ *dar pouca* ~ *aos seus sucessos* play down your achievements 2 (*quantidade*) amount: *a* ~ *da dívida* the amount owed ► *não tem* ~ it doesn't matter *sem* ~ unimportant

importante *adj* important ► *o* ~ *é que...* the main thing is that...

importar¹ *vt* (*Com*) import

importar² *vi* 1 (*ter importância*) matter: *Não importa*. It doesn't matter. 2 (*preocupar*) care (*about sb/sth*): *Pouco me importa*. I couldn't care less. ● **importar-se** *vp* 1 (*incomodar-se*) mind: *Você se importa que eu fume?* Do you mind if I smoke? ◊ *Você se importa de fechar a porta?* Would you mind shutting the door? ◊ *Não me importo de levantar cedo*. I don't mind getting up early. 2 (*preocupar-se*) care (*about sb/sth*): *Ele parece não se* ~ *com os filhos*. H⁺

doesn't seem to care about his children.

impossível *adj, sm* impossible: *Não peça o* ~. Don't ask (for) the impossible.

imposto *sm* tax: *isento de* ~*s* tax-free ► ~ **de Renda** (*abrev* **IR**) income tax ~ **sobre Circulação de Mercadorias e Serviços** (*abrev* **ICMS**) value added tax (*abrev* **VAT**)

impostor/a *sm-sf* impostor

impotente *adj* impotent

imprensa *sf* 1 (*prelo*) printing press 2 (*jornais*) papers [*pl*] 3 (**a imprensa**) (*jornalistas*) the press: ~ *sensacionalista/marrom* gutter press

imprescindível *adj* indispensable

impressão *sf* 1 (*sensação*) impression: *ficar com/causar boa/má* ~ get/make a good/bad impression 2 (*processo*) printing: *pronto para* ~ ready for printing ► ~ **digital** fingerprint *tenho a* ~ **de que...** I get the feeling that...

impressionante *adj* 1 impressive: *um feito* ~ an impressive achievement 2 (*espetacular*) striking: *uma beleza* ~ striking beauty 3 (*comovente*) moving

impressionar *vt* 1 impress: *A eficiência dela me impressiona*. I'm impressed by her efficiency. 2 (*emocionar*) move: *O final me impressionou muito*. I found the ending very moving. 3 (*desagradavelmente*) shock

impressionável *adj* impressionable

impresso *adj* printed

impressora *sf* printer

imprestável *adj* (*inútil*) useless

imprevisível *adj* unpredictable

imprevisto *adj* unforeseen ● *sm*: *Surgiu um* ~. Something unexpected has come up.

imprimir *vt* print

impróprio *adj* unsuitable (*for sth*) ► ~ **para consumo** unfit for human consumption

improvável *adj* unlikely

improvisar *vi* improvise

imprudente *adj* 1 rash 2 (*motorista*) reckless

impulsivo *adj* impulsive

impulso *sm* 1 impulse: *agir por* ~ act on impulse 2 (*empurrão*) boost

impuro *adj* impure

imundície *sf* filth: *Esta cozinha está uma* ~. This kitchen is filthy.

imundo adj filthy

imune adj immune (to sth)

imunidade sf immunity: gozar de ~ diplomática have diplomatic immunity

inabalável adj 1 adamant 2 (crença, opinião) unshakeable

inaceitável adj unacceptable

inacessível adj inaccessible

inacreditável adj unbelievable

inadequado adj inappropriate

inadiável adj pressing: um compromisso ~ a pressing engagement

inadmissível adj unacceptable: um comportamento ~ unacceptable behavior

inalador sm inhaler

inalar vt inhale

inato adj innate

inauguração sf opening, inauguration (fml): a cerimônia de ~ the opening ceremony

inaugurar vt open, inaugurate (fml)

incansável adj tireless

incapaz adj incapable of (doing) sth

incendiar vt set fire to sth ● **incendiar-se** vp catch fire

incendiário/a sm-sf 1 (criminoso) arsonist 2 (revolucionário) agitator

incêndio sm fire: apagar um ~ put out a fire ▶ ~ **premeditado** arson

incenso sm incense

incentivar vt motivate

incentivo sm incentive

incerto adj uncertain

inchaço sm (Med) swelling: O ~ diminuiu. The swelling has gone down.

inchado adj 1 swollen: um pé ~ a swollen foot 2 (estômago) bloated 3 (orgulhoso) full of yourself

inchar vi swell (up): Meu tornozelo inchou. My ankle has swollen up.

incinerar vt 1 incinerate 2 (cadáver) cremate

incisivo adj 1 (cortante) sharp 2 (fig) incisive ● sm incisor

incitar vt incite

inclinar vt 1 tilt 2 (cabeça) nod ● **inclinar(-se)** vi, vp lean: O edifício inclina para o lado. The building leans over to one side.

incluído adj all included ▶ (com) **tudo** ~ all inclusive

incluir vt include: incluindo o serviço including service

inclusive adv including

incógnita sf mystery [pl -ies]

incógnito adj incognito

incolor adj colorless

incomodar vt 1 (importunar) bother: Desculpe por te ~. I'm sorry to bother you. 2 (interromper) disturb ● vi: Não quero ~. I don't want to be a nuisance. ● **incomodar-se** vp 1 ~ (com) (importar-se) care about sth 2 ~ (em) (dar-se ao trabalho) bother (to do sth) ▶ **não** ~ do not disturb você se incomoda se...? do you mind if...?

incômodo adj uncomfortable ● sm 1 (dor) discomfort [U] 2 (chatice) inconvenience: Desculpem o ~. We apologize for any inconvenience. ▶ **se não for** ~ if it's no trouble

incomparável adj (ímpar) unique

incompatível adj incompatible

incompetente adj, smf incompetent

incompleto adj 1 incomplete: informação incompleta incomplete information 2 (por terminar) unfinished

incompreensível adj incomprehensible

incomunicável adj 1 cut off: Ficamos incomunicáveis devido às inundações. We were cut off by the floods. 2 (preso) in solitary confinement

inconfundível adj unmistakable

inconsciente adj, sm unconscious: O doente está ~. The patient is unconscious. ◊ um gesto ~ an unconscious gesture ● adj, smf (irresponsável) irresponsible: Você é um ~. You're so irresponsible.

inconscientemente adv without realizing

incontável adj countless

inconveniente adj 1 (inoportuno, incômodo) inconvenient: uma hora ~ an inconvenient time 2 (pouco apropriado) inappropriate: um comentário ~ an inappropriate comment ● sm 1 (dificuldade, obstáculo) problem: Surgiram alguns ~s. Some problems have arisen. 2 (desvantagem) disadvantage

incorporação sf (admissão) entry (to/into sth)

incorporado adj incorporated into sth

incorreto adj 1 (errado) incorrect 2 (comportamento) improper

incriminar vt incriminate

incrível *adj* incredible

incrustar-se *vp* (*projétil*): *A bala se incrustou na parede.* The bullet embedded itself in the wall.

incubadora *sf* incubator

incubar *vt*, *vi* incubate

inculto *adj* uneducated

incurável *adj* incurable

indagação *sf* inquiry [*pl* -ies]

indecente *adj* **1** (*roupa*) indecent **2** (*espetáculo, gesto, linguagem*) obscene: *uma piada ~* a dirty joke

indeciso *adj* (*pessoa*) indecisive

indefeso *adj* defenseless

indefinido *adj* **1** (*artigo*) indefinite **2** (*cor, idade, forma*) indeterminate

indelicado *adj* impolite

indenizar *vt* pay *sb* compensation (*for sth*)

independência *sf* independence

independente *adj* independent ▶ **~ de...**: *~ do número de alunos* irrespective of the number of students **tornar-se ~** (*país, colônia*) gain independence

indescritível *adj* indescribable

indestrutível *adj* indestructible

indeterminado *adj* **1** (*período*) indefinite: *uma greve por tempo ~* an indefinite strike **2** (*cor, idade, forma*) indeterminate

Índia *sf* India

indiano/a *adj*, *sm-sf* Indian: *os ~s* (the) Indians

indicação *sf* **1** sign **2** (**indicações**) (**a**) (*instruções*) instructions (**b**) (*caminho*) directions: *pedir indicações* ask for directions **3** (*cargo, prêmio*) nomination

indicado *adj* **1** (*adequado*) suitable (*for sth/to do sth*): *o candidato mais ~ para este trabalho* the most suitable candidate for the job **2** (*marcado*) specified: *a data indicada na carta* the date specified in the letter **3** (*aconselhável*) advisable

indicador *sm* **1** indicator **2** (*dedo*) index finger ▶ **~ de gasolina** gas gauge, petrol gauge (*GB*)

indicar *vt* show, indicate (*mais fml*): *~ o caminho* show the way

índice *sm* index ▶ **~ (de assuntos)** table of contents ▶ **~ de audiência** (*TV*) ratings [*pl*] ▶ **~ de natalidade** birth rate

indício *sm* **1** (*sinal*) sign **2** (*pista*) clue

Índico *sm* Indian Ocean

indiferença *sf* indifference (*to sb/sth*)

indiferente *adj* indifferent (*to sb/sth*), not interested (*in sb/sth*) (*mais coloq*) ▶ **isso me, etc. é ~** I, you, etc. don't care **ser ~**: *É ~ que seja branco ou preto.* It doesn't matter whether it's black or white.

indígena *adj* **1** indigenous **2** (*índio*) Indian ● *smf* **1** native **2** (*índio*) Indian

indigestão *sf* indigestion

indignado *adj* indignant (*at/about/over sth*)

indignar *vt* infuriate ● **indignar-se** *vp* get angry (*with sb*) (*about sth*)

indigno *adj* **1** (*desprezível*) contemptible **2** **~ de** unworthy of *sb/sth*

índio/a *adj*, *sm-sf* (American) Indian: *os ~s* (the) Indians

indireta *sf* hint: *dar uma/perceber a ~* drop a/take the hint

indireto *adj* indirect

indiscreto *adj* indiscreet

indiscrição *sf* indiscretion: *Perdoe a minha ~, mas...* Forgive me for asking, but... ◇ *se não for ~ da minha parte* if you don't mind me asking

indispensável *adj* essential ▶ **o ~** the essentials [*pl*]

indisposto *adj* (*maldisposto*) not well

individual *adj* individual

individualista *adj* individualist

indivíduo *sm* **1** individual **2** (*homem*) guy

indomável *adj* fierce

indubitável *adj* undoubted

indulto *sm* pardon: *O juiz lhe concedeu o ~.* The judge pardoned him.

indústria *sf* industry [*pl* -ies]: *~ siderúrgica* iron and steel industry

industrial *adj* industrial ● *smf* industrialist

induzir *vt* (*persuadir*) persuade *sb* to do *sth* ▶ **~ alguém ao erro** mislead *sb*

inédito *adj* **1** (*original*) unheard-of **2** (*livro*) unpublished

ineficaz *adj* ineffective

ineficiente *adj* inefficient

inegável *adj* undeniable

inércia *sf* inertia

inerente *adj* inherent (*in sb/sth*)

inesgotável *adj* **1** (*interminável*) inexhaustible **2** (*incansável*) tireless

inesperado *adj* unexpected

inesquecível *adj* unforgettable

inestimável *adj* invaluable: *ajuda ~* invaluable help

inevitável *adj* inevitable

inexato *adj* inaccurate

inexperiência *sf* inexperience

inexperiente *adj* inexperienced

infalível *adj* infallible

infância *sf* childhood

infantaria *sf* infantry

infantil *adj* 1 (*para crianças*) children's: *literatura ~* children's books 2 (*inocente*) childlike: *um sorriso ~* a childlike smile 3 (*pej*) childish: *Não seja ~.* Don't be so childish.

infecção *sf* infection

infeccioso *adj* infectious

infectar *vt* infect *sb/sth* (*with sth*) ● *vi* become infected

infelicidade *sf* 1 unhappiness 2 (*desgraça*) misfortune

infeliz *adj* 1 unhappy 2 (*inoportuno*) unfortunate ● *smf* unfortunate man

infelizmente *adv* unfortunately

inferior *adj* 1 inferior (*to sb/sth*): *de uma qualidade ~ à sua* inferior in quality to yours 2 (*mais baixo*) lower (*than sth*): *uma taxa de natalidade ~ à do ano passado* a lower birth rate than last year's

inferno *sm* hell: *ir para o ~* go to hell ◊ *tornar a vida de alguém um ~* make life hell for sb

infiel *adj* unfaithful (*to sb/sth*)

infiltrar-se *vp* 1 filter (in/out): *A luz infiltrava-se pelas frestas.* Light was filtering in through the cracks. 2 (*líquido*) seep (in/out): *A água se infiltrou pela parede.* Water was seeping in through the wall.

infinidade *sf* 1 infinity 2 (*grande quantidade*) a great many: *uma ~ de coisas* a great many things

infinitivo *sm* infinitive

infinito *adj* infinite: *uma paciência infinita* infinite patience

inflação *sf* inflation

inflacionário *adj* inflationary

inflamação *sf* inflammation

inflamado *adj* inflamed

inflamar(-se) *vt, vp* 1 (*incendiar-se*) ignite 2 (*Med*) become inflamed

inflamável *adj* inflammable

inflar *vt* (*inchar*) blow *sth* up, inflate (*mais fml*) ● **inflar-se** *vp* inflate

influência *sf* influence (*on/over sb/sth*)

influenciar *vt* influence

influente *adj* influential: *amigos ~s* friends in high places

influir *vt* ~ **em** influence *sb/sth*

informação *sf* 1 information (*on/about sb/sth*) [*U*]: *segundo as informações deles* according to their information 2 (*notícias*) news [*sing*]: *~ esportiva* sports news 3 (*informações*) (*recepção*) information (desk) [*sing*] ▸ **informações telefônicas** directory assistance

informal *adj* 1 (*cerimônia, etc.*) informal 2 (*roupa*) casual

informante *smf* informer

informar *vt* ~ **(de/sobre)** (*notificar*) inform *sb* (of/about *sth*), tell *sb* (about *sth*) (*mais coloq*): *~ alguém do que aconteceu* tell sb what happened 2 (*anunciar*) announce ● **informar-se** *vp* find out (*about sth*)

informática *sf* information technology (*abrev* IT)

infração *sf* 1 violation: *uma ~ de trânsito* a traffic violation 2 (*acordo, contrato, regra*) breach (*of sth*)

infravermelho *adj* infrared

infundado *adj* unfounded

infusão *sf* infusion

ingênuo *adj* 1 (*inocente*) innocent 2 (*crédulo*) naive

ingerir *vt* consume

Inglaterra *sf* England

inglês/esa *adj, sm* English ● *sm-sf* Englishman/woman [*pl* -men/-women]: *os ingleses* the English

ingrato *adj* 1 (*pessoa*) ungrateful 2 (*trabalho, tarefa*) thankless

ingrediente *sm* ingredient

íngreme *adj* steep

ingresso *sm* admission (*to sth*)

inibição *sf* inhibition

inibir *vt* inhibit ● **inibir-se** *vp* feel inhibited

iniciação *sf* 1 introduction (*to sth*): *uma ~ à música* an introduction to music 2 (*rito*) initiation (*into sth*)

inicial *adj, sf* initial

iniciar *vt* 1 (*começar*) begin: *~ a reunião* begin the meeting 2 (*negócio*) start *sth* (up) 3 (*reformas*) initiate ▸ ~ **(a) viagem (para)** set out (for...)

iniciativa *sf*: *ter ~* show initiative ◊ *tomar a ~* take the initiative ◊ *por ~ própria* on your own initiative

início *sm* beginning: *dar ~* begin ◊ *no ~ de...* at the beginning of...

inimigo/a adj, sm-sf enemy [pl -ies] as tropas inimigas the enemy troops

injeção sf shot, injection (mais fml): dar uma ~ em alguém give sb a shot

injetar vt inject

injustiça sf injustice: É uma ~. It's not fair.

injusto adj unfair (on/to sb)

inocência sf innocence

inocente adj 1 innocent: fazer-se de ~ play the innocent ◊ uma brincadeira ~ a harmless joke 2 (ingênuo) naive • smf innocent

inofensivo adj harmless

inoportuno adj: um momento ~ an inopportune moment

inovador adj innovative

inoxidável adj stainless

inquebrável adj unbreakable

inquérito sm investigation: um ~ policial a police investigation

inquietação sf anxiety [pl -ies]

inquieto adj (preocupado) worried (about sb/sth)

inquilino/a sm-sf tenant

insatisfatório adj unsatisfactory

insatisfeito adj dissatisfied (with sb/sth)

inscrever vt 1 (em lista) sign sb up 2 (matricular) enroll 3 (gravar) inscribe • inscrever-se vp 1 (curso, lista) enroll (for/on sth): ~ no judô enroll for judo classes 2 (competição, concurso) enter

inscrição sf 1 (gravura) inscription 2 (registro) registration 3 (curso, exército) enrollment

insegurança sf insecurity [pl -ies]

inseguro adj 1 (pessoa) insecure 2 (perigoso) unsafe 3 (passo, voz) unsteady

insensato adj foolish

insensível adj 1 insensitive (to sth): ~ ao frio insensitive to cold 2 (membro, nervo) numb

inseparável adj inseparable

inseticida sm insecticide

inseto sm insect

insignificante adj insignificant

insinuação sf insinuation

insinuar vt insinuate

insípido adj 1 (comida) bland 2 (pessoa) dull

insistente adj 1 (com palavras) insistent 2 (atitude) persistent

insistir vt, vi insist (on (doing) sth): Ele insistiu que fôssemos. He insisted that we should go.

insolação sf sunstroke [U]: apanhar (uma) ~ get sunstroke

insolente adj insolent

insônia sf insomnia

insosso adj (comida) bland

inspeção sf inspection: realizar uma ~ carry out an inspection

inspecionar vt inspect

inspetor/a sm-sf inspector

inspiração sf inspiration

inspirar vt inspire (sb) (with sth) • inspirar-se vp get inspiration (from sth): Ela se inspirou num fato verídico. She got her inspiration from a real-life event.

instabilidade sf (tempo) uncertainty [pl -ies]

instalação sf 1 installation 2 (instalações) facilities: instalações culturais/esportivas cultural/sports facilities ▶ ~ elétrica (electrical) wiring

instalar vt install • instalar-se vp 1 (em cidade, país) settle (down) 2 (numa casa) move into sth 3 (pânico, medo) spread: O pânico se instalou. Panic spread.

instantâneo adj 1 (rápido) instantaneous 2 (café) instant

instante sm moment: naquele mesmo ~ at that very moment ◊ a qualquer ~ at any moment ◊ por um ~ for a moment ▶ a todo (o) ~ constantly dentro de ~s shortly de um ~ para o outro suddenly

instável adj 1 (pessoa) unstable 2 (tempo) changeable

instinto sm instinct ▶ por ~ instinctively

instituição sf institution

instituto sm institute ▶ ~ de beleza beauty salon ~ Nacional da Previdência Social (INPS) Welfare Department (USA), Department of Social Security (abrev DSS) (GB)

instrução sf 1 (Mil) training 2 (instruções) instructions: instruções de uso instructions for use

instrumental adj instrumental

instrumento sm instrument

instrutor/a sm-sf instructor

insubordinado adj rebellious

insucesso sm failure

insuficiência sf 1 (falta) lack 2 (Med): ~ cardíaca/renal heart/kidney failure 3 (deficiência) inadequacy [pl -ies]

insuficiente adj 1 (escasso) insufficient 2 (deficiente) inadequate • sm (Educ) fail

insulina sf insulin

insultar vt insult

insulto sm insult

insuperável adj 1 (feito, beleza) matchless 2 (dificuldade) insuperable 3 (qualidade, oferta) unbeatable

insuportável adj unbearable

intato adj 1 (não tocado) untouched 2 (não danificado) intact: A reputação dele permanece intata. His reputation remains intact.

íntegra sf ▶ na ~ whole: o meu ordenado na ~ my whole salary

integração sf integration (into sth)

integral adj (completo) comprehensive

integrar-se vp integrate (into sth)

integridade sf integrity

íntegro adj honest

inteirar-se vp 1 (descobrir) find out (about sth) 2 (notícia) hear (about sth)

inteiro adj 1 (completo) whole, entire (mais fml) 2 (intato) intact

intelectual adj, smf intellectual

inteligência sf intelligence

inteligente adj intelligent

intenção sf intention: ter más intenções have evil intentions ▶ com más intenções maliciously fazer algo com boas intenções mean well: Ele o fez com boas intenções. He meant well. ter a ~ de intend to do sth

intencional adj deliberate

intensidade sf 1 intensity 2 (corrente elétrica, vento, voz) strength

intensificar(-se) vt, vp intensify

intensivo adj intensive

intenso adj 1 intense: uma onda de calor ~ intense heat 2 (chuva, neve, trânsito, trabalho) heavy: um ritmo ~ de trabalho a heavy work schedule 3 (dor, crise) severe

interação sf interaction

interativo adj interactive

intercâmbio sm exchange

interceder vi ▶ ~ a (a favor de/por) intervene (on sb's behalf)

interessado adj 1 interested (in doing) sth): Não estou ~. I'm not interested. 2 (disposto) keen (to do sth): Estou ~ em ir. I am keen to go.

interessante adj interesting

interessar vt 1 ~ alguém (em algo) interest sb (in sth) 2 ~ a alguém be interested (in (doing) sth): A arte nos interessa. We're

interested in art. ● **interessar-se** vp 1 (mostrar interesse) show (an) interest in sth 2 (como passatempo) get into (doing) sth: Ela se interessou muito pelo xadrez. She's really gotten into chess. ▶ que me, te, etc. interessa? what's it to me, you, etc.?

interesse sm 1 interest (in sb/sth): suscitar grande ~ arouse a lot of interest ◊ ter ~ pela arte be interested in art 2 (egoísmo) self-interest: por puro ~ purely out of self-interest

interferência sf interference

interferir sm, vi interfere (in sth)

interfone sm intercom

interino adj acting: o diretor ~ da escola the acting principal of the school

interior adj 1 inner: um quarto ~ an inner room 2 (bolso) inside ● sm inner: o ~ de um país the interior of a country

interjeição sf interjection

intermediário/a sm-sf 1 (mediador) mediator 2 (mensageiro) go-between [pl ~s] 3 (Com) middleman [pl -men]

intermédio sm intermediate ▶ por ~ de... through...

interminável adj endless

internacional adj international

internar vt: ser internado no hospital be admitted to the hospital ◊ Eles internaram o pai num asilo. They put their father into a retirement home.

internato sm boarding school

Internet sf (the) Internet

interno/a adj 1 internal: órgãos ~s internal organs 2 (comércio, política, vôo) domestic 3 (face, parte) inner: a parte interna da coxa the inner thigh ● sm-sf (aluno) boarder

interpretação sf interpretation

interpretar vt 1 interpret: ~ a lei interpret the law 2 (Cinema, Teat, Mús) perform ▶ ~ mal misinterpret

intérprete smf 1 interpreter 2 (Cinema, Teat, Mús) performer

interrogar vt question

interrogatório sm interrogation

interromper vt 1 interrupt: Não me interrompa. Don't interrupt me. 2 (trânsito, aula) disrupt

interrupção sf interruption

interruptor sm switch

interurbano adj 1 inter-city: serviços ~s inter-city services 2 (chamada) long-distance

intervalo sm 1 interval: com ~s

de meia hora at half-hourly intervals **2** (*Teat*) intermission **3** (*aula, programa de televisão*) break **4** (*Esporte*) half-time

intervir *vt, vi* **1** intervene (*in sth*) **2** (*falar*) speak

intestino *sm* intestine: *~ delgado/grosso* small/large intestine

intimidade *sf* **1** (*privacidade*) privacy **2** (*familiaridade*) familiarity: *tratar alguém com demasiada ~* be too familiar with sb.

intimidar *vt* intimidate

íntimo *adj* **1** intimate: *uma conversa íntima* an intimate conversation **2** (*amizade, relação*) close: *Eles são amigos ~s.* They're very close friends.

intitulado *adj* (*livro, filme*) called, entitled (*mais fml*)

intolerância *sf* intolerance

intolerante *adj* intolerant

intolerável *adj* intolerable

intoxicação *sf* poisoning: *~ alimentar* food poisoning NOTA "Intoxication" equivale a **embriaguez.**

intragável *adj* **1** (*comida*) inedible **2** (*pessoa*) unbearable

intriga *sf* **1** (*maquinação, romance*) intrigue: *~s políticas* political intrigues **2** (*filme*) plot **3** (*mexerico*) gossip [*U*]: *a última ~* the latest piece of gossip

intrigado *adj* intrigued (*by sth*)

intrincado *adj* complicated

introdução *sf* introduction: *uma ~ à música* an introduction to music

introduzir *vt* insert: *Introduza a moeda na fenda.* Insert the coin into the slot.

intrometer-se *vp* interfere (*in sth*): *~ em assuntos de família* interfere in family affairs

intrometido *adj* interfering

introvertido/a *adj* introverted ● *sm-sf* introvert

intruso/a *sm-sf* intruder

intuição *sf* intuition: *Respondi por ~.* I answered intuitively.

intuir *vt* sense

inúmero *adj* countless: *inúmeras vezes* countless times

inundação *sf* flood

inundar(-se) *vt, vp* flood

inútil *adj* useless: *cacarecos inúteis* useless junk ◊ *É um esforço ~.* It's a waste of time. ◊ *É ~ tentar.* It's pointless trying. ● *smf* good-for-nothing

invadir *vt* invade

invalidez *sf* disability [*pl* -ies]

inválido/a *adj* (*pessoa*) disabled ● *sm-sf* disabled person

invasão *sf* invasion

invasor/a *adj* invading ● *sm-sf* invader

inveja *sf* envy: *Que ~!* I really envy you! ▶ **fazer ~** make sb jealous **ter ~** be jealous (*of sb/sth*)

invejar *vt* envy

invejoso *adj* envious

invenção *sf* **1** invention **2** (*mentira*) lie: *Não é verdade, são invenções dela.* It's not true; she's lying.

invencível *adj* invincible

inventar *vt, vi* **1** (*criar*) invent **2** (*desculpa, história*) make *sth* up: *Você está inventando.* You're just making it up. **3** (*idealizar*) think *sth* up, devise (*mais fml*)

invento *sm* invention

inventor/a *sm-sf* inventor

inverno *sm* winter: *no ~* in (the) winter ◊ *roupa de ~* winter clothes

inverso *adj* **1** (*proporção*) inverse **2** (*ordem*) reverse **3** (*direção*) opposite: *em sentido ~* in the opposite direction

invertebrado *adj, sm* invertebrate

inverter *vt* (*trocar*) reverse: *~ os papéis* reverse roles

invés *sm* ▶ **ao ~ de...** instead of...

investigação *sf* **1** investigation (*into sth*) **2** (*científica, acadêmica*) research [*U*] (*into/on sth*): *realizar um trabalho de ~ sobre algo* do research on sth

investigador/a *sm-sf* investigator

investigar *vt* **1** investigate: *~ um caso* investigate a case **2** (*cientista, acadêmico*) do research (*into/on sth*)

investimento *sm* (*Fin*) investment

investir *vt, vi* (*tempo, dinheiro*) invest (*sth*) (*in sth*): *Investiram dez milhões de dólares na companhia.* They invested ten million dollars in the company.

invicto *adj* unbeaten: *O time continua ~.* The team's still unbeaten.

invisível *adj* invisible

invólucro *sm* wrapper

iodo *sm* iodine

ioga *sf* yoga: *fazer ~* practice yoga

iogurte *sm* yogurt: *~ magro* low-fat yogurt

ir *vi* **1** go: *ir de carro/avião* go by car/plane ◊ *ir a pé* go on foot ◊

Como vão as coisas? How are things going? **2 ir com** (*roupa, cores*) go with(*sth*): *O casaco não vai com a saia.* The jacket doesn't go with the skirt. **3** (*Mat*): *22 e vão dois* 22 and carry two. ◊ *De nove para doze vão três.* Nine from twelve is three. ● *v aux* **1** (+ *infinitivo*) **(a)** be going to do sth: *Vamos vender a casa.* We're going to sell the house. ◊ *Íamos comer quando tocou o telefone.* We were just going to eat when the phone rang. **(b)** (*em ordens*) go and do sth: *Vá falar com ele.* Go and talk to him. **2** (+ *gerúndio*) **(a)** (*iniciar*) start doing sth: *Vá pondo a mesa.* Start setting the table. **(b)** (*indicando simultaneidade*) go on doing sth: *Ela ia comendo enquanto ele falava.* She went on eating while he was talking. ● **ir-se** *vp* leave ▶ **ir contra alguém** go against sb ▶ **dar em** (*rua*) lead to sth ▶ **ir indo**: *Como vai a sua mãe? Vai indo.* How's your mother? Not so bad. ◊ *Vamos indo.* We're doing OK. **vamos...?** (*sugestões*) shall we...?: *Vamos ver?* Shall we go and see? ▶ **vamos** come on: *Vamos, senão perdemos o trem!* Come on or we'll miss the train! ◊ *Vamos, Flamengo!* Come on, Flamengo! **vamos que...** (*temor*) what if...: *Vamos que tenha acontecido alguma coisa com eles.* What if something has happened to them? NOTA Para outras expressões com **ir**, ver o substantivo, adjetivo, etc., p. ex. **ir às compras** EM COMPRA.

íris *sf* iris

Irlanda *sf* Ireland ▶ **~ do Norte** Northern Ireland

irlandês/esa *adj, sm* Irish ● *sm-sf* Irishman/woman [*pl* -men/-women]: *os irlandeses* the Irish

irmandade *sf* **1** (*de homens*) brotherhood **2** (*de mulheres*) sisterhood **3** (*confraria*) association

irmão/ã *sm-sf* **1** brother [*fem* sister]: *a minha irmã mais nova* my youngest sister ◊ *São dois ~s e três irmãs.* There are two boys and three girls. NOTA Para **irmãos**, referindo-se a irmãos e irmãs, diz-se **brothers and sisters**: *Somos seis ~s.* I have five brothers and sisters. **2** (*comunidade religiosa*) brother [*fem* sister]: *o ~ Francisco* Brother Francis ▶ **~ de criação** stepbrother [*fem* stepsister]

ironia *sf* irony [*pl* -ies]: *as ~s da vida* life's little ironies

irônico *adj* ironic

irracional *adj* irrational

irreal *adj* unreal

irreconhecível *adj* unrecognizable

irregular *adj* **1** irregular: *verbos ~es* irregular verbs ◊ *um batimento cardíaco ~* an irregular heartbeat **2** (*anormal*) abnormal: *uma situação ~* an abnormal situation

irremediável *adj* irremediable

irrequieto *adj* restless

irresistível *adj* irresistible: *uma atração/força ~* an irresistible attraction/force ▶ **ter uma vontade ~ de fazer algo** be dying to do sth

irresponsável *adj* irresponsible

irrigação *sf* irrigation

irritante *adj* annoying

irritar *vt* irritate ● **irritar-se** *vp* **1** **~ (com) (por)** get annoyed (*with sb*) (*about sth*): **~ por qualquer coisa** be easily annoyed **2** (*Med*) become irritated

isca *sf* bait

isento *adj* **1** (*não obrigado*) exempt (*from sth*) **2** (*livre*) free (*from sth*): **~ de impostos** tax-free

islâmico *adj* Islamic

isolado *adj* isolated

isolador *adj* insulating ● *sm* insulator

isolante *adj* insulating

isolar *vt* **1** (*separar*) isolate sb/sth (*from sb/sth*) **2** (*deixar incomunicável*) cut sb/sth off (*from sb/sth*): *A aldeia foi isolada pelas cheias.* The village was cut off by the floods. **3** (*com material isolante*) insulate **4** (*polícia*) cordon sth off ▶ **isola** knock on wood

isopor *sm* Styrofoam®, polystyrene (*GB*)

isqueiro *sm* lighter

isso *pron* that, this: *O que é ~?* What's this? ▶ **é isso/isso mesmo** that's right ▶ **que não** definitely not ▶ **não tenho nada com ~** it has nothing to do with me ▶ **para ~** in order to do that ▶ **por ~** so, therefore (*fml*)

istmo *sm* isthmus

isto *pron* this: *Que é ~?* What's this? ▶ **isto é...** that is (to say)...

Itália *sf* Italy

italiano/a *adj, sm-sf, sm* Italian: *os ~s* (the) Italians

itinerário *sm* itinerary [*pl* -ies]

J j

já adv **1** (referindo-se ao passado) already: Você já acabou? Did you finish it already? → YET **2** (referindo-se ao presente) now: Ele estava muito doente mas agora já está bom. He was sick but he's fine now. **3** (em ordens) this minute: Venha aqui já! Come here this minute! **4** (alguma vez) ever: Você já andou de avião? Did you ever fly in an airplane? **5** (uso enfático): Já sei. I know. ◊ Você já vai ver. Just you wait and see. ▸ **é para já** coming up **já vou** coming **já que** since **já vou** coming

jacaré sm alligator

jacinto sm hyacinth

jaguar sm jaguar

jamais adv never: ~ conheci alguém assim. I've never known anyone like him. → ALWAYS

janeiro sm January (abrev **Jan.**): no dia 12 de ~ on January 12 → MAIO

janela sf window

jangada sf raft

jantar¹ sm dinner, supper: Comi uma omelete no ~. I had an omelet for dinner.

jantar² vi have dinner, supper ▸ vt have sth for dinner, supper

Japão sm Japan

japonês/esa adj, sm Japanese ▸ sm-sf Japanese man/woman [pl men/women]: os japoneses the Japanese

jaqueta sf jacket

jardim sm garden: ~ botânico/público botanical/public gardens ▸ ~ **de infância** preschool ~ **de inverno** conservatory [pl -ies] ~ **zoológico** zoo

jardinagem sf gardening

jardineira sf **1** (vaso) window box **2** (peça de vestuário) overalls

jardineiro/a sm-sf gardener

jargão sm jargon

jarra sf **1** (flores) vase **2** (bebida) pitcher, jug (GB)

jarro sm pitcher, jug (GB)

jato sm jet

jaula sf cage

javali sm wild boar [pl wild boar]

jazida sf **1** (Geol) deposit: uma ~ de carvão a coalfield **2** (Arqueologia) site

jazigo sm grave

jeans sm **1** (calça) jeans: uns ~ some jeans/a pair of jeans → PAIR **2** (tecido) denim

jeito sm **1** (modo) way: Não gosto do ~ como ela fala. I don't like the way he talks. **2** (habilidade) skill ▸ **apanhar/pegar o ~** get the hang of sth **com ~** carefully **dar um ~ em** (reparar) fix **dar um (mau) ~ no pé/tornozelo** sprain your foot/ankle **de ~ nenhum** no way **de qualquer ~** any old way: Ele deixa sempre a roupa de qualquer ~. He always leaves his clothes any old way. **ter ~ de** look like: Ele tem cada vez mais o ~ do pai. He looks more and more like his father. **ter ~ para** be good at (doing) sth: ter ~ para a matemática be good at math

jeitoso adj (hábil) skillful

jejum sm fast: 40 dias de ~ 40 days of fasting ▸ **em ~**: Estou em ~. I've had nothing to eat or drink.

jesuíta adj, sm Jesuit

jibóia sf boa (constrictor)

jipe sm Jeep®

joalheiro/a sm-sf jeweler

joalheria sf jewelry store, jeweller's (GB)

joaninha sf ladybug, ladybird (GB)

joelheira sf **1** (Esporte) kneepad **2** (Med) knee support **3** (remendo) knee patch

joelho sm knee ▸ **de ~s** kneeling down: pôr-se de ~s kneel down ◊ Você terá de me pedir de ~s. You'll have to get down on your knees and beg.

jogada sf move

jogador/a sm-sf **1** (competidor) player: ~ de tênis tennis player **2** (apostador) gambler

jogar vt, vi **1** play: ~ bola/futebol play soccer ◊ ~ fora/em casa play away/at home ◊ ~ na loteria buy a lottery ticket ◊ ~ limpo/sujo play fair/dirty **2** (apostar) bet: ~ 30.000 reais num cavalo bet 30,000 reals on a horse **3** (atirar) throw: Jogue os dados. Throw the dice. ◊ ~ algo no lixo throw sth in the garbage ◊ ~ dinheiro fora throw your money away

jogging sm **1** (Esporte) jogging: fazer ~ go jogging **2** (roupa) sweatsuit, tracksuit (GB)

jogo sm **1** game: ~s de vídeo/tabuleiro video/board games ◊ ~ de azar game of chance ◊ ganhar por três ~s a um win by three games to one **2** (azar) gambling **3** (conjunto) set: um

~ **de chaves** a set of keys ▶ **em** ~ at stake: *pôr algo em* ~ put sth at stake ◆ **da velha** tic-tac-toe, noughts and crosses (*GB*) ~ **de palavras** pun ◆ **limpo/sujo** fair/foul play **Jogos Olímpicos** Olympic Games/Olympics (*mais coloq*) **ter** ~ **de cintura** (*ser flexível*) be adaptable

jóia *sf* **1** (*pedra*) jewel **2** (*jóias*) jewelry [*U*]: *As* ~*s estavam no cofre.* The jewelry was in the safe. **3** (*coisa, pessoa*): *Você é uma* ~. You're a treasure.

jóquei *smf* jockey

jornada *sf* **1** day: *uma* ~ *de trabalho de oito horas* an eight-hour working day **2** (*viagem*) journey

jornal *sm* newspaper, paper (*coloq*)

jornaleiro/a *sm-sf* newsdealer, newsagent (*GB*)

jornalismo *sm* journalism

jornalista *smf* journalist

jorrar *vi* gush out

jorro *sm* **1** jet **2** (*muito abundante*) gush: *sair aos* ~*s* gush out

jovem *adj* young: *Ela é a mais* ~ *da família.* She's the youngest in the family. ◆ *smf* **1** (*rapaz, moça*) young man/woman [*pl* men/women] **2** (*jovens*) young people, kids (*coloq*)

juba *sf* mane

jubileu *sm* jubilee

judeu/ia *adj* Jewish ◆ *sm-sf* Jew

judicial *adj: ação* ~ lawsuit

judô *sm* judo: *fazer* ~ practice judo

juiz/íza *sm-sf* **1** (*Jur*) judge **2** (*futebol, boxe*) referee **3** (*tênis, beisebol*) umpire

juízo *sm* **1** (*sensatez*) (common) sense **2** (*opinião*) opinion: *emitir um* ~ give an opinion ◆ *interj* behave ▶ **não estar bom do** ~ not be in your right mind

julgamento *sm* **1** judgment: *Confio no* ~ *das pessoas.* I trust people's judgment. **2** (*Jur*) trial

julgar *vt* **1** judge **2** (*achar*) think: *Ele se julga esperto.* He thinks he's smart. ▶ **mal** misjudge

julho *sm* July (*abrev Jul.*) → MAIO

junho *sm* June (*abrev Jun.*) → MAIO

júnior *smf* (*Esporte*) junior: *Ela joga nos* ~*es.* She plays in the junior team.

juntar *vt* **1** (*pôr lado a lado*) put sb/sth together: *Juntamos as mesas?* Shall we put the tables together? **2** (*unir*) join sth together: *Juntei os dois pedaços.*

I've joined the two pieces (together). **3** (*reunir*) get people together **4** (*adicionar*) add **5** (*dinheiro*) **(a)** (*poupar*) save sth (up): ~ *dinheiro para comprar algo* save up for sth **(b)** (*angariar*) raise ◆ **juntar-se** *vp* **1** (*reunir-se*) gather: *Um monte de gente se juntou à volta dele.* A crowd of people gathered around him. **2** (*para fazer algo*) get together (*to do sth*): *Toda a turma se juntou para comprar o presente.* Everyone in the class got together to buy the present. **3** (*casal*) move in together

junto *adj* **1** together: *todos* ~*s* all together **2** (*próximo*) close together: *As árvores estão muito juntas.* The trees are very close together. ◆ *adv* **1** ~ **a** next to **2** ~ **com** with

Júpiter *sm* Jupiter

juramento *sm* oath

jurar *vt, vi* swear

júri *sm* jury [*pl* -ies]

juro *sm* (**juros**) interest [*U*]: *com 10% de* ~*s* at 10% interest

justamente *adv* **1** (*exatamente*) just **2** (*com justiça*) fairly

justiça *sf* **1** justice: *Espero que seja feita* ~. I hope justice is done. **2** (*retribuição*) law: *Não faça* ~ *com as próprias mãos.* Don't take the law into your own hands. ▶ **fazer** ~ **a alguém**: *O seu comportamento lhe faz* ~. Your behavior does you credit.

justificar *vt* justify

justificável *adj* justifiable

justo *adj* **1** (*razoável*) fair: *uma decisão justa* a fair decision **2** (*correto, exato*) right: *o preço* ~ the right price **3** (*apertado*) tight: *um vestido* ~ a tight dress ◆ *adv* just: *Chegaram* ~ *quando eu estava de saída.* They arrived just as I was leaving.

juvenil *adj* **1** (*caráter*) youthful **2** (*para jovens*): *à moda* ~ young people's fashion **3** (*Esporte*) junior

juventude *sf* **1** (*idade*) youth **2** (*os jovens*) young people: *a* ~ *de hoje* young people today

Kk

karaokê *sm* karaoke
kart *sm* go-cart
kiwi *sm* kiwi

L1

lá¹ *adv* there ▶ **de lá para cá:** *Passei o dia de lá para cá.* I've been running around all day. ◇ *Tenho andado de lá para cá à sua procura.* I've been looking for you everywhere. **lá** (*para*) **dentro/fora** inside/outside: *Vamos lá para fora.* Let's go outside. **lá em cima/embaixo 1** up/down there **2** (*numa casa*) upstairs/downstairs **mais para lá:** *empurrar a mesa mais para lá* push the table further over **para lá de 1** (*mais de*) more than **2** (*para além de*) beyond **sei lá** how should I know

lá² *sm* (*Mús*) A

lã *sf* wool

labareda *sf* flame

lábio *sm* lip

labirinto *sm* **1** labyrinth **2** (*num jardim*) maze

laboratório *sm* laboratory [*pl* -ies], lab (*coloq*)

labuta *sf* work, grind (*coloq*): *a ~ diária* the daily grind

laço *sm* **1** (*laçada*) bow **2** (*fita*) ribbon **3** (*vínculo*) tie: *~s de família/amizade* family ties/ bonds of friendship

lacre *sm* seal

lacrimejar *vi* water

lacrimogêneo *adj*: *gas ~* tear gas

lacuna *sf* **1** (*omissão*) gap **2** (*espaço em branco*) blank: *preencher as ~s* fill in the blanks

ladeira *sf* slope

lado ● *sm* **1** side: *no ~ da caixa* on the side of the box ◇ *ver o ~ bom das coisas* look on the bright side ◇ *Vamos jogar em ~s opostos.* We'll be playing on different sides. ◇ *no outro ~ da cidade* on the other side of town **2** (*lugar*) place: *de um ~ para o outro* from one place to another ◇ *em algum/nenhum ~* somewhere/nowhere **3** (*direção*) way: *Foram por outro ~.* They went a different way. ◇ *olhar para todos os ~s* look in all directions ◇ *Foi cada um por seu ~.* They each went their separate ways. ▶ **ao ~ 1** (*perto*) (very) near **2** (*vizinho*): *o edifício ao ~* the building next door **ao ~ de** next to sb/sth: *Fique ao meu ~.* Stand next to me. **deixar/pôr de ~** set *sth* aside **de ~:** *pôr algo de ~* put sth on its side **de**

~ a ~/de um ~ ao outro from one side to the other **do ~ next door:** *os vizinhos do ~* the next-door neighbors **do ~ de fora** from outside: *do ~ de fora do teatro* from outside the theater **em/por todo o ~** all over the place **estar/ficar do ~ de alguém** be on/take sb's side: *De que ~ você está?* Whose side are you on? **lado a lado** side by side **passar ao ~** (*sem ver*) go straight past *sb/sth* **por outro ~** on the other hand **por todo(s) o(s) ~(s)** all around: *Havia livros por todos os ~s.* There were books everywhere. **por um ~... por outro (~)** on the one hand... on the other (hand)

ladrão **-dra** *sm-sf* **1** thief [*pl* thieves] **2** (*casas*) burglar **3** (*bancos*) robber → **THIEF**

ladrar *vi* bark

ladrilhar *vt* tile

ladrilho *sm* tile

lagarta *sf* caterpillar

lagartixa *sf* gecko [*pl* ~s]

lagarto *sm* lizard

lago *sm* **1** (*natural*) lake **2** (*jardim, parque*) pond

lagoa *sf* **1** (*lago pequeno*) small lake **2** (*laguna*) lagoon

lagosta *sf* lobster

lágrima *sf* tear: *~s de crocodilo* crocodile tears

laguna *sf* lagoon

lajota *sf* **1** (*interior*) floor tile **2** (*exterior*) paving stone

lama *sf* mud

lamacento *adj* muddy

lambada *sf* **1** (*paulada*) blow **2** (*dança*) lambada

lamber *vt* lick ● **lamber-se** *vp* **1** (*pessoa*) lick your lips **2** (*gato*) wash itself

lambreta® *sf* scooter

lambuzar *vt* smear

lamentar *vt* regret: *Lamentamos ter-lhe causado tanto transtorno.* We regret having caused you so much trouble. ◇ *Lamentamos comunicar-lhe que...* We regret to inform you that... ◇ *Lamento muito.* I'm very sorry. ● **lamentar-se** *vp* complain (*about* sth)

lamentável *adj* **1** (*aspecto, condição*) pitiful **2** (*erro, injustiça*) regrettable

lâmina *sf* blade: *~ de barbear* razor blade

lâmpada *sf* (light) bulb: *A ~ queimou.* The bulb has blown. ● **~ fluorescente** fluorescent light

lança *sf* spear

lançamento sm 1 (*míssil, satélite, produto*) launch: *o ~ de seu novo livro* the launch of her new book 2 (*filme, disco*) release 3 (*Esporte*) throw: *~ lateral* throw-in 4 (*bomba*) dropping

lançar vt 1 (*navio, míssil, produto*) launch 2 (*filme, disco*) release 3 (*atirar*) throw 4 (*bomba*) drop ● **lançar-se** vp pounce on sb/sth

lance sm 1 (*arremesso*) throw 2 (*escada*) flight 3 (*leilão*) bid

lancha sf launch

lanchar vt have sth as a snack ● vi have a snack

lanche sm snack

lancheira sf lunch box

lanchonete sf snack bar

lânguido adj languid

lantejoula sf sequin

lanterna sf 1 lantern 2 (*de bolso*) flashlight, torch (*GB*)

lanterninha smf usher [fem usherette]

lapela sf lapel

lápide sf gravestone

lápis sm pencil: *a ~ in* pencil ◇ *~ de cor* colored pencils ▶ *~ de cera* crayon

lapso sm 1 (*esquecimento*) slip 2 (*engano*) mistake

laquê sm hairspray

lar sm 1 (*casa*) home 2 (*família*) family: *formar um ~ start a family* ▶ *~ de idosos* retirement home

laranja sf (*fruto*) orange ● adj, sm (*cor*) orange

laranjada sf orange drink

laranjeira sf orange tree

lareira sf fireplace: *Acenda a ~.* Light the fire.

largar vt 1 (*soltar*) let go of sb/sth: *Largue-me!* Let go of me! 2 (*deixar cair*) drop 3 (*abandonar*) leave: *Ele largou a mulher.* He left his wife. 4 (*drogas*) come off sth

largo adj 1 wide: *uma estrada larga* a wide road 2 (*roupa*) baggy: *um suéter ~ a baggy sweater* ◇ *A cintura é larga demais.* The waist is too big. 3 (*ombros, costas*) broad → BROAD ● sm (*praça*) square

largura sf width: *Quanto mede de ~?* How wide is it? ◇ *Tem um metro de ~.* It's a meter wide.

laringite sf laryngitis

larva sf 1 (*nos alimentos*) maggot 2 (*Zool*) larva

lasanha sf lasagne

lasca sf (*madeira*) splinter

laser sm laser

lástima sf pity: *Que ~!* What a pity!

lata sf 1 (*embalagem*) can, tin (*GB*) 2 (*material*) tin ▶ *de/em ~* canned, tinned (*GB*) *~ de lixo* garbage can, dustbin (*GB*)

latão sm brass

lataria sf (*carroceria*) bodywork

latejar vi throb

lateral adj side: *uma rua ~ a side street* ● sm (*Futebol*): *~ direito* right back

laticínios sm dairy products: *a indústria de ~s* the dairy industry

latido sm bark: *Ouvia-se o ~ de um cão.* You could hear a dog barking.

latifúndio sm large estate

latim sm Latin

latino adj Latin

latir vi bark

latitude sf latitude

lava sf lava

lavabo sm 1 (*lavatório*) sink, washbasin (*GB*) 2 (*banheiro*) bathroom, toilet (*GB*)

lavagem sf laundry ▶ *a seco* dry-cleaning *~ automática* car wash *~ cerebral* brainwashing: *fazer uma ~ cerebral em alguém* brainwash sb

lavanda sf lavender

lavanderia sf 1 laundry [pl -ies] 2 (*tinturaria*) dry-cleaner's ▶ *~ automática* laundromat, launderette (*GB*)

lavar vt 1 wash: *~ a roupa/cabeça* wash your clothes/hair 2 (*dinheiro*) launder ● **lavar-se** vp wash (yourself) ▶ *~ a louça* do the dishes *~ à mão* wash sth by hand *~ a roupa suja em público* wash your dirty linen in public *~ a seco* dry-clean

lavatório sm 1 sink, washbasin (*GB*) 2 (*banheiro*) bathroom, toilet (*GB*)

lavoura sf farm work

lavrador/a sm-sf 1 (*proprietário*) small farmer 2 (*empregado*) farm laborer

lavrar vt plow

laxante adj, sm laxative

lazer sm leisure: *uma viagem de ~ a pleasure trip*

leal adj 1 (*pessoa*) loyal (to sb/sth) 2 (*animal*) faithful (to sb)

lealdade sf loyalty (to sb/sth)

leão/oa sm-sf lion [fem lioness] ● **Leão** sm (*Astrol*) Leo [pl ~s] ▶ **leão-de-chácara** bouncer

lebre sf hare

lecionar vi, vt teach

legal adj **1** (Jur) legal **2** (ótimo) cool: Mas que ~! Cool!

legalizar vt legalize

legenda sf **1** (mapa) key **2** (imagem) caption **3** (legendas) (Cinema, TV) subtitles

legislação sf legislation

legislar vi legislate

legislativo adj: eleições legislativas general election

legítimo adj legitimate ▶ em **legítima defesa** in self-defense

legível adj legible

legume sm vegetable

lei sf **1** law: ir contra a ~ break the law **2** (parlamento) act

leigo adj: Sou ~ no assunto. I know very little about the subject.

leilão sm auction

leitão sm suckling pig

leite sm milk: ~ em pó powdered milk ▶ ~ de coco coconut milk ~ integral/desnatado/semidesnatado whole/skim/two percent milk, full-fat/skimmed/semi-skimmed milk (GB)

leiteiro/a adj dairy: uma vaca leiteira a dairy cow ● sm-sf milkman [pl -men]

leito sm bed

leitor/a sm-sf reader

leitura sf reading

lema sm **1** (Com, Pol) slogan **2** (conduta) motto [pl ~es]

lembrança sf **1** (presente) souvenir **2** (recordação) memory [pl -ies] **3** (idéia) idea **4** (lembranças) regards: dar/mandar ~ give/send sb your regards

lembrar vt **1** ~ algo a alguém remind sb (about sth/to do sth): Lembre-me de comprar pão. Remind me to buy some bread. **2** (por associação) remind sb of sb/sth: Ele me lembra o meu irmão. He reminds me of my brother. → REMIND **lembrar-se** vp (recordar-se) remember ((doing) sth/to do sth): Não me lembro do nome dele. I can't remember his name. ◊ que eu me lembre as far as I remember ◊ Lembro-me de tê-los visto. I remember seeing them. ◊ Lembre-se de pôr a carta no correio. Remember to mail the letter. → REMEMBER

leme sm **1** (objeto) rudder **2** (posição) helm: Quem ia ao ~? Who was at the helm?

lenço sm **1** (mão) handkerchief [pl ~s/-chieves] **2** (cabeça,

pescoço) scarf [pl scarves] ▶ ~ de papel tissue

lençol sm sheet

lenda sf legend

lenha sf firewood

lenhador/a sm-sf woodcutter

lentamente adv slowly

lente sf lens: ~s de contato contact lenses

lentilha sf lentil

lento adj slow

leopardo sm leopard

lepra sf leprosy

leproso/a sm-sf leper

leque sm **1** fan **2** (variedade) range: um amplo ~ de opções a wide range of options

ler vt, vi read: Leia a lista para mim. Read me the list. ◊ ~ em voz baixa read to yourself ▶ ~ a sorte tell sb's fortune ~ nas entrelinhas read between the lines ~ o pensamento read sb's mind ~ os lábios lip-read

lesão sf **1** injury [pl -ies]: lesões graves serious injuries **2** (fígado, rim, cérebro) damage [U] → FERIMENTO

lesar vt (enganar) con sb (out of sth)

lésbica sf lesbian

lesma sf **1** (bicho) slug **2** (pessoa) slowpoke, slowcoach (GB)

leste sm east (abrev E.): a/no ~ in the east ◊ na costa ~ on the east coast

letivo adj school: ano ~ school year

letra sf **1** (alfabeto) letter: ~ maiúscula capital letters **2** (escrita) handwriting: Não entendo a sua ~. I can't read your handwriting. **3** (canção) lyrics [pl] **4** (num cartaz, letreiro) lettering [U] **5** (Letras) (Educ) arts: Faculdade de Letras Arts Faculty ▶ ~ de imprensa block capitals [pl]

letreiro sm **1** (aviso) sign **2** (Cinema) subtitles [pl]

léu sm: andar ao ~ walk aimlessly

leucemia sf leukemia

levantamento sm survey: efetuar um ~ carry out a survey ▶ ~ de pesos weightlifting

levantar vt **1** raise: ~ o braço/o moral/a voz raise your arm/spirits/voice **2** (coisa pesada, tampa) lift sth up **3** (erguer) pick sb/sth up: Levantaram-no entre si. They picked him up between them. ● **levantar-se** vp **1** (ficar de pé) stand up **2** (da cama) get up ▶ ~ (a) âncora weigh anchor ~ pesos

(*Esporte*) do weight training

levantar-se com o pé esquerdo get out on the wrong side of bed ▸ **vôo** take off

levar *vt* **1** take: *Leve-o para a cozinha.* Take it to the kitchen. ◊ *Levarei uns dois dias para consertá-lo.* It'll take me a couple of days to fix it. ◊ *~ alguém para casa* take sb home ◊ *O ladrão levou o vídeo.* The thief took the VCR. **NOTA** Quando a pessoa que fala se oferece para levar algo a quem uma ouve, diz **bring**: *Eu levo para você na sexta.* I'll bring it to you on Friday. **2** (*carga*) carry **3** (*palmada, bofetada*) get: *Fique quieto ou você vai ~ uma palmada.* Be quiet or you'll get a spanking. **4** (*ter*) have: *Eu não levava dinheiro.* I didn't have any cash on me. **5** (*tomar emprestado*) borrow ● *vi* **1** (*conduzir*) lead to *sth* **2** (*levar uma bofetada*) get a slap ▸ **~ a mal** take offense at *sb/sth*: *Não me leve a mal.* Don't take offense. **~ consigo** (*dinheiro, documentos*) have *sth* on you **NOTA** Para outras expressões com **levar**, ver o substantivo, adjetivo, etc., p. ex. **levar bomba** em BOMBA.

leve *adj* **1** light: *comida/roupa ~* light food/clothing ◊ *ter sono ~* sleep lightly **2** (*que quase não se nota*) slight **3** (*ágil*) agile ▸ **de ~ 1** (*superficialmente*) superficially **2** (*levemente*) lightly

lhama *sf* llama

lhe *pron pess* **1** (*ele, ela, coisa*) him/her/it: *Vi o meu chefe mas não ~ chamei.* I saw my boss but didn't speak to him. ◊ *Comprei-lhe um vestido.* I bought her a dress. **2** (*você*) you: *Fiz-lhe uma pergunta.* I asked you a question.

lhes *pron pess* them: *Dei-lhes tudo.* I gave them everything.

libélula *sf* dragonfly [*pl* -ies]

liberado *adj* liberated

liberal *adj, smf* liberal

liberar *vt* free

liberdade *sf* freedom ▸ **~ condicional** parole ▸ **~ de expressão/ imprensa** freedom of speech/ the press ▸ **sob fiança** bail: *ser posto em ~* **sob fiança** be released on bail **pôr em ~** release

libertação *sf* **1** (*país*) liberation **2** (*presos*) release

libertar *vt* **1** (*país*) liberate **2** (*prisioneiro*) release

libra *sf* **1** (*dinheiro*) pound

(*abrev* £): *~s esterlinas* pounds sterling **2** (*peso*) pound (*abrev* **lb.**) → Ver pág. 224 **3** (**Libra**) (*Astrol*) Libra

lição *sf* lesson ▸ **dar uma ~ em alguém** teach sb a lesson

licença *sf* **1** (*autorização*) permission (*to do sth*): *pedir/dar ~* ask/give permission **2** (*documento*) license **3** (*férias*) leave: *Estou de ~.* I'm on leave. ◊ *pedir uma semana de ~* ask for a week off ◊ *~ médica* sick leave ▸ **com ~** excuse me

licenciado/a *sm-sf* graduate (*in sth*): *um ~ pela Universidade de Londres* a graduate of London University

licenciar-se *vp* graduate (*in sth*): *~ na Universidade de Oxford* graduate from the University of Oxford

licenciatura *sf* **1** (*diploma*) degree **2** (*curso*) undergraduate course

licor *sm* liqueur

lidar *vt* **~ com** deal with *sb/sth*

líder *smf* leader

liderança *sf* leadership

liderar *vt* lead

liga *sf* **1** league **2** (*para meias*) garter

ligação *sf* **1** link **2** (*ônibus, trens*) connection: *fazer ~ com algo* connect with *sth* **3** (*amorosa*) affair ▸ **cair/cortar a ~** (*telefone*) be cut off: *De repente caiu a ~.* Suddenly we got cut off. **~ a cobrar** collect call, reverse charge call (*GB*)

ligada *sf* call: *Dê uma ~ para mim.* Give me a call.

ligado *adj* **1** (*televisão, luz*) (switched) on **2** (*interessado*) into *sth*: *Ele é ~ em música rap.* He's into rap music.

ligamento *sm* ligament: *uma ruptura de ~* a torn ligament

ligar *vt* **1** (*televisão, luz*) turn *sth* on **2** (*aparelho na tomada*) plug *sth* in ● *vt, vi* **1** (*unir, relacionar*) connect (*sth*) (*to/with sth*): *~ a impressora ao computador* connect the printer to the computer **2** ~ (*para*) (a) (*telefonar*) call: *~ para a polícia* call the police (b) (*prestar atenção*) take notice of *sb/sth*: *Ela não ligou a mínima para mim.* She took no notice of me. (c) (*dar importância*) care (*about sth*): *Não ligo (para essas coisas).* I don't care (about such things).

ligeiramente *adv* slightly

ligeiro *adj* **1** (*que quase não se*

nota, pouco intenso) slight **2**
(*ágil*) lemon

lima¹ *sf* (*ferramenta*) file

lima² *sf* (*fruta*) lime

limão *sm* **1** (*verde*) lime **2**
(*amarelo*) lemon

limiar *sm* threshold: *no ~ de algo*
on the threshold of sth

limitação *sf* limitation

limitado *adj* limited

limitar *vt* limit ● **limitar-se** *vp*:
Limite-se a responder à pergunta. Just answer the question.

limite *sm* **1** limit: *o ~ de velocidade* the speed limit **2** (*Geog,
Pol*) boundary [*pl* -ies] → BORDER ▸ **passar dos ~s** (*pessoa*) go
too far **sem ~** unlimited

limo *sm* slime

limoeiro *sm* (*fruto amarelo*)
lemon tree **2** (*fruto verde*) lime
tree

limonada *sf* lemonade

limpador *sm* ▸ **– de pára-brisas**
windshield wiper, windscreen
wiper (*GB*)

limpar *vt* **1** clean: *~ os vidros*
clean the windows **2** (*passar
um pano*) wipe **3** (*roubar*) clean
sb/sth out: *Assaltaram a minha
casa e limparam tudo.* They
broke into my house and completely cleaned me out. ●
limpar-se *vp* clean yourself up

limpeza *sf* **1** (*ação de limpar*)
cleaning: *produtos de ~* cleaning products **2** (*asseio*) cleanliness ▸ **– de pele** facial

limpo *adj* **1** clean **2** *um céu ~ a*
clear sky **3** (*sem dinheiro*) broke
● *adv* fair: *jogar ~* play fair ▸
tirar a ~ (*esclarecer*) get to the
bottom of *sth*

lince *sm* lynx

linchar *vt* lynch

lindo *adj* beautiful

língua *sf* **1** (*Anat*) tongue:
mostrar a ~ para alguém stick
your tongue out at sb ◊ *perder a
~* lose your tongue **2** (*idioma*)
language: *Sou formado em ~
Inglesa.* I have a degree in English.▸ **dar com a ~ nos dentes** let
the cat out of the bag **de ~
inglesa, francesa, etc.** Englishspeaking, French-speaking,
etc. **~ materna** mother tongue

linguado *sm* sole [*pl* sole]

linguagem *sf* **1** language **2**
(*falada*) speech

linguarudo/a *sm-sf* gossip

lingüiça *sf* sausage

lingüística *sf* linguistics [*sing*]

linha *sf* **1** line: *uma ~ reta* a

straight line ◊ *~ divisória/de
chegada* dividing/finishing line
2 (*fio*) (piece of) thread **3**
(*estrada de ferro*) track: *a ~ do
trem* the train track ▸ **– aérea**
airline

linho *sm* **1** (*Bot*) flax **2** (*tecido*)
linen

liquidação *sf* **1** (*dívida, conta*)
settlement **2** (*saldo*) sale: *a ~ de
verão* the summer sales

liquidar *vt* **1** (*dívida, conta*) settle
2 (*negócio*) liquidate **3** (*produto*) clear **4** (*matar*) kill

liquidificador *sm* blender,
liquidizer (*GB*)

líquido *adj* **1** liquid **2** (*Econ*) net:
peso/rendimento ~ net weight/
income ● *sm* liquid

lírio *sm* lily [*pl* -ies]

liso *adj* **1** (*plano*) flat **2** (*suave*)
smooth **3** (*sem adornos, de uma
só cor*) plain **4** (*cabelo*) straight
5 (*sem dinheiro*) broke

lisonjear *vt* flatter

lisonjeiro *adj* flattering

lista *sf* **1** list: *~ de compras/
espera* shopping/waiting list **2**
(*telefônica*) phone book **3** (*de
nomes*) roll: *~ eleitoral* electoral
roll

listra *sf* stripe

listrado *adj* striped

literário *adj* literary

literatura *sf* literature

litoral *sm* coastline

litro *sm* liter (*abrev* l): *meio ~* half
a liter

livrar *vt* save *sb/sth* from (*doing*)
sth ● **livrar-se** *vp* **1** (*escapar*) get
out of (*doing*) *sth* **2** (*desembaraçar-se*) get rid of *sb/sth*

livraria *sf* bookstore

livre *adj* free: *Esta cadeira está
~?* Is this seat free? ◊ *Você está
~ amanhã?* Are you free tomorrow? ◊ *~ arbítrio/iniciativa*
free will/enterprise ▸ **~ de
impostos** tax-free

livreiro/a *sm-sf* bookseller

livro *sm* book ▸ **– de bolso** paperback **– didático** textbook

lixa *sf* **1** sandpaper **2** (*unhas*)
emery board

lixar *vt* (*madeira*) sand ● **lixar-se**
vp not care: *Levei bomba, mas
estou pouco me lixando.* I failed
my exams, but I couldn't care
less.

lixeira *sf* garbage can, dustbin
(*GB*)

lixeiro *sm* garbage man, dustman (*GB*)

lixo *sm* garbage, rubbish (*GB*)

[U]: *lata de* ~ garbage can ◇ *jogar algo no* ~ throw sth away

lobo/a *sm-sf* wolf [*pl* wolves]

locadora *sf* rental company [*pl* ~ies] ► ~ **de vídeo** video store

local *adj* local ● *sm* **1** place **2** (*acidente, crime*) scene **3** (*concerto, jogo*) venue **4** (*de interesse histórico, para construção*) site **5** (*instalações*) premises [*pl*]: *O* ~ *é bastante grande.* The premises are pretty big. ► ~ **de nascimento 1** birthplace **2** (*em impressos*) place of birth

localidade *sf* **1** locality [*pl* -ies] **2** (*aldeia*) village **3** (*cidade pequena*) town

localizar *vt* **1** (*encontrar*) locate **2** (*contatar*) get hold of sb

loção *sf* lotion

locutor/a *sm-sf* **1** (*rádio*) announcer **2** (*de noticias*) newscaster, newsreader (*GB*)

lodo *sm* mud

lógico/a *adj* **1** (*normal*) natural: *É* ~ *que você se preocupe.* It's only natural that you're worried. **2** (*Fil*) logical

logo *adv* (*imediatamente*) at once ● *conj* therefore: *Penso,* ~ *existo.* I think therefore I am. ● *até* ~ bye   ~ **depois** soon afterward   ~ **mais** later   ~ **que** as soon as

loja *sf* store, shop (*GB*): ~ *de produtos naturais* health food store ► ~ **de departamentos** department store

lojista *smf* storekeeper, shopkeeper (*GB*)

lombada *sf* **1** (*livro*) spine **2** (*estrada*) ramp

lombo *sm* **1** (*Cozinha*) loin **2** (*Anat*) back

lona *sf* canvas ► **estar na** ~ (*sem dinheiro*) be broke

longa-metragem *sm* feature film

longe *adv* a long way (away) (*from sb/sth*): *Fica muito* ~ *daqui.* It's a long way (away) from here. ► **ao** ~ in the distance   **de** ~ **1** (*distância*) from a distance **2** (*enfático*) by far: *Ela é de* ~ *a melhor.* She's by far the best.   **ir** ~ go far: *Essa menina vai* ~. That girl will go far.   **ir** ~ **demais** go too far ~ **disso** far from it

longitude *sf* longitude

longo *adj* long ► **ao** ~ **de 1** (*espaço*) along... **2** (*tempo*) throughout...

losango *sm* rhombus

lotado *adj* packed

lotar *vt* fill *sth* up

lote *sm* **1** portion **2** (*Com*) batch **3** (*terreno*) plot

loteria *sf* lottery [*pl* -ies]

louça *sf* china

louco/a *adj* crazy, mad (*GB*): *ficar* ~ go crazy ◇ *ser* ~ *por algo* be crazy about sth ● *sm-sf* madman/woman [*pl* -men/-women] ► **estar** ~ **de fome** be starving   **estar** ~ **para fazer algo** be dying to do something   ~ **de pedra** completely nuts

loucura *sf* **1** madness **2** (*disparate*) crazy thing: *É uma* ~ *ir sozinho.* It's crazy to go alone.

louro¹ *sm* **1** (*Cozinha*) bay leaf [*pl* leaves] **2** (*papagaio*) parrot

louro² *adj* fair, blond(e) NOTA Fair é apenas o cabelo louro natural, **blond** é tanto o natural como o pintado: *Ele é* ~. He has fair/blond hair. → BLOND

louvar *vt* praise *sb/sth* (*for sth*)

louvável *adj* praiseworthy

louvor *sm* praise

lua *sf* moon: ~ *cheia/nova* full/new moon ► **estar na** ~/**no mundo da** ~ be miles away

lua-de-mel *sf* honeymoon

luar *sm* moonlight: *ao* ~ in the moonlight

lubrificante *sm* lubricant

lubrificar *vt* lubricate

lúcido *adj* lucid

lucrar *vt* profit (*from sth*)

lucrativo *adj* lucrative

lucro *sm* profit: *dar/ter* ~ make a profit

lugar *sm* **1** place **2** (*posto*) position: *ocupar um* ~ *importante na empresa* have an important position in the firm **3** (*Cinema, Teat, veículo*) seat **4** (*povoação*) village ► **dar** ~ **a algo** cause sth   **em** ~ **nenhum** nowhere, anywhere NOTA Usa-se **nowhere** com o verbo na afirmativa: *Desse modo não iremos a* ~ *nenhum.* At this rate we'll get nowhere. Usa-se **anywhere** com o verbo na negativa: *Não o encontro em nenhuma parte.* I can't find it anywhere. **em primeiro/segundo, etc.** ~ **1** (*posição*) *Em primeiro* ~ *está o espanhol.* The Spaniard is in first place. ◇ *A equipe francesa ficou classificada em último* ~. The French team came last. **2** (*em discurso*) first of all, secondly, etc.: *Em último* ~... Last of all...   ~ **de nascimento** birthplace   **não há** ~ **para dúvida** there's no doubt   **no seu** ~ If I were you   **ter** ~ (*ocorrer*) take place **tomar o ~ de alguém/ algo** (*substituir*) replace sb/sth

lugar-comum *sm* cliché

lúgubre *adj* gloomy

lula *sf* squid [*pl* squid]

luminária *sf* **1** lamp **2** (*de papel*) paper lantern **3** (**luminárias**) (*iluminação de festa*) lights

lunar *adj* lunar

lunático/a *adj, sm-sf* lunatic

lupa *sf* magnifying glass

lustrar *vt* polish

lustre *sm* **1** (*brilho*) shine **2** (*luminária*) chandelier

luta *sf* fight ▸ **~ de boxe** boxing match **~ livre** wrestling

lutador/a *sm-sf* **1** fighter: *Ele é um ~.* He's a real fighter. **2** (*esportista*) wrestler

lutar *vi* **1** fight: *~ pela liberdade/ contra a pobreza* fight for freedom/fight poverty **2** (*Esporte*) wrestle

luto *sm* mourning ▸ **estar de ~** be in mourning (*for sb/sth*)

luva *sf* **1** glove **2** (*com um só dedo*) mitten ▸ **cair como uma ~** fit like a glove

luxo *sm* luxury [*pl* -ies] ▸ **de ~** luxury: *artigos de ~* luxury goods

luxuoso *adj* luxurious

luxúria *sf* lust

luz *sf* **1** light: *acender/apagar a ~* turn the light on/off ◇ *Esta sala tem muita ~.* This room gets a lot of light. **2** (*eletricidade*) electricity: *Ficamos sem ~ durante a tempestade.* The electricity went off during the storm. **3** (*dia*) daylight ▸ **~ apanhar ~** (*rolo fotográfico*) be exposed **dar à ~** give birth (*to sb*) **~ de vela/ do sol** candlelight/sunlight **trazer à ~** bring sth (out) into the open **vir à ~** (*segredo*) come to light

M m

maca *sf* (*Med*) stretcher

maçã *sf* apple ▸ **~ do rosto** cheekbone

macabro *adj* macabre

macacão *sm* **1** (*roupa informal*) jumpsuit **2** (*para trabalho*) coveralls, overalls (*GB*) [*pl*] **3** (*jardineira*) overalls, dungarees (*GB*) [*pl*]

macaco/a *sm-sf* (*animal*) monkey ● *sm* (*carro*) jack

maçaneta *sf* **1** (*porta*) doorknob **2** (*gaveta*) knob

macarrão *sm* macaroni

machado *sm* ax

machismo *sm* machismo

machista *adj, smf* sexist

macho *adj, sm* **1** male: *É ~ ou fêmea? Is it a he or a she?* → FEMALE **2** (*varonil*) macho: *Esse cara é ~.* He's a very macho guy. ● *sm* (*Elet*) plug

machucar *vt* hurt

maciço *adj* **1** (*objeto*) solid **2** (*quantidade*) massive: *uma dose maciça* a massive dose

macieira *sf* apple tree

macio *adj* **1** (*tenro*) tender: *carne macia* tender meat **2** (*suave*) soft: *um colchão ~* a soft mattress

maço *sm* **1** (*tabaco*) pack, packet (*GB*) **2** (*folhas, notas*) bundle

maconha *sf* dope

macrobiótico *adj* macrobiotic

macumba *sf* voodoo: *fazer ~* practice voodoo

madeira *sf* **1** (*material*) wood: *uma ~ de grande qualidade* a high-quality wood ◇ *feito de ~* made of wood **2** (*para construção*) timber: *a ~ do telhado* the roof timbers ▸ **de ~** wooden: *uma viga de ~* a wooden beam

madeixa *sf* (*cabelo*) lock

madrasta *sf* stepmother

madre *sf* ▸ **~ (superiora)** Mother Superior

madrepérola *sf* mother-of-pearl

madrinha *sf* **1** (*batismo*) godmother **2** (*casamento*) woman who acts as a witness at a wedding → CASAMENTO

madrugada *sf*: *às duas da ~* at two in the morning ◇ *na ~ de sexta para sábado* in the early hours of Saturday morning ▸ **de ~** early: *levantar-se de ~* get up early

madrugar *vi* get up early

maduro *adj* **1** (*fruta*) ripe **2** (*de meia-idade*) middle-aged **3** (*sensato*) mature

mãe *sf* mother: *ser ~ de dois filhos* be the mother of two children ◇ *~ solteira/de criação* single/foster mother

maestro *sm* conductor

máfia *sf* mafia: *a ~ da droga* the drugs mafia ◇ *a Máfia* the Mafia

magia *sf* magic: *~ negra* black magic

mágico/a *adj* magic: *poderes ~s* magic powers ● *sm-sf* (*ilusionista*) magician

magistério sm **1** (ensino) teaching: ingressar no ~ start teaching **2** (professores) teachers

magistrado/a sm-sf magistrate

magnata smf tycoon

magnético adj magnetic

magnetismo sm magnetism

magnífico adj wonderful

mago adj magician

mágoa sf (pesar) sorrow

magoar vt hurt: ficar muito magoado com algo be very hurt by sth

magro adj thin, slim NOTA **Thin** é o termo mais geral para magro, usado para pessoas, animais e coisas. **Slim** é só a pessoa magra e com boa aparência. Existe também **skinny**, que significa magricela.

maio sm May NOTA Diz-se "May twelfth" ou "the twelfth of May".

maiô sm swimming suit

maionese sf mayonnaise

maior adj

- **uso comparativo 1** (tamanho) bigger (than sth): ~ do que parece bigger than it looks **2** (importância) greater (than sth)
- **uso superlativo 1** (tamanho) biggest: o ~ dos três the biggest of the three ◊ o ~ dos dois the bigger (one) of the two **2** (importância) greatest: um dos ~es escritores atuais one of today's greatest writers
- **outros usos** (Mús) major: em dó ~ in C major ▸ **a ~ parte (de)** most (of sb/sth): A ~ parte dos católicos. Most of them are Catholics. ~ **de idade** 18 or over: Ela não é ~ de idade. She's under 18.

maioria sf majority [pl -ies]: obter a ~ absoluta get an absolute majority ▸ **a ~ de...** most (of...): a ~ de nós most of us ◊ a ~ dos ingleses most English people → MOST

maioridade sf adulthood

mais adv

- **comparativo** more (than sb/sth): Ela é ~ alta/inteligente do que eu. She's taller/more intelligent than me. ◊ Você viajou ~ do que eu. You've traveled more than I have. ◊ ~ de dois anos more than two years ◊ Gosto ~ do seu. I like yours better. ◊ durar/trabalhar ~ last longer/work harder ◊ São ~ de duas horas It's after two.
- **superlativo** most (in/of...): o edifício ~ antigo da cidade the oldest building in town ◊ o ~

simpático de todos the nicest one of all ◊ a loja que vendeu ~ livros the store that has sold most books NOTA Quando o superlativo se refere a apenas duas coisas ou pessoas, usa-se **more** ou a forma **-er**. Compare: (Dos dois meninos,) quem é o ~ alto? Which boy is taller? ◊ Quem é o menino mais ~ da turma? Who is the tallest child in the class?

- **com pronomes negativos, interrogativos e indefinidos** else: Se você tem ~ alguma coisa para dizer... If you have anything else to say... ◊ ~ alguém? Anyone else? ◊ ~ nada/ninguém nothing more/nobody else ◊ Que ~ posso fazer? What else can I do?
- **outras construções 1** (exclamações): Que cara ~ chato! What a boring guy! **2** (negativas) only: Não sabemos ~ do que aquilo que disseram no rádio. We only know what was reported on the radio. ● sm, prep plus: Dois ~ dois são quatro. Two plus two is four. ▸ **a ~** too much, too many: Você pagou três dólares a ~. You paid three dollars too much. ◊ Há duas cadeiras a ~. There are two chairs too many. ~ **ou menos:** — Que tal vão as coisas? — ~ ou menos. "How are things?" "So-so." ◊ O negócio vai ~ ou menos. Business isn't going too well. ◊ Isto está ~ ou menos acabado. This is more or less finished. ~ **que** nada particularly **por ~ que** however much: Por ~ que você grite... However much you shout... **sem ~ nem menos 1** (sem pensar) just like that: Você decidiu assim, sem ~ nem menos? So you made your mind up, just like that? **2** (sem avisar) out of the blue: Bem, se você lhe disser assim sem ~ nem menos... Well, if you tell him out of the blue like that... NOTA Para outras expressões com **mais**, ver o adjetivo, advérbio, etc., p. ex. **mais além** em ALÉM.

maisena® sf cornstarch, cornflour (GB)

maiúscula sf capital letter: em ~s in capitals

Majestade sf Majesty [pl -ies]: Sua/Vossa ~ His/Your Majesty

major sm major

mal¹ adv **1** badly: comportar-se ~ behave badly ◊ um trabalho ~ pago a poorly/badly paid job ◊ Ouço muito ~. My hearing is

M

very bad. **2** (*qualidade, aspecto*) bad: *Este casaco não fica ~.* This jacket's not bad. **3** (*erradamente, moralmente*) wrong: *Fica ~ você responder à sua mãe.* It's wrong to talk back to your mother. ◊ *responder ~ a uma pergunta* give the wrong answer **4** (*quase não*) hardly: *~ falaram.* They hardly spoke. **5** (*quase nunca*) hardly ever **6** (*pouco mais de*): *~ faz um ano.* It's scarcely a year ago. ▸ **andar/ estar ~ de** (*dinheiro*) be short of *sth* **estar ~** (*saúde*) be/feel sick

mal² *sm* **1** (*dano*) harm: *Ele não fez por ~.* He didn't mean any harm. ◊ *Que ~ eu lhe fiz?* What have I done to upset you? **2** (*Fil*) evil: *o bem e o ~* good and evil **3** (*doença*) disease: *um ~ incurável* an incurable disease **4** (*problema*): *A venda da casa nos salvou de ~es maiores.* The sale of the house saved us from having further problems. ▸ **não há ~ que não venha para bem** every cloud has a silver lining

mal³ *conj* as soon as: *~ eles chegaram, ela saiu.* She left as soon as they arrived.

mala *sf* **1** (*viagem*) (suit)case **2** (*carro*) trunk, boot (*GB*) ▸ **fazer/ desfazer a(s) ~(s)** pack/unpack

mal-agradecido *adj* ungrateful

malagueta *sf* chili [*pl ~es*]

malandro/a *adj* **1** (*preguiçoso*) lazy **2** (*patife*) double-dealing **3** (*astuto*) wily ● *sm-sf* **1** (*preguiçoso*) layabout **2** (*patife*) hustler

malcriado *adj* rude

maldade *sf* wickedness [*U*]: *Foi uma ~ da sua parte.* That was a wicked thing you did.

maldição *sf* curse

maldito *adj* damned: *Estes ~s sapatos me apertam!* These wretched shoes are too tight for me! ● *interj* damn

maldizer *vt* curse

maldoso *adj* **1** (*malicioso*): *Que comentário ~!* What a nasty remark! **2** (*mau*) wicked: *um homem ~* a wicked man

mal-educado *adj* **1** rude: *Que crianças mal-educadas!* What rude children! **2** (*ao falar*) foul-mouthed

mal-entendido *sm* misunderstanding

mal-estar *sm* **1** (*indisposição*): *Sinto um ~ geral.* I don't feel too good. **2** (*inquietação*) unease

malha *sf* **1** (*rede*) mesh **2** (*tricô*)

knitting [*U*] **3** (*roupa de malha*) knitwear [*U*]: *um vestido de ~* a knitted dress **4** (*balé, ginástica*) leotard **5** (*casaco*) sweater

malhado *adj* (*animal*) spotted

mal-humorado *adj* ▸ **estar ~** be in a bad mood **ser ~** be bad-tempered

malícia *sf* malice

malicioso *adj* malicious

maligno *adj* (*Med*) malignant

má-língua *sf* gossip: *As ~s dizem que...* Gossip has it that...

mal-intencionado *adj* malicious

mal-passado *adj* (*bife*) rare

maltratar *vt* mistreat: *Maltrataram-nos física e verbalmente.* We were subjected to physical and verbal abuse.

maluco/a *adj* crazy, mad (*GB*) (*about sb/sth*) ● *sm-sf* madman/ madwoman [*pl* -men/ -women]

maluquice *sf* **1** (*loucura*) madness **2** (*idéia*) crazy idea **3** (*disparate*) crazy thing

malvado *adj* wicked

malvisto *adj*: *ser ~* be frowned upon

mama *sf* breast: *câncer de ~* breast cancer

mamadeira *sf* bottle

mamãe *sf* mom, mum (*GB*) → As crianças pequenas dizem **mommy, mummy** (*GB*).

mamão *sm* papaya

mamar *vi* nurse, feed (*GB*) ▸ **dar de ~** nurse, breastfeed (*GB*)

mamífero *sm* mammal

mamilo *sm* nipple

manada *sf* **1** herd: *uma ~ de cervos* a herd of deer **2** (*gente*) crowd

mancar *vi* limp

mancha *sf* **1** (*sujeira*) stain: *uma ~ de gordura* a grease stain **2** (*pele*) spot ▸ **de óleo** oil slick

manchado *adj* (*sujo*) stained (*with sth*): *~ de sangue/tinta* bloodstained/ink-stained

manchar *vt* (*sujar*) get *sth* dirty ● *vi* stain

manchete *sf* (*jornal*) headline

manco *adj* lame

manda-chuva *smf* big shot

mandado *sm* (*Jur*) warrant: *um ~ de busca* a search warrant

mandamento *sm* (*Relig*) commandment

mandão/ona *adj*, *sm-sf* bossy: *Você é um ~.* You're very bossy.

mandar *vt* **1** (*ordenar*) tell *sb* to do *sth* **2** (*enviar*) send: *Mandei uma carta para você.* I sent you

mandíbula **132**

a letter. **3** (*levar*) have sth done: *Vou ~ limpá-lo*. I'm going to have it cleaned. ● *vi* **1** (*governo*) be in power **2** (*ser o chefe*) be the boss (*coloq*), be in charge: *gostar de ~ nos outros* like to boss people around ▶ **~ alguém passear** tell sb to get lost **~ embora** (*demitir*) fire sb

mandíbula *sf* jaw

maneira *sf* **1** (*modo*) way (of doing sth): *a ~ dela de falar/vestir* her way of speaking/dressing ◊ *Desta ~ é mais fácil.* It's easier this way. **2** (*maneiras*) manners: *boas ~s* good manners ▶ **à minha, etc. ~** my, your, etc. way **de ~ que** (*portanto*) so **de todas as ~s** anyway **~ de ser**: *É a minha ~ de ser.* It's just the way I am. **não haver ~ de**: *Não havia ~ de o carro pegar.* It was impossible to start the car. **que ~ de...**: *Que ~ de dirigir!* What a way to drive!

maneiro *adj* cool (*coloq*)

manejar *vt* **1** handle: *~ uma arma* handle a weapon **2** (*máquina*) operate

manequim *sm* (*vitrina*) mannequin ● *smf* (*pessoa*) model

maneta *adj* **1** (*sem um braço*) one-armed **2** (*sem uma mão*) one-handed

manga¹ *sf* sleeve: *uma camisa de ~ comprida/curta* a long-sleeved/short-sleeved shirt ◊ *em ~s de camisa* in shirtsleeves ▶ **sem ~s** sleeveless

manga² *sf* (*fruta*) mango [*pl* ~es]

mangueira *sf* **1** (*água*) hose **2** (*árvore*) mango tree

manha *sf* **1** (*esperteza, astúcia*) cunning [*U*]: *ter muita ~* be very cunning **2** (*fingimento*) act: *fazer ~* put on an act ◊ *Isso é ~, eu mal toquei nele.* That's (all) an act, I hardly touched him.

manhã *sf* morning: *na ~ seguinte* the following morning ◊ *à uma da ~* at one o'clock in the morning ◊ *O exame é segunda de ~.* The exam is on Monday morning. ◊ *amanhã de ~* tomorrow morning → MORNING

mania *sf* quirk: *Todos nós temos as nossas pequenas ~s.* We all have our little quirks. ◊ *Isso está virando uma ~ sua!* You're getting obsessed about it! ▶ **ter a ~ de fazer algo** have the strange habit of doing sth

maníaco *adj* (*obcecado*) obsessive

manicure *sf* manicure

manifestação *sf* **1** (*protesto*)

demonstration **2** (*expressão*) expression: *uma ~ de apoio* an expression of support

manifestante *smf* demonstrator

manifestar *vt* **1** (*opinião*) express **2** (*mostrar*) show ● **manifestar-se** *vp* demonstrate

manifesto *adj* clear ● *sm* manifesto [*pl* ~s]

manipular *vt* **1** manipulate: *Não se deixe ~.* Don't let yourself be manipulated. **2** (*eleições*) rig

manivela *sf* handle

manjar *sm* delicacy [*pl* -ies]

manobra *sf* maneuver

manobrar *vi* maneuver

mansão *sf* mansion

manso *adj* **1** (*animal*) tame **2** (*pessoa*) meek

manta *sf* blanket

manteiga *sf* butter

manter *vt* **1** (*conservar*) keep: *~ uma promessa* keep a promise ◊ *~ algo vivo* keep sth alive **2** (*economicamente*) support **3** (*afirmar*) maintain ● **manter-se** *vp* (*situação, problema*) remain ▶ **~ a linha/manter-se em forma** keep in shape **~ as aparências** keep up appearances **manter-se firme/em pé** stand firm/remain standing

mantimento *sm* **1** (*manutenção*) maintenance **2** (*mantimentos*) provisions

manual *adj* ● *sm* **1** manual: *~ de instruções* handbook **2** (*Educ*) textbook

manufaturar *vt* manufacture

manuscrito *sm* manuscript

manusear *vt* handle

manutenção *sf* maintenance

mão *sf* **1** hand: *Dê-me a ~.* Hold my hand. ◊ *em boas ~s* in good hands **2** (*pintura*) coat **3** (*animal*) paw ▶ **à ~ 1** (*perto*) at hand: *Você tem o número à ~?* Do you have the number at hand? ◊ *estar à ~* be close by **2** (*manualmente*) by hand: *Deve ser lavado à ~.* It needs to be washed by hand. ◊ *feito à ~* handmade ▶ **à ~ armada** armed: *um assalto à ~ armada* an armed robbery **dar uma ~** give sb a hand **de ~ dadas** hand in hand (with sb) **em ~s**: *Entregue-o em ~s.* Give it to him in person. **fora de ~** out of the way: *Fica fora de ~ para nós.* It's out of our way. **~ de ferro** firm hand **~s ao alto** hands up

mão-aberta *smf* generous person

mão-de-obra *sf* labor

mapa *sm* map: *Está no ~.* It's on the map.

mapa-múndi *sm* world map

maquete *sf* model

maquiador/a *sm-sf* make-up artist

maquiagem *sf* make-up [U]

maquiar *vt* make *sb* up ▶ **maquiar-se** *vp* put on your make-up

máquina *sf* **1** machine: *~ de costura/café* sewing machine/coffee maker **2** (*trem*) engine ▶ **escrever/bater à ~** type **~ de escrever** typewriter **~ de lavar/secar** washing machine/dryer **~ de lavar louça** dishwasher **~ de vender** vending machine **~ fotográfica** camera

maquinaria *sf* machinery

maquinista *smf* engineer, train driver (*GB*)

mar *sm* ocean, sea: *por ~* by sea ◇ *~ adentro* out to sea ▶ **fazer-se ao ~** put out to sea

maracujá *sm* passion fruit

maratona *sf* marathon

maravilha *sf* wonder ▶ **cheirar/ter um sabor que é uma ~** smell/taste wonderful **fazer ~s** work wonders **que ~** how wonderful

maravilhoso *adj* wonderful

marca *sf* **1** (*sinal*) mark **2** (*produtos de limpeza, alimentos, roupa, cigarro*) brand **3** (*carros, motos, eletrodomésticos, computador*) make: *De que ~ é o seu carro?* What make is your car? ▶ **de ~:** *produtos de ~* branded goods **~ registrada** (registered) trademark

marcador *sm* (*Esporte, painel*) scoreboard

marcar *vt* **1** mark: *~ o chão com giz* mark the ground with chalk **2** (*data*) fix **3** (*gado*) brand **4** (*indicar*) say: *O relógio marcava cinco horas.* The clock said five o'clock. **5** (*Esporte*): *~ um gol* score a goal ● *vi* **1** (*Esporte*) score: *~ para o próprio time* score an own goal **2** (*encontrar-se*) meet ▶ **~ encontro (com)** arrange to meet *sb* **~ hora/uma consulta** make an appointment **~ o compasso/ritmo** beat time

marcha *sf* **1** (*bicicleta, carro*) gear: *trocar de ~* shift gear ◇ *um carro com cinco ~s* a car with a five-speed transmission **2** (*Mil, Mús, protesto*) march **3** (*Esporte*) walk ▶ **dar ~ à ré** reverse

marcial *adj* martial

marco¹ *sm* (*estrada*) landmark

marco² *sm* (*moeda*) mark

março *sm* March (*abrev* **Mar.**) → MAIO

maré *sf* **1** tide: *~ alta/baixa* high/low tide ◇ *Subiu/Baixou a ~.* The tide came in/went out. **2** (*série*) run: *uma ~ de sorte* a run of good luck ◇ *uma ~ de desgraças* a series of misfortunes

marfim *sm* ivory

margarida *sf* daisy [*pl* -ies]

margarina *sf* margarine

margem *sf* **1** (*rio, canal*) bank **2** (*numa página*) margin **3** (*oportunidade*) room (*for sth*): *~ para dúvida* room for doubt ▶ **à ~:** *viver à ~ da sociedade* live on the fringes of society ◇ *Eles o deixam à ~ de tudo.* They leave him out of everything.

marginal *smf* (*pessoa*) delinquent ● *sf* (*estrada*) coast road

marginalizado/a *adj* **1** (*pessoa*) marginalized **2** (*zona*) deprived ● *sm-sf* outcast

maricas *sm* fag, poof (*GB*) → Ambas as palavras são consideradas ofensivas. A mais comum é *gay*.

marido *sm* husband

marinha *sf* navy [*pl* -ies] ▶ **a ~ Mercante** the Merchant Marine, the Merchant Navy (*GB*)

marinheiro *sm* sailor

marinho *adj* **1** marine: *vida/poluição marinha* marine life/pollution **2** sea: *ave marinha/sal* ~ seabird/sea salt

marionete *sf* puppet: *teatro de ~s* puppet show

mariposa *sf* moth

marisco *sm* shellfish [U]

marítimo *adj* **1** (*povoação, zona*) coastal **2** (*porto, rota*) sea: *porto ~* seaport

marketing *sm* marketing

marmelada *sf* quince jelly

mármore *sm* marble

marquês/esa *sm-sf* marquis [*fem* marchioness]

marquise *sf* awning

marrom *adj*, *sm* brown

marta *sf* mink

Marte *sm* Mars

martelar *vt*, *vi* **1** hammer *sth* (*in*): *~ um prego* hammer a nail in **2** (*insistir*): *Martelei tanto a canção, que eles acabaram aprendendo.* I went over and over the song with them until they learned it. **3** (*piano*) bang away on *the piano*

martelo *sm* hammer

mártir smf martyr

marxismo sm marxism

marzipã sm marzipan

mas conj but: *devagar ~ com segurança* slowly but surely

mascar vt, vi chew

máscara sf mask

mascarar vt mask

mascote sf mascot

masculino adj **1** male: *a população masculina* the male population **2** (Esporte, moda) men's: *a prova masculina dos 100 metros* the men's 100 meters **3** (característico do homem, Gram) masculine → MALE

massa sf **1** mass: *~ atômica* atomic mass ◊ *uma ~ de gente* a mass of people ◊ *cultura de ~* mass culture **2** (macarrão) pasta **3** (para torta, empada) pastry: *~ folhada* puff pastry **4** (para pão) dough

massacrar vt **1** (chacinar) massacre **2** (estafar) exhaust

massacre sm massacre

massagear vt massage

massagem sf massage: *Você me faz uma ~ nas costas?* Can you massage my back for me?

massagista smf masseur [fem masseuse]

mastigar vt, vi chew

mastro sm **1** (barco) mast **2** (bandeira) flagpole

masturbar-se vp masturbate

mata sf forest

matado adj (malfeito) badly done

matadouro sm slaughterhouse

matança sf slaughter

matar vt kill: *~ o tempo* kill time ▶ **~ a fome:** *Compramos frutas para ~ a fome.* We bought some fruit to keep us going. *~ a tiro* shoot *sb* dead *~ aula* skip class *~ de desgosto* make *sb's* life a misery *~ dois coelhos de uma cajadada* kill two birds with one stone *~ as saudades: para ~ as saudades* for old time's sake ◊ *~ as saudades dos amigos* meet up with your old friends *matar-se de fazer algo* wear yourself out doing *sth*

mate sm (xadrez) mate

matemática sf math, maths (GB), mathematics (fml)

matemático/a adj mathematical ● sm-sf mathematician

matéria sf **1** matter: *~ orgânica* organic matter **2** (disciplina, tema) subject **3** (de estudo) syllabus

material adj material ● sm **1**

(matéria, dados) material: *um ~ resistente ao fogo* fire-resistant material ◊ *Tenho todo o ~ de que necessito para o artigo.* I have all the material I need for the article. **2** (equipamento) equipment [U]: *~ esportivo/de laboratório* sports/lab equipment ▶ *~ didático/educativo* teaching materials [pl]

materialista adj materialistic ● smf materialist

matéria-prima sf raw material

maternal adj motherly, maternal (mais fml)

maternidade sf **1** (condição) motherhood, maternity (mais fml) **2** (hospital) maternity hospital

materno adj **1** (maternal) motherly **2** (parentesco) maternal: *avô ~* maternal grandfather

matilha sf (cães) pack

matinal adj morning: *um vôo ~* a morning flight

matiz sm **1** (cor) shade **2** (nuança) nuance: *~es de significado* nuances of meaning ◊ *um ~ irônico* a touch of irony

mato sm scrubland

matraca sf (tagarela) chatterbox

matrícula sf (inscrição) registration: *Já começaram as ~s.* Registration has begun.

matricular(-se) vt, vp enroll (sb) (in sth)

matrimônio sm marriage → CASAMENTO

matriz sf **1** (fotografia, cópia) original **2** (Mat) matrix [pl matrices]

maturidade sf maturity

matutino adj morning ● sm (jornal) morning paper

mau adj **1** bad: *uma pessoa má* a bad person *~s modos/tempo* bad manners/weather **2** (inadequado) poor: *má alimentação/visibilidade* poor food/visibility ◊ *o ~ estado do terreno* the poor condition of the ground **3** (travesso) naughty **4** em/para (ignorante) bad at (doing) sth: *Sou muito ~ em matemática.* I'm really bad at math.

mau-caráter sm bad guy

maus-tratos sm ill-treatment: *~ contra crianças* ill-treatment of children

maxilar sm jaw

máxima sf **1** (ditado) maxim **2** (temperatura) maximum temperature: *O Rio registrou a ~ de*

37°C. Rio was the hottest place with a temperature of 99°F.

máximo adj, sm maximum: *Temos um prazo ~ de sete dias para pagar.* We have a maximum of seven days in which to pay. ◇ *um ~ de dez pessoas* a maximum of ten people ▸ **ao ~:** *aproveitar os recursos ao ~* make the most of your resources ◇ *Esforcei-me ao ~.* I tried my very best. **no ~** at most

me pron pess **1** (complemento) me: *Você não me viu?* Didn't you see me? ◇ *Dê-me isso.* Give it to me. **2** (reflexivo) (myself): *Eu me vi no espelho.* I saw myself in the mirror. ◇ *Vesti-me.* I got dressed.

meados sm ▸ **em/nos ~ de...** in the middle of...

mecânica sf mechanics [sing]

mecânico/a adj mechanical ● sm-sf mechanic

mecanismo sm mechanism

mecha sf **1** (vela) wick **2** (bomba) fuse **3** (mechas) (penteado) highlights: *fazer ~s* have your hair highlighted

medalha sf medal

média sf **1** average: *em ~* on average **2** (Mat) mean

mediano adj average: *de estatura mediana* of average height

medicamento sm medicine

medicar vt (tratar) treat

medicina sf medicine

médico/a adj medical ● sm-sf doctor: *ir ao ~* go to the doctor's

médico-legista sm forensic expert

medida sf **1** (extensão) measurement: *as ~s duma sala* the measurements of a room **2** (unidade, precauções) measure: *pesos e ~s* weights and measures ◇ *Será preciso tomar ~s a esse respeito.* Something must be done about it. ▸ **à ~ que** as: *à ~ que a doença for avançando* as the illness progresses **(feito) sob ~** (made) to measure **ficar na ~** be a perfect fit **na ~ do possível** as far as possible

medieval adj medieval

médio adj **1** medium: *de tamanho ~* medium size **2** (mediano, normal) average: *temperatura/velocidade média* average temperature/speed **3** (dedo) middle ● sm (Futebol, jogador) midfielder

medíocre adj mediocre

medir vt, vi measure: *~ a sala* measure the room ◇ *A mesa*

mede 1 m de largura. The table measures 1 m wide. ◇ *Quanto você mede?* How tall are you?

meditar vt (refletir) ponder sth: *Ele meditou na resposta.* He pondered his reply. ● vi (fazer meditação) meditate

mediterrâneo adj, sm Mediterranean

medo sm fear (of sb/(doing) sth): *o ~ de voar/do fracasso* fear of flying/failure ▸ **com/por ~ de** for fear of sb/(doing) sth **ficar com ~** be scared of sb/(doing) sth **que ~!** how scary! **sentir ~** be frightened/scared **ter ~** be frightened/scared (of sb/(doing) sth): *ter ~ de cães* be scared of dogs ◇ *Você teve ~ de ser reprovado?* Were you afraid you would fail?

medonho adj **1** (assustador) frightening **2** (horrível) horrible

medroso adj fearful

medula sf marrow: *~ óssea* bone marrow

medusa sf jellyfish [pl jellyfish]

meia sf **1** (curta) sock **2** (de nylon) stocking **3** (meias) (collants) pantyhose, tights (GB)

meia-calça sf (meias-calças) pantyhose, tights (GB)

meia-idade sf middle age: *uma pessoa de ~* a middle-aged person

meia-noite sf midnight

meia-tigela sf ▸ **de ~:** *um ator de ~* a second-rate actor

meia-volta sf ▸ **dar ~** turn around: *Ela deu ~ e voltou para trás.* She turned around and went back.

meigo adj sweet

meio adj (metade de) half a, half an: *meia dúzia* half a dozen ◇ *meia hora* half an hour ◇ half-: *~ adormecido* half asleep ● adv half: *~ adormecido* half asleep ● sm (centro) middle: *no ~ da praça/da manhã* in the middle of the square/morning **2** (ambiente) environment **3** (social) circle: *~s financeiros* financial circles **4** (procedimento, recurso) means [pl means]: *~ de transporte* means of transportation ◇ *ter ~s para comprar algo* have the means to buy sth ● num half [pl halves]: *Dois ~s dão um inteiro.* Two halves make a whole. ◇ *duas horas e meia* two and a half hours ● **meia** num (relógio): *São três e ~.* It's three thirty. ▸ **a meia haste** at half-mast ◇ **de ~ expediente:** *um emprego de*

~ expediente a part-time job
meias medidas half measures
~ ambiente environment
~ de comunicação medium [pl media] **~ mundo** lots of people [pl] **não ser de meias palavras** not beat about the bush **no ~ de** in the middle of sth
meio-de-campo sm midfield: *um jogador* **~** a midfield player
meio-dia sm noon, midday: *a refeição do* **~** the midday meal ◊ *Eles chegaram ao* **~.** They arrived at noon.
meio-fio sm curb, kerb (GB)
meio-irmão, meia-irmã sm-sf half-brother [fem half-sister]
meio-termo sm compromise
mel sm honey
melancia sf watermelon
melancólico adj melancholy
melão sm melon
melhor adj, adv **1** (comparativo) better (than sb/sth): *Eles têm um apartamento* **~** do que o nosso. They have a better apartment than ours. ◊ *Sinto-me* **~.** I feel better. ◊ *quanto antes* **~** the sooner the better ◊ *É* **~** *você levar as chaves.* You'd better take the keys. ◊ *~ do que nunca* better than ever **2** (superlativo) best (in/of/that...): *o meu* **~** *amigo* my best friend ◊ *Ela é a* **~** *da turma.* She's the best in the class. ◊ *o que* **~** *canta* the one who sings best ◊ *fazer o* **~** *possível* do your best ● *sm* best thing: *Se você não sabe, o* **~** *é ficar calado.* If you don't know, the best thing is to keep quiet. ▶ **ou ~** I mean: *cinco, ou* **~,** *seis* five, I mean six
melhora sf improvement (in sb/sth)
melhoramento sm improvement
melhorar vt improve ● vi **1** improve **2** (doente) get better: *Melhore logo!* Get well soon!
melindroso adj **1** (problema, situação) delicate **2** (suscetível) touchy
melodia sf tune
melro sm blackbird
membro sm **1** member: *tornar-se* **~** become a member **2** (Anat) limb
memorável adj memorable
memória sf **1** memory: *ter boa* **~** have a good memory **2** (memórias) (autobiografia) memoirs ▶ **de ~:** *aprender algo de* **~** learn sth by heart **puxar pela ~** try to remember

memorizar vt memorize
menção sf mention
mencionar vt mention ▶ **para não/sem ~...** not to mention...
mendigar vt, vi beg (for sth)
mendigo a sm-sf beggar
menina sf ▶ **a ~ dos olhos de alguém** the apple of sb's eye
meninice sf childhood
menino/a sm-sf boy [fem girl] ▶ **~ do coro** choirboy **~ prodígio** child prodigy [pl -ies] **~ rico** rich kid
menopausa sf menopause
menor adj
● **uso comparativo** smaller (than sth): *O meu jardim é* **~** *do que o seu.* My yard is smaller than yours.
● **uso superlativo** smallest: *o ~ dos dois* the smaller of the two
● **outros usos** (Mús) minor: *em mi* **~** in E minor ◊ *smf* (menor de idade) minor: *Não se serve álcool a* **~es.** We do not serve alcohol to minors. ◊ **~ de idade** under 18 ◊ *Proibida a entrada a ~es de 18 anos.* No entry for under-18s.
menos adv
● **comparativo** less (than sb/sth): *Dê-me* **~.** Give me less. ◊ *Demorei* **~** *do que pensava.* It took me less time than I thought it would. NOTA Com substantivos contáveis a forma mais correta é fewer, embora se use less cada vez mais: *Havia* **~** *gente/carros que ontem.* There were fewer people/cars than yesterday. → LESS
● **superlativo** least (in/of...): *a ~ faladora da família* the least talkative member of the family ◊ *o aluno que* **~** *estuda* the student who works least NOTA Com substantivos contáveis a forma mais correta é fewest, embora se use least cada vez mais: *a turma com* **~** *alunos* the class with fewest students. → LESS ● *prep* (exceto) except **2** (Mat, temperatura) minus: *Cinco* **~** *três* são dois. Five minus three is two. ◊ *Estamos com ~ dez graus.* It's minus ten. ● *sm* (sinal matemático) minus (sign) ▶ **a ~** too little, too few: *Deram-me dez reais a ~.* They gave me ten reals too little. ◊ *três garfos a ~* three forks too few **a ~ que** unless **ao/pelo ~** at least **~ mal** thank goodness
menosprezar vt despise
mensageiro/a sm-sf messenger
mensagem sf message

mensal *adj* monthly: *um salário* ~ a monthly salary

menstruação *sf* menstruation

mental *adj* mental

mentalidade *sf* mentality [*pl* -ies] ▶ **ter uma ~ aberta/fechada** be open-/narrow-minded

mente *sf* mind ▶ **ter algo em ~** have sth in mind

mentir *vi, vt* lie: *Não minta para mim!* Don't lie to me! → LIE²

mentira *sf* lie: *contar/dizer* ~s tell lies ◊ *Isso é* ~! That's a lie! ◊ *uma* ~ *inofensiva* a white lie

mentiroso/a *adj* deceitful ● *sm-sf* liar

menu *sm* menu: *Não estava no* ~. It wasn't on the menu.

mercadinho *sm* convenience store, corner shop (GB)

mercado *sm* market ▶ **~ negro** black market

mercadoria *sf* goods [*pl*]

mercearia *sf* grocery store

merceeiro/a *sm-sf* grocer

mercenário/a *adj, sm-sf* mercenary [*pl* -ies]: *tropas mercenárias* mercenaries

mercúrio *sm* **1** (*Quím*) mercury **2** (**Mercúrio**) (*planeta*) Mercury

merecer *vt* deserve: *Você merece um castigo.* You deserve to be punished.

merecido *adj* well deserved: *uma vitória bem merecida* a well-deserved victory

merengue *sm* (*Cozinha*) meringue

mergulhador/a *sm-sf* **1** diver **2** (*Esporte*) scuba-diver

mergulhar *vi* dive

mergulho *sm* **1** (*ação*) dive **2** (*Esporte*): *praticar* ~ go scuba diving ◊ (*nadando*) dip: *ir dar um* ~ go for a dip

meridiano *sm* meridian

mérito *sm* merit ▶ **ter** ~ be praiseworthy

mero *adj* mere

mês *sm* month: *no* ~ *passado/que vem* last/next month ◊ *no início do* ~ at the beginning of the month ◊ *Fechou num* ~. It closed within a month. ▶ **mês sim, mês não** every other month **por ~** (*em cada mês*) a month: *Quanto você gasta por* ~? How much do you spend a month? **2** (*mensalmente*): *Somos pagos por* ~. We're paid monthly.

mesa *sf* table: *sentar-se à* ~ sit at the table ◊ *pôr/tirar a* ~ set/clear the table ▶ **~ de centro/**jantar coffee/dining table **~ (de escritório/escola)** desk

mesada *sf* allowance

mesa-de-cabeceira *sf* bedside table

meseta *sf* plateau [*pl* ~s/-x]

mesmo/a *adj* **1** (*idêntico*) same: *ao* ~ *tempo* at the same time ◊ *Moro na mesma casa que ele.* I live in the same house as him. ◊ *o* ~ *de sempre* the same as usual ◊ *O* ~, *por favor!* Same again, please! **2** (*uso enfático*): *Eu* ~ *o vi.* I saw it myself. ◊ *em paz consigo* ~ at peace with yourself ◊ *a princesa, ela mesma* the princess herself ● *pron* same one: *Ela é a mesma que veio ontem.* She's the same woman who came yesterday. ● *adv* **1** (*exatamente*) right: *Faço agora* ~. I'll get it done right now. ◊ *Ela saiu agora* ~. She just went out. **2** (*no caso, apesar de*) even: *quando even when* ◊ *nem* ~ not even ◊ *Eles não quiseram vir,* ~ *sabendo que você estava aqui.* They didn't want to come even though they knew you were here. **3** (*de verdade*) really: *É uma maçã* ~! It really is an apple! ◊ **esse** ~ the very same **isso** ~ that's right ~ **assim** even so: ~ *assim, eu não aceitaria.* Even so, I wouldn't accept. ~ **que/se** even if: *Venha,* ~ *que seja tarde.* Come along, even if it's late. **para mim, etc. dá no** ~/**na mesma** It's all the same to me, you, etc. **por isso** ~ that's why

mesquinho *adj* (*avarento*) stingy

mesquita *sf* mosque

mestiço/a *adj, sm-sf* (*person*) of mixed race

mestrado *sm* master's (degree)

mestre/a *sm-sf* **1** (*educador*) teacher **2** (*figura destacada*) master: *um* ~ *do xadrez* a chess master

meta *sf* **1** (*Atletismo*) finishing line **2** (*objetivo*) goal: *alcançar uma* ~ achieve a goal

metade *sf* half [*pl* halves]: ~ *da população* half the population ◊ *partir algo pela* ~ cut sth in half ◊ *Comprei algo a* ~ *do preço.* I bought it half-price. ▶ **na/pela (de):** *Paramos na* ~ *do caminho.* We'll stop halfway. ◊ *A garrafa estava pela* ~. The bottle was half empty.

metáfora *sf* metaphor

metal *sm* metal

metálico *adj* **1** metal: *uma barra*

metálica a metal bar **2** (*brilho, som*) metallic

meteorito *sm* meteorite

meteoro *sm* meteor

meteorológico *adj* weather, meteorological (*fml*): *um boletim* ~ a weather forecast

meteorologista *smf* weather forecaster

meter *vt* **1** put: *Onde você meteu as minhas chaves?* Where did you put my keys? **2** (*introduzir*) introduce **3** (*implicar*) involve ● **meter-se** *vp* **1** (*introduzir-se*) get into sth: ~ *na cama/debaixo do chuveiro* get into bed/the shower **2** (*involver-se, interessar-se*) get involved *in* sth: ~ *na política* get involved in politics **3** (*nos assuntos de outro*) interfere *in* sth: *Eles se metem em tudo.* They interfere in everything. **4** ~ **com** pick on sb ► ~ **a mão em/na cara de alguém** hit sb ~ **medo** frighten sb, scare sb (*mais coloq*) ~ **o bedelho** interfere (*in* sth) ~ **o dedo no nariz** pick your nose ~ **o nariz** poke/stick your nose *into* sth ~ **os pés pelas mãos** get into a tangle **meter-se na vida dos outros** poke your nose into other people's business **meter-se onde não se é chamado** poke your nose in (where it's not wanted)

meticuloso *adj* (*cuidadoso*) meticulous

metido *adj* **1** (*pretensioso*) conceited **2** (*intrometido*) nosy

método *sm* method

metralhadora *sf* machine gun

métrico *adj* metric: *o sistema* ~ the metric system

metro *sm* **1** (*medida*) meter (*abrev* **m**): *os 200* ~*s de nado livre* the 200 meters freestyle ◊ *Vende-se por* ~. It's sold by the meter. ◊ ~ *quadrado* square meter (*fita para medir*) tape measure

metrô *sm* subway, underground (*GB*): *ir de* ~ go on the subway **NOTA** O metrô de Londres chama-se **the tube**.

meu, minha *pron adj* my: *os* ~*s amigos* my friends ● *pron subs* mine: *Este carro é* ~. This car is mine. **NOTA** *Um amigo meu se traduz por* **a friend of mine** *pois significa* um dos meus amigos.

mexer *vt, vi* **1** (*mover*) move: *Não consigo* ~ *as pernas.* I can't move my legs. **2** (a) (*líquido*) stir (b) (*salada*) toss **3** ~ (**em**) (a) (*tocar*) touch: *Não mexa nisso!*

Don't touch it! (b) (*bisbilhotar*) poke around (in sth) **4** ~ **com** (a) (*comover*) affect, get to sb (*coloq*): *Sabe que esse filme mexeu comigo?* The movie really got to me, you know. (b) (*irritar*) tease (c) (*trabalhar*) work with sth: *O seu pai mexe com quê?* What does your father work with? ● **mexer-se** *vp* **1** (*mover-se*) move **2** (*apressar-se*) get a move on: *Mexa-se ou perdemos o trem.* Get a move on or we'll miss the train.

mexericar *vi* gossip

mexerico *sm* gossip [*U*]

mexeriqueiro/a *adj, sm-sf* gossip [*s*]

mexicano/a *adj, sm-sf* Mexican

México *sm* Mexico

mexido *adj*: *ovos* ~*s* scrambled eggs

mexilhão *sm* mussel

mi *sm* (*Mús*) E

miar *vi* meow

miau *sm* meow → GATO

micróbio *sm* microbe, germ (*mais coloq*)

microfone *sm* microphone, mike (*coloq*)

microondas *sm* microwave (oven)

microônibus *sm* minibus

microscópio *sm* microscope

mídia *sf* media

migalha *sf* crumb

migração *sf* migration

migrar *vi* migrate

mijar *vi* piss

mil *num, sm* **1** (a) thousand: ~ *pessoas* a thousand people ◊ *uma conta de cinco* ~ *reais* a bill for five thousand reals **NOTA** Pode-se traduzir **mil** por **one thousand** quando é seguido de outro número: ~ *cento e vinte* one thousand one hundred and twenty, ou quando se deseja dar mais ênfase: *Eu disse* ~, *não dois* ~. I said one thousand, not two. De 1.100 a 1.900 é muito comum usar as formas **eleven hundred, twelve hundred,** etc.: *uma corrida de* ~ *e quinhentos metros* a fifteen hundred meters race. **2** (*anos*): *em 1600* in sixteen hundred ◊ *1713* seventeen thirteen ◊ *o ano 2000* two thousand → Ver pág. 223 ► **às** ~ **maravilhas** wonderfully

milagre *sm* miracle

milênio *sm* millennium

milésimo/a *num, sm* thousandth: *um* ~ *de segundo* a thousandth of a second

milha *sf* mile

milhão *sm* **1** million [*pl* million]: *dois milhões duzentos e dez* two million two hundred and ten **2** (*muitos*): *Tenho um ~ de coisas para fazer.* I have a million things to do. ◊ *milhões de partículas* millions of particles → Ver pág. 223

milhar *sm* **1** thousand [*pl* thousand] **2** (*muitos*): *~es de pessoas* thousands of people ◊ *aos ~es* in their thousands

milho *sm* **1** (*planta*) corn, maize (*GB*) **2** (*grão*) corn on the cob, sweetcorn (*GB*)

milímetro *sm* millimeter (*abrev* **mm**) → Ver pág. 224

milionário/a *sm-sf* millionaire

militar *adj* military ● *smf* soldier: *O meu pai era ~.* My father was in the army.

mim *pron pess* me: *Não gosto de falar de ~ (mesma).* I don't like talking about myself.

mimar *vt* spoil

mímica *sf* mime: *fazer ~* mime

mímico/a *sm-sf* mime

mimo *sm* (*carinho*) fuss [U]: *As crianças precisam de ~s.* children need to be made a fuss of.

mina *sf* **1** mine: *uma ~ de carvão* a coal mine **2** (*lapiseira*) lead ▸ *~* (**de ouro**) (*negócio lucrativo*) gold mine ● (**terrestre**) landmine

mindinho *sm* **1** (*mão*) little finger, pinkie (*coloq*) **2** (*pé*) little toe

mineiro/a *adj* **1** mining: *uma empresa mineira* a mining company **2** (*de Minas Gerais*) (from) Minas Gerais ● *sm-sf* **1** miner **2** (*de Minas Gerais*): *os ~s* the people of Minas Gerais

mineral *adj, sm* mineral

minério *sm* ore: *~ de ferro* iron ore

minguante *adj* (*lua*) waning

minhoca *sf* earthworm

miniatura *sf* miniature

minimizar *vt* **1** minimize **2** (*dar pouca importância*) play *sth* down

mínimo *adj* **1** (*menor*) minimum: *a tarifa mínima* the minimum charge **2** (*insignificante*) minimal ● *sm* minimum ▸ **no ~** at least ◊ *~ que...* the least...: *O ~ que podem fazer é devolver o dinheiro.* The least they can do is give the money back.

minissaia *sf* miniskirt

ministério *sm* (*Pol, Relig*) ministry [*pl* -ies] ▸ *~* **da Fazenda** Treasury Department ◊ *~* **das Relações Exteriores** State

Department, Foreign Office (*GB*)

ministro/a *sm-sf* secretary, minister (*GB*): *o ~ da Educação* the Education Secretary ▸ *~* **da Fazenda** Secretary of the Treasury, Chancellor of the Exchequer (*GB*) ◊ *~* **das Relações Exteriores/do Exterior** Secretary of State, Foreign Secretary (*GB*)

minoria *sf* minority [*pl* -ies]: *ser a ~* be in the minority

minúsculo/a *adj* **1** (*diminuto*) tiny **2** (*letra*) small ● **minúscula** *sf* small letter

minuto *sm* minute: *Espere um ~.* Just a minute.

miolo *sm* **1** (*pão*) crumb **2** (*cérebro*) brain

míope *adj* near-sighted, shortsighted (*GB*)

miopia *sf* near-sightedness, short-sightedness (*GB*)

miragem *sf* mirage

mirante *sm* viewpoint

miserável *adj* **1** miserable: *um quarto/salário ~* a miserable room/income **2** (*pessoa, vida*) wretched ● *smf* (*desgraçado*) wretch

miséria *sf* **1** (*pobreza*) poverty **2** (*quantidade pequena*) pittance

missa *sf* mass: *~ do galo* midnight mass

missão *sf* mission

míssil *sm* missile

missionário/a *sm-sf* missionary [*pl* -ies]

mistério *sm* mystery [*pl* -ies]

misterioso/a *adj* mysterious

misto *adj* (*escola*) coeducational

misto-quente *sm* toasted ham and cheese sandwich

mistura *sf* **1** mixture: *uma ~ de azeite e vinagre* a mixture of oil and vinegar **2** (*tabaco, álcool, café, chá*) blend **3** (*racial, social, musical*) mix

misturar *vt* **1** mix: *~ bem os ingredientes.* Mix the ingredients well. **2** (*desordenar*) get *sth* mixed up **3** (*amalgamar*) blend **4** (*salada*) toss ● **misturar-se** *vp* (*envolver-se*) mix with *sb*: *Ele não quer se misturar com a gente do povoado.* He doesn't want to mix with people from the town.

mito *sm* **1** (*lenda*) myth **2** (*pessoa famosa*) legend: *um ~ do futebol* a soccer legend

mitologia *sf* mythology

miúdo/a *adj* (*pequeno*) small ● **miúdos** *sm* (*ave*) giblets

mixo *adj* **1** (*de má qualidade*)

crummy **2** (*insignificante*) measly

mobília *sf* furniture ▶ **sem ~** unfurnished

mobiliar *vt* furnish

mobiliário *sm* furniture

moçambicano/a *adj*, *sm-sf* Mozambican

Moçambique *sm* Mozambique

mochila *sf* backpack

mocinho/a *sm-sf* good guy

moço/a *sm-sf* young man/ woman [*pl* men/women] ● *adj* young

moda *sf* fashion: *seguir a ~* follow fashion ◊ *sair de ~* go out of fashion ▶ **estar/entrar na ~** be/ become fashionable **fora de ~** old-fashioned

modelo *sm* **1** model: *Ele é um aluno ~.* He's a model student. **2** (*roupa*) style: *Temos vários ~s de casaco.* We have several styles of jacket. ● *smf* (*pessoa*) model

moderação *sf* moderation: *beber com ~* drink in moderation

moderado *adj* moderate

moderar *vt* **1** (*velocidade*) reduce **2** (*violência*) control

modernizar *vt* modernize

moderno *adj* modern

modéstia *sf* modesty

modesto *adj* modest

modificar *vt* **1** (*mudar*) change **2** (*Gram*) modify

modo *sm* **1** (*maneira*) way (*of doing sth*): *um ~ especial de rir* a special way of laughing **2** (*modos*) (*maneiras*): *bons/ maus ~s* good/bad manners ▶ **a/ do meu, etc. ~** my, your, etc. way: *fazer as coisas do meu ~* do things my way **de ~ que** (*portanto*) so **de qualquer ~/de todo ~** anyway **de tal ~ que** so much that: *Ele gritou de tal ~, que perdeu a voz.* He shouted so much that he lost his voice.

módulo *sm* module

moeda *sf* **1** (*metal*) coin: *uma ~ de 50 centavos* a 50 cent coin **2** (*unidade física*) currency [*pl* -ies]: *a ~ francesa* French currency

moedor *sm* **1** (*café*) grinder **2** (*carne*) mincer

moer *vt* **1** (*café, trigo*) grind **2** (*cansar*) wear sb out

mofado *adj* moldy

mofo *sm* mold

mogno *sm* mahogany

moinho *sm* mill ▶ **~ de vento** windmill

moita *sf* ▶ (**fazer algo**) **na ~** (do sth) on the quiet: *Eu os vi sair na ~.* I saw them sneak out.

mola *sf* (*peça de aço*) spring

molar *sm* (*dente*) molar

moldar *vt* mold

molde *sm* **1** (*fôrma*) mold **2** (*costura*) pattern **3** (*para desenhar*) template

moldura *sf* frame

mole *adj* soft

molécula *sf* molecule

moleza *sf* **1** softness **2** (*fraqueza*) weakness **3** (*preguiça*) listlessness ▶ **ser (uma) ~** (*ser fácil*) be a breeze

molhado *adj* wet

molhar *vt* **1** get sb/sth wet: *~ os pés* get your feet wet **2** (*mergulhar*) dip: *~ o pão na sopa* dip bread in soup ● **molhar-se** *vp* get wet

molho¹ *sm* **1** sauce: *~ de tomate* tomato sauce **2** (*de carne*) gravy ▶ **pôr de ~** soak

molho² *sm* (*feixe*) sprig

momento *sm* **1** moment: *Espere um ~.* Just a moment. ◊ *a qualquer ~* at any moment ◊ *neste ~* at this moment ◊ *no ~* for the moment **2** (*período*) time [*U*]: *nestes ~s de crise* at this time of crisis ▶ **a todo o ~** constantly **de um ~ para o outro** suddenly **do ~** contemporary: *os cantores do ~* contemporary singers **em ~ nenhum** never **no ~ em que...** just when...

monarca *smf* monarch

monarquia *sf* monarchy [*pl* -ies]

monetário *adj* monetary

monge, monja *sm-sf* monk [*fem* nun]

monitor *sm* (*Informát*) monitor

monopólio *sm* monopoly [*pl* -ies]

monopolizar *vt* monopolize

monótono *adj* monotonous

monóxido *sm* monoxide: *~ de carbono* carbon monoxide

monstro *sm* monster

monstruoso *adj* monstrous

montado *adj*: *~ num cavalo/ numa motocicleta* riding a horse/a motorcycle

montagem *sf* **1** (*máquina*) assembly: *linha de ~* assembly line **2** (*Cinema*) montage

montanha *sf* **1** mountain: *no alto de uma ~* on the top of a mountain **2** (*tipo de paisagem*) mountains [*pl*]: *Prefiro ~ à praia.* I prefer the mountains to the beach. **3** (*muitos*) a lot of sth

montanha-russa *sf* roller coaster

montanhismo *sm* mountaineering

montanhoso *adj* mountainous

montão *sm* a lot (*of sth*): *um ~ de dinheiro* a lot of money

montar *vt* **1** (*criar*) set sth up: ~ *um negócio* set up a business **2** (*máquina*) assemble **3** (*barraca de camping*) pitch **4** (*cavalo, bicicleta*) get on (*sth*) ● *vi* ride: *Gosto de ~ a cavalo.* I like horseback riding. ◊ *botas/roupa de ~* riding boots/clothes

monte *sm* **1** hill **2** (*nome próprio*) Mount: *o ~ Evereste* Mount Everest **3** (*pilha*) pile ● *um ~ de* (*grande quantidade*) lots of

monumento *sm* monument

morada *sf* home, residence (*fml*)

morador/a *sm-sf* resident

moral *adj* moral ● *sf* **1** (*princípios*) morality **2** (*história*) moral ● *sm* (*ânimo*) morale: ~ *baixo* low morale

morango *sm* strawberry [*pl* -ies]

morar *vi* live

mórbido *adj* morbid

morcego *sm* bat

mordaça *sf* gag

morder *vt, vi* bite: *O cão me mordeu na perna.* The dog bit my leg. ◊ *Mordi a maçã.* I bit into the apple.

mordida *sf* bite

mordomo *sm* butler

moreno *adj* **1** (*pele*) dark **2** (*bronzeado*) tan: *ficar ~* tan

morfina *sf* morphine

moribundo *adj* dying

morno *adj* lukewarm

morrer *vi* die: ~ *de enfarte/num acidente* die of a heart attack/in an accident ● **deixar ~** (*motor*) stall ● **~ afogado** drown ● **~ de calor/frio** be sweltering/freezing (cold) ● **~ de fome** be starving ● **~ de medo/tédio** be scared stiff/bored stiff ● **~ de rir** die laughing ● **~ de vergonha** die of embarrassment ● **~ de vontade de fazer algo** be dying to do sth

morro *sm* **1** hill **2** (*favela*) shanty town

mortadela *sf* bologna

mortal *adj* **1** mortal: *pecado ~* mortal sin **2** (*veneno, inimigo*) deadly ● *smf* mortal

mortalidade *sf* mortality

morte *sf* death

morto/a *adj, sm-sf* dead: *Tinha sido dada por morta.* They had given her up for dead. ◊ *A cidade fica morta durante o*

inverno. The town is dead in winter. ◊ *os ~s na guerra* the war dead ● **estar ~ de vontade de fazer algo** be dying to do sth ● **~ de cansaço** dead tired ● **~ de calor/frio/fome/sede** sweltering/freezing/starving/dying of thirst ● **~ de inveja** green with envy ● **~ de medo** scared/bored stiff ● **~ de raiva/ciúme(s)** eaten up with anger/jealousy ● **~ de vergonha** extremely embarrassed

mosaico *sm* mosaic

mosca *sf* fly [*pl* flies] ● **estar às ~s** be deserted ● **não faz mal a uma ~** he, she, it, etc. wouldn't hurt a fly

mosquito *sm* mosquito [*pl* ~es]

mostarda *sf* mustard

mosteiro *sm* monastery [*pl* -ies]

mostra *sf* **1** (*sinal*) sign: *dar ~s de cansaço* show signs of fatigue **2** (*exposição*) exhibition

mostrar *vt* show: ~ *interesse por algo* show interest in sth ● **mostrar-se** *vp* (*parecer*) seem

motim *sm* mutiny [*pl* -ies]

motivar *vt* **1** (*causar*) cause **2** (*incentivar*) motivate

motivo *sm* reason (*for sth*): *por ~s de saúde* for health reasons ◊ *sem nenhum ~* for no reason

motocicleta (*tb* **moto**) *sf* motorcycle, motorbike (*mais coloq*): *andar de ~* ride a motorcycle

motociclismo *sm* motorcycling

motociclista *smf* motorcyclist

motor *sm* engine, motor → ENGINE

motorista *smf* driver

mouse *sm* (*Informát*) mouse

movediço *adj* unstable

móvel *adj* mobile ● *sm* **1** piece of furniture: *um ~ muito bonito* a beautiful piece of furniture **2** (*móveis*) (*conjunto*) furniture [*U*]: *Os móveis estavam cobertos de pó.* The furniture was covered in dust.

mover(-se) *vt, vp* move: ~ *uma peça de xadrez* move a chess piece ◊ *Não se mova.* Don't move.

movimentado *adj* **1** (*ativo*) busy: *um mês muito ~* a very busy month **2** (*animado*) lively: *um bar ~* a lively bar

movimentar(-se) *vt, vp* move

movimento *sm* **1** movement: *um ligeiro ~ da mão* a slight movement of the hand ◊ *o ~ romântico* the Romantic movement **2** (*andamento*) motion: *pôr algo em ~* set sth in motion

muçulmano/a adj, sm-sf Muslim

mudança sf **1** change (in/of sth): uma ~ de planos/temperatura a change of plan/in temperature **2** (casa) move ▸ **estar de ~** be moving · **de direção/sentido** U-turn

mudar(-se) vt, vi, vp **1** (posição, casa) move: ~ as coisas para outro escritório move your things to another office ◇ mudar-se para longe da família move away from your family **2** (alterar) change: ~ de ideia/opinião change your mind ◇ ~ de assunto change the subject ◇ Ele mudou muito nestes últimos anos. He's changed a lot in the last few years. ▸ **de casa** move · **de roupa** change

mudo adj mute

mugido sm moo

mugir vi **1** (vaca) moo **2** (touro) bellow

muito adj

• orações afirmativas a lot of sth: Tenho ~ trabalho. I have a lot of work. ◇ Havia ~s carros. There were a lot of cars.

• orações negativas e interrogativas **1** (+ substantivo não contável) much, a lot of sth (mais coloq): Ele não tem muita sorte. He doesn't have much luck. ◇ Você toma ~ café? Do you drink a lot of coffee? **2** (+ substantivo contável) many, a lot of sth (mais coloq): Não havia ~s ingleses. There weren't many English people.

• outras construções: Você está com muita fome? Are you very hungry? • pron **1** (em orações afirmativas) a lot: ~s dos meus amigos a lot of my friends **2** (em orações negativas e interrogativas) much [pl many] → MANY • adv **1** a lot: Ele se parece ~ com o pai. He's a lot like his father. ◇ O seu amigo vem ~ aqui. Your friend comes around here a lot. ◇ trabalhar ~ work hard **2** (+ adjetivo ou advérbio, em respostas) very: Eles estão ~ bem/cansados. They're very well/tired. ◇ ~ devagar/cedo very slowly/early ◇ —Você está cansado? —Não ~. "Are you tired?" "Not very." ◇ —Você gostou? —Muito. "Did you like it?" "Very much." **3** (com formas comparativas) much: ~ mais velho/interessante much older/more interesting **4** (muito tempo) a long time: há ~ a long time ago ◇ Eles chegaram ~ antes de nós. They got here

a long time before us. **5** (+ substantivo): Ele é ~ homem. He's a real man. ▸ **~ bem** well done · **quando ~** at the most

mula sf mule

muleta sf crutch

mulher sf **1** woman [pl women] **2** (esposa) wife [pl wives]

multa sf fine: Deram-lhe uma ~. He was fined.

multar vt fine

multidão sf crowd

multinacional adj, sf multinational

multiplicação sf multiplication

multiplicar vt (Mat) multiply: ~ dois por seis multiply two by six

múltiplo adj **1** (não simples) multiple: uma fratura múltipla a multiple fracture **2** (numerosos) numerous: em ~s casos in numerous cases ▸ **múltipla escolha** multiple choice

multirracial adj multiracial

múmia sf mummy [pl -ies]

mundial adj world: o recorde ~ the world record ◇ o ~ world championship: o ~ de Atletismo the World Athletics Championships

mundo sm world: dar a volta ao ~ go around the world ▸ **o ~ do espetáculo** show business · **todo** ~ everybody

munição sf ammunition [U]: ficar sem munições run out of ammunition

municipal adj municipal

município sm municipality [pl -ies]

mural sm mural

muralha sf wall

murcho adj **1** (flor) withered **2** (pessoa) sad

murmurar vt, vi murmur

murmúrio sm murmur

muro sm wall

murro sm punch: dar um ~ em alguém punch sb

musa sf muse

musculação sf working out

muscular adj muscle: uma lesão ~ a muscle injury

músculo sm muscle

musculoso adj muscular

museu sm museum → MUSEUM

musgo sm moss

música sf music: ~ ao vivo live music ◇ ~ de câmara/fundo chamber/background music

musical adj, sm musical

músico/a *sm-sf* musician
mutante *adj, smf* mutant
mutilar *vt* mutilate
mutreta *sf* swindle
mutuamente *adv* each other, one another: *Eles se odeiam* ~. They hate each other.
mútuo *adj* mutual

Nn

nabo *sm* turnip
nação *sf* nation
nacional *adj* 1 (*da nação*) national: *a bandeira* ~ the national flag 2 (*vôo, mercado*) domestic: *o mercado* ~ the domestic market
nacionalidade *sf* 1 nationality [*pl* -ies] 2 (*cidadania*) citizenship
nacionalista *adj, smf* nationalist
nada *pron* nothing, anything
NOTA Usa-se **nothing** com o verbo na afirmativa e **anything** com o verbo na negativa: *Não sobrou* ~. There's nothing left. ◊ *Não quero* ~. I don't want anything. ◊ *Você quer* ~? Don't you want anything? • *adv* at all: *Não está* ~ *claro*. It's not at all clear. • **de** ~ 1 (*sem importância*) little: *É um arranhão de* ~. It's only a little scratch. 2 (*exclamação*) you're welcome • **de especial/do outro mundo** nothing to write home about ~ **disso** no way ~ **mais** 1 (*é tudo*) that's all 2 (*só*) only: *Tenho um,* ~ *mais*. I only have one. **por** ~ **deste mundo**: *Ela não come por* ~ *deste mundo*. She won't eat for love nor money.
nadadeira *sf* (*peixe*) fin
nadador/a *sm-sf* swimmer
nadar *vi* swim: *Não sei* ~. I can't swim. • ~ **de costas/peito** do (the) backstroke/breaststroke ~ **em estilo borboleta/crawl** do (the) butterfly/the crawl
nádega *sf* buttock
nado *sm* stroke: ~ **de costas** backstroke • **a** ~: *atravessar o rio a* ~ swim across the river
naipe *sm* (*cartas*) suit
namorado/a *sm-sf* boyfriend [*fem* girlfriend]: *Você tem namorada?* Do you have a girlfriend? • **ser** ~**s**: *Somos* ~*s há um ano.* We've been going out together for a year.

namorar *vt* go out with *sb* • *vi* go out together
namoro *sm* relationship
não *adv* 1 (*resposta*) no: *Eu disse que* ~. I said no. 2 (*com verbos, advérbios, frases*) not: *Começamos ou* ~? Are we starting or not? ◊ *Claro que* ~. Of course not. ◊ ~ *sei.* I don't know. 3 (*negativa dupla*): *Ele* ~ *sai nunca.* He never goes out. ◊ ~ *sei nada sobre isso.* I know nothing about that. 4 (*palavras compostas*) non-: *não-fumante* non-smoker • *sm* no [*pl* noes]: *um* ~ *categórico* a categorical no • ~ **é, foi, etc.?**: *Hoje é terça,* ~ *é?* Today is Tuesday, isn't it? ◊ *Você comprou,* ~ *comprou?* You did buy it, didn't you?
não-oficial *adj* unofficial
narcótico *sm* (**narcóticos**) drugs
narina *sf* nostril
nariz *sm* nose: *assoar o* ~ blow your nose ◊ *estar com o* ~ *escorrendo* have a runny nose
narrador/a *sm-sf* narrator
narrar *vt* tell
nasal *adj* nasal
nascença *sf* birth: *Ela é cega de* ~. She was born blind.
nascente *adj* (*sol*) rising • *sf* 1 (*água*) spring: *água de* ~ spring water 2 (*rio*) source
nascer *vi* 1 (*pessoa, animal*) be born: *Nasci em 1971.* I was born in 1971. 2 (*sol, rio*) rise 3 (*planta, cabelo, penas*) grow • ~ **para ser ator, cantor, etc.** be a born actor, singer, etc. **o** ~ **do sol** sunrise
nascimento *sm* birth: *data de* ~ date of birth • **de** ~ by birth
natação *sf* swimming
natal *adj* native: *terra* ~ native land • **Natal** *sm* Christmas: *Feliz* ~*!* Merry Christmas! ◊ *no* ~ at Christmas NOTA Nos Estados Unidos e na Grã-Bretanha praticamente não se celebra a véspera/noite de Natal, **Christmas Eve**. O dia mais importante é o 25 de dezembro, **Christmas Day**, quando a família abre os presentes trazidos pelo Papai Noel, **Santa Claus**, **Father Christmas** (GB).
natalidade *sf* birth rate
nativo/a *adj, sm-sf* native
nato *adj* born: *um músico* ~ a born musician
natural *adj* 1 natural: *É* ~*!* It's only natural! 2 (*fruta, flor*) fresh • 3 (*espontâneo*) unaffected: *um gesto* ~ an unaffected

gesture ► **ser ~ de...** (*origem*)
come from...

naturalidade *sf* **1** (*origem*):
de ~ **paulista** born in São Paulo
2 (*simplicidade*): **com a maior ~
do mundo** as if it were the
most natural thing in the
world ► **com ~** naturally

naturalmente *adv* of course

natureza *sf* nature ► **por ~** by
nature

natureza-morta *sf* (*Arte*) still
life [*pl* still lifes]

naufragar *vi* be shipwrecked

naufrágio *sm* shipwreck

náufrago/a *sm-sf* castaway

náusea *sf* nausea ► **dar ~** make
sb feel nauseous **sentir/ter ~** s
feel nauseous

náutico *adj* sailing: **clube ~** sailing club

navalha *sf* **1** (*de barba*) (cut-
throat) razor **2** (*arma*) knife [*pl*
knives]

nave *sf* (*igreja*) nave ► **~ espacial**
spaceship

navegação *sf* navigation

navegador *sm* (*Informát*)
browser

navegar *vi* **1** (*barcos*) sail **2**
(*aviões*) fly ► **~ na Internet** surf
the Net

navio *sm* ship: **~ de guerra** warship

nazista *adj, smf* Nazi

neblina *sf* mist

necessário *adj* necessary: **Farei
o que for ~.** I'll do whatever's
necessary. ◊ **Não leve mais do
que é ~.** Only take what you
need. ◊ **Não é ~ que você venha.**
There's no need for you to
come. ► **se for ~** if necessary

necessidade *sf* **1** (*coisa imprescindível*) necessity [*pl* -ies]: **O
ar condicionado é uma ~.** Air
conditioning is a necessity. **2**
(*de*) need (*for sth/to do sth*):
Não vejo ~ de ir de carro. I don't
see the need to go by car. ◊ **Não
há ~ de autorização.** There's no
need for authorization. ► **passar ~** suffer hardship **sem ~**
needlessly

necessitado/a *adj, sm-sf*
(*pobre*) needy: **os ~s** the needy

necessitar *vt, vi* **~ (de)** need *sth*

necrotério *sm* morgue

negar *vt* **1** (*fato*) deny (*doing*)
sth/that...: **Ele negou ter roubado o quadro.** He denied stealing
the picture. **2** (*autorização,
ajuda*) refuse ● **negar-se** *vp*
refuse *to do sth*

negativa *sf* (*recusa*) refusal

negativo *adj, sm* negative

negligente *adj* careless, negligent (*mais fml*)

negociação *sf* negotiation

negociante *smf* businessman/
woman [*pl* -men/-women]

negociar *vt, vi* negotiate

negócio *sm* **1** (*comércio, assunto*) business: **fazer ~ do** business ◊ **Muitos ~s fracassaram.**
A lot of businesses went bust. ◊
~s são ~s. Business is business.
◊ **Estou aqui a ~s.** I'm here on
business. **2** (*loja*) shop **3** (*troço*)
thing: **Dê-me aquele ~.** Give me
that thing. ► **homem/mulher de
~s** businessman/woman [*pl*
-men/-women] **~ da China**
good business ► **fechar** *um*
deal **o ~ é o seguinte...** here's
the deal...

negro/a *adj, sm* black ● *sm-sf*
black man/woman [*pl* men/
women]: **os ~s** (the) blacks
NOTA Nos Estados Unidos é
preferível usar o termo **African
American**.

nem *conj* **1** (*negativa dupla*) neither... nor...: **~ você ~ eu falamos francês.** Neither you nor I
speak French. ◊ **Ele não disse ~
que sim ~ que não.** He didn't say
yes or no. **2** (*nem sequer*) not
even: **~ ele mesmo sabe quanto
ganha.** Not even he knows how
much he earns. ► **~ eu, etc.** neither am I, do I, have I, etc.:
—Não acredito. — Nem eu.
"I don't believe it." "Neither do
I." **~ que** even if: **~ que me des-
sem dinheiro** not even if they
paid me **~ todos** not everybody / all of them **~ um** not a
single (one): **Não tenho ~ um
real sobrando.** I don't have a
single real left. **~ uma palavra,
um dia, etc.** mais not another
word, day, etc. **que ~:** **correr
que ~** *um louco* run like crazy

nenhum *adj* no, any NOTA Usa-
se **no** com o verbo na afirmativa:
Ainda não chegou ~ aluno. No
students have arrived yet. Usa-
se **any** com o verbo na negativa:
**Ele não prestou nenhuma
atenção.** He didn't pay any
attention. ● *pron* **1** (*entre duas
pessoas ou coisas*) neither,
either NOTA Utiliza-se **neither** com o verbo na afirmativa:
**—Qual dos dois você prefere? —
Nenhum.** "Which one do you
prefer?" "Neither (of them)."
Usa-se **either** com o verbo na
negativa: **Não discuti com ~ dos
dois.** I didn't argue with either
of them. **2** (*entre mais de duas*

pessoas ou coisas) none: *Havia três, mas não sobrou ~.* There were three, but there are none left. ▶ **de maneira nenhuma/ modo** ~ no way (*coloq*), certainly not

neozelandês/esa *adj* New Zealand ● *sm-sf* New Zealander

nervo *sm* **1** nerve: *São os ~s.* It's just nerves. **2** (*carne*) gristle ▶ **ter os ~s à flor da pele** be highly-strung

nervosismo *sm* nervousness

nervoso *adj* **1** nervous: *o sistema ~* the nervous system ◇ *estar/ ficar ~* be nervous/get worked up **2** (*Anat, célula, fibra*) nerve: *tecido ~* nerve tissue

neto/a *sm-sf* grandchild [*pl* grandchildren] [*masc* grandson] [*fem* granddaughter]

Netuno *sm* Neptune

neutro *adj* **1** neutral **2** (*Biol, Gram*) neuter

nevar *v imp* snow

neve *sf* snow

névoa *sf* mist

nevoeiro *sm* fog: *Há muito ~.* It's very foggy.

nicotina *sf* nicotine

ninguém *pron* nobody: *~ sabe disso.* Nobody knows this. ◇ *~ mais estava lá.* There was nobody else there. NOTA Usa-se **anybody** com o verbo na negativa: *Não quer falar com ~.* He won't talk to anybody.

ninhada *sf* (*Zool*) litter

ninharia *sf* (*coisa de pouco valor*): *Para ela, mil dólares é uma ~.* A thousand dollars is nothing to her.

ninho *sm* nest: *fazer um ~* build a nest

nítido *adj* **1** (*claro*) clear **2** (*imagem*) sharp

nitrogênio *sm* nitrogen

nível *sm* **1** level: *~ do mar* sea level ◇ *a todos os níveis* at all levels **2** (*qualidade, preparação*) standard: *um excelente ~ de jogo/vida* an excellent standard of play/living

nivelar *vt* **1** (*terreno, etc.*) level **2** (*desigualdades*) even sth out

nó *sm* knot: *fazer/desfazer um nó* tie/undo a knot ▶ **nó dos dedos** knuckle ● **sentir um nó na garganta** have a lump in your throat

nobre *adj* noble ● *smf* nobleman/woman [*pl* -men/-women]

nobreza *sf* nobility

noção *sf* notion ▶ **ter noções de algo** have a basic grasp of sth

nocaute *sm* knockout

nocivo *adj* harmful (*to sb/sth*)

nódoa *sf* stain

nogueira *sf* walnut tree

noite *sf* night: *às dez da ~* at ten o'clock at night ▶ **à ~** at night: *segunda à ~* on Monday night ● **boa ~** good night NOTA **Good night** é só para a despedida. À chegada, diz-se **good evening**. **da ~** evening: *sessão da ~* evening performance ● **para o dia ~** overnight ● **de ~ 1** (*vestido*) evening **2** (*à noite*) at night **3** (*escuro*) dark: *Já era de ~.* It was already dark. ● **esta ~/hoje à ~** tonight ● **fazer-se ~** get dark ● **~ de Natal/Ano Novo** Christmas Eve/New Year's Eve

noivado *sm* engagement: *anel de ~* engagement ring

noivo/a *sm-sf* **1** (*prometido*) fiancé [*fem* fiancée] **2** (*em casamento, recém-casados*) (*bride*)groom [*fem* bride] → CASAMENTO ▶ **estar ~s** be engaged ● **os ~s 1** (*em casamento*) bride and groom **2** (*recém-casados*) newly-weds

nojento *adj* **1** (*sujo*) filthy **2** (*repugnante*) disgusting

nojo *sm* **1** (*náusea*) nausea **2** (*repugnância*) disgust ▶ **dar ~**: *Rim me dá ~.* I can't stand kidney. ◇ *Este país me dá ~.* This country makes me sick. ● **estar um ~** be filthy ● **que ~** how gross

nômade *adj* nomadic ● *smf* nomad

nome *sm* **1** (**a**) name (**b**) (*em formulários*) first name → MIDDLE NAME **2** (*Gram*) noun: *~ próprio* proper noun ▶ **em ~ de** on behalf of *sb* ● **~ completo** full name ● **~ de batismo/solteira** first/maiden name

nomear *vt* **1** (*mencionar*) mention: *sem o ~* without mentioning his name **2** (*designar alguém para um cargo*) appoint *sb* (*to sth*) **3** (*eleger para prêmio*) nominate *sb* (*for sth*)

nono/a *adj, num, sm* ninth

nora *sf* (*parente*) daughter-in-law [*pl* -ters-in-law]

nordeste *sm* **1** (*ponto cardeal, região*) north-east (*abrev* NE) **2** (*vento, direção*) north-easterly

nordestino/a *adj* north-eastern ● *sm-sf*: *os ~s* the people of the north-east

norma *sf* rule ▶ **(ter) como ~ (não) fazer algo** always/never do sth: *Como ~, não bebo* *durante as refeições.* I never drink at mealtimes.

normal *adj* **1** *(habitual)* normal: *o curso ~ dos acontecimentos* the normal course of events ◊ *É o ~.* That's the normal thing. **2** *(comum)* ordinary: *um emprego ~* an ordinary job **3** *(padrão)* standard: *o procedimento ~* the standard procedure

normalizar *vt (relações, situação)* restore sth to normal • *vi* return to normal

noroeste *sm* **1** *(ponto cardeal, região)* north-west *(abrev* NW) **2** *(direção, vento)* north-westerly

norte *sm* north *(abrev* N.): *a/no ~* in the north ◊ *na costa ~* on the north coast

nortista *adj* northern • *smf* northerner

nos *pron pess* **1** *(complemento)* us: *Eles ~ viram.* They saw us. **2** *(reflexivo)* ourselves: *Nós ~ divertimos.* We enjoyed ourselves. **3** *(recíproco)* each other, one another: *Nós ~ amamos.* We love each other.

nós *pron pess* **1** *(sujeito)* we **2** *(complemento, comparações)* us: *É para ~.* It's for us. ▸ **entre ~** *(confidencialmente)* between ourselves • **mesmos/próprios** (we) ourselves • **somos ~** it's us

nosso/a *pron adj* our: *os ~s amigos* our friends • *pron subs* ours: *Este carro é o ~.* This car is ours. NOTA *Uma amiga nossa se traduz* por a friend of ours *pois significa* uma das nossas amigas.

nostalgia *sf* nostalgia

nostálgico/a *adj* nostalgic

nota *sf* **1** note: *deixar uma ~ para alguém* leave sb a note **2** *(Educ)* grade, mark (GB): *tirar boas ~s* get good grades **3** *(dinheiro)* bill, (bank)note (GB): *~s de dez dólares* ten-dollar bills ▸ **tomar ~** take note *(of sth)*

notar *vt (observar)* notice • **notar-se** *vp (sentir-se)* feel: *Nota-se a tensão.* You can feel the tension. ◊ *Notava-se que ela estava nervosa.* You could tell she was nervous. **2** *(ver-se)*: *Não se nota a idade dele.* He doesn't look his age.

notável *adj* remarkable

notícia *sf* **1** news [U]: *Tenho uma má ~ para lhe dar.* I have some bad news for you. ◊ *As ~s são alarmantes.* The news is alarming. **2** *(Jornal, TV)* news item ▸ **ter ~s de alguém** hear from sb

noticiário *sm* news: *Está na hora do ~.* It's time for the news.

notificar *vt* notify *sb (of sth)*

notório *adj* well known

noturno *adj* **1** night: *serviço ~ de ônibus* night bus service **2** *(aulas)* evening

nova *sf* news [U]: *boas ~s* good news

novamente *adv* again

novato/a *adj* inexperienced • *sm-sf* beginner

Nova Zelândia *sf* New Zealand

nove *num, sm* **1** nine **2** *(data)* ninth

novecentos *num, sm* nine hundred

novela *sf* **1** *(livro)* novella **2** *(TV, rádio)* soap (opera)

novelo *sm* ball: *um ~ de lã* a ball of wool

novembro *sm* November *(abrev* Nov.) → MAIO

noventa *num, sm* ninety

novidade *sf* **1** novelty [*pl* -ies]: *a ~ da situação* the novelty of the situation ◊ *a grande ~ da temporada* the latest thing **2** *(alteração)* change: *Não há ~s com relação ao tempo.* There's no change in the weather. **3** *(notícia)*: *Alguma ~?* Any news?

novilho/a *sm-sf* steer [*fem* heifer]

novo *adj* **1** new **2** *(adicional)* further: *Surgiram ~s problemas.* Further problems arose. **3** *(jovem)* young: *o mais ~ da turma* the youngest in the class ▸ **de ~** again • **em folha** brand new • **o que há de ~?** what's new?

noz *sf* **1** *(fruto)* walnut **2** *(nozes)* *(frutos de casca dura)* nuts [*pl*]

nu *adj* **1** *(pessoa)* naked: *nu em pêlo* stark naked **2** *(parte do corpo, vazio)* bare: *braços nus/paredes nuas* bare arms/walls → NAKED • **pôr a nu** expose

nublado *adj* cloudy

nublar-se *vp (céu)* cloud over

nuca *sf* nape

nuclear *adj* nuclear

núcleo *sm* nucleus [*pl* -lei]

nudez *sf* nudity

nulo *adj* **1** *(inválido)* invalid: *um acordo ~* an invalid agreement **2** *(inexistente)* non-existent

numeração *sf* numbers [*pl*] ▸ **~ arábica/romana** Arabic/Roman numerals [*pl*]

numeral *sm* numeral

numerar *vt* number

número *sm* **1** number: *um ~ de telefone* a phone number ◊ *~ par/ímpar/primo* even/odd/

prime number **2** (*tamanho*) size: *Que ~ você calça?* What size shoe do you take? **3** (*publicação*) issue: *um ~ atrasado* a back issue **4** (*Teat*) act: *um ~ de circo* a circus act ▸ **~ de matrícula** license plate/number plate (*GB*)

numeroso *adj* **1** (*grande*) large: *uma família numerosa* a large family **2** (*muitos*) numerous: *em numerosas ocasiões* on numerous occasions

nunca *adv* never, ever **NOTA** Usa-se **never** com o verbo na afirmativa: *~ estive em Paris.* I've never been to Paris. Usa-se **ever** para exprimir idéias negativas ou com palavras como *nobody, nothing*, etc.: *sem ~ ver o sol* without ever seeing the sun ◊ *~ acontece nada.* Nothing ever happens. → ALWAYS ▸ **mais (do) que ~** more than ever: *Está mais calor do que ~* It's hotter than ever. **~ mais** never again **quase ~** hardly ever

núpcias *sf* wedding [*sing*]

nutrição *sf* nutrition

nutritivo *adj* nutritious

nuvem *sf* cloud ▸ **andar/estar nas nuvens** have your head in the clouds

O o

o¹ *art def* **1** the → THE **2** (*para substantivar*): *o interessante/difícil é...* the interesting/difficult thing is... ▸ **o/a de...** (*posse*): *O da Marisa é melhor.* Marisa's (one) is better. ◊ *Esta bagagem é a do Miguel.* These bags are Miguel's. **2** (*característica*) the one with...: *o de olhos verdes/de barba* the one with green eyes/the beard ◊ *Eu prefiro o de bolinhas.* I'd prefer the one with polka dots. **3** (*vestuário*) the one in...: *o do casaco cinza* the one in the gray coat ◊ *a de vermelho* the one in red **4** (*procedência*) the one from...: *o do Rio* the one from Rio **o/a que...** **1** (*pessoa*) the one (who/that)...: *O que eu vi era mais alto.* The one I saw was taller. **2** (*coisa*) the one (which/that)...: *A que compramos era melhor.* The one (that) we bought was nicer. **3** (*quem quer que*) whoever: *O que chegar primeiro faz o café.* Whoever gets there first has to make the coffee. **o que** which: *o que não é verdade* which isn't true **o que...** what: *Você nem imagina o que foi*

aquilo. You can't imagine what it was like. ◊ *Farei o que você disser.* I'll do whatever you say. **o que é meu** (*posse*) my, your, etc. things: *Tudo o que é meu é seu.* Everything I have is yours.

o² *pron pess* **1** (*ele*) him **2** (*coisa*) it **3** (*você*) you

oásis *sm* oasis [*pl* oases]

obcecado *adj* obsessed (*with sb/sth*)

obedecer *vi* obey: *~ aos pais* obey your parents ◊ *Obedeça!* Do as you're told!

obediência *sf* obedience

obediente *adj* obedient

obeso *adj* obese

obituário *sm* obituary [*pl* -ies]

objetar *vt* object

objetiva *sf* (*Fot*) lens

objetivo *adj* objective ● *sm* **1** (*finalidade*) objective: *~s a longo prazo* long-term objectives **2** (*propósito*) purpose

objeto *sm* (*coisa*, *Gram*) object

oblíquo *adj* oblique

oboé *sm* oboe

obra *sf* **1** work: *uma ~ de arte* a work of art ◊ *as ~ completas de Jorge Amado* the complete works of Jorge Amado **2** (*lugar em construção*) site **3** (*obras*) (*na estrada*) construction [*sing*], roadworks (*GB*)

obra-prima *sf* masterpiece

obrigação *sf* obligation ▸ **ter (a) ~ de** be obliged to do sth

obrigado *adj* obliged: *sentir-se/ver-se ~ a fazer algo* feel obliged to do sth ● *interj* thank you, thanks (*mais coloq*): *Muito ~!* Thank you very much! ● *ser ~ a* have to do sth: *Somos ~s a trocá-lo.* We have to change it.

obrigar *vt* force sb to do sth

obrigatório *adj* compulsory

obsceno *adj* obscene

obscuridade *sf* (*fig*) obscurity

obscuro *adj* (*fig*) obscure: *um poeta ~* an obscure poet

observação *sf* observation: *capacidade de ~* powers of observation ▸ **estar em ~** be under observation

observador/a *adj* observant ● *sm-sf* observer

observar *vt* **1** (*olhar*) watch observe (*fml*) **2** (*notar*) notice: *Você observou do seu estranho nele?* Did you notice anything odd about him? **3** (*comentar*) remark

observatório *sm* observatory [*pl* -ies]

obsessão sf obsession (*with sb/doing sth*)

obstáculo sm obstacle

obstante ▶ **não** ~ nevertheless (*fml*), however

obstinado adj obstinate

obstruir vt block sth (up)

obter vt 1 obtain (*fml*), get: ~ *um empréstimo/o apoio de alguém* get a loan/sb's support 2 (*vitória*) score: ~ *a sua primeira vitória* score your first victory

obturação sf (*dente*) filling

obturar vt fill: *Tenho que ~ um dente.* I have to have a tooth filled.

óbvio adj obvious

ocasião sf 1 (*vez*) occasion: *em várias ocasiões* on several occasions 2 (*oportunidade*) opportunity [*pl* -ies], chance (*mais coloq*) (*to do sth*)

oceano sm ocean

ocidental adj western: *o mundo* ~ the western world ● smf westerner

ocidente sm west: *as diferenças entre o Oriente e o* ~ the differences between East and West

ócio sm leisure

oco adj hollow

ocorrer vi 1 (*acontecer*) happen, occur (*mais fml*): *Não quero que volte a* ~. I don't want it to happen again. 2 (*lembrar*) occur to sb: *Acabe de me* ~ *que...* It has just occurred to me that...

oculista smf (*pessoa*) optician

óculos sm 1 glasses: *um rapaz louro, de* ~ a fair-haired boy with glasses ◊ *usar* ~ wear glasses 2 (*de proteção*) goggles ▶ ~ **escuros** sunglasses

ocultar vt hide sb/sth (*from sb/sth*)

ocupado adj 1 (*pessoa*) busy 2 (*telefone*) busy, engaged (*GB*): *O telefone está* ~. The line's busy. 3 (*banheiro*) occupied, engaged (*GB*) 4 (*lugar, táxi*) taken

ocupar vt 1 (*espaço, tempo*) take up sth: *O artigo ocupa meia página.* The article takes up half a page. 2 (*cargo oficial*) hold 3 (*país*) occupy

odiar vt hate

ódio sm hatred (*for/of sb/sth*) ▶ **ter** ~ **de alguém/algo** hate sb/sth

odioso adj hateful

odor sm odor

oeste sm west (*abrev* **W.**): *a/no* ~ in the west ◊ *na costa* ~ on the west coast

ofegante adj breathless

ofegar vi pant

ofender vt offend ● **ofender-se** vp take offense (*at sth*): *Você se ofende com pouco.* You take offense at the slightest thing.

ofensa sf offense

ofensiva sf offensive

ofensivo adj offensive

oferecer vt 1 offer: ~ *um café a alguém* offer sb a cup of coffee 2 (*dar*) give: *Ele me ofereceu este livro.* He gave me this book. ● **oferecer-se** vp volunteer *to do sth*: ~ *como voluntário* volunteer

oferta sf 1 offer: *uma* ~ *especial* a special offer 2 (*Econ, Fin*) supply: *A procura é maior do que a* ~. Demand outstrips supply. ▶ **em** ~ on sale ~**s de emprego** job vacancies

oficial adj official ● smf (*polícia*) officer

oficina sf 1 workshop: *uma* ~ *de teatro/carpintaria* a theater/carpenter's workshop 2 (*Mec*) garage

ofício sm (*profissão*) trade

oh interj gee

oi interj hi

oitavo adj, num, sm eighth

oitenta num, sm eighty

oito num, sm 1 eight 2 (*data*) eighth

oitocentos num, sm eight hundred

olá interj hi (*coloq*), hello

olaria sf pottery

óleo sm oil: ~ *de girassol* sunflower oil ◊ ~ *lubrificante* lubricating oil ▶ **quadro/pintura a** ~ oil painting

oleoso adj (*pele, cabelo*) greasy

olfato sm sense of smell

olhada sf (*vista de olhos*) glance: *só com uma* ~ at a glance ◊ *dar uma* ~ *em algo* glance at sth ◊ *Uma* ~ *é o suficiente.* Just a quick look will do.

olhar¹ vt (*observar*) watch: *Olhavam as crianças brincando.* They watched the children playing. ● vi look: ~ *para o relógio* look at the clock ◊ ~ *para cima/baixo* look up/down ◊ ~ *nos olhos de alguém* look into sb's eyes ◊ ~ *pela janela* look out of the window ◊ *Ele olhava muito para você.* He kept looking at you. ● **olha** (*surpresa*) hey ▶ ~ **alguém de cima** look down your nose at sb **por onde quer que se olhe** whichever way you look at it

olhar² sm look: *ter um* ~ *inexpressivo* have a blank look

olheiras sf rings under your eyes

olho sm eye: *Ela é morena de ~s verdes.* She has dark hair and green eyes. ◇ *ter um bom ~ para os negócios* have a good eye for business ● **com os ~s vendados** blindfold ◊ **ficar de ~ em** keep an eye out for *sth/sb* ◊ **~ grande** envy ◊ **~ mágico** (*porta*) peephole ◊ **~ roxo** black eye ◊ **o que os ~s não vêem o coração não sente** what the eye doesn't see, the heart doesn't grieve over ◊ **passar os ~s por alto** skim through *sth* ◊ **pôr alguém no ~ da rua** fire sb ◊ **ver com bons ~s** approve of *sth/sth*

olímpico adj Olympic

oliveira sf olive tree

ombro sm shoulder: *carregar algo nos ~s* carry sth on your shoulders

omelete sf omelet

omitir vt leave sth out, omit (*fml*)

onça sf jaguar

onda sf wave: *~ sonora/de choque* sound/shock wave ◇ **estar na ~** be in fashion ◇ **ir na ~** go with the flow

onde pron rel where: *a cidade ~ nasci* the city where I was born ◇ **um lugar ~ morar** a place to live ◇ *a cidade para ~ se dirigem* the city they're heading for ◇ **um morro de ~ se vê o mar** a hill from where you can see the ocean ● adv where: *De ~ você é?* Where are you from? ◇ *Deixe-o ~ você puder.* Leave it wherever you can. ► **não ter ~ cair morto** have nothing to call your own ◇ **por ~?** which way?

ondulação sf 1 (*mar*) swell: *uma ~ forte* a heavy swell 2 (*cabelo*) wave

ondulado adj 1 (*cabelo*) wavy 2 (*superfície*) undulating 3 (*cartão, papel*) corrugated

ônibus sm bus: *apanhar/perder o ~* catch/miss the bus ► **espacial** space shuttle

ontem adv yesterday: *~ à tarde/de manhã* yesterday afternoon/morning ◇ *~ à noite* last night ◇ *o jornal de ~* yesterday's paper

ONU sf UN

onze num, sm 1 eleven 2 (*data*) eleventh

opaco adj opaque

opção sf option: *Ele não tem outra ~.* He has no option.

opcional adj optional

ópera sf opera

operação sf 1 operation: *sub-meter-se a uma ~ cardíaca* have a heart operation ◇ *uma ~ policial* a police operation 2 (*Fin*) transaction

operado adj ► **ser ~** have an operation

operador a sm-sf operator

operar vt, vi operate (on sb): *Tenho que ~ o pé.* I have to have an operation on my foot.

operário a adj 1 (*família, bairro*) working-class 2 (*sindicato*) labor: *o movimento ~* the labor movement ● sm-sf manual worker

opinar vt 1 think 2 (*dar um parecer*): *~ sobre algo* give an opinion on sth

opinião sf opinion: *na minha ~* in my opinion

oponente smf opponent

opor vt offer: *~ resistência a algo* offer resistance to sth ● **opor-se** vp 1 **~ a** oppose *sth*: *~ à reforma* oppose reform 2 (*objetar*) object: *Irei se os meus pais não se opuserem.* I'll go if my parents don't object.

oportunidade sf chance, opportunity [pl -ies] (*mais fml*): *ter a ~ de fazer algo* have the chance to do sth

oportunista smf opportunist

oportuno adj opportune: *um comentário/momento ~* an opportune remark/moment

oposição sf opposition (*to sb/sth*): *o líder da ~* the leader of the opposition

oposto adj, sm opposite (*of sth*): *Ele é o ~ do irmão.* He's the complete opposite of his brother.

opressão sf oppression

opressivo adj oppressive

oprimir vt oppress

optar vt opt for sth / to do sth

ora adv now: *por ~* for now ► **~ essa** come now ◇ **ora..., ora...**: *Ora ele estuda, ~ não estuda.* Sometimes he studies, sometimes he doesn't. ◇ *Ora chove, ~ faz sol.* One minute it's raining, the next it's sunny.

oração sf 1 (*Relig*) prayer: *fazer uma ~* say a prayer 2 (*Gram*) **(a)** sentence **(b)** (*proposição*) clause: *uma ~ subordinada* a subordinate clause

oral adj, sf oral

orar vi pray

órbita sf 1 orbit: *entrar/estar em ~* go into/be in orbit 2 (*olho*) socket

orçamento sm 1 (*gastos*) budget 2 (*estimativa*) estimate:

Pedi que me fizessem um ~. I asked them for an estimate.

ordem *sf* **1** order: *em/por ~ alfabética* in alphabetical order ◇ *dar ordens* give orders ◇ *por ~ do juiz* by order of the court ◇ *a ~ dos franciscanos* the Franciscan order **2** (*associação*) association: *a ~ dos médicos* the medical association

ordenado¹ *sm* **1** pay: *pedir um aumento de ~* ask for a raise **2** (*mensal*) salary [*pl* -ies]

ordenado² *adj* neat

ordenar *vt* **1** put *sth* in order: *~ as fichas alfabeticamente* put the cards in alphabetical order **2** (*mandar*) order *sb to do sth*: *Ele ordenou que eu me sentasse.* He ordered me to sit down.

ordenhar *vt* milk

orelha *sf* ear ▶ **até as ~s** up to your ears (*in sth*): *endividado até as ~s* up to your ears in debt ◇ **em pé** on your guard

orfanato *sm* orphanage

órfão/ã *adj, sm-sf* orphan: *~s de guerra* war orphans ◇ *ser ~* be an orphan ▶ **~ de mãe/pai** motherless/fatherless

orgânico *adj* organic

organismo *sm* **1** (*Biol*) organism **2** (*organização*) organization

organização *sf* organization: *uma ~ internacional* an international organization ◇ *uma ~ juvenil* a youth group ▶ *as Nações Unidas* United Nations

organizador/a *adj* organizing ● *sm-sf* organizer

organizar *vt* organize ● **organizar-se** *vp* (*pessoa*): *~ (melhor)* get yourself (better) organized

órgão *sm* (*Anat, Mús*) organ ▶ **~ genitais/sexuais** genitals

orgulhar *vt* make *sb* proud ● **orgulhar-se** *vp* be proud *of sb/sth*

orgulho *sm* pride: *ferir o ~ de alguém* hurt sb's pride

orgulhoso *adj* proud

oriental *adj* eastern ● *smf* Asian **NOTA** Oriental também existe em inglês, mas pode ser considerada ofensiva.

orientar *vt* **1** (*posicionar*) position **2** (*dirigir*) show *sb* the way **3** (*aconselhar*) advise: *~ a alguém em relação aos cursos* advise sb about courses ● **orientar-se** *vp* (*encontrar o caminho*) find your way around

oriente *sm* east ▶ **o ~ Próximo/Médio/o Extremo ~** the Near/Middle/Far East

orifício *sm* hole: *um ~ de bala* a bullet hole

origem *sf* origin ▶ **dar ~ a** give rise to *sth*

original *adj, sm* original

originar *vt* lead to *sth* ● **originar-se** *vp* start: *O rio se origina nas montanhas.* The river has its source in the mountains.

ornamento *sm* decoration

orquestra *sf* **1** (*música clássica*) orchestra: *~ sinfônica/de câmara* symphony/chamber orchestra **2** (*música popular*) band: *~ de jazz* jazz band

orquídea *sf* orchid

ortografia *sf* spelling: *erros de ~* spelling mistakes

orvalho *sm* dew

os *art, def* the → THE ● *pron pess* them: *Vi-os/as.* I saw them. ▶ **os/as de...** **1** (*posse*): *os da minha avó* my grandmother's **2** (*característico*): *Prefiro os de ponta fina.* I prefer the ones with a fine point. ◇ *Gosto dos com motivo xadrez.* I like the checked ones. **3** (*roupa*): *as de vermelho* the ones in red **4** (*procedência*): *os de Bahia* the ones from Bahia **os/as que...** **1** (*pessoas*) those who: *os que estão aqui* those who are here ◇ *os que têm que madrugar* those of us who have to get up early ◇ *todos os que se candidataram* everyone who applied **2** (*coisas*) the ones (which/that)...: *as que compramos* the ones we bought

oscilar *vi* **1** (*candeeiro, pêndulo*) swing **2** (*preços, temperaturas*) vary (*from sth to sth*): *O preço oscila entre cinco e sete dólares.* The price varies from five to seven dollars.

osso *sm* bone ▶ **os ~s do ofício** part and parcel of the job **ser um ~ duro de roer** **1** (*rigoroso*) be very strict **2** (*difícil*) be a hard nut to crack

ostentar *vt* **1** (*exibir*) show **2** (*alardear*) show *sth* off

ostra *sf* oyster

otário/a *sm-sf* idiot

otimismo *sm* optimism

otimista *adj* optimistic ● *smf* optimist

ótimo *adj* excellent, great (*coloq*)

ou *conj* or ▶ **ou seja** in other words

ouriço-do-mar *sm* sea urchin

ouro *sm* **1** gold: *~ em folha* gold leaf ◇ *ter um coração de ~* have a heart of gold **2** (*ouros*) (*naipe*) diamonds → BARALHO ▶ **nem tudo o que brilha/reluz é** – all that glitters is not gold

ousado *adj* daring

outdoor *sm* billboard, hoarding (GB)

outono *sm* fall, autumn (GB): *no* ~ in the fall

outro/a *pron* another, other (one) [*pl* others] NOTA Usa-se **another** com substantivos no singular e **other** com substantivos no plural: *Não há* ~ *trem até as seis.* There isn't another train until six. ◇ *Você tem* ~? Do you have another (one)? ◇ *Não gosto destes. Você tem* ~s? I don't like these ones. Do you have any others? ◇ *Você tem outras cores?* Do you have any other colors? Também se utiliza **other** em expressões como: *o meu* ~ *irmão* my other brother. **um dia ou** ~ one day or another **O outro/a outra** traduzem-se por "the other one": *Onde está o* ~? Where's the other one? ▶ **em** ~**/noutro lugar, em outra/noutra parte** somewhere else **outra coisa** something else NOTA Em oração negativa, pode-se dizer **nothing else** ou **anything else**, dependendo de haver ou não outra partícula negativa na frase: *Eles não puderam fazer outra coisa.* They couldn't do anything else. ~**s) tanto(s) as** much/as many again: *Ele me pagou 5.000 reais e ainda me deve* ~ *tanto.* He's paid me 5,000 reals and still owes me as much again.

outubro *sm* October (*abrev* **Oct.**) → MAIO

ouvido *sm* 1 (*Anat*) ear: *Diga-me ao* ~. Whisper it in my ear. 2 (*sentido*) hearing ▶ **dar** ~**s** listen (to sb): *Ela nunca me dá* ~s. She never listens to me. **de** ~ by ear: *Toco piano de* ~. I play the piano by ear. **fazer** ~**s de mercador** turn a deaf ear (to sb/sth) **ser todo** ~**s** be all ears **ter bom** ~ have a good ear

ouvinte *smf* 1 listener 2 (*Educ, aluno*) auditor

ouvir *vt* 1 (*perceber sons*) hear: *Não ouvi você entrar.* I didn't hear you come in. 2 (*escutar*) listen (to sb/sth): ~ *o rádio* listen to the radio ▶ **de** ~ **falar**: *Conheço-o de* ~ *falar.* I've heard about him.

ova *sf* (**ovas**) 1 (*Zool*) ~s *de rã* frog spawn [U] 2 (*Cozinha*) roe [U] ▶ **uma** ~ no way

oval *adj* oval

ovário *sm* ovary [*pl* -ies]

ovelha *sf* 1 sheep [*pl* sheep]: *um rebanho de* ~s a flock of sheep 2 (*fêmea*) ewe ▶ ~ **negra** black sheep

overdose *sf* overdose

OVNI *sm* UFO [*pl* ~s]

ovo *sm* egg: *pôr um* ~ lay an egg ◇ ~ *cozido/frito/pochê* hard-boiled/fried/poached egg ◇ ~s *mexidos* scrambled eggs ▶ **de** ~ **virado** in a bad mood

oxidar *vt, vi* rust

oxigênio *sm* oxygen

ozônio *sm* ozone: *a camada de* ~ the ozone layer

Pp

pá *sf* 1 shovel 2 (*Cozinha, porco, vaca*) shoulder ▶ **da pá virada** wild **pá de lixo** dustpan

paciência *sf* 1 patience: *perder a* ~ lose your patience ◇ *A minha* ~ *está chegando ao fim.* My patience is wearing thin. 2 (*jogo de cartas*) solitaire, patience (GB): *jogar* ~ play a game of solitaire ● *interj* oh well ▶ **ter** ~ be patient

paciente *adj, smf* patient

pacífico *adj* 1 peaceful 2 (*oceano*) Pacific ● **Pacífico** *sm* Pacific (Ocean)

pacifista *smf* pacifist

pacote *sm* 1 (*comida*) packet 2 (*embrulho*) package, parcel (GB) → PACKAGE 3 (*Econ, Informát, turismo*) package: ~ *turístico* package tour

pacto *sm* agreement

pactuar *vi* make an agreement (with sb) (to do sth)

padaria *sf* bakery [*pl* -ies]

padeiro *a sm-sf* baker

padrão *adj, sm* 1 (*norma*) standard: *uniforme* ~ regulation uniform 2 (*desenho*) pattern 3 (*modelo*) model ▶ ~ **de vida** standard of living

padrasto *sm* stepfather

padre *sm* 1 priest 2 (*Padre*) (*título*) father: *o* ~ *Rui* Father Rui ◇ *o Santo* ~ the Holy Father

padrinho *sm* 1 (*batismo*) godfather [*pl* godparents] 2 (*casamento*) best man → CASAMENTO

padroeiro *a sm-sf* (*Relig*) patron saint

pagamento *sm* **1** (*ordenado*) pay **2** (*dívida*) payment: *efetuar/fazer um ~* make a payment

pagão/ã *adj, sm-sf* pagan

pagar *vt* pay (for) *sth*: *as dívidas/os impostos* pay your debts/taxes ◇ *os estudos de alguém* pay for sb's education ● *vi* pay: *Pagam bem.* They pay well. ▶ *~ adiantado* pay (*sth*) in advance *~ à vista/em dinheiro* pay (*for sth*) in cash *~ com cheque/cartão de crédito* pay (*for sth*) by check/credit card ◇ *o pato* carry the can (*GB*) *você me paga* you'll pay for this

pager *sm* pager

página *sf* page: *na ~ três* on page three

pai *sm* **1** father: *Ele é ~ de dois filhos.* He is the father of two children. **2** (**pais**) parents, mom and dad (*coloq*)

painel *sm* panel: *~ de controle* control panel

pai-nosso *sm* Our Father: *rezar dois ~s* say two Our Fathers

país *sm* country [*pl* -ies] ▶ *~ de Gales* Wales

paisagem *sf* landscape → SCENERY

paisana *sf* ▶ *à ~* **1** (*militar*) in civilian dress **2** (*polícia*) in plain clothes

paixão *sf* passion ▶ *ter ~ por alguém/algo* be crazy about sb/sth

palácio *sm* palace ▶ *~ da Justiça* Law Courts [*pl*]

paladar *sm* palate

palavra *sf* word: *uma ~ com duas letras* a two-letter word ◇ *Doulhe a minha ~.* I give you my word. ▶ *em outras/poucas ~s* in other/a few words *~ (de honra)* honest *~s cruzadas* crossword: *fazer as ~s cruzadas* do the crossword *ter a última ~* have the last word (*on sth*)

palavrão *sm* swear word: *dizer ~* swear

palco *sm* **1** (*teatro, etc.*) stage: *entrar no/subir ao ~* come onto the stage **2** (*lugar*) scene: *o ~ do crime* the scene of the crime

palerma *adj, smf* fool [*s*]: *Não seja ~.* Don't be a fool.

palestra *sf* **1** talk **2** (*conferência*) lecture

paleta *sf* (*pintor*) palette

paletó *sm* jacket

palha *sf* straw

palhaçada *sf* ▶ *fazer ~s* play the fool

palhaço/a *sm-sf* clown

palheiro *sm* hay loft

pálido/a *adj* pale: *rosa ~* pale pink

palito *sm* (*para os dentes*) toothpick ▶ *estar um ~* be as thin as a rake

palma *sf* palm

palmada *sf* slap: *dar uma ~ em alguém* slap sb

palmeira *sf* palm (tree)

palmo *sm*: *Ele é um ~ mais alto do que eu.* He's several inches taller than me. ▶ *palmo a palmo* inch by inch

pálpebra *sf* eyelid

palpitar *vi* (*coração*) beat

palpite *sm* **1** (*pressentimento*) hunch **2** (*opinião*) opinion ▶ *dar ~* put in your two cents' worth, stick your oar in (*GB*)

pâncreas *sm* pancreas

panda *sm* panda

pandeiro *sm* tambourine

panela *sf* saucepan: *lavar as ~s* do the pots and pans ▶ *~ de pressão* pressure cooker

panfleto *sm* pamphlet

pânico *sm* panic

pano *sm* **1** cloth, material, fabric NOTA **Cloth** é o termo mais geral para pano. Designa tanto o pano usado na confecção de roupas, cortinas, etc., como o material com que é feita determinada coisa: *um saco de ~* a cloth bag. **Material** e **fabric** designam apenas o pano usado na confecção de vestuário e tapeçaria. **Material** e **fabric** são substantivos contáveis e não contáveis, ao passo que **cloth** é não contável quando significa tecido: *Alguns tecidos encolhem ao lavar.* Some materials/fabrics shrink when you wash them. ◇ *Preciso de mais ~/tecido para as cortinas.* I need some more cloth/material/fabric for the curtains. **2** (*Teatro*) curtain: *Subiram o ~.* The curtain went up. ▶ *~ de pó* duster *~ de prato* dish towel, tea towel (*GB*) *por baixo do ~* under the counter

panorama *sm* **1** (*vista*) view **2** (*perspectiva*) prospect

panqueca *sf* pancake

pântano sm marsh

pantera sf panther

pantufa sf slipper

pão sm 1 bread [U]: *Você quer ~?* Do you want some bread? ◊ *~ integral* wholewheat bread ◊ *~ dormido* stale bread → BREAD 2 (*individual*) (a) (*pequeno*) roll: *Eu quero três pães, por favor.* Could I have three rolls, please? (b) (*grande*) (round) loaf [pl loaves]: *~ de fôrma* white loaf ▶ **dizer/ser pão, pão, queijo, queijo** call a spade a spade ~ **doce bun ser um ~** (*homem*) be a hunk

Pão de Açúcar sm Sugar Loaf Mountain

pão-de-ló sm sponge cake

pão-duro sm adj stingy ● sm-sf skinflint

pãozinho sm roll

papa¹ sm pope: *o ~ João Paulo II* Pope John Paul II

papa² sf (*bebê*) baby food ▶ **não ter ~s na língua** not beat around the bush

papagaio sm 1 (*ave*) parrot 2 (*brinquedo*) kite

papai sm dad NOTA As crianças pequenas dizem **daddy**. ▶ ~ **Noel** Santa Claus, Father Christmas

papel sm 1 (*material*) paper [U]: *uma folha de ~* a sheet of paper ◊ *guardanapos de ~* paper napkins ◊ *~ quadriculado/reciclado* graph/recycled paper 2 (*recorte, pedaço*) piece of paper: *anotar algo num ~* note sth down on a piece of paper 3 (*personagem, função*) part, role (*mais fml*): *~ principal/ secundário* leading/supporting role ◊ *fazer o ~ de Otelo* play the part of Othello ◊ *Terá um ~ importante na reforma.* It will play an important part in the reform. ▶ ~ **de alumínio** aluminum foil ~ **de carta/de embrulho** writing/wrapping paper ~ **de parede** wallpaper ~ **higiênico** toilet paper ~ **vegetal 1** (*para cozinhar*) waxed paper, greaseproof paper (GB) 2 (*de desenho*) tracing paper

papelada sf paperwork

papelão sm cardboard: *uma caixa de ~* a cardboard box ▶ **fazer um ~** make a fool of yourself

papelaria sf office supply store, stationer's (GB)

papoula sf poppy [pl -ies]

paquerar vt, vi flirt (with sb)

par adj even: *números ~es* even

numbers ● sm 1 (*em relação amorosa*) couple: *Eles fazem um lindo ~.* They make a really nice couple. 2 (*equipe, coisas*) pair: *o ~ vencedor do torneio* the winning pair in the tournament ◊ *um ~ de meias* a pair of socks 3 (*em jogos, em dança*) partner ▶ **a ~ (de)** up to date (on sth): *Estou a ~ da situação.* I'm up to date on what's happening. **aos pares** two by two: *entrar aos ~es* go in two by two **por alguém a ~** fill sb in (on sth) **sem ~** incomparable

para prep 1 for: *muito difícil ~ mim* too hard for me ◊ *~ que é que você o quer?* What do you want it for? ◊ *Comprei-o ~ meu filho.* I bought it for my son. 2 (a) to: *Dê-o ao seu irmão.* Give it to your brother. 3 + inf to do sth: *Eles vieram ~ ficar.* They came to stay. ◊ *~ não perdê-lo* so as not to miss it 4 (*futuro*): *Preciso dele ~ sexta.* I need it for Friday. ◊ *Deve estar pronto lá ~ o outono.* It ought to be finished by fall. 5 (*em direção a*) to, toward: *Ela foi ~ a cama.* She went to bed. ◊ *dirigir-se ~ a cama* move toward the bed ◊ *Eles já estão indo ~ lá.* They're on their way. ▶ ~ **isso:** *Foi ~ isso que você me chamou?* Is that why you called me? ~ **que... so (that)...:** *Ele os repreendeu ~ que tornassem a fazer o mesmo.* He lectured them so that they wouldn't do it again. ~ **si: dizer algo ~ si próprio** say sth to yourself

parabenizar vt congratulate

parabéns sm 1 best wishes (on...): *~ pelo seu aniversário.* Best wishes on your birthday. ◊ *Parabéns!* Happy Birthday! 2 (*felicitação*) congratulations (on (doing) sth): *Meus ~!* Congratulations! ▶ **dar os ~ 1** (*por determinado êxito*) congratulate sb (on sth) 2 (*por aniversário*) wish sb a happy birthday

parábola sf 1 (*Bíblia*) parable 2 (*Geom*) parábola

parabólica sf satellite dish

pára-brisa sm windshield, windscreen (GB)

pára-choque sm fender, bumper (GB)

parada sf 1 stop: *~ de ônibus* bus stop 2 (*Med*): *~ cardíaca* cardiac arrest ▶ **a ~ de sucessos** the charts

paradeiro sm whereabouts [pl]

parado adj 1 (*imóvel*) motionless 2 (*imobilizado*) at a standstill: *As obras estão paradas já* *faz um mês*. The roadworks have been at a standstill for a month. **3** (*desligado*) switched off

parafuso *sm* screw: *apertar um* ~ tighten a screw

parágrafo *sm* paragraph

Paraguai *sm* Paraguay

paraguaio/a *adj, sm-sf* Paraguayan

paraíso *sm* paradise ▶ ~ **terrestre** heaven on earth

pára-lama *sm* **1** (*bicicleta*) mudguard **2** (*automóvel*) fender, wing (GB)

paralelo *adj, sm* parallel (*to sth*): *linhas paralelas* parallel lines

paralisar *vt* paralyze

paralisia *sf* paralysis [U]

paralítico *adj* paralyzed

parapeito *sm* windowsill

pára-quedas *sm* parachute: *saltar de* ~ parachute

pára-quedista *smf* parachutist

parar *vt, vi* **1** stop: *Pare o carro.* Stop the car. ◊ *O trem não parou.* The train didn't stop. ◊ *Parei para falar com uma amiga.* I stopped to talk to a friend. **2** ~ **de fazer** *algo* stop doing sth ▶ ~ **em** end up: *Foram* ~ *na prisão.* They ended up in prison. **não** ~ be always on the go **sem** ~ non-stop: *trabalhar sem* ~ work non-stop **ser de** ~ **o trânsito** (*muito atraente*) be a stunner

pára-raios *sm* lightning rod, lightning conductor (GB)

parasita *smf* **1** parasite **2** (*pessoa*) freeloader, scrounger (GB)

parceiro/a *sm-sf* partner: *Não posso jogar porque não tenho* ~. I can't play because I don't have a partner. ◊ *Ana veio com o* ~ *dela.* Ana came with her partner.

parcela *sf* **1** portion: *uma* ~ *da população* a sector of the population **2** (*pagamento*) installment

parcial *adj* **1** (*incompleto*) partial **2** (*partidário*) biased

pardal *sm* sparrow

parecer¹ *sm* opinion

parecer² *vi* **1** (*dar a impressão*) seem: *Eles parecem* (*estar*) *muito seguros.* They seem very certain. ◊ *Parece que foi ontem.* It seems like only yesterday. **2** (*ter aspecto*) **(a)** **+ adj** look: *Ela parece mais jovem do que é.* She looks younger than she is. **(b)** **+ substantivo** look like *sb/sth*: *Ela parece uma atriz.* She looks like

an actress. ● *vt* (*opinar*) think: *Pareceu-me que ele não tinha razão.* I thought he was wrong. ● **parecer-se** *vp* **1** (*pessoas*) **(a)** (*fisicamente*) look alike, look like *sb*: *Eles se parecem muito.* They look very much alike. ◊ *Você se parece com a sua irmã.* You look like your sister. **(b)** (*em caráter*) be like *sb*: *Ele se parece muito com o pai.* He's just like his father. **2** (*coisas*) be similar (*to sth*) ▶ **até parece que…**: *Até parece que sou milionário!* Anyone would think I was a millionaire!

parecido *adj* **1** (*pessoas*) alike, like *sb*: *Vocês são tão* ~*s!* You're so alike! ◊ *Você é muito parecida com a sua mãe.* You're very like your mother. **2** (*coisas*) similar (*to sth*): *Esse vestido é* ~ *com o meu.* That dress is similar to mine. ▶ **(ou) algo** ~ (or) something like that

parede *sf* wall: ~ *divisória* partition wall ◊ *Há uma foto na* ~. There's a photo on the wall. ▶ **as** ~**s têm ouvidos** walls have ears

parente/a *sm-sf* relation: ~ *próximo/afastado* close/distant relation ▶ **ser** ~ (**de alguém**) be related (to sb)

parentesco *sm* relationship ▶ **ter** ~ **com alguém** be related to sb

parêntese *sm* (*sinal*) parentheses, brackets (GB) [*pl*]: *entre* ~*s* in parentheses

parir *vt, vi* give birth (*to sb/sth*)

parlamentar *adj* parliamentary ● *smf* Congressman/woman [*pl* -men/-women], Member of Parliament (GB)

parlamento *sm* parliament

pároco *sm* parish priest

paródia *sf* parody [*pl* -ies]

paróquia *sf* **1** (*igreja*) parish church **2** (*comunidade*) parish

parque *sm* **1** (*jardim*) park **2** (*de bebê*) playpen ▶ ~ **de camping** campsite ~ **de diversões/temático** amusement/theme park ~ **infantil** playground

parquímetro *sm* parking meter

parreira *sf* vine

parte *sf* **1** part: *três* ~*s iguais* three equal parts ◊ *Em que* ~ *da cidade você mora?* Which part of town do you live in? **2** (*pessoa*) party [*pl* -ies]: *a* ~ *contrária* the opposing party ▶ **à** ~ **1** (*de lado*) aside: *Porei estes papéis à* ~. I'll put these documents aside. **2** (*separadamente*) separate(ly): *Para estas coisas, faça uma conta à* ~. Give me a separate bill for these items. ◊ *Vou pagar isto* ~ I'll pay for this separately. **3** (*exceto*) apart from *sb/sth* **4** *um mundo à* ~ a different world **a** ~ **de baixo/cima** the bottom/top **a** ~ **de trás/da frente** the back/front **da** ~ **de alguém** on behalf of *sb* **da** ~ **de quem?** (*ao telefone*) who's calling? **dar** ~: **report**: *dar* ~ *de alguém à polícia* report *sb* to the police **de minha, etc.** ~ as far as I, you are, etc. concerned: *De nossa* ~ *não há nenhum problema.* As far as we're concerned, there's no problem. **em/por toda(s) a(s)** ~**(s)** everywhere **por** ~ **sth** by bit: *consertar o telhado por* ~ repair the roof bit by bit **tomar** ~ take part (*in sth*)

parteira *sf* midwife [*pl* -wives]

participação *sf* participation: *a* ~ *do público* audience participation

participante *adj*: *os países* ~*s* the participating countries ● *smf* participant

participar *vi* participate, take part (*mais coloq*) (*in sth*)

partícula *sf* particle

particular *adj* **1** (*privado*) private: *aulas* ~*es* private classes **2** (*característico*) characteristic: *um sabor* ~ a characteristic taste ▶ **em** ~ **1** (*especialmente*) in particular **2** (*confidencialmente*) in private

particularmente *adv* particularly

partida *sf* **1** (*saída*) departure: ~*s nacionais* domestic departures ◊ *o painel de* ~*s* the departures board ◊ *estar de* ~ be leaving **2** (*corrida*) start **3** (*jogo*) game: *jogar uma* ~ *de xadrez* have a game of chess

partidário/a *adj* in favor of (*doing*) *sth* ● *sm-sf* supporter

partido *sm* (*Pol*) party [*pl* -ies] ▶ **tirar** ~ **de alguém/algo** take advantage of *sb/sth* **tomar o** ~ **de alguém** side with *sb*

partilhar *vt* share

partir *vt* **1** break **2** (*com faca*) cut *sth* (up): *o bolo* cut the cake **3** (*com as mãos*) break *sth* (off): *Você me parte um pedaço de pão?* Could you break me off a piece of bread? **4** (*noz*) crack **5** (*rachar*) split ● *vi* (*ir-se embora*) leave (*for...*): *Ela parte amanhã para Cuiabá.* She's leaving for Cuiabá tomorrow. ● **partir(-se)**

vi, **vp 1** (*quebrar*) break **2** (*corda*) snap ▶ **a** ~ **de...** (*on*): *a* ~ *das nove da noite* from 9 p.m. on ◊ *a* ~ *de então* from then on ◊ *a* ~ *de amanhã* starting from tomorrow

partitura *sf* score

parto *sm* birth

Páscoa *sf* Easter

pasmado *adj* amazed (*at/by sth*)

passa *sf* (*uva*) raisin

passada *sf* step ▶ **dar uma** ~ **em** stop by..., call in at... (*sb*)

passado¹ *adj* **1** (*carne*): *bem* ~/ ~ *demais* well done/overdone ◊ *mal* ~ rare NOTA Para um bife no ponto, diz-se **medium rare**. **2** (*fruta*) bad **3** (*peixe*) off

passado² *adj* **1** (*dia, semana, mês, verão, etc.*) last **2** (*Gram, época*) past: *séculos* ~*s* past centuries ● *sm* past

passageiro/a *sm-sf* passenger

passagem *sf* **1** passage: *a* ~ *do tempo* the passage of time **2** (*acesso*): *Por aqui não há* ~. There's no way through. ◊ ~ *proibida* no access ▶ **de** ~ in passing ~ **de ano** New Year's Eve ~ **de nível** grade crossing, level crossing (*GB*) ~ **subterrânea** underpass

passaporte *sm* passport

passar **1** *vt*, *vi* pass: *Pode me* ~ *esse livro?* Could you pass me that book, please? ◊ ~ *o tempo* pass the time ◊ *A moto passou a toda a velocidade.* The motorcycle passed at top speed. ◊ *Passaram três horas.* Three hours passed. ◊ *Já passou um ano desde que ele escreveu.* It's a year since he wrote. ◊ *Como o tempo passa!* How time flies! ◊ *Esse ônibus passa pelo museu.* That bus goes past the museum. ◊ ~ *por alguém na rua* pass *sb* in the street **2** *vt* (*período de tempo*) spend: *Passamos a tarde conversando.* We spent the afternoon talking. **3** *vt* (*ponte, rio, fronteira*) cross **4** *vt*, *vi* (*filme, programa*) show: *O que é que está passando na televisão esta noite?* What's on TV tonight? **5** *vt* (*a ferro*) iron: *É a minha vez de* ~ *a roupa.* It's my turn to do the ironing. **6** *vt* (*doença, vírus*) pass *sth* on **7** *vt* (*aplicar*) apply **8** *vi* (*ir*) go: *Amanhã passo pelo banco.* I'll go to the bank tomorrow. **9** *vi* (*terminar*) be over: *Não chore mais.* Don't cry, it's all over now. ◊ *A dor de cabeça dela já passou.* Her headache's better now. **10** (*Educ*) pass: *Passei em física na primeira.* I passed physics first time. ◊ *Passei de ano.* I've (now) moved up a year. ● **passar-se** *vp* **1** (*acontecer*) happen: *Passou-se o mesmo comigo.* The same thing happened to me. **2** (*romance, filme*) be set (*in…*) ▶ **como tem passado?** how have you been? **fazer-se ~ por…** pass yourself off as *sb/sth* **não ~ de…** be nothing but…: *Tudo isto não passa de um grande mal-entendido.* The whole thing's nothing but a misunderstanding. **o (que é) que se passa?** what's the matter? ~ **alguém para trás 1** (*negócios*) con sb **2** (*romance*) cheat on sb ~ **bem 1** (*sobreviver*) do without *sb/sth*: *Passo bem sem a sua ajuda.* I can do without your help. **2** (*omitir*) skip: ~ **sem comer** skip a meal ~ **por 1** (*confundir-se*) pass for *sb/sth*: *Essa garota passa facilmente por italiana.* That girl could easily pass for an Italian. **2** (*atravessar*) go through *sth*: ~ **por maus bocados** have a hard time NOTA Para outras expressões com **passar**, ver o substantivo, adjetivo, etc., p. ex. **passar um carão** em CARÃO.

pássaro *sm* bird ▶ **mais vale um ~ na mão que dois voando** a bird in the hand is worth two in the bush

passatempo *sm* hobby [*pl* -ies]: *como/por* ~ as a hobby

passe *sm* **1** (*trem*) season ticket **2** (*autorização*) pass: *entrar sem* ~ get in without a pass **3** (*Futebol*) pass

passear *vi* walk: ~ *pela praia* walk along the beach ◊ *levar o cachorro para* ~ take the dog for a walk

passeata *sf* march: *fazer uma* ~ hold a march

passeio *sm* **1** (*a pé*) walk: *dar um* ~ go for a walk **2** (*de bicicleta, a cavalo*) ride **3** (*de carro*) drive **4** (*rua*) sidewalk, pavement (*GB*)

passivo/a *adj* passive: *na voz passiva* in the passive

passo *sm* **1** step: ~ *a* ~ step by step ◊ *dar um* ~ *atrás/em frente* take a step back/forward ◊ *um* ~ *para a paz* a step towards peace **2** (*ruído*) footstep: *ouvir* ~*s* hear footsteps **3** (*ritmo*) pace: *a* ~ *de cágado* at a snail's pace ◊ *Neste* ~ *não vamos chegar lá nunca.* We'll never get

---

there at this rate. ▶ **ao ~ que…** while… **ficar a ~s** *Fica a dois ~s daqui.* It's just around the corner from here.

pasta¹ *sf* **1** (*maleta*) briefcase **2** (*da escola*) school bag **3** (*cartolina, plástico*) binder **4** (*Informát*) folder **5** (*médico*) (doctor's) bag **6** (*Pol*) portfolio

pasta² *sf* paste ▶ ~ **de dentes** toothpaste

pastar *vi* graze

pastel *sm* **1** (*para comer*) pastry [*pl* -ies] **2** (*Arte*) pastel

pastilha *sf* (*doce*) pastille ▶ ~ **para a garganta/tosse** throat lozenge/cough drop

pasto *sm* pasture

pastor/a *sm-sf* **1** (*guardador de gado*) shepherd [*fem* -ess] **2** (*sacerdote*) minister ▶ ~ **alemão** German shepherd

pata *sf* (*pé de animal*) **(a)** (*quadrúpede com unhas*) paw: *O cachorro machucou a* ~. The dog hurt its paw. **(b)** (*casco*) hoof [*pl* ~s/hooves] **2** *Ver* PATO

patada *sf* kick: *Ele deu uma* ~ *na mesa.* He kicked the table. ◊ *levar uma* ~ be kicked

patamar *sm* **1** (*escada*) landing **2** (*nível*) level

patavina *sf* ▶ **não entender/ saber** ~ not understand/know a thing: *Não sei* ~ *de francês.* I don't know a word of French.

patê *sm* pâté

patente *sf* patent

paternal *adj* fatherly, paternal (*mais fml*)

paternidade *sf* fatherhood, paternity (*fml*)

paterno/a *adj* **1** (*paternal*) fatherly **2** (*parentesco*) paternal: *avô* ~ paternal grandfather

pateta *smf* halfwit

patife *sm* scoundrel

patim *sm* **1** roller skate: *patins em linha* in-line skates **2** (*de lâmina*) ice skate

patinação *sf* skating: ~ *no gelo/ artística* ice skating/figure skating

patinador/a *sm-sf* skater

patinar *vi* skate

patinho/a *sm-sf* duckling

pátio *sm* **1** courtyard **2** (*escola*) playground

pato/a *sm-sf* duck NOTA Falando só do macho, diz-se **drake**.

patrão/oa *sm-sf* boss

pátria *sf* (*native*) country [*pl* -ies]

patrício/a *sm-sf* (*compatriota*)

P

fellow countryman/woman [*pl* -men/-women]

patrimônio *sm* **1** (*herança*) heritage: ~ **nacional** national heritage **2** (*bens*) property [U]

patriota *smf* patriot

patriótico *adj* patriotic

patriotismo *sm* patriotism

patrocinador/a *sm-sf* sponsor

patrocinar *vt* sponsor

patrocínio *sm* sponsorship

patrono/a *sm-sf* (*Relig*) patron saint

patrulha *sf* patrol: **carro de ~** patrol car

patrulhar *vt, vi* patrol

pau *sm* **1** stick **2** (*paus*) (*naipe*) clubs → BARALHO ▶ **a dar com o ~** loads of sth: **gente a dar com o ~** loads of people **de ~** wooden

paulista *adj, smf* (person from) São Paulo State: **os ~s** the people of São Paulo State

paulistano/a *adj, sm-sf* (person from) São Paulo: **os ~s** the people of São Paulo

pausa *sf* pause: **fazer uma ~** pause

pausado/a *adj* slow

pauta *sf* **1** (*discussão*) agenda **2** (*Mús*) stave

pauzinhos *sm* (*talher*) chopsticks

pavão/oa *sm-sf* peacock [*fem* peahen]

pavilhão *sm* **1** (*exposição*) pavilion: **o ~ da França** the French pavilion **2** (*Esporte*) gym

pavimentar *vt* pave

pavimento *sm* **1** (*rua*) surface **2** (*andar*) story [*pl* -ies]

pavio *sm* (*vela*) wick ▶ **ter o ~ curto** have a short fuse

pavor *sm* terror ▶ **ter ~ de alguém/algo** be terrified of sb/sth

paz *sf* peace: **plano de ~** peace plan ◊ **em tempo(s) de ~** in peacetime ▶ **deixar em ~** leave sb/sth alone **fazer as ~es** make it up (with sb)

pé *sm* **1** foot [*pl* feet]: **o pé direito/esquerdo** your right/left foot ◊ **ter o pé chato** have flat feet **2** (*estátua, coluna*) pedestal **3** (*copo*) stem **4** (*abajur*) stand **5** (*mesa, cadeira*) leg ▶ **ao pé da letra** literally **ao pé de** near: **Sentamos ao pé da lareira.** We sat by the fire. **dar no pé** (*fugir*) run off **dar pé 1** (*em água*) **Não dá pé.** I'm out of my depth. **2** (*ser possível*): **Amanhã não dá pé.** I can't make it tomorrow. **dos pés à cabeça** from top to toe **estar de pé ~**

standing (up) **ficar de pé stand up** ▶ **ficar no pé de alguém** nag sb **não ter pé nem cabeça** be absurd

peão *sm* **1** (*trabalhador rural*) farm laborer **2** (*xadrez*) pawn

peça *sf* **1** (*xadrez, Mús, etc.*) piece **2** (*Mec*) part: **uma ~ sobressalente** a spare part ▶ **~ de roupa/vestuário** garment **~ (teatral ou de teatro)** play

pecado *sm* sin

pecador/a *sm-sf* sinner

pecar *vi* sin ▶ **~ por** be too...: **Você peca por confiar demais.** You're too trusting.

pechincha *sf* bargain

pechinchar *vi* haggle

peculiar *adj* **1** (*especial*) special **2** (*característico*) particular

pedacinho *sm* ▶ **fazer em ~s** (*papel, tecido*) tear sth to shreds

pedaço *sm* piece: **um ~ de bolo/pão** a piece of cake/bread ◊ **cortar algo em ~s** cut sth into pieces ◊ **cair aos ~s** fall to pieces

pedágio *sm* toll

pedagogia *sf* education

pedagógico *adj* educational

pedal *sm* pedal

pedalar *vi* pedal

pedalinho *sm* (*embarcação*) pedalo [*pl* ~s]

pedante *adj* pretentious

pé-de-pato *sm* (*nadador, mergulhador*) flipper

pedestre *smf* pedestrian

pediatra *smf* pediatrician

pedicuro/a *sm-sf* podiatrist

pedido *sm* **1** request (*for sth*): **a ~ de alguém** at sb's request **2** (*Com*) order ▶ **~ de casamento** marriage proposal

pedinte *smf* beggar

pedir *vt* **1** ask (*sb*) for sth: **~ a conta** ask for the bill ◊ **~ ajuda aos vizinhos** ask the neighbors for help **2** (*autorização, favor, quantidade*) ask (*sb*) (*sth*): **pedir um favor a alguém** ask sb a favor ◊ **Eles estão pedindo mil dólares.** They're asking a thousand dollars. **3** + **algo que faça/para fazer algo** ask sb to do sth: **Ele me pediu que esperasse/para esperar.** He asked me to wait. **4** (*encomendar*) order: **Como entrada pedimos sopa.** For first course we ordered soup. ▶ **~ desculpa/perdão** apologize (*to sb*) (*for sth*) **~ demissão** resign **~ emprestado** borrow: **Ele me pediu o**

carro emprestado. He borrowed my car. ~ **esmola** beg

pedra *sf* **1** stone: *uma ~ preciosa* a precious stone ◇ *um muro de ~* a stone wall **2** (*lápide*) tombstone **3** (*granizo*) hailstone ▸ *de ~* (*insensível*) hard-hearted ~ **de gelo** ice cube **ser uma ~ no sapato de alguém** be a thorn in sb's side

pedrada *sf*: *Receberam-no a ~s.* They threw stones at him.

pedreira *sf* quarry [*pl* -ies]

pedreiro *sm* **1** (*mason*) stonemason **2** (*que põe tijolos*) bricklayer

pegada *sf* **1** (*pessoa*) footprint **2** (*animal*) track

pegado *adj* (*muito perto*) right next to *sb/sth*

pegajoso *adj* sticky

pegar *vt* **1** catch: *Aposto que você não me pega!* I bet you can't catch me! ◇ ~ *uma bola* catch a ball ◇ ~ *alguém roubando* catch sb stealing ◇ ~ *um resfriado* catch a cold **2** (*levar*) take: *Pegue os livros que quiser.* Take as many books as you like. **3** (*agarrar, segurar*) take hold of *sth*: *Pegue nesse lado que eu pego neste.* You take hold of that side and I'll take this one. **4** (*hábito, vício, sotaque*) pick up ▸ *vi* **1** (*motor, carro*) start **2** (*mentira, desculpa*): *Não vai ~.* Nobody will believe that. **3** (*idéia, moda*) catch on **4** (*colar-se*) stick **5** (*doença*) be catching ● **pegar-se** *vp* (*brigar*) come to blows (*with sb*) ▸ **pegar e...** up and *do sth*: *Peguei e fui-me embora.* I upped and left.

peito *sm* **1** chest: *dores no ~* chest pains **2** (*mamas, pessoas*) (a) (*busto*) bust (b) (*mama*) breast **3** (*ave*): ~ *de frango* chicken breast ▸ **no ~ (e na raça)** whatever it takes ~ **do pé** instep

peitoril *sm* **1** ledge **2** (*janela*) window sill

peixaria *sf* fish market

peixe *sm* fish [*pl* fish]: *Vou comprar* ~. I'm going to buy some fish. ◇ ~*s de água doce* freshwater fish ▸ **FISH** ◇ **como um ~ fora d'água** like a fish out of water ~ **dourado** goldfish [*pl* goldfish]

peixe-espada *sm* swordfish

peixeiro a *sm-sf* fish seller

Peixes (*Astrol*) Pisces

pelada *sf* game (*of soccer*)

pelado *adj* **1** (*nu*) naked **2** (*sem dinheiro*) broke

pele *sf* **1** (*Anat*) skin: ~ *branca/morena* fair/dark skin ◇ *um tapete de* ~ *de carneiro* a sheepskin rug ◇ *cor-da-pele* skin **2** (*com pêlo*) fur: *um casaco de* ~ a fur coat ▸ **arriscar/salvar a ~** risk/save your neck **cair na ~ de alguém** make fun of sb **só e o osso** nothing but skin and bone

pelicano *sm* pelican

película *sf* **1** movie, film (*GB*) **2** (*Fot*) film

pêlo *sm* **1** hair: *ter ~s nas pernas* have hair on your legs **2** (*pele de animal*) coat

pelota *sf* ball ▸ **dar ~** pay attention *to sth*

pelotão *sm* platoon

pelúcia *sf* plush

peludo *adj* **1** hairy **2** (*animal*) furry

pena¹ *sf* (*ave*) feather: *um travesseiro de ~s* a feather pillow

pena² *sf* **1** (*tristeza*) sorrow: *Essas crianças me dão tanta ~.* I feel so sorry for these children. **2** (*lástima*) pity: *Que ~ que você não possa vir!* What a pity you can't come! **3** (*condenação*) sentence: *Ele foi condenado a uma ~ de cinco anos.* He was given a five-year sentence. ◇ **cumprir ~** serve a term in prison ▸ **vale a pena.../não vale a pena...** it's worth there's no point in doing *sth*: *vale a ~ lê-lo.* It's worth reading. ◇ *Não vale a ~ gritar.* There's no point in shouting. ~ **de morte** death penalty

penal *adj* penal

penalidade *sf* penalty [*pl* -ies]

pênalti *sm* (*Esporte*) penalty [*pl* -ies]: *cobrar/conceder um ~* take/concede a penalty ◇ *marcar um (gol de) ~* score (from) a penalty

penca *sf* (*bananas, etc.*) bunch

pendente *adj* **1** (*assunto, dívida, problema*) outstanding **2** (*decisão, veredicto*) pending ● *sm* pendant

pendurado *adj* hanging *on/from sth*

pendurar *vt* **1** hang *sth* (*from/on sth*) ▸ **ENFORCAR(-SE) 2** (*roupa*) hang *sth* up **3** (*pagamento*) buy *sth* on credit ▸ ~ **as chuteiras** (*aposentar-se*) retire

peneira *sf* sieve

penetra *smf* gatecrasher: *entrar de ~ numa festa* crash a party

penetrante *adj* **1** penetrating: *um olhar* ~ a penetrating look **2** (*frio, vento*) bitter

penetrar *vt, vi* **1** (*entrar*) enter, get into *sth* (*mais coloq*): *A água* *penetrou no porão.* The water got into the basement. **2** (*bala, flecha, som*) pierce

penhasco *sm* cliff

penhor *sm* pledge

penhorar *vt* pawn

penicilina *sf* penicillin

penico *sm* potty [*pl* -ies]

península *sf* peninsula

pênis *sm* penis

penitência *sf* penance: *fazer ~* do penance

penitenciária *sf* prison

penoso *adj* **1** (*assunto, tratamento*) painful **2** (*trabalho, estudo*) difficult

pensamento *sm* thought

pensão *sf* **1** (*aposentadoria*) pension: *uma ~ de viúva* a widow's pension **2** (*residencial*) boarding house ● **alimentícia** maintenance ● ~ **completa/meia** ~ full/half board

pensar *vt, vi* **1** ~ **(em)** think (about/of *sb/(doing) sth*): *Pense num número.* ◊ *No que você está pensando?* What are you thinking about? ◊ *Você só pensa em si próprio.* You only ever think of yourself. ◊ *Estamos pensando em casar.* We're thinking of getting married. **2** (*opinar*) think *sth of sb/sth*: *Não pense mal deles.* Don't think badly of them. **3** (*ter decidido*): *Pensava ir amanhã.* I was thinking of going tomorrow. ▶ **nem** ~ **no way** *pensando bem...* on second thoughts... ● **na morte da bezerra** daydream *sem ~ duas vezes* without a second thought

pensativo *adj* thoughtful

pensionista *smf* pensioner

pente *sm* comb

penteadeira *sf* dressing table

penteado *adj*: *Você ainda não está penteada?* Haven't you done your hair yet? ● **sm** hairstyle ▶ **andar/estar bem/mal ~**: *Ela estava muito bem penteada.* Her hair looked really nice. ◊ *Ele anda sempre mal ~.* His hair always looks messy.

pentear *vt* **1** comb *sb's* hair: *Deixe-me ~ você.* Let me comb your hair. **2** (*cabeleireiro*) do *sb's* hair ● **pentear-se** *vp* comb your hair

penugem *sf* **1** (*ave*) down **2** (*pêlo*) fluff

penúltimo *adj* penultimate (*fml*), second to last: *o ~ capítulo* the penultimate chapter ◊

a penúltima parada the second to last stop

penumbra *sf* half-light

pepino *sm* cucumber

pequeno *adj* **1** small: *um ~ problema/detalhe* a small problem/ detail ◊ *O quarto é ~ demais.* The room is too small. → SMALL **2** (*criança*) little: *quando eu era ~* when I was little **3** (*pouco importante*) minor: *umas pequenas alterações* a few minor changes

pêra *sf* pear

perante *prep* **1** before: ~ *as câmaras/o juiz* before the cameras/the judge **2** (*face a*) in the face of *sth*: ~ *as dificuldades* in the face of adversity

perceber *vt* realize

percentagem *sf* Ver PORCENTAGEM

percevejo *sm* **1** (*preguinho*) thumbtack, drawing pin (*GB*) **2** (*inseto*) bedbug

percorrer *vt* **1** travel around...: *Percorremos a França de trem.* We traveled around France by train. **2** (*distância*) cover: ~ *150 km* cover 150 km

percurso *sm* route

percussão *sf* percussion

perda *sf* **1** loss: *A partida dele foi uma grande ~.* His leaving was a great loss. **2** (*tempo*) waste: *uma ~ de tempo* a waste of time ▶ ~**s e danos** damages ~**s e ganhos** profit and loss

perdão *sm* forgiveness ● **interj** sorry → EXCUSE

perdedor/a *adj* losing: *a equipe perdedora* the losing team ● *sm-sf* loser: *ser um bom/mau ~* be a good/bad loser

perder *vt* **1** lose: ~ *altura/peso* lose height/weight ◊ *Perdi o relógio.* I lost my watch. **2** (*meio de transporte, oportunidade, filme*) miss: ~ *o ônibus/avião* miss the bus/plane ◊ *Não perca esta oportunidade!* Don't miss this opportunity! **3** (*desperdiçar*) waste: ~ *tempo* waste time ◊ *sem ~ um minuto* without wasting a minute ● *vi* **1** lose (*at sth*): ~ *no xadrez* lose at chess **2** (*sair prejudicado*) lose out: *Você é que perde.* It's your loss. ● **perder-se** *vp* get lost: *Se não levar um mapa, você vai se perder.* You'll get lost if you don't take a map. ▶ **nem ~ uma** (*ser muito esperto*) be sharp as a tack ~ **a cabeça/o juízo** lose your head ~ **a calma/as estribeiras** lose your temper

~ **a vontade** go off the idea (of doing sth): *Perdi a vontade de sair.* I went off the idea of going out. ~ **de vista** lose sight of *sb/sth* ~ **o costume** (*mania* stop (doing sth)): ~ **o costume de roer as unhas** stop biting your nails ~ **o rastro** lose track *of sb/sth* **pôr algo a** ~ ruin sth **sair perdendo** lose out

perdido *adj* **1** lost: *Estou* ~. I'm lost. **2** (*extraviada*) stray: *uma bala perdida* a stray bullet

perdiz *sf* partridge

perdoar *vt* **1** forgive *sb* (for doing sth)): *Jamais perdoarei o que ele fez.* I'll never forgive him for what he did. **2** (*dívida, obrigação, sentença*) let *sb* off *sth*: *Ela me perdoou o dinheiro que eu lhe devia.* She let me off the money I owed her.

peregrinação *sf* pilgrimage: *fazer* ~ go on a pilgrimage

peregrino *a sm-sf* pilgrim

pereira *sf* pear tree

perene *adj* **1** everlasting **2** (*Bot*) perennial

perfeito *adj* perfect: *sair* ~ turn out perfectly

perfil *sm* **1** (*pessoa*) profile: *Ele é mais bonito de* ~. He's better-looking in profile. **2** (*edifício, montanha*) outline

perfilar *vt* **1** (*traçar o perfil*) draw the outline of sth **2** (*alinhar*) line sth up **3** (*aprumar*) stand sth up straight ● **perfilar-se** *vp* stand up straight

perfumado *adj* scented

perfumar *vt* perfume ● **perfumar-se** *vp* put perfume on

perfume *sm* perfume

perfurador *sm* hole punch

pergunta *sf* question: *responder a/fazer uma* ~ answer/ask a question

perguntar *vt, vi* **1** ask **2** ~ **(por) (a)** (*ao procurar alguém/algo*) ask for *sb/sth*: *Esteve um homem aqui perguntando por você.* A man was here asking for you. **(b)** (*ao interessar-se por alguém*) ask after *sb*: *Pergunte pelo filho dela.* Ask after her son. **(c)** (*ao interessar-se por algo*) ask about *sth*: *Perguntei-lhe pelo exame.* I asked her about the exam. ● **perguntar-se** *vp* wonder

periferia *sf* (*cidade*) outskirts [*pl*]

perigo *sm* danger: *em/fora de* ~ in/out of danger

perigoso *adj* dangerous

perímetro *sm* perimeter

periódico *adj* periodic ● *sm* **1** (*revista*) magazine **2** (*jornal*) newspaper

período *sm* period ● ~ **escolar** semester, term (*GB*)

peripécia *sf* **1** (*imprevisto*) incident **2** (*aventura*) adventure: *uma viagem cheia de* ~s a very eventful trip

periquito *sm* parakeet

perito *a adj, sm-sf* expert (*at/in* (doing) sth)

permanecer *vi* remain, be: ~ *pensativo/sentado* remain thoughtful/seated ◇ ~ *acordado toda a noite* be awake all night

permanente *adj* permanent ● *sf* (*cabelo*) perm: *fazer* ~ have your hair permed

permissão *sf* permission: *pedir* ~ *para fazer algo* ask permission to do sth

permitir *vt* **1** (*deixar*) let *sb* (do sth): *Permita-me ajudá-lo.* Let me help you. ◇ *Não me permitiriam.* They wouldn't let me. **2** (*autorizar*) allow *sb* to do sth: *Não permitem que ninguém entre sem gravata.* No one is allowed in without a tie. → ALLOW ► **permitir-se o luxo** (to sth): *Permiti-me o luxo de jantar fora.* I treated myself to a meal out.

permutação *sf* **1** (*Mat*) permutation **2** (*troca*) exchange

perna *sf* leg: *quebrar a* ~ break your leg ◇ *cruzar/esticar as* ~s cross/stretch your legs ◇ ~ *de carneiro* leg of lamb ► **com as** ~s **cruzadas** cross-legged **de** ~s **para o ar** in a mess

pernil *sm* (*porco*) leg

pernilongo *sm* mosquito [*pl* ~es]

pérola *sf* pearl

perpendicular *adj, sf* perpendicular

perpétuo *adj* perpetual

perplexo *adj* puzzled ► **deixar alguém** ~ leave sb speechless

perseguição *sf* **1** pursuit: *A polícia foi em* ~ *aos assaltantes.* The police went in pursuit of the robbers. **2** (*Pol, Relig*) persecution

perseguir *vt* **1** pursue: ~ *um carro/objetivo* pursue a car/an objective **2** (*Pol, Relig*) persecute

perseverança *sf* determination

persiana *sf* blind: *subir/baixar as* ~s raise/lower the blinds

persistente *adj* persistent

persistir *vi* persist (*in (doing) sth*)

personagem *sm* character: *o ~ principal* the main character

personalidade *sf* personality [*pl* -ies]

perspectiva *sf* **1** perspective **2** (*vista*) view **3** (*para o futuro*) prospect: *boas ~s* good prospects

perspicácia *sf* insight

perspicaz *adj* perceptive

persuadir *vt* persuade *sb* (*to do sth*) ● **persuadir-se** *vp* become convinced (*of sth/that...*)

persuasivo *adj* persuasive

pertencente *adj*: *os países ~s ao Mercosur* the countries belonging to Mercosur

pertencer *vi* belong *to sb/sth*

pertences *sm* belongings

pertinente *adj* relevant

perto *adv* near(by): *Vivemos muito ~.* We live very near. → NEAR ▶ **de ~** close up: *Deixe-me vê-lo de ~.* Let me see it close up. *~ de 1* (*a pouca distância*) near: *~ daqui* near here here **2** (*quase*) nearly: *O trem atrasou ~ de uma hora.* The train was nearly an hour late.

perturbar *vt* **1** (*atrapalhar*) disturb **2** (*assediar*) hassle **3** (*abalar*) unsettle

Peru *sm* Peru

peru/a *sm-sf* turkey

perua *sf* (*veículo*) station wagon, estate car (*GB*)

peruano/a *adj*, *sm-sf* Peruvian

peruca *sf* wig

perverso *adj* (*malvado*) wicked

perverter *vt* pervert

pervertido/a *sm-sf* pervert

pesadelo *sm* nightmare

pesado *adj* heavy: *uma mala/comida pesada* a heavy suitcase/meal ◊ *uma atmosfera pesada* an oppressive atmosphere

pêsames *sm*: *Os meus ~.* My deepest condolences. ▶ **dar os ~** offer *sb* your condolences

pesar¹ *vt*, *vi* weigh: *Quanto você pesa?* How much do you weigh? ◊ *Isto pesa é bem!* This weighs a ton! ◊ *Não pesa nada!* It hardly weighs a thing! ▶ **na consciência** weigh on your conscience

pesar² *sm* (*tristeza*) sorrow

pesca *sf* fishing: *ir à ~* go fishing

pescador/a *sm-sf* fisherman/woman [*pl* -men/-women]

pescar *vi* fish: *Eles tinham ido ~.* They'd gone fishing. ● *vt* catch: *~ uma truta* catch a trout

pescoço *sm* neck: *Estou com dor no ~.* My neck hurts.

peso *sm* weight: *ganhar/perder ~* put on/lose weight ◊ *vender algo por ~* sell sth by weight ◊ *~ bruto/líquido* gross/net weight ◊ *Tiraram um grande ~ de cima de mim.* That's a great weight off my mind. ▶ **de ~ 1** (*pessoa*) influential **2** (*assunto*) weighty

pesqueiro *adj* fishing: *um porto ~* a fishing port ● *sm* (*barco*) fishing boat

pesquisa *sf* **1** research: *~ de mercado* market research **2** (*Informát*) search

pesquisador/a *sm-sf* researcher

pesquisar *vt* **1** research **2** (*Informát*) search

pêssego *sm* peach

pessegueiro *sm* peach tree

pessimismo *sm* pessimism

pessimista *adj* pessimistic ● *smf* pessimist

péssimo *adj* terrible

pessoa *sf* person [*pl* people]: *milhares de ~s* thousands of people ▶ **em ~** in person **por ~** per head: *1.000 reais por ~* 1,000 reals per head **ser (uma) boa ~/~ de bem**: *Eles são muito boas ~s.* They're very nice.

pessoal *adj* personal ● *sm* staff

pestana *sf* eyelash ▶ **tirar uma ~** have forty winks

pestanejar *vi* blink ▶ **sem ~**: *Ele escutou a notícia sem ~.* He heard the news without batting an eyelid.

peste *sf* **1** (*doença*) plague: *~ bubônica* bubonic plague **2** (*pessoa, animal*) pest: *Ele é uma ~.* He's a pest.

pesticida *sm* pesticide

pétala *sf* petal

petição *sf* petition: *elaborar uma ~* draw up a petition ▶ **em ~ de miséria** in a terrible state

petiscar *vt* (*comer*) nibble

petisco *sm* delicacy [*pl* -ies]

petroleiro *sm* oil tanker

petróleo *sm* oil: *~ bruto* crude oil

pia *sf* sink

piada *sf* joke: *contar uma ~* tell a joke

pianista *smf* pianist

piano *sm* piano [*pl* -s]: *tocar algo ao ~* play sth on the piano ▶ **~ de cauda** grand piano

pião *sm* top

piar *vi* chirp

picada *sf* **1** (*alfinete, agulha*) prick **2** (*mosquito, cobra*) bite **3**

(abelha, vespa) sting: levar uma ~ get stung

picadeiro sm 1 (circo) (circus) ring 2 (escola de equitação) riding school

picante adj 1 (Cozinha) hot: um molho ~ a hot sauce 2 (anedota) risqué

picar vt 1 prick 2 (mosquito, cobra) bite 3 (abelha, vespa) sting 4 (hortaliça) chop sth (up) • vi 1 (planta espinhosa): Tenha cuidado que elas picam. Be careful, they're prickly. 2 (produzir comichão): Este suéter pica. This sweater is itchy.

pichação sf 1 (piche) pitch 2 (grafite) graffiti [U] 3 (crítica) criticism

pichar vt 1 (cobrir com piche) cover with pitch 2 (grafitar) spray sth with graffiti 3 (criticar) criticize

piche sm pitch

picles sm pickles

pico sm 1 (ponta aguda) point 2 (cume) peak: os ~s cobertos de neve the snow-covered peaks • e ~ 1 odd: dois mil reais e ~ two thousand odd reals ◇ Ele tem trinta anos e ~. He's thirty something. 2 (hora) just after: Eram umas duas e ~. It was just after two.

picolé sm Popsicle®, ice lolly [pl -ies] (GB)

picuinha sf ► fazer/ficar de ~ be spiteful

piedade sf 1 (compaixão) mercy (on sb): Senhor, tende ~. Lord have mercy. 2 (devoção) piety

piedoso adj (religioso) devout

piegas adj sappy, soppy (GB)

pifar vi (estragar) break down

pijama sm pajamas, pyjamas (GB) [pl]: um ~ a pair of pajamas ► PAIR

pilantra smf crook

pilar sm pillar

pilha sf 1 (monte) pile: uma ~ de jornais a pile of newspapers 2 (Elet) battery [pl -ies]: Acabaram as ~s. The batteries are dead. ► uma ~ de nervos a bundle of nerves

pilotar vt 1 (avião) fly 2 (carro) drive

piloto sm 1 (avião) pilot 2 (carro) racing driver ► automático automatic pilot

pílula sf pill

pimenta sf pepper

pimenta-malagueta sf chili [pl ~es]

pimentão sm pepper: ~ verde/vermelho green/red pepper

pinça sf 1 tweezers [pl] 2 (gelo) tongs [pl] 3 (Med) calipers [pl] ► PAIR 4 (caranguejo, etc.) pincer

pincel sm paintbrush ► ~ de barba shaving brush

pinga sf sugar cane liquor

pingar vi 1 (gotejar) drip 2 (estar encharcado) be dripping wet • v imp (chover) drizzle

pingente sm pendant

pingo sm (gota) drop

pingue-pongue sm ping-pong

pingüim sm penguin

pinha sf (pinheiro) pine cone

pinhal sm pine wood

pinhão sm pine nut

pinheiro sm pine (tree)

pino sm (Mec) pin

pinta sf 1 (mancha, bola) dot 2 (aspecto) look: Não gosto da ~ deste cara. I don't like the look of this guy. ► ter ~ de look like sth: Esse cara tem ~ de galã de cinema. That guy looks like a movie star.

pintado adj painted: As paredes estão pintadas de azul. The walls are painted blue. ► ~ à mão handpainted

pintar vt, vi paint: ~ as unhas paint your nails ◇ uma parede de vermelho paint a wall red ◇ ~ a óleo/aquarela paint in oils/watercolors • vt color sth (in): O garoto pintou a casa de azul. The little boy colored the house blue. ◇ Ele desenhou uma bola e depois pintou-a. He drew a ball and then colored it in. • pintar-se vp (maquilar-se) put your make-up on: Não me pinto. I don't wear make-up. ◇ demais wear too much make-up ◇ ~ o cabelo dye your hair: ~ o cabelo de castanho dye your hair dark brown ► ~ o sete 1 (traquinar) mess around 2 (divertir-se) paint the town red ► ~ os lábios/olhos put on your lipstick/eye make-up

pinto sm chick

pintor/a sm-sf painter

pintura sf painting

pio sm (som) cheep ► não dar um ~ not say a word

piolho sm louse [pl lice]

pioneiro/a adj pioneering • sm-sf pioneer: um ~ da cirurgia plástica a pioneer of plastic surgery

pior adj, adv (comparativo) worse (than sb/sth): Este carro é ~ do que aquele. This car is worse than that one. ◊ *Sinto-me ~ hoje.* I feel worse today. ◊ *Ela cozinha ainda ~ do que a mãe.* She's an even worse cook than her mother. ● *adj, adv, smf* ~ **(de)** (*superlativo*) worst (in/of...): *Sou o ~ corredor do mundo.* I'm the worst runner in the world. ◊ **o ~ de tudo** the worst of all ◊ **o que canta** ~ the one who sings worst ▶ **o ~ é que... the worst** thing is (that)...

piorar *vt* make *sth* worse ● *vi* get worse: *Ele piorou muito desde a última vez em que o vi.* He's much worse since I saw him last.

pipa *sf* 1 (*barril*) barrel 2 (*papagaio*) kite

pipoca *sf* popcorn

pique *sm* ▶ **ir a ~** (*barco*) sink 2 (*arruinar-se*) go bust

piquenique *sm* picnic: *fazer um ~* go for a picnic

pirado *adj*: *ser* ~ be nuts

pirâmide *sf* pyramid

piranha *sf* piranha

pirar *vi* (*ficar maluco*) go nuts ● **pirar(-se)** *vi, vp* (*fugir*) clear off

pirata *adj, smf* pirate

piratear *vt* 1 (*disco, vídeo*) pirate 2 (*sistema informático*) hack into *sth*

pires *sm* saucer

pirilampo *sm* firefly [*pl* -ies]

piromaníaco/a *sm-sf* arsonist

pirralho/a *sm-sf* kid

pirueta *sf* pirouette

pirulito *sm* lollipop

pisada *sf* 1 (*som*) footstep 2 (*marca*) footprint

pisar *vt* 1 step on/in *sth*: *no pé de alguém* step on sb's foot ◊ *~ numa poça de água* step in a puddle 2 (*terra*) stomp *sth* down, tread *sth* down (GB) 3 (*acelerador, freio*) put your foot on *sth* 4 (*dominar*) walk all over *sb*: *Não deixe que pisem em você.* Don't let people walk all over you. 5 (*contundir*) bruise ● *vi* tread ▶ ~ **em brasa** be in a very difficult situation ▪ **na bola** overstep the mark **ver por onde se pisa** tread carefully

piscadela *sf* wink

pisca-pisca *sm* turn signal, indicator (GB)

piscar *vt* 1 (*olho*) wink (*at sb*) 2 (*farol*) flash ● *vi* 1 (*olhos*) blink 2 (*luz*) flicker

piscina *sf* swimming pool

piso *sm* floor ▶ ~ **salarial** minimum wage

pista *sf* 1 (*rastro*) track(s):

seguir a ~ de um animal follow an animal's tracks 2 (*dado*) clue 3 (*corridas*) track: *uma ~ ao ar livre/coberta* an outdoor/indoor track 4 (*Esporte, faixa, rodovia*) lane: *o atleta na ~ dois* the athlete in lane two 5 (*Aeronáut*) runway ▶ **na ~ de alguém** on sb's trail ▪ **de dança** dance floor ▪ **de esqui** ski slope ▪ **de patinação** skating rink ~ **dupla** divided highway, dual carriageway (GB)

pistache *sm* pistachio [*pl* ~s]

pistola *sf* gun ▶ ~ **de ar comprimido** airgun

pistolão *sm* (*contato*) contacts ▶ **servir de** ~ pull strings for *sb*

pitada *sf* (*sal*) pinch

pitoresco *adj* picturesque

pitu *sm* crayfish [*pl* crayfish]

pivete *sm* (*menino ladrão*) street urchin

pizza *sf* pizza

pizzaria *sf* pizzeria

placa *sf* 1 (*lâmina, Geol*) plate: *~s de aço* steel plates ◊ *A ~ na porta diz "dentista".* The plate on the door says "dentist". 2 (*comemorativa*) plaque 3 (*em estrada*) sign 4 (*carro*) license plate, number plate (GB)

placar *sm* scoreboard

plaina *sf* (*ferramenta*) plane

planador *sm* glider

planalto *sm* plateau [*pl* ~s/-x]

planar *vi* glide

planejamento *sm* planning: *~ familiar* family planning

planejar *vt* plan

planeta *sm* planet

planície *sf* plain

plano *adj* flat ● *sm* 1 (*desígnio*) plan: *Mudei de ~s.* I've changed my plans. ◊ *Você tem ~s para sábado?* Do you have anything planned for Saturday? 2 (*nível*) level: *As casas foram construídas em ~s diferentes.* The houses were built on different levels. ◊ *no ~ pessoal* on a personal level 3 (*Cinema*) shot

planta *sf* 1 (*Bot*) plant 2 (*desenho*) (a) (*cidade, etc.*) map (b) (*Arquit*) plan 3 (*do pé*) sole

plantação *sf* plantation

plantado *adj* ▶ **deixar alguém** ~ stand *sb* up

plantão *sm* (*turno*) shift ▶ **de** ~ on duty

plantar *vt* plant

plástico *adj* plastic: *cirurgia plástica* plastic surgery ● *sm* plastic: *um recipiente de* ~

a plastic container ◊ *um ~* a plastic sheet

plastificar *vt* laminate

plataforma *sf* platform

plátano *sm* plane tree

platéia *sf* **1** (*teatro*) the orchestra **2** (*público*) audience

platina *sf* platinum

plebiscito *sm* referendum: *realizar um ~* hold a referendum

pleno *adj* full ▸ **em ~...** (right) in the middle of...: *em ~ inverno* in the middle of winter ◊ *em ~ centro da cidade* right in the center of the city ◊ *em plena luz do dia* in broad daylight **em plena forma** in peak condition

plural *adj, sm* plural

Plutão *sm* Pluto

plutônio *sm* plutonium

pneu *sm* tire: *~ furado* flat (tire)

pneumonia *sf* pneumonia [*U*]: *apanhar uma ~* catch pneumonia

pó *sm* **1** (*sujeira*) dust: *cheio de pó* covered in dust ◊ *levantar pó* kick up the dust **2** (*Cozinha, Quím, cosmético*) powder: *pó de arroz* face powder ▸ **tirar o pó (de)** dust (*sth*)

pobre *adj* poor ● *smf* poor man/woman [*pl* men/women]: *os ~s* the poor ▸ **o ~ de...**: *o ~ do Henrique* poor old Henrique

pobreza *sf* poverty

poça *sf* (*charco*) puddle

pocilga *sf* pigsty [*pl* -ies]

poço *sm* well: *um ~ de petróleo* an oil well

podar *vt* prune

poder¹ *v aux* **1** can do *sth*; be able to do *sth*: *Posso escolher Londres ou Rio.* I can choose London or Rio. ◊ *Eu não podia acreditar.* I couldn't believe it. ◊ *Desde então ele não pode andar.* He hasn't been able to walk since then. → CAN¹ **2** (*ter autorização*) can, may (*mais fml*): *Posso falar com o André?* Can I talk to André? ◊ *Posso sair?* May I go out? → MAY **3** (*probabilidade*) may, could, might NOTA O uso de may, could e might depende do grau de probabilidade da ação: could e might exprimem menos probabilidade que may: *Eles podem chegar a qualquer momento.* They may arrive at any time. ◊ *Poderia ser perigoso.* It could/might be dangerous. ▸ **até não ~ mais**: *Gritamos até não ~ mais.* We shouted as loud as we could. **não ~ deixar de** can't/

couldn't help *doing sth*: *Não pude deixar de ouvir os vizinhos discutindo.* I couldn't help hearing the neighbors quarreling. **não ~ mais** (*estar cansado*) be exhausted **~ com** cope with *sth*: *Não posso com essa criança.* I can't cope with this child. **pode-se/não se pode**: *Pode-se usar bermuda?* Is it all right if I wear bermuda shorts? ◊ *Não se pode fumar aqui.* You can't smoke in here. **pode ser (que...)** maybe: *Pode ser que sim, pode ser que não.* Maybe, maybe not.

poder² *sm* power: *tomar o ~* seize power ◊ *~ aquisitivo* purchasing power ▸ **~ judicial/legislativo** judicial branch/legislature **ter algo em seu ~** have *sth* in your possession

poderoso *adj* powerful

podre *adj* rotten: *uma maçã/sociedade ~* a rotten apple/society

poeira *sf* dust

poeirada *sf* cloud of dust

poeirento *adj* dusty

poema *sm* poem

poesia *sf* **1** poetry **2** (*poema*) poem

poeta *sm* poet

poético *adj* poetic

poetisa *sf* poet

pois *conj* well: *Não está com vontade de sair? ~ então não saia.* You don't feel like going out? Well, don't then. ▸ **~ é** (*ao concordar*) that's right **~ não?** (*numa loja*) can I help you?

polar *adj* polar

polegada *sf* inch (*abrev* in.) → Ver pág. 224

polegar *sm* thumb

poleiro *sm* **1** (*pássaros*) perch **2** (*galinhas*) roost

polêmico a *adj* controversial ● **polêmica** *sf* controversy [*pl* -ies]

pólen *sm* pollen

polícia *smf* police officer ● *sf* police [*pl*]: *~ de choque/rodoviária* riot/traffic police

policial *adj* police: *força ~* police force ● *sm* police officer

poliglota *adj, smf* polyglot

polígono *sm* polygon

polimento *sm* polish: *dar um ~ nos móveis* give the furniture a polish

pólio (*tb* **poliomielite**) *sf* polio: *contrair ~* catch polio

polir *vt* polish

politécnico *adj* polytechnic

política sf **1** politics [sing]: entrar para a ~ go into politics **2** (posição, programa) policy [pl -ies]: ~ externa foreign policy

político/a adj political: um partido ~ a political party • sm-sf politician: um ~ de esquerda a left-wing politician

pólo sm **1** (Geog, Fís) pole: o ~ sul the South Pole **2** (Esporte) polo: ~ aquático water polo

polpa sf pulp

poltrona sf (cadeira) armchair

poluição sf pollution

poluir vt, vi pollute

polvilhar vt sprinkle sth (with sth)

polvo sm octopus

pólvora sf gunpowder

pomada sf ointment

pombo/a sm-sf **1** pigeon **2** (branca) dove

pomo-de-adão sm Adam's apple

pomposo adj pompous

poncho sm poncho [pl ~s]

ponderar vt, vi reflect (on sth)

pônei sm pony [pl -ies]

ponta sf **1** (faca, arma, pena, lápis) point **2** (língua, dedo, ilha, iceberg) tip: as ~s dos dedos fingertips **3** (extremo, cabelo) end: ~s quebradas split ends ◊ na outra ~ da mesa at the other end of the table **4** (futebol) winger ▶ de ~ a ~/de uma ~ à outra: de uma ~ à outra de São Paulo from one end of São Paulo to the other na ~ da língua on the tip of your tongue na ~ dos pés on tiptoe: andar na ~ dos pés walk on tiptoe ◊ Entrei na ~ dos pés. I tiptoed in. uma ~ de a touch of: uma ~ de inveja a touch of envy

pontada sf twinge

pontapé sm kick: Dei-lhe um ~. I kicked him. ▶ ~ inicial (futebol) kick-off

pontaria sf aim: fazer ~ take aim ▶ ter boa/má ~ be a good/bad shot

ponte sf bridge: ~ suspensa suspension bridge ▶ ~ aérea shuttle service ~ levadiça drawbridge

ponteiro sm hand: ~ dos segundos second hand

pontiagudo adj pointed

pontinha sf: uma ~ de sal/humor a pinch of salt/touch of humor

ponto sm **1** point: em todos os ~s do país all over the country ◊ Passemos ao ~ seguinte. Let's move on to the next point. ◊ perder por dois ~s lose by two

points ◊ o seu ~ fraco his weak point ◊ o ~ alto da noite the high point of the evening **2** (sinal de pontuação) period, full stop (GB) **3** (grau) extent: Até que ~ isso é verdade? To what extent is this true? **4** (Costura, Med) stitch: Dê um ~ nessa bainha. Put a stitch in the hem. ◊ Levei três ~s. I had three stitches. **5** (parada) stop: ~ de ônibus bus stop ▶ ao ~ (carne) medium rare em ~ exactly: São duas em ~. It's two o'clock exactly. • e ~ final and that's that ~ estar a ~ de fazer algo ◊ be about to do sth: Está a ~ de terminar. It's about to finish. **2** (por pouco) nearly do sth: Ele esteve a ~ de perder a vida. He nearly lost his life. ~ de ebulição/fusão boiling/melting point ~ de exclamação/interrogação exclamation point/question mark ~ de partida starting point ~ de táxi cabstand, taxi rank (GB) ~ de venda point of sale ~ de vista point of view ~ e vírgula semicolon ~ final period ~ morto (carro) neutral **2** (negociações) deadlock ~ parágrafo new paragraph **ponto por ponto** (pormenorizadamente) down to the last detail

pontuação sf punctuation: sinais de ~ punctuation marks

pontual adj punctual **NOTA** Usa-se **punctual** para a qualidade ou virtude de uma pessoa: É importante ser ~. It's important to be punctual. Para a idéia de chegar a tempo, usa-se a expressão **on time**: Procure ser ~. Try to get there on time. ◊ Ele nunca é ~. He's never on time.

popa sf stern

população sf population: a ~ ativa the working population

popular adj popular

por prep
• **lugar 1** (verbos de movimento): circular pela direita drive on the right ◊ Você vai passar ~ uma farmácia? Are you going past a drugstore? ◊ passar pelo centro de Paris go through the center of Paris ◊ Passo pela sua casa. I'll drop by your house. ◊ viajar pela Europa travel around Europe ◊ ~ aqui/ali this/that way **2** (verbos como pegar, agarrar) by: Peguei-o pelo braço. I grabbed him by the arm.
• **tempo 1** (duração) for: só ~ uns dias only for a few days → FOR **2** (perto de) about: Chegarei lá

pelas oito. I'll arrive (at) about eight.

● **causa:** *Foi cancelado ~ causa do mau tempo.* It was canceled because of bad weather. ◊ *fazer algo ~ dinheiro* do sth for money ◊ *Ele foi despedido ~ furto/ser preguiçoso.* He was sacked for stealing/being lazy. ◊ *~ ciúme/costume* out of jealousy/habit

● **agente por:** *assinado ~...* signed by... ◊ *pintado ~ Dali* painted by Dali

● **para com/a favor de:** *sentir carinho ~ alguém* feel affection for sb ◊ *~ que time você torce?* Which team are you rooting for?

● **expressões numéricas:** *Mede 7 ~ 2.* It measures 7 by 2. ◊ *50 reais ~ hora/~ pessoa* 50 reals an hour/per person

● **outras construções 1** *(meio, modo):* ~ *correio/avião* by mail/air ◊ *~ escrito* in writing ◊ *vender algo ~ metro* sell sth by the meter **2** *(freqüência): uma vez ~ ano* once a year **3** *(substituição): Ela irá ~ mim.* She'll go instead of me. ◊ *Comprei-o ~ um milhão de reais.* I bought it for a million reals. **4** *(sucessão)* by: *um ~ um* one by one **5 + adj/ adv** however: *~ mais simples que...* However simple... ◊ *~ mais que você trabalhe...* However hard you work... **6** *(inacabado): Os pratos estão ~ lavar.* The dishes haven't been done. ◊ *deixar o trabalho ~ acabar* leave the work unfinished ▶ *~ isso* so: *Tenho muito trabalho, ~ isso vou chegar tarde.* I've a lot of work to do, so I won't be there until later. *~ mim, etc.* as far as I am, you are, etc. concerned *~ que/quê?* why: *~ que não?* Why not? ◊ *sem saber ~ quê* without knowing why

pôr *vt* **1** put: *Ponha os livros sobre a mesa.* Put the books on the table. ◊ *~ o lixo na rua* put out the garbage **2** *(parte do corpo)* stick sth out: *Não ponha a língua de fora.* Don't stick your tongue out. ◊ *~ a cabeça para fora da janela* stick your head out of the window **3** *(ligar): ~ o rádio para tocar* turn on the radio **4** *(vestir, estender)* put sth on: *O que é que eu ponho?* What shall I put on? ◊ *~ a toalha na mesa* put the tablecloth on the table **5** *(disco, etc.): ~ um CD* play a CD **6** *(relógio): ~ o despertador para as seis* set the alarm for six **7**

(servir) give: *Pode ~ mais um pouco de sopa, por favor?* Could you give me a little more soup please? **8** *~ um ovo* lay an egg ● **pôr-se** *vp* **1** *(colocar-se)* stand: *Ponha-se ao meu lado.* Stand next to me. **2** *(sol)* set **3** *~* a start doing sth/to do sth: *~ a correr* start to run ◊ *~ a chorar* burst into tears NOTA Para expressões com **pôr**, ver o substantivo, adjetivo, etc., p. ex. **pôr no correio** em CORREIO.

porão *sm* **1** hold: *no ~ do navio* in the ship's hold **2** *(casa)* basement

porca *sf* **1** *(parafuso)* nut **2** *(animal)* sow → PORCO

porção *sf* *(comida)* portion: *meia ~* a small portion

porcaria *sf* **1** *(sujeira)* filth **2** *(algo de má qualidade)* garbage, rubbish (GB) [U]: *O filme é uma ~.* The movie is garbage. **3** *(comida)* junk food [U]: *Pare de comer ~s.* Stop eating junk food. ▶ *que ~...*: *Que ~ de tempo!* What lousy weather!

porcelana *sf* china, porcelain *(mais fml)*: *um prato de ~* a china plate

porcentagem *sf* percentage

porco *adj* *(sujo)* filthy ● *sm-sf* **1** *(animal)* pig NOTA **Pig** é o substantivo genérico. **Boar** é o macho e **sow** a fêmea. Os porquinhos e os leitões são **piglets**. **2** *(pessoa)* slob ● *sm* *(carne)* pork: *lombo de ~* loin of pork → CARNE

porco-espinho *sm* porcupine

porém *conj* however

pormenor *sm* detail

pormenorizado *adj* detailed

pormenorizar *vt* **1** *(contar em pormenores)* give details of sth **2** *(especificar)* specify

pornografia *sf* pornography

pornográfico *adj* pornographic

poro *sm* pore

poroso *adj* porous

porque *conj* because

porquê *sm* reason *(for sth)*: *o ~ da greve* the reason for the strike

porquinho-da-índia *sm* guinea pig

porre *sm* ▶ *tomar um ~* get wasted

porta *sf* door: *a ~ da frente/dos fundos* the front/back door ◊ *Há alguém à ~.* There's somebody at the door. ▶ *~ corrediça/ giratória* sliding/revolving door *sair ~ afora* clear off

porta-aviões sm aircraft carrier

porta-jóias sm jewelry box

porta-malas sm trunk, boot (GB)

porta-níqueis sm change purse, purse (GB)

portanto adv therefore

portão sm gate ▶ ~ **de embarque** gate

portaria sf **1** (entrada) entrance (hall) **2** (decreto) decree

portar-se vp behave: Porte-se bem. Be good.

portátil adj portable

porta-voz smf spokesperson [pl ~s/-people]: o ~ da oposição the spokesperson for the opposition. NOTA Esta é a forma preferida actualmente, embora também se use **spokesman** e **spokeswoman**.

porte sm **1** (custo de envio) postage: ~ e embalagem postage and packing **2** (corpo) **(a)** (mulher) figure: ter um ~ bonito have a nice figure **(b)** (homem) body ▶ ~ **registrado** registered mail

porteiro a sm-sf **1** (edifício público) custodian, caretaker (GB) **2** (edifício residencial) superintendent, porter (GB)

porto sm port: um ~ pesqueiro a fishing port

Portugal sm Portugal

português/esa adj, sm Portuguese • sm-sf Portuguese man/woman [pl men/women]: os portugueses the Portuguese

porventura adv by chance

posar vi pose

pós-escrito sm postscript (abrev P.S.)

posição sf position

positivo adj positive: O resultado do teste foi ~. The test was positive.

posse sf **1** (possessão) possession: ter ~ de algo be in possession of sth **2** (posses) (dinheiro) wealth [sing]: ter muitas ~s be very wealthy ▶ **tomar** ~ (cargo) take up office

possessivo adj possessive

possesso adj furious ▶ **ficar** ~ fly into a rage

possibilidade sf possibility [pl -ies] ▶ **ter (muita)** ~ **de...** have a (good) chance of doing sth

possível adj **1** possible **2** (potencial) potential: um ~ acidente a potential accident ▶ **fazer (todo)** o ~ **para** do your best to do sth

possuir vt (ser dono de) own

posta sf (peixe) piece

postal adj postal • sm postcard

postar vt (pessoa) post sb (to...): O cônsul passou um ano postado em Lima. The consul was posted to Lima for a year. • **postar-se** vp position yourself

poste sm pole: ~ telegráfico telegraph pole ▶ ~ **de alta tensão** tower, pylon (GB) ~ **de luz** lamp post

pôster sm poster

posterior adj **1** (tempo): um acontecimento ~ a subsequent event ◇ os anos ~es à guerra the post-war years **2** (lugar): na parte ~ do ônibus at the back of the bus ◇ a fila ~ à sua the row behind yours

postiço adj false: dentadura postiça false teeth

posto sm **1** (lugar) place: Todos a ~s! Places, everyone! **2** (emprego) position: Ofereceram-lhe um novo ~. They offered him a new position. ▶ ~ **de gasolina** gas station, petrol station (GB) ~ **de saúde** health center

potável adj: água ~ drinking water

potência sf power: ~ atômica/econômica atomic/economic power ◇ as grandes ~s the Great Powers ▶ **de alta/grande** ~ powerful

potente adj powerful

potro a sm-sf foal NOTA Foal é o substantivo genérico. O macho é **colt** e a fêmea **filly**.

pouco adj **1** (+ substantivo não contável) little, not much (mais coloq): Eles demonstram ~ interesse. They show little interest. ◇ Tenho ~ dinheiro. I don't have much money. **2** (+ substantivo contável) few, not many (mais coloq): em poucas ocasiões on very few occasions ◇ Ele tem ~s amigos. He doesn't have many friends. ▶ **FEW, LESS** • pron little [pl few]: Vieram muito ~s. Very few came. • adv **1** not much: Ele come ~ para o seu tamanho. He doesn't eat much for someone his size. **2** (pouco tempo) not long: Eu a vi há ~. I saw her not long ago. **3** (+ adj) not very: Ele é ~ esperto. He's not very smart. ▶ **aos** ~ gradually **fazer** ~ **de** make fun of sb/sth **por** ~ **não...** nearly: Por ~ ele não me atropelou. He nearly ran me over. **pouco a pouco** little by little ~ **mais de** only just (coloq), barely: Ela tem ~ mais de dois anos. She's only just turned two. ~ **mais/menos**

(de) just over/under um ~ a little: um ~ mais/melhor a little more/better ◇ um ~ de açúcar a little sugar ◇ Espere um ~. Wait a little. NOTA Para outras expressões com pouco, ver o substantivo, adjetivo, etc., p. ex. **ser pouca coisa** em COISA.

poupador/a adj thrifty ● sm-sf saver

poupança sf savings [pl]

poupar vt, vi **1** (economizar) save: ~ tempo/dinheiro save time/money **2** (vida) spare: ~ a vida de alguém spare sb's life

pousada sf inn

pousar vt, vi land (on sth)

povo sm people [pl]: o ~ brasileiro the Brazilian people

povoação sf **1** (conjunto de pessoas) population **2** (localidade) **(a)** (cidade pequena) town **(b)** (aldeia) village

povoado sm village

praça sf **1** (espaço aberto) square: a ~ principal the main square **2** (mercado) market (place)

prado sm meadow

praga sf **1** (maldição) curse: rogar uma ~ a alguém put a curse on sb **2** (abundância de coisas importunas) plague

praguejar vi swear

praia sf beach

prancha sf plank ▶ ~ de windsurfe windsurfer

prata sf silver: um anel de ~ a silver ring

prateado adj **1** (cor) silver **2** (banhado a prata) silver-plated

prateleira sf shelf [pl shelves]

prática sf **1** practice: Em teoria funciona, mas na ~... It's all right in theory, but in practice... ◇ pôr algo em ~ put sth into practice **2** (Educ, aula) practical

praticamente adv practically

praticante adj practising

praticar vt **1** practice: ~ medicina practice medicine **2** (esporte) play

prático adj practical

prato sm **1** (utensílio) plate: ~ raso/de sobremesa dinner/dessert plate **2** (iguaria) dish: o ~ típico do país the national dish **3** (parte de uma refeição) course: o ~ principal the main course **4** (pratos) (Mús) cymbals ▶ pôr tudo em ~s limpos get things out into the open ~ fundo/de sopa soup bowl

praxe sf custom

prazer sm pleasure: Tenho o ~ de lhes apresentar... It is my pleasure to introduce... ▶ muito prazer/prazer em conhecê-lo pleased to meet you

prazo sm (período): o ~ de matrícula the enrollment period ◇ Temos um ~ de dois meses para pagar. We have two months to pay. ◇ O ~ acaba amanhã. The deadline's tomorrow. ▶ a curto/médio/longo ~ in the short/medium/long term ~ de validade expiration date, sell-by date (GB)

preâmbulo sm **1** (prólogo) introduction **2** (rodeios): Deixe de ~s. Stop beating around the bush.

precaução sf precaution: por ~ as a precaution ◇ tomar precauções take precautions ▶ com ~ carefully

precaver-se vp take precautions (against sb/sth)

precavido adj prepared: Vim ~ para qualquer coisa. I came prepared for anything.

precedente adj preceding ● sm precedent: abrir ~ make a precedent

preceder vt go/come before sb/sth, precede (fml): O adjetivo precede o substantivo. The adjective comes before the noun.

preceito sm rule

precioso adj precious: uma pedra preciosa a precious stone

precipício sm precipice

precipitação sf haste

precipitado adj hasty: uma decisão precipitada a hasty decision

precipitar-se vp **1** (não pensar) be hasty: Pense bem, não se precipite. Think it over. Don't be hasty. **2** (atirar-se) throw yourself out of sth **3** ~ sobre/em direção a (correr) rush toward sb/sth

precisão sf accuracy ▶ com ~ accurately

precisar vt **1** need: Precisamos de mais duas cadeiras. We need two more chairs. ◇ Você não precisa vir. You don't need to come. **2** (especificar) specify: ~ até o último detalhe specify every last detail

preciso adj **1** (exato) precise **2** (necessário) necessary: Não foi ~ recorrermos aos bombeiros. There was no need to call the fire department. ◇ É ~ que você venha. You must come.

preço sm price: a ~ fixo at a fixed price ◇ Qual é o ~ do quarto de casal? How much is the double room?

precoce adj 1 (criança) precocious 2 (prematuro) premature: calvície ~ premature balding

preconceito sm prejudice

predador adj predatory ● sm predator

prédio sm 1 (edifício) building 2 (apartamentos) apartment building, block of flats (GB)

predizer vt predict

predominante adj predominant

preencher vt (formulário, ficha) fill sth in

pré-escolar adj pre-school: crianças em idade ~ pre-school children

pré-fabricado adj prefabricated

prefácio sm preface

prefeito/a sm-sf mayor

prefeitura sf 1 (prédio) city hall, town hall (GB) 2 (cargo): Quem está na ~ da cidade atualmente? Who's the current mayor?

preferência sf preference ▶ de ~ preferably

preferencial adj preferential: tratamento ~ preferential treatment ● sf (rua) main street

preferido/a adj, sm-sf favorite

preferir vt prefer sb/sth (to sb/sth): Prefiro chá a café. I prefer tea to coffee. ◊ Prefiro estudar de manhã. I prefer to study in the morning. NOTA Ao perguntar o que uma pessoa prefere, diz-se **would prefer** quando se trata de duas coisas e **would rather** quando se trata de duas ações, por exemplo: Você prefere chá ou café? Would you prefer tea or coffee? ◊ Você prefere ir ao cinema ou ver um vídeo? Would you rather go to the movies or watch a video? Ao responder, deve-se dizer **I would rather**, **he/she would rather**, etc. ou **I'd rather**, **he'd/she'd rather**, etc.: —Você prefere chá ou café? —Prefiro chá. "Would you prefer tea or coffee?" "I'd rather have tea." **Would rather** é sempre seguido do infinitivo sem **to**.

preferível adj preferable ▶ ser ~ be better (to do sth): É ~ que você não entre agora. It'd be better if you didn't go in now.

prefixo sm 1 prefix 2 (de DDD) area code

prega sf 1 fold: O tecido caía formando ~s. The fabric fell in folds. 2 (saia) pleat

pregar¹ vt, vi (Relig) preach

pregar² vt 1 (prego) hammer sth into sth 2 (fixar algo com pregos) nail sth to sth 3 (botão) sew a button on ▶ não ~ olho not sleep a wink ~ um susto em alguém give sb a fright ~ uma peça play a dirty trick on sb

prego sm nail

preguiça sf laziness: Depois de comer me dá ~. I always feel sleepy after lunch. ◊ Que ~ de trabalhar! It's such a pain having to work!

preguiçoso/a adj lazy ● sm-sf lazybones

pré-histórico adj prehistoric

prejudicar vt 1 damage: A seca prejudicou as colheitas. The drought damaged the crops. 2 (interesses) prejudice

prejudicial adj harmful (to sb/sth) 2 (saúde) bad (for sb/sth): O tabaco é ~ à saúde. Cigarettes are bad for your health.

prejuízo sm 1 (em negócio): loss: A empresa teve muitos ~s. The company suffered many losses. 2 (dano) harm [U]: causar ~ a alguém cause sb harm

preliminar adj preliminary ● sf (Esporte) preliminary [pl -ies]

prematuro adj premature

premiado/a adj 1 (escritor, livro) prizewinning 2 (número, títulos) winning ● sm-sf prizewinner

premiar vt 1 award sb a prize: Premiaram o ator (com um Oscar). The actor was awarded an Oscar. 2 (recompensar) reward: ~ alguém pelo seu esforço reward sb for their efforts

prêmio sm 1 prize: ganhar o primeiro ~ win first prize ◊ ~ de consolação consolation prize 2 (recompensa) reward

pré-natal adj prenatal, antenatal (GB)

prender vt 1 (atar) tie sb/sth (up): Ela prendeu o cachorro a um banco. She tied the dog to a bench. 2 (cabelo) tie your hair back 3 (com alfinetes) pin sth (to/on sth): Prendi a manga com alfinetes. I pinned the sleeve on. 4 (deter) arrest 5 (encarcerar) imprison 6 (Mil) take sb prisoner 7 (imobilizar) obstruct ● prender-se vp 1 (agarrar-se) get caught: A minha manga se prendeu na porta. My sleeve got caught in the door. 2 (amarrar-se) get tied down ▶ ~ a atenção grab sb's attention ~ o intestino make sb constipated

prenhe adj pregnant

prensa sf press

prensar vt press

preocupação sf worry [pl -ies]

preocupar vt worry: *Minha saúde me preocupa.* I'm worried about my health. • **preocupar-se** vp worry (*about sb/sth*)

preparação sf **1** preparation **2** (*treino*) training

preparado adj **1** (*pronto*) ready **2** (*pessoa*) qualified

preparar vt prepare, get *sb/sth* ready (*mais coloq*): ~ *o jantar* get supper ready • **preparar-se** vp prepare for *sth*: ~ *para fazer o teste de direção* practice for your driving test

preparativos sm preparations

preparo sm preparation ▸ ~ **físico** physical fitness

preposição sf preposition

presa sf (*caça*) prey [U]

prescindir vt ~ **de 1** (*privar-se*) do without *sth*: *Não posso* ~ *do carro.* I can't do without the car. **2** (*desfazer-se*) dispense with *sb*

presença sf presence ▸ ~ **de espírito** presence of mind

presenciar vt **1** (*testemunhar*) witness **2** (*estar presente*) attend

presente sm present • adj present (*at sth*): *entre os* ~*s na reunião* among those present at the meeting

presentear vt give: ~ *alguém com um buquê de flores* give sb a bunch of flowers

presépio sm (*natalino*) crib

preservativo sm **1** (*camisinha*) condom **2** (*em comida*) preservative

presidência sf **1** presidency [pl -ies]: *a* ~ *de um país* the presidency of a country (*clube, comitê, empresa, partido*) chair

presidencial adj presidential

presidente/a sm-sf **1** (*Pol, companhia*) president **2** (*clube, comitê, empresa, partido*) chair(person) NOTA Estas são as formas preferidas atualmente, embora também se usem **chairman** e **chairwoman**.

presidiário/a sm-sf convict

presidir vt **1** preside *at/over sth* **2** ~ *uma reunião* chair a meeting

preso/a adj **1** (*atado*) tied up **2** (*prisioneiro*): *estar* ~ be in prison **3** (*imobilizado*) stuck: *Meu sapato ficou* ~ *na grade.* My shoe got caught in the grating. • sm-sf prisoner

pressa sf hurry: *Não tem* ~. There's no hurry. ▸ **às** ~**s** hurriedly **estar com/ter** ~ be in a hurry

presságio sm omen

pressão sf pressure: *a* ~ *atmosférica* atmospheric pressure

pressentimento sm feeling: *Tenho um mau* ~. I have a bad feeling about it.

pressentir vt **1** (*sentir antecipadamente*) sense: ~ *o perigo* sense danger **2** (*prever*) have a feeling (*that...*)

pressionar vt **1** (*apertar*) press: *Pressione a tecla duas vezes.* Press the key twice. **2** (*forçar*) put pressure on sb (*to do sth*)

prestação sf (*pagamento*) installment: *pagar algo a/em* ~ pay for sth in installments

prestar vi, vt (*servir*) do: *Isso presta para quê?* What's that for? NOTA Para dizer *não prestar* use-se **be no good**: *Joguei fora as canetas que não prestavam.* I threw away all the pens that were no good. **2** (*pessoa*) be good (*as sth*): *Eu não prestaria para professora.* I'd be no good as a teacher. **3** (*serviço*) provide **4** (*exame*) take **5** (*Jur*): ~ *declarações/juramento* give evidence/take an oath ▸ **não** ~ **para nada** be completely useless ~ **atenção** pay attention **prestar-se ao ridículo** lay yourself open to ridicule

prestativo adj helpful

prestes adj ~ **a** about to do sth: *Eu estava* ~ *a sair quando tocou o telefone.* I was just about to go out when the phone rang.

prestígio sm prestige: *de* ~ prestigious

presumido adj vain

presumível adj alleged: *o* ~ *criminoso* the alleged criminal

presunçoso/a sm-sf big-head • adj (*convencido*) big-headed

presunto sm cured ham

pretender vt intend to do sth / doing sth: *Ele não pretende ficar aqui, né?* He's not intending to stay here, is he? ◇ *Se você pretende ir sozinha, pode esquecer.* If you're thinking of going alone, forget it.

pretexto sm excuse: *arranjar um* ~ *para não fazer algo* find an excuse not to do sth

preto adj, sm black: *vestir-se de* ~ wear black

prevalecer vi prevail (*over sb/sth*)

prevenção sf **1** (precaução) prevention **2** (parcialidade) bias

prevenido adj **1** (preparado) prepared: estar ~ para algo be prepared for sth **2** (prudente) prudent

prevenir vt **1** (evitar) prevent **2** (avisar) warn sb about sth

prever vt foresee

previdência sf ► - **Social** welfare, social security (GB)

previdente adj far-sighted

prévio adj previous: experiência prévia previous experience ◊ sem aviso ~ without prior warning

previsão sf forecast: a ~ do tempo the weather forecast

prezado adj (em correspondência) Dear: Prezado Senhor/ Prezada Senhora Dear Sir/ Dear Madam

primário adj **1** primary: cor primária primary color **2** (Educ) elementary, primary (GB): professor ~ elementary school teacher

primavera sf spring: na ~ in (the) spring

primeira sf **1** (automóvel) first (gear): Engatei a ~ e saí a toda a velocidade. I put it into first and sped off. **2** (classe) first class: viajar de ~ travel first class ► de ~ top-class: um restaurante de ~ a top-class restaurant na ~ first time: Eu me sai bem na ~. I got it right first time.

primeira-dama sf first lady

primeiro adj first (abrev **1st**): à primeira vista at first glance ◊ o dia ~ de maio the first of May ● num, sm **1** (one): Fomos os ~s a sair. We were the first (ones) to leave. **2** (melhor) top: Você é o ~ da turma. You're top of the class. ● adv first ► de primeira necessidade absolutely essential em ~ lugar first of all ~ plano foreground ~s socorros first aid [U]

primeiro-ministro, primeira-ministra sm-sf prime minister

primitivo/a adj primitive

primo/a sm-sf cousin: ~ de primeiro grau first cousin

princesa sf princess

principal adj main, principal (mais fml): prato/oração ~ main meal/clause ◊ Isso é o ~. That's the main thing. ◊ o ~ país produtor de ouro the principal gold-producing country

príncipe sm prince **NOTA** Quando se trata de um casal de príncipes, diz-se **prince and**

princess: Os ~s nos receberam no palácio. The prince and princess received us at the palace. ► - **encantado** Prince Charming

principiante smf beginner

princípio sm **1** (início) beginning: desde o ~ from the beginning ◊ do ~ ao fim from beginning to end ◊ no ~ do ano at the beginning of the year ◊ no ~ de maio in early May **2** (conceito, moral) principle ► a ~ at first em/por ~ in/on principle

prioridade sf priority [pl -ies]

prisão sf **1** (local) prison: ir para a ~ go to prison **2** (detenção) arrest **3** (clausura) imprisonment: ~ perpétua life imprisonment ◊ 10 meses de ~ 10 months' imprisonment ► - de ventre constipation: ter/ficar com ~ de ventre be/become constipated

prisioneiro/a sm-sf prisoner: fazer ~s take prisoners

privacidade sf privacy

privado adj private

privar vt deprive sb/sth (of sth) ●
privar-se vp ~ de do without sth

privatizar vt privatize

privilegiado adj **1** (excepcional) exceptional **2** (favorecido) privileged: as classes privilegiadas the privileged classes

privilégio sm privilege

pró sm ► os ~s e os contras the pros and cons

proa sf bow(s)

probabilidade sf likelihood, probability [pl -ies] (mais fml) ► contra todas as ~s against all the odds

problema sm problem: ~ seu! That's your problem!

procedência sf origin

procedente adj ~ de from: o trem ~ do Rio the train from Rio

proceder vt (originar-se) come from...: A língua portuguesa procede do latim. Portuguese comes from Latin. ● vi (comportar-se) behave: ~ corretamente behave properly

procedimento sm **1** (método) procedure: de acordo com os ~s de praxe according to established procedure **2** (comportamento) behavior

processador sm: ~ de dados/ texto data/word processor

processamento sm: ~ de dados/ textos data/word processing

processar vt **1** (classificar) file **2** (Informát) process **3** (Jur)

(a) (*indivíduo*) sue sb (for sth) (b) (*Estado*) prosecute sb (for (doing) sth)

processo sm **1** process **2** (*Jur*) (a) (*ação civil*) lawsuit **2** (*divórcio, falência*) proceedings [pl]

procissão sf procession

procura sf **1** search (for sth) **2** (*Com*) demand: *oferta e ~* supply and demand ▶ **andar à ~ de...** be looking for sb/sth

procurar vt **1** look for sb/sth: *~ trabalho* look for work **2** (*sistematicamente*) search for sb/sth: *Usam cães para ~ drogas.* They use dogs to search for drugs. **3** (*num livro, numa lista*) look up: *~ uma palavra no dicionário* look a word up in the dictionary **4** ~ **fazer algo** try to do sth **5** ~ **(em)** (*look (in/through sth*) ▶ ~ **uma agulha num palheiro** look for a needle in a haystack **procura-se**: *Procura-se apartamento.* Apartment wanted.

prodígio sm prodigy [pl -ies]

produção sf **1** production: *a ~ de aço* steel production **2** (*industrial, artística*) output

produtivo adj productive

produto sm product: *~s de beleza/limpeza* beauty/cleaning products ▶ **~s agrícolas** agricultural produce [U] **~s alimentícios** foodstuffs → PRODUCT

produtor/a sm-sf adj: *países ~es de petróleo* oil-producing countries ● **sm-sf** producer ● **produtora** sf production company [pl -ies]

produzir vt produce

proeza sf exploit ▶ **ser uma grande ~** be quite a feat

profecia sf prophecy [pl -ies]

proferir vt **1** (*palavra, frase*) utter **2** (*discurso*): *~ um discurso* give a speech **3** ~ *insultos* hurl insults **4** ~ *uma acusação* make an accusation **5** (*Jur*): *~ uma sentença* pass sentence

professor/a sm-sf **1** teacher: *um ~ de inglês* an English teacher **2** (*em universidade*) professor, lecturer (*GB*)

profeta/isa sm-sf prophet

profissão sf profession → WORK

profissional adj, smf professional

profundidade sf depth: *a 50 metros de ~* at a depth of 50 meters ◊ *Tem 5 metros de ~.* It's 5 meters deep.

profundo adj deep: *uma voz profunda* a deep voice

prognóstico sm (*Med*) prognosis [pl -noses]: *Qual é o ~ dos especialistas?* What do the specialists think?

programa sm **1** (*TV, Informát, etc.*) program: *um ~ de televisão* a TV program **2** (*matéria de uma disciplina*) syllabus **3** (*plano*) plan: *Você tem ~ para sábado?* Do you have anything planned for Saturday?

programação sf **1** (*TV, rádio*) programs [pl]: *a ~ infantil* children's programs **2** (*Informát*) programming **3** (*de cinema, etc., em jornal*) listings [pl]

programador/a sm-sf (*Informát*) programmer

programar vt **1** (*elaborar*) plan **2** (*dispositivo*) set: *~ o vídeo* set the VCR ● vt, vi (*Informát*) program

progredir vi make progress: *~ muito* make good progress

progressivo adj progressive

progresso sm progress [U]: *fazer ~* make progress

proibição sf ban (on sth)

proibido adj forbidden: *fruto ~* forbidden fruit ◊ *dirigir em sentido ~* drive the wrong way ▶ ~ **fixar cartazes** post no bills ~ **fumar** no smoking

proibir vt **1** not allow sb to do sth, forbid sb to do sth (*fml*): *Proibiram-na de comer doces.* She's not allowed to eat candy. ◊ *O meu pai me proibiu de sair à noite.* My father has forbidden me to go out at night. **2** (*oficialmente*) ban sb/sth (from (doing) sth): *Proibiram o trânsito no centro da cidade.* Traffic has been banned from downtown.

projetar vt **1** (*refletir*): *~ uma imagem numa tela* project an image onto a screen **2** (*Cinema*) show: *~ slides/um filme* show slides/a movie

projétil sm projectile

projeto sm **1** project **2** (*plano*) plan: *Você tem algum ~ para o futuro?* Do you have any plans for the future? ▶ ~ **de lei** bill

projetor sm **1** (*lâmpada*) spotlight **2** (*slides, etc.*) projector

prol sm ▶ **em ~ de** in favor of sb/sth: *a organização em ~ dos cegos* the society for the blind

prolongamento sm extension

prolongar vt (*tempo*) prolong (*fml*), make sth longer: *~ a vida de um doente* prolong a patient's life ● **prolongar-se** vp (*demorar demais*) drag on

promessa sf promise: *cumprir/*

fazer uma ~ keep/make a promise

prometer vt promise: *Eu te prometo que vou voltar.* I promise I'll be back. ◊ *uma jovem que promete* a young woman with great promise

promissor adj promising

promoção sf promotion ▶ **em ~** on special offer

promotor/a sm-sf promoter ▶ **~ público** district attorney, public prosecutor (GB)

promover vt promote: *Promoveram-no a capitão.* He was promoted to captain.

pronome sm pronoun

prontificar-se vp offer to do sth

pronto adj 1 (*preparado*) ready (*for* sth/*to do* sth): *Está tudo ~ para a festa.* Everything is ready for the party. ◊ *~ para sair* ready to leave 2 (*cozido*) done: *O frango ainda não está ~.* The chicken isn't done yet. • interj 1 (*bom!*) right (then) 2 (*e acabou!*) so there: *Pois agora não vou, ~!* Well, now I'm not going, so there!

pronto-socorro sm emergency room, casualty (department) (GB)

pronúncia sf pronunciation

pronunciar vt pronounce • **pronunciar-se** vp speak out ▶ **~ (a) sentença** pass sentence

propaganda sf 1 (*publicidade*) advertising: *fazer ~ de um produto* advertise a product 2 (*material publicitário*) leaflets [pl]: *A caixa do correio estava cheia de ~.* The mailbox was full of advertising leaflets. ◊ *distribuir ~ na rua* hand out flyers in the street 3 (*Pol*) propaganda: *~ eleitoral* election propaganda

propenso adj prone to (*do*) sth

propina sf (*gorjeta*) tip

propor vt (*medida, plano*) propose: *Eu te proponho um acordo.* I have a deal to put to you. • **propor-se** vp 1 (*oferecer-se*) offer to *do* sth 2 (*decidir-se*) set out to *do* sth: *Eu me propus a acabá-lo.* I set out to finish it.

proporção sf 1 (*relação, tamanho*) proportion 2 (*Mat*) ratio: *A ~ é de um rapaz para três moças.* The ratio of boys to girls is one to three.

propósito sm 1 (*intenção*) intention: *bons ~s* good intentions 2 (*objetivo*) purpose: *O ~ desta reunião é...* The purpose of this meeting is... ▶ **a ~** by the way **de ~** on purpose

proposta sf proposal: *A ~ foi recusada.* The proposal was turned down.

propriedade sf property [pl -ies]: *~ particular* private property ◊ *as ~s medicinais das plantas* the medicinal properties of plants

proprietário/a sm-sf 1 owner 2 (*de casa alugada*) landlord [*fem* landlady] [pl ~es]

próprio adj 1 (*de cada um*) my, your, etc. own: *Tudo o que você faz é em benefício ~.* Everything you do is for your own benefit. 2 (*mesmo*) himself [*fem* herself] [pl themselves]: *O ~ pintor inaugurou a exposição.* The painter himself opened the exhibition. 3 (*característico*) typical *of* sb 4 (*conveniente*) suitable: *Esse filme não é ~ para menores de 18 anos.* This movie isn't suitable for under 18s. ▶ **o/a próprio/a** the very same

prorrogação sf 1 (*prazo*) extension 2 (*Esporte*) extra time

prosa sf prose

prospecto sm (*propaganda*) leaflet

prosperar vi prosper

prosperidade sf prosperity

próspero adj prosperous

prostituta sf prostitute

protagonista smf main character

protagonizar vt star in sth: *~ um filme* star in a film

proteção sf protection

proteger vt protect sb/sth (*against/from* sb/sth): *O chapéu te protege do sol.* Your hat will protect you from the sun.

proteína sf protein

protestante adj, smf Protestant

protestar vt, vi (*reivindicar*) protest (*against/about* sth): *~ contra uma lei* protest against a law

protesto sm protest: *Ignoraram os ~s dos alunos.* They ignored the students' protests. ◊ *uma carta de ~* a letter of protest

protetor adj protective (*towards* sb) • sm 1 (*solar*) sunscreen 2 (*defensor*) protector

protótipo sm prototype: *o ~ dos novos motores* the prototype for the new engines

protuberante adj (*olhos*) bulging

prova sf 1 test: *uma ~ de aptidão/francês* an aptitude/French test 2 (*Mat*) proof 3 (*Esporte*): *as ~s de dardo* the javelin competition **4** (*amostra*) token: *uma ~ de amor* a token of love **5** (*Jur*) evidence [*U*]: *Não há ~s contra mim.* There's no evidence against me. ▸ **à - d'água/ de bala/de som** waterproof/ bulletproof/soundproof **pôr alguém à ~** put sb to the test ▸ **- final** final (exam): *As ~s finais começam hoje.* Finals start today.

provar *vt* **1** (*demonstrar*) prove **2** (*comida, bebida*) try: *Nunca provei caviar.* I've never tried caviar. ◇ *Prove isto. Falta sal?* Try this. Does it need more salt? **3** (*roupa*) try *sth* on

provável *adj* probable: *É muito ~ que chova.* It's probably going to rain. ◇ *É ~ que ele não esteja em casa.* He probably won't be in. ▸ **pouco ~** unlikely

provavelmente *adv* probably

proveito *sm* benefit ▸ **bom ~** enjoy your meal **tirar ~** benefit *from sth*: *tirar o máximo ~ de algo* get the most out of sth

provérbio *sm* proverb

proveta *sf* test tube: *bebê de ~* test-tube baby

providência *sf* (*medida*) measure

província *sf* province

provinciano *adj* provincial

provir *vi* come *from sth*: *A sidra provém da maçã.* Cider comes from apples.

provisório *adj* provisional

provocação *sf* provocation: *resistir a provocações* resist provocation

provocar *vt* **1** (*desafiar*) provoke **2** (*causar*) cause: *~ um acidente* cause an accident **3** *~ um incêndio* start a fire

proximidade *sf* nearness, proximity (*mais fml*): *a ~ do mar* the proximity of the sea

próximo *adj* **1** (*seguinte*) next: *a próxima parada* the next stop ◇ *o ~ mês/a próxima terça* next month/Tuesday **2** (*relativo a tempo*): *O Natal está ~.* It will soon be Christmas. ◇ *as próximas eleições* the forthcoming elections **3** (*relativo a intimidade*) close (*to sb/sth*): *um parente ~* a close relative ◇ *fontes próximas da família* sources close to the family **4** (*relativo a distância*) near *sb/sth*: *um povoado ~ de Goiás* a village near Goiás → NEAR ● *sm* neighbor: *amar o ~* love your neighbor

prudência *sf* caution ▸ **com ~** carefully

prudente *adj* **1** (*cuidadoso*) careful **2** (*sensato*) sensible: *um homem/uma decisão ~* a sensible man/decision

pseudônimo *sm* pseudonym

psicologia *sf* psychology

psicólogo/a *sm-sf* psychologist

psicoterapeuta *smf* (psycho) therapist

psicoterapia *sf* (psycho) therapy

psiquiatra *smf* psychiatrist

psiquiatria *sf* psychiatry

psiu *interj* (*silêncio!*) sh!

pub *sm* bar

puberdade *sf* puberty

púbis *sm* pubis

publicação *sf* publication ▸ **de ~ semanal**: *uma revista de ~ semanal* a weekly magazine

publicar *vt* **1** publish: *~ um romance* publish a novel **2** (*divulgar*) publicize

publicidade *sf* **1** publicity: *Fizeram muita ~ do caso.* The case had a lot of publicity. **2** (*propaganda*) advertising

publicitário *adj* advertising: *uma campanha publicitária* an advertising campaign

público *adj* public: *a opinião pública* public opinion ◇ *transporte ~* public transportation ● *sm* **1** public: *O ~ é a favor da lei.* The public is in favor of the law. ◇ *aberto ao ~* open to the public ◇ *falar em ~* speak in public **2** (*espectadores*) audience

pudim *sm* pudding ▸ **~ de leite** caramel custard

pudor *sm* shame

puericultura *sf* child care

pugilismo *sm* boxing

pugilista *smf* boxer

puir *vt* wear *sth* out: *A suéter dele está puída nos cotovelos.* His sweater is worn at the elbows.

pular *vi* jump

pulga *sf* flea ▸ **estar/ficar com a ~ atrás da orelha** smell a rat

pulmão *sm* lung

pulmonar *adj* lung: *uma infecção ~* a lung infection

pulo *sm* jump: *dar ~s de alegria* jump for joy ▸ **dar um ~ a/até** stop by...: *dar um ~ até o mercado para comprar leite* stop by the market for some milk

pulôver *sm* sweater

púlpito *sm* pulpit

pulsação *sf* (*coração*) pulse: *O número de pulsações aumenta* *após o exercício*. Your pulse rate increases after exercise.

pulseira sf **1** (*bracelete*) bracelet **2** (*relógio*) strap

pulso sm **1** (*Anat*) wrist **2** (*Med*) pulse: *tomar o ~ de alguém* take sb's pulse

pulverizador sm spray

pulverizar vt **1** (*vaporizar*) spray sth (*with sth*) **2** (*destroçar*) pulverize

puma sm puma

punhado sm handful: *um ~ de arroz* a handful of rice

punhal sm dagger

punhalada sf stab

punho sm **1** (*mão fechada*) fist **2** (*manga*) cuff ► **3** (*bastão*) handle **4** (*espada*) hilt

punir vt penalize

punk adj, smf punk

pupila sf pupil

purê sm purée: *~ de maçã* apple purée ◊ *~ (de batata)* mashed potato

pureza sf purity

purgatório sm purgatory

purificar vt purify

puritanismo sm puritanism

puritano/a adj **1** (*pudico*) puritanical **2** (*Relig*) Puritan ● sm-sf Puritan

puro adj **1** pure: *ouro ~* pure gold **2** (*enfático*) simple: *a pura verdade* the simple truth ► **por ~ acaso/pura** casualidade by sheer chance

puro-sangue sm thoroughbred

púrpura sf purple

pus sm pus

puxa interj **1** (*surpresa*) wow **2** (*irritação*) darn **3** (*desapontamento*) what a pity

puxado adj (*difícil, cansativo*) hard: *O exame foi bem ~.* The test was really hard.

puxador sm (*porta, gaveta*) handle

puxão sm tug: *dar um ~ no cabelo de alguém* give sb's hair a tug

puxar vt **1** pull **2** *~ a* look like sb: *Ele puxa um pouco pela mãe.* He looks a little like his mother. **3** *~ para*: *O cabelo dele puxa para o louro.* He has blondish hair. ◊ *cor-de-rosa puxando para o vermelho* pinkish red ► *a* **brasa para a sua sardinha** look out for number one

puxa-saco adj, smf: *Não dê uma de ~.* Don't be such a creep.

Q q

quadra sf court: *~ de tênis* tennis court

quadrado adj square ● sm **1** square **2** (*figura, formulário*) box

quadragésimo/a num, sm fortieth

quadril sm hip

quadrilha sf gang

quadrinhos sm (*revista, jornal*) comic strip [*sing*]

quadro sm **1** (*sala de aula*) (black)board **2** (*Arte*) painting **3** (*funcionários*) staff ► **de avisos** bulletin board, noticeboard (*GB*)

quádruplo/a num quadruple ● sm four times: *Qual é o ~ de quatro?* What's four times four?

qual pron rel **1** (*pessoa*) whom: *Tenho dez alunos, dois dos quais são ingleses.* I have ten students, two of whom are English. → WHOM **2** (*coisa, animal*) which: *Ela comprou vários livros, entre os quais um dicionário.* She bought several books, among which was a dictionary. ● pron interr **1** what: *~ é a capital do Brasil?* What's the capital of Brazil? **2** (*entre vários*) which (one): *~ você prefere?* Which one do you prefer? → WHAT

qualidade sf quality [*pl* -ies] ► **na ~ de** as: *na ~ de porta-voz* as a spokesperson

qualificação sf qualification

qualificar-se vp qualify (*as sth*)

qualquer pron **1** any: *Tome ~ ônibus que vá para o centro.* Catch any bus that goes downtown. ◊ *em ~ caso* in any case → SOME **2** (*qualquer que seja*) any old: *Pegue um trapo ~.* Just use any old cloth. ● **em ~ lugar/parte** anywhere ~ **coisa** anything: *Discutem por ~ coisa.* They argue over the slightest thing. ~ **um/uma 1** (*qualquer pessoa*) anybody: *~ um pode se enganar.* Anybody can make a mistake. **2** (*entre dois*) either (one): *~ um dos dois serve.* Either (of them) will do. ◊ *— Qual dos dois livros eu devo levar? — Qualquer um.* "Which of the two books should I take?" "Either one (of them)." **3** (*entre mais de dois*) any (one): *~ uma dessas cidades* in any one of those cities **um/uma ~**

(pessoa sem importância) a nobody: *Ele não passa de um ~.* He's just a nobody.

quando *adv, conj* **1** when: *~ é que é a sua prova?* When's your exam? ◊ *Passe na casa ~ quiser.* Stop by my house whenever you want. **2** *(simultaneidade)* as: *Eu o vi ~ eu estava saindo.* I saw him as I was leaving. ▶ **de quando em quando** from time to time **desde ~?** since when…?: *Desde ~ você se interessa por esporte?* Since when have you been interested in sports? **~ muito** at (the) most: *Havia uns dez ~ muito.* There were ten of them at the most. **~ quer que…** whenever…

quantia *sf* amount

quantidade *sf* **1** amount: *uma pequena ~ de tinta* a small amount of paint **2** *(pessoas, objetos)* number: *Havia uma grande ~ de gente.* There were a large number of people. ◊ *Que ~ de carros!* What a lot of cars! **3** *(magnitude)* quantity ▶ **em ~** in huge amounts

quanto/a *pron*

● **uso interrogativo 1** *(substantivo não contável)* how much: *~ dinheiro você gastou?* How much money did you spend? ◊ *De ~ você precisa?* How much do you need? **2** *(substantivo contável)* how many: *Quantas pessoas estavam lá?* How many people were there?

● **uso exclamativo** *~ vinho!* What a lot of wine! ◊ *~s turistas!* What a lot of tourists!

● **outras construções** *Faça ~s testes forem necessários.* Do whatever tests are necessary. ◊ *Vou fazer quantas vezes forem necessárias.* I'll do it as many times as I have to. ◊ *Eu lhe dei o ~ tinha.* I gave him everything I had. ◊ *Chore o ~ quiser.* Cry as much as you like. ● *adv* **1** *(uso interrogativo)* how much **2** *(uso exclamativo)* ~ *eu gosto deles!* I'm so fond of them! ▶ **~ a…** as for… **(o)** *~* **antes** as soon as possible **~ é/custa?** how much is it? **~ mais/menos…** the more/less…: *~ mais ele tem, mais quer.* The more he has, the more he wants. ◊ *~ mais eu penso no assunto, menos eu entendo.* The more I think about it, the less I understand it. **~ tempo/~s dias, meses, etc.?** how long…?: *~ tempo levou para você chegar lá?* How long did it take you to get

there? ◊ *Há ~s anos você vive aqui?* How long have you been living here?

quarenta *num, sm* forty

quaresma *sf* Lent

quarta(-feira) *sf* Wednesday *(abrev Wed.)* ▶ DOMINGO ▶ **~ de Cinzas** Ash Wednesday

quartas-de-final *sf* quarter-finals

quarteirão *sm (casas)* block

quartel *sm* **1** *(caserna)* barracks **2** *entrar para o ~* do your military service ▶ **~ do corpo de bombeiros** fire station

quartel-general *sm* headquarters *(abrev HQ)*

quarto¹ *sm* **1** room *(de dormir)* bedroom ▶ **~ de despejo/hóspedes** boxroom/guestroom **~ de solteiro** single room

quarto² *adj, num, sm* fourth *(abrev 4th)* ● *sm (quantidade)* quarter: *um ~ de hora* a quarter of an hour ◊ **quarta** *sf (marcha)* fourth (gear) ▶ **~ crescente/minguante** first/last quarter

quase *adv* **1** *(frases afirmativas)* nearly, almost: *~ cai.* I almost fell. ◊ *Estava ~ cheio.* It was nearly full. → NEARLY **2** *(frases negativas)* hardly: *~ nunca a vejo.* I hardly ever see her. ◊ *Não sobrou ~ nada.* There was hardly anything left. ▶ **~ sempre** nearly always

quatorze *num, sm* **1** fourteen **2** *(data)* fourteenth

quatro *num, sm* four **2** *(data)* fourth

quatrocentos *num, sm* four hundred

que¹ *pron*

● **interrogação** what: *~ horas são?* What time is it? NOTA Quando há poucas possibilidades, deve-se usar **which**: *~ carro vamos usar hoje? O seu ou o meu?* Which car shall we take today? Yours or mine?

● **exclamação 1** *(+ substantivos contáveis no plural e não-contáveis)* what: *~ casas lindas!* What lovely houses! ◊ *~ coragem!* What courage! ◊ *Não sei o ~ você quer.* I don't know what you want. **2** *(+ substantivos contáveis no singular)* what a: *~ vida!* What a life! **3** *(+ substantivo traduzido por adjetivo)* how: *~ raiva/horror!* How annoying/awful! ◊ *~ interessante!* How interesting! ● *adv* how: *~ interessante!* How interesting! ▶ **~ tal? 1** *(como é/são?)* what is/are sb/sth like?: *~ tal foi o filme?* What was the movie like? **2** (*sugestão*): ~ *tal um café?* How about a coffee?

que[2] *pron rel*

● **sujeito 1** (*pessoas*) who: *o homem ~ esteve aqui ontem* the man who was here yesterday **2** (*coisas*) that, which: *o carro ~ está estacionado na praça* the car that's parked in the square ◇ *Este edifício, ~ antes foi sede de Governo, hoje é uma escola.* This building, which previously housed the government, is now a school.

● **complemento NOTA** É preferível não traduzir **que** quando este funciona como complemento, apesar de ser correto usar **that/who** com pessoas e **that/which** com coisas: *a revista ~ você me emprestou* the magazine (that/which) you lent me ◇ *o rapaz ~ você conheceu em Roma* the boy (that/who) you met in Rome.→ WHOM

que[3] *conj* **1** (*orações subordinadas*) (that): *Ele disse ~ viria esta semana.* He said (that) he would come this week. ◇ *Quero ~ você veja.* I want you to see it. **2** (*comparações*): *Meu irmão é mais alto (do) ~ você.* My brother's taller than you. **3** (*resultado*) (that): *Estava tão cansada ~ adormeci.* I was so tired (that) I fell asleep. **4** (*outras construções*): *Aumenta o rádio ~ não estou ouvindo nada.* Turn the radio up — I can't hear a thing. ◇ *Não havia dia em ~ não chovesse.* There wasn't a single day when it didn't rain.

quê *interj* what

quebra-cabeça *sm* puzzle: *fazer um ~* do a (jigsaw) puzzle

quebra-mar *sm* breakwater

quebra-nozes *sm* nutcracker

quebrar *vt, vi* break: ~ *uma promessa/um vidro* break a promise/window ▶ ~ **a cabeça** rack your brains: *Tenho quebrado a cabeça para resolver esse problema.* I've been racking my brains trying to solve this problem. ▶ ~ **a cara de alguém** smash sb's face in ~ **o gelo** break the ice

queda *sf* **1** fall: *uma ~ de três metros* a three-meter fall ◇ *a ~ do governo* the fall of the government ◇ *uma ~ dos preços* a fall in prices **2** (*temperatura*) drop *in* **3** (*cabelo*) loss: *a ~ de cabelo* hair loss ▶ ~ **d'água** waterfall **ter (uma)** ~ **por doces** have a sweet tooth

queijo *sm* cheese: ~ *ralado* grated cheese

queimada *sf* forest fire

queimado *adj* **1** burned **2** (*bronzeado*) tanned **3** (*calcinado*) charred

queimadura *sf* **1** burn: ~*s de segundo grau* second-degree burns **2** (*com líquido fervente*) scald ▶ ~ **solar** sunburn [U]

queimar *vt* burn ● *vi* **1** *Está queimando!* It's very hot! **2** (*fusível*) blow ● **queimar-se** *vp* **1** (*pessoa*) burn yourself (*on sth*) **2** (*com o sol*) burn: ~ *facilmente* burn easily

queixa *sf* complaint: *fazer ~ de alguém* complain about sb ▶ **apresentar uma** ~ report sth to the police

queixar-se *vp* complain (*about sb/sth*)

queixo *sm* chin

quem *pron rel* **1** (*sujeito*) who: ~ *me disse foi o meu irmão.* It was my brother who told me. **2** (*complemento*) ● Em inglês é preferível não traduzir **quem** quando este funciona como complemento, apesar de ser correto usar **who** ou **whom**: ~ *eu quero ver é a minha mãe.* I want my mother I want to see. ◇ *O rapaz com ~ eu vi ontem é primo dela.* The boy (who) I saw her with yesterday is her cousin. **3** (*qualquer um*) whoever: *Convide ~ você quiser.* Invite whoever you want. ◇ ~ *estiver a favor levante a mão.* Those in favor, raise your hands. ◇ *O João, o Zé ou ~ quer que seja.* João, Zé or whoever. ● *pron interr* who: ~ *é?* Who is it? ◇ ~ *é que você viu?* Who did you see? ◇ *De ~ você está falando?* Who are you talking about? → WHOM ▶ **de quem...?** (*posse*) whose...?: *De ~ é este casaco?* Whose coat is this? ▶ **me dera** if only: *Quem me dera ganhar na loteria!* If only I could win the lottery! ▶ ~ **quer que** whoever: ~ *quer que seja culpado será castigado.* Whoever is responsible will be punished.

quente *adj* **1** hot: *água ~* hot water ◇ *um dia ~* a hot day **2** (*morno*) warm: *uma cama/noite ~* a warm bed/night → FRIO

quer *conj* ▶ **quer... quer...** whether... or...: ~ *chova ~ não chova* whether it rains or not ◇ ~ *queira, ~ não (queira)* whether you like it or not

querer *vt* **1** want: *Qual você*

quer? Which one do you want? ◇ *Ele que vamos à casa dele.* He wants us to go to his house. ◇ *Como entrada, quero sopa de peixe.* I'd like fish soup to start with. → WANT 2 (*amar*) love • *vi* want to: *Não quero.* I don't want to. ▶ **por** ~ (*de propósito*) on purpose ▶ **dizer** ~ mean: *O que quer dizer isto?* What does this mean? **queria eu...** I, he, etc. would like to: *Queria eu saber por que é que você chega sempre atrasado.* I'd like to know why you're always late. **sem** ~: *Desculpe, foi sem ~.* Sorry, it was an accident.

querido/a *adj* dear • *sm-sf*: *Meu ~!* Sweetheart!

querosene *sm* kerosene

questão *sf* **1** question: *em* ~ in question ◇ *fora de* ~ out of the question **2** (*assunto, problema*) matter: *em* ~ *de horas* in a matter of hours ◇ *uma* ~ *de vida ou morte* a matter of life or death ▶ **a** ~ **é...** the thing is... **fazer** ~ (**de**) insist on *doing sth*: *Ele fez* ~ *de pagar.* He insisted on paying. **pôr algo em** ~ question sth

questionário *sm* questionnaire

quicar *vi* (*bola*) bounce: *Esta bola quica muito.* This ball is very bouncy.

quieto/a *adj* **1** (*imóvel*) still: *estar/ficar* ~ keep still **2** (*em silêncio*) quiet

quilo *sm* kilo [*pl* ~s] (*abrev* **kg**) → Ver pág. 224

quilômetro *sm* kilometer (*abrev* **km**) → Ver pág. 224

quilowatt *sm* kilowatt (*abrev* **kw.**)

química *sf* chemistry

químico/a *adj* chemical • *sm-sf* chemist

quina *sf* (*aresta*) edge: *a* ~ *da mesa* the edge of the table

quinhentos *num, sm* five hundred

quinta(-feira) *sf* Thursday (*abrev* **Thur(s).**) → DOMINGO ▶ ~ **Santa** Maundy Thursday

quintal *sm* backyard

quinto/a *adj, num, sm* fifth • **quinta** *sf* (*marcha*) fifth (gear)

quinze *num, sm* **1** fifteen **2** (*data*) fifteenth **3** (*hora*) a quarter: *às* ~ *para as dez* at a quarter to/of ten ◇ *É uma e* ~. It's a quarter after one. ▶ ~ **dias** fortnight: *Vamos ficar* ~ *dias.* We're staying for a fortnight.

quinzena *sf*: *a segunda* ~ *de junho* the last two weeks of June

quiosque *sm* newsstand

quitar *vt* (*pagar*) pay *sth* off: ~ *uma dívida* pay *sth* off a debt

quite *adj* even (*with sb*): *Assim estamos* ~s. That way we're even.

quota *sf Ver* COTA

R r

rã *sf* frog

rabanete *sm* radish

rabino *sm* rabbi

rabiscar *vt, vi* **1** (*desenhar*) doodle **2** (*escrever*) scribble

rabisco *sm* **1** (*desenho*) doodle **2** (*escrita*) scribble

rabo *sm* **1** (*animal*) tail **2** (*pessoa*) backside ▶ **pelo/com o** ~ **do olho** out of the corner of your eye

rabo-de-cavalo *sm* (*cabelo*) ponytail

rabugento *adj* grumpy

raça *sf* **1** (*humana*) race **2** (*animal*) breed ▶ **de** ~ (*cão*) pedigree **2** (*cavalo*) thoroughbred

ração *sf* (*para gado*) fodder

racha *sf* (*fenda*) crack

rachar *vt* (*lenha*) chop • *vi* (*fender*) crack

racial *adj* racial: *discriminação* ~ racial discrimination ◇ *relações raciais* race relations

raciocinar *vi* think

raciocínio *sm* reasoning

racional *adj* rational

racionamento *sm* rationing: ~ *de água* water rationing

racionar *vt* ration

racismo *sm* racism

racista *adj, sm,f* racist

radar *sm* radar [*U*]: ~*es inimigos* enemy radar

radiador *sm* radiator

radiante *adj* **1** (*brilhante*) bright: *O sol estava* ~. The sun was shining brightly. **2** (*pessoa*) radiant: ~ *de alegria* radiant with joy

radical *adj, sm,f* radical

rádio¹ *sm* (*Quím*) radium

rádio² *sm* radio [*pl* ~s]: *falar no* ~ speak on the radio ◇ *ouvir* ~ listen to the radio

radioativo *adj* radioactive

radiodespertador *sm* clock radio

radiografia *sf* X-ray: *fazer/tirar uma* ~ take an X-ray

radiogravador *sm* radio cassette player

radionovela *sf* (radio) serial

radiotáxi *sm* minicab

raia *sf* **1** (*linha*) line: *passar da ~* go over the line **2** (*pista*) racetrack

rainha *sf* queen

raio¹ *sm* **1** ray: *um ~ de sol* a ray of sunshine **2** (*Meteor*) lightning [*U*] ▶ **~ laser** laser beam **~s X** X-rays

raio² *sm* **1** (*Geom*) radius [*pl* radii] **2** (*roda*) spoke ▶ **num ~**: *Não havia uma única casa num ~ de dez quilômetros.* There were no houses within ten kilometers.

raiva *sf* **1** (*ira*) rage: *Que ~!* I was furious! **2** (*Med*) rabies [*sing*] ▶ **dar(uma) ~** drive *sb* crazy **ter-de alguém** hate *sb*: *Ela tem uma ~ dele!* She really hates him.

raivoso *adj* **1** (*furioso*) furious: *Ele respondeu ~.* He replied furiously. **2** (*Med*) rabid: *um cachorro ~* a rabid dog

raiz *sf* root ▶ **até a ~ (dos cabelos)** sick and tired *of sb/sth* ▶ **~ quadrada/cúbica** square/cube root

rajada *sf* **1** (*vento*) gust **2** *uma ~ de balas* a burst of gunfire

ralador *sm* grater

ralar *vt* grate

ralhar *vt* reprimand *sb* (*for doing*) *sth*

ralo¹ *sm* drain

ralo² *adj* **1** (*sopa, etc.*) thin **2** (*cabelo*) thinning

rama *sf* foliage

ramal *sm* **1** (*ferroviário*) branch line **2** (*telefônico*) extension

ramo *sm* **1** (*flores*) bunch **2** (*árvore, ciência*) branch: *um ~ de árvore* the branch of a tree ◊ *um ~ da filosofia* a branch of philosophy **3** (*setor*) field

rampa *sf* ramp

rancor *sm* resentment

rancoroso *adj* resentful

rançoso *adj* rancid

ranger *vi* (*porta, soalho*) creak ● *vt* (*dentes*) grind

rangido *sm* (*porta*) creak

ranhura *sf* groove

rapaz *sm* young man

rapidez *sf* speed ▶ **com ~** quickly

rápido *adj* **1** (*breve*) quick: *fazer uma chamada rápida* make a quick phone call **2** (*veloz*) fast: *um corredor ~* a fast runner → FAST ● *adv* quickly

raposa *sf* fox

raptar *vt* kidnap

rapto *sm* kidnapping

raptor/a *sm-sf* kidnapper

raquete *sf* racket: *uma ~ de tênis* a tennis racket

raro *adj* (*pouco comum*) rare

rascunho *sm* draft: *um ~ de uma redação* a rough draft of an essay

rasgar(-se) *vt, vp* tear: *~ a saia num prego* tear your skirt on a nail ◊ *Este tecido se rasga com facilidade.* This material tears easily. ◊ *Ele rasgou a carta.* He tore up the letter.

raso *adj* **1** (*plano*) flat **2** (*colher, medida*) level **3** (*pouco profundo*) shallow

raspar *vt* **1** (*superfície*) scrape *sth* (*off sth*): *~ a tinta do chão* scrape the paint off the floor **2** (*tocar levemente*) graze **3** (*rapar*) shave: *~ a cabeça/as pernas* shave your head/legs ◊ *~ a barba* shave your beard off

rasteira *sf* ▶ **passar uma ~** trip: *Você passou uma ~ nele.* You tripped him.

rastejante *adj* **1** (*planta*) trailing **2** (*animal*) crawling

rastejar *vi* crawl

rasto *sm* **1** (*marca, pista*) trail **2** (*barco*) wake **3** (*avião*) vapor trail ▶ **de ~s**: *Ele se aproximou de ~s.* He crawled over. **sem deixar ~** without a trace

rasurar *vt* cross *sth* out

ratazana *sf* rat

ratificar *vt* ratify

ratoeira *sf* trap

razão *sf* reason (*for doing*) *sth*: *sem ~* without reason ▶ **com ~** rightly so **dar ~ a alguém** admit *sb* is right **ter/não ter ~** be right/wrong

razoável *adj* reasonable

ré *sm* (*Mús*) D ● *sf* (*marcha*) reverse

reabastecer(-se) *vt, vi, vp* (*veículo*) refuel

reabilitação *sf* **1** rehabilitation: *programas para a ~ de delinquentes* rehabilitation programs for criminals **2** (*prédio*) renovation

reabilitar *vt* **1** rehabilitate **2** (*prédio*) renovate

reação *sf* reaction

readmitir *vt* reinstate *sb*: *Readmitiram-no na empresa.* The company reinstated him.

reagir *vi* **1** react (*to sb/sth*) **2** (*doente*) respond (*to sb/sth*)

real¹ *adj* (*de reis*) royal ● *sm* (*moeda brasileira*) real: *mil reais* a thousand reais

real² *adj* **1** real: *o mundo ~ the real world* ◇ *em tempo ~* real time **2** *(caso, história)* true

realçar *vt* **1** *(cor, beleza)* bring sth out **2** *(dar ênfase)* enhance

realidade *sf* reality [*pl* -ies] ▶ na ~ actually

realismo *sm* realism

realista *adj* realistic ● *smf* realist

realização *sf* **1** *(projeto, trabalho)* : *Eu me encarrego da ~ do plano.* I'll take charge of carrying out the plan. **2** *(objetivo, sonho)* fulfillment

realizar *vt* **1** *(levar a cabo)* carry sth out: *~ um projeto* carry out a project **2** *(sonho, objetivo)* fulfill **3** *(reunião)* hold ● **realizar-se** *vp* **1** *(tornar-se realidade)* come true: *Os meus sonhos se realizaram.* My dreams came true. **2** *(pessoa)* be fulfilled **3** *(reunião, evento)* take place

realmente *adv* really

reanimar *vt* revive ● *vi* **1** *(fortalecer)* get your strength back **2** *(voltar a si)* regain consciousness

reatar *vt* *(restabelecer)* resume

reativar *vt* revive

reator *sm* reactor: *~ nuclear* nuclear reactor

rebaixamento *sm (Esporte)* relegation *(GB)*

rebaixar *vt* **1** humiliate **2** *(Esporte)* relegate *(GB)* ● **rebaixar-se** *vp* lower yourself: *~ a ponto de fazer algo* lower yourself by doing sth

rebanho *sm* **1** *(ovelhas)* flock **2** *(gado)* herd

rebate *sm* ▶ ~ falso false alarm

rebelde *adj* rebel: *bases/tropas ~s* rebel bases/troops **2** *(espírito)* rebellious ● *smf* rebel

rebelião *sf* rebellion

rebentar *vi* **1** *(bomba)* explode **2** *(balão, pneu, pessoa)* burst **3** *(guerra, epidemia)* break out **4** *(escândalo, tempestade)* break ● *vt (balão)* burst

rebobinar *vt* rewind

rebocar *vt* tow

reboque *sm* **1** *(ato)*: *a ~ on tow* ◇ *um carro com um trailer a ~* a car towing a trailer **2** *(veículo)* tow truck, breakdown truck *(GB)*

rebote *sm (Esporte)* rebound: *no ~* on the rebound

rebuliço *sm* **1** *(ruído)* racket **2** *(atividade)*: *o ~ da capital* the hustle and bustle of the capital

recado *sm* message: *deixar (um) ~* leave a message

recaída *sf* relapse: *ter uma ~* have a relapse

recanto *sm* corner

recear *vt* fear

receber *vt* **1** get, receive *(fml)*: *Recebi a sua carta.* I got your letter. **2** *(pessoa)* welcome **3** *(pagamento)*: *Ainda não recebi o pagamento por aquilo.* I still haven't been paid for that. ◇ *Recebemos na quinta!* We get paid on Thursday! **4** *(notícia)*: *~ a notícia com resignação* take the news philosophically

receio *sm* fear

receita *sf* **1** *(rendimentos)* **(a)** *(instituição)* income **(b)** *(Estado, município)* revenue: *Departamento da ~ Federal* Internal Revenue Service **2** *(Med)* prescription: *Só se vende mediante ~ médica.* Only available on prescription. **3** *(Cozinha)* recipe *(for sth)*

receitar *vt* prescribe

recém-casado/a *adj, sm-sf* newly-wed: *os ~s* the newlyweds

recém-nascido/a *adj* newborn ● *sm-sf* newborn baby [*pl* -ies]

recenseamento *sm* census

recente *adj* recent

recepção *sf* reception

recepcionista *smf* receptionist

recessão *sf* recession

recheio *sm* **1** *(pastel, bolo)* filling **2** *(carne, verduras)* stuffing

rechonchudo *adj* plump

recibo *sm* receipt

reciclagem *sf* recycling

reciclar *vt* recycle

reciclável *adj* recyclable

recife *sm* reef

recipiente *sm* receptacle

recital *sm* recital

recitar *vt* recite

reclamação *sf* complaint: *fazer/apresentar uma ~* make/lodge a complaint

reclamar *vt* demand: *~ justiça* demand justice ● *vi* complain

reclinar-se *vp (pessoa)* lean back *(against/on sb/sth)*

reclinável *adj*: *um banco ~* a reclining seat

recluso/a *sm-sf* **1** *(solitário)* recluse **2** *(prisioneiro)* prisoner

recobrar *vt* recover, get sth back *(mais coloq)*: *Tenho certeza de que ele irá ~ a visão.* I'm sure he'll recover his sight. ◇ *~ a memória* get your memory back

recolher *vt* collect ● **recolher-se** *vp (ir dormir)* go to bed

recomendação *sf* recommendation: *Fomos por ~ do meu irmão.* We went on my brother's recommendation.

recomendar *vt* recommend

recompensa *sf* reward: *como ~ por algo* as a reward for sth

recompensar *vt* reward *sb* (*for sth*)

reconciliar-se *vp* make up (*with sb*)

reconhecer *vt* **1** recognize **2** (*admitir*) admit

reconhecimento *sm* recognition

reconstruir *vt* **1** rebuild **2** (*fatos, evento*) reconstruct

recordação *sf* **1** (*memória*) memory [*pl* -ies]: *Ela tem boas recordações de algo* have happy memories of sth **2** (*turismo*) souvenir

recordar(-se) *vt, vp* remember, recall (*fml*): *Recordo-me de tê-lo visto.* I remember seeing it. ◊ *~ o passado* recall the past

recorde *sm* record: *bater/deter um ~* break/hold a record

recordista *smf* record holder

recorrer *vi* **1** (*utilizar*) resort to *sth* **2** (*pedir ajuda*) turn to *sb*: *Eu não tinha ninguém a quem ~.* I had no one to turn to. **3** (*Jur*) appeal

recortar *vt* cut *sth* out: *~ uma foto de uma revista* cut a photo out of a magazine

recreio *sm* **1** (*pausa*) recess, break (*GB*): *Às onze saímos para o ~.* Recess is at eleven. **2** (*local*) playground ► **de ~** recreational

recruta *smf* recruit

recuar *vi* **1** (*retroceder*) go back **2** (*desistir*) back down

recuperar *vt* **1** regain (*fml*), get *sth* back: *~ o dinheiro* get the money back **2** (*saúde*) recover **3** (*tempo, aulas*) make *sth* up: *Você vai ter que ~ as horas de trabalho.* You'll have to make up the time. ● **recuperar-se** *vp* recover (*from sth*): *~ de uma doença* recover from an illness

recurso *sm* **1** (*meio*) resort **2** (**recursos**) resources: *~s humanos/naturais* human/natural resources **3** (*Jur*) appeal

recusa *sf* refusal to *do sth*

recusar(-se) *vt, vp* refuse (*to do sth*): *~ um convite* refuse an invitation ◊ *Recusei-me a acreditar.* I refused to believe it.

redação *sf* (*trabalho escolar*) assignment

redator/a *sm-sf* (*Jornal*) editor

rede *sf* **1** (*Esporte, caça, pesca*) net: *~ de segurança* safety net **2** (*Informát, comunicações*) network: *a ~ rodoviária/de computadores* the road/computer network **3** (*de dormir*) hammock **4** (*organizações, sucursais*) chain ► **cair na ~** fall into the trap *~ de arame* wire netting

rédea *sf* rein ► **dar ~ (larga)** give free rein to *sb/sth*

redemoinho *sm* **1** (*em rio*) whirlpool **2** (*de vento*) whirlwind

redigir *vt* write

redondo *adj* round: *em números ~s* in round numbers

redor *sm* ► **ao/em ~ (de)** around: *as pessoas ao meu ~* the people around me ◊ *em ~ da casa* around the house

redução *sf* reduction

reduzido *adj* **1** (*pequeno*) small **2** (*limitado*) limited

reduzir *vt* reduce: *~ o preço em 15%* reduce the price by 15 per cent ● **reduzir-se** *vp* ► *Tudo se reduz a...* It all boils down to... ► *~ a velocidade* slow down

reeleger *vt* re-elect

reembolsar *vt* **1** (*quantidade paga*) refund **2** (*gastos*) reimburse

reembolso *sm* refund ► *~ postal* collect on delivery (*abrev* COD)

reencarnação *sf* reincarnation

refazer *vt* **1** redo **2** *~ a vida* rebuild your life

refeição *sf* meal: *uma ~ ligeira* a light meal

refeitório *sm* (*escola, fábrica*) canteen

refém *smf* hostage

referência *sf* reference (*to sb/sth*): *ter boas ~s* have good references ◊ *Com ~ à sua carta...* With reference to your letter... ► *fazer ~ a* refer to *sb/sth*

referendo *sm* referendum

referente *adj* *~ a* regarding *sb/sth*

referir-se *vp* refer to *sb/sth*

refinaria *sf* refinery [*pl* -ies]

refletir *vt, vi* reflect (*on sth*)

reflexo *adj* reflex: *um ato ~* a reflex action ● *sm* **1** reflection: *Vi o meu ~ no espelho.* I saw my reflection in the mirror. **2** (*reação*) reflex: *ter bons ~s* have good reflexes **3** (**reflexos**) (*cabelo*) highlights

reforçar *vt* reinforce

reforço *sm* reinforcement

reforma sf 1 reform: ~ *agrária* land reform 2 (*edifício*) alteration

reformar vt 1 reform: ~ *uma lei/um delinqüente* reform a law/a delinquent 2 (*edifício*) make alterations to sth

reformatório sm reform school

refrescante adj refreshing

refrescar vt 1 (*esfriar*) cool 2 (*memória*) refresh ● **refrescar-se** vp freshen up

refresco sm fruit cordial

refrigerante sm soft drink

refrigerar vt refrigerate

refugiado/a sm-sf refugee: *um campo de ~s* a refugee camp

refugiar-se vp take refuge (*from sth*)

refúgio sm refuge: *um ~ na montanha* a mountain refuge

regar vt water

regatear vt, vi haggle (*over/about sth*)

regateio sm bargaining

regenerar(-se) vt, vp regenerate

regente adj, smf regent

reger vt 1 (*país, sociedade*) rule 2 (*orquestra*) conduct

região sf region

regime sm 1 (*Pol, normas*) regime 2 (*dieta*) diet: *estar de ~* be on a diet

regimento sm regiment

regional adj regional

registrar vt 1 register: ~ *um nascimento/uma carta* register a birth/a letter 2 (*alteração, acontecimento*) record: ~ *informação* record information ● **registrar-se** vp register: ~ *num hotel* check into a hotel

registro sm 1 (*inscrição*) registration 2 (*livro*) register

regozijar-se vp be delighted *at/with sth*

regra sf rule: *Isso vai contra as ~s.* It's against the rules. ▸ **em ~** as a general rule

regressar vi go/come back: ~ *ao seu país* go back to your own country ◊ *Acho que regressam amanhã.* I think they'll be back tomorrow.

regresso sm return: *no meu ~ à cidade* on my return to the city

régua sf ruler

regulamento sm regulations [*pl*]

regular¹ vt regulate

regular² adj regular: *verbos ~es* regular verbs

regularidade sf regularity ▸ **com ~** regularly

rei sm (*monarca*) king NOTA Para *os reis*, referindo-se ao rei e à rainha, diz-se **the king and queen.** ▸ **os ~s Magos** the Three Wise Men

reinado sm reign

reinar vi reign

reincidir vi relapse (*into (doing) sth*)

reiniciar vt 1 resume 2 (*Informát*) reboot

reino sm 1 kingdom: *o ~ animal* the animal kingdom 2 (*âmbito*) realm ▸ **o Reino Unido** the United Kingdom (*abrev* U.K.)

reivindicação sf demand (*for sth*)

reivindicar vt (*exigir*) demand: ~ *um aumento salarial* demand a raise

rejeitar vt (*recusar*) reject

relação sf 1 relationship (*with sb/sth*): *manter relações com alguém* have a relationship with sb 2 (*ligação*) connection (*between...*) ▸ **com/em ~ a** in/with relation to sb/sth **relações públicas** public relations (*abrev* PR) **ter relações** (*sexuais*) **com alguém** have sexual relations, sex (*coloq*) (*with sb*)

relacionado adj related (*to sth*)

relacionamento sm (*relação*) relationship: *o nosso ~ com os vizinhos* our relationship with our neighbors

relacionar vt relate sth (*to/with sth*); link sth (*to sth*) (*mais coloq*): *Os médicos relacionam os problemas do coração com o estresse.* Doctors link heart disease to stress. ● **relacionar-se** vp mix (*with sb*)

relâmpago sm lightning [U]: *Um ~ e um trovão anunciaram a tempestade.* A flash of lightning and a clap of thunder heralded the storm. ◊ *uma viagem/visita ~* a lightning trip/visit

relance sm ▸ **de ~**: *Só a vi de ~.* I only caught a glimpse of her.

relatar vt relate

relatividade sf relativity

relativo adj 1 (*não absoluto*) relative: *Bem, isso é ~.* Well, it's all relative. 2 ~ **a** relating (*to sb/sth*)

relato sm 1 (*narrativa*) narrative 2 (*descrição*) account: *fazer um ~ dos acontecimentos* give an account of events

relatório sm report: *o ~ anual da empresa* the company's annual report

relaxado adj (*preguiçoso*) lazy

relaxamento sm relaxation

relaxar vt, vi relax

relevância sf (*importância*) importance

relevo sm **1** (*Geog*) relief: *um mapa em ~* a relief map ◊ *uma região com ~ acidentado* an area with a rugged landscape **2** (*importância*) importance

religião sf religion

religioso/a adj religious ● sm-sf monk [*fem* nun]

relinchar vi neigh

relíquia sf relic

relógio sm **1** clock: *Que horas são no ~ da cozinha?* What time does the kitchen clock say? ◊ *uma corrida contra o ~* a race against the clock **2** (*de pulso, de bolso*) watch: *Meu ~ está atrasado.* My watch is slow. **3** meter: *o ~ do gás* the gas meter

reluzir vi shine

relva sf grass

remar vi row

rematar vt (*terminar*) finish sb/sth off

remate sm **1** (*acabamento*) border **2** (*final*) end

remediar vt remedy

remédio sm remedy [*pl* -ies]. cure (*mais coloq*) (*for sth*) ▶ **não ter outro ~** (*senão...*) have no choice (but to...)

remendar vt mend

remendo sm patch

remessa sf **1** (*ação*) sending **2** (*Com*) consignment **3** (*dinheiro*) remittance ▶ **~ a cobrar** cash on delivery (*abrev* COD)

remetente smf sender

remexer vt **1 ~ em** (*gavetas, papéis*) rummage in/through sth: *~ nas coisas de alguém* rummage through sb's things **2 ~ em** (*assunto*) bring sth up **3** (*terra*) turn the soil over

remo sm **1** (*instrumento*) **(a)** (*grande*) oar **(b)** (*pequeno*) paddle **2** (*Esporte*) rowing: *praticar ~* row ▶ **a ~**: *atravessar o rio a ~* row across the river

remontar vt (*evento, tradição*) date back to sth

remorso sm remorse

remoto/a adj remote: *uma aldeia/possibilidade remota* a remote village/possibility

remover vt remove

Renascimento sm Renaissance

renda¹ sf (*Fin*) income

renda² sf (*tecido*) lace

render vt **1** (*dinheiro*) bring sth in **2** (*juros*) earn **3** (*preço*) reach

● vi **1** (*ser lucrativo*) pay off **2** (*dar para muito*): *Arroz rende muito.* Rice goes a long way. ● **render-se** vp (*Mil*) surrender (*to sb/sth*)

rendição sf surrender

rendimento sm **1** (*Fin*) income **2** (*atuação*) performance

renovação sf **1** renewal: *a data de ~* the renewal date **2** (*decoração, equipamento*) renovation

renovar vt **1** renew: *~ um contrato/o passaporte* renew a contract/your passport **2** (*equipamento, decoração*) renovate **3** (*modernizar*) modernize

rentável adj profitable: *um negócio ~* a profitable deal

rente adj **~ a** level with sth: *~ ao chão* along the floor ● adv: *Ela cortou o cabelo bem ~.* She cropped her hair.

renunciar vt **1** renounce: *~ uma herança/um direito* renounce an inheritance/a right **2** (*cargo*) resign from sth

reparar vt **1** (*consertar*) repair **2** (*remediar*) remedy: *~ a situação* remedy the situation **3 ~ em/que** notice: *Reparei que a camisa dele estava molhada.* I noticed (that) his shirt was wet.

reparo sm **1** (*reparação*) repair: *Esta casa necessita de ~s.* This house is in need of repair. **2** (*comentário*) critical remark ▶ **fazer ~s** (*criticar*) find fault with sb/sth

repartição sf (*administração*) department

repartir vt **1** (*dividir*) share sth out: *~ o trabalho* share out the work **2** (*distribuir*) distribute

repente sm outburst: *De vez em quando lhe dão uns ~s.* Now and then he has these outbursts. ▶ **de ~** suddenly

repentino/a adj sudden

repercussão sf repercussion

repertório sm repertoire

repetição sf repetition

repetir vt **1** repeat: *Pode ~?* Could you repeat that please? ◊ *Não vou ~.* I'm not going to tell you again. **2** (*servir-se de mais comida*) have another helping (*of sth*) ● **repetir-se** vp **1** (*acontecimento*) happen again: *Que isto não se repita!* And don't let it happen again! **2** (*pessoa*) repeat yourself

repicar vt, vi (*sino*) chime

repleto/a adj full (*of sb/sth*)

replicar vt, vi retort

repolho sm cabbage

repor vt 1 (no devido lugar) put sth back 2 (substituir) replace

reportagem sf 1 (TV, rádio) documentary [pl -ies] 2 (Jornal) article

repórter smf reporter ▶ ~ fotográfico press photographer

repousar vi 1 rest: Você precisa ~. You need to rest. 2 (jazer) lie: Os seus restos repousam neste cemitério. His remains lie in this cemetery. → LIE²

repouso sm 1 (descanso) rest 2 (paz) peace: Não tenho um momento de ~. I don't have a moment's peace.

repreender vt reproach sb (for doing) sth

represa sf 1 (em rio) weir 2 (barragem) dam

represália sf reprisal

representação sf 1 representation 2 (Teat) performance

representante smf representative

representar vt 1 (organização, país) represent 2 (quadro, estátua) depict 3 (simbolizar) symbolize 4 (Teat) (a) (peça teatral) perform (b) (papel) play: ~ o papel de Otelo play the part of Othello

representativo adj representative

repressão sf repression

repressivo adj repressive

reprimenda sf reprimand

reprimido adj repressed

reprodução sf reproduction

reproduzir(-se) vt, vp reproduce

reprovação sf (em exame) failure: o índice de reprovações the failure rate

reprovar vt (em exame) fail: ser reprovado em duas disciplinas fail two subjects

réptil sm reptile

república sf republic

republicano/a adj, sm-sf republican

repugnante adj revolting

reputação sf reputation: ter boa/má ~ have a good/bad reputation

requentar vt warm sth up

requerente smf 1 (candidato) applicant (for sth) 2 (que faz reclamação) claimant

requerimento sm request (for sth)

requintado adj (gosto, objeto) exquisite

requisito sm requirement (for sth/to do sth)

rês sf (farm) animal

reserva sf 1 (hotel, viagem, restaurante) reservation: fazer uma ~ make a reservation 2 (recursos naturais) reserve(s): uma boa ~ de petróleo good oil reserves 3 (parque natural) reserve ● smf (Esporte) reserve ▶ de ~ spare: um filme de ~ a spare roll of film

reservado adj (pessoa) reserved

reservar vt 1 (guardar) save: Reserve um lugar para mim. Save me a place. 2 (pedir antecipadamente) reserve, book (mais coloq)

reservatório sm 1 (tanque) tank 2 (abastecimento de cidade, etc.) reservoir

resfriado sm cold: pegar um ~ catch a cold

resfriar(-se) vi, vp catch a cold

resgatar vt 1 (salvar) rescue sb (from sth) 2 (recuperar) recover sth (from sb/sth)

resgate sm (pagamento) ransom ▶ exigir/pedir ~ por alguém hold sb to ransom

resguardar(-se) vt, vp shelter (sb/sth) (from sth)

residência sf residence

residencial adj residential

residente smf resident

resíduos sm waste [U]: ~s tóxicos toxic waste

resistência sf 1 (oposição, defesa) resistance: Ele não ofereceu qualquer ~. He offered no resistance. 2 (pessoa) stamina: ter pouca ~ have very little stamina 3 (material) strength

resistir vt ~ a 1 (suportar) withstand 2 (peso) take: A ponte não resistirá ao peso daquele caminhão. The bridge can't take the weight of that truck. ● vi 1 (tentação) resist 2 (manter-se firme) hold on 3 (debater-se) struggle

resmungar vi, vt grumble (about sth)

resolver vt 1 (problema, mistério, caso) solve 2 ~ fazer algo decide to do sth ● **resolver-se** vp (decidir-se) make up your mind (to do sth)

respectivo adj respective

respeitar vt 1 (considerar) respect sb/sth (for sth): ~ a opinião dos outros respect other people's opinions 2 (código, sinal) obey

respeitável adj respectable: uma pessoa/quantidade ~ a respectable person/amount

respeito *sm* respect (*for sb/sth*) ▶ **com ~ a/a ~ de** with regard to *sb/sth* **dizer ~** (a) concern: *Esse assunto não te diz ~.* This matter doesn't concern you.

respeitoso *adj* respectful

respiração *sf* 1 (*respiramento*) breathing: *exercícios de ~* breathing exercises 2 (*fôlego*) breath: *ficar sem ~* be out of breath ◇ *conter a ~* hold your breath ▶ **~ artificial** artificial respiration **• boca a boca** mouth-to-mouth resuscitation

respirar *vt, vi* breathe: *~ fundo* take a deep breath

resplandecente *adj* shining

resplandecer *vi* shine

responder *vt, vi* 1 (*dar uma resposta*) answer, reply (*to sb*) (*mais fml*): *~ a uma carta/pergunta* answer a letter/question ◇ *Ele respondeu que não tinha nada a ver com o assunto.* He replied that he had nothing to do with it. 2 (*reagir*) respond to *sth*: *~ a um tratamento* respond to treatment 3 **~ por** answer for *sb/sth*: *Não respondo por mim!* I won't answer for my actions! 4 (*replicar*) answer *sb* back: *Não me responda!* Don't answer (me) back!

responsabilidade *sf* responsibility [*pl* -ies]

responsabilizar *vt* hold *sb* responsible (*for (doing) sth*) ● **responsabilizar-se** *vp* bear responsibility (*for (doing) sth*)

responsável *adj* 1 responsible (*for sth*): *Quem é o ~ por este caos?* Who is responsible for this chaos? 2 (*de confiança*) reliable ● *smf*: *o ~ pelas obras* the person in charge of the building work ◇ *Os responsáveis se entregaram.* Those responsible gave themselves up.

resposta *sf* 1 answer, reply [*pl* -ies] (*mais fml*): *Eu quero uma ~ à minha pergunta.* I want an answer to my question. ◇ *Não tivemos nenhuma ~.* We didn't receive a single reply. 2 (*reação*) response (*to sth*): *uma ~ favorável* a favorable response

ressaca *sf* 1 (*bebedeira*) hangover: *estar de ~* have a hangover 2 (*mar*) undertow

ressaltar *vt* (*mencionar*) point *sth* out

ressecado *adj* 1 (*terra*) parched 2 (*pele*) dry

ressentimento *sm* resentment

ressentir-se *vp* take offense (*at sth*)

ressoar *vi* 1 (*metal, voz*) ring 2 (*retumbar*) resound

ressurreição *sf* resurrection

ressuscitar *vi* (*Relig*) rise from the dead ● *vt* (*Med*) resuscitate

restabelecer *vt* 1 restore: *~ a ordem* restore order 2 (*diálogo, negociações*) resume ● **restabelecer-se** *vp* recover (*from sth*)

restar *vi* 1 (*haver*) remain: *Resta ver se...* It remains to be seen whether... 2 (*ter*) have *sth* left: *Não me resta nenhum dinheiro.* I don't have any money left.

restauração *sf* restoration

restaurante *sm* restaurant

restaurar *vt* restore

resto *sm* 1 rest: *O ~ eu te conto amanhã.* I'll tell you the rest tomorrow. 2 (*Mat*) remainder 3 (**restos**) (a) (*Arqueologia, etc.*) remains (b) (*comida*) leftovers

restrição *sf* restriction: *restrições à liberdade de expressão* restrictions on freedom of speech

restringir *vt* restrict

resultado *sm* 1 result: *como ~ da luta* as a result of the fight 2 (*num concurso*) score: *o ~ final* the final score ▶ **dar/não dar ~** be successful/unsuccessful

resultar *vt* result (*in/from sth*)

resumir *vt* 1 summarize 2 (*concluir*) sum *sth* up: *Resumindo,...* To sum up,...

resumo *sm* summary [*pl* -ies]: *~ informativo* news summary ▶ **em ~** in short

resvalar *vi* 1 slip 2 (*veículo*) skid

reta *sf* 1 (*linha*) straight line 2 (*estrada*) straight stretch ▶ **~ final 1** (*Esporte*) home stretch 2 (*fig*) closing stages [*pl*]

retalho *sm* (*tecido*) remnant

retangular *adj* rectangular

retângulo *sm* rectangle

retardado *adj* 1 delayed: *de ação retardada* delayed-action 2 (*pessoa*) retarded NOTA **Retarded** pode ser considerado ofensivo. É preferível dizer que a pessoa retardada tem **special needs** ou a **learning disability**.

retardatário/a *sm-sf* straggler

reter *vt* 1 (*guardar*) keep 2 (*memorizar*) remember 3 (*deter*) hold: *~ alguém contra a sua vontade* hold sb against their will

retificar *vt* rectify

retina *sf* retina

retirada *sf* (*Mil*) retreat

retirar vt withdraw sth (from sb/ sth): ~ as tropas/a licença de alguém withdraw troops/sb's license • vi (Mil) retreat • **retirar-se** vp (ir-se embora, desistir) withdraw (from sth): ~ de uma luta/da política withdraw from a fight/from politics

retiro sm retreat

reto adj straight: em linha reta in a straight line • sm rectum

retomar vt resume: ~ o trabalho resume work

retoque sm finishing touch: dar os últimos ~s em algo put the finishing touches to sth

retornar vi go back

retorno sm return: o ~ à normalidade the return to normality

retrasado adj second to last: na semana retrasada the week before last

retratar vt 1 (pintar) paint sb's portrait 2 (Fot) take a picture of sb/sth 3 (descrever) portray

retrato sm 1 (quadro) portrait 2 (fotografia) photograph 3 (descrição) portrayal ▶ ~ falado composite picture

retribuir vt return: ~ um favor return a favor

retrovisor sm rear-view mirror

retumbante adj 1 (tremendo) resounding: um fracasso ~ a resounding flop 2 (recusa) emphatic

retumbar vt resound

réu, ré sm-sf the accused

reumatismo sm rheumatism

reunião sf 1 meeting: ~ de cúpula summit (meeting) 2 (encontro) reunion: uma ~ de ex-alunos a school reunion

reunir vt 1 gather sb/sth together 2 (informação) collect 3 (dinheiro) raise 4 ~ qualidades de liderança, etc. have leadership, etc. qualities • **reunir-se** vp meet

reveillon sm New Year's Eve party [pl -ies]

revelação sf 1 revelation 2 (Fot) developing 3 (pessoa, fato) discovery [pl -ies]: a ~ do ano the discovery of the year

revelar vt 1 reveal: ~ um segredo reveal a secret 2 (Fot) develop 3 (interesse, talento) show

rever vt 1 (pessoa, lugar) see sb/ sth again 2 (fazer revisão) check

reverência sf bow: fazer (uma) ~ a alguém bow to sb

reversível adj reversible

reverso sm (moeda) reverse

revés sm 1 (contratempo) setback: sofrer um ~ suffer a setback 2 (Esporte) backhand

revestir vt (cobrir) cover

revezamento sm (Esporte): uma corrida de ~ a relay race

revezar vt (substituir) take over from sb • **revezar-se** vp (fazer por turnos) take turns (doing sth)

revirar vt mess sth up

reviravolta sf U-turn

revisão sf 1 (Educ) revision [U]: fazer revisões do revision ◇ fazer uma ~ de algo revise sth 2 (verificação, inspeção) check 3 (veículo) service

revista sf 1 (publicação) magazine 2 (inspeção) search 3 (Teat) revue 4 (Mil) review ▶ ~ em quadrinhos comic (book)

revistar vt search

reviver vt, vi revive

revolta sf revolt

revoltado adj (all) worked up: O povo anda ~ com as eleições. People are all worked up about the elections.

revoltante adj outrageous

revoltar-se vp 1 rebel (against sb/sth) 2 (indignar-se) be outraged (by sth)

revolto adj (desarrumado) messy

revolução sf revolution

revolucionar vt revolutionize

revolucionário/a adj, sm-sf revolutionary [pl -ies]

revólver sm revolver

rezar vt: ~ uma oração say a prayer • vi pray (for sb/sth)

riacho sm stream

rico/a adj rich: uma família rica a rich family ◇ ~ em minerais rich in minerals • sm-sf rich man/ woman [pl men/women]: os ~s the rich

ricochetear vi ricochet (off sth)

ridicularizar vt ridicule

ridículo adj ridiculous

rifa sf 1 (sorteio) raffle 2 (bilhete) raffle ticket

rifar vt raffle

rígido adj 1 (teso) rigid 2 (severo) strict

rigoroso adj 1 (severo) strict 2 (minucioso) thorough 3 (castigo, inverno) harsh

rijo adj tough

rim sm kidney

rima sf rhyme

rimar vi rhyme

rímel sm mascara: pôr ~ put on mascara

ringue sm ring

rinoceronte sm rhino [pl ~s]

rinque sm rink: ~ de patinação ice-skating rink

rio sm river NOTA Escreve-se **river** com maiúscula quando precede o nome de um rio: o ~ Amazonas the River Amazon. ▶ ~ **abaixo/acima** downstream/upstream

riqueza sf **1** (dinheiro) [U]: acumular ~s amass wealth **2** (qualidade) richness: a ~ do terreno the richness of the land

rir vi laugh: desatar a ~ burst out laughing ▶ ~ **com alguém** joke around with sb ~ **de alguém/algo** laugh at sb/sth: De que você está rindo? What are you laughing at?

risada sf laugh

riscar vt **1** (rasurar) cross sth out: ~ os verbos cross out the verbs **2** (folha, livro) scribble on sth: O Zé riscou o meu livro. Zé scribbled on my book. **3** (superfície) scratch: Não risque o meu carro. Don't scratch my car. **4** (fósforo) strike

risco[1] sm **1** line: fazer um ~ draw a line **2** (rasura) crossing-out [pl crossings-out] (GB) **3** (linha delimitadora) mark

risco[2] sm risk: correr o ~ de fazer algo run the risk of doing sth

riso sm **1** laugh: um ~ nervoso a nervous laugh **2** (risos) laughter [U]: um ataque de ~ a fit of laughter ◊ os ~s das crianças the children's laughter

risonho adj **1** (cara) smiling **2** (pessoa) cheerful

ritmo sm **1** (Mús) rhythm, beat (mais coloq): acompanhar o ~ keep in time with the beat **2** (velocidade) rate: o ~ do crescimento the growth rate ◊ Se continuar neste ~ não vou durar muito. I won't last long if I carry on at this rate. **ter ~ 1** (pessoa) have a good sense of rhythm **2** (melodia) have a good beat

rito sm rite

ritual sm ritual

rival adj, smf rival

rixa sf **1** (briga) fight **2** (discussão) argument

robô sm robot

robusto adj robust

roçar vt **1** brush against sth: Rocei no vestido dela. I brushed against her dress. **2** (raspar) rub (against) sth: O pára-lamas roça na roda. The fender rubs

against the wheel. ● vi (folhas secas, papel) rustle

rocha sf rock

rochedo sm cliff

rochoso adj rocky

roda sf **1** wheel: ~ dianteira/traseira front/back wheel **2** (pessoas) circle: fazer uma ~ form a circle ▶ ~ **gigante** Ferris wheel, big wheel (GB)

rodada sf (Esporte, bebidas) round

rodar vt, vi **1** (girar) turn **2** (girar rapidamente) spin ● vt (filme) film, shoot (mais coloq)

rodear vt surround sb/sth (with sb/sth)

rodeio sm ▶ **ficar com/fazer ~s** beat around the bush

rodela sf slice: uma ~ de limão a slice of lemon ◊ Corte-o em ~s. Cut it in slices.

rodovia sf highway, motorway (GB) NOTA Usa-se **highway** sobretudo no oeste dos Estados Unidos. No leste diz-se **freeway** e no sul, **interstate**.

rodoviário/a adj road ● **rodoviária** sf bus station

roedor sm rodent

roer vt gnaw (at/on) sth ▶ ~ **as unhas** bite your nails

rogado adj ▶ **fazer-se de** ~ play hard to get

rogar vt **1** (suplicar) beg (sb) for sth; beg (sth) of sb: Roguei-lhes que me soltassem. I begged them to let me go. **2** (rezar) pray: Roguemos a Deus. Let us pray.

roído adj: ~ de ciúme(s)/raiva consumed with jealousy/anger

rojão sm (foguete) rocket

rolar vi **1** roll: As pedras rolaram pelo precipício. The rocks rolled down the cliff. **2** (andar de um lado para o outro) go around: Faz um mês que esta carta está rolando pelo escritório. This letter has been going around the office for a month.

roldana sf pulley

roleta sf roulette

rolha sf cork: tirar a ~ de uma garrafa uncork a bottle

rolo sm **1** roll: ~s de papel higiênico toilet rolls **2** (Fot) roll of film **3** (cabelo) roller **4** (embrulhada): Que ~! What a mess! ◊ Meteram-no num grande ~. They got him into trouble. ▶ ~ **de pastel** rolling pin

romã sf pomegranate

romance sm **1** (Liter) novel:

~ *policial* detective novel 2 (*namoro*) romance

romancista *smf* novelist

romano/a *adj, sm-sf* Roman

romântico/a *adj, sm-sf* romantic

romper *vt* 1 tear: ~ *um ligamento* tear a ligament 2 (*contrato, acordo*) break: ~ *um noivado* break off an engagement 3 ~ **com alguém** (*namorados*) break up with sb ●**romper-se** *vp* 1 tear 2 (*corda*) snap ▶ **ao ~ da aurora** at daybreak

roncar *vi* 1 snore 2 (*barriga*) rumble

ronda *sf* round ▶**fazer a ~ 1** (*polícia*) walk the beat 2 (*soldado, vigia*) be on patrol

ronrom *sm* purr: *Ouvia-se o ~ do gato.* You could hear the cat purring.

ronronar *vi* purr

roqueiro *sm* rock musician

rosa *sf* rose ●*adj, sm* (*cor*) pink

rosário *sm* (*Relig*) rosary [*pl* -ios]: *rezar o ~* say the rosary

rosbife *sm* roast beef

rosca *sf* 1 (*pão*) (ring-shaped) roll 2 (*parafuso*) thread

rosé *adj* rosé

roseira *sf* rose bush

rosnar *vi* (*cão*) growl

rosto *sm* face: *a expressão no seu ~* the look on his face

rota *sf* route: *Que ~ vamos tomar?* What route will we take?

rotação *sf* rotation

rotatividade *sf* turnover: *~ de pessoal* staff turnover

roteiro *sm* 1 (*itinerário*) itinerary [*pl* -ios] 2 (*Cinema*) script

rotina *sf* routine: *a ~ diária* the daily routine ◊ *inspeções de ~* routine inspections

rótula *sf* kneecap

rotular *vt* label: ~ *uma caixa put a label on a box* ◊ ~ *alguém de imbecil* label sb a fool

rótulo *sm* label

roubar *vt* 1 (*pessoa, banco, loja*) rob 2 (*dinheiro, objetos*) steal: *Roubaram o meu relógio.* They stole my watch. 3 (*casa*) burglarize ● *vi* steal: *Ele foi expulso da escola por ~.* He was expelled for stealing. → ROB

roubo *sm* 1 (*banco, loja, pessoa*) robbery [*pl* -ios]: *Fui vítima de um ~.* I was robbed. 2 (*objetos*) theft: ~ *de carros* car theft 3 (*preço excessivo*) rip-off: *Isso é um ~!* What a rip-off!

rouco *adj* hoarse: *Fiquei ~ de tanto gritar.* I shouted myself hoarse.

roupa *sf* 1 (*de pessoas*) clothes [*pl*]: ~ *infantil/usada* children's / second-hand clothes ◊ *Que ~ eu ponho?* What shall I wear? 2 ~ *de cama* bed linens ▶ ~ **de baixo** underwear ~ **esportiva** sportswear

roupão *sm* bathrobe

rouxinol *sm* nightingale

roxo *adj* 1 (*de frio*) blue 2 (*de pancadas*) black and blue ●*adj, sm* (*cor*) purple

rua *sf* street (*abrev* St.): *uma ~ de pedestres* a pedestrian street ◊ *Fica na ~ Bahia.* It's on Bahia Street. ◊ ~ *acima/abaixo* up/down the street NOTA Se se menciona o número da casa ou porta, usa-se a preposição **at**: *Moro no número 49 da ~ Bahia.* I live at 49 Bahia Street. → STREET ● *interj* (get) out ▶ **botar/pôr na ~ 1** (*expulsar*) throw sb out 2 (*despedir*) fire sb

rubéola *sf* German measles [*sing*]

rubi *sm* ruby [*pl* -ies]

ruborizar-se *vp* blush

rude *adj* coarse

ruela *sf* backstreet

ruga *sf* wrinkle

rúgbi *sm* rugby

rugido *sm* roar

rugir *vi* roar

ruído *sm* noise

ruidoso *adj* noisy

ruim *adj* (*mau*) bad

ruína *sf* 1 ruin: *em ~s* in ruins ◊ ~ *econômica* financial ruin ◊ *levar alguém à ~* ruin sb 2 (*desmoronamento*) collapse

ruir *vi* collapse

ruivo/a *adj* red-haired ● *sm-sf* redhead

rum *sm* rum

rumo *sm* 1 (*caminho, direção*) direction 2 (*avião, barco*) course: *O navio partiu ~ ao sul.* The ship set course southward. ▶ ~ **a** bound for: *O navio ia ~ a Recife.* The ship was bound for Recife. **sem ~** adrift

rumor *sm* 1 (*notícia*) rumor: *Corre o ~ de que eles vão se casar.* There's a rumor going around that they're getting married. 2 (*murmúrio*) murmur

rural *adj* rural

Rússia *sf* Russia

russo/a *adj, sm-sf, sm* Russian: *os ~s* (the) Russians

rústico *adj* rustic

Ss

sábado *sm* Saturday (*abrev* **Sat.**)
▶ ~ **de Aleluia** Holy Saturday
→ DOMINGO

sabão *sm* soap: *uma barra de* ~
a bar of soap

sabedoria *sf* wisdom

saber *vt* **1** know: *Não sei nada de
arte.* I don't know anything
about art. ◊ *Eu sabia que ele
voltaria.* I knew he would be
back. ◊ *Já sei!* I know! **2** ~ *fazer
algo* (*ser capaz*) can: *Você sabe
nadar?* Can you swim? **3** ~ *de*
(*ter notícias*) hear of *sb/sth*:
Nunca mais soube dele. That
was the last I heard of him. **4**
(*descobrir*) find *sth* out: *Eu
soube hoje.* I found out today. ● *
vi* know: *Nunca se sabe.* You
never know. ◊ *Como é que eu
podia* ~? How should I know? ▶
que eu saiba as far as I know
NOTA Para outras expressões
com **saber**, ver o substantivo,
adjetivo, etc., p. ex.e **saber algo
de cor** em COR[1].

sabichão/ona *sm-sf* know-it-
all, know-all (GB)

sábio *adj* wise

sabonete *sm* soap [U]: *um* ~
a bar of soap

sabor *sm* (*gosto*) taste: *Tem um
~ estranho.* It has a strange
taste. ◊ *A água não tem* ~. Water
is tasteless. **2** (*aromatizante*)
flavor: *Que* ~ *você quer?* Which
flavor would you like? ◊ *um
iogurte com* ~ *de banana* a
banana-flavored yogurt

saborear *vt* **1** (*comida, bebida*)
savor **2** (*vitória, férias, sol*)
enjoy

saboroso *adj* delicious

sabotagem *sf* sabotage

sabotar *vt* sabotage

saca *sf* sack

sacada *sf* balcony [*pl* -ies]

sacar *vt* (*entender*) understand
● *vi* (*Esporte*) serve

sacarina *sf* saccharin

saca-rolhas *sm* corkscrew

sacerdote *sm* priest

saciar *vt* **1** (*fome, ambição, desejo*) satisfy **2** (*sede*) quench

saco *sm* **1** (*geral*) bag: *um* ~ *de plástico*
a plastic bag ◊ ~ *de dormir/
viagem* sleeping/travel bag **2**
(*arroz, etc.*) sack **3** (*inconveniente*) pain: *Que* ~! What a pain!

sacramento *sm* sacrament

sacrificar *vt* sacrifice ● **sacri-**

ficar-se *vp* make sacrifices: *Os
meus pais se sacrificaram
muito.* My parents made a lot of
sacrifices.

sacrifício *sm* sacrifice

sacudir *vt* **1** shake: ~ *a areia da
toalha* shake the sand off your
towel **2** (*com mão, escova*)
brush *sth* (off): ~ *o pó do casaco*
brush the dust off your coat

sádico/a *adj* sadistic ● *sm-sf*
sadist

safar-se *vp* **1** (*desembaraçar-se*)
get by: *fazer apenas o suficiente
para se safar* do just enough to
get by **2** (*escapar*) get away

safira *sf* sapphire

safra *sf* harvest

Sagitário *sm* Sagittarius

sagrado *adj* **1** (*Relig*) holy: *a
Bíblia Sagrada* the Holy Bible **2**
(*intocável*) sacred: *Os domingos
para mim são* ~s. My Sundays
are sacred.

saia *sf* skirt

saída *sf* **1** way out: *à* ~ *do cinema*
on the way out of the movie
theater **2** (*porta*) exit: *a* ~ *de
emergência* the emergency exit
3 (*avião, trem*) departure

saiote *sm* short skirt

sair *vt, vi* **1** (*partir*) leave: *Saí de
casa às duas.* I left home at two.
◊ *O trem sai da plataforma seis.*
The train leaves from track six.
2 (*ir/ir para fora*) go/come
out: *Saí para ver o que se passava.* I went out to see what was
going on. ◊ *Ele não queria* ~ *do
banheiro.* He wouldn't come out
of the bathroom. **3** (*cair, abandonar*) come off: *Saiu uma peça.*
A piece came off. ◊ *O carro saiu
da estrada.* The car went off the
road. **4** (*socialmente*) go out:
~ *para jantar* go out for dinner
◊ *Ela está saindo com um aluno.*
She's going out with a student.
5 (*líquido*) leak **6** (*produto, flor,
sol*) come out: *O CD sai em abril.*
The CD is coming out in April.
◊ *O sol saiu à tarde.* The sun
came out in the afternoon. **7**
(*resultar*) turn out: *Que tal saiu
a receita?* How did the recipe
turn out? **8** ~ **de** (*superar*): ~ *de
uma situação difícil* get through
a tricky situation **9** ~ **a alguém**
(*parecer-se*) take after *sb* **10** ~
a/por (*custar*): *Sai a 60 dólares o
metro.* It works out at 60 dollars
a meter. ● **sair-se** *vp* (*obter
êxito*) get on: ~ *bem na escola*
get on well at school
▶ **sair-se bem/mal** do
well/badly NOTA Para outras
expressões com **sair**, ver o

substantivo, adjetivo, etc., p. ex. **sair perdendo** em PERDER.

sal sm salt: ~ *fino/grosso* table/sea salt ◇ *sem* ~ unsalted ▶ **sais de banho** bath salts

sala sf **1** (casa) room: ~ *de espera/operações/reuniões* waiting/operating/meeting room ◇ ~ *de jantar* dining room **2** ~ (*de estar*) living room **3** (Cinema): *A ~ 1 é a maior.* Screen 1 is the biggest. ▶ ~ **de aula** classroom

salada sf salad: ~ *mista/de frutas* mixed/fruit salad

salame sm salami

salão sm **1** (casa) living room **2** (hotel) lounge ▶ ~ **de beleza** beauty salon

salário sm salary [pl -ies] ▶ ~ **mínimo** minimum wage

saldar vt (conta, dívida) settle

saldo sm (de uma conta) balance ▶ **estar com/ter** ~ **negativo** be in the red

salgado adj **1** (gosto) salty **2** (em oposição a doce) savory

salgueiro sm willow

saliva sf saliva

salmão sm salmon [pl salmon] ● adj, sm (cor) salmon (pink)

salmo sm psalm

salmoura sf brine

salpicar vt **1** (sujar) splash sb/sth (with sth): *Um carro salpicou a minha calça.* A car splashed my pants. **2** (polvilhar) sprinkle

salsa sf parsley

salsicha sf frankfurter

saltar vt jump: *O cavalo saltou a cerca.* The horse jumped the fence. ● vi **1** jump: *Saltaram na água/pela janela.* They jumped into the water/out of the window. ◇ ~ *sobre alguém* jump on sb **2** (ônibus) get off ▶ ~ **à vista/aos olhos** be obvious ▶ ~ **de alegria** jump for joy

salto¹ sm **1** jump: *Atravessei o riacho com um* ~. I jumped over the stream. **2** (pássaro, coelho, canguru) hop **3** (trampolim) dive **4** (salto vigoroso, progresso) leap **5** (bola) bounce ▶ **dar** ~**s** (pular) bounce ▶ ~ **de vara** pole vault ▶ ~ **em altura/distância** high/long jump

salto² sm (calçado) heel: *Ela nunca usa* ~ (alto). She never wears high heels. ▶ **de** ~ (alto) high-heeled

salva¹ sf (planta) sage

salva² sf (tiro) salvo [pl ~es] ▶ ~ **de palmas** round of applause

salvação sf salvation

salvador/a sm-sf savior

salvamento sm rescue

salvar vt save ● **salvar-se** vp **1** (sobreviver) survive **2** (escapar) escape ▶ **salve-se quem puder** every man for himself

salva-vidas sm **1** (pessoa) lifeguard **2** (barco) lifeboat

salvo adj safe: *estar a* ~ be safe ◇ *pôr-se a* ~ reach safety ● prep except ▶ ~ **se...** unless...

samambaia sf fern

samba sm samba

sanção sf **1** (castigo) sanction: *sanções econômicas* economic sanctions **2** (multa) fine **3** (aprovação) ratification

sancionar vt **1** sanction (confirmar) ratify

sandália sf sandal

sanduíche sm sandwich: *um* ~ *de queijo* a cheese sandwich

sangrar vt, vi bleed: *Estou sangrando pelo nariz.* I have a nosebleed.

sangrento adj **1** (luta) bloody **2** (ferida) bleeding

sangue sm blood: *dar* ~ give blood

sangue-frio sm: *Admiro o seu* ~. I admire her calm manner. ▶ **a** ~ in cold blood **ter** ~ keep calm

sanguíneo adj blood: *grupo* ~ blood group

sanidade sf health: ~ *mental* mental health

sanitário adj **1** (saúde) health: *medidas sanitárias* health measures **2** (higiene) sanitary

santo/a adj **1** (Relig) holy **2** (enfático): *todo* ~ *dia* every single day ● sm-sf **1** saint: *Essa mulher é uma santa.* That woman is a saint. **2** (título) Saint (abrev St.): ~ *André* Saint Andrew

santuário sm shrine

São adj Saint (abrev St.): ~ *João* Saint John

são adj **1** healthy **2** (de espírito) sane ▶ ~ **e salvo** safe and sound

sapataria sf shoe store

sapateado sm tap-dancing

sapatilha sf shoe: ~ *de balé/pano/escalada* ballet/canvas/climbing shoe

sapato sm shoe: ~*s de salto alto* high-heeled shoes

sapo sm toad

saque sm **1** (cidade) sack **2** (roubo) looting **3** (Esporte) serve **4** (de dinheiro) withdrawal

saquear vt **1** (cidade) sack **2** (roubar) loot **3** (despensa) raid

saraivada sf hail: uma ~ de balas a hail of bullets

sarampo sm measles [sing]

sarar vi **1** (ferida) heal (over/up) **2** (doente) recover

sarcástico adj sarcastic

sarda sf freckle

sardinha sf sardine

sargento sm sergeant

satélite sm satellite

satisfação sf satisfaction: Sinto ~ em poder fazer isso. I'm pleased to be able to do it.

satisfatório adj satisfactory

satisfazer vt **1** satisfy: ~ a fome/curiosidade satisfy your hunger/curiosity **2** (sede) quench **3** (ambição, sonho) fulfill **4** (pessoa) satisfy: Nada o satisfaz. He's never satisfied. **5** (agradar) please sb ● vi be satisfactory

satisfeito adj **1** satisfied (with sth): um cliente ~ a satisfied customer **2** (contente) pleased (with sb/sth): Estou ~ com o meu rendimento. I'm pleased with my performance. **3** (saciado): Não quero mais, estou ~. No more, thank you — I'm fine. **5** **dar-se por ~**: Eu me daria por ~ com um seis. I'd be happy with a pass. **~ consigo mesmo/próprio** self-satisfied

saturado adj **1** (impregnado) saturated (with sth) **2** (farto) sick of sth

Saturno sm Saturn

saudação sf **1** greeting **2** (saudações) (em carta) best wishes, regards (mais fml)

saudade (saudades) sf **1** (casa, país) homesickness [U]: sentir ~s de casa be homesick **2** (pessoa) longing [U] **3** (passado, infância) nostalgia [U] ♢ **deixar ~s** be missed: Ele vai deixar ~s. He'll be missed. **sentir/ter ~s de** miss sb/sth

saudar vt say hello (to sb), greet (mais fml)

saudável adj healthy

saúde sf health: bem/mal de ~ in good/poor health ♢ **~ pública** public health ▸ **à saúde** (brinde) cheers **saúde!** (ao espirrar) bless you! → ATXIM

sauna sf sauna

saxofone sm saxophone (abrev sax)

scanner sm scanner

se¹ pron pess

• **reflexivo** **1** (ele, ela, coisa)

himself, herself, itself: Ela se machucou. She hurt herself. **2** (você, vocês) yourself [pl yourselves]: Sentem-se. Sit down. **3** (eles, elas) themselves

• **recíproco** each other, one another: Eles se amam. They love each other.

• **apassivador**: Registraram-se três mortes. Three deaths were recorded. ♢ Não se aceitam cartões de crédito. We don't take credit cards. ♢ Diz-se que... It's said (that)...

• **impessoalidade**: Vive-se bem aqui. People live well here.

se² conj **1** if: Se chover, não vamos. If it rains, we won't go. ♢ Se eu fosse rico, compraria uma moto. If I were rich, I'd buy a motorbike. NOTA Na linguagem falada atual, é comum usar-se "if I/he/she/it was". **2** (dúvida) whether: Não sei se fico ou se saio. I don't know whether to stay or go. **3** (desejo) if only: Se você tivesse me dito antes! If only you'd told me before! ▸ **se bem que** although

sé sf cathedral

seboso adj greasy

seca sf (falta de chuva) drought

secador sm dryer: ~ de cabelo/roupa hairdryer/clothes dryer

secamente adv (dizer, responder) coldly

seção sf **1** (Arquit, Mat, etc.) section **2** (loja) department: ~ masculina menswear department **3** (jornal, revista): a ~ de esportes the sports pages ▸ **~ eleitoral** polling station

secar vt dry ● vi **1** dry **2** (planta, rio, terra, ferida) dry up

seco adj **1** dry: um clima ~ a dry climate **2** (frutos, flores) dried **3** (sem vida) dead: folhas secas dead leaves **4** (som, pancada) sharp **5** (pessoa) cold **6** (resposta) curt

secretaria sf (escola) admissions office ▸ **~ de Estado** government department

secretariado sm **1** (curso) secretarial course **2** (organismo) secretariat: o ~ da ONU the UN secretariat **3** (sede) secretary's office

secretário/a sm-sf secretary [pl -ies] ▸ **secretária eletrônica** answering machine **secretária particular** personal assistant (abrev PA)

secreto adj secret

século sm **1** (cem anos) century [pl -ies]: no ~ XX in the 20th century **2** (**séculos**) ages: *Há ~s que eu sabia disso!* I've known that for ages!

secundário *adj* secondary

seda *sf* silk

sedativo *sm* sedative

sede¹ *sf* thirst ▶ **ter/estar com ~** be thirsty

sede² *sf* **1** headquarters (*abrev* HQ) **2** (*Esporte*) venue

sediar *vt* host: *~ as Olimpíadas* host the Olympics

sedimento *sm* sediment

sedoso *adj* silky

sedução *sf* **1** (*sexual*) seduction **2** (*encanto*) allure

sedutor/a *adj* **1** (*sentido sexual*) seductive **2** (*encantador*) alluring ● *sm-sf* seducer

seduzir *vt* **1** (*sexualmente*) seduce **2** (*desencaminhar*) lead sb astray

segmento *sm* segment

segredo *sm* secret: *em ~* in secret

segregar *vt* (*separar*) segregate sb/sth (*from sb/sth*)

seguido/a *adj: quatro vezes seguidas* four times in a row ▶ **em seguida 1** (*depois, agora*) next: *E em ~ temos o noticiário.* And next we have the news. **2** (*imediatamente*) right away

seguidor/a *sm-sf* follower

seguinte *adj* next: *no dia ~* the next day

seguir *vt* **1** follow: *Siga-me.* Follow me. **2** (*carreira*) pursue: *~ a carreira de médico* pursue a medical career **3** (*regras, ordens*) abide by sth ● *vi* go on (*doing sth*): *Siga até a praça.* Go on till you reach the square. ● **seguir-se** *vp* ensue (*fml*): *Seguiram-se dez anos de paz.* There ensued ten years of peace. ▶ **a ~** (*depois*) afterwards **a seguir a…** after…

segunda(-feira) *sf* Monday (*abrev* Mon.)

segundo¹ *prep* according to sb/sth: *~ ela/o plano* according to her/the plan ● *conj* **1** (*de acordo com o que*) according to what…: *~ ouvi dizer* from what I heard said **2** (*à medida que*) as: *~ forem entrando* as they come in

segundo² *sm* (*tempo*) second

segundo³ *adj, num, sm* second (*abrev* 2nd) ● **segunda** *sf* (*marcha*) second (gear) ▶ **de segunda** second-hand **ter segundas intenções** have ulterior motives

segurança *sf* **1** (*contra aciden-* *tes*) safety: *a ~ pública/nas estradas* public/road safety **2** (*contra roubo, etc., garantia*) security: *controles de ~* security checks **3** (*certeza*) certainty **4** (*confiança*) confidence ● *smf* (*pessoa*) security guard ▶ **com ~** (*agir, afirmar, etc.*) confidently

segurar *vt* **1** (*agarrar*) hold: *~ bem o guarda-chuva* hold the umbrella tight **2** (*prender*) fasten: *~ papéis com um clipe* fasten papers together with a paper clip **3** (*com uma companhia de seguros*) insure sb/sth (*against sth*) ● **segurar-se** *vp* (*agarrar-se*) hold on (*to sth*)

seguro *adj* **1** (*sem risco*) safe: *um lugar ~* a safe place **2** (*convencido*) sure **3** (*firme, bem apertado*) secure: *O gancho não estava bem ~.* The hook wasn't secure. **4** (*atado*) fastened: *A bagagem estava bem segura.* The baggage was tightly fastened. **5** (*preso*): *Dois policiais o tinham bem ~.* Two policemen were holding him down. ● *sm* insurance [U]: *adquirir um ~ de vida* take out life insurance ◊ *pôr algo no ~* insure sth ▶ **de si** confident

seio *sm* (*mama*) breast

seis *num, sm* **1** six **2** (*data*) sixth

seiscentos *num, sm* six hundred

seita *sf* sect

seiva *sf* (*Bot*) sap

seixo *sm* pebble

sela *sf* saddle

selar¹ *vt* **1** (*fechar*) seal: *~ um envelope/uma amizade* seal an envelope/a friendship **2** (*pôr selo*) stamp

selar² *vt* (*cavalo*) saddle sth (up)

seleção *sf* **1** selection **2** (*equipe*) (national) squad: *a ~ brasileira de futebol* the Brazilian soccer squad ◊ *~ mirim* youth squad

selecionar *vt* select

seleto *adj* select: *um grupo ~* a select group

selim *sm* (*bicicleta*) saddle

selo *sm* **1** (*correios*) stamp **2** (*lacre*) seal ▶ **~ fiscal** official stamp

selva *sf* jungle

selvagem *adj* **1** wild: *animais selvagens* wild animals **2** (*povo, tribo*) uncivilized

selvageria *sf* savagery

sem *prep* without: *~ pensar* without thinking ◊ *Saíram ~ ninguém os ver.* They left without anybody seeing them.

semáforo *sm* traffic light: *um ~ vermelho* a red light

semana *sf* week: *a ~ passada/que vem* last/next week ◇ *duas vezes por ~* twice a week ◇ *hoje faz uma ~* a week ago today ◇ *de hoje a uma ~* in a week's time ◇ *~ sim, ~ não* every other week

semanal *adj* **1** (*a cada semana*) weekly: *uma revista ~* a weekly magazine **2** (*por semana*): *Temos uma hora ~ de educação física.* We have one hour of P.E. a week.

semear *vt* sow: *~ trigo/uma terra* sow wheat/a field

semelhança *sf* similarity [*pl* -ies] ▸ **à ~ de** just like: *à ~ do que aconteceu no ano passado* just like last year

semelhante *adj* **1** (*parecido*) similar (*to sb/sth*) **2** (*tal*): *Como você pôde fazer coisa ~?* How could you do such a thing?

sêmen *sm* semen

semente *sf* **1** (*planta*) seed **2** (*fruta*) pip

semestral *adj*: *uma publicação ~* a half-yearly publication

semestre *sm* **1** (*period of*) six months: *durante o primeiro ~ de 1999* in the first six months of 1999 **2** (*Educ*) semester

semicírculo *sm* semicircle

semifinal *sf* semifinal

semifinalista *smf* semifinalist

seminário *sm* **1** (*aula*) seminar **2** (*Relig*) seminary [*pl* -ies]

sem-número *sm*: *um ~ de pessoas* hundreds of people

sempre *adv* always: *Vivi ~ com os meus primos.* I've always lived with my cousins. → ALWAYS ▸ **como ~** as usual **de ~** (*habitual*) usual: *no lugar de ~* in the usual place **o de ~** the usual thing **para ~ 1** (*permanentemente*) for good: *Estou deixando o Brasil para ~.* I'm leaving Brazil for good. **2** (*eternamente*) forever: *O nosso amor é para ~.* Our love will last forever. ▸ **que... whenever...**: *~ que saímos de férias você fica doente.* Whenever we go on vacation you get sick. ▸ **reto/em frente** straight on: *Siga ~ em frente.* Go straight on.

sem-terra *smf* landless person

sem-teto *smf* homeless person: *os ~* the homeless

sem-vergonha *smf* scoundrel

senado *sm* senate

senador/a *sm-sf* senator

senão *conj* or else: *Cale-se, ~ vai apanhar.* Shut up, or else you'll

get in trouble. ◇ *É melhor você vender agora, ~ vai perder dinheiro.* You'd better sell now, otherwise you'll lose money. ● *prep* but: *Você não faz nada ~ criticar.* You do nothing but criticize. ● *sm* fault: *encontrar ~ em algo* find fault with sth

senha *sf* password

senhor/a *sm-sf* **1** man [*fem* lady] [*pl* -ies] **2** (+ *sobrenome*) Mr. [*fem* Mrs.] [*pl* Mr. and Mrs.]: *O ~ Lopes está?* Is Mr. Lopes in? ◇ *o ~ e Senhora Silva* Mr. and Mrs. Silva **3** (+ *cargo*): *o ~ Prefeito* the mayor **4** (*para chamar a atenção*): *(Minha) Senhora!* Deixou cair o bilhete. Excuse me! You've dropped your ticket. **5** (*de cortesia*) sir [*fem* madam] [*pl* -ies]: *Bom dia, ~.* Good morning, sir. ◇ *Senhoras e ...es...* Ladies and gentlemen... ▸ **não ~/senhora** no way **sim ~/senhora** too right ● **Senhor** *sm* Lord ● **senhora** *sf* (*esposa*) wife [*pl* wives] ● *adj* lavish: *dar uma senhora festa* hold a lavish party

senhorio/a *sm-sf* landlord [*fem* landlady] [*pl* -ies]

senhorita *sf* Miss, Ms. NOTA Usa-se **Miss** com o sobrenome ou com o nome e sobrenome: *"Miss Jones"* ou *"Miss Mary Jones"*, mas nunca só com o nome: *Telefone à Srta. Helena/à Srta. Helena Almeida.* Call Helena/Miss Helena Almeida. Usa-se **Ms.** tanto para mulheres casadas quanto solteiras quando não se conhece (ou não se quer diferenciar) o seu estado civil.

senil *adj* senile: *ficar ~* go senile

sensação *sf* feeling ▸ **causar ~** cause a sensation

sensacional *adj* sensational

sensatez *sf* good sense

sensato *adj* sensible

sensibilidade *sf* sensitivity [*pl* -ies]

sensibilizar *vt* (*comover*) touch

sensível *adj* **1** sensitive (*to sth*): *pele ~* sensitive skin ◇ *uma criança muito ~* a very sensitive child **2** (*grande*) noticeable: *uma melhora ~* a noticeable improvement

senso *sm* sense: *~ de humor* sense of humor ▸ **(bom) ~** (*sensatez*) (common) sense: *Você não tem o menor bom ~.* You're totally lacking in common sense. **ter o bom ~ de...** be sensible enough to...

sensual *adj* sensual

sentado *adj* sitting, seated (*mais fml*): *~ à mesa* sitting at the table ◇ *Ficaram ~s.* They remained seated.

sentar *vt sit sb (down): Ele sentou o bebê no carrinho.* He sat the baby down in its stroller. ● **sentar-se** *vp sit (down): Sente-se, por favor.* Sit down, please. ◇ *~ no chão* sit (down) on the floor

sentença *sf (Jur)* sentence ▶ **passar uma ~** pass sentence (on sb)

sentenciar *vt* sentence sb (to sth)

sentido¹ *sm* **1** sense: *os cinco ~s* the five senses ◇ *Não faz ~.* It doesn't make sense. **2** *(significado)* meaning **3** *(direção)* direction: *uma rua de ~ único* a one-way street ◇ *~ proibido* no entry ● *interj* attention ▶ **perder/recuperar os ~s** lose/regain consciousness **pôr-se em ~** stand to attention **sem ~** **1** *(sem lógica)* meaningless **2** *(sem propósito)* pointless **sem ~s** unconscious

sentido² *adj* hurt: *estar ~ com algo* be hurt about sth

sentimental *adj* **1** sentimental: *valor ~* sentimental value **2** *vida ~* love life

sentimento *sm* feeling

sentinela *sf* **1** *(Mil)* sentry *[pl -ies]* **2** *(vigia)* lookout: *estar de ~* be on the lookout

sentir *vt* **1** feel: *~ frio/fome* feel cold/hungry **2** *(lamentar)* be sorry *(about sth/that)...: Sinto muito não te poder te ajudar.* I'm really sorry (that) I can't help you. ● **sentir-se** *vp* feel: *~ bem* feel fine

separação *sf* separation

separado *adj* **1** *(estado civil)* separated **2** *(diferentes)* separate: *levar vidas separadas* lead separate lives ▶ **em ~** separately

separar *vt* **1** separate *sb/sth (from sth)* **2** *(distanciar)* move *sb/sth* away *(from sb/sth)* **3** *(guardar)* put sth aside: *Separe um pão para mim.* Put a loaf aside for me. ● **separar-se** *vp* separate, split up *(coloq): Ela se separou do marido.* She separated from her husband. ◇ *Nós nos separamos no meio do caminho.* We split up halfway.

sepultar *vt* bury

sepultura *sf* grave

seqüência *sf* sequence

sequer *adv* even: *Você nem ~ me contou.* You didn't even tell me.

seqüestrador/a *sm-sf* **1** *(de*

pessoa) kidnapper **2** *(de avião)* hijacker

seqüestrar *vt* **1** *(pessoa)* kidnap **2** *(avião)* hijack

seqüestro *sm* **1** *(pessoa)* kidnapping **2** *(avião)* hijacking

ser¹ *v lig, vt* **1** be: *Ela é alta.* She's tall. ◇ *Sou de Cuiabá.* I'm from Cuiabá. ◇ *Dois e dois são quatro.* Two and two are four. ◇ *São sete horas.* It's seven o'clock. ◇ *— Quanto é? — São 320 reais.* "How much is it?" "(It's) 320 reais." ◇ *— Quem é? — É a Ana.* "Who's that?" "It's Ana." ◇ *Na minha família somos seis.* There are six of us in my family. NOTA Usa-se o artigo indefinido **a/an** antes de profissões em orações com o verbo "be": *Ele é médico/engenheiro.* He's a doctor/an engineer. **2** ~ *de (material)* be made of sth: *É de ferro.* It's made of iron. **3** ~ *sobre (filme, livro)* be about sth: *O filme é sobre o quê?* What's the movie about? **4** ~ *de (equipe)* support sth: *Eles são do Flamengo.* They're Flamengo fans. ● *v aux* be: *Ele será julgado sexta-feira.* He will be tried on Friday. ▶ **a não ~ que...** unless... **como se (isso) fosse pouco** to top it all **é que...:** *É que não tenho vontade.* I just don't feel like it. **o que seja** whatever you say in other words: *No dia 17, ou seja, terça passada.* The 17th, in other words last Tuesday. **se eu fosse...** if I were... **seja como for/seja o que for/seja quem for** no matter how/what/who **se não é/fosse por** if it weren't for sb/sth **se não fosse ele:** *Se não fosse ele, teriam me matado.* If it weren't for him, I would have been killed. **sou eu, etc.** it's me, you, etc. NOTA Para outras expressões com **ser**, ver o substantivo, adjetivo, etc., p. ex. **ser o cúmulo** em CÚMULO.

ser² *sm* being: *um ~ humano/vivo* a human/living being

serão *sm* night shift ▶ **fazer ~** work nights

sereia *sf* mermaid

sereno *adj, sm* calm ● *sm* dew

série *sf* series *[pl -ies]: uma ~ de desastres* a series of disasters ◇ *uma nova ~ de televisão* a new TV series → SERIES

seringa *sf* syringe

sério *adj* **1** serious: *um livro/assunto ~* a serious book/matter **2** *(responsável)* reliable: *um homem de negócios ~* a reliable

businessman 3 (*honrado*) honest ● *adv* seriously: *levar algo a* ~ take sth seriously ◊ *Você está falando* ~? Are you serious? ► **tirar alguém do** ~ drive sb up the wall

sermão *sm* (*Relig*) sermon ► **dar/pregar (um)** ~ give sb a lecture

serpentina *sf* streamer

serra *sf* **1** (*ferramenta*) saw **2** (*região*) mountains [*pl*]: *uma casa na* ~ a house in the mountains **3** (*Geog*) mountain range

serragem *sf* sawdust

serralheiro/a *sm-sf* locksmith

serrar *vt* saw *sth* (up): ~ *madeira* saw up wood

serrote *sm* (hand)saw

servente *sm* (*trabalhador*) laborer

serviço *sm* **1** service: ~ *de ônibus* bus service ◊ *fazer o* ~ *militar* do (*your*) military service **2** (*trabalho*) work: *chegar atrasado ao* ~ be late for work **3** (*tarefa*) job: *Tenho um* ~ *para você.* I have a job for you. ► **de** ~ on duty: *estar de* ~ be on duty ◊ *o médico de* ~ the doctor on duty ~ **de Emergência** (*em hospital*) emergency room ~ **fúnebre** funeral ~ **público** civil service

servidor *sm* (*Informát*) server

servir *vt, vi* **1** serve: ~ *na marinha* serve in the navy **2** ~ **de/como/para** serve as *sth/to do sth*: *Serviu para esclarecer as coisas.* ◊ *A caixa me serviu de mesa.* I used the box as a table. **3** (*usar-se*) be (used) *for doing sth*: *Serve para cortar.* It's used for cutting. ◊ *Para que é que serve?* What's it for? **4** (*atuar como*) act as *sth*: ~ *de intermediário* act as an intermediary **5** (*roupa*) fit: *Estas calças não me servem.* These pants don't fit me. **6** (*comida, bebida*) serve: *Demoraram muito para nos* ~. They took a long time to serve us. ◊ *Sirvo-lhe um pouco mais?* Would you like some more? ● **servir-se** *vp* (*comida*) help yourself (*to sth*): *Sirva-se.* Help yourself. ► **não** ~ **1** (*utensílio*) be no good (*for doing sth*) **2** (*pessoa*) be no good *at doing sth*

sessão *sf* **1** session: ~ *de treino/encerramento* training/closing session **2** (*Cinema*) showing **3** (*Teat*) performance

sessenta *num, sm* sixty ► **os anos** ~ the sixties

sesta *sf* nap: *fazer/tirar uma* ~ take a nap

seta *sf* arrow

sete *num, sm* **1** seven **2** (*data*) seventh ► **ter** ~ **vidas** have nine lives

setecentos *num, sm* seven hundred

setembro *sm* September (*abrev* **Sept.**) → MAIO

setenta *adj, num, sm* seventy

sétimo/a *adj, num, sm* seventh

setor *sm* **1** (*zona, indústria*) sector **2** (*grupo de pessoas*) section: *um pequeno* ~ *da população* a small section of the population

seu, sua *pron adj* **1** (*de você, de vocês*) your **2** (*dele*) his **3** (*dela*) her **4** (*deles/delas*) their **5** (*de objeto, animal, conceito*) its **6** (*impessoal*) their: *Cada um tem a sua opinião.* Everyone has their own opinion. ● *pron subs* **1** (*de você, vocês*) yours **2** (*dele*) his **3** (*dela*) hers **4** (*deles, delas*) theirs NOTA *Um amigo seu* se traduz por a friend of yours/his/hers/theirs pois significa *um dos seus amigos.*

severo/a *adj* **1** (*rígido*) strict (*with sb*) **2** (*castigo, crítica*) harsh **3** (*intenso*) severe: *um golpe* ~ a severe blow

sexagésimo/a *num, sm* sixtieth

sexo *sm* sex

sexta-(feira) *sf* Friday (*abrev* **Fri.**) → DOMINGO ► **Santa** S~ Good Friday ~ **treze** Friday the thirteenth

sexto/a *adj, num, sm* sixth: ~ *sentido* sixth sense ◊ *Moro no* ~. I live on the sixth floor.

sexual *adj* **1** sexual: *assédio* ~ sexual harassment **2** *educação/vida* ~ sex education/life

sexualidade *sf* sexuality

shopping (center) *sm* (shopping) mall

si¹ *sm* (*Mús*) B

si² *pron pess reflexivo* **1** (*a*) (*você*) yourself (*b*) (*vocês*) yourselves → YOU **2** (*ele*) himself **3** (*ela*) herself **4** (*coisa*) itself: *O problema se resolveu por si (mesmo).* The problem resolved itself. **5** (*eles, elas*) themselves ► **em si (mesmo)** in itself

siamês *adj* ► **gêmeos/irmãos siameses** Siamese twins

siderurgia *sf* iron and steel industry

siderúrgica *sf* steelworks [*sing*]

siderúrgico *adj: o setor* ~ *brasileiro* the Brazilian iron and steel sector

sidra *sf* cider

sigiloso *adj* confidential

sigla *sf* acronym: *Qual é a ~ de...?* What's the acronym for...? ◊ *UE é a ~ da União Européia.* UE stands for "União Européia".

significado *sm* meaning

significar *vt* mean: *O que significa esta palavra?* What does this word mean? ◊ *Ele significa muito para mim.* He means a lot to me.

significativo *adj* significant: *um ~ aumento de salário* a significant raise

signo *sm* sign: *os ~s do zodíaco* the signs of the zodiac

sílaba *sf* syllable

silenciar *vt* **1** (*pessoa*) silence **2** (*escândalo*) hush *sth* up

silêncio *sm* silence: *A turma estava em ~ absoluto.* There was total silence in the classroom. ◊ *Silêncio!* Silence!

silenciosamente *adv* very quietly

silencioso *adj* **1** (*em silêncio, calado*) silent: *A casa estava completamente silenciosa.* The house was totally silent. **2** (*tranqüilo*) quiet: *uma rua muito silenciosa* a very quiet street ● *sm* (*Mec*) muffler, silencer (*GB*)

silhueta *sf* silhouette

silício *sm* silicon: *uma plaqueta de ~* a silicon chip

silicone *sm* silicone

silvestre *adj* wild

silvo *sm* (*cobra*) hiss

sim *adv, sm* yes: — *Você quer um pouco mais? —Quero ~.* "Would you like a bit more?" "Yes, please."

simbólico *adj* symbolic

simbolizar *vt* symbolize

símbolo *sm* symbol

simétrico *adj* symmetrical

similar *adj* similar (*to sb/sth*)

símio/a *sm-sf* ape

simpatia *sf* (*atração*) liking ▸ **ter ~ por alguém** like sb

simpático *adj* nice: *Ele me pareceu muito ~.* I thought he was very nice. **NOTA** Sympathetic não significa "simpático", mas compreensivo, solidário.

simpatizante *smf* sympathizer: *ser ~ do partido liberal* be a liberal party sympathizer

simpatizar *vt* (*gostar de*) like *sb/sth*: *Simpatizei com ele/o jeito dele.* I liked him/the look of him. ◊ *Simpatizamos com o*

Partido Verde. Our sympathies lie with the Green Party.

simples *adj* **1** simple: *O problema não é tão ~ como parece.* The problem's not as simple as it looks. ◊ *uma refeição ~* a simple meal **2** (*mero*): *É uma ~ formalidade.* It's just a formality. **3** (*único*) single

simplicidade *sf* simplicity

simplificar *vt* simplify

simultâneo *adj* simultaneous

sina *sf* fate

sinagoga *sf* synagogue

sinal *sm* **1** sign: *sinais de trânsito* road signs ◊ *É um bom/mau ~.* It's a good/bad sign. ◊ *em ~ de protesto* as a sign of protest **2** (*marca*) mark **3** (*telefone*) tone: *o ~ de discar/de ocupado* the dial tone/busy signal **4** (*na pele*) mole **5** (*de nascença*) birthmark ▸ **dar ~/sinais** show signs of (*doing*) *sth* **fazer ~** signal (*to sb*) (*to do sth*): *Ele me fez ~ para entrar.* He signaled to me to come in. **~ de via preferencial** Yield sign, Give Way sign (*GB*) **~ luminoso** flare

sinalização *sf* (*rodoviária*) road signs [*pl*]

sinalizar *vt* signpost

sinceridade *sf* sincerity

sincero *adj* sincere

sincronizar *vt* synchronize

sindicato *sm* (*labor*) union: *o ~ dos mineiros* the miners' union

síndico *sm* building manager

síndrome *sf* syndrome ▸ **~ de abstenção** withdrawal symptoms [*pl*] **~ de deficiência imunológica adquirida** acquired immune deficiency syndrome (*abrev* AIDS)

sinfonia *sf* symphony [*pl* -ies]

sinfônico *adj* **1** (*música*) symphonic **2** *orquestra sinfônica* symphony orchestra

singelo *adj* simple

singular *adj* (*Gram*) singular

sinistro *adj* sinister

sino *sm* bell: *Soaram os ~s.* The bells rang out.

sinônimo *adj* synonymous (*with sth*) ● *sm* synonym

síntese *sf* synthesis: *fazer uma ~* sum up

sintético *adj* **1** (*resumido*) concise **2** (*artificial*) synthetic

sintetizador *sm* synthesizer

sintoma *sm* symptom

sintonizador *sm* tuner

sintonizar *vt, vi* tune (*sth*) in (*to sth*): *~ a BBC* tune in to the BBC

sirene *sf* siren: ~ *da polícia* police siren

sísmico *adj* seismic

sistema *sm* system: ~ *político/ operacional* political/operating system ◊ *o* ~ *solar* the solar system

sisudo *adj* serious

site *sm* website

sítio *sm* **1** (*chácara*) small property in the country **2** (*cerco*) siege: *estado de* ~ state of siege

situação *sf* situation: *deixar alguém numa* ~ *difícil* put sb in an awkward situation

situado *adj* situated

situar *vt* **1** (*colocar, edificar*) place: *Situaram as tropas em volta do edifício*. They placed the troops around the building. **2** (*em mapa*): *Situe Angola no mapa*. Find Angola on the map. **3** (*romance, filme*) set sth in... ● **situar-se** *vp* **1** (*pôr-se*) position yourself **2** (*estar situado*) be situated

skate *sm* skateboard

slide *sm* slide: *um* ~ *a cores* a color slide

slogan *sm* slogan

smoking *sm* tuxedo [*pl* ~s], tux (*coloq*), dinner jacket (*GB*)

só *adj* **1** (*sem companhia*) alone: *estar só em casa* be alone in the house **2** (*solitário*) lonely: *uma pessoa muito só* a very lonely person ◊ *sentir-se só* feel lonely ● *adv* only: *Só trabalho aos sábados*. I only work on Saturdays. ◊ *Só te peço uma coisa*. I'm asking you just one thing. ▶ **não só... como/mas também...** not only... but also...

soalho *sm* wooden floor

soar *vi* **1** (*alarme, sirene*) go off **2** (*campainha, sino, telefone*) ring **3** (*parecer*) sound: *Como te soa isto?* How does this sound to you?

sob *prep* under

soberano/a *adj, sm-sf* sovereign

sobra *sf* **1** (*excesso*) surplus **2** (*sobras*) leftovers ▶ **de** ~ **1** (*suficiente*) plenty of (*sth*): *Há tempo/comida de* ~. There's plenty of time/food. **2** (*em demasia*) too much/many...: *ter trabalho de* ~ have too much work

sobrancelha *sf* eyebrow

sobrar *vi* **1** (*restar*) be left (over): *Sobrou queijo de ontem*. There's some cheese left (over) from last night. ◊ *Sobraram-me dois doces*. I have two pieces of candy left. **2** (*haver mais do que*

o necessário) be too much/ many: *Sobram dois pratos*. There are two plates too many. **3** (*estar de mais*) be in the way: *Estamos sobrando aqui*. We're in the way here.

sobre *prep* **1** (*em cima de*) on: ~ *a mesa* on the table **2** (*por cima, sem tocar*) over: *Voamos* ~ *o Rio*. We flew over Rio. **3** (*a respeito de*): *um filme* ~ *a Escócia* a movie about Scotland **4** (*num total de*) out of: *oito* ~ *dez* eight out of ten

sobreaviso *sm* ▶ **estar/ficar de** ~ be on your guard

sobrecarregar *vt* overload

sobreloja *sf* (*edifício*) mezzanine

sobremesa *sf* dessert: *O que a gente tem de* ~? What's for dessert?

sobrenatural *adj* supernatural

sobrenome *sm* family/last name, surname (*GB*)

sobressair *vi* stick out, protrude (*fml*)

sobressalente *adj* spare

sobressaltar *vt* startle

sobressalto *sm* (*susto*) fright

sobretudo¹ *sm* overcoat

sobretudo² *adv* especially
→ **SPECIALLY**

sobrevivência *sf* survival

sobrevivente *adj* surviving ● *smf* survivor

sobreviver *vi* survive

sobrinho/a *sm-sf* nephew [*fem* niece] NOTA Para *sobrinhos* referindo-se a *sobrinhos* e *sobrinhas*, diz-se **nephews and nieces**: *Quantos* ~*s você tem?* How many nephews and nieces do you have?

sóbrio *adj* sober

social *adj* social

socialismo *sm* socialism

socialista *adj, smf* socialist

sociável *adj* sociable

sociedade *sf* **1** society [*pl* -ies]: *a* ~ *de consumo* the consumer society **2** (*Com*) company [*pl* -ies] ▶ ~ **anônima** public corporation, public limited company (*abrev* plc) (*GB*) ~ **limitada** limited company (*abrev* Ltd)

sócio/a *sm-sf* **1** (*clube*) member: *tornar-se* ~ *de um clube* join a club **2** (*Com*) partner

sociologia *sf* sociology

sociólogo/a *sm-sf* sociologist

soco *sm* punch: *dar um* ~ *no rosto de alguém* punch sb in the face

socorrer vt help

socorro sm help: um pedido de ~ a cry for help • interj help

soda sf **1** (bicarbonato) baking soda, bicarbonate of soda (GB) **2** (bebida) soda (water) ▶ ~ (limonada) soda, (fizzy) lemonade (GB)

sofá sm couch, sofa

sofá-cama sm sofa bed

sofisticado adj sophisticated

sofrer vt, vi **1** suffer (from sth): ~ uma derrota/lesão suffer a defeat/an injury ◊ ~ de dor de cabeça/nas costas suffer from headaches/backache **2** (ter) have: ~ um acidente/do coração have an accident/heart trouble ◊ A cidade sofre com problemas de trânsito. The city has traffic problems. **3** (mudança) undergo ▶ ~ **uma desilusão** be disappointed: ~ uma desilusão amorosa be unlucky in love

sofrimento sm suffering

sofrível adj (aceitável) passable

sogro/a sm-sf father-in-law [fem mother-in-law] [pl parents-in-law/in-laws (mais coloq)]

soja sf soybean, soya (GB)

sol¹ sm sun: sentar-se ao ~ sit in the sun ◊ uma tarde de ~ a sunny afternoon ▶ **de sol a sol** from morning to night fazer ~ be sunny tomar ~ sunbathe

sol² sm (Mús) G

sola sf sole: sapatos com ~ de borracha rubber-soled shoes

solar¹ adj (do sol) solar

solar² sm manor (house)

solavanco sm jolt

soldado sm soldier

soldar vt solder

soleira sf (porta) threshold

solene adj solemn

soletrar vt spell

solfejo sm music theory

solicitação sf request

solicitar vt request

solícito adj (prestativo) helpful

solidão sf loneliness, solitude (mais fml)

solidariedade sf solidarity

solidário adj supportive: ser ~ com alguém support sb

solidez sf solidity

solidificar vt, vi **1** solidify **2** (água) freeze

sólido adj, sm solid

solista smf soloist

solitário adj **1** (sozinho) solitary: levar uma vida solitária lead a solitary life **2** (lugar) lonely

solo¹ sm **1** (superfície da terra) ground **2** (terra) soil

solo² sm (Mús) solo [pl ~s]

soltar vt **1** (largar) let go of sb/ sth: Solte essa criança! Let go of that child! **2** (deixar cair) drop **3** (libertar) set sb/sth free, release (mais fml) **4** (cão) set a dog loose **5** (cabo, corda, grito) let sth out: Solte um pouco a corda. Let the rope out a little. ◊ ~ um suspiro de alívio heave a sigh of relief **6** (fumo, cheiro) give sth off: A chaminé solta muita fumaça. The chimney gives off a lot of smoke. **7** (velas) unfurl • **soltar-se** vp **1** (desprender-se) come/work loose **2** (botão) come undone ▶ ~ **o cabelo** let your hair down ~ **(um) palavrão** swear

solteirão/ona sm-sf bachelor [fem spinster]

solteiro/a adj single • sm-sf single man/woman [pl men/ women]

solto adj loose: um parafuso ~ a loose screw ◊ Uso sempre o cabelo ~. I always wear my hair loose.

solução sf solution (to sth)

soluçar vi **1** (chorar) sob **2** (Med) hiccup

solucionar vt solve

soluço sm **1** (ao chorar) sob **2** (Med) hiccup: estar com ~(s) have the hiccups

solúvel adj soluble

solvente adj, sm solvent

som sm sound: Esta parede tem um ~ oco. This wall sounds hollow.

soma sf sum: fazer uma ~ do a sum

somar vt, vi add: Some dois mais cinco. Add two and five.

sombra sf **1** (ausência de sol) shade: sentar-se à/na ~ sit in the shade ◊ A árvore fazia ~ no carro. The car was shaded by the tree. ◊ Você está fazendo ~. You're keeping the sun off me. **2** (silhueta) shadow: projetar uma ~ cast a shadow ◊ Ela não é nem a ~ do que era. She's a shadow of her former self. **3** (para olhos) eyeshadow ▶ **sem ~ de dúvida** undoubtedly

sombreado adj shady

sombrinha sf **1** (guarda-sol) sunshade **2** (guarda-chuva) umbrella

somente adv Ver só

sonâmbulo/a sm-sf sleepwalker

sonda sf (Med) probe ▶ **espacial** space probe

sondagem sf (opinião, mercado) poll: uma ~ de opinião an opinion poll

sondar vt 1 (pessoa) sound sb out (about/on sth) 2 (opinião, mercado) test ▶ **~ o terreno** (averiguar) see how the land lies

soneca sf nap: tirar uma ~ take a nap

sonhador a sm-sf dreamer

sonhar vt, vi dream (about sb/ sth); (of doing sth): Ontem à noite sonhei com você. I dreamed about you last night. ◇ ~ **em ser famoso** dream of becoming famous ▶ **nem sonhando** no chance ~ **acordado** daydream ~ **com os anjos** sweet dreams

sonho sm 1 (dormindo, aspiração) dream 2 (Cozinha) doughnut ▶ **de ~**: uma casa de ~ a dream home **nem em ~** no chance

sonífero sm sleeping pill

sono sm 1 (descanso) sleep: por falta de ~ due to lack of sleep ◇ Não deixe que isso lhe tire o ~. Don't lose any sleep over it. 2 (sonolência) drowsiness: Estes comprimidos dão ~. These pills make you drowsy. ▶ **caindo/ morrendo de ~** dead on your feet **estar com/ter ~** be sleepy

sonolento adj sleepy

sonoro adj 1 (Tec) sound: efeitos ~s sound effects 2 (voz) loud

sopa sf soup

soprano sf soprano [pl ~s]

soprar vt 1 (para apagar algo) blow sth out 2 (para esfriar algo) blow on sth ▶ vi blow

sopro sm 1 blow: Ele apagou todas as velas com um ~ só. He blew out all the candles in one go. 2 (vento) gust

soquete sf sock

sórdido adj sordid

soronegativo adj HIV-negative

soropositivo adj HIV-positive

sorridente adj smiling

sorrir vi smile (at sb)

sorriso sm smile

sorte sf 1 luck: Boa ~ no exame! Good luck with your exam! ◇ dar/trazer boa/má ~ bring good/bad luck ◇ Que ~! What a stroke of luck! ◇ o meu número de ~ my lucky number 2 (destino) fate ▶ **à ~** at random **por ~** fortunately ~ **(grande)** (loteria) first prize **ter (pouca/má) ~** be (un)lucky: ter a má ~ de… be

unlucky enough to… **tirar à ~** draw lots for sth

sortear vt 1 (tirar à sorte) draw lots for sth 2 (rifar) raffle

sorteio sm 1 (loteria) draw 2 (rifa) raffle

sortido adj (variado) assorted

sortimento sm selection

sorver vt, vi 1 sip 2 (com um canudo) suck

sorvete sm 1 ice cream: ~ de chocolate chocolate ice cream 2 (feito com água) sorbet

sorveteria sf ice cream parlor

S.O.S. sm SOS: enviar um ~ send out an SOS

sósia smf double

soslaio sm ▶ **de ~**: olhar alguém de ~ look at sb out of the corner of your eye

sossegado adj quiet: deixar alguém ~ leave sb in peace

sossegar vt, vi calm (sb/sth) down

sossego sm peace (and quiet)

sótão sm attic

sotaque sm accent

sova sf beating

sovaco sm armpit

sovina adj (pessoa) stingy ● smf miser

sozinho adj 1 (sem companhia) alone: estar ~ em casa be alone in the house 2 (sem ajuda) by myself, yourself, etc.: Ele já come ~. He can eat by himself now. → ALONE

squash sm squash

standard adj, sm standard

status sm status

stress sm stress: sofrer de ~ suffer from stress

suado adj sweaty

suar vi sweat ▶ **~ em bicas** drip with sweat ~ **sangue** sweat blood

suave adj 1 (cor, luz, música, pele, roupa, voz) soft 2 (superfície) smooth 3 (brisa, pessoa, curva, descida, som, exercícios) gentle 4 (castigo, clima, sabor) mild 5 (chuva, vento) light

subconsciente adj, sm subconscious

subdesenvolvido adj underdeveloped

subdesenvolvimento sm underdevelopment

subentender vt assume: Pelo que você diz, subentende-se que não gostou dela. From what you say, I take it you didn't like her.

subestimar vt underestimate

subida sf 1 (ação) ascent 2

(*ladeira*) slope: *no alto desta ~ at the top of this slope* **3** (*aumento*) rise (*in sth*): *uma ~ de preços* a rise in prices

subir *vt* **1** (*ir/vir para cima*) go/come up: *~ uma rua* go up a street **2** (*montanha, escada*) climb **3** (*pôr mais para cima*) put *sth* up **4** (*levantar*) lift *sth* up: *~ a bagagem para o trem* lift the baggage onto the train **5** (*levar*) take/bring *sth* up: *~ as malas até o quarto* take the suitcases up to the room **6** (*preços*) put *sth* up, raise (*mais fml*) **7** (*persiana*) raise ● *vi* **1** (*ir/vir para cima*) go/come up: *~ até o último andar* go up to the top floor **2** (*trepar*) climb: *~ em árvores* climb trees **3** (*temperatura, rio*) rise **4** (*maré*) come in **5** (*preços*) go up (in price): *A gasolina subiu.* Gasoline has gone up. **6** (*transporte público, cavalo, bicicleta*) get on (*sth*)
▶ **~ à cabeça (de alguém)** (*bebida, sucesso, cargo*) go to sb's head **~ pelas paredes** (*ficar furioso*) hit the roof

súbito *adj* sudden

subjetivo *adj* subjective

subjuntivo *sm* subjunctive

sublinhar *vt* underline

sublocar *vt* sublet

submarino *adj* underwater ● *sm* submarine

submergir *vt* submerge

submeter *vt* **1** (*dominar*) subdue **2** (*expor*) subject *sb/sth* to *sth*: *~ os presos a torturas* subject prisoners to torture **3** (*procurar aprovação*) submit *sth* (*to sb/sth*): *~ algo a votação* put *sth* to the vote ● **submeter-se** *vp* **1** (*aceitar*) submit to *sth*: *~ às exigências de alguém* submit to sb's demands **2** (*sofrer*) undergo: *~ a uma operação* undergo an operation

submisso *adj* submissive

subnutrido *adj* undernourished

subordinado/a *adj, sm-sf* subordinate

subornar *vt* bribe

suborno *sm*: *tentativa de ~* attempted bribery ◊ *aceitar ~s* accept/take bribes

subsidiar *vt* subsidize

subsídio *sm* subsidy [*pl* -ies]

subsistir *vi* subsist (*on sth*)

subsolo *sm* basement

substância *sf* substance

substancial *adj* substantial

substantivo *sm* noun

substituição *sf* **1** (*permanente*)

replacement **2** (*temporária, Esporte*) substitution

substituir *vt* **1** (*permanentemente*) replace *sb/sth* (*with sb/sth*) **2** (*tomar o lugar de*) stand in for *sb*: *O meu ajudante vai me ~*. My assistant will stand in for me.

substituto/a *sm-sf, adj* **1** (*permanente*) replacement **2** (*suplente*) substitute: *um professor ~* a substitute teacher

subterrâneo *adj* underground

subtração *sf* (*Mat*) subtraction

subtrair *vt* subtract (*fml*), take *sth* away: *~ 3 de 7* take 3 away from 7

subúrbio *sm* **1** (*arredores*) suburb **2** (*bairro pobre*) poor area

sucata *sf* scrap: *vender um carro para ~* sell a car for scrap

sucedâneo/a *sm-sf* substitute (*for sth*)

suceder *vi* (*acontecer*) happen (*to sb/sth*) ● *vt* (*cargo, trono*) succeed: *O filho vai sucedê-lo no trono*. His son will succeed to the throne.

sucessão *sf* succession

sucessivamente *adv* successively

sucesso *sm* **1** (*êxito*) success: *ter ~* be successful **2** (*Mús, Cinema*) hit: *os seus últimos ~s de bilheteria* his latest box-office hits

sucessor/a *sm-sf* successor (*to sb/sth*)

suco *sm* juice: *~ de laranja feito na hora* freshly squeezed orange juice

suculento *adj* **1** juicy **2** (*carne*) succulent

sucursal *sf* branch

sudeste *sm* **1** (*ponto cardeal, região*) south-east (*abrev* SE) **2** (*vento, direção*) south-easterly

súdito/a *sm-sf* subject: *um ~ britânico* a British subject

sudoeste *sm* **1** (*ponto cardeal, região*) south-west (*abrev* SW) **2** (*vento, direção*) southwesterly

suéter *sm* sweater

suficiente *adj* enough: *Não há arroz ~.* There isn't enough rice. ◊ *Serão ~s?* Will there be enough? ◊ *Ganho o ~ para viver.* I earn enough to live on.

sufocante *adj* stifling: *Estava um calor ~.* It was stiflingly hot.

sufocar *vt* **1** (*asfixiar*) suffocate **2** (*rebelião*) put *sth* down ● *vi* **1** (*calor*) suffocate **2** (*respirar mal*) get out of breath

sufoco *sm* **1** (*calor*): *Que ~!* It's so

hot in here! **2** (*preocupação, agitação*) hassle (*coloq*)

sugerir *vt* suggest *doing sth/ that…*: *um Ele sugeriu que fôssemos embora*. He suggested (that) we leave. ◇ *Sugiro que vamos ao cinema*. I suggest we go to the movies.

sugestão *sf* suggestion

suicidar-se *vp* commit suicide

suicídio *sm* suicide

sujar *vt* get *sth* dirty: *~ o vestido de óleo* get oil on your dress ● **sujar-se** *vp* get dirty

sujeira *sf* dirt ▶ **fazer ~** make a mess

sujeitar *vt* subject *sb/sth to sth* ● **sujeitar-se** *vp* (*arriscar-se*) risk *sth*: *~ a ser multado* risk a fine

sujeito *adj* subject *to sth*: *~ às regras* subject to the rules ● *sm* **1** (*tipo*) character **2** (*Gram*) subject

sujo *adj* dirty

sul *sm* south (*abrev* **S.**): *a/no ~* in the south ◇ *na costa ~* on the south coast

sulco *sm* **1** (*Agricultura, rugo*) furrow **2** (*água*) wake **3** (*disco, metal*) groove

sulista *adj* southern ● *smf* southerner

sultão/ana *sm-sf* sultan

suma *sf* ▶ **em ~** in short

sumarento *adj* juicy

sumariar *vt* summarize

sumo *sm* (fruit) juice

sunga *sf* swimming trunks [*pl*] → PAIR

suor *sm* sweat

superar *vt* **1** (*dificuldade, problema*) overcome (*fml*), get over *sth* **2** (*rival, recorde*) beat **3** (*prova*) pass **4** (*fazer melhor*) surpass: *~ as expectativas* surpass expectations ◇ *O time brasileiro superou os italianos no jogo*. The Brazilian team outplayed the Italians. ● **superar-se** *vp* outdo yourself

superestimar *vt* overestimate

superficial *adj* superficial

superfície *sf* **1** surface: *a ~ da água* the surface of the water **2** (*Mat, extensão*) area

supérfluo *adj* **1** superfluous: *detalhes ~s* superfluous details **2** (*despesas*) unnecessary

superior *adj* **1** higher (*than sb/ sth*): *um número 20 vezes ~ ao normal* a figure 20 times higher than normal ◇ *ensino ~* higher education **2** (*qualidade, Mil*) superior (*to sb/sth*): *Ele era ~ ao rival*. He was superior to his

rival. **3** (*posição*) top: *o canto ~ esquerdo* the top left-hand corner ◇ *o lábio ~* the upper lip **4** (*oficial*) senior ● *sm* superior

superioridade *sf* superiority

superlotado *adj* packed

supermercado *sm* supermarket

superpovoado *adj* overpopulated

superstição *sf* superstition

supersticioso *adj* superstitious

supervisionar *vt* supervise

suplemento *sm* supplement

súplica *sf* plea

suplicar *vt* beg (*sb*) (*for sth*): *Eu lhe suppliquei que não o fizesse*. I begged him not to do it.

suplício *sm* **1** (*tortura*) torture [*U*]: *Estes saltos são um ~*. These high heels are torture. **2** (*experiência*) ordeal: *Aquelas horas de incerteza foram um ~*. Those hours of uncertainty were an ordeal.

supor *vt* suppose: *Suponho que sim/não*. I suppose so/not. ▶ **supondo/suponhamos que…** supposing…

suportar *vt* **1** (*pessoa, situação*) put up with *sb/sth*: *~ o calor* put up with the heat NOTA Em frase negativa, usa-se muito **stand**: *Não a suporto*. I can't stand her. ◇ *Não suporto ter que esperar*. I can't stand waiting. **2** (*peso, pressão, dor*) withstand **3** (*sustentar*) support: *As vigas suportam o telhado*. The beams support the roof.

suporte *sm* **1** support **2** (*prateleira*) bracket

suposição *sf* supposition

supositório *sm* suppository [*pl -ies*]

suposto *adj* (*presumível*) alleged

supremacia *sf* supremacy (*over sb/sth*)

supremo *adj* supreme

suprimir *vt* **1** (*omitir, excluir*) leave *sth* out **2** (*abolir*) abolish: *~ uma lei* abolish a law

surdez *sf* deafness

surdo/a *adj* deaf: *ficar ~* go deaf ● *sm* (*surdo*) deaf person: *uma escola especial para ~s* a special school for the deaf ▶ **fazer-se de ~** pretend not to hear   **~ como uma porta** as deaf as a post

surdo-mudo/surda-muda *adj* deaf and dumb ● *sm-sf* deaf mute

surfe *sm* surfing: *fazer/praticar ~* go surfing

surfista *smf* surfer

surgir vi 1 (aparecer) appear 2 (problema, complicação) arise: *Espero que não surja nenhum problema.* I hope no problems arise.

surpreendente adj surprising

surpreender vt 1 surprise: *Surpreende-me que ele ainda não tenha chegado.* I'm surprised he hasn't arrived yet. 2 (apanhar desprevenido) catch sb (unawares): *Surpreenderam os assaltantes.* They caught the robbers unawares. ◊ ~ alguém roubando catch sb stealing

surpreendido adj surprised

surpresa sf surprise ▶ **apanhar de** ~ take sb by surprise **fazer uma** ~ **(a)** surprise sb

surra sf thrashing: *O Vasco deu uma* ~ *neles.* Vasco gave them a real thrashing.

surrado adj threadbare

surtir vt ▶ ~ **efeito** produce an effect

surto sm (epidemia, violência) outbreak

suscetível adj 1 (melindroso) touchy 2 ~ **de** (capaz) liable to do sth

suspeita sf suspicion

suspeitar vt, vi suspect: *Suspeitam que o jovem seja um terrorista.* They suspect the young man of being a terrorist. ▶ **eu já suspeitava** just as I thought

suspeito/a adj suspicious ● smsf suspect

suspender vt 1 (aluno, jogo) suspend: *O árbitro suspendeu o jogo durante uma hora.* The referee suspended the game for an hour. 2 (adiar) postpone

suspense sm suspense

suspensórios sm suspenders, braces (GB)

suspirar vi sigh

suspiro sm 1 (ai) sigh 2 (Cozinha) meringue

sussurrar vt, vi whisper

sussurro sm whisper

sustenido adj (Mús) sharp

sustentar vt 1 (suster) support, hold sth up [mais coloq] 2 (manter) maintain

sustento sm 1 (alimento) sustenance 2 (suporte, apoio) support

susto sm 1 (medo, sobressalto) fright: *Que* ~ *você me deu/pregou!* Oh, you gave me a fright! 2 (falso alarme) scare

sutiã sm bra

sutil adj subtle

T t

tabacaria sf tobacconist's

tabaco sm tobacco

tabefe sm (bofetada) slap

tabela sf 1 (lista, índice) table: ~ **de equivalências** conversion table 2 ~ **de preços** price list 3 (marcador) scoreboard

tablete sm (chocolate) bar

tabu sm [pl ~s]: **um tema/ uma palavra** ~ a taboo subject/ word

tábua sf 1 (madeira) plank: *uma ponte feita de* ~s a bridge made from planks 2 (madeira polida, prancha) board: ~ **de passar roupa** ironing board

tabuleiro sm board: ~ **de xadrez** chessboard

tabuleta sf sign

taça sf 1 (copo) (champagne) glass: *uma* ~ **de champanhe** a glass of champagne 2 (Taça) (Esporte) Cup

tacada sf 1 (bilhar) shot 2 (Golfe) stroke

tachinha sf thumbtack, drawing pin (GB)

taco sm 1 (bilhar) cue 2 (Golfe) (golf) club

tagarela adj talkative ● smf 1 (falador) chatterbox 2 (indiscreto) gossip

tagarelar vi chatter

tagarelice sf chatter [U]

tal adj 1 (+ substantivos contáveis no plural e não contáveis) such: *em tais situações* in such situations ◊ *uma questão de* ~ *gravidade* a matter of such importance 2 (+ substantivos contáveis no singular) such a: *Como você pode dizer* ~ *coisa?* How can you say such a thing? ▶ **em** ~ **caso** in that case **o/a** ~ the so-called: *A* ~ *esposa não era mais do que a cúmplice dele.* His so-called wife was only his accomplice. ~ **como** (do modo) the way: *Escreve-se* ~ *como se diz.* It's spelled the way it sounds. ~ **e qual**: *Ele é* ~ *e qual o pai.* He's exactly like his father. **tal pai tal filho** like father like son **um/uma** ~ **de** a: *Telefonou um* ~ *de Luís Sá.* A Luís Sá called for you.

talão sm stub ▶ ~ **de cheques** checkbook

talco sm talc

talento sm talent: *ter* ~ *para algo* have a talent for sth

talhar vt **1** (madeira, pedra) carve **2** (vidro) cut ● vi (leite, creme) curdle

talher sm silverware, cutlery (GB) [U]: pôr os ~es put out the silverware ◊ usar os ~es use a knife and fork

talho sm cut

talismã sm good luck charm

talo sm stem

talvez adv maybe

tamanco sm clog

tamanduá sm anteater

tamanho adj such: Nunca ouvi tamanha estupidez. I never heard anything so stupid. ● sm size: Que ~ de camisa você veste? What size shirt do you wear? ◊ Que ~ tem a caixa? What size is the box? ◊ ser do/ter o mesmo ~ be the same size

tâmara sf date

também adv also, too, as well NOTA Too e as well vão no final da frase: Eu ~ quero ir. I want to go too/as well. Also é mais informal e coloca-se antes do verbo principal, ou depois, se é um verbo auxiliar: ~ vendem sapatos. They also sell shoes. ◊ Conheci os pais de Jane ~. I've also met Jane's parents. ● eu ~ me too → não neither, nor, either: —Não vi esse filme. — Eu ~ não. "I didn't see that movie." "Neither did I./Me neither." ◊ —Não gosto. —Eu ~ não. "I don't like it." "Nor do I./Neither do I./I don't either." ◊ Eu ~ não fui. I didn't go either. → NEITHER

tambor sm drum: tocar ~ play the drums

tampa sf **1** lid **2** (garrafa, tubo) top: ~ de rosca screw top **3** (Tec, banheira, ralo) plug

tampão sm (higiênico) tampon

tampouco adv neither, nor, either → NEITHER

tangente adj, sf tangent

tangerina sf tangerine

tanque sm **1** (reservatório, Mil) tank **2** (de lavar roupa) sink ► ~ de gasolina gas tank, petrol tank (GB)

tanto pron **1** (referente a substantivo não contável) so much: Não ponha ~ arroz para mim. Don't give me so much rice. ◊ Nunca tinha passado tanta fome. I'd never been so hungry. **2** (referente a substantivo contável) so many: Havia tantas pessoas lá! There were so many people there! ◊ Por que você

comprou ~s? Why did you buy so many? ● adv **1** so much: Comi ~ que não posso me mexer. I ate so much that I can't move. **2** Não corra ~. Don't run so fast. ► às/até as tantas in/until the small hours de tantas em tantas horas, semanas, etc. every so many hours, weeks, etc. ~ e ~ great: Ele é um cara e ~. He's a great guy. ~ e ~s (+ quantidade, com idade) odd: quarenta e tantas pessoas forty-odd people ~ tanto... como... **1** (em comparações) **(a)** (+ substantivo não contável) as much... as...: Bebi tanta cerveja como você. I drank as much beer as you. **(b)** (+ substantivo contável) as many... as...: Não temos ~s amigos como antes. We don't have as many friends as we used to. **2** (os dois) both... and...: ~ ele como a irmã sabiam. He and his sister both knew. ~ faz (dá na mesma) it's all the same ~ melhor so much the better ~ pior too bad ~ quanto/quantos... **1** (quantidade) as much/as many as...: ~s quantos forem necessários as many as are needed **2** (tempo) as long as... um ~ (bastante) pretty, rather (GB) É um ~ ~ caro. It's pretty expensive.

tão adv **1** (+ adjetivo/advérbio) so: É ~ difícil que... It's so hard that... ◊ Não acho que ele seja ~ ingênuo assim. I don't think he's that naive. **2** (+ substantivo) such: Eu não esperava um presente ~ caro. I wasn't expecting such an expensive present. ► tão... como... as... as...: Ele é ~ elegante como o pai. He's as elegant as his father.

tão-só (tb tão-somente) adv only

tapa sm (amigável) pat: um ~ nas costas a pat on the back **2** (bofetada) slap

tapar vt **1** (cobrir) cover sb/sth (with sth) **2** (com tampa) put the lid on sth **3** (com tampa de rosca) put the cap on sth **4** (caixa) close **5** (buraco, goteira) stop sth (up) **6** (a vista) block sb's view (of sth)

tapete sm **1** (grande) carpet **2** (pequeno) rug **3** (capacho) mat

tarado /a adj crazy about sb/sth ● sm-sf sex maniac

tarântula sf tarantula

tarde¹ sf afternoon, evening: O concerto é à ~. The concert is in the afternoon/evening. ◊ Eles chegaram domingo à ~. They

arrived on Sunday afternoon/
evening. ◇ *hoje/amanhã à* ~
this/tomorrow afternoon/
evening ◇ *às duas da* ~ at two
o'clock in the afternoon ◇ *a
programação da* ~ afternoon
viewing NOTA Usa-se **afternoon** para o período do meio-
dia até, aproximadamente, as
seis da tarde e **evening** para o
período das seis até a hora de
dormir. → MORNING ▸ **boa** ~
good afternoon/evening

tarde² *adv* late: *levantar-se* ~ get
up late ◇ *Vou-me embora, que já
é* ~. I'm off; it's getting late. ◇ *É
* ~ *para telefonar.* It's too late to
call them.

tarefa *sf* **1** task: *uma* ~ *impossível* an impossible task **2**
(obrigação) duty [*pl* -ies] ▸
~**s domésticas** housework [*U*]

tarifa *sf* tariff

tartaruga *sf* **1** *(terra)* tortoise **2**
(mar) turtle NOTA Nos Esta-
dos Unidos usa-se apenas a
palavra **turtle**.

tática *sf* **1** tactics [*pl*]: *a* ~ *de
guerra dos romanos* Roman
military tactics ◇ *uma mudança
de* ~ a change of tactics **2**
(manobra) tactic: *uma brilhante
* ~ *eleitoral* a brilliant electoral
tactic

tato *sm* **1** *(sentido)* sense of
touch: *ter um* ~ *muito desenvolvido* have a highly developed
sense of touch ◇ *reconhecer
algo pelo* ~ recognize sth by
touch **2** *(habilidade)* tact: *Que
falta de* ~! How tactless!

tatuagem *sf* tattoo [*pl* ~s]

taxa *sf* **1** *(índice)* rate: ~ *de câmbio* exchange rate **2** *(imposto)*
tax ▸ ~**s escolares** tuition fees

táxi *sm* taxi, cab *(coloq)*

taxista *smf* taxi driver, cab
driver *(coloq)*

tchau *interj* bye

te *pron pess* you: *Ele te viu?* Did
he see you?

teatral *adj* **1** *(comportamento,
pessoa)* theatrical **2** *(relativo ao
teatro)* theater: *companhia* ~
theater company

teatro *sm* theater

teatrólogo/a *sm-sf* playwright

tecer *vt* **1** weave **2** *(aranha,
bicho-da-seda)* spin

tecido *sm* **1** *(pano)* fabric → PANO
2 *(Anat)* tissue

tecla *sf* key: *apertar uma* ~ press
a key

tecladista *smf* keyboard player

teclado *sm* keyboard

técnica *sf* *(método)* technique

técnico/a *adj* technical ● *sm-sf* **1**
technician **2** *(Esporte)* manager

tecnologia *sf* technology [*pl*
-ies]: ~ *de ponta* state of the art
technology

tédio *sm* boredom

teia *sf* web ▸ ~ **de aranha** spider
web, cobweb *(GB)*

teimosia *sf* stubbornness

teimoso *adj* stubborn

tela *sf* **1** *(TV, Informát)* screen:
uma ~ *de computador* a com-
puter screen **2** *(Arte)* canvas

telecomunicações *sf* telecommunications

teleférico *sm* **1** *(cabine)* cable
car **2** *(cadeira)* chairlift

telefonar *vt, vi* telephone, call
(mais coloq)

telefone *sm* **1** *(aparelho)* telephone, phone *(mais coloq)*: *Ela
está ao* ~. She's on the phone. ◇
atender o ~ answer the phone ◇
*Ana, ~! Phone for you, Ana! ◇ O
* ~ *dá sinal de ocupado.* The line's
busy. **2** *(número)* phone number ▸ ~ **celular** cellular phone,
cell phone *(coloq)*, mobile
(phone) *(GB)* ~ **público** (public) payphone ~ **sem fio** cordless phone

telefonema *sm* phone call

telefônico *adj* telephone, phone
(coloq): *fazer uma chamada
telefônica* make a phone call

telefonista *smf* (telephone)
operator

telegrama *sm* telegram

telejornal *sm* news [*sing*]: *A que
horas é o* ~? What time is the
news on?

telenovela *sf* soap (opera)

teleobjetiva *sf* telephoto lens

telepatia *sf* telepathy

telescópio *sm* telescope

telespectador/a *sm-sf* viewer

teletexto *sm* teletext

televisão *sf* television *(abrev
TV)*: *aparecer na* ~ be on television ◇ *Ligue/desligue a* ~. Turn
the TV on/off. ◇ *O que é que há
hoje à noite na* ~? What's on TV
tonight? ◇ *ver* ~ watch television ▸ ~ **a cabo** cable TV

telha *sf* (roof) tile ▸ **como/o que
me der na** ~ however/whatever
I, you, etc. want: *Faço como me
der na* ~. I do it however I want.

telhado *sm* roof

tema *sm* **1** subject **2** *(Mús)*
theme

temática *sf* subject matter

temer *vt, vi* **1** be afraid *(of sb/*

(doing) sth; ~ **enganar-se** be afraid of making mistakes ◇ *Eu não disse nada, pois temi que ele se zangasse.* I didn't say it for fear of making him angry. **2** ~ **por** fear for *sb/sth*: *Temi pela segurança das crianças.* I feared for the children's safety.

temível *adj* frightening

temor *sm* fear

temperado *adj (clima)* mild

temperamento *sm* temperament

temperar *vt* **1** *(comida)* season **2** *(salada)* dress

temperatura *sf* temperature

tempero *sm* **1** *(comida)* seasoning **2** *(salada)* dressing

tempestade *sf* storm: *Vem aí uma* ~. There's a storm brewing. ▶ **de** ~ stormy: *época de* ~ stormy season **uma** ~ **num copo d'água** a tempest in a teapot, a storm in a teacup *(GB)*

tempestuoso *adj* stormy

templo *sm* temple

tempo *sm* **1** time: *no* ~ *dos romanos* in Roman times ◇ *Há* ~ *que moro aqui.* I've been living here for some time. ◇ *no meu* ~ *livre* in my free time ◇ *passar o* ~ pass the time ◇ *Ele acabou ao mesmo* ~ *que eu.* He finished at the same time as I did. ◇ *Há quanto* ~ *você estuda inglês?* How long have you been studying English? **2** *(meteorológico)* weather: *Ontem fez bom/mau* ~. The weather was good/bad yesterday. **3** *(Gram)* tense **4** *(Esporte)* half *[pl halves]*: *o primeiro* ~ the first half ▶ **com o** ~ in time: *Com o* ~ *você vai entender.* You'll understand in time. **com** ~ **1** *(de sobra)*: *Avise-me com* ~. Let me know in good time. **2** *(longamente)* at length **de** ~**(s) em** ~**(s)** from time to time **em** ~ **integral**: *trabalhar em* ~ *integral* work full time **estar em** ~ be in time: *Ainda está em* ~ *de você enviá-lo.* You're still in time to send it. **pouco** ~ **depois** soon afterwards

têmpora *sf (Anat)* temple

temporada *sf* **1** *(período de tempo)* time: *Ele esteve doente durante uma longa* ~. He was sick for a long time. ◇ *passar uma* ~ *no estrangeiro* spend some time abroad **2** *(época)* season: *a* ~ *de beisebol* the baseball season

temporal *sm* storm

temporário *adj* temporary

tenaz *adj* tenacious ● **tenazes** *sf* tongs ⊳ PAIR

tenda *sf* tent

tendão *sm* tendon

tendência *sf* **1** tendency *[pl -ies]*: *ter* ~ *para fazer algo* have a tendency to do sth **2** *(moda)* trend: *as últimas* ~*s da moda* the latest fashion trends

tender *vt* tend *to do sth*

tenente *sm* lieutenant

tênis *sm* **1** *(jogo)* tennis **2** *(calçado)* sneaker, trainer *(GB)* ▶ ~ **de mesa** table tennis

tenista *smf* tennis player

tenor *sm* tenor

tenro *adj* tender: *um bife* ~ a tender steak

tensão *sf* **1** tension: *a* ~ *de uma corda* the tension of a rope ◇ *Havia uma grande* ~ *durante o jantar.* There was a lot of tension during dinner. **2** *(elétrica)* voltage: *cabos de alta* ~ high-voltage cables

tenso *adj* tense

tentação *sf* temptation: *resistir à* ~ *de fazer algo* resist the temptation to do sth

tentáculo *sm* tentacle

tentador *adj* tempting

tentar *vt* **1** *(experimentar)* try *(sth/to do sth)*: *O que é que ele está tentando nos dizer?* What's he trying to tell us? **2** *(seduzir)* tempt: *A idéia de ir de férias está me tentando.* The idea of going on vacation is very tempting.

tentativa *sf* attempt: *na primeira* ~ at the first attempt

tênue *adj* faint

teologia *sf* theology *[pl -ies]*

teor *sm* **1** *(carta)* contents *[sing]* **2** *(gordura)* content **3** *(discurso)* tenor ▶ ~ **alcoólico**: *Este vinho tem baixo* ~ *alcoólico.* This wine has a low alcoholic content.

teoria *sf* theory *[pl -ies]*: *em* ~ in theory

teórico *adj* theoretical

tépido *adj* lukewarm

ter *vt*
● **posse** have NOTA Existem duas formas para *ter* no presente: **have** e **have got**. **Have** é mais comum nos Estados Unidos e é sempre acompanhado de um auxiliar nas orações negativas e interrogativas: *Você tem irmãos?* Do you have any brothers or sisters? ◇ *Ele não tem dinheiro nenhum.* He doesn't have any money. **Have got** não necessita de um auxiliar nas orações negativas e

interrogativas: Have you got any brothers or sisters? He hasn't got any money. Nos outros tempos verbais usa-se **have**: *Quando era pequena, eu tinha uma bicicleta.* I had a bike when I was little.

● **estado, atitude 1** (*idade, tamanho*) be: *A minha filha tem dez anos.* My daughter is ten (years old). ◊ *Tem um metro de comprimento.* It's a meter long. **2** (*sentir, ter determinada atitude*) be NOTA Quando "ter" significa "sentir", usa-se o verbo be com um adjetivo, enquanto em português se usa um substantivo: *Tenho muita fome.* I'm very hungry. ◊ ~ *calor/frio/sede/medo* be hot/cold/thirsty/frightened ◊ *Tenho um grande carinho pela sua mãe.* I'm very fond of your mother. ◊ ~ *cuidado/paciência* be careful/patient. **3** (*dor, doença*) have: ~ *pneumonia/dor de dente/febre* have pneumonia/a toothache/a fever **4** (*amor, raiva, ódio*) *Ela tem um ódio tremendo dele.* She really hates him. ◊ ~ *carinho por alguém* care about sb ● *v aux* **1 ~ que/de fazer algo** have to do sth: ~ *que lhe embora imediatamente* have to leave right away ◊ *Você tem que dizer a ele.* You must tell him. → MUST **2** + *particípio: Eles têm tudo planejado.* They've got it all planned. ◊ *Eles tinham-me dito que viriam.* They had told me they would come. ► **não tem de quê** you're welcome **se tivesse…** if…: *Se eu tivesse sabido antes, não teria dito nada.* If I had known, I wouldn't have said anything. ~ **a ver** (*assunto*) have to do with sb/sth: *Mas o que é que isso tem a ver com o assunto?* What's that got to do with anything? ◊ *Isso não tem nada a ver.* That's got nothing to do with it. NOTA Para outras expressões com ter, ver o substantivo, adjetivo, etc., p. ex. **ter graça** em GRAÇA.

terapeuta *sf* therapist

terapia *sf* therapy [*pl* -ies]: ~ *de grupo* group therapy

terça(-feira) *sf* Tuesday (*abrev* Tue(s).) → DOMINGO ► ~ **gorda** Mardi Gras, Shrove Tuesday (*GB*) NOTA Na Grã-Bretanha também se chama **Pancake Day** porque é tradicional comer panquecas.

terceiro/a *num* third (*abrev* **3rd**) ● (**terceiros**) *sm*: *seguro contra ~s* third-party insurance ● **terceira** *sf* (*marcha*) third (gear) ► **terceira idade**: *atividades para a terceira idade* activities for senior citizens

terço *sm, num* (*quantidade*) third: *dois ~ do país* two thirds of the country ◊ **a/uma terça parte** a third ● *sm* (*Relig*) rosary [*pl* -ies]: *rezar o ~* say the rosary

terçol *sm* sty [*pl* sties]

termas *sf spa* [*sing*]

térmico *adj* thermal

terminação *sf* ending

terminal *adj, sm* terminal: *doentes terminais* terminally ill patients ◊ ~ *de passageiros* passenger terminal

terminar *vt, vi* **1 ~ (de fazer algo)** finish (doing sth) **2 ~ (em)** end (in *sth*): *As festas terminam na segunda que vem.* The festivities end next Monday. ◊ *A manifestação terminou em tragédia.* The demonstration ended in tragedy.

termo *sm* **1** term: *em ~s gerais* in general terms **2** (*fim*) end

termômetro *sm* thermometer ► **pôr o ~ take** sb's temperature

terno *sm* suit

terno *adj* tender

terra *sf* **1** (*por oposição ao mar, campo, terreno*) land [U]: *viajar por* ~ travel by land ◊ *cultivar a* ~ work the land ◊ *Ele vendeu as* ~*s da família.* He sold his family's land. **2** (*para plantas, terreno*) soil: *uma* ~ *fértil* fertile soil **3** (*chão*) ground: *cair por* ~ fall to the ground **4** (*pátria*) home: *costumes da minha* ~ customs from back home **5** (*Terra*) (*planeta*) earth: *A* ~ *é um planeta.* The Earth is a planet. **6** (*eletricidade*) ground, earth (*GB*): *O fio está ligado à* ~. The cable is grounded. **7** (*lugar*) place: *viajar por muitas* ~*s* travel around many places ► **a vista** land ahoy ~ **firme** dry land ~ **natal** homeland ~ **Santa** the Holy Land

terraço *sm* terrace

terremoto *sm* earthquake, quake (*coloq*)

terreno *sm* **1** (*terra*) land [U]: *um ~ muito fértil* very fertile land ◊ *comprar um* ~ buy some land **2** (*fig*) field: *o* ~ *da biologia* the field of biology ► ~ **baldio** wasteland

térreo *sm* ground floor NOTA Na Grã-Bretanha, o *andar térreo* é **ground floor**, o primeiro andar, **first floor**, etc. Nos Estados Unidos o térreo pode ser **ground floor** ou **first floor**. O primeiro andar é o **second floor** e assim sucessivamente.

terrestre adj land: um animal/ataque ~ a land animal/attack

território sm territory [pl -ies]

terrível adj terrible

terror sm terror ▸ **de ~** horror: um filme de ~ a horror movie

terrorismo sm terrorism

terrorista adj, smf terrorist

tese sf thesis [pl theses]

teso adj stiff

tesoura sf scissors [pl]: uma ~ nova some new scissors/a pair of new scissors → PAIR

tesoureiro/a sm-sf treasurer

tesouro sm **1** treasure: um ~ escondido hidden treasure ◊ Você é um ~! You're a treasure! **2** (Tesouro) Treasury: o ~ Nacional the Treasury

testa sf (Anat) forehead

testamento sm **1** (Jur) will: fazer um ~ make a will **2** (Testamento) o Antigo/Novo ~ the Old/New Testament

testar vt **1** (pôr à prova, Educ) test **2** (experimentar) try sth out: ~ o computador try out the computer **3** (carro) test-drive

teste sm test: fazer o ~ de gravidez have a pregnancy test ▸ **~ antidoping** drug test: O resultado do seu ~ antidoping foi positivo. He tested positive.

testemunha sf witness ▸ **~ de algo** witness sth ▸ **~ ocular** eyewitness

testemunhar vt (presenciar) witness ▸ vi (Jur) testify

testemunho sm (Jur) evidence: dar o seu ~ give evidence

testículo sm testicle

teta sf teat

teto sm **1** ceiling **2** (carro) roof

tétrico adj gloomy

teu, tua pron adj your: os ~s amigos your friends ● pron subs yours: Estes livros são ~s. These books are yours. NOTA Um amigo teu se traduz por a **friend of yours** ou pois significa um dos teus amigos.

têxtil adj textile

texto sm text

textualmente adv word for word

textura sf texture

tez sf complexion

ti pron pess you

tiete smf fan: Sou ~ do REM. I'm an REM fan.

tigela sf bowl

tigre sm tiger NOTA Falando só da fêmea, diz-se **tigress**.

tijolo sm brick

til sm tilde

tilintar vt **1** (campainha) jingle **2** (moedas) clink ● sm **1** (campainha) jingle **2** (moedas) clink

timão sm rudder

timbre sm **1** (voz) pitch: um ~ de voz alto a high-pitched voice **2** (papel) heading

time sm team

tímido adj shy

tímpano sm (ouvido) eardrum

tingir vt dye: ~ algo de vermelho dye sth red

tinta sf **1** (de pintar) paint: ~ a óleo oil paint ◊ ~ fresca wet paint **2** (de escrever) ink: um desenho a ~ an ink drawing **3** (para tingir, para o cabelo) dye

tintim interj cheers ▸ **~ por ~** blow-by-blow: Ela me contou a história ~ por ~. She gave me a blow-by-blow account.

tinto adj (vinho) red ● sm red wine

tinturaria sf **1** (lavanderia) laundry [pl -ies] **2** (lavanderia a seco) dry cleaner's

tio/a sm-sf uncle [fem aunt]: em casa dos meus ~s at my uncle and aunt's house

típico adj **1** (característico) typical (of sb/sth) **2** (tradicional) traditional: um traje ~ a traditional costume

tipo sm **1** kind (of sth): o ~ nervoso the nervous kind ◊ todo o ~ de gente all kinds of people **2** (pessoa) guy: Que ~ mais feio! What an ugly guy! **3** (letra) typeface

tique sm twitch

tira¹ sf **1** (papel, pano) strip: cortar algo em ~s cut sth into strips **2** (sapato) strap **3** (história em quadrinhos) comic strip

tira² smf (polícia) cop

tiracolo sm ▸ **a ~ 1** (bolsa) over your shoulder **2** (pessoa) in tow: com os filhos a ~ with her children in tow

tiragem sf (jornal, revista) circulation

tira-gosto sm appetizer

tirano/a sm-sf tyrant

tirar vt **1** take sth off/down, remove (mais fml): Tire o preço/os sapatos. Take the price tag/your shoes off. ◊ Ele tirou o cartaz. He took the poster down.

2 (*para fora*) take sb/sth out (*of sth*): ~ *uma pasta da gaveta* take a folder out of the drawer **3** (*Mat, subtrair*) take sth away (*from sb/sth*): *Se você tira um de três...* If you take one (away) from three... **4** (*mancha*) remove **5** (*conseguir*) get: *Quanto foi que você tirou em matemática?* What did you get in math? **6** (*roubar*) steal **7** (*cópia*) make **8** (*foto, radiografia*) take **9** (*mesa*) clear ▸ **não ~ os olhos de (cima de)** not take your eyes off sb/sth NOTA Para outras expressões com **tirar**, ver o substantivo, adjetivo, etc., p. ex. **tirar partido de algo** em PARTIDO.

tiritar *vi* (*dentes*): ~ *de frio* chatter

tiro *sm* **1** (*disparo*) shot **2** (*Futebol*) kick: ~ *livre* free kick ▸ **dar um ~** shoot: *Ele deu um ~ em si mesmo.* He shot himself. **dar um ~** take a risk **sair o ~ pela culatra** backfire **ser ~ e queda** be a sure thing ▸ **com arco** archery

tiroteio *sm* **1** (*entre polícia e criminosos*) shoot-out **2** (*ruído de disparos*) shooting [U]: *Ouvi um ~ na rua.* I heard shooting in the street. **3** (*durante uma guerra*) fighting

titio/a *sm-sf* uncle [*fem* auntie]

titular *adj*: *a equipe ~* the first team ◊ *um jogador ~* a first team player ● *smf* (*passaporte, conta bancária*) holder

título *sm* **1** title: *Que ~ você deu ao seu romance?* What's the title of your novel? ◊ *lutar pelo ~* fight for the title **2** (*Fin*) bond

toa *sf* ▸ **à ~ 1** (*ao acaso*) aimlessly **2** (*sem motivo*) for nothing: *Não é à ~ que ele é considerado o melhor jogador.* Not for nothing is he considered the best player. **3** (*desocupado*) at a loose end

toalete *sf*: *fazer a ~* get washed and dressed ● *sm* (*banheiro*) restroom, toilet (*GB*)

toalha *sf* towel: ~ *de banho* bath towel ▸ **~ absorvente** sanitary napkin, sanitary towel (*GB*) ~ **de mesa** tablecloth

tobogã *sm* slide
toca-CD *sm* CD player
toca-discos *sm* record player
toca-fitas *sm* tape deck
tocar *vt* **1** touch **2** (*apalpar*) feel: *Posso ~ o tecido?* Can I feel the fabric? **3** (*Mús*) play: ~ *piano* play the piano **4** (*sino, campai-*

nha) ring **5** (*buzina, sirene*) sound **6** ~ **em** (*assunto, tema*) touch on sth **7** ~ **a** be up to sb to do sth: *Não toca a mim decidir.* It's not up to me to decide. ● *vi* **1** (*Mús*) play **2** (*campainha, telefone*) ring ▸ **no que me, etc. toca** as far as I'm, you're, etc. concerned

tocha *sf* torch
toco *sm* **1** (*cigarro*) butt **2** (*árvore*) stump
todavia *conj* however

todo *adj* **1** all: *Fiz o trabalho ~.* I did all the work. ◊ *Limparam todas as casas da aldeia.* They cleaned up all the buildings in the village. NOTA Com substantivo contável no singular, é preferível usar the **whole**: *limpar o edifício* ~ clean the whole building **2** (*cada*) every: *Levanto-me ~s os dias às sete.* I get up at seven every day. → EVERY ● *pron* **1** all: ~ *gostamos da peça.* All of us/We all liked the play. **2** (*toda a gente*) everyone: ~*s dizem o mesmo.* Everyone says the same thing. NOTA **Everybody** e **everyone** são acompanhados do verbo no singular, mas podem ser seguidos de um pronome no plural (p. ex. "their"): ~*s têm os seus lápis?* Does everybody have their pencils? ● *sm* whole: considerado como um ~ taken as a whole ▸ **ao ~** altogether: *Ao ~ somos dez.* There are ten of us altogether. **de ~** totally: *Não sou de ~-maluca.* I'm not totally nuts. **no ~** all in all **por o ~ Brasil, ~ o mundo, etc.** throughout Brazil, the world, etc. NOTA Para outras expressões com **todo**, ver o substantivo, adjetivo, etc., p. ex. **em todo o caso** em CASO.

toldo *sm* **1** (*marquise*) awning **2** (*tenda grande*) marquee

tolerar *vt* **1** (*suportar*) bear, tolerate (*fml*): *Ele não tolera pessoas como eu.* He can't bear people like me. **2** (*consentir*): *O governo tolera a corrupção.* The government turns a blind eye to corruption.

tolice *sf* silly thing

tolo/a *adj* dumb, stupid NOTA No inglês americano **stupid** é um pouco mais forte que **dumb**: *uma desculpa tola* a dumb excuse ◊ *Não seja ~, e pare de chorar.* Don't be so stupid and stop crying. No inglês britânico, diz-se **silly** ou **stupid**. ● *sm-sf* fool ▶ **fazer-se de ~** act dumb

tom *sm* **1** tone: *Não me fale nesse ~!* Don't you take that tone of voice with me! ◇ *~ de discar* dial tone **2** (*cor*) shade **3** (*Mús*) key ▶ **ser de bom ~** be the done thing

tomada *sf* **1** (*macho*) plug: *~ de três pernas* three-pin plug ◇ *~ dupla/tripla* double/triple adaptor plug **2** (*fêmea*) outlet, socket (*GB*)

tomar *vt* take: *~ uma ducha* take a shower ◇ *~ notas/precauções* take notes/precautions ◇ *As crianças tomam muito o meu tempo.* The children take up a lot of my time. **2** (*decisão*) make **3** (*beber*) ▶ **tome** there: *Tome, é para você!* Here, it's for you! NOTA Para outras expressões com **tomar**, ver o substantivo, adjetivo, etc., p. ex. **tomar conta** em CONTA.

tomate *sm* tomato [*pl* ~es]

tombar *vt* knock *sth* down ● *vi* fall down

tombo *sm* (*queda*) fall

tona *sf* ▶ **vir à ~** emerge

tonalidade *sf* **1** (*cor*) shade **2** (*Mús*) key

tonelada *sf* ton

tônico *adj* (*sílaba*) stressed ● *sm* tonic

tonto *adj* **1** (*zonzo*) dizzy: *estar/ficar ~* feel/get dizzy ◇ *Esses comprimidos me deixaram ~.* Those pills made me dizzy. **2** (*tolo*) dumb → TOLO

tontura *sf* dizziness ▶ **estar com/ter ~** feel dizzy

topar *vt* **~ com** bump into *sb/sth*

tópico *sm* main point

topo *sm* top

toque *sm* **1** (*pancada pequena*) tap **2** (*acabamento*) touch: *dar o ~ final em algo* put the finishing touches on *sth* **3** (*campainha*) ring **4** (*telefone*) call ▶ **dar um ~ em alguém 1** (*mencionar*) mention *sth* to *sb* **2** (*avisar*) have a word with *sb* ▶ **de recolher** curfew

tórax *sm* thorax

torcedor/a *sm-sf* fan

torcer *vt* **1** twist: *~ o braço de alguém* twist *sb*'s arm **2** (*Med*) sprain: *~ o tornozelo* sprain your ankle **3** (*roupa*) **(a)** (*à mão*) wring *sth* out **(b)** (*na máquina de lavar*) spin **4** *~ por* (*time, partido*) root for *sb/sth* **5** *~ por alguém/para que...* keep your fingers crossed for *sb/*

that...: *Torça para que eu consiga o emprego.* Keep your fingers crossed that I get the job. ▶ **~ o nariz** turn your nose up (*at sth*)

torcicolo *sm* crick in your neck

tormento *sm* torment

tornar *vt* **1** (*fazer*) make: *O livro tornou-o famoso.* The book made him famous. **2** (*transformar*) turn *sth* into *sth* ● *vi* **~ a fazer algo** do *sth* again ● **tornar-se** *vp* become: *Ele se tornou um déspota.* He became a tyrant. ▶ **tornar-se realidade** come true

torneio *sm* tournament

torneira *sf* faucet, tap (*GB*): *abrir/fechar a ~* turn the faucet on/off

torniquete *sm* tourniquet

torno *sm* ▶ **em ~ de 1** (*em volta de*) around: *em ~ da cidade* around the city **2** (*aproximadamente*) about

tornozelo *sm* ankle

torpedo *sm* torpedo [*pl* ~es]

torrada *sf* toast [*U*]: *Queimei as ~s.* I burned the toast. ◇ *uma ~* a slice of toast

torradeira *sf* toaster

torrão *sm* lump: *um ~ de açúcar* a sugar lump

torrar *vt* **1** (*pão, frutos secos*) toast **2** (*café*) roast **3** (*dinheiro*) blow ● *vi* (*ao sol*) roast

torre *sf* **1** tower: *~ de controle* control tower **2** (*eletricidade, telecomunicações*) antenna, mast (*GB*) (*xadrez*) rook, castle ▶ **~ de vigia** watchtower

torrencial *adj* torrential: *chuvas torrenciais* torrential rain

torresmo *sm* crackling [*U*]

torso *sm* torso [*pl* ~s]

torta *sf* tart, pie → PIE

torto *adj* **1** (*dentes, nariz, linha*) crooked **2** (*quadro, roupa*) lopsided ▶ **a ~ e a direito** left, right and center

tortura *sf* torture

torturar *vt* torture

tosar *vt* **1** (*ovelha*) shear **2** (*cabelo*) crop

tosse *sf* cough: *A fumaça do cigarro me dá ~.* Cigarette smoke makes me cough.

tossir *vi* **1** cough **2** (*para aclarar a voz*) clear your throat

tostão *sm* ▶ **um ~ furado:** *não ter um ~ furado* be broke ◇ *não valer um ~ furado* not be worth a penny

total *adj* ▶ total: *um sucesso/fracasso ~* a total success/failure ● *sm* total ▶ **no ~** altogether

totalizar vt add sth up

totalmente adv totally

touca sf bonnet ► ~ **de banho 1** (piscina) swimming cap **2** (ducha) shower cap

toucinho sm bacon

toupeira sf **1** (animal) mole **2** (pessoa) idiot

tourada sf bullfight

toureiro/a sm-sf bullfighter

touro sm **1** bull **2** (Touro) (Astrol) Taurus ► **agarrar/pegar o ~ à unha** take the bull by the horns

tóxico adj toxic ● sm drug

toxicomania sf drug addiction

toxicômano/a sm-sf drug addict

trabalhador/a adj hard-working ● sm-sf worker: ~**es qualificados** skilled workers

trabalhar vi, vt work: Nunca trabalhei como professora. I've never worked as a teacher. ◊ Em que trabalha a sua irmã? What does your sister do? ◊ ~ **a terra** work the land

trabalho sm **1** work: ~ **pesado/agrícola** hard/farm work ◊ usar Internet no ~ use Internet at work ◊ **sem** ~ out of work **2** (emprego) job: um ~ **bem pago** a well-paid job ◊ **ficar sem** ~ lose your job → WORK **3** (na escola) assignment: **fazer um** ~ **sobre algo** do an assignment on sth ► **dar** ~ give sb trouble: Estas crianças dão muito ~. These kids are a real handful. **dar-se ao** ~ **de** take the trouble to do sth ► ~ **de casa** (Educ) homework [U] ◊ **de/em equipe** teamwork ◊ ~ **de parto** labor ◊ ~ **doméstico** housework ◊ ~ **forçado** hard labor ◊ ~**s manuais** arts and crafts

traça sf moth

tração sf **1** (com) ~ **nas quatro rodas** four-wheel drive

traçar vt **1** (linha, mapa) draw **2** (plano, projeto) draw sth up

traço sm **1** dash **2** (personalidade) characteristic: os ~**s distintivos da sua obra** the distinctive features of her work **3** (lápis, pincel) stroke **4** (traços) (rosto) features ► **sem deixar** ~(s) without a trace

tradição sf tradition

tradicional adj traditional

tradução sf translation (from sth) (into sth): **fazer uma** ~ **do inglês para o russo** do a translation from English into Russian

tradutor/a sm-sf translator

traduzir vt, vi translate (sth)

(from sth) (into sth) → INTERPRET

tráfego sm traffic

traficante smf: um ~ **de armas/drogas** an arms/drug dealer

traficar vt, vi deal (in sth): ~ **drogas** deal in drugs

tráfico sm traffic ► ~ **de drogas** drug trafficking

tragada sf (cigarro) drag: **dar uma** ~ **num cigarro** take a drag on a cigarette

tragar vt **1** (bebida) swallow **2** (fumaça) inhale **3** (tolerar) bear, tolerate (fml)

tragédia sf tragedy [pl -ies]

trágico adj tragic

trago sm mouthful ► **tomar um** ~ have a drink

traição sf **1** betrayal: **cometer uma** ~ **contra os amigos** betray your friends **2** (contra o Estado) treason: **alta** ~ high treason

traidor/a sm-sf traitor

trailer sm **1** (veículo) trailer, caravan (GB) **2** (Cinema) preview, trailer (GB)

training sm sweatsuit, tracksuit (GB)

trair vt **1** betray: ~ **um companheiro/uma causa** betray a friend/a cause **2** (nervos) let sb down: Os nervos me traíram. My nerves let me down. ● **trair-se** vp give yourself away

trajar vt wear: ~ **terno e gravata** wear a suit and tie

traje sm **1** (de um país, de uma região) dress **2** (de carnaval) costume ► ~ **a rigor** evening dress ◊ ~ **de banho/mergulho** swimsuit/wetsuit ◊ ~ **espacial** spacesuit

trajeto sm route: o ~ **do ônibus** the bus route

trajetória sf trajectory [pl -ies]

trama sf (intriga) plot

tramar vt plot: **estar tramando algo** be up to something

trâmite sm procedure: **seguir os** ~**s normais** follow the normal procedure

trampolim sm **1** (ginasta) trampoline **2** (Natação) diving board

tranca sf **1** (porta) bolt **2** (carro) lock

trança sf braid, plait (GB)

trancar vt lock sb/sth (up): ~ **o carro** lock the car

tranquilidade sf **1** calm: um **ambiente de** ~ an atmosphere of calm ◊ a ~ **do campo** the peace and quiet of the countryside **2** (espírito) peace of mind

tranqüilizante sm tranquilizer
tranqüilizar vt **1** calm sb down **2** (aliviar) reassure: *As notícias tranqüilizaram-no.* The news reassured him. • **tranqüilizar-se** vp calm down
tranqüilo adj **1** calm **2** (lugar) peaceful
transa sf **1** (acordo) deal **2** (caso amoroso) love affair
transar vi **1** (lidar) deal **2** (ter relações sexuais) have sex
transatlântico sm (ocean) liner
transbordante adj overflowing (with sth)
transbordar vi **1** (rio) burst its banks **2** (passar das bordas) overflow
transcrição sf transcription
transeunte smf passer-by [pl passers-by]
transferência sf transfer: ~ *bancária* credit transfer
transferir vt transfer
transformador sm transformer
transformar vt transform sb/ sth (into sth) • **transformar-se** vp turn into sb/sth: *A rã transformou-se num príncipe.* The frog turned into a prince.
transfusão sf transfusion: ~ *de sangue* blood transfusion
transição sf transition
transitar vi circulate
transitivo adj transitive
trânsito sm traffic ► **proibido no through traffic**
transmissão sf **1** (TV, rádio) broadcast **2** (Tec) transmission
transmitir vt **1** transmit (fml), pass sth on (to sb): ~ *uma doença* transmit a disease ◊ ~ *a notícia a alguém* pass the news on to sb **2** (TV, rádio) broadcast ► ~ **pela televisão** televise
transparecer vi **1** (verdade) come out **2** (emoção, sentimento) be apparent ► **deixar** ~ (emoção, sentimento) show
transparente adj **1** transparent **2** (roupa) see-through: *uma blusa* ~ a see-through blouse
transpiração sf perspiration
transpirar vi perspire
transplantar vt transplant
transplante sm transplant
transportador/a sm-sf carrier
transportar vt carry
transporte sm transportation, transport (GB): ~ *público/coletivo* public transportation
transtornar vt upset
transtorno sm disruption
transversal adj transverse: *eixo*

~ *transverse axis* ◊ *A Rua Pamplona é* ~ *à Avenida Paulista.* Rua Pamplona crosses Avenida Paulista.
trapaça sf swindle
trapacear vt, vi swindle
trapaceiro/a smf trapeze artist
trapézio sm **1** (circo) trapeze **2** (Geom) trapezoid, trapezium (GB)
trapo sm old rag ► **estar um** ~ be a wreck: *Mal chegou aos 50 anos e já está um* ~. He's only 50, but he's a wreck already.
traquéia sf windpipe, trachea (fml)
trás adv ► **deixar para** ~ leave sb/ sth behind **de** ~ (da traseira) back: *a porta de* ~ the back door **de** ~ **para frente** backwards: *Você está com o suéter de* ~ *para frente.* Your sweater is on backwards. **ficar para** ~: *Não fique para* ~. Don't get left behind. ◊ *ficar para* ~ *nos estudos* fall behind in your studies **para** ~ backward: *andar para* ~ walk backward ◊ *voltar para* ~ go back **por** ~ behind
traseira sf back: *a* ~ *do carro* the back of the car
traseiro adj back: *a porta traseira* the back door • sm behind, backside (coloq)
traste sm **1** (coisa) junk [U]: *uma loja cheia de* ~*s* a store full of junk **2** (pessoa) useless: *Ela é um* ~. She's really useless.
tratado sm (Pol) treaty [pl -ies]
tratamento sm treatment: *um* ~ *contra o acne* a treatment for acne
tratar vt **1** treat: *Gostamos que nos tratem bem.* We like people to treat us well. **2** (discutir, lidar) deal with sb/sth: *Trataremos destas questões amanhã.* We will deal with these matters tomorrow. ◊ *Não gosto de* ~ *com esse tipo de gente.* I don't like dealing with people like that. **3** (ter por assunto) be about sb/ sth: *O filme trata do mundo do espetáculo.* The movie is about show business. **4** (assunto, problema) sort sth out • **tratar-se** vp (cuidar-se) **1** take care of yourself **2** ~ **de** be about sb/sth
trato sm **1** treatment **2** (acordo) deal: *fazer um* ~ make a deal
trator sm tractor
trauma sm trauma
traumatismo sm ► ~ **craniano** concussion
travar vt (carro) stop • vi (roda) lock ► ~ **conhecimento com**

alguém make sb's acquaintance ~ **conversa** strike up a conversation (*with sb*)

trave *sf* (*Esporte*) crossbar

travessa *sf* **1** (*rua*) side street: *Fica numa* ~ *da Avenida Ipiranga.* It's in a side street off Avenida Ipiranga. **2** (*prato*) dish **3** (*cabelo*) slide

travessão *sm* dash

travesseiro *sm* pillow

travesso *adj* naughty

travessura *sf* mischief [*U*]: *Esse garoto só faz* ~*s.* That boy is always up to mischief.

travesti *sm* transvestite

trazer *vt* **1** bring: *Traga uma toalha.* Bring a towel (with you). **2** (*causar*) cause

trecho *sm* **1** (*caminho*) stretch: *um* ~ *perigoso* a dangerous stretch of road **2** (*texto*) passage

treco *sm* ▸ **ter um** ~ get sick, be taken ill (*GB*)

trégua *sf* **1** (*hostilidade*) truce: *romper uma* ~ break a truce **2** (*incômodo*) rest, respite (*fml*)

treinador/a *sm-sf* **1** trainer **2** (*Esporte*) coach

treinamento (*tb* **treino**) *sm* training

treinar(-se) *vt, vi, vp* train (*sb/sth*) (*as/in sth*)

trela *sf* leash, lead (*GB*) ▸ **dar** ~ **a alguém** lead sb on

treliça *sf* trellis

trem *sm* train: *apanhar/perder o* ~ catch/miss the train ◇ *estação de* ~ railroad/train station ◇ *viajar de* ~ travel by train ◇ ~ **de carga** freight train, goods train (*GB*)

tremendo *adj* **1** (*terrível*) terrible: *um* ~ *desgosto/uma dor tremenda* a terrible blow/pain **2** (*impressionante*) terrific: *um sucesso* ~ a terrific success

tremer *vi* **1** tremble: ~ *de medo* tremble with fear **2** (*edifício, móveis*) shake: *O terremoto fez* ~ *a cidade inteira.* The quake shook the whole city. ▸ ~ **como vara verde** be shaking like a leaf ▸ ~ **de frio** shiver

tremor *sm* tremor: *um* ~ *de terra* an earth tremor

trenó *sm* **1** sled, sledge (*GB*) **2** (*de cavalos, renas*) sleigh

trepadeira *sf* vine

trepar *vt, vi* climb up *sth*

três *num, sm* **1** three **2** (*data*) third

trevas *sf* darkness [*U*]

trevo *sm* (*Bot*) clover

treze *num, sm* **1** thirteen **2** (*data*) thirteenth

trezentos *num, sm* three hundred

triangular *adj* triangular

triângulo *sm* triangle: ~ *equi-látero/retângulo* equilateral/right(-angled) triangle

tribo *sf* tribe

tribuna *sf* platform

tribunal *sm* court: *levar alguém a* ~ take sb to court ◇ *comparecer perante o* ~ appear before the court ◇ *o Supremo* ~ the Supreme Court

tributação *sf* taxation

tributo *sm* **1** (*imposto*) tax **2** (*homenagem*) tribute

tricampeão/eã *sm-sf* three-time champion

triciclo *sm* tricycle, trike (*coloq*)

tricô *sm* knitting: *fazer* ~ knit

tricotar *vt, vi* knit

trigêmeos/as *sm-sf* triplets

trigo *sm* wheat

trilha *sf* (*caminho*) track ▸ ~ **sonora** soundtrack

trilho *sm* (*carril*) rail

trimestral *adj* quarterly

trimestre *sm* quarter

trincheira *sf* trench

trinco *sm* (*porta*) latch ▸ **sair dos** ~**s** (*porta*) come off its hinges

trindade *sf* trinity

trinque *sm* ▸ **nos** ~**s** (*bem vestido*) dressed up to the nines

trinta *num, sm* **1** thirty **2** (*data*) thirtieth

trio *sm* trio [*pl* ~s]

tripa *sf* **1** (*Cozinha*) tripe [*U*] **2** (*intestinos*) gut ▸ **fazer das** ~**s coração** make a great effort

triplicar *vt* treble

triplo/a *num* triple: *salto* ~ triple jump ● *sm* three times: *Nove é o* ~ *de três.* Nine is three times three. ◇ *o* ~ *do tamanho do outro* three times bigger than the other one ◇ *Ele ganha o* ~ *do meu salário.* He earns three times as much as me.

tripulação *sf* crew

tripulante *smf* crew member

tripular *vt* (*avião, barco*) man

triste *adj* **1** sad (*about sth*): *sentir-se* ~ feel sad **2** (*deprimente, deprimido*) gloomy: *um quarto* ~ a gloomy room

tristeza *sf* **1** sadness **2** (*melancolia*) gloom

triturar *vt* (*alimentos*) grind

triunfal *adj* **1** (*entrada*) triumphal **2** (*regresso*) triumphant

triunfante adj (gesto, expressão) triumphant

triunfar vi 1 (ganhar) win: ~ a qualquer preço win at any price 2 ~ **contra** triumph over sb/sth

triunfo sm 1 (Pol, Mil) victory [pl -ies] 2 (feito pessoal, proeza) triumph: um ~ da engenharia a triumph of engineering

trivial adj trivial

trivialidade sf triviality [pl -ies]

triz sm ▸ **por um** ~: Apanhei o trem por um ~. I almost missed the train. ◇ **escapar por um** ~ have a narrow escape

troca sf exchange: uma ~ de impressões an exchange of views ▸ **em ~ (de)** in return for (doing) sth: não receber nada em ~ get nothing in return ◇ **em ~ de você me ajudar** in return for you helping me

troça sf mockery: um tom de ~ a mocking tone ▸ **fazer** ~ make fun of sb/sth

trocadilho sm pun

trocado sm loose change

trocador/a sm-sf (ônibus) conductor

trocar vt 1 (dinheiro) change sth (into sth): ~ reais por dólares change reals into dollars 2 (permutar) exchange: ~ prisioneiros exchange prisoners ◇ Se não ficar bem, você pode ~. You can exchange it if it doesn't fit. 3 (veículo) trade sth in (for sth) 4 (confundir) mix sth up: Ele não presta atenção e troca tudo. He doesn't pay attention and mixes everything up. 5 ~ **de** change: ~ de emprego/trem/sapatos change jobs/trains/your shoes ● **trocar-se** vp get changed ▸ ~ **tiros** exchange gunfire

troco sm 1 change: Deram-me o ~ errado. They gave me the wrong change. ◇ **Tem ~ para 50 reais?** Do you have change for 50 reais? ◇ troco (dinheiro trocado) loose change ▸ **dar o** ~ (a alguém) (responder) reply in kind

troço sm ▸ **ter um** ~ be (very) upset: Quase tive um ~ quando recebi as notas. I was really upset when I got my results.

troféu sm trophy [pl -ies]

tromba sf (Zool) 1 (elefante) trunk 2 (inseto) proboscis 3 (focinho) snout ▸ **ficar/estar de** ~ be in/get into a bad mood

trombada sf crash: dar/levar uma ~ have a crash

trombadinha sf child thief

trombone sm trombone

trombose sf thrombosis

trompete sm trumpet

tronco sm trunk

trono sm throne: subir ao ~ come to the throne ◇ o herdeiro do ~ the heir to the throne

tropa sf troop: as ~s the troops

tropeção sm stumble ▸ **dar um** ~ trip

tropeçar vt, vi 1 (cair) trip (over sth) 2 (problemas) come up against sth: ~ em um problema come up against a problem

tropical adj tropical

trópico sm tropic

trotar vi trot

trote sm trot: ir a ~ go at a trot

trouxa sf (roupa) bundle ● smf (pessoa) sucker

trovão sm thunder [U]: um ~ a clap of thunder ◇ raios e trovões thunder and lightning

trovejar v imp thunder

trovoada sf thunder

trunfo sm 1 (jogo de cartas) trump 2 (vantagem) asset: A experiência é o teu ~. Experience is your greatest asset.

truque sm trick

truta sf trout [pl trout]

tu pron pess you

tubarão sm shark

tuberculose sf tuberculosis (abrev TB)

tubo sm 1 (cano) pipe 2 (recipiente) tube: um ~ de pasta de dentes a tube of toothpaste ▸ ~ **de ensaio** test tube

tudo pron 1 all: É ~ por hoje. That's all for today. ◇ no fim de ~ after all 2 (todas as coisas) everything: ~ o que eu te disse era verdade. Everything I told you was true. 3 (qualquer coisa) anything: O meu cão come de ~. My dog eats anything. ▸ **dar/fazer** ~ **por algo** give/do your all for sth ~ **bem/bom?** how are things?

tufão sm typhoon

tule sm net

tulipa sf tulip

tumba sf 1 grave 2 (mausoléu) tomb

tumor sm tumor: ~ benigno/cerebral benign/brain tumor

túmulo sm grave

tumulto sm 1 (algazarra) hubbub 2 (movimento) bustle 3 (motim) rioting [U]

túnel sm tunnel: passar por um ~ go through a tunnel

turbante sm turban

turbilhão *sm* whirlwind

turbulência *sf* turbulence

turismo *sm* tourism ▶ **fazer ~ 1** (*por país*) travel: *fazer ~ pela África* travel around Africa **2** (*por cidade*) go sightseeing

turista *smf* tourist

turma *sf* class

turnê *sf* tour ▶ **estar em/fazer (uma)** ~ be/go on tour

turno *sm* **1** (*trabalho*) shift: *~ do dia/da noite* day/night shift ◇ *trabalhar em ~* do shift work **2** (*vez*) turn ▶ **em ~s** in turns: *A limpeza é feita em ~s.* We take turns cleaning.

turquesa *adj, sf* turquoise

turra *sf* ▶ **às ~s**: *Eles andam sempre às ~s.* They're always arguing.

turvar *vt* **1** (*líquido*) make sth cloudy **2** (*relações, assunto*) cloud • **turvar-se** *vp* **1** (*líquido*) become cloudy **2** (*relações, assunto*) become confused

turvo *adj* **1** (*líquido*) cloudy **2** (*relações*) troubled **3** (*assunto*) murky

tutor/a *sm-sf* (*Jur*) guardian

U u

ufa *interj* phew: *Ufa, que calor!* Phew, it's hot!

ufo *sm* UFO [*pl* ~s]

uh *interj* (*nojo*) ugh

uísque *sm* whiskey, whisky (GB)

uivar *vi* howl

uivo *sm* howl

úlcera *sf* ulcer

ultimamente *adv* recently

ultimato *sm* ultimatum

último/a *adj* **1** last: *em ~ caso/ recurso* as a last resort ◇ *estes ~s dias* the last few days ◇ *pela última vez* for the last time **2** (*mais recente*) latest: *andar na última moda* be fashionably dressed **3** (*mais alto*) top: *no ~ andar* on the top floor **4** (*mais baixo*) bottom: *estar em ~ lugar na liga* be bottom of the league • *sm-sf* **1** last (one): *Fomos os ~s a chegar.* We were the last (ones) to arrive. **2** (*mencionado em último lugar*) latter ▶ **à/na última hora** at the last moment **a última gota** the last straw **em última análise** at the end of the day **por ~** finally

ultrapassado *adj* outdated

ultrapassar *vt* **1** (*quantidade,* *limite, medida*) exceed: *~ os 170 km por hora* exceed 170 km an hour **2** (*veículo, pessoa*) pass, overtake (GB): *O carro me ultrapassou na curva.* The car passed me on the bend.

ultravioleta *adj* ultraviolet

um, uma¹ *art indef* **1** a, an NOTA Usa-se an antes de vogal ou som vocálico: *uma árvore* a tree ◇ *um braço* an arm ◇ *uma hora* an hour **2** (*uns*) some: *Preciso de uns sapatos novos.* I need some new shoes. ◇ *Compre umas bananas.* Get some bananas. ◇ *Você tem uns olhos muito bonitos.* You have beautiful eyes. **3** (*uso enfático*): *Está fazendo um calor!* It's so hot! ◇ *Estou com uma fome!* I'm starving! ◇ *Tive umas férias e tanto!* What a vacation I had!

um, uma² *num* one: *Eu disse um quilo e não dois.* I said one kilo, not two. ◇ *à uma (hora)* at one (o'clock) • *pron* **1** one: *Como ele não tinha gravata, eu lhe emprestei uma.* He didn't have a tie, so I lent him one. **2** (*uns*): *Uns gostam, outros não.* Some (people) like it, some don't. ▶ **um ao outro** each other, one another: *Ajudaram-se uns aos outros.* They helped each other. **um a um** one by one

umbigo *sm* navel

umedecer *vt* moisten • *vi* get wet

umidade *sf* **1** damp: *Esta parede tem ~.* This wall is damp. **2** (*atmosfera*) humidity

úmido *adj* **1** damp: *uma casa úmida/um pano* ~ a damp house/cloth **2** (*ar, calor*) humid: *um país* ~ a humid country → MOIST

unânime *adj* unanimous

unha *sf* **1** (*mão*) (finger)nail: *roer as ~s* bite your nails **2** (*pé*) toenail **3** (*garra*) claw ▶ **ser ~ e carne** be inseparable

união *sf* **1** union: *a ~ monetária* monetary union **2** (*unidade*) unity: *A ~ é a nossa melhor arma.* Unity is our best weapon. **3** (*ato*) joining (together): *a ~ das duas partes* the joining together of the two parts

único/a *adj* **1** (*um só*) only: *a única exceção* the only exception **2** (*sem paralelo*) unique: *uma peça única* a unique piece • *sm-sf* only one: *Ela é a única que* *sabe nadar.* She's the only one who can swim.

unidade *sf* **1** unit: ~ *de medida* unit of measurement **2** (*união*) unity: *falta de* ~ lack of unity ▶ ~ **de Terapia Intensiva** intensive care (unit)

unido *adj* close: *Eles são muito* ~*s.* They're very close.

unificar *vt* unify

uniforme *adj* **1** uniform: *de tamanho* ~ of uniform size **2** (*superfície*) even ● *sm* uniform ▶ **com/de** ~: *alunos com* ~ children in school uniform ◊ *soldados de* ~ uniformed soldiers

unir *vt* **1** (*interesses, pessoas*) unite: *os objetivos que nos unem* the aims that unite us **2** (*peças, objetos*) join **3** (*estrada, ferrovia*) link ● **unir-se** *vp* join: ~ *ao grupo* join the group

universal *adj* **1** universal **2** *a história/literatura* ~ world history/literature

universidade *sf* university [*pl* -ies]: *entrar para a* ~ go to college/university (*GB*)

universitário/a *adj* university ● *sm-sf* (*estudante*) college/university student

universo *sm* universe

untar *vt* (*com manteiga, óleo, etc.*) grease

urânio *sm* uranium

Urano *sm* Uranus

urbanização *sf* housing development

urbano *adj* urban

urgência *sf* emergency [*pl* -ies]: *em caso de* ~ in case of emergency

urgente *adj* **1** urgent: *um pedido/trabalho* ~ an urgent order/job **2** (*correio*) express

urina *sf* urine

urinar *vi* urinate ● **urinar-se** *vp* wet yourself

urna *sf* **1** (*cinzas*) urn **2** (*Pol*) ballot box

urso/a *sm-sf* bear ▶ ~ **de pelúcia** teddy bear

urso-branco *sm* polar bear

urtiga *sf* nettle

urubu *sm* vulture

Uruguai *sm* Uruguay

uruguaio/a *adj*, *sm-sf* Uruguayan

urze *sf* heather

usado *adj* **1** (*de segunda mão*) second-hand: *roupa usada* second-hand clothes **2** (*gasto*) worn out: *sapatos* ~*s* worn-out shoes

usar *vt* **1** (*utilizar*) use **2** (*óculos,*

roupa, penteado) wear: ~ *óculos/perfume* wear glasses/perfume

usina *sf* factory [*pl* -ies] ▶ ~ **hidrelétrica/termonuclear** hydroelectric/nuclear power plant

uso *sm* use: *instruções de* ~ instructions for use ▶ **de** ~ **diário/everyday** ▶ *botas de* ~ *diário* everyday boots

usuário/a *sm-sf* user

utensílio *sm* **1** (*ferramenta*) tool **2** (*cozinha*) utensil ▶ ~*s* **de cozinha** kitchenware [*U*]

útero *sm* womb

útil *adj* useful

utilidade *sf* usefulness ▶ **ter muita** ~ be very useful

utilitário *sm* (*veículo*) Jeep™

utilizar *vt* use

uva *sf* grape

V v

vaca *sf* **1** (*animal*) cow **2** (*carne*) beef → CARNE

vacina *sf* vaccine: *a* ~ *contra a pólio* the polio vaccine

vacinar *vt* vaccinate *sb/sth* (*against sth*)

vácuo *sm* vacuum

vadio *adj* (*pessoa*) idle

vaga *sf* **1** (*emprego*) vacancy [*pl* -ies]: ~*s de emprego* job vacancies **2** (*num curso*) place: *Não há mais* ~. There are no places left.

vagabundo/a *adj* (*de má qualidade*) shoddy ● *sm-sf* bum

vaga-lume *sm* (*pirilampo*) glowworm

vagão *sm* car: ~ *de carga/passageiros* freight/passenger car

vagão-leito *sm* sleeping car

vagão-restaurante *sm* dining car

vagar¹ *sm* ▶ **com mais** ~ at a more leisurely pace **com** ~ at your leisure

vagar² *vi* wander: ~ *pelas ruas da cidade* wander around the city streets

vagaroso *adj* slow

vagem *sf* string bean, French bean (*GB*)

vagina *sf* vagina

vago *adj* vague

vaia *sf* booing

vaiar *vt* boo

vaidade *sf* vanity [*pl* -ies]

vaidoso *adj* vain

vaivém sm swinging

vala sf ditch ▶ ~ **comum** common grave

vale¹ sm (Geog) valley

vale² sm 1 (cupom) coupon, voucher (GB) 2 (recibo) receipt ▶ ~ **postal** money order, postal order (GB)

valente adj brave

valentia sf courage

valer vt 1 (custar) cost 2 (ter um valor) be worth: Uma libra vale mais ou menos 1,50 dólar. A pound is worth about $1·50. ● vi 1 (ser permitido) be allowed: Não vale colar. No cheating. 2 (documento) be valid: Este passaporte não vale mais. This passport is no longer valid. ● **valer-se** vp use: ~ de todos os meios para fazer algo use every means possible to do sth ▶ **isso não vale** (não é justo) that's not fair **não ~ para nada** be useless **para ~** (a sério) for real **vale mais...**: Vale mais dizer a verdade. It's better to tell the truth.

valete sm (baralho) jack → BARALHO

validade sf validity

válido adj valid

valioso adj valuable

valor sm 1 value: ter um grande ~ sentimental have great sentimental value ◇ um objeto de ~ a valuable object 2 (preço) price: As jóias alcançaram um ~ alto. The jewels fetched a high price. 3 (pessoa) worth: mostrar o seu ~ show your worth ▶ **dar ~** a value sth **sem ~** worthless

valsa sf waltz

válvula sf valve

vampiro sm vampire

vandalismo sm vandalism

vândalo/a sm-sf vandal

vanguarda sf 1 (Mil) vanguard 2 (Arte) avant-garde: teatro de ~ avant-garde theater

vantagem sf advantage: Morar aqui tem muitas ~s. Living here has many advantages. ◇ levar ~ sobre alguém have an advantage over sb ◇ tirar ~ de algo take advantage of sth

vão adj vain: uma tentativa vã a vain attempt ● sm gap ▶ **em ~** in vain **~ da escada** stairwell **~ da porta** doorway

vapor sm 1 steam: um ferro a ~ a steam iron 2 (Quím) vapor: ~es tóxicos toxic vapors ▶ **a todo o ~** flat out

vaquinha sf (dinheiro em comum) pot, kitty [pl -ies] (GB)

vara sf 1 (pau) stick 2 (Esporte) pole ▶ ~ **de pescar** fishing rod

varal sm (corda) clothesline

varanda sf balcony [pl -ies]: ir para a ~ go out onto the balcony

varar vt (perfurar) pierce ▶ ~ **a noite** stay up all night

varejo sm retail trade: vender a ~ retail

vareta sf rod

variação sf variation: ligeiras variações de pressão slight variations in pressure

variar vt, vi 1 (tornar variado, ser variado) vary: Os preços variam de acordo com a loja. Prices vary depending on the shop. 2 (mudar) change: Não varia no plural. It doesn't change in the plural. ▶ **para ~** for a change

variável adj changeable ● sf variable

variedade sf variety [pl -ies]

varinha sf ▶ ~ **de condão** magic wand

varíola sf smallpox

vários adj, pron several: em várias ocasiões on several occasions

variz sf varicose vein

varredor/a sm-sf sweeper: ~ de rua street sweeper

varrer vt, vi sweep

vascular vt go through sth: ~ as gavetas go through the drawers

vasilha sf vessel

vaso sm 1 (plantas) flowerpot 2 (Anat, Bot) vessel: ~s capilares/sanguíneos capillary/blood vessels ▶ ~ **sanitário** toilet bowl

vassoura sf 1 broom 2 (de bruxa) broomstick

vasto adj vast

vazamento sm (gás, água) leak

vazio adj empty ● sm void

veado sm 1 (animal) deer [pl deer] NOTA Deer é o substantivo genérico. Stag (ou buck) é o macho e doe, a fêmea. O filhote é fawn. 2 (carne) venison

vedação sf (tapume) fence

vedar vt 1 (com cerca) fence off 2 (recipiente) seal 3 (acesso) block

vedete sf star: uma ~ de cinema a movie star

vegetação sf vegetation

vegetal adj vegetable: óleo ~ vegetable oil ● sm vegetable

vegetar vi 1 (Bot) grow 2 (pessoa) be a vegetable

vegetariano/a *adj, sm-sf* vegetarian: *ser* ~ be a vegetarian

veia *sf* vein

veículo *sm* vehicle ▶ ~ **de comunicação** medium [*pl* media]

veio *sm* **1** (*rocha*) vein **2** (*mina*) seam **3** (*madeira*) grain

vela¹ *sf* **1** candle: *acender/apagar uma* ~ light/put out a candle **2** (*Mec*) spark plug

vela² *sf* **1** (*barco, moinho*) sail **2** (*Esporte*) sailing: *praticar* ~ go sailing

velar *vt* **1** (*cadáver*) keep vigil (*over sb*) **2** (*doente*) sit up with *sb* **3** ~ **por** take care of *sb/sth*

veleiro *sm* sailing boat

velharia *sf* (*traste*) old thing

velhice *sf* old age

velho/a *adj* old: *estar/ficar* ~ look/get old ◊ *Sou mais* ~ *do que o meu irmão.* I'm older than my brother. ◊ *O mais* ~ *da turma* the oldest (one) in the class ◊ *o mais* ~ *dos dois irmãos* the older of the two brothers ● *sm-sf* **1** old man/woman [*pl* men/women] **2** (**velhos**) old people

velhote *sm-sf* old man/woman [*pl* men/women]

velocidade *sf* (*rapidez*) speed: *trens de alta* ~ high-speed trains ▶ **a toda** ~ at top speed ~ **máxima** (*nas estradas*) speed limit

velódromo *sm* velodrome, cycle track [*mais coloq*]

veloz *adj* fast → FAST

veludo *sm* velvet ▶ ~ **cotelê** corduroy

vencedor/a *adj* **1** winning: *a equipe vencedora* the winning team **2** (*Mil*) victorious ● *sm-sf* **1** winner: *o* ~ *da prova* the winner of the competition **2** (*Mil*) victor

vencer *vt* **1** (*Esporte*) beat **2** (*Mil*) defeat **3** (*superar*) overcome: *O sono me venceu.* I was overcome with sleep. ● *vi* **1** win **2** (*prazo*) expire **3** (*pagamento*) be due: *O pagamento do empréstimo vence hoje.* Repayment of the loan is due today.

vencido/a *adj* beaten ● *sm-sf* loser ▶ **dar-se por** ~ give in

vencimento *sm* **1** (*data de pagamento*) due date: *Quando é o* ~ *do aluguel?* When's the rent due? **2** (*fim de prazo*) expiration date, expiry date (*GB*) **3** (*salário*) salary [*pl* -ies] ▶ **não dar** ~ **a**: *Não dão* ~ *às encomendas.* They can't keep up with all the orders.

venda *sf* sale: *à* ~ for sale ▶ **pôr à** ~: *pôr a casa à* ~ put the house on the market ~ **por correspondência** mail order

vendar *vt* blindfold

vendaval *sm* gale

vendedor/a *sm-sf* **1** seller **2** (*caixeiro-viajante*) salesman/woman [*pl* -men/-women] **3** (*em loja*) salesclerk, shop assistant (*GB*)

vender *vt* sell: *Vão* ~ *o apartamento de cima.* The upstairs apartment is for sale. ▶ ~ **aos montes** sell like hotcakes ~ **gato por lebre** take *sb* in **vende-se** for sale

veneno *sm* poison

venenoso *adj* poisonous

veneta *sf* ▶ **dar na** ~ take it into your head to do *sth*: *Deu-me na* ~ *ir fazer compras.* I took it into my head to go shopping. ◊ *Ele só faz o que lhe dá na* ~. He only does what he wants to.

veneziana *sf* shutter

Venezuela *sf* Venezuela

venezuelano/a *adj, sm-sf* Venezuelan

ventania *sf* gale

ventar *vi*: *Está ventando (demais).* It's (much too) windy.

ventilação *sf* ventilation

ventilador *sm* ventilator

vento *sm* wind

ventre *sm* **1** (*abdome*) stomach **2** (*útero*) womb

ventríloquo/a *sm-sf* ventriloquist

Vênus *sm* Venus

ver¹ *sm* opinion: *a meu* ~ in my opinion

ver² *vt* **1** see: *Há muito tempo que não a vejo.* I haven't seen her for a long time. ◊ *Não vejo por quê.* I don't see why. ◊ *Você está vendo aquela casa?* Can you see that house over there? **2** (*televisão*) watch **3** (*examinar*) look at *sth*: *Preciso* ~ *com mais calma.* I need more time to look at it. ● *vi* see: *Espere, vou* ~. Wait — I'll go and see. ◊ *Vamos* ~. Let's see. ● **ver-se** *vp* (*encontrar-se*) be: *Eu nunca tinha me visto em tal situação.* I'd never been in a situation like that. ▶ **dar para** ~ (*prever*): *Dava mesmo para* ~ *que isso iria acontecer.* I could see it coming **para você** ~ **so there** **vai** ~ **que...** maybe: *Vai* ~ *que eles se perderam.* Maybe they were lost. **veja só...**: *Veja só, casar com aquele imprestável!* Imagine marrying that good-for-nothing! NOTA

Para outras expressões com **ver**, ver o substantivo, adjetivo, etc., p. ex. **ver para crer** en CRER.

veranista *smf* vacationer, holiday-maker (GB)

verão *sm* summer: *no ~* in (the) summer ◊ *as férias de ~* the summer vacation

verbal *adj* verbal

verbete *sm* entry [pl -ies]

verbo *sm* verb

verdade *sf* truth: *Diga a ~.* Tell the truth. ▶ **não é ~?**: *Esta marca é melhor, não é ~?* This brand's better, isn't it? ◊ *Você não gosta de leite, não é ~?* You don't like milk, do you? **ser ~** be true **verdade?** really?

verdadeiro *adj* true: *a verdadeira história* the true story

verde *adj* **1** (cor) green **2** (fruta) unripe: *Ainda estão ~s.* They're not ripe yet. ● **sm** green

verdura *sf* vegetables [pl]

verdureiro *sm* greengrocer's

vereador/a *sm-sf* (town) councillor

veredicto *sm* verdict

vergonha *sf* **1** (timidez) shyness **2** (embaraço) embarrassment: *Que ~!* How embarrassing! **3** (sentimento de culpa, pudor) shame: *não ter ~ na cara* have no shame ◊ *ter ~ de confessar algo* be ashamed to admit sth ▶ **ter/ficar com ~ 1** (ser tímido) be shy **2** (sentir embaraço) be embarrassed: *Tenho ~ de perguntar a ele.* I'm too embarrassed to ask him. **ter ~ de alguém/algo** be ashamed of sb/sth

vergonhoso *adj* disgraceful

verídico *adj* true

verificar *vt* check

verme *sm* worm

vermelho *adj, sm* red ▶ **no ~** in the red **ficar ~ (como um tomate)** go (as) red (as a beet)

verniz *sm* **1** (para madeira) varnish **2** (couro) patent leather

verruga *sf* wart

versão *sf* version ▶ **em ~ original** (filme) with subtitles

verso¹ *sm* back: *no ~ do cartão* on the back of the card

verso² *sm* **1** (linha de poema) line **2** (poema) verse **3** (gênero literário) poetry

vértebra *sf* vertebra [pl -brae]

vertebrado *adj, sm* vertebrate

vertical *adj* **1** vertical: *uma linha ~* a vertical line **2** (posição) upright: *em posição ~* in an upright position

vértice *sm* vertex [pl -tices]

vertigem *sf* vertigo: *sentir/ter ~* have vertigo ▶ **dar ~** make sb dizzy

vesgo *adj* cross-eyed

vesícula *sf* ▶ **~ (biliar)** gall bladder

vespa *sf* **1** (inseto) wasp **2** (Vespa®) scooter

véspera *sf* day before (sth): *na ~ (do exame)* the day before (the exam) NOTA Usa-se **eve** para a véspera de festa religiosa ou de acontecimento importante: *a ~ de Natal* Christmas Eve ◊ *na ~ das eleições* on the eve of the election ▶ **em/nas ~s de** just before sth

vestiário *sm* **1** (teatro, etc.) coat check, cloakroom (GB) **2** (Esporte) locker room, changing room (GB)

vestibular *sm* university entrance examination

vestíbulo *sm* **1** (entrada) hall **2** (teatro, cinema, hotel) foyer

vestido *sm* dress: *~ de noiva* wedding dress ▶ **~ de noite** evening gown

vestígio *sm* trace

vestir *vt* **1** dress: *Vesti as crianças.* I got the children dressed. **2** (levar) wear: *~ um terno* wear a suit **3** (tamanho) take: *~ calças tamanho quarenta* take size forty pants ● **vestir(-se)** *vi, vp ~ (de)* dress (in sth): *~ bem/de branco* dress well/in white ● **vestir-se** *vp* get dressed

vestuário *sm* clothing

veterano/a *adj, sm-sf* veteran

veterinária *sf* veterinary science

veterinário/a *sm-sf* veterinarian, vet (GB)

veto *sm* veto [pl -es]

véu *sm* veil

vexame *sm* disgrace ▶ **dar ~** make a fool of yourself

vez *sf* **1** time: *duas/três ~es por ano* twice/three times a year ◊ *Ganho três ~es mais do que ele.* I earn three times as much as he does. ◊ *3 ~es 3 são 9.* 3 times 3 is 9. **2** (turno) turn ▶ **às vezes** sometimes **~ da ~ (individualmente)** in turns **de uma (só) ~** in one go **de uma ~ (por todas)** once and for all: *Responda de uma ~!* Hurry up and answer! **para o/for good:** *Ele foi embora de ~.* He left for good. **de ~ em quando** from time to time **em ~ de** instead of sb/ (doing) sth **era uma vez...** once upon a time there was...

muitas/poucas vezes often/sel-
dom **outra** → again **por sua** →
in turn **uma** → once **uma** → na
vida, **outra na morte** once in a
blue moon **um de cada** → one
at a time

via *sf* **1** (*estrada*) road **2** (*vias*)
(*Med*) tract [*sing*]: ~s respirató-
rias respiratory tract ► (*por*) ~
aérea (*correios*) (by) airmail
por ~ das dúvidas just in case
~ férrea railroad, railway
(*GB*) **Via Láctea** Milky Way ► **satélite**: *uma ligação ~ satélite* a satellite link

viagem *sf* journey, trip, travel
NOTA Não confundir as pala-
vras **travel**, **journey**, **trip**, **voyage** e **tour**. **Travel** é o incontável e refere-se à atividade de
viajar em geral: *As suas atividades favoritas são a leitura e
viagens.* Her main interests are
reading and travel. **Journey** e
trip referem-se a uma viagem
específica. **Journey** apenas
denota o deslocamento de um
lugar a outro: *A ~ foi cansativa.*
The journey was exhausting,
enquanto **trip** denota também a
estadia: *uma ~ de negócios* a
business trip. **Voyage** é uma
viagem longa por mar e **tour** é
uma viagem organizada, com
paradas em vários lugares: *uma
~ pela Terra Santa* a tour
around the Holy Land. ► **boa ~**
have a good trip **estar/partir
de ~** be/go away **~ de intercâmbio** exchange visit

viajante *sf* **1** (*turista*) traveler
2 (*passageiro*) passenger

viajar *vi* travel: *~ de avião/carro*
travel by plane/car

viatura *sf* vehicle

viável *adj* feasible

víbora *sf* viper

vibrar *vi* vibrate ► *~ de alegria* be
thrilled

vice-campeão/ã *sm-sf* runner-
up [*pl* -ers-up]

vice-presidente/a *sm-sf* vice-
president

vice-versa *adv* vice versa

viciado/a *adj* addicted (*to sth*) ●
sm-sf addict

viciar-se *vp* get addicted (*to sth*)

vício *sm* **1** vice: *Não tenho ~s.* I
don't have any vices. **2** (*hábito*)
addiction: *O jogo se transfor-
mou num ~* Gambling became
an addiction. ► **adquirir/ter o ~
de algo** get/be addicted to sth

vicioso *adj* vicious

vida *sf* **1** life [*pl* lives]: *Como é
que vai a ~?* How's life? ◇ *a ~*

noturna do Rio Rio night life ◇
para toda a ~ for life **2** (*sustento*) living: *ganhar a ~* make a
living ► **com ~** alive **isto é que
é ~** this is the life **sem ~** life-
less **uma ~ de cão** a dog's life

videira *sf* vine

vidente *smf* clairvoyant

vídeo *sm* **1** video [*pl* ~s] **2** (*aparelho*) VCR, video (*GB*) ► **filmar/
gravar em ~** videotape

videocassete *sm* videotape

videoclipe *sm* video [*pl* ~s]

videoclube *sm* video store

vidraça *sf* (window) pane

vidraceiro/a *sm-sf* glazier

vidrado *adj* nuts (*about sb/sth*)

vidrar *vt* (*cerâmica*) glaze

vidro *sm* **1** glass: *uma garrafa de
~* a glass bottle **2** (*carro*) window: *Baixe/suba o ~.* Open/
close the window. **3** (*vidraça*)
(window)pane

viga *sf* **1** (*madeira*, *concreto*)
beam **2** (*metal*) girder

vigarice *sf* rip-off

vigarista *smf* con man

vigente *adj* current ► **ser ~** be in
force

vigia *sf* **1** (*vigilância*) watch:
ficar de ~ keep watch **2** (*barco*)
porthole ● *smf* (*pessoa*) guard

vigiar *vt* **1** (*prestar atenção*,
tomar conta) keep an eye on *sb/
sth* **2** (*guardar*) guard: *~ a fron-
teira/os presos* guard the bor-
der/prisoners

vigilância *sf* surveillance

vigor *sm* vigor ► **entrar em ~**
come into force

vigorar *vi* (*lei*) be in force

vila *sf* **1** (*povoado*) small town **2**
(*casa*) villa **3** (*conjunto de
casas*) housing development
► *~* **olímpica** Olympic village

vime *sm* wicker

vinagre *sm* vinegar

vinagrete *adj*, *sm* vinaigrette

vinco *sm* crease

vínculo *sm* link

vingança *sf* revenge

vingar *vt* avenge ● **vingar-se** *vp*
take revenge (*on sb*) (*for sth*)

vinha *sf* vineyard

vinho *sm* wine: *um copo de ~* a
glass of wine ◇ *~ branco/tinto/
de mesa* white/red/table wine

vinícola *adj* (*indústria* ~)
wine industry ◇ *região ~* wine-
growing region

vinicultor/a *sm-sf* wine-grower

vinte *num*, *sm* **1** twenty **2** (*data*)
twentieth: *o século ~* the twen-
tieth century

viola sf 1 (acústica) guitar 2 (tipo de violino) viola

violação sf 1 (estupro) rape 2 (leis, profanação) violation

violador/a sm-sf rapist

violar vt 1 (estuprar) rape 2 (transgredir) break 3 (profanar) violate

violência sf violence

violento adj violent

violeta adj, sm-sf violet

violinista sm-sf violinist

violino sm violin

violoncelo sm cello [pl ~s]

vir vt, vi 1 come: Venha aqui! Come here! 2 (voltar) be back: Eu já venho. I'll be back soon. 3 (chegar) arrive ● v aux ~ fazendo algo have been doing sth: Há anos que venho te dizendo isto. I've been telling you this for years. ▶ que vem next: terça que vem next Tuesday NOTA Para outras expressões com **vir**, ver o substantivo, adjetivo, etc., p. ex. **vir à tona** em TONA.

vira-casaca smf traitor

virada sf por uma ~ para a esquerda turn left

vira-lata adj, sm (cão) mongrel

virar vt 1 turn: ~ a cabeça turn your head ◊ Ele me virou as costas. He turned his back on me. 2 (derrubar) knock sth over ● vi 1 ~ a (dobrar) turn: ~ à direita/esquerda turn right/left 2 (carro) turn off 3 (tempo) change ● **virar-se** vp 1 turn (towards sb/sth): Ela se virou e olhou para mim. She turned around and looked at me. ◊ ~ para alguém turn towards sb 2 (sair de dificuldades) manage (to do sth): Você vai ter que se ~ de alguma forma. You'll have to manage somehow. ▶ ~ a cara look the other way ▶ ~ a casaca be a traitor ▶ ~ de cabeça para baixo turn sth upside down ~ de cabeça para cima overturn

virgem adj 1 virgin: ser ~ be a virgin ◊ florestas virgens virgin forests ◊ azeite extra ~ extra virgin olive oil 2 (cassete) blank ● smf virgin: a ~ Maria the Virgin Mary ● **Virgem** sm (Astrol) Virgo [pl ~s]

virgindade sf virginity

vírgula sf 1 (pontuação) comma 2 (Mat) point: dez ~ cinco (10,5) ten point five (10.5)

viril adj manly, virile (fml)

virilha sf groin

virilidade sf manliness

virtual adj virtual: a realidade ~ virtual reality

virtualmente adv virtually

virtude sf virtue

virtuoso adj (honesto) virtuous ● sm virtuoso [pl ~s]

virus sm virus

visão sf 1 (vista) (eye)sight: perder a ~ de um olho lose the sight of one eye 2 (ponto de vista) view 3 (alucinação) vision 4 (instinto): um político com ~ a far-sighted politician

visar vt, vi aim (at sb/sth): ~ fazer algo aim to do sth

viscoso adj viscous

viseira sf visor

visibilidade sf visibility: pouca ~ poor visibility

visita sf 1 visit: horário de ~ (s) visiting hours 2 (visitante) visitor ▶ **fazer uma** ~ pay sb a visit

visitante adj visiting: a equipe ~ the visiting team ● smf visitor

visitar vt visit

visível adj visible

visom sm mink

vista sf 1 ser operado da ~ have an eye operation ◊ As cenouras fazem bem à ~. Carrots are good for your eyesight. 2 (panorama) view: a ~ do meu quarto the view from my room ◊ com ~ para o mar overlooking the sea ▶ à ~ cash payment: pagar algo à ~ pay cash for sth ▶ até a ~ see you around/later (dar/passar) uma ~ de olhos (have) a look (at sb/sth): Uma ~ de olhos é o suficiente. Just a quick look will do. **deixar algo à** ~: Deixe-o à ~. Leave it where I can see it. **em** ~ **de** in view of sth **fazer** ~ **grossa** turn a blind eye (to sth) **ter a** ~ **cansada** be far-sighted

visto¹ sm visa: ~ de entrada/saída entry/exit visa

visto² adj ~ **pelo** ~ apparently ~ **que** since

vistoso adj eye-catching

visual adj visual

vital adj 1 (Biol) life: o ciclo ~ the life cycle 2 (decisivo) vital

vitalidade sf vitality

vitamina sf 1 vitamin 2 (bebida) (milk)shake

vitelo/a sm-sf calf [pl calves] ● **vitela** sf (carne) veal → CARNE

viticultura sf wine growing

vítima sf 1 victim: ser ~ de algo be the victim of sth 2 (mortal) casualty [pl -ies]

vitória sf 1 victory [pl -ies] 2 (Esporte) win: uma ~ fora de casa an away win

vitorioso *adj* victorious ► sair ~ triumph

vitrina *sf* store window

viúvo/a *adj* widowed ● *sm-sf* widower [*fem* widow]

viva *sm* cheer ● *interj*: Viva, passei! Hooray! I passed! ◊ ~ o rei! Long live the king!

viveiro *sm* **1** (*plantas*) nursery [*pl* -ies] **2** (*peixes*) fish farm **3** (*aves*) aviary [*pl* -ies]

viver *vt, vi* live: *Ele viveu quase setenta anos.* He lived for almost seventy years. ◊ *Como você vive bem!* What a nice life you have! ◊ *Viva a sua vida.* Live your own life. ◊ *Vivemos com 200 dólares por mês.* We live on 200 dollars a month. ► ~ às custas de alguém live off sb ~ rindo, brigando, etc. be always laughing, quarreling, etc.

víveres *sm* provisions

vivo *adj* **1 (a)** (+ *substantivo*) living: *seres ~s/línguas vivas* living beings/languages **(b)** (*depois de ser ou estar*) alive: *Ele ainda é ~?* Is he still alive? **2** (*esperto*) smart **3** (*luz, cor, olhos*) bright **4** (*cheio de vida*) lively ► **ao ~** (*transmissão*) live ~ **ou morto** dead or alive

vizinhança *sf* **1** (*bairro*) neighborhood: *uma escola da ~* a neighborhood school **2** (*vizinhos*) residents [*pl*]

vizinho/a *adj* neighboring: *países ~s* neighboring countries ● *sm-sf* neighbor

voador *adj* flying

voar *vi* **1** fly: *~ até Roma via Lisboa* fly to Rome via Lisbon ◊ *O tempo voa.* Time flies. **2** (*com o vento*) blow away: *O chapéu dele voou pelos ares.* His hat blew away. ► **voando** (*depressa*) in a rush: *Saí voando.* I rushed off.

vocabulário *sm* vocabulary [*pl* -ies]

vocação *sf* vocation

vocal *adj* vocal

vocalista *smf* lead singer

você *pron pess* you: *~s devem ir.* You should go. ► ~ **mesmo/próprio** you yourself ~**s mesmos/próprios** you yourselves

vodca *sf* vodka

vogal *sf* (*letra*) vowel ● *smf* (*pessoa*) member

volante *sm* (*veículo*) steering wheel

voleibol *sm* volleyball

volt *sm* volt

volta *sf* **1** (*regresso*) return: *Vejo você na ~.* I'll see you when I get back. **2** (*Esporte*) lap: *dar três ~s na pista* do three laps of the track ► **dar a ~ ao mundo** go around the world **dar a ~ em algo** (*virar*) turn sth over **dar uma ~ 1** (*a pé*) go for a walk: *dar uma ~ no quarteirão* go for a walk around the block **2** (*de carro*) go for a drive **dar ~s em algo** turn sth: *dar duas ~s na chave* turn the key twice **em ~** around: *Havia muita gente em dele.* There were a lot of people around him. **estar de ~** be back **por ~ de 1** (*cerca de*) about: *Éramos por ~ de cem.* There were about a hundred of us. **2** (*no tempo*) around: *por ~ do Natal* around Christmas →AROUND ~ **e meia** every now and then

voltagem *sf* voltage

voltar *vi* **1** (*regressar*) go/come back: *Voltei para casa.* I went back home. ◊ *Volte aqui.* Come back here. ◊ *A que horas você volta?* What time will you be back? **2** ~ **a fazer algo** do sth again: *Não volte a dizer isso.* Don't say that again. ● *vt* turn: *~ a cabeça* turn your head ◊ *Ele me voltou as costas.* He turned his back on me. ● **voltar-se** *vp* turn around ► ~ **a si** come around ~ **atrás (com a palavra)** go back (on your word)

volume *sm* **1** volume: *o primeiro ~* the first volume ◊ *diminuir/aumentar o ~* turn the volume down/up **2** (*embrulho*) package, parcel (*GB*)

volumoso *adj* bulky: *É muito ~?* Does it take up much space?

voluntário/a *adj* voluntary ● *sm-sf* volunteer

volúvel *adj* changeable

vomitar *vt* throw sth up ● *vi* throw up, vomit (*mais fml*)

vômito *sm*

vontade *sf* **1** will: *não ter própria* have no will of your own ◊ *contra a minha ~* against my will **2** (*desejo*) wishes [*pl*]: *respeitar a ~ de alguém* respect sb's wishes ► **à ~ 1** (*como em sua própria casa*) be at home: *Esteja/Fique à ~.* Make yourself at home. **2** (*com liberdade*) quite happily: *Aqui as crianças podem brincar à ~.* The children can play here quite happily. **boa ~** goodwill **dar ~ de fazer algo** make sb want to do sth **de boa/má ~** willingly/reluctantly **estar com/ter ~** feel like (doing) sth: *Estou com ~ de* *comer algo.* I feel like having something to eat. ◇ *Faço porque tenho ~.* I'm doing it because I want to.

vôo *sm* flight: *o ~ Rio-São Paulo* the Rio-São Paulo flight ◇ *~s domésticos* domestic flights ▸ **~ livre** gliding

vós *pron* pess you

vosso/a *pron adj* your ● *pron subs* yours

votação *sf* vote

votar *vi* vote (*for/against sb/sth*)

voto *sm* **1** (*Pol*) vote: *~ nulo* spoiled vote **2** (*Relig*) vow **3** (*votos*) (*em carta*) wishes: *~ de felicidade* best wishes ▸ **fazer ~s** hope: *Faço ~s de que esteja bem.* I hope you're well.

vovô/ó *sm-sf* grandpa [*fem* grandma]

voz *sf* voice: *em ~ alta/baixa* in a loud/quiet voice

vulcão *sm* volcano [*pl* ~s/~es]

vulgar *adj* vulgar

vulnerável *adj* vulnerable

vulto *sm* figure: *Vi um ~ se mexendo.* I saw a figure moving.

W w

walkie-talkie *sm* walkie-talkie

walkman® *sm* Walkman®

watt *sm* watt: *uma lâmpada de 60 ~s* a 60-watt light bulb

w.c. *sm* bathroom, toilet (*GB*)

windsurfe *sm* windsurfing: *praticar ~* go windsurfing

windsurfista *smf* windsurfer

X x

xadrez *sm* **1** (*jogo*) chess **2** (*tabuleiro e peças*) chess set **3** (*prisão*) slammer **4** (*tecido*) check: *uma blusa ~* a check blouse

xale *sm* shawl

xampu *sm* shampoo [*pl* ~s]: *~ anticaspa* dandruff shampoo

xará *smf* namesake: *Somos ~s!* We have the same name!

xarope *sm* syrup: *~ para a tosse* cough syrup

xeque *sm* (*xadrez*) check

xeque-mate *sm* (*xadrez*) checkmate: *dar ~* checkmate

xereta *adj* nosy

xérox *sm* **1** (*cópia*) photocopy [*pl* -ies] **2** (*máquina*) photocopier

xícara *sf* cup: *uma ~ de café* a cup of coffee

xilofone *sm* xylophone

xixi *sm* pee ▸ **fazer ~** (have a) pee

xô *interj* shoo

xodó *sm* pet: *Ele é o ~ do professor.* He's the teacher's pet.

Z z

zangado *adj* mad (*at sb*) (*about sth*)

zangar *vt* make *sb* mad ● **zangar-se** *vp* be mad (*at sb*) (*about sth*)

zarolho *adj* **1** (*cego de um olho*) one-eyed **2** (*estrábico*) cross-eyed

zarpar *vi* set sail (*for...*): *~ para Malta* set sail for Malta

zás *interj* bang

zebra *sf* zebra

zelador/a *sm-sf* caretaker

zé-ninguém *sm* ▸ **ser um ~** be a nobody

zero *num*, *sm* **1** zero [*pl* ~s], nought (*GB*): *~ vírgula cinco* zero point five **2** (*temperaturas, grau*) zero: *abaixo de ~* below zero ◇ *Está dez graus abaixo de ~.* It's ten below. **3** (*números de telefone*) zero, O (*GB*) → Ver pág. 223. **4** (*Esporte*) **(a)** nothing: *um a ~* one to nothing **(b)** (*Tênis*) love ▸ **começar/partir do ~** start from scratch • **ser um ~ à esquerda (em) 1** (*não saber nada*) be useless (*at (doing) sth*) **2** (*não ser importante*) be a nobody

ziguezague *sm* zigzag: *andar em ~* zigzag

zinco *sm* zinc

zodíaco *sm* zodiac: *os signos do ~* the signs of the zodiac

zombar *vt* make fun of *sb/sth*

zona *sf* **1** (*área*) area: *~ industrial/residencial* industrial/residential area **2** (*Anat, Geog, Mil*) zone: *~ de fronteira* border zone ▸ **~ norte, etc.** north, etc.: *a ~ sul da cidade* the south of the city • *~s* **verdes** green spaces

zonzo *adj* dizzy

zoologia *sf* zoology

zoológico *sm* zoo [*pl* ~s]

zoom *sm* zoom lens

zumbi *adj*, *smf* zombie: *parecer um ~* go around like a zombie

zumbido *sm* **1** (*inseto, ouvidos*) buzzing [*U*] **2** (*máquina*) humming [*U*]

zumbir *vi* buzz

zunzum *sm* (*boato*) rumor

223

Expressões numéricas

Numerais

	Cardinais		Ordinais
1	one	1st	first
2	two	2nd	second
3	three	3rd	third
4	four	4th	fourth
5	five	5th	fifth
6	six	6th	sixth
7	seven	7th	seventh
8	eight	8th	eighth
9	nine	9th	ninth
10	ten	10th	tenth
11	eleven	11th	eleventh
12	twelve	12th	twelfth
13	thirteen	13th	thirteenth
14	fourteen	14th	fourteenth
15	fifteen	15th	fifteenth
16	sixteen	16th	sixteenth
17	seventeen	17th	seventeenth
18	eighteen	18th	eighteenth
19	nineteen	19th	nineteenth
20	twenty	20th	twentieth
21	twenty-one	21st	twenty-first
30	thirty	30th	thirtieth
40	forty	40th	fortieth
50	fifty	50th	fiftieth
60	sixty	60th	sixtieth
70	seventy	70th	seventieth
80	eighty	80th	eightieth
90	ninety	90th	ninetieth
100	a/one hundred	100th	hundredth
101	a/one hundred and one	101st	hundred and first
200	two hundred	200th	two hundredth
1,000	a/one thousand	1,000th	thousandth
10,000	ten thousand	10,000th	ten thousandth
1,000,000	a/one million	1,000,000th	millionth

* Em inglês se usa uma vírgula para marcar o milhar, por exemplo 25,000.

Frações e decimais

½	a half	$\frac{1}{10}$	a/one tenth
⅓	a/one third	$\frac{1}{16}$	a/one sixteenth
¼	a quarter	1½	one and a half
⅛	an/one eighth	2⅓	two and a third

0.1 (zero) (GB nought) point one
0.25 (zero) (GB nought) point two five
1.75 one point seven five

* Em inglês se usa um ponto para marcar os decimais.

Expressões matemáticas

+	plus	%	per cent
−	minus	3^2	three squared
×	times ou multiplied by	5^3	five cubed
÷	divided by	6^{10}	six to the power of ten
=	equals		

Moeda americana e inglesa

EUA	Valor da moeda/nota	Nome da moeda/nota
1¢	a cent	a penny
5¢	five cents	a nickel
10¢	ten cents	a dime
25¢	twenty-five cents	a quarter
$1	a dollar	a dollar bill/coin
$5	five dollars	a five-dollar bill
$10	ten dollars	a ten-dollar bill
$50	fifty dollars	a fifty-dollar bill
$100	a hundred dollars	a hundred-dollar bill

Reino Unido	Valor da moeda/nota	Nome da moeda/nota
1p	a penny*	a penny
2p	two pence*	a two-pence piece
5p	five pence*	a five-pence piece
10p	ten pence*	a ten-pence piece
20p	twenty pence*	a twenty-pence piece
50p	fifty pence*	a fifty-pence piece
£1	a pound	a pound (coin)
£2	two pounds	a two-pound coin
£5	five pounds	a five-pound note
£10	ten pounds	a ten-pound note
£50	fifty pounds	a fifty-pound note

* É muito comum usar a palavra *p* /piː/ no lugar de *penny* e *pence*.

Pesos e medidas

Peso

	Sistema americano	Sistema métrico
	1 ounce (oz.)	= 28.35 grams (g)
16 ounces	= 1 pound (lb.)	= 0.454 kilogram (kg)
2,000 pounds	= 1 ton (t.)	= 0.907 metric ton (m.t.)

Comprimento

	Sistema americano	Sistema métrico
	1 inch (in.)	= 25.4 millimeters (mm)
12 inches	= 1 foot (ft.)	= 30.48 centimeters (cm)
3 feet	= 1 yard (yd.)	= 0.914 meter (m)
1,760 yards	= 1 mile	= 1.609 kilometers (km)

Superfície

	Sistema americano	Sistema métrico
	1 square inch (sq in.)	= 6.452 square centimeters
144 square inches	= 1 square foot (sq ft.)	= 929.03 square centimeters
9 square feet	= 1 square yard (sq yd.)	= 0.836 square meter
4,840 square yards	= 1 acre	= 0.405 hectare
640 acres	= 1 square mile	= 2.59 square kilometers/ 259 hectares

Expressões de tempo

Datas

Como escrevê-las:
4/15/02 (*GB* 15/4/02)   April 15, 2002 (*GB* 15 April 2002)

Como dizê-las:
April fifteenth, two thousand and two
The fifteenth of April/ April the fifteenth, two thousand
   and two (*GB*)

Como dizer os anos:
1900 nineteen hundred   2002 two thousand and two
1999 nineteen ninety-nine   2050 two thousand and fifty

Horas

10:00   ten o´clock

11:10   ten after eleven
           eleven ten

5:15   (a) quarter after five
          five fifteen

11:40   twenty to twelve
           eleven forty

6:30   half past six
          six thirty

14:07   seven after two
           two o seven

3:45   quarter to four
          three forty-five

12:00   twelve o´clock
           twelve noon/midnight

*O "relógio de vinte e quatro horas" em geral é apenas para
horários de ônibus, trens e aviões. Para especificar que são 06:00
e não 18:00, pode-se dizer *six o'clock in the morning* ou *six a.m.*
18.00 seria *six o'clock in the evening* ou *six p.m.*

O telefone

637-2335	*six three seven, two three three five*
(617) 731-0293	*area code* six one seven, seven three one,*
(x321)	*zero** two nine three, extension* three two one*

* *area code* = DDD   *extension* = ramal
** Em inglês britânico, o número 0 também é pronunciado "ou":
   o two nine three

Nomes geográficos

Africa /ˈæfrɪkə/	African /ˈæfrɪkən/
Algeria /ælˈdʒɪəriə/	Algerian /ælˈdʒɪəriən/
America /əˈmerɪkə/	American /əˈmerɪkən/
Angola /æŋˈɡəʊlə/	Angolan /æŋˈɡəʊlən/
Antarctica /ænˈtɑːktɪkə/	Antarctic /ænˈtɑːktɪk/
(the) Arctic /ˈɑːktɪk/	Arctic /ˈɑːktɪk/
Argentina /ˌɑːdʒənˈtiːnə/	Argentinian /ˌɑːdʒənˈtɪniən/, Argentine /ˌɑːdʒəntaɪn/
Asia /ˈeɪʒə, ˈeɪʃə/	Asian /ˈeɪʒn, ˈeɪʃn/
(the) Atlantic /ətˈlæntɪk/	Atlantic /ətˈlæntɪk/
Australia /ɒːˈstreɪliə, ɑːˈs-/	Australian /ɒːˈstreɪliən, ɑːˈs-/
Austria /ˈɒːstriə, ˈɑːs-/	Austrian /ˈɒːstriən, ˈɑːs-/
Barbados /bɑːˈbeɪdɒs/	Barbadian /bɑːˈbeɪdiən/
Belgium /ˈbeldʒəm/	Belgian /ˈbeldʒən/
Bolivia /bəˈlɪviə/	Bolivian /bəˈlɪviən/
Brazil /brəˈzɪl/	Brazilian /brəˈzɪliən/
Cameroon /ˌkæməˈruːn/	Cameroonian /ˌkæməˈruːniən/
Canada /ˈkænədə/	Canadian /kəˈneɪdiən/
Cape Verde /ˌkeɪp ˈvɜːrd/	Cape Verdean /ˌkeɪp ˈvɜːrdiən/
Chile /ˈtʃɪli/	Chilean /ˈtʃɪliən/
China /ˈtʃaɪnə/	Chinese /ˌtʃaɪˈniːz/
Colombia /kəˈlʌmbiə/	Colombian /kəˈlʌmbiən/
Croatia /krəʊˈeɪʃə/	Croatian /krəʊˈeɪʃən/
Cuba /ˈkjuːbə/	Cuban /ˈkjuːbən/
Cyprus /ˈsaɪprəs/	Cypriot /ˈsɪpriət/
(the) Czech Republic /ˌtʃek rɪˈpʌblɪk/	Czech /tʃek/
Denmark /ˈdenmɑːk/	Danish /ˈdeɪnɪʃ/, Dane /deɪn/
(the) Dominican Republic /dəˌmɪnɪkən rɪˈpʌblɪk/	Dominican /dəˈmɪnɪkən/
Ecuador /ˈekwədɒːr/	Ecuadorian /ˌekwəˈdɔːriən/
Egypt /ˈiːdʒɪpt/	Egyptian /iˈdʒɪpʃn/
England /ˈɪŋɡlənd/	English /ˈɪŋɡlɪʃ/, Englishman, Englishwoman
Ethiopia /ˌiːθiˈəʊpiə/	Ethiopian /ˌiːθiˈəʊpiən/
Europe /ˈjʊərəp/	European /ˌjʊərəˈpiːən/
Finland /ˈfɪnlənd/	Finnish /ˈfɪnɪʃ/, Finn /fɪn/
France /frɑːns; GB frɑːns/	French /frentʃ/, Frenchman, Frenchwoman
Germany /ˈdʒɜːrməni/	German /ˈdʒɜːrmən/
Great Britain /ˌɡreɪt ˈbrɪtn/	British /ˈbrɪtɪʃ/, Briton /ˈbrɪtn/
Greece /ɡriːs/	Greek /ɡriːk/
Guinea /ˈɡɪmi/	Guinean /ˈɡɪniən/
Guyana /ɡaɪˈænə/	Guyanese /ˌɡaɪəˈniːz/
Haiti /ˈheɪti/	Haitian /ˈheɪʃn/
Holland /ˈhɒlənd/ → (the) Netherlands	
Hungary /ˈhʌŋɡəri/	Hungarian /hʌŋˈɡeəriən/
Iceland /ˈaɪslənd/	Icelandic /aɪsˈlændɪk/
India /ˈɪndiə/	Indian /ˈɪndiən/
Indonesia /ˌɪndəˈniːʒə/	Indonesian /ˌɪndəˈniːʒn/
Iran /ɪˈrɑːn/	Iranian /ɪˈreɪniən/
Iraq /ɪˈrɑːk/	Iraqi /ɪˈrɑːki/
(the Republic of) Ireland /ˈaɪələnd/	Irish /ˈaɪərɪʃ/, Irishman, Irishwoman
Israel /ˈɪzreɪl/	Israeli /ɪzˈreɪli/
Italy /ˈɪtəli/	Italian /ɪˈtæliən/
Jamaica /dʒəˈmeɪkə/	Jamaican /dʒəˈmeɪkən/
Japan /dʒəˈpæn/	Japanese /ˌdʒæpəˈniːz/

Jordan /ˈdʒɔːrdn/	Jordanian /dʒɔːrˈdeɪniən/
Kenya /ˈkenjə/	Kenyan /ˈkenjən/
Korea /kəˈriːə/ **North Korea, South Korea**	North Korean /ˌnɔːrθ kəˈriːən/ South Korean /ˌsaʊθ kəˈriːən/
Lebanon /ˈlebənən; *GB* -nən/	Lebanese /ˌlebəˈniːz/
Libya /ˈlɪbiə/	Libyan /ˈlɪbiən/
Malaysia /məˈleɪʒə/	Malaysian /məˈleɪʒn/
Mexico /ˈmeksɪkoʊ/	Mexican /ˈmeksɪkən/
Morocco /məˈrɑkoʊ/	Moroccan /məˈrɑkən/
Mozambique /ˌmoʊzæmˈbiːk/	Mozambican /ˌmoʊzæmˈbiːkən/
Nepal /nɪˈpɑl/	Nepalese /ˌnepəˈliːz/
(the) Netherlands /ˈneðərləndz/	Dutch /dʌtʃ/, Dutchman, Dutchwoman
New Zealand /ˌnuː ˈziːlənd; *GB* ˌnjuː/	New Zealander /ˌnuː ˈziːləndər; *GB* ˌnjuː/
Nigeria /naɪˈdʒɪəriə/	Nigerian /naɪˈdʒɪəriən/
Northern Ireland /ˌnɔːrðərn ˈaɪərlənd/	Northern Irish /ˌnɔːrðərn ˈaɪrɪʃ/
Norway /ˈnɔːrweɪ/	Norwegian /nɔːrˈwiːdʒən/
Oceania /ˌoʊsiˈɑːniə/	Oceanian /ˈoʊsiɑːniən/
(the) Pacific /pəˈsɪfɪk/	Pacific /pəˈsɪfɪk/
Pakistan /ˈpækɪstæn; *GB* ˌpɑːkɪˈstɑn/ ˌpɑːkɪˈstɑːn/	Pakistani /ˌpækɪˈstæni; *GB* /ˌpɑːkɪˈstɑːni/
Paraguay /ˈpærəgwaɪ/	Paraguayan /ˌpærəˈgwaɪən/
Peru /pəˈruː/	Peruvian /pəˈruːviən/
(the) Philippines /ˈfɪlɪpiːnz/	Philippine /ˈfɪlɪpiːn/, Filipino /ˌfɪlɪˈpiːnoʊ/
Poland /ˈpoʊlənd/	Polish /ˈpoʊlɪʃ/, Pole /poʊl/
Portugal /ˈpɔːrtʃʊgl/	Portuguese /ˌpɔːrtʃuˈgiːz/
Romania /ruˈmeɪniə/	Romanian /ruˈmeɪniən/
Russia /ˈrʌʃə/	Russian /ˈrʌʃn/
Saudi Arabia /ˌsaʊdi əˈreɪbiə/	Saudi /ˈsaʊdi/, Saudi Arabian /ˌsaʊdi əˈreɪbiən/
Scotland /ˈskɒtlənd/	Scottish /ˈskɒtɪʃ/, Scots /ˈskɒts/, Scot /skɒt/, Scotsman, Scotswoman
Singapore /ˈsɪŋəpɔːr; *GB* sɪŋəˈpɔːr/	Singaporean /ˌsɪŋəˈpɔːriən, ˌsɪŋgə-/
Slovakia /sloʊˈvækiə/	Slovak /ˈsloʊvæk/
South Africa /ˌsaʊθ ˈæfrɪkə/	South African /ˌsaʊθ ˈæfrɪkən/
Spain /speɪn/	Spanish /ˈspænɪʃ/, Spaniard /ˈspænɪərd/
Sweden /ˈswiːdn/	Swedish /ˈswiːdɪʃ/, Swede /swiːd/
Switzerland /ˈswɪtsərlənd/	Swiss /swɪs/
Syria /ˈsɪriə/	Syrian /ˈsɪriən/
Taiwan /taɪˈwɑn/	Taiwanese /ˌtaɪwəˈniːz/
Tanzania /ˌtænzəˈniːə/	Tanzanian /ˌtænzəˈniːən/
Tunisia /tuˈniːʒə; *GB* tjuˈnɪziə/	Tunisian /tuˈniːʒn; *GB* tjuˈnɪziən/
Turkey /ˈtɜːrki/	Turkish /ˈtɜːrkɪʃ/, Turk /tɜːrk/
Uganda /juːˈgændə/	Ugandan /juːˈgændən/
(the) United States of America /juˌnaɪtɪd ˌsteɪts əv əˈmerɪkə/	American /əˈmerɪkən/
Uruguay /ˈjʊərəgwaɪ/	Uruguayan /ˌjʊərəˈgwaɪən/
Venezuela /ˌvenəˈzweɪlə/	Venezuelan /ˌvenəˈzweɪlən/
Vietnam /vietˈnɑm; *GB* -ˈnæm/	Vietnamese /vietnəˈmiːz/
Wales /weɪlz/	Welsh /welʃ/, Welshman, a Welshwoman
Zimbabwe /zɪmˈbɑbwi/	Zimbabwean /zɪmˈbɑbwiən/

Falsos cognatos

A palavra em inglês...	significa em português...
actual	exato; verdadeiro
agenda	pauta, ordem do dia
assign	designar; indicar
barracks	quartel
beef	carne de vaca
baton	cassetete; batuta; bastão
cap	gorro; barrete; tampa
carton	caixa
casual	esporte; ocasional; superficial; sem importância; descontraido, informal
cigar	charuto
collar	colarinho; coleira
college	centro de ensino superior, universidade; faculdade
comprehensive	abrangente
compromise	acordo
be constipated	estar com prisão de ventre
contempt	desprezo
costume	traje
curse	ofensa; maldição; praga
data	dados; informação
deception	trapaça, fraude
dent	amassado
disgust	repugnância
enroll	inscrever
eventual	final
exquisite	refinado
fabric	tecido
flock	rebanho; bando
grip	ato de agarrar; controle; pressão; cabo
intend	pretender, ter a intenção de
intoxication	embriaguez
library	biblioteca
lunch	almoço
notorious	de má reputação
parent	mãe; pai
pretend	fingir; ter pretensões
push	empurrar; apertar; promover
record	registrar, anotar; gravar; marcar
resume	reatar; retomar
sensible	sensato
sort	tipo; pessoa
straight	reto; em ordem; direto; puro
stranger	desconhecido; forasteiro
sympathetic	compreensivo, solidário
trap	armadilha

e não...	que em inglês é...
atual	current; present-day
agenda	diary
assinar	sign; subscribe
barraca	tent; stall
bife	steak
batom	lipstick
capa	cover; sleeve; cape; cloak
cartão	card; cardboard
casual	chance
cigarro	cigarette
colar	necklace
colégio	school
compreensivo	understanding
compromisso	commitment; agreement; engagement
estar constipado	have a cold
contente	happy; pleased
costume	habit; custom
curso	course; degree
data	date
decepção	disappointment
dente	tooth
desgosto	sorrow
enrolar	roll sth up; curl; deceive, con
eventual	accidental
esquisito	strange
fábrica	factory
floco	flake
gripe	flu
entender	understand
intoxicação	poisoning
livraria	bookstore
lanche	snack
notório	well known
parente	relation
pretender	intend
puxar	pull
recordar	remember, recall
resumir	summarize; sum sth up
sensível	sensitive; noticeable
sorte	luck; fate
estreito	narrow
estrangeiro	foreigner
simpático	nice
trapo	old rag

Verbos irregulares

Infinitivo	Passado	Particípio	Infinitivo	Passado	Particípio
be	was/were	been	leave	left	left
bear	bore	borne	lend	lent	lent
beat	beat	beaten	let	let	let
become	became	become	lie[2]	lay	lain
begin	began	begun	light	lit,	lit,
bend	bent	bent		lighted	lighted
bite	bit	bitten	lose	lost	lost
blow	blew	blown	make	made	made
break	broke	broken	mean	meant	meant
bring	brought	brought	meet	met	met
build	built	built	pay	paid	paid
burn	burned,	burned,	put	put	put
	burnt	burnt	quit	quit,	quit,
burst	burst	burst	read	read	read
buy	bought	bought	ride	rode	ridden
catch	caught	caught	ring[2]	rang	rung
choose	chose	chosen	rise	rose	risen
come	came	come	run	ran	run
cost	cost,	cost,	say	said	said
	costed	costed	see	saw	seen
cut	cut	cut	seek	sought	sought
deal	dealt	dealt	sell	sold	sold
do[1]	did	done	send	sent	sent
draw	drew	drawn	set	set	set
dream	dreamed,	dreamed,	shake	shook	shaken
	dreamt	dreamt	shine	shone	shone
drink	drank	drunk	shoot	shot	shot
drive	drove	driven	show	showed	shown
eat	ate	eaten	shut	shut	shut
fall	fell	fallen	sing	sang	sung
feed	fed	fed	sink	sank	sunk
feel	felt	felt	sit	sat	sat
fight	fought	fought	sleep	slept	slept
find	found	found	speak	spoke	spoken
fly	flew	flown	spend	spent	spent
forbid	forbade	forbidden	spell	spelled,	spelled,
forget	forgot	forgotten		spelt	spelt
forgive	forgave	forgiven	spill	spilled,	spilled,
freeze	froze	frozen		spilt	spilt
get	got	gotten;	spin	spun	spun
		(GB) got	stand	stood	stood
give	gave	given	steal	stole	stolen
go	went	gone	stick	stuck	stuck
grow	grew	grown	sting	stung	stung
hang	hung,	hung,	strike	struck	struck
	hanged	hanged	swear	swore	sworn
have	had	had	swim	swam	swum
hear	heard	heard	take	took	taken
hide	hid	hidden	teach	taught	taught
hit	hit	hit	tear[2]	tore	torn
hold	held	held	tell	told	told
hurt	hurt	hurt	think	thought	thought
keep	kept	kept	throw	threw	thrown
know	knew	known	wake	woke	woken
lay[1]	laid	laid	wear	wore	worn
lead[2]	led	led	win	won	won
learn	learned,	learned,	write	wrote	written
	learnt	learnt			

A a

A, a /eɪ/ s (pl **A's, a's** /eɪz/) **1** A, a: *A as in apple* A de abelha **2** (Educ) (nota) A **3** (Mús) lá

a /ə, eɪ/ (tb **an** /ən, æn/) art indef **NOTA** Corresponde aos artigos um, uma em português, exceto em: **1** (números): *a hundred people* cem pessoas **2** (profissões): *My mother is a lawyer.* Minha mãe é advogada. **3** por: *50¢ a dozen* 50 centavos a dúzia **4** (com desconhecidos) um(a) tal (de)

aback /əˈbæk/ adv: *I was taken aback.* Isso me pegou de surpresa.

abandon /əˈbændən/ vt abandonar

abbess /ˈæbes/ s abadessa

abbey /ˈæbi/ s abadia

abbot /ˈæbət/ s abade

abbreviate /əˈbriːvieɪt/ vt abreviar **abbreviation** s **1** abreviação **2** abreviatura

ABC /ˌeɪ biː ˈsiː/ s **1** abecedário **2** abecê

abdicate /ˈæbdɪkeɪt/ vt, vi abdicar: ~ (all) responsibility renunciar a toda responsabilidade

abdomen /ˈæbdəmən/ s abdome **abdominal** /æbˈdɒmɪnl/ adj abdominal

abduct /æbˈdʌkt, əb-/ vt seqüestrar **abduction** s seqüestro

abide /əˈbaɪd/ vt suportar: *I can't ~ them.* Não os suporto. ■ **abide by sth** **1** acatar algo **2** (promessa) cumprir algo

ability /əˈbɪləti/ s (pl -ies) **1** (talento) capacidade, capacidade **2** habilidade

ablaze /əˈbleɪz/ adj **1** em chamas: *set sth* ~ colocar fogo em algo **2** **be ~ with sth** resplandecer com algo

able /ˈeɪbl/ adj **1** **be ~ to do sth** poder fazer algo: *They are not yet ~ to swim.* Eles ainda não sabem nadar. → CAN¹ **2** (-er, -est) capaz

abnormal /æbˈnɔːrml/ adj anormal **abnormality** /ˌæbnɔːrˈmæləti/ s (pl -ies) anomalia, anormalidade

aboard /əˈbɔːrd/ adv, prep a bordo (de)

abode /əˈboʊd/ s (fml) domicílio

abolish /əˈbɒlɪʃ/ vt abolir **abolition** s abolição

abominable /əˈbɑmənəbl; GB -mɪn-/ adj abominável

abort /əˈbɔːrt/ vt, vi abortar: *They aborted the launch.* Eles cancelaram o lançamento.

abortion /əˈbɔːrʃn/ s aborto (intencional): *have an* ~ abortar

abortive /əˈbɔːrtɪv/ adj fracassado

abound /əˈbaʊnd/ vi ~ (with sth) abundar, ser rico (em algo)

about /əˈbaʊt/ adv **1** mais ou menos, aproximadamente **2** cerca de: *at ~ half past seven* pelas sete e meia ● **AROUND 3** por perto/aqui: *There are no jobs ~ at the moment.* Não há empregos no momento. **4** quase **5** (esp GB) de um lado para o outro **6** (esp GB) aqui e ali: *People were standing ~ in the street.* Havia pessoas paradas na rua. **NOTA** Para o uso de **about** em PHRASAL VERBS, ver o verbo, p. ex. **lie about** em LIE. ▶ **be about to do sth** estar prestes a fazer algo ● prep **1** por: *She's somewhere ~ the place.* Ela está em algum lugar por aqui. **2** sobre: *What's the book ~?* Do que trata o livro? **3** [com adj]: angry/happy ~ sth zangado/feliz com algo **4** (característica): *There's something ~ her I like.* Há algo nela que me atrai. ▶ **how/what about?**: *What ~ his car?* E o carro dele? ◇ *How ~ going swimming?* Que tal irmos nadar?

above /əˈbʌv/ adv, prep acima (de): *the apartment ~ the store* o apartamento acima da loja ◇ *children aged ten and ~* crianças de dez anos para cima ▶ **above all** acima de tudo

abrasive /əˈbreɪsɪv/ adj **1** (pessoa) grosso **2** áspero: ~ paper (papel de) lixa

abreast /əˈbrest/ adv: *cycle two* ~ andar de bicicleta lado a lado com alguém ▶ **keep abreast of sth** manter-se a par de algo

abridged /əˈbrɪdʒd/ adj resumido

abroad /əˈbrɔːd/ adv no exterior: *go* ~ viajar para o exterior

abrupt /əˈbrʌpt/ adj **1** (mudança) repentino, abrupto **2** (pessoa) brusco

absence /ˈæbsəns/ s ausência, falta: *in the ~ of new evidence* na falta de novas provas

absent /ˈæbsənt/ adj **1** ausente **2** distraído

absentee /ˌæbsənˈtiː/ s ausente

absent-minded adj distraído

absolute /ˈæbsəluːt/ *adj* absoluto

absolutely /ˈæbsəluːtli/ *adv* **1** absolutamente: *You are ~ right.* Você está com toda a razão. ◊ *It's ~ essential that...* É imprescindível que... **2** [*frases negativas*]: *~ nothing* nada em absoluto **3** /ˌæbsəˈluːtli/ (*concordando com algo*) sem dúvida

absolve /əbˈzɒlv/ *vt* absolver

absorb /əbˈsɔːb/ *vt* **1** absorver, assimilar **2** ~ *a shock* amortecer um choque

absorbed /əbˈsɔːbd/ *adj* absorto

absorbing /əbˈsɔːbɪŋ/ *adj* envolvente, absorvente

absorption /əbˈsɔːpʃn/ *s* **1** absorção **2** assimilação

abstain /əbˈsteɪn/ *vi* abster-se

abstract /ˈæbstrækt/ *adj* abstrato ● *s* obra de arte abstrata ▶ **in the abstract** em abstrato

absurd /əbˈsɜːd/ *adj* absurdo: *look ~* ficar ridículo **absurdity** *s* (*pl* -**ies**) absurdo

abundance /əˈbʌndəns/ *s* abundância

abundant /əˈbʌndənt/ *adj* abundante

abuse /əˈbjuːz/ *vt* **1** abusar de **2** insultar **3** maltratar ● /əˈbjuːs/ *s* abuso: *human rights abuses* violação aos direitos humanos **2** [*U*] insultos: *They shouted ~ at him.* Eles o insultaram aos gritos. **3** [*U*] maus tratos **abusive** *adj* ofensivo, grosseiro

academic /ˌækəˈdemɪk/ *adj* **1** acadêmico **2** teórico ● *s* acadêmico/a

academy /əˈkædəmi/ *s* (*pl* -**ies**) academia

accelerate /əkˈseləreɪt/ *vt, vi* acelerar **acceleration** *s* aceleração **accelerator** *s* acelerador

accent /ˈæksent, -sənt/ *s* **1** sotaque **2** ênfase **3** acento (*gráfico*)

accentuate /əkˈsentʃueɪt/ *vt* **1** acentuar **2** ressaltar **3** agravar

accept /əkˈsept/ *vt, vi* **1** aceitar: *The machine only accepts coins.* A máquina só funciona com moedas. **2** admitir

acceptable /əkˈseptəbl/ *adj* aceitável

acceptance /əkˈseptəns/ *s* **1** aceitação **2** aprovação

access /ˈækses/ *s* acesso

accessible /əkˈsesəbl/ *adj* acessível

accessory /əkˈsesəri/ *s* (*pl* -**ies**) **1** acessório **2** ~ **(to sth)** cúmplice (de algo)

accident /ˈæksɪdənt/ *s* **1** aci-

dente **2** acaso ▶ **by accident 1** acidentalmente, sem querer **2** por acaso **3** por descuido **accidental** /ˌæksɪˈdentl/ *adj* **1** acidental **2** casual

acclaim /əˈkleɪm/ *vt* aclamar ● *s* [*U*] aclamação: *receive critical ~* ser elogiado pelos críticos

accommodate /əˈkɒmədeɪt/ *vt* alojar, acomodar

accommodations /əˌkɒməˈdeɪʃnz/ (*GB* **accommodation**) *s* [*pl*] alojamento, acomodação

accompaniment /əˈkʌmpənimənt/ *s* acompanhamento

accompany /əˈkʌmpəni/ *vt* (*pt, pp* -**ied**) acompanhar

accomplice /əˈkʌmplɪs; *GB* əˈkʌm-/ *s* cúmplice

accomplish /əˈkʌmplɪʃ; *GB* əˈkʌm-/ *vt* realizar

accomplished /əˈkʌmplɪʃt; *GB* əˈkʌm-/ *adj* consumado, talentoso

accomplishment /əˈkʌmplɪʃmənt; *GB* əˈkʌm-/ *s* **1** realização **2** talento

accord /əˈkɔːd/ *s* acordo ▶ **in accord (with sb/sth)** de acordo (com alguém/algo) **of your own accord** por sua livre vontade ● (*fml*) **1** *vi* concordar **2** *vt* outorgar, conceder

accordance /əˈkɔːdns/ *s* ▶ **in accordance with sth** de acordo com algo

accordingly /əˈkɔːdɪŋli/ *adv* **1** portanto **2** *act* ~ agir de acordo

according to *prep* segundo

accordion /əˈkɔːdiən/ *s* acordeão

account /əˈkaʊnt/ *s* **1** (*Fin*) conta: *checking* ~ conta corrente **2** fatura **3** (**accounts**) [*pl*] contabilidade **2** relato, descrição ▶ **by/from all accounts** pelo que dizem **of no account** sem qualquer importância **on account of sth** por causa de algo **on no account; not on any account** por nenhum motivo, de forma alguma **on this/that account** por esta/aquela razão **take account of sth; take sth into account** ter/levar algo em conta **a ~ for sth** prestar contas de algo

accountable /əˈkaʊntəbl/ *adj* ~ **(to sb) (for sth)** responsável (perante alguém) (por algo) **accountability** /əˌkaʊntəˈbɪləti/ *s* responsabilidade da qual se deve prestar contas

accountant /əˈkaʊntənt/ *s* contador/a

accounting /əˈkaʊntɪŋ/ (*GB*

accountancy /əˈkaʊntənsi/ *s* contabilidade

accumulate /əˈkjuːmjələrt/ *vt, vi* acumular(-se) **accumulation** *s* acumulação

accuracy /ˈækjərəsi/ *s* precisão

accurate /ˈækjərət/ *adj* preciso, exato

accusation /ˌækjuˈzeɪʃn/ *s* acusação

accuse /əˈkjuːz/ *vt* acusar **the accused** *s* (*pl* **the accused**) o acusado/a **accusingly** *adv* acusadoramente

accustomed /əˈkʌstəmd/ *adj* acostumado: *be ~ to sth* estar acostumado com algo ◊ *become/grow ~ to sth* acostumar-se a/com algo

ace /eɪs/ *s* ás

ache /eɪk/ *s* dor ● *vi* doer

achieve /əˈtʃiːv/ *vt* **1** (*objetivo*) atingir **2** obter **achievement** *s* realização

aching /ˈeɪkɪŋ/ *adj* dolorido

acid /ˈæsɪd/ *s* ácido ● *adj* **1** (*tb* **acidic** /əˈsɪdɪk/) ácido **2** acre **acidity** /əˈsɪdəti/ *s* acidez

acid rain *s* chuva ácida

acknowledge /əkˈnɒlɪdʒ/ *vt* **1** reconhecer **2** acusar recebimento de *She didn't even ~ me.* Ela nem demonstrou ter notado minha presença. **acknowledg(e)ment** *s* **1** reconhecimento **2** prova de recebimento **3** agradecimento (*em livro, etc.*)

acne /ˈækni/ *s* acne

acorn /ˈeɪkɔːn/ *s* (*Bot*) bolota

acoustic /əˈkuːstɪk/ *adj* acústico **acoustics** /*pl*/ acústica

acquaintance /əˈkweɪntəns/ *s* **1** amizade, conhecimento **2** conhecido/a ▶ **make sb's acquaintance/make the acquaintance of sb** (*fml*) conhecer alguém (*pela primeira vez*) **acquainted** *adj* familiarizado: *become/get ~ with sb* (vir a) conhecer alguém

acquiesce /ˌækwiˈes/ *vi* (*fml*) ~ **(in sth)** consentir (algo/em fazer algo); aceitar (algo) **acquiescence** *s* consentimento

acquire /əˈkwaɪər/ *vt* **1** adquirir **2** obter

acquisition /ˌækwɪˈzɪʃn/ *s* aquisição

acquit /əˈkwɪt/ *vt* (**-tt-**) absolver **acquittal** *s* absolvição

acre /ˈeɪkər/ *s* acre (4,047 metros quadrados) ▶ Ver pág. 224

acrobat /ˈækrəbæt/ *s* acrobata

across /əˈkrɒs; *GB* əˈkrɒs/ *adv, prep* **1** de um lado a outro: *swim*

~ *atravessar a nado* ◊ *walk ~ the border* atravessar a fronteira a pé **2** ao outro lado: *We were ~ in no time.* Chegamos ao outro lado num segundo. ◊ *from ~ the room* do outro lado da sala **3** sobre, ao longo de **4** de largura: *The river is half a mile ~.* O rio tem um quilômetro de largura. **5** ~ **from** em frente de NOTA Para o uso de **across** em PHRASAL VERBS ver o verbo, p. ex. **come across** em COME.

acrylic /əˈkrɪlɪk/ *adj, s* acrílico

act /ækt/ *s* **1** ato: *a circus* ~ um número de circo (*Jur*) decreto ▶ **get your act together** (*coloq*) organizar-se **in the act of doing sth** no ato de fazer algo **put on an act** fingir ● **1** *vi* atuar **2** *vi* comportar-se **3** *vt* (*Teat*) fazer o papel de

acting /ˈæktɪŋ/ *s* teatro, atuação: *his ~ career* sua carreira de ator ● *adj* interino NOTA Usa-se somente antes de substantivos.

action /ˈækʃn/ *s* **1** ação: *in* ~ em ação ◊ *This machine is out of* ~. Esta máquina não está funcionando. **2** [*U*] medidas **3** ato ▶ **put sth into action** colocar algo em prática

activate /ˈæktɪveɪt/ *vt* ativar

active /ˈæktɪv/ *adj* ativo: *take an ~ part in sth* participar ativamente de algo

activity /ækˈtɪvəti/ *s* (*pl* **-ies**) **1** atividade **2** agitação

actor /ˈæktər/ *s* (*fem* **actress** /ˈæktrəs/) ator, atriz NOTA Atualmente usa-se o termo **actor** tanto como feminino quanto como masculino.

actual /ˈæktʃuəl/ *adj* **1** exato: *What were his ~ words?* O que ele disse exatamente? **2** verdadeiro: *based on ~ events* baseado em fatos reais ◊ *in ~ fact* na realidade **3** the ~ *city center* o centro da cidade propriamente dito NOTA Para **atual**, diz-se **current** ou **present-day**.

actually /ˈæktʃuəli/ *adv* **1** na realidade, de fato: *He's ~ very bright.* Na verdade ele é muito inteligente. **2** exatamente: *What did she ~ say?* O que ela disse exatamente? **3** *Actually, my name's Sue.* A propósito, meu nome é Sue. **4** (*para enfatizar*): *You ~ met her?* Você a conheceu mesmo? ◊ *He ~ expected me to leave.* Ele até esperava que eu fosse embora.

acupuncture /ˈækjʊpʌŋktʃər/ *s* acupuntura

acute /əˈkjuːt/ *adj* **1** extremo: *become more ~* agravar-se **2** agudo: *~ angle/pain* ângulo agudo/dor aguda **3** *(remorso, etc.)* profundo

ad /æd/ *s (coloq)* anúncio *(publicidade)*

AD /ˌeɪ ˈdiː/ *abrev* depois de Cristo

adamant /ˈædəmənt/ *adj ~ (about/in sth)* firme, categórico quanto a algo

adapt /əˈdæpt/ *vt, vi* adaptar (-se) **adaptable** *adj* adaptável **adaptation** *s* adaptação

adaptor /əˈdæptər/ *s* adaptador

add /æd/ *vt* **1** adicionar **2** *~ sth (together/up)* somar algo ■ **add sth on (to sth)** acrescentar algo (a algo) **add to sth 1** aumentar algo **2** ampliar algo **add up** *(coloq)* encaixar: *His story doesn't ~ up.* A história dele não faz sentido. **add up to sth** totalizar algo: *The bill adds up to $40.* A conta dá um total de 40 dólares.

adder /ˈædər/ *s* víbora

addict /ˈædɪkt/ *s* viciado/a: *drug ~* toxicômano **addicted** /əˈdɪktɪd/ *adj* viciado **addiction** /əˈdɪkʃn/ *s* vício: *drug ~* toxicomania **addictive** /əˈdɪktɪv/ *adj* que vicia

addition /əˈdɪʃn/ *s* **1** incorporação **2** aquisição **3** *(Mat)* adição ▸ **in addition (to sth)** além disso, além de algo **additional** *adj* adicional

additive /ˈædətɪv/ *s* aditivo

address /ˈædres; *GB* əˈdres/ *s* **1** endereço **2** discurso ● *vt* **1** endereçar **2** *~ sb* dirigir-se a alguém **3** *~ (yourself to) sth* dedicar-se a algo

adept /əˈdept/ *adj* hábil

adequate /ˈædɪkwət/ *adj* **1** adequado **2** aceitável

adhere /ədˈhɪər/ *vi (fml)* aderir **adherence** *s* **1** adesão **2** observância **adherent** *s* adepto/a

adhesive /ədˈhiːsɪv/ *adj, s* adesivo

adjacent /əˈdʒeɪsnt/ *adj* adjacente

adjective /ˈædʒɪktɪv/ *s* adjetivo

adjoining /əˈdʒɔɪnɪŋ/ *adj* adjacente

adjourn /əˈdʒɜːrn/ *vt* adiar **2** *vt, vi (reunião)* suspender(-se)

adjust /əˈdʒʌst/ **1** *vt* ajustar, regular **2** *vt, vi ~ (sth) (to sth)* adaptar algo, adaptar-se (a algo) **adjustment** *s* **1** ajuste, modificação **2** adaptação

administer /ədˈmɪnɪstər/ *vt* **1** administrar **2** dirigir **3** *(castigo)* aplicar

administration /ədˌmɪnɪˈstreɪʃn/ *s* administração, direção

administrative /ədˈmɪnɪstreɪtɪv/ *adj* administrativo

administrator /ədˈmɪnɪstreɪtər/ *s* administrador/a

admirable /ˈædmərəbl/ *adj* admirável

admiral /ˈædmərəl/ *s* almirante

admiration /ˌædməˈreɪʃn/ *s* admiração

admire /ədˈmaɪər/ *vt* admirar, elogiar **admirer** *s* admirador/a **admiring** *adj* cheio de admiração

admission /ədˈmɪʃn/ *s* **1** entrada, admissão **2** confissão

admit /ədˈmɪt/ **(-tt-) 1** *vt, vi* confessar: *~ to a mistake* reconhecer um erro **2** *vt* deixar entrar, admitir **admittedly** *adv*: *Admittedly...* Deve-se admitir que...

adolescent /ˌædəˈlesnt/ *adj, s* adolescente **adolescence** *s* adolescência

adopt /əˈdɒpt/ *vt* adotar **adopted** *adj* adotivo **adoption** *s* adoção

adore /əˈdɔːr/ *vt* adorar

adorn /əˈdɔːrn/ *vt* adornar

adrenalin /əˈdrenəlɪn/ *s* adrenalina

adrift /əˈdrɪft/ *adj* à deriva

adult /əˈdʌlt, ˈædʌlt/ *adj* adulto, maior (de idade) ● *s* adulto/a

adultery /əˈdʌltəri/ *s* adultério

adulthood /ˈædʌlthʊd/ *s* idade adulta

advance /ədˈvæns; *GB* -ˈvɑːns/ *s* **1** avanço **2** adiantamento ▸ **in advance 1** com antecedência **2** adiantado ● *adj* antecipado: *~ warning* aviso prévio ● **1** *vi* avançar **2** *vt* adiantar **advanced** *adj* avançado **advancement** *s* **1** desenvolvimento **2** promoção

advantage /ədˈvæntɪdʒ; *GB* -ˈvɑːn-/ *s* **1** vantagem **2** benefício ▸ **take advantage of sth 1** aproveitar-se de algo **2** tirar proveito de algo **take advantage of sb/sth take advantage of sb/sth** abusar de alguém/algo **advantageous** /ˌædvənˈteɪdʒəs/ *adj* vantajoso

advent /ˈædvent/ *s* **1** advento **2** (Advent) Advento

adventure /ədˈventʃər/ *s* aventura **adventurer** *s* aventureiro/a **adventurous** *adj* **1** aventureiro **2** arriscado

adverb /ˈædvɜːrb/ *s* advérbio

adversary /ˈædvərseri; *GB* -səri/

s (*pl* **-ies**) adversário/a

adverse /'ædvɜːrs/ *adj* **1** adverso **2** negativo **adversely** *adv* negativamente

adversity /əd'vɜːrsəti/ *s* (*pl* **-ies**) adversidade

advert /'ædvɜːrt/ *s* (GB) anúncio (*publicidade*)

advertise /'ædvərtaiz/ **1** *vt* anunciar **2** *vi* fazer propaganda **3** *vi* ~ **for sb/sth** procurar alguém/algo por anúncio **advertisement** /,ædvər'taizmənt; GB əd'vɜːtɪsmənt/ *s* ~ (**for sb/sth**) anúncio (de alguém/algo)

advertising *s* **1** publicidade: ~ *campaign* campanha publicitária **2** anúncios

advice /əd'vais/ *s* [U] conselho: *a piece of* ~ um conselho ◊ *take legal* ~ consultar um advogado

advisable /əd'vaizəbl/ *adj* aconselhável

advise /əd'vaiz/ *vt, vi* **1** aconselhar, recomendar: ~ *sb to do sth* aconselhar alguém a fazer algo ◊ *You would be well advised to...* Seria aconselhável você... **2** assessorar **advisor** (*GB* **adviser**) *s* conselheiro/a, assessor/a **advisory** *adj* consultivo/a

advocacy /'ædvəkəsi/ *s* **1** ~ **of sth** apoio a algo; defesa de algo **2** advocacia

advocate /'ædvəkeit/ *vt* apoiar, defender

aerial /'eəriəl/ *s* (GB) antena (TV) ● *adj* aéreo

aerobics /ə'roubiks/ *s* [*sing*] ginástica, aeróbica

aerodynamic /,eəroʊdar'næmik/ *adj* aerodinâmico/a

aeroplane /'eərəplein/ (GB) *s* avião

aesthetic /es'θetik/ *adj* estético

affair /ə'feər/ *s* **1** assunto: *current affairs* assuntos de atualidade ◊ *Department of Foreign Affairs* Ministério das Relações Exteriores ◊ *the Watergate* ~ o caso Watergate **2** acontecimento **3** caso (*amoroso*)

affect /ə'fekt/ *vt* **1** afetar, influir em **2** comover

affection /ə'fekʃn/ *s* afeto **affectionate** *adj* afetuoso/a

affinity /ə'finəti/ *s* (*pl* **-ies**) afinidade

affirm /ə'fɜːrm/ *vt* afirmar

afflict /ə'flikt/ *vt* afligir: *be afflicted with* sofrer de

affluent /'æfluənt/ *adj* rico **affluence** *s* riqueza

afford /ə'fɔːrd/ *vt* **1** permitir-se (o luxo de) **2** proporcionar

affordable *adj* acessível

afield /ə'fiːld/ *adv* ➤ **far/further afield** afastado: *from as far as...* de lugares tão distantes como...

afloat /ə'floʊt/ *adj* **1** à tona **2** a bordo

afraid /ə'freid/ *adj* **1** be ~ (**of sb/ sth**); be ~ (**to do sth**) ter medo (de alguém/algo); (de fazer algo) **2** be ~ **for sb** temer por alguém ➤ **I'm afraid (that...)** Acho que..., Sinto muito, mas...: *I'm* ~ *so/not.* Temo que sim/não.

afresh /ə'freʃ/ *adv* de novo

after /'æftər; GB 'ɑːf-/ *adv* **1** depois: *the day* ~ o dia seguinte **2** atrás: *She came running* ~. Ela veio correndo atrás. ● *prep* **1** depois de: ~ *lunch/doing your homework* depois do almoço/ de fazer a tarefa de casa **2** após, atrás: *time* ~ *time* repetidas vezes **3** (*busca*): *What are you* ~? O que você está procurando? **4** *We named him* ~ *you.* Demos a ele o seu nome. ➤ **after all** depois de tudo, afinal (de contas) ● *conj* depois que

aftermath /'æftərmæθ; GB 'ɑːf-/ *s* [U] conseqüências ➤ **in the aftermath of** no período subseqüente a

afternoon /,æftər'nuːn; GB ,ɑːf-/ *s* tarde: *tomorrow* ~ amanhã de tarde ◊ *good* ~ boa tarde → MORNING, TARDE[1]

afterthought /'æftərθɔːt; GB 'ɑːf-/ *s* ocorrência/reflexão posterior: *As an afterthought...* Pensando melhor...

afterwards /'æftərwədz; GB 'ɑːf-/ (*USA* **afterward**) *adv* depois, mais tarde: *shortly/soon* ~ logo depois

again /ə'gen, ə'gein/ *adv* outra vez, novamente: *once* ~ mais uma vez ◊ *never* ~ nunca mais ◊ ~ *and* ~ repetidamente ➤ **then/ there again** por outro lado

against /ə'genst, ə'geinst/ *prep* contra: *Put the piano* ~ *the wall.* Ponha o piano encostado à parede. **NOTA** Para o uso de **against** em PHRASAL VERBS ver o verbo, p. ex. **come up against** em COME.

age /eidʒ/ *s* **1** idade **2** velhice: *It improves with* ~. Melhora com o tempo/a idade. **3** época, era **4** eternidade: *It's ages since I saw her.* Faz um tempão que não a vejo. ➤ **age of consent** maioridade **come of age** atingir a maioridade **under**

age muito jovem, menor (de idade) • *vt, vi* (*part pres* **aging** *pt, pp* **aged**) envelhecer

aged /'eɪdʒd/ *adj* **1** *He died ~ 81.* Ele morreu aos 81 anos. **2** /'eɪdʒɪd/ idoso, velho • **the aged** /'eɪdʒɪd/ *s* [*pl*] os idosos

agency /'eɪdʒənsi/ *s* (*pl* -ies) agência, organização

agenda /ə'dʒendə/ *s* pauta, ordem do dia

agent /'eɪdʒənt/ *s* agente, representante

aggravate /'ægrəveɪt/ *vt* **1** agravar **2** irritar **aggravating** *adj* irritante **aggravation** *s* **1** irritação **2** agravamento

aggression /ə'ɡreʃn/ *s* [*U*] agressão, agressividade

aggressive /ə'ɡresɪv/ *adj* agressivo

agile /'ædʒl; *GB* 'ædʒaɪl/ *adj* ágil **agility** /ə'dʒɪləti/ *s* agilidade

aging /'eɪdʒɪŋ/ *adj* envelhecido • *s* envelhecimento

agitated /'ædʒɪteɪtɪd/ *adj* agitado: *get ~* agitar-se **agitation** *s* agitação, perturbação

ago /ə'ɡoʊ/ *adv* atrás: *How long ~ did she die?* Há quanto tempo ela morreu? ◊ *as long ~ as 1950* já em 1950 NOTA **Ago** é usado com o *simple past* e o *past continuous*, mas nunca com o *present perfect*: *She arrived a few minutes ~.* O *past perfect* utiliza-se **before** ou **earlier**: *She had arrived two days before.*

agonize /'ægənaɪz/ *vi* ~ (**about/over sth**) atormentar-se (por com algo) **agonized** *adj* agoniado **agonizing** *adj* **1** angustiante **2** (*dor*) horroroso

agony /'ægəni/ *s* (*pl* -ies) agonia: *be in ~* sofrer dores horrorosas/estar agonizante

agree /ə'ɡriː/ **1** *vi* ~ (**with sb**) (**on about sth**) estar de acordo, concordar (com alguém) (sobre algo) **2** *vi* ~ (**to sth**) consentir (em algo); concordar (com algo) **3** *vt, vi* chegar a um acordo: *It was agreed that...* Concordou-se que... **4** *vt* (*relatório, etc.*) aprovar ▪ **agree with sb** fazer bem a alguém (*comida, clima*) **agreeable** *adj* **1** agradável **2** ~ (**to sth**) de acordo (com algo)

agreement /ə'ɡriːmənt/ *s* **1** conformidade, acordo: *in ~ with* de acordo com **2** convênio, acordo **3** contrato

agriculture /'ægrɪkʌltʃər/ *s* agricultura **agricultural** /ˌægrɪ'kʌltʃərəl/ *adj* agrícola

ah /ɑ/ *interj* oh

ahead /ə'hed/ *adv* **1** adiante, à frente: *She looked (straight) ~.* Ela olhou para frente. **2** próximo ▸ **be ahead** estar na frente, levar vantagem NOTA Para o uso de **ahead** em PHRASAL VERBS ver o verbo, p. ex. **press ahead** em PRESS. • *prep* ~ **of sb/ sth 1** na frente de alguém/algo: *directly ~ of us* bem na nossa frente **2** antes de alguém/algo

aid /eɪd/ *s* **1** ajuda **2** auxílio **3** apoio: *in ~ of sth* em apoio a algo • *vt* ajudar, facilitar

AIDS /eɪdz/ *abrev de* **acquired immune deficiency syndrome** AIDS (= síndrome de imunodeficiência adquirida)

ailment /'eɪlmənt/ *s* indisposição, doença

aim /eɪm/ **1** *vt, vi* ~ (**sth**) (**at sb/ sth**) apontar (algo) (para alguém/algo) **2** *vi* ~ **sth at sb/ sth** dirigir algo contra alguém/algo: *be aimed at sth* ter algo como objetivo ◊ *She aimed a blow at his head.* Ela visou a cabeça dele para dar uma pancada. **3** *vi* ~ **at/for sth** aspirar a algo **4** *vi* ~ **to do sth** ter a intenção de fazer algo • *s* **1** objetivo **2** pontaria: *take ~* apontar

aimless /'eɪmləs/ *adj* sem objetivo/propósito **aimlessly** *adv* sem rumo

ain't /eɪnt/ (*coloq*) **1** = AM/IS/ARE NOT *Ver* BE **2** = HAS/HAVE NOT *Ver* HAVE

air /eər/ *s* ar: ~ *fares* tarifas aéreas ◊ *by ~* por via aérea ▸ **give yourself/put on airs** dar-se ares (de superioridade) **in the air**: *There's something in the ~.* Há algo no ar. **on air** (*TV, etc.*) no ar **up in the air**: *The plan is still up in the ~.* O plano ainda está no ar. • *vt* **1** arejar **2** (*queixa, etc.*) manifestar

air conditioning *s* ar condicionado **air-conditioned** *adj* com ar condicionado

aircraft /'eərkræft; *GB* -krɑːft/ *s* (*pl* **aircraft**) avião

airfield /'eərfiːld/ *s* campo de pouso

air force *s* força aérea

air hostess *s* aeromoça

airline /'eərlaɪn/ *s* companhia aérea **airliner** *s* avião de passageiros

airmail /'eərmeɪl/ *s*: *by ~* por via aérea

airplane /'eərpleɪn/ *s* avião

airport /'eərpɔːrt/ *s* aeroporto

air raid *s* ataque aéreo

airtight /'eərtaɪt/ *adj* hermético

aisle /aɪl/ s **1** nave (de igreja) **2** corredor

akin /əˈkɪn/ adj ~ **to sth** semelhante a algo

alarm /əˈlɑːrm/ s **1** alarme: *raise/ sound the* ~ dar o alarme **2** (*tb* ~ **clock**) (relógio) despertador **3** (*tb* ~ **bell**) campainha de alarme ● vt alarmar: *be/become alarmed* alarmar-se ● *alarming adj* alarmante

alas /əˈlæs/ interj que desgraça, ai

albeit /ˌɔːlˈbiːɪt/ conj (*fml*) embora

album /ˈælbəm/ s álbum

alcohol /ˈælkəhɒl/; GB -hɒl/ s álcool: *alcohol-free* sem álcool **alcoholic** /ˌælkəˈhɒlɪk/ adj alcoólico ● s alcoólatra

ale /eɪl/ s cerveja

alert /əˈlɜːrt/ adj alerta ● s alerta: *bomb* ~ alerta de bomba ◊ *be on the* ~ estar alerta ● vt ~ **sb (to sth)** alertar alguém (de algo)

algae /ˈældʒiː/; GB *tb* ˈælɡiː/ s algas

algebra /ˈældʒɪbrə/ s álgebra

alibi /ˈæləbaɪ/ (*pl* ~s) s álibi

alien /ˈeɪliən/ adj **1** estranho **2** estrangeiro **3** alheio ● s **1** (*fml*) estrangeiro/a **2** extraterrestre **alienate** vt alienar

alight /əˈlaɪt/ adj: *be* ~ estar em chamas ◊ *set sth alight* fazer algo pegar fogo

align /əˈlaɪn/ vt **1** alinhar **2** ~ **yourself with sb/sth** (*Pol*) aliar-se a alguém/algo

alike /əˈlaɪk/ adj **1** parecido: *be/ look* ~ parecer-se ◊ *No two are* ~. Não há dois iguais. ● adv igualmente, do mesmo modo: *It appeals to young and old* ~. Atrai tanto a velhos quanto a jovens.

alive /əˈlaɪv/ adj [*nunca antes de substantivo*] vivo, com vida: *keep yourself/stay* ~ sobreviver ▸ **alive and kicking** mais vivo do que nunca **keep sth alive 1** (*tradição*) conservar algo **2** (*recordação*) manter algo vivo na mente

all /ɔːl/ adj todos: ~ *four of us* nós quatro **2** *deny* ~ *knowledge of sth* negar qualquer conhecimento de algo ● **on all fours** de quatro ● pron tudo, todos: *All I want is...* Tudo o que quero é... ◊ *All of us liked it*. Todos nós gostamos. ▸ **all in all** no geral **all the more** tanto mais, ainda mais **at all**: *if it's at* ~ *possible* se houver a menor possibilidade **in all** no total ● adv **1** totalmente: ~ *in white* todo de

branco **2** muito: ~ *excited* todo emocionado **3** (*Esporte*): *The score is two* ~. Estão empatados em dois a dois. ▸ **all along** o tempo todo **all but** quase: ~ *but impossible* quase impossível **all over 1** por toda parte **2** *That's her* ~ *over*. Isso é típico dela. **all the better** tanto melhor **all too** demasiado **be all for sth** estar/ser totalmente a favor de algo

all-around adj **1** geral **2** (*pessoa*) completo

allege /əˈledʒ/ vt alegar **alleged** adj suposto **allegedly** adv supostamente **allegation** /ˌæləˈɡeɪʃn/ s alegação, denúncia (*sem provas*)

allegiance /əˈliːdʒəns/ s lealdade

allergic /əˈlɜːrdʒɪk/ adj alérgico

allergy /ˈælərdʒi/ s (*pl* -ies) alergia

alleviate /əˈliːvieɪt/ vt aliviar **alleviation** s alívio

alley /ˈæli/ (*tb* **alleyway**) s passagem

alliance /əˈlaɪəns/ s aliança

allied /ˈælaɪd, əˈlaɪd/ adj **1** relacionado **2** aliado

alligator /ˈælɪɡeɪtər/ s aligátor

allocate /ˈæləkeɪt/ vt alocar **allocation** s distribuição

allot /əˈlɒt/ vt (-tt-) designar **allotment** s distribuição **2** parcela

all-out adj total ● adv ▸ **go all out** fazer todo o possível

allow /əˈlaʊ/ vt **1** ~ **sb/sth to do sth** permitir a alguém/algo que faça algo: *Dogs are not allowed.* É proibida a entrada de cães. **NOTA** Utiliza-se **allow** tanto no inglês formal quanto no coloquial e a forma passiva **be allowed** é muito comum. Usa-se **permit**, mais formal, principalmente na linguagem escrita, e **let**, informal, no inglês falado. **2** conceder **3** reservar, calcular **4** admitir ● **allow for sth** levar algo em conta **allowable** adj admissível, permitido

allowance /əˈlaʊəns/ s **1** limite permitido **2** ajuda de custo, mesada ▸ **make allowances for sb/sth** abrir concessão a alguém/levar algo em consideração

alloy /ˈælɔɪ/ s (*Quím*) liga

all right adj, adv **1** bem: *Did you get here* ~? Foi fácil para você chegar até aqui? **2** *The food was* ~. A comida não estava má. **3** de acordo **4** *That's him* ~. Tenho certeza de que é ele.

all-time adj de todos os tempos

ally /əˈlaɪ/ vt, vi (pt, pp **-ied**) ~ (yourself) with/to sb/sth aliar-se a alguém/algo ● /ˈælaɪ/ s (pl **-ies**) aliado/a

almond /ˈɑːmənd, ˈɔːl-/ s 1 amêndoa 2 (tb ~ tree) amendoeira

almost /ˈɔːlməʊst/ adv quase
→ NEARLY

alone /əˈləʊn/ adj, adv 1 só: Are you ~? Você está sozinha? NOTA Alone é a palavra neutra e não se utiliza antes de substantivo; lonely é usado em qualquer posição e tem conotações negativas: I want to be ~. Quero ficar sozinho. ◇ feel very lonely sentir-se muito só ◇ a lonely house uma casa solitária. 2 somente: You ~ can help me. Só você pode me ajudar. ▶ **leave/let sb/sth alone** deixar alguém/algo em paz

along /əˈlɒŋ; GB əˈlɒŋ/ prep por, ao longo de ● adv: I was driving ~. Eu estava dirigindo. ◇ Bring some friends ~. Traga alguns amigos com você. NOTA É comum utilizar-se along com verbos de movimento em tempo contínuo quando não se menciona o destino do movimento. Geralmente não se traduz para o português. ▶ **along with** junto com **come along** venha NOTA Para o uso de along em PHRASAL VERBS, ver o verbo, p. ex. **get along** em GET.

alongside /əˌlɒŋˈsaɪd; GB əˌlɒŋ-/ prep, adv junto a, ao lado/longo de: A car drew up ~. Um carro parou ao nosso lado.

aloud /əˈlaʊd/ adv 1 em voz alta 2 (bem) alto

alphabet /ˈælfəbet/ s alfabeto

alphabetical /ˌælfəˈbetɪkl/ adj alfabético

already /ɔːlˈredi/ adv já: Surely you're not going ~! Você não está indo assim tão cedo! → YET

alright /ɔːlˈraɪt/ = ALL RIGHT

also /ˈɔːlsəʊ/ adv também, além disso → TAMBÉM

altar /ˈɔːltər/ s altar

alter /ˈɔːltər/ 1 vt, vi alterar 2 vt ajustar **alteration** s 1 alteração 2 ajuste

alternate /ˈɔːltərnət; GB ɔːlˈtɜːnət/ adj alternado ● /ˈɔːltərneɪt/ vt, vi alternar

alternative /ɔːlˈtɜːrnətɪv/ s alternativa, opção ● adj alternativo

although /ɔːlˈðəʊ/ conj embora

altitude /ˈæltɪtuːd; GB -tjuːd/ s altitude

altogether /ˌɔːltəˈɡeðər/ adv 1 completamente 2 no total 3 Altogether, it was disappointing. No geral, foi decepcionante.

aluminum /əˈluːmɪnəm/ (GB **aluminium** /ˌæljəˈmɪniəm/) s alumínio

always /ˈɔːlweɪz/ adv sempre NOTA A posição dos advérbios de freqüência always, never, usually, etc. depende do verbo que os acompanha. Vão depois de verbos auxiliares e modais e diante dos demais verbos: I am ~ tired. ◇ I have never visited her. ◇ I usually go shopping on Mondays.

am /əm, m, æm/ Ver BE

a.m. /ˌeɪ ˈem/ abrev da manhã → P.M.

amalgam /əˈmælɡəm/ s amálgama

amalgamate /əˈmælɡəmeɪt/ vt, vi amalgamar, fundir(-se)

amateur /ˈæmətər, -tʃʊər/ adj, s amador/a

amaze /əˈmeɪz/ vt assombrar **amazement** s assombro **amazing** adj espantoso

ambassador /æmˈbæsədər/ s embaixador/a

amber /ˈæmbər/ adj, s âmbar

ambiguity /ˌæmbɪˈɡjuːəti/ s (pl **-ies**) ambigüidade

ambiguous /æmˈbɪɡjuəs/ adj ambíguo

ambition /æmˈbɪʃn/ s ambição

ambitious /æmˈbɪʃəs/ adj ambicioso

ambulance /ˈæmbjələns/ s ambulância

ambush /ˈæmbʊʃ/ s emboscada

amen /ɑːˈmen, eɪˈmen/ interj, s amém

amend /əˈmend/ vt emendar, corrigir **amendment** s emenda

amends /əˈmendz/ s [pl] ▶ **make amends (to sb) (for sth)** compensar (alguém) (por algo)

amenities /əˈmenətiz; GB əˈmiːnətiz/ s 1 comodidades 2 (GB) instalações (públicas)

amiable /ˈeɪmiəbl/ adj amigável, amável

amicable /ˈæmɪkəbl/ adj amistoso

amid /əˈmɪd/ (tb **amidst** /əˈmɪdst/) prep (fml) entre, em meio de

ammunition /ˌæmjuˈnɪʃn/ s [U] 1 munição 2 argumentos (para discutir)

amnesty /ˈæmnəsti/ s (pl **-ies**) anistia

among /əˈmʌŋ/ (tb **amongst** /əˈmʌŋst/) prep entre (mais de duas coisas): I was ~ the last to leave. Fui dos últimos a sair.

amount /ə'maʊnt/ vi ~ **to sth** 1 chegar a algo: *Our information doesn't ~ to much.* Não temos muitas informações. **2** equivaler a algo ● s **1** quantidade **2** (*fatura*) total **3** (*dinheiro*) soma ▸ **any amount of** uma grande quantidade de: *any ~ of money* todo o dinheiro necessário

amphibian /æm'fɪbiən/ adj, s anfíbio

amphitheater (GB **-theatre**) /'æmfɪθɪətər/ s anfiteatro

ample /'æmpl/ adj **1** abundante **2** (*suficiente*) bastante **3** (*extenso*) amplo **amply** adv amplamente

amplify /'æmplɪfaɪ/ vt (pt, pp -ied) **1** amplificar **2** (*relato, etc.*) aumentar **amplifier** s amplificador

amuse /ə'mjuːz/ vt **1** entreter **2** distrair, divertir **amusement** s **1** diversão, distração **2** atração ◇ *~ arcade* salão de fliperama ◇ *~ park* parque de diversões **amusing** adj divertido, engraçado

an Ver **A**

anaemia (GB) = ANEMIA

anaesthetic (GB) = ANESTHETIC

analogy /ə'næləʤi/ s (pl -ies) analogia

analysis /ə'næləsɪs/ s (pl -yses /-əsiːz/) **1** análise **2** psicanálise ▸ **in the last/final analysis** em última análise

analyst /'ænəlɪst/ s analista

analytic(al) /ˌænə'lɪtɪk(l)/ adj analítico

analyze (GB **-lyse**) /'ænəlaɪz/ vt analisar

anarchist /'ænərkɪst/ adj, s anarquista

anarchy /'ænərki/ s anarquia **anarchic** /ə'nɑrkɪk/ adj anárquico

anatomy /ə'nætəmi/ s (pl -ies) anatomia

ancestor /'ænsestər/ s antepassado **ancestral** /æn'sestrəl/ adj ancestral **ancestry** /'ænsestri/ s (pl -ies) ascendência

anchor /'æŋkər/ s **1** âncora: *at ~* ancorado **2** suporte ● vt, vi ancorar

ancient /'eɪnʃənt/ adj **1** antigo **2** (*coloq*) velhíssimo

and /ænd, ənd/ conj **1** e: *one hundred ~ three* cento e três ◇ *bread ~ butter* pão com manteiga **2** [com verbos em vez de to]: *Come ~ help me.* Venha ajudar-me.

3 [com comparativo]: *bigger ~ bigger* cada vez maior **4** (*repetição*): *They shouted ~ shouted.* Eles gritaram sem parar. ◇ *I've tried ~ tried.* Eu tentei várias vezes.

anecdote /'ænɪkdoʊt/ s (conto) anedota

anemia /ə'niːmiə/ s anemia **anemic** adj anêmico

anesthetic /ˌænəs'θetɪk/ s anestesia: *give sb an ~* anestesiar alguém

angel /'eɪnʤl/ s anjo

anger /'æŋgər/ s raiva ● vt irritar

angle /'æŋgl/ s ângulo: *at an ~* inclinado

angling /'æŋglɪŋ/ s pesca (com vara)

angry /'æŋgri/ adj (-ier, -iest) **1** ~ (at/about sth); ~ (with sb) com raiva (de algo/alguém): *get ~* ficar com raiva ◇ *make sb ~* irritar alguém **2** (*céu*) tempestuoso **angrily** adv com raiva

anguish /'æŋgwɪʃ/ s angústia **anguished** adj angustiado

angular /'æŋgjələr/ adj **1** angular **2** anguloso, ossudo

animal /'ænɪml/ s animal

animate /'ænɪmət/ adj animado (vivo) ● /'ænɪmeɪt/ vt animar

ankle /'æŋkl/ s tornozelo

anniversary /ˌænɪ'vɜrsəri/ s (pl -ies) aniversário

announce /ə'naʊns/ vt anunciar (tornar público) **announcement** s aviso, anúncio (em público): *make an ~* anunciar algo **announcer** s (TV, etc.) apresentador/a

annoy /ə'nɔɪ/ vt irritar, incomodar **annoyance** s irritação, incômodo: *much to our ~* para nosso aborrecimento **annoyed** adj irritado, incomodado: *get ~* irritar-se/incomodar-se **annoying** adj irritante

annual /'ænjuəl/ adj anual **annually** adv anualmente

anonymity /ˌænə'nɪməti/ s anonimato

anonymous /ə'nɑnɪməs/ adj anônimo

another /ə'nʌðər/ adj (um) outro: ~ *one* mais um → OUTRO ● pron (um) outro NOTA O plural do pron *another* é *others*. Ver tb ONE ANOTHER

answer /'ænsər/ GB /'ɑːnsə(r)/ s **1** resposta: *There was no ~.* Ninguém atendeu. ◇ *in ~ to sth* em resposta a algo **2** solução **3** (*Mat*) resultado ▸ **have/know all the answers**

saber tudo (sobre um assunto) ● **1** *vt*, *vi* responder (a): ~ *the door* atender a porta **2** *vt* (*pedido*) ouvir ■ **answer back** replicar (*com insolência*) **answer for sb/ sth** responder por alguém/algo **answer to sb (for sth)** responder a alguém (por algo), prestar contas a alguém

answering machine (*GB tb* answerphone /'ænsərfoʊn; *GB* 'ɑːn-/) *s* secretária eletrônica

ant /ænt/ *s* formiga

antagonism /æn'tægənɪzəm/ *s* antagonismo **antagonistic** *adj* hostil

antenna /æn'tenə/ *s* **1** (*pl* **-nae** /-niː/) (*inseto*) antena **2** (*pl* **-nas**) (*USA*) (*TV, etc.*) antena

anthem /'ænθəm/ *s* hino

anthology /æn'θɑlədʒi/ *s* (*pl* **-ies**) antologia

anthropology /ˌænθrə'pɑlədʒi/ *s* antropologia **anthropological** /ˌænθrəpə'lɑdʒɪkl/ *adj* antropológico **anthropologist** /ˌænθrə'pɑlədʒɪst/ *s* antropólogo/a

antibiotic /ˌæntibaɪ'ɑtɪk/ *adj*, *s* antibiótico

antibody /'æntibɑdi/ *s* (*pl* **-ies**) anticorpo

anticipate /æn'tɪsɪpeɪt/ *vt* **1** prever: *as anticipated* como previsto **2** ~ **sth/sb/doing sth** antecipar-se a alguém/algo

anticipation /ænˌtɪsɪ'peɪʃn/ *s* **1** previsão **2** expectativa

antics /'æntɪks/ *s* palhaçadas

antidote /'æntidoʊt/ *s* ~ **(for/to sth)** antídoto (contra algo)

antiquated /'æntɪkweɪtɪd/ *adj* antiquado

antique /æn'tiːk/ *s* (*objeto*) antigüidade ● *adj* antigo (*ger valioso*) **antiquity** /æn'tɪkwəti/ *s* (*pl* **-ies**) antigüidade

antithesis /æn'tɪθəsɪs/ *s* (*pl* **-theses** /-θəsiːz/) antítese

antler /'æntlər/ *s* **1** [*U*] chifre de cervo, rena, alce **2** (**antlers**) [*pl*] galhada

anus /'eɪnəs/ *s* (*pl* **-es**) ânus

anxiety /æŋ'zaɪəti/ *s* (*pl* **-ies**) **1** ansiedade, preocupação **2** ~ **for sth/to do sth** ânsia de (fazer) algo

anxious /'æŋkʃəs/ *adj* **1** ~ **(about sth)** preocupado (com algo): ~ *moment* momento de preocupação **2** ~ **to do sth** ansioso para fazer algo **anxiously** *adv* ansiosamente

any /'eni/ *adj*, *pron* → SOME

● **orações interrogativas 1** *Do you have* ~ *cash?* Você tem di-

nheiro? **2** um pouco (de): *Do you know* ~ *French?* Você sabe um pouco de francês? **3** algum: *Are there* ~ *problems?* Há algum problema? NOTA Neste sentido, o substantivo só vai para o plural em inglês.

● **orações negativas 1** *He doesn't have* ~ *friends.* Ele não tem amigos. ◇ *There isn't* ~ *left.* Não sobrou nenhum. → **NENHUM 2** [*uso enfático*]: *We won't do you* ~ *harm.* Nós não vamos lhe fazer mal algum.

● **orações condicionais 1** *If I had* ~ *relatives...* Se eu tivesse parentes... **2** um pouco de: *If he's got* ~ *sense, he won't go.* Se ele tiver um mínimo de bom senso, não irá. **3** algum NOTA Neste sentido, o substantivo só vai para o plural em inglês: *If you see* ~ *mistakes, tell me.* Se você vir algum erro, diga-me. NOTA Em muitas orações condicionais, pode-se empregar **some** em vez de **any**: *If you need some help, tell me.* Se precisar de ajuda, diga-me.

● **orações afirmativas 1** qualquer: *Take* ~ *one you like.* Pegue qualquer um que você quiser. **2** todo: *Give her* ~ *help she needs.* Dê-lhe toda a ajuda de que ela precisar.

● *adv* [*antes de comparativo*] mais: *She doesn't work here* ~ *longer.* Ela não trabalha mais aqui.

anybody /'enibɑdi/ *pron* **1** [*em orações interrogativas*] alguém: *Is* ~ *else coming?* Há mais alguém vindo? **2** [*em orações negativas*] ninguém → NOBODY **3** [*em orações afirmativas e comparativas*] qualquer pessoa: *Invite* ~ *you like.* Convide quem você quiser. ◇ *He spoke more than* ~. Ele falou mais do que qualquer outra pessoa. → EVERYBODY, SOMEBODY

anyhow /'enihaʊ/ *adv* **1** (*coloq* **any old how**) de qualquer maneira, descuidadamente **2** de qualquer forma, mesmo assim

anymore /ˌeni'mɔːr/ *adv* (*GB* **any more**): *She doesn't live here* ~. Ela não mora mais aqui.

anyone /'eniwʌn/ *Ver* ANYBODY

anyplace /'enipleɪs/ *Ver* ANYWHERE

anything /'eniθɪŋ/ *pron* **1** [*em orações interrogativas*] algo: *Is there* ~ *in this?* Há alguma verdade nestes boatos? **2** [*em orações negativas*] nada **3** [*em* orações afirmativas e comparativas] qualquer coisa, tudo: *It's better than ~ I've ever seen.* É melhor do que qualquer (outra) coisa que eu tenha visto. → NOBODY, SOMETHING ▶ **anything but:** *It was ~ but pleasant.* Foi tudo menos agradável. ◇ *"Are you tired?" "Anything but."* —Você está cansado? —De maneira alguma. **if anything:** *I'm a pacifist, if ~.* Eu sou um pacifista, para falar a verdade.

anyway /'eniweɪ/ *Ver* ANYHOW (2)

anywhere /'eniweəʳ/ *adv, pron* **1** [*em orações interrogativas*] em/ a algum lugar **2** [*em orações negativas*] em/a lugar nenhum: *I don't have ~ to stay.* Não tenho onde ficar. **3** [*em orações afirmativas e comparativas*] (em/a) qualquer lugar: ~ *you like* onde você quiser ◇ *more beautiful than ~* mais bonito do que qualquer outro lugar → NOBODY, SOMEWHERE

apart /ə'pɑːt/ *adv* **1** *The men were ten meters ~.* Os homens estavam a dez metros um do outro. ◇ *They are a long way ~.* Estão muito distantes um do outro. **2** à parte **3** (*em*) separado: *They live ~.* Eles vivem separados. ◇ *I can't pull them ~.* Não consigo separá-los. ▶ **take sth apart 1** desmontar algo **2** despedaçar algo

apart from *prep* exceto por, além de

apartment /ə'pɑːtmənt/ *s* apartamento

apathy /'æpəθi/ *s* apatia **apathetic** /ˌæpə'θetɪk/ *adj*

ape /eɪp/ *s* macaco ▶ *vt* imitar

apologetic /əˌpɒlə'dʒetɪk/ *adj* de desculpa: ~ *look* olhar de desculpa ◇ *be ~ (about sth)* desculpar-se (por algo)

apology /ə'pɒlədʒi/ *s* (*pl* **-ies**) (pedido de) desculpa: *make no ~ for sth* não se desculpar por algo **apologize** /ə'pɒlədʒaɪz/ *vi* desculpar-se

apostle /ə'pɒsl/ *s* apóstolo

appal (*USA tb* **appall**) /ə'pɔːl/ *vt* (-ll-) estarrecer **appalling** *adj* estarrecedor, horrível

apparatus /ˌæpə'ræetəs; *GB* -'reɪtəs/ *s* [U] aparelho

apparent /ə'pærənt/ *adj* evidente **2** aparente **apparently** *adv* ao que parece: *Apparently not.* Aparentemente, não.

appeal /ə'piːl/ *vi* **1** ~ **to sb to do sth;** ~ **(to sb) for sth** implorar a

alguém para que faça algo; algo (a alguém) **2** appelar **3** ~ **(to sb)** atrair alguém **4** ~ **(against sth)** recorrer (de algo) ▶ *s* **1** ~ **(for sth)** apelo (de algo) **2** súplica **3** atração **4** recurso: ~*(s) court* tribunal de apelação **appealing** *adj* **1** atraente **2** suplicante

appear /ə'pɪəʳ/ *vi* **1** aparecer **2** parecer **3** comparecer **appearance** *s* **1** aparição **2** aparecimento ▶ **keep up appearances** manter as aparências

appendicitis /əˌpendə'saɪtɪs/ *s* apendicite

appendix /ə'pendɪks/ (*pl* **-dices** /-dɪsiːz/) *s* apêndice

appetite /'æpɪtaɪt/ *s* apetite: *give sb an ~* abrir o apetite de alguém

applaud /ə'plɔːd/ *vt, vi* aplaudir **applause** *s* [U] aplausos: *a big round of ~* uma grande salva de palmas

apple /'æpl/ *s* **1** maçã **2** (*tb* ~ **tree**) macieira

appliance /ə'plaɪəns/ *s* aparelho: *electrical appliances* eletrodomésticos ◇ *kitchen appliances* utensílios de cozinha

applicable /'æplɪkəbl, ə'plɪkəbl/ *adj* aplicável, apropriado

applicant /'æplɪkənt/ *s* requerente, candidato/a (*a uma vaga, a um emprego*)

application /ˌæplɪ'keɪʃn/ *s* **1** solicitação: ~ *form* formulário para requerimento/inscrição **2** aplicação

applied /ə'plaɪd/ *adj* aplicado

apply /ə'plaɪ/ (*pt, pp* **-ied**) **1** *vt, vi* ~ **(to sb/sth)** aplicar, aplicar-se (a alguém/algo) **2** *vt* (*força, etc.*) empregar: ~ *the brakes* frear **3** *vi* ~ **(for sth)** solicitar (algo); inscrever-se (em algo) ▶ **apply yourself (to sth)** dedicar-se (a algo)

appoint /ə'pɔɪnt/ *vt* **1** nomear **2** (*fml*) (*hora, lugar*) marcar **appointment** *s* **1** nomeação **2** posto **3** compromisso (*profissional*) **4** consulta (*médico, etc.*)

appraisal /ə'preɪzl/ *s* avaliação

appreciate /ə'priːʃieɪt/ **1** *vt* apreciar **2** *vt* agradecer **3** *vt* compreender **4** *vi* valorizar-se **appreciation** *s* **1** apreciação **2** agradecimento **3** valorização **appreciative** *adj* **1** ~ **(of sth)** agradecido (por algo) **2** (*olhar, etc.*) de admiração **3** (*reação*) favorável, caloroso

apprehend /ˌæprɪ'hend/ *vt* apreender **apprehension** *s* apreensão **apprehensive** *adj* apreensivo

apprentice /ə'prentɪs/ s **1** aprendiz **2** principiante apprenticeship s aprendizagem

approach /ə'prəʊtʃ/ **1** vt, vi aproximar-se (de) **2** vt ~ sb procurar alguém (para pedir/oferecer algo) **3** vt abordar ● s **1** chegada **2** aproximação **3** acesso **4** enfoque

appropriate /ə'prəʊprɪət/ adj **1** apropriado, adequado **2** oportuno appropriately ● adv apropriadamente, adequadamente ● /ə'prəʊprɪeɪt/ vt apropriar-se de

approval /ə'pruːvl/ s aprovação, autorização ▸ on approval sob condição

approve /ə'pruːv/ **1** vt aprovar **2** vi ~ (of sth) aprovar (algo); estar de acordo (com algo) **3** vi ~ (of sb): I don't ~ of him. Não o tenho em bom conceito. approving adj aprovador

approximate /ə'prɒksɪmət/ adj aproximado ● /ə'prɒksɪmeɪt/ vi ~ to sth aproximar-se de algo approximately adv aproximadamente

apricot /'eɪprɪkɒt/ s **1** damasco **2** (tb ~ tree) damasqueiro **3** cor de damasco

April /'eɪprəl/ s (abrev Apr.) abril → MAY

apron /'eɪprən/ s avental

apt /æpt/ adj (~er, ~est) apropriado ▸ be apt to do sth ter tendência a fazer algo aptly adv apropriadamente

aptitude /'æptɪtuːd; GB -tjuːd/ s aptidão

aquarium /ə'kweərɪəm/ s aquário

Aquarius /ə'kweərɪəs/ s Aquário

aquatic /ə'kwætɪk/ adj aquático

arable /'ærəbl/ adj cultivável: ~ land terra de cultivo

arbitrary /'ɑːbɪtreri; GB 'ɑːbɪtrəri/ adj arbitrário

arbitrate /'ɑːbɪtreɪt/ vt, vi arbitrar arbitration s árbitro

arc /ɑːk/ s arco

arcade /ɑː'keɪd/ s **1** galeria: amusement ~ salão de fliperama **2** arcada

arch /ɑːtʃ/ s arco ● vt, vi arquear(-se)

archaic /ɑː'keɪɪk/ adj arcaico

archbishop /ˌɑːtʃ'bɪʃəp/ s arcebispo

archeology (GB **archae-**) /ˌɑːki'ɒlədʒi/ s arqueologia **archeological** (GB **archae-**) /ˌɑːkiə'lɒdʒɪkl/ adj arqueológico **archeologist** (GB **archae-**)

/ˌɑːki'ɒlədʒɪst/ s arqueólogo/a

archer /'ɑːtʃər/ s arqueiro/a archery s arco-e-flecha

architect /'ɑːkɪtekt/ s arquiteto/a

architecture /'ɑːkɪtektʃər/ s arquitetura architectural /ˌɑːkɪ'tektʃərəl/ adj arquitetônico

archive /'ɑːkaɪv/ s arquivo

archway /'ɑːtʃweɪ/ s arco (arquitetônico)

ardent /'ɑːdnt/ adj ardente, entusiasta

ardor (GB **-our**) /'ɑːdər/ s fervor

arduous /'ɑːdʒʊəs; GB -dju-/ adj árduo

are /ər, ɑː/ Ver BE

area /'eərɪə/ s **1** superfície **2** área **3** (Geog) região: ~ manager gerente regional **4** recinto

area code s prefixo (de DDD)

arena /ə'riːnə/ s **1** estádio **2** (circo) picadeiro **3** arena **4** âmbito

aren't /ɑːnt/ = ARE NOT Ver BE

arguable /'ɑːgjuəbl/ adj **1** It is ~ that... Pode-se argumentar que... **2** discutível arguably adv provavelmente

argue /'ɑːgjuː/ **1** vi discutir **2** vt, vi ~ (for/against sth) argumentar (a favor de/contra algo)

argument /'ɑːgjumənt/ s **1** discussão: have an ~ discutir **2** ~ (for/against sth) argumento (a favor de/contra algo)

arid /'ærɪd; GB 'ærɪd/ adj árido

Aries /'eəriːz/ s Áries

arise /ə'raɪz/ vi (pt arose pp arisen /ə'rɪzn/) **1** (problema, etc.) surgir: should the need ~ se houver necessidade **2** (oportunidade) aparecer **3** (questão) levantar-se **4** (antiq) levantar-se

aristocrat /ə'rɪstəkræt; GB 'ærɪst-/ s aristocrata aristocratic /ˌærɪstə'krætɪk/ adj aristocrático aristocracy /ˌærɪ'stɒkrəsi/ s (pl -ies) aristocracia

arithmetic /ə'rɪθmətɪk/ s aritmética: mental ~ = cálculo mental

ark /ɑːk/ s arca

arm /ɑːm/ s **1** braço: ~ in ~ (with sb) de braços dados NOTA Os nomes das partes do corpo geralmente são precedidas por um adjetivo possessivo (my, your, etc.). **2** manga ● vt, vi ~ (yourself) (with sth) armar(-se) com/de algo

armament /'ɑːməmənt/ s armamento

armchair /ɑːm'tʃeər/ s poltrona, cadeira de braços

armed /ɑːmd/ adj armado: ~ *robbery* assalto à mão armada
armed forces (tb **armed services**) s forças armadas
armistice /ˈɑːmɪstɪs/ s armistício
armor (GB **-our**) /ˈɑːmə(r)/ s [U] **1** *suit of* ~ armadura **2** blindagem
armored (GB **-oured**) adj **1** blindado **2** encouraçado
armpit /ˈɑːmpɪt/ s axila
arms /ɑːmz/ s [pl] **1** armas: ~ *race* corrida armamentista **2** brasão ▶ **be up in arms** (about/over sth) estar em pé de guerra (por algo)
army /ˈɑːmi/ s (pl **-ies**) exército
arose /əˈrəʊz/ pret de ARISE
around /əˈraʊnd/ • prep **1** mais ou menos, aproximadamente **2** cerca de: ~ *1850* por volta de 1850 NOTA Em expressões temporais, **about** é precedido pelas preposições **at, on, in**, enquanto **around** não requer preposição: *around/at about five o'clock* ◊ *around/on about June 15*. **3** por perto/aqui • adv **1** daqui para lá, por aqui: *I was dashing* ~ *all day*. Eu corri de lá para cá o dia todo. **2** ao redor NOTA Para o uso de **around** em PHRASAL VERBS, ver o verbo, p. ex. **lie around** em LIE[2] • prep **1** por: *travel* ~ *the world* viajar pelo mundo inteiro **2** ao redor de
arouse /əˈraʊz/ vt **1** suscitar **2** excitar (sexualmente) **3** despertar
arrange /əˈreɪndʒ/ vt **1** dispor **2** arrumar **3** organizar **4** ~ for sb to do sth providenciar para que alguém faça algo **5** ~ to do sth combinar de fazer algo **6** (Mús) fazer arranjo de
arrangement s **1** disposição **2** arranjo **3** acordo **4** (**arrangements**) preparativos
arrest /əˈrest/ vt **1** (criminoso) deter, prender **2** (fml) (inflação, etc.) conter **3** (atenção) atrair • s **1** detenção: *be under* ~ estar detido/preso **2** *cardiac* ~ parada cardíaca
arrival /əˈraɪvl/ s **1** chegada **2** *new/recent arrivals* recém-chegados
arrive /əˈraɪv/ vi **1** chegar NOTA Usa-se **arrive in** quando se chega a país ou cidade: *When did you* ~ *in England?* Usa-se **arrive at** quando o verbo é seguido de referência a um local específico, como um edifício, estação, etc.: *We'll phone you as soon as we* ~ *at the airport.*

"Chegar em casa" traduz-se por *arrive home* ou *get home.* **2** (coloq) (êxito) chegar lá (em cima)
arrogant /ˈærəgənt/ adj arrogante arrogance s arrogância
arrow /ˈærəʊ/ s flecha, seta
arson /ˈɑːsn/ s incêndio premeditado
art /ɑːt/ s **1** arte: *work of* ~ obra de arte **2** (**the arts**) as belas-artes **3** (**arts**) [pl] (estudos) humanas **4** astúcia
artery /ˈɑːtəri/ s (pl **-ies**) artéria
arthritis /ɑːˈθraɪtɪs/ s artrite arthritic adj artrítico
artichoke /ˈɑːtɪtʃəʊk/ s alcachofra
article /ˈɑːtɪkl/ s **1** artigo **2** *articles of clothing* peças de roupa/vestuário
articulate /ɑːˈtɪkjuleɪt/ vt, vi articular • /ɑːˈtɪkjələt/ adj que se exprime com clareza
artificial /ˌɑːtɪˈfɪʃl/ adj artificial
artillery /ɑːˈtɪləri/ s artilharia
artisan /ˈɑːtɪzn; GB ˌɑːtɪˈzæn/ s artesão
artist /ˈɑːtɪst/ s artista
artistic /ɑːˈtɪstɪk/ adj artístico
artwork /ˈɑːtwɜːk/ s arte-final
as /əz, æz/ prep **1** como: *Treat me as a friend.* Trate-me como um amigo. ◊ *work as a waiter* trabalhar como/de garçom **2** *as a child* quando (era/se é) criança NOTA Em comparações e exemplos se utiliza **like**: *a car like yours* ◊ *romantic poets like Byron*. • adv **as... as** tão... quanto/como: *as soon as possible* o quanto antes ◊ *I earn as much as her/as she does.* Ganho tanto quanto ela. • conj **1** enquanto **2** uma vez que, como: *as you weren't there...* como você não estava lá... **3** (tal) como ▶ **as for sb/sth** em relação a alguém/algo: *As for you, you can go now.* Quanto a você, pode ir agora. **as from/of**: *as from/of May 12* a partir de 12 de maio **as if/as though** como se **as it is** em situação da situação **as many 1** tantos: *I didn't win as many as him.* Não ganhei tantos quanto ele. ◊ *You ate three times as many as I did.* Você comeu três vezes mais do que eu. **2** outros tantos: *four jobs in as many months* quatro empregos no mesmo número de meses **as many as...**: *as many as ten people* até dez pessoas **as much:** *I don't have as much as you.* Não tenho tanto quanto você. ◊

I thought as much. Foi o (mesmo) que eu pensei. **as much/many again** outro(s) tanto(s) **as to sth/as regards sth** quanto a/em relação a algo **as yet** até agora

asbestos /æs'bestəs, əz'bestəs/ s amianto

ascend /ə'send/ (*fml*) **1** *vi* ascender **2** *vt* subir (a)

ascendancy /ə'sendənsi/ s influência, ascendência

ascent /ə'sent/ s **1** ascensão **2** subida

ascertain /ˌæsər'tem/ *vt* (*fml*) averiguar

ascribe /ə'skraɪb/ *vt* atribuir

ash /æʃ/ s **1** (*tb* ~ **tree**) freixo **2** cinza

ashamed /ə'ʃeɪmd/ *adj* envergonhado: *be ~ to do sth* estar com vergonha de fazer algo

ashore /ə'ʃɔːr/ *adv, prep* em/à terra: *go ~* desembarcar

ashtray /'æʃtreɪ/ s cinzeiro

Ash Wednesday s Quarta-feira de Cinzas

aside /ə'saɪd/ *adv* **1** para um lado **2** de reserva, de lado ● s aparte

aside from *prep* (*esp USA*) exceto por, além de

ask /æsk; *GB* ɑːsk/ **1** *vt, vi* ~ (**sb**) (**sth**) perguntar (algo) (a alguém): ~ *a question* fazer uma pergunta **2** *vt, vi* ~ (**sb**) **for sth**; ~ **sb to do sth** pedir algo (a alguém); a alguém que faça algo **3** *vt* convidar: ~ **sb out/round** convidar alguém para sair/para vir à sua casa ▸ **ask for trouble/it** (*coloq*) procurar sarna para se coçar **don't ask me** (*coloq*) eu é que sei, sei lá **for the asking**: *The job is yours for the asking.* Basta pedir e o emprego é seu. ■ **ask after sb** perguntar como alguém está ■ **ask for sb** pedir para ver/conversar com alguém

asleep /ə'sliːp/ *adj* adormecido: *fall ~* adormecer ◇ *fast/sound ~* dormindo profundamente NOTA Não se usa *asleep* antes de substantivos; portanto, para traduzir "um bebê adormecido" diz-se *a sleeping baby*.

asparagus /ə'spærəgəs/ s [*U*] aspargo(s)

aspect /'æspekt/ s **1** (*situação, etc.*) aspecto **2** (*Arquit*) orientação

asphalt /'æsfɔːlt; *GB* -fælt/ s asfalto

asphyxiate /əs'fɪksieɪt/ *vt* asfixiar

aspiration /ˌæspə'reɪʃn/ s aspiração

aspire /ə'spaɪər/ *vi* aspirar: *aspiring musicians* músicos aspirantes

aspirin /'æsprɪn, 'æspərɪn/ s aspirina

ass /æs/ s **1** asno **2** (*idiota*) burro

assailant /ə'seɪlənt/ s (*fml*) agressor/a

assassin /ə'sæsn; *GB* -sɪn/ s assassino/a **assassinate** *vt* assassinar **assassination** s assassinato ➤ ASSASSINAR

assault /ə'sɔːlt/ *vt* **1** agredir **2** (*sexualmente*) violar ● s **1** agressão **2** ~ (**on sb/sth**) ataque (contra alguém/algo) **3** (*sexual*) violação

assemble /ə'sembl/ **1** *vt, vi* reunir(-se) **2** *vt* (*Mec*) montar

assembly /ə'sembli/ s (*pl* -**ies**) **1** assembléia **2** (*escola*) reunião matinal **3** (*montagem*) ~ **line** linha de montagem

assert /ə'sɜːrt/ *vt* **1** afirmar **2** (*direitos, etc.*) fazer valer ▸ **assert yourself** impor-se **assertion** s afirmação

assertive /ə'sɜːrtɪv/ *adj* firme, confiante

assess /ə'ses/ *vt* **1** avaliar **2** calcular **assessment** s avaliação **assessor** s avaliador/a

asset /'æset/ s **1** qualidade, vantagem: *be an ~ to sb/sth* ser de valor para alguém/algo **2** (*assets*) (*Com*) bens

assign /ə'saɪn/ *vt* **1** designar **2** ~ **sth to sb/sth** indicar alguém para algo

assignment /ə'saɪnmənt/ s **1** (*escola*) trabalho **2** missão

assimilate /ə'sɪmɪleɪt/ **1** *vt* assimilar **2** *vi* ~ **into sth** incorporar-se a algo

assist /ə'sɪst/ *vt, vi* (*fml*) ajudar, assistir **assistance** s (*fml*) **1** ajuda **2** auxílio

assistant /ə'sɪstənt/ s **1** ajudante, assistente **2** vendedor/a **3** ~ *manager* subgerente

associate /ə'səʊʃieɪt, -sieɪt/ **1** *vt* associar **2** *vi* ~ **with sb** tratar, envolver-se com alguém ● s /ə'səʊʃiət, -siət/ s sócio/a

association /əˌsəʊsi'eɪʃn/ s **1** associação **2** envolvimento

assorted /ə'sɔːrtɪd/ *adj* **1** variado **2** sortido

assortment /ə'sɔːrtmənt/ s sortimento

assume /ə'suːm; *GB* ə'sjuːm/ *vt* **1** supor **2** dar por certo **3** (*significado*) adquirir **4** (*controle,* *expressão*) assumir

assumption /ə'sʌmpʃn/ s 1 suposição 2 (*de poder, etc.*) tomada

assurance /ə'ʃʊərəns; *GB* ə'ʃɔːrəns/ s 1 garantia 2 confiança

assure /ə'ʃʊər/ vt 1 ~ (**yourself that...**) assegurar(-se) (de que...) 2 vt ~ **sb of sth** garantir algo a alguém; convencer alguém de algo **assured** adj ~ (**of sth**) seguro (quanto a algo)

asterisk /'æstərɪsk/ s asterisco

asthma /'æzmə; *GB* 'æsmə/ s asma **asthmatic** /æz'mætɪk/ *GB* æs-/ adj, s asmático/a

astonish /ə'stɒnɪʃ/ vt assombrar **astonishing** adj assombroso **astonishingly** adv incrivelmente **astonishment** s assombro

astound /ə'staʊnd/ vt deixar atônito **astounding** adj incrível

astray /ə'streɪ/ adv ▶ **go astray** extraviar-se

astride /ə'straɪd/ prep a cavalo, (montado) sobre

astrology /ə'strɒlədʒi/ s astrologia

astronaut /'æstrənɔːt/ s astronauta

astronomy /ə'strɒnəmi/ s astronomia **astronomer** s astrônomo/a **astronomical** /ˌæstrə'nɒmɪkl/ adj astronômico

astute /ə'stuːt; *GB* ə'stjuːt/ adj astuto

asylum /ə'saɪləm/ s 1 asilo (*político*) 2 (*antiq*) hospício

at /æt, ət/ prep 1 (*posição*) em, a: *at home* em casa → EM 2 (*tempo*): *at 3.35* às 3h 35 ◇ *at times* às vezes ◇ *at night* à noite ◇ *at the moment* no momento 3 (*preço, freqüência, velocidade*) a: *at full volume* no máximo volume ◇ *two at a time* de dois em dois 4 *stare at sb* olhar fixamente para alguém 5 (*reação*): *surprised at sth* surpreso com algo ◇ *At this, she fainted.* Nesse momento, ela desmaiou. 6 (*atividade*) em: *She's at work.* Ela está trabalhando. ◇ *children at play* crianças brincando

ate /eɪt/ *GB* /et/ pret de EAT

atheism /'eɪθiɪzəm/ s ateísmo **atheist** s ateu, atéia

athlete /'æθliːt/ s atleta

athletic /æθ'letɪk/ adj atlético **athletics** s [*sing*] atletismo

atlas /'ætləs/ s 1 atlas 2 (*de estradas*) mapa

ATM /ˌeɪ tiː 'em/ s caixa

automático

atmosphere /'ætməsfɪər/ s 1 atmosfera 2 ambiente

atom /'ætəm/ s 1 átomo 2 (*fig*) pingo

atomic /ə'tɒmɪk/ adj atômico

atrocious /ə'trəʊʃəs/ adj 1 atroz 2 péssimo **atrocity** /ə'trɒsəti/ s (*pl* -**ies**) atrocidade

attach /ə'tætʃ/ vt 1 atar 2 juntar 3 (*documentos*) anexar 4 ~ *importance to sth* dar importância a algo **attached** adj: *be* ~ *to sb/sth* ter carinho por alguém/algo **attachment** s 1 acessório 2 apego 3 (*Informát*) anexo

attack /ə'tæk/ s ~ (**on sb/sth**) ataque (contra alguém/algo) ● vt, vi atacar **attacker** s atacante

attain /ə'teɪn/ vt alcançar, conseguir **attainment** s obtenção, realização

attempt /ə'tempt/ vt tentar ● s 1 ~ (**at doing/to do sth**) tentativa (de fazer algo) 2 tentativa: *attempted* adj: ~ *robbery* tentativa de roubo

attend /ə'tend/ 1 vt, vi comparecer (a): ~ *school* ir à escola ◇ ~ *a meeting* participar de uma reunião 2 vi ~ **to sb/sth** ocupar-se de/com alguém/algo **attendance** s 1 assistência 2 comparecimento ▶ **in attendance** presente

attendant /ə'tendənt/ s encarregado/a

attention /ə'tenʃn/ s, interj atenção

attentive /ə'tentɪv/ adj atento

attic /'ætɪk/ s sótão

attitude /'ætɪtuːd; *GB* -tjuːd/ s atitude

attorney /ə'tɜːrni/ s 1 (*USA*) advogado/a → ADVOGADO 2 procurador/a

Attorney-General s 1 (*USA*) procurador/a geral do Estado 2 (*GB*) procurador/a público/a

attract /ə'trækt/ vt atrair 2 (*atenção*) chamar **attraction** s 1 atração 2 atrativo **attractive** adj atraente

attribute /'ætrɪbjuːt/ s atributo ● /ə'trɪbjuːt/ vt atribuir

aubergine /'əʊbərʒiːn/ s berinjela ● adj roxo

auction /'ɔːkʃn/ s leilão ● vt leiloar **auctioneer** /ˌɔːkʃə'nɪər/ s leiloeiro/a

audible /'ɔːdəbl/ adj audível

audience /'ɔːdiəns/ s 1 (*teatro, etc.*) público 2 (*TV, rádio*) audiência 3 ~ **with sb** audiência com alguém audit /'ɔːdɪt/ s auditoria • vt fazer auditoria de

audition /ɔː'dɪʃn/ s audição • vi apresentar-se em uma audição

auditor /'ɔːdɪtər/ s auditor/a

auditorium /ˌɔːdɪ'tɔːriəm/ s auditório

August /'ɔːgəst/ s (abrev Aug.) agosto ➤ MAY

aunt /ænt/ GB ɑːnt/ s tia: my ~ and uncle meus tios meu tio auntie (tb aunty) s (coloq) titia

au pair /ˌoʊ 'peər/ s au pair (pessoa, em geral estrangeira, que mora com uma família em troca de serviços domésticos)

austere /ɔː'stɪər/ adj austero

austerity /ɔː'sterəti/ s austeridade

authentic /ɔː'θentɪk/ adj autêntico authenticity /ˌɔː'θen'tɪsəti/ s autenticidade

author /'ɔːθər/ s autor/a

authoritarian /ɔːˌθɒrɪ'teəriən/ adj, s autoritário/a

authoritative /ɔː'θɒrətətɪv; GB -tətɪv/ adj 1 de grande autoridade, confiável 2 autoritário

authority /ɔː'θɒrəti/ s (pl -ies) autoridade ▸ have it on good authority that... saber de fonte segura que...

authorize /'ɔːθəraɪz/ vt autorizar authorization /ˌɔːθərɪ'zeɪʃn; GB -raɪz-/ s autorização

autobiography /ˌɔːtəbaɪ'ɒɡrəfi/ s (pl -ies) autobiografia autobiographical /ˌɔːtəˌbaɪə'ɡræfɪkl/ adj autobiográfico

autograph /'ɔːtəɡræf; GB -ɡrɑːf/ s autógrafo • vt autografar

automate /'ɔːtəmeɪt/ vt automatizar

automatic /ˌɔːtə'mætɪk/ adj automático • s 1 pistola automática 2 carro hidramático automatically adv automaticamente automation /ˌɔːtə'meɪʃn/ s automação

automobile /'ɔːtəməbiːl/ s automóvel

autonomous /ɔː'tɒnəməs/ adj autônomo autonomy s autonomia

autopsy /'ɔːtɒpsi/ s (pl -ies) autópsia

autumn /'ɔːtəm/ s (GB) outono

auxiliary /ɔːɡ'zɪliəri/ adj, s auxiliar, assistente

avail /ə'veɪl/ s ▸ to no avail em vão

available /ə'veɪləbl/ adj disponível

avalanche /'ævəlæntʃ; GB -lɑːnʃ/ s avalanche

avant-garde /ˌævɒŋ 'ɡɑːd/ adj vanguardista

avenue /'ævənuː; GB -njuː/ s 1 (abrev Ave.) avenida, alameda 2 (fig) caminho

average /'ævərɪdʒ/ s média: on ~ em média • adj 1 médio 2 comum 3 medíocre • vt ter uma média de ■ average out: It averages out at 10%. Sai a uma média de 10%.

aversion /ə'vɜːrʒn/ s aversão

avert /ə'vɜːrt/ vt 1 (olhar) desviar 2 (crise, etc.) evitar

aviation /ˌeɪvi'eɪʃn/ s aviação

avid /'ævɪd/ adj ávido

avocado /ˌævə'kɑːdoʊ, ˌæv-/ s (pl ~s) abacate

avoid /ə'vɔɪd/ vt 1 ~ (doing) sth evitar (fazer) algo 2 eximir-se de

await /ə'weɪt/ vt (fml) 1 estar à espera de 2 aguardar

awake /ə'weɪk/ adj 1 acordado 2 ~ to sth consciente de algo • vt, vi (pt awoke pp awoken) (fml) acordar NOTA O verbo mais comum é wake (sb) up.

awaken /ə'weɪkən/ vt, vi (fml) despertar

award /ə'wɔːrd/ vt conceder • s prêmio, recompensa

aware /ə'weər/ adj consciente, ciente: as far as I am ~ que eu saiba ◊ make sb ~ of sth informar alguém de algo awareness s 1 consciência 2 conhecimento

away /ə'weɪ/ adv 1 (distância): The hotel is two kilometers ~. O hotel está a dois quilômetros. ◊ It's a long way ~. Fica bem longe daqui. ◊ Christmas is only a week ~. Falta apenas uma semana para o Natal. ◊ She's ~ this week. Ela está fora esta semana. 2 (com verbos de movimento): He limped ~. Ele se foi mancando. 3 [uso enfático]: I was working ~ all night. Passei toda a noite trabalhando. ◊ The snow had melted ~. A neve havia derretido completamente. NOTA Para o uso de away em PHRASAL VERBS, ver o verbo, p. ex. get away em GET.

awe /ɔː/ s admiração, temor: be in ~ of sb sentir-se intimidado por alguém awesome adj impressionante

awful /'ɔːfl/ adj 1 horrível 2 an ~ lot of money um monte de dinheiro awfully adv terrivelmente: I'm ~ sorry. Sinto muitíssimo.

awkward /'ɔːkwərd/ adj 1 inoportuno, incômodo

2 (*pessoa*) difícil **3** desajeitado **4** embaraçoso

awoke /əˈwoʊk/ *pret de* AWAKE

awoken /əˈwoʊkən/ *pp de* AWAKE

ax (GB **axe**) /æks/ *s* machado ▶ **have an ax to grind** ter um interesse pessoal ● *vt* **1** (*serviço, etc.*) cortar **2** (*pessoal, etc.*) despedir

axis /ˈæksɪs/ *s* (*pl* **axes** /ˈæksiːz/) eixo

axle /ˈæksl/ *s* eixo (*rodas*)

aye (*tb* **ay**) /aɪ/ *interj, s* (*antiq*) sim: *The ~s have it.* Ganharam os que estavam a favor. NOTA *Aye* é comum na Escócia e no norte da Inglaterra.

Bb

B, b /biː/ *s* (*pl* **B's, b's** /biːz/) **1** B, b **2** (*Educ*) (nota) B **3** (*Mús*) si

babble /ˈbæbl/ *s* **1** fala ininteligível, burburinho (*bebê*) ● *vt, vi* falar de maneira confusa, balbuciar

babe /beɪb/ *s* (*coloq*) garota (*brotinho*)

baby /ˈbeɪbi/ *s* (*pl* **-ies**) bebê: *newborn ~* recém-nascido ◊ *~ girl* menina **2** (*animal*) filhote **3** (*esp USA, coloq*) benzinho

babysit /ˈbeɪbisɪt/ *vi* (**-tt-**) (*pt, pp* **-sat**) cuidar de uma criança **babysitter** *s* babá

bachelor /ˈbætʃələr/ *s* solteirão

back /bæk/ *s* **1** parte de trás **2** dorso **3** (*página, etc.*) verso **4** costas **5** (*cadeira*) encosto ▶ **at the back of your/sb's mind** no fundo (da mente de alguém) **back to back** de costas um para o outro **back to front** de trás para frente **be glad, etc. to see the back of sb/sth** alegrar-se por se ver livre de alguém/algo **be on sb's back** (*fig*) estar em cima de alguém **behind sb's back** pelas costas (de alguém) **get/have your own back (on sb)** (GB, *coloq*) vingar-se de alguém) **get/put sb's back up** irritar alguém **have your back to the wall** estar encurralado ● *adj* **1** traseiro: *the ~ door* a porta dos fundos **2** (*fascículo*) atrasado ▶ *adv* **1** (*movimento, posição*) para trás: *Stand well ~.* Mantenha-se afastado. ◊ *a mile ~* uma milha atrás **2** (*de volta*) de volta: *He smiled ~ (at her).* Ele lhe sorriu de volta ◊ *on the way ~* na volta ◊ *go there and ~* ir lá e

voltar **3** (*tempo*) lá (por): *a few years ~* há alguns anos ▶ **back and forth** de lá para cá NOTA Para o uso de *back* em PHRASAL VERBS, ver o verbo, p. ex. go **back** em GO ● *vt* **1** apoiar alguém ▶ **back ~ sb / sth (up)** apoiar alguém **2** *vt* financiar **3** *vt* apostar em **4** *vi* **~ (up)** dar marcha a ré ■ **back away (from sb / sth)** retroceder (diante de alguém / algo) **back down / off** desistir **back on to sth** (GB) *Our house backs on to the river.* A parte de trás da nossa casa dá para o rio. **back out (of an agreement, etc.)** voltar atrás (em um acordo, etc.)

backache /ˈbækeɪk/ *s* dor nas costas

backbone /ˈbækboʊn/ *s* **1** coluna vertebral **2** firmeza

backdrop /ˈbækdrɑp/ (GB *tb* **backcloth** /ˈbækklɔːθ; GB -klɒθ/) *s* pano de fundo

backfire /bækˈfaɪər/ *vi* **1** engasgar **2 ~ (on sb)** sair (a alguém) o tiro pela culatra

background /ˈbækɡraʊnd/ *s* **1** fundo **2** contexto **3** antecedentes (*classe social, etc.*)

backing /ˈbækɪŋ/ *s* **1** apoio **2** (*Mús*) acompanhamento

backlash /ˈbæklæʃ/ *s* reação violenta

backlog /ˈbæklɔːɡ/ *s* acúmulo: *a huge ~ of work* um monte de trabalho acumulado

backpack /ˈbækpæk/ *s* mochila

back seat *s* assento traseiro ▶ **take a back seat** passar para o segundo plano

backside /ˈbæksaɪd/ *s* traseiro

backstage /ˌbækˈsteɪdʒ/ *adv* nos bastidores

backup /ˈbækʌp/ *s* **1** apoio, reserva **2** (*Informát*) cópia

backward /ˈbækwərd/ *adj* **1** para trás **2** atrasado

backward(s) /ˈbækwərd(z)/ *adv* **1** para trás **2** de costas **3** de trás para frente ▶ **backward(s) and forward(s)** de um lado para o outro

backyard /ˌbækˈjɑːrd/ *Ver* YARD (1), (2)

bacon /ˈbeɪkən/ *s* toicinho

bacteria /bækˈtɪəriə/ *s* [*pl*] bactérias

bad /bæd/ *adj* (*comp* **worse** *superl* **worst**) **1** mau: *It's ~ for your health.* Não faz bem à saúde. ◊ *I'm ~ at math.* Eu sou ruim em matemática. **2** (*erro, acidente, etc.*) grave **3** (*dor de cabeça, etc.*) forte ▶ **be in sb's bad books** (GB) estar na lista negra de alguém **go through/ hit a bad patch** (*coloq*) passar por uma fase ruim **too bad** *It's too ~ you can't come.* (É uma) pena que você não possa vir. **2** pior para você, que pena

badge /bædʒ/ s **1** distintivo, crachá **2** símbolo

badger /'bædʒər/ s texugo

bad language s linguagem chula

badly /'bædli/ adv (*comp* **worse** *superl* **worst**) **1** mal **2** *The house was ~ damaged.* A casa estava bastante danificada. **3** com urgência ▸(**not) be badly off** (não) estar mal (de dinheiro)

badminton /'bædmɪntən/ s espécie de tênis com peteca

bad-tempered *adj* mal-humorado

baffle /'bæfl/ vt **1** confundir, desnortear **2** frustrar **baffling** *adj* desnorteante

bag /bæg/ s bolsa, saco, sacola ▸**bags of sth** (*coloq*) montanhas de algo **be in the bag** (*coloq*) estar no papo

baggage /'bægɪdʒ/ s bagagem

baggy /'bægi/ adj (**-ier, -iest**) folgado (*roupa*)

bag lunch s (*USA*) almoço/ sanduíche que se leva de casa

bagpipes /'bægpaɪps/ s [*pl*] gaita de foles

baguette /bæ'get/ s baguete

bail /beɪl/ s (liberdade sob) fiança: *go/stand ~ (for sb)* (*GB*) pagar a fiança (de alguém)

bailiff /'beɪlɪf/ s oficial de justiça

bait /beɪt/ s isca

bake /beɪk/ vt, vi assar **baker** s padeiro/a **bakery** s (pl **-ies**) (*GB* **baker's**) padaria

balance /'bæləns/ s **1** equilíbrio **2** (*Fin*) saldo, balanço **3** balança ▸**on balance** (*GB*) considerando-se tudo ● vt, vi equilibrar (-se) **2** vt manter algo em equilíbrio **3** vt compensar, contrabalançar **4** vt, vi (*contas*) (fazer) acertar

balcony /'bælkəni/ s (pl **-ies**) **1** sacada (*Teat*) balcão

bald /bɔːld/ adj careca

ball /bɔːl/ s **1** (*Esporte*) bola **2** esfera **3** novelo **4** baile ▸**be on the ball** (*coloq*) estar por dentro **have a ball** (*coloq*) divertir-se muito **start/set the ball rolling** começar

ballad /'bæləd/ s balada

ballet /'bæleɪ/ s balé

ballet dancer s bailarino/a

balloon /bə'luːn/ s balão

ballot /'bælət/ s votação: *absentee ~* voto postal

ballot box s urna (*eleitoral*)

ballpoint pen /ˌbɔːlpɔɪnt 'pen/ s (caneta) esferográfica

ballroom /'bɔːlruːm/ s salão de baile

bamboo /ˌbæm'buː/ s bambu

ban /bæn/ vt (**-nn-**) proibir ● s ~ **(on sth)** proibição (de algo)

banana /bə'nænə; *GB* bə'nɑːnə/ s banana

band /bænd/ s **1** faixa, fita **2** escala **3** (*Mús*) banda **4** (*de ladrões, etc.*) bando

bandage /'bændɪdʒ/ s faixa (de gaze) ● vt enfaixar

Band-Aid® s (*USA*) band-aid

bandwagon /'bændwægən/ s ▸**climb/jump on the bandwagon** entrar na onda

bang /bæŋ/ **1** vt golpear: ~ *your fist on the table* dar um murro na mesa ◊ *I banged the box down on the floor.* Atirei a caixa no chão. **2** vt, vi (*porta, etc.*) bater: ~ *your head (against/on sth)* bater a cabeça (contra/em) **3** vi ~ **into sb/sth** chocar-se contra alguém/algo ● s **1** golpe **2** explosão ● adv **1** (*GB*) (*coloq*) exato, completamente ▸**bang goes sth** (*GB*) acabar-se algo: ~ *went his hopes of promotion.* E lá se foram as esperanças dele de promoção. **go bang** (*coloq*) explodir ● interj pum

banger /'bæŋər/ s **1** lingüiça **2** rojão **3** calhambeque: *an old ~* uma lata velha

bangs /bæŋz/ s [*pl*] franja (de cabelo)

banish /'bænɪʃ/ vt desterrar, expulsar

banister /'bænɪstər/ s corrimão

bank /bæŋk/ s **1** banco: ~ *balance/statement* saldo/extrato bancário ◊ *~ account* conta bancária **2** barranca (*rio, lago*) ● vt **1** depositar (em banco) **2** vi ter conta (em um banco) ■ **bank on sb/sth** contar com alguém/algo **banker** s banqueiro/a

bank holiday s (*GB*) feriado (nacional)

bankrupt /'bæŋkrʌpt/ adj falido: *go ~* falir **bankruptcy** s falência

banner /'bænər/ s faixa (de passeata), estandarte

banning /'bænɪŋ/ s proibição

banquet /'bæŋkwɪt/ s banquete

baptize /'bæptaɪz; *GB* bæp'taɪz/ vt batizar **baptism** /'bæptɪzəm/ s batismo

bar /bɑr/ s **1** barra **2** (*café, etc.*)

bar 3 (*Mús*) compasso 4 barreira ▶ **behind bars** (*coloq*) atrás das grades ● *vt* (**-rr-**) ~ **sb from doing sth** impedir alguém de fazer algo ▶ **bar the way** barrar o caminho ● *prep* exceto

barbarian /bɑːˈbeəriən/ s bárbaro/a barbaric /bɑːˈbærɪk/ adj bárbaro

barbecue /ˈbɑːbɪkjuː/ s churrasqueira, churrasco

barbed wire /ˌbɑːbd ˈwaɪər/ s arame farpado

barber /ˈbɑːbər/ s barbeiro

barbershop /ˈbɑːbərʃɒp/ (GB barber's) s barbearia

bare /beər/ adj (-er, -est) 1 nu → NAKED 2 só ◇ *floors pisos sem carpete* ◇ *room* ~ *of furniture* sala sem móveis 4 the ~ *essentials* o mínimo essencial barely *adv* mal

barefoot /ˈbeəfʊt/ adv descalço

bargain /ˈbɑːgən/ s 1 trato 2 pechincha ▶ **into the bargain** além disso ● *vi* 1 negociar 2 pechinchar ▶ **bargain for sth**: *He got more than he bargained for.* Ele recebeu mais do que esperava. bargaining s 1 negociação 2 regateio

barge /bɑːdʒ/ s barcaça

bar graph s gráfico de barras

baritone /ˈbærɪtəʊn/ s barítono

bark /bɑːk/ s 1 casca (*árvore*) 2 latido ● *vi* 1 latir 2 ~ (*at sb/sth*) gritar barking s latidos

barley /ˈbɑːli/ s cevada

barmaid /ˈbɑːmeɪd/ s garçonete

barman /ˈbɑːmən/ s (pl **-men**) barman

barometer /bəˈrɒmɪtər/ s barômetro

baron /ˈbærən/ s barão

baroness /ˈbærənəs/ s baronesa

barracks /ˈbærəks/ s quartel

barrage /ˈbærɑːʒ; GB ˈbærɑːʒ/ s 1 (*Mil*) barragem de artilharia 2 (*perguntas, etc.*) bombardeio 3 (*rio*) barragem

barrel /ˈbærəl/ s 1 barril 2 cano (*arma*)

barren /ˈbærən/ adj estéril, árido

barricade /ˌbærɪˈkeɪd/ s barricada ● *vt* bloquear (com uma barricada): ~ *yourself in* defender-se com barricadas

barrier /ˈbæriər/ s barreira

barrister /ˈbærɪstər/ s (GB) advogado/a (*que trabalha nos tribunais*) → ADVOGADO

barrow /ˈbærəʊ/ s carrinho (*de mão*)

bartender /ˈbɑːtendər/ s

barman

base /beɪs/ s base ● *vt* 1 basear(-se) 2 **(be based in/at)** ter base em

baseball /ˈbeɪsbɔːl/ s beisebol

basement /ˈbeɪsmənt/ s 1 porão 2 subsolo

bash /bæʃ/ *vt, vi* (*coloq*) golpear com força: ~ *your head, etc.* (*against/on/into sth*) bater a cabeça, etc. (*contra/em algo*) ● *s* golpe forte ▶ **have a bash (at sth)** (GB, *coloq*) experimentar (algo)

basic /ˈbeɪsɪk/ adj 1 fundamental 2 básico ● **basics** s [pl] o básico basically *adv* basicamente

basin /ˈbeɪsn/ s 1 pia (de banheiro) 2 bacia

basis /ˈbeɪsɪs/ s (pl **bases** /ˈbeɪsiːz/) base: *on the* ~ *of sth* baseando-se em algo ◇ *do sth on a monthly* ~ fazer algo todo mês

basket /ˈbɑːskɪt; GB ˈbɑːskɪt/ s cesta, cesto

basketball /ˈbɑːskɪtbɔːl; GB ˈbɑːs-/ s basquete

bass /beɪs/ s 1 (*cantor*) baixo 2 grave 3 (*tb* ~ **guitar**) baixo (elétrico) 4 contrabaixo ● adj grave

bat /bæt/ s 1 bastão (*beisebol, etc.*) 2 morcego ● *vt, vi* (**-tt-**) dar tacada (em) ▶ **not bat an eye** (*coloq*) não pestanejar

batch /bætʃ/ s lote

bath /bɑːθ; GB bɑːθ/ s 1 banho 2 banheira ● *vt* (GB) dar banho em

bathe /beɪð/ *vt* 1 lavar 2 *vi* tomar banho de mar, rio, etc.

bathroom /ˈbɑːθruːm; GB ˈbɑːθ-/ s banheiro → TOILET

baton /bəˈtɒn; GB ˈbætn, ˈbætɒn/ s 1 cassetete 2 (*Mús*) batuta 3 (*Esporte*) bastão

battalion /bəˈtæliən/ s batalhão

batter /ˈbætər/ s 1 *vt* espancar: ~ *sb to death* matar alguém a pancadas 2 *vt, vi* ~ **(at/on) sth** dar murro em algo ▶ **batter sth down** amassar algo batterred adj estropiado

battery /ˈbætəri/ s (pl **-ies**) 1 bateria, pilha 2 ~ **hen** galinha criada industrialmente

battle /ˈbætl/ s batalha, luta ● *vi* lutar: ~ *on* seguir lutando

battlefield /ˈbætlfiːld/ (*tb* **battleground**) s campo de batalha

battlements /ˈbætlmənts/ s ameias

battleship /ˈbætlʃɪp/ s encouraçado

bauble /ˈbɔːbl/ s bugiganga

bawl /bɔːl/ 1 vi berrar 2 vt gritar

bay /beɪ/ s 1 baía 2 *loading* ~ zona de abastecimento 3 (tb ~ **tree**) loureiro 4 cavalo baio ▸hold/keep sb/sth at bay manter alguém/algo à distância • vi uivar

bayonet /ˈbeɪənət/ s baioneta

bay window s janela (*saliente*)

bazaar /bəˈzɑːr/ s bazar (*beneficente*)

BC /ˌbiː ˈsiː/ abrev antes de Cristo

be /bi, biː/ (pt **was/were** pp **been**) → Para os usos de be com there ver THERE.

• v intransitivo 1 ser: *Be quick!* Anda logo! ◇ *I was late.* Cheguei atrasado. 2 (*estado*) estar NOTA Compare as duas orações: *He's bored.* Ele está entediado. ◇ *He's boring.* Ele é chato. Com adjetivos terminados em -ed, como *interested, tired,* etc., o verbo be expressa um estado e se traduz como "estar". Com adjetivos terminados em -ing, como *interesting, tiring,* etc., expressa uma qualidade e se traduz como "ser": *I'm right, aren't I?* Estou certo, não? ◇ *I'm hot/afraid.* Estou com calor/medo. ◇ *Are you in a hurry?* Está com pressa? NOTA Em português usa-se estar com com substantivos como fome, frio, etc.; em inglês usa-se be com o adjetivo correspondente. 3 (*localização*) estar 4 (*origem*) ser 5 [*só em tempos perfeitos*] visitar: *I've never been to Spain.* Nunca fui à Espanha. NOTA Às vezes been é usado como particípio de go. ► GO 6 (*idade*) ter: *He is ten (years old).* Ele tem dez anos. ► OLD, YEAR 7 (*tempo*): *It's cold/hot.* Está frio/quente. 8 (*medida*): *He is six feet tall.* Ele mede 1,80 m. 9 (*hora*) ser: *It's two o'clock.* São duas horas. 10 (*preço*) custar

• v auxiliar 1 [*com particípios para formar a voz passiva*]: *He was killed in the war.* Ele foi morto na guerra. ◇ *It is said that he is/He is said to ~ rich.* Dizem que ele é/é rico. 2 [*com -ing para formar os tempos contínuos*]: *I'm just coming!* Estou indo! 3 [*com infinitivo*]: *I am to inform you that...* Devo informar-lhe que... ◇ *They were to be married.* Eles iam se casar. NOTA Para expressões com be, ver o substantivo, adjetivo, etc., p. ex. be a drain on sth em DRAIN. ■be through (to sb/sth) (GB) estar

falando (ao telefone) (com alguém/algo) **be through (with sb/sth)** terminar (com alguém/algo de fazer algo)

beach /biːtʃ/ s praia • vt encalhar

beacon /ˈbiːkən/ s 1 farol 2 (*fogueira*) sinal 3 radiofarol

bead /biːd/ s 1 conta 2 (beads) [pl] colar de contas 3 (*de suor, etc.*) gota

beak /biːk/ s bico

beaker /ˈbiːkər/ s 1 proveta (*descartável*) 2 (GB) copo de plástico com bico

beam /biːm/ s 1 viga 2 (*de luz*) feixe, facho • vi sorrir de alegria • vt transmitir (*programa*)

bean /biːn/ s 1 feijão: *lima beans* favas 2 (*café, cacau*) grão

bear /beər/ s urso • (pt **bore** pp **borne**) 1 vt suportar 2 vt (*assinatura, etc.*) levar 3 vt (*peso*) sustentar 4 vt (*despesas*) responsabilizar-se por 5 vt (*responsabilidade*) assumir 6 vt: *It won't ~ close examination.* Não resistirá a um exame detalhado. 7 vt (*fml*) dar à luz 8 vt (*colheita, resultado*) produzir 9 vi (*estrada, etc.*) tomar uma determinada direção ▸**bear a grudge** guardar rancor **bear a resemblance to sb/sth** parecer com alguém/algo **bear little relation to sth** ter pouco a ver com algo **bear sb/sth in mind** ter alguém/algo em mente, lembrar alguém/algo ■**bear sb/sth out** confirmar algo/a suspeita de alguém **bear with sb** ter paciência com alguém **bearable** adj tolerável

beard /bɪərd/ s barba **bearded** adj barbado

bearer /ˈbeərər/ s 1 portador/a 2 (*de documento*) titular

bearing /ˈbeərɪŋ/ s (Náut) marcação ▸get/take your bearings (GB) orientar-se **have a bearing on sth** ter relação com algo

beast /biːst/ s animal, besta: *wild ~* fera

beat /biːt/ (pt **beat** pp **beaten** /ˈbiːtn/) 1 vt golpear: *~ sb up* dar uma surra em alguém 2 vt, vi bater: *~ the record* bater o recorde 3 vt (*tambor*) tocar 4 vt derrotar 5 vt: *Nothing beats home cooking.* Não há nada melhor do que comida caseira. ▸**beat about the bush** fazer rodeios **off the beaten track** (num lugar) fora do mapa • s 1 ritmo 2 (*tambor*) toque 3 (*polícia*) ronda **beating** s 1 surra 2 (porta, etc.) batida ▶ **take a lot of/ some beating** ser difícil de superar

beautiful /ˈbjuːtɪfl/ adj **1** lindo **2** magnífico **beautifully** adv maravilhosamente

beauty /ˈbjuːti/ s (pl -ies) beleza

beaver /ˈbiːvər/ s castor

because /bɪˈkɒz; GB -ˈkɒz/ conj porque because of prep por causa de, devido a

beckon /ˈbekən/ **1** vi acenar **2** vt chamar através de sinais

become /bɪˈkʌm/ vi (pt became /bɪˈkeɪm/ pp become) **1** [+ substantivo] tornar-se, transformar-se em, fazer-se **2** [+ adj] ficar, virar: ~ aware of sth dar-se conta de algo ● **become of sb/ sth**: What will ~ of me? O que será de mim?

bed /bed/ s **1** cama NOTA Não se usa o artigo definido nas expressões: go to ~ It's time for ~. **2** (tb river/sea ~) fundo (rio, mar) **3** (flores) canteiro

bed and breakfast (tb abrev B & B) s quarto com café da manhã

bedding /ˈbedɪŋ/ s (GB **bed-clothes** /ˈbedkləʊðz/) [pl] roupa de cama

bedroom /ˈbedruːm/ s quarto (de dormir)

bedside /ˈbedsaɪd/ s: ~ table mesa-de-cabeceira

bedsit /ˈbedsɪt/ s (GB) (apartamento) conjugado

bedspread /ˈbedspred/ s colcha

bedtime /ˈbedtaɪm/ s hora de dormir

bee /biː/ s abelha

beech /biːtʃ/ (tb ~ **tree**) s faia

beef /biːf/ s carne de vaca: roast ~ rosbife Ver ← CARNE

beefburger /ˈbiːfbɜːrɡər/ s hambúrguer

beehive /ˈbiːhaɪv/ Ver HIVE

been /biːn/ GB tb biːn/ pp de BE

beer /bɪər/ s cerveja

beet /biːt/ (GB **beetroot** /ˈbiːtruːt/ s beterraba

beetle /ˈbiːtl/ s besouro

before /bɪˈfɔːr/ adv antes: the day/week ~ o dia/a semana anterior ♦ prep **1** antes de: the day ~ yesterday anteontem **2** diante de, na frente de: He puts his work ~ everything. Ele põe o trabalho na frente de tudo. ♦ conj antes que

beforehand /bɪˈfɔːrhænd/ adv de antemão

beg /beg/ (-gg-) **1** vt, vi ~ (sth/for sth) (from sb) mendigar (algo) (a alguém) **2** vt ~ sb to do sth

implorar a alguém que faça algo ▶ **beg sb's pardon 1** pedir perdão a alguém **2** pedir a alguém que repita o que disse **beggar** s mendigo/a

begin /bɪˈgɪn/ vt, vi (-nn-) (pt **began** /bɪˈɡæn/ pp **begun** /bɪˈɡʌn/) começar ▶ **to begin with 1** para começar **2** a princípio **beginner** s principiante **beginning** s **1** começo **2** origem

behalf /bɪˈhæf; GB -ˈhɑːf/ s ▶ **in behalf of sb/in sb's behalf** (GB **on behalf of sb/on sb's behalf**) em nome de alguém

behave /bɪˈheɪv/ vi ~ **well, badly, etc. (towards sb)** comportar-se bem, mal, etc. (com alguém): Behave yourself! Comporte-se!

behavior (GB -**our**) /bɪˈheɪvjər/ s comportamento

behind /bɪˈhaɪnd/ prep **1** atrás de: What's ~ this sudden change? O que há por trás dessa mudança repentina? **2** ~ schedule estar atrasado (em relação a um plano) **3** a favor de ♦ adv **1** atrás: leave sth ~ deixar algo para trás ◇ He was shot from ~. Atiraram nele pelas costas. **2** ~ **(in/with sth)** atrasado (com algo) ● s traseiro

being /ˈbiːɪŋ/ s **1** ser **2** existência: come into ~ originar-se

belated /bɪˈleɪtɪd/ adj tardio

belch /beltʃ/ vi arrotar ● s arroto

belief /bɪˈliːf/ s **1** crença **2** confiança, fé **3** opinião ▶ **beyond belief** inacreditável **in the belief that...** pensando que...

believe /bɪˈliːv/ vt, vi ~ **(in) sth** crer, acreditar (em algo) ▶ **believe it or not** acredite se quiser **believable** adj acreditável **believer** s crente, pessoa que crê: be a great/firm ~ in sth ser grande partidário de algo

bell /bel/ s **1** sino, sineta **2** campainha

bell-bottoms (USA) calça boca-de-sino

bellow /ˈbeləʊ/ **1** vi urrar **2** vt, vi berrar ● s **1** urro **2** berro

belly /ˈbeli/ s (pl -ies) (coloq) barriga **2** pança

belong /bɪˈlɒŋ; GB -ˈlɒŋ/ vi **1** pertencer **2** ser o lugar adequado: Where does this ~? Onde se guarda isso? **belongings** s pertences

below /bɪˈləʊ/ prep abaixo de, debaixo de ♦ adv abaixo, embaixo

belt /belt/ s **1** cinto **2** (Mec) cinta, correia **3** (Geog) zona ▶ **below the belt**: That remark hit below *the ~*. Aquele comentário foi um golpe baixo.

bemused /bɪˈmjuːzd/ *adj* perplexo

bench /bentʃ/ *s* 1 (*assento*) banco 2 (*GB, Pol*): *He started his career on the back ~*. Ele começou a carreira como deputado. 3 (**the bench**) a magistratura

benchmark /ˈbentʃmɑːk/ *s* ponto de referência

bend /bend/ (*pt, pp* **bent**) 1 *vt, vi* curvar(-se) 2 *vi* ~ (**down**) agachar-se, inclinar-se ● *s* 1 curva 2 (*cano*) dobra

beneath /bɪˈniːθ/ *prep* (*fml*) 1 abaixo/debaixo de 2 indigno de ● *adv* debaixo

benefactor /ˈbenɪfæktər/ *s* benfeitor/a

beneficial /ˌbenɪˈfɪʃl/ *adj* benéfico

benefit /ˈbenɪfɪt/ *s* 1 benefício: *be of ~ to...* ser benéfico para... 2 subsídio: *unemployment ~* auxílio-desemprego 3 ação beneficente ▸ **give sb the benefit of the doubt** dar uma segunda chance a alguém ● (*pt, pp* -**fited**, *USA tb* -**tt**-) 1 *vt* beneficiar 2 *vi* ~ (**from/by sth**) beneficiar-se, tirar proveito (de algo)

benevolent /bəˈnevələnt/ *adj* 1 benevolente 2 caridoso **benevolence** *s* benevolência

benign /bɪˈnaɪn/ *adj* benigno

bent /bent/ *pret, pp de* **BEND** ■ **be bent on (doing) sth** estar decidido a (fazer) algo ● *s* habilidade, inclinação

bequeath /bɪˈkwiːð/ *vt* (*fml*) legar

bequest /bɪˈkwest/ *s* (*fml*) legado

bereaved /bɪˈriːvd/ *adj* (*fml*) de luto ● *s* **the bereaved** [*pl*] os enlutados **bereavement** *s* luto

beret /ˈbereɪ/ *GB* /ˈbereɪ/ *s* boina

berry /ˈberi/ *s* (*pl* -**ies**) baga

berserk /bəˈsɜːk/ *adj* louco de raiva: *go ~* perder a cabeça

berth /bɜːθ/ *s* 1 (*navio*) beliche 2 (*trem*) cabine 3 (*Náut*) ancoradouro ● *vt, vi* atracar

beset /bɪˈset/ *vt* (-**tt**-) (*pt, pp* **beset**) (*fml*) assediar: *~ by doubts* roído de dúvidas

beside /bɪˈsaɪd/ *prep* junto de, ao lado de ▸ **beside yourself (with sth)** fora de si (por causa de algo)

besides /bɪˈsaɪdz/ *prep* além de, exceto ● *adv* além disso

besiege /bɪˈsiːdʒ/ *vt* 1 sitiar 2 assediar

best /best/ *adj* (*superl de* **good**) melhor ▸ **best before**: ~ *before May 2004* consumir antes de maio de 2004 **best wishes**: *Best wishes, Ann.* Abraços, Ann. ◇ *Give her my ~ wishes.* Dê lembranças a ela. **I'd, you'd, etc. best (do sth)** é melhor (que se faça algo) ● *adv* (*superl de* **well**) 1 mais bem, melhor 2 *best-known* mais famoso ▸ **as best you can** o melhor que puder ● **the best** *s* 1 o/a melhor: *We're the ~ of friends.* Somos ótimos amigos. 2 o melhor: *be at its/your ~* estar em seu melhor momento ▸ **at best** na melhor das hipóteses **do/try your (level/very) best** fazer o melhor possível **make the best of sth** tirar o melhor partido possível de algo **to the best of your belief/knowledge** que você saiba

best man *s* padrinho (de casamento) → CASAMENTO

bestseller /ˌbestˈselər/ *s* sucesso de vendas, best-seller

bet /bet/ *vt* (-**tt**-) (*pt, pp* **bet** *ou* **betted**) ~ (**on**) **sth** apostar (em) algo ▸ **I bet (that)...** (*coloq*): *I ~ you he doesn't come.* Aposto (com você) que ele não vem. ● *s* aposta: *place a ~* apostar

betray /bɪˈtreɪ/ *vt* 1 trair 2 (*segredo*) revelar **betrayal** *s* traição

better /ˈbetər/ *adj* (*comp de* **good**) melhor: *get ~* melhorar ▸ **be little/no better than...**: *He is no ~ than a thief.* Ele não passa de um ladrão. **have seen/known better days** estar gasto, não ser mais o que era ● *adv* 1 (*comp de* **well**) melhor 2 mais ▸ **be better off (without sb/sth)** estar melhor (sem alguém/algo): *He'd be ~ off leaving now.* Seria melhor (para ele) que ele fosse agora. **better late than never** antes tarde do que nunca **better safe than sorry** melhor prevenir do que remediar **I'd, you'd, etc. better (do sth)** é melhor (que se faça algo): *I'd ~ be going now.* É melhor eu ir agora. ● *s* (algo) melhor, mais ▸ **get the better of sb** levar vantagem sobre alguém: *His shyness got the ~ of him.* A timidez o venceu.

betting shop *s* (*GB*) casa de apostas

between /bɪˈtwiːn/ *prep* entre (*duas coisas/pessoas*) ● *adv* (*tb* **in ~**) no meio

beverage /ˈbevrɪdʒ/ *s* bebida

beware /bɪˈweər/ *vi* ~ (**of sb/sth**) ter cuidado (com alguém/algo)

bewilder /bɪ'wɪldər/ *vt* confundir
bewildered *adj* perplexo
bewildering *adj* desorientador
bewilderment *s* perplexidade

bewitch /bɪ'wɪtʃ/ *vt* enfeitiçar, encantar

beyond /bɪ'jɑnd/ *prep, adv* além (de) ▸ **be beyond sb** (*coloq*): *It's ~ me.* Está além da minha compreensão.

bias /'baɪəs/ *s* **1** ~ **towards sb/sth**; ~ **against sb/sth** predisposição em relação a alguém/algo; preconceito contra alguém/algo **2** parcialidade biased (*tb* -ss-) *adj* parcial

bib /bɪb/ *s* **1** babadouro **2** parte superior de um avental

Bible /'baɪbl/ *s* Bíblia biblical (*tb* Biblical) *adj* bíblico

bibliography /ˌbɪbli'ɑgrəfi/ *s* (*pl* -ies) bibliografia

biceps /'baɪseps/ *s* (*pl* biceps) bíceps

bicker /'bɪkər/ *vi* bater boca

bicycle /'baɪsɪk(ə)l/ *s* bicicleta

bid /bɪd/ *vi* (-dd-) (*pt, pp* bid) **1** (*leilão*) fazer uma oferta *s* **2** (*Com*) licitar *s* **1** (*leilão*) lance **2** (*Com*) licitação **3** tentativa: *He made a ~ for freedom.* Ele tentou obter a liberdade. bidder *s* lançador/a, licitante

bide /baɪd/ *vt* ▸ **bide your time** esperar pelo momento certo

biennial /baɪ'eniəl/ *adj* bienal

big /bɪg/ (**bigger, biggest**) *adj* **1** grande: *the biggest desert in the world* o maior deserto do mundo NOTA Big e large são sinônimos, mas **big** é menos formal. **2** maior, mais velho **3** importante **4** (*erro*) grave ▸ **a big cheese/fish/shot** (*coloq*) um manda-chuva **big business**: *This is ~ business.* É um negócio da China. **the big time** (*coloq*) o estrelato *adv* (*coloq*) sem limitações: *think ~* pensar grande

big-head *s* (*coloq*) presunçoso/a big-headed *adj* presunçoso

bigamy /'bɪgəmi/ *s* bigamia

bigoted /'bɪgətɪd/ *adj* fanático, intolerante

bike /baɪk/ *s* (*coloq*) **1** bicicleta **2** moto

bikini /bɪ'ki:ni/ *s* biquíni

bilingual /ˌbaɪ'lɪŋgwəl/ *adj* bilíngüe

bill /bɪl/ *vt* **1** ~ **sb for sth** apresentar a conta de algo a alguém **2** anunciar (*num programa*) *s* **1** conta, fatura **2** programa (*cinema, etc.*) **3** projeto de lei **4** (*nota.*) **ten-dollar** ~ nota de dez dólares **5** bico (*ave*) ▸ **fill/fit the bill** preencher os requisitos

billboard /'bɪlbɔːrd/ *s* outdoor

billiards /'bɪliərdz/ *s* [*sing*] bilhar billiard *adj*: ~ **ball/ table** bola/mesa de bilhar

billing /'bɪlɪŋ/ *s*: *get top/star* ~ encabeçar o elenco

billion /'bɪljən/ *adj, s* bilhão

bin /bɪn/ *s* **1** lata, caixa: *waste-paper* ~ cesta de lixo **2** (*GB*) lata de lixo

binary /'baɪnəri/ *adj* binário

bind /baɪnd/ *vt* (*pt, pp* bound) **1** atar: ~ *sb's hands together* deixar alguém de mãos atadas **2** unir, ligar **3** ~ **sb/yourself (to sth)** obrigar alguém/obrigar-se (a fazer algo) *s* (*coloq*) **1** *What a* ~! Que saco! **2** dificuldade: *be in a* ~ estar em apuros

binder /'baɪndər/ *s* fichário

binding /'baɪndɪŋ/ *s* **1** encadernação **2** debrum *s adj* ~ **(on/upon sb)** obrigatório (a alguém)

binge /bɪndʒ/ *s* (*coloq*) farra *vi* **1** empanturrar-se **2** beber até cair

bingo /'bɪŋgoʊ/ *s* bingo

binoculars /bɪ'nɑkjələrz/ *s* [*pl*] binóculo

biochemist /ˌbaɪoʊ'kemɪst/ *s* bioquímico/a biochemistry *s* bioquímica biochemical *adj* bioquímico

biography /baɪ'ɑgrəfi/ *s* (*pl* -ies) biografia biographer *s* biógrafo/a biographical /ˌbaɪə'græfɪkl/ *adj* biográfico

biology /baɪ'ɑlədʒi/ *s* biologia biological /ˌbaɪə'lɑdʒɪkl/ *adj* biológico biologist /baɪ'ɑlədʒɪst/ *s* biólogo/a

bird /bɜːrd/ *s* ave, pássaro

biro® (*tb* Biro) /'baɪroʊ/ (*GB*) *s* (*pl* ~s) (caneta) esferográfica

birth /bɜːrθ/ *s* **1** nascimento **2** natalidade **3** parto **4** descendência, origem ▸ **give birth to sb/sth** dar à luz alguém/algo

birthday /'bɜːrθdeɪ/ *s* aniversário

birthplace /'bɜːrθpleɪs/ *s* lugar de nascimento

biscuit /'bɪskɪt/ *s* biscoito

bishop /'bɪʃəp/ *s* bispo

bit /bɪt/ *s* **1** (*GB*) bocado, pedacinho **2** (*Informát*) bite **3** freio (*para cavalo*) ▸ **a bit um pouco**: *I've got a ~ of shopping to do.* Tenho que fazer umas comprinhas. **a bit much** (*coloq*) além do limite **bit by bit** pouco a pouco **bits and pieces** (*coloq*) troços **do your**

bit (*coloq*) fazer a sua parte **not a bit**; **not one (little) bit** nem um pouco **to bits**: *pull/tear sth to bits* fazer algo em pedaços ◇ *fall to bits* despedaçar-se ◇ *take sth to bits* desmontar algo

bitch /bɪtʃ/ *s* cadela → **cão**

bite /baɪt/ (*pt* **bit** /bɪt/ *pp* **bitten** /ˈbɪtn/) **1** *vt*, *vi* ~ **(into sth)** morder (algo): ~ *your nails* roer as unhas **2** *vt* (*inseto*) picar ● *s* **1** mordida **2** bocado **3** picada

bitter /ˈbɪtər/ *adj* (~**er**, ~**est**) **1** amargo **2** ressentido **3** gélido ● *s* (*GB*) cerveja amarga bitterly *adv* amargamente: *It's* ~ *cold.* Faz um frio de rachar. bitterness *s* amargura

bizarre /bɪˈzɑːr/ *adj* **1** bizarro **2** esquisito

black /blæk/ *adj* (~**er**, ~**est**) **1** negro, preto: ~ *eye* olho roxo **2** escuro **3** (*café, chá*) puro ● *s* **1** preto **2** (*pessoa*) negro/a ■ **black out** perder a consciência

blackbird /ˈblækbɜːrd/ *s* melro

blackboard /ˈblækbɔːrd/ *s* quadro-negro

blackcurrant /ˌblækˈkʌrənt/ *s* groselha negra

blacken /ˈblækən/ *vt* **1** (*reputação, etc.*) manchar **2** escurecer

blacklist /ˈblæklɪst/ *s* lista negra ● *vt* pôr na lista negra

blackmail /ˈblækmeɪl/ *s* chantagem ● *vt* chantagear blackmailer *s* chantagista

blacksmith /ˈblæksmɪθ/ (*GB tb* **smith**) *s* ferreiro

bladder /ˈblædər/ *s* bexiga

blade /bleɪd/ *s* **1** lâmina **2** (*ventilador, remo*) pá **3** (*grama*) folha

blame /bleɪm/ *vt* **1** ~ **sb (for sth)/** **sth on sb** culpar alguém (por algo) **2** [*frases negativas*]: *You can't* ~ *him for being annoyed.* Não é à toa que ele ficou chateado. ▶ **be to blame (for sth)** ser culpado (de algo) ● *s* culpa

bland /blænd/ *adj* (~**er**, ~**est**) insosso

blank /blæŋk/ *adj* **1** em branco **2** (*parede*) nu **3** (*cassete*) virgem **4** sem expressão ● *s* **1** espaço em branco, lacuna **2** cartucho sem bala

blanket /ˈblæŋkɪt/ *s* cobertor ● *adj*: ~ *ban on sth* proibição geral a algo ● *vt* cobrir (*por completo*)

blare /bleər/ *vi* ~ **(out)** retumbar, buzinar

blasphemy /ˈblæsfəmi/ *s* blasfêmia blasphemous *adj* blasfemo

blast /blæst; *GB* blɑːst/ *s* **1** explosão **2** estrondo **3** rajada ● *vt* dinamitar ■ **blast off** ser lançado (*foguete*) ● *interj* (*GB*) droga blasted *adj* (*coloq*) maldito

blatant /ˈbleɪtnt/ *adj* descarado

blaze /bleɪz/ *s* **1** incêndio **2** fogueira **3** [*sing*]: *a* ~ *of color/publicity* uma explosão de cores/um estouro publicitário ● *vi* **1** arder **2** resplandecer **3** *eyes blazing* olhos chispando (de raiva)

blazer /ˈbleɪzər/ *s* blazer: *school* ~ paletó de uniforme escolar

bleach /bliːtʃ/ *vt* alvejar ● *s* água sanitária

bleachers /ˈbliːtʃərz/ *s* [*pl*] arquibancada descoberta

bleak /bliːk/ *adj* (~**er**, ~**est**) **1** (*paisagem*) desolado **2** (*tempo*) sombrio, cinzento e deprimente **3** desanimador bleakly *adv* desoladamente bleakness *s* desolação

bleed /bliːd/ *vi* (*pt, pp* **bled** /bled/) sangrar bleeding *s* hemorragia

blemish /ˈblemɪʃ/ *s* mancha ● *vt* manchar

blend /blend/ **1** *vt*, *vi* misturar **2** *vi* mesclar-se ■ **blend in (with sth)** combinar (com algo) ● *s* mistura blender *s* liquidificador

bless /bles/ *vt* (*pt, pp* **blessed** /blest/) abençoar ▶ **be blessed with sth** ter a sorte de possuir algo **bless you!** que Deus te abençoe **2** saúde (*ao espirrar*) → **ATXIM**

blessed /ˈblesɪd/ *adj* **1** sagrado **2** abençoado **3** (*coloq*): *the whole* ~ *day* todo o santo dia

blessing /ˈblesɪŋ/ *s* [*sing*] **1** bênção **2** aprovação ▶ **it's a blessing in disguise** há males que vêm para bem

blew /bluː/ *pret de* **BLOW**

blind /blaɪnd/ *adj* cego ● *vt* **1** ofuscar **2** cegar ● *s* **1** persiana **2** (**the blind**) [*pl*] os cegos blindly *adv* cegamente blindness *s* cegueira

blindfold /ˈblaɪndfəʊld/ *vt* vendar os olhos a ● *s* venda (*para os olhos*) ● *adv* com os olhos vendados

blink /blɪŋk/ *vi* piscar ● *s* piscada

bliss /blɪs/ *s* [*U*] êxtase blissful *adj* extasiante

blister /ˈblɪstər/ *s* bolha

blistering /ˈblɪstərɪŋ/ *adj* causticante

blitz /blɪts/ *s* **1** bombardeio aéreo **2** (*coloq*) ~ **(on sth)** blitz (contra algo)

blizzard /ˈblɪzərd/ s nevasca

bloated /ˈbloʊtɪd/ adj inchado

blob /blɑb/ s 1 pingo (líquido espesso) 2 mancha

bloc /blɑk/ s (Pol) bloco

block /blɑk/ s 1 bloco 2 quarteirão 3 (apartamentos) prédio 4 (ingressos, ações, etc.) pacote: a ~ reservation uma reserva coletiva 5 obstáculo: a ~ mental um bloqueio mental ◆ vt 1 bloquear 2 tapar, entupir 3 impedir

blockade /blɑˈkeɪd/ s (Mil) bloqueio ● vt bloquear

blockage /ˈblɑkɪdʒ/ s 1 obstrução 2 bloqueio 3 impedimento

blockbuster /ˈblɑkbʌstər/ s sucesso de vendas (filme, livro)

block capitals (tb **block letters**) s maiúsculas

bloke /bloʊk/ s (GB, coloq) cara, sujeito

blond (tb **blonde**) /blɑnd/ adj (~er, ~est) louro ● s louro/a NOTA Usa-se **blonde** apenas para o sexo feminino. → LOURO

blood /blʌd/ s sangue: ~ group grupo sanguíneo ◇ ~ pressure pressão arterial

bloodshed /ˈblʌdʃed/ s derramamento de sangue

bloodshot /ˈblʌdʃɑt/ adj injetado de sangue

blood sports [pl] caça

bloodstream /ˈblʌdstriːm/ s corrente sanguínea

bloody /ˈblʌdi/ adj (-ier, -iest) 1 ensangüentado 2 sanguinolento 3 sangrento ● adj, adv (GB, coloq): That ~ car! Maldito carro!

bloom /bluːm/ s flor ● vi florescer

blossom /ˈblɑsəm/ s flor (árvore) ● vi florescer

blot /blɑt/ s mancha ● vt (-tt-) 1 borrar, rasurar 2 secar ■ **blot sth out** (memória, etc.) apagar algo (vista, luz, etc.) tapar algo

blotch /blɑtʃ/ s mancha (na pele)

blouse /blaʊs; GB blauz/ s blusa

blow /bloʊ/ (pt blew pp blown /bloʊn/) 1 vi soprar 2 vt, vi (ação do vento): The wind blew them ashore. O vento os levou para a terra. ◇ ~ sb/sth down/over derrubar alguém/algo ◇ ~ away vento ser carregado para longe ◇ The door blew shut/open. A porta se fechou/abriu (com o vento). 3 vt, vi (apito) tocar, soar ▶ **blow it** droga **blow your nose** assoar o nariz ■ **blow sth out** apagar algo **blow over** passar (tempestade, escândalo) **blow up 1** explodir 2 (tempestade, escândalo)

estourar 3 (coloq) perder a paciência **blow sth up 1** (dinamitar) demolir algo 2 (balão, etc.) encher algo 3 (Fot) ampliar algo 4 (coloq) exagerar algo ● s ~ (to sb/sth) golpe (para alguém/algo): at one ~/at a single ~ de um golpe só ▶ a **blow-by-blow account** um relato tintim por tintim **come to blows (over sth)** cair de tapas (por causa de algo)

blue /bluː/ adj 1 azul 2 (coloq) triste 3 (filme) pornô ● s 1 azul 2 (the blues) [pl] (Mús) os blues 3 (the blues) [pl] a depressão ▶ **out of the blue** sem mais nem menos

blueberry /ˈbluːberi; GB -bəri/ s (pl -ies) arando (fruta)

blue-collar adj [antes de substantivo] de classe operária

bluejay /ˈbluːdʒeɪ/ s gaio (espécie de corvo)

blueprint /ˈbluːprɪnt/ s ~ (for sth) anteprojeto (de algo)

bluff /blʌf/ vi blefar ● s blefe

blunder /ˈblʌndər/ s erro crasso ● vi cometer um erro crasso

blunt /blʌnt/ vt embotar, cegar ● adj (~er, ~est) 1 sem fio, cego 2 obtuso: a ~ instrument instrumento sem fio 3 curto e grosso: be ~ falar sem rodeios 4 (comentário) brusco

blur /blɜːr/ s borrão ● vt (-rr-) 1 embaçar 2 atenuar blurred adj embaçado

blurt /blɜːrt/ ■ **blurt sth out** falar algo sem pensar

blush /blʌʃ/ vi corar ● s rubor blusher s ruge

boar /bɔːr/ s (pl boar ou ~s) 1 javali 2 varrão → PORCO

board /bɔːrd/ s 1 tábua 2 quadronegro 3 quadro de avisos 4 tabuleiro 5 cartolina 6 the ~ (of directors) diretoria 7 full/half ~ pensão completa/meia pensão ▶ **above board** acima de qualquer suspeita **across the board** em todos os níveis: a 10% increase across the ~ um aumento geral de 10% **on board** a bordo ● 1 vt ~ sth (up/over) cobrir algo com tábuas 2 vi embarcar 3 vt subir em

boarder /ˈbɔːrdər/ s 1 (colégio) interno/a 2 (pensão) hóspede

boarding card (tb **boarding pass**) s cartão de embarque

boarding house s pensão

boarding school s internato

boardwalk /ˈbɔːrdwɔːk/ s passarela de madeira na praia

boast /bəʊst/ **1** *vi* gabar-se **2** *vt* (*fml*) ostentar ● *s* ostentação **boastful** *adj* **1** exibido **2** vaidoso

boat /bəʊt/ *s* **1** barco **2** bote: ~ *race* regata **3** navio NOTA Boat e ship têm significados muito semelhantes, mas **boat** geralmente se refere a embarcações menores.

bob /bɒb/ *vi* (-bb-) ~ (**up and down**) balouçar (*na água*)

bobby /ˈbɒbi/ *s* (*pl* -ies) (GB, *coloq*) tira (*policial*)

bode /bəʊd/ *vt* (*fml*) pressagiar ▶ **bode ill/well (for sb/sth)** ser de mau/bom agouro (para alguém/algo)

bodice /ˈbɒdɪs/ *s* corpete

bodily /ˈbɒdɪli/ *adj* do corpo, corporal ● *adv* à força

body /ˈbɒdi/ *s* (*pl* -ies) **1** corpo **2** cadáver **3** grupo: *government* ~ órgão do governo ▶ **body and soul** de corpo e alma

bodybuilding /ˈbɒdibɪldɪŋ/ *s* musculação

bodyguard /ˈbɒdigɑːd/ *s* **1** guarda-costas **2** (*grupo*) escolta

bodywork /ˈbɒdiwɜːk/ *s* [U] carroceria

bog /bɒɡ/ *s* **1** pântano **2** (GB, *coloq*) privada ■ **get bogged down 1** encrencar-se **2** atolar-se **boggy** *adj* lamacento

bogeyman /ˈbəʊɡimæn/ (GB) = **BOOGEYMAN**

bogus /ˈbəʊɡəs/ *adj* falso, fraudulento

boil /bɔɪl/ **1** *vt, vi* ferver **2** *vt* cozinhar ■ **boil down to** resumir-se a algo **boil over** transbordar ● *s* furúnculo ▶ **be on the boil** (GB) estar fervendo ▶ **keep sth boiling** (GB) *fig* fervendo: ~ *point* ponto de ebulição ◊ ~ *hot* pelando

boiler /ˈbɔɪlər/ *s* caldeira, aquecedor ▶ **boiler suit** macacão

boisterous /ˈbɔɪstərəs/ *adj* animado, alvoroçado

bold /bəʊld/ *adj* (~er, ~est) **1** ousado, valente **2** nítido, claro **3** (*cor*) vivo **4** (*tipo*): *in* ~ em negrito ▶ **be so bold (as to do sth)** (*fml*) atrever-se (a fazer algo) **boldly** *adv* **1** corajosamente **2** audaciosamente **3** resolutamente **boldness** *s* **1** coragem **2** audácia, atrevimento

bolster /ˈbəʊlstər/ *vt* **1** ~ **sth** (**up**) sustentar algo **2** ~ **sb** (**up**) apoiar a alguém

bolt /bəʊlt/ *s* **1** trinco **2** parafuso **3** ~ *of lightning* raio (*de relâmpago*) ▶ **make a bolt for it** tentar escapar ● **1** *vt* passar o trinco,

trancar **2** *vt* ~ **A to B**; ~ **A and B together** prender A a B **3** *vi* (*cavalo*) disparar **4** *vi* sair em disparada **5** *vt* ~ **sth** (**down**) (GB) comer algo às pressas

bomb /bɒm/ *s* **bomba** ▶ **go like a bomb** (GB, *coloq*) ser rápido como um foguete ● **1** *vt, vi* bombardear **2** *vt, vi* plantar uma bomba (*num edifício, etc.*) **3** *vi* ~ **along, down, up, etc.** (GB, *coloq*) andar a mil por hora

bombard /bɑmˈbɑːd/ *vt* **1** bombardear **2** (*perguntas, etc.*) assediar **bombardment** *s* bombardeio

bomber /ˈbɑmər/ *s* **1** bombardeiro **2** pessoa que planta bombas

bombing /ˈbɑmɪŋ/ *s* **1** bombardeio **2** atentado com explosivos

bombshell /ˈbɑmʃel/ *s*: *The news came as a* ~. A notícia estourou como uma bomba.

bond /bɒnd/ *vt* unir ● *s* **1** acordo **2** laço **3** (*Fin*) título **4** (**bonds**) correntes

bone /bəʊn/ *s* **1** osso: ~ *marrow* medula óssea **2** (*peixe*) espinha ▶ **a bone of contention** o pomo da discórdia **bone dry** completamente seco ▶ **have a bone to pick with sb** ter contas para acertar com alguém ▶ **make no bones about sth** falar de algo sem rodeios ● *vt* desossar

bonfire /ˈbɑnfaɪər/ *s* fogueira

Bonfire Night *s* (GB) NOTA No dia 5 de novembro, na Grã-Bretanha, a tentativa de incêndio do Parlamento, em 1605, é lembrada com fogueiras e fogos de artifício.

bonnet /ˈbɑnɪt/ *s* **1** (*bebê*) touca **2** (*mulher*) chapéu (*tipo touca*) **3** (GB) capô

bonus /ˈbəʊnəs/ *s* **1** bônus **2** bênção

bony /ˈbəʊni/ *adj* **1** ósseo **2** cheio de espinhas **3** ossudo

boo /buː/ *vt, vi* vaiar ● *s* (*pl* ~s) vaia ● *interj* u!

booby trap *s* armadilha (explosiva)

boogeyman /ˈbuːɡimæn/ *s* (*pl* -men) bicho-papão

book /bʊk/ *s* **1** livro **2** caderno (*de exercícios*) **3** (*cheques*) talão **4** (**the books**) as contas: *do the books* fazer a contabilidade ▶ **be in sb's good books** (GB) gozar do favor de alguém ▶ **do sth by the book** fazer algo como manda o figurino ● **1** *vt, vi* reservar, fazer uma reserva: ~ *in* registrar-se **2** *vt* contratar **3** *vt* (*coloq*) (*polícia*) fichar **4** *vt* (*Esporte*) penalizar ▶ **be booked up 1** ter a lotação esgotada **2** (*coloq*): *I'm booked up.* Não tenho hora na agenda.

bookcase /'bʊkkeɪs/ *s* estante

booking /'bʊkɪŋ/ *s* (*esp GB*) reserva: ~ *office* bilheteria

booklet /'bʊklət/ *s* livreto, apostila

bookmaker /'bʊkmeɪkə(r)/ (*tb* **bookie**) *s* banqueiro/a (de apostas)

bookseller /'bʊkˌselə(r)/ *s* livreiro/a

bookshelf /'bʊkʃelf/ *s* (*pl* **-shelves** /-ʃelvz/) estante de livros

bookstore /'bʊkstɔ:r/ (*GB* **bookshop**) *s* livraria

boom /bu:m/ *vi* estrondear, retumbar ● *s* estrondo

boost /bu:st/ *vt* **1** aumentar **2** (*moral*) levantar ● *s* **1** aumento **2** estímulo

boot /bu:t/ *s* **1** bota **2** (*GB*) porta-malas

booth /bu:θ; *GB* bu:ð/ *s* **1** barraca, tenda **2** cabine

booty /'bu:ti/ *s* saque

booze /bu:z/ *s* (*coloq*) birita ● *v* (*coloq*): *go out boozing* tomar um porre

border /'bɔ:rdə(r)/ *s* **1** fronteira **NOTA** Border e frontier designam a divisão entre países ou estados, mas border só se aplica a fronteiras naturais: *The river forms the ~ between the two countries. Boundary*, por sua vez, refere-se a divisões entre áreas menores, como municípios. **2** (*jardim*) canteiro à borda, margem ● *vt* limitar-se com, fazer fronteira com ▶ **border on sth** chegar às raias de algo

borderline /'bɔ:rdərlaɪn/ *s* linha divisória ▶ **a borderline case** um caso de difícil diagnóstico

bore /bɔ:r/ *pret de* BEAR ● *vt* **1** entediar **2** perfurar ● *s* **1** (*pessoa*) chato/a **2** chatice, aporrinhação **3** calibre **bored** *adj* entediado **boredom** *s* tédio **boring** *adj* chato

born /bɔ:rn/ *nascido* ▶ **be born** nascer: *He was ~ blind.* Ele é cego de nascença. ● *adj* [*antes de substantivo*] nato

borne /bɔ:rn/ *pp de* BEAR

borough /'bʌroʊ; *GB* -rə/ *s* município

borrow /'bɑːroʊ/ *vt* ~ **sth (from sb/sth)** pedir (algo) emprestado (a alguém/algo) ► Em português

costuma-se mudar a estrutura e empregar o verbo "emprestar" precedido de pronome: *Could I ~ a pen?* Você me empresta uma caneta? **borrower** *s* (*esp Fin*) pessoa que pede algo emprestado **borrowing** *s*: *public sector ~* empréstimo ao governo

bosom /'bʊzəm/ *s* **1** peito, busto **2** seio

boss /bɔːs; *GB* bɒs/ *s* (*coloq*) chefe ● *vt* ~ **sb about/around** (*pej*) dar ordens a alguém: *mandar em alguém* **bossy** *adj* (**-ier, -iest**) (*pej*) mandão

botany /'bɒtəni/ *s* botânica **botanical** /bə'tænɪkl/ (*tb* **botanic**) *adj* botânico **botanist** /'bɒtənɪst/ *s* botânico/a

both /boʊθ/ *pron, adj* ambos/as, os dois/as duas: ~ *of us* nós dois ● *adv* **both... and...** não só... como também...: ~ *you and me* tanto você quanto eu

bother /'bɒðər/ **1** *vt* incomodar **2** *vt, vi* preocupar(-se): ~ *about sb/sth* preocupar-se com alguém/algo **3** *vi* ~ **(to do sth)** dar-se ao trabalho de fazer algo ▶ **I can't be bothered (to do sth)** (*GB*) não estou com a mínima vontade (de fazer algo) **I'm not bothered** (*GB*) não estou nem aí ● *s* incômodo ● *interj* (*GB*) que saco

bottle /'bɒtl/ *s* **1** garrafa: *bottle-opener* abridor de garrafas **2** frasco **3** mamadeira ● *vt* **1** engarrafar **2** armazenar em frascos

bottle bank *s* (*GB*) área de coleta de garrafas para reciclagem

bottom /'bɒtəm/ *s* **1** (*colina, página, escada*) pé **2** fundo **3** (*Anat*) traseiro ● *adj* [*antes de substantivo*] **4** último **5** *He's ~ of the class.* Ele é o último da classe. **6** parte inferior (*biquíni, etc.*) ▶ **be at the bottom of sth** estar por trás de algo **get to the bottom of sth** desvendar algo

bough /baʊ/ *s* ramo

bought /bɔ:t/ *pret, pp de* BUY

boulder /'boʊldər/ *s* rocha

bounce /baʊns/ **1** *vt, vi* quicar, saltar **2** *vi* (*coloq*) (*cheque*) ser devolvido ■ **bounce back** (*coloq*) recuperar-se ● *s* salto

bouncer /'baʊnsər/ *s* leão-de-chácara

bound /baʊnd/ *pret, pp de* BIND ● *adj* **1 be ~ to do sth:** *You're ~ to pass the exam.* Você certamente passará no exame. **2** obrigado (*por lei/dever*) **3** ~ **for...** com destino a... ▶ **bound up with sth**

ligado a algo ● *vi* pular ● *s* pulo

boundary /'baʊndri/ *s* (*pl* **-ies**) limite, fronteira → BORDER

boundless /'baʊndləs/ *adj* sem limites

bounds /baʊndz/ *s* limites ▸ **out of bounds** interdito

bouquet /bu'keɪ/ *s* buquê

bourgeois /ˌbʊər'ʒwɑː/ *adj*, *s* burguês

bout /baʊt/ *s* **1** período **2** (*enfermidade*) ataque **3** (*boxe*) combate

bow¹ /boʊ/ *s* **1** laço **2** (*Esporte*, *violino*) arco

bow² /baʊ/ **1** *vi* curvar-se, fazer reverência **2** *vt* (*cabeça*) inclinar, abaixar ● *s* **1** reverência **2** (*tb* **bows** [*pl*]) proa

bowel /'baʊəl/ *s* **1** [*freq pl*] intestino(s) **2** (**bowels**) (*fig*) entranhas

bowl /boʊl/ *s* **1** tigela: *fruit ~* fruteira ◇ *sugar ~* açucareiro **2** bacia **3** taça **4** (*banheiro*) privada **5** bola de madeira **6** (**bowls**) [*sing*] jogo semelhante a boliche ● *vt*, *vi* arremessar (a bola)

bowler /'boʊlər/ *s* (*GB*) **1** (*Esporte*) lançador/a **2** (*tb* **~ hat**) chapéu-coco

bowling /'boʊlɪŋ/ *s* [*U*] jogo de boliche

bow tie *s* gravata borboleta

box /bɑks/ *s* **1** caixa **2** estojo (*jóias, etc.*) **3** (*Teat*) camarote **4** (*GB*) (*telefone*) cabine **5** (**the box**) (*coloq, GB*) a TV ● *vt* **1** dar tapa a **2** *vi* lutar boxe/com os punhos **3** *vt* ~ **sth (up)** encaixotar algo

boxer /'bɑksər/ *s* **1** boxeador/a **2** bóxer

boxers /'bɑksərz/ (*tb* **boxer shorts**) *s* [*pl*] cueca (*samba-canção*)

boxing /'bɑksɪŋ/ *s* boxe

Boxing Day *s* (*GB*) 26 de dezembro (*feriado na Inglaterra*) → NATAL

box number *s* caixa postal

box office *s* bilheteria

boy /bɔɪ/ *s* **1** menino **2** filho: *She's got a ~ and two girls.* Ela tem um menino e duas meninas. **3** moço

boycott /'bɔɪkɒt/ *vt* boicotar ● *s* boicote

boyfriend /'bɔɪfrend/ *s* namorado

boyhood /'bɔɪhʊd/ *s* meninice, juventude (*rapazes*)

boyish /'bɔɪʃ/ *adj* juvenil: *a ~ figure* tipo de menino

bra /brɑ/ *s* sutiã

brace /breɪs/ *vt* ~ **yourself (for sth)** preparar-se (para algo difícil) ■ **brace up** (*USA*) animar-se

bracing *adj* revigorante

bracelet /'breɪslət/ *s* bracelete

braces /'breɪsɪz/ *s* [*pl*] **1** (*para os dentes*) aparelho **2** (*GB*) suspensório(s)

bracket /'brækɪt/ *s* **1** (*GB* **square ~**) colchete **2** (*GB*) parêntese: *in brackets* entre parênteses **3** suporte angular fixo à parede **4** categoria: *the 20-30 age ~* a faixa etária entre 20 e 30 anos ● *vt* **1** colocar entre parênteses **2** categorizar

brag /bræg/ *vi* (-**gg-**) ~ **(about sth)** gabar(-se) (de algo)

braid /breɪd/ *s* trança

brain /breɪn/ *s* **1** cérebro **2** (**brains**) miolos **3** mente ▸ **have sth on the brain** (*coloq*) estar com algo na cabeça **brainless** *adj* desmiolado, burro **brainy** *adj* (-**ier, -iest**) (*coloq*) inteligente

brainwash /'breɪnwɒʃ/ *vt* ~ **sb (into doing sth)** fazer lavagem cerebral em alguém (*para que faça algo*) **brainwashing** *s* lavagem cerebral

brake /breɪk/ *s* freio ● *vt*, *vi* frear

bramble /'bræmbl/ *s* amoreira silvestre

bran /bræn/ *s* farelo de trigo

branch /brɑːntʃ; *GB* brɑːntʃ/ *s* **1** ramo **2** filial, agência ■ **branch off** *vi* desviar-se **2** bifurcar-se ■ **branch out (into sth)** expandir-se (em algo) (*ramo, atividade*)

brand /brænd/ *s* **1** marca (*cigarros, roupas, etc.*) **2** tipo ● *vt* **1** (*gado*) marcar **2** ~ **sb/sth (as sth)** estigmatizar alguém/algo (como algo)

brandish /'brændɪʃ/ *vt* brandir

brand new *adj* novo em folha

brandy /'brændi/ *s* conhaque

brash /bræʃ/ *adj* grosseiro, impetuoso **brashness** *s* grosseria

brass /bræs; *GB* brɑːs/ *s* **1** latão **2** (*Mús*) metais

brat *s* pirralho

bravado /brə'vɑːdoʊ/ *s* bravata

brave /breɪv/ *vt* **1** desafiar **2** enfrentar (*com bravura*) ● *adj* (-**er, -est**) valente

brawl /brɔːl/ *s* briga

Brazil nut *s* castanha-do-pará

breach /briːtʃ/ *s* **1** quebra: *~ of confidence/faith* abuso de confiança **2** (*lei*) violação **3** (*relações*) rompimento ● *vt* **1** (*con-*

trato, promessa) quebrar **2** (*lei*) violar **3** (*muro, etc.*) abrir brecha em

bread /bred/ s pão: *a loaf of* ~ um pão NOTA Usa-se o plural **breads** para tipos diferentes de pão, não para vários pães.

breadcrumbs /ˈbredkrʌmz/ s [pl] farinha de rosca: *fish in* ~ peixe empanado

breadth /bredθ/ s **1** amplitude **2** largura

break /breɪk/ s **1** abertura **2** intervalo, férias curtas, recreio: *coffee* ~ pausa para o café **3** interrupção, mudança **4** (*coloq*) golpe de sorte ◊ **give sb a break** dar trégua a alguém **make a break (for it)** escapar (*esp. da prisão*) ◊ **(pt broke pp broken) 1** vt quebrar: ~ *a promise* quebrar uma promessa ◊ *Her waters broke.* A bolsa de águas (da parturiente) se rompeu. **2** vi despedaçar-se **3** vt (*lei*) violar **4** vt (*recorde*) bater **5** vt (*queda*) amortecer **6** vt (*viagem*) interromper **7** vt fazer uma pausa **8** vt (*moral, etc.*) destruir **9** vt (*maus hábitos*) abandonar **10** vt (*código*) decifrar **11** vt (*cofre*) arrombar **12** vt (*tempo*) virar **13** vi (*tempestade, escândalo*) irromper **14** vt (*história, etc.*) revelar: ~ *the news (to sb)* dar a (má) notícia (a alguém) **15** vi (*voz*) mudar de tom, engrossar ▸ **break it up** basta **break the bank** (*coloq*): *A meal out won't* ~ *the bank.* Jantar fora não vai nos arruinar. **break your back (to do sth)** matar-se (para fazer algo) ■ **break away (from sth)** escapar (*de algo*), romper (*com algo*) **break down 1** (*carro, etc.*) quebrar **2** (*pessoa*) descontrolar-se: *He broke down and cried.* Ele se descontrolou e se pôs a chorar. **3** (*negociações*) falhar **break sth down 1** derrubar algo **2** analisar algo **3** decompor algo **break in/ into sth 1** (*ladrão*) invadir algo **2** (*mercado*) introduzir-se em algo **3** começar a fazer algo: ~ *into a run* disparar a correr ◊ ~ *into a cold sweat* começar a suar frio **break off** parar de falar **break sth off 1** partir algo **2** romper algo (*compromisso*) **break out 1** (*epidemia*) surgir **2** irromper **3** começar **4** cobrir-se repentinamente de: ~ *out in a rash* ficar coberto de manchas **break through sth** abrir caminho através de algo **break up 1** (*GB*)

dissolver-se **2** (*relação*) terminar **3** (*GB*): *School breaks up on 9 July.* As aulas terminam em 9 de julho. **break (up) with sb** terminar (*relação*) com alguém **break sth up** terminar algo, fazer algo fracassar

breakdown /ˈbreɪkdaʊn/ s **1** avaria **2** (*saúde*) crise: *nervous* ~ colapso nervoso **3** análise

breakfast /ˈbrekfəst/ s café da manhã

break-in s arrombamento

breakthrough /ˈbreɪkθruː/ s avanço (*pesquisa, etc.*)

breast /brest/ s seio, peito (*mulher*): ~ *cancer* câncer de mama

breath /breθ/ s fôlego, hálito, respiração: *take a deep* ~ respirar fundo ◊ *out of/short of* ~ sem fôlego ◊ *a breath of fresh air* um sopro de ar fresco **take sb's breath away** deixar alguém boquiaberto ◊ *under your breath* sussurrar (*algo*) ◊ ~ *(to sb)* dizer uma palavra (sobre algo) (a alguém) **breathing** s respiração

breathe /briːð/ **1** vi respirar **2** vt, vi ~ *(in/out)* inspirar, expirar ▸ **breathe down sb's neck** (*fig*) estar em cima de alguém **breathe life into sth/sb** dar vida a algo/alguém **not breathe a word (of/about sth) (to sb)** não dizer uma palavra (sobre algo) (a alguém)

breathless /ˈbreθləs/ adj ofegante, sem fôlego

breathtaking /ˈbreθteɪkɪŋ/ adj impressionante

breed /briːd/ (*pt, pp bred* /bred/) **1** vi reproduzir-se **2** vt criar **3** vt provocar, gerar ■ s raça, casta

breeze /briːz/ s brisa

brew /bruː/ **1** vt (*cerveja*) produzir **2** vt (*chá, etc.*) preparar **3** vi formar-se: *Trouble is brewing.* Está se armando um problema. **brewery** /ˈbruːəri/ s cervejaria

bribe /braɪb/ s suborno ■ vt ~ **sb (into doing sth)** subornar alguém (para que faça algo) **bribery** s suborno (*ato*)

brick /brɪk/ s tijolo ■ **brick sth in/ up** fechar algo com tijolos

bride /braɪd/ s noiva: *the* ~ *and groom* os noivos → CASAMENTO

bridegroom /ˈbraɪdɡruːm/ s *Ver* GROOM (2)

bridesmaid /ˈbraɪdzmeɪd/ s dama de honra → CASAMENTO

bridge /brɪdʒ/ s **1** ponte **2** vínculo ■ vt ▸ **bridge a/the gap between...** reduzir as diferenças entre...

bridle /ˈbraɪdl/ s freio (*cavalo*)

brief /briːf/ *adj* (~er, ~est) breve, curto ▶ **in brief** em poucas palavras • *s* instruções • *vt* instruir, dar instruções **briefly** *adv* 1 brevemente 2 em poucas palavras

briefcase /'briːfkeɪs/ *s* pasta executiva

briefs /briːfs/ *s* [*pl*] 1 calcinha 2 cueca → PAIR

bright /braɪt/ (~er, ~est) *adj* 1 brilhante, luminoso 2 (*cor*) vivo, berrante 3 radiante, alegre 4 inteligente • *adv* com brilho

brighten /'braɪtn/ *vt, vi* ~ (sth) (up) animar-se, animar algo 2 *vi* ~ (up) (*tempo*) clarear

brightly /'braɪtli/ *adv* 1 com brilho 2 ~ *lit* com muita luz ◇ ~ *painted* pintado com cores vivas 3 radiantemente, alegremente

brightness /'braɪtnəs/ *s* 1 brilho, luminosidade 2 alegria 3 inteligência

brilliant /'brɪliənt/ *adj* 1 brilhante 2 (*GB*) genial **brilliance** *s* 1 brilho 2 talento

brim /brɪm/ *s* 1 borda 2 aba (*chapéu*)

bring /brɪŋ/ *vt* (*pt, pp* brought) → LEVAR 1 trazer 2 levar: ~ *sth* (*out*) *into the open* levar algo a público ◇ ~ *sb to justice* levar alguém à justiça (*ações judiciais*) instaurar ▶ **be able to bring yourself to do sth**: *I couldn't ~ myself to tell her.* Eu não tive coragem de dizer-lhe. **bring sth home to sb** (*GB*) deixar algo claro para alguém **bring sth to a close** concluir algo **bring sb/ sth to life** animar alguém/ algo **bring sb/sth up to date** atualizar alguém/algo **bring tears to sb's eyes/a smile to sb's face** fazer alguém chorar/sorrir **bring up the rear** estar em último lugar ■ **bring sth about/on (yourself)** provocar algo para si próprio **bring sb around/to** fazer alguém voltar a si **bring sth back** 1 restaurar algo 2 fazer pensar em algo 3 devolver algo **bring sth down** 1 derrubar algo, derrotar algo 2 (*preços, etc.*) reduzir algo **bring sth forward** adiantar algo **bring sth in** introduzir algo (*lei*) **bring sth off** (*coloq*) conseguir algo (difícil) **bring sth out** 1 produzir algo (*produto*) 2 publicar algo (*livro*) 3 realçar algo (*significado*) **bring sb round/over (to sth)** (*GB*) convencer alguém (de algo) **bring sb/sth together** reconciliar, reunir alguém/algo

sb up criar alguém **bring sth up** 1 vomitar algo 2 mencionar algo

brink /brɪŋk/ *s* borda: *on the* ~ *of war* à beira da guerra

brisk /brɪsk/ *adj* (~er, ~est) 1 enérgico 2 (*negócio*) ativo

brittle /'brɪtl/ *adj* 1 quebradiço 2 frágil

broach /brəʊtʃ/ *vt* abordar (*um assunto*)

broad /brɔːd/ *adj* (~er, ~est) 1 largo (*sorriso*) amplo 3 (*esquema, etc.*) geral, amplo NOTA Para a distância entre dois extremos, **wide** é mais comum: *The gate is four meters wide.* **Broad** é usado para características geográficas: *a ~ expanse of desert* e em frases como: ~ *shoulders.* ▶ **in broad daylight** em plena luz do dia

broad bean *s* (*GB*) fava

broadcast /'brɔːdkæst; *GB* 'brɔːdkɑːst/ (*pt, pp* broadcast) 1 *vt* (*TV, etc.*) transmitir 2 *vt* difundir 3 *vt* emitir • *s* transmissão: *party political* ~ horário eleitoral

broaden /'brɔːdn/ *vt, vi* ~ (out) ampliar(-se)

broadly /'brɔːdli/ *adv* 1 *smiling* ~ com um amplo sorriso 2 de maneira geral: ~ *speaking* falando em termos gerais

broccoli /'brɒkəli/ *s* brócolis

brochure /'brəʊʃər; *GB* 'brəʊʃə(r)/ *s* brochura, folheto (*turístico, publicitário*)

broil /brɔɪl/ *vt* grelhar

broke /brəʊk/ *pret de* BREAK • *adj* (*coloq*) sem dinheiro, quebrado: *go* ~ quebrar (*negócio*)

broken /'brəʊkən/ *pp de* BREAK • *adj* 1 quebrado, interrompido 2 (*coração*) partido

broker /'brəʊkər/ *s* corretor/a de bolsa de valores

bronchitis /brɒŋ'kaɪtɪs/ *s* [*U*] bronquite

bronze /brɒnz/ *s* bronze • *adj* de bronze, da cor do bronze

brooch /brəʊtʃ/ *s* broche

brood /bruːd/ *vi* ~ (on/over sth) remoer algo

brook /brʊk/ *s* riacho

broom /bruːm/ *s* vassoura **broomstick** *s* (cabo de) vassoura

broth /brɒθ; *GB* brɒθ/ *s* [*U*] caldo

brother /'brʌðər/ *s* 1 irmão: *brothers and sisters* irmãos 2 confrade **brotherhood** *s* 1 irmandade 2 confraria **brotherly** *adj* fraternal

brother-in-law *s* (*pl* -ers-in-law) cunhado

brought /brɔːt/ *pret, pp de* BRING

brow /brau/ *s* **1** (*Anat*) testa NOTA A palavra **forehead** é mais comum. **2** (*ger pl*) sobrancelha **3** (*colina*) cimo

brown /braun/ *adj* (**-er, ~est**) **1** marrom **2** (*pêlo*) castanho **3** (*pele*) moreno **4** (*açúcar*) mascavo **5** (*GB*): ~ *bread* pão integral **6** ~ *paper* papel pardo ● *s* marrom ● *vt, vi* (*Cozinha*) dourar(-se) **brownish** *adj* pardacento, acastanhado

brownie /'brauni/ *s* **1** (**Brownie**) (*menina*) bandeirante **2** biscoito de chocolate

browse /brauz/ *vi* **1** ~ (*through sth*) passar os olhos (por algo), folhear (algo) **2** pastar

browser /'brauzər/ *s* (*Informát*) navegador

bruise /bruːz/ *s* machucado ● *vt, vi* machucar(-se) **bruising** *s* [*U*] (*GB*): *He had a lot of* ~. Ele tinha muitas contusões.

brush /brʌʃ/ *s* **1** escova **2** pincel **3** broxa **4** escovada **5** ~ *with sb* briga com alguém ● *vt* **1** escovar **2** varrer **3** ~ *past/against sb/sth* roçar(-se) (com) alguém/algo ■ **brush sth aside** fazer pouco caso de algo **brush sth up/brush up on sth** desenferrujar algo (*idioma, etc.*)

brusque /brʌsk; *GB* bruːsk/ *adj* (*pessoa*) brusco

Brussels sprout /'brʌsl spraut/ *s* couve-de-bruxelas

brutal /'bruːtl/ *adj* brutal **brutality** /bruː'tæləti/ *s* (*pl* **-ies**) brutalidade

brute /bruːt/ *s* **1** besta **2** bruto ● *adj* bruto **brutish** *adj* brutal

bubble /'bʌbl/ *s* bolha ● *vi* borbulhar **bubbly** *adj* (**-ier, -iest**) **1** efervescente **2** (*pessoa*) animado

bubble bath *s* espuma para banho, banho de espuma

bubblegum /'bʌblgʌm/ *s* chiclete

buck /bʌk/ *s* **1** (*USA, coloq*) dólar **2** (*ger pl*) (*coloq*) grana **3** macho (*coelho, veado*) → COELHO, VEADO ► **make a fast/quick buck** ganhar dinheiro fácil **the buck stops here** a responsabilidade pára aqui ● *vi* corcovear ► **buck the trend** ir contra a corrente ■ **buck sb up** (*coloq*) animar alguém

bucket /'bʌkɪt/ *s* balde

buckle /'bʌkl/ *s* fivela ● *vt* afivelar **2** *vi* (*pernas*) dobrar-se **3** *vt, vi* (*metal*) deformar(-se)

bud /bʌd/ *s* (*Bot*) broto

Buddhism /'buːdɪzəm, 'bʊ-/ *s* budismo **Buddhist** *adj, s* budista

budding /'bʌdɪŋ/ *adj* nascente

buddy /'bʌdi/ *s* (*pl* **-ies**) (*USA, coloq*) amigo (*íntimo*)

budge /bʌdʒ/ **1** *vt, vi* mover(-se) **2** *vi* ceder

budgerigar /'bʌdʒərɪgɑr/ *s* (*GB*) periquito

budget /'bʌdʒɪt/ *s* orçamento: ~ *deficit* déficit orçamentário ● **1** *vt* orçar **2** *vi* (*gastos*) planejar **3** *vi* ~ *for sth* reservar dinheiro para algo **budgetary** *adj* orçamentário

buff /bʌf/ *s* aficionado/a: *a movie* ~ um fanático por cinema ● *adj, s* bege

buffalo /'bʌfələu/ *s* (*pl* **buffalo** *ou* ~**es**) búfalo

buffer /'bʌfər/ *s* **1** proteção **2** (*estrada*) pára-choque **3** (*Informát*) memória intermediária **4** (*GB, coloq*) (*tb old* ~) velhote

buffet¹ /bə'feɪ; *GB* 'bufeɪ/ *s* **1** lanchonete: ~ *car* vagão-restaurante **2** bufê

buffet² /'bʌfɪt/ *vt* **1** esbofetear **2** (*vento*) fustigar **buffeting** *s* bofetada

bug /bʌg/ *s* **1** inseto **2** (*coloq*) infecção **3** (*Informát*) defeito **4** (*coloq*) microfone para escuta clandestina ● *vt* (**-gg-**) **1** grampear (*telefone, etc.*) **2** (*coloq, esp USA*) irritar

buggy /'bʌgi/ *s* (*pl* **-ies**) carrinho de bebê

build /bɪld/ *vt* (*pt, pp* **built**) **1** construir **2** criar ■ **build sth in 1** embutir algo **2** incorporar algo **build on sth** partir (dos resultados) de algo **build up 1** intensificar-se **2** acumular-se **build sb/sth up** elogiar alguém/algo **build sth up 1** ampliar algo **2** (*negócio*) expandir algo

builder /'bɪldər/ *s* construtor/a, pedreiro

building /'bɪldɪŋ/ *s* **1** edifício **2** construção

building site *s* local de construção, obra

building society *s* (*GB*) sociedade de crédito imobiliário

build-up *s* **1** aumento gradual **2** acúmulo **3** ~ (*to sth*) preparação (para algo) **4** publicidade

built¹ /bɪlt/ *pret, pp de* BUILD

built-in *adj* **1** embutido **2** incorporado

built-up *adj* (*GB*) urbanizado

bulb /bʌlb/ *s* **1** (*Bot*) bulbo **2** lâmpada elétrica

bulge /bʌldʒ/ *s* **1** protuberância **2**

(*coloq*) aumento (temporário) ●
vi inchar (*bolso, etc.*)

bulk /bʌlk/ *s* **1** volume: ~ *buying*
compra no atacado **2** massa
3 the bulk of sth (*of sth*) a maior parte
(de algo) ▸ **in bulk 1** em grandes
quantidades **2** a granel **bulky**
adj (**-ier, -iest**) volumoso

bull /bʊl/ *s* **1** touro **2** (*GB*) Ver
BULLSEYE

bulldoze /ˈbʊldəʊz/ *vt* **1** (*escavadeira*) aplainar **2** derrubar

bullet /ˈbʊlɪt/ *s* (*arma*) bala

bulletin /ˈbʊlətɪn/ *s* **1** comunicado **2** boletim: ~ *board* quadro
de avisos

bulletproof /ˈbʊlɪtpruːf/ *adj*
à prova de balas

bullfight /ˈbʊlfaɪt/ *s* tourada
bullfighter *s* toureiro/a **bull-
fighting** *s* tauromaquia

bullfrog /ˈbʊlfrɒɡ/ *s* rã-touro

bullion /ˈbʊliən/ *s* ouro/prata
(*em lingotes*)

bullring /ˈbʊlrɪŋ/ *s* praça de
touros

bullseye /ˈbʊlzaɪ/ *s* mosca (*do
alvo*)

bully /ˈbʊli/ *s* (*pl* **-ies**) valentão
● *vt* (*pt, pp* **-ied**) provocar, intimidar

bum /bʌm/ *s* **1** (*coloq*) (*GB*)
bunda **2** (*USA*) vagabundo
■ **bum around** (*coloq*) vaga-
bundear

bumblebee /ˈbʌmblbiː/ *s*
abelhão

bump /bʌmp/ **1** *vt* chocar **2** *vi*
~ **into sb/sth** chocar(-se) contra
alguém/algo ■ **bump into sb**
topar com alguém **bump sb off**
(*coloq*) matar alguém ● *s* **1**
baque **2** sacudida **3** (*Anat*)
inchaço **4** protuberância
5 (*carro*) parte amassada

bumper /ˈbʌmpər/ *s* pára-
choque: ~ *car* carrinho de batida (*parque de diversões*) ● *adj*: a
~ *crop* uma colheita abundante

bumpy /ˈbʌmpi/ *adj* (**-ier, -iest**)
1 (*superfície*) desigual **2** (*estrada*) acidentado **3** (*vôo*) turbulento

bun /bʌn/ *s* **1** pãozinho doce
2 (*cabelo*) coque

bunch /bʌntʃ/ *s* **1** (*uvas, etc.*)
cacho **2** (*ervas, etc.*) maço
3 ramalhete **4** (*chaves*) molho
5 (*coloq*) grupo ● *vt, vi* agrupar
(-se), aglomerar(-se)

bundle /ˈbʌndl/ *s* **1** (*roupas*)
trouxa **2** feixe (*notas, etc.*)
maço ● *vt* ~ **sth** (**together/up**)
empacotar algo

bung /bʌŋ/ *s* rolha ● *vt* **1** arrolhar

2 (*GB, coloq*) jogar: *Don’t ~ your
clothes on the floor.* Não jogue
suas roupas no chão.

bungalow /ˈbʌŋɡələʊ/ *s* bangalô

bungle /ˈbʌŋɡl/ **1** *vt* estragar, pôr
a perder **2** *vi* fracassar, fazer
malfeito

bunk /bʌŋk/ *s* beliche ▸ **do
a bunk** (*GB, coloq*) sumir

bunny /ˈbʌni/ (*tb* ~ **rabbit**)
s coelhinho

bunting /ˈbʌntɪŋ/ *s* [*U*]
bandeirolas

buoy /bɔɪ; *GB* bɔɪ/ *s* bóia ■ **buoy
sb up** animar alguém **buoy sth
up** manter algo à tona

buoyant /ˈbɔɪənt/ *adj* (*Econ*)
em alta

burble /ˈbɜːbl/ *vi* **1** (*riacho*) murmurar **2** ~ (**on**) (**about sth**) (*GB*)
palrar (sobre algo)

burden /ˈbɜːdn/ *s* **1** carga
2 fardo ● *vt* **1** carregar **2** sobrecarregar **burdensome** *adj* incômodo, opressivo

bureau /ˈbjʊərəʊ/ *s* (*pl* ~**s** *ou* ~**x**
/-rəʊz/) **1** (*GB*) escrivaninha
2 (*USA*) cômoda **3** (*esp USA,
Pol*) repartição pública **4** (*GB*)
agência

bureaucracy /bjʊəˈrɒkrəsi/ *s*
(*pl* **-ies**) burocracia **bureaucrat**
/ˈbjʊərəkræt/ *s* burocrata
bureaucratic /ˌbjʊərəˈkrætɪk/
adj burocrático

burger /ˈbɜːɡər/ *s* (*coloq*)
hambúrguer

burglar /ˈbɜːɡlər/ *s* arrom-
bador/a: ~ *alarm* alarme contra
roubo → THIEF **burglarize** (*GB*
burgle) *vt* roubar (*de uma casa*)
→ ROB **burglary** *s* (*pl* **-ies**) roubo
(*de uma casa*) → THEFT

burgundy /ˈbɜːɡəndi/ *s* **1** (*tb* **Burgundy**) borgonha **2** (*cor*) vinho

burial /ˈberiəl/ *s* enterro

burly /ˈbɜːli/ *adj* (**-ier, -iest**)
corpulento

burn /bɜːn/ (*pt, pp* **burnt** /bɜːnt/
ou **burned**) → DREAM **1** *vt, vi*
queimar(-se): *to be badly burned*
sofrer queimaduras graves **2** *vi*
arder: *burning building* edifício
em chamas ◇ ~ *to do sth/for sth*
(*GB*) estar morrendo de vontade de fazer algo **3** *vi* sentir
muito calor **4** *vi*: *He left the lamp
burning.* Ele deixou a luz acesa.
5 *vt*: *The furnace burns oil.* A caldeira funciona com petróleo. ● *s*
queimadura

burner /ˈbɜːnər/ *s* boca (*fogão*)

burning /ˈbɜːnɪŋ/ *adj* **1** ardente **2**
intenso **3** urgente

burp /bɜːp/ **1** *vi* arrotar **2** *vt* fazer

arrotar ● s arroto

burrow /'bɜːrəʊ/ s toca ● vt cavar (toca)

burst /bɜːrst/ vt, vi (pt, pp burst) **1** arrebentar **2** estourar **3** romper: *The river ~ its banks.* O rio transbordou. ▶ **be bursting to do sth** estar morrendo de vontade de fazer algo **burst into tears** cair no choro **burst open** abrir-se de repente **burst out laughing** desatar a rir ▶ **burst into/out of sth**: *~ into/out of a room* irromper em/sair de repente de uma sala ● s **1** (raiva, etc.) ataque **2** (tiros) rajada **3** (aplausos) salva

bury /'beri/ vt (pt, pp **-ied**) **1** enterrar **2** sepultar **3** (faca, etc.) cravar **4** *She buried her face in her hands.* Ela escondeu o rosto nas mãos.

bus /bʌs/ s ônibus (urbano)

bush /bʊʃ/ s **1** arbusto: *rose ~* roseira **2** (the bush) mato **bushy** adj **1** (barba) cerrado **2** (rabo) peludo **3** frondoso

busily /'bɪzɪli/ adv atarefadamente

business /'bɪznəs/ s **1** [U] negócios: *on ~* a negócios ◇ *~ card* cartão de visitas ◇ *~ studies* estudos de administração **2** negócio, empresa **3** *It's none of your ~!* Não é da sua conta! **4** (em uma reunião): *any other ~* e outros assuntos ▶ **business before pleasure** primeiro a obrigação, depois a diversão **get down to business** ir ao que interessa **go out of business** falir **have no business doing sth** não ter direito de fazer algo

businesslike /'bɪznəslaɪk/ adj **1** prático **2** profissional

businessman /'bɪznəsmæn/ s (fem businesswoman) (pl -men, -women) homem/mulher de negócios

busk /bʌsk/ vi (GB) tocar música em local público (para arrecadar dinheiro) **busker** s (GB) músico que toca na rua

bust /bʌst/ vt, vi (pt, pp **bust** ou **busted**) (coloq) romper(-se) → DREAM ● s busto ● adj (coloq) quebrado ▶ **go bust** falir

bustle /'bʌsl/ vi ~ (about) apressar(-se) ● s ruído, alvoroço **bustling** adj alvoroçado

busy /'bɪzi/ adj (-ier, -iest) **1** ocupado **2** movimentado **3** (temporada) agitado **4** (programa) apertado **5** *The line is ~.* A linha está ocupada. ● vt ~ **yourself with (doing) sth** ocupar-se com algo

busybody /'bɪzibɑdi/ s (pl -ies) intrometido/a

but /bʌt, bət/ conj **1** mas **2** senão: *What could I do – cry?* O que eu podia fazer senão chorar? ● prep exceto: *nobody ~ you* ninguém, exceto você ▶ **we can but hope, try, etc.** só nos resta esperar, tentar, etc.

butcher /'bʊtʃər/ s **1** açougueiro/a **2** carniceiro/a ● vt **1** (animal) abater e carnear **2** (pessoa) matar brutalmente **butcher's** s açougue

butler /'bʌtlər/ s mordomo

butt /bʌt/ s **1** tonel **2** culatra **3** (cigarro) toco **4** (coloq) bunda **5** (coloq): *be the ~ of a joke* ser o alvo duma piada ● vt dar cabeçadas em ▶ **butt in** (coloq) interromper, intrometer-se

butter /'bʌtər/ s manteiga ● vt untar com manteiga

butterfly /'bʌtərflaɪ/ s (pl -ies) borboleta ▶ **have butterflies (in your stomach)** estar com frio na barriga

buttock /'bʌtək/ s nádega

button /'bʌtn/ s botão ● vt, vi ~ (sth) (up) abotoar-se, abotoar algo

buttonhole /'bʌtnhoʊl/ s casa de botão

buttress /'bʌtrəs/ s contraforte

buy /baɪ/ vt (pt, pp bought) ~ sth for sb; ~ sb sth comprar algo para alguém ● s compra **buyer** s comprador/a

buzz /bʌz/ s **1** zumbido **2** (vozes) burburinho **3** prazer, excitação: *I get a real ~ out of flying.* Eu adoro viajar de avião. **4** (coloq) telefonema ● vi zumbir ■ **buzz off** (coloq) vá embora

buzzard /'bʌzərd/ s tipo de falcão

buzzer /'bʌzər/ s campainha elétrica

by /baɪ/ prep **1** por: *ten (multiplied) by six* dez vezes seis **2** ao lado de, junto a **3** antes de: *be home by ten o'clock* estar em casa antes das dez **4** de: *by day/night* de dia/noite ◇ *by boat/car* de barco/carro ◇ *two by two* de dois em dois **5** *by my watch* segundo meu relógio **6** com: *pay by check* pagar com cheque **7** a: *little by little* pouco a pouco **8** by doing sth: *Let me begin by saying...* Permitam-me que comece dizendo... ◇ *by working hard* à custa de muito trabalho ▶ **have/keep sth by you** ter/manter algo à mão ● adv ▶ **by and by**

logo, em pouco tempo **by the by** a propósito *go, drive, etc.* **by** passar por/diante *keep/put sth by* deixar algo de reserva

bye /baɪ/ (tb **bye-bye** /ˌbaɪˈbaɪ, bəˈbaɪ/) *interj* tchau

by-election s (GB) eleição parcial

bygone /ˈbaɪgɒn/ adj passado

bypass /ˈbaɪpæs/; GB -pɑːs/ s **1** desvio **2** (*heart* ~) ponte de safena ● vt **1** contornar **2** evitar

by-product s **1** subproduto **2** conseqüência

bystander /ˈbaɪstændər/ s circunstante, espectador/a

C c

C, c /siː/ s (pl **C's, c's** /siːz/) **1** C,c **2** (*Educ*) (nota) C **3** (*Mús*) dó

cab /kæb/ s **1** táxi **2** cabine (*caminhão, etc.*)

cabbage /ˈkæbɪdʒ/ s couve, repolho

cabin /ˈkæbɪn/ s **1** (*Náut*) camarote **2** (*avião*) cabine **3** cabana

cabinet /ˈkæbɪnət/ s **1** armário: *drinks* ~ *bar* **2** (**the Cabinet**) o gabinete

cable /ˈkeɪbl/ s **1** cabo **2** amarra

cable car s teleférico

cackle /ˈkækl/ s **1** cacarejo **2** gargalhada ● *vi* **1** cacarejar **2** dar uma gargalhada

cactus /ˈkæktəs/ s (pl **-es** ou **cacti** /ˈkæktaɪ/) cacto

cadet /kəˈdet/ s cadete

Caesarean /sɪˈzeəriən/ (*tb* ~ **section**) s cesariana

café /ˈkæfeɪ/; GB /ˈkæfeɪ/ s café (*bar*)

cafeteria /ˌkæfəˈtɪəriə/ s cantina

caffeine /ˈkæfiːn/ s cafeína

cage /keɪdʒ/ s gaiola, jaula ● vt engaiolar, enjaular

cagey /ˈkeɪdʒi/ adj (**-ier, -iest**) (*coloq*) fechado: *He's very ~ about his family.* Ele é muito reservado sobre a família.

cake /keɪk/ s bolo ▶ **have your cake and eat it too** (*coloq*) associar e chupar cana

caked /keɪkt/ adj ~ **with sth** empastado de algo

calamity /kəˈlæməti/ s (pl **-ies**) calamidade

calculate /ˈkælkjuleɪt/ vt calcular ▶ **be calculated to do sth** ser programado para fazer algo *calculating* adj calculista

calculation s cálculo

calculator /ˈkælkjuleɪtər/ s calculadora

caldron = CAULDRON

calendar /ˈkælɪndər/ s calendário: ~ *month* mês civil

calf /kæf; GB kɑːf/ s (pl **calves**) **1** barriga da perna **2** bezerro → CARNE **3** cria (*foca, etc.*)

caliber (GB **calibre**) /ˈkælɪbər/ s calibre

call /kɔːl/ s **1** grito, chamada **2** (*ave*) canto **3** visita **4** ligação telefônica **5** ~ **for sth** (*Com*) demanda para algo ▶ **(be) on call** (estar) de plantão ● **1** *vt, vi* ~ **sth (out)**; ~ **(out) (to sb) (for sth)** gritar algo, chamar (alguém) (para algo): *She called for help.* Ela gritou por ajuda. ◇ ~ *a taxi* chamar um táxi **2** *vt, vi* telefonar: *Please* ~ *me at six.* Por favor me ligue às seis. **3** *vt: What's your dog called?* Como se chama seu cachorro? **4** *vi* (*GB*) ~ **(in/round) (on sb)**; ~ **(in/round) (at…)** visitar (alguém), passar (em…) **5** *vi* (*GB*) (*trem*) parar **6** *vt* (*reunião, etc.*) convocar ▶ **call it a day** (*coloq*) dar por encerrado: *Let's* ~ *it a day.* Chega por hoje. ■ **call by** (*coloq*) dar uma passada: *Could you* ~ *by later?* Pode passar por aqui mais tarde? **call for sb** buscar alguém **call for sth** requerer algo **call sth off** cancelar, romper algo **call sb out** convocar, chamar alguém **call sb up 1** (*esp USA*) ligar para alguém **2** (*GB*) recrutar alguém

caller /ˈkɔːlər/ s **1** pessoa que chama ao telefone **2** visita

callous /ˈkæləs/ adj cruel

calm /kɑːm/ adj (**-er, -est**) calmo ● s calma ● *vt, vi* ~ **(sb) (down)** acalmar-se, acalmar alguém

calorie /ˈkæləri/ s caloria

calves /kævz; GB kɑːvz/ *plural de* CALF

came /keɪm/ *pret de* COME

camel /ˈkæml/ s **1** camelo **2** bege

camera /ˈkæmərə/ s câmara

camouflage /ˈkæməflɑːʒ/ s camuflagem ● vt camuflar

camp /kæmp/ s acampamento: concentration ~ campo de concentração • vi: go camping acampar • adj 1 (pessoa) afeminado 2 (estilo) exagerado

campaign /kæm'peɪn/ s campanha • vi fazer campanha campaigner s militante

campsite /'kæmpsaɪt/ (tb **camp-ground**) s área de camping

campus /'kæmpəs/ s cidade universitária

can[1] /kən, kæn/ v modal (neg **cannot** /'kænɒt/ ou **can't** /kænt; GB kɑːnt/ pt **could** neg **could not** ou **couldn't**) NOTA Can é um verbo modal, seguido de infinitivo sem to. As orações interrogativas e negativas são formadas sem o auxiliar do. Só possui a forma presente e pretérita: can't swim. Não sei nadar. ◊ He couldn't do it. Ele não conseguiu fazer isso. Também possui um valor condicional: Could you come? Você pode vir? Para outras formas, deve-se usar be able to: Will you be able to come? Você vai poder vir? ◊ I'd like to be able to go. Gostaria de poder ir.
• **possibilidade de poder**
• **conhecimento saber**: Can you swim? Você sabe nadar?
• **permissão poder**: You can't go swimming today. Você não pode ir nadar hoje. → MAY
• **oferecimento, pedido, etc. poder**: We ~ eat here, if you want. Podemos comer aqui, se você quiser. ◊ Could you help us? Pode me ajudar? → MUST
• **com verbos de percepção**: You ~ see it everywhere. Se vê isso em todo lugar. ◊ I ~ smell something burning. Sinto um cheiro de queimado.
• **incredulidade**: I can't believe it. Não acredito.

can[2] /kæn/ s lata: can-opener abridor de latas • vt (-nn-) enlatar

canal /kə'næl/ s canal

canary /kə'neəri/ s (pl -ies) canário

cancel /'kænsl/ vt, vi (-l-, GB -ll-) 1 cancelar 2 anular ■ **cancel (sth) out** invalidar (algo) cancellation s cancelamento

Cancer /'kænsər/ s Câncer

cancer /'kænsər/ s câncer

candid /'kændɪd/ adj franco

candidate /'kændɪdət; GB -dət/ s candidato/a candidacy s candidatura

candle /'kændl/ s vela

candlelight /'kændllaɪt/ s luz de vela

candlestick /'kændlstɪk/ s 1 castiçal 2 candelabro

candy /'kændi/ s (pl -ies) doce

cane /keɪn/ s 1 (Bot) cana 2 bambu 3 vara, bengala

canister /'kænɪstər/ s 1 lata (café, etc.) 2 estojam

canned /kænd/ adj enlatado

cannibal /'kænɪbl/ s canibal

cannon /'kænən/ s canhão

canoe /kə'nuː/ s canoa canoeing s canoagem

canopy /'kænəpi/ s (pl -ies) 1 toldo 2 dossel 3 abóbada

canteen /kæn'tiːn/ s 1 cantina 2 (GB) cantil

canvas /'kænvəs/ s 1 lona 2 (Arte) tela

canvass /'kænvəs/ vt, vi angariar votos: ~ for/on behalf of sb fazer campanha para alguém 2 vt (opinião) sondar

canyon /'kænjən/ s desfiladeiro

cap /kæp/ s 1 gorro 2 barrete 3 tampa • vt (-pp-) superar ▶ **to cap it all** para completar

capability /ˌkeɪpə'bɪləti/ s (pl -ies) 1 capacidade, aptidão 2 potencial

capable /'keɪpəbl/ adj capaz

capacity /kə'pæsəti/ s (pl -ies) 1 capacidade: filled to ~ lotado 2 nível máximo de produção: at full ~ a todo vapor 3 in your ~ as sth em sua qualidade de algo

cape /keɪp/ s 1 capa 2 (Geog) cabo

caper /'keɪpər/ vi ~ (about) saltitar • s 1 (coloq) truque, travessura 2 alcaparra

capillary /'kæpəleri; GB kə-'pɪləri/ s (pl -ies) vaso capilar

capital /'kæpɪtl/ s 1 (tb ~ city) capital 2 (tb ~ letter) maiúscula 3 (Arquit) capitel 4 (Fin) capital: ~ gains ganhos de capital ▶ **make capital (out) of sth** tirar vantagem de algo • adj 1 capital: ~ punishment pena de morte 2 maiúsculo capitalism s capitalismo capitalist adj, s capitalista capitalize vt capitalizar ■ **capitalize on sth** tirar partido de algo

capitulate /kə'pɪtʃuleɪt/ vi capitular

capricious /kə'prɪʃəs/ adj caprichoso

Capricorn /'kæprɪkɔːrn/ s Capricórnio

capsize /kæp'saɪz; GB kæp'saɪz/ vt, vi (embarcação) virar(-se)

capsule /'kæpsl; GB -sju:l/ s cápsula

captain /'kæptən/ s 1 capitão/ã 2 (avião) comandante ● vt capitanear, comandar captaincy s comando

caption /'kæpʃn/ s 1 cabeçalho, título 2 (ilustração) legenda

captivate /'kæptɪveɪt/ vt cativar captivating adj cativante

captive /'kæptɪv/ adj cativo: take/hold sb ~ capturar alguém/manter alguém em cativeiro ● s prisioneiro/a captivity /kæp'tɪvəti/ s cativeiro

captor /'kæptər/ s captor/a

capture /'kæptʃər/ vt 1 capturar 2 (interesse, etc.) atrair 3 (Mil) tomar 4 ~ sb's heart conquistar o coração de alguém 5 (Arte) captar ● s 1 captura 2 (cidade) conquista

car /kɑr/ s 1 carro 2 vagão

caramel /'kærəmǝl, 'kɑrmǝl/ s 1 caramelo (açúcar queimado) 2 cor de caramelo

carat = KARAT

caravan /'kærəvæn/ s 1 (GB) trailer 2 carroção 3 caravana (camelos)

carbohydrate /ˌkɑrbə'haɪdreɪt/ s carboidrato

carbon /'kɑrbən/ s carbono: ~ paper papel-carbono

carbon copy s (pl -ies) 1 cópia de papel-carbono 2 réplica: She's a ~ of her sister. Ela é a cara da irmã.

carburetor /'kɑrbəˌreɪtər/ (GB **carburettor** /ˌkɑːbə'retə(r)/) s carburador

carcass (tb carcase) /'kɑrkəs/ s 1 carcaça 2 restos de um animal pronto para o consumo

card /kɑrd/ s 1 cartão 2 ficha: ~ index fichário 3 (de sócio, etc.) carta 4 carta (baralho) 5 [U] cartolina ▶ get your cards/give sb their cards (coloq) ser despedido/despedir alguém on the cards (coloq) provável

cardboard /'kɑrdbɔːrd/ s papelão

cardholder /'kɑːrdhəʊldər/ s titular do cartão (de crédito)

cardiac /'kɑrdiæk/ adj cardíaco

cardigan /'kɑrdɪɡən/ s cardigã

cardinal /'kɑrdɪnl/ adj 1 cardeal 2 fundamental ● s cardeal

care /keər/ s 1 ~ (over sth/in doing sth) cuidado (com algo/ao fazer algo): child ~ provision instalações para crianças (creche, etc.) ◊ take sb into/put sb in ~ (GB) colocar alguém em

cuidados de uma instituição 2 atenção 3 preocupação ▶ care of sb (correspondência) aos cuidados de alguém take care of sb/sth encarregar-se, cuidar de alguém/algo: take ~ of yourself cuidar-se that takes care of that isso encerra o assunto ● vi 1 ~ (about sth) importar-se (com algo): See if I ~. Para mim tanto faz. 2 ~ to do sth querer fazer algo ▶ for all I, you, etc. care pouco me, te, etc. importa I, you, etc. couldn't care less não estou, está, etc. nem aí ■ care for sb 1 ter afeição por alguém 2 cuidar de alguém care for sth 1 gostar de algo 2 querer algo

career /kə'rɪər/ s carreira ● vi correr a toda velocidade

carefree /'keərfri/ adj despreocupado

careful /'keərfl/ adj 1 be ~ (about/of/with sth) ter cuidado (com algo) 2 cuidadoso carefully adv com cuidado: listen/think ~ escutar com atenção/pensar bem

careless /'keərləs/ adj ~ (about sth) descuidado, desatento (com algo)

carer /'keərər/ s (GB) acompanhante (de pessoa idosa ou doente)

caress /kə'res/ s carícia ● vt acariciar

caretaker /'keərteɪkər/ s (GB) zelador/a ● adj interino

cargo /'kɑrɡoʊ/ s (pl ~s ou ~es) 1 carga 2 carregamento

caricature /'kærɪkətʃər/ s caricatura ● vt caricaturar

caring /'keərɪŋ/ adj afetuoso, humanitário

carnation /kɑr'neɪʃn/ s cravo (flor)

carnival /'kɑrnɪvl/ s carnaval

carnivore /'kɑrnɪvɔːr/ s carnívoro carnivorous /kɑr'nɪvərəs/ adj carnívoro

carol /'kærəl/ s cântico natalino

car park (GB) s estacionamento

carpenter /'kɑrpəntər/ s carpinteiro/a carpentry s carpintaria

carpet /'kɑrpɪt/ s tapete, carpete ● vt acarpetar carpeting s [U] tapeçaria

carriage /'kærɪdʒ/ s 1 carruagem 2 (GB) vagão 3 (correio) porte carriageway s pista

carrier /'kæriər/ s 1 (trans)portador/a 2 transportadora (empresa)

carrier bag s (GB) saco (plástico, papel)

carrot /'kærət/ s 1 cenoura 2 recompensa

carry /'kæri/ (*pt, pp* -**ied**) 1 *vt* carregar: ~ *a gun* portar uma arma → WEAR 2 *vt* sustentar 3 *vt* (*votação*) aprovar 4 *vt*: ~ *yourself well* ter um porte elegante 5 *vi* projetar-se: *Her voice carries well.* Ela tem uma boa projeção de voz. ▶ **carry the can** (**for sth**) (*GB, coloq*) levar a culpa (por algo) **carry the day** sair vitorioso **carry weight** pesar (numa decisão) ■ **carry sth away** 1 entusiasmar alguém/algo 2 *Don't get carried away.* Não se deixe levar. **carry sb/sth off** ganhar, conquistar alguém/algo **carry sth off** 1 sair-se bem em algo 2 realizar algo **carry on** (**with sb**) (*coloq*) ter um caso (com alguém) **carry on** (**with/ doing sth**) (*coloq*) continuar (com algo/a fazer algo): ~ *on a conversation* manter uma conversa **carry sth out** 1 (*promessa, ordem*) cumprir algo 2 (*plano*) levar algo a cabo **carry sth through** levar algo até o fim

carryall /'kæriɔːl/ s saco de viagem

cart /kɑːrt/ s carroça ● *vt* transportar (em carroça) ■ **cart sth about/around** (*coloq*) carregar algo para cima e para baixo **cart sb/sth off** (*coloq*) carregar alguém/algo

carton /'kɑːrtn/ s caixa (*de papelão*)

cartoon /kɑːr'tuːn/ s 1 charge, cartum 2 história em quadrinhos 3 desenho animado 4 (*Arte*) esboço **cartoonist** s caricaturista, cartunista

cartridge /'kɑːrtrɪdʒ/ s 1 cartucho 2 (*câmara, etc.*) carretel

carve /kɑːrv/ 1 *vt, vi* esculpir 2 *vt, vi* talhar 3 *vt* gravar 4 *vt, vi* (*carne*) trinchar ■ **carve sth out** (**for yourself**): ~ *out a career for yourself* fazer carreira para si mesmo **carve sth up** (*coloq*) repartir algo **carving** s escultura, obra de talha

cascade /kæ'skeɪd/ s cascata

case /keɪs/ s 1 caso: *It's a ~ of…* Trata-se de… 2 argumento: *There is a ~ for…* Há razões para… ◊ *make* (*out*) *a ~* (*for sth*) apresentar argumentos a favor (de algo) 3 (*Jur*) processo: *the ~ for the defense/prosecution* a causa para a defesa/acusação 4 estojo 5 caixa (*embalagem*) 6 caixote (*vinho*) 7 mala ▶ **in any case** em todo caso (**just**) **in case** se por acaso, no caso de

cash /kæʃ/ s dinheiro (em espécie): ~ *card* cartão de saque ◊ ~ *machine/register* caixa automática / registradora ◊ ~ *flow* fluxo de caixa ▶ **cash down** pagamento à vista **cash on delivery** (*abrev* COD) pagamento contra entrega ● *vt*: ~ *a check* descontar um cheque ■ **cash in** (**on sth**) lucrar (com algo) **cash sth in** trocar algo

cashier /kæ'ʃɪər/ s caixa (*pessoa*)

cash machine (*GB tb* **cash dispenser**) s caixa automático

cashmere /ˌkæʃ'mɪər/ s cashmere

casino /kə'siːnoʊ/ s (*pl* ~**s**) cassino

cask /kæsk; *GB* kɑːsk/ s barril

casket /'kæskɪt; *GB* 'kɑːskɪt/ s 1 (*GB*) caixa (*para jóias, etc.*) 2 (*USA*) caixão

casserole /'kæsəroʊl/ s 1 (*tb* - **dish**) panela de barro 2 ensopado

cassette /kə'set/ s fitacassete: ~ *deck/player/recorder* toca-fitas

cast /kæst; *GB* kɑːst/ s 1 (*Teat*) elenco 2 (*Med*): *My arm's in a* ~. Meu braço está engessado. 3 (*Arte*) molde ● *vt* (*pt, pp* **cast**) 1 (*Teat*): ~ *sb as Hamlet* dar a alguém o papel de Hamlet 2 atirar, lançar 3 ~ *an eye over sth* dar uma olhada rápida em algo 4 (*sombra*) projetar 5 ~ *your vote* votar ▶ **cast a spell on/ sth** lançar um feitiço em alguém/algo **cast doubt** (**on sth**) lançar suspeita (sobre algo) ■ **cast around/about for sth** buscar algo às pressas **cast sb/sth aside** colocar alguém/algo de lado **cast sth off** desfazer-se de algo

castaway /'kæstəweɪ; *GB* 'kɑːst-/ s náufrago/a

caste /kæst; *GB* kɑːst/ s casta

cast iron s ferro fundido ● *adj* 1 de ferro (fundido) 2 (*álibi*) forte

castle /'kæsl; *GB* 'kɑːsl/ s 1 castelo 2 (*xadrez*) torre

castrate /'kæstreɪt; *GB* kæ'streɪt/ *vt* castrar **castration** s castração

casual /'kæʒuəl/ *adj* 1 (*roupa*) esporte 2 (*trabalho*) ocasional 3 superficial: *a ~ acquaintance* um conhecido ◊ *a ~ glance* uma espiada 4 (*comentário*) sem importância 5 (*comportamento*) descontraído, informal: ~ *sex* sexo sem compromisso **casually** *adv* 1 casualmente 2 informalmente 3 temporariamente 4 descontraídamente

casualty /'kæʒuəlti/ s (pl **-ies**) vítima, ferido/a

cat /kæt/ s **1** gato ► GATO **2** felino

catalogue (USA tb **-log**) /'kætəlɒg; GB -lɔg/ s **1** catálogo **2** a ~ of disasters uma série de desastres ● vt catalogar cataloguing s catalogação

catalyst /'kætəlɪst/ s catalisador

catapult /'kætəpʌlt/ s estilingue, catapulta

cataract /'kætərækt/ s catarata

catarrh /kə'tɑr/ s (GB) catarro

catastrophe /kə'tæstrəfi/ s catástrofe catastrophic /ˌkætə'strɒfɪk/ adj catastrófico

catch /kætʃ/ (pt, pp caught) **1** vt, vi apanhar: ~ sb off balance apanhar alguém desprevenido **2** vt pegar, agarrar: ~ sb doing sth pegar alguém fazendo algo **3** vt surpreender **4** vt (USA, coloq) ver **5** vt ~ sth (in/on sth) prender algo (em/com algo) **6** vt (Med) ser contagiado por, pegar **7** vt ouvir, compreender **8** vi: ~ fire pegar fogo ► catch it (coloq): You'll ~ it! Você vai se dar mal! **catch sb's attention/eye** chamar a atenção de alguém **catch sight/a glimpse of sb/sth** avistar alguém/algo **catch your breath 1** recuperar o fôlego **2** ficar sem respiração **catch your death (of cold)** (coloq) pegar uma pneumonia ■ **catch at sth** agarrar-se a algo **catch on** (coloq) entrar na moda, pegar **catch on (to sth)** (coloq) entender (algo) **catch sb out 1** apanhar alguém fazendo algo errado **2** (Esporte) eliminar alguém no passe de bola **be caught up in sth** estar envolvido em algo **catch up (on sth)** pôr (algo) em dia **catch up (with sb/)** (GB) **catch sb up** alcançar alguém ● s **1** ação de apanhar (especialmente bola) **2** captura **3** pesca **4** (coloq): He's a good ~. Ele é um bom partido. **5** trinco, fecho **6** armadilha: It's a catch-22 (situation). Se correr o bicho pega, se ficar o bicho come. catcher s apanhador/a catching adj contagioso catchy adj (**-ier**, **-iest**) que pega fácil, fácil de memorizar

catchment area s (GB) distrito (coberto por escola, hospital, etc.)

catchphrase /'kætʃfreɪz/ s frase feita

catechism /'kætəkɪzəm/ s catecismo

categorical /ˌkætə'gɒrɪkl; GB -'gɒr-/ (tb **categoric**) adj **1** categórico **2** terminante **3** (regra) final categoricamente adv categoricamente

category /'kætəgɔri; GB -gəri/ s (pl **-ies**) categoria categorize vt classificar

cater /'keɪtər/ vi abastecer: ~ for all tastes satisfazer a todos os gostos catering s serviço de bufê

caterpillar /'kætərpɪlər/ s lagarta

catfish /'kætfɪʃ/ s bagre

cathedral /kə'θidrəl/ s catedral

Catholic /'kæθlɪk/ adj, s católico/a Catholicism /kə'θɑləsɪzəm/ s catolicismo

cattle /'kætl/ s [pl] gado

caught /kɔt/ pret, pp de CATCH

cauldron /'kɔldrən/ s caldeirão

cauliflower /'kɔlɪflaʊər; GB 'kɒlɪ-/ s couve-flor

cause /kɔz/ vt causar ● s **1** causa **2** ~ (for sth) motivo (de/para algo)

causeway /'kɔzweɪ/ s estrada ou caminho elevado

caustic /'kɔstɪk/ adj **1** cáustico **2** mordaz

caution /'kɔʃn/ **1** vt, vi advertir **2** vt avisar ● s **1** precaução, cautela: exercise extreme ~ agir de forma extremamente cautelosa **2** aviso ► **throw/fling caution to the wind** fazer algo sem pensar nas consequências cautionary adj de advertência

cautious /'kɔʃəs/ adj ~ (about/of sth) cauteloso (com algo): ~ driver motorista precavido cautiously adv cautelosamente

cavalry /'kævlri/ s cavalaria

cave /keɪv/ s caverna, gruta ■ **cave in 1** desabar **2** ceder

cavern /'kævərn/ s caverna cavernous adj cavernoso

cavity /'kævəti/ s (pl **-ies**) **1** cavidade **2** cárie

CD /ˌsi: 'di:/ s CD

cease /sis/ vt, vi (fml) cessar: ~ to do sth parar de fazer algo

ceasefire /'sisfaɪər/ s cessar-fogo

ceaseless /'sisləs/ adj incessante

cede /sid/ vt ceder

ceiling /'silɪŋ/ s **1** teto **2** altura máxima **3** limite

celebrate /'selɪbreɪt/ **1** vt celebrar **2** vi festejar **3** vt (fml) homenagear celebrated adj célebre celebration s comemoração celebratory /'seləbrəˌtɔri/ adj comemorativo, festivo

celebrity /sə'lebrəti/ s (pl **-ies**) celebridade

celery /'seləri/ s aipo

cell /sel/ s **1** cela **2** célula

cellar /'selər/ s **1** porão **2** adega

cellist /'tʃelɪst/ s violoncelista

cello /'tʃeloʊ/ s (pl **~s**) violoncelo

cellular /'seljʊlər/ adj celular

cellular phone (coloq **cell phone**) s celular

cement /sɪ'ment/ s cimento ● vt **1** cimentar **2** fortalecer

cemetery /'semətri/, GB -tri/ s (pl **-ies**) cemitério (municipal)

censor /'sensər/ s censor ● vt censurar censorship s [U] censura

censure /'senʃər/ vt censurar ● s censura (reprimenda)

census /'sensəs/ s censo

cent /sent/ s cêntimo

centennial /sen'teniəl/ s centenário

center /'sentər/ s **1** centro **2** núcleo **3** (tb ~ **forward**) (Esporte) centroavante ● vt, vi centrar(-se) ■ center sth on/upon/around sb/sth concentrar algo em alguém/algo

center back s zagueiro

centre (GB) = CENTER

century /'sentʃəri/ s (pl **-ies**) século

cereal /'sɪəriəl/ s cereal

cerebral /sə'ri:brəl/; GB 'serəbrəl/ adj cerebral

ceremony /'serəmoʊni; GB -məni/ s (pl **-ies**) cerimônia ceremonial /ˌserɪ'moʊniəl/ adj, s cerimonial

certain /'sɜːrtn/ adj certo: to a ~ extent até certo ponto ◊ make certain (that...)/of (doing) sth assegurar-se (de que...) It is ~ that he'll be elected. Ele certamente será eleito. **2** determinado **3** tal: a ~ Mr. Brown um tal de Sr. Brown ► for certain com certeza ● pron ~ of...: ~ of those present alguns dos presentes certainly adv **1** com certeza **2** (como resposta) claro certainty s (pl **-ies**) certeza

certificate /sər'tɪfɪkət/ s certificado: doctor's ~ atestado médico **2** certidão

certify /'sɜːrtɪfaɪ/ vt (pt, pp **-ied**) **1** certificar **2** (tb ~ **insane**): He was certified (insane). Ele foi declarado louco. certification s atestado

chain /tʃeɪn/ s **1** corrente: in chains acorrentado ◊ ~ reaction reação em cadeia **2** (Geog) cordilheira ● vt ~ sb/sth (up) prender alguém/algo com corrente

chainsaw /'tʃeɪnsɔː/ s serra elétrica

chain-smoke vi fumar um cigarro atrás do outro

chair /tʃeər/ s **1** cadeira: Pull up a ~. Sente-se. ◊ easy ~ poltrona **2** (the chair) (reunião) a presidência, o/a presidente **3** (the electric) chair) a cadeira elétrica **4** cátedra ● vt presidir (reunião)

chairperson /'tʃeərpɜːrsn/ s presidente/a NOTA Esta é a forma preferida atualmente, embora também se usem **chairman** e **chairwoman**.

chalet /ʃæ'leɪ/ s chalé

chalk /tʃɔːk/ s [ger não contável] **1** (Geol) greda **2** giz ■ chalk sth up pôr algo na conta (de alguém)

chalkboard /'tʃɔːkbɔːrd/ s quadro-negro

challenge /'tʃæləndʒ/ s desafio ● vt **1** desafiar **2** interpelar **3** (autoridade, etc.) contestar challenger s **1** desafiante **2** concorrente challenging adj estimulante, desafiante

chamber /'tʃeɪmbər/ s câmara

champagne /ʃæm'peɪn/ s champanhe

champion /'tʃæmpiən/ s **1** campeão/ã **2** (causa) defensor/a ● vt defender championship s campeonato

chance /tʃæns; GB tʃɑːns/ s **1** acaso: by (any) ~ por acaso **2** casualidade: ~ meeting encontro casual **3** probabilidade **4** oportunidade **5** risco: take a ~ (on sth) correr o risco (de algo) ◊ take ~s arriscar-se ► on the (off) chance por via das dúvidas the chances are (that)... (coloq) o mais provável é que... ● vt ~ doing sth correr o risco de fazer algo ► chance your arm/luck (coloq) arriscar-se ■ chance on/upon sb/sth encontrar com alguém/encontrar algo por acaso

chancellor /'tʃænsələr; GB 'tʃɑːns-/ s **1** chanceler: Chancellor of the Exchequer (GB)

Ministro da Fazenda **2** (*universidade*) reitor/a honorário/a

chandelier /ˌʃændəˈlɪər/ *s* lustre

change /tʃeɪndʒ/ **1** *vt, vi* mudar **2** *vt* ~ **sb/sth (into sth)** transformar alguém/algo (em algo) **3** *vi* ~ **from sth (in)to sth;** ~ **over (from sth to sth)** passar de algo para algo ▶ **change hands** trocar de dono **change places (with sb) 1** trocar de lugar (com alguém) **2** colocar-se no lugar de (alguém) **change your mind** mudar de idéia **change your tune** (*coloq*) virar a casaca ■ **change back into sth 1** vestir algo outra vez **2** voltar a ser algo **change into sth 1** passar para algo **2** transformar-se em algo ▶ **1** mudança **2** troca: *a ~ of socks* um par de meias extra **3** baldeação **4** [*U*] (*dinheiro*) trocado, troco ▶ **a change for the better/worse** uma mudança para melhor/pior **a change of heart** uma mudança de atitude **for a change** para variar **make a change** mudar o estado das coisas **the change of life** a menopausa **changeable** *adj* variável

changeover /ˈtʃeɪndʒoʊvər/ *s* transição

changing room *s* cabine de provas, vestiário

channel /ˈtʃænl/ *s* **1** canal **2** (*rio, etc.*) leito **3** via ● *vt* (**-ll-**, *USA tb* **-l-**) **1** canalizar **2** sulcar

chant /tʃænt; *GB* tʃɑːnt/ *s* **1** (*Relig*) cântico **2** toada, canção ● *vt, vi* **1** (*Relig*) cantar **2** entoar, cantarolar

chaos /ˈkeɪɑs/ *s* [*U*] caos: *cause ~* causar confusão **chaotic** /keɪˈɑtɪk/ *adj* caótico

chap /tʃæp/ *s* (*coloq, GB*) (*sujeito*) cara

chapel /ˈtʃæpl/ *s* capela

chaplain /ˈtʃæplɪn/ *s* capelão

chapped /tʃæpt/ *adj* rachado

chapter /ˈtʃæptər/ *s* **1** capítulo **2** época ▶ **chapter and verse** nos mínimos detalhes

char /tʃɑr/ *vt, vi* (**-rr-**) carbonizar

character /ˈkærəktər/ *s* **1** caráter: ~ *references* referências pessoais ◊ ~ *assassination* difamação **2** (*pessoa*) peça, figura **3** (*Cinema, livro*) personagem: *main ~* protagonista **4** reputação ▶ **in/out of character** típico/atípico

characteristic /ˌkærəktəˈrɪstɪk/ *adj* característico ● *s* traço, característica **characteristically** *adv*: *His answer was ~ frank.* Ele

respondeu com a franqueza habitual.

characterize /ˈkærəktəraɪz/ *vt* **1** retratar **2** caracterizar **characterization** *s* caracterização

charade /ʃəˈreɪd; *GB* ʃəˈrɑːd/ *s* farsa, charada

charcoal /ˈtʃɑrkoʊl/ *s* carvão (vegetal) **2** (*tb* ~ **gray**) cinza escuro

charge /tʃɑrdʒ/ *s* **1** acusação: *bring/press charges against sb* processar alguém **2** preço: *free of ~* grátis **3** encargo: *Who's in ~?* Quem é o encarregado? ◊ *in/under sb's ~* sob os cuidados de alguém ◊ *take ~ (of sth)* assumir a responsabilidade (por algo) ◊ *have ~ of sth* ser responsável por algo **4** (*Mil*) carga **5** (*Esporte*) ataque **6** investida **7** carga (*elétrica ou de arma*) ● **1** *vt* ~ **sb (with sth)** acusar alguém (de algo) **2** *vt, vi* ~ **(at) (sb/sth)** lançar-se (contra alguém/algo): *The children charged up the stairs.* As crianças correram escada acima. **3** *vt, vi* ~ **(at sb/sth)** investir (contra alguém/algo) **4** *vt, vi* cobrar: ~ *sth (up) to sb* pôr algo na conta de alguém **5** *vt* (*revólver, pilha*) carregar **6** *vt* (*fml*) incumbir **chargeable** *adj* **1** passível de acusação **2** ~ **to sb** debitado na conta de alguém

chariot /ˈtʃærɪət/ *s* biga

charisma /kəˈrɪzmə/ *s* carisma **charismatic** /ˌkærɪzˈmætɪk/ *adj* carismático

charitable /ˈtʃærətəbl/ *adj* **1** caridoso **2** bondoso **3** beneficente

charity /ˈtʃærəti/ *s* (*pl* **-ies**) **1** caridade **2** compaixão **3** instituição de caridade: *for ~* com fins beneficentes

charm /tʃɑrm/ *s* **1** charme **2** amuleto: ~ *bracelet* pulseira de berloques **3** feitiço ● *vt* encantar: *a charmed life* uma vida afortunada ■ **charm sth from/out of sb/sth** conseguir algo de alguém/algo por meio de charme **charming** *adj* encantador, charmoso

chart /tʃɑrt/ *s* **1** carta de navegação **2** gráfico: *flow ~* fluxograma **3** (**the charts**) [*pl*] parada de sucessos ● *vt* mapear: ~ *the progress of sth* traçar a evolução de algo

charter /ˈtʃɑrtər/ *s* **1** estatuto: *royal ~* (*GB*) autorização real **2** frete: ~ *flight/plane* vôo/avião fretado ● *vt* **1** conceder autorização a **2** fretar **chartered** *adj*

chase /tʃeɪs/ *vt, vi* perseguir: ~ *(after) women* correr atrás de mulheres ◇ ~ *about, around, etc.* correr de lá para cá ■ **chase sb/ sth away, off, etc.** botar alguém/ algo para fora **chase sth up** (*GB, coloq*) localizar algo ● *s* **1** perseguição **2** caça

chasm /ˈkæzəm/ *s* abismo

chassis /ˈʃæsi/ *s* (*pl* chassis /ˈʃæsiz/) chassi

chaste /tʃeɪst/ *adj* **1** casto **2** (*estilo*) sóbrio

chastened /ˈtʃeɪsnd/ *adj* escaldado **2** (*voz*) submisso **chastening** *adj* que serve de lição

chastity /ˈtʃæstəti/ *s* castidade

chat /tʃæt/ *s* bate-papo: ~ *show* (*GB*) programa de entrevistas ● *vi* (-tt-) bater papo ■ **chat sb up** (*GB, coloq*) cantar alguém **chatty** *adj* (-ier, -iest) **1** conversador **2** (*tom*) informal

chatter /ˈtʃætər/ *vi* **1** ~ *(away/on)* tagarelar **2** (*macaco*) chiar **3** (*pássaro*) chilrar **4** (*dentes*) tiritar ● *s* tagarelice

chauffeur /ˈʃoʊfɜːr; *GB* ˈʃəʊfə(r)/ *s* chofer ● *vt* ~ *sb around* levar alguém num carro

chauvinism /ˈʃoʊvɪnɪzəm/ *s* chauvinismo **chauvinist** *s, adj* chauvinista

cheap /tʃiːp/ *adj* (~er, ~est) *adj* **1** barato **2** econômico **3** de má qualidade **4** vulgar **5** (*coloq, USA*) pão-duro ● *adv* (*coloq*) barato ► **be going cheap** (*coloq*) estar em oferta **not come cheap** (*coloq*): *Success doesn't come* ~. O sucesso não vem de graça. ► **on the cheap** (*coloq*) abaixo do custo **cheapen** *vt* **1** baixar o preço de **2** ~ *yourself* rebaixar-se **cheaply** *adv* barato, por baixo preço

cheat /tʃiːt/ **1** *vt* enganar: ~ *sb (out) of sth* defraudar alguém de algo **2** *vi* (*colégio*) colar **3** *vi* trapacear ■ **cheat on sb** ser infiel a alguém ● *s* **1** trapaceiro/a **2** trapaça, fraude

check /tʃek/ *vt* **1** verificar, revisar **2** *vt, vi* examinar **3** *vt* deter **4** *vi* controlar(-se) ■ **check in (at...); check into...** registrar-se (*hotel, aeroporto*) **check sth in** entregar algo (*bagagem*) **check sth off** ticar algo de uma lista **check out (of...)** pagar a conta e partir (*de um hotel*) **check sb/ sth out; check (up) on sb/sth**

investigar alguém/algo ● *s* **1** verificação, revisão **2** investigação **3** xeque **4** cheque **5** (*restaurante*) conta ► **hold/keep sth in check** conter/controlar algo **checked** (*tb* check) *adj* xadrez (*tecido*)

checkbook /ˈtʃekbʊk/ *s* talão de cheques

checkers /ˈtʃekərz/ *s* [*sing*] (jogo de) damas

check-in *s* check-in

checklist /ˈtʃeklɪst/ *s* lista

check mark *s* tique

checkmate /ˈtʃekmeɪt/ *s* xeque-mate

checkout /ˈtʃekaʊt/ *s* **1** caixa (*numa loja*) **2** ato de pagar a conta num hotel e partir

checkpoint /ˈtʃekpɔɪnt/ *s* (ponto de) controle

check-up *s* **1** exame (*médico*) **2** revisão

cheek /tʃiːk/ *s* **1** bochecha **2** (*GB*) descaramento: *What (a) ~!* Que cara-de-pau! **cheeky** *adj* (-ier, -iest) (*GB*) atrevido

cheer /tʃɪər/ **1** *vt, vi* aclamar, dar vivas a: ~ *sb on* torcer por alguém **2** *vt* ~ *sb/sth (up)* animar, alegrar alguém/algo: *Cheer up!* Anime-se! ● *s* ovação, aplauso: *Three ~s for...!* Três vivas para...! **cheerful** *adj* **1** alegre, bem-disposto **2** agradável **cheery** *adj* (-ier, -iest) alegre, animado

cheering /ˈtʃɪərɪŋ/ *s* [*U*] aclamação ● *adj* reconfortante

cheerio /ˌtʃɪəriˈoʊ/ *interj* (*GB*) tchau

cheerleader /ˈtʃɪərliːdər/ *s* animador/a (*de torcida*)

cheers /tʃɪərz/ *interj* (*GB*) **1** saúde **2** tchau **3** obrigado

cheese /tʃiːz/ *s* queijo

cheesecake /ˈtʃiːzkeɪk/ *s* torta de queijo

cheetah /ˈtʃiːtə/ *s* chita

chef /ʃef/ *s* cozinheiro-chefe, cozinheira-chefe

chemical /ˈkemɪkl/ *adj* químico ● *s* produto químico

chemist /ˈkemɪst/ *s* **1** químico/a **2** (*GB*) farmacêutico/a **chemist's** *s* (*GB*) farmácia → PHARMACY

chemistry /ˈkemɪstri/ *s* química

cheque /tʃek/ *s* = CHECK (4)

cheque book (*GB*) = CHECKBOOK

cherish /ˈtʃerɪʃ/ *vt* **1** valorizar **2** (*pessoa*) estimar, cuidar **3** (*esperança*) acalentar **4** guardar com carinho

cherry /'tʃeri/ s (pl -ies) 1 cereja 2 (tb ~ tree) cerejeira 3 (tb ~ red) (cor) vermelho cereja

cherub /'tʃerəb/ s querubim

chess /tʃes/ s xadrez

chest /tʃest/ s 1 caixa: ~ of drawers cômoda 2 peito (tórax) ▸ get it/something off your chest (coloq) desabafar

chestnut /'tʃesnʌt/ s 1 castanha 2 castanheira 3 (coloq) história ou piada surrada ● adj, s (cor) castanho

chew /tʃu:/ vt ~ sth (up) mastigar algo ■ chew sth over (coloq) ruminar algo

chewing gum s [U] chiclete

chick /tʃik/ s 1 pinto 2 (coloq) garota

chicken /'tʃikin/ s 1 frango 2 galinha 3 (coloq) covarde ■ chicken out (coloq) dar para trás ● adj (coloq) medroso

chickenpox /'tʃikinpɑks/ s catapora

chickpea /'tʃikpi:/ s grão-de-bico

chicory /'tʃikəri/ s [U] 1 endívia 2 chicória

chief /tʃi:f/ s chefe ● adj principal chiefly adv principalmente

chieftain /'tʃi:ftən/ s chefe (tribo)

child /tʃaild/ s (pl children /'tʃildrən/) 1 criança: ~ benefit (GB) salário-família ◇ ~ care puericultura ◇ childminder babá que cuida de crianças em sua própria casa ◇ children's clothes/TV roupa/programação infantil 2 filho/a: an only ~ um filho único 3 (fig) produto ▸ child's play (coloq) moleza childbirth s parto childhood s infância childish adj 1 infantil 2 imaturo: be ~ portar-se como criança childless adj sem filhos childlike adj de (uma) criança

chili (GB chilli) /'tʃili/ s (pl -es) (tb ~ pepper) pimenta-malagueta

chill /tʃil/ s 1 frio 2 resfriado: catch/get a ~ resfriar-se 3 calafrio ● vt gelar: ~ sb to the bone/marrow congelar alguém até os ossos 2 vt, vi esfriar, refrigerar chilling adj terrorizante chilly adj (-ier, -iest) frio

chime /tʃaim/ s 1 badalada 2 carrilhão ● vi badalar ■ chime in (with sth) (coloq) interromper uma conversa (dizendo algo)

chimney /'tʃimni/ s chaminé: ~ piece consolo da lareira

chimpanzee /,tʃimpæn'zi:/ (coloq chimp) s chimpanzé

chin /tʃin/ s queixo ▸ keep your chin up (coloq) manter o moral alto

china /'tʃainə/ s 1 porcelana 2 louça

chink /tʃiŋk/ s fresta ▸ a chink in sb's armor o ponto fraco de alguém

chip /tʃip/ s 1 pedaço 2 (madeira) lasca 3 rachadura 4 (GB) batata frita 5 batata frita (de saco) 6 (cassino) ficha 7 (Elet) (micro)chip ▸ a chip off the old block (coloq) filho de peixe, peixinho é ◇ have a chip on your shoulder (coloq) ter complexo de inferioridade ● vt, vi lascar, rachar ■ chip away at sth quebrar algo pedaço por pedaço, destruir algo pouco a pouco chip in (with sth) (coloq) 1 interromper uma conversa (dizendo algo) 2 (dinheiro) contribuir (com algo) chippings s [pl] 1 cascalho 2 (tb wood ~) lascas de madeira

chipmunk /'tʃipmʌŋk/ s tâmia (gênero de esquilo americano)

chirp /tʃɜ:rp/ s 1 gorjeio 2 cricri ● vi 1 gorjear 2 fazer cricri chirpy adj animado (pessoa)

chisel /'tʃizl/ s cinzel ● vt cinzelar, talhar: finely chiseled features feições bem delineadas

chivalry /'ʃivəlri/ s 1 cavalaria 2 cavalheirismo

chive /tʃaiv/ s [ger pl] cebolinha

chloride /'klɔ:raid/ s cloreto

chlorine /'klɔ:ri:n/ s cloro

chock-a-block /,tʃɑk ə 'blɑk/ adj ~ (with sth) abarrotado (de algo)

chock-full /,tʃɑk 'fʊl/ adj repleto

chocolate /'tʃɑklət/ s 1 chocolate 2 bombom ● adj (cor) de chocolate

choice /tʃɔis/ s 1 escolha: make a ~ escolher 2 seleção 3 possibilidade: If I had the choice... Se dependesse de mim... ▸ out of/from choice por decisão própria ● adj (-er, -est) 1 de qualidade 2 seleto

choir /'kwaiər/ s coro

choke /tʃoʊk/ 1 vi ~ (on sth) engasgar-se (com algo): ~ to death morrer engasgado 2 vt sufocar 3 vt ~ sth (up) obstruir algo ■ choke sth back conter algo ● s afogador

cholera /'kɑlərə/ s cólera

cholesterol /kə'lestərɑl; GB -rɒl/ s colesterol

choose /tʃu:z/ (pt chose pp chosen) 1 vt, vi escolher, selecionar 2 vt ~ sb/sth as sth eleger alguém/algo como algo 3 vt, vi

(to do sth) decidir (fazer algo) **4** *vi* preferir: *whenever I ~* quando me convém **choosy** *adj* (**-ier**, **-iest**) (*coloq*) exigente, difícil de agradar

chop /tʃɑp/ *vt* (**-pp-**) **1 ~ sth (up) (into sth)** cortar algo (em pedaços); picar algo: *~ sth in two* partir algo pela metade **2** (*GB, coloq*) reduzir ▶ **chop and change** mudar de opinião a toda hora ∎ **chop sth down** abater algo ∎ **chop sth off** cortar algo aos golpes ● *s* **1** machadada **2** golpe **3** (*carne*) costeleta

chopper /ˈtʃɑpər/ *s* **1** machadinha **2** cutelo **3** (*coloq*) helicóptero **choppy** *adj* (**-ier**, **-iest**) agitado (*mar*)

chopsticks /ˈtʃɑpstɪks/ *s* pauzinhos (*com que se come*)

choral /ˈkɔːrəl/ *adj* coral (*coro*)

chord /kɔːrd/ *s* acorde

chore /tʃɔːr/ *s* tarefa (*do dia-a-dia*): *household ~s* afazeres domésticos

choreography /ˌkɔːriˈɑɡrəfi; *GB* ˌkɒri-/ *s* coreografia **choreographer** *s* coreógrafo/a

chorus /ˈkɔːrəs/ *s* **1** coro: *~ girl* corista **2** refrão ▶ **in chorus** em coro ● *vt* cantar em coro

chose /tʃəʊz/ *pret de* CHOOSE

chosen /ˈtʃəʊzn/ *pp de* CHOOSE

Christ /kraɪst/ *s* Cristo

christen /ˈkrɪsn/ *vt* batizar **christening** *s* batismo

Christian /ˈkrɪstʃən/ *adj*, *s* cristão/ã **Christianity** /ˌkrɪstiˈænəti/ *s* cristianismo

Christian name *s* (pre)nome

Christmas /ˈkrɪsməs/ *s* Natal → NATAL

chrome /krəʊm/ *s* cromo

chromium /ˈkrəʊmiəm/ *s* cromo: *chromium-plated* cromado

chromosome /ˈkrəʊməsəʊm/ *s* cromossomo

chronic /ˈkrɑnɪk/ *adj* **1** crônico **2** (*pessoa*) inveterado

chronicle /ˈkrɑnɪkl/ *s* crônica ● *vt* registrar

chrysalis /ˈkrɪsəlɪs/ *s* crisálida

chubby /ˈtʃʌbi/ *adj* (**-ier**, **-iest**) gorducho

chuck /tʃʌk/ *vt* (*coloq*) **1** jogar **2 ~ sth (in/up)** (*GB*) abandonar algo ∎ **chuck sb/sth out** (*coloq*) botar alguém para fora/jogar algo fora

chuckle /ˈtʃʌkl/ *vi* rir consigo mesmo ● *s* riso contido

chum /tʃʌm/ *s* (*coloq*) camarada

chunk /tʃʌŋk/ *s* pedaço grande **chunky** *adj* (**-ier**, **-iest**) massudo, atarracado

church /tʃɜːrtʃ/ *s* igreja: *~ hall* salão paroquial ◇ *go to ~* ir à missa/ao culto → SCHOOL

churchyard /ˈtʃɜːrtʃjɑːrd/ *s* (*GB*) adro, cemitério de igreja

churn /tʃɜːrn/ **1** *vt*, *vi* **~ (sth) (up)** (*água, etc.*) agitar algo; agitar-se **2** *vi* (*estômago*) virar ∎ **churn sth out** (*coloq*) produzir algo em série

chute /ʃuːt/ *s* **1** calha (*para mercadorias, etc.*) **2** (*GB*) (*USA* **water slide**) tobogã

cider /ˈsaɪdər/ *s* sidra

cigar /sɪˈɡɑːr/ *s* charuto

cigarette /ˌsɪɡəˈret/ *s* cigarro

cinder /ˈsɪndər/ *s* cinza

cinema /ˈsɪnəmə/ *s* (*GB*) cinema

cinnamon /ˈsɪnəmən/ *s* canela

circle /ˈsɜːrkl/ *s* **1** círculo **2** (*Teat*) balcão ▶ **go around in circles** andar em círculos ● *vt* **1** dar uma volta/voltas em **2** rodear **3** marcar com um círculo

circuit /ˈsɜːrkɪt/ *s* **1** turnê **2** volta **3** pista **4** (*Elet*) circuito

circular /ˈsɜːrkjələr/ *adj* redondo, circular ● *s* circular

circulate /ˈsɜːrkjəleɪt/ *vt*, *vi* circular

circulation /ˌsɜːrkjəˈleɪʃn/ *s* **1** circulação **2** tiragem

circumcise /ˈsɜːrkəmsaɪz/ *vt* circuncidar **circumcision** /ˌsɜːrkəmˈsɪʒn/ *s* circuncisão

circumference /sərˈkʌmfərəns/ *s* circunferência

circumstance /ˈsɜːrkəmstæns/ *s* **1** circunstância **2** (**circumstances**) [*pl*] situação econômica ▶ **in/under no circumstances**/**under the circumstances** de jeito algum **in/under the circumstances** em tais circunstâncias

circus /ˈsɜːrkəs/ *s* circo

cistern /ˈsɪstərn/ *s* **1** caixa d'água **2** reservatório

cite /saɪt/ *vt* **1** citar **2** (*USA*) fazer menção a

citizen /ˈsɪtɪzn/ *s* cidadão/ã **citizenship** *s* cidadania

citrus /ˈsɪtrəs/ *adj* cítrico

city /ˈsɪti/ *s* (*pl* **-ies**) **1** cidade **2** (**the City**) a City (*centro financeiro de Londres*)

civic /ˈsɪvɪk/ *adj* **1** municipal: *~ center* sede municipal **2** cívico

civil /ˈsɪvl/ *adj* **1** civil: *~ strife* dissensão social ◇ *the ~ service* (*GB*) a Administração Pública ◇ *~ servant* funcionário público **2** cortês

civilian /səˈvɪliən/ *s* civil

civilization /ˌsɪvələˈzeɪʃn; *GB* -əlaɪˈz-/ *s* civilização

civilized /'sɪvəlaɪzd/ *adj*
civilizado

clad /klæd/ *adj* (*fml*) ~ (**in sth**)
vestido (de algo)

claim /kleɪm/ **1** *vt, vi* ~ (**for sth**)
exigir algo **2** *vt* afirmar, alegar
3 *vt* (*atenção*) merecer **4** *vt*
(*vidas*) tomar ● *s* **1** ~ (**for sth**);
~ (**against sb/sth**) reivindicação
(por algo); reclamação (em
relação a alguém/algo) **2** ~ (**on
sb/sth**); ~ (**to sth**) direito (sobre
alguém/algo); (a algo) **3** afirmação, alegação **claimant** *s*
requerente

clam /klæm/ *s* amêijoa ■ **clam up**
(*coloq*) calar a boca

clamber /'klæmbər/ *vi* trepar
(*com dificuldade*)

clammy /'klæmi/ *adj* (**-ier, -iest**)
úmido, pegajoso

clamor (*GB* **-our**) /'klæmər/
s clamor, rebuliço ● *vi* **1** clamar
2 ~ **for** sth exigir algo aos gritos
3 ~ **against** sth protestar aos
gritos contra algo

clamp /klæmp/ *s* **1** grampo
2 fixador **3** bloqueador (*para
carro estacionado ilegalmente*)
● *vt* **1** segurar **2** prender com
bloqueador ■ **clamp down on
sb/sth** (*coloq*) impor restrições
a alguém/algo

clampdown /'klæmpdaʊn/ *s*
~ (**on sth**) restrição (a algo);
medidas drásticas (contra algo)

clan /klæn/ *s* clã

clandestine /klæn'destɪn/ *adj*
(*fml*) clandestino

clang /klæŋ/ *s* tinido ● *vt, vi* tinir

clank /klæŋk/ *vi* retinir
(*correntes, etc.*)

clap /klæp/ *vt, vi* (**-pp-**) aplaudir:
~ *your hands* (*together*) bater
palmas ◇ ~ *sb on the back* (*GB*)
dar um tapinha nas costas de
alguém ● *s* **1** aplauso **2** *a* ~ *of
thunder* uma trovoada **clapping**
s aplausos

clarify /'klærəfaɪ/ *vt* (*pt, pp* **-ied**)
esclarecer **clarification** *s* esclarecimento

clarinet /ˌklærə'net/ *s* clarinete

clarity /'klærəti/ *s* clareza

clash /klæʃ/ **1** *vi* chocar-se (*com
ruído*) **2** *vi* ~ (**with sb**) (**on/over
sth**) enfrentar (alguém); diver-
gir fortemente (de alguém)
(sobre algo) **3** *vi* (*datas*) coincidir **4** *vi* (*cores*) destoar ● *s*
1 estrondo **2** luta **3** ~ (**on/over
sth**) divergência (a respeito de
algo): ~ *of interests* conflito de
interesses

clasp /klæsp/; *GB* klɑːsp/ *s* fecho
● *vt* abraçar

class /klæs; *GB* klɑːs/ *s* **1** classe:
They're in ~. Eles estão na sala
de aula. **2** categoria: *They are
not in the same* ~. Eles não se
comparam. ◇ *in a* ~ *of your/its
own* sem par ● *vt* classificar

classic /'klæsɪk/ *adj, s* clássico,
típico

classical /'klæsɪkl/ *adj* clássico

classification /ˌklæsɪfɪ'keɪʃn/ *s*
1 classificação **2** categoria

classify /'klæsɪfaɪ/ *vt* (*pt, pp* **-ied**)
classificar **classified** *adj* **1** clas-
sificado **2** confidencial

classmate /'klæsmeɪt; *GB* klɑːs-/
s colega de classe

classroom /'klæsruːm; *GB*
klɑːs-/ *s* sala de aula

classy /'klæsi; *GB* klɑːsi/ *adj*
(**-ier, -iest**) cheio de estilo, clas-
sudo

clatter /'klætər/ *s* (*tb* **clattering**
/-ərɪŋ/) **1** estardalhaço **2** (*trem*)
ruído (ao sacolejar) ● *vt, vi*
fazer estardalhaço (*com pratos,
etc.*) **2** *vi* (*trem*) sacolejar ruidosamente

clause /klɔːz/ *s* **1** (*Gram*) oração
2 (*Jur*) cláusula

claw /klɔː/ *s* **1** garra **2** (*gato*)
unha **3** (*caranguejo*) pinça ● *vt*
arranhar

clay /kleɪ/ *s* argila

clean /kliːn/ *adj* (~**er**, ~**est**)
1 limpo **2** (*Esporte*) que joga
limpo **3** em branco ▶ **make a
clean break** (**with sth**) romper
definitivamente (com algo) ● *vt,
vi* ~ (**sth**) (**up**) limpar (algo); ~ *sth
from/off sth* tirar algo de algo ◇
~ *up your image* melhorar a
própria imagem ■ **clean sth out**
(*coloq*) depenar alguém **clean
sth out** fazer uma limpeza
caprichada em algo **cleaning** *s*
limpeza **cleanliness** /'klenlinəs/
s limpeza (*qualidade*) **cleanly**
adv perfeitamente

clean-cut /kliːn/ *adj* **1** alinhado **2** íntegro (*feições*) bem definido

cleaner /'kliːnər/ *s* **1** (*produto*)
limpador **2** faxineiro/a
3 (**cleaners**) tinturaria

cleanse /klenz/ *vt* **1** limpar
profundamente **2** purificar
cleanser *s* **1** produto de limpeza
2 creme de limpeza

clean-shaven *adj* de cara
rapada

clean-up *s* limpeza geral

clear /klɪər/ (~**er**, ~**est**) *adj*
1 claro: *make sth* ~ deixar algo
claro **2** (*céu, estrada*) limpo,
desanuviado **3** transparente **4**
nítido **5** (*consciência*) tranqüilo
6 livre: ~ *of debt* sem dívidas

▶(as) clear as day claro como água (as) clear as mud nada claro ● *adv* claramente ● *s* in the clear (coloq) 1 fora de suspeita 2 fora de perigo ● **v** 1 vt ~ (up) (*tempo*) desanuviar-se, clarear 2 vt ~ sth (up) (*dúvida*) esclarecer algo 3 vt desentupir 4 vt (*pessoas*) dispersar 5 vt absolver: ~ *your name* limpar seu nome 6 vt (*obstáculo*) transpor 7 vt, vi ~ (*sth*) away/up desobstruir (algo): ~ *the table* tirar a mesa ▶ clear the air esclarecer as coisas ■ clear off (coloq) cair fora clear sth out arrumar algo ▶ keep/stay/steer clear (of sb/sth) evitar alguém/algo

clearance /'klɪərəns/ *s* 1 despejo: *a ~ sale* uma liquidação 2 vão 3 autorização 4 compensação (*cheque*)

clear-cut *adj* bem definido

clear-headed *adj* sensato

clearing /'klɪərɪŋ/ *s* clareira

clearly /'klɪərli/ *adv* claramente

clear-sighted *adj* lúcido

cleavage /'kliːvɪdʒ/ *s* decote

clef /klef/ *s* (*Mús*) clave

clench /klentʃ/ *vt* cerrar (*punhos, dentes*)

clergy /'klɜːrdʒi/ *s* [pl] clero

clergyman /'klɜːrdʒimən/ *s* (pl -men) 1 clérigo 2 pastor anglicano → PRIEST

clerical /'klerɪkl/ *adj* 1 de escritório: ~ *staff* pessoal administrativo 2 (*Relig*) eclesiástico

clerk /klɑːrk; *GB* klɑːk/ *s* 1 auxiliar de escritório 2 escrevente 3 (*USA*) (*tb* desk ~) recepcionista 4 (*USA*) (*em loja*) funcionário/a

clever /'klevər/ *adj* (~er, ~est) 1 esperto 2 habilidoso: *be ~ at sth* ter aptidão para algo 3 engenhoso 4 malandro ▶ be too clever ser presunçoso cleverness *s* esperteza, habilidade

cliché /kliːʃeɪ/ *s* clichê

click /klɪk/ *s* 1 clique 2 estalido 3 batida (de saltos) ● *vi* 1 (*Informát, etc.*) clicar, fazer clique: ~ *open* abrir(-se) com um estalido 2 vt: ~ *your heels/fingers* bater os saltos/estalar os dedos 3 vi (*amizade*) entrosar 4 vi dar-se conta

client /'klaɪənt/ *s* cliente

clientele /ˌklaɪənˈtel; *GB* ˌkliːɒnˈtel/ *s* clientela

cliff /klɪf/ *s* penhasco, precipício

climate /'klaɪmət/ *s* clima: *the social* ~ a situação social

climax /'klaɪmæks/ *s* clímax

climb /klaɪm/ *vt, vi* 1 escalar: *go climbing* praticar alpinismo 2 subir: *The road climbs steeply.* A estrada é muito íngreme. 3 ~ (up) (sth) trepar (em algo) 4 (*sociedade*) ascender ■ climb down 1 voltar atrás 2 descer climb out of sth 1 ~ *out of bed* levantar-se da cama 2 descer de algo ● *s* 1 escalada, subida 2 ladeira

climber /'klaɪmər/ *s* alpinista

clinch /klɪntʃ/ *vt* 1 (*negócio, etc.*) fechar 2 ganhar 3 (*vitória, etc.*) assegurar: *That clinched it.* Foi o que faltava para decidir.

cling /klɪŋ/ *vi* (*pt, pp* **clung**) agarrar-se, grudar-se: ~ *to each other* dar-se um abraço apertado clinging *adj* 1 (*tb* clingy) (*roupa*) justo 2 (*pessoa*) grudento

clinic /'klɪnɪk/ *s* clínica

clinical /'klɪnɪkl/ *adj* 1 clínico 2 impassível

clink /klɪŋk/ 1 *vi* tilintar 2 *vt*: ~ *glasses* tocar as taças num brinde

clip /klɪp/ *s* 1 clipe 2 (*cabelo*) grampo ● *vt* (-pp-) 1 cortar 2 ~ sth (on) to sth/together prender algo a algo (com um grampo/clipe)

clique /kliːk/ *s* panelinha (*grupo de pessoas*)

cloak /kloʊk/ *s* manto ● *vt* encobrir: *cloaked in secrecy* envolto em mistério

cloakroom /'kloʊkruːm/ *s* 1 vestiário 2 (*GB*) toalete → TOILET

clock /klɑːk/ *s* 1 relógio (*de parede ou de mesa*) 2 (coloq) medidor de quilometragem 3 (coloq) taxímetro ▶ around the clock vinte e quatro horas por dia ● *vt* cronometrar ■ clock in/on; clock off/out (*trabalho*) marcar o ponto (ao chegar)/(ao sair) clock sth up registrar algo, acumular algo clockwise *adv*, *adj* em sentido horário

clockwork /'klɑːkwɜːrk/ *adj* que funciona como um relógio ● *s* mecanismo (*com de relógio*) ▶ like clockwork às mil maravilhas, conforme o planejado

clog /klɑːg/ *s* tamanco ● *vt, vi* ~ (**sth**) (up) entupir algo, entupir-se, emperrar(-se)

cloister /'klɔɪstər/ *s* claustro

clone /kloʊn/ *s* clone ● *vt* clonar

close¹ /kloʊs/ (~er, ~est) *adj* 1 (*parente*) próximo 2 íntimo: ~ *to sb* chegado a alguém 3 (*vínculos, etc.*) estreito 4 (*vigilância*) rigoroso 5 (*exame*) minucioso 6 (*Esporte*) acirrado 7 (*tempo*)

close

C

276

abafado **8** ~ **to sth** próximo de algo, perto de algo: *to be quase chorando* ▸ *it/that was a* **close call/shave** (*coloq*) escapou por um triz ■ **keep a close eye/ watch on sb/sth** manter alguém/algo sob forte vigilância ● *adv* (*tb* ~ **by**) perto: ~ *together* lado a lado ▸ **close on** quase **closely** *adv* **1** de perto **2** atentamente **3** minuciosamente **closeness** *s* **1** proximidade **2** intimidade

close² /klouz/ *vt, vi* **1** fechar(-se) **2** terminar ▸ **close your mind to sth** recusar-se a considerar algo ■ **close down 1** (*empresa*) falir **2** encerrar (*a transmissão*) **close sth down** fechar algo (*empresa, etc.*) **close in** (*dia*) ficar mais curto **close in (on sb/ sth)** (*névoa, inimigo, etc.*) baixar em cima (*de alguém/algo*) ● *s* fim: *come/draw to a ~* chegar ao fim do: *closed adj* fechado

close-knit *adj* muito unido (*comunidade, etc.*)

closet /ˈklɑzɪt/ *s* (*esp USA*) armário

close-up *s* primeiro plano

closing /ˈklouzɪŋ/ *adj* **1** final **2** ~ *time/date* horário/data de encerramento

closure /ˈklouʒər/ *s* fechamento

clot /klɑt/ *s* **1** coágulo **2** (*GB, coloq*) imbecil

cloth /klɔːθ; *GB* klɒθ/ *s* **1** tecido → TECIDO **2** pano

clothe /klouð/ *vt* ~ **sb/yourself (in sth)** vestir alguém, vestir-se (de algo)

clothes /klouz; *GB* klouðz/ *s* [*pl*] roupa

clothing /ˈklouðɪŋ/ *s* vestuário

cloud /klaud/ *s* nuvem ● **1** *vt* ofuscar **2** *vt* complicar **3** *vi* (*expressão*) anuviar-se ■ **cloud over** (*tempo*) anuviar-se **cloudless** *adj* sem nuvens **cloudy** *adj* (*-ier, -iest*) nublado

clout /klaut/ *s* (*coloq*) **1** cascudo **2** influência ● *vt* (*GB, coloq*) dar um cascudo em

clove /klouv/ *s* **1** cravo (*especiaria*) **2** ~ *of garlic* dente de alho

clover /ˈklouvər/ *s* trevo

clown /klaun/ *s* palhaço/a

club /klʌb/ *s* **1** clube **2** boate **3** porrete **4** taco (*golfe*) **5** (**clubs**) (*naipe*) paus → BARALHO ● *vt, vi* (*-bb-*) dar uma porretada ▸ **go clubbing** ir à boate ■ **club together (to do sth)** cotizar-se (para fazer algo)

clue /kluː/ *s* **1** ~ (**to sth**) pista de algo **2** indício **3** (*palavra cruza-*

da) definição ▸ **not have a clue** (*coloq*) **1** não fazer a menor idéia **2** ser inútil (*para algo*)

clump /klʌmp/ *s* grupo (*plantas, etc.*)

clumsy /ˈklʌmzi/ *adj* (*-ier, -iest*) **1** desajeitado **2** malfeito

clung /klʌŋ/ *pret, pp de* CLING

cluster /ˈklʌstər/ *s* grupo ■ **cluster/be clustered (together) around sb/sth** apinhar-se ao redor de alguém/algo

clutch /klʌtʃ/ *vt* **1** apertar, segurar com força **2** ~ (**at) sth** agarrar(-se) (a) algo ● *s* **1** embreagem **2** (**clutches**) [*pl*] garras

clutter /ˈklʌtər/ *s* desordem, bagunça ● *vt* ~ **sth (up)** entulhar algo

coach /koutʃ/ *s* **1** (*GB*) ônibus **2** (*GB*) vagão **3** carruagem **4** treinador/a **5** professor/a particular ● **1** *vt* (*Esporte*) treinar **2** *vt, vi* ~ (**sb**) (**for/in sth**) dar aulas particulares (de algo) (a alguém) **coaching** *s* treinamento, preparação

coal /koul/ *s* **1** carvão **2** brasa

coalfield /ˈkoulfiːld/ *s* região carbonífera

coalition /ˌkouəˈlɪʃn/ *s* coalizão

coarse /kɔːrs/ *adj* (*-er, -est*) **1** (*areia, etc.*) grosso **2** áspero **3** vulgar, grosseiro

coast /koust/ *s* costa ● *vi* **1** ir em ponto morto **2** ir sem pedalar **coastal** *adj* costeiro

coastguard /ˈkoustɡɑːrd/ *s* guarda costeira

coastline /ˈkoustlaɪn/ *s* litoral

coat /kout/ *s* **1** casaco, sobretudo: ~ *hanger* cabide **2** (*white coat*) guarda-pó **3** (*animal*) pêlo, lã **4** (*pintura*) camada ● *vt* ~ **sth (in/with sth)** cobrir, revestir algo (de algo) **coating** *s* revestimento

coax /kouks/ *vt* **1** ~ **sb into/out of (doing) sth**; ~ **sb to do sth** convencer alguém (a fazer/deixar de fazer algo) **2** ~ **sth out of/from sb** conseguir algo de alguém

cobble /ˈkɑbl/ *s* (*tb* **cobblestone**) *s* pedra de calçamento

cobweb /ˈkɑbweb/ *s* teia de aranha

cocaine /kouˈkeɪn/ *s* cocaína

cockney /ˈkɑkni/ *adj, s* (*nativo/a*) do leste de Londres

cockpit /ˈkɑkpɪt/ *s* cabine (*de piloto*)

cockroach /ˈkɑkroutʃ/ *s* barata

cocktail /ˈkɑkteɪl/ *s* coquetel

cocoa /ˈkoukou/ *s* **1** cacau **2** (*bebida*) chocolate

coconut /'koʊkənʌt/ s coco

cocoon /kə'ku:n/ s **1** casulo **2** (fig) manto

cod /kɒd/ (pl **cod**) s bacalhau

code /koʊd/ s **1** código **2** palavra chave: ~ *name* codinome

coercion /koʊ'ɜːrʃn/ s coerção

coffee /'kɒfi; GB 'kɒfi/ s **1** café **2** cor de café

coffin /'kɔːfin; GB 'kɒf-/ s caixão

cog /kɒg/ s dente (de roda)

cogent /'koʊdʒənt/ adj convincente

coherent /koʊ'hɪərənt/ adj **1** coerente **2** inteligível

coil /kɔɪl/ s **1** rolo **2** (serpente) rosca **3** DIU ● **1** vt ~ **sth** (**up**) enrolar algo **2** vt, vi ~ (**yourself**) **up** (**around sth**) enroscar-se (em algo)

coin /kɔɪn/ s moeda ● vt cunhar

coincide /,koʊɪn'saɪd/ vi coincidir

coincidence /koʊ'ɪnsɪdəns/ s **1** coincidência **2** (fml) convergência

coke /koʊk/ s **1** (**Coke**®) Coca-Cola® **2** (colog) coca **3** coque

cold /koʊld/ adj (~er, ~est) frio: *I'm cold.* Estou com frio. ◇ *It's cold today.* Está frio hoje. ◇ *get* ~ esfriar/ficar frio ▶ *be* FRIO ▶ *get/ have cold feet* (colog) ficar com ter medo ● s **1** frio **2** resfriado: *catch* (*a*) ~ resfriar-se

cold-blooded adj **1** (Biol) de sangue frio **2** insensível

coliseum /,kɒlɪ'siːəm/ s estádio

collaboration /kə,læbə'reɪʃn/ s colaboração

collapse /kə'læps/ vi **1** desabar, despencar **2** desmaiar **3** (negócio, etc.) fracassar **4** (móvel, etc.) dobrar ● s **1** fracasso **2** queda **3** (Med) colapso

collar /'kɒlər/ s **1** colarinho **2** coleira

collateral /kə'lætərəl/ s garantia

colleague /'kɒliːg/ s colega (trabalho)

collect /kə'lekt/ **1** vt recolher: *collected works* obras completas **2** vt ~ **sth** (**up/together**) juntar, reunir algo **3** vt (dados) coletar **4** vt (fundos) arrecadar **5** vt (selos, etc.) colecionar **6** vi (multidão) reunir-se **7** vi acumular ● adj, adv (USA) a cobrar (chamada) **collection** s **1** coleção **2** coleta **3** ajuntamento, grupo **collector** s colecionador/a

collective /kə'lektɪv/ adj, s coletivo

college /'kɒlɪdʒ/ s centro de ensino superior **2** (USA) universidade **3** (GB) faculdade (Oxford, Cambridge, etc.)

collide /kə'laɪd/ vi colidir

colliery /'kɒliəri/ s (pl -ies) (GB) mina de carvão

collision /kə'lɪʒn/ s colisão

collusion /kə'luːʒn/ s conluio

colon /'koʊlən/ s **1** cólon **2** dois pontos

colonel /'kɜːrnl/ s coronel

colonial /kə'loʊniəl/ adj colonial

colony /'kɒləni/ s (pl -ies) colônia

color (GB -our) /'kʌlər/ s **1** cor: *color-blind* daltônico **2** (colors) [pl] (Mil) bandeira ▶ *be/feel off color* (colog) estar indisposto ● **1** vt, vi ~ (**sth**) (**in**) colorir algo **2** vt influenciar algo **3** deturpar ■ **color up** (**at sth**) corar (por algo) **colored** adj **1** *cream-colored* (de cor) creme **2** (pessoa) de cor **3** deturpado **colorful** adj **1** colorido, vibrante **2** (vida) fascinante **coloring** s **1** colorido **2** tez **3** corante **colorless** adj **1** incolor, sem cor **2** sem graça

colossal /kə'lɒsl/ adj colossal

colt /koʊlt/ s potro ▶ POTRO

column /'kɒləm/ s coluna

coma /'koʊmə/ s coma

comb /koʊm/ s **1** pente **2** (enfeite) travessa ● **1** vt pentear **2** vt, vi ~ (**through**) **sth** (**for sb/ sth**) vasculhar algo (em busca de alguém/algo)

combat /'kɒmbæt/ s [U] combate ● vt combater

combination /,kɒmbɪ'neɪʃn/ s combinação

combine /kəm'baɪn/ **1** vt, vi combinar(-se) **2** vi (Com) unir-se **3** vt (qualidades) reunir

come /kʌm/ vi (pt **came** pp **come**) **1** vir **2** chegar **3** percorrer **4** (posição) ser: ~ *first* o primeiro **5** ~ *undone* desatar-se **6** ~ *to/into* + substantivo: ~ *to a halt* parar ◇ ~ *into a fortune* herdar uma fortuna ▶ *come to nothing; not come to anything* não dar em nada *come what may* aconteça o que acontecer *when it comes to* (*doing*) *sth* quando se trata de (fazer) algo NOTA Para expressões com **come**, ver o substantivo, adjetivo, etc., p. ex. *come of age* em AGE. ■ **come about** (**that...**) ocorrer, suceder (que...) **come across sb/sth** encontrar com alguém/encontrar algo por acaso **come along 1** chegar, aparecer **2** vir também **3** progredir **come apart** desfazer-se **come away** (**from**

sth) desprender-se (de algo) **come away (with sth)** partir, ir-se embora (com algo) **come back** voltar **come by sth** 1 conseguir algo 2 adquirir algo **come down** 1 baixar 2 vir abaixo **come forward** oferecer-se **come from...** ser de... **come in** 1 entrar 2 chegar **come in for sth** (*crítica, etc.*) receber algo **come off** 1 (*mancha*) sair 2 (*peça*): *Does it ~ off?* Isso sai? 3 (*coloq*) dar certo (*plano*) **come off (sth)** soltar-se (de algo) **come on** 1 entrar em cena 2 *Come on!* Vamos! 3 progredir **come out** 1 sair 2 revelar(-se) 3 declarar-se homossexual **come out with sth** dizer algo surpreendente **come over (to...)** (*GB tb* **come round (to...)**) dar uma passada (em...) **come over sb** apossar-se de alguém: *I can't think what came over me.* Não sei o que me deu. **come through (sth)** sobreviver (a algo) **come to sth** 1 somar algo 2 chegar a algo **come up** 1 (*planta, sol*) desabrochar, nascer 2 (*assunto*) surgir **come up against sth** esbarrar em algo **come up to sb** acercar-se de alguém

comeback /'kʌmbæk/ s: make/ stage a ~ regressar à cena

comedian /kə'miːdiən/ s comediante

comedy /'kɒmədi/ s (*pl* -ies) 1 comédia 2 comicidade

comet /'kɒmɪt/ s cometa

comfort /'kʌmfət/ s 1 bem-estar, conforto 2 consolo 3 (**comforts**) comodidades • *vt* consolar

comfortable /'kʌmfətəbl; *GB* -ftəbl/ *adj* 1 confortável 2 (*vitória*) fácil 3 (*margem*) amplo **comfortably** *adv* (*ganhar*) facilmente ▶ **be comfortably off** viver bem (financeiramente)

comforter /'kʌmfətər/ (*USA*) s edredom

comic /'kɒmɪk/ *adj* cômico • s 1 (*GB* ~ **book**) revista em quadrinhos, gibi 2 humorista

coming /'kʌmɪŋ/ s 1 chegada 2 (*Relig*) vinda • *adj* próximo

comma /'kɒmə/ s vírgula

command /kə'mɑːnd; *GB* -'mɑːnd/ 1 *vt* ordenar 2 *vt, vi* mandar (em) 3 *vt* (*recursos*) dispor de 4 *vt* (*vista*) possuir 5 *vt* (*respeito*) inspirar 6 *vt* (*atenção*) atrair • s 1 ordem 2 (*Informát, Mil*) comando

3 (*idioma*) domínio **commander** s 1 (*Mil*) comandante 2 chefe

commemorate /kə'meməreɪt/ *vt* comemorar

commence /kə'mens/ *vt, vi* (*fml*) começar

commend /kə'mend/ *vt* 1 elogiar 2 (*GB, fml*) recomendar **commendable** *adj* louvável

comment /'kɒment/ s comentário • *vi* comentar

commentary /'kɒmənteri; *GB* -tri/ s (*pl* -**ies**) comentário

commentator /'kɒmenteɪtər/ s comentarista

commerce /'kɒmɜːs/ s comércio NOTA A palavra mais comum é **trade**.

commercial /kə'mɜːrʃl/ *adj* 1 comercial 2 (*direito*) mercantil 3 (*TV, etc.*) patrocinado por publicidade → **TELEVISION** • s anúncio

commission /kə'mɪʃn/ s 1 comissão 2 encargo • *vt* 1 encarregar 2 encomendar

commissioner /kə'mɪʃənər/ s comissário/a (*encarregado de um departamento*)

commit /kə'mɪt/ *vt* (-tt-) 1 cometer 2 confiar: ~ *sth to memory* memorizar algo 3 ~ **yourself (to (doing) sth)**; ~ **yourself (on sth)** comprometer-se (a (fazer) algo); (com alguém) **commitment** s 1 ~ (**to sth/to do sth**) (*com algo/de fazer algo*) compromisso 2 comprometimento

committee /kə'mɪti/ s comitê

commodity /kə'mɒdəti/ s (*pl* -**ies**) 1 mercadoria 2 (*Fin*) (**commodities**) commodities

common /'kɒmən/ *adj* 1 habitual 2 comum: ~ *sense* bom senso 3 ordinário, vulgar ▶ **in common** em comum • s 1 (*tb* ~ **land**) terra comunitária 2 (**the Commons**) (*GB*) a Câmara dos Comuns **commonly** *adv* geralmente

commonplace /'kɒmənpleɪs/ *adj* trivial

commotion /kə'məʊʃn/ s comoção

communal /kə'mjuːnl, 'kɒmjənl/ *adj* comunal

commune /'kɒmjuːn/ s comuna

communicate /kə'mjuːnɪkeɪt/ *vt, vi* comunicar(-se) **communication** s 1 comunicação 2 mensagem

communion /kə'mjuːniən/ (*tb* **Holy Communion**) s comunhão

communiqué /kə,mjuːnə'keɪ; *GB* kə'mjuːnɪkeɪ/ s comunicado

communism /'kɒmjunɪzəm/

C   comprise

s comunismo **communist** *adj*,
s comunista

community /kəˈmjuːnəti/
s (*pl* **-ies**) **1** comunidade:
~ *center* centro comunitário
2 (*de estrangeiros*) colônia

commute /kəˈmjuːt/ *vi* viajar
(diariamente) para o trabalho
commuter *s* pessoa que viaja de
casa para o trabalho

compact /kəmˈpækt/ *adj* compacto ● /ˈkɒmpækt/ *s* (*tb* **powder**
~) estojo de pó-de-arroz

compact disc *s* CD

companion /kəmˈpæniən/ *s*
companheiro/a **companionship**
s companheirismo

company /ˈkʌmpəni/ *s* (*pl* **-ies**)
1 companhia **2** (*Com*) empresa
▶ **keep sb company** fazer companhia a alguém

comparable /ˈkɒmpərəbl/ *adj*
comparável

comparative /kəmˈpærətɪv/ *adj*
1 comparativo **2** relativo

compare /kəmˈpeər/ *vt*, *vi*
comparar(-se)

comparison /kəmˈpærɪsn/ *s*
comparação

compartment /kəmˈpɑːtmənt/
s compartimento

compass /ˈkʌmpəs/ *s* **1** bússola
2 (*tb* **compasses** [*pl*]) compasso

compassion /kəmˈpæʃn/ *s*
compaixão **compassionate** *adj*
compassivo

compatible /kəmˈpætəbl/ *adj*
compatível

compel /kəmˈpel/ *vt* (**-ll-**) (*fml*)
1 obrigar **2** forçar **compelling**
adj **1** irresistível **2** (*motivo, etc.*)
convincente

compensate /ˈkɒmpenseɪt/ **1** *vt*,
vi compensar **2** *vt* indenizar
compensation *s* **1** compensação
2 indenização

compete /kəmˈpiːt/ *vi* competir

competent /ˈkɒmpɪtənt/ *adj*
competente **competence** *s* competência, capacidade

competition /ˌkɒmpəˈtɪʃn/
s competição, concurso **1** (**the
competition**) a concorrência

competitive /kəmˈpetətɪv/ *adj*
competitivo

competitor /kəmˈpetɪtər/ *s*
competidor/a, concorrente

compile /kəmˈpaɪl/ *vt* compilar

complacency /kəmˈpleɪsnsi/
s ~ (**about sb/sth**) satisfação
consigo próprio (em relação a
alguém/algo) **complacent** *adj*
satisfeito consigo mesmo

complain /kəmˈpleɪn/ *vi*
queixar-se **complaint** *s*

1 queixa, reclamação **2** (*Med*)
doença

complement /ˈkɒmplɪmənt/
s **1** ~ (**to sth**) complemento
(*de/para algo*) **2** lotação ● *vt*
complementar **complementary**
/ˌkɒmplɪˈmentəri/ *GB* -tri/ *adj*
complementar

complete /kəmˈpliːt/ *vt* **1** completar **2** terminar **3** preencher
● *adj* **1** completo **2** total **3** absoluto **4** terminado **completely** *adv*
completamente **completion** *s* **1**
conclusão **2** finalização de um
contrato de venda (*residência*)

complex /kəmˈpleks/; *GB*
ˈkɒmpleks/ *adj* complexo
● *s* complexo

complexion /kəmˈplekʃn/ *s* **1** tez
2 (*fig*) caráter

compliance /kəmˈplaɪəns/
s conformidade: *in* ~ *with...* de
acordo com...

complicate /ˈkɒmplɪkeɪt/ *vt*
complicar **complicated** *adj* complicado **complication** *s* complicação

compliment /ˈkɒmplɪmənt/ *s*
1 elogio **2** (**compliments**) [*pl*]
(*fml*) cumprimentos ● *vt* ~ **sb**
(**on sth**) cumprimentar alguém
(*por algo*) **complimentary**
/ˌkɒmplɪˈmentəri/ (*GB*)-tri/ *adj* **1**
lisonjeiro **2** (*entrada, etc.*)
grátis

comply /kəmˈplaɪ/ *vi* ~ (**with sth**)
agir/estar em conformidade

component /kəmˈpəʊnənt/
s **1** componente **2** (*Mec*) peça
● *adj*: ~ *parts* peças integrantes

compose /kəmˈpəʊz/ *vt* **1** (*Mús*)
compor **2** redigir **3** (*idéias*) pôr
no lugar **4** ~ **yourself** acalmar-se
composed *adj* sereno **composer**
s compositor/a

composition /ˌkɒmpəˈzɪʃn/
s **1** composição **2** redação

compost /ˈkɒmpɒst/ *s* adubo

composure /kəmˈpəʊʒər/ *s* serenidade

compound /ˈkɒmpaʊnd/ *adj*,
s composto ● *s* recinto
● /kəmˈpaʊnd/ *vt* agravar

comprehend /ˌkɒmprɪˈhend/ *vt*
compreender (*inteiramente*),
abranger **comprehensible** *adj*
compreensível **comprehension**
s compreensão

comprehensive /ˌkɒmprɪˈhensɪv/ *adj* abrangente

comprehensive school *s* (*GB*)
escola secundária estatal

compress /kəmˈpres/ *vt*
1 comprimir **2** condensar
compression *s* compressão

comprise /kəmˈpraɪz/ *vt*

1 constar de **2** formar

compromise /'kɒmprəmaɪz/ s acordo ● **1** vi chegar a um acordo **2** vt comprometer *compromising adj* comprometedor

compulsion /kəm'pʌlʃn/ s compulsão **2** desejo irresistível

compulsive /kəm'pʌlsɪv/ adj **1** (filme, etc.) absorvente, fascinante **2** compulsivo **3** (jogador) inveterado

compulsory /kəm'pʌlsəri/ adj compulsório: ~ purchase expropriação

computer /kəm'pjuːtər/ s computador: ~ programmer programador *computerize* vt informatizar *computing* s informática

comrade /'kɒmræd; GB -reɪd/ s **1** (Pol) camarada **2** companheiro/a

con /kɒn/ s (coloq) trapaça: ~ artist/man trapaceiro ● vt (coloq) (-nn-) ~ sb (out of sth) trapacear alguém (tirando algo)

conceal /kən'siːl/ vt **1** ocultar **2** dissimular

concede /kən'siːd/ vt **1** conceder **2** ~ that... admitir que...

conceit /kən'siːt/ s presunção *conceited adj* presunçoso

conceivable /kən'siːvəbl/ adj concebível *conceivably* adv possivelmente

conceive /kən'siːv/ vt, vi **1** conceber **2** ~ (of) sth imaginar algo

concentrate /'kɒnsntreɪt/ vt, vi concentrar(-se) *concentration* s concentração

concept /'kɒnsept/ s conceito

conception /kən'sepʃn/ s **1** concepção **2** idéia

concern /kən'sɜːrn/ vt **1** as far as I am concerned no que me diz respeito/quanto a mim **2** referir-se a **3** ~ yourself with sth involver-se com algo **4** preocupar ● s **1** preocupação **2** interesse **3** negócio *concerned adj* preocupado ▶ be concerned with sth tratar de algo *concerning prep* **1** a respeito de **2** no que se refere a

concert /'kɒnsərt/ s concerto

concerted /kən'sɜːrtɪd/ adj **1** coordenado **2** (esforço) conjunto

concerto /kən'tʃɜːrtoʊ/ s (pl ~s) concerto (peça musical)

concession /kən'seʃn/ s **1** desconto para determinadas pessoas **2** (Fin) concessão

conciliation /kənˌsɪli'eɪʃn/ s conciliação *conciliatory* /kən-

'sɪliətɔːri/ adj conciliador

concise /kən'saɪs/ adj conciso

conclude /kən'kluːd/ **1** vt, vi concluir **2** vt ~ that... chegar à conclusão de que... *conclusion* s conclusão *conclusive adj* conclusivo

concoct /kən'kɒkt/ vt **1** (freq pej) fabricar **2** (desculpa) inventar **3** (plano, etc.) tramar *concoction* s **1** mixórdia **2** mistura

concord /'kɒŋkɔːrd/ s harmonia

concourse /'kɒŋkɔːrs/ s saguão (edifício)

concrete /'kɒŋkriːt/ adj concreto, tangível ● s concreto

concur /kən'kɜːr/ vi (-rr-) (fml) ~ (with sb/sth) (in sth) concordar (com alguém/algo) (sobre algo) *concurrence* s acordo *concurrent adj* simultâneo *concurrently* adv ao mesmo tempo

concussion /kən'kʌʃn/ s concussão cerebral

condemn /kən'dem/ vt **1** condenar **2** (edifício) declarar impróprio para uso *condemnation* s condenação

condensation /ˌkɒnden'seɪʃn/ s **1** condensação **2** resumo

condense /kən'dens/ vt, vi **1** condensar(-se) **2** resumir(-se)

condescend /ˌkɒndɪ'send/ vi dignar-se

condition /kən'dɪʃn/ s **1** estado, condição: on ~ (that...) com a condição de que... **2** be out of ~ estar fora de forma **3** requisito **4** (conditions) circunstâncias, condições ▶ on no condition (fml) de modo algum ● vt **1** condicionar, determinar **2** acondicionar *conditional adj* condicional: be ~ on/upon sth depender de algo *conditioner* s condicionador

condolence /kən'doʊləns/ s [ger pl] condolência: send your condolences dar os pêsames

condom /'kɒndəm; GB 'kɒndɒm/ s preservativo, camisinha

condominium /ˌkɒndə'mɪniəm/ s condomínio

condone /kən'doʊn/ vt **1** tolerar **2** sancionar

conducive /kən'duːsɪv; GB -'djuːs-/ adj propício

conduct /'kɒndʌkt/ s **1** conduta **2** gestão ● /kən'dʌkt/ vt **1** guiar **2** dirigir **3** (investigação) levar a cabo **4** (orquestra) reger **5** ~ yourself (fml) comportar-se **6** (Elet) conduzir *conductor* s **1** (Mús) maestro **2** (GB) (ônibus) cobrador/a **3** (trem) fiscal **4** (*Elet*) condutor

cone /koʊn/ s **1** cone **2** (*sorvete*) casquinha **3** (*Bot*) pinha

confectioner's sugar s açúcar para glacê

confectionery /kənˈfekʃənəri; (*GB*)-nəri/ s [U] doces

confederation /kənˌfedəˈreɪʃn/ s confederação

confer /kənˈfɜːr/ (**-rr-**) **1** vi deliberar **2** vi conferenciar **3** vt ~ **sth (on)** conferir algo (a)

conference /ˈkɑnfərəns/ s **1** congresso: ~ **hall** sala de conferência **2** reunião

confess /kənˈfes/ vt, vi ~ **(to) (sth)** confessar(-se) (algo) **confession** s confissão

confide /kənˈfaɪd/ vt confiar (*segredos, etc.*): ~ **in sb** fazer confidências a alguém

confidence /ˈkɑnfɪdəns/ s **1** confiança: ~ **trick** conto-do-vigário **2** confidência: **take sb into your** ~ confidenciar a alguém **confident** adj **1** seguro (de si) **2** be ~ **of sth/that...** confiar em algo/ter confiança em que... **confidential** /ˌkɑnfɪˈdenʃl/ adj **1** confidencial **2** (*tom, etc.*) de confiança **confidently** adv com confiança

confine /kənˈfaɪn/ vt **1** confinar, encarcerar: *confined to bed* acamado **2** limitar **confined** adj restrito (*espaço*) **confinement** s detenção

confines /ˈkɑnfaɪnz/ s (*fml*) confins

confirm /kənˈfɜːrm/ vt confirmar **confirmed** adj inveterado **confirmation** /ˌkɑnfərˈmeɪʃn/ s confirmação

confiscate /ˈkɑnfɪskeɪt/ vt confiscar

conflict /ˈkɑnflɪkt/ s conflito ♦ /kənˈflɪkt/ vi ~ **(with sth)** divergir (de algo) **conflicting** adj divergente: ~ **evidence** provas discrepantes

conform /kənˈfɔːrm/ vi **1** adaptar-se **2** seguir as regras **conformist** s conformista **conformity** s (*fml*) conformidade: in ~ **with sth** de acordo com algo

confront /kənˈfrʌnt/ vt confrontar **confrontation** s confronto

confuse /kənˈfjuːz/ vt **1** confundir **2** desorientar **3** complicar **confused** adj **1** confuso **2** desorientado **confusing** adj confuso **confusion** s confusão

congeal /kənˈdʒiːl/ vi coagular-se, solidificar-se

congenial /kənˈdʒiːniəl/ adj

1 agradável **2** ~ **(to sb)** atraente (para alguém) **3** ~ **(to sth)** propício (a algo)

congenital /kənˈdʒenɪtl/ adj congênito

congested /kənˈdʒestɪd/ adj ~ **(with sth)** congestionado (de algo) **congestion** s congestionamento, congestão

conglomerate /kənˈglɑmərət/ s conglomerado (*empresas*)

congratulate /kənˈgrætʃuleɪt/ vt parabenizar **congratulation** s **1** felicitação **2** (**congratulations**) parabéns

congregate /ˈkɑŋgrɪgeɪt/ vi reunir-se **congregation** s congregação

congress /ˈkɑŋgrəs; *GB* -gres/ s congresso **congressional** /kənˈgreʃənl/ adj de congresso

Congressman /ˈkɑŋgrəsmən (*GB*)-gres-/ s (*fem* **Congresswoman**) (*pl* **-men, -women**) deputado/a federal

conical /ˈkɑnɪkl/ adj cônico

conifer /ˈkɑnɪfər/ s conífera

conjecture /kənˈdʒektʃər/ s conjetura

conjunction /kənˈdʒʌŋkʃn/ s (*Gram*) conjunção ▶ **in conjunction with** junto com

conjure /ˈkʌndʒər/ vi fazer truques mágicos ■ **conjure sth up 1** evocar algo **2** fazer algo aparecer através de mágica **3** (*espírito*) invocar **conjurer** s mágico/a

connect /kəˈnekt/ **1** vt, vi conectar(-se) **2** vt (*aposentos*) comunicar **3** vt: *connected by marriage* aparentados por casamento **4** vt relacionar **5** vt (*telefone*) ligar **connection** s **1** ligação **2** relação **3** (*transporte*) conexão ▶ **have connections** ter contatos **in connection with** com relação a

connoisseur /ˌkɑnəˈsɜːr/ s conhecedor/a

conquer /ˈkɑŋkər/ vt **1** conquistar **2** derrotar **conqueror** s **1** conquistador/a **2** vencedor/a

conquest /ˈkɑŋkwest/ s conquista

conscience /ˈkɑnʃəns/ s (*moral*) consciência: *have sth on your* ~ estar com a consciência pesada sobre algo

conscientious /ˌkɑnʃiˈenʃəs/ adj consciencioso: ~ **objector** pessoa que tem objeções de consciência

conscious /ˈkɑnʃəs/ adj **1** consciente **2** intencional **consciously** adv deliberadamente **consciousness** s **1** percepção **2** consciência

conscript /'kɒnskrɪpt/ s recruta **conscription** s serviço militar (obrigatório)

consecrate /'kɒnsɪkreɪt/ vt consagrar

consecutive /kən'sekjətɪv/ adj consecutivo

consent /kən'sent/ vi ~ **(to sth)** consentir (em algo) ● s consentimento

consequence /'kɒnsɪkwəns; (GB)-kwəns/ s **1** [ger pl] conseqüência **2** (fml) importância

consequent /'kɒnsɪkwənt; (fml)/ **1** resultante **2** ~ **on/upon sth** que resulta de algo **consequently** adv por conseguinte

conservation /ˌkɒnsər'veɪʃn/ s conservação, proteção: ~ area zona preservada

conservative /kən'sɜːrvətɪv/ adj, s (tb **Conservative**) conservador/a

conservatory /kən'sɜːrvətɔːri; GB -tri/ s (pl -ies) **1** jardim-de-inverno **2** (Mús) conservatório

conserve /kən'sɜːrv/ vt **1** conservar **2** economizar **3** proteger

consider /kən'sɪdər/ vt **1** considerar: ~ doing sth pensar em fazer algo **2** levar em consideração

considerable /kən'sɪdərəbl/ adj considerável **considerably** adv consideravelmente, muito

considerate /kən'sɪdərət/ adj ~ **(towards sb/sth)** atencioso (com alguém/algo)

consideration /kənˌsɪdə'reɪʃn/ s **1** consideração: It is under ~. Está sendo considerado. ◊ take sth into ~ levar algo em consideração **2** fator

considering /kən'sɪdərɪŋ/ conj considerando que

consign /kən'saɪn/ vt entregar: consigned to oblivion relegado ao esquecimento **consignment** s **1** consignação **2** remessa

consist /kən'sɪst/ v ■ **consist of sth** consistir em algo, compor-se de algo

consistency /kən'sɪstənsi/ s (pl -ies) **1** consistência **2** coerência

consistent /kən'sɪstənt/ adj **1** coerente **2** ~ **(with sth)** de acordo (com algo) **consistently** adv **1** regularmente **2** coerentemente

consolation /ˌkɒnsə'leɪʃn/ s consolação, consolo

console /kən'soʊl/ vt consolar **consolidate** /kən'sɒlɪdeɪt/ vt, vi consolidar(-se)

consonant /'kɒnsənənt/ s consoante

consortium /kən'sɔːrtiəm/ s (pl -tia /-tiə/) consórcio

conspicuous /kən'spɪkjuəs/ adj **1** visível: make yourself ~ fazer-se notar **2** be ~ for sth ter fama de algo **3** notável ▶ be conspicuous by your/its absence ser notado por sua ausência **conspicuously** adv notavelmente

conspiracy /kən'spɪrəsi/ s (pl -ies) **1** conspiração **2** trama conspiratorial /kənˌspɪrə'tɔːriəl/ adj conspirador

conspire /kən'spaɪər/ vi conspirar

constable /'kʌnstəbl; GB 'kʌn-/ s (GB) policial

constant /'kɒnstənt/ adj **1** constante, contínuo **2** (amigo, etc.) fiel ● s constante **constantly** adv constantemente

constipation /ˌkɒnstɪ'peɪʃn/ s prisão de ventre **constipated** adj com prisão de ventre

constituency /kən'stɪtjuənsi/ s (pl -ies) **1** eleitorado **2** (GB) distrito eleitoral

constituent /kən'stɪtjuənt/ s **1** (Pol) constituinte **2** componente

constitute /'kɒnstɪtuːt; GB -tjuːt/ vt constituir

constitution /ˌkɒnstɪ'tuːʃn; GB -'tjuːʃn/ s constituição **constitutional** adj constitucional

constraint /kən'streɪnt/ s **1** coação **2** restrição

constrict /kən'strɪkt/ vt **1** apertar **2** comprimir

construct /kən'strʌkt/ vt construir **construction** s construção: under ~ em construção

construe /kən'struː/ vt interpretar (o significado de)

consul /'kɒnsl/ s cônsul

consulate /'kɒnsələt; GB -sjəl-/ s consulado

consult /kən'sʌlt/ vt, vi consultar: consulting room consultório **consultant** s **1** consultor/a **2** (Med) especialista **consultancy** s consultoria **consultation** s consulta

consume /kən'suːm; GB -'sjuːm/ vt consumir: consumed with envy tomado de inveja **consumer** s consumidor/a

consummate /kən'sʌmət/ adj (fml) **1** consumado **2** (habilidade, etc.) extraordinário ● /'kɒnsəmeɪt/ vt (fml) **1** completar **2** (matrimônio) consumar

consumption /kən'sʌmpʃn/ s

1 consumo **2** (*antiq*) tuberculose

contact /'kɒntækt/ s contato ● vt contatar

contagious /kən'teɪdʒəs/ adj contagioso

contain /kən'teɪn/ vt conter: ~ *yourself* controlar-se container s **1** recipiente **2** ~ *ship* navio container

contaminate /kən'tæmɪneɪt/ vt contaminar

contemplate /'kɒntəmpleɪt/ **1** vt, vi contemplar, meditar **2** vt considerar: ~ *doing sth* pensar em fazer algo

contemporary /kən'temprəri; GB -prəri/ adj contemporâneo ● s (*pl* -ies) contemporâneo/a

contempt /kən'tempt/ s **1** desprezo: *beneath* ~ desprezível ao extremo **2** (*tb* ~ *of court*) desacato (ao tribunal) contemptible adj desprezível contemptuous adj desdenhoso

contend /kən'tend/ **1** vi ~ (**with** sth) lutar (contra algo): *problems to* ~ *with* problemas a enfrentar **2** vi competir **3** vt afirmar contender s adversário/a

content¹ /'kɒntent/ (*tb* contents [*pl*]) s conteúdo: *table of* ~s índice

content² /kən'tent/ adj contente, satisfeito ● vt ~ *yourself with sth* contentar-se com algo contented adj satisfeito contentment s contentamento

contention /kən'tenʃn/ s **1** disputa: *in* ~ *for...* na luta por... **2** discórdia

contentious /kən'tenʃəs/ adj **1** controvertido **2** altercador

contest /kən'test/ vt **1** contestar **2** impugnar **3** (*prêmio, etc.*) disputar ● /'kɒntest/ s **1** competição **2** concorrência, luta contestant /kən'testənt/ s concorrente

context /'kɒntekst/ s contexto

continent /'kɒntɪnənt/ s **1** (*Geog*) continente **2** (**the Continent**) (GB) o continente europeu continental /,kɒntɪ'nentl/ adj continental

contingency /kən'tɪndʒənsi/ s (*pl* -ies) **1** eventualidade **2** contingência: ~ *plan* plano de emergência

contingent /kən'tɪndʒənt/ s **1** contingente: *the German* ~ *at the conference* os representantes alemães à conferência

continual /kən'tɪnjuəl/ adj contínuo continually adv continuamente NOTA Continual cos-

tuma descrever ações que se repetem sucessivamente e que, em geral, têm um aspecto negativo: *His continual phone calls started to annoy her.* **Continuous** é usado para descrever ações ininterruptas: *There has been a continuous improvement in his work.* ◇ *It has been raining continuously for three days.*

continuation /kən,tɪnju'eɪʃn/ s continuação

continue /kən'tɪnju:/ vt, vi continuar continued adj contínuo continuing adj continuando

continuity /,kɒntɪ'nu:əti; GB -'nju:-/ s continuidade

continuous /kən'tɪnjuəs/ adj constante, contínuo continuously adv continuamente, sem parar → CONTINUAL

contort /kən'tɔːt/ vt, vi contorcer(-se)

contour /'kɒntʊər/ s contorno

contraband /'kɒntrəbænd/ s contrabando

contraception /,kɒntrə'sepʃn/ s contracepção contraceptive adj, s anticoncepcional

contract /'kɒntrækt/ s contrato: *under* ~ contratado ● /kən'trækt/ **1** vt contratar **2** vt contrair **3** vi contrair-se, encolher-se **4** vi ~ **with** sb fazer um contrato com alguém contractor s contratante, empreiteiro/a

contraction /kən'trækʃən/ s contração

contradict /,kɒntrə'dɪkt/ vt contradizer contradiction s contradição contradictory adj contraditório

contrary /'kɒntrəri; GB -trəri/ adj contrário ● adv ~ **to** sth contrariamente, contrário a algo ● **the contrary** s o contrário ▶ **on the contrary** pelo contrário

contrast /kən'træst; GB -'trɑːst/ vt, vi contrastar ● /'kɒntræst; GB -trɑːst/ s contraste

contribute /kən'trɪbjuːt/ **1** vt, vi contribuir **2** vt, vi ~ (**sth**) **to** (*artigo*) escrever (algo) para algo **3** vi ~ **to** (*debate*) participar de algo contributor s **1** contribuinte **2** (*publicação*) colaborador/a contributory adj **1** que contribui **2** contributivo

contribution /,kɒntrɪ'bjuːʃn/ s **1** contribuição, participação **2** (*publicação*) artigo

control /kən'trəʊl/ s **1** controle, comando **2** (**controls**) comandos ▶ **be out of control 1** estar fora de controle: *Her car went out of* ~. O carro dela perdeu a direção.

2 rebelar-se • vt **1** controlar, mandar em **2** dirigir **3** ~ **yourself** controlar-se **4** (lei) supervisionar **5** (gastos, etc.) conter

controversial /ˌkɒntrəˈvɜːʃl/ adj controvertido, polêmico

controversy /ˈkɒntrəvɜːrsi/ s (pl -ies) ~ (about/over sth) controvérsia (a respeito de algo)

convene /kənˈviːn/ vt convocar

convenience /kənˈviːniəns/ s **1** comodidade: public ~ banheiro público **2** conveniência

convenient /kənˈviːniənt/ adj **1** if it's ~ (for you) se lhe convier **2** (momento) apropriado **3** prático **4** à mão **5** ~ for sth bem situado em relação a algo **conveniently** adv convenientemente

convent /ˈkɒnvənt; GB -vənt/ s convento

convention /kənˈvenʃn/ s **1** congresso **2** convenção **conventional** adj convencional: ~ wisdom sabedoria popular

converge /kənˈvɜːrdʒ/ vi **1** convergir **2** ~ (on sth) encontrar-se (em algo) **convergence** s convergência

conversant /kənˈvɜːrsnt/ adj (fml) ~ with sth versado em algo: become ~ with sth familiarizar-se com algo

conversation /ˌkɒnvərˈseɪʃn/ s conversação: make ~ puxar conversa/conversar

converse¹ /kənˈvɜːrs/ vi (fml) conversar

converse² /ˈkɒnvɜːrs/ the converse s o contrário **conversely** adv inversamente

conversion /kənˈvɜːrʒn; GB kənˈvɜːʃn/ s conversão

convert /kənˈvɜːrt/ vt, vi converter(-se): The sofa converts (in)to a bed. O sofá vira cama. • /ˈkɒnvɜːt/ s convertido/a

convertible /kənˈvɜːrtəbl/ adj conversível • s conversível (carro)

convey /kənˈveɪ/ vt **1** (fml) levar, transportar **2** comunicar, expressar **3** (saudações) enviar **4** (propriedade) transferir **conveyor** (tb ~ belt) s correia transportadora

convict /kənˈvɪkt/ vt ~ sb (of sth) condenar alguém (por algo) • /ˈkɒnvɪkt/ s presidiário/a **conviction** s **1** condenação **2** convicção: lack ~ não ser convincente

convince /kənˈvɪns/ vt convencer **convinced** adj convicto **convincing** adj convincente

convulse /kənˈvʌls/ vt convul-

sionar: convulsed with laughter morto de rir **convulsion** s [ger pl] convulsão

cook /kʊk/ **1** vi cozinhar **2** vt preparar: The fish isn't cooked. O peixe não está cozido. ▸ **cook the books** (coloq) burlar a contabilidade ■ **cook sth up** (coloq): ~ up an excuse inventar uma desculpa • s cozinheiro/a

cookbook /ˈkʊkbʊk/ s livro de receitas

cooker /ˈkʊkər/ s (GB) fogão

cookery /ˈkʊkəri/ s (GB) culinária: Oriental ~ cozinha oriental

cookie /ˈkʊki/ s biscoito (doce)

cooking /ˈkʊkɪŋ/ s cozinha: do the ~ fazer a comida

cool /kuːl/ adj (~er, ~est) **1** fresco → FRIO **2** (coloq) calmo: keep ~ ficar calmo **3** ~ (about/with towards sb) indiferente (a algo/alguém) **4** (acolhida) frio **5** (coloq) legal: ~ guy cara legal • vt, vi **1** ~ (sth) (down/off) esfriar algo, esfriar-se **2** ~ (sb) down/off acalmar(-se) (alguém) ▸ the cool s frescor ▸ keep/lose your cool (coloq) manter/perder a calma

cooperate /koʊˈɑːpəreɪt/ vi ~ (with sb) (in doing/to do sth); ~ (on sth) cooperar (com alguém) (para fazer algo); (em algo) **cooperation** s cooperação

cooperative /koʊˈɑːpərətɪv/ adj **1** cooperativo **2** disposto a colaborar • s cooperativa

coordinate /koʊˈɔːrdɪneɪt/ vt coordenar

cop /kɒp/ s (coloq) tira

cope /koʊp/ vi ~ (with sth) dar conta (de algo); enfrentar algo: I can't ~. Não posso mais.

copious /ˈkoʊpiəs/ adj (fml) copioso

copper /ˈkɑːpər/ s **1** cobre **2** (coloq, GB) tira (policial)

copy /ˈkɑːpi/ s (pl -ies) **1** cópia **2** exemplar **3** (revista, etc.) número **4** texto, originais • vt (pt, pp -ied) **1** copiar **2** fotocopiar **3** imitar

copyright /ˈkɑːpiraɪt/ s direitos autorais • adj registrado, protegido por direitos autorais

coral /ˈkɔːrəl; GB ˈkɒrəl/ s coral • adj de coral

cord /kɔːrd/ s **1** corda **2** fio elétrico **3** veludo cotelê **4** (cords) calças de veludo cotelê

cordon /ˈkɔːrdn/ s cordão ■ **cordon sth off** isolar algo

corduroy /ˈkɔːrdərɔɪ/ s veludo cotelê

core /kɔːr/ s 1 (*fruta*) caroço 2 núcleo ▶ **to the core** até a medula

cork /kɔːrk/ s cortiça, rolha

corkscrew /ˈkɔːrkskruː/ s saca-rolhas

corn /kɔːrn/ s 1 (*USA*) milho 2 (*GB*) cereal 3 calo

corncob /ˈkɔːrnkɑb/ s espiga de milho

corner /ˈkɔːrnər/ s 1 (*dentro*) canto 2 (*fora*) esquina 3 (*tb ~ kick*) escanteio ▶ (**just) around the corner** a um pulo daqui ● 1 vt encurralar 2 vi fazer uma curva 3 vt (*mercado*) monopolizar

cornerstone /ˈkɔːrnərstoʊn/ s pedra angular

cornstarch /ˈkɔːrnstɑrtʃ/ s farinha de milho

corollary /ˈkɔːrəleri; GB kəˈrɒləri/ s (*fml*) corolário

coronation /ˌkɔːrəˈneɪʃn; GB ˌkɒr-/ s coroação

coroner /ˈkɔːrənər/ s magistrado/a (*que investiga mortes suspeitas*)

corporal /ˈkɔːrpərəl/ s (*Mil*) cabo ● adj: ~ **punishment** castigo corporal

corporate /ˈkɔːrpərət/ adj 1 coletivo 2 corporativo

corporation /ˌkɔːrpəˈreɪʃn/ s 1 municipalidade, junta 2 corporação

corps /kɔːr/ s (pl corps /kɔːz/) (*Mil*) corpo

corpse /kɔːrps/ s cadáver

correct /kəˈrekt/ adj correto ● vt corrigir

correlation /ˌkɔːrəˈleɪʃn; GB ˌkɒr-/ s correlação

correspond /ˌkɔːrəˈspɒnd; GB ˌkɒr-/ vi 1 coincidir 2 equivaler 3 corresponder-se correspondence s correspondência corresponding adj correspondente

corridor /ˈkɔːrɪdɔːr; GB ˈkɒr-/ s corredor

corrosion /kəˈroʊʒn/ s corrosão

corrugated /ˈkɔːrəɡeɪtɪd/ adj corrugado, ondulado

corrupt /kəˈrʌpt/ adj 1 corrupto 2 depravado ● vt corromper, depravar corruption s corrupção

cosmetic /kɒzˈmetɪk/ adj cosmético: ~ **surgery** operação plástica cosmetics s cosméticos

cosmopolitan /ˌkɒzməˈpɒlɪtən/ adj, s cosmopolita

cost /kɔːst; GB kɒst/ vt 1 (pt, pp cost) custar, valer 2 (pt, pp costed) (*Com*) estimar, orçar ▶ **cost a bomb** (*GB*) custar um dinheirão ● vt **whatever the ~** custe o que custar ◇ **cost-effective** rentável 2 (**costs**) custas, gastos ▶ **at all costs** a qualquer custo **costly** adj (-ier, -iest) caro

costume /ˈkɑstuːm; GB -tjuːm/ s 1 traje 2 (**costumes**) [pl] (*Teat*) vestuário

cosy (*GB*) = COZY

cot /kɑt/ s 1 (*USA*) cama de campanha 2 (*GB*) berço

cottage /ˈkɑtɪdʒ/ s chalé, casa (*de campo*)

cotton /ˈkɑtn/ s 1 algodão: ~ **wool** algodão (*de farmácia*) 2 fio (*de algodão*)

couch /kaʊtʃ/ s sofá ● vt (*fml*) expressar

cough /kɔːf; GB kɒf/ vt, vi ~ (**sth up**) tossir (*algo para fora*) ■ **cough (sth) up** (*GB, coloq*) soltar (*algo*) ● s tosse

could /kəd, kʊd/ pret de CAN[1]

council /ˈkaʊnsl/ s 1 câmara municipal, distrito: ~ *flat/house* (*GB*) apartamento/casa em conjunto habitacional 2 conselho councilor (*GB* -ll-) s conselheiro/a, vereador/a

counsel /ˈkaʊnsl/ s 1 (*fml*) conselho 2 (pl counsel) advogado/a → ADVOGADO ● vt (-l-, GB -ll-) (*fml*) aconselhar counseling (*GB* -ll-) s aconselhamento, orientação counselor (*GB* -ll-) s 1 assessor/a, conselheiro/a 2 (*USA ou Irl*) advogado/a

count /kaʊnt/ s conde ● 1 vt, vi ~ (**sth) (up)**; ~ (**as sth**) contar (*algo*); (*como algo*) 2 vi ~ (**for sth**) importar, valer (*para algo*): ~ **towards sth** contribuir para algo 3 vt: ~ *yourself lucky* considerar-se com sorte ▶ **count the cost (of sth)** sofrer as consequências (*de algo*) ■ **count down** fazer contagem regressiva **count sb/sth in/out** incluir/excluir alguém/algo **count on sb/sth** contar com alguém/algo

countdown /ˈkaʊntdaʊn/ s contagem regressiva

countenance /ˈkaʊntənəns/ vt (*fml*) aprovar

counter /ˈkaʊntər/ 1 vi replicar, contestar 2 vt responder a ● s 1 (*jogo*) ficha 2 contador 3 balcão (*bar, loja*) 4 (*cozinha*) superfície de trabalho ● adv ~ **to sth** ao contrário de algo

counteract /ˌkaʊntərˈækt/ vt (re)agir contra, contrapor-se a

counter-attack s contra-ataque

counterfeit /ˈkaʊntərfɪt/ adj falsificado

counterpart /'kaʊntərpɑːrt/
s **1** contrapartida **2** equivalente

counterproductive /ˌkaʊntərprə-
'dʌktɪv/ adj contraproducente

countess /'kaʊntəs/ s condessa

countless /'kaʊntləs/ adj
inumerável

country /'kʌntri/ s (pl -ies)
1 país **2** [sing] pátria **3** (tb
the ~) o campo, o interior **4**
zona, terra

countryman /'kʌntrimən/ s
(fem **countrywoman**) (pl -men,
-women) **1** compatriota
2 homem/mulher do campo

countryside /'kʌntrisaɪd/ s [U]
1 campo, interior **2** paisagem

county /'kaʊnti/ s (pl -ies) con-
dado

coup /kuː/ s (pl ~s /kuːz/) **1** (tb
~ d'état /kuː deɪ'tɑ/ pl ~s
d'état) golpe (de Estado) **2** golpe

couple /'kʌpl/ s **1** casal (relacionamento amoroso) **2** a ~ (of)
um par de; uns/umas, alguns/
algumas • vt **1** associar a: cou-
pled with sth junto com algo
2 acoplar

coupon /'kuːpɑn/ s cupom, vale

courage /'kʌrɪdʒ/ s coragem
courageous /kə'reɪdʒəs/ adj
corajoso

courgette /kʊər'ʒet/ s
abobrinha

courier /'kʊriər/ s **1** guia turístico (pessoa) **2** mensageiro

course /kɔːrs/ s **1** curso, trans-
curso **2** (avião, rio) rumo: on/off
~ dentro/fora do curso **3** ~ (in/
on sth) (Educ) curso (de algo) **4**
(Med) tratamento **5** (golfe)
campo **6** (corrida) pista **7**
(comida) prato ▸ **course of
action** linha de ação   **in the
course of sth** no decorrer de
algo   **of course** é claro

court /kɔːrt/ s **1** ~ (of law) tribunal: a ~ case um processo
(jurídico) ◇ ~ order ordem judicial ◇ go to ~ (over sth) entrar na
justiça (por algo) ◇ take sb to ~
processar alguém **2** (Esporte)
quadra **3** (Court) corte (de um
monarca) • vt **1** cortejar **2** (perigo, etc.) expor-se a

courteous /'kɜːrtiəs/ adj cortês

courtesy /'kɜːrtəsi/ s (pl -ies)
cortesia: (by) ~ of sb (por)
cortesia/gentileza de alguém

court martial s (pl ~s martial)
corte marcial

courtship /'kɔːrtʃɪp/ s noivado

courtyard /'kɔːrtjɑːrd/ s pátio

cousin /'kʌzn/ (tb first ~) s primo
(irmão), prima (irmã)

cove /koʊv/ s enseada

covenant /'kʌvənənt/ s
convênio, pacto

cover /'kʌvər/ vt **1** ~ sb/sth in/
with sth; ~ sth (up/over) (with
sth) cobrir alguém/algo (de/
com algo) **2** vt (timidez, etc.)
dissimular **3** vt incluir **4** vt tratar
de, encarregar-se de **5** vi ~ for sb
substituir alguém ■ **cover (sth)
up** encobrir (algo) **cover up for
sb** dar cobertura a alguém • s
1 abrigo: take ~ (from sth)
resguardar-se (de algo) **2** coberta
3 (livro, etc.) capa: from ~ to ~ da
primeira à última página **4** (the
covers) as cobertas (de cama)
5 ~ (for sth) disfarce (para algo)
6 identidade falsa **7** (Mil) proteção **8** ~ (for sb) substituição
(para/de alguém) **9** ~ (against
sth) seguro (contra algo)
▸ **under cover of sth** sob a proteção de algo: under ~ of darkness protegido pela escuridão
coverage s cobertura (fatos,
notícias, etc.) **covering** s **1**
cobertura, revestimento **2** capa

covert /'koʊvɜːrt; GB 'kʌvət/ adj
1 secreto **2** (olhar) furtivo

cover-up s acobertamento

covet /'kʌvət/ vt cobiçar

cow /kaʊ/ s vaca ↗ CARNE

coward /'kaʊərd/ s covarde **cowardice** s [U] covardia **cowardly**
adj covarde

cowboy /'kaʊbɔɪ/ s **1** vaqueiro
2 (GB, coloq) trambiqueiro
(comerciante, etc.)

co-worker s colega de trabalho

coy /kɔɪ/ adj (~er, ~est) **1**
(que pretende ser) recatado
2 reservado

cozy /'koʊzi/ adj (-ier, -iest)
1 acolhedor **2** confortável

crab /kræb/ s caranguejo

crack /kræk/ s **1** rachadura
2 defeito **3** fenda e estalo,
estampido ▸ **the crack of dawn**
(coloq) o raiar do dia • **1** vt, vi
rachar **2** vt ~ sth (open) quebrar
algo (para abrir) **3** vi ~ (open)
romper(-se) **4** vt ~ sth (on/
against sth) bater algo (contra
algo) **5** vt, vi estalar **6** vi
desmoronar **7** vt resolver, decifrar **8** vi (voz) mudar **9** vt
(piada) contar ▸ **get cracking**
(GB, coloq) pôr mãos à obra
■ **crack down (on sb/sth)** tomar
medidas enérgicas (contra
alguém/algo) **crack up** (coloq)
ter um colapso (físico, mental)

crackdown /'krækdaʊn/ s ~ (on
sth) medidas enérgicas (contra
algo)

287

c

creep

cracker /'krækər/ s **1** bolacha de água e sal **2** bombinha de São João **3** (*tb* Christmas ~) (*GB*) embrulho em forma de tubo que estala ao se romper

crackle /'krækl/ *vi* crepitar, estalar ● s (*tb* crackling) crepitação, estalido

cradle /'kreɪdl/ s berço (*com balanço*) ● *vt* ninar

craft /krɑːft; *GB* kræft/ s **1** artesanato **2** técnica **3** ofício **4** nave ● *vt* produzir artesanalmente, elaborar

craftsman /'krɑːftsmən; *GB* 'krɑːfts-/ s (*pl* -men) **1** artesão/ã **2** artista **craftsmanship** s **1** artesanato **2** arte

crafty /'krɑːfti; *GB* 'krɑːfti/ *adj* (-ier, -iest) astuto

crag /kræg/ s penhasco **craggy** *adj* escarpado

cram /kræm/ **1** *vt* ~ A into B enfiar A em B (*com força*) **2** *vi* ~ into sth meter-se com dificuldade em, abarrotar algo **3** *vi* (*coloq*) rachar de estudar (antes de provas)

cramp /kræmp/ s [U] **1** (*muscular*) cãibra **2** ((*stomach*) cramps) cólicas estomacais **3** grampo ● *vt* (*movimento, etc.*) impedir, atrapalhar **cramped** *adj* **1** espremido **2** apertado

crane /kreɪn/ s **1** (*ave*) grou **2** (*Mec*) guindaste

crank /kræŋk/ s **1** (*Mec*) manivela **2** (*coloq*) excêntrico/a **cranky** /'kræŋki/ *adj* **1** excêntrico **2** ranzinza

crash /kræʃ/ s **1** estrondo **2** acidente, batida (*veículo*): ~ helmet capacete (de proteção) **3** (*Com*) quebra **4** (*bolsa de valores*) queda ● **1** *vi* (*carro*) sofrer um acidente **2** *vt*, *vi* ~ (sth) (into sth) bater (algo) (em/contra algo): ~ your car bater o carro ● *adj* (*curso, dieta*) intensivo

crash landing s aterrissagem forçada

crass /kræs/ *adj* estúpido

crate /kreɪt/ s **1** caixote **2** engradado (*garrafas*)

crater /'kreɪtər/ s cratera

crave /kreɪv/ *vt*, *vi* ~ (for) sth estar com desejo de algo **craving** s ~ (for sth) ânsia, vontade (de algo)

crawl /krɔːl/ *vi* **1** ~ (along) engatinhar, arrastar-se **2** (*coloq*) ~ (to sb) bajular (alguém) ► **crawling with sth** coberto de algo ● s **1** passo de tartaruga **2** (*natação*) crawl

crayfish /'kreɪfɪʃ/ s (*pl* crayfish)

lagostim

crayon /'kreɪən/ s **1** creiom **2** (*Arte*) pastel

craze /kreɪz/ s moda, febre

crazy /'kreɪzi/ *adj* (-ier, -iest) (*coloq*) **1** louco **2** disparatado **3** ~ paving (*GB*) pavimento de pedras irregulares

creak /kriːk/ *vi* ranger, estalar

cream /kriːm/ s **1** nata, creme: ~ cheese queijo cremoso **2** pomada **3** (the cream (of the crop)) a nata (de algo) ● *adj*, s (*cor*) creme **creamy** ● *adj* (-ier, -iest) cremoso *vt* bater/amassar até tornar cremoso ■ **cream sth off** selecionar (as melhores pessoas ou coisas)

crease /kriːs/ s vinco, prega ● *vt*, *vi* amarrotar

create /kri'eɪt/ *vt* criar, produzir: ~ a fuss armar uma confusão **creation** s criação **creative** *adj* criativo

creator /kri'eɪtər/ s criador/a

creature /'kriːtʃər/ s criatura: living ~ ser vivo ◊ ~ of habit pessoa metódica ◊ ~ comforts necessidades básicas

crèche /kreʃ/ s (*GB*) creche

credentials /krə'denʃlz/ s **1** credenciais **2** qualificações

credibility /,kredə'bɪləti/ s credibilidade

credible /'kredəbl/ *adj* crível, verossímil

credit /'kredɪt/ s **1** crédito, empréstimo bancário: on ~ pelo crediário ◊ creditworthy solvente **2** be in ~ (*GB*) ter saldo (positivo) **3** (*contabilidade*) haver **4** mérito **5** (credits) (*filme, etc.*) créditos ► a credit to sb/sth uma honra para alguém/ algo **do sb credit** dar o devido crédito a alguém ● *vt* ~ sb/sth with sth atribuir o mérito de algo a alguém/algo **2** (*Fin*) creditar **3** acreditar em **creditable** *adj* louvável **creditor** s credor/a

credit card s cartão de crédito

creed /kriːd/ s credo

creek /kriːk; *GB* kriːk/ s **1** (*USA*) riacho **2** (*GB*) enseada ► be up the creek (without a paddle) (*coloq*) estar em dificuldades

creep /kriːp/ *vi* (*pt, pp* crept /krept/) **1** mover-se furtivamente, insinuar-se: ~ up on sb pegar alguém desprevenido **2** A feeling of drowsiness crept over him. Uma sensação de torpor o invadiu. **3** (*planta*) trepar ● s (*coloq*) bajulador ► give sb the creeps (*coloq*) dar calafrios em alguém **creepy** *adj* (-ier,

-iest (*coloq*) repugnante

cremation /krəˈmeɪʃn/ *s* cremação

crematorium /ˌkriːməˈtɔːriəm/ *s* crematório

crêpe /kreɪp/ *s* crepe, panqueca

crescendo /krəˈʃendəʊ/ (*pl* **~s**) **1** (*Mús*) crescendo **2** ponto máximo

crescent /ˈkresnt/ *s* **1** crescente, meia-lua **2** rua em forma de semicírculo

cress /kres/ *s* agrião

crest /krest/ *s* **1** crista **2** (*colina*) topo **3** (*Heráldica*) timbre

crestfallen /ˈkrestfɔːlən/ *adj* cabisbaixo

crevice /ˈkrevɪs/ *s* fenda (*em rocha*)

crew /kruː/ *s* **1** tripulação **2** equipe

crew cut *s* corte de cabelo à escovinha

crib /krɪb/ *s* **1** manjedoura **2** berço **3** plágio, cola ● *vt, vi* plagiar, colar

cricket /ˈkrɪkɪt/ *s* **1** (*Zool*) grilo **2** (*Esporte*) críquete **cricketer** *s* jogador/a (*de críquete*)

crime /kraɪm/ *s* **1** delito, crime **2** delinquência

criminal /ˈkrɪmɪnl/ *adj* criminoso: ~ *damage* dano culposo ◇ ~ *record* antecedentes criminais **2** (*direito*) penal **3** imoral ● *s* delinquente, criminoso/a

crimson /ˈkrɪmzn/ *adj* carmim

cringe /krɪndʒ/ *vi* **1** encolher-se (*de medo*) **2** morrer de vergonha

cripple /ˈkrɪpl/ *s* aleijado/a ● *vt* **1** aleijar **2** prejudicar seriamente **crippling** *adj* **1** que deixa inválido **2** (*dívida*) descomunal

crisis /ˈkraɪsɪs/ *s* (*pl* **crises** /-siːz/) crise

crisp /krɪsp/ *adj* (**~er, ~est**) **1** crocante **2** (*frutas, etc.*) fresco **3** ~ *new bank notes* notas novinhas em folha ◇ ~ *white shirt* camisa branca impecável **4** (*tempo*) seco e frio **5** (*modos*) incisivo ● *s* (*tb* **potato** ~) (*GB*) batata frita (*de saco*) **crisply** *adv* incisivamente **crispy** *adj* (**-ier, -iest**) crocante

criterion /kraɪˈtɪəriən/ *s* (*pl* **-ria** /-rɪə/) critério

critic /ˈkrɪtɪk/ *s* **1** crítico/a **2** detrator/a **critical** *adj* **1** crítico: ~ *acclaim* reconhecimento da crítica **2** crucial **critically** *adv* **1** de maneira crítica **2** ~ *ill* gravemente enfermo

criticism /ˈkrɪtɪsɪzəm/ *s* [*ger* U] crítica

criticize /ˈkrɪtɪsaɪz/ *vt* criticar

critique /krɪˈtiːk/ *s* análise crítica

croak /krəʊk/ *vi* **1** coaxar **2** rouquejar ● *s* (*tb* **croaking**) coaxo

crochet /ˈkrəʊʃeɪ; *GB* ˈkrəʊʃeɪ/ *s* crochê

crockery /ˈkrɒkəri/ *s* [U] louça

crocodile /ˈkrɒkədaɪl/ *s* crocodilo

crocus /ˈkrəʊkəs/ *s* açafrão

crony /ˈkrəʊni/ *s* (*pl* **-ies**) comparsa

crook /krʊk/ *s* (*coloq*) trapaceiro/a **crooked** /ˈkrʊkɪd/ *adj* (**~er, ~est**) **1** torto **2** tortuoso **3** (*coloq*) desonesto

crop /krɒp/ *s* **1** colheita, produção **2** cultivo **3** safra ● *vt* (**-pp-**) **1** tosar **2** pastar ■ **crop up** aparecer (*inesperadamente*)

croquet /ˈkrəʊkeɪ; *GB* ˈkrəʊkeɪ/ *s* croqué

cross /krɔːs; *GB* krɒs/ *s* **1** cruz **2** cruzamento, misto ● *vt, vi* cruzar(-se), atravessar: *Shall we ~ over?* Passamos para o outro lado? **2** *vt* ~ *yourself* persignar-se **3** *vt* contrariar **4** *vt* (*Zool, Bot*) cruzar ► **cross your fingers (for me)** torça (por mim) **cross your mind** passar pela cabeça, ocorrer a alguém ■ **cross sb/sth off/out/through** riscar/tirar/cancelar alguém/algo ● *adj* (**~er, ~est**) **1** zangado: *get* ~ zangar-se **2** (*vento*) contrário

crossbar /ˈkrɔːsbɑːr; *GB* ˈkrɒs-/ *s* **1** barra (*de bicicleta*) **2** (*Esporte*) trave (*do gol*)

crossbow /ˈkrɔːsbəʊ; *GB* ˈkrɒs-/ *s* (*arco*) besta

cross-country *adj, adv* através de campos e matas

cross-examine *vt* interrogar

cross-eyed *adj* estrábico

crossfire /ˈkrɔːsfaɪər; *GB* ˈkrɒs-/ *s* fogo cruzado: *get caught in the* ~ ficar entre dois fogos

crossing /ˈkrɔːsɪŋ; *GB* ˈkrɒs-/ *s* **1** travessia **2** (*GB*) (*estrada*) cruzamento **3** passagem de nível **4** faixa para pedestres **5** *border* ~ fronteira

cross-legged *adj, adv* de/com pernas cruzadas

crossly /ˈkrɔːsli; *GB* ˈkrɒs-/ *adv* com irritação

crossover /ˈkrɔːsəʊvər; *GB* ˈkrɒs-/ *s* **1** passagem **2** transição

cross purposes *s* ► **at cross purposes**: *We're (talking) at* ~. Há um mal-entendido entre nós.

cross-reference s (texto) remissão

crossroads /'krɔ:sroʊdz; GB 'krɒs-/ s cruzamento, encruzilhada

cross-section s 1 secção (transversal) 2 amostra representativa

crosswalk /'krɔ:swɔ:k; GB 'krɒs-/ s faixa para pedestres

crossword /'krɔ:swɜ:rd; GB 'krɒs-/ (tb ~ puzzle) s palavras cruzadas

crotch /krɑtʃ/ s virilha

crouch /kraʊtʃ/ vi agachar-se, curvar-se

crow /kroʊ/ s 1 corvo ▸ **as the crow flies** em linha reta ● vi 1 cantar 2 ~ (over sth) gabar-se de algo

crowbar /'kroʊbɑr/ s pé-de-cabra

crowd /kraʊd/ s 1 multidão 2 público 3 (the crowd) a(s) massa(s) 4 (coloq) gente, turma (de amigos) ● vt ~ (espaço) abarrotar ■ **crowd around (sb/sth)** amontoar-se (ao redor de alguém/algo) **crowd (sb/sth) in** amontoar alguém/algo, apinhar-se **crowded** adj 1 lotado, abarrotado 2 repleto

crown /kraʊn/ s 1 coroa: ~ prince príncipe herdeiro 2 (cabeça, colina) topo 3 (chapéu) copa ● vt coroar

crucial /'kru:ʃl/ adj crucial

crucifix /'kru:səfɪks/ s crucifixo

crucify /'kru:sɪfaɪ/ vt (pt, pp -ied) crucificar

crude /kru:d/ adj (-er, -est) 1 bruto 2 grosseiro

crude oil s óleo cru

cruel /kru:əl/ adj (-ller, -llest) ~ (to sb/sth) cruel (com alguém/algo) **cruelty** s (pl -ies) crueldade

cruise /kru:z/ vi 1 fazer um cruzeiro 2 (avião, carro) ir (em velocidade constante) ● s cruzeiro **cruiser** s 1 cruzador 2 (tb cabin cruiser) lancha a motor com cabine

crumb /krʌm/ s migalha

crumble /'krʌmbl/ 1 vt, vi ~ (away) desfazer(-se), desmoronar(-se) 2 vt, vi (Cozinha) desmanchar(-se) **crumbly** adj (-ier, -iest) que se desfaz, farelento

crumple /'krʌmpl/ vt, vi ~ (sth) (up) amassar, enrugar algo

crunch /krʌntʃ/ 1 vt morder (ruidosamente) 2 vt, vi esmigalhar ● s mastigação ruidosa, ruído áspero **crunchy** adj (-ier, -iest) crocante

crusade /kru:'seɪd/ s cruzada **crusader** s 1 (Hist) cruzado 2 combatente

crush /krʌʃ/ vt 1 esmagar: be crushed to death morrer esmagado 2 ~ sth (up) (rocha, etc.) triturar algo: crushed ice gelo picado 3 (alho, tecido) amassar 4 (fruta) espremer 5 moer 6 (ânimo) abater 7 ~ sb 1 aglomeração 2 ~ (on sb) (coloq) breve paixão (por alguém): have a ~ on sb ter uma queda por alguém 3 suco **crushing** adj arrasador

crust /krʌst/ s casca (pão) **crusty** adj (-ier, -iest) (de casca) crocante

crutch /krʌtʃ/ s 1 muleta 2 apoio

crux /krʌks/ s xis (da questão)

cry /kraɪ/ (pt, pp **cried**) 1 vi ~ (over sb/sth) chorar (por alguém/algo) 2 vt, vi ~ (out) gritar ▸ **cry your eyes/heart out** chorar amargamente **it's no use crying over spilt milk** não adianta chorar pelo leite derramado ■ **cry off** dar para trás **cry out for sth** exigir/implorar por algo ● s (pl cries) 1 grito 2 choro: have a (good) ~ desabafar-se chorando **crying** adj ▸ **a crying shame** uma verdadeira lástima

crybaby /'kraɪbeɪbi/ s chorão

crypt /krɪpt/ s cripta

cryptic /'krɪptɪk/ adj críptico

crystal /'krɪstl/ s cristal ▸ **crystal clear 1** cristalino **2** claro como o dia

cub /kʌb/ s 1 (leão, etc.) filhote 2 lobinho 3 (the Cub Scouts) os lobinhos (escoteiros)

cube /kju:b/ s 1 cubo 2 cubinho **cubic** adj cúbico

cubicle /'kju:bɪkl/ s 1 cubículo 2 provador 3 (piscina) vestiário 4 vaso sanitário, privada

cuckoo /'kʊku:/ s (pl ~s) cuco

cucumber /'kju:kʌmbər/ s pepino

cuddle /'kʌdl/ vt, vi abraçar(-se), afagar: ~ up (to sb) aconchegar-se a alguém ● s abraço, afago **cuddly** adj (-ier, -iest) (coloq) mimoso, fofo: ~ toy brinquedo de pelúcia

cue /kju:/ s 1 sinal 2 (Teat) deixa: take your ~ from sb pegar a deixa de alguém 3 exemplo 4 (tb billiard/pool ~) taco ▸ **(right) on cue** no momento exato ● vt ~ sb (in) dar o sinal/a deixa a alguém

cuff /kʌf/ s 1 (*roupa*) punho 2 tapa ▶ **off the cuff** de improviso • *vt* dar um tapa em

cuff link s abotoadura

cuisine /kwɪˈziːn/ s culinária

cul-de-sac /ˈkʌl də sæk/ s (*pl ~s*) rua sem saída

cull /kʌl/ *vt* 1 (*informação*) colher (de várias fontes) 2 (*animais*) matar (*para controlar o número*)

culminate /ˈkʌlmɪneɪt/ *vi* (*fml*) culminar **culmination** s auge

culottes /kjuːˈlɒts/ s [*pl*] saia-calça

culprit /ˈkʌlprɪt/ s acusado/a

cult /kʌlt/ s 1 ~ (**of sb/sth**) culto (a alguém/algo) 2 moda

cultivate /ˈkʌltɪveɪt/ *vt* cultivar **cultivated** *adj* 1 culto 2 refinado **cultivation** s cultivo

culture /ˈkʌltʃər/ s 1 cultura: ~ *shock* choque cultural 2 (*Biol*) cultura **cultural** *adj* cultural **cultured** *adj* 1 culto 2 ~ *pearl* pérola cultivada

cum /kʌm/ *prep* (*GB*) kitchen-cum-dining room cozinha com sala de jantar

cumbersome /ˈkʌmbərsəm/ *adj* 1 incômodo 2 volumoso 3 emperrado

cumulative /ˈkjuːmjələtɪv/ *adj* 1 acumulado 2 cumulativo

cunning /ˈkʌnɪŋ/ *adj* 1 astuto 2 engenhoso 3 (*USA*) (*pessoa*) atraente • s [*U*] astúcia, manha **cunningly** *adv* astuciosamente

cup /kʌp/ s 1 xícara: *paper ~* copo de papel 2 taça: *World Cup* Copa do Mundo ▶ (**not**) **be sb's cup of tea** (*coloq*) (não) fazer o gênero de alguém • *vt* (*mãos*) juntar em concha: *a hand over sth* cobrir algo com a mão ◊ *~ your chin in your hands* apoiar o queixo nas mãos

cupboard /ˈkʌbərd/ s armário

cupful /ˈkʌpfʊl/ s (*quantidade*) xícara

curate /ˈkjʊərət/ s (*igreja anglicana*) cura

curative /ˈkjʊərətɪv/ *adj* medicinal

curator /ˈkjʊərətər; *GB* kjʊəˈreɪtə(r)/ s curador/a (*museu, etc.*)

curb /kɜːrb/ s 1 freio 2 meio-fio • *vt* refrear

curdle /ˈkɜːrdl/ *vt, vi* coalhar

cure /kjʊər/ *vt* 1 curar 2 sanar • s 1 cura, restabelecimento 2 remédio

curfew /ˈkɜːrfjuː/ s toque de recolher

curious /ˈkjʊəriəs/ *adj* curioso

curiosity /ˌkjʊəriˈɒsəti/ s (*pl -ies*) 1 curiosidade 2 coisa rara

curl /kɜːrl/ s 1 cacho 2 espiral • 1 *vt, vi* cachear(-se), enrolar(-se) 2 *vi*: *The smoke curled upwards.* A fumaça subiu em espiral. ■ **curl up** 1 cachear(-se) 2 (*sentar-se/deitar-se*) espiral(-se) 2 encolher **curly** *adj* (**-ier, -iest**) ondulado

currant /ˈkʌrənt/ s 1 uva passa 2 groselha

currency /ˈkʌrənsi/ s (*pl -ies*) 1 moeda (*sistema*) 2 uso corrente: *gain ~* generalizar-se/ entrar em uso

current /ˈkʌrənt/ s corrente • *adj* 1 atual: ~ *affairs* (assuntos de atualidades) 2 generalizado **currently** *adv* atualmente

curriculum /kəˈrɪkjələm/ s currículo (*escolar*)

curriculum vitae /kəˌrɪkjələm ˈviːtaɪ/ s curriculum vitae

curry /ˈkʌri/ s (*pl -ies*) (*prato ao*) caril • *vt* (*pret, pp -ied*) ▶ **curry favor (with sb)** bajular (alguém)

curse /kɜːrs/ s 1 ofensa 2 maldição 3 praga 4 (**the curse**) (*antiq*) as regras (*menstruação*) • *vt, vi* 1 xingar 2 amaldiçoar ▶ **be cursed with sth** estar tomado por algo

cursory /ˈkɜːrsəri/ *adj* apressado, superficial

curt /kɜːrt/ *adj* (*tom*) abrupto

curtail /kɜːrˈteɪl/ *vt* reduzir **curtailment** s 1 limitação 2 interrupção

curtain /ˈkɜːrtn/ s 1 cortina 2 (*Teat*) pano de boca 3 (**curtains**) (*coloq*) [*pl*] o fim

curtsy (*tb* **curtsey**) /ˈkɜːrtsi/ *vi* (*pt, pp -ied ou* **curtseyed**) (*somente mulheres*) fazer uma reverência • s (*pl -ies ou -eys*) reverência

curve /kɜːrv/ s curva • *vi* 1 curvar(-se) 2 fazer uma curva **curved** *adj* 1 curvo 2 (*tb* **curving**) em curva, arqueado

cushion /ˈkʊʃn/ s 1 almofada 2 colchão • *vt* 1 amortecer 2 ~ **sb/sth** (**against sth**) proteger alguém/algo (de algo)

custard /ˈkʌstərd/ s [*U*] creme (de baunilha)

custodian /kʌˈstoʊdiən/ s 1 guardião/ã 2 depositário/a

custody /ˈkʌstədi/ s custódia

custom /ˈkʌstəm/ s 1 costume, hábito 2 clientela **customary** *adj* habitual: *It is ~ to...* É costume... • s cliente

customs /ˈkʌstəmz/ s [*pl*] 1 (*tb*

~ **duty**) impostos aduaneiros **2** (*tb the* ~) a alfândega

cut /kʌt/ (**-tt-**) (*pt, pp* **cut**) **1** *vt, vi* cortar(-se): ~ *sth in half* cortar algo ao meio **2** *vt* (*pedra*) lapidar, talhar **3** *vt* ferir **4** *vt* reduzir, recortar **5** *vt* (*motor*) desligar ▸ **cut it/that out** (*coloq*) chega, deixa disso **cut in/things fine** deixar pouca margem (de tempo) **cut sb/sth short** interromper alguém/algo ■ **cut across sth** **1** atravessar algo **2** cortar caminho (por um atalho) **cut back** (**on sth**) reduzir (algo) consideravelmente **cut sth back** podar algo **cut down** (**on sth**): ~ *down on smoking* fumar menos **cut sth down 1** cortar/ derrubar algo **2** reduzir algo **cut in** (**on sb/sth**) cortar (*outro carro*) **2** interromper (alguém/ algo) **cut sb off** **1** desdar alguém **2** (*telefone*): *I've been ~ off.* Cortaram a linha. **cut sth off 1** cortar algo: ~ *20 seconds off the record* diminuir o recorde em 20 segundos **2** isolar alguém/algo: *be ~ off* ficar incomunicável **cut sth out 1** cortar algo **2** (*informação*) omitir algo **3** deixar (de fazer) algo *be cut out for sth/to be sth* (*coloq*) ser feito para algo **cut sth up** cortar, picar algo ● *s* **1** corte **2** redução **3** (*carne*) peça **4** (*coloq*) (*lucros*) parte ▸ **a cut above sb/sth** (*coloq*) (algo) superior a alguém/algo

cutback /'kʌtbæk/ *s* redução, corte

cute /kjuːt/ *adj* (**-er, -est**) (*coloq*) atraente, engraçadinho

cutlery /'kʌtləri/ *s* [*U*] talheres

cutlet /'kʌtlət/ *s* **1** costeleta (*carne*) **2** posta (*peixe*)

cut-off (*tb* ~ **point**) *s* limite

cut-rate *adj, adv* de oferta

cut-throat *adj* sem piedade

cutting /'kʌtɪŋ/ *s* **1** recorte **2** (*Bot*) muda ● *adj* **1** cortante **2** mordaz

cv /ˌsiː 'viː/ *abrev de* **curriculum vitae**

cyanide /'saɪənaɪd/ *s* cianeto

cycle /'saɪkl/ *s* **1** ciclo **2** série **3** bicicleta ● *vi*: *go cycling* andar de bicicleta **cyclic(al)** /'saɪklɪk(l)/ *adj* cíclico **cycling** *s* ciclismo **cyclist** *s* ciclista

cyclone /'saɪkloʊn/ *s* ciclone

cylinder /'sɪlɪndər/ *s* **1** cilindro **2** (*gás*) tambor **cylindrical** /sə'lɪndrɪkl/ *adj* cilíndrico

cymbal /'sɪmbl/ *s* (*Mús*) prato

cynic /'sɪnɪk/ *s* cínico/a, desconfiado/a **cynical** *adj* cínico

cynicism *s* cinismo

cypress /'saɪprəs/ *s* cipreste

cyst /sɪst/ *s* quisto

cystic fibrosis /ˌsɪstɪk faɪ'broʊsɪs/ *s* fibrose pulmonar

czar (*tb* **tsar**) /zɑːr/ *s* czar

czarina (*tb* **tsarina**) /zɑː'riːnə/ *s* czarina

Dd

D, d /diː/ *s* (*pl* **D's, d's** /diːz/) **1** D, d **2** (*Educ*) (nota) D **3** (*Mús*) ré

dab /dæb/ *vt, vi* (**-bb-**) ~ (**at**) **sth** tocar algo levemente: ~ *sth on/ off* colocar/retirar algo com leves toques ● *s* toque, pincelada (de tinta)

dad /dæd/ (*tb* **daddy** /'dædi/) *s* (*coloq*) papai

daffodil /'dæfədɪl/ *s* narciso

daft /dæft; *GB* dɑːft/ *adj* (**-er, -est**) (*coloq*) tolo, ridículo

dagger /'dægər/ *s* adaga ▸ **look daggers at sb** lançar um olhar fulminante a alguém

daily /'deɪli/ *adj* cotidiano ● *adv* todo dia, diariamente ● *s* (*pl* **-ies**) diário (*jornal*)

dairy /'deəri/ *s* (*pl* **-ies**) **1** leiteria **2** usina de leite

dairy farm *s* fazenda de gado leiteiro **dairy farming** *s* indústria de laticínios

dairy products *s* laticínios

daisy /'deɪzi/ *s* (*pl* **-ies**) margarida

dale /deɪl/ *s* vale

dam /dæm/ *s* represa, barragem ● *vt* represar

damage /'dæmɪdʒ/ *vt* **1** danificar **2** prejudicar **3** estragar ● *s* **1** [*U*] dano, prejuízo: *brain* ~ lesão cerebral **2** (**damages**) [*pl*] indenização (por perdas e danos) **damaging** *adj* prejudicial

Dame /deɪm/ *s* (*GB*) dama (título honorífico)

damn /dæm/ *vt* condenar (ao inferno), amaldiçoar ● (*tb* **damned**) *adj* (*coloq*) maldito ● *interj* droga **damning** *adj* contundente **damnation** /dæm'neɪʃn/ *s* condenação

damp /dæmp/ *adj* (**-er, -est**)

úmido → MOIST • s umidade • vt (tb **dampen**) 1 molhar, umedecer 2 ~ **sth (down)** esfriar, sufocar algo: ~ **sb's enthusiasm** acabar com o entusiasmo de alguém

dance /dæns; GB dɑ:ns/ vt, vi dançar • s dança, baile **dancer** s dançarino/a bailarino/a

dandelion /ˈdændɪlaɪən/ s dente-de-leão

dandruff /ˈdændrʌf/ s caspa

danger /ˈdeɪndʒər/ s perigo: *be in ~ of sth* correr o risco de algo **dangerous** adj 1 perigoso 2 nocivo

dangle /ˈdæŋgl/ vi balançar

dank /dæŋk/ adj (~er, ~est) frio e úmido

dare /deər/ 1 v modal, vi (neg **dare not** ou **daren't** /ˈdeərnt/ ou **don't/doesn't dare** pt **dared not** ou **didn't dare**) (em orações negativas e interrogativas) atrever-se a: *How ~ you!* Como se atreve? ◇ *Don't (you) ~ tell her!* Não ouse contar para ela! 2 vt desafiar ▶ **I dare say...** eu diria... **NOTA** Quando **dare** é verbo modal, é seguido de infinitivo sem *to* e dispensa o auxiliar *do* nas orações negativas, interrogativas e no passado: *Nobody dared speak.* ◇ *I daren't ask for a day off.*

daring /ˈdeərɪŋ/ s atrevimento, ousadia • adj atrevido, ousado

dark /dɑrk/ **the dark** ◊ escuridão ▶ **before/after dark** antes/depois do anoitecer • adj (~er, ~est) 1 escuro: *glasses* óculos escuros ◇ *get ~* escurecer/anoitecer 2 (pessoa) moreno 3 secreto, obscuro 4 triste, de mau agouro: ~ *days* tempos difíceis ▶ **a dark horse** uma pessoa de talentos ocultos

darken /ˈdɑrkən/ vt, vi escurecer

darkly /ˈdɑrkli/ adv 1 ameaçadoramente 2 pessimistamente

darkness /ˈdɑrknəs/ s escuridão, trevas: *in ~* no escuro

darkroom /ˈdɑrkru:m/ s (Fot) quarto escuro

darling /ˈdɑrlɪŋ/ s querido/a

dart /dɑrt/ s dardo • vi precipitar-se: ~ *away/off* sair em disparada

dash /dæʃ/ s 1 ~ **(of sth)** pingo, pitada (de algo) 2 travessão 3 corrida curta e rápida: *100-meter ~* 100 metros rasos ▶ **make a ~ for sth** precipitar-se para cima de algo • vi apressar-se 2 vi disparar: ~ *upstairs* subir as escadas correndo/em disparada 3 vt acabar com ▶ **dash sth off** rabiscar algo com pressa

dashboard /ˈdæʃbɔ:rd/ s painel (de carro)

data /ˈdeɪtə; GB ˈdeɪtə (GB) ˈdɑ:tə/ s [U] 1 (Informát) dados 2 informação

database /ˈdeɪtəbeɪs/ s banco de dados

date /deɪt/ s 1 data: *What's the ~?* Que dia é hoje? 2 época 3 (coloq) encontro (romântico) 4 (coloq) pessoa com quem se tem encontro (romântico) 5 tâmara ▶ **to date** até hoje **up to date** 1 em dia 2 atualizado • vt datar **dated** adj 1 fora de moda 2 datado

daughter /ˈdɔ:tər/ s filha

daughter-in-law s (pl **-ers-in-law**) nora

daunting /ˈdɔ:ntɪŋ/ adj desencorajador

dawn /dɔ:n/ s amanhecer, madrugada: *from ~ till dusk* do nascer ao pôr-do-sol • vi amanhecer

day /deɪ/ s 1 dia: *by ~* de dia ◇ *~ by/after ~* dia a/após dia ◇ *the ~ after tomorrow* depois de amanhã ◇ *the ~ before yesterday* anteontem ◇ *from one ~ to the next* de um dia para o outro 2 jornada (de trabalho, etc.) 3 (days) [pl] época ▶ **day in, day out** entra dia, sai dia **one/some day; one of these days** algum dia, um dia destes **these days** hoje em dia **to this day** até hoje

daycare center s (USA) creche

daydream /ˈdeɪdri:m/ s devaneio • vi sonhar acordado, devanear

daylight /ˈdeɪlaɪt/ s luz do dia: *in ~* de dia

day off s dia livre/de folga

day return s (GB) passagem de ida e volta para o mesmo dia

daytime /ˈdeɪtaɪm/ s dia (entre o nascer e o pôr-do-sol)

day-to-day adj diário

day trip s excursão de um dia

daze /deɪz/ s ▶ **in a daze** aturdido, confuso **dazed** adj aturdido, confuso

dazzle /ˈdæzl/ vt ofuscar, deslumbrar

dead /ded/ adj 1 morto 2 (folhas) seco 3 (perna, etc.) dormente 4 (bateria) descarregado 5 *The line's gone* ~. O telefone está mudo. • adv absolutamente • s ▶ **in the/at dead of night** em plena noite **deaden** vt 1 (som) abafar 2 (dor) aliviar

dead end s beco sem saída

dead heat s empate

deadline /'dedlaɪn/ s data limite

deadlock /'dedlɒk/ s impasse

deadly /'dedli/ adj (-ier, -iest) mortal, fatal

deaf /def/ adj (~er, ~est) surdo: ~ **and dumb** surdo-mudo **deafen** vt ensurdecer **deafening** adj ensurdecedor **deafness** s surdez

deal /di:l/ vt, vi (pt, pp dealt /delt/) (golpe, cartas) dar → BARALHO ■ **deal in sth** comercializar algo: ~ **in drugs** traficar drogas **deal with sb 1** tratar com alguém **2** castigar alguém **3** ocupar-se com alguém **deal with sth 1** resolver algo **2** lidar com algo (tema) tratar de algo ● s **1** trato **2** contrato ● **a good/great deal** muito, uma boa quantia: It's a good ~ warmer today. Está bem mais quente hoje.

dealer /'di:lər/ s **1** vendedor/a, comerciante **2** (drogas, armas) traficante **3** (cartas) carteador/a

dealing /'di:lɪŋ/ s **have dealings with sb/sth** ter negócios, tratar com alguém/algo

dean /di:n/ s **1** deão **2** decano

dear /dɪər/ adj (~er, ~est) **1** querido/a (carta): Dear Sir Caro/Prezado senhor ◊ Dear Jason,... Caro/Querido Jason,... **3** (GB) caro ● **oh dear** oh, meu Deus ● s querido/a **dearly** adv muito

death /deθ/ s morte: ~ **certificate** certidão de óbito ◊ **beat sb to** ~ matar alguém a pauladas ◊ **put sb to** ~ executar alguém **deathly** adj (-ier, -iest) mortal: ~ **cold** frio como um cadáver

debase /dɪ'beɪs/ vt ~ **(yourself)** degradar(-se)

debatable /dɪ'beɪtəbl/ adj discutível

debate /dɪ'beɪt/ s debate ● vt, vi debater

debit /'debɪt/ s débito ● vt debitar, cobrar

debris /də'bri:; GB 'deɪbri:/ s [U] escombros

debt /det/ s dívida: be in ~ estar endividado **debtor** s devedor/a

decade /'dekeɪd; GB dɪ'keɪd/ s década

decadent /'dekədənt/ adj decadente **decadence** s decadência

decaffeinated /ˌdi:'kæfɪneɪtɪd/ adj descafeinado

decay /dɪ'keɪ/ vi **1** cariar **2** decompor-se **3** decair ● s [U]

1 cárie **2** decomposição

deceased /dɪ'si:st/ adj (fml) falecido ● **the deceased** s o/a falecido/a

December /dɪ'sembər/ s (abrev **Dec.**) dezembro → MAY

decency /'di:snsi/ s decência, decoro

decent /'di:snt/ adj **1** decente **2** aceitável **3** amável

deception /dɪ'sepʃn/ s trapaça, fraude

deceptive /dɪ'septɪv/ adj enganoso

decide /dɪ'saɪd/ **1** vi decidir(-se) **2** vi ~ **on sb/sth** optar por alguém/algo **3** vt determinar **decided** adj **1** inquestionável **2** ~ **(about sth)** decidido (quanto a algo)

decimal /'desɪml/ adj, s decimal

decipher /dɪ'saɪfər/ vt decifrar

decision /dɪ'sɪʒn/ s decisão

decisive /dɪ'saɪsɪv/ adj **1** decisivo **2** decidido

deck /dek/ s **1** (Náut) convés **2** (ônibus) andar **3** (USA) baralho **4** toca-fitas

deckchair /'dektʃeər/ s espreguiçadeira

declaration /ˌdeklə'reɪʃn/ s declaração

declare /dɪ'kleər/ **1** vt declarar **2** vi pronunciar-se

decline /dɪ'klaɪn/ **1** vt, vi (Gram) declinar **2** vi negar-se ● s **1** declínio **2** decadência, deterioração

decompose /ˌdi:kəm'pəʊz/ vt, vi decompor(-se), apodrecer

décor /'deɪkɔːr; GB 'deɪkɔː(r)/ s [U] decoração

decorate /'dekəreɪt/ vt **1** decorar, ornamentar **2** pintar **3** condecorar **decoration** s **1** decoração **2** ornamento **3** condecoração

decorative /'dekərətɪv/ adj decorativo

decoy /'di:kɔɪ/ s isca

decrease /dɪ'kri:s/ **1** vi diminuir **2** vt reduzir ● /'di:kri:s/ s diminuição, redução

decree /dɪ'kri:/ s decreto ● vt decretar

decrepit /dɪ'krepɪt/ adj decrépito

dedicate /'dedɪkeɪt/ vt dedicar(-se) **dedication** s **1** dedicação **2** dedicatória

deduce /dɪ'du:s; GB dɪ'dju:s/ vt deduzir (teoria, etc.)

deduct /dɪˈdʌkt/ vt deduzir (*impostos*, *etc.*) **deduction** s dedução

deed /diːd/ s **1** (*fml*) ação, obra **2** ato, feito **3** (*Jur*) escritura

deem /diːm/ vt (*fml*) considerar

deep /diːp/ (~er, ~est) adj **1** profundo, fundo: *The pool is one meter* ~. A piscina tem um metro de profundidade. **2** (*voz*, *etc.*) grave **3** (*cor*) intenso **4** ~ in sth concentrado em algo ● adv muito profundo, em profundidade ▸ **deep down** (*coloq*) lá no fundo **go/run deep** (*crenças*) estar muito enraizado deeply adv profundamente, muitíssimo

deepen /ˈdiːpən/ vt, vi aprofundar, aumentar

deep freeze s congelador

deer /dɪər/ s (pl deer) cervo → VEADO

default /dɪˈfɔːlt/ s **1** descumprimento **2** revelia ▸ **by default** por não comparecimento ● vi **1** não comparecer **2** ~ (on sth) deixar de cumprir (algo) ● adj (*Informát*) (por) padrão

defeat /dɪˈfiːt/ vt **1** derrotar **2** (*objetivos*, *etc.*) frustrar ● s derrota: *admit* ~ dar-se por vencido

defect /ˈdiːfekt, dɪˈfekt/ s defeito → MISTAKE ● adj defeituoso /dɪˈfekt/ vi **1** ~ (from sth) desertar (de algo) **2** ~ to sth passar para algo **defection** s deserção **defector** s desertor/a

defense (GB defence) /dɪˈfens/ s **1** defesa **2** (the defense) (*judiciário*) a defesa defenseless adj indefeso **defend** /dɪˈfend/ vt defender, proteger **defendant** acusado/a, réu/ré **defense** /dɪˈfensɪv/ adj (on the) ~ (about sth) na defensiva (contra/sobre algo)

defer /dɪˈfɜːr/ vt (-rr-) **1** ~ sth to sth adiar algo para algo **2** ~ (on sth) acatar algo **a deference** /ˈdefərəns/ s deferência: *in* ~ *to sb/sth* por respeito a alguém/algo

defiance /dɪˈfaɪəns/ s desafio, desobediência **defiant** adj desafiador

deficiency /dɪˈfɪʃnsi/ s (pl -ies) deficiência **deficient** adj deficiente

define /dɪˈfaɪn/ vt definir

definite /ˈdefɪnət/ adj **1** definido, concreto **2** seguro, definitivo **definitely** adv **1** definitivamente **2** indubitavelmente, sem dúvida alguma

definition /ˌdefɪˈnɪʃn/ s definição

definitive /dɪˈfɪnətɪv/ adj definitivo

deflate /diːˈfleɪt/ vt, vi desinchar, desinflar

deflect /dɪˈflekt/ vt desviar

deforestation /diːˌfɒrɪˈsteɪʃn/ s desmatamento

deform /dɪˈfɔːrm/ vt deformar **deformed** adj deformado **deformity** s (pl -ies) deformidade

defrost /ˌdiːˈfrɔːst; GB ˌdiːˈfrɒst/ vt descongelar

deft /deft/ adj habilidoso

defunct /dɪˈfʌŋkt/ adj (*fml*) morto, extinto

defuse /ˌdiːˈfjuːz/ vt **1** (*bomba*) desativar **2** (*crise*) atenuar

defy /dɪˈfaɪ/ vt (pt, pp -ied) desafiar, desobedecer a

degenerate /dɪˈdʒenəreɪt/ vi degenerar(-se) **degeneration** s degeneração

degrade /dɪˈɡreɪd/ vt degradar **degradation** s degradação

degree /dɪˈɡriː/ s **1** grau **2** diploma, título: ~ *course* curso universitário ▸ **by degrees** pouco a pouco

deity /ˈdeɪəti/ s (pl -ies) divindade

dejected /dɪˈdʒektɪd/ adj desanimado

delay /dɪˈleɪ/ **1** vt atrasar **2** vi adiar, atrasar-se: *Don't* ~! Não (se) demore! **3** vt retardar ● s atraso: *without* ~ sem demora a **delaying** adj: ~ *tactics* táticas de retardamento

delegate /ˈdelɪɡət/ s delegado/a, representante ● /ˈdelɪɡeɪt/ vt delegar **delegation** s delegação

delete /dɪˈliːt/ vt **1** apagar, riscar **2** (*Informát*) excluir **deletion** s omissão, eliminação

deliberate /dɪˈlɪbərət/ adj deliberado ● /dɪˈlɪbəreɪt/ vi (*fml*) deliberar **deliberation** s [ger pl] deliberação

delicacy /ˈdelɪkəsi/ s (pl -ies) **1** delicadeza **2** manjar

delicate /ˈdelɪkət/ adj **1** delicado: ~ *china* porcelana fina **2** (*cor*) suave

delicatessen /ˌdelɪkəˈtesn/ s casa de frios, etc. (*especializada em produtos importados*)

delicious /dɪˈlɪʃəs/ adj delicioso

delight /dɪˈlaɪt/ s delícia ▸ **take delight in (doing) sth** sentir prazer em (fazer) algo ● **1** vt encantar **2** vi ~ in (doing) sth sentir prazer de (fazer) algo **delighted** adj: ~ (at/with sth); ~ (to do sth) encantado (com algo);

delightful /dɪˈlaɪtfl/ *adj* encantador

delinquent /dɪˈlɪŋkwənt/ *adj*, *s* delinqüente delinquency *s* delinqüência

delirious /dɪˈlɪriəs/ *adj* delirante: ~ with joy louco de alegria delirium *s* delírio

deliver /dɪˈlɪvər/ *vt* 1 entregar 2 (*recado*) dar 3 (*discurso, etc.*) fazer 4 (*Med*) fazer o parto 5 (*golpe*) dar delivery *s* (*pl* -ies) 1 entrega 2 parto

delta /ˈdeltə/ *s* delta

delude /dɪˈluːd/ *vt* enganar, iludir

deluge /ˈdeljuːdʒ/ *s* (*fml*) tromba d'água, dilúvio ● *vt* inundar

delusion /dɪˈluːʒn/ *s* engano, ilusão

de luxe /dəˈlʌks/ *adj* de luxo

demand /dɪˈmɑːnd; *GB* -ˈmænd/ *s* 1 ~ (for sb to do sth) exigência (de que alguém faça algo) 2 ~ (for sb/sth) demanda, procura (por alguém/algo): *in* ~ (muito) solicitado ● **on demand** a pedidos ● *vt* 1 exigir 2 requerer demanding *adj* exigente

demise /dɪˈmaɪz/ *s* (*fml*) 1 fracasso 2 falecimento

demo /ˈdeməʊ/ *s* (*pl* ~s) (*coloq*) manifestação

democracy /dɪˈmɒkrəsi/ *s* (*pl* -ies) democracia democrat /ˈdeməkræt/ *s* democrata democratic /ˌdeməˈkrætɪk/ *adj* democrático

demographic /ˌdeməˈgræfɪk/ *adj* demográfico

demolish /dɪˈmɒlɪʃ/ *vt* demolir demolition *s* demolição

demon /ˈdiːmən/ *s* demônio demonic *adj* demoníaco

demonstrate /ˈdemənstreɪt/ *vt* 1 demonstrar 2 *vi* manifestar-se demonstration *s* 1 demonstração 2 manifestação

demonstrative /dɪˈmɒnstrətɪv/ *adj* 1 carinhoso, expressivo 2 (*Gram*) demonstrativo demonstrator /ˈdemənstreɪtər/ *s* manifestante

demoralize /dɪˈmɒrəlaɪz/ *GB* -ˈmɒr-/ *vt* desmoralizar

demure /dɪˈmjʊər/ *adj* recatado

den /den/ *s* toca

denial /dɪˈnaɪəl/ *s* ~ (of sth) negação (de algo); recusa (em fazer algo)

denim /ˈdenɪm/ *s* brim

denomination /dɪˌnɒmɪˈneɪʃn/ *s* 1 seita 2 denominação

denounce /dɪˈnaʊns/ *vt* denunciar

dense /dens/ *adj* (-er, -est) 1 denso 2 (*coloq*) burro density *s* (*pl* -ies) densidade

dent /dent/ *s* amassado ● *vt, vi* amassar(-se) (*esp carro*)

dental /ˈdentl/ *adj* dental

dentist /ˈdentɪst/ *s* dentista

denunciation /dɪˌnʌnsiˈeɪʃn/ *s* denúncia, crítica

deny /dɪˈnaɪ/ *vt* (*pt, pp* -ied) 1 negar 2 desmentir

deodorant /diˈəʊdərənt/ *s* desodorante

depart /dɪˈpɑːt/ *vi* (*fml*) partir

department /dɪˈpɑːtmənt/ *s* (*abrev* Dept.) 1 departamento, seção 2 ministério department- /ˌdiːpɑːtˈmentl/ *adj* departamental

department store *s* loja de departamentos

departure /dɪˈpɑːtʃər/ *s* partida

depend /dɪˈpend/ *vi* 1 ~ on/upon sb/sth contar com alguém/ algo; confiar em alguém/algo 2 ~ on sb/sth depender de alguém/algo ▸ that depends; it (all) depends (isso) depende dependable *adj* confiável

dependent /dɪˈpendənt/ *adj* dependente ● *s* (*GB tb* -ant) dependente dependence *s* ~ (on/upon sb/sth) dependência (de alguém/algo)

depict /dɪˈpɪkt/ *vt* representar, descrever

depleted /dɪˈpliːtɪd/ *adj* exaurido

deplore /dɪˈplɔːr/ *vt* 1 condenar 2 lamentar

deploy /dɪˈplɔɪ/ *vt* dispor em formação de combate

deport /dɪˈpɔːt/ *vt* deportar deportation *s* deportação

depose /dɪˈpəʊz/ *vt* destituir

deposit /dɪˈpɒzɪt/ *vt* 1 (*dinheiro*) depositar 2 ~ sth (with sb) deixar algo (a cargo de alguém) ● *s* 1 (*Fin*) depósito: ~ account conta remunerada 2 (*aluguel*) fiança 3 ~ (on sth) sinal, entrada (para comprar algo) 4 sedimento

depot /ˈdiːpəʊ; *GB* ˈdepəʊ/ *s* 1 depósito, armazém 2 garagem 3 (*USA*) (estação) terminal

depress /dɪˈpres/ *vt* deprimir depression *s* depressão

deprivation /ˌdeprɪˈveɪʃn/ *s* pobreza, privação

deprive /dɪˈpraɪv/ *vt* privar deprived *adj* necessitado

depth /depθ/ *s* profundidade ▸ **in depth** a fundo, em profundidade deputation /ˌdepjuˈteɪʃn/ s delegação

deputize /ˈdepjətaɪz/ vi ~ (for sb) representar alguém

deputy /ˈdepjəti/ s (pl -ies) 1 substituto/a, suplente: ~ chairman vice-presidente 2 (Pol) deputado/a

deranged /dɪˈreɪndʒd/ adj transtornado, louco

deregulation /ˌdiːregjuˈleɪʃn/ s liberação (preços, etc.)

derelict /ˈderəlɪkt/ adj (casa, etc.) abandonado

deride /dɪˈraɪd/ vt ridicularizar, zombar de

derision /dɪˈrɪʒn/ s escárnio derisive /dɪˈraɪsɪv/ adj ridicularizante derisory /dɪˈraɪsəri/ adj irrisório

derivation /ˌderɪˈveɪʃn/ s derivação derivative /dɪˈrɪvətɪv/ s derivado

derive /dɪˈraɪv/ 1 vt obter, tirar: ~ comfort from sth achar consolo em algo 2 vi derivar

derogatory /dɪˈrɒgətəri; GB -tri/ adj depreciativo

descend /dɪˈsend/ vt, vi (fml) descer: in descending order em ordem decrescente descendant s descendente

descent /dɪˈsent/ s 1 descida 2 ascendência

describe /dɪˈskraɪb/ vt descrever, qualificar description s descrição

desert /ˈdezət/ s deserto ● /dɪˈzɜːt/ 1 vt abandonar 2 vi (Mil) desertar deserted adj deserto deserter s desertor/a

deserve /dɪˈzɜːv/ vt merecer deserving adj digno

design /dɪˈzaɪn/ s 1 desenho 2 projeto 3 design ● vt 1 desenhar 2 projetar

designate /ˈdezɪgneɪt/ vt 1 (fml) designar 2 nomear

designer /dɪˈzaɪmər/ s projetista, estilista

desirable /dɪˈzaɪrəbl/ adj desejável

desire /dɪˈzaɪər/ s 1 desejo 2 ~ (for sth/to do sth) vontade (de algo/fazer algo) ● vt desejar

desk /desk/ s escrivaninha: information ~ balcão de informações

desktop /ˈdesktɒp/ adj: ~ computer computador (de mesa) ◊ ~ publishing editoração eletrônica

desolate /ˈdesələt/ adj 1 deserto 2 desolado desolation s 1 desolação 2 abandono

despair /dɪˈspeər/ vi (fml) perder as esperanças ● s desespero despairing adj desesperado

despatch /dɪˈspætʃ/ = DISPATCH

desperate /ˈdespərət/ adj 1 desesperado 2 desesperador despicable /dɪˈspɪkəbl/ adj desprezível

despise /dɪˈspaɪz/ vt desprezar

despite /dɪˈspaɪt/ prep apesar de

despondent /dɪˈspɒndənt/ adj desanimado

despot /ˈdespɒt/ s déspota

dessert /dɪˈzɜːt/ s sobremesa

dessertspoon /dɪˈzɜːtspuːn/ s 1 colher de sobremesa 2 (tb dessertspoonful) colher de sobremesa (medida)

destination /ˌdestɪˈneɪʃn/ s destino (trem, etc.)

destined /ˈdestɪnd/ adj (fml) destinado: ~ to fail condenado ao fracasso

destiny /ˈdestəni/ s (pl -ies) destino (sina)

destitute /ˈdestɪtjuːt; GB -tjuːt/ adj indigente

destroy /dɪˈstrɔɪ/ vt destruir destroyer s contratorpedeiro

destruction /dɪˈstrʌkʃn/ s destruição destructive adj destrutivo

detach /dɪˈtætʃ/ vt separar detachable adj destacável

detached /dɪˈtætʃt/ adj 1 imparcial 2 indiferente 3 (casa) separado

detachment /dɪˈtætʃmənt/ s 1 imparcialidade 2 desapego 3 (Mil) destacamento

detail /ˈdiːteɪl/ s detalhe, pormenor: in ~ detalhadamente ▶ go into detail(s) entrar em detalhes ● vt detalhar detailed adj detalhado

detain /dɪˈteɪn/ vt deter detainee s detido/a

detect /dɪˈtekt/ vt 1 detectar 2 descobrir detectable adj detectável detection s detecção: escape ~ passar despercebido

detective /dɪˈtektɪv/ s detetive: ~ story história policial

detention /dɪˈtenʃn/ s detenção

deter /dɪˈtɜːr/ vt (-rr-) dissuadir

detergent /dɪˈtɜːdʒənt/ adj, s detergente

deteriorate /dɪˈtɪəriəreɪt/ vi deteriorar(-se), piorar deterioration s deterioração

determination /dɪˌtɜːmɪˈneɪʃn/ s determinação

determine /dɪˈtɜːmɪn/ vt determinar, decidir: determining factor fator determinante determined *adj* determinado

determiner /dɪˈtɜːrmɪnər/ s (*Gram*) determinante

deterrent /dɪˈtɜːrənt/; *GB* -ˈter-/ s **1** impedimento **2** *nuclear* ~ força nuclear de dissuasão

detest /dɪˈtest/ *vt* detestar

detonate /ˈdetəneɪt/ *vt, vi* detonar

detour /ˈdiːtʊər/ s desvio

detract /dɪˈtrækt/ *vi* ~ from sth diminuir (o valor de) algo: ~ from sb's enjoyment of sth diminuir o prazer de alguém em algo

detriment /ˈdetrɪmənt/ s ▸ **to the detriment of sb/sth** em detrimento de alguém/algo **detrimental** /ˌdetrɪˈmentl/ *adj* prejudicial

devalue /ˌdiːˈvæljuː/ *vt, vi* desvalorizar(-se) **devaluation** s desvalorização

devastate /ˈdevəsteɪt/ *vt* **1** devastar **2** (*pessoa*) desolar: be devastated by sth ficar arrasado com algo **devastating** *adj* **1** devastador **2** arrasador **devastation** s devastação

develop /dɪˈveləp/ **1** *vt, vi* desenvolver **2** *vt* (*plano*) elaborar **3** *vt* (*doença*) contrair **4** *vt* (*Fot*) revelar **5** *vt* urbanizar **developed** *adj* desenvolvido **developer** s fomentador/a, construtor/a **developing** *adj* em desenvolvimento

development /dɪˈveləpmənt/ s **1** desenvolvimento, evolução: There has been a new ~. Aconteceu algo novo. **2** urbanização **3** (*tb developing*) (*Fot*) revelação

deviant /ˈdiːviənt/ *adj, s* **1** transviado/a **2** pervertido/a

deviate /ˈdiːvieɪt/ *vi* desviar-se **deviation** s desvio: a ~ from the rules uma divergência das regras

device /dɪˈvaɪs/ s **1** aparelho, dispositivo **2** esquema, estratagema

devil /ˈdevl/ s demônio, diabo: You lucky ~! Seu sortudo!

devious /ˈdiːviəs/ *adj* **1** desonesto **2** tortuoso

devise /dɪˈvaɪz/ *vt* idealizar, elaborar

devoid /dɪˈvɔɪd/ *adj* desprovido, isento

devolution /ˌdevəˈluːʃn; ˌdiːv-/ s **1** descentralização **2** (*de poderes*) delegação

devote /dɪˈvəʊt/ *vt* **1** ~ sth/yourself to sb/sth dedicar algo; dedicar-se a alguém/algo **2** (*recursos*) destinar **devoted**

---

adj fiel, devotado: ~ to each other leais um ao outro

devotee /ˌdevəˈtiː/ s devoto/a

devotion /dɪˈvəʊʃn/ s **1** dedicação **2** devoção

devour /dɪˈvaʊər/ *vt* devorar

devout /dɪˈvaʊt/ *adj* **1** devoto **2** sincero **devoutly** *adv* **1** com devoção **2** sinceramente

dew /duː; *GB* djuː/ s orvalho

dexterity /dekˈsterəti/ s destreza

diabetes /ˌdaɪəˈbiːtiːz/ s diabetes **diabetic** *adj, s* diabético/a

diabolic /ˌdaɪəˈbɒlɪk/ (*tb* **diabolical**) *adj* diabólico

diagnose /ˈdaɪəgnəʊs; *GB* ˌdaɪəgˈnəʊz/ *vt* diagnosticar **diagnosis** /ˌdaɪəgˈnəʊsɪs/ s (*pl* **-noses** /-ˈnəʊsiːz/) diagnóstico **diagnostic** *adj* diagnóstico

diagonal /daɪˈægənl/ *adj, s* diagonal **diagonally** *adv* diagonalmente

diagram /ˈdaɪəgræm/ s diagrama

dial /ˈdaɪəl/ s **1** mostrador **2** (*telefone*) disco **3** (*relógio*) face ● *vt* (*-l-*, *GB* -ll-) discar

dialect /ˈdaɪəlekt/ s dialeto

dialling code (*GB*) s prefixo (de DDD)

dialogue (*USA tb* -log) /ˈdaɪələːg; *GB* -lɒg/ s diálogo

dial tone (*GB* **dialling tone**) s sinal de discar

diameter /daɪˈæmɪtər/ s diâmetro

diamond /ˈdaɪmənd, ˈdaɪə-/ s **1** diamante **2** losango **3** ~ jubilee sexagésimo aniversário **4** (**diamonds**) (*naipe*) ouros → BARALHO

diaper /ˈdaɪpər/ s fralda

diaphragm /ˈdaɪəfræm/ s diafragma

diarrhea (*GB* **diarrhoea**) /ˌdaɪəˈrɪə/ s diarréia

diary /ˈdaɪəri/ s (*pl* -ies) **1** diário **2** (*GB*) agenda

dice /daɪs/ s (*pl dice*) (*jogo*) dado ● *vt* cortar em cubinhos

dictate /ˈdɪkteɪt/ *vt, vi* **1** ditar **2** *vi* ~ to sb impor algo a alguém **dictation** s ditado

dictator /ˈdɪkteɪtər; *GB* dɪkˈteɪtə(r)/ s ditador/a **dictatorship** s ditadura

dictionary /ˈdɪkʃəneri; *GB* -nri/ s (*pl* -ies) dicionário

did /dɪd/ *pret de* DO

didactic /daɪˈdæktɪk/ *adj* (*fml*) didático

didn't /ˈdɪd(ə)nt/ = DID NOT *Ver* DO¹

die /daɪ/ s (*jogo*) dado ● *vi* (*pt, pp*

died part pres **dying**) morrer ▶ **be dying for sth/to do sth** morrer de vontade de fazer algo ∎ **die away 1** desvanecer **2** (*ruído*) desaparecer aos poucos **die down 1** apagar-se, diminuir gradualmente **2** amainar **die off** morrer um após o outro **die out 1** (*Zool*) extinguir(-se) **2** desaparecer

diesel /ˈdiːzl/ s diesel

diet /ˈdaɪət/ s dieta: *go on a ~* começar uma dieta → LOW-CALORIE ● vi estar de dieta **dietary** adj **1** dietético **2** alimentar

differ /ˈdɪfər/ vi **1** diferir, ser diferente **2** não concordar, discordar

difference /ˈdɪfrəns/ s diferença ▶ **it makes all the difference** isto muda tudo **it makes no difference** dá no mesmo

different /ˈdɪfrənt/ adj ~ **(from sb/sth)** (*USA to* than **sth**) diferente, distinto (de alguém/algo) **differently** adv de (uma) maneira diferente/distinta

differentiate /ˌdɪfəˈrenʃieɪt/ vt, vi distinguir, diferenciar **differentiation** s diferenciação

difficult /ˈdɪfɪkəlt/ adj difícil **difficulty** s (pl **-ies**) **1** dificuldade **2** apuro, aperto: *make difficulties for sb* colocar obstáculos a alguém

diffident /ˈdɪfɪdənt/ adj (*pessoa*) inseguro **diffidence** s insegurança

dig /dɪɡ/ vt, vi (**-gg-**) (pt, pp **dug**) **1** cavar: ~ *sb/sth out* retirar alguém/algo (cavando) **2** ~ (**sth**) **into sth** cravar algo em algo ▶ **dig your heels in** manter-se firme (*opinião, etc.*) ∎ **dig in** (*coloq*) (*comida*) atacar **dig sth up 1** arrancar algo da terra **2** desenterrar algo **3** (*terra*) preparar algo ● s escavação **digger** s escavadeira

digest /daɪˈdʒest/ vt **1** resumo **2** condensação ● /daɪˈdʒest/, /dɪ-/ vt, vi digerir **digestion** s digestão

digit /ˈdɪdʒɪt/ s dígito **digital** adj digital

dignified /ˈdɪɡnɪfaɪd/ adj digno

dignitary /ˈdɪɡnɪtəri; GB -təri/ s dignitário/a

dignity /ˈdɪɡnəti/ s dignidade

digression /daɪˈɡreʃn/ s digressão

dike /daɪk/ s **1** dique **2** barragem

dilapidated /dɪˈlæpɪdeɪtɪd/ adj **1** arruinado **2** deteriorado

dilemma /dɪˈlemə, daɪ-/ s dilema

dilute /daɪˈluːt; GB daɪˈljuːt/ vt **1** diluir **2** suavizar

dim /dɪm/ adj (**dimmer, dimmest**) **1** (*luz*) fraco, tênue **2** (*lembrança, etc.*) vago **3** (*perspectivas*) pouco promissor, sombrio **4** (*coloq*) (*pessoa*) estúpido **5** (*visão*) turvo ● (**-mm-**) **1** vt diminuir **2** vi apagar-se pouco a pouco **3** vt, vi empanar (o brilho de), turvar **4** vt (*USA*) (*faróis de um carro*) abaixar

dime /daɪm/ s (*Can, USA*) (moeda de) 10 centavos

dimension /dɪˈmenʃn, daɪ-/ s dimensão

diminish /dɪˈmɪnɪʃ/ vt, vi diminuir **diminishing** adj minguante

diminutive /dɪˈmɪnjətɪv/ adj diminuto ● adj, s diminutivo

dimly /ˈdɪmli/ adv **1** fracamente **2** vagamente **3** (*ver*) apenas

dimple /ˈdɪmpl/ s covinha (*do rosto*)

din /dɪn/ s [sing] **1** alarido **2** barulhada

dine /daɪn/ vi (*fml*) ~ (**on sth**) comer (algo): ~ *out* jantar fora **diner** s **1** comensal **2** (*USA*) pequeno restaurante

dinghy /ˈdɪŋɡi/ s (pl **-ies**) **1** bote **2** (*GB*) barco inflável

dingy /ˈdɪndʒi/ adj (**-ier, -iest**) **1** lúgubre **2** encardido

dining room s sala de jantar

dinner /ˈdɪnər/ s jantar (de gala), almoço: *have* ~ almoçar/comer ◇ ~ *party* jantar entre amigos

dinner jacket s (*GB*) smoking

dinosaur /ˈdaɪnəsɔːr/ s dinossauro

diocese /ˈdaɪəsɪs/ s diocese

dioxide /daɪˈɑksaɪd/ s dióxido

dip /dɪp/ (**-pp-**) **1** vt mergulhar, molhar **2** vi descer **3** (*GB*) vt (*faróis de um carro*) abaixar ● s **1** (*coloq*) mergulho **2** (*Geog*) depressão **3** declive **4** (*preços*) baixa **5** (*Cozinha*) molho (*para molhar alimentos*)

diploma /dɪˈploumə/ s diploma

diplomacy /dɪˈ ploʊməsi/ s diplomacia **diplomat** /ˈdɪpləmæt/ s diplomata **diplomatic** /ˌdɪpləˈmætɪk/ adj diplomático **diplomatically** adv diplomaticamente

dire /ˈdaɪər/ adj (**-er, -est**) **1** (*fml*) terrível **2** (*coloq*) fatal ▶ **in dire straits** numa situação calamitosa

direct /dɪˈrekt, daɪ-/ vt dirigir: *Could you ~ me to...?* Poderia indicar-me o caminho para...? ● adj **1** direto **2** franco **3** exato

• **adv 1** diretamente: *The train goes ~ to London.* O trem vai direto para Londres. **2** pessoalmente

direct debit *s* (*GB*) débito automático

direction /dɪˈrekʃn, daɪ-/ *s* **1** direção, sentido **2** (**directions**) instruções: *ask for directions* pedir orientação

directive /dɪˈrektɪv, daɪ-/ *s* diretriz

directly /dɪˈrektli, daɪ-/ *adv* **1** diretamente: *~ opposite (sth)* bem em frente (a algo) **2** imediatamente

directness /dɪˈrektnəs, daɪ-/ *s* franqueza

director /dɪˈrektər, daɪ-/ *s* diretor/a

directorate /dɪˈrektərət, daɪ-/ *s* **1** quadro de diretores, diretoria **2** diretório

directory /dəˈrektəri, daɪ-/ *s* (*pl* **-ies**) catálogo, lista (*telefônica*)

dirt /dɜːrt/ *s* **1** sujeira **2** terra **3** (*coloq*) obscenidade: *the ~ about the movie stars* os podres dos astros do cinema

dirty /ˈdɜːrti/ *vt, vi* (*pt, pp* **-ied**) sujar(-se) • *adj* (**-ier, -iest**) **1** sujo: *~ word* palavrão **2** (*coloq*) injusto: *~ trick* golpe baixo

disability /ˌdɪsəˈbɪləti/ *s* (*pl* **-ies**) **1** incapacidade **2** (*Med*) invalidez

disabled /dɪsˈeɪbld/ *adj* incapacitado • **the disabled** *s* [*pl*] os inválidos

disadvantage /ˌdɪsədˈvæntɪdʒ; *GB* -ˈvɑːn-/ *s* desvantagem disadvantaged *adj* desfavorecido disadvantageous *adj* desvantajoso

disagree /ˌdɪsəˈɡriː/ *vi* discordar: *He disagreed with her on what to do.* Ele discordava dela quanto ao que fazer. ■ **disagree with sb** (*comida, clima*) fazer mal a alguém disagreeable *adj* desagradável disagreement *s* **1** desacordo **2** discussão

disappear /ˌdɪsəˈpɪər/ *vi* desaparecer disappearance *s* desaparecimento

disappoint /ˌdɪsəˈpɔɪnt/ *vt* **1** decepcionar, desapontar **2** (*esperanças*) frustrar disappointed *adj* ~ (**in/with sb/sth**); ~ (**about/at/by sth**) decepcionado (com alguém/algo); desapontado (com algo) disappointing *adj* decepcionante disappointment *s* decepção

disapproval /ˌdɪsəˈpruːvl/ *s* desaprovação

disapprove /ˌdɪsəˈpruːv/ *vi* **1** ~ (**of sth**) desaprovar (algo) **2** ~ (**of sb**) ter má opinião (de alguém) disapproving *adj* de desaprovação

disarm /dɪsˈɑːrm/ *vt, vi* desarmar(-se) disarmament *s* desarmamento

disassociate /ˌdɪsəˈsəʊʃieɪt/ = DISSOCIATE

disaster /dɪˈzæstər; *GB* -ˈzɑː-/ *s* desastre, calamidade disastrous *adj* desastroso, catastrófico

disband /dɪsˈbænd/ *vt, vi* (*grupo*) dissolver(-se)

disbelief /ˌdɪsbɪˈliːf/ *s* descrença

disc /dɪsk/ *s* disco

discard /dɪsˈkɑːrd/ *vt* descartar, desfazer-se de

discern /dɪˈsɜːrn/ *vt* **1** perceber **2** discernir discernible /dɪˈsɜːrnəbl/ *adj* perceptível

discharge /dɪsˈtʃɑːrdʒ/ *vt* **1** (*resíduos*) descarregar, despejar **2** (*Mil*) dispensar **3** (*Med*) dar alta **4** (*dever*) cumprir • /ˈdɪstʃɑːrdʒ/ *s* **1** descarga **2** (*resíduo*) emissão **3** (*Mil*) dispensa **4** (*Jur*): *conditional ~* liberdade condicional **5** (*Med*) supuração **6** (*paciente*) alta

disciple /dɪˈsaɪpl/ *s* discípulo/a

discipline /ˈdɪsəplɪn/ *s* disciplina • *vt* disciplinar disciplinary *adj* disciplinar

disc jockey *s* disc-jóquei

disclose /dɪsˈkləʊz/ *vt* (*fml*) revelar disclosure /dɪsˈkləʊʒər/ *s* revelação (*segredo*)

discolor (*GB* **-our**) /dɪsˈkʌlər/ *vt, vi* descolorir

discomfort /dɪsˈkʌmfərt/ *s* [*U*] desconforto, incômodo

disconcerted /ˌdɪskənˈsɜːrtɪd/ *adj* desconcertado disconcerting *adj* desconcertante

disconnect /ˌdɪskəˈnekt/ *vt* **1** desconectar **2** (*luz, etc.*) cortar disconnected *adj* desconexo, incoerente

discontent /ˌdɪskənˈtent/ (*tb* **discontentment**) *s* descontentamento discontented *adj* descontente

discontinue /ˌdɪskənˈtɪnjuː/ *vt* suspender

discord /ˈdɪskɔːrd/ *s* **1** (*fml*) discórdia **2** (*Mús*) dissonância discordant /dɪsˈkɔːdənt/ *adj* **1** discordante **2** (*som*) dissonante

discount /ˈdɪskaʊnt/ *s* desconto • /dɪsˈkaʊnt/ *vt* **1** descartar, ignorar **2** (*Com*) descontar discourage /dɪsˈkʌrɪdʒ/ vt 1 desencorajar 2 desaconselhar 3 dissuadir discouraging adj desanimador

discover /dɪsˈkʌvər/ vt descobrir discovery s (pl -ies) descoberta

discredit /dɪsˈkredɪt/ vt desacreditar

discreet /dɪˈskriːt/ adj discreto

discrepancy /dɪsˈkrepənsi/ s (pl -ies) discrepância

discretion /dɪˈskreʃn/ s 1 discrição 2 discernimento ▶ at sb's discretion a critério de alguém

discriminate /dɪˈskrɪmɪneɪt/ vi 1 distinguir 2 discriminar: ~ in favor of sb favorecer alguém discriminating adj perspicaz discrimination s 1 discernimento, bom gosto 2 discriminação

discuss /dɪˈskʌs/ vt discutir, tratar de discussion s discussão, debate

disdain /dɪsˈdeɪn/ s desdém

disease /dɪˈziːz/ s enfermidade, doença NOTA Em geral, usa-se disease para enfermidades específicas como heart disease ou Parkinson's disease. Illness se refere à enfermidade como um estado ou o período em que se está doente. Ver exemplos em ILLNESS. diseased adj enfermo

disembark /ˌdɪsɪmˈbɑːrk/ vi desembarcar

disenchanted /ˌdɪsɪnˈtʃæntɪd; GB -ˈtʃɑːntɪd/ adj desiludido

disentangle /ˌdɪsɪnˈtæŋɡl/ vt 1 desembaraçar, desenredar 2 livrar

disfigure /dɪsˈfɪɡjər; GB -ɡə(r)/ vt desfigurar

disgrace /dɪsˈɡreɪs/ vt desonrar: ~ yourself cair em desgraça ● s 1 desgraça, desonra: in ~ with sb desacreditado perante alguém 2 a ~ (to sb/sth) uma vergonha (para alguém/algo) disgraceful adj vergonhoso

disgruntled /dɪsˈɡrʌntld/ adj 1 ~ (at/about sth) desgostoso (por/com algo) 2 descontente

disguise /dɪsˈɡaɪz/ vt disfarçar, dissimular ● s disfarce: in ~ disfarçado

disgust /dɪsˈɡʌst/ s repugnância

dish /dɪʃ/ s 1 prato 2 (para servir) travessa: wash/do the dishes lavar a louça ■ dish sth out 1 (comida) servir algo 2 (dinheiro, folhetos) distribuir algo em grandes quantidades dish sth up servir algo

disheartened /dɪsˈhɑːrtnd/ adj

desanimado disheartening adj desanimador

disheveled (GB dishevelled) /dɪˈʃevld/ adj 1 (cabelo) despenteado 2 (aparência) desalinhado

dishonest /dɪsˈɑnɪst/ adj 1 desonesto 2 fraudulento dishonesty s desonestidade

dishonor (GB -our) /dɪsˈɑnər/ s desonra ● vt desonrar dishonorable (GB -our-) adj desonroso

dishwasher /ˈdɪʃwɑʃər/ s máquina de lavar louça

disillusion /ˌdɪsɪˈluːʒn/ s (tb disillusionment) desilusão, decepção ● vt desiludir, decepcionar

disinfect /ˌdɪsɪnˈfekt/ vt desinfetar disinfectant s desinfetante

disintegrate /dɪsˈɪntɪɡreɪt/ vt, vi desintegrar(-se) disintegration s desintegração

disinterested /dɪsˈɪntrəstɪd/ adj desinteressado

disjointed /dɪsˈdʒɔɪntɪd/ adj desconexo

disk /dɪsk/ s disco

disk drive s unidade de disco

diskette /dɪsˈket/ s disquete

dislike /dɪsˈlaɪk/ vt não gostar de, ter aversão a ● s ~ (of sb/sth) aversão (a/por alguém/algo); antipatia (por alguém/algo): take a ~ to sb/sth antipatizar com alguém

dislocate /ˈdɪsloʊkeɪt; GB -lək-/ vt deslocar dislocation s deslocamento

dislodge /dɪsˈlɑdʒ/ vt desalojar, deslocar

disloyal /dɪsˈlɔɪəl/ adj ~ (to sb/sth) desleal (com alguém/algo) disloyalty s deslealdade

dismal /ˈdɪzməl/ adj 1 triste, sombrio 2 (coloq) péssimo

dismantle /dɪsˈmæntl/ vt 1 desmontar, desfazer 2 desmantelar

dismay /dɪsˈmeɪ/ s ~ (at sth) consternação (ante algo) ● vt consternar

dismember /dɪsˈmembər/ vt desmembrar

dismiss /dɪsˈmɪs/ vt 1 demitir, dispensar 2 descartar, desconsiderar dismissal s 1 demissão 2 repúdio dismissive adj desdenhoso

dismount /dɪsˈmaʊnt/ vi desmontar, apear(-se)

disobedient /ˌdɪsəˈbiːdiənt/ adj ~ (to sb/sth) desobediente (com alguém/algo) disobedience s desobediência

disobey /ˌdɪsəˈbeɪ/ *vt, vi* desobedecer

disorder /dɪsˈɔːrdər/ *s* desordem

disorderly *adj* **1** desarrumado **2** desordeiro **3** tumultuado

disorganized /dɪsˈɔːrɡənaɪzd/ *adj* desorganizado

disorient /dɪsˈɔːriənt/ (*GB* **disorientate**) /dɪsˈɔːriənteɪt/ *vt* desorientar

disown /dɪsˈoʊn/ *vt* repudiar

dispatch /dɪˈspætʃ/ *vt* (*fml*) **1** enviar **2** (*em reunião*) despachar ● *s* **1** envio **2** (*Jornal*) matéria enviada (*por agência*)

dispel /dɪˈspel/ *vt* (**-ll-**) dissipar

dispense /dɪˈspens/ *vt* dispensar ■ **dispense with sb/sth** prescindir de alguém/algo

disperse /dɪˈspɜːrs/ *vt, vi* dispersar(-se) **dispersal** (*tb* **dispersion**) *s* dispersão

displace /dɪsˈpleɪs/ *vt* **1** deslocar **2** substituir

display /dɪˈspleɪ/ *vt* **1** expor, exibir (na tela) **2** (*emoção, etc.*) mostrar ● *s* **1** exibição **2** demonstração **3** (*Informát*) (informação apresentada na) tela ▸ **on display** em exposição

disposable /dɪˈspoʊzəbl/ *adj* **1** descartável **2** (*Fin*) disponível

disposal /dɪˈspoʊzl/ *s* **1** eliminação **2** uso **3** (*Com*) venda ▸ **at sb's disposal** à disposição de alguém

disposed /dɪˈspoʊzd/ *adj* disposto: **ill/well ~ towards sb** mal/bem disposto em relação a alguém

disposition /ˌdɪspəˈzɪʃn/ *s* índole, temperamento

disproportionate /ˌdɪsprəˈpɔːrʃənət/ *adj* desproporcional

disprove /ˌdɪsˈpruːv/ *vt* refutar (*teoria, etc.*)

dispute /dɪˈspjuːt/ *s* **1** discussão **2** conflito, controvérsia ▸ **in dispute 1** em discussão **2** (*Jur*) em litígio ● *vt* **1** discutir, colocar em dúvida **2** disputar

disqualify /dɪsˈkwɒlɪfaɪ/ *vt* (*pt, pp* **-ied**) desqualificar: **~ sb from doing sth** impedir alguém de fazer algo

disregard /ˌdɪsrɪˈɡɑːrd/ *vt* ignorar (*conselho, erro*) ● *s* indiferença, desconsideração

disreputable /dɪsˈrepjətəbl/ *adj* **1** de má reputação **2** indecoroso

disrepute /ˌdɪsrɪˈpjuːt/ *s* descrédito

disrespect /ˌdɪsrɪˈspekt/ *s* desrespeito

disrupt /dɪsˈrʌpt/ *vt* (inter)romper **disruption** *s* transtorno, interrupção

disruptive /dɪsˈrʌptɪv/ *adj* destruidor, perturbador

dissatisfaction /ˌdɪsˌsætɪsˈfækʃn/ *s* insatisfação

dissatisfied /dɪˈsætɪsfaɪd/ *adj* insatisfeito

dissent /dɪˈsent/ *s* discordância **dissenting** *adj* discordante, contrário

dissertation /ˌdɪsərˈteɪʃn/ *s* dissertação

dissident /ˈdɪsɪdənt/ *adj, s* dissidente

dissimilar /dɪˈsɪmɪlər/ *adj* diferente

dissociate /dɪˈsoʊʃieɪt/ *vt* **1 ~ yourself from sb/sth** desligar-se de alguém/algo **2** desassociar

dissolve /dɪˈzɒlv/ **1** *vt* dissolver(-se) **2** *vi* desvanecer(-se)

dissuade /dɪˈsweɪd/ *vt* dissuadir

distance /ˈdɪstəns/ *s* distância: **in the ~** ao longe ● *vt* distanciar **distant** *adj* distante

distaste /dɪsˈteɪst/ *s* **~ (for sb/sth)** aversão (a alguém/algo) **distasteful** *adj* desagradável

distill (*GB* **distil**) /dɪˈstɪl/ *vt* (**-ll-**) destilar **distillery** *s* destilaria

distinct /dɪˈstɪŋkt/ *adj* **1** claro, nítido **2** distinto: **as ~ from sth** em contraposição a algo **distinction** *s* **1** distinção **2** honra **distinctive** *adj* peculiar

distinguish /dɪˈstɪŋɡwɪʃ/ **1** *vt, vi* distinguir **2** **~ yourself** destacar-se

distort /dɪˈstɔːrt/ *vt* distorcer, deformar **distortion** *s* distorção

distract /dɪˈstrækt/ *vt* desviar a atenção de **distracted** *adj* distraído, preocupado **distraction** *s* distração: **drive sb to ~** levar alguém à loucura

distraught /dɪˈstrɔːt/ *adj* consternado

distress /dɪˈstres/ *s* **1** sofrimento **2** desgraça **3 ~ signal** sinal de perigo **distressed** *adj* aflito **distressing** *adj* angustiante

distribute /dɪˈstrɪbjuːt/ *vt* distribuir **distribution** *s* distribuição **distributor** *s* distribuidor/a

district /ˈdɪstrɪkt/ *s* **1** distrito, região **2** zona

distrust /dɪsˈtrʌst/ *s* desconfiança ● *vt* desconfiar de **distrustful** *adj* desconfiado

disturb /dɪsˈtɜːrb/ *vt* perturbar, interromper: **I'm sorry to ~ you.** Desculpe incomodá-lo. **disturbance** *s* **1** perturbação: **cause a ~** perturbar a ordem **2** distúrbio disturbed *adj* perturbado

disturbing *adj* inquietante

disuse /dɪs'juːs/ *s* desuso

disused *adj* abandonado

ditch /dɪtʃ/ *s* valeta ◆ *vt* (*coloq*) abandonar, livrar-se de

dither /'dɪðər/ *vi* (*coloq*) vacilar

ditto /'dɪtoʊ/ *s* idem NOTA Refere-se ao símbolo ("), usado para evitar repetições em listas.

dive /daɪv/ *vi* (*pt* dove *ou* dived (GB) *pp* dived) 1 ~ (down) (for sth) mergulhar (em busca de algo) 2 (*submarino*) submergir 3 (*avião*) picar 4 ~ (into/under sth) meter-se (em/debaixo de algo): ~ *for cover* procurar abrigo (rapidamente) ◆ *s* mergulho

diver *s* mergulhador/a

diverge /daɪ'vɜːrdʒ/ *vi* 1 (*estradas*) separar-se 2 (*fml*) (*opiniões*) divergir divergence *s* divergência divergent *adj* divergente

diverse /daɪ'vɜːrs/ *adj* diversificado diversification *s* diversificação diversify *vt, vi* (*pt, pp -ied*) diversificar(-se)

diversion /daɪ'vɜːrʒn; GB -'vɜːʃn/ *s* 1 desvio 2 distração

diversity /daɪ'vɜːrsəti/ *s* diversidade

divert /daɪ'vɜːrt/ *vt* 1 desviar 2 distrair

divide /dɪ'vaɪd/ 1 *vt* ~ sth (out/up) dividir, repartir algo 2 *vi* ~ (up) into sth dividir-se em algo 3 *vt* separar 4 *vt* ~ sth by sth (*Mat*) dividir algo por algo dividido dividido

divided highway *s* (USA) rodovia

dividend /'dɪvɪdend/ *s* dividendo

divine /dɪ'vaɪn/ *adj* divino

diving /'daɪvɪŋ/ *s* mergulho, salto

diving board *s* trampolim

division /dɪ'vɪʒn/ *s* 1 divisão 2 departamento (*empresa*) divisional *adj* divisório

divorce /dɪ'vɔːrs/ *s* divórcio ◆ *vt* divorciar-se *de*: get divorced divorciar-se divorcé /dɪˌvɔːr'seɪ/ *s* divorciado /dɪˌvɔːr'siː/ *s* divorciado/a

divulge /daɪ'vʌldʒ/ *vt* divulgar

DIY /ˌdiː aɪ 'waɪ/ *abrev* de do it yourself

dizzy /'dɪzi/ *adj* (-ier, -iest) vertiginoso dizziness *s* tontura, vertigem

DJ /'diː dʒeɪ/ *abrev* de disc jockey

do¹ /duː/ (3ª pess sing pres does *pt* did *pp* done)
● *vt, vi* fazer NOTA Usa-se do quando se fala de uma atividade

sem dizer exatamente do que se trata, acompanhado, por exemplo, de palavras como *something*, *nothing*, etc.: *Are you doing anything tomorrow?* Você vai fazer alguma coisa amanhã? ◊ *I've got nothing to do.* Não tenho nada para fazer. ◊ *What can I do for you?* Em que posso servi-lo? ◊ *Do as you please.* Faça como quiser.

● do + the, my, etc. + -ing *vt* (*obrigações*) fazer: *do the washing up* lavar (a) louça ◊ *do the ironing* passar (a) roupa

● do + (the, my, etc.) + substantivo *vt*: *do a test/a course* (GB) fazer uma prova/um curso ◊ *do business* fazer negócios ◊ *do your duty* cumprir sua obrigação ◊ *do your hair/have your hair done* fazer um penteado/ir ao cabeleireiro

● outros usos 1 *vt*: *do your best* fazer o melhor possível ◊ *do good* fazer o bem 2 *vi* servir, bastar: *Will $10 do?* $10 será suficiente? 3 *vi*: *Will Friday do?* Pode ser na sexta? 4 *vi*: *He did badly on the test.* Ele foi mal no exame.

▶ be/have to do with sb/sth ter a ver com alguém/algo *it/that will never/won't do*: *It (simply) won't do.* Não pode ser. ◊ *It would never do to...* Não daria para... that does it (*coloq*) chega *that's done it* (GB, *coloq*) era só o que faltava *that will do* basta NOTA Para outras expressões com do, ver os verbetes do substantivo, adjetivo, etc., p. ex. do your bit em BIT. ■ do away with sth desfazer-se de algo, abolir algo do sth up 1 abotoar, fechar algo (*roupas*) 2 (GB) embrulhar algo 3 (GB) reformar algo (*casa*) do with sb/sth 1 *We could do with a holiday.* Umas férias não fariam bem. 2 *She won't have anything to do with him.* Ela não quer nada com ele. do without (sb/sth) passar sem (alguém/algo) NOTA Ver exemplos em MAKE.

● *v aux* NOTA Não se traduz o auxiliar do, pois indica apenas o tempo e/ou a pessoa do verbo principal da oração.

● orações interrogativas e negativas: *Do you speak French?* Você fala francês? ◊ *She didn't go to Paris.* Ela não foi a Paris.

● question tags 1 [*oração afirmativa*] [*do + n*t + sujeito (*pron pessoal*)]: *John lives here, doesn't he?* John mora aqui, não mora/não é? 2 [*oração* *negativa*]: **do + sujeito (pron pessoal)?:** *Mary doesn't know, does she?* Mary não sabe, sabe? **3** [*oração afirmativa*]: **do + sujeito (pron pessoal)?:** *You told them, did you?* Você contou para eles, não é?

• **em afirmativas com uso enfático:** *He does look tired.* Ele parece realmente cansado. ◊ *Oh, do be quiet!* Ah, fique quieto!

• **para evitar repetições:** *She knows more than he does.* Ela sabe mais do que ele. ◊ *"Who won?" "I did."* —Quem ganhou? —Eu. —Eu. ◊ *Peter didn't go and neither did I.* Peter não foi e eu também não.

do² /duː/ s (pl **dos** ou **do's** /duːz/) ▸ **do's and don'ts** regras

docile /ˈdɒsaɪl/ adj **dóceis** /ˈdɒsaɪl/ adj

dock /dɒk/ s **1** doca **2** (GB) banco dos réus • vt, vi (*Náut*) atracar **2** vi chegar de barco **3** vt, vi (*Aeronáut*) acoplar(-se) **4** vt reduzir **5** vt cortar

doctor /ˈdɒktər/ s (*abrev* **Dr.**) **1** médico/a **2** ~ **(of sth)** (*título*) doutor/a (em algo) • vt (*coloq*) **1** falsificar **2** alterar

doctorate /ˈdɒktərət/ s doutorado

doctrine /ˈdɒktrɪn/ s doutrina

document /ˈdɒkjumənt/ s documento • vt documentar

documentary /ˌdɒkjuˈmentəri/ adj documental • s (pl **-ies**) documentário

dodge /dɒdʒ/ vt, vi esquivar-se: ~ *awkward questions* fugir de perguntas embaraçosas

dodgy /ˈdɒdʒi/ adj (-ier, -iest) (GB, coloq) suspeito: *a ~ situation* uma situação delicada ◊ *a ~ wheel* uma roda defeituosa

doe /dəʊ/ s cerva, rena, lebre (fêmea) → COELHO, VEADO

does /dəz, dʌz/ *Ver* DO

doesn't /ˈdʌznt/ = DOES NOT *Ver* DO

dog /dɒɡ/ s cachorro • vt (-gg-) perseguir

dogged /ˈdɒɡɪd/ adj tenaz **doggedly** adv tenazmente

doggie (*tb* **doggy**) /ˈdɒɡi/ GB /ˈdɒɡi/ s (coloq) cachorrinho

dogsbody /ˈdɒɡzbɒdi/ GB /ˈdɒɡ-/ s (pl **-ies**) (GB) pau para toda obra

do it yourself s faça-você-mesmo

the dole /dəʊl/ s (GB, coloq) seguro-desemprego: *on the ~* desempregado

doll /dɒl/ s boneca

dollar /ˈdɒlər/ s dólar

dolly /ˈdɒli/ s (pl **-ies**) bonequinha

dolphin /ˈdɒlfɪn/ s golfinho

domain /dəʊˈmeɪn/ s **1** propriedade, domínio **2** campo (de conhecimento): *outside my ~* fora de minha competência

dome /dəʊm/ s cúpula, abóbada **domed** adj abobadado

domestic /dəˈmestɪk/ adj **1** doméstico **2** nacional **domesticated** adj **1** domesticado **2** caseiro

dominant /ˈdɒmɪnənt/ adj dominante **dominance** s predominância

dominate /ˈdɒmɪneɪt/ vt, vi dominar **domination** s domínio, dominação

domineering /ˌdɒmɪˈnɪərɪŋ/ adj dominador

dominion /dəˈmɪniən/ s domínio

domino /ˈdɒmɪnəʊ/ s (pl **~es**) (pedra de) dominó: *play dominoes* jogar dominó

donate /dəʊˈneɪt/ GB /dəʊˈneɪt/ vt doar **donation** s **1** donativo **2** doação

done /dʌn/ pp de DO¹ • adj pronto (*comida, etc.*)

donkey /ˈdɒŋki, ˈdɔːn-/ s asno

donor /ˈdəʊnər/ s doador/a

don't /dəʊnt/ = DO NOT *Ver* DO¹

donut /ˈdəʊnʌt/ s sonho (*doce*)

doom /duːm/ s **1** (*fml*) perdição: *send sb to his ~* condenar alguém à morte **2** pessimismo **doomed** adj condenado

door /dɔːr/ s porta ▸ **(from) door to door** de casa em casa: *door-to-door salesman* vendedor ambulante ▸ **out of doors** ao ar livre

doorbell /ˈdɔːrbel/ s campainha (*porta*)

doormat /ˈdɔːrmæt/ s capacho

doorstep /ˈdɔːrstep/ s degrau da porta ▸ **on your doorstep** a um passo (da sua casa)

doorway /ˈdɔːrweɪ/ (*tb* **door**) s vão (porta)

dope /dəʊp/ s (coloq) **1** imbecil **2** (*droga*) fumo • vt dopar, drogar

dope test s teste antidoping

dormant /ˈdɔːrmənt/ adj inativo

dormitory /ˈdɔːrmətɔːri/ GB /-tri/ s (pl **-ies**) (*tb* **dorm**) **1** (USA) residência universitária **2** (GB) dormitório

dosage /ˈdəʊsɪdʒ/ s dosagem

dose /dəʊs/ s dosagem, dose

dot /dɒt/ s ponto ▸ **on the dot**

(*coloq*) na hora exata: *5 o'clock on the* ~ 5 em ponto ● *vt* (**-tt-**) colocar um ponto (sobre), pontilhar ▶ **dot your the i's and cross your/the t's** dar os últimos retoques

dote /doʊt/ *vi* ~ **on sb/sth** adorar alguém/algo **doting** *adj* devotado

double /'dʌbl/ *adj* duplo: ~ *figures* número de dois algarismos ◇ *She earns* ~ *what he does.* Ela ganha o dobro do que ele ganha. ● *adv*: *see* ~ ver em dobro ◇ *bent* ~ curvado/dobrado (em dois) ◇ *fold a blanket* ~ dobrar um cobertor no meio ● *s* **1** dobro, dobro **2** (*Cinema*) dublê **3** (*bebida*) dose dupla **4** (**doubles**) [*pl*] (*Esporte*) duplas ● **1** *vt, vi* duplicar **2** *vt* ~ **sth** (**up/over/across/back**) dobrar algo (em dois) **3** *vi* ~ **as sth** fazer as vezes de algo ■ **be doubled up**: *be doubled up with laughter/pain* morrer de rir/dobrar-se de dor **double back** dar meia volta

double-barrelled *adj* **1** de cano duplo **2** (*GB*) (*sobrenome*) composto

double bass *s Ver* BASS (4)

double bed *s* cama de casal

double-breasted *adj* (*roupa*) transpassado

double-check *vt* verificar novamente

double-cross *vt* enganar

double-decker /ˌdʌbl 'dekər/ *s* (*GB*) ônibus de dois andares

double-edged *adj* **1** de fio duplo **2** de duplo sentido

double glazed *adj* (*GB*) com vidro duplo

double glazing *s* (*GB*) janela com vidro duplo

doubly /'dʌbli/ *adv* duplamente: *make* ~ *sure of sth* tornar a assegurar-se de algo

doubt /daʊt/ *s* dúvida: *in* ~ duvidoso ▶ **beyond a/all/any doubt** sem dúvida alguma; **without (a) doubt** sem dúvida ● *vt, vi* duvidar **doubter** *s* cético/a **doubtless** *adv* sem dúvida

doubtful /'daʊtfl/ *adj* duvidoso, incerto: *be* ~ *about (doing) sth* ter dúvidas quanto a (fazer) algo **doubtfully** *adv* sem convicção

dough /doʊ/ *s* massa

doughnut = DONUT

dour /dʊər/ *adj* severo, austero

douse /daʊs/ *vt* jogar (*água*)

dove¹ /dʌv/ *s* pomba

dove² /doʊv/ (*USA*) *pret de* DIVE

dowdy /'daʊdi/ *adj* (**-ier, -iest**) **1** malvestido **2** sem graça

down /daʊn/ *s* **1** penugem **2** buço ● *prep* abaixo: *run your eyes* ~ *a list* percorrer uma lista de cima a baixo ◇ ~ *the corridor on the right* descendo o corredor, à direita ● *adv* **1** para baixo: *Inflation is* ~ *this month.* A inflação abaixou este mês. **2** *I'm $50* ~. Estou com 50 dólares a menos. ◇ *Ten* ~, *five to go.* Dez a menos, faltam cinco. **3** (*Informát*): *The computer's* ~. O computador teve uma pane. ▶ **be/feel down** (*coloq*) sentir-se deprimido **down with sb/sth** abaixo alguém/algo NOTA Para o uso de **down** em PHRASAL VERBS, ver o verbo, por exemplo, go **down** em GO.

down and out *s* mendigo/a

downcast /'daʊnkæst; *GB* -kɑːst/ *adj* deprimido

downfall /'daʊnfɔːl/ *s* queda: *Drink will be your* ~. A bebida será sua ruína.

downgrade /'daʊngreɪd/ *vt* rebaixar

downhearted /ˌdaʊn'hɑːtɪd/ *adj* desanimado

downhill /ˌdaʊn'hɪl/ *adv, adj* morro abaixo ▶ **be (all) downhill (from here/there)** ser moleza (de agora/dali em diante) **go downhill** ir de mal a pior, decair

download /ˌdaʊn'loʊd/ *vt* (*Informát*) baixar

downmarket /ˌdaʊn'mɑːkɪt/ *adj* de massa, vulgar

downpour /'daʊnpɔːr/ *s* toró

downright /'daʊnraɪt/ *adj* total ● *adv* completamente

downside /'daʊnsaɪd/ *s* desvantagem

Down's syndrome *s* síndrome de Down

downstairs /ˌdaʊn'steərz/ *adv* (*escadas*) em/para baixo ● *adj* no andar de baixo ● *s* [*sing*] andar(es) inferior(es)

downstream /ˌdaʊn'striːm/ *adv* rio abaixo

down-to-earth *adj* prático

downtown /ˌdaʊn'taʊn/ *adv* (*esp USA*) ao/no centro (da cidade)

downtrodden /'daʊntrɒdn/ *adj* oprimido

downturn /'daʊntɜːn/ *s* queda

downward /'daʊnwərd/ *adj* para baixo: ~ *tendência* tendência a baixar ● *adv* (*tb* **downwards**) para baixo

downy /'daʊni/ *adj* coberto por

penugem/buço

dowry /'dauri/ s (pl **-ies**) dote (de casamento)

doze /dəuz/ vi dormitar ■ **doze off** cochilar ● s cochilo

dozen /'dʌzn/ s (abrev **doz**) dúzia

dozy /'dəuzi/ adj (-ier, -iest) (GB) sonolento

drab /dræb/ adj monótono, sem graça

draft /dræft; GB drɑːft/ s **1** esboço, rascunho: ~ *bill* (ante)projeto de lei **2** (Fin) ordem de pagamento, letra de câmbio **3** (**the draft**) (USA) a convocação (para o Exército) **4** corrente (de ar) ● adj de barril: ~ *beer* chope ● vt **1** esboçar, rascunhar **2** ~ *sb/sth* (**in**) (tb Mil) convocar alguém/algo

draftsman /'dræftsmən; GB 'drɑːfts-/ s (pl **-men**) desenhista

drafty /'dræfti/ adj (-ier, -iest) com muita corrente (de ar)

drag /dræg/ (**-gg-**) **1** vt, vi ~ (**on**) arrastar(-se) **2** vi (tempo) passar lentamente **3** vt (Náut) dragar ● s **1** (**a drag**) (coloq) peso, chato/a **2** (coloq): *man dressed in ~* homem vestido de mulher

dragon /'drægən/ s dragão

dragonfly /'drægənflaɪ/ s libélula

drain /dreɪn/ s **1** esgoto **2** bueiro ► **be a drain on sth** consumir/ exaurir algo ● vt **1** (pratos, etc.) escorrer **2** drenar ● **be/feel drained** estar/sentir-se esgotado ■ **drain away 1** perder-se **2** consumir-se (lentamente)

drainage s drenagem

draining board s superfície para escorrer louça

drainpipe /'dreɪnpaɪp/ s cano de esgoto

drama /'drɑːmə/ s **1** peça de teatro **2** teatro: ~ *school/student* escola/estudante de arte dramática **3** drama **dramatic** /drə'mætɪk/ adj dramático **dramatically** adv radicalmente

dramatist /'dræmətɪst/ s dramaturgo/a **dramatization** s dramatização **dramatize** vt, vi dramatizar

drank /dræŋk/ pret de DRINK

drape /dreɪp/ vt **1** ~ *sth* **across/ around/over sth** (tecido) jogar algo sobre algo **2** ~ *sb/sth* (**in/ with sth**) cobrir, envolver alguém/algo (com/em algo) **drapes** (tb **draperies**) s cortinas

drastic /'dræstɪk/ adj **1** drástico **2** grave **drastically** adv drasticamente

draught (GB) = DRAFT **draughty** (GB) = DRAFTY

draughts /drɑːfts/ (GB) (jogo de) damas

draughtsman (GB) = DRAFTS-MAN

draw /drɔː/ s **1** (GB) [gen sing] sorteio **2** (GB) empate ● (pt **drew** pp **drawn**) **1** vt, vi desenhar, traçar **2** vi: ~ *level with sb* alcançar alguém ◊ ~ *near* aproximar-se **3** vt (cortinas) correr **4** vt tirar: ~ *comfort/ inspiration from sth* consolar-se com/inspirar-se em algo ◊ ~ *a distinction* fazer uma distinção ◊ ~ *an analogy* estabelecer uma analogia **5** vt (salário, etc.) receber **6** vt provocar, causar **7** vt ~ *sb* (**to sb/sth**) atrair alguém (para alguém/algo) **8** vi (Esporte) empatar ■ **draw back** retroceder, retirar-se **draw sth back** retirar, puxar algo **draw in** (GB) (trem) entrar na estação **draw on/upon sth** fazer uso de algo **draw out 1** (dia) alongar-se **2** (GB) (trem) sair da estação **draw up** estacionar **draw sth up 1** redigir/preparar algo **2** aproximar algo

drawback /'drɔːbæk/ s ~ (**of/to** (**doing**) **sth**) inconveniente, desvantagem de (fazer) algo

drawer /drɔːr/ s gaveta

drawing /'drɔːɪŋ/ s **1** desenho, esboço **2** sorteio

drawing pin s (GB) tachinha

drawing room s (GB, antiq) sala de visitas

drawl /drɔːl/ s fala arrastada

drawn /drɔːn/ pp de DRAW ● adj contraído, tenso

dread /dred/ s terror ● vt temer **dreadful** adj **1** terrível, espantoso **2** péssimo, horrível: *How ~!* Que horror! **dreadfully** adv **1** terrivelmente **2** muito: *I'm ~ sorry.* Sinto muitíssimo.

dream /driːm/ s sonho: *have a ~ about sth* sonhar com algo ● (pt, pp **dreamt** /dremt/ ou **dreamed**) **1** vt, vi ~ (**about/of** (**doing**) **sth**) sonhar (com algo/em fazer algo) **2** vt imaginar **NOTA** Alguns verbos possuem formas regulares e irregulares para o pretérito e o particípio passado: **spell**: **spelled/spelt**, **spill**: **spilled/spilt**, etc. No inglês britânico, preferem-se as formas irregulares; no inglês americano, as regulares. **dreamer** s sonhador/a **dreamy** adj (-ier, -iest) **1** sonhador, distraído

2 vago dreamily *adv* distraidamente

dreary /'drɪəri/ *adj* (**-ier**, **-iest**) **1** deprimente **2** chato

dredge /dredʒ/ *vt, vi* dragar dredge(r) *s* draga

drench /drentʃ/ *vt* ensopar: *be drenched to the skin/drenched through* molhar-se até os ossos/encharcar-se

dress /dres/ *s* **1** vestido **2** [U] roupa • **1** *vt, vi* vestir-se: *dressed in sth* vestido com/de algo NOTA Para o ato de vestir-se, diz-se **get dressed**. **2** *vt* colocar curativo **3** *vt* (*salada*) temperar ■ **dress (sb) up** as **sb/sth**) fantasiar-se, fantasiar alguém de alguém/algo **dress sth up** disfarçar algo **dress up** arrumar-se

dress circle *s* (*GB*) (*Teat*) balcão nobre

dresser /'dresər/ *s* **1** armário de cozinha **2** (*USA*) (*GB* **dressing table**) cômoda

dressing /'dresɪŋ/ *s* **1** curativo **2** tempero (de salada)

dressing gown *s* roupão

dressing room *s* vestiário, camarim

dressmaker /'dresmeɪkər/ (*tb* **dress designer**) *s* costureira dressmaking *s* corte e costura

dress rehearsal *s* (*Teat*) ensaio geral

drew /druː/ *pret* de DRAW

dribble /'drɪbl/ **1** *vi* babar **2** *vt, vi* driblar

dried /draɪd/ *pret, pp* de DRY • *adj* seco

drier = DRYER

drift /drɪft/ *vi* **1** flutuar **2** (*areia, neve*) amontoar-se **3** ir à deriva: *~ into (doing) sth* fazer algo por acaso/inércia • *s* [U] idéia geral drifter *s* vagabundo/a

drill /drɪl/ • *s* **1** broca: *power ~* furadeira elétrica **2** treinamento (de rotina) **3** exercício (repetitivo) • *vt* **1** furar, perfurar **2** treinar

drily = DRYLY

drink /drɪŋk/ *s* bebida: *a ~ of water* um gole d'água ◊ *go for a ~* sair para beber ◊ *soft ~* refresco/refrigerante • *vt, vi* (*pt* **drank** *pp* **drunk**) beber: *~ (a toast) to sb/sth* fazer um brinde a alguém/algo ▸ **drink (to) sb's health** beber à saúde de alguém ■ **drink sth down/up** beber de um trago/gole **drink sth in** absorver algo drinker *s* bebedor/a drinking *s* a bebida, o consumo de álcool

drinking water *s* água potável

drip /drɪp/ *vi* (**-pp-**) pingar, gotejar: *be dripping with sth* estar molhado/coberto de algo • *s* **1** gota, gotejar **2** (*Med*) tubo (para soro)

drive /draɪv/ • *vt, vi* (*pt* **drove** *pp* **driven** /'drɪvn/) **1** *vt, vi* dirigir **2** *vi* andar de carro: *~ away/off* ir embora de carro **3** *vt* levar (de carro) **4** *vt*: *~ cattle* conduzir gado ◊ *~ sb crazy* deixar alguém louco ◊ *~ sb to drink* levar alguém à bebida **5** *vt* forçar: *~ sb on* impulsionar alguém ▸ **be driving at sth**: *What are you driving at?* O que você está insinuando? **drive a hard bargain** negociar duro ■ **drive sb/sth back/off** afugentar alguém/algo • *s* **1** passeio, viagem (*de carro*): *go for a ~* dar uma volta de carro **2** entrada da garagem (*em uma casa*) **3** impulso **4** campanha **5** (*Mec*) mecanismo de transmissão: *four-wheel ~* tração nas quatro rodas ◊ *left-hand ~ car* carro com o volante à esquerda **6** (*Informát*): *disk/hard ~* unidade de disco/disco rígido

drive-in *s* (*USA*) drive-in

driver /'draɪvər/ *s* motorista: *train ~* maquinista ▸ **be in the driver's seat** estar no controle

driver's license (*GB* **driving licence**) *s* carteira de motorista

driveway /'draɪvweɪ/ *s* entrada da garagem (*em uma casa*)

driving school *s* auto-escola

driving test *s* exame para tirar carteira

drizzle /'drɪzl/ *s* garoa • *vi* garoar

drone /droʊn/ *vi* zumbir: *~ on about sth* falar sobre algo em tom monótono • *s* zumbido

drool /druːl/ *vi* **~ (over sb/sth)** babar por alguém/algo

droop /druːp/ *vi* **1** pender **2** (*flor*) murchar **3** desanimar drooping (*tb* **droopy**) *adj* **1** penso, caído **2** (*flor*) murcho

drop /drɑp/ *s* **1** gota, pingo: *a ~ of wine* um pouquinho de vinho **2** [*sing*] queda: *a sheer ~* um precipício ▸ **at the drop of a hat** sem pensar duas vezes **(only) a drop in the bucket** apenas uma gota no oceano • (**-pp-**) **1** *vi* cair: *I feel ready to ~.* Estou morto de cansaço. ◊ *work till you ~* matar-se de trabalhar **2** *vt* deixar cair, derrubar: *~ anchor* lançar âncora **3** *vt, vi* diminuir, reduzir **4** *vt ~ sb/sth (off)* deixar alguém/algo em algum lugar **5** *vt* excluir

6 vt ~ sb romper relações com alguém **7** vt ~ sth (*hábito, etc.*) deixar (de fazer) algo: *Can we ~ the subject?* Vamos mudar de assunto? ▸ **drop a hint (to sb)/ drop (sb) a hint** dar uma indireta (a alguém) **drop dead** (*coloq*) cair morto: *Drop dead!* Vá pro inferno! **drop sb a line** (*coloq*) mandar uma carta a alguém ∎ **drop back/behind** ficar para trás **drop by/in/over:** *Why don't you ~ by?* Por que você não dá um pulo lá em casa? ◇ ~ *in for lunch* passar para o almoço **drop in on sb** fazer uma visitinha a alguém **drop off** (*coloq*) cochilar **drop out (of sth)** retirar-se de algo: ~ *out of (college/society)* sair da universidade/afastar-se da sociedade

dropout /'drɒpaʊt/ s **1** marginal **2** estudante que abandona os estudos

droppings /'drɒpɪŋz/ s [*pl*] excremento (*animais*)

drought /draʊt/ s seca

drove /drəʊv/ *pret de* DRIVE

drown /draʊn/ vt, vi afogar(-se) ∎ **drown sb/sth out** encobrir alguém/algo: *drowned out by the music* abafado pela música

drowsy /'draʊzi/ adj (-**ier**, -**iest**) sonolento

drudgery /'drʌdʒəri/ s [U] trabalho monótono

drug /drʌg/ s **1** remédio, medicamento: ~ *company* empresa farmacêutica **2** droga: ~ *abuse* uso de drogas ● vt (-**gg**-) drogar

drugstore /'drʌgstɔːr/ s (*USA*) farmácia que também vende lanches, etc.

drum /drʌm/ s **1** (*Mús*) tambor, bateria **2** barril ● (-**mm**-) **1** tocar tambor, batucar **2** vt, vi ~ (**sth**) **on sth** tamborilar (com algo) em algo ∎ **drum sth into sb/ into sb's head** martelar algo na cabeça de alguém **drum sb out (of sth)** expulsar alguém (de algo) **drum sth up** lutar para conseguir algo (*apoio, etc.*): ~ *up interest in sth* levantar o interesse em algo **drummer** s baterista

drumstick /'drʌmstɪk/ s **1** (*Mús*) baqueta **2** (*Cozinha*) perna (*frango*)

drunk /drʌŋk/ pp *de* DRINK ● adj bêbado: ~ *with joy* ébrio de felicidade ◇ *get* ~ embriagar-se ▸ **drunk and disorderly:** *charged with being* ~ *and disorderly* acusado de embriaguez e mau comportamento ● s (*tb* **drunkard**) bêbado/a

drunken /'drʌŋkən/ adj bêbado: ~ *driving* dirigir embriagado **drunkenness** s embriaguez

dry /draɪ/ adj (**drier**, **driest**) **1** seco: *Today will be ~.* Hoje não vai chover. **2** árido **3** (*humor*) irônico ● vt, vi (*pt, pp* **dried**) ~ (**sth**) (**out/up**) secar, enxugar algo; secar-se

dry-clean vt lavar a seco **dry-cleaner's** s tinturaria **dry-cleaning** s lavagem a seco

dryer /'draɪər/ s secador

dry land s terra firme

dryly /'draɪli/ adv secamente

dryness /'draɪnəs/ s **1** secura **2** aridez **3** ironia

dual /'duːəl; *GB* 'djuːəl/ adj duplo **dual carriageway** s (*GB*) rodovia

dub /dʌb/ vt (-**bb**-) dublar **dubbing** s dublagem

dubious /'duːbiəs; *GB* 'djuː-/ adj **1** be ~ about sth ter dúvidas a respeito de algo **2** (*attitude*) suspeito **3** (*honra*) duvidoso **dubiously** adv **1** de maneira suspeita **2** em tom duvidoso

duchess (*tb* **Duchess** *em títulos*) /'dʌtʃəs/ s duquesa

duck /dʌk/ s pato → PATO ● **1** vi abaixar(-se) (a cabeça) **2** vt mergulhar: ~ *sb* dar caldo em alguém **3** vt, vi ~ (**out of**) **sth** livrar-se de algo

duct /dʌkt/ s **1** (*Anat*) canal **2** (*gás, etc.*) tubo

dud /dʌd/ adj (*coloq*) **1** defeituoso **2** inutilizável **3** (*cheque*) sem fundos ● s (*coloq*): *This battery is a ~.* Esta pilha está com defeito.

due /duː; *GB* djuː/ adj **1** ~ (**to sb/ sth**) devido (a alguém/algo): *Our thanks are ~ to...* Devemos nossos agradecimentos a... ◇ *It's all ~ to her efforts.* Tudo se deve a seus esforços. **2** *She's ~ back soon.* Ela deve chegar logo. ◇ *Payment is ~ on the fifth.* O pagamento vence no dia cinco. **3** ~ (**for**) **sth**: *I'm ~ (for) a holiday.* Mereço umas férias. ▸ **in due course** em seu devido tempo ● **dues** s [*pl*] cota ▸ **give sb their due** ser justo com alguém ● adv: ~ *south* exatamente ao/para o sul

duel /'duːəl; *GB* 'djuːəl/ s duelo

duet /du'et; *GB* dju'et/ s (*Mús*) duo

duffel coat /'dʌfl kəʊt/ s (*GB*) casaco de lã (*com capuz*)

dug /dʌg/ *pret, pp de* DIG

duke (tb **Duke** em títulos) /duːk; GB djuːk/ s duque

dull /dʌl/ adj (~er, ~est) 1 nublado 2 (cor) apagado, opaco 3 (luz) sombrio: a ~ glow um brilho amortecido 4 (ruído) abafado 5 (dor) indefinido 6 chato, monótono **dully** adv desanimadamente

duly /ˈduːli; GB ˈdjuːli/ adv 1 devidamente 2 no tempo devido

dumb /dʌm/ adj (~er, ~est) 1 (coloq) bobo 2 mudo **dumbly** adv sem falar

dumbfounded (tb dumfounded) /dʌmˈfaʊndɪd/ (tb dumbstruck /ˈdʌmstrʌk/) adj atônito

dummy /ˈdʌmi/ s (pl -ies) 1 manequim 2 imitação 3 (GB) chupeta 4 (coloq) imbecil ● adj falso: ~ run ensaio

dump /dʌmp/ vt, vi 1 jogar (fora), despejar 2 (coloq) abandonar 3 desfazer-se de ● s 1 depósito (de lixo) 2 (coloq) espelunca

dumpling /ˈdʌmplɪŋ/ s bolinho de massa cozido

dumps /dʌmps/ s [pl] ▸ (down) in the dumps (coloq) deprimido

dune /duːn; GB djuːn/ s duna

dung /dʌŋ/ s esterco

dungarees /ˌdʌŋɡəˈriːz/ s [pl] jardineira (roupa)

dungeon /ˈdʌndʒən/ s masmorra

duo /ˈduːəʊ; GB ˈdjuːəʊ/ s (pl ~s) duo

dupe /duːp; GB djuːp/ vt enganar

duplicate /ˈduːplɪkeɪt; GB ˈdjuː-/ vt 1 copiar 2 repetir ● /ˈduːplɪkət; GB ˈdjuː-/ adj, s duplicado: ~ (letter) cópia (da carta)

durable /ˈdʊərəbl; GB ˈdjʊə-/ adj durável ● (consumer) durables s eletrodomésticos **durability** /ˌdʊərəˈbɪləti; GB ˌdjʊə-/ s durabilidade

duration /duˈreɪʃn; GB djuː-/ s duração ▸ for the duration (coloq) pelo tempo que durar

duress /dʊˈres; GB djuː-/ s: under ~ sob coação

during /ˈdʊərɪŋ; GB ˈdjʊər-/ prep durante → DURANTE

dusk /dʌsk/ s crepúsculo: at ~ ao anoitecer

dusky /ˈdʌski/ adj (-ier, -iest) moreno

dust /dʌst/ s pó ● 1 vt, vi ~ (sb/sth down/off) tirar (o) pó (de alguém/algo) 2 vt ~ sth with sth polvilhar algo com algo

dustbin /ˈdʌstbɪn/ (GB) Ver BIN (2)

dustcloth /ˈdʌstklɔːθ/ s pano de pó

dustman /ˈdʌstmən/ s (pl -men) (GB) lixeiro

dustpan /ˈdʌstpæn/ s pá de lixo

dusty /ˈdʌsti/ adj (-ier, -iest) empoeirado

Dutch /dʌtʃ/ adj ▸ Dutch courage (coloq) coragem causada por bebida **go Dutch (with sb)** dividir a conta (com alguém)

dutiful /ˈduːtɪfl; GB ˈdjuː-/ adj (fml) obediente

duty /ˈduːti; GB ˈdjuːti/ s (pl -ies) 1 dever, obrigação 2 função: ~ officer oficial de plantão ◇ be on/off ~ estar/não estar de plantão/serviço 3 ~ (on sth) imposto sobre algo

duty-free adj isento (de impostos de importação)

duvet /ˈduːveɪ; GB ˈduːveɪ/ s edredom

dwarf /dwɔːrf/ s (pl ~s ou dwarves /dwɔːrvz/) anão ● vt tornar menor: a house dwarfed by skyscrapers uma casa apequenada pelos arranha-céus

dwell /dwel/ vi (pt, pp dwelled ou dwelt /dwelt/ (GB)) (antiq) morar ▪ dwell on/upon sth 1 insistir em algo, estender-se sobre algo (assunto) 2 deixar-se obcecar por algo **dwelling** (tb dwelling place) s residência

dwindle /ˈdwɪndl/ vi diminuir, reduzir-se

dye /daɪ/ vt, vi (3ª pess sing pres dyes pt, pp dyed part pres dyeing) tingir ● s corante

dying /ˈdaɪɪŋ/ adj 1 (pessoa) agonizante 2 (palavras, etc.) último: a ~ breed uma espécie em extinção

dynamic /daɪˈnæmɪk/ adj dinâmico

dynamics /daɪˈnæmɪks/ s [pl] dinâmica

dynamism /ˈdaɪnəmɪzəm/ s dinamismo

dynamite /ˈdaɪnəmaɪt/ s dinamite ● vt dinamitar

dynamo /ˈdaɪnəməʊ/ s (pl ~s) dínamo

dynasty /ˈdaɪnəsti; GB ˈdɪ-/ s (pl -ies) dinastia

dysentery /ˈdɪsənteri; GB -tri/ s disenteria

dyslexia /dɪsˈleksiə/ s dislexia **dyslexic** adj, s disléxico/a

dystrophy /ˈdɪstrəfi/ s distrofia

Ee

E, e /iː/ s (pl **E's**, **e's** /iːz/) **1 E**, **e 2** (GB) (Educ) (nota) E **3** (Mús) mi

each /iːtʃ/ adj cada NOTA Geralmente se traduz **each** como "cada (um/uma)" e **every** como "todo(s)". Uma exceção importante ocorre quando se expressa a repetição de algo em intervalos fixos de tempo: The Olympics are held every four years. → EVERY ● pron cada um (de dois ou mais): ~ for himself cada um por si ● adv cada (um de): We have two ~. Temos dois cada um.

each other pron um ao outro (mutuamente)

eager /'iːgər/ adj **1** ~ (for sth/to do sth) ávido (por algo); ansioso (para fazer algo): ~ to please preocupado em agradar **eagerly** adv com impaciência **eagerness** s ânsia, entusiasmo

eagle /'iːgl/ s águia

ear /ɪər/ s **1** orelha → ARM **2** ouvido **3** espiga ▶ be all ears (coloq) ser todo ouvidos up to your ears in sth até o pescoço de/com algo

earache /'ɪəreɪk/ s dor de ouvido

eardrum /'ɪərdrʌm/ s tímpano

earl /ɜːrl/ s conde

early /'ɜːrli/ (-ier, -iest) adj **1** precoce **2** (morte) prematuro **3** antecipado **4** ~ memory recordação antiga ◇ at an ~ age cedo (na vida) ◇ He's in his ~ twenties. Ele tem pouco mais de 20 anos. ● adv **1** (mais) cedo: as ~ as 1988 já em 1988 **2** prematuramente **3** ~ last week no começo da semana passada ▶ at the earliest não antes de early bird madrugador: The ~ bird gets the worm. Deus ajuda quem cedo madruga. early on logo no começo: earlier on anteriormente it's early days (yet) (esp GB) é muito cedo ainda the early hours a madrugada

earmark /'ɪərmɑːrk/ vt destinar

earn /ɜːrn/ vt **1** (dinheiro) ganhar **2** render (juros, etc.) **3** merecer

earnest /'ɜːrnɪst/ adj **1** (caráter) sério **2** (desejo, etc.) fervoroso ▶ in earnest **1** de verdade **2** a sério **earnestly** adv com empenho **earnestness** s fervor, seriedade

earnings /'ɜːrnɪŋz/ s ganhos

earphones /'ɪərfoʊnz/ s fones de ouvido

earring /'ɪərɪŋ/ s brinco

earshot /'ɪərʃɑːt/ s ▶ out of/within earshot longe/perto dos ouvidos (de alguém)

earth /ɜːrθ/ s **1** (the Earth) a Terra **2** (Geol) terra **3** (Elet) fio terra ▶ charge/cost/pay the earth (GB, coloq) cobrar/custar/pagar uma fortuna come back/down to earth (with a bang/bump) (coloq) colocar os pés no chão how/what, etc. on earth (coloq): What on ~ are you doing? Que diabo você está fazendo? ● vt (GB) (Elet) ligar o fio terra

earthly /'ɜːrθli/ adj **1** terreno **2** (coloq) possível: You haven't an ~ chance of winning. Você não tem a mais remota possibilidade de vencer.

earthquake /'ɜːrθkweɪk/ s terremoto

earthworm /'ɜːrθwɜːrm/ s minhoca

ease /iːz/ s **1** facilidade **2** conforto **3** alívio ▶ at (your) ease à vontade ● vt **1** aliviar: ~ sb's conscience/mind tranqüilizar (a consciência/mente de) alguém **2** reduzir, diminuir **3** amenizar **4** vt (restrição) afrouxar ▶ ease (sb/sth) across, along, etc. sth mover (alguém/algo) cuidadosamente através, ao longo de algo ease off/up tornar-se menos intenso ease up on sb/sth ser mais moderado com alguém/algo

easel /'iːzl/ s (Arte) cavalete

easily /'iːzəli/ adv **1** facilmente **2** certamente **3** muito provavelmente

east /iːst/ s **1** (tb the east, the East) (abrev E.) (o) leste: eastbound em direção ao leste **2** (the East) (o) Oriente ● adj (do) leste ● adv para o leste

Easter /'iːstər/ s Páscoa

eastern (tb Eastern) /'iːstərn/ adj (do) leste, oriental

eastward(s) /'iːstwərd(z)/ adv em direção ao leste

easy /'iːzi/ (-ier, -iest) adj **1** fácil **2** tranqüilo ▶ I'm easy (coloq, esp GB) tanto faz (para mim) ● adv ▶ easier said than done fácil de falar, fazer é que é difícil go easy on/with sb/sth (coloq) ir devagar com alguém/algo take it easy calma take things easy relaxar

easygoing /ˌiːziˈgoʊɪŋ/ adj tolerante, fácil de lidar

eat /iːt/ *vt, vi* (*pt* **ate** *pp* **eaten** /ˈiːtn/) comer: ~ *out* comer fora ▸ **be eaten up with sth** estar/estar tomado por algo **eat sb eating sb**: *What's eating you?* O que está atormentando você? **eat out of sb's hand**: *She had him eating out of her hand.* Ela o tinha na palma da mão. **eat your words** engolir suas palavras/o que disse ▪ **eat away at sth/eat sth away 1** erodir algo **2** consumir algo **eat into sth 1** corroer, desgastar algo **2** consumir algo (*reservas*) **eat (sth) up** comer tudo **eat sth up** devorar algo: *This car eats up gas!* Este carro bebe um monte de gasolina. **eater** *s: He's a big* ~. Ele é um comilão.

eavesdrop /ˈiːvzdrɒp/ *vi* (**-pp-**) ~ **(on sb/sth)** escutar escondido (alguém/algo)

ebb /eb/ *vi* ~ **(away) 1** (*maré*) baixar **2** diminuir ● **the ebb** *s* a vazante ▸ **on the ebb** em decadência ■ **the ebb and flow (of sth)** o ir e vir (de algo)

ebony /ˈebəni/ *s* ébano

echo /ˈekoʊ/ *s* (*pl* **~es**) **1** eco **2** arremedo ● *vt* ~ **1** (*back*) repetir, refletir algo **2** *vi* ecoar

ecological /ˌiːkəˈlɒdʒɪkl/ *adj* ecológico **ecologically** *adv* ecologicamente

ecology /iːˈkɒlədʒi/ *s* ecologia **ecologist** *s* ecologista

economic /ˌiːkəˈnɒmɪk, ˌekə-/ *adj* **1** (*política, etc.*) econômico **2** rentável

economical /ˌiːkəˈnɒmɪkl, ˌekə-/ *adj* (*aparelho, etc.*) econômico NOTA Ao contrário de **economic**, **economical** pode ser qualificado por palavras como *more, less, very, etc.* ▸ **be economical with the truth** não contar toda a verdade **economically** *adv* economicamente

economics /ˌiːkəˈnɒmɪks, ˌekə-/ *s* [*sing*] economia **economist** *s* economista

economize /ɪˈkɒnəmaɪz/ *vi* ~ **(on sth)** economizar (algo)

economy /ɪˈkɒnəmi/ *s* (*pl* **-ies**) economia: *make economies* economizar ◇ ~ *size* embalagem econômica

ecstasy /ˈekstəsi/ *s* (*pl* **-ies**) êxtase: *be in/go into* ~ *(over sth)* extasiar-se (com algo) **ecstatic** /ɪkˈstætɪk/ *adj* extasiado

edge /edʒ/ *s* **1** fio (*faca, etc.*) **2** borda **3** ~ **(on/over sb/sth)** vantagem (*sobre alguém/algo*) ▸ **be on edge** estar com os ner-

vos à flor da pele **take the edge off sth** suavizar, reduzir algo ● *vt, vi* ladear ▸ **edge (your way)** along, away, etc. avançar, aproximar-se, etc. pouco a pouco

edgy /ˈedʒi/ *adj* (*coloq*) nervoso

edible /ˈedəbl/ *adj* comestível

edit /ˈedɪt/ *vt* **1** editar **2** revisar **edition** /ɪˈdɪʃn/ *s* edição

editor /ˈedɪtər/ *s* editor/a (*livro, jornal, etc.*)

educate /ˈedʒukeɪt/ *vt* educar (*academicamente*): *He was educated abroad.* Ele estudou no exterior. **educated** *adj* culto ▸ **an educated guess** uma suposição fundamentada

education /ˌedʒuˈkeɪʃn/ *s* **1** educação, ensino **2** pedagogia **educational** *adj* educativo, pedagógico

eel /iːl/ *s* enguia

eerie /ˈɪəri/ *adj* (**-ier, -iest**) misterioso, horripilante

effect /ɪˈfekt/ *s* efeito: *for* ~ para impressionar ▸ **come into effect** entrar em vigor **in effect** na realidade **take effect 1** surtir efeito **2** entrar em vigor **to no effect** em vão ▸ **to this effect** com este propósito ● *vt* (*fml*) efetuar

effective /ɪˈfektɪv/ *adj* **1** ~ **(in doing sth)** eficaz (para fazer algo) **2** de grande efeito **effectively** *adv* **1** eficazmente **2** efetivamente **effectiveness** *s* eficácia

effeminate /ɪˈfemɪnət/ *adj* efeminado

efficient /ɪˈfɪʃnt/ *adj* **1** (*pessoa*) eficiente **2** (*máquina, etc.*) eficaz **efficiency** *s* eficiência **efficiently** *adv* eficientemente

effort /ˈefət/ *s* **1** esforço: *make an* ~ esforçar-se **2** realização

e. g. /ˌiː ˈdʒiː/ *abrev* por exemplo (= p. ex.)

egg /eg/ *s* **1** ovo **2** (*Biol*) óvulo ▸ **put all your eggs in one basket** arriscar tudo (em uma só coisa) ■ **egg sb on (to do sth)** provocar/incitar alguém (a fazer algo)

eggplant /ˈegplænt; *GB* -plɑːnt/ *s* berinjela

eggshell /ˈegʃel/ *s* casca de ovo

ego /ˈiːgoʊ/ *s* ego: *boost sb's* ~ levantar o moral de alguém

eight /eɪt/ *adj, pron, s* oito **eighth 1** *adj* oitavo **2** *pron, adv* o(s)/a(s) oitavo(s)/oitava(s) **3** *s* oitava parte, oitavo

eighteen /ˌeɪˈtiːn/ *adj, pron, s* dezoito **eighteenth 1** *adj* décimo oitavo **2** *pron, adv* o(s) décimo(s) oitavo(s), a(s) décima(s) oitava(s) **3** s décima oitava parte, dezoito avos

eighty /'eɪti/ adj, pron, s oitenta **eightieth** /'eɪtiəθ/ adj, pron octogésimo **2** s octogésima parte, oitenta avos

either /'aɪðər; GB 'i:ðər/ adj **1** qualquer um dos dois **2** ambos **3** [em orações negativas] nenhum dos dois ● pron **1** qualquer, um ou outro **2** nenhum → NENHUM ● adv **1** tampouco, também não **2** (either... or...) ou... ou..., nem... nem... → NEITHER.

eject /i'dʒekt/ vt **1** (fml) expulsar **2** vt expelir ● vt ejetar

elaborate /ɪ'læbərət/ adj complicado ● /ɪ'læbəreɪt/ **1** vi dar detalhes **2** vt elaborar

elapse /ɪ'læps/ vi (fml) (tempo) decorrer

elastic /ɪ'læstɪk/ adj **1** elástico **2** flexível ● s elástico

elastic band s elástico

elated /i'leɪtɪd/ adj exultante

elbow /'elboʊ/ s cotovelo

elder /'eldər/ adj, pron, s mais velho NOTA Os comparativos mais comuns de **old** são **older** e **oldest**: He is older than me. ◊ the oldest building in the city. Ao comparar as idades dos membros de uma família, costuma-se usar **elder** e **eldest**: my elder brother ◊ the elder of the two brothers. **Elder** e **eldest** não se usam com **than** e só podem anteceder o substantivo. elderly adj idoso

eldest /'eldɪst/ adj, pron o mais velho → ELDER

elect /ɪ'lekt/ vt eleger election s eleição electoral adj eleitoral electorate s eleitorado

electric /ɪ'lektrɪk/ adj **1** elétrico **2** eletrizante electrical adj elétrico → ELECTRIC electrician /ˌɪlek'trɪʃn/ s eletricista electricity /ɪˌlek'trɪsəti/ s eletricidade electrification /ɪˌlek'trɪsəti/ s eletrificação electrify /ɪ'lektrɪfaɪ/ vt (pt, pp **-ied**) **1** eletrificar **2** eletrizar

electrocute /ɪ'lektrəkju:t/ vt eletrocutar

electrode /ɪ'lektroʊd/ s eletrodo

electron /ɪ'lektrɒn/ s elétron

electronic /ˌɪlek'trɒnɪk/ adj eletrônico electronics s [sing] eletrônica

elegant /'elɪgənt/ adj elegante elegance s elegância

element /'elɪmənt/ s elemento

elementary /ˌelɪ'mentəri/ adj elementar: ~ school escola primária

elephant /'elɪfənt/ s elefante

elevator /'elɪveɪtər/ s elevador

eleven /ɪ'levn/ adj, pron, s onze **eleventh** /ɪ'levnθ/ adj décimo primeiro **2** pron, adv o(s) décimo(s) primeiro(s), a(s) décima(s) primeira(s) **3** s a décima primeira parte, onze avos

elicit /ɪ'lɪsɪt/ vt (fml) obter (esp com dificuldade)

eligible /'elɪdʒəbl/ adj: be ~ for sth ter direito a algo ◊ be ~ to do sth estar qualificado/capacitado para fazer algo ◊ an ~ bachelor um bom partido

eliminate /ɪ'lɪmɪneɪt/ vt **1** eliminar **2** erradicar

elk /elk/ s alce

elm /elm/ (tb ~ tree) s olmo

elope /i'loʊp/ vi fugir com o/a amante

eloquent /'eləkwənt/ adj eloqüente

else /els/ adv [com pronomes indefinidos, interrogativos ou negativos e com advérbio]: Did you see anybody ~? Você viu mais alguém? ◊ anyone ~ qualquer outra pessoa ◊ somebody ~ outra pessoa ◊ nobody ~ mais ninguém ◊ Anything ~? Mais alguma coisa? ◊ What ~? Que mais? ▸ or else ou então, senão elsewhere adv em/para outro lugar

elude /i'lu:d/ vt **1** escapar de **2** Her name eludes me. Não consigo me lembrar do nome dela. elusive adj esquivo

emaciated /i'meɪʃieɪtɪd/ adj emaciado

email (tb **e-mail**) /'i:meɪl/ s correio eletrônico NOTA A maneira de dizer o endereço de correio eletrônico "sjones@oup.com" é "s jones at oup dot com". ● vt enviar por correio eletrônico

emanate /'eməneɪt/ vi emanar, provir

emancipation /ɪˌmænsɪ'peɪʃn/ s emancipação

embankment /ɪm'bæŋkmənt/ s aterro

embargo /ɪm'bɑːrgoʊ/ s (pl **-es**) embargo

embark /ɪm'bɑːrk/ vt, vi **1** embarcar **2** ~ on sth envolver-se em algo

embarrass /ɪm'bærəs/ vt envergonhar, atrapalhar embarrassing adj embaraçoso embarrassment s **1** vergonha **2** (pessoa) estorvo embassy /'embəsi/ s (pl -ies) embaixada

embedded /ɪm'bedɪd/ adj **1** encravado, embutido **2** (dentes) cravado

ember /'embər/ s tição

embezzlement /ɪm'bezlmənt/ s desfalque

embittered /ɪm'bɪtərd/ adj amargurado

embody /ɪm'bɑdi/ vt (pt, pp **-ied**) (fml) encarnar, incorporar embodiment s personificação

embrace /ɪm'breɪs/ **1** vt, vi abraçar **2** vt (oportunidade) agarrar **3** vt abarcar ● s abraço

embroider /ɪm'brɔɪdər/ vt, vi bordar embroidery s [U] bordado

embryo /'embrioʊ/ s (pl ~s /-oʊz/) embrião

emerald /'emərəld/ s esmeralda

emerge /i'mɜːrdʒ/ vi emergir, surgir: It emerged that... Descobriu-se que... emergence s surgimento

emergency /i'mɜːrdʒənsi/ s (pl -ies) emergência

emigrate /'emɪgreɪt/ vi emigrar emigrant s emigrante emigration s emigração

eminent /'emɪnənt/ adj eminente

emission /i'mɪʃn/ s emissão

emit /i'mɪt/ vt (-tt-) **1** emitir **2** (odor, etc.) soltar

emotion /i'moʊʃn/ s emoção emotional adj emocional, emotivo emotive adj emotivo

empathy /'empəθi/ s empatia

emperor /'empərər/ s imperador

emphasis /'emfəsɪs/ s (pl -ases /-əsiːz/) ênfase emphatic adj enfático

emphasize /'emfəsaɪz/ vt enfatizar

empire /'empaɪər/ s império

employ /ɪm'plɔɪ/ vt empregar employee s empregado/a employer s empregador/a employment s emprego → WORK

empress /'empris/ s imperatriz

empty /'empti/ adj **1** vazio **2** vão, inútil ● (pt, pp -ied) **1** vt ~ sth (out) esvaziar, jogar algo **2** vt (habitação, etc.) desalojar **3** vi esvaziar-se emptiness s **1** vazio **2** inutilidade

empty-handed adj de mãos vazias

enable /i'neɪbl/ vt ~ sb to do sth permitir, possibilitar a alguém fazer algo

enact /i'nækt/ vt (fml) **1** (Teat) representar **2** realizar

enamel /ɪ'næml/ s (dentes, etc.) esmalte

enchanting /ɪn'tʃæntɪŋ; GB -'tʃɑːnt-/ adj encantador

encircle /ɪn'sɜːrkl/ vt rodear

enclose /ɪn'kloʊz/ vt **1** ~ sth (with sth) cercar algo (de algo) **2** anexar: I enclose.../Please find enclosed... Segue anexo... enclosure s **1** documento anexo **2** cercado

encore /'ɑŋkɔːr/ interj bis ● s repetição

encounter /ɪn'kaʊntər/ vt (fml) deparar(-se) com ● s encontro

encourage /ɪn'kɜːrɪdʒ/ vt **1** ~ sb (in sth/to do sth) animar alguém (a fazer) algo **2** estimular encouragement s estímulo encouraging adj encorajador

encyclopedia (tb -paedia) /ɪn,saɪklə'piːdiə/ s enciclopédia

end /end/ s **1** final, extremo: from ~ to ~ de ponta a ponta **2** (bastão, etc.) ponta, extremidade **3** the east ~ of town a região leste da cidade **4** fim: at the ~ of ◊ (be) at an ~ (estar/haver) terminado **5** propósito **6** (Esporte) lado (do campo/quadra) ▸ be at the end of your rope não aguentar mais in the end no final ◊ on end **1** em pé **2** for days on ~ por dias a fio ● vt, vi terminar, acabar end up (as sth/doing sth) acabar (sendo/fazendo algo) end up (in...) ir parar (em...) (lugar)

endanger /ɪn'deɪndʒər/ vt colocar em perigo

endear /ɪn'dɪər/ vt (fml) ~ sb/ yourself to sb tornar(-se) querido por alguém; conquistar a simpatia de alguém endearing adj afetuoso

endeavor (GB -vour) /ɪn'devər/ s (fml) empenho ● vi (fml) empenhar-se

ending /'endɪŋ/ s final

endless /'endləs/ adj interminável, infinito

endorse /ɪn'dɔːrs/ vt **1** aprovar **2** endossar endorsement s **1** aprovação **2** endosso **3** (em carta de motorista) nota de advertência

endow /ɪn'daʊ/ vt dotar endowment s **1** doação **2** (talento) dom

endurance /ɪn'dʊərəns; GB -'djʊə-/ s resistência

endure /ɪn'dʊər; GB ɪn'djʊə(r)/ **1** vt suportar NOTA Em negativas é mais comum utilizar-se can't bear ou can't stand. **2** vi perdurar enduring adj duradouro

enemy /'enəmi/ *s* (*pl* **-ies**) inimigo/a

energy /'enədʒi/ *s* (*pl*-ies) energia **energetic** /ˌenə'dʒetik/ *adj* enérgico

enforce /ɪn'fɔːrs/ *vt* fazer cumprir (*lei*) **enforcement** *s* aplicação

engage /ɪn'geɪdʒ/ **1** *vt* (*fml*) contratar **2** *vt* (*fml*) (*pensamentos, etc.*) ocupar **3** *vt* (*fml*) (*atenção*) prender **4** *vi* (*Mec*) encaixar(-se) ■ **engage in sth** dedicar-se a algo **engage sb in sth** envolver alguém em algo **engaged** *adj* **1** ocupado, comprometido **2** (*GB*) (*telefone*) ocupado **3 ~ (to sb)** comprometido (com alguém): *get ~* ficar noivo **engaging** *adj* atraente

engagement /ɪn'geɪdʒmənt/ *s* **1** (compromisso de) noivado **2** compromisso

engine /'endʒɪn/ *s* **1** motor NOTA Em geral usa-se **engine** para o motor de um veículo e **motor** para o de eletrodomésticos. **2** (*tb* **locomotive**) locomotiva: *~ driver* maquinista

engineer /ˌendʒɪ'nɪər/ *s* **1** engenheiro/a **2** técnico/a **3** maquinista ● *vt* (*coloq*) maquinar **2** construir

engineering /ˌendʒɪ'nɪərɪŋ/ *s* engenharia

engrave /ɪn'greɪv/ *vt* gravar **engraving** *s* **1** gravação **2** (*Arte*) gravura

engrossed /ɪn'groʊst/ *adj* absorto

enhance /ɪn'hæns; *GB* -'hɑːns/ *vt* **1** aumentar, melhorar **2** realçar

enjoy /ɪn'dʒɔɪ/ *vt* **1 ~ doing sth** gostar de fazer algo **2** desfrutar de: *Enjoy your meal!* Bom apetite! **3 ~ yourself** divertir-se **enjoyable** *adj* agradável, divertido **enjoyment** *s* satisfação, prazer

enlarge /ɪn'lɑːrdʒ/ *vt* ampliar **enlargement** *s* ampliação

enlighten /ɪn'laɪtn/ *vt* **~ sb (about/as to/on sth)** esclarecer (algo) a alguém **enlightened** *adj* **1** culto **2** (*política*) esclarecido **enlightenment** *s* (*fml*) esclarecimento **2** (**the Enlightenment**) o Iluminismo

enlist /ɪn'lɪst/ **1** *vi* (*Mil*) alistar-se **2** *vt* recrutar

enmity /'enməti/ *s* inimizade

enormous /ɪ'nɔːrməs/ *adj* enorme **enormously** *adv* enormemente, muitíssimo

enough /ɪ'nʌf/ *adj, pron* suficiente, bastante: *That's ~!* Basta!

▶ **have had enough (of sb/sth)** estar farto (de alguém/algo) ● *adv* (o) bastante NOTA **Enough** sempre vem depois do adjetivo e **too** diante deste: *You're not old enough./You're too young.* ▶ **curiously, oddly, strangely etc. enough** o curioso/estranho, etc. é que...

enquire = INQUIRE

enrage /ɪn'reɪdʒ/ *vt* enfurecer

enrich /ɪn'rɪtʃ/ *vt* enriquecer

enrol (*esp GB* **enrol**) /ɪn'roʊl/ *vt, vi* (**-ll-**) inscrever **enrollment** *s* inscrição, matrícula

ensure (*GB*) = INSURE (2)

entangle /ɪn'tæŋgl/ *vt* enredar **entanglement** *s* enredamento

enter /'entər/ **1** *vt* entrar em: *The thought never entered my head.* A idéia nunca me passou pela cabeça. **2** *vt* **~ (for) sth** inscrever-se em algo **3** *vt* matricular-se em **4** *vt* ingressar em **5** *vt* anotar ■ **enter into sth 1** (*negociações*) iniciar algo **2** (*um acordo*) chegar a algo **3** ter a ver com algo

enterprise /'entərpraɪz/ *s* **1** (*atividade*) empresa, empreendimento **2** espírito empreendedor **enterprising** *adj* empreendedor

entertain /ˌentər'teɪn/ **1** *vt, vi* receber (convidados) **2** *vt, vi* entreter **3** *vt* (*idéia*) cogitar **entertainer** *s* artista de variedades **entertaining** *adj* interessante **entertainment** *s* entretenimento, diversão

enthralling /ɪn'θrɔːlɪŋ/ *adj* cativante

enthusiasm /ɪn'θuːziæzəm; *GB* -'θjuː-/ *s* entusiasmo **enthusiast** *s* entusiasta **enthusiastic** /ɪnˌθuːzi'æstɪk; *GB* -ˌθjuː-/ *adj* entusiasmado

entice /ɪn'taɪs/ *vt* atrair

entire /ɪn'taɪər/ *adj* inteiro, todo **entirely** *adv* completamente **entirety** *s* totalidade

entitle /ɪn'taɪtl/ *vt* **1 ~ sb to (do) sth** dar direito a alguém (de fazer algo) **2** entitular **entitlement** *s* direito

entity /'entəti/ *s* (*pl* **-ies**) entidade

entrance /'entrəns/ *s* **1** entrada **2** admissão

entrant /'entrənt/ *s* participante

entrepreneur /ˌɑːntrəprə'nɜːr/ *s* empresário/a

entrust /ɪn'trʌst/ *vt* **~ sb with sth** confiar algo a alguém

entry /'entri/ *s* (*pl* **-ies**) **1** entrada, ingresso **2** (*diário*) anotação

3 (*dicionário*) verbete

enunciate /ɪ'nʌnsieɪt/ *vt, vi* pronunciar

envelop /ɪn'veləp/ *vt* envolver

envelope /'envələʊp, 'ɒn-/ *s* envelope

enviable /'enviəbl/ *adj* invejável **envious** *adj* invejoso: *be ~ of sb* ter inveja de alguém

environment /ɪn'vaɪrənmənt/ *s* **1** ambiente **2 (the environment)** o meio ambiente **environmental** /ɪn,vaɪrən'mentl/ *adj* ambiental **environmentalist** *s* ambientalista

envisage /ɪn'vɪsɪdʒ/ *vt* prever, imaginar

envoy /'envɔɪ, 'ɒn-/ *s* enviado/a

envy /'envi/ *s* inveja ● *vt* (*pt, pp* **-ied**) invejar

enzyme /'enzaɪm/ *s* enzima

ephemeral /ɪ'femərəl/ *adj* (*fml*) efêmero

epic /'epɪk/ *s* épico ● *adj* épico

epidemic /,epɪ'demɪk/ *s* epidemia

epilepsy /'epɪlepsi/ *s* epilepsia **epileptic** /,epɪ'leptɪk/ *adj, s,* epiléptico/a

episode /'epɪsəʊd/ *s* episódio

epitaph /'epɪtæf; *GB* -tɑːf/ *s* epitáfio

epitome /ɪ'pɪtəmi/ *s*: *the ~ of sth* a mais pura expressão de algo

epoch /'epɒk; *GB* 'iːpɒk/ *s* (*fml*) época

equal /'iːkwəl/ *adj, s* igual: *~ opportunities* igualdade de oportunidades ◊ *feel ~ to a task* sentir-se à altura de uma tarefa ▶ **be on equal terms** ter uma relação de igual para igual ● *vt* (**-l-**) (*GB* **-ll-**) **1** igualar(-se) **2** (*Mat*): *7 plus 9 equals 16. 7* mais 9 é igual a 16. **equality** /ɪ'kwɒləti/ *s* igualdade **equally** *adv* igualmente

equate /ɪ'kweɪt/ *vt* equiparar

equation /ɪ'kweɪʒn/ *s* (*Mat*) equação

equator /ɪ'kweɪtə(r)/ *s* equador

equilibrium /,iːkwɪ'lɪbriəm, ,ek-/ *s* equilíbrio

equinox /'iːkwɪnɒks, 'ek-/ *s* equinócio

equip /ɪ'kwɪp/ *vt* (**-pp-**) equipar, preparar **equipment** *s* [U] equipamento

equitable /'ekwɪtəbl/ *adj* (*fml*) equitativo

equivalent /ɪ'kwɪvələnt/ *adj, s* equivalente

era /'ɪərə, 'eərə/ *s* era

eradicate /ɪ'rædɪkeɪt/ *vt* erradicar

erase /ɪ'reɪs; *GB* ɪ'reɪz/ *vt* apagar **eraser** *s* borracha (*de apagar*)

erect /ɪ'rekt/ *vt* erigir ● *adj* **1** erguido **2** ereto **erection** *s* ereção

erode /ɪ'rəʊd/ *vt* erodir

erotic /ɪ'rɒtɪk/ *adj* erótico

errand /'erənd/ *s*: *run ~s for sb* fazer serviço de rua para alguém (*ir às compras, etc.*)

erratic /ɪ'rætɪk/ *adj* irregular

error /'erə(r)/ *s* (*fml*) erro: *The letter was sent to you in ~.* A carta lhe foi enviada por engano. NOTA Mistake é mais comum do que error. Mas em algumas construções usa-se apenas error: *human error* ◊ *an error of judgement.* → MISTAKE.

erupt /ɪ'rʌpt/ *vi* **1** entrar em erupção **2** (*violência*) irromper

escalate /'eskəleɪt/ *vt, vi* **1** aumentar **2** intensificar(-se) **escalation** *s* escalada

escalator /'eskəleɪtə(r)/ *s* escada rolante

escapade /'eskəpeɪd, ,eskə'peɪd/ *s* aventura

escape /ɪ'skeɪp/ **1** *vt, vi* escapar: *~ unharmed* sair ileso ◊ *~ (sb's) notice* passar despercebido (a alguém) **2** *vi* (*gás, etc.*) vazar ● *s* **1** fuga: *make your ~* fugir **2** (*gás, líquido*) vazamento

escort /'eskɔːt/ *s* **1** escolta **2** (*fml*) acompanhante ● /ɪ'skɔːt/ *vt* **1** acompanhar **2** (*Mil*) escoltar

especially /ɪ'speʃəli/ *adv* especialmente, sobretudo → SPECIALLY

espionage /'espiənɑːʒ/ *s* espionagem

essay /'eseɪ/ *s* **1** ensaio **2** (*escolar*) redação

essence /'esns/ *s* essência **essential** *adj* **1** imprescindível **2** fundamental **essentially** *adv* basicamente

establish /ɪ'stæblɪʃ/ *vt* **1** estabelecer(-se) **2** determinar **established** *adj* **1** (*negócio*) sólido **2** (*religião*) oficial **establishment** *s* **1** fundação **2** estabelecimento **3 (the Establishment)** o "establishment", o sistema

estate /ɪ'steɪt/ *s* **1** propriedade **2** (*bens*) patrimônio **3** *Ver* HOUSING ESTATE

estate agent *s* (*GB*) corretor de imóveis

estate (car) *s* (*GB*) carro tipo perua

esteem /ɪ'stiːm/ *s* ▶ **hold sb/sth in high/low esteem** ter uma boa/má opinião de alguém/algo

estimate /'estɪmət/ s **1** estimativa **2** avaliação **3** orçamento ● /'estɪmeɪt/ vt estimar

estimation /ˌestɪ'meɪʃn/ s opinião

estranged /ɪ'streɪndʒd/ adj: be ~ from sb estar brigado com/ separado de alguém

estuary /'estʃuəri/ GB -uari/ s (pl -ies) estuário

etching /'etʃɪŋ/ s gravura (a água-forte)

eternal /ɪ'tɜːrnl/ adj eterno **eternity** s eternidade

ether /'iːθər/ s éter **ethereal** /ɪ'θɪriəl/ adj etéreo

ethics /'eθɪks/ s [sing] ética **ethical** adj ético

ethnic /'eθnɪk/ adj étnico

ethos /'iːθɒs/ s (fml) mentalidade

etiquette /'etɪket, -kɪt/ s (regras) etiqueta

euro /'jʊroʊ/ s (pl -s) euro

evacuate /ɪ'vækjueɪt/ vt evacuar (pessoas) **evacuee** /ɪˌvækju'iː/ s evacuado/a

evade /ɪ'veɪd/ vt sonegar

evaluate /ɪ'væljueɪt/ vt avaliar

evaporate /ɪ'væpəreɪt/ vt, vi evaporar(-se) **evaporation** s evaporação

evasion /ɪ'veɪʒn/ s evasão **evasive** adj evasivo

eve /iːv/ s véspera: on the ~ of sth à(s) véspera(s) de algo

even /'iːvn/ adv **1** [uso enfático] até, (nem) mesmo: He didn't ~ open the letter. Ele nem sequer abriu a carta. **2** [com adj ou adv comparativo] ainda: ~ less ainda menos ▸ **even if/though** ainda que, mesmo que **even so** mesmo assim, não obstante ● adj **1** (superfície) plano, liso **2** (cor) uniforme **3** (temperatura) uniforme **4** (competição, pontuação) igual **5** (número) par ■ **even out** nivelar(-se) **even sth out** dividir algo equitativamente **even sth up** equilibrar algo

evening /'iːvnɪŋ/ s **1** (final de) tarde, noite: an ~ class uma aula noturna ◇ ~ meal jantar ◇ ~ paper jornal vespertino → MORNING, TARDE¹ **2** entardecer ▸ **good evening** boa noite → NOITE

evenly /'iːvənli/ adv **1** de maneira uniforme **2** equitativamente

event /ɪ'vent/ s evento, acontecimento ▸ **at all events/in any event** em todo caso **in the event** no final **in the event of sth** na eventualidade de algo **eventful** adj memorável

eventual /ɪ'ventʃuəl/ adj final **eventually** adv finalmente

ever /'evər/ adv nunca: for ~ (and ~) para sempre ◇ Has it ~ happened before? Isto já aconteceu antes? ▸ **ever since** desde então → ALWAYS, NUNCA

every /'evri/ adj cada, todos: ~ (single) time toda vez NOTA Usa-se **every** para designar todos os elementos de um grupo em conjunto: Every player was in top form. Usa-se **each** para designar cada um individualmente: The Queen shook hands with each player after the game. → EACH. ▸ **every last...** até o último... **every now and again/then** de vez em quando **every other**: ~ other week uma semana sim, outra não **every so often** de tempos em tempos

everybody /'evribɑdi/ (tb **everyone** /'evriwʌn/) pron todos, todo mundo NOTA **Everybody**, **anybody** e **somebody** são usados com o verbo no singular, mas substituídos por pronomes no plural, exceto em linguagem formal: Somebody has left their coat behind.

everyday /'evrideɪ/ adj cotidiano, de todos os dias: for/in ~ use para uso diário/de uso corrente NOTA Só se usa **everyday** antes de substantivo, e não se deve confundir com a expressão **every day**, que significa "todos os dias".

everything /'evriθɪŋ/ pron tudo

everywhere /'evriwear/ adv (em/por) toda parte/todo lugar

evict /ɪ'vɪkt/ vt despejar (de casa, etc.)

evidence /'evɪdəns/ s [U] (Jur) **1** prova **2** testemunho **evident** adj evidente **evidently** adv obviamente

evil /'iːvl/ adj mau ● s (fml) mal

evocative /ɪ'vɑkətɪv/ adj evocativo

evoke /ɪ'voʊk/ vt evocar

evolution /ˌevə'luːʃn/ GB /ˌiːv-/ s evolução

evolve /ɪ'vɑlv/ vi evoluir

ewe /juː/ s ovelha

exact /ɪg'zækt/ adj exato

exacting /ɪg'zæktɪŋ/ adj exigente

exactly /ɪg'zæktli/ adv exatamente ● interj exato

exaggerate /ɪgˈzædʒəreɪt/ vt exagerar **exaggerated** adj exagerado **exaggeration** s exagero

exam /ɪgˈzæm/ s exame

examination /ɪgˌzæmɪˈneɪʃn/ s **1** (fml) exame **2** investigação **examine** vt **1** examinar, investigar **2** (Jur) interrogar

example /ɪgˈzɑːmpl; GB -ˈzɑːmpl/ s exemplo: for ~ por exemplo ► **set a good example** dar bom exemplo

exasperate /ɪgˈzæspəreɪt; GB -ˈzɑːs-/ vt exasperar **exasperation** s exasperação

excavate /ˈekskəveɪt/ vt, vi escavar **excavation** s escavação

exceed /ɪkˈsiːd/ vt exceder(-se) (em), superar **exceedingly** adv extremamente

excel /ɪkˈsel/ vi (-ll-) sobressair (-se)

excellent /ˈeksələnt/ s excelente, ótimo **excellence** s excelência

except /ɪkˈsept/ prep ~ (for) sb/ sth exceto alguém/algo **exception** s exceção: make an ~ abrir uma exceção ► **take exception to sth** fazer objeção a algo **exceptional** adj excepcional

excerpt /ˈeksɜːpt/ s (livro, filme, etc.) passagem

excess /ɪkˈses, ˈekses/ s excesso **excessive** adj excessivo

exchange /ɪksˈtʃeɪndʒ/ s **1** troca, intercâmbio **2** (Fin) câmbio ● vt trocar

the Exchequer /ɪksˈtʃekər/ s (GB) Ministério da Fazenda

excite /ɪkˈsaɪt/ vt excitar **excitable** adj excitável **excited** adj entusiasmado, excitado **excitement** s entusiasmo, excitação **exciting** adj estimulante

exclaim /ɪkˈskleɪm/ vi exclamar **exclamation** s exclamação

exclamation point (GB **exclamation mark**) s ponto de exclamação

exclude /ɪkˈskluːd/ vt excluir **exclusion** s exclusão

exclusive /ɪkˈskluːsɪv/ adj **1** exclusivo **2** ~ of sb/sth excluindo alguém/algo

excursion /ɪkˈskɜːʒn; GB -ˈʃn/ s excursão

excuse /ɪkˈskjuːs/ s desculpa ● /ɪkˈskjuːz/ vt **1** desculpar **2** dispensar NOTA Usa-se **excuse me** para interromper ou abordar alguém: Excuse me, sir! Na Grã-Bretanha diz-se **sorry** para pedir desculpas por algo: I'm sorry I'm late. ◊ Did I hit you? I'm sorry! Em inglês americano

usa-se **excuse me** em vez de **sorry**.

execute /ˈeksɪkjuːt/ vt executar **execution** s execução **executioner** s carrasco/a

executive /ɪgˈzekjətɪv/ s executivo/a

exempt /ɪgˈzempt/ adj dispensado ● vt eximir **exemption** s isenção

exercise /ˈeksəsaɪz/ s exercício ● **1** vi fazer exercício **2** vt exercer

exert /ɪgˈzɜːt/ vt **1** exercer **2** ~ **yourself** esforçar-se **exertion** s esforço

exhaust /ɪgˈzɔːst/ s **1** (tb ~ fumes) fumaça de escapamento **2** (tb ~ pipe) (cano de) escapamento ● vt esgotar **exhausted** adj exausto **exhausting** adj esgotante **exhaustion** s exaustão **exhaustive** adj exaustivo

exhibit /ɪgˈzɪbɪt/ s objeto em exposição ● **1** vt, vi expor **2** vt demonstrar

exhibition /ˌeksɪˈbɪʃn/ s exposição, demonstração

exhilarating /ɪgˈzɪləreɪtɪŋ/ adj estimulante **exhilaration** s euforia

exile /ˈeɡzaɪl, ˈeksaɪl/ s **1** exílio **2** exilado/a ● vt exilar

exist /ɪgˈzɪst/ vi **1** existir **2** ~ (on sth) sobreviver (à base de/com algo) **existence** s existência **existing** adj existente

exit /ˈeksɪt/ s saída

exotic /ɪgˈzɒtɪk/ adj exótico

expand /ɪkˈspænd/ vt, vi **1** dilatar(-se) **2** expandir(-se) ■ **expand on sth** desenvolver (uma história)

expanse /ɪkˈspæns/ s (área) extensão

expansion /ɪkˈspænʃn/ s **1** expansão **2** desenvolvimento

expansive /ɪkˈspænsɪv/ adj expansivo

expatriate /ˌeksˈpeɪtriət; GB -ˈpæt-/ s expatriado/a

expect /ɪkˈspekt/ vt **1** esperar → ESPERAR **2** (esp GB) supor: "Will you be late?" "I ~ so." — Você vai chegar tarde? —Acho que sim. **expectant** adj cheio de expectativa: ~ **mother** mulher grávida **expectancy** s expectativa **expectation** s expectativa

expedition /ˌekspəˈdɪʃn/ s expedição

expel /ɪkˈspel/ vt (-ll-) **1** expulsar **2** expelir

expend /ɪkˈspend/ vt (fml) (tempo, dinheiro) empregar

expendable /ɪkˈspendəbl/ *adj* (*fml*) **1** descartável **2** dispensável

expenditure /ɪkˈspendɪtʃər/ *s* gasto(s)

expense /ɪkˈspens/ *s* gasto(s) **expensive** *adj* caro

experience /ɪkˈspɪəriəns/ *s* experiência ● *vt* experimentar **experienced** *adj* experiente

experiment /ɪkˈsperɪmənt/ *s* experimento ● *vi* fazer experimentos

expert /ˈekspɜːrt/ *adj, s* especialista **expertise** /ˌekspɜːrˈtiːz/ *s* conhecimento especializado, perícia

expire /ɪkˈspaɪər/ *vi* (*data*) vencer, caducar **expiration** (*GB* **expiry**) *s* (prazo de) validade

explain /ɪkˈsplein/ *vt* explicar, esclarecer **explanation** *s* explicação, esclarecimento **explanatory** /ɪkˈsplænətɔːri; *GB* -tri/ *adj* explanatório

explicit /ɪkˈsplɪsɪt/ *adj* explícito

explode /ɪkˈsploʊd/ *vt, vi* explodir

exploit /ɪkˈsplɔɪt/ *vt* explorar (*pessoas, recursos*): ~ *sb's generosity* abusar da generosidade de alguém ● *s* proeza **exploitation** *s* exploração

explore /ɪkˈsplɔːr/ *vt, vi* explorar (*um lugar*) **exploration** *s* exploração, investigação **explorer** *s* explorador/a

explosion /ɪkˈsploʊʒn/ *s* explosão **explosive** *adj, s* explosivo

export /ˈekspɔːrt/ *s* (artigo de) exportação ● /ɪkˈspɔːt/ *vt, vi* exportar

expose /ɪkˈspoʊz/ *vt* **1** ~ (**yourself**) **expor**(-se) **2** desmascarar (*ignorância, etc.*): revelar **exposed** *adj* exposto **exposure** *s* **1** exposição: *die of* ~ morrer de (exposição ao) frio **2** (*de falta*) revelação

express /ɪkˈspres/ *adj* **1** expresso **2** (*serviço*) rápido ● *adv* **1** por entrega rápida **2** de trem expresso ● *vt* expressar ● *s* **1** (*tb* ~ **train**) trem expresso **2** serviço de entrega rápida

expression /ɪkˈspreʃn/ *s* **1** expressão **2** demonstração: *as an* ~ *of his gratitude* como mostra de sua gratidão **3** expressividade

expressive /ɪkˈspresɪv/ *adj* expressivo

expressly /ɪkˈspresli/ *adv* expressamente

expressway /ɪkˈspresweɪ/ *s* rodovia

expulsion /ɪkˈspʌlʃn/ *s* expulsão

exquisite /ˈekskwɪzɪt, ɪkˈskwɪzɪt/ *adj* refinado

extend /ɪkˈstend/ *vt* **1** estender, prolongar **2** *vi* estender-se: ~ *as far as sth* chegar até algo **3** *vt* (*prazo*) prorrogar **4** *vt* (*boas vindas*) dar

extension /ɪkˈstenʃn/ *s* **1** extensão **2** ampliação, anexo **3** prolongação **4** (*prazo*) prorrogação **5** (*Telec*) ramal

extensive /ɪkˈstensɪv/ *adj* **1** extenso, amplo **2** (*danos*) grande **3** (*uso*) freqüente **extensively** *adv* **1** extensivamente: *He traveled* ~ *in Europe.* Ele viajou por toda a Europa. **2** (*usar*) freqüentemente

extent /ɪkˈstent/ *s* alcance, grau: *the full* ~ *of the losses* o valor total das perdas ▸**to a large/great extent** em grande parte **to a lesser extent** em menor grau **to some/what extent** até certo/que ponto

exterior /ɪkˈstɪəriər/ *adj* exterior ● *s* **1** exterior **2** (*pessoa*) aspecto

exterminate /ɪkˈstɜːrmɪneɪt/ *vt* exterminar **extermination** *s* extermínio

external /ɪkˈstɜːrnl/ *adj* externo, exterior

extinct /ɪkˈstɪŋkt/ *adj* extinto: *become* ~ extinguir-se

extinguish /ɪkˈstɪŋgwɪʃ/ *vt* extinguir NOTA A expressão mais comum **é put sth out**. **extinguisher** *s* extintor (*incêndio*)

extort /ɪkˈstɔːrt/ *vt* **1** (*dinheiro*) extorquir **2** (*confissão*) arrancar (à força) **extortion** *s* extorsão

extortionate /ɪkˈstɔːrʃənət/ *adj* **1** exorbitante **2** excessivo

extra /ˈekstrə/ *adj* **1** adicional, extra: ~ *charge* sobrecarga/sobretaxa ◊ *Wine is* ~. O vinho não está incluído (na conta). **2** de sobra (*Esporte*): ~ *time* prorrogação ● *adv* super, extra: *pay* ~ pagar a mais ● *s* **1** adicional **2** (*Cinema*) figurante

extract /ɪkˈstrækt/ *vt* **1** extrair **2** arrancar ● /ˈekstrækt/ *s* **1** extrato **2** (*texto, filme, etc.*) passagem

extraordinary /ɪkˈstrɔːrdəneri; *GB* -dnri/ *adj* extraordinário

extravagant /ɪkˈstrævəgənt/ *adj* **1** extravagante **2** exagerado **extravagance** *s* extravagância

extreme /ɪkˈstriːm/ *adj, s* extremo **extremely** *adv* extremamente **extremist** *s* extremista **extremity** /ɪkˈstremɪti/ *s* (*pl* **-ies**) extremidade, extremo

extricate /'ekstrikeit/ vt (fml)
livrar

extrovert /'ekstrəvə:rt/ s
extrovertido/a

exuberant /ig'zu:bərənt/, GB
-'zju:-/ adj exuberante

exude /ig'zu:d/, GB ig'zju:d/ vt, vi
1 (fml) exsudar 2 irradiar

eye /ai/ s 1 olho: sharp eyes vista
afiada → ARM 2 (agulha) buraco
▶ before your very eyes diante
do seu nariz in the eyes of sb/
in sb's eyes na opinião de
alguém in the eyes of the law
de acordo com a lei ▶ keep an
eye on sb/sth dar uma olhada
em alguém/algo (not) see eye
to eye with sb (não) concordar
plenamente com alguém up
to your eyes in sth até o pescoço
de/com algo ● vt (part pres
eyeing) olhar

eyeball /'aibɔ:l/ s globo ocular

eyebrow /'aibrau/ s sobrancelha

eye-catching adj vistoso

eyelash /'ailæʃ/ s cílio

eye level adj à altura dos olhos

eyelid /'ailid/ s pálpebra

eyesight /'aisait/ s visão

eyewitness /'aiwitnəs/ s testemunha ocular

Ff

F, f /ef/ s (pl F's, f's /efs/) 1 F, f
2 (Educ) (nota) F 3 (Mús) fá

fable /'feibl/ s fábula

fabric /'fæbrik/ s 1 tecido
→ TECIDO 2 the ~ of society a
estrutura da sociedade

fabulous /'fæbjələs/ adj 1 fabuloso 2 lendário

façade /fə'sad/ s fachada

face /feis/ s 1 face, rosto: to sb's ~
na cara de alguém ◊ ~ down/up
virado para baixo/cima 2 lado:
rock ~ parede de pedra 3 mostrador (relógio) 4 superfície
▶ face to face cara a cara in the
face of sth 1 apesar de algo
2 diante de algo make faces/a
face fazer careta on the face
of it (coloq) aparentemente
put a brave, etc. face on it/on sth
aceitar algo corajosamente ● vt
1 estar de frente para 2 ter vista
para: a house facing the park
uma casa que dá para o parque
3 enfrentar 4 afrontar: ~ the
facts encarar os fatos 5 (sentença, etc.) correr o risco de receber 6 revestir ▶ face up to sb/sth
enfrentar alguém/algo

faceless /'feisləs/ adj anônimo

facelift /'feislift/ s 1 cirurgia
plástica (facial) 2 reforma (de
edifício, etc.)

facet /'fæsit/ s faceta

facetious /fə'si:ʃəs/ adj
engraçadinho

face value s valor nominal
▶ accept/take sth at (its) face
value levar algo ao pé da letra

facial /'feiʃl/ adj facial ●
s limpeza de pele

facile /'fæsil/, GB -sail/ adj
simplista

facilitate /fə'siliteit/ vt (fml)
facilitar

facility /fə'siləti/ s 1 facilidade
2 (facilities) [pl]: sports/banking
facilities instalações desporti-
vas/serviços bancários

fact /fækt/ s fato: in ~ na verdade
▶ facts and figures dados concretos the facts of life informações sobre sexuali-
dade (para crianças)

factor /'fæktər/ s fator

factory /'fæktəri/ s (pl -ies)
fábrica

factual /'fæktʃuəl/ adj baseado
em fatos

faculty /'fæklti/ s (pl -ies)
1 faculdade 2 (USA) corpo
docente (de uma universidade)

fad /fæd/ s 1 mania 2 moda

fade /feid/ vt, vi 1 descolorir(-se)
2 desbotar 3 (flor) murchar
■ fade away desaparecer aos
poucos

fag /fæg/ s 1 (USA, pej) bicha
2 (GB, coloq) cigarro

fail /feil/ vt 1 vt reprovar 2 vi fracassar: ~ in your duty faltar ao
dever 3 vi ~ to do sth: The letter
failed to arrive. A carta não
chegou. ◊ He never fails to
write. Ele nunca deixa de
escrever. 4 vi (forças, motor)
falhar 5 vi (saúde) deteriorar-
se 6 vi (colheita) arruinar-se 7
vi (negócio) quebrar ● s reprovação ▶ without fail sem falta

failing /'feilin/ s 1 falha 2 fraqueza ● prep na falta de: Failing
this... Se isto não for possível...

failure /'feiljər/ s 1 fracasso
2 reprovação 3 falha: heart ~
parada cardíaca 4 ~ to do sth:
His ~ to answer puzzled her. Ela
estranhou que ele deixasse de
lhe responder.

faint /feint/ adj (~er, ~est) 1 leve
2 (som) fraco 3 (semelhança)
ligeiro 4 zonzo: feel ~ sentir-se
tonto ● vi desmaiar ● s desmaio

faintly adv 1 debilmente 2 vagamente

fair /feər/ s feira: fun ~ parque de diversões ● adj (~er, ~est) 1 ~ (to/on sb) justo, imparcial (com alguém) 2 (tempo) bom 3 (cabelo) louro → LOURO 4 (idéia) (suficientemente) bom: a ~ size bastante grande ▶ fair and square 1 merecidamente 2 claramente   fair game presa fácil   fair play jogo limpo (more than) your fair share of sth: He has more than his ~ share- of problems. Ele tem mais problemas do que merece.

fair-haired adj louro

fairly /ˈfeəli/ adv 1 justamente 2 [antes de adj ou adv] bastante: It's ~ easy. É bem fácil ◊ It's ~ good. Não está nada mau. ◊ ~ quickly razoavelmente rápido NOTA Os advérbios fairly e pretty (e rather e quite na Grã-Bretanha) modificam a intensidade das palavras que os acompanham e podem significar "bastante", "até certo ponto" ou "não muito". Fairly é o de grau mais baixo.

fairy /ˈfeəri/ s (pl -ies) fada

faith /feɪθ/ s fé: put your ~ in sb/sth confiar em alguém/algo ▶ in bad/good faith de má-/boa- fé

faithful /ˈfeɪθfl/ adj fiel, leal   faithfully adv fielmente

fake /feɪk/ s imitação ● adj false ● 1 vt falsificar 2 vt, vi fingir

falcon /ˈfælkən; GB ˈfɔːl-/ s falcão

fall /fɔːl/ s 1 queda 2 baixa 3 ~ of snow nevasca 4 outono 5 [ger pl] (Geog) catarata ● vi (pt fell pp fallen) 1 ~ (over) cair 2 baixar NOTA Fall pode ter o sentido de "tornar-se", "ficar", "pôr-se": ~ asleep pegar no sono ◊ ~ ill ficar doente. ▶ fall in love (with sb) apaixonar-se por alguém   fall short of sth ficar aquém de algo   fall victim to sth sucumbir a algo, ficar doente com algo ■ fall apart fazer-se em pedaços   fall back retroceder   fall back on sb/sth recorrer a alguém/algo   fall behind (sb/sth) ficar para trás/atrás (de alguém/algo)   fall behind with sth atrasar (pagamento/execução de algo)   fall down 1 cair 2 (plano) falhar   fall for sb (coloq) ficar caído por alguém   fall for sth (coloq) acreditar em algo: He fell for it immediately. Ele caiu na história na mesma hora.   fall in 1 (teto) despencar 2 (Mil) entrar em formação   fall off diminuir   fall on/upon sb recair sobre

alguém   fall out (with sb) brigar (com alguém)   fall over sb/sth tropeçar em alguém/algo   fall through fracassar

fallen /ˈfɔːlən/ pp de FALL ● adj caído

false /fɔːls/ adj 1 falso 2 (dentes) postiço 3 fraudulento ▶ a false move um passo em falso   a false start (Esporte) saída nula 2 tentativa frustrada

falsify /ˈfɔːlsɪfaɪ/ vt (pt, pp -ied) falsificar

falter /ˈfɔːltər/ vi 1 vacilar 2 (voz) titubear

fame /feɪm/ s fama

familiar /fəˈmɪliər/ adj 1 familiar (conhecido) 2 familiarizado   familiarity /fəˌmɪliˈærəti/ s 1 ~ with conhecimento de algo 2 familiaridade

family /ˈfæməli/ s (pl -ies) família: ~ name sobrenome ◊ ~ tree árvore genealógica → FAMÍLIA

famine /ˈfæmɪn/ s fome → FOME

famous /ˈfeɪməs/ adj famoso

fan /fæn/ s 1 leque 2 ventilador 3 fã, torcedor/a ● vt (-nn-) 1 ~ (yourself) abanar(-se) 2 atiçar ■ fan out espalhar-se em forma(de) leque

fanatic /fəˈnætɪk/ s fanático/a   fanatic(al) adj fanático

fanciful /ˈfænsɪfl/ adj 1 extravagante 2 (pessoa) fantasista

fancy /ˈfænsi/ s 1 capricho 2 fantasia ▶ catch/take sb's fancy agradar a alguém   take a fancy to sb/sth ficar interessado em alguém/algo ● adj extravagante: nothing ~ nada luxuoso/exagerado ● vt (pt, pp -ied) 1 imaginar 2 (GB, coloq) querer 3 (GB, coloq) gostar de: I don't ~ him. Ele não me atrai. ▶ fancy (that) quem diria, imagine   fancy yourself as sth (GB, coloq) achar-se algo

fancy dress s [U] (GB) (roupa) fantasia

fantastic /fænˈtæstɪk/ adj fantástico

fantasy /ˈfæntəsi/ s (pl -ies) fantasia

far /fɑːr/ (comp farther ou further superl farthest ou furthest) adj 1 mais distante: the ~ end o outro extremo 2 oposto ◊ the ~ (antig) distante ● adv 1 longe: ~ away muito longe ◊ How~ is it? A que distância fica? NOTA Neste sentido é usado em orações negativas ou interrogativas. Em orações afirmativas a long way é muito mais comum. 2 [com

prep ou comparativo] muito
▸ **as far as** até ◂ **as/so far as
tanto quanto**: *as ~ as I know* que
eu saiba ◂ **as/so far as sb/sth is
concerned** no que se refere a
alguém/algo ◂ **be far from
(doing) sth** estar longe de
(fazer) algo ◂ **by far** consideravelmente: *She is by ~ the best.*
Ela é de longe a melhor. ◂ **far
and wide** por todo lugar ◂ **far
from it** (*coloq*) longe disso ◂ **go
too far** ir longe demais ◂ **so far
1** até agora **2** até certo ponto

faraway /'fɑːrəweɪ/ *adj* **1** remoto
2 (*expressão*) distraído

fare /feər/ *s* preço de passagem
● *vi* (*fml*): *~ well/badly* sair-se
bem/mal

farewell /ˌfeər'wel/ *interj* (*antiq,
fml*) adeus ● *s* despedida: *bid/
say ~ to sb/sth* despedir-se de
alguém/algo

farm /fɑːrm/ *s* fazenda ● *vt* **1**, *vi*
cultivar **2** *vt* (*animais*) criar

farmer /'fɑːrmər/ *s* fazendeiro/a,
agricultor/a

farmhouse /'fɑːrmhaʊs/ *s* sede
(de fazenda)

farming /'fɑːrmɪŋ/ *s* agricultura,
cultivo

farmyard /'fɑːrmjɑːrd/ *s* terreiro
(de fazenda)

far-sighted *adj* **1** previdente
2 hipermetrope

fart /fɑːrt/ *s* (*coloq*) peido ● *vi*
(*coloq*) peidar

farther /'fɑːrðər/ = FURTHER

farthest /'fɑːrðɪst/ = FURTHEST

fascinate /'fæsɪneɪt/ *vt* fascinar
fascinating *adj* fascinante

fascism /'fæʃɪzəm/ *s* fascismo
fascist *adj*, *s* fascista

fashion /'fæʃn/ *s* **1** moda: *be in/
out of ~* estar na moda/fora de
moda **2** [U] maneira ● *vt*
amoldar, fazer

fashionable /'fæʃnəbl/ *adj* da
moda

fast /fæst; *GB* fɑːst/ (*~er, ~est*) *adj*
1 rápido NOTA Só se usa fast
para descrever uma pessoa ou
coisa que se move a grande
velocidade: *a ~ horse/car/run-
ner*; **quick** refere-se a algo que
se realiza em um curto espaço
de tempo: *a quick decision/visit.*
2 (*relógio*) adiantado **3** firme
4 (*cor*) que não desbota ● *adv*
1 depressa, rapidamente **2**
~ asleep dormindo profundamente ● *vi* jejuar ● *s* jejum

fasten /'fæsn; *GB* 'fɑːsn/ **1** *vt ~
sth (down/together)* prender algo
2 *vt ~ sth (up)* fechar, fixar algo
3 *vi* fechar-se, prender-se

fastidious /fæˈstɪdiəs, fə-/ *adj*
meticuloso, exigente

fat /fæt/ *adj* (**fatter, fattest**)
gordo: *You're getting ~.* Você
está engordando. NOTA Há
palavras menos diretas que fat,
p. ex. **chubby, stout, plump** e
overweight. ● *s* **1** gordura
2 banha

fatal /'feɪtl/ *adj* **1** ~ **(to sb/sth)**
mortal (para alguém/algo)
2 (*fml*) fatídico fatality /fə'tæləti/
s (*pl* -**ies**) vítima (mortal)

fate /feɪt/ *s* destino fated *adj* pre-
destinado fateful *adj* fatal

father /'fɑːðər/ *s* pai: *Father
Christmas* (*GB*) Papai Noel
→ NATAL ● *s* **1** ▸ like
father, like son tal pai, tal filho

father-in-law *s* (*pl* -**ers-in-law**)
sogro

fatigue /fə'tiːg/ *s* fadiga ● *vt*
fatigar

fatten /'fætn/ *vt* **1** cevar **2** (*alimento*): *Butter is very fattening.*
Manteiga engorda muito.

fatty /'fæti/ *adj* **1** (*Med*) adiposo
2 (-**ier, -iest**) gorduroso

faucet /'fɔːsət/ *s* torneira

fault /fɔːlt/ *vt* criticar ● *s*
1 defeito, falha → MISTAKE
2 culpa: *be at ~* ser culpado
3 (*Tênis*) falta **4** (*Geol*) falha
faultless /'fɔːltləs/ *adj* sem
defeito, impecável

faulty /'fɔːlti/ *adj* (-**ier, -iest**)
defeituoso

fauna /'fɔːnə/ *s* fauna

favor (*GB* -**our**) /'feɪvər/ *s* favor:
in ~ of (doing) sth a favor de
(fazer) algo ● *vt* **1** favorecer
2 preferir, ser partidário de
favorable (*GB* -**our-**) /'feɪvərəbl/
adj **1** favorável **2** ~ **(to/toward
sb/sth)** a favor de (alguém/
algo)

favorite (*GB* -**our-**) /'feɪvərɪt/
s favorito/a ● *adj* preferido

fawn /fɔːn/ *s* cervo (com menos
de um ano) → VEADO ● *adj*,
s bege

fax /fæks/ *s* fax ● *vt* **1** ~ **sb** passar
um fax a alguém **2** ~ **sth** enviar
algo por fax

fear /fɪər/ *vt* temer ● *s* temor: *in ~
of sb/sth* com medo de alguém/
algo ▸ **for fear of (doing) sth/
that...)** por/com medo de
(fazer) algo/de...

fearful /'fɪərfl/ *adj* terrível

fearless /'fɪərləs/ *adj* intrépido

fearsome /'fɪərsəm/ *adj* terrível

feasible /'fiːzəbl/ *adj* viável feasi-
bility /ˌfiːzə'bɪləti/ *s* viabilidade

feast /fiːst/ *s* **1** banquete

2 (*Relig*) festa, festividade ● *vi* banquetear-se

feat /fiːt/ *s* proeza

feather /ˈfeðər/ *s* pena

feature /ˈfiːtʃər/ *s* **1** característica **2** (*TV*) programa (especial) **3** longa-metragem **4** (**features**) [*pl*] feições ● *vt: featuring Tom Hanks* apresentando (como ator principal) Tom Hanks ► **featureless** *adj* sem traços marcantes

February /ˈfebruəri; *GB* -uəri/ *s* (*abrev* **Feb.**) fevereiro → MAY

federal /ˈfedərəl/ *adj* federal

federation /ˌfedəˈreɪʃn/ *s* federação

fed up *adj* ~ (**about/with sb/sth**) (*coloq*) farto, cheio (de alguém/algo)

fee /fiː/ *s* **1** [*ger pl*] honorários **2** cota (*de clube*) **3** *school fees* anuidade/mensalidade escolar

feeble /ˈfiːbl/ *adj* (**-er**, **-est**) **1** débil **2** (*desculpa, argumento*) fraco

feed /fiːd/ (*pt, pp* **fed** /fed/) **1** *vt* ~ (**on sth**) alimentar(-se) (de algo) **2** *vt* dar de comer a **3** *vt* (*dados, etc.*) fornecer ● *s* **1** alimento **2** ração

feedback /ˈfiːdbæk/ *s* (*informação*) retorno

feel /fiːl/ (*pt, pp* **felt**) **1** *vt* sentir, tocar: ~ *the cold* ser sensível ao frio ◇ *She felt the water.* Ela experimentou a temperatura da água. **2** *vi* sentir-se: ~ *cold/hot/hungry* estar com frio/calor/fome **3** *vt* achar de **4** *vi* (*coisa*) parecer: *It feels like leather.* Parece de couro. ► **feel like…: I ~ like I'm going to throw up.** Acho que vou vomitar. **feel like (doing) sth** ter vontade de fazer algo **feel sorry for sb/ for yourself** sentir pena de alguém/de si mesmo **feel good** sentir-se bem **feel your way** andar/mover-se às apalpadelas, ir com cautela **feel about (for sth)** procurar (algo) às apalpadelas **feel for sb** sentir pena de alguém **feel up to (doing) sth** sentir-se capaz de (fazer) algo ● *s*: *Let me have a* ~. Deixe-me tocá-lo. ► **get the feel of (doing) sth** (*coloq*) pegar o jeito de (fazer) algo **have a feel for sth** ter jeito para algo

feeling /ˈfiːlɪŋ/ *s* **1** sensação **2** opinião **3** [*ger pl*] sentimento **4** sensibilidade ► **bad/ill feeling** ressentimento

feet /fiːt/ *plural de* FOOT

fell /fel/ *pret de* FALL ● *vt*

1 (*árvore*) cortar **2** derrubar

fellow /ˈfeloʊ/ *s* **1** companheiro: ~ *countryman* compatriota **2** (*GB, coloq*) cara

fellowship /ˈfeloʊʃɪp/ *s* **1** companheirismo **2** associação **3** bolsa de pesquisa

felt /felt/ *pret, pp de* FEEL ● *s* feltro

female /ˈfiːmeɪl/ *adj* **1** feminino NOTA Aplica-se às características físicas das mulheres: *the* ~ *figure.* **2** fêmea NOTA **Female** e **male** especificam o sexo de pessoas ou animais: *a female/male friend, rabbit, etc.* **3** ~ *equality* a igualdade da mulher ● *s* fêmea

feminine /ˈfemənɪn/ *adj, s* feminino (*próprio da mulher*) NOTA Usa-se **feminine** para as qualidades consideradas típicas da mulher.

feminism /ˈfemənɪzəm/ *s* feminismo **feminist** *s* feminista

fence /fens/ *s* **1** cerca **2** alambrado ● **1** *vt* cercar **2** *vi* praticar esgrima **fencing** *s* esgrima

fend /fend/ *v* ■ **fend for yourself** cuidar de si mesmo **fend sb/sth off** defender-se de alguém/algo

fender /ˈfendər/ *s* **1** (*lareira*) guarda-fogo **2** (*Náut*) defensa **3** pára-lama

ferment /fərˈment/ *vt, vi* fermentar ● /ˈfɜːrment/ *s* ebulição

fern /fɜːrn/ *s* samambaia

ferocious /fəˈroʊʃəs/ *adj* feroz

ferocity /fəˈrɑsəti/ *s* ferocidade

ferry /ˈferi/ *s* (*pl* **-ies**) **1** ferry-boat: *car* ~ barcaça para carros **2** balsa ● *vt* (*pt, pp* **-ied**) transportar

fertile /ˈfɜːrtl; *GB* -taɪl/ *adj* **1** fértil **2** frutífero

fertility /fərˈtɪləti/ *s* fertilidade

fertilization /ˌfɜːrtələˈzeɪʃn/ *s* fertilização

fertilize /ˈfɜːrtəlaɪz/ *vt* **1** fertilizar **2** adubar **fertilizer** *s* **1** fertilizante **2** adubo

fervent /ˈfɜːrvənt/ (*tb* **fervid** /ˈfɜːrvɪd/) *adj* ardente

fester /ˈfestər/ *vi* infectar(-se)

festival /ˈfestɪvl/ *s* **1** festival **2** (*Relig*) festa

fetch /fetʃ/ *vt* **1** trazer **2** buscar **3** atingir (*preço*)

fête /feɪt/ *s* (*GB*) tipo de quermesse ao ar livre

fetus /ˈfiːtəs/ *s* feto

feud /fjuːd/ *s* rixa (*famílias/classes*) ● *vi* ter rixa

feudal /ˈfjuːdl/ *adj* feudal **feudalism** *s* feudalismo

fever /ˈfiːvər/ s febre **feverish** adj febril

few /fjuː/ adj, pron **1** (~er, ~est) poucos: every ~ minutes no/com intervalo de alguns minutos ◊ fewer than six menos de seis → LESS **2** (a few) alguns/algumas, uns/umas NOTA Few tem sentido negativo e equivale a "pouco". A few tem sentido mais positivo, equivalendo a "uns, alguns": Few people turned up. Veio pouca gente. ◊ I've got a ~ friends coming for dinner. Alguns amigos estão vindo para jantar. ► **a good few; quite/not a few** um bom número (de), muitos **few and far between** escasso

fiancé /fiˈɒnseɪ; GB fiˈɒnseɪ/ s (fem **fiancée**) noivo/a

fib /fɪb/ s (coloq) mentira ● vi (coloq) contar lorota

fiber (GB **fibre**) /ˈfaɪbər/ s fibra **fibrous** adj fibroso

fickle /ˈfɪkl/ adj **1** (tempo) instável **2** (pessoa) volúvel

fiction /ˈfɪkʃn/ s ficção

fiddle /ˈfɪdl/ s (coloq) **1** violino **2** fraude ● vt **1** (coloq) falsificar **2** vi tocar violino **3** vi ~ (about) **with sth** brincar com algo (nas mãos) ■ **fiddle around** perder tempo **fiddler** s violinista

fiddly /ˈfɪdli/ adj (GB, coloq) complicado

fidelity /fɪˈdeləti/ s fidelidade NOTA A palavra mais comum é **faithfulness**.

field /fiːld/ s campo

fiend /fiːnd/ s **1** demônio **2** (coloq) entusiasta **fiendish** adj (coloq) diabólico

fierce /fɪərs/ adj (~er, ~est) **1** feroz **2** (oposição) intenso

fifteen /ˌfɪfˈtiːn/ adj, pron, s quinze **fifteenth 1** adj décimo quinto **2** pron, adv o(s) décimo(s) quinto(s), a(s) décima(s) quinta(s) **3** s décima quinta parte, quinze avos

fifth /fɪfθ/ (abrev **5th**) adj quinto ● pron, adv o(s) quinto(s)/a(s) ~ s **1** quinta parte, quinto **2** (the fifth) o dia cinco **3** (tb ~ gear) quinta (marcha)

fifty /ˈfɪfti/ adj, pron, s cinquenta: the fifties os anos cinquenta ◊ be in your fifties ter cinquenta e poucos anos (de idade) ► **go fifty-fifty** dividir meio a meio **fiftieth 1** adj, pron quinquagésimo **2** s quinquagésima parte, cinquenta avos

fig /fɪg/ s **1** figo **2** (tb ~ tree) figueira

fight /faɪt/ s **1** luta, briga: give up without a ~ desistir sem lutar ◊ A ~ broke out in the bar. Saiu uma briga no bar. **2** combate NOTA Quando se trata de um conflito prolongado, usa-se **fighting**: There has been heavy/fierce fighting in the capital. ► **put up a good/poor fight** colocar muito/pouco empenho em algo ● (pt, pp **fought**) **1** vi, vt ~ (about/over sth); ~ (for sth) lutar (por algo): ~ a battle (against sth) travar uma batalha (contra algo) **2** vi, vt ~ (sb/with sb) (about/over sth) brigar (com alguém) (por algo) **3** vt combater ► **fight it out**: They must ~ it out between them. Eles devem resolver isso entre si. **fight tooth and nail** lutar com unhas e dentes **fight your way across, into, etc.** abrir caminho (à força) através de/por algo ■ **fight back** contra-atacar **fight sb/sth off** repelir/rechaçar alguém/algo

fighter /ˈfaɪtər/ s **1** lutador/a, combatente **2** (avião de) caça

figure /ˈfɪɡjər; GB ˈfɪɡə(r)/ s **1** número **2** [ger sing] quantia **3** (pessoa de destaque) figura **4** corpo: have a good ~ ter tipo bonito **5** silhueta ► **put a figure on sth** dar o número de algo, pôr preço em algo ● vi figurar **2** vt calcular: It's what I figured. É o que eu pensava. ■ **it/that figures** compreende-se/faz sentido ■ **figure sth out** entender/descobrir algo

file /faɪl/ s **1** pasta (suspensa, para arquivo) **2** arquivo: on ~ arquivado **3** lixa ● vt ~ sth (away) arquivar algo **2** vt (reclamação, etc.) registrar **3** vt lixar **4** vi ~ (past sth) desfilar (em fila) (diante de algo) **5** vi ~ in/out entrar/sair em fila **filing cabinet** s (móvel) arquivo

fill /fɪl/ **1** vt, vi encher(-se) **2** vt (buraco, etc.) fechar **3** vt (dente) obturar **4** vt (cargo) ocupar ■ **fill in (for sb)** substituir (alguém) **fill sth in/out** preencher algo **fill sb in (on sth)** colocar alguém a par (de algo)

fillet /ˈfɪlɪt/ s filé

filling /ˈfɪlɪŋ/ s **1** obturação **2** recheio

film /fɪlm/ s **1** película **2** (esp GB) cinema: film-maker cineasta **3** filme ● vt filmar **filming** s filmagem

filter /ˈfɪltər/ s filtro ● vt, vi filtrar(-se)

filth /fɪlθ/ s **1** imundície **2** obscenidade

filthy /ˈfɪlθi/ adj (-ier, -iest) **1** imundo **2** obsceno **3** (coloq) desagradável

fin /fɪn/ s nadadeira, barbatana

final /ˈfaɪnl/ s **1** (Esporte) final **2** (finals) exames finais • adj **1** último, final **2** definitivo: I'm not coming, and that's ~. Eu não vou, e assunto encerrado.

finally /ˈfaɪnəli/ adv **1** por último **2** finalmente **3** por fim

finance /ˈfaɪnæns, fəˈnæns/ s finança: ~ company (companhia) financeira ◇ ~ minister ministro da Fazenda ◇ ♦ vt financiar **financial** /faɪˈnænʃl, fəˈn-/ adj financeiro: ~ year (GB) ano fiscal

find /faɪnd/ vt (pt, pp found) **1** encontrar, achar **2** procurar: They came to ~ work. Eles vieram em busca de trabalho. **3** ~ sb guilty declarar alguém culpado ▶ find fault (with sb/sth) encontrar problemas/falhas (em alguém/algo) find your feet acostumar-se find your way encontrar/descobrir o caminho ∎ find (sth) out informar-se (de), descobrir (algo) find sb out descobrir/desmascarar alguém (por algo errado) finding s **1** descoberta, resultado **2** decisão

fine /faɪn/ adj (-er, -est) **1** excelente: I'm ~. Estou bem. ◇ You're a ~ one to talk! (GB) Veja só quem fala! **2** fino **3** (traços) delicado **4** (tempo) bom: a ~ day um lindo dia **5** (diferença) sutil • adv (coloq) bem ▶ one fine day um certo dia • s multa • vt multar

fine art (tb the fine arts) s as belas-artes

finger /ˈfɪŋɡər/ s dedo (da mão) ▶ all fingers and thumbs atrapalhado (com as mãos) put your finger on sth apontar algo (com precisão) (problema, etc.)

fingernail /ˈfɪŋɡərneɪl/ s unha (da mão)

fingerprint /ˈfɪŋɡərprɪnt/ s impressão digital

fingertip /ˈfɪŋɡərtɪp/ s ponta do dedo ▶ have sth at your fingertips ter algo à mão

finish /ˈfɪnɪʃ/ **1** vt, vi terminar **2** vt ~ sth (off/up) (comida) acabar (com) algo ∎ finish up: He could ~ up dead. Ele poderia acabar morto. • s acabamento

finish(ing) line s linha de chegada

fir /fɜːr/ (tb ~ tree) s abeto

fire /ˈfaɪər/ **1** vt, vi disparar: ~ at sb/sth atirar em alguém/algo **2** vt (insultos) soltar **3** vt (pessoa) demitir **4** vt (imaginação) estimular • s **1** fogo **2** fogueira **3** incêndio **4** disparo(s) ▶ be/come under fire **1** estar/vir sob fogo inimigo **2** ser bastante criticado **on fire** em chamas **set fire to sth/set sth on fire** botar fogo em algo

firearm /ˈfaɪərɑːrm/ s [ger pl] arma de fogo

fire engine s carro de bombeiros

fire escape s escada de incêndio

fire extinguisher (tb **extinguisher**) s extintor de incêndio

firefighter /ˈfaɪərfaɪtər/ s bombeiro/a

fireman /ˈfaɪərmən/ s (pl -men) (GB) bombeiro

fireplace /ˈfaɪərpleɪs/ s lareira

fire station s quartel dos bombeiros

firewood /ˈfaɪərwʊd/ s lenha

firework /ˈfaɪərwɜːrk/ s fogo de artifício

firing /ˈfaɪərɪŋ/ s tiroteio: ~ line linha de fogo ◇ ~ squad pelotão de fuzilamento

firm /fɜːrm/ s firma, empresa • adj (-er, -est) firme ▶ a firm hand mão/pulso firme **be on firm ground** pisar terreno seguro

first /fɜːrst/ (abrev **1st**) adj primeiro ▶ at first hand em primeira mão **first name** (pre)nome **first night** estréia **first thing**: ~ thing in the morning/evening de manhã cedo/no começo da noite **first things first** primeiro o mais importante • adv **1** primeiro: come ~ chegar primeiro **2** pela primeira vez **3** em primeiro lugar **4** antes ▶ at first come, first served por ordem de chegada **first of all 1** antes de tudo **2** em primeiro lugar **put sb/sth first** pôr alguém/algo em primeiro lugar • pron o(s) primeiro(s), a(s) primeira(s) ▶ s **1** (the first) o dia primeiro **2** (tb ~ gear) primeira (marcha) ▶ from first to last do princípio ao fim **from the (very) first** desde o primeiro momento

first aid s primeiros socorros

first class s **1** primeira (classe) **2** correio de entrega rápida • adv de primeira classe: send sth ~ enviar algo pelo serviço de entrega rápida do correio

first-hand *adj, adv* de primeira mão

firstly /ˈfɜːstli/ *adv* em primeiro lugar

first-rate *adj* de primeira (categoria)

fish /fɪʃ/ *s* peixe ▶ **have bigger/ other fish to fry** ter coisas mais importantes para fazer **like a fish out of water** como um peixe fora d'água ● *vt, vi* pescar

fisherman /ˈfɪʃərmən/ *s* (*pl* **-men**) pescador

fishing /ˈfɪʃɪŋ/ *s* pesca

fishmonger /ˈfɪʃmʌŋɡər/ *s* (GB) peixeiro/a **a fishmonger's** peixaria

fishy /ˈfɪʃi/ *adj* (**-ier, -iest**) **1** de peixe **2** (*coloq*) suspeito: *There's something ~ going on.* Aqui há dente de coelho.

fist /fɪst/ *s* punho **fistful** *s* punhado

fit /fɪt/ *s* **1** ataque (*riso, choro, etc.*) **2** (*roupas*): *be a good/tight ~* ficar bem/justo ▶ **have/throw a fit**: *She'll have/throw a ~!* Ela vai ter um ataque! ● *(-tt-)* (*pt, pp* **fit, GB fitted**) **1** *vt, vi* caber **2** *vt* servir **3** *vt* equipar **4** *vt* ~ **sth on(to)sth** colocar algo em algo **5** *vt*: *~ a description* enquadrar-se em uma descrição ▶ **fit (sb) like a glove** cair como uma luva (em alguém) ■ **fit in (with sb/sth)** ajustar-se (a alguém/em algo) ● *adj* (**fitter, fittest**) **1** em condições, adequado: *a meal ~ for a king* uma refeição digna de um rei **2** ~ **to do sth** (*coloq*) pronto (para fazer algo) **3** em (boa) forma: *keep ~* (GB) manter-se em forma ▶ **(as) fit as a fiddle** em ótima forma

fitness /ˈfɪtnəs/ *s* boa forma (física)

fitted /ˈfɪtɪd/ *adj* **1** (*carpete*) instalado **2** (*armários*) embutido **3** (*quarto*) mobiliado **4** (*cozinha*) feita sob medida

fitting /ˈfɪtɪŋ/ *adj* apropriado ● *s* **1** acessório, peça **2** prova: *~ room* provador

five /faɪv/ *adj, pron, s* cinco: *all ~ of them* todos os cinco ◊ *There were ~ of us.* Éramos cinco. **fiver** *s* (GB, *coloq*) nota de cinco (libras)

fix /fɪks/ *s* (*coloq*) dificuldade: *be in/get yourself into a ~* estar/meter-se numa enrascada ● *vt* **1** fixar **2** consertar **3** estabelecer **4** (*comida*) preparar **5** (*coloq*) (*eleições, etc.*) manipular **6** (*reunião*) marcar **7** (*coloq*)

acertar as contas com ■ **fix on sb/sth** decidir-se por alguém/algo **fix sb up (with sth)** (*coloq*) providenciar algo para alguém **fix sth up 1** consertar algo **2** reformar algo

fixed /fɪkst/ *adj* fixo

fixture /ˈfɪkstʃər/ *s* **1** acessório fixo de uma casa **2** evento esportivo **3** (*coloq*) pessoa/algo integrante de um lugar

fizz /fɪz/ *vi* **1** efervescer **2** chiar

fizzy /ˈfɪzi/ *adj* (**-ier, -iest**) com gás

flabby /ˈflæbi/ *adj* (*coloq*) (**-ier, -iest**) flácido

flag /flæɡ/ *s* **1** bandeira **2** bandeirola ● *vi* (**-gg-**) fraquejar

flagrant /ˈfleɪɡrənt/ *adj* flagrante

flair /fleər/ *s* **1** [*sing*] talento **2** estilo

flake /fleɪk/ *s* floco ● *vi* ~ (**off/ away**) descascar(-se)

flamboyant /flæmˈbɔɪənt/ *adj* **1** (*pessoa*) extravagante **2** chamativo

flame /fleɪm/ *s* chama

flammable /ˈflæməbl/ *adj* inflamável

flan /flæn/ *s* torta (*doce, sem cobertura*)

flank /flæŋk/ *s* **1** (*pessoa*) lado **2** (*tb Mil*) flanco ● *vt* flanquear

flannel /ˈflænl/ *s* **1** flanela **2** (GB) toalhinha de (lavar o) rosto

flap /flæp/ *s* **1** (*livro*) orelha (*da capa*) **2** (*bolso*) aba **3** (*mesa*) borda dobrável **4** (*Aeronáut*) flap ● *(-pp-)* **1** *vt, vi* agitar(-se) **2** *vt* (*asas*) bater

flare /fleər/ *s* **1** labareda **2** clarão **3** (**flares**) [*pl*] (GB) calça boca-de-sino ● *vi* **1** relampejar **2** explodir (em): *Tempers flared.* Os ânimos se exaltaram. ■ **flare up 1** (*fogo*) avivar-se **2** (*conflito*) rebentar **3** (*problema*) reaparecer

flash /flæʃ/ *s* **1** clarão: *~ of lightning* relâmpago **2** lampejo: *~ of genius* lance de gênio **3** (*Fot*) flash ▶ **a flash in the pan** um sucesso passageiro **in a/like a flash** num piscar de olhos ● *vi* **1** relampejar, brilhar: *It flashed on and off.* Ele acendeu e apagou. **2** *vt* piscar (*luz*): *~ your headlights* piscar os faróis do carro **3** *vt* mostrar rapidamente (*imagem*) ■ **flash by, past, through, etc.** passar/cruzar como um raio

flashlight /ˈflæʃlaɪt/ *s* (USA) lanterna

flashy /ˈflæʃi/ *adj* (**-ier, -iest**) chamativo

flask /flæsk; GB flɑːsk/ s **1** garrafa térmica **2** garrafa de bolso

flat /flæt/ s **1** (esp GB) apartamento **2** the ~ of sth (GB) a parte plana de algo: the ~ of your hand a palma da mão **3** [gen pl] (Geog): mud flats brejo **4** (Mús) bemol **5** (USA, coloq) pneu furado ● adj (flatter, flattest) **1** plano, liso **2** (pneu) furado **3** (GB) (bateria) descarregado **4** (bebida) choco **5** (Mús) desafinado **6** (preço, etc.) único ● adv: lie down ~ deitar-se completamente esticado ● **flat out** (trabalhar, correr, etc.) a toda **in 10 seconds, etc. flat** em apenas 10 segundos, etc.

flatly /ˈflætli/ adv completamente

flatten /ˈflætn/ **1** vt ~ (sth) (out) alisar algo **2** vt derrotar, arrasar **3** vi ~ (out) aplainar-se

flatter /ˈflætər/ vt **1** adular: I was flattered by your invitation. Fiquei lisonjeado com seu convite. **2** (roupa, penteado) favorecer **3** ~ yourself (that) ter a ilusão (de que) flattering adj lisonjeiro, favorecedor

flaunt /flɔːnt/ vt alardear

flavor (GB -our) /ˈfleɪvər/ s sabor, gosto ● vt condimentar

flaw /flɔː/ s **1** defeito **2** falha **flawed** adj defeituoso **flawless** adj impecável

flea /fliː/ s pulga

fleck /flek/ s **1** partícula, pingo (pó, cor)

flee /fliː/ (pt, pp **fled** /fled/) **1** vi fugir **2** vt abandonar

fleet /fliːt/ s frota

flesh /fleʃ/ s **1** carne **2** (de fruta) polpa ▶ **flesh and blood** corpo humano: It was more than ~ and blood could stand. Foi mais forte do que qualquer pessoa agüentaria. **in the flesh** em pessoa **your own flesh and blood** (parente) do seu próprio sangue

flew /fluː/ pret de **FLY**

flex /fleks/ s fio elétrico ● vt flexionar **flexible** /ˈfleksəbl/ adj flexível

flick /flɪk/ s **1** pancadinha rápida **2** ~ of the wrist movimento de pulso ● vt **1** acertar **2** ~ sth (off, on, etc.) mover/bater em algo rapidamente ▶ **flick through (sth)** folhear (algo) rapidamente

flicker /ˈflɪkər/ vi **1** tremeluzir **2** vislumbrar ● s **1** tremulação **2** vislumbre

flight /flaɪt/ s **1** vôo **2** fuga: take (to) ~ fugir **3** (aves) bando (escadas) lance

flight attendant s comissário/a de bordo

flimsy /ˈflɪmzi/ adj (-ier, -iest) **1** (tecido) fino **2** fraco

flinch /flɪntʃ/ vi **1** retroceder **2** ~ from (doing) sth esquivar-se diante de (fazer) algo

fling /flɪŋ/ vt (pt, pp **flung**) **1** ~ sth (at sth) lançar algo (contra algo): ~ your arms around sb lançar os braços ao redor do pescoço de alguém **2** empurrar/jogar (com força): He flung the door open. Ele abriu a porta de um só golpe. ● s **1** farra **2** aventura amorosa

flint /flɪnt/ s **1** pederneira **2** pedra (isqueiro)

flip /flɪp/ (-pp-) **1** vt lançar: ~ a coin tirar cara ou coroa **2** vt, vi ~ (sth) (over) virar (algo) **3** vi (coloq) ficar uma fera

flippant /ˈflɪpənt/ adj irreverente

flirt /flɜːrt/ vi flertar ● s namorador/eira

flit /flɪt/ vi (-tt-) esvoaçar

float /floʊt/ **1** vi flutuar **2** vi boiar **3** vt fazer flutuar **4** vt (idéia) propor ● s **1** bóia **2** flutuador **3** carro alegórico

flock /flɑk/ s **1** rebanho (ovelhas, cabras) **2** bando (aves, pessoas) ● vi **1** agrupar-se **2** ~ into/to sth ir em bando a algo

flog /flɑg/ vt (-gg-) **1** açoitar **2** ~ sth (off) (GB, coloq) vender algo ▶ **flog a dead horse** esforçar-se por nada

flood /flʌd/ s **1** inundação **2** the **Flood** o Dilúvio **3** enxurrada ● vt, vi inundar(-se) ▶ **flood in** chegar em enormes quantidades

flooding /ˈflʌdɪŋ/ s [U] inundação

floodlight /ˈflʌdlaɪt/ s holofote ● vt (pt, pp **-lit** /-lɪt/) iluminar com holofote

floor /flɔːr/ s **1** assoalho: on the ~ no chão **2** andar **3** (mar, vale) fundo ● vt **1** derrubar ao chão **2** confundir

floorboard /ˈflɔːrbɔːrd/ s tábua (assoalho)

flop /flɑp/ s (coloq) fracasso ● vi (-pp-) **1** despencar **2** (coloq) fracassar

floppy /ˈflɑpi/ adj (-ier, -iest) frouxo, flexível

floppy disk (tb **floppy**) s disquete

flora /ˈflɔːrə/ s [pl] flora

floral /ˈflɔːrəl/ adj floral: ~ tribute coroa de flores

florist /ˈflɔːrɪst; GB ˈflɒr-/

s florista florist's s floricultura

flounder /'flaʊndər/ vi **1** vacilar, atrapalhar-se **2** debater-se **3** mover-se com dificuldade

flour /'flaʊər/ s farinha

flourish /'flʌrɪʃ/ s **1** vi prosperar **2** vt (arma) brandir ● s floreio

flow /floʊ/ s **1** fluxo **2** corrente **3** circulação **4** escoamento ● vi (pt, pp -ed) **1** fluir: ~ into the sea desaguar no mar ◇ ~ in/into sth chegar a algo num fluxo contínuo **2** circular **3** deslizar **4** ~ in/out (maré) subir/baixar

flower /'flaʊər/ s flor: ~ bed canteiro (de flores) ● vi florescer

flowering /'flaʊərɪŋ/ s florescimento ● adj que dá flores

flowerpot /'flaʊərpɒt/ s vaso de (plantar) flores

flown /floʊn/ pp de FLY

flu /fluː/ s (coloq) gripe

fluctuate /'flʌktʃueɪt/ vi flutuar, variar

fluent /'fluːənt/ adj **1** She's ~ in Russian. Ela fala russo com fluência. ◇ speak ~ French dominar o francês **2** (orador) eloqüente **3** (estilo) articulado

fluff /flʌf/ s **1** felpa: a piece of ~ uma felpa **2** penugem fluffy adj (-ier, -iest) **1** felpudo, coberto de penugem **2** macio

fluid /'fluːɪd/ adj **1** fluido **2** (plano) flexível **3** (situação) instável **4** (estilo, movimento) gracioso, solto ● s **1** líquido **2** (Quím) fluido

fluke /fluːk/ s (coloq) (golpe de) sorte

flung /flʌŋ/ pret, pp de FLING

flunk /flʌŋk/ vt (coloq) (Educ) ser reprovado

flurry /'flʌri/ s (pl -ies) **1** (vento) rajada **2** (chuva) pancada **3** nevada **4** ~ (of sth) (atividade, emoção) onda (de algo)

flush /flʌʃ/ s rubor: hot ~ onda de calor ● **1** vi ruborizar-se **2** vt (privada) dar descarga

fluster /'flʌstər/ vt aturdir: get flustered ficar nervoso

flute /fluːt/ s flauta

flutter /'flʌtər/ **1** vi (pássaros) esvoaçar, inquietar-se **2** vi (asas) agitar(-se) **3** vi tremular **4** vt agitar ● s **1** (asas) bater **2** pestanejar ▶ all of a/in a flutter numa grande agitação

fly /flaɪ/ s (pl flies) **1** mosca **2** (GB flies [pl]) braguilha ● (pt flew pp flown) **1** vi voar: ~ away/off sair voando **2** vi ir/viajar de avião: ~ in/out/back chegar/partir/voltar de avião **3** vt pilotar **4** vt

transportar (de avião) **5** vi ir rápido: I must ~. Eu tenho de correr. **6** vi (repentinamente): The wheel flew off. A roda saiu em disparada. ◇ The door flew open. A porta abriu-se de repente. **7** vi estar solto no ar **8** vt hastear **9** vt (pipa) soltar ▶ fly high ir longe ■ fly at sb lançar-se sobre alguém

flying /'flaɪɪŋ/ s vôo ● adj voador ▶ get off to a flying start começar bem

flying saucer s disco voador

flyover /'flaɪoʊvər/ s viaduto

foal /foʊl/ s potro → POTRO

foam /foʊm/ s **1** espuma **2** (tb ~ rubber) espuma (de enchimento) ● vi espumar

focus /'foʊkəs/ s foco: in ~/out of ~ enfocado/desfocado ● (-s- ou -ss-) **1** vt, vi enfocar **2** vt concentrar: ~ your attention/mind on sth concentrar-se em algo

fodder /'fɒdər/ s forragem

foetus (GB) = FETUS

fog /fɒg; GB fɒg/ s neblina ● vi (-gg-) ~ (up) embaçar(-se)

foggy /'fɒgi; GB 'fɒgi/ adj (-ier, -iest) nevoento: a ~ day um dia de neblina

foil /fɔɪl/ s **1** lâmina/folha (de metal): aluminum ~ papel-alumínio ● vt frustrar

fold /foʊld/ s, vt, vi dobrar(-se), fechar(-se): ~ sth back/down/up fechar/dobrar algo **2** vi (negócio) falir **3** vi (peça de teatro) sair de cartaz ▶ fold your arms cruzar os braços ● s **1** prega **2** cercado

folder /'foʊldər/ s pasta (Informát, etc.)

folding /'foʊldɪŋ/ adj dobrável NOTA Só se usa antes de substantivo: ~ table/bed.

folk /foʊk/ s **1** pessoas: country ~ gente do campo (folks) [pl] (coloq) pessoal **2** (folks) [pl] (coloq) pais, parentes ● adj folclórico, popular

follow /'fɒloʊ/ vt, vi **1** ~ (on) seguir: ~ the crowd ir com/acompanhar a maioria **2** entender **3** ~ (on) (from sth) resultar, ser a conseqüência (de algo) ▶ as follows o seguinte ■ follow sth through prosseguir com algo até o fim ■ follow sth up complementar, acompanhar algo

follower /'fɒloʊər/ s seguidor/a

following /'fɒloʊɪŋ/ adj seguinte ● s **1** (the following) o(s) seguinte(s) **2** seguidores ● prep após, depois de

follow-up s continuação

fond /fɒnd/ adj (~er ~est) **1** [antes de substantivo] carinhoso: ~ memories lembranças queridas **2** be ~ of sb ter carinho por alguém **3** be ~ of (doing) sth gostar muito de (fazer) algo **4** (esperança) ingênuo

fondle /ˈfɒndl/ vt acariciar

food /fuːd/ s alimento, comida ▶ food for thought algo em que pensar

food processor s processador de alimentos

foodstuffs /ˈfuːdstʌfs/ s gêneros alimentícios

fool /fuːl/ s bobo ▶ act/play the fool fazer-se de bobo be no/nobody's fool não ser (nenhum) bobo make a fool of yourself/sb fazer papel/alguém de bobo • **1** vi gracejar **2** vt enganar ■fool around/about perder tempo: Stop fooling about! Pare de brincar!

foolish /ˈfuːlɪʃ/ adj **1** bobo **2** ridículo

foolproof /ˈfuːlpruːf/ adj infalível

foot /fʊt/ s **1** (pl feet) pé: on ~ a pé → ARM **2** (pl feet ou foot) (abrev ft.) (medida) pé (30,48 cm) → Ver pág. 224 ▶ fall/land on your feet safar-se de uma situação difícil (por sorte) put your feet up descansar put your foot down bater o pé (contra algo) put your foot in it dar uma fora • vt ▶ foot the bill (for sth) pagar a conta (de algo)

football /ˈfʊtbɔːl/ s **1** (USA) futebol americano **2** (GB) futebol **3** bola (de futebol)

football player s jogador/a de futebol (GB tb **footballer**) s jogador/a de futebol

footing /ˈfʊtɪŋ/ s [U] **1** equilíbrio **2** situação: on an equal ~ em igualdade de condições

footnote /ˈfʊtnəʊt/ s nota de rodapé

footpath /ˈfʊtpɑːθ; GB -pɑːθ/ s trilha, caminho para pedestres

footprint /ˈfʊtprɪnt/ s [ger pl] pegada

footstep /ˈfʊtstep/ s passo

footwear /ˈfʊtweər/ s [U] calçados

for /fər, fɔːr/ prep **1** para: What's it ~? Para que é isso? ◊ It's time ~ supper. Está na hora de jantar. **2** por **3** (em expressões temporais) durante, por: I haven't seen him ~ two days. Eu não o vejo há dois dias. NOTA Quando for se traduz por "há", "faz", pode ser confundido com since,

"desde". As duas palavras são usadas para expressar o tempo que dura a ação do verbo, mas for especifica a duração da ação e since o início da ação: I've been living here ~ three months. ◊ I've been living here since May. Em ambos os casos se usa o "present perfect", nunca o presente. → AGO **4** ~ (doing) sth a favor de (fazer) algo **5** [com infinitivo]: There's no need ~ you to go. Você não precisa ir. ◊ It's impossible ~ me to do it. É impossível para mim fazê-lo. **6** (outros usos): I ~ Irene (GB) I de ilha ◊ ~ miles and miles por milhas e milhas ◊ What does he do ~ a job? Com o que ele trabalha? ▶ be (in) for it (GB, coloq): He's ~ it now! Agora ele está frito! for all: ~ all his wealth apesar de toda a sua riqueza NOTA Para o uso de for em PHRASAL VERBS, ver o verbo, p. ex. look for em LOOK. • conj (fml) visto que

forbid /fərˈbɪd/ vt (pt forbade /fərˈbæd, -ˈbeɪd; GB fəˈbæd/ pp forbidden /fərˈbɪdn/) proibir forbidding adj imponente, amedrontador

force /fɔːrs/ s **1** força: by ~ à força ▶ in force em vigor: come into ~ entrar em vigor • vt forçar, obrigar: ~ sth on sb impor algo a alguém

forcible /ˈfɔːrsəbl/ adj **1** à força **2** convincente forcibly adv **1** à força **2** energicamente

ford /fɔːrd/ s vau • vt vadear

fore /fɔːr/ adj dianteiro • s proa ▶ be/come to the fore destacar-se

forearm /ˈfɔːrɑːrm/ s antebraço

forecast /ˈfɔːrkæst; GB -kɑːst/ vt (pt, pp forecast ou forecasted) prever • s previsão

forefinger /ˈfɔːrfɪŋɡər/ s (dedo) indicador

forefront /ˈfɔːrfrʌnt/ s ▶ at/in the forefront of sth à frente de algo

foreground /ˈfɔːrɡraʊnd/ s primeiro plano

forehead /ˈfɔːrhed, -ɪd; GB ˈfɒrɪd/ s testa

foreign /ˈfɔːrən; GB ˈfɒr-/ adj **1** estrangeiro **2** exterior: Foreign Office/Secretary (GB) Ministério/Ministro das Relações Exteriores **3** (fml) ~ to sb/sth estranho a alguém/algo foreigner /ˈfɔːrənər; GB ˈfɒrənə(r)/ s estrangeiro/a

foremost /ˈfɔːrməʊst/ adj mais

importante ● adv principalmente

forerunner /'fɔːrʌnər/ s precur-
sor/a

foresee /fɔːr'siː/ vt (pt **foresaw**
/-'sɔː/ pp **foreseen** /-'siːn/) prever
foreseeable adj previsível:
for/in the ~ future em futuro
próximo

foresight /'fɔːrsaɪt/ s previsão

forest /'fɔːrɪst/ GB 'fɒr-/ s floresta

foretell /fɔːr'tel/ vt (pt, pp **fore-
told** /-'toʊld/) (fml) profetizar

forever /fə'revər/ adv 1 (GB **for
ever**) para sempre 2 constantemente 3 It takes her ~ to get
dressed. Ela leva uma eternidade para se vestir.

foreword /'fɔːrwɜːrd/ s prefácio

forge /fɔːrdʒ/ s forja ● vt 1 forjar
2 falsificar 3 (laços) estabelecer
■**forge ahead** progredir com
rapidez

forgery /'fɔːrdʒəri/ s (pl **-ies**) falsificação

forget /fər'get/ (pt **forgot** /-'gɒt/
pp **forgotten** /-'gɒtn/) 1 vt, vi ~
(**sth/to do sth**); ~ (**about sb/sth**)
esquecer(-se) (de algo/fazer
algo); (de alguém/algo) 2 vt
deixar de pensar em ▸ **not for-
getting**... sem esquecer de...
forgetful adj 1 esquecido 2 descuidado

forgive /fər'gɪv/ vt (pt **forgave**
/-'geɪv/ pp **forgiven** /-'gɪvn/) perdoar **forgiveness** s perdão **for-
giving** adj clemente

fork /fɔːrk/ s 1 garfo 2 forcado 3
bifurcação ● vi 1 bifurcar-se 2
(pessoa): ~ left virar à esquerda
■**fork out** (**for/on sth**) (coloq)
soltar grana para algo

form /fɔːrm/ s 1 forma 2 formulário 3 formalidades 4 (GB)
(Educ) série ▸ **in/off form** em
forma/fora de forma ● vt 1 formar 2 vi formar-se

formal /'fɔːrml/ adj 1 cerimoni-
oso 2 formal 3 (declaração)
oficial

formality /fɔːr'mæləti/ s (pl **-ies**)
1 cerimônia 2 trâmite: legal for-
malities formalidades legais

formally /'fɔːrməli/ adv 1 oficialmente 2 formalmente

format /'fɔːrmæt/ s formato

formation /fɔːr'meɪʃn/ s
formação

former /'fɔːrmər/ adj 1 anterior 2
antigo: in ~ times em tempos
passados 3 primeiro (de duas
coisas) ● **the former** pron aquilo,
aquele/-la, aqueles/-las

formerly /'fɔːrmərli/ adv anteriormente

formidable /'fɔːrmɪdəbl/ adj
1 extraordinário, formidável
2 (tarefa) tremendo

formula /'fɔːrmjələ/ s (pl **-s**
(uso científico) **-lae** /'fɔːrmjuliː/)
fórmula

forsake /fər'seɪk/ vt (pt **forsook**
/-'sʊk/ pp **forsaken** /-'seɪkən/) 1
renunciar a 2 abandonar

fort /fɔːrt/ s forte

forth /fɔːrθ/ adv (fml) para
frente/diante: from that day ~
daquele dia em diante ▸ **and (so
on and) so forth** e assim por
diante

forthcoming /fɔːrθ'kʌmɪŋ/ adj
1 próximo 2 disponível 3
(pessoa) prestativo NOTA Nos
sentidos 2 e 3, não se usa antes
de substantivo.

forthright /'fɔːrθraɪt/ adj
1 (pessoa) direto 2 (oposição)
enérgico

fortieth Ver FORTY

fortification /fɔːrtɪfɪ'keɪʃn/ s
fortalecimento, fortificação

fortify /'fɔːrtɪfaɪ/ vt (pt, pp **forti-
fied**) 1 fortificar 2 ~ **sb/yourself**
fortalecer alguém; forta-
lecer-se

fortnight /'fɔːrtnaɪt/ s (GB)
quinzena

fortnightly /'fɔːrtnaɪtli/ adj (GB)
quinzenal ● adv quinzenal-
mente

fortress /'fɔːrtrəs/ s fortaleza

fortunate /'fɔːrtʃənət/ adj
afortunado: be ~ ter sorte
fortunately adv felizmente

fortune /'fɔːrtʃən/ s 1 fortuna 2
sorte

forty /'fɔːrti/ adj, pron, s
quarenta **fortieth** 1 adj, pron
quadragésimo 2 s quadragé-
sima parte, quarenta avos

forward /'fɔːrwərd/ adj 1 para
frente 2 dianteiro: ~ position
posição avançada 3 ~ planning
planejamento para o futuro 4
atrevido ● adv 1 (tb **forwards**)
para frente 2 em diante ● vt
remeter: please ~ favor enviar
(para novo endereço) ◇ for-
warding address endereço novo
para onde enviar as cartas ● s
(Esporte) atacante

fossil /'fɒsl/ s fóssil

foster /'fɒstər/ vt 1 fomentar
2 acolher em uma família: ~
parents pais de criação

fought /fɔːt/ pret, pp de FIGHT

foul /faʊl/ adj 1 sujo 2 (odor,
sabor) nojento 3 (caráter,
tempo) horrível ● s (Esporte)
falta ● vt (Esporte) cometer

uma falta contra ∎ **foul sth up** estragar algo

foul play s **1** crime violento **2** (*Esporte*) jogo sujo

found /faʊnd/ *pret, pp de* FIND ● *vt* **1** fundar **2** fundamentar: *founded on fact* baseado em fatos

foundation /faʊnˈdeɪʃn/ s **1** fundação **2** fundamento **3** (*tb* ~ **cream**) (*maquiagem*) base

founder /ˈfaʊndər/ s fundador/a

fountain /ˈfaʊntɪn; *GB* -tən/ s fonte, bebedouro

fountain pen s caneta-tinteiro

four /fɔːr/ *adj, pron, s* quatro

fourteen /ˌfɔːrˈtiːn/ *adj, pron, s* quatorze **fourteenth 1** *adj* décimo quarto **2** *pron, adv* o(s) décimo(s) quarto(s), a(s) décima(s) quarta(s) **3** s décima quarta parte, quatorze avos

fourth /fɔːrθ/ (*abrev* **4th**) *adj* quarto ● *pron, adv* o(s)/a(s) quarto(s)/a(s) ● s **1** quarto, quarto (**the fourth**) o dia quatro **3** (*tb* ~ **gear**) quarta (*marcha*)

fowl /faʊl/ s (*pl* **fowl** *ou* ~**s**) ave (*doméstica*)

fox /fɑks/ s raposa

foyer /ˈfɔɪer; *GB* ˈfɔɪeɪ/ s hall de entrada

fraction /ˈfrækʃn/ s fração

fracture /ˈfræktʃər/ s fratura ● *vt, vi* fraturar(-se)

fragile /ˈfrædʒl; *GB* -dʒaɪl/ *adj* frágil

fragment /ˈfrægmənt/ s fragmento ● /ˈfrægˈment/ *vt, vi* fragmentar(-se)

fragrance /ˈfreɪɡrəns/ s fragrância, aroma

fragrant /ˈfreɪɡrənt/ *adj* aromático

frail /freɪl/ *adj* fraco NOTA Aplica-se sobretudo a idosos ou doentes.

frame /freɪm/ s **1** moldura **2** armação, estrutura ▸ **frame of mind** estado de espírito ● *vt* **1** emoldurar **2** (*pergunta, etc.*) formular **3** (*coloq*) incriminar (*pessoa inocente*): *I've been framed.* Caí numa cilada.

framework /ˈfreɪmwɜːrk/ s **1** armação, estrutura **2** sistema

franc /fræŋk/ s (*moeda*) franco

frank /fræŋk/ *adj* franco

frantic /ˈfræntɪk/ *adj* frenético, desesperado

fraternal /frəˈtɜːrnl/ *adj* fraternal

fraternity /frəˈtɜːrnəti/ s (*pl* -**ies**) **1** fraternidade **2** irmandade,

confraria

fraud /frɔːd/ s **1** fraude **2** impostor/a

fraught /frɔːt/ *adj* **1** ~ **with sth** cheio, carregado de algo **2** tenso: *She sounded* ~. Pela voz, ela parecia preocupada.

fray /freɪ/ *vt, vi* desgastar(-se), desfiar(-se)

freak /friːk/ s (*coloq*) excêntrico, anomalia

freckle /ˈfrekl/ s sarda **freckled** *adj* sardento

free /friː/ *adj* (**freer** /ˈfriːər/, **freest** /ˈfriːɪst/) **1** livre: ~ *speech* liberdade de expressão ◇ *set sb* ~ colocar alguém em liberdade ◇ *of your own* ~ *will* por vontade própria **2** (*sem prender*) solto **3** gratuito: ~ *of charge* grátis **4** ~ **with sth** generoso com algo **5** atrevido ▸ **feel free** sinta-se/ esteja à vontade **free and easy** descontraído **get, have, etc. a free hand** ter total liberdade (*para fazer algo*) ● *vt* **1** libertar **2** livrar **3** soltar ● *adv* **1** livremente **2** generosamente, copiosamente

freedom /ˈfriːdəm/ s **1** ~ (**of sth**) ~ (**to do sth**) liberdade (de algo); (*para fazer algo*) **2** ~ **from sth** imunidade contra algo

freemason /ˈfriːmeɪsn/ *Ver* MASON (2)

free-range *adj*: ~ *eggs* ovos de galinha caipira

freeway /ˈfriːweɪ/ s rodovia → RODOVIA

freeze /friːz/ (*pt* **froze** *pp* **frozen**) **1** *vt, vi* gelar: *I'm freezing!* Estou morrendo de frio! ◇ *freezing point* ponto de solidificação **2** *vt, vi* (*comida, preços, etc.*) congelar **3** *vt, vi* paralisar(-se): *Freeze!* Não se mova! ● s **1** frio intenso (*abaixo de zero*) **2** (*preços, etc.*) congelamento

freezer /ˈfriːzər/ s congelador

freight /freɪt/ s frete

French fry s batata frita

French window (*USA tb* **French door**) s porta envidraçada

frenzied /ˈfrenzid/ *adj* frenético, enlouquecido

frenzy /ˈfrenzi/ s frenesi

frequency /ˈfriːkwənsi/ s (*pl* -**ies**) freqüência

frequent /ˈfriːkwənt/ *adj* freqüente ● /frɪˈkwent/ *vt* freqüentar

frequently /ˈfriːkwəntli/ *adv* freqüentemente → ALWAYS

fresh /freʃ/ *adj* (-**er**, -**est**) **1** novo, outro **2** recente **3** fresco **4**

freshen 330

(*água*) doce **freshly** *adv*: ~ baked recém-saído do forno **freshness** *s* **1** frescor **2** novidade

freshen /ˈfreʃn/ **1** *vt* ~ **sth (up)** dar nova vida a algo **2** *vt, vi* ~ **(yourself) up** lavar(-se) **3** *vi* (*vento*) refrescar

freshman /ˈfreʃmən/ *s* (*pl* -men) (*USA*) (*GB* **fresher**) calouro

freshwater /ˈfreʃwɔːtər/ *adj* de água doce

fret /fret/ *vi* (-tt-) ~ **(about/at/over sth)** ficar ansioso (com algo)

friar /ˈfraɪər/ *s* frade

friction /ˈfrɪkʃn/ *s* **1** fricção, roçar **2** desavença

Friday /ˈfraɪdeɪ, -di/ *s* (*abrev* **Fri.**) sexta(-feira) → MONDAY ▸ **Good Friday** Sexta-feira Santa

fridge /frɪdʒ/ *s* (*coloq*) geladeira

fried /fraɪd/ *pret, pp de* FRY ● *adj* frito

friend /frend/ *s* **1** amigo/a, colega **2** ~ **of/to sth** amante de algo ▸ **be/make friends (with sb)** ser/tornar-se amigo (de alguém) **have friends in high places** ter grandes contatos/pistolões **make friends** fazer amigos

friendly /ˈfrendli/ *adj* (-ier, -iest) **1** simpático NOTA Sympathetic se traduz por "solidário", "compreensivo". **2** (*relação*) amigável **3** (*conselho*) de amigo **4** (*ambiente*) acolhedor **5** (*jogo*) amistoso **friendliness** *s* cordialidade

friendship /ˈfrendʃɪp/ *s* amizade

fright /fraɪt/ *s* susto

frighten /ˈfraɪtn/ *vt* assustar **frightened** *adj* assustado: *be ~ of sth* ter medo de algo **frightening** *adj* assustador

frightful /ˈfraɪtfl/ *adj* **1** horrível **2** (*GB*) a ~ mess uma bagunça terrível **frightfully** *adv* (*GB, coloq*): *I'm ~ sorry.* Sinto muitíssimo.

frigid /ˈfrɪdʒɪd/ *adj* frígido

frill /frɪl/ *s* **1** babado **2** [*ger pl*] adorno

fringe /frɪndʒ/ *s* **1** franja **2** margem ● *adj*: ~ *theater* teatro alternativo ◇ ~ *benefits* benefícios adicionais ● *vt* ▸ **be fringed by/with sth** estar cercado by algo

frisk /frɪsk/ **1** *vt* revistar **2** *vi* saltar **frisky** *adj* brincalhão

frivolity /frɪˈvɒləti/ *s* frivolidade

frivolous /ˈfrɪvələs/ *adj* frívolo

frock /frɒk/ *s* vestido

frog /frɒɡ; *GB* frɒɡ/ *s* rã

from /frəm, frʌm/ *prep* **1** *de* (*procedência*): *the train ~ London* o trem (procedente) de Londres

◇ **take sth away** ~ **sb** tirar algo de alguém **2** (*tempo, situação*) desde: ~ *above/below* de cima/baixo ◇ ~ *time to time* de vez em quando → SINCE **3** por: ~ *choice* (*GB*) (*USA* by choice) por escolha **4** *choose from two options* escolher entre duas opções **5** *Wine is made* ~ *grapes.* Vinho é feito de uvas. **6** (*Mat*): *7 ~ 28 is/ are 21.* 28 menos 7 são 21. ▸ **from… on**: ~ *now/then on* de agora/dali em diante NOTA Para o uso de **from** em PHRASAL VERBS, ver o verbo, p. ex. **hear from** em HEAR.

front /frʌnt/ *s* **1** the ~ **(of sth)** a frente, a parte dianteira (de algo) **2 (the front)** (*Mil*) frente de combate **3** fachada **4** terreno: *on the financial* ~ na área econômica ● *adj* dianteiro, da frente ● *adv* ▸ **in front** em frente: *the row in* ~ a fila de frente **in front of 1** diante de **2** ante NOTA Em frente de se traduz por **across from** ou **opposite** quando os objetos estão frente a frente. ▸ **up front** (*coloq*) (*pagamento*) adiantado

front cover *s* capa (*livro, etc.*)

front door *s* porta da frente/de entrada

frontier /frʌnˈtɪər; *GB* ˈfrʌntɪə(r)/ *s* fronteira → BORDER

front page *s* primeira página

front row *s* primeira fila

frost /frɔːst; *GB* frɒst/ *s* **1** geada **2** gelo (da geada) ● *vt, vi* cobrir com geada **frosty** *adj* (-ier, -iest) **1** gelado **2** coberto de geada **3** frio

froth /frɔːθ; *GB* frɒθ/ *s* espuma (*cerveja, etc.*) ● *vi* espumar

frown /fraun/ *vi* franzir as sobrancelhas/o cenho ■ **frown on/upon sth** desaprovar algo

froze /frəʊz/ *pret de* FREEZE

frozen /ˈfrəʊzn/ *pp de* FREEZE

fruit /fruːt/ *s* **1** [*ger U*] fruta(s) **2** fruto

fruitful /ˈfruːtfl/ *adj* proveitoso

fruition /fruˈɪʃn/ *s* realização: *come to* ~ realizar-se

fruitless /ˈfruːtləs/ *adj* infrutífero

frustrate /ˈfrʌstreɪt; *GB* frʌˈstreɪt/ *vt* frustrar, desbaratar

fry /fraɪ/ *vt, vi* (*pt, pp* **fried**) fritar **frying pan** *s* frigideira ▸ **out of the frying pan into the fire** sair da frigideira para o fogo

fuel /ˈfjuːəl/ *s* **1** combustível **2** estímulo

fugitive /ˈfjuːdʒətɪv/ *s* fugitivo/a

fulfill (GB **fulfil**) /fʊlˈfɪl/ vt (-ll-) **1** (*promessa, dever*) cumprir **2** (*tarefa, função*) realizar **3** (*desejo, requisitos*) satisfazer

full /fʊl/ adj (~er, ~est) **1** ~ (of sth) cheio (de algo) **2** ~ of sth tomado por algo **3** ~ (up) satisfeito (*depois de comer*) **4** (*informações*) completo: in ~ detalhadamente **5** (*discussões*) extenso **6** (*sentido*) amplo **7** (*investigação*) detalhado **8** (*roupa*) folgada ► (at) full blast/speed a toda (velocidade) come full circle voltar ao ponto de partida full of yourself: be ~ of yourself ser cheio de si in full swing em plena atividade to the full (GB) ao máximo ● adv **1** ~ in the face bem no rosto **2** muito: know ~ well that... saber muito bem que...

full board s pensão completa

full-length adj **1** (*espelho*) de corpo inteiro **2** (*roupa*) longo

full stop (GB) s ponto final (*Ortografia*)

full-time adj, adv (de) período integral

fully /ˈfʊli/ adv **1** completamente **2** de todo **3** ~ two hours duas horas completas

fumble /ˈfʌmbl/ vi ~ (with sth) manusear desajeitadamente (algo)

fume /fjuːm/ s [ger pl] fumaça: *poisonous fumes* gases tóxicos ● vi estar furioso

fun /fʌn/ s **1** diversão: *have ~ divertir-se ◇ take the ~ out of sth* tirar a graça de algo ► make fun of sb/sth ridicularizar alguém/algo ● adj divertido

function /ˈfʌŋkʃn/ s **1** função **2** cerimônia ● vi **1** funcionar **2** ~ as sth fazer as vezes de algo

fund /fʌnd/ s fundo ● vt financiar

fundamental /ˌfʌndəˈmentl/ adj fundamental ● s [ger pl] fundamento(s)

funeral /ˈfjuːnərəl/ s **1** funeral: ~ *parlor* (casa) funerária ◇ ~ *director* agente funerário **2** cortejo fúnebre

fungus /ˈfʌŋɡəs/ s (pl -gi /-gaɪ, -dʒaɪ/) fungo

funnel /ˈfʌnl/ s **1** funil **2** chaminé ● vt (-l-, GB -ll-) colocar com funil

funny /ˈfʌni/ adj (-ier, -iest) **1** engraçado, divertido **2** esquisito: *funnily enough* por estranho que pareça

fur /fɜːr/ s **1** pêlo (*animal*) **2** pele: ~ *coat* casaco de peles

furious /ˈfjʊəriəs/ adj **1** furioso **2** violento **3** (*debate*) acalorado

furiously adv violentamente, furiosamente

furnace /ˈfɜːrnɪs/ s caldeira

furnish /ˈfɜːrnɪʃ/ vt **1** mobiliar **2** ~ sb/sth with sth prover algo a alguém/algo **furnishings** s [pl] mobília

furniture /ˈfɜːrnɪtʃər/ s [U] mobília, móveis: *piece of ~* móvel

furrow /ˈfʌroʊ/ s sulco ● vt sulcar: *furrowed brow* rosto preocupado

furry /ˈfɜːri/ adj (-ier, -iest) **1** peludo **2** de/como pele

further /ˈfɜːrðər/ adj (comp de far) **1** mais distante **2** mais: *until ~ notice* até novo aviso ● adv **1** mais distante: *How much ~ is it to Oxford?* Quanto falta para (chegar a) Oxford? **2** além disso: *Further to my letter...* Em relação à minha carta... **3** *hear nothing ~* não ter mais notícias NOTA Farther e further são formas comparativas de far, mas só são sinônimos quando se referem a distâncias: *Which is further/farther?*

furthermore /ˌfɜːrðərˈmɔːr/ adv além disso

furthest /ˈfɜːrðɪst/ adj, adv (superl de far) o mais distante

fury /ˈfjʊəri/ s fúria

fuse /fjuːz/ s **1** fusível **2** pavio **3** estopim, detonador ● **1** vi fundir(-se) **2** vi (*fusível, etc.*) queimar **3** vt ~ sth (together) soldar algo

fusion /ˈfjuːʒn/ s fusão

fuss /fʌs/ s [U] alvoroço, preocupação exagerada ► make a fuss of/over sb/sth dar muita atenção a alguém/algo make, kick up, etc. a fuss (about/over sth) fazer um escândalo/uma cena (por algo) ● vi **1** ~ (about) preocupar-se (com ninharias) **2** ~ over sb dar muita atenção a alguém

fussy /ˈfʌsi/ adj (-ier, -iest) **1** meticuloso **2** ~ (about sth) exigente (com algo)

futile /ˈfjuːtl; GB -taɪl/ adj inútil

future /ˈfjuːtʃər/ s futuro: *in (the) ~* no futuro/de agora em diante ● adj futuro

fuze (USA) = FUSE (3)

fuzzy /ˈfʌzi/ adj (-ier, -iest) **1** felpudo **2** borrado **3** (*mente*) confuso

Gg

G, g /dʒiː/ s (pl **G's, g's** /dʒiːz/) **1** G, g **2** (Mús) sol

gable /ˈgeɪbl/ s empena

gadget /ˈgædʒɪt/ s aparelho

gag /gæg/ s **1** mordaça **2** piada (de comediante) • vt (-gg-) amordaçar

gage (USA) = GAUGE

gaiety /ˈgeɪəti/ s alegria

gain /geɪn/ s **1** lucro **2** aumento • **1** vt ganhar, obter **2** vt aumentar, ganhar: ~ two kilograms engordar dois quilos **3** vi ~ by/from (doing) sth beneficiar-se de (fazer) algo **4** vi (relógio) adiantar(-se) ● **gain on sb/sth** aproximar-se de alguém/algo

gait /geɪt/ s [sing] (modo de) andar

galaxy /ˈgæləksi/ s (pl -ies) galáxia

gale /geɪl/ s **1** vendaval **2** (no mar) temporal

gallant /ˈgælənt/ adj **1** valente **2** (antiq) /gəˈlænt/ galante gallantry s valentia

gallery /ˈgæləri/ s (pl -ies) **1** (tb art ~) galeria de arte → MUSEUM **2** (comercial, Teat) galeria

galley /ˈgæli/ s **1** cozinha (de avião ou barco) **2** (Náut) galé

gallon /ˈgælən/ s (abrev gall) galão NOTA Um galão equivale a 3,8 litros nos EUA e 4,5 litros na Grã-Bretanha.

gallop /ˈgæləp/ vt, vi galopar ● s galope

the gallows /ˈgæləʊz/ s a forca

gamble /ˈgæmbl/ vt, vi jogar (a dinheiro) ● **gamble on (doing) sth** apostar em/arriscar (fazer) algo ● s **1** jogada **2** be a ~ ser arriscado gambler s jogador/a gambling s jogo (de azar)

game /geɪm/ s **1** jogo **2** partida (games) [pl] (GB) educação física **4** [U] caça (carne) ● adj: Are you ~? Você topa?

gammon /ˈgæmən/ s (GB) [U] presunto defumado

gander /ˈgændə(r)/ s ganso (macho)

gang /gæŋ/ s **1** quadrilha **2** turma ● **gang up on sb** juntar-se contra alguém

gangster /ˈgæŋstə(r)/ s gângster

gangway /ˈgæŋweɪ/ s **1** passadiço **2** (GB) corredor (entre fileiras, etc.)

gaol /dʒeɪl/ s = JAIL

gap /gæp/ s **1** vão **2** espaço **3** intervalo **4** separação **5** lacuna

gape /geɪp/ vi **1** ~ (at sb/sth) olhar boquiaberto (para alguém/algo) **2** abrir-se gaping adj enorme

garage /ˈgærɑːʒ, -rɑːdʒ; GB ˈgærɑːʒ, ˈgærɪdʒ/ s **1** garagem **2** oficina mecânica **3** posto de gasolina e borracharia

garbage /ˈgɑːbɪdʒ/ s **1** lixo **2** besteira

garbage man s lixeiro

garbled /ˈgɑːbld/ adj confuso

garden /ˈgɑːdn/ s jardim: vegetable ~ horta ● vi trabalhar num jardim gardener s jardineiro/a gardening s jardinagem

gargle /ˈgɑːgl/ vi fazer gargarejo

garish /ˈgeərɪʃ/ adj (cor) berrante

garland /ˈgɑːlənd/ s grinalda

garlic /ˈgɑːlɪk/ s [U] alho

garment /ˈgɑːmənt/ s (fml) traje

garnish /ˈgɑːnɪʃ/ vt decorar (comida) ● s guarnição (de um prato)

garrison /ˈgærɪsn/ s guarnição (militar)

gas /gæs/ s **1** gás **2** [U] (tb gasoline /ˈgæsəliːn/) gasolina: ~ station posto de gasolina **3** [U] (Med) gases ● vt (-ss-) asfixiar com gás

gash /gæʃ/ s ferida profunda

gasp /gɑːsp; GB gɑːsp/ vi **1** dar um grito sufocado ou arfar: ~ for air fazer esforço para respirar **2** vt ~ sth (out) dizer algo com voz entrecortada ● s arfada, grito sufocado

gate /geɪt/ s **1** portão, porteira **2** (estádio, etc.) arrecadação, público (pagante)

gatecrash /ˈgeɪtkræʃ/ vt, vi entrar de penetra gatecrasher s penetra

gateway /ˈgeɪtweɪ/ s **1** entrada **2** ~ to sth passaporte para algo

gather /ˈgæðə(r)/ **1** vi reunir-se: ~ around aproximar-se ◊ ~ around sb/sth agrupar-se em torno de alguém/algo **2** vi (multidão) formar-se **3** vt ~ sb/sth (together) reunir alguém/algo **4** vt deduzir **5** vt (flores, etc.) colher **6** vt ~ sth (up) recolher algo **7** vt ~ sth (in) (costura) franzir algo **8** vt (velocidade) ganhar gathering s encontro

gaudy /ˈgɔːdi/ adj (-ier, -iest) espalhafatoso

gauge /geɪdʒ/ s **1** medida **2** (ferrovia) bitola **3** medidor ● vt **1** calcular **2** julgar

gaunt /gɔːnt/ adj abatido

gauze /gɔːz/ s gaze

gave /geɪv/ *pret de* GIVE

gay /geɪ/ *adj* 1 homossexual 2 (*antiq*) alegre ● s homossexual

gaze /geɪz/ *vi* ~ (**at sb/sth**) contemplar/olhar fixamente (alguém/algo) ● s olhar intenso

GCSE /ˌdʒi: si: es 'i:/ *abrev* (*GB*) General Certificate of Secondary Education diploma de segundo grau britânico

gear /gɪər/ s 1 equipamento 2 (*carro*) marcha: *out of* ~ em ponto morto ◊ *change* ~ trocar de marcha 3 (*Mec*) engrenagem ■ **gear sth to/towards sth** adaptar algo a algo **gear (sb/sth) up (to do/for sth)** preparar (alguém/algo) (para (fazer) algo)

gearbox /'gɪəbɒks/ s caixa de câmbio

geese /gi:s/ *plural de* GOOSE

gem /dʒem/ s 1 pedra preciosa 2 (*fig*) jóia

Gemini /'dʒemɪnaɪ/ s Gêmeos

gender /'dʒendər/ s 1 (*Gram*) gênero 2 classificação sexual

gene /dʒi:n/ s gene

general /'dʒenrəl/ *adj* geral ▶ **in general** em geral ● s general

generalize /'dʒenrəlaɪz/ *vi* generalizar generalization s generalização

generally /'dʒenrəli/ *adv* geralmente, em geral

general practice s (*GB*) clínica geral

general election s eleições gerais

general practitioner s (*GB*) clínico geral

general-purpose *adj* de uso geral

generate /'dʒenəreɪt/ *vt* gerar generation s 1 geração 2 produção (*eletricidade, etc.*)

generator /'dʒenəreɪtər/ s gerador

generosity /ˌdʒenə'rɒsəti/ s generosidade

generous /'dʒenərəs/ *adj* 1 generoso 2 (*porção*) abundante

genetic /dʒə'netɪk/ *adj* genético genetics s [*sing*] genética

genial /'dʒi:niəl/ *adj* afável

genital /'dʒenɪtl/ *adj* genital genitals (*tb* genitalia /ˌdʒenɪ-'teɪliə/) s [*pl*] genitália

genius /'dʒi:niəs/ s gênio: *have a* ~ *for sth* ter talento para algo

genocide /'dʒenəsaɪd/ s genocídio

gent /dʒent/ s 1 (**the Gents**) [*sing*] (*GB, colog*) banheiro público masculino 2 (*antiq*) cavalheiro

genteel /dʒen'ti:l/ *adj* refinado gentility /dʒen'tɪləti/ s fineza

gentle /'dʒentl/ *adj* (**-er, -est**) 1 (*pessoa*) amável, benévolo 2 suave 3 (*animal*) manso gentleness s 1 amabilidade 2 suavidade 3 mansidão gently *adv* 1 suavemente 2 (*cozinhar*) em fogo brando 3 (*persuadir*) aos poucos

gentleman /'dʒentlmən/ s (*pl* -men) cavalheiro

genuine /'dʒenjuɪn/ *adj* 1 autêntico 2 sincero

geography /dʒi'ɒgrəfi/ s geografia geographer /dʒi'ɒgrəfər/ s geógrafo/a geographical /ˌdʒi:ə-'græfɪkl/ *adj* geográfico

geology /dʒi'ɒlədʒi/ s geologia geological /ˌdʒi:ə'lɒdʒɪkl/ *adj* geológico geologist /dʒi-'ɒlədʒɪst/ s geólogo/a

geometry /dʒi'ɒmətri/ s geometria geometric(al) /ˌdʒi:ə-'metrɪk(l)/ *adj* geométrico

geriatric /ˌdʒeri'ætrɪk/ *adj*, s geriátrico/a

germ /dʒɜ:rm/ s germe, micróbio

gesture /'dʒestʃər/ s gesto ● *vi* fazer um gesto, indicar com um gesto

get /get/ (**-tt-**) (*pt* got *pp* gotten, *GB* got)

● **get + n/pron** *vt* receber, obter, conseguir: ~ *a shock* levar um susto ◊ ~ *bad headaches* sofrer de fortes dores de cabeça ◊ *I didn't* ~ *the joke*. Eu não entendi a piada.

● **get + objeto + infinitivo ou -ing** *vt* **get sb/sth doing sth/to do sth** fazer com que, conseguir que alguém/algo faça algo: ~ *the car to start* fazer o carro pegar

● **get + objeto + particípio** *vt* (*com coisas que queremos que outra pessoa faça para nós*): ~ *your hair cut* cortar o cabelo (no cabeleireiro) ◊ ~ *your watch repaired* levar o relógio para consertar

● **get + objeto + adj** *vt* (*conseguir que algo se torne/faça...*): ~ *sth right* acertar algo ◊ ~ *the children ready for school* aprontar as crianças para a escola ◊ ~ (*yourself*) *ready* arrumar-se

● **get + adj** *vi* tornar-se, ficar: ~ *wet* molhar-se ◊ ~ *better* melhorar/recuperar-se

● **get + particípio** *vi*: ~ *tired of sth* ficar farto de algo ◊ ~ *used to sth* acostumar-se com algo ◊ ~ *lost* perder-se NOTA Algumas combinações comuns de **get + particípio** se traduzem por verbos pronominais: ~ *bored* entediar-se ◊ ~ **drunk** ficar bêbado ◊ ~ **married** casar-se. Para conjugá-los, usa-se a forma correspondente de **get**: *She soon got used to that.* Ela logo se acostumou com aquilo. ◊ *I'm getting dressed.* Estou me vestindo. **Get + particípio** também expressam ações que ocorrem ou se realizam de forma acidental, inesperada ou repentina: *I got caught in a heavy rainstorm.* Fui pego por uma forte tempestade. ◊ *He got hit by a ball.* Ele levou uma bolada.

● outros usos **1** *vi* ~ **to do sth** chegar a fazer algo: ~ **to know sb** (vir a) conhecer alguém **2** *vt, vi* (**have got (to do) sth**) ter (que fazer) algo **3** *vi* ~ **to...** (*movimento*) chegar a... ● **get away from it all** (*coloq*) ficar longe de tudo, conseguir algo **get (sb) nowhere**; **not get (sb) anywhere** não levar alguém a lugar algum **get there** chegar lá, conseguir algo NOTA Para expressões com **get**, ver o substantivo, adjetivo, etc., p. ex. **get the hang of it** em HANG.

■ **get about/around 1** sair, mover-se **2** (*notícia, etc.*) circular **get sth across (to sb)** comunicar algo (a alguém), fazer (alguém) entender algo **get ahead (of sb)** ultrapassar (alguém) **get along (with sb) (together)** dar-se bem (com alguém) **get around to (doing) sth** encontrar tempo para (fazer) algo **get at sb** pegar no pé (de alguém) **get at sth** insinuar algo **get away (from...)** afastar-se (de...) **get away with (doing)** sth sair impune de (fazer) algo **get back** regressar **get sth back** recuperar algo **get back at sb** vingar-se de alguém **get behind (with sth)** atrasar-se (com/em algo) **get by** (conseguir) passar **get down 1** baixar 2 (*crianças*) levantar-se da mesa **get sb down** deprimir alguém **get down to (doing) sth** começar a fazer algo: *Let's ~ down to business.* Vamos aos negócios. **get in; get into sth 1** (*trem, etc.*) chegar (a algum lugar) **2** (*pessoa*) voltar (para casa) **3** entrar (em algo) (*carro*) **get in with sb** entrar em recolher algo **get off (sth)** sair (de algo) **get sth off (sth)** tirar algo (de algo) **get off with sb** (*GB, coloq*) envolver-se com alguém (*romanticamente*) **get on 1** (*GB*) (*USA* **do well**) ter sucesso **2** (*tb* **get along**) conseguir fazer, virar-se **get sth on** vestir algo

get on; get onto sth entrar (em algo) **get on to sth** passar a considerar algo **get on (with sb) (together)** (*GB*) (*USA* **get along**) dar-se bem (com alguém) **get on with sth** prosseguir com algo **get out (of sth)** sair (de algo): *Get out (of here)!* Fora daqui! **get out of (doing) sth** livrar-se de (fazer) algo **get sth out of sb/sth** tirar algo de alguém/algo **get over sth 1** superar algo **2** esquecer algo **3** recuperar-se de algo **get round** (*GB*) convencer alguém **get through (to sb)** conseguir falar (com alguém) (*por telefone*), fazer-se entender (por alguém) **get through sth 1** consumir/usar algo **2** (*tarefa*) terminar algo **get together (with sb)** reunir-se (com alguém) **get sb/sth together** reunir alguém, montar algo **get up** levantar-se **get sb up** acordar alguém **get up to sth 1** chegar a algo **2** meter-se em algo

getaway /'getəweɪ/ *s* fuga

ghastly /'gæstli; *GB* 'gɑː-/ *adj* (**-ier**, **-iest**) medonho

ghetto /'getəʊ/ *s* (*pl* ~**s** *ou* ~**es**) gueto

ghost /ɡəʊst/ *s* fantasma **ghostly** *adj* (**-ier**, **-iest**) fantasmagórico

ghost story *s* história de terror

giant /'dʒaɪənt/ *s* gigante

gibberish /'dʒɪbərɪʃ/ *s* bobagem

giddy /'gɪdi/ *adj* (**-ier**, **-iest**) **1** zonzo **2** vertiginoso

gift /gɪft/ *s* **1** presente **2** dom **3** (*coloq*) moleza ● **have the gift of the gab** ter muita lábia **gifted** *adj* talentoso

gift certificate (*tb* **gift voucher**) *s* vale-presente

gift-wrap *vt* embrulhar para presente

gig /gɪg/ *s* (*coloq*) apresentação (*música*)

gigantic /dʒaɪˈgæntɪk/ *adj* gigantesco

giggle /'gɪgl/ *vi* ~ **(at sb/sth)** dar risadinhas (de alguém/algo) ● *s* **1** risinho **2** gozação: *I only did it for a ~.* Eu só fiz isso de brincadeira. **3** (**the giggles**) [*pl*]: *a fit of the giggles* um ataque de riso

gilded /'gɪldɪd/ (*tb* **gilt** /gɪlt/) *adj* dourado

gimmick /'gɪmɪk/ *s* **1** recurso publicitário **2** acessório promocional

gin /dʒɪn/ *s* gim

ginger /'dʒɪndʒər/ *s* gengibre ● *adj* (*GB*) castanho-avermelhado (*cabelo*)

gingerly /'dʒɪndʒərli/ *adv* cautelosamente

gipsy = GYPSY

giraffe /dʒəˈræf; GB -ˈrɑːf/ s girafa

girl /gɜːrl/ s menina, garota

girlfriend /ˈgɜːrlfrend/ s 1 namorada 2 (esp USA) amiga

gist /dʒɪst/ s ▸ get the gist of sth captar o essencial de algo

give /gɪv/ s ▸ give and take concessões mútuas • (pt gave pp given) 1 vt ~ sth (to sb); ~ (sb) sth dar algo (a alguém): ~ a lecture dar uma palestra 2 vi fazer doação 3 vi ceder 4 vt (tempo, etc.) dedicar 5 vt (doença) passar 6 vt conceder: I'll ~ you that. Admito que você está certo. ▸ don't give me that não me venha com essa give or take sth: an hour, ~ or take a few minutes uma hora, mais ou menos not give a damn, a hoot, etc. (about sb/sth) (coloq) não dar a mínima (a alguém/algo) NOTA Para expressões com give, ver o substantivo, adjetivo, etc., p. ex. give rise to sth em RISE. ■ give sb/sth away delatar alguém/algo give sth away entregar algo (de presente) give (sb) back sth; give sth back (to sb) devolver algo (a alguém) give in (to sb/sth) entregar os pontos (a alguém/algo) give sth in entregar algo give sth out distribuir algo give up desistir, render-se give up (doing) sth deixar algo/de fazer algo: ~ up hope perder as esperanças ◇ ~ up smoking parar de fumar

given /ˈgɪvn/ pp de GIVE • adj, prep dado

given name s (pre)nome

glad /glæd/ adj (gladder, gladdest) 1 be ~ (about sth/to do sth) estar contente (com algo/por fazer algo) 2 be ~ to do sth ter prazer em fazer algo: I'd be ~ to help. Será um prazer ajudar. 3 be ~ of sth estar grato por algo NOTA Glad e pleased se referem a circunstâncias ou fatos concretos: Are you glad/pleased about getting a job? Você está contente de ter conseguido um emprego? Happy descreve um estado mental e pode preceder um substantivo: Are you happy in your new job? Você está contente em seu novo emprego? ◇ a happy occasion uma ocasião feliz/alegre ◇ happy memories boas lembranças. gladly adv com prazer

glamor (GB -our) /ˈglæmər/ s glamour glamorous adj glamouroso

glance /glæns; GB glɑːns/ vi ~ at/down/over/through sth dar uma olhada em algo • s olhada (rápida) ▸ at a glance num relance

gland /glænd/ s glândula

glare /gleər/ s 1 luz/brilho ofuscante 2 olhar penetrante • vi ~ at sb/sth olhar ferozmente para alguém/algo glaring adj 1 (erro) evidente 2 (expressão) feroz 3 ofuscante glaringly adv: ~ obvious extremamente óbvio

glass /glæs; GB glɑːs/ s 1 [U] vidro: a pane of ~ uma vidraça 2 copo 3 (glasses) óculos → PAIR

glaze /gleɪz/ s 1 verniz para vitrificação 2 calda de açúcar ou de ovos para dar brilho a assados e tortas • vt 1 vitrificar 2 pincelar com calda de açúcar/ovos ■ glaze over apagar-se glazed adj 1 (olhos) inexpressivo 2 vitrificado

gleam /gliːm/ s 1 lampejo 2 vislumbre (emoção, etc.) • vi brilhar gleaming adj reluzente

glean /gliːn/ vt obter (informação)

glee /gliː/ s regozijo gleeful adj eufórico gleefully adv com euforia

glen /glen/ s vale estreito

glide /glaɪd/ s deslizamento • vi 1 deslizar 2 planar glider s planador

glimmer /ˈglɪmər/ s 1 luz trêmula 2 vislumbre: ~ of hope raio de esperança

glimpse /glɪmps/ s vislumbre, olhada • vt vislumbrar

glint /glɪnt/ vi brilhar • s 1 lampejo 2 brilho

glisten /ˈglɪsn/ vi reluzir (esp superfície molhada)

glitter /ˈglɪtər/ vi reluzir • s brilho

gloat /gloʊt/ vi ~ (about/over sth) regozijar-se (com algo)

global /ˈgloʊbl/ adj 1 mundial 2 global

globe /gloʊb/ s globo (terrestre)

gloom /gluːm/ s 1 penumbra 2 tristeza 3 pessimismo gloomy adj (-ier, -iest) 1 escuro, sombrio 2 (prognóstico) pouco promissor 3 deprimido, melancólico

glorious /ˈglɔːriəs/ adj 1 glorioso 2 esplêndido

glory /ˈglɔːri/ s 1 glória 2 esplendor • vi ~ in sth orgulhar-se de algo

gloss /glɔs, glɑs/ s 1 brilho (superfície) 2 (tb ~ paint) tinta brilhante 3 (fig) falso brilho

4 ~ (on sth) glosa (de algo) ■ **gloss over sth** tratar de algo por alto, encobrir algo **glossy** *adj* (**-ier, -iest**) lustroso

glossary /ˈɡlɒsəri/ *s* (*pl* **-ies**) glossário

glove /ɡlʌv/ *s* luva

glow /ɡləʊ/ *vi* **1** incandescer-se **2** reluzir **3** (*rosto*) enrubescer **4** (*esp saúde*) irradiar ● *s* **1** luz suave **2** rubor **3** arrebatamento

glucose /ˈɡluːkəʊs/ *s* glicose

glue /ɡluː/ *s* cola (adesiva) ● *vt* (*part pres* **gluing**) colar

glutton /ˈɡlʌtn/ *s* **1** glutão **2 ~ for sth** (*coloq*) maníaco por algo: *be a ~ for punishment* adorar sofrer

gnarled /nɑːld/ *adj* **1** retorcido **2** nodoso

gnaw /nɔː/ *vt, vi* **1 ~ (at) sth** roer algo **2 ~ (at) sb** atormentar alguém

gnome /nəʊm/ *s* gnomo

go /ɡəʊ/ ● *s* (*pl* **goes** /ɡəʊz/) **1** (*GB*) (*jogo*) vez **2** (*coloq*) [*U*] energia ▸ **be on the go** (*coloq*) ter pique **have a go (at (doing) sth)** (*coloq*) tentar (fazer) algo ● *vi* (*3ª pess sing pres* **goes** /ɡəʊz/ *pt* **went** *pp* **gone**) **1** ir NOTA **Been** é usado para dizer que alguém foi a um lugar e já voltou: *Have you ever been to London?* Você já foi (alguma vez) a Londres? *Gone* implica que essa pessoa ainda não regressou: *John's gone to Peru. He'll be back in May.* John foi para o Peru. Voltará em maio. **2** ir-se (embora) **3** partir **4** **go + -ing**: *go swimming/camping* ir nadar/acampar **5** **go for a + substantivo**: *go for a walk* ir dar um passeio **6** (*progresso*) ir, sair(-se): *Everything went well.* Deu tudo certo. **7** (*máquina*) funcionar **8** tornar-se: *go crazy/pale* ficar louco/pálido **9** fazer (*um som*): *How does that song go?* Como é mesmo aquela música? **10** desaparecer, terminar: *My headache's gone.* Minha dor de cabeça passou. ◊ *Is it all gone?* Acabou tudo? **11** falhar, estragar **12** (*tempo*) passar ▸ **be going to do sth** ir fazer algo: *We're going to buy a house.* Vamos comprar uma casa. NOTA Para expressões com *go*, ver o substantivo, adjetivo, etc., p. ex. **go astray** em ASTRAY. ■ **go about 1** [*com adj ou -ing*] andar (por aí): *go about naked* andar pelado **2** (*boato*) circular **go about (doing) sth**: *How should I go about telling him?* Como eu

deveria contar a ele? **go ahead (with sth)** ir em frente (com algo) **go along with sb/sth** concordar com alguém/algo **go around 1** ser suficiente para todos **2** *Ver* GO ABOUT **go away 1** ir-se (embora), ir viajar **2** (*mancha, etc.*) desaparecer **go back** voltar **go back on sb/sth** faltar com algo (*promessa, etc.*) **go by 1** passar: *as time goes by* com o (passar do) tempo **2** seguir (*regra*) **go down 1** (*barco*) afundar **2** (*sol*) pôr-se **go down (with sth)** (*filme, etc.*) ser recebido (por alguém) **go down with sth** cair de cama com algo **go for sb** atacar alguém **go for sb/sth** ser válido para alguém: *That goes for you too.* Isso vale para você também. **go in** entrar **go in for (doing) sth** interessar-se por (fazer) algo **go into sth** entrar em algo (*profissão, detalhes*) **go off 1** ir-se (embora) **2** (*arma*) disparar **3** explodir **4** (*alarme*) soar **5** (*luz, etc.*) apagar-se **6** (*alimentos*) estragar **7** ocorrer: *It went off well.* Correu tudo bem. **go off sb/sth** perder o interesse em alguém/algo **go off with sth** levar algo (que não lhe pertence) **go on 1** seguir em frente **2** (*luz*) acender-se **3** acontecer **4** continuar, durar **go on (about sb/sth)** não parar de falar (de alguém/algo) **go on (with (doing) sth)** continuar (com algo a fazer algo) **go out 1** sair **2** (*luz*) apagar-se **go over sth 1** examinar algo **2** revisar algo **go over to sth** passar para algo (*opinião*) **go through** ser aprovado (*lei*) **go through sth 1** revisar algo **2** repassar algo **3** passar por algo **go through with sth** levar algo a cabo **go together** combinar (com algo) **go up 1** subir **2** (*edifício*) erguer **3** explodir **go with sth** combinar com algo **go without (sth)** passar sem algo

goad /ɡəʊd/ *vt* **~ sb (into doing sth)** provocar alguém (a fazer algo)

go-ahead *s* sinal verde ● *adj* empreendedor

goal /ɡəʊl/ *s* **1** gol **2** meta **goalkeeper** (*tb coloq* **goalie**) *s* goleiro/a **goalpost** *s* trave de gol

goat /ɡəʊt/ *s* bode, cabra

gobble /ˈɡɒbl/ *vt* **~ sth (up/down)** devorar algo

go-between *s* intermediário/a

god /ɡɒd/ *s* **1** deus **2** (*God*) Deus

godchild /ˈɡɒdtʃaɪld/ *s* (*masc*

godson /-sʌn/ (*fem* **god-daughter**) (*pl* **godchildren** /-tʃɪldrən/) afilhado/a

goddess /ˈɡɑdes/ s deusa

godparent /ˈɡɑdpeərənt/ s (*masc* **godfather** /ˈɡɑdfɑðər/) (*fem* **godmother** /ˈɡɑdmʌðər/) padrinho, madrinha (*de batismo*)

godsend /ˈɡɑdsend/ s dádiva do céu

goggles /ˈɡɑglz/ s óculos de natação/proteção

going /ˈɡoʊɪŋ/ s **1** [*U*] partida (*de um lugar*) **2** *Good ~!* Bom tempo! ◊ *That was good ~.* Essa foi rápida. ◊ *The path was rough ~.* O caminho estava em mau estado. ▶ **get out while the going is good** ir embora enquanto as coisas andam bem ● *adj* **a going concern** um negócio próspero **the going rate** a tarifa atual

gold /ɡoʊld/ s ouro ▶ **(be) as good as gold** (comportar-se) como um anjo

gold dust s ouro em pó

golden /ˈɡoʊldən/ *adj* **1** de ouro **2** dourado

goldfish /ˈɡoʊldfɪʃ/ (*pl* **goldfish**) s peixinho dourado

golf /ɡɑlf/ s golfe ~ **club** s **1** clube de golfe **2** taco de golfe **golfer** s golfista

gone /ɡɔːn; *GB* ɡɒn/ *pp* de **GO** ● *prep* (*GB*) *It was ~ midnight.* Já passava da meia-noite.

gonna /ˈɡʊnə, ˈɡɑnə/ (*coloq*) = **GOING TO** ver **GO**

good /ɡʊd/ *adj* (*comp* **better** *superl* **best**) **1** ~ **(at sth)** bom (em algo): *Vegetables are ~ for you.* Legumes são bons para a saúde. **2** ~ **to sb** bom para, amável para com alguém ▶ **as good as** praticamente **good for you, etc.** (*coloq*) muito bem **NOTA** Para expressões com **good**, ver o substantivo, adjetivo, etc., p. ex. **a good many** em MANY. ● *s* **1** bem **2** **(the good)** [*pl*] os bons ▶ **be no good (doing sth)** não adiantar nada (fazer algo) **do sb good** fazer bem a alguém **for good** para sempre

goodbye /ˌɡʊdˈbaɪ/ *interj, s* adeus: *say ~* despedir-se **NOTA** Para despedidas mais informais, usam-se **bye, cheerio** (*GB*) e **cheers** (*GB*).

good-humored (*GB* -oured) *adj* **1** afável **2** bem-humorado

good-looking *adj* bonito

good-natured *adj* **1** amável **2** de bom coração

goodness /ˈɡʊdnəs/ s **1** bondade **2** valor nutritivo ● *interj* céus

goods /ɡʊdz/ s [*pl*] **1** bens **2** artigos, mercadorias

goodwill /ˌɡʊdˈwɪl/ s boa vontade

goose /ɡuːs/ s (*pl* **geese**) ganso

gooseberry /ˈɡuːsberi; *GB* ˈɡʊzbəri/ s (*pl* -**ies**) uva-espim

goose pimples (*tb* **goose bumps**) s [*pl*] pele arrepiada

gorge /ɡɔːrdʒ/ s (*Geog*) garganta

gorgeous /ˈɡɔːrdʒəs/ *adj* **1** magnífico **2** (*coloq*) lindo

gorilla /ɡəˈrɪlə/ s gorila

gory /ˈɡɔːri/ *adj* (-ier, -iest) **1** ensanguentado **2** sangrento

go-slow s (*GB*) greve branca

gospel /ˈɡɑspl/ s evangelho

gossip /ˈɡɑsɪp/ s **1** [*U*] fofoca **2** fofoqueiro/a ● *vi* fofocar

got /ɡɑt/ *pret, pp* de **GET**

Gothic /ˈɡɑθɪk/ *adj* gótico

gotten /ˈɡɑtn/ (*USA*) *pp* de **GET**

gouge /ɡaʊdʒ/ *vt* furar ■ **gouge sth out** arrancar algo (*com dedos ou ferramenta*)

govern /ˈɡʌvərn; *GB* ˈɡʌvn/ **1** *vt, vi* governar **2** *vt* (*ação*) reger **governing** *adj* regulador

governess /ˈɡʌvərnəs/ s governanta

government /ˈɡʌvərnmənt/ s governo **governmental** /ˌɡʌvərnˈmentl; *GB* ˌɡʌvn-/ *adj* governamental

governor /ˈɡʌvərnər/ s **1** governador/a **2** diretor/a

gown /ɡaʊn/ s **1** vestido longo **2** (*Educ, Jur*) toga **3** (*Med*) avental

GP /ˌdʒiː ˈpiː/ s clínico geral

grab /ɡræb/ (-**bb**-) **1** *vt* ~ **(at sb/sth)** (*tb* ~ **(hold of sb/sth)**) agarrar alguém/algo **2** *vt* (*atenção*) chamar **3** *vt* arrancar ● *s* ▶ **make a grab for/at sth** tentar agarrar algo

grace /ɡreɪs/ s **1** graça, elegância **2** prazo extra: *five days' ~* cinco dias a mais de prazo **3** *say ~* rezar em agradecimento (*pela refeição*) ● *vt* **1** enfeitar **2** honrar **graceful** *adj* **1** gracioso, elegante **2** (*cortês*) delicado

gracious /ˈɡreɪʃəs/ *adj* **1** afável **2** elegante, luxuoso

grade /ɡreɪd/ s **1** categoria **2** (*Educ*) nota **3** (*Educ*) série **4** (*Geog*) declive ▶ **make the grade** (*coloq*) atingir a média ● *vt* **1** classificar **2** (*Educ*) dar nota (*a exame*) **grading** s classificação

grade crossing s passagem de nível

gradient /ˈɡreɪdiənt/ s (*Geog*) declive

gradual /'grædʒuəl/ *adj* **1** gradual **2** (*inclinação*) suave gradually *adv* gradativamente, aos poucos

graduate /'grædʒuət/ s **1** (*USA*) diplomado/a **2** (*GB*) formado/a /'grædʒueit/ **1** (*USA*) ● *vi* graduar-se **2** *vi* (*GB*) formar-se **3** *vt* graduar graduation *s* graduação

graffiti /grə'fi:ti/ s [*U*] grafite

graft /græft; *GB* grɑ:ft/ s ● enxerto ● *vt* enxertar

grain /grein/ s **1** [*U*] cereais **2** grão **3** veio (*da madeira*) ▶ be/go against the grain ser/ir contra a natureza

gram (*GB* gramme) /græm/ s (*abrev* g) grama → Ver pág. 224

grammar /'græmər/ s gramática

grammar school s **1** (*USA, antiq*) escola primária **2** (*GB*) escola de segundo grau

grammatical /grə'mætıkl/ *adj* **1** gramatical **2** (*gramaticalmente*) correto

gramophone /'græməfoʊn/ s (*antiq*) gramofone

grand /grænd/ *adj* (~er, ~est) **1** magnífico, grandioso **2** (*coloq, Irl*) estupendo **3** (Grand) (*títulos*) grão ● s (*pl* grand) (*coloq*) mil dólares/libras

grandad /'grændæd/ s (*coloq*) vovô

grandchild /'græntʃaɪld/ s (*pl* -children) neto/a

granddaughter /'grændɔ:tər/ s neta

grandeur /'grændʒər/ s grandiosidade

grandfather /'grænfɑ:ðər/ s avô

grandma /'grænmɑ/ s (*coloq*) vovó

grandmother /'grænmʌðər/ s avó

grandpa /'grænpɑ/ s (*coloq*) vovô

grandparent /'grænpeərənt/ s avô, avó

grand piano s piano de cauda

grandson /'grænsʌn/ s neto

grandstand /'grændstænd/ s (*Esporte*) tribuna (de honra)

granite /'grænıt/ s granito

granny /'græni/ s (*pl* -ies) (*coloq*) vovó

grant /grænt; *GB* grɑ:nt/ *vt* conceder ▶ take sb/sth for granted não dar valor a alguém/algo, dar algo por certo ● s **1** subvenção **2** (*Educ*) bolsa de estudos

grape /greip/ s uva

grapefruit /'greipfru:t/ s (*pl* grapefruit *ou* ~s) toranja

grapevine /'greipvain/ s **1**

videira **2** (the grapevine) boatos: *hear sth on the* ~ ouvir algo por aí

graph /græf/ s gráfico: ~ *paper* papel quadriculado

graphic /'græfık/ *adj* **1** gráfico **2** (*relato, etc.*) vívido graphics *s* [*pl*]: *computer* ~ imagens de computador

grapple /'græpl/ *vi* atracar-se

grasp /græsp; *GB* grɑ:sp/ *vt* **1** agarrar **2** (*oportunidade*) aproveitar **3** compreender ● s **1** controle: *within/beyond the* ~ *of...* dentro/fora do alcance/poder de... **2** conhecimento grasping *adj* ganancioso

grass /grɑs; *GB* grɑ:s/ s grama

grasshopper /'græshɑpər; *GB* 'grɑ:s-/ s gafanhoto

grassland /'græslænd; *GB* 'grɑ:s-/ (*tb* grasslands [*pl*]) s pasto(s)

grass roots s [*pl*] (comunidades de) bases

grassy /'græsi; *GB* 'grɑ:-/ *adj* (-ier, -iest) coberto de grama

grate /greit/ **1** *vt* ralar **2** *vi* ranger **3** ~ vi (on sb/sth) irritar (alguém/algo) ● s grelha (*lareira*)

grateful /'greitfl/ *adj* agradecido, grato

grater /'greitər/ s ralador

gratitude /'grætıtu:d; *GB* -tju:d/ s gratidão

grave /greiv/ *adj* (-er, -est) (*fml*) grave ● s túmulo

gravel /'grævl/ s cascalho

graveyard /'greivjɑrd/ s cemitério (*ao redor de uma igreja*)

gravity /'grævəti/ s **1** (*Fís*) gravidade **2** (*fml*) seriedade

gravy /'greivi/ s molho (*feito com o caldo da carne assada*)

gray /grei/ *adj* (~er, ~est) **1** cinza **2** (*cabelo*) branco: *go/turn* ~ ficar grisalho ● s cinza

graze /greiz/ **1** *vi* pastar **2** *vt* (*pele*) raspar **3** *vt* roçar ● s arranhão

grease /gri:s/ s **1** gordura **2** (*Mec*) lubrificante **3** brilhantina ● *vt* **1** lubrificar **2** untar greasy /'gri:si/ *adj* (-ier, -iest) gorduroso

great /greit/ *adj* (~er, ~est) **1** grande, grandioso: *the world's greatest player* o melhor jogador do mundo **2** (*idade*) avançado **3** (*cuidado*) muito **4** (*coloq*) magnífico: *We had a* ~ *time.* Nós nos divertimos imensamente. ◇ *It's* ~ *to see you!* Que bom te ver! **5** ~ at sth muito bom em algo **6** (*coloq*) muito: *a* ~ *big* *dog* um cachorro enorme ▶ **great minds think alike** os gênios se entendem ● s (*coloq*): *a jazz ~* um grande astro do jazz **greatly** *adv* muito **greatness** s grandeza

great-grandfather s bisavô

great-grandmother s bisavó

greed /gri:d/ s 1 ganância 2 gula **greedily** *adv* 1 gananciosamente 2 vorazmente **greedy** *adj* (**-ier -iest**) 1 ~ (**for sth**) ganancioso (de algo) 2 guloso

green /gri:n/ *adj* (**~er -est**) verde ● s 1 verde 2 (**greens**) verduras 3 parque público (gramado) **greenery** s verde, folhagem

greengrocer /'gri:ngrəʊsər/ s (GB) verdureiro/a **greengrocer's** s quitanda

greenhouse /'gri:nhaʊs/ s estufa de plantas: *~ effect* efeito estufa

greet /gri:t/ *vt* 1 cumprimentar 2 receber **greeting** s 1 saudação: *season's greetings* votos de boas-festas 2 recepção

grenade /grə'neɪd/ s granada (*de mão*)

grew /gru:/ *pret de* GROW

grey (*esp* GB) = GRAY

greyhound /'greɪhaʊnd/ s galgo

grid /grɪd/ s 1 grade 2 (GB) (*eletricidade, gás*) rede 3 linhas de coordenadas

grief /gri:f/ s ~ (**over/at sth**) pesar (por algo) ▶ **come to grief** (GB, *coloq*) 1 fracassar 2 sofrer um acidente

grievance /'gri:vns/ s 1 (*motivo de*) queixa 2 reivindicação

grieve /gri:v/ (*fml*) 1 *vt* causar grande dor a 2 ~ (**for/over/ about sb/sth**) chorar a perda (*de alguém/algo*) 3 *vi* ~ **at/ about/over sth** lamentar(-se), afligir-se por algo

grill /grɪl/ s 1 grelha 2 grelhado ● 1 *vt, vi* grelhar 2 *vt* crivar de perguntas

grille (*tb* **grill**) /grɪl/ s grade (*de proteção*)

grim /grɪm/ *adj* (**grimmer, grimmest**) 1 (*pessoa*) carrancudo 2 (*lugar*) lúgubre, macabro 3 deprimente, desagradável

grimace /'grɪmas, grɪ'meɪs/ s careta ● *vi* ~ (**at sb/sth**) fazer careta (*para alguém/algo*)

grime /graɪm/ s sujeira **grimy** *adj* (**-ier -iest**) encardido

grin /grɪn/ *vi* (**-nn-**) ~ (**at sb/sth**) sorrir de orelha a orelha (*para alguém/algo*) ▶ **grin and bear it**

aguentar firme (*sem reclamar*) ● s sorriso largo

grind /graɪnd/ (*pt, pp* ground) 1 *vt, vi* moer, triturar 2 *vt* afiar 3 *vt* (*dentes*) ranger ▶ **grind to a halt/ standstill** parar aos poucos ● s (*coloq*): *the daily ~* a rotina diária

grip /grɪp/ (**-pp-**) 1 *vt, vi* agarrar (**-se**) 2 *vt* (*atenção*) absorver ● s 1 ~ (**on sb/sth**) ato de agarrar (*a alguém/algo*) 2 controle, pressão 3 cabo ▶ **come/get to grips with sb/sth** lidar/atracar-se com alguém/algo **gripping** *adj* fascinante

grit /grɪt/ s 1 areia grossa 2 coragem, determinação ● *vt* (**-tt-**) cobrir com areia ▶ **grit your teeth** 1 cerrar os dentes 2 tomar coragem

groan /grəʊn/ *vi* 1 gemer 2 (*móveis, etc.*) ranger 3 ~ (**on**) (**about/over sth**) reclamar (*de algo*) 4 ~ (**at sb/sth**) queixar-se (*de alguém/algo*) ● s 1 gemido 2 queixa 3 rangido

grocer /'grəʊsər/ s merceeiro/a **grocer's** (*tb* **grocery shop/store**) mercearia, armazém **groceries** s comestíveis

groggy /'grɒgi/ *adj* (**-ier -iest**) tonto

groin /grɔɪn/ s virilha

groom /gru:m/ s 1 cavalariço 2 noivo ● *vt* 1 (*cavalo*) cuidar de 2 (*pêlo*) escovar 3 preparar

groove /gru:v/ s ranhura, sulco

grope /grəʊp/ *vi* 1 mover-se às cegas 2 ~ (**about**) **for sth** procurar algo às apalpadelas

gross /grəʊs/ s (*pl* **~es** *ou* **gross**) grosa (*doze dúzias*) ● *adj* (**~er, ~est**) 1 repulsivamente gordo 2 grosseiro 3 (*exagero*) flagrante 4 (*erro*) crasso 5 (*injustiça*) grave 6 (*total, peso*) bruto ● *vt* totalizar, atingir (*valor bruto*) **grossly** *adv* extremamente

grotesque /grəʊ'tesk/ *adj* grotesco

grouch /graʊtʃ/ s rabugice

grouchy /'graʊtʃi/ *adj* rabugento

ground /graʊnd/ *pret, pp de* GRIND ● *vt* 1 (*avião*) impedir que decole 2 (*coloq*) proibir de sair ● s 1 chão, terra 2 terreno 3 campo (*de esportes*) 4 (**grounds**) jardins, terreno (*ao redor de uma casa*) 5 (*ger pl*) motivo(s) 6 (**grounds**) [*pl*] borra ▶ **get off the ground** 1 iniciar-se com êxito 2 decolar **give/lose ground (to sb/sth)** ceder/perder terreno (*para alguém/algo*) **on the ground** no chão, entre as massas

to the ground (*destruir*) completamente ● *adj* moído **grounding** *s* [*sing*] ▸ **(in sth)** fundamentos (de algo) **groundless** *adj* infundado

ground floor *s* andar térreo **ground-floor** *adj* [*antes de substantivo*] do/no andar térreo

group /gru:p/ *s* grupo ● *vt, vi* ~ **(together)** agrupar(-se) **grouping** *s* agrupamento, comissão

grouse /graʊs/ *s* (*pl* **grouse**) galo silvestre

grove /grəʊv/ *s* arvoredo

grovel /ˈgrɒvl/ *vi* (**-l-**, *GB* **-ll-**) ~ **(to sb)** humilhar-se (ante alguém) **grovelling** *adj* servil

grow /grəʊ/ (*pt* **grew** *pp* **grown**) **1** *vi* crescer **2** *vt* (*cabelo*) deixar crescer **3** *vt* cultivar **4** *vi* tornar-se: ~ *old/rich* envelhecer/ enriquecer **5** *vi*: ~ *to rely on sb* passar a depender de alguém cada vez mais ■ **grow into sth** tornar-se algo **grow on sb** tornar-se cada vez mais atraente para alguém **grow up 1** desenvolver-se **2** crescer: *Oh, ~ up!* Deixe de ser criança! **growing** *adj* crescente

growl /graʊl/ *vi* rosnar ● *s* rosnado

grown /grəʊn/ *pp de* GROW ● *adj* adulto

grown-up *adj* adulto ● *s* adulto/a

growth /grəʊθ/ *s* **1** crescimento **2** aumento **3** formação **4** tumor

grub /grʌb/ *s* **1** larva **2** (*coloq*) (*comida*) bóia

grubby /ˈgrʌbi/ *adj* (**-ier, -iest**) (*coloq*) sujo

grudge /grʌdʒ/ *vt* ~ **sb sth** *s* invejar alguém por algo **2** regatear algo a alguém: ~ *doing sth* fazer algo de má vontade ● *s* ressentimento: *bear sb a* ~ *against sth* guardar rancor de alguém **grudgingly** *adv* de má vontade

grueling (*GB* **-ll-**) /ˈgru:əlɪŋ/ *adj* penoso

gruesome /ˈgru:səm/ *adj* horrível

gruff /grʌf/ *adj* **1** brusco **2** áspero

grumble /ˈgrʌmbl/ *vi* resmungar: ~ *about/at sth* queixar-se de algo ● *s* queixa

grumpy /ˈgrʌmpi/ *adj* (**-ier, -iest**) (*coloq*) resmungão

grunt /grʌnt/ *vi* grunhir ● *s* grunhido

guarantee /ˌgærənˈti:/ *s* garantia ● *vt* **1** garantir **2** avalizar

guard /gɑːd/ *vt* **1** proteger, guardar **2** vigiar ■ **guard against sth** prevenir-se contra algo ● *s* **1** guarda, vigilância **2** guarda, sentinela **3** (*grupo de soldados*) guarda **4** dispositivo de segurança **5** (*GB*) (*Ferrovia*) guarda-freios ▸ **be off/on your guard** estar desprevenido/alerta **guarded** *adj* cauteloso

guardian /ˈgɑːdiən/ *s* **1** guardião: ~ *angel* anjo da guarda **2** tutor/a

guerrilla (*tb* **guerilla**) /ɡəˈrɪlə/ *s* guerrilheiro/a: ~ *warfare* guerrilha

guess /ges/ *vt, vi* **1** adivinhar **2** ~ **(at)** (*sth*) imaginar (algo) **3** (*coloq, esp USA*) crer: *I* ~ *so/not.* Suponho que sim/não. ● *s* suposição: *make a* ~ *at sth* tentar adivinhar algo ◇ **guesswork** conjecturas ▸ **it's anybody's guess** ninguém sabe

guest /gest/ *s* **1** convidado/a **2** hóspede: ~ *house* pensão ▸ **be my guest** pois não

guidance /ˈgaɪdns/ *s* orientação

guide /gaɪd/ *s* **1** (*pessoa*) guia **2** (*tb* **guidebook**) guia (*de turismo*) **3** (*GB*) (*tb* **Girl Guide**) (*USA* **Girl Scout**) (*menina*) bandeirante ● *vt* **1** guiar, orientar: ~ *sb to sth* levar alguém a algo **2** influenciar **guided** *adj* acompanhado (*por guia*)

guideline /ˈgaɪdlaɪn/ *s* diretriz, pauta

guilt /gɪlt/ *s* culpa, culpabilidade **guilty** *adj* (**-ier, -iest**) culpado

guinea pig /ˈgɪni pɪg/ *s* cobaia

guise /gaɪz/ *s* disfarce

guitar /gɪˈtɑː(r)/ *s* violão: *electric* ~ guitarra elétrica

gulf /gʌlf/ *s* **1** golfo **2** abismo

gull /gʌl/ *s* gaivota

gullible /ˈgʌləbl/ *adj* crédulo

gulp /gʌlp/ **1** *vt* ~ **sth (down)** engolir algo apressadamente **2** *vi* engolir saliva/um seco ● *s* trago

gum /gʌm/ *s* **1** (*Anat*) gengiva **2** goma, resina **3** chiclete

gun /gʌn/ *s* arma (*de fogo* ■ **gun sb down** matar/ferir alguém a tiros

gunfire /ˈgʌnfaɪə(r)/ *s* tiroteio

gunman /ˈgʌnmən/ *s* (*pl* **-men**) pistoleiro

gunpoint /ˈgʌnpɔɪnt/ *s* ▸ **at gunpoint** sob a ameaça de uma arma

gunpowder /ˈgʌnpaʊdə(r)/ *s* pólvora

gunshot /ˈgʌnʃɒt/ *s* disparo

gurgle /ˈgɜːɡl/ ● *vi* gorgolejar

gush /gʌʃ/ *vi* **1** ~ **(out)** jorrar **2** ~ **(over sb/sth)** falar/escrever com muito entusiasmo (de/sobre alguém/algo

gust /gʌst/ s rajada (*vento*)

gusto /ˈgʌstoʊ/ s entusiasmo

gut /gʌt/ s **1** (**guts**) [*pl*] (*coloq*) tripas, barriga **2** (**guts**) [*pl*] coragem **3** intestino: ~ *reaction* reação instintiva ● *vt* (**-tt-**) **1** destripar **2** destruir por dentro

gutter /ˈgʌtər/ s **1** sarjeta: *the ~ press* a imprensa marrom **2** calha

guy /gaɪ/ s (*coloq*) sujeito: *Hi guys!* Oi, pessoal!

guzzle /ˈgʌzl/ vt ~ **sth** (**down/up**) (*coloq*) encher a cara, empanturrar-se de algo

gym /dʒɪm/ s **1** (*tb* **gymnasium** /dʒɪmˈneɪziəm/) ginásio (*de esportes*) **2** (*tb* **gymnastics** /dʒɪmˈnæstɪks/ [*sing*]) ginástica (*olímpica*)

gymnast /ˈdʒɪmnæst/ s ginasta

gynecologist (*GB* **gynae-**) /ˌgaɪnəˈkɒlədʒɪst/ s ginecologista

gypsy /ˈdʒɪpsi/ s (*pl* **-ies**) cigano/a

H h

H, h /eɪtʃ/ s (*pl* **H's**, **h's** /ˈeɪtʃɪz/) H, h

habit /ˈhæbɪt/ s hábito

habitation /ˌhæbɪˈteɪʃn/ s habitação

habitual /həˈbɪtʃuəl/ adj habitual

hack /hæk/ vt, vi **1** ~ (**at**) **sth** cortar algo aos golpes **2** ~ (**into**) (**sth**) (*Informát*) invadir algo ilegalmente hacking s invasão ilegal de um sistema

had /həd, hæd/ *pret, pp de* HAVE

hadn't /ˈhæd(ə)nt/ = HAD NOT *Ver* HAVE

haemoglobin (*GB*) = HEMOGLOBIN

haemorrhage (*GB*) = HEMORRHAGE

haggard /ˈhægərd/ adj abatido

haggle /ˈhægl/ vi ~ (**over/about**) **sth** pechinchar (por algo)

hail /heɪl/ **1** vt chamar (*atrair a atenção*) **2** vt ~ **sb/sth as sth** aclamar alguém/algo como algo **3** vi cair granizo ● s **1** granizo **2** saraivada

hailstone /ˈheɪlstoʊn/ s pedra (*granizo*)

hailstorm /ˈheɪlstɔːrm/ s tempestade de granizo

hair /heər/ s **1** cabelo, fio de cabelo **2** pêlo

hairbrush /ˈheərbrʌʃ/ s escova (*cabelo*)

haircut /ˈheərkʌt/ s corte de cabelo: *have/get a ~* cortar o cabelo (no cabeleireiro)

hairdo /ˈheərduː/ s (*pl* **~s**) (*coloq*) penteado

hairdresser /ˈheərdresər/ (*tb* **hair stylist**) s cabeleireiro/a hairdresser's (*GB*) s salão de cabeleireiro hairdressing s arte de cortar e pentear cabelos

hairdryer /ˈheərdraɪər/ (*tb* **hairdrier**) s secador (*cabelo*)

hairpin /ˈheərpɪn/ s grampo de cabelo: ~ *curve/turn* curva em U

hairstyle /ˈheərstaɪl/ s penteado

hairy /ˈheəri/ adj (**-ier, -iest**) peludo, cabeludo

half /hæf; *GB* hɑːf/ s (*pl* **halves**) metade, meio: *two and a ~ hours* duas horas e meia ◊ *break sth in ~* partir algo ao meio ► **go halves** (**with sb**) dividir a conta meio a meio (com alguém) ● adj, pron metade de, meio ► **half (past) one, two, etc.** uma, duas, etc. e meia ● adv meio: ~ *built* construído pela metade

half board s meia pensão

half-brother s meio-irmão

half-hearted adj pouco entusiasmado **half-heartedly** adv sem entusiasmo

half-sister s meia-irmã

half-term (*GB*) semana de férias na metade de um período de aulas

half-time s (*Esporte*) meio tempo

halfway /ˈhæfweɪ; *GB* ˌhɑːf-/ adj, adv a meio caminho, na metade

halfwit /ˈhæfwɪt; *GB* ˈhɑːf-/ s estúpido/a

hall /hɔːl/ s **1** vestíbulo **2** (*concertos, etc.*) sala **3** (*tb* ~ **of residence**) (*GB*) residência universitária

hallmark /ˈhɔːlmɑrk/ s **1** (*metais preciosos*) marca de qualidade **2** marca característica

Halloween /ˌhæləˈwiːn/ s NOTA Halloween é a noite de fantasmas e bruxas no dia 31 de outubro. É costume esvaziar uma abóbora, desenhar um rosto nela e colocar uma vela dentro. As crianças se fantasiam e passam pelas casas, pedindo doces ou dinheiro e dizendo **trick or treat** ("dê algo para a gente ou faremos uma traquinagem").

hallucination /həˌluːsɪˈneɪʃn/ s alucinação

hallway /ˈhɔːlweɪ/ s **1** vestíbulo

2 (USA) corredor

halo /ˈheɪloʊ/ s (pl ~s ou ~es) auréola

halt /hɔːlt/ s parada, interrupção ● vt, vi deter(-se): *Halt!* Alto!

halting /ˈhɔːltɪŋ/ adj vacilante

halve /hæv/ *GB* hɑːv/ vt **1** dividir na metade **2** reduzir à metade

halves /hævz/ *GB* hɑːvz/ *plural de* HALF

ham /hæm/ s presunto

hamburger /ˈhæmbɜːrɡər/ s hambúrguer

hamlet /ˈhæmlət/ s vilarejo

hammer /ˈhæmər/ s martelo ● vt **1** martelar: *~ sth in* pregar algo (com martelo) **2** (coloq) arrasar

hammock /ˈhæmək/ s rede (de dormir)

hamper /ˈhæmpər/ vt tolher, impedir ● s (GB) cesta (piquenique, Natal)

hamster /ˈhæmstər/ s hamster

hand /hænd/ s **1** mão **2** letra manuscrita, caligrafia **3** (relógio) ponteiro **4** peão, peoa, operário/a **5** (Náut) tripulante **6** (baralho) jogada **7** (medida) palmo ▸ *by hand* à mão: *delivered by ~* entregue em mão **(close/near)** *at hand* à mão, perto *give/lend sb a hand* dar uma mão a alguém *hand in hand* **1** de mãos dadas **2** (fig) junto *hands up* mãos ao alto *in hand* **1** de reserva **2** sob controle *on hand* à disposição *on the one hand... on the other (hand)...* por um lado... por outro lado... *out of hand* **1** descontrolado **2** sem pensar (duas vezes) *to hand* à mão ● vt passar ■ *hand sth back* devolver algo *hand sth in* entregar algo *hand sth out* distribuir algo

handbag /ˈhændbæɡ/ s bolsa (de mão)

handbook /ˈhændbʊk/ s manual, guia

handbrake /ˈhændbreɪk/ s freio de mão

handcuff /ˈhændkʌf/ vt algemar ● *handcuffs* s algemas

handful /ˈhændfʊl/ s punhado ▸ *be a (real) handful* (coloq) ser insuportável: *The children are a real ~.* As crianças são difíceis de controlar.

handicap /ˈhændikæp/ s **1** (Med) deficiência (física ou mental) **2** (Esporte) desvantagem ● vt (-pp-) prejudicar *handicapped* adj deficiente (físico ou mental)

handicrafts /ˈhændikræfts/ *GB* -krɑːfts/ s [pl] artesanato

handkerchief /ˈhæŋkərtʃɪf, -tʃiːf/ s (pl ~s ou -chieves /-tʃiːvz/) lenço (de bolso)

handle /ˈhændl/ s **1** (ferramenta) cabo **2** (mala) alça **3** (xícara) asa **4** (porta, etc.) maçaneta ● vt **1** manusear **2** (máquinas) operar **3** (pessoas) tratar **4** suportar

handlebars /ˈhændlbɑːrz/ s [pl] guidão

handmade /ˌhændˈmeɪd/ adj feito à mão, artesanal NOTA Podem-se formar adjetivos compostos para todas as habilidades manuais, p. ex. **handbuilt** (construído à mão), **handknitted** (tricotado à mão), etc.

handout /ˈhændaʊt/ s **1** donativo **2** folheto **3** comunicado

handshake /ˈhændʃeɪk/ s aperto de mão

handsome /ˈhænsəm/ adj **1** atraente NOTA Refere-se principalmente a homens. **2** (presente) generoso

handwriting /ˈhændraɪtɪŋ/ s **1** escrita **2** caligrafia

handwritten /ˌhændˈrɪtn/ adj escrito à mão

handy /ˈhændi/ adj (-ier, -iest) **1** prático **2** à mão **3** conveniente

hang /hæŋ/ (pt, pp hung) **1** vt pendurar **2** vi estar pendurado **3** vi (roupa, cabelo) cair **4** vt, vi (pt, pp hanged) enforcar **5** vi pender ■ *hang about/around* (coloq) ficar/esperar sem fazer nada *hang on* segurar (firme), aguardar *hang (sth) out* estender algo (roupa no varal) *hang up (on sb)* (coloq) bater o telefone (na cara de alguém) ▸ s ▸ *get the hang of sth* (coloq) pegar o jeito de algo

hangar /ˈhæŋər/ s hangar

hanger /ˈhæŋər/ s (tb **clothes ~**) s cabide

hang-glider s asa-delta **hanggliding** s vôo de asa-delta

hangman /ˈhæŋmən/ s (pl -men) **1** carrasco (de forca) **2** (jogo) forca

hangover /ˈhæŋoʊvər/ s ressaca (de bebida)

hang-up s (coloq) complexo

haphazard /hæpˈhæzərd/ adj ao acaso

happen /ˈhæpən/ vi acontecer: *if you ~ to go into town* se por acaso, você for ao centro ▸ *as it happens* para falar a verdade *happening* s acontecimento

happy /ˈhæpi/ adj (-ier, -iest) **1** feliz **2** contente → GLAD *happily* adv **1** com satisfação **2** felizmente *happiness* s felicidade

harass /həˈræs, ˈhærəs/ vt assediar, atormentar **harassment** s assédio

harbor (GB **-our**) /ˈhɑrbər/ s porto ● vt **1** abrigar **2** (dúvidas, etc.) nutrir

hard /hɑrd/ (**~er, ~est**) adj **1** duro **2** difícil **3** cansativo, intenso: ~ worker pessoa trabalhadora **4** severo, cruel **5** (bebida) alcoólico ▸ **hard cash** dinheiro vivo **hard luck** (coloq) azar **have/give sb a hard time** dar trabalho a alguém **take a hard line (on/over sth)** adotar uma linha dura (a respeito de algo) **the hard way** o caminho mais difícil ● adv **1** (trabalhar, chover) muito, com força: try ~ esforçar-se **2** (vencer) com dificuldade **3** (olhar) fixamente ▸ **be hard put to do sth** ter dificuldade em fazer algo **be hard up** estar duro (sem dinheiro)

hardback /ˈhɑrdbæk/ s livro de capa dura

hard disk (tb **hard drive**) s (Informát) disco rígido

harden /ˈhɑrdn/ vt, vi endurecer(-se): hardened criminal criminoso calejado **hardening** s endurecimento

hardly /ˈhɑrdli/ adv **1** apenas: I ~ know her. Eu mal a conheço. **2** dificilmente: It's ~ surprising. Não chega a surpreender. **3** ~ anybody/ever quase ninguém/nunca

hardship /ˈhɑrdʃɪp/ s privação

hardware /ˈhɑrdwɛər/ s **1** ferramentas **2** (Mil) armamentos **3** (Informát) hardware

hard-working adj trabalhador

hardy /ˈhɑrdi/ adj (**-ier, -iest**) robusto

hare /hɛər/ s lebre

harm /hɑrm/ s dano, mal: do more ~ than good fazer mais mal do que bem ◊ (There's) no ~ done. Não aconteceu nada (de mal). ▸ **come to harm**: You'll come to no ~. Não lhe acontecerá nada (de mal). **out of harm's way** em lugar seguro ● vt **1** prejudicar **2** danificar **harmful** adj nocivo, prejudicial **harmless** adj **1** inócuo **2** inocente, inofensivo

harmony /ˈhɑrməni/ s (pl ~ies) harmonia

harness /ˈhɑrnəs/ s [sing] arreios ● vt **1** arrear **2** (recursos) aproveitar

harp /hɑrp/ s harpa ■ **harp on (about) sth** falar repetidamente sobre algo

harsh /hɑrʃ/ adj (**~er, ~est**) **1** áspero **2** duro **3** (luz) forte **4** (cor) berrante **5** estridente **6** (clima, etc.) rigoroso **7** (castigo) severo **harshly** adv severamente

harvest /ˈhɑrvɪst/ s colheita ● vt colher

has /həz, hæz/ Ver HAVE

hasn't /ˈhæz(ə)nt/ = HAS NOT Ver HAVE

hassle /ˈhæsl/ s (coloq) **1** trabalheira: It's a big ~. Dá muito trabalho. **2** discussão: Don't give me any ~! Deixe-me em paz! ● vt (coloq) perturbar

haste /heɪst/ s pressa: in ~ com pressa **hasten** /ˈheɪsn/ vi **1** apressar-se **2** vt acelerar **hastily** adv apressadamente **hasty** adj (**-ier, -iest**) apressado

hat /hæt/ s chapéu

hatch /hætʃ/ **1** vi ~ (**out**) sair do ovo **2** vt, vi chocar **3** vt ~ **sth (up)** tramar algo ● s **1** portinhola **2** abertura (para passar comida)

hate /heɪt/ vt **1** odiar **2** lamentar: I ~ to bother you, but... Desculpe incomodá-lo, mas... ● s **1** ódio **2** (coloq): One of my pet hates is... Uma das coisas que mais odeio é... **hateful** adj odioso **hatred** s ódio

haul /hɔːl/ vt puxar, arrastar ● s **1** percurso: long-haul flight vôo de longa distância **2** (quantidade) rede (de peixes) **3** ganho, despojo

haunt /hɔːnt/ vt **1** (fantasma) assombrar **2** freqüentar **3** (pensamento) atormentar ● s lugar predileto **haunted** adj (casa) assombrado

have /həv, hæv/ v aux NOTA Como auxiliar do "present perfect", o verbo **have** geralmente não se traduz e toda a expressão pode ser traduzida ou no passado ou no presente, conforme o caso: I've lived here since last year. Moro aqui desde o ano passado. ◊ "I've finished my work." "So have I." —Eu terminei meu trabalho. —Eu também. ◊ He's gone home, hasn't he? Ele foi para casa, não foi? ● vt **1** (tb **have got**) ter: ~ flu estar com gripe → TER **2** ~ **(got) sth to do;** ~ **(got) to do sth** ter algo a fazer; ter que fazer algo **3** tomar: ~ a coffee tomar um café NOTA A estrutura **have + substantivo** às vezes se traduz apenas por um verbo em português: ~ a wash lavar-se **4** ~ **sth done** fazer/mandar fazer algo: ~ your hair *cut* cortar o cabelo (no cabeleireiro) ◊ *She had her bag stolen.* Roubaram a bolsa dela. **5** *I won't ~ it!* Não aceitarei isso. ▸ **have had it** (*coloq*): *The TV has had it.* A TV já deu o que tinha que dar. **have it (that)**: *Rumor has it that...* Dizem que... ◊ *As luck would ~ it...* O destino quis que... **have to do with sb/algo** NOTA Para expressões com **have**, ver o substantivo, adjetivo, etc., p. ex. **have a sweet tooth** em SWEET. ■ **have sth back**: *Let me ~ the book back soon.* Devolva-me logo o livro. **have sb on** (*GB*, *coloq*) ridicularizar alguém: *You're having me on!* Você está me gozando! **have sth on** vestir: *He's got a tie on.* Ele está de gravata. **2** (*GB*) estar ocupado: *Have you got anything on today?* Você tem algum plano para hoje?

haven /'heɪvn/ s refúgio

haven't /'hæv(ə)nt/ = HAVE NOT Ver HAVE

havoc /'hævək/ s devastação: *wreak/cause/play ~ with sth* fazer estragos em algo

hawk /hɔ:k/ s falcão

hay /heɪ/ s feno: *~ fever* alergia ao pólen

hazard /'hæzəd/ s perigo ● *vt* ▸ **hazard a guess** arriscar um palpite **hazardous** *adj* arriscado

haze /heɪz/ s bruma

hazel /'heɪzl/ s aveleira ● *adj* castanho-claro

hazelnut /'heɪzlnʌt/ s avelã

hazy /'heɪzi/ *adj* (**-ier, -iest**) **1** brumoso **2** vago **3** (*pessoa*) confuso

he /hi:/ *pron* ele → YOU ● s: *Is it a he or a she?* É macho ou fêmea?

head /hed/ *vt* **1** liderar **2** (*Futebol*) cabecear ■ **head for sth** dirigir-se a algo ● *s* **1** cabeça: *It never entered my ~.* Isso nunca me ocorreu. → ARM **2** (*a/per head*) por cabeça: *ten dollars a ~* dez dólares por pessoa **3** *the ~ of the table* a cabeceira da mesa **4** chefe **5** (*masc tb* headmaster /,hed'mɑːstər/) (*fem tb* headmistress /,hed'mɪstrəs/) (*GB*) diretor/a (*escola*) ▸ **be/go above/over your head** estar acima da sua compreensão **go to your head** subir à cabeça de alguém **head first** de cabeça **heads or tails?** cara ou coroa? **not make head or tail of sth** não conseguir entender algo

headache /'hedeɪk/ s dor de cabeça

heading /'hedɪŋ/ s cabeçalho, divisão de texto

headlight /'hedlaɪt/ (*tb* headlamp) s farol (*veículo*)

headline /'hedlaɪn/ s **1** manchete **2** (**the headlines**) [*pl*] resumo das principais notícias

head office s escritório central

head-on *adj, adv* de frente

headphones /'hedfoʊnz/ s fones de ouvido

headquarters /,hed'kwɔːrtəz/ s (*abrev* **HQ**) **1** sede **2** quartel-general

head start s: *have a ~ over sb* ter uma vantagem sobre alguém

headway /'hedweɪ/ s ▸ **make headway** avançar/progredir

heal /hiːl/ **1** *vi* cicatrizar **2** *vt* curar

health /helθ/ s saúde: *~ foods* alimentos naturais

healthy /'helθi/ *adj* (**-ier, -iest**) **1** são **2** saudável

heap /hiːp/ s montão, pilha ● *vt* ~ **sth (up)** empilhar algo

hear /hɪər/ (*pt, pp* heard /hɜːrd/) **1** *vt, vi* ouvir: *~ of/sb/sth* ouvir falar de alguém/algo **2** *vt* escutar **3** *vi* ~ **about sth** ficar sabendo de algo **4** *vt* (*Jur*) dar audiência ■ **hear from sb** ter notícias de alguém

hearing /'hɪərɪŋ/ s **1** (*tb* sense of ~) audição **2** (*Jur*) audiência

heart /hɑːrt/ s **1** coração **2** *the ~ of the matter* o xis da questão **3** (*alface, etc.*) miolo **4** (**hearts**) (*naipe*) copas → BARALHO ▸ **at heart** em essência **by heart** de memória/cor **set your heart on (having/doing) sth** desejar (ter/fazer) algo ardentemente **take heart** animar-se **take sth to heart** levar algo a sério **your/sb's heart sinks**: *When I saw the line my ~ sank.* Quando vi a fila, perdi o ânimo.

heartbeat /'hɑːrtbiːt/ s batimento cardíaco

heartbreak /'hɑːrtbreɪk/ s sofrimento **heartbreaking** *adj* angustiante **heartbroken** *adj* de coração partido

hearten /'hɑːrtn/ *vt* animar **heartening** *adj* animador

heartfelt /'hɑːrtfelt/ *adj* sincero

hearth /hɑːrθ/ s **1** lareira **2** lar

heartless /'hɑːrtləs/ *adj* desumano

hearty /'hɑːrti/ *adj* (**-ier, -iest**) **1** cordial: *a ~ welcome* uma recepção calorosa **2** (*pessoa*) expansivo (*às vezes demais*) **3** (*comida*) abundante

heat /hi:t/ s **1** calor **2** (Esporte) prova classificatória ▶ **be in heat** (GB **be on heat**) estar no cio **in the heat of the moment** no auge da irritação ● vt, vi ~ (**sth**) (**up**) aquecer (algo); aquecer-se **heated** adj **1** aquecido: centrally ~ com aquecimento central **2** (discussão, etc.) inflamado **heater** s aquecedor

heath /hi:θ/ s charneca

heathen /ˈhi:ðn/ s pagão/ã

heather /ˈheðər/ s urze

heating /ˈhi:tɪŋ/ s calefação

heatwave /ˈhi:tweɪv/ s onda de calor

heave /hi:v/ **1** vt, vi ~ (**at/on sth**) arrastar, levantar, puxar algo (com esforço) **2** vt (coloq) lançar (algo pesado) ● s puxão, empurrão

heaven (tb **Heaven**) /ˈhevn/ s (Relig) céu

heavenly /ˈhevnli/ adj **1** (Relig) celestial **2** (astro) celeste **3** (coloq) divino

heavily /ˈhevɪli/ adv **1** bem, muito: rain ~ chover forte **2** pesadamente

heavy /ˈhevi/ adj (**-ier, -iest**) **1** pesado: How ~ is it? Quanto pesa? **2** intenso: ~ drinker pessoa que bebe muito ▶ **with a heavy hand** com mão firme

heavyweight /ˈheviweɪt/ s **1** (Esporte) peso pesado **2** pessoa de peso

heckle /ˈhekl/ vt, vi perturbar um orador

hectare /ˈhekteər/ s hectare → Ver pág. 224

hectic /ˈhektɪk/ adj frenético

he'd /hi:d/ **1** = HE HAD Ver HAVE **2** = HE WOULD Ver WOULD

hedge /hedʒ/ s **1** sebe **2** proteção ● vt, vi esquivar-se

hedgehog /ˈhedʒhɔːɡ; GB -hɒɡ/ s ouriço

heed /hi:d/ vt (fml) prestar atenção a ● s ▶ **take heed** (**of sth**) dar atenção (a algo)

heel /hi:l/ s **1** calcanhar **2** (sapato) salto

hefty /ˈhefti/ adj (**-ier, -iest**) **1** robusto **2** pesado **3** (golpe) forte

height /haɪt/ s **1** altura **2** estatura **3** (Geog) altitude **4** auge: at/in the ~ of summer em pleno verão **5** the ~ of fashion a última moda → ALTO

heighten /ˈhaɪtn/ vt, vi intensificar

heir /eər/ s ~ (**to sth**) herdeiro (de algo)

heiress /ˈeərəs/ s herdeira

held /held/ pret, pp de HOLD

helicopter /ˈhelɪkɒptər/ s helicóptero

hell /hel/ s inferno NOTA Hell não é acompanhado por artigo. ▶ **a/one hell of a...** (coloq): a ~ of a shock um susto terrível **what, where, who, etc. the hell...?** (coloq): Who the ~ is he? Quem diabos é ele? **hellish** adj infernal

he'll /hi:l/ = HE WILL Ver WILL

hello /həˈloʊ/ interj, s **1** olá **2** (telefone) alô

helm /helm/ s timão

helmet /ˈhelmɪt/ s capacete

help /help/ **1** vt, vi ajudar: Help! Socorro! ◊ Ver ajuda? ◊ May I ~ you? Em que posso servi-lo? **2** vt ~ **yourself** (**to sth**) servir-se (de) algo ▶ **a helping hand**: give/lend (sb) a helping hand dar uma mão (a alguém) **can't help sth**: He can't ~ it. Ele não consegue evitar. ◊ I couldn't ~ laughing. Não pude deixar de rir. **it can't/couldn't be helped** não há/havia remédio ■ **help (sb) out** dar uma mão (a alguém) ● s [U] **1** ajuda: It wasn't much ~. Não ajudou muito. **2** assistência

helper /ˈhelpər/ s ajudante

helpful /ˈhelpfl/ adj **1** prestativo **2** atencioso **3** útil

helping /ˈhelpɪŋ/ s porção (comida)

helpless /ˈhelpləs/ adj **1** indefeso **2** incapaz

helter-skelter /ˌheltər ˈskeltər/ s tobogã (em espiral) ● adj atabalhoado

hem /hem/ s bainha ● vt (**-mm-**) fazer a bainha em ■ **hem sb/sth in 1** cercar alguém/algo **2** encurralar alguém

hemisphere /ˈhemɪsfɪər/ s hemisfério

hemoglobin /ˌhiːməˈɡloʊbɪn/ s hemoglobina

hemorrhage /ˈhemərɪdʒ/ s hemorragia

hen /hen/ s galinha

hence /hens/ adv **1** desde já: two years ~ daqui a dois anos **2** daí, portanto

henceforth /ˌhensˈfɔːrθ/ adv (fml) de agora em diante

hepatitis /ˌhepəˈtaɪtɪs/ s hepatite

her /hɜːr, ɜːr, ər/ pron **1** [objeto direto] a, ela **2** [objeto indireto] lhe, a ela **3** [depois de prep e do verbo be] ela: She took it with ~. Ela o levou consigo. ● adj poss dela → HER

herald /ˈherəld/ s mensageiro/a

• vt anunciar (*chegada, início*)
heraldry s heráldica

herb /ɜːrb; GB hɜːb/ s erva **herbal**
adj herbáceo: ~ *tea* chá de ervas

herd /hɜːrd/ s rebanho, manada
• vt conduzir (*rebanho*)

here /hɪər/ adv aqui: *They'll be ~
soon.* Eles vão chegar logo.
NOTA Nas orações que
começam com **here** o verbo
segue o sujeito, se este for um
pronome: *Here they are, at last!*
◇ *Here it is, on the table!* Mas
precede, se o sujeito for um
substantivo: *Here comes the
bus.* ▸ **here and there** aqui e ali
here you are aqui está • interj 1
ei 2 (*oferecendo algo*) tome 3
presente

hereditary /hə'redɪteri; GB -tri-/
adj hereditário

heresy /'herəsi/ s (pl **-ies**)
heresia

heritage /'herɪtɪdʒ/ s patrimônio

hermit /'hɜːrmɪt/ s ermita

hero /'hɪəroʊ/ s (pl **-es**) 1 protagonista 2 herói, heroína **heroic**
/hə'roʊɪk/ adj heróico **heroism**
/'heroʊɪzəm/ s heroísmo

heroin /'heroʊɪn/ s heroína
(*droga*)

heroine /'heroʊɪn/ s heroína
(*pessoa*)

herring /'herɪŋ/ s (pl **herring** ou
~s) arenque

hers /hɜːrz/ pron poss o(s)/a(s)
dela: *a friend of ~* um amigo
dela

herself /hɜːr'self/ pron 1 [uso
reflexivo] se 2 [uso enfático] ela
mesma 3 [depois de prep] si
(mesma)

he's /hiːz/ 1 = HE IS *Ver* BE 2 = HE
HAS *Ver* HAVE

hesitant /'hezɪtənt/ adj hesitante

hesitate /'hezɪteɪt/ vi 1 hesitar:
Don't ~ to call. Não deixe de
telefonar. 2 vacilar **hesitation** s
hesitação

heterogeneous /ˌhetərə-
'dʒiːniəs/ adj heterogêneo

heterosexual /ˌhetərə'sekʃuəl/
adj, s heterossexual

hexagon /'heksəgən; GB -gən/ s
hexágono

heyday /'heɪdeɪ/ s auge

hi /haɪ/ interj (coloq) oi

hibernate /'haɪbərneɪt/ vi hibernar **hibernation** s hibernação

hiccup (tb **hiccough**) /'hɪkʌp/ s 1
soluço 2 (coloq) problema

hidden /'hɪdn/ pp de HIDE • adj
oculto, escondido

hide /haɪd/ s pele (*animal*) • (pt
hid /hɪd/ pp **hidden**) 1 vi escon-

der-se 2 vt ocultar

hide-and-seek /ˌhaɪd n 'siːk/ s
esconde-esconde

hideous /'hɪdiəs/ adj horrendo

hiding /'haɪdɪŋ/ s (coloq) surra
▸ **be in/go into hiding** estar
escondido, esconder-se

hierarchy /'haɪərɑːrki/ s (pl **-ies**)
hierarquia

hieroglyphic /ˌhaɪərə'glɪfɪk/ s
hieróglifo

hi-fi /'haɪ faɪ/ adj, s alta-fideli-
dade

high /haɪ/ s pico • (~er, ~est) adj
1 alto: *be X meters, feet, etc.* ~
medir/ter X metros, pés, etc. de
altura ◇ *How ~ is it?* Qual é a
altura ◇ *high-level* de
alto nível → ALTO 2 elevado: *I
have it on the highest authority.*
Sei de fonte segura/da mais
alta fonte. 3 *friends in ~ places*
amigos influentes 3 *have a ~
opinion of sb* ter alguém em alta
estima ◇ *~ hopes* grandes
expectativas 4 (*vento*) forte 5
the ~ point of the evening o melhor
momento da noite 6 (*som*)
agudo 7 *in ~ summer* em pleno
verão ◇ *~ season* alta temporada 8 (coloq) • **(on sth)** intoxi-
cado (de algo) (*drogas, álcool*) •
adv alto, a grande altura ▸ **high
and dry** em apuros

highbrow /'haɪbraʊ/ adj (freq
pej) intelectual

high-class adj de categoria

High Court s (GB) Tribunal
Superior

higher education s ensino
superior

high jump s salto em altura

highland /'haɪlənd/ s [ger pl]
região montanhosa

highlight /'haɪlaɪt/ s 1 ponto alto
2 [ger pl] mecha • vt ressaltar

highly /'haɪli/ adv 1 muito, extremamente 2 *think/speak ~ of sb*
ter alguém em alta estima/falar
muito bem de alguém

highly strung adj tenso, irritadiço

Highness /'haɪnəs/ s: *your/his/
her ~* Vossa/Sua Alteza

high-powered adj 1 de alta
potência 2 dinâmico 3 *a ~ job*
um cargo com muito poder

high pressure s alta pressão

high-pressure adj estressante

high-rise s edifício alto, espigão
• adj 1 com muitos andares 2 de
um espigão

H

high school s (esp USA) escola secundária

high street s rua principal

high-tech adj de alta tecnologia

high tide (tb **high water**) s maré alta

highway /ˈhaɪweɪ/ s 1 (esp USA) rodovia → RODOVIA 2 via pública: *Highway Code* Código Nacional de Trânsito

hijack /ˈhaɪdʒæk/ vt 1 seqüestrar 2 monopolizar ● s seqüestro **hijacker** s seqüestrador/a (avião)

hike /haɪk/ s excursão a pé ● vi fazer uma excursão a pé **hiker** s caminhante

hilarious /hɪˈleəriəs/ adj hilariante

hill /hɪl/ s 1 colina, monte 2 ladeira, subida **hilly** adj montanhoso

hillside /ˈhɪlsaɪd/ s encosta

hilt /hɪlt/ s punho (espada) ▸ **(up) to the hilt** 1 completamente 2 incondicionalmente

him /hɪm/ pron 1 [objeto direto] o, ele 2 [objeto indireto] lhe, a ele 3 [depois de prep e do verbo **be**] ele: *He took it with ~.* Ele o levou consigo.

himself /hɪmˈself/ pron 1 [uso reflexivo] se 2 [uso enfático] ele mesmo 3 [depois de prep] ele (mesmo)

hinder /ˈhɪndər/ vt retardar, atrapalhar: *Our work was hindered by bad weather.* O nosso trabalho foi dificultado pelo mau tempo.

hindrance /ˈhɪndrəns/ s obstáculo

hindsight /ˈhaɪndsaɪt/ s: *with the benefit of)/in* ~ em retrospectiva

Hindu /ˈhɪnduː; GB hɪnˈduː/ adj, s hindu **Hinduism** s hinduísmo

hinge /hɪndʒ/ s dobradiça ■ **hinge on sth** depender de algo

hint /hɪnt/ s 1 insinuação 2 indício 3 dica ● 1 vi ~ **at sth** fazer alusão a algo 2 vt, vi insinuar

hip /hɪp/ s quadril

hippo /ˈhɪpəʊ/ (pl ~s) (tb **hippopotamus** /ˌhɪpəˈpɒtəməs/) s hipopótamo

hire /ˈhaɪər/ vt 1 alugar 2 contratar → ALUGAR ● s aluguel: *Bicycles for* ~. Alugam-se bicicletas. ◇ ~ *purchase* compra a prazo

his /hɪz/ adj poss dele ● pron poss o(s)/a(s) dele: *a friend of* ~ um amigo dele

hiss /hɪs/ 1 vi sibilar 2 vt, vi vaiar ● s silvo

historian /hɪˈstɔːriən/ s historiador/a

historic /hɪˈstɒrɪk; GB -ˈstɔːr-/ adj histórico **historical** adj histórico

history /ˈhɪstri/ s (pl -ies) 1 história 2 (Med, etc.) histórico

hit /hɪt/ vt (-tt-) (pt, pp **hit**) 1 bater (com) 2 acertar: *He's been* ~ *in the leg by a bullet.* Ele foi atingido por uma bala na perna. 3 colidir com 4 (Mil) atingir, afetar: *the areas* ~ *by the drought* as zonas atingidas pela seca ▸ **hit it off (with sb)** (coloq): *Pete and Sue* ~ *it off immediately.* Pete e Sue se entrosaram de saída. **hit the nail on the head** acertar na mosca ■ **hit back (at sb/sth)** revidar a alguém/algo **hit out (at sb/sth)** desferir golpes (em alguém/algo) ● s 1 golpe 2 sucesso

hit-and-run adj: ~ *driver* motorista que atropela alguém e foge

hitch /hɪtʃ/ vt, vi: ~ (a ride/lift) pegar carona ■ **hitch sth up** (calças, etc.) arregaçar ● s problema

hitchhike /ˈhɪtʃhaɪk/ vi pedir carona **hitchhiker** s pessoa que viaja de carona

hi-tech = HIGH-TECH

hive /haɪv/ s colméia

hoard /hɔːd/ s 1 tesouro 2 provisão ● vt acumular

hoarding /ˈhɔːdɪŋ/ s outdoor

hoarse /hɔːs/ adj rouco

hoax /həʊks/ s trote: ~ *bomb warning* alerta de bomba falso

hob /hɒb/ s placa de aquecimento (de fogão)

hockey /ˈhɒki/ s 1 (USA) (GB **ice** ~) hóquei sobre o gelo 2 (GB) (USA **field** ~) hóquei

hog /hɒɡ; GB hɒɡ/ s porco ● vt (coloq) monopolizar

hoist /hɔɪst/ vt içar

hold /həʊld/ (pt, pp **held**) 1 vt segurar, prender na mão: ~ *sth on/down* segurar algo ◇ ~ *hands (with sb)* ficar de mãos dadas (com alguém) 2 vi ~ **on (to sb/sth)** agarrar-se (a alguém/algo) 3 vt, vi (peso) agüentar 4 vt (criminoso, etc.) deter 5 vt (opinião) sustentar 6 vt acomodar: *It won't* ~ *you all.* Não vai haver lugar para todos. 7 vt (cargo) ocupar 8 vt (conversação) manter 9 vt (reunião, eleições) realizar 10 vt (possuir) ter 11 vt (fml) considerar 12 vt (oferta, etc.) ser válido 13 vt (título) ostentar 14 vi (ao telefone) esperar

▶**don't hold your breath** é melhor esperar sentado **hold fast firm to sth** aferrar-se a algo **hold firm to sth** manter-se fiel a algo **hold it** (*coloq*) espere **hold sb to ransom** chantagear alguém **hold sb/sth in contempt** desprezar alguém/algo **hold the line** aguardar na linha **hold your breath** prender a respiração ■**hold sth against sb** ter algo contra alguém **hold sb/sth back** conter alguém/algo **hold sth back** ocultar algo **hold forth** (*pej*) discursar **hold out 1** durar **2** agüentar **hold up (a bank, etc.)** assaltar (um banco, etc.) **hold sb/sth up** atrasar alguém/algo **hold with sth** concordar com algo ● **s 1** *keep a firm ~ of sth* manter-se agarrado a algo ◇ *take ~ of sb/sth* agarrar alguém/algo **2** (*judô*) chave **3** influência, controle **4** (*barco, avião*) porão ▶**get hold of sth** contatar alguém

holdall /'hoʊldɔːl/ s saco de viagem

holder /'hoʊldər/ s **1** titular **2** portador/a **3** suporte

hold-up s **1** (*trânsito*) engarrafamento **2** atraso **3** assalto

hole /hoʊl/ s **1** buraco **2** orifício **3** furo **4** toca **5** (*coloq*) aperto

holiday /'hɒlədeɪ/ s **1** feriado **2** férias ● vi passar as férias **holidaymaker** s pessoa que está de férias

holiness /'hoʊlinəs/ s santidade

hollow /'hɒloʊ/ adj **1** oco **2** (*rosto, olhos*) fundo **3** (*som*) surdo **4** (*pessoa*) falso ● s **1** buraco **2** cavidade **3** depressão ● vt ~ **sth out** escavar algo

holly /'hɒli/ s azevinho

holocaust /'hɒləkɔːst/ s holocausto

holster /'hoʊlstər/ s coldre

holy /'hoʊli/ adj (-ier, -iest) **1** santo **2** sagrado **3** bento

homage /'hɒmɪdʒ, 'ɒm-/ s [U] (*fml*) homenagem

home /hoʊm/ s **1** casa, lar **2** (*de idosos, etc.*) asilo **3** (*fig*) berço **4** (*Zool*) hábitat **5** (*corrida*) meta ▶ **at home 1** em casa **2** à vontade **3** no meu, seu, etc. país ● adj **1** familiar: ~ *comforts* comodidades do lar **2** caseiro **3** nacional: *the ~ Office* o Ministério do Interior **4** (*Esporte*) de/em casa **5** natal ● adv **1** *go ~* ir para casa **2** (*fixar, prender, etc.*) até o fundo ▶ **hit/strike home** acertar em cheio **home and dry** fora de perigo

homeland /'hoʊmlænd/ s terra natal

homeless /'hoʊmləs/ adj sem lar ● **the homeless** s [pl] os desabrigados

homely /'hoʊmli/ adj (-ier, -iest) **1** (*GB*) simples, despretensioso **2** (*lugar*) caseiro **3** (*USA*) feio

homemade /ˌhoʊm'meɪd/ adj caseiro, feito em casa

home page s página home

homesick /'hoʊmsɪk/ adj saudoso (de casa): *be/feel ~* ter/sentir saudade de casa

homework /'hoʊmwɜːrk/ s [U] (*colégio*) dever de casa

homicide /'hɒmɪsaɪd/ s homicídio **homicidal** /ˌhɒmɪ'saɪdl/ adj homicida

homogeneous /ˌhoʊmə'dʒiːniəs/ adj homogêneo

homosexual /ˌhoʊmə'sekʃuəl/ adj, s homossexual **homosexuality** /ˌhoʊməsekʃu'æləti/ s homossexualismo

honest /'ɒnɪst/ adj **1** honesto **2** sincero **3** (*salário*) digno honestly adv **1** honestamente **2** de verdade, francamente

honesty /'ɒnəsti/ s **1** honestidade **2** franqueza

honey /'hʌni/ s **1** mel **2** (*coloq, USA*) querido/a

honeymoon /'hʌnimuːn/ s lua-de-mel

honk /hɒŋk, hʌŋk/ vt, vi buzinar

honor (*GB* -our) /'ɒnər/ s **1** honra **2** condecoração **3** (honors) [pl] distinção: (*first class*) *honors degree* diploma (com distinção) **4** (*my/his/her Honor*) Vossa/Sua Excelência ▶ **in honor of sb/ sth; in sb's/sth's honor** em homenagem a alguém/algo ● vt **1** honrar **2** condecorar **3** (*opinião, etc.*) respeitar

honorable (*GB* -our-) /'ɒnərəbl/ adj **1** honrado **2** honroso

honorary /'ɒnəreri; *GB* 'ɒnərəri/ adj honorário

hood /hʊd/ s **1** capuz **2** capô

hoof /huːf/ s (pl ~s ou **hooves**) casco

hook /hʊk/ s **1** gancho **2** anzol ▶ **let/get sb off the hook** (*coloq*) tirar alguém de um aperto **off the hook** fora do gancho (*telefone*) ● vt, vi enganchar, fisgar ▶ **be hooked on (sb/sth)** (*coloq*) estar vidrado (em alguém), ser/ficar viciado (em algo)

hooligan /'huːlɪɡən/ s vândalo/a **hooliganism** s vandalismo

hoop /huːp/ s arco

hooray /huˈreɪ/ *interj* = HURRAH

hoot /huːt/ s **1** pio **2** buzinada ● **1** *vi* piar **2** *vi* buzinar **3** *vt* (*buzina*) tocar

Hoover® /ˈhuːvər/ (*GB*) s aspirador de pó **hoover** *vt*, *vi* passar o aspirador (em)

hooves /huːvz/ s plural de HOOF

hop /hɒp/ *vi* (**-pp-**) **1** (*pessoa*) pular num pé só **2** (*animal*) saltitar ● s **1** pulo **2** lúpulo

hope /həʊp/ s esperança ● *vt*, *vi* ~ **(for sth)** esperar (algo) **· I should hope not** era só o que faltava → ESPERAR

hopeful /ˈhəʊpfl/ *adj* **1** otimista: *be* ~ *that...* ter esperança de que... **2** (*situação*) promissor **hopefully** *adv* **1** com esperança **2** com sorte

hopeless /ˈhəʊpləs/ *adj* **1** inútil **2** (*tarefa*) impossível **hopelessly** *adv* irremediavelmente

horde /hɔːd/ s horda: *hordes of people* um bando de gente

horizon /həˈraɪzn/ s **1** horizonte **2** (**horizons**) [*ger pl*] perspectiva

horizontal /ˌhɒrɪˈzɒntl/; *GB* ˌhɒr-/ *adj*, s horizontal

hormone /ˈhɔːməʊn/ s hormônio

horn /hɔːn/ s **1** chifre **2** (*Mús*) trompa **3** buzina

horoscope /ˈhɒrəskəʊp/; *GB* ˈhɒr-/ s horóscopo

horrendous /hɒˈrendəs/; *GB* hɒr-/ *adj* **1** horrendo **2** (*coloq*) tremendo

horrible /ˈhɒrəbl/; *GB* ˈhɒr-/ *adj* horrível

horrid /ˈhɒrɪd/; *GB* ˈhɒrɪd/ *adj* horrível, antipático

horrific /həˈrɪfɪk/ *adj* horripilante, espantoso

horrify /ˈhɒrɪfaɪ/; *GB* ˈhɒr-/ *vt* (*pt*, *pp* **-ied**) horrorizar **horrifying** *adj* horripilante

horror /ˈhɒrər/; *GB* ˈhɒr-/ s horror: ~ *movie* filme de terror

horse /hɔːs/ s cavalo

horseback rider /ˈhɔːsbæk raɪdər/ s cavaleiro

horseman /ˈhɔːsmən/ s (*fem* **horsewoman**) (*pl* -**men** -**women**) cavaleiro, amazona

horsepower /ˈhɔːspaʊər/ s (*abrev* **hp**) cavalo-vapor

horseshoe /ˈhɔːsʃuː/ s ferradura

horticulture /ˈhɔːtɪkʌltʃər/ s horticultura **horticultural** /ˌhɔːtɪˈkʌltʃərəl/ *adj* hortícola

hose /həʊz/ (*GB tb* **hosepipe**) s mangueira

hospice /ˈhɒspɪs/ s hospital (*para moribundos*)

hospitable /həˈspɪtəbl, ˈhɒspɪtəbl/ *adj* hospitaleiro

hospital /ˈhɒspɪtl/ s hospital

hospitality /ˌhɒspɪˈtæləti/ s hospitalidade

host /həʊst/ s **1** montão: *a* ~ *of admirers* um monte de admiradores **2** anfitrião **3** (*TV*) apresentador **4** (*the Host*) a hóstia ● *vt* sediar: ~ *the World Cup* sediar a Copa do Mundo

hostage /ˈhɒstɪdʒ/ s refém

hostel /ˈhɒstl/ s hospedaria: *youth* ~ albergue da juventude

hostess /ˈhəʊstəs/ s **1** anfitriã **2** (*TV*) apresentadora **3** cicerone

hostile /ˈhɒstaɪl; *GB* -taɪl/ *adj* **1** hostil **2** (*território*) inimigo

hostility /hɒˈstɪləti/ s hostilidade

hot /hɒt/ *adj* (**hotter, hottest**) **1** quente: *I'm* ~. Estou com calor. → FRIO **2** calorento: *It's very* ~. Faz muito calor. **3** picante

hot dog s cachorro-quente

hotel /həʊˈtel/ s hotel

hotly /ˈhɒtli/ *adv* ardentemente, energicamente

hound /haʊnd/ s cão de caça ● *vt* acossar

hour /ˈaʊər/ s **1** hora: *on the* ~ na hora exata **2** (**hours**) [*pl*] horário: *after hours* depois do expediente **3** momento **hourly** *adv*, *adj* de hora em hora

house /haʊs/ s **1** casa **2** (*Teat*) sala de espetáculos: *There was a full* ~. Lotou o teatro. ▶ **on the house** cortesia da casa ● /haʊz/ *vt* hospedar

household /ˈhaʊshəʊld/ s: *a large* ~ uma casa cheia de gente (*família, empregados, etc.*) ◇ ~ *chores* tarefas domésticas **householder** s dono/a da casa

housekeeper /ˈhaʊskiːpər/ s governanta **housekeeping** s **1** administração do lar **2** despesas domésticas

the House of Commons s (*GB*) a Câmara dos Comuns

the House of Lords s (*GB*) a Câmara dos Lordes

the House of Representatives s (*USA*) a Câmara dos Deputados

the Houses of Parliament s o Parlamento (*britânico*)

housewife /ˈhaʊswaɪf/ s (*pl* -**wives**) dona-de-casa

housework /ˈhaʊswɜːk/ s [*U*] trabalhos domésticos

housing /ˈhaʊzɪŋ/ s [*U*] habitação, alojamento

housing development (GB **housing estate**) s (USA) loteamento, conjunto residencial

hover /'hʌvər; GB 'hɒvə(r)/ vi 1 pairar/ficar suspenso (no ar) 3 (pessoa) rondar

how /haʊ/ adv interr como: How are you? Como vai? ◇ How old are you? Quantos anos você tem? ◇ How fast were you going? A que velocidade você ia? ▸ **how about?**: How about it? Que tal? **how come...?** como é que...? **how do you do?** (fml) muito prazer NOTA How do you do? é usado em apresentações formais e se responde com how do you do? Por outro lado, **how are you?** é empregado em situações informais e a pessoa responde conforme esteja se sentindo: fine, very well, not too well, etc. **how many?** quantos?; as? **how much?** quanto? ● adv que...!: How cold it is! Que frio! ◇ How you've grown! Como você cresceu! ● conj como

however /haʊ'evər/ adv 1 contudo 2 por mais que: ~ strong you are por mais forte que você seja ● conj como: however you like como você quiser ● adv interr como

howl /haʊl/ s 1 uivo 2 grito ● vi 1 uivar 2 berrar

hub /hʌb/ s 1 (roda) cubo 2 centro

hubbub /'hʌbʌb/ s vozeio

huddle /'hʌdl/ vi 1 aconchegar-se 2 apinhar-se ● s aglomerado

hue /hjuː/ s 1 matiz 2 cor ▸ **hue and cry** clamor público

huff /hʌf/ s: in a ~ com raiva

hug /hʌg/ s abraço ● vt (-gg-) abraçar

huge /hjuːdʒ/ adj enorme

hull /hʌl/ s casco (navio)

hullo = HELLO

hum /hʌm/ s 1 zumbido 2 (vozes) murmúrio ● (-mm-) 1 vi zumbir 2 vt, vi cantarolar com a boca fechada 3 vi (coloq): ~ with activity ferver de atividade

human /'hjuːmən/ adj, s humano

humane /hjuː'meɪn/ adj humano, compassivo

humanity /hjuː'mænəti/ s 1 humanidade 2 (humanities) humanidades **humanitarian** /hjuːˌmænɪ'teəriən/ adj humanitário

humble /'hʌmbl/ adj (-er, -est) humilde ● vt: ~ yourself ter uma atitude humilde

humid /'hjuːmɪd/ adj úmido **humidity** /hjuː'mɪdəti/ s umidade NOTA **Humid** e **humidity** só se referem à umidade atmosférica. → MOIST

humiliate /hjuː'mɪlieɪt/ vt humilhar **humiliating** adj humilhante **humiliation** s humilhação

humility /hjuː'mɪləti/ s humildade

hummingbird /'hʌmɪŋbɜːd/ s beija-flor

humor (GB **-our**) /'hjuːmər/ s 1 humor 2 graça ● vt agradar

humorous /'hjuːmərəs/ adj humorístico, divertido

hump /hʌmp/ s corcova

hunch /hʌntʃ/ vt, vi ~ (sth) (up) curvar algo/curvar-se ● s palpite

hundred /'hʌndrəd/ adj, pron cem, cento ● s cento, centena **hundredth** 1 adj, pron centésimo 2 s centésima parte

hung /hʌŋ/ pret, pp de HANG

hunger /'hʌŋgər/ s fome → FOME ■ **hunger for/after sth** ansiar por/ter sede de algo

hungry /'hʌŋgri/ adj (-ier, -iest) faminto: I'm ~. Estou com fome.

hunk /hʌŋk/ s naco

hunt /hʌnt/ vt, vi caçar, ir à caça 2 ~ (for sb/sth) andar à procura (de alguém/algo) ● s 1 caça 2 perseguição, busca **hunter** s caçador/a

hunting /'hʌntɪŋ/ s caça

hurdle /'hɜːrdl/ s 1 barreira 2 obstáculo

hurl /hɜːrl/ vt 1 arremessar 2 (insultos, etc.) proferir

hurrah /hə'rɑː/ interj ~ (for sb/sth) viva (alguém/algo)

hurricane /'hɜːrɪkeɪn; GB 'hʌrɪkən/ s furacão

hurried /'hɜːrid/ adj apressado

hurry /'hɜːri/ s pressa: be in a ~ estar com pressa ● vt, vi (pt, pp -ied) andar depressa ■ **hurry up** (coloq) apressar-se

hurt /hɜːrt/ (pt, pp hurt) 1 vt ferir, machucar: get ~ machucar-se 2 vi doer: My leg hurts. Estou com dor na perna. 3 vt ofender 4 vt (reputação, etc.) prejudicar, causar dano **hurtful** adj cruel, prejudicial

hurtle /'hɜːrtl/ vi despencar-se

husband /'hʌzbənd/ s marido

hush /hʌʃ/ s [sing] silêncio ■ **hush sb/sth up** calar alguém/algo

husky /'hʌski/ adj (-ier, -iest) rouco ● s (pl -ies) cão esquimó

hustle /'hʌsl/ vt empurrar ● s ▸ **hustle and bustle** corre-corre

hut /hʌt/ s cabana

hybrid /'haɪbrɪd/ adj, s híbrido

hydrant /'haɪdrənt/ s hidrante

hydraulic /haɪ'drɔːlɪk/ adj hidráulico

hydroelectric /ˌhaɪdrəʊ'lektrɪk/ adj hidroelétrico

hydrogen /'haɪdrədʒən/ s hidrogênio

hyena (tb hyaena) /haɪ'iːnə/ s hiena

hygiene /'haɪdʒiːn/ s higiene hygienic adj higiênico

hymn /hɪm/ s hino religioso

hype /haɪp/ s (coloq) propaganda (exagerada) ■ hype sth (up) (coloq) exagerar os fatos sobre algo

hypermarket /'haɪpəmɑːkɪt/ s (GB) hipermercado

hyphen /'haɪfn/ s hífen

hypnosis /hɪp'nəʊsɪs/ s hipnose

hypnotic /hɪp'nɒtɪk/ adj hipnótico

hypnotism /'hɪpnətɪzəm/ s hipnotismo hypnotist s hipnotizador/a

hypnotize /'hɪpnətaɪz/ vt hipnotizar

hypochondriac /ˌhaɪpə'kɒndriæk/ s hipocondríaco/a

hypocrisy /hɪ'pɒkrəsi/ s hipocrisia

hypocrite /'hɪpəkrɪt/ s hipócrita hypocritical /ˌhɪpə'krɪtɪkl/ adj hipócrita

hypothesis /haɪ'pɒθəsɪs/ s (pl -eses /-əsiːz/) hipótese

hypothetical /ˌhaɪpə'θetɪkl/ adj hipotético

hysteria /hɪ'stɪəriə/ s histeria

hysterical /hɪ'sterɪkl/ adj 1 histérico 2 (coloq) hilariante

hysterics /hɪ'sterɪks/ s [pl] 1 crise de histeria 2 (coloq) ataque de riso

I i

I, i /aɪ/ s (pl I's, i's /aɪz/) I, i

I /aɪ/ pron eu → YOU

ice /aɪs/ s gelo ● vt cobrir com glacê

iceberg /'aɪsbɜːg/ s iceberg

icebox /'aɪsbɒks/ s (USA, antiq) geladeira

ice cream s sorvete

ice lolly /ˌaɪs 'lɒli/ s (pl -ies) (GB) picolé

ice rink Ver RINK

ice skate s patim de gelo ● vi patinar sobre gelo ice skating s patinação sobre o gelo

icicle /'aɪsɪkl/ s pingente de gelo

icing /'aɪsɪŋ/ s glacê

icon /'aɪkɒn/ s ícone

icy /'aɪsi/ adj (-ier, -iest) 1 gelado 2 glacial

I'd /aɪd/ 1 = I HAD Ver HAVE 2 = I WOULD Ver WOULD

idea /aɪ'dɪə/ s 1 idéia: have no ~ não ter a menor idéia ◇ get/have the ~ that... ter a impressão de que... 2 sugestão ▸ get the idea entender give sb ideas dar esperança a alguém

ideal /aɪ'diːəl/ adj ideal ● s ideal

idealism /aɪ'diːəlɪzəm/ s idealismo idealist s idealista idealistic /ˌaɪdɪə'lɪstɪk/ adj idealista

idealize /aɪ'diːəlaɪz/ vt idealizar

ideally /aɪ'diːəli/ adv de preferência: be ~ suited complementar-se de forma ideal ◇ Ideally, they should all help. O ideal seria que todos ajudassem.

identical /aɪ'dentɪkl/ adj idêntico

identification /aɪˌdentɪfɪ'keɪʃn/ s identificação: ~ papers documentos de identidade

identify /aɪ'dentɪfaɪ/ vt (pt, pp -ied) identificar

identity /aɪ'dentəti/ s (pl -ies) identidade: case of mistaken ~ erro de identificação

ideology /ˌaɪdi'ɒlədʒi/ s (pl -ies) ideologia

idiom /'ɪdiəm/ s 1 expressão idiomática 2 idioma

idiosyncrasy /ˌɪdiə'sɪŋkrəsi/ s idiossincrasia

idiot /'ɪdiət/ s idiota idiotic /ˌɪdi'ɒtɪk/ adj estúpido

idle /'aɪdl/ adj (-er, -est) 1 preguiçoso 2 ocioso 3 (máquina) parado 4 inútil: ~ threat ameaça vazia ■ idle sth away desperdiçar algo (tempo) idleness s ociosidade

idol /'aɪdl/ s ídolo idolize vt idolatrar

idyllic /aɪ'dɪlɪk; GB ɪ'd-/ adj idílico

i.e. /ˌaɪ 'iː/ abrev isto é

if /ɪf/ conj 1 se 2 quando, sempre que: if in doubt em caso de dúvida 3 (tb even if) mesmo que ▸ if I were you se eu fosse você, no seu lugar if only quem dera: If only I had known! Se eu soubesse! if so se assim for, em caso afirmativo

igloo /'ɪgluː/ s (pl ~s) iglu

ignite /ɪg'naɪt/ vt, vi incendiar(-se) ignition s 1 combustão 2 (Mec) ignição

ignominious /ˌɪgnə'mɪniəs/ adj vergonhoso

ignorance /'ɪgnərəns/ s
ignorância

ignorant /'ɪgnərənt/ adj ignorante: *be ~ of sth* desconhecer
algo

ignore /ɪg'nɔːr/ vt 1 não fazer
caso de, não dar ouvidos a 2
ignorar

ikon = ICON

ill /ɪl/ adj 1 (GB) doente: *feel ~*
sentir-se mal 2 mau • adj
NOTA Emprega-se muito em
palavras compostas, p. ex. **ill-
equipped** despreparado e **ill-
advised** imprudente. ▸ill at
ease constrangido, pouco à
vontade • s (fml) infortúnio

I'll /aɪl/ 1 = I SHALL Ver SHALL
2 = I WILL Ver WILL

illegal /ɪ'liːgl/ adj ilegal

illegible /ɪ'ledʒəbl/ adj ilegível

illegitimate /ˌɪlə'dʒɪtɪmət/ adj
ilegítimo

ill feeling s rancor

ill health s saúde precária

illicit /ɪ'lɪsɪt/ adj ilícito

illiterate /ɪ'lɪtərət/ adj 1 analfa-
beto 2 ignorante

illness /'ɪlnəs/ s doença: *mental ~*
doença mental ◊ *absences due
to ~* ausência por motivos de
saúde → DISEASE

illogical /ɪ'lɒdʒɪkl/ adj ilógico

ill-treatment s [U] maus-tratos

illuminate /ɪ'luːmɪneɪt/ vt iluminar illuminating adj esclarece-
dor illumination s 1 iluminação
2 (illuminations) (GB) luminárias

illusion /ɪ'luːʒn/ s ilusão (*idéia
falsa*): *be under an ~* ter ilusão

illusory /ɪ'luːsəri/ adj ilusório

illustrate /'ɪləstreɪt/ vt ilustrar
illustration s 1 ilustração 2
exemplo

illustrious /ɪ'lʌstriəs/ adj ilustre

image /'ɪmɪdʒ/ s imagem
imagery s imagens

imaginary /ɪ'mædʒɪnəri; GB
-məri/ adj imaginário

imagination /ɪˌmædʒɪ'neɪʃn/ s
imaginação imaginative
/ɪ'mædʒɪnətɪv/ adj imaginativo

imagine /ɪ'mædʒɪn/ vt
imaginar(-se)

imbalance /ɪm'bæləns/ s dese-
quilíbrio

imbecile /'ɪmbəsl; GB -siːl/ s
imbecil

imitate /'ɪmɪteɪt/ vt imitar

imitation /ˌɪmɪ'teɪʃn/ s 1 imitação
2 cópia, reprodução

immaculate /ɪ'mækjələt/ adj 1
imaculado 2 impecável

immaterial /ˌɪmə'tɪəriəl/ adj
irrelevante

immature /ˌɪmə'tʊər, -'tʃʊər; GB
-tjʊə(r)/ adj imaturo

immeasurable /ɪ'meʒərəbl/ adj
incomensurável

immediate /ɪ'miːdiət/ adj 1 imediato 2 (*parentes*) mais próximo 3 (*necessidade, etc.*) urgente

immediately /ɪ'miːdiətli/ adv 1
imediatamente 2 diretamente •
conj (GB) assim que

immense /ɪ'mens/ adj imenso

immerse /ɪ'mɜːrs/ vt submergir
immersion s imersão

immigrant /'ɪmɪgrənt/ adj, s imigrante

immigration /ˌɪmɪ'greɪʃn/ s imigração

imminent /'ɪmɪnənt/ adj iminente

immobile /ɪ'moʊbl; GB -baɪl/ adj
imóvel

immobilize /ɪ'moʊbəlaɪz/ vt imobilizar

immoral /ɪ'mɔːrəl; GB ɪ'mɒrəl/
adj imoral

immortal /ɪ'mɔːrtl/ adj 1 imortal
2 (*fama*) eterno immortality
/ˌɪmɔːr'tæləti/ s imortalidade

immovable /ɪ'muːvəbl/ adj 1 fixo
2 inflexível

immune /ɪ'mjuːn/ adj imune
immunity s imunidade

immunize /'ɪmjunaɪz/ vt imuni-
zar immunization s imunização

imp /ɪmp/ s 1 diabinho 2 (*criança*) capeta

impact /'ɪmpækt/ s 1 impacto 2
(*carro*) choque

impair /ɪm'peər/ vt prejudicar:
impaired vision vista fraca
impairment s deterioração

impart /ɪm'pɑːrt/ vt 1 conferir 2
comunicar

impartial /ɪm'pɑːrʃl/ adj
imparcial

impasse /'ɪmpæs; GB 'æmpɑːs/ s
impasse

impassioned /ɪm'pæʃnd/ adj
fervoroso

impassive /ɪm'pæsɪv/ adj
impassível

impatience /ɪm'peɪʃns/ s impaciência

impatient /ɪm'peɪʃnt/ adj impaciente

impeccable /ɪm'pekəbl/ adj
impecável

impede /ɪm'piːd/ vt impedir,
retardar

impediment /ɪm'pedɪmənt/ s 1 ~
(**to sb/sth**) obstáculo (para
alguém/algo) 2 (*fala*) defeito

impel /ɪmˈpel/ vt (-ll-) impelir

impending /ɪmˈpendɪŋ/ adj iminente

impenetrable /ɪmˈpenɪtrəbl/ adj impenetrável, incompreensível

imperative /ɪmˈperətɪv/ adj 1 imprescindível 2 (tom de voz) autoritário • s imperativo

imperceptible /ˌɪmpəˈseptəbl/ adj imperceptível

imperfect /ɪmˈpɜːrfɪkt/ adj, s defeituoso

imperial /ɪmˈpɪəriəl/ adj imperial imperialism s imperialismo

impersonal /ɪmˈpɜːrsənl/ adj impessoal

impersonate /ɪmˈpɜːrsəneɪt/ vt 1 personificar 2 fazer-se passar por

impertinent /ɪmˈpɜːrtɪnənt/ adj impertinente

impetus /ˈɪmpɪtəs/ s ímpeto

implausible /ɪmˈplɔːzəbl/ adj implausível

implement /ˈɪmplɪmənt/ s instrumento • vt 1 implementar 2 pôr em prática (lei) aplicar implementation s 1 implementação (lei) aplicação

implicate /ˈɪmplɪkeɪt/ vt envolver

implication /ˌɪmplɪˈkeɪʃn/ s 1 implicação 2 conexão (com delito)

implicit /ɪmˈplɪsɪt/ adj 1 implícito 2 absoluto

implore /ɪmˈplɔːr/ vt implorar

imply /ɪmˈplaɪ/ vt (pt, pp implied) 1 dar a entender 2 sugerir

import /ɪmˈpɔːrt/ vt 1 importar 2 trazer • /ˈɪmpɔːrt/ s importação

important /ɪmˈpɔːrtnt/ adj importante: vitally ~ de suma importância importance s importância

impose /ɪmˈpoʊz/ vt 1 ~ sth (on sb/sth) impor algo (a alguém/algo) 2 ~ on/upon sb/sth abusar (da hospitalidade) de alguém/algo imposing adj imponente imposition s 1 imposição (restrição, etc.) 2 incômodo

impossible /ɪmˈpɑsəbl/ adj 1 impossível 2 insuportável • the impossible s o impossível impossibility /ɪmˌpɑsəˈbɪləti/ s impossibilidade

impotence /ˈɪmpətəns/ s impotência impotent adj impotente

impoverished /ɪmˈpɑvərɪʃt/ adj empobrecido

impractical /ɪmˈpræktɪkl/ adj não prático

impress /ɪmˈpres/ vt 1 impressi-

onar 2 vt ~ sth on/upon sb incutir algo em alguém 3 vi causar boa impressão

impression /ɪmˈpreʃn/ s 1 impressão 2 imitação (de pessoa)

impressive /ɪmˈpresɪv/ adj impressionante

imprison /ɪmˈprɪzn/ vt encarcerar imprisonment s encarceramento

improbable /ɪmˈprɑbəbl/ adj improvável

impromptu /ɪmˈprɑmptuː; GB -tjuː/ adj improvisado

improper /ɪmˈprɑpər/ adj 1 incorreto 2 impróprio 3 (transação) desonesto

improve /ɪmˈpruːv/ 1 vt, vi melhorar 2 vi ~ on/upon sth aperfeiçoar algo improvement s 1 ~ (on/in sth) melhora (de algo) 2 melhoria

improvise /ˈɪmprəvaɪz/ vt, vi improvisar

impulse /ˈɪmpʌls/ s impulso: on ~ sem pensar

impulsive /ɪmˈpʌlsɪv/ adj impulsivo

I'm /aɪm/ = I AM Ver BE

in /ɪn/ s ▸ the ins and outs (of sth) os pormenores (de algo) • prep 1 em: in here aqui dentro 2 [depois de superlativo] de: the best store in town a melhor loja da cidade 3 (tempo) de: in the daytime de dia 4 I'll see you in two days. Vejo você daqui a dois dias. ◇ He did it in two days. Ele o fez em dois dias. 5 one in ten people uma em cada dez pessoas 6 (descrição): the girl in glasses a garota de óculos ◇ covered in mud coberto de lama ◇ Speak in English. Fale em inglês. 7 + ing: In saying that, you're contradicting yourself. Ao dizer isso, você se contradiz. ▸ in that já que • adv 1 be in estar (em casa) 2 be/get in chegar ◇ Applications must be in by... Os formulários devem ser entregues até... 3 na moda ▸ be in for sth (coloq) estar a ponto de passar por algo desagradável: He's in for a surprise! Que surpresa ele vai levar! be/get in on sth (coloq) estar por dentro de algo, inteirar-se de algo have (got) it in for sb (coloq): He's got it in for me. Ele tem implicância comigo. NOTA Para o usao de in em PHRASAL VERBS, ver o verbo, p. ex. go in em go.

inability /ˌɪnəˈbɪləti/ s incapacidade

inaccessible /ˌɪnækˈsesəbl/ adj 1 inacessível 2 incompreensível

inaccurate /ɪnˈækjərət/ adj inexato

inaction /ɪnˈækʃn/ s inatividade

inadequate /ɪnˈædɪkwət/ adj 1 inadequado 2 incapaz

inadvertently /ˌɪnədˈvɜːrtəntli/ adv inadvertidamente

inappropriate /ˌɪnəˈproʊpriət/ adj inapropriado

inaugural /ɪnˈɔːgjərəl/ adj 1 inaugural 2 (discurso) de posse

inaugurate /ɪˈnɔːgjəreɪt/ vt 1 empossar 2 inaugurar

incapable /ɪnˈkeɪpəbl/ adj 1 incapaz 2 incapacitado

incapacity /ˌɪnkəˈpæsəti/ s incapacidade

incense /ˈɪnsens/ s incenso

incensed /ɪnˈsenst/ adj furioso

incentive /ɪnˈsentɪv/ s incentivo

incessant /ɪnˈsesnt/ adj incessante incessantly adv sem parar

incest /ˈɪnsest/ s incesto

inch /ɪntʃ/ s (abrev in.) polegada (25,4 milímetros) → ver pág. 224 ► not give an inch não ceder nem um milímetro

incidence /ˈɪnsɪdəns/ s incidência, taxa

incident /ˈɪnsɪdənt/ s incidente: without ~ sem maiores problemas

incidental /ˌɪnsɪˈdentl/ adj 1 eventual, casual 2 sem importância, secundário 3 ~ to sth inerente a algo incidentally adv 1 a propósito 2 incidentalmente

incisive /ɪnˈsaɪsɪv/ adj 1 incisivo 2 (tom) mordaz 3 (mente) perspicaz

incite /ɪnˈsaɪt/ vt incitar

inclination /ˌɪnklɪˈneɪʃn/ s 1 inclinação 2 ~ to/for/towards sth disposição, tendência para (fazer) algo 3 ~ to do sth desejo de fazer algo

incline /ɪnˈklaɪn/ vt, vi inclinar (-se) ● /ˈɪnklaɪn/ s declive inclined adj be ~ to do sth 1 desejar fazer algo; estar disposto a fazer algo 2 ser/estar propenso a (fazer) algo

include /ɪnˈkluːd/ vt incluir including prep inclusive

inclusion /ɪnˈkluːʒn/ s inclusão

inclusive /ɪnˈkluːsɪv/ adj 1 incluído: be ~ of sth incluir algo 2 inclusive

incoherent /ˌɪnkoʊˈhɪərənt/ adj incoerente

income /ˈɪŋkʌm/ s rendimentos:

~ tax imposto de renda

incoming /ˈɪnkʌmɪŋ/ adj entrante, novo

incompetent /ɪnˈkɑːmpɪtənt/ adj, s incompetente

incomplete /ˌɪnkəmˈpliːt/ adj incompleto

incomprehensible /ɪnˌkɑːmprɪˈhensəbl/ adj incompreensível

inconceivable /ˌɪnkənˈsiːvəbl/ adj inconcebível

inconclusive /ˌɪnkənˈkluːsɪv/ adj inconcluso: The meeting was ~. Não se decidiu nada na reunião.

incongruous /ɪnˈkɑːŋgruəs/ adj incongruente

inconsiderate /ˌɪnkənˈsɪdərət/ adj sem consideração

inconsistent /ˌɪnkənˈsɪstənt/ adj 1 inconsistente 2 incoerente

inconspicuous /ˌɪnkənˈspɪkjuəs/ adj pouco visível: make yourself ~ não chamar a atenção

inconvenience /ˌɪnkənˈviːniəns/ s 1 [U] inconveniente 2 estorvo ● vt incomodar

inconvenient /ˌɪnkənˈviːniənt/ adj 1 inconveniente 2 inoportuno

incorporate /ɪnˈkɔːrpəreɪt/ vt 1 ~ sth (in/into sth) incorporar algo (a algo); incluir algo (em algo) 2 (Com): incorporated company sociedade anônima

incorrect /ˌɪnkəˈrekt/ adj incorreto

increase /ˈɪŋkriːs/ s ~ (in sth) aumento (de algo): on the ~ em alta ● vt, vi 1 aumentar 2 elevar(-se) increasing adj crescente increasingly adv cada vez mais

incredible /ɪnˈkredəbl/ adj incrível

indecisive /ˌɪndɪˈsaɪsɪv/ adj 1 indeciso 2 inconcludente

indeed /ɪnˈdiːd/ adv 1 (GB) [uso enfático]: Thank you very much ~! Muitíssimo obrigado! 2 realmente: Did you ~? É mesmo? 3 (fml) de fato

indefensible /ˌɪndɪˈfensəbl/ adj injustificável

indefinite /ɪnˈdefɪnət/ adj 1 vago 2 indefinido indefinitely adv indefinidamente

indelible /ɪnˈdeləbl/ adj indelével

indemnity /ɪnˈdemnəti/ s 1 indenização 2 seguro

independence /ˌɪndɪˈpendəns/ s independência

independent /ˌɪndɪˈpendənt/ adj

1 independente **2** (*colégio*) particular

in-depth *adj* detalhado

indescribable /ˌɪndɪˈskraɪbəbl/ *adj* indescritível

index /ˈɪndeks/ s **1** (*pl* ~es) índice: ~ *finger* dedo indicador ◊ *index-linked* vinculado ao índice do custo de vida **2** (*pl* ~es) (*tb* **card** ~) (*arquivo*) ficha **3** (*pl* **indices** /ˈɪndɪsiːz/) (*Mat*) expoente

indicate /ˈɪndɪkeɪt/ **1** *vt* indicar **2** *vi* indicar com o pisca-pisca

indication /ˌɪndɪˈkeɪʃn/ s **1** indicação **2** indício

indicative /ɪnˈdɪkətɪv/ *adj* indicativo

indicator /ˈɪndɪkeɪtər/ s **1** indicador **2** pisca-pisca

indictment /ɪnˈdaɪtmənt/ s **1** acusação **2** incriminação **3** crítica

indifference /ɪnˈdɪfrəns/ s indiferença

indifferent /ɪnˈdɪfrənt/ *adj* **1** indiferente **2** medíocre

indigenous /ɪnˈdɪdʒənəs/ *adj* (*fml*) nativo, indígena

indigestion /ˌɪndɪˈdʒestʃən/ s indigestão

indignant /ɪnˈdɪgnənt/ *adj* indignado

indignation /ˌɪndɪgˈneɪʃn/ s indignação

indignity /ɪnˈdɪgnəti/ s humilhação

indirect /ˌɪndəˈrekt, -daɪˈr-/ *adj* indireto **indirectly** *adv* indiretamente

indiscreet /ˌɪndɪˈskriːt/ *adj* indiscreto

indiscretion /ˌɪndɪˈskreʃn/ s indiscrição

indiscriminate /ˌɪndɪˈskrɪmɪnət/ *adj* indiscriminado

indispensable /ˌɪndɪˈspensəbl/ *adj* indispensável

indisputable /ˌɪndɪˈspjuːtəbl/ *adj* irrefutável

indistinct /ˌɪndɪˈstɪŋkt/ *adj* indistinto

individual /ˌɪndɪˈvɪdʒuəl/ *adj* **1** distinto **2** individual **3** particular ● s indivíduo **individually** *adv* **1** separadamente **2** individualmente

individualism /ˌɪndɪˈvɪdʒuəlɪzəm/ s individualismo

indoctrination /ɪnˌdɒktrɪˈneɪʃn/ s doutrinação

indoor /ˈɪndɔːr/ *adj* interno, interior: ~ (*swimming*) *pool* piscina coberta

indoors /ˌɪnˈdɔːrz/ *adv* dentro

(*de casa, etc.*)

induce /ɪnˈduːs; *GB* ɪnˈdjuːs/ *vt* **1** induzir **2** causar

induction /ɪnˈdʌkʃn/ s iniciação: ~ *course* curso de introdução

indulge /ɪnˈdʌldʒ/ **1** *vt* satisfazer: ~ *yourself* (*with sth*) dar-se ao capricho (de algo) **2** *vi* ~ (*in sth*) dar-se ao luxo de algo

indulgence /ɪnˈdʌldʒəns/ s **1** tolerância **2** vício, prazer **indulgent** *adj* indulgente

industrial /ɪnˈdʌstriəl/ *adj* **1** industrial **2** de trabalho: ~ *unrest* agitação de trabalhadores **industrialist** s (*pessoa*) industrial

industrialization /ɪnˌdʌstriəlɪˈzeɪʃn/; *GB* -laɪˈz-/ s industrialização **industrialize** /ɪnˈdʌstriəlaɪz/ *vt* industrializar

industrious /ɪnˈdʌstriəs/ *adj* trabalhador

industry /ˈɪndəstri/ s (*pl* -ies) **1** indústria **2** (*fml*) diligência

inedible /ɪnˈedəbl/ *adj* incomestível

ineffective /ˌɪnɪˈfektɪv/ *adj* **1** ineficaz **2** ineficiente

inefficiency /ˌɪnɪˈfɪʃnsi/ s ineficiência **inefficient** *adj* **1** ineficiente **2** incompetente

ineligible /ɪnˈelɪdʒəbl/ *adj* **be ~** (*for sth/to do sth*) não ter direito (a algo/a fazer algo)

inept /ɪˈnept/ *adj* inepto

inequality /ˌɪnɪˈkwɒləti/ s (*pl* -ies) desigualdade

inert /ɪˈnɜːrt/ *adj* inerte

inertia /ɪˈnɜːrʃə/ s inércia

inescapable /ˌɪnɪˈskeɪpəbl/ *adj* inelutável

inevitable /ɪnˈevɪtəbl/ *adj* inevitável **inevitably** *adv* inevitavelmente

inexcusable /ˌɪnɪkˈskjuːzəbl/ *adj* imperdoável

inexhaustible /ˌɪnɪgˈzɔːstəbl/ *adj* inesgotável

inexpensive /ˌɪnɪkˈspensɪv/ *adj* econômico

inexperience /ˌɪnɪkˈspɪəriəns/ s inexperiência **inexperienced** *adj* inexperiente: ~ *in sth* sem experiência em algo

inexplicable /ˌɪnɪkˈsplɪkəbl/ *adj* inexplicável

infallible /ɪnˈfæləbl/ *adj* infalível **infallibility** /ɪnˌfæləˈbɪləti/ s infalibilidade

infamous /ˈɪnfəməs/ *adj* infame

infancy /ˈɪnfənsi/ s **1** infância **2** *Cinema was still in its* ~. O cinema ainda estava dando os primeiros passos.

infant /'ɪnfənt/ s (fml) criança pequena: ~ school (GB) pré-primária ◇ ~ mortality rate taxa de mortalidade infantil • adj principiante

infantile /'ɪnfəntaɪl/ adj infantil

infantry /'ɪnfəntri/ s infantaria

infatuated /ɪn'fætʃueɪtɪd/ adj be ~ (with/by sb/sth) ter paixonite (por alguém/algo) infatuation s paixonite

infect /ɪn'fekt/ vt 1 infectar 2 contagiar infection s infecção infectious adj contagioso

infer /ɪn'fɜːr/ vt (-rr-) 1 deduzir 2 inferir inference /'ɪnfərəns/ s conclusão: by ~ por dedução

inferior /ɪn'fɪəriər/ adj, s inferior inferiority /ɪn,fɪəri'ɔːrəti/ s inferioridade

infertile /ɪn'fɜːtl; GB -taɪl/ adj estéril infertility /,ɪnfɜː'tɪləti/ s infertilidade

infest /ɪn'fest/ vt infestar infestation s infestação

infidelity /,ɪnfɪ'deləti/ s infidelidade

infiltrate /'ɪnfɪltreɪt/ vt, vi infiltrar(-se)

infinite /'ɪnfɪnət/ adj infinito infinitely adv muito

infinitive /ɪn'fɪnətɪv/ s infinitivo

infinity /ɪn'fɪnəti/ s 1 infinidade 2 infinito

infirm /ɪn'fɜːrm/ adj enfermo infirmity s (pl -ies) 1 enfermidade 2 fraqueza

infirmary /ɪn'fɜːrməri/ s (pl -ies) enfermaria

inflamed /ɪn'fleɪmd/ adj 1 (Med) inflamado 2 exaltado

inflammable /ɪn'flæməbl/ adj inflamável

inflammation /,ɪnflə'meɪʃn/ s inflamação

inflate /ɪn'fleɪt/ vt, vi inflar(-se) inflation /ɪn'fleɪʃn/ s inflação

inflexible /ɪn'fleksəbl/ adj inflexível

inflict /ɪn'flɪkt/ vt ~ sth (on sb) infligir, causar algo (a alguém)

influence /'ɪnfluəns/ s 1 influência: under the ~ of alcohol sob o efeito de álcool 2 prestígio • vt 1 ~ sth influir em algo 2 ~ sb influenciar alguém

influential /,ɪnflu'enʃl/ adj influente

influenza /,ɪnflu'enzə/ (fml) s gripe

influx /'ɪnflʌks/ s afluxo

inform /ɪn'fɔːrm/ 1 vt informar 2 vi ~ against/on sb delatar alguém informants s informante

informal /ɪn'fɔːrml/ adj 1 informal, extra-oficial 2 (pessoa, tom) sem cerimônia 3 (traje) de passeio

information /,ɪnfər'meɪʃn/ s [U] informação: a piece of ~ uma informação

information technology s informática

informative /ɪn'fɔːrmətɪv/ adj informativo

informer /ɪn'fɔːrmər/ s informante

infrastructure /'ɪnfrəstrʌktʃər/ s infra-estrutura

infrequent /ɪn'friːkwənt/ adj infreqüente

infringe /ɪn'frɪndʒ/ vt infringir

infuriate /ɪn'fjʊərieɪt/ vt enfurecer infuriating adj de dar raiva

ingenious /ɪn'dʒiːniəs/ adj engenhoso

ingenuity /,ɪndʒə'nuːəti; GB -'njuː-/ s engenhosidade

ingrained /,ɪn'greɪnd/ adj arraigado

ingredient /ɪn'griːdiənt/ s ingrediente

inhabit /ɪn'hæbɪt/ vt habitar

inhabitant /ɪn'hæbɪtənt/ s habitante

inhale /ɪn'heɪl/ 1 vi inalar 2 vi (fumante) tragar 3 vt aspirar

inherent /ɪn'hɪərənt/ adj inerente inherently adv inerentemente

inherit /ɪn'herɪt/ vt herdar inheritance s herança

inhibit /ɪn'hɪbɪt/ vt 1 impedir 2 dificultar inhibited adj inibido inhibition s inibição

inhospitable /,ɪnhɒ'spɪtəbl/ adj 1 inospitaleiro 2 inóspito

inhuman /ɪn'hjuːmən/ adj desumano

initial /ɪ'nɪʃl/ adj, s inicial • vt (-l-, GB -ll-) rubricar initially adv no início, inicialmente

initiate /ɪ'nɪʃieɪt/ vt 1 (fml) iniciar 2 (processo) abrir initiation s iniciação

initiative /ɪ'nɪʃətɪv/ s iniciativa

inject /ɪn'dʒekt/ vt injetar injection s injeção

injure /'ɪndʒər/ vt ferir → FERIMENTO injured adj 1 ferido 2 (tom) ofendido

injury /'ɪndʒəri/ s (pl -ies) 1 ferimento → FERIMENTO 2 dano ▶ injury time (Esporte) desconto

injustice /ɪn'dʒʌstɪs/ s injustiça

ink /ɪŋk/ s tinta

inkling /'ɪŋklɪŋ/ s [sing] idéia vaga

inland /'ɪnlənd/ adj interior • /,ɪn'lænd/ adv para o interior

Inland Revenue s (GB) Receita (Federal)

in-laws s [pl] família do marido/ da esposa

inlet /'ɪnlet/ s **1** enseada **2** entrada

in-line skates s [pl] patins (em linha)

inmate /'ɪnmeɪt/ s presidiário/a, internado/a

inn /ɪn/ s **1** (USA) estalagem **2** (GB) taverna

innate /ɪ'neɪt/ adj inato

inner /'ɪnər/ adj **1** interior **2** íntimo

innermost /'ɪnərməʊst/ adj **1** mais íntimo **2** mais profundo

innocent /'ɪnəsnt/ adj inocente innocence s inocência

innocuous /ɪ'nɑkjuəs/ adj inofensivo **2** inócuo

innovate /'ɪnəveɪt/ vi inovar innovation s inovação innovative (tb innovatory) adj inovador

innuendo /,ɪnju'endəʊ/ s insinuação

innumerable /ɪ'nuːmərəbl; GB ɪ'njuː-/ adj inumerável

inoculate /ɪ'nɑkjuleɪt/ vt vacinar inoculation s vacinação

input /'ɪnpʊt/ s **1** contribuição **2** (Informát) entrada

inquest /'ɪnkwest/ s ~ (on sb/into sth) inquérito (judicial) (a respeito de alguém/algo)

inquire /ɪn'kwaɪə(r)/ (fml) **1** vt perguntar **2** vi pedir informação inquiring adj **1** (mente) curioso **2** (olhar) inquisitivo

inquiry /'ɪnkwəri; GB ɪn'kwaɪəri/ s (pl -ies) (fml) **1** pergunta **2** (inquiries) [pl] seção de informações **3** investigação

inquisition /,ɪnkwɪ'zɪʃn/ s **1** inquérito **2** (the Inquisition) a Inquisição

inquisitive /ɪn'kwɪzətɪv/ adj curioso

insane /ɪn'seɪn/ adj louco insanity /ɪn'sænəti/ s loucura

insatiable /ɪn'seɪʃəbl/ adj insaciável

inscribe /ɪn'skraɪb/ vt inscrever inscribed adj gravado inscription /ɪn'skrɪpʃn/ s inscrição, dedicatória

insect /'ɪnsekt/ s inseto insecticide /ɪn'sektɪsaɪd/ s inseticida

insecure /,ɪnsɪ'kjʊər/ adj inseguro insecurity s insegurança

insensitive /ɪn'sensətɪv/ adj **1** insensível **2** (ato) imune insensitivity /,ɪn,sensə'tɪvəti/ s insensibilidade

inseparable /ɪn'seprəbl/ adj inseparável

insert /ɪn'sɜːrt/ vt inserir

inside /ɪn'saɪd/ s **1** interior **2** (insides) (coloq) entranhas ▸ **inside out 1** do avesso **2** de alto a baixo: know sth ~ out conhecer algo como a palma da mão ● adj [antes de substantivo] **1** interior, interno: the ~ pocket o bolso de dentro **2** interno: ~ information informação obtida dentro da própria organização ● prep (USA ~ of) dentro de ● adv dentro: Let's go ~. Vamos entrar. insider s alguém de dentro (empresa, grupo)

insight /'ɪnsaɪt/ s **1** perspicácia **2** ~ (into sth) percepção (de algo)

insignificant /,ɪnsɪg'nɪfɪkənt/ adj insignificante insignificance s insignificância

insincere /,ɪnsɪn'sɪər/ adj insincero insincerity s insinceridade

insinuate /ɪn'sɪnjueɪt/ vt insinuar insinuation s insinuação

insist /ɪn'sɪst/ vi **1** insistir **2** ~ on (doing) sth teimar em (fazer) algo

insistence /ɪn'sɪstəns/ s insistência insistent adj insistente

insofar /,ɪnsəʊ'fɑːr æz/ conj na medida em que

insolent /'ɪnsələnt/ adj insolente insolence s insolência

insomnia /ɪn'sɑmniə/ s insônia

inspect /ɪn'spekt/ vt inspecionar inspection s fiscalização inspector s **1** inspetor/a **2** fiscal

inspiration /,ɪnspə'reɪʃn/ s inspiração

inspire /ɪn'spaɪər/ vt inspirar

instability /,ɪnstə'bɪləti/ s instabilidade

install /ɪn'stɔːl/ vt instalar

installation /,ɪnstə'leɪʃn/ s instalação

installment (GB **instalment**) /ɪn'stɔːlmənt/ s **1** fascículo **2** (televisão) capítulo **3** ~ (on sth) prestação (de algo)

instance /'ɪnstəns/ s caso ▸ **for instance** por exemplo

instant /'ɪnstənt/ s instante ● adj **1** imediato **2** ~ coffee café solúvel instantly adv imediatamente

instantaneous /,ɪnstən'teɪniəs/ adj instantâneo

instead /ɪn'sted/ adv em vez disso instead of prep em vez de

instigate /'ɪnstɪgeɪt/ vt instigar instigation s instigação

instill (GB **instil**) /ɪn'stɪl/ vt (-ll-) incutir

instinct /'ɪnstɪŋkt/ s instinto instinctive /ɪn'stɪŋktɪv/ adj instintivo

institute /'ɪnstɪtuːt; *GB* -tjuːt/ *s* instituto, associação ● *vt* (*fml*) instituir

institution /ˌɪnstɪ'tuːʃn; *GB* -'tjuːʃn/ *s* instituição institutional *adj* institucional

instruct /ɪn'strʌkt/ *vt* **1** instruir **2** dar instruções

instruction /ɪn'strʌkʃn/ *s* **1** instrução **2** ensino

instructive /ɪn'strʌktɪv/ *adj* instrutivo

instructor /ɪn'strʌktər/ *s* instrutor/a

instrument /'ɪnstrəmənt/ *s* instrumento

instrumental /ˌɪnstrə'mentl/ *adj* **1** be ~ in doing sth contribuir decisivamente para algo **2** (*Mús*) instrumental

insufferable /ɪn'sʌfrəbl/ *adj* insuportável

insufficient /ˌɪnsə'fɪʃnt/ *adj* insuficiente

insular /'ɪnsələr/ *adj* bitolado

insulate /'ɪnsəleɪt; *GB* -sjul-/ *vt* isolar insulation *s* isolamento

insult /'ɪnsʌlt/ *s* insulto ● *vt* /ɪn'sʌlt/ *vt* insultar insulting *adj* insultante

insurance /ɪn'ʃʊərəns; *GB* -'ʃɔːr-/ *s* [U] seguro (*Fin*)

insure /ɪn'ʃʊər/ *vt* **1** segurar **2** assegurar

intake /'ɪnteɪk/ *s* **1** admissão: *We have an annual ~ of 20.* Admitimos 20 a cada ano. **2** consumo

integral /'ɪntɪɡrəl/ *adj* essencial

integrate /'ɪntɪɡreɪt/ *vt, vi* integrar(-se) integration *s* integração

integrity /ɪn'teɡrəti/ *s* integridade

intellectual /ˌɪntə'lektʃuəl/ *adj, s* intelectual intellectually *adv* intelectualmente

intelligence /ɪn'telɪdʒəns/ *s* inteligência intelligent *adj* inteligente intelligently *adv* inteligentemente

intend /ɪn'tend/ *vt* **1 ~ to do sth** pretender, ter a intenção de fazer algo **2** intended for sb/sth destinado a alguém/algo: *They're not intended for eating.* Não são para comer. **3 ~ sb to do sth:** *I ~ you to take over.* Tenho planos de que você assuma o cargo. ◊ *You weren't intended to hear that.* Não era para você ter ouvido aquilo. **4 ~ sth as sth:** *It was intended as a joke.* Era para ser uma piada.

intense /ɪn'tens/ *adj* (-er, -est) **1**

intenso 2 (*pessoa*) sério intensely *adv* intensamente intensify *vt, vi* (*pt, pp* -ied) intensificar(-se) intensity *s* intensidade

intensive /ɪn'tensɪv/ *adj* intensivo

intent /ɪn'tent/ *adj* **1** atento **2 ~ on doing sth** decidido a fazer algo **3 ~ on (doing) sth** absorto em (fazendo) algo ● *s* ▸ **to all intents (and purposes)** para todos os efeitos

intention /ɪn'tenʃn/ *s* intenção intentional *adj* intencional intentionally *adv* de propósito

intently /ɪn'tentli/ *adv* atentamente

interact /ˌɪntər'ækt/ *vi* **1** (*pessoas*) interagir **2** (*coisas*) mesclar-se interaction *s* **1** relacionamento (*pessoas*) **2** interação interactive *adj* interativo

intercept /ˌɪntər'sept/ *vt* interceptar

interchange /ˌɪntər'tʃeɪndʒ/ *vt* intercambiar ● /'ɪntərtʃeɪndʒ/ *s* intercâmbio interchangeable /ˌɪntər'tʃeɪndʒəbl/ *adj* intercambiável

interconnect /ˌɪntərkə'nekt/ *vi* **1** interligar-se **2** (*tb* intercommunicate) comunicar-se entre si interconnected *adj* interligado interconnection *s* conexão

intercourse /'ɪntərkɔːrs/ *s* (*fml*) relações sexuais

interest /'ɪntrəst/ *s* **1** interesse (por algo): *in sb's ~* interesse de alguém ◊ *It is of no ~ to me.* Não me interessa. **2** passatempo: *her main ~ in life* o que mais lhe interessa na vida **3** (*Fin*) juro(s) ▸ **in the interest(s) of sth** pelo bem de algo: *in the ~(s) of safety* por motivo de segurança ● *vt* interessar: *~ sb in sth* fazer com que alguém se interesse por algo

interested /'ɪntrəstɪd/ *adj* interessado: *be ~ in sth* interessar-se por algo

interesting /'ɪntrəstɪŋ/ *adj* interessante interestingly *adv* curiosamente

interfere /ˌɪntər'fɪər/ *vi* **1** intrometer-se **2 ~ with sth** mexer em algo **3 ~ with sth** dificultar algo interference *s* [U] **1** intromissão **2** (*rádio*) interferência **3** (*USA*) (*Esporte*) obstrução interfering *adj* intrometido

interim /'ɪntərɪm/ *adj* provisório ● *s* ▸ **in the interim** neste ínterim

interior /ɪn'tɪəriər/ *adj, s* interior

interlude /'ɪntərluːd/ *s* intervalo

intermediate /ˌɪntərˈmiːdiət/ adj intermediário

intermission /ˌɪntərˈmɪʃn/ s intervalo (Teat)

intern /ɪnˈtɜːrn/ vt internar

internal /ɪnˈtɜːrnl/ adj interno, interior **internally** adv internamente, interiormente

international /ˌɪntərˈnæʃnəl/ adj internacional • s (GB) (Esporte) 1 partida internacional 2 jogador/a internacional **internationally** adv internacionalmente

Internet /ˈɪntərnet/ s Internet

interpret /ɪnˈtɜːrprɪt/ vt 1 interpretar, entender 2 traduzir NOTA **Interpret** refere-se à tradução oral e **translate** à tradução escrita. **interpretation** s interpretação **interpreter** s intérprete

interrelated /ˌɪntərɪˈleɪtɪd/ adj inter-relacionado

interrogate /ɪnˈterəgeɪt/ vt interrogar **interrogation** s 1 interrogação 2 interrogatório **interrogator** s interrogador/a

interrogative /ˌɪntəˈrɒgətɪv/ adj interrogativo

interrupt /ˌɪntəˈrʌpt/ vt, vi interromper **interruption** s interrupção

intersect /ˌɪntərˈsekt/ vi cruzar-se **intersection** s cruzamento

interspersed /ˌɪntərˈspɜːrst/ adj entremeado

intertwine /ˌɪntərˈtwaɪn/ vt, vi entrelaçar(-se)

interval /ˈɪntərvl/ s intervalo

intervene /ˌɪntərˈviːn/ vi 1 intervir 2 (tempo) decorrer 3 interpor-se **intervening** adj interveniente

intervention /ˌɪntərˈvenʃn/ s intervenção

interview /ˈɪntərvjuː/ s entrevista • vt entrevistar **interviewee** s entrevistado/a **interviewer** s entrevistador/a

interweave /ˌɪntərˈwiːv/ vt, vi (pt **-wove** /-ˈwoʊv/ pp **-woven** /-ˈwoʊvn/) entrelaçar(-se)

intestine /ɪnˈtestɪn/ s intestino

intimacy /ˈɪntɪməsi/ s intimidade

intimate /ˈɪntɪmət/ adj 1 íntimo 2 (amizade) estreito 3 (conhecimento) profundo • /ˈɪntɪmeɪt/ vt (fml) insinuar **intimation** s (fml) insinuação

intimidate /ɪnˈtɪmɪdeɪt/ vt intimidar **intimidation** s intimidação

into /ˈɪntuː/ prep 1 em, dentro de:

come ~ a room entrar numa sala 2 para: go ~ town ir ao centro 3 (tempo, distância): long ~ the night noite adentro ◇ far ~ the distance até perder de vista 4 (Mat): 12 ~ 144 goes 12 times. 144 dividido por 12 é 12. ▸ **be into sth** (coloq): She's ~ football. Ela é ligada em futebol. NOTA Para o uso de **into** em PHRASAL VERBS, ver o verbo, p. ex. **look into** em LOOK.

intolerable /ɪnˈtɑlərəbl/ adj intolerável

intolerance /ɪnˈtɑlərəns/ s intolerância

intolerant /ɪnˈtɑlərənt/ adj intolerante

intonation /ˌɪntəˈneɪʃn/ s entonação

intoxicated /ɪnˈtɑksɪkeɪtɪd/ adj (fml) embriagado

intoxication /ɪnˌtɑksɪˈkeɪʃn/ s embriaguez

intrepid /ɪnˈtrepɪd/ adj intrépido

intricate /ˈɪntrɪkət/ adj complexo

intrigue /ˈɪntriːg, ɪnˈtriːg/ s intriga • /ɪnˈtriːg/ 1 vi fazer intriga 2 vt intrigar **intriguing** adj intrigante

intrinsic /ɪnˈtrɪnzɪk/ adj intrínseco

introduce /ˌɪntrəˈduːs; GB -ˈdjuːs/ vt 1 apresentar → APRESENTAR 2 ~ **sb to sth** iniciar alguém em algo 3 introduzir

introduction /ˌɪntrəˈdʌkʃn/ s 1 apresentação 2 ~ **(to sth)** prólogo (de algo) 3 iniciação 4 introdução (produto, reforma, etc.)

introductory /ˌɪntrəˈdʌktəri/ adj 1 introdutório 2 (oferta) de lançamento

introvert /ˈɪntrəvɜːrt/ s introvertido/a

intrude /ɪnˈtruːd/ vi 1 importunar 2 intrometer-se **intruder** s intruso/a **intrusion** s 1 invasão 2 intromissão **intrusive** adj intruso

intuition /ˌɪntuˈɪʃn; GB -tjuː-/ s intuição

intuitive /ɪnˈtuːɪtɪv; GB -ˈtjuː-/ adj intuitivo

inundate /ˈɪnʌndeɪt/ vt inundar

invade /ɪnˈveɪd/ vt, vi invadir **invader** s invasor/a

invalid /ˈɪnvəlɪd/ s inválido/a • /ɪnˈvælɪd/ adj nulo

invalidate /ɪnˈvælɪdeɪt/ vt invalidar

invaluable /ɪnˈvæljuəbl/ adj inestimável

invariably /ɪnˈveəriəbli/ adv

invariavelmente

invasion /ɪnˈveɪʒn/ s invasão

invent /ɪnˈvent/ vt inventar **invention** s 1 invenção 2 invento **inventive** adj 1 inventivo 2 imaginativo **inventiveness** s inventividade **inventor** s inventor/a

inventory /ˈɪnvəntɔːri; GB -tri/ s (pl -ies) 1 inventário 2 (USA) balanço (comercial)

invert /ɪnˈvɜːrt/ vt inverter: in inverted commas (GB) entre aspas

invertebrate /ɪnˈvɜːrtɪbrət/ adj, s invertebrado

invest /ɪnˈvest/ vt, vi investir

investigate /ɪnˈvestɪgeɪt/ vt, vi investigar

investigation /ɪnˌvestɪˈgeɪʃn/ s ~ (into sth) investigação (de algo)

investigative /ɪnˈvestɪgeɪtɪv; GB -gətɪv/ adj: ~ journalism jornalismo de investigação

investigator /ɪnˈvestɪgeɪtər/ s investigador/a

investment /ɪnˈvestmənt/ s investimento

investor /ɪnˈvestər/ s investidor/a

invigorating /ɪnˈvɪgəreɪtɪŋ/ adj revigorante

invincible /ɪnˈvɪnsəbl/ adj invencível

invisible /ɪnˈvɪzəbl/ adj invisível

invitation /ˌɪnvɪˈteɪʃn/ s convite

invite /ɪnˈvaɪt/ vt 1 convidar: ~ sb in/out convidar alguém para entrar/sair ◇ ~ trouble procurar encrenca 2 (sugestões) pedir ■ **invite sb back 1** convidar alguém a voltar consigo para casa **2** retribuir um convite **invite sb over/around** convidar alguém para sua casa ● /ˈɪnvaɪt/ s (coloq) convite **inviting** /ɪnˈvaɪtɪŋ/ adj **1** convidativo **2** apetitoso

invoice /ˈɪnvɔɪs/ s ~ (for sth) fatura (de algo) ● vt ~ **sb/sth** faturar (mercadorias) a alguém/algo

involuntary /ɪnˈvɒləntəri; GB -tri/ adj involuntário

involve /ɪnˈvɒlv/ vt **1** implicar: The job involves me moving. O trabalho exige que eu mude. **2** envolver **3** meter, enredar **4** be/get involved with sb (pej) estar ligado com alguém **5** be/get involved with sb (emocionalmente) estar envolvido, envolver-se com alguém **involved** adj complicado **involvement** s **1** ~ (in sth) envolvimento, participação (em algo) **2** ~ (with sb) compromisso

(com alguém)

inward /ˈɪnwərd/ adj **1** interior, íntimo: give an ~ sigh suspirar para si mesmo **2** (direção) para dentro ● adv (tb **inwards**) para dentro **inwardly** adv **1** por dentro **2** (suspirar, sorrir) para si

IQ /ˌaɪ ˈkjuː/ abrev de **intelligence quotient** quociente de inteligência

iris /ˈaɪrɪs/ s íris

iron /ˈaɪərn; GB ˈaɪən/ s **1** ferro **2** ferro de passar roupa ● vt passar roupa ■ **iron sth out 1** alisar algo **2** (problema) resolver algo **ironing** s roupa passada ou para passar: do the ~ passar roupa

ironic /aɪˈrɒnɪk/ adj irônico **ironically** adv ironicamente

irony /ˈaɪrəni/ s (pl -ies) ironia

irrational /ɪˈræʃənl/ adj irracional **irrationality** /ɪˌræʃəˈnæləti/ s irracionalidade **irrationally** adv de forma irracional

irrelevant /ɪˈreləvənt/ adj irrelevante: ~ remarks observações descabidas **irrelevance** s irrelevância

irresistible /ˌɪrɪˈzɪstəbl/ adj irresistível **irresistibly** adv irresistivelmente

irrespective of /ˌɪrɪˈspektɪv əv/ prep independentemente de, sem levar em conta

irresponsible /ˌɪrɪˈspɒnsəbl/ adj irresponsável **irresponsibility** /ˌɪrɪˌspɒnsəˈbɪləti/ s irresponsabilidade **irresponsibly** adv de forma irresponsável

irrigation /ˌɪrɪˈgeɪʃn/ s irrigação

irritable /ˈɪrɪtəbl/ adj irritável **irritability** /ˌɪrɪtəˈbɪləti/ s irritabilidade **irritably** adv com irritação

irritate /ˈɪrɪteɪt/ vt irritar **irritating** adj irritante **irritation** s irritação

the IRS /ˌaɪ ɑːr ˈes/ abrev de **the Internal Revenue Service** Receita Federal

is /ɪz, s, z/ Ver BE

Islam /ˈɪzlɑːm, ɪzˈlɑːm/ s islã, islamismo

island /ˈaɪlənd/ s (abrev **I, Is**) ilha **islander** s ilhéu/oa

isle /aɪl/ s (abrev **I, Is**) ilha NOTA Usa-se sobretudo em nomes de lugares, p. ex.: the Isle of Man.

isn't /ˈɪznt/ = IS NOT Ver BE

isolate /ˈaɪsəleɪt/ vt isolar **isolated** adj isolado **isolation** s isolamento ▶ **in isolation (from sb/ sth)** isolado (de alguém/algo), fora do contexto

issue /ˈɪʃuː; GB ˈɪsjuː/ s **1** questão **2** emissão **3** (revista, etc.) número ▶ **make an issue (out) of**

sth levar algo a sério: *Let's not make an ~ of it.* Vamos deixar isso para trás. • **1** *vt* distribuir **2** *vt ~ sth* prover alguém de algo **3** *vt* (*visto, etc.*) expedir **4** *vt* publicar **5** *vt* (*selos, etc.*) emitir **6** *vi* ~ **from sth** (*fml*) emanar de algo

it /ɪt/ *pron*

• como sujeito e objeto **NOTA** It refere-se a animal ou coisa. Também se usa para designar um bebê. **1** [*como sujeito*] ele, ela: *"Who is it?" "It's me."* —Quem é?—Sou eu. → YOU **2** [*como objeto direto*] o, a: *Did you buy it?* Você comprou (isso/aquilo)? **3** [*como objeto indireto*] lhe: *Give it some milk.* Dá um pouco de leite para ele/ela. **4** [*depois de prep*]: *That box is heavy. What's inside it?* Essa caixa está pesada. O que é que tem dentro?

• orações impessoais **NOTA** Em muitos casos it não tem significado e é usado como sujeito gramatical em orações que, em português, costumam ser impessoais. Em geral, não se traduz. **1** (*tempo, distância e time*): *It's ten past one.* É uma e dez. ◊ *It's two miles to the beach.* São duas milhas até a praia. ◊ *It's hot.* Está calor. **2** (*em outras construções*): *Does it matter what color the hat is?* Faz diferença a cor do chapéu? ◊ *It's Jim who's the smart one, not his brother.* O Jim é que é o esperto, não o irmão. ▸ **that's it 1** é isso aí **2** é tudo **3** é assim mesmo **that's just it** aí é que está o problema **this is it** chegou a hora

italics /ɪˈtælɪks/ *s* [*pl*] itálico

itch /ɪtʃ/ *s* coceira • *vi* coçar: *My leg itches.* Estou com coceira na perna. ◊ *itching to do sth* louco para fazer algo **itchy** *adj*: *My skin is ~.* Estou com coceira na pele.

it'd /ɪtəd/ **1** = IT HAD Ver HAVE **2** = IT WOULD Ver WOULD

item /ˈaɪtəm/ *s* **1** item **2** (*tb news* ~) notícia

itinerary /aɪˈtɪnərəri; GB -rəri/ *s* (*pl* -**ies**) itinerário

it'll /ɪtl/ = IT WILL Ver WILL

it's /ɪts/ **1** = IT IS Ver BE **2** = IT HAS Ver HAVE

its /ɪts/ *adj poss* dele(s)/dela(s)/ seu(s)/sua(s) (*coisa, animal ou bebê*)

itself /ɪtˈself/ *pron* **1** [*uso reflexivo*] se **2** [*uso enfático*] ele/a mesmo/a **3** *She is kindness ~.*

Ela é a bondade personificada. ▸ **by itself 1** por si **2** sozinho **in itself** em si

I've /aɪv/ = I HAVE Ver HAVE

ivory /ˈaɪvəri/ *s* marfim

ivy /ˈaɪvi/ *s* hera

Jj

J, j /dʒeɪ/ *s* (*pl* **J's, j's** /dʒeɪz/) J, j

jab /dʒæb/ *vt, vi* (**-bb-**) espetar: ~ *sth into sth* fincar algo em algo • *s* **1** injeção **2** espetada **3** murro

jack /dʒæk/ *s* **1** (*Mec*) macaco **2** (*baralho*) valete → BARALHO

jackal /ˈdʒækl/ *s* chacal

jackdaw /ˈdʒækdɔː/ *s* gralha

jacket /ˈdʒækɪt/ *s* **1** jaqueta **2** paletó **3** (*livro*) sobrecapa

jackpot /ˈdʒækpɒt/ *s* sorte grande

jade /dʒeɪd/ *adj, s* jade

jaded /ˈdʒeɪdɪd/ *adj* enfastiado

jagged /ˈdʒægɪd/ *adj* denteado, pontiagudo

jaguar /ˈdʒægwɑːr/ *s* jaguar

jail /dʒeɪl/ *s* cadeia

jam /dʒæm/ *s* **1** geléia **2** obstrução: *traffic* ~ engarrafamento **3** (*coloq*) aperto • (**-mm-**) **1** *vt* ~ **sth into/under sth** forçar algo dentro/debaixo de algo **2** *vt, vi* amontoar(-se) **3** *vt, vi* apinhar (-se), obstruir **4** *vt* (*rádio*) interferir

jangle /ˈdʒæŋgl/ *vt, vi* soar de maneira estridente

janitor /ˈdʒænɪtər/ *s* zelador/a

January /ˈdʒænjueri; GB -juəri/ *s* (*abrev* **Jan.**) janeiro → MAY

jar /dʒɑːr/ *s* **1** frasco, pote **2** jarro • (**-rr-**) **1** *vi* ~ (**on sb/sth**) irritar (alguém/algo) **2** *vi* ~ (**with sth**) destoar (de algo) **3** *vt* ferir

jargon /ˈdʒɑːrgən/ *s* jargão

jasmine /ˈdʒæzmɪn/ *s* jasmim

jaundice /ˈdʒɔːndɪs/ *s* icterícia **jaundiced** *adj* amargurado

javelin /ˈdʒævlɪn/ *s* dardo

jaw /dʒɔː/ *s* maxilar

jazz /dʒæz/ *s* jazz ▪ **jazz sth up** animar algo **jazzy** *adj* (*coloq*) espalhafatoso

jealous /ˈdʒeləs/ *adj* **1** ciumento: *He's very ~ of her friends.* Ele tem muito ciúme dos amigos dela. **2** invejoso: *be very ~ of sth* estar com muita inveja de algo **jealousy** *s* (*pl* -**ies**) ciúme, inveja

jeans /dʒiːnz/ *s* [*pl*] jeans → PAIR

Jeep® /dʒiːp/ *s* jipe

jeer /dʒɪər/ *vt, vi* ~ (**at**) (**sb/sth**)

1 zombar (de alguém/algo) **2** vaiar (alguém/algo) • s zombaria, vaia

Jell-O® /ˈdʒeloʊ/ (USA) s gelatina

jelly /ˈdʒeli/ s (pl -ies) **1** (GB) gelatina **2** geléia

jellyfish /ˈdʒelifɪʃ/ s (pl jellyfish) (Zool) água-viva

jeopardy /ˈdʒepərdi/ s perigo
jeopardize vt pôr em perigo

jerk /dʒɜːrk/ s **1** solavanco **2** (coloq) idiota • vt, vi sacudir

Jesus /ˈdʒiːzəs/ (tb ~ Christ) Jesus Cristo

jet /dʒet/ s **1** (tb ~ aircraft) (avião) jato **2** (água, gás) jorro **3** azeviche

jetty /ˈdʒeti/ s (pl -ies) cais, quebra-mar

Jew /dʒuː/ s judeu/ia

jewel /ˈdʒuːəl/ s **1** jóia **2** pedra preciosa jeweler (GB -ll-) s joalheiro/a jewelry (GB -ll-) s [U] jóias jewelry shop/store (GB jeweller's) s joalheria

Jewish /ˈdʒuːɪʃ/ adj judaico

jigsaw /ˈdʒɪɡsɔː/ (tb ~ puzzle) s quebra-cabeça

jingle /ˈdʒɪŋɡl/ s **1** [sing] tilintar **2** anúncio cantado • vt, vi tilintar

jinx /dʒɪŋks/ s azarão • vt (coloq) trazer azar

job /dʒɑb/ s **1** trabalho, emprego: out of a ~ desempregado → WORK **2** tarefa **3** dever, responsabilidade ▸ **a good job** (coloq): It's a good ~ (that) you've come. Ainda bem que você veio.

jobcenter /ˈdʒɑbsentər/ s (GB) agência de empregos (do governo)

jobless /ˈdʒɑbləs/ adj desempregado

jockey /ˈdʒɑki/ s jóquei

jog /dʒɑɡ/ s [sing] **1** sacudidela **2** go for a ~ fazer cooper a (-gg-) **1** vt empurrar de leve **2** vi fazer cooper ▸ **jog sb's memory** refrescar a memória de alguém

jogging /ˈdʒɑɡɪŋ/ s cooper jogger s corredor/a

join /dʒɔɪn/ s **1** junção **2** costura • **1** vt unir, juntar **2** vi ~ up (with sb/sth) juntar-se (com alguém/algo); unir-se a alguém/algo **3** vt ~ sb reunir-se com alguém **4** vt, vi (clube, etc.) associar-se (a) **5** vt, vi (empresa) entrar (em) **6** vt (organização) ingressar em ▸ **join in (sth)** participar (de algo)

joiner /ˈdʒɔɪnər/ s (GB) marceneiro/a

joint /dʒɔɪnt/ adj conjunto, coletivo • s **1** (Anat) articulação **2**

junta **3** quarto de carne **4** (coloq) espelunca **5** (coloq) baseado jointed adj articulada

joke /dʒoʊk/ s **1** piada: The new laws are a ~. As novas leis são uma piada. **2** brincadeira: play a ~ on sb pregar uma peça em alguém ▸ vi brincar ▸ **joking apart** falando sério

joker /ˈdʒoʊkər/ s **1** brincalhão **2** (coloq) palhaço/a **3** (cartas) curinga

jolly /ˈdʒɑli/ adj (-ier -iest) alegre • adv (GB, coloq) muito

jolt /dʒoʊlt/ **1** vi sacolejar **2** vt sacudir • s **1** sacudida **2** susto

jostle /ˈdʒɑsl/ vt, vi empurrar(-se)

jot /dʒɑt/ v (-tt-) ▪ jot sth down anotar algo

journal /ˈdʒɜːrnl/ s **1** revista, jornal (especializado) **2** diário journalism s jornalismo journalist s jornalista

journey /ˈdʒɜːrni/ s viagem, trajeto → VIAGEM

joy /dʒɔɪ/ s **1** alegria **2** deleite joyful adj alegre joyfully adv alegremente

joystick /ˈdʒɔɪstɪk/ s alavanca de controle, joystick

jubilant /ˈdʒuːbɪlənt/ adj jubiloso jubilation s júbilo

jubilee /ˈdʒuːbɪliː/ s jubileu

Judaism /ˈdʒuːdeɪɪzəm; GB -deɪɪzəm/ s judaísmo

judge /dʒʌdʒ/ s **1** juiz, juíza **2** árbitro **3** ~ (of sth) entendido/a (em algo) • vt, vi julgar, considerar

judgment (GB **judgement**) /ˈdʒʌdʒmənt/ s julgamento, juízo: use your own ~ agir de acordo com a sua própria consciência

judicious /dʒuˈdɪʃəs/ adj judicioso judiciously adv judiciosamente

judo /ˈdʒuːdoʊ/ s judô

jug /dʒʌɡ/ s **1** bilha **2** (GB) jarro

juggle /ˈdʒʌɡl/ vt, vi **1** fazer malabarismos **2** ~ (with) sth virar-se do avesso para algo: She juggles home, career and children. Ela dá conta da casa, do trabalho e dos filhos.

juice /dʒuːs/ s suco juicy adj (-ier, -iest) **1** suculento **2** (coloq) (história, etc.) picante

July /dʒuˈlaɪ/ s (abrev **Jul.**) julho → MAY

jumble /ˈdʒʌmbl/ vt ~ sth (up) misturar algo • s **1** bagunça **2** (GB) objetos vendidos em bazar de caridade

jumbo /ˈdʒʌmbəʊ/ *adj* (*coloq*) (de tamanho) gigante

jump /dʒʌmp/ **s 1** salto **2** alta ● **1** *vt, vi* saltar: ~ *rope* pular corda ◊ ~ *up* levantar-se com um salto **2** *vi* sobressaltar-se: *It made me* ~. Isso me deu um susto. **3** *vi* aumentar ▸ **jump the queue** (*GB*) furar a fila **jump to conclusions** tirar conclusões precipitadas **jump to it** (*coloq*) de uma vez ● **jump at sth** agarrar uma oportunidade com unhas e dentes

jumper /ˈdʒʌmpər/ **s 1** (*USA*) avental **2** (*GB*) suéter **3** saltador/a

jumpy /ˈdʒʌmpi/ *adj* (**-ier -iest**) (*coloq*) nervoso

junction /ˈdʒʌŋkʃn/ **s 1** cruzamento **2** entroncamento

June /dʒuːn/ **s** (*abrev* **Jun.**) junho → **MAY**

jungle /ˈdʒʌŋɡl/ **s** selva

junior /ˈdʒuːniər/ *adj* **1** subalterno **2** (*abrev* **Jr.**) júnior **3** ~ *school* (*GB*) escola primária ● ~ *high school* (*USA*) ginásio ● **s 1** subalterno/a **2** [*precedido de adj poss*]: *He's three years her* ~. Ele é três anos mais novo do que ela. **3** (*USA*) estudante no penúltimo ano do segundo grau **4** (*GB*) aluno/a da escola primária

junk /dʒʌŋk/ **s** [*U*] **1** (*coloq*) traste **2** ferro-velho, velharias

junk food **s** (*coloq, pej*) comida, lanche sem valor nutritivo

junk mail **s** propaganda não solicitada entregue em casa

Jupiter /ˈdʒuːpɪtər/ **s** Júpiter

juror /ˈdʒʊərər/ **s** jurado/a

jury /ˈdʒʊəri/ **s** (*pl* **-ies**) júri

just /dʒʌst/ *adv* **1** exatamente, exatamente: *That's* ~ *it*! É isso mesmo! ◊ ~ *here* aqui mesmo **2** ~ **as** bem na hora em que: *It's* ~ *as I thought.* É exatamente como imaginei. **3** ~ **as... as...** tão... quanto... **4 have ~ done sth** acabar de fazer algo: *"Just married"* "Recém-casados" **5** (*GB*) (*tb* **only** ~): *I can (only)* ~ *reach the shelf.* Por pouco não alcanço a prateleira. **6** ~ **over/ under** um pouco mais/menos (de) **7** já: *I'm* ~ *going.* Já vou. **8 be** ~ **about/going to do sth** estar prestes a fazer algo: *I was* ~ *about/~ going to call you.* Eu já ia te telefonar. **9** simplesmente: *It's* ~ *one of those things.* Não é nada de mais. **10** somente: *Just let me say something!* Deixe-me só dizer uma coisa! ◊ ~ *for fun*

só de brincadeira ▸ **it is just as well (that...)** ainda bem que... **just about** (*coloq*) quase: *I know* ~ *about everyone.* Conheço praticamente todo mundo. **just in case** no caso de, por via das dúvidas **just like 1** igual a: *It was* ~ *like old times.* Foi como nos velhos tempos. **2** *It's* ~ *like her to be late.* É típico dela se atrasar. **just like that** sem mais nem menos **just now 1** no momento **2** agora mesmo ● *adj* **1** justo **2** merecido

justice /ˈdʒʌstɪs/ **s 1** justiça **2** juiz, juíza ▸ **do justice to sb/sth** fazer justiça a alguém/algo **do yourself justice**: *He didn't do himself* ~ *in the exam.* Ele poderia ter se saído muito melhor na prova.

justifiable /ˌdʒʌstɪˈfaɪəbl, ˈdʒʌstɪfaɪəbl/ *adj* justificável **justifiably** *adv* justificadamente

justify /ˈdʒʌstɪfaɪ/ *vt* (*pt, pp* **-ied**) justificar

justly /ˈdʒʌstli/ *adv* justamente, com razão

jut /dʒʌt/ *v* (**-tt-**) ● **jut out** sobressair

juvenile /ˈdʒuːvənl; *GB* ˈdʒuːvənaɪl/ **s** jovem, menor ● *adj* **1** juvenil **2** pueril

juxtapose /ˌdʒʌkstəˈpəʊz/ *vt* (*fml*) justapor **juxtaposition** **s** justaposição

K k

K, k /keɪ/ **s** (*pl* **K's, k's** /keɪz/) K, k

kaleidoscope /kəˈlaɪdəskəʊp/ **s** caleidoscópio

kangaroo /ˌkæŋɡəˈruː/ **s** (*pl* **~s**) canguru

karat /ˈkærət/ **s** quilate

karate /kəˈrɑːti/ **s** caratê

kebab /kəˈbæb/ **s** churrasquinho

keel /kiːl/ **s** quilha ● **keel over** desmaiar, emborcar

keen /kiːn/ *adj* (**~er, ~est**) **1** entusiasmado **2 be ~ (to do sth/ that...)** ter muita vontade (de fazer algo/de que...); ter entusiasmo (para fazer algo) **3** (*interesse*) grande **4** aguçado, agudo ▸ **be keen on sb/sth** (*esp GB*) gostar de alguém/algo **keenly** *adv* **1** com entusiasmo **2** profundamente

keep /kiːp/ (*pt, pp* **kept**) **1** *vi* ficar, permanecer: *Keep still!* Não se mexa! ◊ *Keep quiet!* Cale-se! **2** *vi* ~ **(on) doing sth** continuar a fazer algo; não parar de fazer algo **3** vt [com adj, adv ou -ing] manter, causar: ~ warm manter-se aquecido ◇ ~ sb waiting fazer alguém esperar ◇ ~ sb amused/happy entreter/alegrar alguém **4** vt atrasar **5** vt conservar: ~ a secret guardar um segredo **6** vt ficar com: Keep the change. Fique com o troco. **7** vt (negócio) ter, ser proprietário de **8** vt (animais) criar, ter **9** vi (alimentos) conservar-se (fresco) **10** vt (diário) escrever **11** vt (contas, etc.) anotar **12** vt (pessoa) sustentar **13** vt: ~ a meeting comparecer **14** vt (promessa) cumprir NOTA Para expressões com keep, ver o substantivo, adjetivo, etc., p. ex. keep your word em WORD. ■ keep (sb) away (from sb/sth) manter-se afastado, manter (alguém/algo) afastado (de alguém/algo) keep sth (back) from sb ocultar algo de alguém keep sth down manter algo num nível baixo keep sb from (doing) sth impedir alguém de fazer algo keep (yourself) from doing sth evitar fazer algo keep off (sth) manter-se afastado (de algo), não tocar (em algo): Keep off the grass. Não pise na grama. keep sb/sth off (sb/sth) não deixar alguém/algo se aproximar (de alguém/algo): Keep your hands off me! Não me toque! keep on (at sb) (about sb/sth) ficar em cima de (alguém) (sobre alguém/algo) keep (sb/sth) out (of sth) não entrar, impedir (alguém/algo) de entrar (em algo) keep (yourself) to yourself ficar na sua keep sth to yourself guardar algo para si keep up (with sb/sth) manter-se no mesmo nível (de alguém/algo) keep sth up manter o padrão de algo, continuar a fazer algo ● s sustento

keeper /'ki:pər/ s **1** guarda **2** zelador/a

keeping /'ki:pɪŋ/ s ► in/out of keeping (with sth) em harmonia/desarmonia (com algo) in sb's keeping sob os cuidados de alguém

kennel /'kenl/ s **1** casa de cachorro **2** canil

kept /kept/ pret, pp de KEEP

kerb (GB) = CURB

kerosene /'kerəsi:n/ s (USA) querosene

ketchup /'ketʃəp/ s ketchup

kettle /'ketl/ s (GB) chaleira

key /ki:/ s **1** chave: the ~ to good health a chave da boa saúde **2** (Mús) clave **3** tecla ● adj chave ●

vt **key sth (in)** teclar, digitar algo

keyboard /'ki:bɔ:rd/ s teclado

keyhole /'ki:hoʊl/ s buraco da fechadura

khaki /'kɑki/ adj, s cáqui

kick /kɪk/ **1** vt dar um pontapé em **2** vt chutar **3** vi espernear **4** vi dar coice(s) ► kick the bucket (coloq) bater as botas ■ kick off (of sth) (coloq) botar alguém para fora (de algo) ● s **1** pontapé, chute **2** (coloq): for kicks por curtição

kick-off s pontapé inicial

kid /kɪd/ s **1** (coloq) garoto/a: How are the kids? Como vão as crianças? **2** (coloq, esp USA) his ~ sister a irmã mais nova dele **3** cabrito **4** pelica ● (-dd-) **1** vt, vi (coloq) brincar **2** vt ~ yourself enganar a si mesmo

kidnap /'kɪdnæp/ vt (-pp-) seqüestrar kidnapper s seqüestrador/a kidnapping s seqüestro

kidney /'kɪdni/ s rim

kill /kɪl/ vt, vi matar: She was killed in a car crash. Ela morreu num acidente de carro. ► kill time matar o tempo ■ kill sb/sth off dar fim em alguém, aniquilar algo ● s (animal abatido) presa ► go/move in for the kill atacar killer s assassino/a

killing /'kɪlɪŋ/ s assassinato ► make a killing faturar uma boa nota

kiln /kɪln/ s forno para tijolos

kilogram /'kɪləgræm/ (GB -gramme, kilo /'ki:loʊ/) s (abrev kg) quilograma → Ver pág. 224

kilometer (GB -metre) /kɪ-'amitər/ s (abrev km) quilômetro → Ver pág. 224

kilt /kɪlt/ s saiote escocês

kin /km/ s [pl] (antiq) família, parente

kind /kaɪnd/ adj (~er, ~est) amável ● s tipo, classe: the best of its ~ o melhor do gênero ► in kind **1** em espécie **2** (fig) na mesma moeda **kind of** (coloq) de certo modo: ~ of scared um pouco assustado

kindly /'kaɪndli/ adv **1** amavelmente **2** Kindly leave me alone! Por favor me deixe em paz! ► not take kindly to sb/sth não gostar de alguém/algo ● adj (-ier, -iest) amável

kindness /'kaɪndnəs/ s **1** amabilidade, bondade **2** favor

king /kɪŋ/ s rei

kingdom /'kɪŋdəm/ s reino

kingfisher /ˈkɪŋfɪʃər/ s martim-pescador

kinship /ˈkɪnʃɪp/ s parentesco

kiosk /ˈkiːɒsk/ s quiosque, banca

kipper /ˈkɪpər/ s (GB) arenque defumado

kiss /kɪs/ vt, vi beijar(-se) ● s beijo ▸ **the kiss of life** (GB) respiração boca-a-boca

kit /kɪt/ s 1 equipamento 2 kit para montar

kitchen /ˈkɪtʃɪn/ s cozinha

kite /kaɪt/ s pipa, papagaio

kitten /ˈkɪtn/ s gatinho → GATO

kitty /ˈkɪti/ s (pl -ies) (coloq) vaquinha

knack /næk/ s jeito: get the ~ of sth aprender o macete de algo

knapsack /ˈnæpsæk/ s mochila

knead /niːd/ vt amassar (barro, massa de pão)

knee /niː/ s joelho ▸ **be/go (down) on your knees** estar/ficar ajoelhado

kneecap /ˈniːkæp/ s rótula

kneel /niːl/ vi (pt, pp kneeled, GB tb knelt /nelt/) → DREAM ~ **(down)** ajoelhar-se

knew /nuː; GB njuː/ pret de KNOW

knickers /ˈnɪkərz/ s [pl] (GB) calcinha → PAIR

knife /naɪf/ s (pl knives /naɪvz/) faca ● vt esfaquear

knight /naɪt/ s 1 cavaleiro 2 (xadrez) cavalo ● vt conceder o título de Sir **knighthood** s título de cavaleiro/Sir

knit /nɪt/ (-tt-) (pt, pp knit ou (esp GB knitted) 1 vt tricotar 2 vi fazer tricô 3 Ver CLOSE-KNIT **knitting** s trabalho de tricô: ~ needle agulha de tricô

knitwear /ˈnɪtweər/ s roupa de malha ou lã (tricotada)

knob /nɒb/ s 1 maçaneta 2 (gaveta) puxador 3 (televisão, etc.) botão

knock /nɒk/ s 1 There was a ~ at the door. Bateram na porta. 2 golpe ● 1 vt, vi bater: ~ at/on the door bater na porta 2 vt (coloq) criticar ▸ **knock on wood** (USA) bater na madeira ■ **knock sb down** derrubar, atropelar alguém **knock sth down** demolir algo **knock off (sth)** (coloq): ~ off (work) terminar o expediente **knock sth off** fazer um desconto em algo **knock sb/sth off (sth)** derrubar alguém/algo (de algo) **knock sb out** nocautear alguém 2 (coloq) deixar alguém impressionado **knock sb/sth over** derrubar alguém/algo

knockout /ˈnɒkaʊt/ s 1 nocaute 2 ~ **tournament** competição com eliminatórias

knot /nɒt/ s 1 nó 2 grupo (pessoas) ● vt (-tt-) dar um nó em, atar

know /noʊ/ s ▸ **be in the know** (coloq) estar por dentro ● (pt **knew** pp **known** /noʊn/) 1 vt, vi saber: ~ how to swim saber nadar ◇ Not that I ~ of. Que eu saiba, não. ◇ Let me ~ if... Avise-me se... 2 vt conhecer: get to ~ sb conhecer bem alguém ▸ **for all you know** pelo (pouco) que se sabe **God/goodness/Heaven knows** sabe Deus **know best** saber o que se está fazendo **know better (than that/than to do sth)**: You ought to ~ better! Você não aprende mesmo! **you never know** nunca se sabe

knowing /ˈnoʊɪŋ/ adj: a ~ smile um sorriso de cumplicidade **knowingly** adv de propósito

knowledge /ˈnɒlɪdʒ/ s [U] 1 conhecimento: not to my ~ que eu saiba, não 2 saber ▸ **in the knowledge that...** sabendo que... **knowledgeable** adj versado

knuckle /ˈnʌkl/ s nó dos dedos ■ **knuckle down (to sth)** (coloq) pôr mãos à obra **knuckle under** (coloq) ceder

Koran /kəˈræn; GB -ˈrɑːn/ s Alcorão

Ll

L, l /el/ s (pl **L's**, **l's** /elz/) L, l

label /ˈleɪbl/ s rótulo, etiqueta ● vt (-l-, GB -ll-) 1 etiquetar 2 sb/sth as sth rotular alguém/algo de algo

labor (GB -our) /ˈleɪbər/ s [U] 1 trabalho: ~ relations relações trabalhistas 2 mão-de-obra 3 parto 4 **(Labor)** (tb the Labor Party) o Partido Trabalhista ● vi trabalhar duro **labored** (GB -our-) adj 1 difícil 2 forçado **laborer** (GB -our-) s operário/a

laboratory /ˈlæbrətɔːri; GB ləˈbɒrətri/ s (pl -ies) laboratório

laborious /ləˈbɔːriəs/ adj 1 laborioso 2 elaborado

labyrinth /ˈlæbərɪnθ/ s labirinto

lace /leɪs/ s 1 renda 2 cadarço ● vt amarrar (sapatos)

lack /læk/ vt carecer de ▸ **be lacking** faltar **be lacking in sth** carecer de algo ● s [sing] falta

lacquer /ˈlækər/ s laca

lacy /'leɪsi/ *adj* rendado

lad /læd/ *s* (*coloq*) rapaz

ladder /'lædər/ *s* **1** escada (de mão) **2** fio corrido (*em meia*) **3** escala (*social, profissional*)

laden /'leɪdn/ *adj* ~ (**with sth**) carregado (de algo)

lady /'leɪdi/ *s* (*pl* -**ies**) **1** senhora **2** dama **3** (**Lady**) lady (*título de nobreza*) **4** (**Ladies**) [*sing*] (*GB*) (*USA* **ladies room**) banheiro feminino

ladybug /'leɪdibʌg/ (*GB* **ladybird** /'leɪdibɜːd/) *s* joaninha

lag /læg/ *vi* (-**gg-**) ~ **behind** (**sb/sth**) ficar para trás (*em relação* a alguém/algo) • *s* (*tb* **time** ~) defasagem

lager /'lɑːgər/ *s* cerveja (clara)

lagoon /ləˈguːn/ *s* **1** lagoa **2** laguna

laid /leɪd/ *pret, pp de* LAY¹

laid-back *adj* (*coloq*) descontraído

lain /leɪn/ *pp de* LIE²

lake /leɪk/ *s* lago

lamb /læm/ *s* cordeiro → CARNE

lame /leɪm/ *adj* **1** manco **2** pouco convincente

lament /ləˈment/ *vt, vi* ~ (**for/over sb/sth**) lamentar(-se) (de alguém/algo)

lamp /læmp/ *s* lâmpada

lamp post *s* poste

lampshade /'læmpʃeɪd/ *s* abajur

land /lænd/ *s* **1** terra **2** terreno(s), terra(s): *a plot of ~* um lote **3** (**the land**) solo **4** país ● **1** *vt, vi* desembarcar **2** *vt, vi* pousar **3** *vi* aterrissar **4** *vi* cair **5** *vt* (*coloq*) conseguir ■ **land sb with sb/sth** (*coloq*) impingir algo a alguém: *I got landed with the washing up.* Deixaram a louça para eu lavar.

landing /'lændɪŋ/ *s* **1** aterrissagem **2** desembarque **3** (*escada*) patamar

landlady /'lændleɪdi/ *s* (*pl* -**ies**) **1** senhoria **2** (*GB*) proprietária (*pub, pensão*)

landlord /'lændlɔːrd/ *s* **1** senhorio **2** (*GB*) proprietário (*pub, pensão*)

landmark /'lændmɑːrk/ *s* **1** ponto de referência **2** marco

landmine /'lændmaɪn/ *s* mina (terrestre)

landowner /'lændoʊnər/ *s* proprietário de terras

landscape /'lændskeɪp/ *s* paisagem → SCENERY

landslide /'lændslaɪd/ *s* **1** desabamento (*de terra*) **2** (*tb* ~ **victory** (*pl* -**ies**)) vitória esma-

gadora (*eleições*)

lane /leɪn/ *s* **1** senda **2** viela **3** pista **4** (*Esporte*) raia

language /'læŋgwɪdʒ/ *s* **1** linguagem: *bad* ~ palavrões **2** idioma, língua

lantern /'læntərn/ *s* lanterna

lap /læp/ *s* **1** colo **2** (*Esporte*) volta **● 1** *vi* marulhar **2** *vt* ~ **sth** (**up**) beber água às lambidas ■ **lap sth up** (*coloq*) regalar-se de algo

lapel /ləˈpel/ *s* lapela

lapse /læps/ *s* **1** erro, lapso **2** ~ (**into sth**) deslize (em algo) **3** (*tempo*) intervalo ● *vi* **1** decair: ~ *into silence* calar-se **2** (*Jur*) caducar

laptop /'læptɒp/ *s* laptop

larder /'lɑːrdər/ *s* (*GB*) despensa

large /lɑːrdʒ/ *adj* (-**er**, -**est**) **1** grande **2** amplo → BIG ■ **at large 1** à solta **2** em geral: *the world at* ~ o mundo inteiro **by and large** de modo geral

largely /'lɑːrdʒli/ *adv* em grande parte

large-scale *adj* **1** em grande escala, extenso **2** (*mapa*) ampliado

lark /lɑːrk/ *s* cotovia

laser /'leɪzər/ *s* laser

lash /læʃ/ *s* **1** chicotada **2** cílio ● *vt* **1** chicotear **2** (*rabo*) sacudir com força ■ **lash out at sb/sth** atacar alguém/algo violentamente **2** insurgir-se contra alguém/algo

lass /læs/ (*tb* **lassie** /'læsi/) *s* moça (*esp na Escócia e no norte da Inglaterra*)

last /læst; *GB* lɑːst/ *adj* **1** último → LATE **2** passado: *the night before* ~ anteontem à noite ■ **as a/in the last resort** em último caso **have the last laugh** levar a melhor **have the last word** ter a última palavra ● **the last** *s* **1** o/a último/a: *the* ~ *but one* (*GB*) o penúltimo **2** o/a anterior ■ **(long) last** finalmente ● *adv* **1** último **2** da última vez ■ **last but not least** por último, porém não menos importante ■ *vi* **1** durar **2** continuar **lasting** *adj* durável, duradouro **lastly** *adv* por último

last name *s* sobrenome

latch /lætʃ/ *s* **1** tranca **2** trinco ■ **latch on (to sth)** (*coloq*) captar algo (*explicação, etc.*)

late /leɪt/ (-**er**, -**est**) *adj* **1** atrasado: *be* ~ atrasar-se **2** *in the* ~ *20th century* no final do século XX ◇ *in her* ~ *twenties* beirando os trinta **3** (**latest**) o mais recente **NOTA Latest** significa "mais recente", "mais novo": *the latest technology*. O adjetivo **last** significa o último de uma série. **4** [*antes de substantivo*] falecido ▶ **at the latest** o mais tardar ▶ *adv* tarde: *arrive an hour ~* chegar uma hora atrasado ▶ **later on** mais tarde

lately /'leɪtli/ *adv* ultimamente

latitude /'lætɪtuːd; *GB* -tjuːd/ *s* latitude

the latter /'lætər/ *pron* este último

laugh /læf; *GB* lɑːf/ *vi* rir(-se) ■ **laugh at sb/sth 1** rir de alguém/algo **2** zombar de alguém/algo ● *s* **1** riso, gargalhada **2** (*coloq*): *What a ~!* Que engraçado! ◇ *be good for a ~* se divertido **laughable** *adj* risível **laughter** *s* [U] risada: *roar with ~* dar gargalhadas

launch /lɔːntʃ/ *vt* lançar (ao mar) ■ **launch into sth** (*discurso, etc.*) dar início a algo ● *s* **1** lançamento **2** lancha

laundromat /'lɔːndrəmæt/ (*GB* **launderette** /lɔːn'dret/) *s* lavanderia self-service

laundry /'lɔːndri/ *s* (*pl* **-ies**) **1** roupa para lavar: *do the ~* lavar roupa **2** lavanderia

lava /'lɑːvə/ *s* lava

lavatory /'lævətɔːri/ *s* (*pl* **-ies**) (*GB, fml*) banheiro → TOILET

lavender /'lævəndər/ *s* alfazema

lavish /'lævɪʃ/ *adj* **1** generoso **2** abundante

law /lɔː/ *s* **1** (*tb* **the ~**) lei **2** (*carreira*) direito ▶ **law and order** a ordem pública **lawful** *adj* legítimo

lawn /lɔːn/ *s* gramado

lawsuit /'lɔːsuːt/ *s* ação judicial

lawyer /'lɔːjər/ *s* advogado/a → ADVOGADO

lay[1] /leɪ/ *pret de* LIE[2] ● *vt, vi* (*pt, pp* **laid**) **1** colocar, pôr: *~ sth aside* colocar algo de lado **2** instalar **3** cobrir → LIE[2] **4** (*ovos*) pôr ▶ **lay claim to sth** reivindicar algo **lay your cards on the table** pôr as cartas na mesa ■ **lay sth down 1** (*armas*) depor algo **2** estipular **lay sb off** demitir alguém **lay sth on sb 1** (GB) instalar algo **2** (*coloq*) prover algo **lay sth out 1** exibir algo **2** (*argumento*) expor algo **3** (*jardim, cidade*) planejar algo

lay[2] /leɪ/ *adj* leigo

lay-by *s* (GB) acostamento (*estrada*)

layer /'leɪər/ *s* **1** camada **2** (*Geol*)

estrato **layered** *adj* em camadas

lazy /'leɪzi/ *adj* (**-ier, -iest**) **1** vadio **2** preguiçoso

lead[1] /liːd/ *s* **1** iniciativa **2** (*competição*) vantagem: *in the ~* na frente **3** (*Teat*) papel principal **4** (*cartas*): *It's your ~*. Você começa. **5** (*indício*) pista **6** (*cão*) coleira **7** (*Elet*) fio ● (*pt, pp* **led**) **1** *vt, vi* levar, conduzir: *~ the way* mostrar o caminho ◇ *This road leads back to town*. Esta estrada vai dar na cidade. **2** *vi* ~ **to sth** dar lugar a algo **3** *vi* estar na frente **4** *vt* encabeçar **5** *vt, vi* (*cartas*) começar a partida ▶ **lead up to sth** conduzir a algo **leader** *s* líder **leadership** *s* **1** liderança **2** chefia **leading** *adj* principal

lead[2] /led/ *s* chumbo **leaded** *adj* com chumbo

leaf /liːf/ *s* (*pl* **leaves**) folha ▶ **take a leaf out of sb's book** seguir o exemplo de alguém **leafy** *adj* (**-ier, -iest**) frondoso: *~ vegetables* verduras

leaflet /'liːflət/ *s* folheto

league /liːg/ *s* **1** liga **2** (*coloq*) classe ▶ **in league (with sb)** em conluio (com alguém)

leak /liːk/ *s* **1** buraco, goteira **2** vazamento **3** divulgação ● **1** *vi* gotejar, vazar **2** *vi* (*gás, líquido*) escapar **3** *vt* deixar escapar

lean /liːn/ *adj* (**-er, -est**) **1** esguio **2** (*carne*) magro ● (*pt, pp* **leaned** ou **leant** /lent/ (GB)) **1** *vi* inclinar(-se), debruçar(-se) **2** *vi* ~ **against/on sth** encostar(-se) em algo **leaning** *s* inclinação

leap /liːp/ *vi* (*pt, pp* **leaped** ou *esp* GB **leapt** /lept/) **1** pular **2** (*coração*) disparar ● *s* salto

leap year *s* ano bissexto

learn /lɜːrn/ *vt, vi* (*pt, pp* **learned** ou **learnt** /lɜːrnt/ (GB)) → DREAM **1** aprender **2** ~ (*of/about*) sth ficar sabendo de algo ▶ **learn your lesson** aprender com um erro **learner** *s* aprendiz/a, principiante **learning** *s* **1** aprendizagem **2** erudição

lease /liːs/ *s* arrendamento ● *vt* ~ **sth (to/from sb)** arrendar algo (a alguém)

least /liːst/ *pron* (*superl de* little) menos: *It's the ~ I can do*. É o mínimo que eu posso fazer. ▶ **not in the least** de maneira nenhuma ● *adj* menor ● *adv* menos ▶ **at least** pelo menos, no mínimo **not least** especialmente

leather /'leðər/ *s* couro

leave /li:v/ (pt, pp left) **1** vt, vi deixar: ~ sth behind deixar algo para trás/esquecer algo **2** vt, vi ir-se de (sair de (be left): You've only got a day left. Só te falta um dia. ◇ be left over sobrar ● s licença (férias): on ~ de licença

▶at your leisure quando lhe convier

leaves /li:vz/ plural de LEAF

lecture /'lektʃər/ s **1** palestra: ~ theater anfiteatro **2** (repri-menda) sermão ● **1** vi dar uma palestra **2** vt ~ sb passar um sermão em alguém **lecturer** s **1** (GB) ~ (in sth) (universi-dade) professor/a (de algo) **2** conferencista

leisurely /'li:ʒəli; GB 'leʒəli/ adj pausado, relaxado ● adv tran-qüilamente

lemon /'lemən/ s limão

lemonade /ˌleməˈneɪd/ s limonada

led /led/ pt, pp de LEAD[1]

ledge /ledʒ/ s **1** saliência: the window ~ o peitoril da janela **2** (Geog) recife

leek /li:k/ s alho-poró

left /left/ pt, pp de LEAVE ● adj esquerdo ● adv à esquerda ● s **1** esquerda **2 (the Left)** (Pol) a esquerda

lend /lend/ vt (pt, pp lent) emprestar

length /leŋθ/ s **1** comprimento, extensão **2** duração: for some ~ of time por bastante tempo ▶go to any, great, etc. lengths (to do sth) fazer todo o possível (para realizar algo) **lengthen** vt, vi alongar(-se) **lengthy** adj (-ier, -iest) demorado

left-hand adj à/da esquerda: on the ~ side do lado esquerdo **left-handed** adj canhoto

left luggage office s (GB) depó-sito de bagagem

leftover /'leftoʊvər/ adj [antes de substantivo] restante **leftovers** s sobras (comida)

lenient /'li:niənt/ adj **1** indul-gente **2** tolerante

lens /lenz/ s **1** objetiva **2** lente

lent /lent/ pt, pp de LEND ● **Lent** s quaresma

lentil /'lentl/ s lentilha

Leo /'li:oʊ/ s (pl ~s) Leão

leopard /'lepərd/ s leopardo

lesbian /'lezbiən/ s lésbica

leg /leg/ s **1** perna → ARM **2** (viagem, etc.) etapa ▶give sb a leg up (coloq) ajudar alguém a subir em algo ▶not have a leg to stand on (coloq) não ter como se justificar

less /les/ adj, adv, pron menos NOTA Como comparativo de little, less acompanha normal-mente substantivos não contá-veis: "I've got very little money." "I have even ~ money (than you)." **Fewer** é o comparativo de few e é usado com substantivos no plural: fewer accidents, people, etc. No inglês falado usa-se mais less. ▶less and less cada vez menos ▶the less... the less... quanto menos..., menos... **lessen 1** vi diminuir **2** vt reduzir **lesser** adj menor

legacy /'legəsi/ s (pl -ies) **1** lega-do **2** patrimônio

legal /'li:gl/ adj legal: take ~ action abrir um processo legal-ity /li'gæləti/ s legalidade **legal-ization** s legalização **legalize** vt legalizar

lesson /'lesn/ s **1** aula **2** lição

let /let/ vt (-tt-) (pt, pp let) deixar, permitir: ~ sb do sth deixar alguém fazer algo ◇ ~ sb in/out deixar alguém entrar/sair Ver nota em ALLOW. NOTA Usa-se let us + infinitivo sem to para fazer sugestões. Normalmente utiliza-se a contração informal let's: Let's go! Vamos! Na nega-tiva, usa-se let's not: Let's not argue. Não vamos brigar. → ALUGAR ▶let alone: I can't afford new clothes, ~ alone a vacation. Não tenho dinheiro para comprar roupa, quanto mais para férias. ▶let fly at sb/ sth atacar alguém/algo ▶let fly with sth disparar algo ▶let off steam (coloq) desabafar(-se) ▶let sb know sth informar alguém sobre algo ▶let sb/sth go; let go of sb/sth soltar alguém/algo ▶let sth/sth loose

legend /'ledʒənd/ s lenda **legendary** adj legendário

leggings /'legɪŋz/ s [pl] legging

legible /'ledʒəbl/ adj legível

legion /'li:dʒən/ s legião

legislate /'ledʒɪsleɪt/ vi legislar **legislation** s legislação **legisla-tive** adj legislativo **legislature** s (fml) assembléia legislativa

legitimacy /lɪ'dʒɪtɪməsi/ s legiti-midade

legitimate /lɪ'dʒɪtɪmət/ adj **1** legítimo **2** válido

leisure /'li:ʒər; GB 'leʒə(r)/ s lazer: ~ center centro de lazer (e esporte) ◇ ~ time tempo livre

libertar alguém/algo **let's face it** (coloq) convenhamos **let sth slip** deixar escapar algo **let the cat out of the bag** dar com a língua nos dentes **let the matter drop/rest** pôr um fim no assunto **let us say** digamos ■ **let sb down** decepcionar alguém **let sb off (sth)** perdoar alguém (de algo) **let sth off 1** disparar algo 2 (*fogos de artifício*) soltar algo

let² /let/ *vt* (-**tt**-) (*pt, pp* let) (*GB*) alugar: *to ~* aluga(m)-se → ALUGAR

lethal /'liːθl/ *adj* letal

lethargy /'leθərdʒi/ *s* letargia lethargic /lə'θɑːrdʒɪk/ *adj* letárgico

let's /lets/ = LET US *Ver* LET¹

letter /'letər/ *s* 1 letra 2 carta ▸ **to the letter** ao pé da letra

letter box *s* 1 (*GB*) caixa do correio 2 fenda na porta da casa para a correspondência

letter carrier *s* carteiro/a

lettuce /'letɪs/ *s* alface

leukemia (*GB* -**kae**-) /luː'kiːmiə/ *s* leucemia

level /'levl/ *adj* 1 plano 2 ~ (**with sb/sth**) no mesmo nível (de alguém/algo) ● *s* nível ● *vt* (-**l-**, *GB* -**ll-**) 1 nivelar ■ **level sth at sb/ sth** dirigir algo a alguém/algo (*críticas, etc.*) **level off/out** estabilizar-se

level crossing (*GB*) *s* passagem de nível

lever /'levər; *GB* 'liːvə(r)/ *s* alavanca **leverage** *s* 1 influência 2 potência/sistema de alavanca

levy /'levi/ *vt* (*pt, pp* -**ied**) cobrar (*impostos, etc.*) ● *s* 1 cobrança 2 imposto

liability /ˌlaɪə'bɪləti/ *s* (*pl* -**ies**) 1 responsabilidade 2 (*coloq*) desvantagem **liable** *adj* 1 ~ (**for sth**) responsável (por algo) 2 ~ (**to sth**) sujeito a algo 3 ~ **to do sth** propenso a algo 4 ~ **to do sth** suscetível de fazer algo

liaison /li'eɪzn; *GB* li'eɪzn/ *s* 1 vínculo 2 caso amoroso

liar /'laɪər/ *s* mentiroso/a

libel /'laɪbl/ *s* difamação

liberal /'lɪbərəl/ *adj* 1 (*tb* **Liberal**) liberal 2 livre

liberate /'lɪbəreɪt/ *vt* libertar **liberated** *adj* liberado **liberation** *s* liberação

liberty /'lɪbərti/ *s* (*pl* -**ies**) liberdade ▸ **take liberties** faltar com o respeito

Libra /'liːbrə/ *s* Libra

library /'laɪbreri; *GB* -brəri/ *s* (*pl* -**ies**) biblioteca **librarian** /laɪ'breəriən/ *s* bibliotecário/a

lice /laɪs/ *plural de* LOUSE

license (*GB* **licence**) /'laɪsns/ *s* 1 licença: *driver's ~* carteira de motorista ◇ ~ *plate* placa (de carro) 2 (*fml*) permissão

lick /lɪk/ *vt* lamber ● *s* lambida

licorice /'lɪkərɪs; *GB* -ɪʃ/ *s* alcaçuz

lid /lɪd/ *s* 1 tampa 2 pálpebra

lie¹ /laɪ/ *vi* (*pt, pp* lied *part pres* lying) mentir ● *s* mentira: *tell lies* mentir

lie² /laɪ/ *vi* (*pt* lay *pp* lain *part pres* lying) 1 ~ (**down**) deitar-se, jazer 2 estar: *The problem lies in...* O problema reside em... 3 estender-se ■ **lie about/around 1** vadiar 2 estar à toa: *leave your clothes lying around* deixar suas roupas espalhadas por aí **lie back** recostar-se **lie in** (*GB*) ficar na cama até tarde NOTA Compare os verbos lie e lay. O verbo **lie** (lay, lain, lying) é intransitivo e significa "estar deitado": *I lay down on the bed for a while.* É importante não confundir com **lie** (lied, lied, lying), que significa "mentir". Por outro lado, **lay** (laid, laid, laying) é transitivo e significa "colocar sobre": *She laid her dress on the bed.*

lieutenant /luː'tenənt; *GB* lef't-/ *s* tenente

life /laɪf/ (*pl* lives) *s* 1 vida: *late in ~* com uma idade avançada 2 (*tb* ~ *imprisonment*) prisão perpétua ▸ **come to life** animar-se **take your (own) life** suicidar-se

lifebelt /'laɪfbelt/ *s* cinto salvavidas

lifeboat /'laɪfboʊt/ *s* barco salvavidas

life expectancy *s* expectativa de vida

lifeguard /'laɪfɡɑːrd/ *s* salvavidas

lifelong /'laɪflɔːŋ; *GB* -lɒŋ/ *adj* que dura a vida inteira

life preserver (*tb* **life jacket**) *s* colete salva-vidas

lifestyle /'laɪfstaɪl/ *s* estilo de vida

lifetime /'laɪftaɪm/ *s* existência: *It lasts a ~.* Dura toda a vida. ▸ **the chance, etc. of a lifetime** uma oportunidade, etc. única

lift /lɪft/ 1 *vt* ~ **sb/sth (up)** levantar alguém/algo 2 *vt* (*embargo, etc.*) suspender 3 *vi* (*nuvens, etc.*) dispersar-se ■ **lift off** decolar ● *s* 1 estímulo 2 (*GB*) elevador 3 carona

light /laɪt/ s **1** luz **2** ((traffic) **lights**) [pl] semáforo **3** (a light): *Have you got a ~?* Tem fogo? ▸ **come to light** vir à luz **in the light of sth** considerando algo **set light to sth** botar fogo em algo ● (~er, ~est) adj **1** iluminado **2** (cor) claro **3** leve: *two kilograms lighter* dois quilos a menos **4** (golpe, vento) brando ● adv: *travel ~* viajar com pouca bagagem ● (pt, pp lit ou lighted) **1** vt, vi acender(-se) **2** vt iluminar, clarear NOTA Geralmente usa-se **lighted** como adjetivo antes do substantivo: *a lighted candle*, e **lit** como verbo: *He lit the candle.* ▪ **light up (with sth)** iluminar-se (de algo) (rosto, olhos)

light bulb Ver BULB

lighten /'laɪtn/ vt, vi **1** iluminar (-se) **2** tornar(-se) mais leve **3** descontrair(-se)

lighter /'laɪtər/ s isqueiro

light-headed adj tonto

light-hearted adj **1** despreocupado **2** (comentário) despretensioso

lighthouse /'laɪthaʊs/ s farol

lighting /'laɪtɪŋ/ s iluminação

lightly /'laɪtli/ adv **1** ligeiramente, levemente **2** suavemente **3** às pressas ▸ **get off/escape lightly** (coloq) livrar a cara

lightness /'laɪtnəs/ s **1** claridade **2** leveza **3** suavidade **4** agilidade

lightning /'laɪtnɪŋ/ s [U] relâmpago

lightweight /'laɪtweɪt/ s peso leve (boxe) ● adj **1** leve **2** (boxeador) peso leve

like /laɪk/ prep **1** como, igual a: *look/be ~ sb* parecer-se com alguém **2** (exemplo) (tal) como **3** like + -ing como + infinitivo ● conj (coloq) **1** como **2** como se ● vt gostar ▸ **if you like** se você quiser **likeable** adj agradável

likely /'laɪkli/ adj (-ier, -iest) provável: *It isn't ~ to rain.* Não é provável que chova. ◇ *She's very ~ to call me.* É bem capaz de ela me ligar. **2** apropriado ● adv ▸ **not likely** (coloq) nem pensar **likelihood** s [sing] probabilidade

liken /'laɪkən/ vt (fml) ~ **sth to sth** comparar algo com algo

likeness /'laɪknəs/ s semelhança: *a family ~* traços de parentesco

likewise /'laɪkwaɪz/ adv (fml) **1** da mesma forma **2** também

liking /'laɪkɪŋ/ s ▸ **take a liking to**

sb simpatizar com alguém **to sb's liking** (fml) do agrado de alguém

lilac /'laɪlæk/ s lilás

lily /'lɪli/ s (pl -ies) lírio

lima bean /'laɪmə biːn/ s (USA) fava

limb /lɪm/ s braço, perna (pessoa)

lime /laɪm/ s **1** cal **2** limão, limeira ● adj, s (tb ~ **green**) (cor) verde-limão

limelight /'laɪmlaɪt/ s: *be in the ~* estar em evidência

limestone /'laɪmstoʊn/ s pedra calcária

limit /'lɪmɪt/ s limite ▸ **within limits** até certo ponto ● vt limitar **limitation** s limitação **limited** adj limitado **limiting** adj restritivo **limitless** adj ilimitado

limousine /ˌlɪməˈziːn, 'lɪməziːn/ s limusine

limp /lɪmp/ adj **1** mole **2** débil ● vi mancar ● s: *have a ~* ser/estar coxo

line /laɪn/ vt **1** ~ **sth (with sth)** revestir algo (de algo) **2** enfileirar(-se): ~ *up (for sth)* fazer fila (para algo) **lined** adj **1** enrugado **2** (papel) pautado **3** forrado **lining** s **1** forro **2** revestimento s **1** linha, reta: *a clothes ~* uma corda para estender roupa ◇ *~ drawing* desenho a lápis ou a pena **2** fila **3** (lines) [pl] (Teat): *learn your lines* decorar seu texto **4** (lines) cópias (castigo escolar) **5** linha telefônica **6** [sing]: *the official ~* o parecer oficial ▸ **along/on the same, etc. lines** no mesmo estilo **in line with sth** de acordo com algo

linen /'lɪnən/ s **1** linho **2** roupa (branca) de cama

liner /'laɪnər/ s transatlântico

linger /'lɪŋɡər/ vi **1** (pessoa) demorar-se **2** persistir

linguist /'lɪŋɡwɪst/ s **1** poliglota **2** lingüista **linguistic** /lɪŋˈɡwɪstɪk/ adj lingüístico **linguistics** s [sing] lingüística

link /lɪŋk/ s **1** elo **2** laço **3** vínculo **4** conexão ● vt unir: ~ *arms* dar o braço **2** relacionar ▪ **link up (with sb/sth)** unir-se (com alguém/algo)

lion /'laɪən/ s leão

lip /lɪp/ s lábio

lip-read vi (pt, pp **lip-read** /-red/) ler os lábios

lipstick /'lɪpstɪk/ s batom

liqueur /lɪˈkɜːr/; GB -ˈkjʊər/ s licor

liquid /'lɪkwɪd/ s líquido ● adj líquido **liquidize** vt liqüidificar **liquidizer** s liqüidificador

liquor /'lɪkər/ s bebida alcoólica: ~ store loja de bebidas

liquorice (GB) = LICORICE

lisp /lɪsp/ s ceceio ● vt, vi cecear

list /lɪst/ s lista ● vt 1 enumerar 2 listar

listen /'lɪsn/ vi 1 ~ (to sb/sth) escutar (alguém/algo) 2 ~ to sb/ sth dar ouvidos a alguém/algo ■ listen out for sth prestar atenção a algo **listener** s 1 (rádio) ouvinte 2 a good ~ uma pessoa que sabe escutar os outros

lit /lɪt/ pret, pp de LIGHT

liter (GB litre) /'li:tər/ s (abrev l) litro

literacy /'lɪtərəsi/ s alfabetização

literal /'lɪtərəl/ adj literal **literally** adv literalmente

literary /'lɪtəreri; GB -rəri/ adj literário

literate /'lɪtərət/ adj alfabetizado

literature /'lɪtərətʃər; GB -tʃə(r)/ s 1 literatura 2 folhetos

litter /'lɪtər/ s 1 lixo: ~ bin lata de lixo 2 (Zool) ninhada ● vt: Papers littered the floor. Havia papéis espalhados pelo chão.

little /'lɪtl/ adj NOTA O comparativo de **little** é pouco freqüente; normalmente usa-se **smaller** e **smallest**. 1 pequeno: my ~ brother meu irmão caçula ◇ ~ finger dedo mindinho ◇ Poor ~ thing! Pobrezinho! 2 pouco ► LESS NOTA **Little** tem um sentido negativo e equivale a "pouco". **A little** tem uma acepção muito mais positiva e significa "um pouco de". Compare as seguintes frases: I have ~ hope. Tenho pouca esperança. ◇ Always carry a ~ money. Tenha sempre um pouco de dinheiro com você. ● s, pron pouco: There was ~ anyone could do. Havia pouco que se pudesse fazer. ◇ I only want a ~. Só quero um pouquinho. ● adv pouco ► **little by little** pouco a pouco **little or nothing** quase nada

live¹ /lɪv/ vi 1 morar 2 ~ (for/on sth) viver (para/de algo) 3 permanecer vivo ■ **live on** continuar a viver **live through sth** sobreviver a algo **live up to sth** corresponder às expectativas **live with sth** tolerar algo

live² /laɪv/ adj 1 vivo 2 (bomba, etc.) ativado 3 (Elet) eletrizado

4 (show) ao vivo ● adv ao vivo

livelihood /'laɪvlihʊd/ s (meio de) vida

lively /'laɪvli/ adj (-ier, -iest) 1 (pessoa) vivo 2 animado

liver /'lɪvər/ s fígado

lives /laɪvz/ plural de LIFE

livestock /'laɪvstɑk/ s criação (animais)

living /'lɪvɪŋ/ s sustento: make a ~ ganhar a vida ◇ What do you do for a ~? O que você faz na vida? ◇ cost of ~ custo de vida ● adj [antes de substantivo] vivo ► **in/within living memory** de que se tem notícia

living room s sala de estar

lizard /'lɪzərd/ s lagarto

load /loʊd/ s 1 carga 2 **loads (of sth)** [pl] (coloq) um monte (de algo) ► **a load of (old) rubbish, etc.** (coloq): What a ~ of rubbish! Quanta asneira! ● vt 1 ~ sth (into/onto sb/sth); ~ (sth) (up) (with sth) carregar (alguém/ algo de algo) 2 vt ~ sb/sth (down) atulhar alguém/algo **loaded** adj carregado: a ~ question uma pergunta capciosa

loaf /loʊf/ s [pl **loaves** /loʊvz/] pão (de forma, redondo, etc.)

loan /loʊn/ s empréstimo

loathe /loʊð/ vt abominar **loathing** s repugnância

lobby /'lɑbi/ s (pl -ies) 1 vestíbulo 2 (Pol) grupo de pressão ● vt (pt, pp -ied) pressionar

lobster /'lɑbstər/ s lagosta

local /'loʊkl/ adj 1 local, do lugar: ~ authority município 2 (Med) localizado: ~ anesthetic anestesia local **locally** adv na vizinhança

locate /'loʊkeɪt; GB ləʊ'keɪt/ vt 1 localizar 2 situar

location /loʊ'keɪʃn/ s 1 local 2 localização 3 (pessoa) paradeiro ► **on ~** em externas (filmagem)

loch /lɑk, lɑx/ s (Escócia) lago

lock /lɑk/ s 1 fechadura 2 eclusa ● vt, vi 1 trancar 2 (volante, etc.) travar ■ **lock sth away/up** guardar algo a sete chaves **lock sb up** trancafiar alguém

locker /'lɑkər/ s armário com chave

lodge /lɑdʒ/ s 1 casa do guarda (numa propriedade), (caça, pesca, etc.) cabana 3 portaria ● vi alojar-se **lodger** s (GB) hóspede, inquilino/a **lodging** s 1 alojamento: board and ~ (GB) casa e comida 2 **lodgings** [pl] (GB) quarto mobiliado

loft /lɒft; GB lɒft/ s sótão

log /lɒg; GB lɔːg/ s **1** tronco **2** lenha **3** diário de bordo/de vôo (**-gg-**) registrar ■ **log in/on** (*Informát*) iniciar a sessão **log off/out** (*Informát*) encerrar a sessão

logic /lɒdʒɪk/ s lógica **logical** *adj* lógico

logo /loʊgoʊ/ s (*pl* **~s**) logotipo

lollipop /lɒlipɒp/ s pirulito

lonely /loʊnli/ *adj* **1** só → ALONE **2** solitário **loneliness** s solidão **loner** s solitário/a

long¹ /lɒŋ; GB lɒŋ/ (**~er** /lɒŋgər/, **~est** /lɒŋgɪst/) *adj* **1** comprido: *It's two meters ~.* Tem dois metros de comprimento. ◊ *~ time* (*tempo*): *a ~ time ago* há muito tempo ◊ *How ~ is the vacation?* Quanto tempo duram as férias? ▶ **at the longest** no máximo **in the long run** no final das contas ● *adv* **1** muito (*tempo*): *Stay as ~ as you like.* Fique o tempo que quiser. ◊ *for ~* por muito tempo **2** todo: *all day ~* o dia inteiro ▶ **as/so long as** contanto que **no/any longer**: *I can't stay any longer.* Não posso ficar mais.

long² /lɒŋ; GB lɒŋ/ *vi* **1** **~ to do sth** ansiar por (fazer) algo **2** **~ for sb to do sth** desejar que alguém faça algo **longing** s desejo

long-distance *adj, adv* de longa distância: *phone ~* fazer um telefonema interurbano

longitude /lɒndʒɪtuːd; GB -tjuːd/ s longitude

long jump s salto em distância

long-life *adj* de duração prolongada

long-range *adj* **1** a longo prazo **2** de longo alcance

long-sighted *adj* hipermetrope

long-standing *adj* muito antigo

long-suffering *adj* resignado

long-term *adj* a longo prazo

loo /luː/ s (*pl* **~s**) (*GB, coloq*) banheiro → TOILET

look /lʊk/ s **1** olhada **2** *have a ~ for sth* buscar algo **3** aspecto **4** estilo **5** *looks* [*pl*] físico: *good looks* boa aparência ● *vi* **1** **~ (at sb/sth)** olhar (para alguém/algo): *~ sb up and down* olhar para alguém de cima a baixo **2** parecer **3** **~ onto sth** dar para algo ▶ **don't look a gift horse in the mouth** de cavalo dado não se olham os dentes **look on the bright side** ver o lado bom das coisas **look your age** aparentar a idade que se tem **not look yourself** parecer abatido/

cansado ■ **look after yourself/sb** cuidar-se/cuidar de alguém **look around 1** olhar para trás **2** dar uma comparada **look around sth** visitar algo **look at sth 1** examinar algo **2** considerar algo **look back** (**on sth**) recordar algo **look down on sb/sth** desprezar alguém/algo **look for sb/sth** procurar alguém/algo **look forward to (doing) sth** aguardar (fazer) algo com ansiedade **look into sth** investigar algo **look on** assistir **look out 1** *Look out!* Cuidado! **2** **~ out for sb/sth** estar à espreita de alguém/algo **look sth over** checar algo **look up 1** procurar algo à vista **2** (*coloq*) melhorar **look up to sb** admirar alguém **look sth up** procurar algo (*dicionário, livro*)

lookout /lʊkaʊt/ s vigia ▶ **be on the lookout for sb/sth; keep a lookout for sb/sth** estar à espreita de alguém/algo

loom /luːm/ s tear ● *vi* **1** **~ (up)** surgir **2** ameaçar

loony /luːni/ *adj, s* (*pl* **-ies**) (*coloq*) maluco/a

loop /luːp/ s **1** curva **2** (*com nó*) laço ● **1** *vi* laçadas **2** *vt*: *~ sth round/over sth* enrolar algo ao redor de algo

loophole /luːphoʊl/ s escapatória: *a legal ~* uma saída legal

loose /luːs/ *adj* (**-er** **-est**) **1** solto: *~ change* (dinheiro) trocado **2** frouxo **3** (*vestido*) folgado **4** (*moral*) corrupto ▶ **be at a loose end** estar sem ter o que fazer ● *s* ▶ **on the loose** à solta **loosely** *adv* **1** sem apertar **2** aproximadamente

loosen /luːsn/ **1** *vt, vi* afrouxar, soltar(-se) **2** *vt* (*controle*) relaxar ■ **loosen up 1** descontrair-se **2** (*Esporte*) aquecer-se

loot /luːt/ s saque ● *vt, vi* saquear **looting** s saque

lop /lɒp/ *vt* (**-pp-**) podar ■ **lop sth off** cortar algo

lopsided /ˌlɒpˈsaɪdɪd/ *adj* **1** torto **2** destorcido

lord /lɔːrd/ s **1** senhor **2** (**the Lord**) o Senhor: *the Lord's Prayer* o pai-nosso **3** (**the Lords**) (*GB*) a Câmara dos Lordes **4** (*Lord*) (*GB*) lorde **lordship** s ▶ **your/his Lordship** Vossa/Sua Senhoria

lorry /lɒri; GB lɒri/ s (*pl* **-ies**) (*GB*) caminhão

lose /luːz/ (*pt, pp* **lost**) **1** *vt, vi* perder: *~ your way* perder-se **2** *vt* **~ sb sth** fazer alguém perder algo: *It lost us the game.* Isso nos custou a partida. **3** vi (relógio) atrasar-se ▶ **lose sight of sb/sth** perder alguém/algo de vista: *We must not ~ sight of the fact that...* Devemos ter em mente o fato de que... **lose your mind** enlouquecer ▶ **lose out (on sth)/(to sb/sth)** (coloq) sair perdendo (em algo)/(em relação a alguém/algo) **loser** *s* fracassado/a

loss /lɔːs; GB lɒs/ *s* perda ▶ **be at a loss** estar desorientado

lost /lɔːst; GB lɒst/ *pret, pp de* LOSE ● *adj* perdido: *She got ~.* Ela se perdeu. ▶ **get lost** (coloq) cai fora

lost and found *s* (objetos) achados e perdidos

lot /lɑt/ ▶ **a lot, lots** *pron* (coloq) muito ● **a lot of, lots of** *adj* (coloq) muito(s): *pile of people* uma porção de gente ◇ *What a ~ of presents!* Quantos presentes! → MANY ● *adv* muito: *Thanks a ~.* Muito obrigado. ● *s* **1** (the (whole) lot) (esp GB) tudo **2** (GB) grupo: *What do you ~ want?* O que é que vocês querem? ◇ *I don't go out with that ~.* Não ando com essa turma. **3** lote **4** sorte (destino)

lotion /ˈloʊʃn/ *s* loção

lottery /ˈlɑtəri/ *s* (pl -ies) loteria

loud /laʊd/ (~ -est) *adj* **1** alto **2** (grito) forte **3** (cor) berrante ● *adv* alto ▶ **out loud** em voz alta

loudspeaker /ˈlaʊdspiːkər/ *s* alto-falante

lounge /laʊndʒ/ *vi* ~ (**about/around**) preguiçar ● *s* **1** sala de estar **2** salão

louse /laʊs/ *s* (pl lice) piolho

lousy /ˈlaʊzi/ *adj* (-ier, -iest) péssimo

lout /laʊt/ *s* (GB) arruaceiro

lovable /ˈlʌvəbl/ *adj* adorável

love /lʌv/ *s* **1** amor: *in ~ with sb* apaixonado por alguém NOTA Para pessoas, diz-se love for somebody; para coisas, love of something. **2** (Esporte) zero ▶ **give/send sb your love** dar/mandar lembranças a alguém **make love (to sb)** fazer amor (com alguém) ● *vt* **1** amar **2** adorar: *I'd ~ to come.* Gostaria muito de ir.

love affair *s* caso (amoroso)

lovely /ˈlʌvli/ *adj* (-ier, -iest) **1** lindo **2** encantador **3** muito agradável: *We had a ~ time.* Nós nos divertimos bastante.

lovemaking /ˈlʌvmeɪkɪŋ/ *s* relações sexuais

lover /ˈlʌvər/ *s* amante

loving /ˈlʌvɪŋ/ *adj* carinhoso
lovingly *adv* amorosamente

low /loʊ/ (~ -est) *adj* **1** baixo: *lower lip* lábio inferior ◇ *lower case* minúsculas **2** (som) grave **3** abatido ▶ **keep a low profile** procurar passar despercebido ● *adv* baixo ▶ *s* baixa

low-alcohol *adj* de baixo teor alcoólico

low-calorie *adj* baixo em calorias NOTA Low-calorie é o termo usual para produtos de baixo teor calórico ou "light". Para bebidas usa-se **diet**: *diet drinks*.

low-cost *adj* barato

lower /ˈloʊər/ *vt, vi* abaixar(-se)

low-fat *adj* magro

low-key *adj* discreto

lowlands /ˈloʊləndz/ *s* planícies

loyal /ˈlɔɪəl/ *adj* leal, fiel **loyalist** *s* legalista **loyalty** *s* (pl -ies) lealdade

luck /lʌk/ *s* sorte: *in/out of ~* com/sem sorte ▶ **no such luck** que nada!

lucky /ˈlʌki/ *adj* (-ier, -iest) **1** sortudo **2** *It's ~ she's still here.* Por sorte ela ainda está aqui. ◇ *a ~ number* um número de sorte **luckily** *adv* por sorte

ludicrous /ˈluːdɪkrəs/ *adj* ridículo

luggage /ˈlʌɡɪdʒ/ *s* [U] bagagem: *~ rack* bagageiro

lukewarm /ˌluːkˈwɔːrm/ *adj* morno

lull /lʌl/ *vt* **1** acalmar **2** acalentar ● *s* calmaria

lumber /ˈlʌmbər/ **1** *vt* ~ **sb with sb/sth** empurrar alguém/algo para cima de alguém **2** *vi* mover-se pesadamente **lumbering** *adj* desajeitado, pesado

lump /lʌmp/ *s* **1** pedaço: *sugar ~* torrão de açúcar **2** coágulo **3** (Med) caroço, galo ● *vt* ~ **sth together** juntar alguém/algo indiscriminadamente **lumpy** *adj* (-ier, -iest) **1** encaroçado **2** (colchão, etc.) disforme

lump sum *s* quantia paga de uma só vez

lunacy /ˈluːnəsi/ *s* [U] loucura

lunatic /ˈluːnətɪk/ *s* louco/a

lunch /lʌntʃ/ *s* almoço: *have ~* almoçar ● *vi* almoçar

lunchtime /ˈlʌntʃtaɪm/ *s* a hora do almoço

lung /lʌŋ/ *s* pulmão

lurch /lɜːrtʃ/ *s* guinada ● *vi* **1** cambalear **2** dar uma guinada

lure /lʊər/ *s* atrativo ● *vt* atrair

lurid /ˈlʊərɪd/ *adj* **1** (cor) berrante

2 sensacionalista

lurk /lɜːrk/ vi espreitar

luscious /ˈlʌʃəs/ adj apetitoso

lush /lʌʃ/ adj (vegetação) exuberante

lust /lʌst/ s **1** luxúria **2** ~ **for sth** ânsia por algo • vi ~ **after/for sb/sth** cobiçar algo; desejar alguém

luxurious /lʌɡˈʒʊəriəs/ adj luxuoso

luxury /ˈlʌkʃəri/ s (pl -ies) luxo

lying Ver LIE[1,2]

lyrical /ˈlɪrɪkl/ adj lírico

lyrics /ˈlɪrɪks/ s [pl] letra (de canção)

M m

M, m /em/ s (pl **M's, m's** /emz/) M, m

mac (tb **mack**) /mæk/ s (GB, coloq) Ver MACKINTOSH

macabre /məˈkɑːbrə/ adj macabro

macaroni /ˌmækəˈrouni/ s [U] macarrão

machine /məˈʃiːn/ s máquina

machine gun /məˈʃiːn ɡʌn/ s metralhadora

machinery /məˈʃiːnəri/ s maquinaria

mackintosh /ˈmækɪntɒʃ/ s (GB) capa (de chuva)

mad /mæd/ adj (**madder, maddest**) **1** (coloq, esp USA) ~ (**at/with sb**) furioso (com alguém) **2** ~ (**about sb/sth**) louco (por alguém/algo): go ~ ficar louco ▸ **like mad** (coloq) como um louco **madly** adv loucamente: ~ **in love with sb** perdidamente apaixonado por alguém **madness** s loucura

madam /ˈmædəm/ s [sing] (fml) senhora

maddening /ˈmædnɪŋ/ adj exasperante

made /meɪd/ pret, pp de MAKE

magazine /ˈmæɡəziːn; GB ˌmæɡəˈziːn/ s revista

maggot /ˈmæɡət/ s larva

magic /ˈmædʒɪk/ s magia: like ~ como que por magia • adj mágico **magical** adj mágico **magician** /məˈdʒɪʃn/ s mágico/a

magistrate /ˈmædʒɪstreɪt/ s magistrado/a, juiz: the magistrates' court o Juizado de Paz

magnet /ˈmæɡnət/ s ímã magnetic /mæɡˈnetɪk/ adj magnético **magnetism** /ˈmæɡnətɪzəm/ s magnetismo magnetize vt magnetizar

magnificent /mæɡˈnɪfɪsnt/ adj magnífico magnificence s magnificência

magnify /ˈmæɡnɪfaɪ/ vt, vi (pt, pp -ied) aumentar magnification s ampliação

magnifying glass s lupa

magnitude /ˈmæɡnɪtuːd; GB -tjuːd/ s magnitude

mahogany /məˈhɒɡəni/ adj, s mogno

maid /meɪd/ s empregada

maiden /ˈmeɪdn/ (tb **maid**) s (antiq) donzela

maiden name s nome de solteira NOTA Nos países de língua inglesa, muitas mulheres casadas usam só o nome do marido.

mail /meɪl/ s [U] correio: ~ **order** venda por correspondência NOTA No inglês britânico, **post** é mais usual do que **mail**, embora **mail** seja bastante comum, sobretudo em palavras compostas como **email, junk mail** e **air-mail**. • vt mandar pelo correio

mailbox /ˈmeɪlbɑːks/ (USA) s caixa do correio

mailman /ˈmeɪlmæn/ s (USA) (pl **-men**) carteiro

maim /meɪm/ vt mutilar

main /meɪn/ adj principal: the ~ **thing** o principal ▸ **in the main** em geral mainly • adv principalmente s **1** (água, gás) cano principal **2** (the mains) [pl] (GB) rede elétrica

mainland /ˈmeɪnlænd/ s terra firme, continente

main line s (Ferroviária) linha principal

mainstream /ˈmeɪnstriːm/ s tendência dominante

maintain /meɪnˈteɪn/ vt **1** manter **2** conservar: well maintained bem cuidado **3** sustentar

maintenance /ˈmeɪntənəns/ s **1** manutenção **2** pensão alimentícia

maize /meɪz/ (GB) s milho NOTA Milho cozido é **sweet-corn**.

majestic /məˈdʒestɪk/ adj majestoso

majesty /ˈmædʒəsti/ s (pl -ies) majestade

major /ˈmeɪdʒər/ adj **1** muito importante, principal: ~ **changes** mudanças consideráveis ◇ a ~ **problem** um problema sério **2** (*Mús*) maior ● **s 1** major **2** (*USA*) (*universidade*) matéria principal ● *vi* ~ **in sth** especializar-se em algo

majority /məˈdʒɒrəti; *GB* -ˈdʒɔːr-/ *s* (*pl* -**ies**) **1** maioria **2** [*antes de substantivo*] majoritário

make /meɪk/ *s* marca (*carros*, *etc.*) ● *vt* (*pt, pp* **made**) **1** fazer: ~ *a noise/hole/list* fazer barulho/um buraco/uma lista ◇ ~ *plans/an offer* fazer planos/uma oferta ◇ ~ *sb a coffee* fazer um café para alguém ◇ ~ *an impression* impressionar ◇ ~ *a note of sth* anotar algo ◇ ~ *a mistake* cometer um erro ◇ ~ *an excuse for* dar uma desculpa ◇ ~ *sth (from/out of sth)* fazer algo (com/de algo): *made in Japan* fabricado no Japão **3** ~ **sth into sth** converter algo em algo ◇ **4** ~ **sb/sth + adj/subst**: ~ *sb angry* irritar alguém ◇ ~ *things worse* piorar as coisas ◇ *He made my life hell.* Ele tornou minha vida um inferno. **5** ~ **sb/sth (do) sth** fazer algo de alguém; com que alguém/algo faça algo NOTA A menos que **make** esteja na voz passiva, o verbo que o segue no infinitivo não leva to: *I let ~ him do it.* ◇ *You've made her feel guilty.* ◇ *He was made to wait at the police station.* **6** tornar-se: *He'll ~ a good teacher.* Ele vai ser um bom professor. **7** (*dinheiro*) ganhar **8** (*coloq*) (*conseguir*): *Can you ~ it (to the party)?* Você vai poder vir (à festa)? ▶ **make do with sth** contentar-se (com algo) **make it** (*coloq*) triunfar **make the most of sth** aproveitar algo ao máximo NOTA Para expressões com **make**, ver o substantivo, adjetivo, etc., p. ex. **make love** em LOVE. ■ **be made for sb/each other** ser feito para alguém/serem feitos um para o outro **make for sb/sth** dirigir-se para alguém/algo: *What do you ~ of it?* O que você acha disso? **make for sth** contribuir para (melhorar) algo **make sth of sb/sth** ter uma opinião sobre alguém/algo **make off (with sth)** fugir (com algo) **make sb/sth out 1** compreender alguém/algo **2** distinguir alguém/algo: ~ *sb's writing* decifrar a letra de alguém **make sth out: ~ *out a check* fazer um cheque **make up (with sb)** fazer as pazes (com alguém) **make (sb)/(yourself) up** maquilar alguém, maquilar-se **make sth up 1** constituir algo **2** inventar algo

make up for sth compensar algo

maker /ˈmeɪkər/ *s* fabricante

makeshift /ˈmeɪkʃɪft/ *adj* improvisado

make-up *s* [*U*] **1** maquilagem **2** constituição **3** caráter

making /ˈmeɪkɪŋ/ *s* fabricação ▶ **be the making of sb** ser a chave do êxito de alguém **have the makings of sth 1** ter potencial para algo **2** ter as condições para tornar-se algo

male /meɪl/ *adj* **1** masculino NOTA Aplica-se às características físicas dos homens: *The voice is deeper than the female.* **2** macho → FEMALE ● *s* macho

malice /ˈmælɪs/ *s* maldade **malicious** /məˈlɪʃəs/ *adj* mal-intencionado

malignant /məˈlɪgnənt/ *adj* maligno

mall /mɔːl/ *s* centro comercial

malnutrition /ˌmælnuːˈtrɪʃn; *GB* -ˈnjuː-/ *s* desnutrição

malt /mɔːlt/ *s* malte

mammal /ˈmæml/ *s* mamífero

mammoth /ˈmæməθ/ *s* mamute ● *adj* colossal

man /mæn/ *s* (*pl* **men**) homem: *a young* ~ um rapaz ▶ **the man in/on the street** o cidadão comum NOTA **Man** e **mankind** são usados com o significado geral de "todos os homens e mulheres". Mas muitos consideram esse uso discriminatório e preferem usar **humanity**, **the human race** (singular) ou **humans**, **human beings**, **people** (plural). ● *vt* (**-nn-**) **1** prover de pessoal **2** tripular

manage /ˈmænɪdʒ/ **1** *vt* gerenciar **2** *vt* (*propriedades*) administrar **3** *vi* arranjar-se: *I can't ~ on $50 a week.* Não consigo viver com 50 dólares por semana. **4** *vt, vi*: ~ *to do sth* conseguir fazer algo ◇ *Can you ~ all of it?* Você dá conta disso tudo? ◇ *Can you ~ six o'clock?* Dá para você vir às seis? ◇ *I couldn't ~ another mouthful.* Não pude dar nem mais uma garfada. **manageable** *adj* **1** manejável **2** acessível, dócil

management /ˈmænɪdʒmənt/ *s* direção, gestão: ◇ *a ~ committee* um comitê/conselho administrativo ◇ *a ~ consultant* um consultor em administração

manager /ˈmænɪdʒər/ *s* **1** diretor/a, gerente **2** administrador/a **3** (*Teat*) empresário/a **4** (*Esporte*) técnico/a **managerial** /ˌmænəˈdʒɪəriəl/ *adj* admini-

strativo, gerencial
managing director s diretor/a geral
mandate /'mændeɪt/ s mandato
mandatory /'mændətɔːri; GB -təri/ adj obrigatório
mane /meɪn/ s 1 crina 2 juba
maneuver /mə'nuːvər/ s manobra
manfully /'mænfəli/ adv valentemente
mangle /'mæŋgl/ vt mutilar
manhood /'mænhʊd/ s virilidade
mania /'meɪniə/ s mania **maniac** adj, s maníaco/a
manic /'mænɪk/ adj 1 maníaco 2 frenético
manicure /'mænɪkjʊər/ s manicure
manifest /'mænɪfest/ vt manifestar **manifestation** s manifestação **manifestly** adv visivelmente
manifesto /ˌmænɪ'festoʊ/ s (pl ~s) manifesto
manifold /'mænɪfoʊld/ adj (fml) múltiplo
manipulate /mə'nɪpjuleɪt/ vt manipular **manipulation** s manipulação **manipulative** adj manipulador
mankind /ˌmæn'kaɪnd/ s humanidade → MAN
manly /'mænli/ adj (-ier, -iest) másculo
man-made adj artificial
manned /mænd/ adj tripulado
mannequin /'mænɪkən/ s manequim
manner /'mænər/ s 1 maneira 2 atitude, comportamento 3 (manners) [pl] educação: good/bad manners boa/má educação ◇ He has no manners. Ele é muito mal-educado.
mannerism /'mænərɪzəm/ s maneirismo
manoeuvre (GB) = MANEUVER
manor /'mænər/ s 1 (terra) senhorio 2 (tb ~ house) solar
manpower /'mænpaʊər/ s mão-de-obra
mansion /'mænʃn/ s mansão
manslaughter /'mænslɔːtər/ s homicídio involuntário
mantelpiece /'mæntlpiːs/ s consolo da lareira
manual /'mænjuəl/ adj manual ● s manual **manually** adv manualmente
manufacture /ˌmænju'fæktʃər/ vt fabricar **manufacturer** s fabricante
manure /mə'nʊər/ s estrume

manuscript /'mænjuskrɪpt/ adj, s manuscrito
many /'meni/ adj, pron muito/a, -os/as: In ~ ways, I regret it. Sob vários pontos de vista, lamento o que aconteceu. ◇ ~ a time muitas vezes **NOTA** Muito se traduz conforme o substantivo ao qual acompanha ou substitui. Em frases afirmativas usa-se **a lot (of)**: She's got a lot of money. ◇ Lots of people are poor. Em frases negativas e interrogativas usa-se **many** ou **a lot of** quando o substantivo é contável: I haven't seen ~ women as bosses. Usa-se **much** ou **a lot of** quando o substantivo é não-contável: I haven't eaten much (food). → **MUITO** ▶ **a good/great many** muitíssimos
map /mæp/ s mapa ▶ **put sb/sth on the map** tornar alguém/algo conhecido ◇ **Quick ~!** Marcha acelerada! ◇ **~ sth out** 1 planejar algo 2 (idéia) expor algo
maple /'meɪpl/ s bordo
marathon /'mærəθən; GB -θən/ s maratona: The meeting was a real ~. A reunião foi exaustiva.
marble /'mɑːrbl/ s 1 mármore 2 bola de gude
March /mɑːrtʃ/ s (abrev **Mar.**) março → MAY
march /mɑːrtʃ/ vi 1 marchar: ~ in entrar marchando ◇ ~ up! Marcha acelerada! ◇ ~ up to sb abordar alguém com resolução 2 ~ sb away/off conduzir alguém à força 3 ~ past (sb) desfilar (diante de alguém) ▶ **get your marching orders** ser despedido
mare /meər/ s égua
margarine /'mɑːrdʒərən; GB ˌmɑːdʒə'riːn/ s margarina
margin /'mɑːrdʒɪn/ s margem **marginal** adj 1 menor (importância) 2 (notas) de margem **marginally** adv ligeiramente
marina /mə'riːnə/ s marina
marine /mə'riːn/ adj 1 marinho 2 marítimo ● s fuzileiro naval
marital /'mærɪtl/ adj conjugal: ~ status estado civil
maritime /'mærɪtaɪm/ adj marítimo
mark /mɑːrk/ s 1 marca 2 sinal 3 (GB, Educ) nota 4 marco (moeda) ▶ **be up to the mark** (GB) corresponder às expectativas **make your mark** ganhar nome **on your marks, (get) set, go!** ficar em posição, preparar, vai! ● vt 1 marcar 2 assinalar 3 (exames) corrigir ▶ **mark time 1**

(*Mil*) marcar passo **2** fazer hora **mark my words** pode escrever o que eu estou dizendo ● **mark sth up/down** aumentar/baixar o preço de algo **marked** /mɑːkt/ *adj* marcante **markedly** /ˈmɑːkɪdli/ *adv* marcadamente

marker /ˈmɑːkər/ *s* marcador: *a ~ buoy* uma bóia de sinalização

market /ˈmɑːkɪt/ *s* mercado: *~ research* pesquisa de mercado ▶ **in the market for sth** interessado em comprar algo **on the market** no mercado: *put sth on the ~* colocar algo à venda ● *vt* **1** vender **2** *~ sth (to sb)* promover a venda de algo (para alguém) **marketable** *adj* comercializável

marketing /ˈmɑːkɪtɪŋ/ *s* marketing

marketplace /ˈmɑːkɪtpleɪs/ *s* mercado

marmalade /ˈmɑːməleɪd/ *s* geléia (*frutos cítricos*)

maroon /məˈruːn/ *adj, s* vinho (*cor*)

marooned /məˈruːnd/ *adj* abandonado (p. ex. numa ilha deserta)

marquee /mɑːˈkiː/ *s* (*USA*) toldo

marriage /ˈmærɪdʒ/ *s* **1** matrimônio **2** casamento → CASAMENTO

married /ˈmærid/ *adj* *~ (to sb)* casado (com alguém): *get ~* casar-se ◇ *a ~ couple* um casal

marrow /ˈmæroʊ/ *s* **1** medula **2** abóbora

marry /ˈmæri/ *vt, vi* (*pt, pp* **-ied**) casar(-se)

Mars /mɑːz/ *s* Marte

marsh /mɑːʃ/ *s* pântano

marshal /ˈmɑːʃl/ *s* **1** marechal **2** (*USA*) espécie de xerife ● *vt* (**-l-**, *GB* **-ll-**) **1** (*tropas*) formar **2** (*idéias, dados*) ordenar

marshy /ˈmɑːʃi/ *adj* (**-ier, -iest**) pantanoso

martial /ˈmɑːʃl/ *adj* marcial

Martian /ˈmɑːʃn/ *adj, s* marciano

martyr /ˈmɑːtər/ *s* mártir **martyrdom** *s* martírio

marvel /ˈmɑːvl/ *s* prodígio ● *vi* (**-l-**, *GB* **-ll-**) *~ at sth* maravilhar-se com algo **marvelous** (*GB* **-ll-**) *adj* excelente: *have a ~ time* divertir-se à beça ◇ (*That's*) *~!* Que maravilha!

Marxism /ˈmɑːksɪzəm/ *s* marxismo **Marxist** *adj, s* marxista

marzipan /ˈmɑːzɪpæn/ *s* marzipã

mascara /mæˈskærə; *GB* mæˈskɑːrə/ *s* rímel

mascot /ˈmæskɑt/ *s* mascote

masculine /ˈmæskjəlɪn/ *adj, s* masculino **NOTA Masculine** se refere a qualidades consideradas típicas do homem. **masculinity** /ˌmæskjuˈlɪmɪti/ *s* masculinidade

mash /mæʃ/ *s* (*GB, coloq*) purê (de batatas) ● *vt* **1** *~ sth (up)* esmagar algo **2** fazer purê de

mask /mæsk; *GB* mɑːsk/ *s* máscara, disfarce ● *vt* **1** mascarar **2** tapar **3** disfarçar **masked** *adj* **1** mascarado **2** encapuzado

mason /ˈmeɪsn/ *s* **1** pedreiro **2** (*tb* **Mason**) maçom **masonic** (*tb* **Masonic**) /məˈsɑnɪk/ *adj* maçônico

masonry /ˈmeɪsənri/ *s* alvenaria

masquerade /ˌmæskəˈreɪd; *GB* ˌmɑːsk-/ *s* farsa ● *vi* *~ as sth* fazer-se passar por algo; disfarçar-se de algo

mass /mæs/ *s* **1** *~ (of sth)* massa (de algo) **2** montão, grande quantidade **3** [*função adjetiva*]: *a ~ grave* uma sepultura coletiva ◇ *~ hysteria* histeria coletiva ◇ *~ media* meios de comunicação de massa **4 (the masses)** [*pl*] as massas **5** (**Mass**) (*Relig, Mús*) Missa ▶ **be a mass of sth** estar coberto/cheio de algo **the (great) mass of...** a (grande) maioria de... ● *vt, vi* **1** reunir (-se) (*em massa*) **2** (*Mil*) concentrar(-se)

massacre /ˈmæsəkər/ *s* massacre ● *vt* massacrar

massage /məˈsɑʒ; *GB* ˈmæsɑːʒ/ *vt* fazer massagem em ● *s* massagem

massive /ˈmæsɪv/ *adj* **1** enorme, monumental **2** maciço **massively** *adv* extremamente

mass production *s* produção em massa **mass produce** *vt* produzir em massa

mast /mæst; *GB* mɑːst/ *s* **1** mastro **2** (*televisão*) torre

master /ˈmæstər; *GB* ˈmɑːs-/ *s* **1** dono, patrão **2** mestre **3** (*Náut*) capitão **4** (*filme*) original **5** *~ bedroom* quarto principal ◇ *a ~ plan* um plano infalível ● *vt* **1** dominar **2** controlar **masterful** *adj* **1** autoritário **2** (*tb* **masterly** /ˈmæstərli/) magistral

mastermind /ˈmæstərmaɪnd; *GB* ˈmɑːs-/ *s* cabeça ● *vt* planejar

masterpiece /ˈmæstərpiːs; *GB* ˈmɑːs-/ *s* obra-prima

Master's (*tb ~ degree*) *s* mestrado

mastery /ˈmæstəri; *GB* ˈmɑːs-/ *s* **1** domínio **2** controle

masturbate /ˈmæstərbeɪt/ *vi*

masturbar-se masturbation s masturbação

mat /mæt/ s 1 esteira, capacho 2 colchonete 3 descanso para pratos 4 emaranhamento

match /mætʃ/ s 1 (*Esporte*) partida 2 igual 3 complemento 4 fósforo ▶ a good match um bom partido **find/meet your match** encontrar alguém à sua altura ● 1 vt, vi combinar com 2 vt fazer jogo (com): *matching shoes and handbag* sapatos e bolsa da mesma cor 3 vt igualar ■ **match up** coincidir **match up to sb/sth** equiparar-se a alguém/algo **match sth up (with sth)** juntar algo (a algo)

matchbox /ˈmætʃbɒks/ s caixa de fósforos

mate /meɪt/ s 1 (*GB, coloq*) colega, pessoa, companheiro/a 2 ajudante 3 (*Náut*) imediato 4 (*Zool*) macho ou fêmea 5 (*tb* check-mate) s xeque-mate ● vt, vi acasalar(-se)

material /məˈtɪəriəl/ s 1 material: *raw materials* matérias-primas 2 tecido ♢ → TECIDO ● adj material **materially** adv substancialmente

materialism /məˈtɪəriəlɪzəm/ s materialismo **materialist** s materialista **materialistic** /məˌtɪəriəˈlɪstɪk/ adj materialista

materialize /məˈtɪəriəlaɪz/ vi concretizar-se

maternal /məˈtɜːnl/ adj 1 maternal 2 (*familiares*) materno

maternity /məˈtɜːnəti/ s maternidade

mathematics /ˌmæθəˈmætɪks/ (*coloq* math, *GB* maths) s [*sing*] matemática **mathematical** adj matemático **mathematician** /ˌmæθəməˈtɪʃn/ s matemático/a

matinée /ˈmætɪneɪ; *GB* ˈmætɪneɪ/ s matinê

mating /ˈmeɪtɪŋ/ s acasalamento: ~ *season* época de cio

matrimony /ˈmætrɪməʊni; *GB* -məni/ s (*fml*) matrimônio **matrimonial** /ˌmætrɪˈməʊniəl/ adj matrimonial

matron /ˈmeɪtrən/ s (*GB, antiq*) enfermeira-chefe

matt (*USA* matte) /mæt/ adj 1 fosco 2 (*tb* paint) tinta mate

matted /ˈmætɪd/ adj emaranhado

matter /ˈmætə(r)/ s 1 assunto 2 (*Fís*) matéria 3 material: *printed* ~ impressos ▶ **a matter of hours, days, etc.** coisa de horas, dias, etc. **a matter of opinion/** **life and death** uma questão de opinião/ de vida ou morte **as a matter of course** como de costume **as a matter of fact** na verdade **be the matter (with sb/sth)** (*coloq*) estar incomodando alguém/algo: *What's the ~ with him?* O que ele tem? ♢ *Is anything the ~?* O que é que há? ♢ *What's the ~ with my dress?* O que há de errado com o meu vestido? **for that matter** quanto a isso **no matter who, what, etc.**: *no* ~ *what he says* não importa o que ele disser ♢ *no* ~ *how rich he is* por mais rico que ele seja ♢ *no* ~ *what* aconteça o que acontecer **take matters into your own hands** agir por conta própria ● vi importar

matter-of-fact adj 1 prosaico 2 (*pessoa*) objetivo 3 prático

mattress /ˈmætrəs/ s colchão

mature /məˈtʊə(r); *GB* -ˈtʃʊə(r)/ adj 1 maduro 2 (*Com*) vencido ● 1 vi amadurecer 2 vi (*Com*) vencer 3 vt tornar maduro **maturity** s maturidade

maul /mɔːl/ vt 1 maltratar 2 (*fera*) estraçalhar

mausoleum /ˌmɔːsəˈliːəm/ s mausoléu

mauve /məʊv/ adj, s malva

maverick /ˈmævərɪk/ s inconformista

maxim /ˈmæksɪm/ s máxima

maximize /ˈmæksɪmaɪz/ vt maximizar

maximum /ˈmæksɪməm/ s (*pl* maxima /ˈmæksɪmə/) (*abrev* max.) máximo ● adj máximo

May /meɪ/ s maio: *on* ~ *1st* no dia primeiro de maio ♢ *every/next* ~ todo o ano em maio/em maio do ano que vem NOTA Os nomes dos meses se escrevem com maiúscula.

may /meɪ/ v modal (*pt* might *neg* might not *ou* mightn't, *GB*)) NOTA May é um verbo modal, seguido de infinitivo sem to. As orações interrogativas e negativas são formadas sem o auxiliar do. Tem apenas duas formas: presente, may, e passado, might. 1 (*permissão*) poder: *You* ~ *as well go home.* Vale mais a pena você ir para casa. NOTA Para pedir permissão, may é mais polido do que can, embora can seja muito mais usual: *Can I come in?* ♢ *May I get down from the table?* ♢ *I'll take a seat, if I* ~. No passado usa-se could muito mais do que might: *She asked if she could come in.* 2 (*possibili-*

dade) pode ser que → PODER¹
► **be that as it may** seja como for

maybe /'meɪbi/ *adv* talvez

mayhem /'meɪhem/ *s* caos

mayonnaise /ˌmeɪə'neɪz; *GB* 'meɪəneɪz/ *s* maionese

mayor /'meɪər; *GB* meə(r)/ *s* prefeito/a **mayoress** /'meə'res/ *s* **1** (*tb* lady ~) prefeita **2** esposa do prefeito

maze /meɪz/ *s* labirinto

me /mi:/ *pron* **1** [*complemento*] me **2** [*depois de prep*] mim **3** [*depois do verbo* be] eu: *Hello, it's me.* Oi, sou eu.

meadow /'medəʊ/ *s* prado

meager (*GB* -**gre**) /'mi:gər/ *adj* escasso, magro

meal /mi:l/ *s* refeição ► **make a meal of sth** (*coloq*) perder tempo com algo

mean /mi:n/ *s* meio-termo **2** (*Mat*) média ● *adj* (~**er**, ~**est**) **1** ~ **(to sb)** mesquinho (com alguém) **2** (*GB*) avarento **3** médio ● *vt* (*pt, pp* meant /ment/) **1** querer dizer **2** ~ **sth (to sb)** significar algo (para alguém): *That name doesn't ~ anything to me.* Esse nome não me diz nada. **3** implicar: *His new job means him traveling more.* Seu novo emprego acarreta mais viagem. **4** pretender: *I didn't ~ to.* Não tive a intenção. ◊ *I meant to wash the car.* Era para eu lavar o carro. **5** falar a sério: *She meant it as a joke.* Ela falou de brincadeira. ► **be meant for each other** serem feitos um para o outro **I mean** (*coloq*) quero dizer: *We went there on Tuesday, I – Thursday.* Fomos lá na terça, quero dizer, quinta. **mean business** estar para brincadeiras **mean well** ter boas intenções

meander /mi'ændər/ *vi* **1** serpentear **2** perambular **3** (*conversa*) divagar

meaning /'mi:nɪŋ/ *s* significado **meaningful** *adj* significativo **meaningless** *adj* sem sentido

means /mi:nz/ *s* (*pl* means) **1** meio: *a ~ to an end* um meio para se atingir um fim **2** [*pl*] recursos (*financeiros*) ► **by all means** claro que sim

meantime /'mi:ntaɪm/ *adv* ► **in the meantime** nesse ínterim

meanwhile /'mi:nwaɪl/ *adv* enquanto isso

measles /'mi:zlz/ *s* sarampo

measurable /'meʒərəbl/ *adj* **1** mensurável **2** notável

measure /'meʒər/ *vt, vi* ~ **(sb/sth)**

(up) medir (alguém/algo): ~ *sb up for a suit* tirar as medidas de alguém para fazer um terno ■ **measure up (to sth)** estar à altura (de algo) ● *s* medida: *make sth to* ~ fazer algo sob medida ► **for good measure** para arrematar **half measures**: *do things by half measures* fazer as coisas pela metade

measured /'meʒərd/ *adj* **1** comedido **2** pausado

measurement /'meʒərmənt/ *s* **1** medição **2** medida

meat /mi:t/ *s* carne

meatball /'mi:tbɔ:l/ *s* almôndega

meaty /'mi:ti/ *adj* (-**ier**, -**iest**) **1** carnudo **2** substancial

mechanic /mə'kænɪk/ *s* mecânico/a **mechanical** *adj* mecânico **mechanically** *adv* mecanicamente: *be ~ minded* ter jeito para máquinas

mechanics /mə'kænɪks/ *s* **1** [*sing*] mecânica **2** (**the mechanics**) [*pl*] mecanismo

mechanism /'mekənɪzəm/ *s* mecanismo

medal /'medl/ *s* medalha **medalist** (*GB* -**ll**-) *s* (*Esporte*) ganhador/a de medalha

medallion /mə'dæliən/ *s* medalhão

meddle /'medl/ *vi* (*pej*) **1** intrometer-se **2** ~ **with sth** mexer em algo

media /'mi:diə/ *s* **1** (**the media**) [*pl*] os meios de comunicação, mídia: ~ *studies* comunicação (*disciplina*) **2** *plural de* MEDIUM

mediaeval = MEDIEVAL

mediate /'mi:dieɪt/ *vi* mediar **mediation** *s* mediação **mediator** *s* mediador/a

medic /'medɪk/ *s* (*coloq*) **1** médico/a **2** estudante de medicina

medical /'medɪkl/ *adj* **1** médico: ~ *student* estudante de medicina **2** clínico ● *s* exame médico

medication /ˌmedɪ'keɪʃn/ *s* medicação

medicine /'medɪsn; *GB* 'medsn/ *s* **1** medicina **medicinal** /mə'dɪsɪnl/ *adj* medicinal

medieval /ˌmedi'i:vl/ *adj* medieval

mediocre /ˌmi:di'əʊkər/ *adj* medíocre **mediocrity** /ˌmi:di'ɑkrəti/ *s* **1** mediocridade **2** (*pessoa*) medíocre

meditate /'medɪteɪt/ *vi* meditar **meditation** *s* meditação

medium /'mi:diəm/ *s* **1** (*pl* media) meio-termo **2** (*pessoa*) médium **3** (*pl* media) meio ● *adj* (tamanho) médio

medley /'medli/ s miscelânea

meek /mi:k/ adj (~er, ~est) manso **meekly** adv submissamente

meet /mi:t/ s 1 (esp USA) (Esporte) competição 2 (GB) reunião de caçadores • (pt, pp **met**) 1 vt, vi ~ (up) (with sb) encontrar, encontrar-se (com alguém): Our eyes met. Nossos olhares se cruzaram. ◊ Will you ~ me at the station? Você vai me esperar na estação? 2 vi ~ (with sb) reunir-se (com alguém) 3 vi conhecer(-se): I'd like you to meet... Gostaria de lhe apresentar... 4 vt, vi enfrentar(-se) 5 vt (requisito) satisfazer: They failed to ~ payments on their loan. Não conseguiram pagar o empréstimo. ▶meet sb's eye olhar alguém nos olhos

meeting /'mi:tɪŋ/ s 1 encontro 2 reunião 3 (Esporte) competição 4 (Pol) assembléia

megaphone /'megəfoun/ s megafone

melancholy /'melənkəli/ s melancolia • adj 1 melancólico 2 triste

mêlée /'meɪleɪ; GB 'meleɪ/ s briga, tumulto

mellow /'meloʊ/ adj (~er, ~est) 1 (cor, etc.) suave 2 (som) melodioso 3 (vinho) envelhecido 4 (atitude) amadurecido 5 (coloq) alegre (devido à bebida) • 1 vt, vi (pessoa) abrandar(-se) 2 vi (vinho) envelhecer

melodious /mə'loʊdiəs/ adj melodioso

melodrama /'melədrɑːmə/ s melodrama **melodramatic** /ˌmelədrə'mætɪk/ adj melodramático

melody /'melədi/ s (pl ~ies) melodia **melodic** /mə'lɑdɪk/ adj melódico

melon /'melən/ s melão

melt /melt/ 1 vt, vi derreter: melting point ponto de fusão 2 vi desfazer-se 3 vt, vi ~ (away): ~ (sth) (down) fundir(-se) 4 vt dissolver 5 vt, vi enternecer(-se) **melting** s 1 derretimento 2 fundição

melting pot s cadinho (raças, culturas, etc.) ▶in the melting pot em processo de mudança

member /'membər/ s 1 (tb Anat) membro: ~ of Parliament deputado 2 (clube) sócio/a membership's 1 apply for ~ candidatar-se a sócio ◊ ~ card carteira de sócio 2 (número de) sócios

membrane /'membreɪn/ s membrana

memento /mə'mentoʊ/ s (pl ~es ou ~s) lembrança

memo /'memoʊ/ s (pl ~s) memorando: an inter-office ~ uma circular interna

memoirs /'memwɑrz/ s memórias

memorabilia /ˌmemərə'bɪliə/ s [pl] recordações

memorable /'memərəbl/ adj memorável

memorandum /ˌmemə'rændəm/ s (pl -anda /-də/) 1 memorando 2 nota 3 (Jur) minuta

memorial /mə'mɔːriəl/ s ~ (to sb/ sth) monumento comemorativo (de alguém/algo)

memorize /'meməraɪz/ vt decorar

memory /'meməri/ s (pl ~ies) 1 memória: from ~ de cabeça 2 recordação

men /men/ plural de MAN

menace /'menəs/ s 1 ~ (to sb/sth) ameaça (para alguém/algo) 2 (a menace) (coloq) uma praga • vt ameaçar **menacing** adj ameaçador

menagerie /mə'nædʒəri/ s coleção de feras para exibição

mend /mend/ 1 vt consertar 2 vi recuperar-se ▶mend your ways emendar-se • s remendo ▶on the mend (coloq) melhorando **mending** s 1 reparo (roupa) 2 roupas por consertar

menfolk /'menfoʊk/ s os homens (da família)

meningitis /ˌmenɪn'dʒaɪtɪs/ s meningite

menopause /'menəpɔːz/ s menopausa

menstruation /ˌmenstru'eɪʃn/ s menstruação **menstrual** /'menstruəl/ adj menstrual

menswear /'menzweər/ s roupa masculina

mental /'mentl/ adj 1 mental: ~ hospital hospital psiquiátrico 2 (coloq) pirado **mentally** adv mentalmente: ~ ill/disturbed doente mental

mentality /men'tæləti/ s (pl ~ies) mentalidade

mention /'menʃn/ vt mencionar: worth mentioning digno de nota ▶don't mention it não há de quê not to mention... para não falar de... • s menção

mentor /'mentɔːr/ s mentor/a

menu /'menjuː/ s menu

meow /mi'aʊ/ interj miau • s miado • vi miar

mercantile /ˈmɜːkəntiːl; GB -tɪl, -taɪl/ *adj* mercantil

mercenary /ˈmɜːrsəneri; GB -nəri/ *adj* **1** mercenário **2** interesseiro ● *s* (*pl* **-ies**) mercenário/a

merchandise /ˈmɜːrtʃəndaɪz; GB -daɪs/ *s* [U] mercadoria(s) **merchandising** *s* promoção

merchant /ˈmɜːrtʃənt/ *s* **1** atacadista (*que comercia com o exterior*) **2** (*Hist*) mercador **3** ~ **bank** banco mercantil ◊ ~ **navy** marinha mercante

Mercury /ˈmɜːrkjəri/ *s* Mercúrio

mercury /ˈmɜːrkjəri/ *s* mercúrio

mercy /ˈmɜːrsi/ *s* **1** piedade, misericórdia: ~ *killing* eutanásia **2** *It's a ~ that...* É uma sorte que... ▶ **at the mercy of sb/sth** à mercê de alguém/algo **merciful** *adj* ~ **(to/towards sb)** misericordioso (com alguém) **2** (*sucesso*) afortunado **mercifully** *adv* **1** misericordiosamente **2** felizmente **merciless** *adj* ~ **(to/towards sb)** impiedoso (com alguém)

mere /mɪər/ *adj* mero, simples: *He's a ~ child.* Ele não passa de uma criança. ◊ *the ~ thought of him* só de pensar nele **merely** *adv* simplesmente, apenas

merge /mɜːrdʒ/ *vt, vi* **1** (*Com*) fundir(-se) **2** mesclar(-se), unir(-se) **merger** *s* fusão (*empresas*)

meringue /məˈræŋ/ *s* merengue

merit /ˈmerɪt/ *s* mérito ● *vt* (*fml*) merecer

mermaid /ˈmɜːrmeɪd/ *s* sereia

merry /ˈmeri/ *adj* (**-ier, -iest**) **1** alegre: *Merry Christmas!* Feliz Natal! **2** (*coloq*) alegre (*devido à bebida*) ▶ **make merry** (*antiq*) divertir-se **merriment** *s* (*fml*) regozijo

merry-go-round *s* carrossel

mesh /meʃ/ *s* **1** malha: *wire ~* aramado **2** (*Mec*) engrenagem **3** rede ● *vi* ~ **(with sth) 1** encaixar (em algo) **2** encaixar (em algo)

mesmerize /ˈmezməraɪz/ *vt* hipnotizar

mess /mes/ *s* **1** bagunça **2** (*coloq*) cocô **3** confusão **4** desleixado **5** (*Mil*) (*USA tb* ~ **hall**) refeitório ● *vt* (*USA, coloq*) bagunçar ■ **mess about/around 1** vadiar **2** fazer algo de forma despreocupada **mess sb around**; **mess about/around with sb/sth** enrolar alguém, mexer com algo **mess sb up** (*coloq*) fazer mal a alguém (*emocionalmente*) **mess sth up 1** sujar, desarrumar

algo: *Don't ~ up my hair!* Não me despenteie! **2** fazer algo mal feito **mess with sb/sth** mexer com alguém/algo

message /ˈmesɪdʒ/ *s* **1** recado **2** mensagem ▶ **get the message** (*coloq*) sacar

messenger /ˈmesɪndʒər/ *s* mensageiro/a

Messiah (*tb* **messiah**) /məˈsaɪə/ *s* Messias

messy /ˈmesi/ *adj* (**-ier, -iest**) **1** sujo **2** desarrumado **3** (*fig*) enrolado

met /met/ *pret, pp de* MEET

metabolism /məˈtæbəlɪzəm/ *s* metabolismo

metal /ˈmetl/ *s* metal: *metalwork* trabalho em metal **metallic** /məˈtælɪk/ *adj* metálico

metamorphose /ˌmetəˈmɔːrfouz/ *vt, vi* metamorfosear(-se) **metamorphosis** /ˌmetəˈmɔːrfəsɪs/ *s* (*pl* **-oses** /-əsiːz/) metamorfose

metaphor /ˈmetəfɔːr; GB -fə(r)/ *s* metáfora **metaphorical** /ˌmetəˈfɔːrɪkl; GB -ˈfɒr-/ *adj* metafórico

metaphysics /ˌmetəˈfɪzɪks/ *s* [*sing*] metafísica **metaphysical** *adj* metafísico

meteor /ˈmiːtiər/ *s* meteoro **meteoric** /ˌmiːtiˈɔːrɪk; GB -ˈɒr-/ *adj* meteórico

meteorite /ˈmiːtiəraɪt/ *s* meteorito

meter /ˈmiːtər/ *s* **1** (*abrev* **m**) metro → *Ver pág.* 224 **2** medidor **metric** /ˈmetrɪk/ ● *adj* métrico *vt* medir

methane /ˈmiːθeɪn/ *s* metano

method /ˈmeθəd/ *s* método **methodical** /məˈθɒdɪkl/ *adj* metódico **methodology** *s* metodologia

Methodist /ˈmeθədɪst/ *adj, s* metodista

methylated spirits /ˌmeθəleɪtɪd ˈspɪrɪts/ (*GB, coloq* **meths**) *s* álcool metílico

meticulous /məˈtɪkjələs/ *adj* meticuloso

metre (*GB*) = METER (1)

metric /ˈmetrɪk/ → METER

metropolis /məˈtrɒpəlɪs/ *s* metrópole **metropolitan** /ˌmetrəˈpɒlɪtən/ *adj* metropolitano

mice /maɪs/ *plural de* MOUSE

micro /ˈmaɪkroʊ/ (*tb* **microcomputer**) *s* microcomputador

microbe /ˈmaɪkroʊb/ *s* micróbio

microchip /ˈmaɪkroʊtʃɪp/ *s* (micro)chip

microcosm /ˈmaɪkrəkɒzəm/ *s* microcosmo

micro-organism *s* microorganismo

microphone /'maikrəfəʊn/ s
microfone

microprocessor /,maikrəʊ-
'prəʊsesər/ s microprocessador

microscope /'maikrəskəʊp/
s microscópio **microscopic**
/,maikrə'skɒpik/ adj micro-
scópico

microwave /'maikrəweiv/ s 1
microonda 2 (tb ~ oven) (forno
de) microondas

mid /mid/ adj: in mid-July em
meados de julho ◊ *mid-morn-
ing* (no) meio da manhã ◊ *mid-
life crisis* crise da meia-idade

mid-air s: in ~ em pleno ar
◊ *leave sth in ~* deixar algo sem
resolver

midday /,mid'dei/ s meio-dia

middle /'midl/ s 1 (**the middle**)
o meio 2 (coloq) cintura ▶ **in the
middle of nowhere** (coloq)
no fim do mundo ● adj central,
médio: ~ *management* executi-
vos de nível intermediário
▶ (**follow/take**) **a middle course**
(seguir/ficar em) um meio-
termo **the middle ground** a ala
moderada

middle age s meia-idade **middle-aged** adj de meia-idade

middle class s classe média
middle-class adj de classe
média

middleman /'midlmæn/ s (pl
-**men**) intermediário

middle name s segundo nome
NOTA Nos países de língua
inglesa, geralmente usam-se
dois nomes e um sobrenome.

middle-of-the-road adj
moderado

middleweight /'midlweit/ s
(Boxe) peso médio

midfield /mid'fi:ld/ s meio-de-
campo **midfielder** s (jogador de)
meio-de-campo

midge /midʒ/ s mosquito

midget /'midʒit/ s anão, anã

midnight /'midnait/ s meia-noite

midriff /'midrif/ s abdome

midst /midst/ s meio: in our ~
entre nós

midsummer /,mid'samər/ s
época do solstício de verão (21
de junho)

midway /,mid'wei/ adv no meio,
meio caminho

midweek /,mid'wi:k/ s o meio da
semana ● adv no meio da
semana

midwife /'midwaif/ s (pl -**wives**
/-waivz/) parteira **midwifery**
/mid'wifəri/ s trabalho de parteira

midwinter /,mid'wintər/ s época
do solstício de inverno (21 de
dezembro)

miffed /mift/ adj (coloq)
chateado

might¹ /mait/ v modal (neg **might
not** ou **mightn't** /'maitnt/) **1** pret
de **MAY** **2** (possibilidade) poder
(ser que): I ~ be able to. Talvez
eu possa. **3** (fml): Might I make
a suggestion? Eu poderia fazer
uma sugestão? ◊ And who ~
she be? E quem será ela? ◊
You ~ have told me! Você
poderia ter me dito! → **MAY**,
PODER¹

might² /mait/ s [U] força, poder:
military ~ poderio militar
mightily adv extremamente
mighty adj (-ier, -iest) **1** poderoso, potente **2** imenso

migraine /'maigrein; GB
'mi:grein/ s enxaqueca

migrant /'maigrənt/ adj **1**
migrante **2** (ave) migratório ● s
migrante

migrate /mai'greit; GB mai'greit/
vi migrar **migratory** /'mai-
grətɔri; GB mai'greitəri/ adj
migratório

mike /maik/ s microfone

mild /maild/ adj (~er, ~est) **1**
(caráter) meigo **2** (clima)
ameno **3** (sabor, etc.) suave **4**
(enfermidade, castigo) leve
mildly adv levemente, um tanto
▶ **to put it mildly** para não dizer
outra coisa

mildew /'mildu:; GB 'mildju:/ s
mofo

mild-mannered adj gentil

mile /mail/ s milha → Ver pág. 224
▶ **be miles away** (coloq) estar
longe (em pensamento/son-
hando) **miles better** (coloq)
muito melhor **miles from any-
where/nowhere** no fim do
mundo **see/tell sth a mile off**
(coloq) ver/notar algo de longe
mileage s **1** milhagem **2** (coloq)
vantagem: The press got a lot of
~ out of the story. A imprensa
explorou muito essa história.

milestone /'mailstəʊn/ s marco

milieu /'mi:ljɜ:/ s meio social

militant /'militənt/ adj, s militante

military /'militəri; GB -tri/ adj
militar ● s **the military** os
militares

militia /mə'liʃə/ s milícia **militia-
man** s (pl -**men**) miliciano

milk /milk/ s leite: ~ products laticínios ● vt **1** ordenhar **2** tirar,
extrair (desonestamente) **milky**

adj (-ier, -iest) **1** com bastante leite **2** leitoso

milkman /ˈmɪlkmən/ s (pl -men) leiteiro

the Milky Way s a Via Láctea

mill /mɪl/ s **1** moinho **2** moedor **3** fábrica: steel ~ siderúrgica ● vt moer ■ **mill about/around** circular (confusamente em grupo) **miller** s moleiro/a

millennium /mɪˈleniəm/ s (pl -ia /-ɪə/ ou -iums) milênio

millet /ˈmɪlɪt/ s painço

million /ˈmɪljən/ adj, s milhão ▸ **one in a million** uma raridade **millionth** adj milionésimo **2** s milionésima parte

millionaire /ˌmɪljəˈneər/ s milionário/a

millstone /ˈmɪlstəʊn/ s mó ▸ **a millstone around your/sb's neck** um peso sobre os ombros (de alguém)

mime /maɪm/ s mímica: a ~ artist um mímico ● vt, vi fazer mímica, imitar

mimic /ˈmɪmɪk/ vt (pt, pp mimicked part pres -ck-) arremedar ● s imitador/a **mimicry** s imitação

mince /mɪns/ vt moer (carne) ▸ **not mince (your) words** não fazer rodeios ● s (GB) carne moída

mincemeat /ˈmɪnsmiːt/ s recheio de frutas secas: mince(meat) pie torta de Natal recheada com frutas secas ▸ **make mincemeat of sb/sth** (coloq) fazer picadinho de alguém/algo

mind /maɪnd/ s **1** espírito **2** mente: mind-boggling incrível **3** pensamento: My ~ was on other things. Minha cabeça estava em outras coisas. **4** juízo ▸ **come/spring to mind** ocorrer a alguém **have a mind of your own** ter opinião própria **have half a mind (GB a good mind) to do sth** estar com (muita) vontade de fazer algo **have sb/sth in mind (for sth)** ter alguém/algo em mente (para algo) **in two minds about (doing) sth** (GB) indeciso quanto a (fazer) algo **in your mind's eye** na sua imaginação **keep your mind on sth** concentrar-se em algo **make up your mind** decidir(-se) **on your mind?** What's on your ~? Com que você está preocupado? **out of your mind** (coloq) louco, fora de si **put/set your/sb's mind at ease/rest** tranqüilizar-se / tranqüilizar

alguém **put/set your mind to sth** concentrar-se em, dedicar-se a algo **take your/sb's mind off sth** distrair-se/distrair alguém de algo ▸ **to my mind** no meu parecer ● **1** vt cuidar de **2** vt, vi: I don't ~. Eu não me importo. ◇ Would you ~ going tomorrow? Você se importaria de ir amanhã? **3** vt preocupar-se com: Don't ~ him. Não se importe com ele. **4** (GB) vt, vi ter cuidado com ▸ **do you mind?** Você se importa(ria)? **mind (you)** (GB, coloq) veja bem **mind your own business** não se meter onde não é chamado **never mind** não tem importância **never you mind** (coloq) nem pergunte ■ **mind out (for sb/sth)** ter cuidado (com alguém/algo) **minder** s (GB) **1** pessoa que cuida de outra pessoa **2** guarda-costas **mindful** adj (fml) consciente **mindless** adj idiota, descuidado

mine /maɪn/ pron poss meu(s), minha(s): a friend of ~ um amigo meu **s mina**: ~ worker mineiro ● vt **1** extrair (minerais) **2** minar **3** colocar minas em **miner** s mineiro/a

minefield /ˈmaɪnfiːld/ s **1** campo minado **2** terreno perigoso

mineral /ˈmɪnərəl/ s mineral

mingle /ˈmɪŋgl/ **1** vi misturar (-se) (às pessoas) (festa, etc.): ~ with the guests juntar-se aos convidados. **2** vt combinar

miniature /ˈmɪnətʃər/ s miniatura

minibus /ˈmɪnibʌs/ s microônibus

minicab /ˈmɪnikæb/ s (GB) radiotáxi

minimal /ˈmɪnɪməl/ adj mínimo

minimize /ˈmɪnɪmaɪz/ vt minimizar

minimum /ˈmɪnɪməm/ s (pl minima /-mə/) (abrev min.) mínimo ● adj mínimo

mining /ˈmaɪnɪŋ/ s mineração

minister /ˈmɪnɪstər/ s **1** (GB) ministro/a **2** ministro (protestante) → PRIEST ● vi (fml) atender **ministerial** /ˌmɪnɪˈstɪəriəl/ adj ministerial

ministry /ˈmɪnɪstri/ s (pl -ies) **1** (GB) (Pol) ministério **2** (the ministry) o clero (protestante): enter/go into the ~ tornar-se pastor

mink /mɪŋk/ s visom

minor /ˈmaɪnər/ adj **1** secundário: ~ repairs pequenos reparos ◇ ~ injuries ferimentos leves

2 (*Mús*) menor • *s* menor (de idade)

minority /maɪˈnɔːrəti; *GB* -ˈnɒr-/ *s* (*pl* -ies) minoria: *be in the ~* estar na minoria ◇ *~ vote* voto minoritário

mint /mɪnt/ *s* **1** hortelã **2** bala de menta **3** a Casa da Moeda **4** [*sing*] (*coloq*) fortuna • *s* **in mint condition** em perfeitas condições • *vt* cunhar (moeda)

minus /ˈmaɪnəs/ *prep* **1** menos **2** (*coloq*) sem **3** abaixo de zero • *s* **1** (*tb ~ sign*) sinal de menos **2** (*coloq*) desvantagem: *the pluses and minuses* os prós e os contras

minute¹ /ˈmɪnɪt/ *s* **1** minuto **2** momento, instante **3** nota (*oficial*) **4** (minutes) [*pl*] ata (*reunião*) • **not for a minute** nem por um segundo **the minute (that)...** assim que...

minute² /maɪˈnjuːt; *GB* -ˈnjuːt/ (*-er*, *-est*) **1** minúsculo **2** minucioso **minutely** *adv* minuciosamente

miracle /ˈmɪrəkl/ *s* milagre: *a ~ cure* uma cura milagrosa • **do/work miracles** (*coloq*) fazer milagres **miraculous** /mɪˈrækjələs/ *adj* milagroso

mirage /mɪˈrɑːʒ/ *s* miragem

mirror /ˈmɪrər/ *s* **1** espelho **2** (*no carro*) retrovisor **3** (*fig*) reflexo • **mirror image** réplica exata, imagem invertida • *vt* refletir

mirth /mɜːrθ/ *s* (*fml*) **1** riso **2** alegria

misadventure /ˌmɪsədˈventʃər/ *s* **1** (*fml*) desgraça (*GB*) (*Jur*): *death by ~* morte acidental

misbehave /ˌmɪsbɪˈheɪv/ *vi* comportar-se mal **misbehavior** (*GB* **-our**) *s* mau comportamento

miscalculation /ˌmɪskælkjuˈleɪʃn/ *s* erro de cálculo

miscarriage /ˈmɪskærɪdʒ, ˌmɪsˈkær-/ *s* aborto (*espontâneo*) • **miscarriage of justice** erro judicial

miscellaneous /ˌmɪsəˈleɪniəs/ *adj* variado: *~ items* artigos diversos

mischief /ˈmɪstʃɪf/ *s* **1** travessura **2** dano **mischievous** /ˈmɪstʃɪvəs/ *adj* travesso

misconceive /ˌmɪskənˈsiːv/ *vt* (*fml*) interpretar mal **misconception** *s* ideia equivocada: *a popular ~* um erro comum

misconduct /ˌmɪsˈkɒndʌkt/ *s* (*fml*) **1** (*Jur*) má conduta **2** (*Com*) má administração

miser /ˈmaɪzər/ *s* sovina **miserly** *adj* **1** avarento **2** mísero

miserable /ˈmɪzrəbl/ *adj* **1** triste **2** desprezível **3** horrível **miserably** *adv* **1** tristemente **2** miseravelmente: *fail ~* ser um fracasso total

misery /ˈmɪzəri/ *s* (*pl* -ies) **1** tristeza, sofrimento: *a life of ~* uma vida miserável **2** [*ger pl*] tormento **3** (*GB*, *coloq*) rabugento/a • **put sb out of their misery** acabar com o sofrimento de alguém

misfortune /ˌmɪsˈfɔːrtʃən/ *s* desgraça

misgiving /ˌmɪsˈɡɪvɪŋ/ *s* [*ger pl*] dúvida (*apreensão*)

misguided /ˌmɪsˈɡaɪdɪd/ *adj* equivocado: *~ generosity* generosidade mal empregada

mishap /ˈmɪshæp/ *s* contratempo

misinform /ˌmɪsɪnˈfɔːrm/ *vt* informar mal

misinterpret /ˌmɪsɪnˈtɜːrprɪt/ *vt* interpretar mal **misinterpretation** *s* interpretação errônea

misjudge /ˌmɪsˈdʒʌdʒ/ *vt* **1** julgar mal **2** calcular mal

mislay /ˌmɪsˈleɪ/ *vt* (*pt*, *pp* -laid /-ˈleɪd/) extraviar, pôr em lugar errado

mislead /ˌmɪsˈliːd/ *vt* (*pt*, *pp* misled /-ˈled/) induzir alguém em erro: *Don't be misled by...* Não se deixe enganar por... **misleading** *adj* enganoso

mismanagement /ˌmɪsˈmænɪdʒmənt/ *s* má administração

misogynist /mɪˈsɒdʒɪnɪst/ *s* misógino

misplaced /ˌmɪsˈpleɪst/ *adj* **1** mal colocado **2** imerecido **3** fora de propósito

misprint /ˈmɪsprɪnt/ *s* erro de impressão

misread /ˌmɪsˈriːd/ *vt* (*pt*, *pp* misread /-ˈred/) **1** ler mal **2** interpretar mal

misrepresent /ˌmɪsreprɪˈzent/ *vt* *~ sb* deturpar as palavras de alguém

Miss /mɪs/ *s* senhorita
→ SENHORITA

miss /mɪs/ **1** *vt*, *vi* não acertar, errar: *You can't ~ it.* Você não tem como errar. ◇ *~ your footing* tropeçar **2** *vt* não ver/entender **3** *vt* perder, não chegar a tempo para **4** *vt* sentir saudades de **5** *vt* evitar: *narrowly ~ hitting sth* não bater em algo por pouco • **not miss much/a trick** (*coloq*) ser muito vivo ■ **miss out (on sth)** perder (a oportunidade de) algo **miss sb/sth out** (*GB*) deixar alguém/algo de fora • *s* falha, tiro errado ►**give sth a miss** (*GB, coloq*) decidir não fazer algo

missile /'mɪsl; *GB* 'mɪsaɪl/ s **1** projétil **2** (*Mil*) míssil

missing /'mɪsɪŋ/ *adj* **1** extraviado **2** que falta: *He has a tooth* ~. Ele não tem um dente. **3** desaparecido

mission /'mɪʃn/ s missão

missionary /'mɪʃəneri; *GB* -nri/ s (*pl* -ies) missionário/a

mist /mɪst/ s **1** névoa **2** bruma ● *vt, vi* ~ **(sth) over/up** embaçar (algo)

mistake /mɪ'steɪk/ s erro: *make a* ~ errar ◊ *by* ~ por engano **NOTA Mistake e error** têm o mesmo significado, mas **error** é mais formal. **Mistake** indica culpa: *It's all your fault.* Também indica uma imperfeição: *an electric fault* ◊ *He has faults.* **Defect** é uma imperfeição mais grave: *a speech defect* ● *vt* (*pt* **mistook** /mɪ'stʊk/ *pp* **mistaken** /mɪ'steɪkən/) **1** equivocar-se a respeito de: *I mistook your meaning.* Eu entendi mal o que você queria dizer. **2** ~ **sb/sth for sb/sth** confundir alguém/algo (com alguém/algo) **mistaken** *adj* equivocado: *if I'm not* ~ se não me engano **mistakenly** *adv* por engano

mister /'mɪstər/ s (*abrev* **Mr.**) Senhor

mistletoe /'mɪsltoʊ/ s visco

mistreat /ˌmɪs'triːt/ *vt* maltratar

mistress /'mɪstrəs/ s **1** amante **2** (*de situação, animal*) dona **3** (*esp GB*) professora **4** senhora

mistrust /ˌmɪs'trʌst/ *vt* desconfiar de ● s desconfiança

misty /'mɪsti/ *adj* (-ier, -iest) **1** com cerração **2** embaçado

misunderstand /ˌmɪsʌndər-'stænd/ *vt, vi* (*pt, pp* -**stood** /-'stʊd/) compreender/interpretar mal **misunderstanding** s **1** mal-entendido **2** desavença

misuse /ˌmɪs'juːs/ s **1** emprego incorreto **2** (*fundos*) malversação **2** abuso

mitigate /'mɪtɪgeɪt/ *vt* (*fml*) mitigar

mitten /'mɪtn/ s mitene

mix /mɪks/ **1** *vt, vi* misturar(-se): ~ *sth in* adicionar algo ◊ *a drink* preparar uma bebida **2** *vi* ~ **(with sb/sth)** relacionar-se com alguém/algo ●**be/get mixed up in sth** estar metido/meter-se em algo ■**mix sb/sth up (with sb/sth)** confundir alguém/algo (com alguém/

algo) ● s **1** mistura **2** preparado **mixed** *adj* **1** misto: ~ *feelings* sentimentos desencontrados **2** sortido **3** (*tempo*) variável **mixer** s **1** batedeira **2** *be a good* ~ ser sociável **mixture** s **1** mistura **2** combinação **mix-up** s (*coloq*) confusão

moan /moʊn/ **1** *vt, vi* gemer **2** *vi* ~ **(about sth)** (*coloq*) queixar-se (de algo) ● s **1** gemido **2** (*coloq*) queixa

moat /moʊt/ s fosso (*castelo*)

mob /mɑb/ s **1** turba **2** (*coloq*) quadrilha (*criminosos*) **3** (**the Mob**) a Máfia ● *vt* (**-bb-**) acossar

mobile /'moʊbl, -bɪl; *GB* -baɪl/ *adj* (*tb* ~ **phone**) celular ● *adj* **1** móvel: ~ *library* biblioteca itinerante ◊ ~ *home* trailer **2** (*rosto*) versátil **mobility** /moʊ-'bɪləti/ s mobilidade

mobilize /'moʊbəlaɪz/ **1** *vt, vi* (*Mil*) mobilizar(-se) **2** *vt* organizar

mock /mɑk/ *vt, vi* zombar: *a mocking smile* um sorriso de zombaria ● *adj* **1** fictício: ~ *battle* batalha simulada **2** falso, de imitação **mockery** s [*U*] **1** zombaria **2** paródia ●**make a mockery of sth** ridicularizar algo

mode /moʊd/ s (*fml*) **1** (*transporte*) meio **2** (*produção*) modo **3** (*de pensar*) forma

model /'mɑdl/ s **1** modelo **2** maquete: ~ *car* carro em miniatura ● *vt, vi* (-**l**-, *GB* -**ll**-) **1** posar como/ser modelo: ~ *an outfit* desfilar um conjunto **2** *vt* ~ **yourself/sth on sb/sth** tomar alguém/algo como modelo **modeling** (*GB* -**ll**-) s **1** modelagem **2** trabalho de modelo

modem /'moʊdem/ s modem

moderate /'mɑdərət/ *adj* **1** moderado **2** regular ● s moderado/a ● /'mɑdəreɪt/ *vt, vi* moderar(-se): *a moderating influence* uma influência moderadora **moderation** s moderação

modern /'mɑdərn/ *adj* moderno **modernity** /mə'dɜːrnəti/ s modernidade **modernize** *vt, vi* modernizar(-se)

modest /'mɑdɪst/ *adj* **1** ~ **(about sth)** modesto (em relação a algo) **2** pequeno: *a* ~ *price* um preço módico **3** recatado **modesty** s modéstia

modify /'mɑdɪfaɪ/ *vt* (*pt, pp* -**ied**) modificar **NOTA** O verbo mais comum é **change**.

module /'mɑdʒuːl; *GB* mə'djuːl/ s módulo **modular** *adj* modular

mogul /'moʊgl/ s magnata

moist /mɔɪst/ adj úmido **NOTA**
Moist e damp se traduzem por
"úmido" mas damp é mais
usado e pode ter sentido mais
negativo: damp walls ◊ Use
a damp cloth. ◊ cold damp
weather. ◊ cold damp
weather. **moisten** /ˈmɔɪsn/
vt, vi umedecer(-se) **moisture**
/ˈmɔɪstʃər/ s umidade **moistur-
ize** vt hidratar **moisturizer** s
(creme) hidratante

molar /ˈmoʊlər/ s molar

mold (mould) /moʊld/ vt, vi molde(-se) ●
s **1** molde **2** mofo **moldy** adj
mofado

mole /moʊl/ s **1** pinta **2** (Zool)
toupeira **3** informante

molecule /ˈmɒlɪkjuːl/ s molécula
molecular /məˈlekjələr/ adj
molecular

molest /məˈlest/ vt agredir/
molestar sexualmente

mollify /ˈmɒlɪfaɪ/ vt (pt, pp -ied)
acalmar

molten /ˈmoʊltən/ adj fundido

mom /mɑm/ s (coloq) mamãe

moment /ˈmoʊmənt/ s momento,
instante: at the ~ atualmente ◊ I
shall only be a ~. Não vou
demorar. ▶ at a moment's notice
imediatamente, sem avisar
for the moment por enquanto
not for a/one moment nem por
um segundo the moment of
truth a hora da verdade the
moment (that)... assim que ...

momentary /ˈmoʊmənteri;
GB -tri/ adj momentâneo **moment-
arily** adv **1** momentaneamente
2 (US) imediatamente

momentous /məˈmentəs,
moʊˈm-/ adj de enorme importância

momentum /məˈmentəm,
moʊˈm-/ s **1** ímpeto **2** (Fís) momento: gain/gather ~ ganhar
velocidade

mommy /ˈmɑmi/ s (pl -ies)
mamãe

monarch /ˈmɑnərk; GB -ɑːk/ s
monarca **monarchy** s (pl -ies)
monarquia

monastery /ˈmɑnəsteri; GB -tri/
s (pl -ies) mosteiro

monastic /məˈnæstɪk/ adj
monástico

Monday /ˈmʌndeɪ, -di/ s (abrev
Mon.) segunda(-feira): last/
next ~ segunda passada/que
vem ◊ the ~ before last/after
next duas segundas atrás/
daqui a duas segundas ◊ ~
morning/evening segunda de
manhã/noite ◊ ~ week/a week
on ~ na outra segunda ◊ See you
~. Até segunda. **NOTA** Os

nomes dos dias da semana se
escrevem com maiúscula.

monetary /ˈmʌnɪteri; GB -tri/ adj
monetário

money /ˈmʌni/ s dinheiro ▶ get
your money's worth receber boa
qualidade (compra, serviço)

monitor /ˈmɑnɪtər/ s **1** monitor **2**
(eleições) supervisor/a ● vt **1**
observar **2** controlar monitor-
ing s supervisão

monk /mʌŋk/ s monge

monkey /ˈmʌŋki/ s **1** macaco **2**
(coloq) capetinha (criança)

monogamy /məˈnɑgəmi/ s
monogamia **monogamous** adj
monogâmico

monolithic /ˌmɒnəˈlɪθɪk/ adj
monolítico

monologue (USA tb **-log**)
/ˈmɒnəlɔːg; GB -lɒg/ s monólogo

monopoly /məˈnɑpəli/ s (pl -ies)
monopólio **monopolize** vt
monopolizar

monoxide /məˈnɑksaɪd/ s
monóxido

monsoon /ˌmɑnˈsuːn/ s monção

monster /ˈmɑnstər/ s monstro
monstrous /ˈmɑnstrəs/ adj
monstruoso

monstrosity /mɑnˈstrɑsəti/ s (pl
-ies) monstruosidade

month /mʌnθ/ s mês

monthly /ˈmʌnθli/ adj mensal ●
adv mensalmente ● s (pl -ies)
publicação mensal

monument /ˈmɑnjumənt/ s
monumento **monumental**
/ˌmɑnjuˈmentl/ adj **1** monumental **2** excepcional **3** enorme

moo /muː/ vi mugir

mood /muːd/ s **1** humor: be in the
~ for (doing) sth estar a fim de
(fazer) algo **2** mau humor: in a ~
mal-humorado **3** ambiente **4**
(Gram) modo **moody** adj (-ier,
-iest) **1** de humor instável **2**
mal-humorado

moon /muːn/ s lua ▶ over the
moon (coloq) louco de contente
● vi ~ (about/around) (coloq)
ficar/andar sem fazer nada

moonlight /ˈmuːnlaɪt/ s luar ● vi
(pt, pp ~ed) (coloq) fazer um
bico (trabalho) **moonlit** adj
enluarado

Moor /mʊər/ s mouro/a **Moorish**
adj mourisco

moor /mʊər/ (tb **moorland**
/ˈmʊərlənd/) s charneca ● vt, vi
(Náut) amarrar **mooring** s **1**
(moorings) amarras **2** ancoradouro

moose /muːs/ s (pl moose)
alce americano

mop /mɒp/ s **1** esfregão **2** (*cabelo*) madeixa ● vt (**-pp-**) **1** esfregar **2** ~ **sth (up)** enxugar algo

mope /məʊp/ vi deprimir-se: ~ *around* andar deprimido

moped /ˈməʊped/ s bicicleta motorizada

moral /ˈmɒrəl/ GB ˈmɒrəl/ s **1** moral **2** (**morals**) [*pl*] moralidade ● adj moral moralistic /ˌmɒrəˈlɪstɪk/ adj moralista morality /məˈrælətɪ/ s moral, moralidade: *standards of* ~ padrões morais moralize vi dar lição de moral morally adv moralmente, honradamente

morale /məˈrɑːl/ GB məˈrɑːl/ s moral (*ânimo*)

morbid /ˈmɔːbɪd/ adj **1** mórbido **2** (*Med*) patológico morbidity /mɔːˈbɪdəti/ s **1** morbidez **2** (*Med*) patologia

more /mɔː(r)/ adj, adv, pron mais: *I hope we'll see* ~ *of you.* Espero ver você com mais frequência. ◊ *That's* ~ *like it.* Assim, sim! NOTA É usado para formar o comparativo de *adjs* e *advs* de duas ou mais sílabas. ▶ **be more than happy, glad, etc. to do sth** ter o maior prazer em fazer algo **more and more** cada vez mais **more or less** mais ou menos: ~ *or less finished* quase pronto **the more… the more…** quanto mais…, mais… **what is more** além disso

moreover /mɔːˈrəʊvə(r)/ adv além disso

morgue /mɔːɡ/ s necrotério

morning /ˈmɔːnɪŋ/ s **1** manhã: *in the* ~ de/pela manhã NOTA Com **morning**, **afternoon** e **evening**, usa-se a preposição in para indicar o período do dia: *at three o'clock in the afternoon*, e **on** para nos referirmos a um ponto no calendário: *on a cool May* ~ ◊ *on Sunday afternoon* ◊ *on the* ~ *of 4 September.* Mas, junto com **tomorrow**, **this**, **that** e **yesterday**, não se usa preposição: *They'll leave this evening.* ◊ *I saw her yesterday* ~. **2** madrugada **3** [*antes de substantivo*] da manhã: *the* ~ *papers* os jornais matutinos ▶ **good morning** bom dia NOTA Em situações informais, muitas vezes se diz simplesmente **Morning!** ao invés de **Good morning!**

moron /ˈmɔːrɒn/ s (*coloq*) imbecil

morose /məˈrəʊs/ adj carrancudo morosely adv com mau humor

morphine /ˈmɔːfiːn/ s morfina

morsel /ˈmɔːsl/ s bocado (*comida*)

mortal /ˈmɔːtl/ s mortal ● adj mortal mortality /mɔːˈtæləti/ s **1** mortalidade **2** mortandade

mortar /ˈmɔːtə(r)/ s **1** argamassa **2** (*Mil*) morteiro **3** pilão

mortgage /ˈmɔːɡɪdʒ/ s hipoteca ● vt hipotecar

mortify /ˈmɔːtɪfaɪ/ vt (*pt*, *pp* **-ied**) humilhar

mortuary /ˈmɔːtʃʊeri/ GB ˈmɔːtʃəri/ s (*pl* **-ies**) sala/capela mortuária

mosaic /məʊˈzeɪk/ s mosaico

Moslem /ˈmɒzləm/ = MUSLIM

mosque /mɒsk/ s mesquita

mosquito /məsˈkiːtəʊ/ s (*pl* **-es**) mosquito: ~ *net* mosquiteiro

moss /mɒs; GB mɒs/ s musgo

most /məʊst/ adj **1** mais, a maior parte de **2** a maioria de, quase todos ● pron **1** I ate (the) ~. Fui eu quem comeu mais. ◊ *the* ~ *I can offer you* o máximo que eu posso oferecer a você **2** a maioria de: ~ *of the day* a maior parte do dia NOTA **Most** é o superlativo de **much** e de **many**, usado tanto com substantivos não contáveis quanto com substantivos no plural: *Who's got* ~ *time?* ◊ ~ *children*. Mas, diante de pronomes, de substantivos precedidos por *the* ou de adjetivos possessivos ou demonstrativos, usa-se **most of**: ~ *of my friends* ◊ ~ *of us* ◊ ~ *of these records*. ● adv **1** mais NOTA Usa-se para formar o superlativo de locuções adverbiais, adjetivos e advérbios de duas ou mais sílabas: *What upset me the* (the) ~ *was that…* O que mais me aborreceu foi que… ◊ ~ *of all* sobretudo **2** muito: ~ *likely* muito provavelmente ▶ **at (the) most** no máximo mostly adv principalmente, em geral

moth /mɒθ; GB mɒθ/ s **1** mariposa **2** (*tb* **clothes** ~) traça

mother /ˈmʌðə(r)/ s mãe ● vt criar (como mãe) **2** mimar motherhood s maternidade (*estado*) mother-in-law s (*pl* **-ers-in-law**) sogra motherly adj maternal mother-to-be s (*pl* **-ers-to-be**) futura mamãe mother tongue língua materna

motif /məʊˈtiːf/ s **1** desenho **2** tema

motion /ˈməʊʃn/ s **1** movimento: ~ *picture* filme (de cinema) ◊ *put/set sth in motion* colocar algo em funcionamento **2** (*em*

reunião) moção ▶ **go through the motions (of doing sth)** fingir (fazer algo) ● *vt, vi* ~ **(to/for sb to do sth)** fazer sinal (a alguém para que faça algo): ~ *sb in* fazer sinal para alguém entrar motionless *adj* imóvel

motivate /'moʊtɪveɪt/ *vt* motivar

motive /'moʊtɪv/ s ~ **(for sth)** motivo (de algo): *have an ulterior* ~ ter segundas intenções NOTA A tradução mais comum de "motivo" é **reason**.

motor /'moʊtər/ s **1** motor: ~ *boat* lancha a motor → ENGINE **2** (GB, *antiq*) carro: ~ *racing* corrida automobilística **motoring** s automobilismo **motorist** s motorista **motorize** *vt* motorizar

motorcycle /'moʊtərsaɪkl/ (GB **motorbike** /'moʊtərbaɪk/) s motocicleta

motorway /'moʊtərweɪ/ (GB) s rodovia

mottled /'mɑtld/ *adj* mosqueado

motto /'mɑtoʊ/ s (*pl* ~**es**) lema

mould(y) (GB) = MOLD

mound /maʊnd/ s **1** montículo **2** monte (*de coisas*)

mount /maʊnt/ s **1** (*Geog*) monte **2** suporte **3** (*animal*) montaria **4** moldura ● **1** *vt* (*cavalo*) montar em **2** *vt* emoldurar **3** *vt* organizar **4** *vt* instalar **5** *vi* ~ **(up) (to sth)** aumentar (até atingir algo) **mounting** *adj* crescente

mountain /'maʊntn; GB -ntən/ s montanha **mountaineer** /ˌmaʊntɪˈnɪər/ s alpinista **mountaineering** /ˌmaʊntɪˈnɪərɪŋ/ s alpinismo **mountainous** /'maʊntənəs/ *adj* montanhoso

mountain bike s mountain bike

mountainside /'maʊntənsaɪd/ s encosta

mourn /mɔːrn/ **1** *vi* lamentar (-se) **2** *vi* estar de luto **3** *vt*: ~ *sb* chorar a morte de alguém **mourner** s pessoa que comparece a enterro ou velório **mournful** *adj* triste **mourning** s luto

mouse /maʊs/ s (*pl* **mice** /maɪs/) **1** camundongo **2** (*Informát*) mouse **mousetrap** s ratoeira

mousse /muːs/ s mousse

moustache (*esp GB*) = MUSTACHE

mouth /maʊθ/ s **1** boca **2** (*rio*) foz **mouthful** s **1** (*comida*) bocado **2** trago

mouthpiece /'maʊθpiːs/ s **1** bocal **2** porta-voz

movable /'muːvəbl/ *adj* móvel

move /muːv/ s **1** movimento **2**

(*casa, etc.*) mudança **3** (*jogo*) vez **4** medida ▶ **get a move on** (*coloq*) apressar-se **make a move 1** agir **2** ir(-se) embora ● **1** *vi* mover(-se): *Don't* ~! Não se mexa! ◊ ~ *about/around* andar de lá para cá ◊ *It's your turn to* ~. É a sua vez de jogar. **2** *vt, vi* mudar(-se) de local, transportar: ~ *house* mudar(-se) (*da casa*) ◊ *He has been moved to London.* Ele foi enviado para Londres. **3** *vt* comover **4** *vt* ~ *sb* **(to do sth)** convencer alguém (a fazer algo) ■ **move (sth) away** afastar-se, afastar algo **move forward** avançar **move in** instalar-se **move on** prosseguir (*viagem*) **move out** mudar-se

movement /'muːvmənt/ s **1** movimento **2** ~ **(towards/away from sth)** tendência (*em direção a algo/a afastar-se de algo*) **3** (*Mec*) mecanismo

movie /'muːvi/ s (*esp USA*) filme (*de cinema*): ~ *theater* cinema

moving /'muːvɪŋ/ *adj* **1** móvel **2** comovente

mow /moʊ/ *vt* (*pt* mowed *pp* mown /moʊn/ ou mowed) cortar (*grama*) ■ **mow sb down** aniquilar alguém **mower** s cortador (*de grama*)

MP /ˌem 'piː/ *abrev* (GB) **Member of Parliament** deputado/a

Mr. /'mɪstər/ *abrev* senhor (= Sr.)

Mrs. /'mɪsɪz/ *abrev* senhora (= Sra.)

Ms. /mɪz, məz/ *abrev* senhora (= Sra.) → SENHORITA

much /mʌtʃ/ *adj* muito: *so* ~ *traffic* tanto tráfego ● *pron* muito: *How* ~ *is it?* Quanto é? ◊ *too* ~ demais ◊ *as* ~ *as you can* quanto você puder ◊ *for* ~ *of the day* pela maior parte do dia → MANY ● *adv* muito: *Much to her surprise...* Para grande surpresa dela... ◊ ~ *the same* praticamente igual ◊ ~ *too cold* frio demais ▶ **much as** por mais que **not much of a...**: *He's not* ~ *of an actor.* Ele não é grande coisa como ator.

muck /mʌk/ s **1** esterco **2** (*coloq, esp GB*) porcaria ■ **muck about/around** (*coloq*) perder tempo **muck sth up** (*coloq*) estragar algo **mucky** *adj* (*-ier, -iest*) sujo

mucus /'mjuːkəs/ s muco

mud /mʌd/ s lama: **mudguard** pára-lama **muddy** *adj* (*-ier, -iest*) **1** lamacento: ~ *footprints* pegadas de barro **2** turvo

muddle /'mʌdl/ *vt* **1** ~ **sth (up)** misturar, bagunçar algo **2** ~ **sb/**

sth **(up)** confundir alguém/algo ● s **1** desordem **2** ~ **(about/over sth)** confusão (com algo) muddled adj confuso

muffin /ˈmʌfɪn/ s tipo de bolo

muffled /ˈmʌfld/ adj **1** (grito, voz) abafado **2** ~ **(up)** (em roupa) enrolado

muffler /ˈmʌflər/ s **1** cachecol **2** (carro) silenciador

mug /mʌg/ s **1** caneca **2** (coloq) (rosto) cara **3** (coloq) otário ● **a mug's game** (GB) uma perda de tempo ● vt (-gg-) assaltar mugger s assaltante mugging s assalto

muggy /ˈmʌgi/ adj (-ier -iest) (tempo) abafado

mulberry /ˈmʌlberi; GB ˈmʌlbəri/ s **1** (tb ~ tree/bush) amoreira **2** amora **3** cor de amora

mule /mjuːl/ s **1** mula **2** chinelo (de quarto)

mull /mʌl/ v ■ mull sth over refletir sobre algo

multicolored (GB -our-) /ˈmʌltikʌlərd/ adj multicor

multilingual /ˌmʌltiˈlɪŋgwəl/ adj poliglota

multinational /ˌmʌltiˈnæʃnəl/ adj, s multinacional

multiple /ˈmʌltɪpl/ adj múltiplo ● s múltiplo

multiple sclerosis /ˌmʌltɪpl skləˈroʊsɪs/ s esclerose múltipla

multiplex /ˈmʌltɪpleks/ (GB tb ~ cinema) s cinema com várias salas de projeção

multiplication /ˌmʌltɪplɪˈkeɪʃn/ s multiplicação: ~ table tabuada

multiplicity /ˌmʌltɪˈplɪsəti/ s multiplicidade

multiply /ˈmʌltɪplaɪ/ vt, vi (pt, pp -ied) multiplicar(-se)

multi-purpose adj para diversas finalidades

multitude /ˈmʌltɪtuːd; GB -tjuːd/ s (fml) multidão

mum (GB) = MOM

mumble /ˈmʌmbl/ vt, vi murmurar, resmungar

mummy /ˈmʌmi/ s (pl -ies) **1** (GB, coloq) mamãe **2** múmia

mumps /mʌmps/ s [sing] caxumba

munch /mʌntʃ/ vt, vi ~ **(on)** sth mastigar algo

mundane /mʌnˈdeɪn/ adj comum, mundano

municipal /mjuːˈnɪsɪpl/ adj municipal

munitions /mjuːˈnɪʃnz/ s munições

mural /ˈmjʊərəl/ s (Arte) mural

murder /ˈmɜːrdər/ s **1** assassi-

nato **2** (coloq) um pesadelo ▶ **get away with murder** (coloq) escapar impune ● vt assassinar → ASSASSINAR murderer s assassino/a murderous adj **1** homicida: a ~ look um olhar fulminante **2** (coloq) (muito desagradável) de matar

murky /ˈmɜːrki/ adj (-ier, -iest) **1** lúgubre **2** obscuro

murmur /ˈmɜːrmər/ s murmúrio: without a ~ sem um pio ● vt, vi murmurar

muscle /ˈmʌsl/ s **1** músculo: Don't move a ~! Não mexa um dedo! **2** (fig) poder ■ **muscle in (on sth)** (coloq) intrometer-se (em algo) muscular /ˈmʌskjələr/ adj **1** muscular **2** musculoso

muse /mjuːz/ s musa ● **1** vi ~ **(about/over sth)** refletir (sobre algo) **2** vt: "How strange," he mused. -Que estranho-disse ele, pensativo.

museum /mjuˈziəm/ s museu NOTA **Museum** é o museu em que se expõem peças históricas, científicas, etc. (**Art) gallery** é o museu em que se expõem quadros e esculturas.

mushroom /ˈmʌʃruːm/ s cogumelo ● vi crescer/dar como praga

mushy /ˈmʌʃi/ adj **1** pastoso **2** (coloq) piegas

music /ˈmjuːzɪk/ s **1** música: a piece of ~ uma peça musical/ uma música ◇ ~ hall teatro de variedades **2** partitura musical adj musical: be ~ ter talento para música musical (tb ~ comedy (pl -ies)) s (comédia) musical musician musica/o musicianship s habilidade musical

musk /mʌsk/ s (perfume de) almíscar

musket /ˈmʌskɪt/ s mosquete musketeer s mosqueteiro

Muslim /ˈmʌzləm; GB ˈmʊzlɪm/ adj, s muçulmano/a

muslin /ˈmʌzlɪn/ s musselina

mussel /ˈmʌsl/ s mexilhão

must /mʌst/ s (coloq): It's a ~. É imprescindível. ◇ His new book is a ~. Você não pode deixar de ler o último livro dele. ● /məst, mʌst/ v modal (neg must not ou mustn't /ˈmʌsnt/) NOTA **Must** é um verbo modal, seguido de infinitivo sem to. As orações interrogativas e negativas são formadas sem o auxiliar do: Must you go? ◇ We mustn't tell her. **Must** tem apenas o presente: I ~ leave early. Para outros tempos, usa-se **have to**: *He'll have to come tomorrow.* ◇ *We had to eat quickly.*

● **obrigação e proibição** dever, ter que/de NOTA Emprega-se **must** para dar ordens ou para fazer alguém (ou a pessoa que fala) seguir determinado comportamento: *The children ~ be back by four.* ◇ *I ~ quit smoking.* Quando a ordem é imposta por um agente externo, p. ex. uma lei, etc., usa-se **have to**: *The doctor says I have to quit smoking.* ◇ *You have to send it today.* Em negativas, **must not** ou **mustn't** expressam proibição: *You mustn't open the door.* Mas **haven't got to** ou **don't have to** indicam ausência de obrigação: *You don't have to go if you don't want to.*

● **sugestão, conselho** ter que: *You ~ come to lunch.* Você tem que vir almoçar. NOTA Na maioria dos casos, para sugestões e conselhos usa-se **ought to** ou **should**.

● **probabilidade** dever: *You ~ be hungry.* Você deve estar com fome. ▶ **if I, you, etc. must** se não há outro jeito

mustache /'mʌstæʃ/ s bigode
mustard /'mʌstərd/ s 1 mostarda 2 (cor de) mostarda
muster /'mʌstər/ 1 *vt, vi* reunir (-se) 2 *vt* juntar: *~ (up) enthusiasm* ganhar entusiasmo ◇ *~ a smile* conseguir sorrir
musty /'mʌsti/ *adj* (**-ier, -iest**) 1 mofado 2 bolorento, obsoleto
mutant /'mjuːtənt/ *adj, s* mutante
mutate /'mjuːteɪt; GB mjuː'teɪt/ *vi* transformar-se **mutation** *s* mutação
mute /mjuːt/ *adj* mudo ● s 1 (*Mús*) surdina 2 (*antiq, pessoa*) mudo/a ● *vt* 1 abafar (*som*) 2 (*Mús*) colocar surdina em **muted** *adj* 1 (*som*) abafado 2 (*cor*) apagado 3 (*crítica, etc.*) velado 4 (*Mús*) em surdina
mutilate /'mjuːtɪleɪt/ *vt* mutilar
mutiny /'mjuːtəni/ *s* (*pl* **-ies**) motim **mutinous** *adj* 1 rebelde 2 amotinado
mutter /'mʌtər/ 1 *vt, vi* falar entre os dentes, murmurar 2 *vi* ~ (**about/against/at sb/sth**) resmungar (de alguém/algo)
mutton /'mʌtn/ s (carne de) carneiro → CARNE
mutual /'mjuːtʃuəl/ *adj* 1 mútuo 2 comum **mutually** *adv* mutuamente

muzzle /'mʌzl/ s 1 focinho 2 focinheira 3 (*arma de fogo*) boca ● *vt* 1 colocar focinheira em 2 amordaçar
my /maɪ/ *adj poss* meu, minha
myopia /maɪ'oʊpiə/ s miopia **myopic** /maɪ'ɒpɪk/ *adj* míope
myriad /'mɪriəd/ s miríade ● *adj* inúmero: *~ problems* inúmeros problemas
myself /maɪ'self/ *pron* 1 [*uso reflexivo*] me: *I said to myself...* Eu disse a mim mesmo... 2 [*uso enfático*] eu mesmo/a ▶ (**all**) by **myself** sozinho
mysterious /mɪ'stɪəriəs/ *adj* misterioso
mystery /'mɪstri/ s (*pl* **-ies**) 1 mistério 2 ~ *tour* viagem surpresa ◇ *the ~ assailant* o agressor anônimo 3 (*romance*) policial, de mistério
mystic /'mɪstɪk/ s místico/a ● *adj* (*tb* **mystical**) místico **mysticism** s misticismo, mística
mystification /ˌmɪstɪfɪ'keɪʃn/ s 1 mistério, perplexidade 2 confusão (*deliberada*)
mystify /'mɪstɪfaɪ/ *vt* (*pt, pp* **-ied**) deixar perplexo **mystifying** *adj* intrigante
mystique /mɪ'stiːk/ s [*sing*] (ar de) mistério
myth /mɪθ/ s mito **mythical** *adj* mítico, fictício
mythology /mɪ'θɒlədʒi/ s mitologia **mythological** /ˌmɪθə'lɒdʒɪkl/ *adj* mitológico

N n

N, n /en/ s (*pl* **N's, n's** /enz/) N, n
nag /næg/ *vt, vi* (**-gg-**) ~ (**at**) **sb** 1 atazanar alguém 2 dar bronca em alguém 3 (*dor, suspeita*) incomodar alguém **nagging** *adj* 1 (*dor, suspeita*) persistente 2 (*pessoa*) ranzinza
nail /neɪl/ s 1 unha 2 prego ■ **nail sb down** (**to sth**) conseguir que alguém se comprometa (com algo), conseguir uma resposta concreta de alguém (sobre algo) **nail sth to sth** pregar algo em algo
naive (*tb* **naïve**) /naɪ'iːv/ *adj* ingênuo
naked /'neɪkɪd/ *adj* 1 nu NOTA Há três traduções para "nu": **bare**, **naked** e **nude**. **Bare** refere-se às partes do corpo: *bare arms*, **naked** geralmente se

refere ao corpo todo: *a naked body* e **nude**, a nus artísticos e eróticos: *a nude figure*. **2** (lâmpada) sem cúpula **3** puro ▶ **with the naked eye** a olho nu

name /neɪm/ *s* **1** nome **2** sobrenome **3** reputação **4** personalidade ▶ **by name** de nome **by/ of the name of** (*fml*) chamado **in the name of sb/sth** em nome de alguém/algo ● *vt* **1** ~ **sb/sth sth** chamar alguém/algo de algo **2** ~ **sb/sth (after sb)** dar nome a alguém; colocar em alguém/algo o nome de alguém **3** nomear **4** (*data, etc.*) fixar ▶ **you name it** qualquer coisa (que você imaginar)

nameless /ˈneɪmləs/ *adj* anônimo, sem nome

namely /ˈneɪmli/ *adv* a saber

namesake /ˈneɪmseɪk/ *s* xará

nanny /ˈnæni/ *s* (*pl* **-ies**) (*GB*) babá

nap /næp/ *s* soneca

nape /neɪp/ *s* (*tb* ~ **of the neck**) *s* nuca

napkin /ˈnæpkɪn/ (*GB tb* **table ~**) *s* guardanapo

nappy /ˈnæpi/ *s* (*pl* **-ies**) (*GB*) fralda

narcotic /nɑːrˈkɑtɪk/ *adj*, *s* narcótico

narrate /ˈnæreɪt; *GB* nəˈreɪt/ *vt* narrar **narrator** *s* narrador/a

narrative /ˈnærətɪv/ *s* **1** relato **2** narrativa ● *adj* narrativo

narrow /ˈnæroʊ/ *adj* (**-er, -est**) **1** estreito **2** limitado **3** (*vantagem*) pequeno ▶ **have a narrow escape** escapar por pouco ● *vt*, *vi* estreitar(-se), diminuir ■ **narrow (sth) down to sth** reduzir algo a algo **narrowly** *adv* por pouco

narrow-minded *adj* intolerante

nasal /ˈneɪzl/ *adj* **1** nasal **2** (*voz*) anasalado

nasty /ˈnæsti; *GB* ˈnɑːs-/ *adj* (**-ier, -iest**) **1** desagradável **2** (*odor*) repugnante **3** (*pessoa*) antipático: *be ~ to sb* tratar alguém mal **4** (*situação, etc.*) feio **5** grave, perigoso

nation /ˈneɪʃn/ *s* nação

national /ˈnæʃnəl/ *adj* nacional: ~ *service* serviço militar ● *s* cidadão **nationally** *adv* nacionalmente

National Health Service *s* (*GB*) (*abrev* **NHS**) sistema estatal de saúde

National Insurance *s* (*GB*) previdência social

nationalism /ˈnæʃnəlɪzəm/ *s*

nacionalismo **nationalist** *adj*, *s* nacionalista

nationality /ˌnæʃəˈnæləti/ *s* (*pl* **-ies**) nacionalidade

nationalize /ˈnæʃnəlaɪz/ *vt* nacionalizar

nationwide /ˌneɪʃnˈwaɪd/ *adj*, *adv* em escala nacional

native /ˈneɪtɪv/ *s* **1** nativo/a, natural **2** (*freq pej*) indígena **3** *The tapir is a ~ of Brazil.* O tapir é originário do Brasil. ● *adj* **1** natal **2** indígena, nativo **3** inato **4** ~ **to...** originário de...

natural /ˈnætʃərəl/ *adj* **1** natural **2** nato

naturalist /ˈnætʃərəlɪst/ *s* naturalista

naturally /ˈnætʃərəli; *GB* ˈnætʃrəli/ *adv* **1** naturalmente **2** evidentemente

nature /ˈneɪtʃər/ *s* **1** (*tb* **Nature**) natureza **2** caráter: *good-* ~ bom coração **3** [*U*] índole ▶ **in the nature of sth** da mesma natureza de algo

naughty /ˈnɔːti/ *adj* (**-ier, -iest**) **1** travesso: *be* ~ comportar-se mal **2** malicioso, picante

nausea /ˈnɔːziə/ *s* náusea **nauseating** /ˈnɔːzieɪtɪŋ/ *adj* asqueroso

nautical /ˈnɔːtɪkl/ *adj* náutico

naval /ˈneɪvl/ *adj* naval

nave /neɪv/ *s* nave (*igreja*)

navel /ˈneɪvl/ *s* umbigo

navigate /ˈnævɪgeɪt/ **1** *vt*, *vi* navegar (por) **2** *vi* (*em carro*) dar a direção **3** *vt* (*barco*) dirigir **navigation** *s* navegação **navigator** *s* navegador/a

navy /ˈneɪvi/ *s* **1** (*pl* **-ies**) frota **2** (**the navy, the Navy**) a Marinha **3** (*tb* ~ **blue**) azul-marinho

Nazi /ˈnɑːtsi/ *s* nazista

near /nɪər/ *adj* (**~ -er, -est**) *adj* próximo **NOTA** Antes de substantivo usa-se o adjetivo **nearby** em vez de **near**: *a nearby village*. Mas com outras formas do adjetivo, como o superlativo, temos de usar **near**: *the nearest store*. ● *prep* perto de: *Is there a bank ~ here?* Há um banco por aqui? ◇ ~ *the beginning* próximo do começo ● *adv* perto: *get nearer* aproximar-se *We are getting* ~ *to Christmas.* Estamos nos aproximando do Natal. **NOTA** A expressão *I live nearby* é mais comum do que *I live near*, mas **nearby** não pode ser modificado por **quite**, **very**, etc.: *I live quite near.* ▶ **not be anywhere near**; **be nowhere near** não chegar nem perto, não se parecer em nada ● *vt* aproximar(-se) (de)

nearby /ˈnɪərˈbaɪ/ *adj* próximo ● *adv* perto → NEAR

nearly /ˈnɪərli/ *adv* quase NOTA Com freqüência, **almost** e **nearly** são intercambiáveis. Mas apenas **almost** pode qualificar outro advérbio terminado em -ly: *almost completely* e apenas **nearly** pode ser qualificado por outros advérbios: *I very nearly left.* ▸ **not nearly** nem (de perto)

near-sighted *adj* míope

neat /niːt/ *adj* (~er, ~est) **1** em ordem, arrumado **2** (*pessoa*) organizado **3** (*letra*) caprichado **4** (*coloq, esp USA*) genial **5** (*GB*) (*líquidos*) puro (*sem água*) **neat·ly** *adv* **1** organizadamente, asseadamente **2** habilmente

necessarily /ˌnesəˈserəli/ *adv* necessariamente

necessary /ˈnesəseri; GB -səri/ *adj* **1** necessário **2** inevitável

necessitate /nəˈsesɪteɪt/ *vt* (*fml*) requerer

necessity /nəˈsesəti/ *s* (*pl* -ies) **1** necessidade **2** artigo de primeira necessidade

neck /nek/ *s* **1** pescoço **2** (*roupa*) gola ▸ **neck and neck (with sb/ sth)** emparelhado (com alguém/algo) **up to your neck in sth** até o pescoço em algo

necklace /ˈnekləs/ *s* colar

neckline /ˈneklaɪn/ *s* decote

necktie /ˈnektaɪ/ *s* gravata

nectarine /ˌnektəˈriːn/ *s* nectarina

need /niːd/ *v modal* (*neg* **need not** *ou* **needn't** /ˈniːdnt/ (GB)/) (*obrigação*) precisar: *You needn't have come.* Você não precisava ter vindo. NOTA Quando é verbo modal, **need** é seguido de infinitivo sem *to* e as orações interrogativas e negativas são formadas sem o auxiliar *do*. ● *vt* **1** necessitar: *It needs painting.* Está precisando de uma pintura. **2** ~ **to do sth** ter que fazer algo: *Do we ~ to leave now?* Precisamos sair agora? NOTA Neste sentido, é possível usar o verbo modal, que seria mais formal: *Need we really leave so early?* ● *s* ~ **(for sth)** necessidade (de algo): *be in ~ of sth* necessitar algo ▸ **if need be** se (for) necessário

needle /ˈniːdl/ *s* agulha

needless /ˈniːdləs/ *adj* desnecessário ▸ **needless to say** nem é preciso dizer que

needlework /ˈniːdlwɜːrk/ *s* [U] costura, bordado

needy /ˈniːdi/ *adj* necessitado

negative /ˈnegətɪv/ *adj* negativo ● *s* (*Fot*) negativo

neglect /nɪˈglekt/ *vt* **1** negligenciar **2** ~ **to do sth** esquecer(-se) de fazer algo ● *s* abandono

negligent /ˈneglɪdʒənt/ *adj* negligente **negligence** *s* negligência

negligible /ˈneglɪdʒəbl/ *adj* insignificante

negotiate /nɪˈgoʊʃieɪt/ **1** *vi, vt* negociar **2** *vt* (*obstáculo*) contornar **negotiation** *s* negociação

neigh /neɪ/ *vi* relinchar ● *s* relincho

neighbor (GB **-our**) /ˈneɪbər/ *s* **1** vizinho/a **2** próximo/a **neighborhood** (GB **-our-**) *s* **1** bairro **2** vizinhança **neighboring** (GB **-our-**) *adj* contíguo

neither /ˈnaɪðər, ˈniːðər/ *adj, pron* nenhum → NENHUM ● *adv* **1** nem, também não NOTA Quando **neither** significa "tampouco/nem" pode ser substituído por **nor**. Com ambos utiliza-se a estrutura: **neither/nor** + **v aux/v modal** + **sujeito**: *I don't go.* "*Neither/nor did I.*" ◇ *I can't swim and neither/nor can my brother.* **Either** pode significar "tampouco/também não", mas requer um verbo na negativa e ocupa uma posição diferente na oração: *I don't like it, and I can't afford it either.* ◇ *My sister didn't go either.* ◇ "*I haven't seen that movie.*" "*I haven't either.*" **2** (**neither... nor**) nem... nem

neon /ˈniːɑːn/ *s* néon

nephew /ˈnefjuː; GB tb ˈnevjuː/ *s* sobrinho (*homem*)

Neptune /ˈneptuːn; GB -tjuːn/ *s* Netuno

nerd /nɜːrd/ *s* (*coloq, pej*) **1** *He's a bit of a nerd.* Ele é meio chato. ◇ *I feel like a nerd.* Eu me sinto um idiota. **2** (*tb* **computer ~**): *He's a computer nerd.* Ele é obcecado com computadores.

nerve /nɜːrv/ *s* **1** nervo: *nerve-racking* desesperador **2** coragem **3** (*coloq*): *You've got some ~!* Você é cara-de-pau! ▸ **get on your/sb's nerves** (*coloq*) dar nos nervos de alguém

nervous /ˈnɜːrvəs/ *adj* ~ **(about/ of (doing) sth)** nervoso (com a idéia de fazer algo) **nervousness** *s* nervosismo

nest /nest/ *s* ninho

nestle /ˈnesl/ **1** *vi* acomodar(-se), aconchegar(-se) **2** *vi* (*vilarejo*) estar situado **3** *vt, vi* ~ **(sth) against/on sb/sth** recostar algo, recostar-se a alguém/algo

net /net/ s **1** rede **2** [U] tela: ~ *curtains* cortinas de filó ● *adj* (tb **nett**) **1** (*peso, salário*) líquido **2** (*resultado*) final **netting** s rede: *wire* ~ tela de arame ◊ **netball** /ˈnetbɔːl/ s tipo de basquete

nettle /ˈnetl/ s urtiga

network /ˈnetwɜːrk/ s rede, sistema ● **1** *vt* interligar (em rede) **2** *vi* fazer (uma rede de) contatos

neurotic /nʊəˈrɒtɪk; *GB* njʊ-/ *adj, s* neurótico/a

neutral /ˈnuːtrəl; *GB* ˈnjuː-/ *adj* neutro ● *s* (*marcha*) ponto morto

never /ˈnevər/ *adv* **1** nunca **2** *That will* ~ *do.* Isto não serve (de maneira alguma). ► **well, I never (did)** veja(m) só → ALWAYS, NUNCA

nevertheless /ˌnevərðəˈles/ *adv* (*fml*) no entanto

new /nuː; *GB* njuː/ *adj* (~**er**, ~**est**) novo: *a* ~ *lease on life* uma nova vida ◊ *What's* ~? Quais as novidades? ► **(as) good as new** como novo **newly** *adv* recém **newness** s novidade

newcomer /ˈnuːkʌmər; *GB* ˈnjuː-/ s recém-chegado/a

news /nuːz; *GB* njuːz/ s [U] **1** notícia(s), novidade(s): *a piece of* ~ uma notícia **2** (*the news*) o noticiário

newsdealer /ˈnuːzdiːlər; *GB* ˈnjuː-/ (*GB* **newsagent** /ˈnuːzeɪdʒənt; *GB* ˈnjuː-/) s jornaleiro/a

newspaper /ˈnuːzpeɪpər; *GB* ˈnjuː-/ s jornal (impresso)

newsstand /ˈnuːzstænd; *GB* ˈnjuːz-/ s banca de jornais

new year s ano novo

next /nekst/ *adj* **1** próximo, seguinte: ~ *month* o mês que vem ◊ *It's not ideal, but it's the* ~ *best thing.* Não é o ideal, mas é o melhor possível. **2** (*contíguo*) ao lado de ● **next to** *prep* **1** ao lado de, junto a **2** depois de **3** ~ *to nothing* quase nada ◊ ~ *to last* penúltimo ● *adv* **1** depois, agora **2** *when we* ~ *meet* na próxima vez em que nos encontrarmos **3** *the* ~ *oldest* o próximo em idade ● **the next** s [*sing*] o/a seguinte, o/a próximo/a ► **next of kin** parente(s) mais próximo(s)

next door *adj, adv*: *next-door neighbor* vizinho ao lado ◊ *the room next door* o quarto vizinho

nibble /ˈnɪbl/ *vt, vi* ~ **(at sth)** mordiscar, lambiscar (algo)

nice /naɪs/ *adj* (~**er**, ~**est**) **1** ~ **(to**

sb) simpático, amável (com alguém) ► **Sympathetic** se traduz por "compassivo". **2** bonito **3** agradável: *have a* ~ *time* divertir-se ◊ *It smells* ~. Tem cheiro bom. **4** (*tempo*) bom ► **nice and...** (*coloq*) bem: ~ *and warm* bem quentinho **nicely** *adv* **1** (muito) bem **2** de maneira amável/agradável

niche /nɪtʃ, niːʃ/ s **1** nicho **2** oportunidade, lugar

nick /nɪk/ s **1** entalhe, pequeno corte **(the nick)** (*GB, coloq*) a delegacia, a prisão ► **in the nick of time** na hora H ● *vt* **1** entalhar **2** roubar

nickel /ˈnɪkl/ s **1** níquel **2** (*Can, USA*) moeda de 5 centavos

nickname /ˈnɪkneɪm/ s apelido ● *vt* apelidar

nicotine /ˈnɪkətiːn/ s nicotina

niece /niːs/ s sobrinha

night /naɪt/ s **1** noite: ~ *school* escola noturna ◊ *at/by* ~ à/de noite **2** (*Teat*) apresentação: *opening* ~ noite de estréia ► **good night** boa noite, até manhã (*como despedida*) → NOITE

nightclub /ˈnaɪtklʌb/ s Ver CLUB (2)

nightfall /ˈnaɪtfɔːl/ s anoitecer

nightgown /ˈnaɪtɡaʊn/ (*tb* **nightie** (*coloq*)) s camisola

nightingale /ˈnaɪtɪŋɡeɪl; *GB* -tɪŋɡ-/ s rouxinol

nightlife /ˈnaɪtlaɪf/ s vida noturna

nightly /ˈnaɪtli/ *adv* toda noite ● *adj* **1** noturno **2** de todas as noites

nightmare /ˈnaɪtmeər/ s pesadelo **nightmarish** *adj* apavorante

night-time s noite

nil /nɪl/ s **1** (*GB*) (*Esporte*) zero **2** nada

nimble /ˈnɪmbl/ *adj* (~**er**, ~**est**) **1** ágil **2** (*mente*) esperto

nine /naɪn/ *adj, pron, s* nove **ninth 1** *adj* nono **2** *pron, adv* o(s)/a(s) nono(s)/a(s) **3** s nona parte, nono

nineteen /ˌnaɪnˈtiːn/ *adj, pron, s* dezenove **nineteenth 1** *adj* décimo nono **2** *pron, adv* o(s)/a(s) décimo(s) nono(s), a(s) décima(s) nona(s) **3** s décima nona parte, dezenove avos

ninety /ˈnaɪnti/ *adj, pron, s* noventa **ninetieth 1** *adj, pron* nonagésimo **2** s nonagésima parte, noventa avos

nip /nɪp/ (-**pp**-) **1** *vt* beliscar **2** *vi*

(*coloq*) correr: ~ *out* sair por um momento

nipple /'nɪpl/ s mamilo

nitrogen /'naɪtrədʒən/ s nitrogênio

no /nəʊ/ *adj* [antes de substantivo] **1** nenhum: *No two people are the same* Não há duas pessoas iguais. ♦ **NENHUM 2** *No smoking.* Proibido fumar. **3** (para enfatizar): *She's no fool.* Ela não é nenhuma tola. ♦ *It's no joke.* Não é brincadeira. ● *adv* [antes de adj comparativo e adv] não ● *interj* não

nobility /nəʊ'bɪləti/ s nobreza

noble /'nəʊbl/ *adj, s* (-er /'nəʊblər/, -est /'nəʊblɪst/) nobre

nobody /'nəʊbədi/ *pron* ninguém NOTA Não se podem utilizar duas negativas na mesma oração. Como **nobody, nothing** e **nowhere** são negativas, o verbo sempre fica no afirmativo: *Nobody saw him.* ♦ *She said nothing.* ♦ *Nothing happened.* Com o verbo na negativa, usa-se **anybody, anything** e **anywhere**: *I didn't see anybody.* ♦ *She didn't say anything.* ● *s* (pl -ies) joão-ninguém

nocturnal /nɒk'tɜ:rnl/ *adj* noturno

nod /nɒd/ (-dd-) *vt, vi* afirmar com a cabeça: *He nodded in agreement.* Ele disse sim com a cabeça. **2** *vi* saudar com a cabeça (a alguém) **3** *vt, vi* indicar/fazer sinal com a cabeça **4** *vi* pescar (dormindo) ■ **nod off** (*coloq*) cochilar ● *s* movimento da cabeça ▸ **give (sb) the nod** dar permissão (a alguém) para fazer algo

noise /nɔɪz/ *s* ruído ▸ **make a noise (about sth)** fazer escândalo (por algo) **noisily** *adv* ruidosamente, escandalosamente **noisy** *adj* (-ier -iest) **1** ruidoso **2** barulhento

nomad /'nəʊmæd/ s nômade **nomadic** /nəʊ'mædɪk/ *adj* nômade

nominal /'nɒmɪnl/ *adj* nominal **nominally** *adv* de nome, na aparência

nominate /'nɒmɪneɪt/ *vt* **1** nomear **2** ~ **sth (as sth)** designar algo (como algo) **nomination** *s* nomeação

nominee /ˌnɒmɪ'ni:/ s candidato/a, pessoa indicada

none /nʌn/ *pron* **1** nenhum/a **2** [com substantivos ou pronomes não contáveis] nada **3** (*fml*) ninguém ▸ **none but** apenas

none other than nada mais nada menos do que ● *adv* **1** [the+ comparativo]: *I'm* ~ *the wiser.* Continuo sem entender nada. ♦ *He's* ~ *the worse for it.* Não lhe fez mal. **2** [too+ adj/adv]: ~ *too clean* não muito limpo

nonetheless /ˌnʌnðə'les/ *adv* todavia

non-existent /ˌnɒn ɪɡ'zɪstənt/ *adj* inexistente

non-fiction /ˌnɒn 'fɪkʃn/ s (livros de) não-ficção

no one *Ver* NOBODY

nonsense /'nɒnsens; GB -sns/ s [U] **1** absurdo(s) **2** tolice **nonsensical** /nɒn'sensɪkl/ *adj* absurdo

non-stop /ˌnɒn 'stɒp/ *adj* **1** (vôo, etc.) direto **2** ininterrupto ● *adv* **1** diretamente, sem escalas **2** sem parar

noodle /'nu:dl/ s macarrão tipo espaguete

noon /nu:n/ s meio-dia

noose /nu:s/ s nó corrediço, laço

nor /nɔ:r/ *conj, adv* **1** nem: *Nor do I.* Nem eu. **2** tampouco → NEITHER

norm /nɔ:rm/ s norma

normal /'nɔ:rml/ *adj, s* normal: *Things are back to* ~. As coisas voltaram ao normal. **normally** *adv* normalmente → ALWAYS

north /nɔ:rθ/ s (tb **the north, the North**) (abrev **N.**) (o) norte: *northbound* em direção ao norte ● *adj* (do) norte ● *adv* para o norte

north-east s (abrev **NE**) nordeste ● *adj* (do) nordeste ● *adv* para o nordeste **north-eastern** *adj* (do) nordeste

northern (tb **Northern**) /'nɔ:rðərn/ *adj* do norte **northerner** s nortista

northward(s) /'nɔ:rθwərd(z)/ *adv* em direção ao norte

north-west s (abrev **NW**) noroeste ● *adj* (do) noroeste ● *adv* para o noroeste **north-western** *adj* (do) noroeste

nose /nəʊz/ s **1** nariz **2** faro ■ **nose about/around** bisbilhotar

nostalgia /nɒ'stældʒə/ s nostalgia

nostril /'nɒstrəl/ s narina

nosy (tb **nosey**) /'nəʊzi/ *adj* (-ier, -iest) (*coloq*) xereta

not /nɒt/ *adv* não: *I hope* ~. Espero que não. ♦ ~ *even...* Nem mesmo... NOTA **Not** forma a negativa com verbos auxiliares e modais (be, do, have, can, must, etc.) e muitas vezes é usado como a contração -n't: *She is not/isn't going.* ◇ *We did not/didn't go.* ◇ *I must not/mustn't go.* A forma não contraída (**not**) é mais formal ou enfática e coloca a negativa dos verbos subordinados: *He warned me not to be late.* ◇ *I suppose not.* ▸**not as...as all that** não tão... assim: *He's not as rich as all that.* Ele não é tão rico assim. **not at all 1** (*resposta*) de nada **2** nada, nem um pouco **not that...**: *It's ~ that I mind...* Não que eu me importe...

notably /'nɒʊtəbli/ *adv* particularmente

notary public /'nɒʊtəri pʌblɪk/ *s* (*pl* notaries public) tabelião/ã (público/a)

notch /nɒtʃ/ *s* **1** entalhe **2** grau ■ **notch sth up** (*coloq*) conseguir algo

note /nɒʊt/ *s* **1** nota (*tb Mús*): notepaper papel de carta ◇ banknote nota (de dinheiro) **2** (*piano, etc.*) tecla **3** tom: *an optimistic* ~ um tom otimista ● *vt* **1** notar, observar **2** ~ **sth (down)** anotar algo **noted** *adj* ~ **(for/as sth)** conhecido (por (ser) algo)

notebook /'nɒʊtbʊk/ *s* caderno

noteworthy /'nɒʊtwɜːrθi/ *adj* digno de nota

nothing /'nʌθɪŋ/ *pron* **1** nada → NOBODY **2** zero ▸**for nothing 1** grátis **2** em vão **have nothing to do with sb/sth** não ter nada a ver com alguém/algo **nothing much** nada de mais

notice /'nɒʊtɪs/ *s* **1** anúncio: noticeboard (GB) quadro de avisos **2** aviso: *until further* ~ até segunda ordem ◇ *give one month's* ~ avisar com um mês de antecedência **3** (*carta de*) demissão ▸**take no notice/not take any notice (of sb/sth)** não dar atenção (a alguém/algo) ● *vt* **1** dar-se conta **2** prestar atenção a, notar **noticeable** *adj* perceptível, evidente

notify /'nɒʊtɪfaɪ/ *vt* (*pt, pp* -ied) notificar

notion /'nɒʊʃn/ *s* noção, idéia

notorious /nɒʊ'tɔːriəs/ *adj* ~ **(for/as sth)** de má reputação (por (ser) algo)

notwithstanding /ˌnɒtwɪθ-'stændɪŋ/ *prep* (*fml*) apesar de ● *adv* (*fml*) ainda assim

nought /nɔːt/ *s* (GB) zero

noun /naʊn/ *s* substantivo

nourish /'nɜːrɪʃ/ *vt* **1** nutrir **2** (*fml*) (*fig*) alimentar **nourishing** *adj* nutritivo

novel /'nɒvl/ *adj* original ● *s* romance **novelist** ▸*s* romancista

novelty /'nɒvlti/ *s* (*pl* -ies) novidade

November /nɒʊ'vembər/ *s* (*abrev* **Nov.**) novembro → MAY

novice /'nɒvɪs/ *s* **1** novato/a **2** noviço/a

now /naʊ/ *adv* **1** agora **2** então ▸**(every) now and again/then** de vez em quando ● *conj* **now (that...)** agora que...

nowadays /'naʊədeɪz/ *adv* hoje em dia

nowhere /'nɒʊweər/ *adv* a/em lugar nenhum: *There's* ~ *to park.* Não há lugar para estacionar. ▸**NOBODY** ▸**be nowhere to be found/seen** não se encontrar em lugar algum

nozzle /'nɒzl/ *s* bocal

nuance /'nuːɑːns; GB 'njuː-/ *s* matiz

nuclear /'nuːkliər; GB 'njuː-/ *adj* nuclear

nucleus /'nuːkliəs; GB 'njuː-/ *s* (*pl* -lei /-liaɪ/) núcleo

nude /nuːd; GB njuːd/ *adj* nu (*artístico, erótico*) → NAKED ● *s* nu (*artístico*) ▸**in the nude** nu **nudity** *s* nudez

nudge /nʌdʒ/ *vt* **1** dar uma cotovelada em **2** empurrar gentilmente

nuisance /'nuːsns; GB 'njuː-/ *s* **1** incômodo **2** (*pessoa*) chato/a: *Stop making a* ~ *of yourself.* Pare de amolar.

null /nʌl/ *adj* ▸**null and void** nulo

numb /nʌm/ *adj* (*parte do corpo*) dormente: ~ *with shock* paralisado de susto ● *vt* **1** entorpecer **2** paralisar

number /'nʌmbər/ *s* **1** (*abrev* **No**) número **2 a** ~ **of...** vários, certos ● *vt* **1** numerar **2** ser em número **3** ~ **sth** (*fechamento*) ascender a: *We numbered 20 in all.* Éramos 20 no total.

number plate *s* (GB) placa (*de carro*)

numerical /nuː'merɪkl; GB njuː-/ *adj* numérico

numerous /'nuːmərəs; GB 'njuː-/ *adj* (*fml*) numeroso

nun /nʌn/ *s* freira

nurse /nɜːrs/ *s* **1** enfermeiro/a **2** (*tb* nursemaid) babá ● *vt* **1** cuidar de **2** *vt, vi* (*mãe*) amamentar **3** *vi* (*bebê*) mamar **4** *vt* abraçar **5** *vt* (*sentimentos*) alimentar **nursing** *s* **1** enfermagem: ~ *home* asilo para idosos **2** cuidado (*enfermos*)

nursery /'nɜːrsəri/ s (pl -ies) 1 creche: ~ school escola maternal ◇ ~ rhyme canção infantil 2 quarto de crianças 3 viveiro (plantas)

nurture /'nɜːrtʃər/ vt 1 (criança) criar 2 alimentar 3 fomentar

nut /nʌt/ s 1 noz: Brazil ~ castanha-do-pará 2 porca (parafuso) 3 (coloq) (GB tb nutcase /'nʌtkeɪs/ (tb nutter)) maluco/a 4 fanático/a

nutcrackers /'nʌtkrækərz/ s [pl] quebra-nozes

nutmeg /'nʌtmeg/ s noz-moscada

nutrient /'nuːtriənt; GB 'njuː-/ s nutriente

nutrition /nuː'trɪʃn; GB 'njuː-/ s nutrição nutritional adj nutritivo nutritious adj nutritivo

nuts /nʌts/ adj (coloq) 1 maluco 2 ~ about sth/sb louco por alguém/algo

nutshell /'nʌtʃel/ s casca (noz) ▸in a nutshell em poucas palavras

nutty adj (-ier, -iest) 1 a ~ flavor um sabor de castanhas 2 (coloq) maluco

nylon /'naɪlɑn/ s náilon

nymph /nɪmf/ s ninfa

O o

O, o /oʊ/ s (pl O's, o's /oʊz/) 1 O, o 2 zero

oak /oʊk/ (tb ~ tree) s carvalho

oar /ɔːr/ s remo

oasis /oʊ'eɪsɪs/ s (pl oases /-siːz/) oásis

oath /oʊθ/ s 1 juramento: on/under ~ sob juramento 2 palavrão

oats /oʊts/ s [pl] (grãos de) aveia

obedient /oʊ'biːdiənt; GB ə'biːd-/ adj obediente obedience s obediência

obese /oʊ'biːs/ adj (fml) obeso

obey /oʊ'beɪ; GB ə'beɪ/ vt, vi obedecer

obituary /oʊ'bɪtʃueri; GB ə'bɪtʃuəri/ s (pl -ies) obituário

object /'ɑbdʒɪkt/ s 1 objeto 2 objetivo ● /əb'dʒekt/ vi ~ (to sth/sb) objetar (a alguém/algo): If he doesn't ~. Se ele não tiver nada contra.

objection /əb'dʒekʃn/ s objeção

objective /əb'dʒektɪv/ adj, s objetivo: remain ~ manter a objetividade

obligation /,ɑblɪ'geɪʃn/ s 1 obrigação 2 (Com) compromisso

obligatory /ə'blɪgətɔːri; GB -tri/ adj (fml) obrigatório

oblige /ə'blaɪdʒ/ vt 1 obrigar 2 ~ sb (with sth/by doing sth) fazer um favor, satisfazer a alguém (fazendo algo) obliged adj agradecido obliging adj atencioso

obliterate /ə'blɪtəreɪt/ vt eliminar

oblivion /ə'blɪviən/ s esquecimento

oblivious /ə'blɪviəs/ adj não consciente

oblong /'ɑblɔːŋ; GB -lɒŋ/ s retângulo ● adj retangular

oboe /'oʊboʊ/ s oboé

obscene /əb'siːn/ adj obsceno

obscure /əb'skjʊər/ adj 1 obscuro 2 desconhecido ● vt obscurecer

observation /,ɑbzər'veɪʃn/ s observação

observatory /əb'zɜːrvətɔːri; GB -tri/ s (pl -ies) observatório

observe /əb'zɜːrv/ vt 1 observar 2 (fml) (festividade) celebrar observer s observador/a observant adj observador

obsess /əb'ses/ vt obcecar obsession s obsessão obsessive adj obsessivo

obsolete /'ɑbsəliːt/ adj obsoleto

obstacle /'ɑbstəkl/ s obstáculo

obstetrician /,ɑbstə'trɪʃn/ s obstetra

obstinate /'ɑbstɪnət/ adj obstinado

obstruct /əb'strʌkt/ vt obstruir obstruction s obstrução

obtain /əb'teɪn/ vt obter obtainable adj obtenível

obvious /'ɑbviəs/ adj óbvio obviously adv obviamente

occasion /ə'keɪʒn/ s 1 ocasião 2 acontecimento 3 oportunidade

occasional /ə'keɪʒənl/ adj esporádico: She reads the ~ book. Ela lê um livro ocasionalmente. occasionally adv de vez em quando → ALWAYS

occupant /'ɑkjəpənt/ s ocupante

occupation /,ɑkju'peɪʃn/ s 1 ocupação 2 profissão → WORK

occupational /,ɑkju'peɪʃənl/ adj 1 profissional 2 (terapia) ocupacional

occupier /'ɑkjupaɪər/ s ocupante

occupy /'ɑkjupaɪ/ vt (pt, pp -ied) 1 ocupar 2 ~ yourself (in doing sth/with sth) ocupar-se (fazendo algo/com algo)

occur /əˈkɜːr/ *vi* (**-rr-**) **1** ocorrer **2** existir

occurrence /əˈkʌrəns/ *s* **1** acontecimento, caso **2** aparecimento **3** freqüência

ocean /ˈoʊʃn/ *s* oceano

o'clock /əˈklɑk/ *adv*: *six* ~ seis horas

October /ɑkˈtoʊbər/ *s* (*abrev* **Oct.**) outubro → MAY

octopus /ˈɑktəpəs/ *s* polvo

odd /ɑd/ *adj* **1** (**-er, -est**) estranho **2** (*número*) ímpar **3** (*artigo de um par*) **4** restante, a mais **5** *thirty-odd* trinta e poucos ▸ *twelve pounds* ~ doze libras e pouco **6** *have the* ~ *beer* tomar uma cerveja de vez em quando ▸ *be the odd man/one out* ser o único sem par, ser diferente

oddity /ˈɑdəti/ *s* (*pl* **-ies**) **1** (*tb* **oddness**) peculiaridade **2** excentricidade **3** (*pessoa*) excêntrico/a

oddly /ˈɑdli/ *adv* de maneira estranha: ~ *enough...* Curiosamente...

odds /ɑdz/ *s* [*pl*] **1** probabilidades: *The* ~ *are that...* O mais provável é que... **2** apostas ▸ *be at odds (with sb)* (*on/over sth*) desentender-se (com alguém) (a respeito de algo) *it makes no odds* (*GB, coloq*) dá no mesmo **odds and ends** (*coloq*) coisas sem valor, quinquilharias

odor (*GB* **-our**) /ˈoʊdər/ *s* (*fml*) odor: *body* ~ cheiro de suor NOTA Geralmente implica cheiro desagradável.

of /əv, ʌv/ *prep* **1** de: *It was very kind of him.* Foi muito gentil da parte dele. ◇ *the first of May* o dia primeiro de maio ◇ *What did she die of?* Do que ela morreu? **2** (*com possessivos*) de: *a friend of John's* um amigo de John ◇ *a cousin of mine* um primo meu **3** (*com quantidades*): *There were five of us.* Éramos cinco. ◇ *most of all* acima de tudo

off /ɔːf; *GB* ɒf/ *adj* (*GB*) **1** (*comida*) estragado **2** (*leite*) azedado ● *adv* **1** (*distância*): *five miles* ~ a cinco milhas ◇ *not far* ~ não muito distante **2** *You left the lid* ~. Você deixou destampado. ▸ *with her shoes* ~ descalça **3** *I must be* ~. Tenho que ir embora. **4** *The meeting is* ~. A reunião está cancelada. **5** (*luz,*

máquina) desligado **6** (*torneira*) fechado **7** *a day* ~ um dia de folga **8** *five per cent* ~ cinco por cento de desconto ▸ *be off (for sth)* (*GB, coloq*): *How are you* ~ *for cash?* Como você está de dinheiro? **off and on** os tempos em tempos ● *prep* **1** de: *fall* ~ *sth* cair de algo **2** *a street* ~ *the main road* uma rua que sai da principal **3** ~ *the coast* a certa distância da costa **4** (*GB*) sem vontade de: ~ *your food* sem fome ▸ **come off it** pare com isso NOTA Para o uso de **off** em PHRASAL VERBS, ver o verbo, p. ex. **go off** em GO.

off-duty *adj* de folga

offend /əˈfend/ *vt* ofender: *be offended* ofender-se offender *s* **1** infrator/a **2** criminoso/a

offense (*GB* **offence**) /əˈfens/ *s* **1** delito **2** ofensa: *take* ~ *at sth* ofender-se por algo

offensive /əˈfensɪv/ *adj* **1** ofensivo **2** repugnante ● *s* ofensiva

offer /ˈɔːfər; *GB* ˈɒf-/ *vt, vi* oferecer ● *s* oferta **offering** *s* **1** oferecimento **2** oferenda

offhand /ˌɔːfˈhænd; *GB* ˌɒf-/ *adv* de improviso, sem pensar ● *adj* brusco

office /ˈɔːfɪs; *GB* ˈɒf-/ *s* **1** escritório: ~ *hours* horário de expediente **2** consultório **3** cargo: *take* ~ tomar posse ▸ **in office** no poder

officer /ˈɔːfɪsər; *GB* ˈɒf-/ *s* **1** (*exército*) oficial **2** funcionário/a **3** (*tb* **police** ~) policial

official /əˈfɪʃl/ *adj* oficial ● *s* funcionário/a **officially** *adv* oficialmente

off-licence *s* (*GB*) loja de bebidas

off-peak *adj* **1** de baixa temporada **2** de menor consumo

off-putting *adj* (*coloq*) **1** desconcertante **2** (*pessoa*) desagradável

offset /ˌɔːfˈset; *GB* ˌɒf-/ *vt* (**-tt-**) (*pt, pp* **offset**) compensar

offshore /ˌɔːfˈʃɔːr; *GB* ˌɒf-/ *adj* **1** (*ilha*) próximo da costa **2** (*brisa*) terrestre **3** (*pesca*) costeira

offside /ˌɔːfˈsaɪd; *GB* ˌɒf-/ *adj, adv* (*Esporte*) impedido

offspring /ˈɔːfsprɪŋ; *GB* ˈɒf-/ *s* (*pl* **offspring**) (*fml*) **1** filho(s), descendência **2** cria

often /ˈɔːfn; *GB* ˈɒfn/ *adv* **1** muitas vezes: *How* ~ *do you see her?* Com que freqüência você a vê? **2** geralmente → ALWAYS

oh /oʊ/ *interj* **1** ó, ah **2** *Oh yes I*

will. Com certeza eu vou! ◇ *Oh no you won't!* Ah, não vai, não!

oil /ɔɪl/ s **1** petróleo: *oilfield* campo petrolífero ◇ ~ *rig* plataforma de petróleo ◇ ~ *tanker* petroleiro **2** óleo **3** (*Arte*) tinta a óleo ● vt lubrificar *oily adj* (**-ier**, **-iest**) **1** oleoso **2** engordurado

OK (*tb* **okay**) /ˌoʊˈkeɪ/ *adj* (*coloq*) bom ● *adv* (*coloq*) bem ● *interj* tudo bem ● vt aprovar ● s consentimento, aprovação

old /oʊld/ *adj* (**-er**, **-est**) → ELDER **1** velho: ~ *age* velhice ◇ ~ *people* os idosos ◇ *the* ~ *Testament* o Antigo Testamento **2** *How* ~ *are you?* Quantos anos você tem? NOTA Para falar "tenho dez anos", diz-se *I am ten* ou *I am ten years old.* Mas "um menino de dez anos" é a *boy of ten* ou a *ten-year-old boy.* ✦ YEAR **3** antigo ● **the old** s [*pl*] os idosos

old-fashioned *adj* **1** fora de moda **2** tradicional

olive /ˈɑlɪv/ s **1** azeitona: ~ *oil* azeite ◇ ~ *(tb* ~ *tree*) oliveira ● *adj* **1** (*tb* ~ *green*) verde-oliva **2** (*pele*) azeitonado

the Olympic Games (*tb the* **Olympics**) s as Olimpíadas

omelet (*tb* **omelette**) /ˈɑmlət/ s omelete

omen /ˈoʊmen/ s presságio

ominous /ˈɑmɪnəs/ *adj* agourento

omission /oʊˈmɪʃn/ s omissão, ausência

omit /oʊˈmɪt/ vt (**-tt-**) **1** ~ *doing/to do sth* deixar de fazer algo **2** omitir

omnipotent /ɑmˈnɪpətənt/ *adj* onipotente

on /ɑn, ɔn/ *adv* **1** (*continuidade*): *play on* continuar tocando ◇ *further on* mais adiante ◇ (*roupa, etc.*) vestido: *I have my glasses on.* Estou de óculos. **3** (*máquinas, etc.*) ligado **4** (*torneira*) aberto **5** programado: *When is the movie on?* A que horas começa o filme? ● **on and on** sem parar ● **on and off de** tempos em tempos ● *prep* **1** em, sobre **2** (*transporte*): *go on foot/on the train* ir a pé/de trem **3** (*datas*): *on Sunday/May 3* no domingo/no dia três de maio **4** (*tb* **upon**) [+ *-ing*]: *on arriving home* ao chegar em casa **5** (*a respeito de*) sobre **6** (*consumo*): *be on drugs* estar tomando drogas ◇ *live on fruit/on \$20 a week* viver de frutas/com 20 dólares por semana **7** em (*atividade, etc.*) de:

on vacation/on duty de férias/de serviço NOTA Para o uso de **on** em PHRASAL VERBS, ver os verbetes dos verbos correspondentes, p. ex. **get on** em GET.

once /wʌns/ *conj* uma vez que: *Once he'd gone...* Assim que ele saiu... ● *adv* uma vez ● **at once 1** imediatamente **2** de uma só vez **once again/more** mais uma vez **once and for all** de uma vez por todas **once in a while** de vez em quando **once or twice** algumas vezes **once upon a time** era uma vez

oncoming /ˈʌnkʌmɪŋ, ˈɔːn-/ *adj* em direção contrária

one /wʌn/ *adj* (a) **2** único **3** *of* ~ *mind* da mesma opinião ● *pron* **1** [*depois de adj*]: *the little ones* os pequenos ◇ *I prefer this/that* ~. Prefiro este/aquele. ◇ *Which* ~? Qual? ● *another* ~ (um) outro ◇ *It's better than the old* ~. É melhor que o antigo. **2** o(s), a(s): *the* ~ *at the end* o que está no final **3** um(a): *I need a pen. Do you have* ~? Preciso de uma caneta. Você tem uma? **4** [*sujeito indeterminado*] (*fml*): *One must be sure.* Deve-se estar seguro. ● YOU ● **(all) in one** tudo em um **one by one** um a um **one or two** alguns

one another *pron* uns aos outros, um ao outro

one-off *adj, s* (*algo*) excepcional/único

oneself /wʌnˈself/ *pron* **1** [*uso reflexivo*]: *cut* ~ cortar-se **2** [*uso enfático*] mesmo: *do it* ~ fazer sozinho

one-way *adj* **1** (*rua*) de mão única **2** (*passagem*) de ida

ongoing /ˈɑngoʊɪŋ/ *adj* **1** em andamento **2** atual

onion /ˈʌnjən/ s cebola

online /ˌɑnˈlaɪn/ *adj, adv* (*Informát*) conectado

onlooker /ˈɑnlʊkər/ s espectador/a

only /ˈoʊnli/ *adv* somente, apenas ● **not only... but also** não só... mas também **only just 1** I've ~ *just arrived.* Acabo de chegar. **2** *I can* ~ *just see.* Eu mal consigo ver. ● *adj* único: *an* ~ *child* filho único ● *conj* (*coloq*) só que, mas

onset /ˈɑnset/ s início

onslaught /ˈɑnslɔːt/ s ~ (**on sb/sth**) investida violenta (contra alguém/algo)

onto (*tb* **on to**) /ˈɑntə, ˈɑntu/ *prep* em, sobre, a ● **be onto sb** (*coloq*) estar atrás de alguém **be onto**

sth ter descoberto algo importante

onward /'ɑnwərd, 'ɔːn-/ adj (fml) para diante/frente: your ~ journey a continuação da sua viagem ● adv (tb onwards) 1 para frente 2 em diante

ooze /uːz/ 1 vt, vi ~ (with) sth soltar, exsudar algo 2 vi ~ from/out of sth vazar de algo

opaque /ou'peɪk/ adj opaco

open /'oupən/ adj 1 aberto 2 (vista) desimpedido 3 público 4 leave sth ~ deixar algo em aberto ▸ in the open air ao ar livre ● 1 vt, vi ~ (sth) (out/up) abrir-se, abrir algo 2 vt começar 3 vt, vi (edifício, etc.) inaugurar ■ open into/onto sth dar (acesso) para (um lugar) open sth out abrir algo open up (coloq) abrir-se, soltar-se ■ the open s o ar livre ▸ come (out) into the open vir a público **opener** s abridor **openly** adv abertamente **openness** s franqueza

open-air adj ao ar livre

opening /'oupənɪŋ/ s 1 abertura 2 começo 3 (tb ~ night) (Teat) estréia 4 inauguração 5 (trabalho) vaga 6 oportunidade ● adj primeiro

open-minded adj de mente aberta

opera /'ɑprə/ s ópera

operate /'ɑpəreɪt/ 1 vt, vi funcionar, operar 2 vt (serviço) oferecer 3 vt (negócio) dirigir 4 vi ~ (on sb) (for sth) (Med) operar (alguém) (de algo): operating room sala de cirurgia

operation /,ɑpə'reɪʃn/ s 1 operação 2 funcionamento ▸ be in/come into operation 1 estar/entrar em funcionamento 2 (Jur) estar/entrar em vigor **operational** adj 1 operacional 2 em funcionamento

operative /'ɑpərətɪv, 'ɑprə-/ adj 1 em funcionamento 2 (Jur) em vigor 3 (Med) operatório ● s operário/a

operator /'ɑpəreɪtər/ s operador/a: switchboard ~ telefonista

opinion /ə'pɪnɪən/ s opinião, parecer: in my ~ na minha opinião

opponent /ə'pounənt/ s oponente 2 be an ~ of sth ser contrário a algo

opportunity /,ɑpər'tuːnəti; GB 'tjuːn-/ s (pl -ies) ~ for (doing) sth; ~ (to do sth) oportunidade (de fazer algo): take the ~ of doing sth aproveitar a oportunidade para fazer algo

oppose /ə'pouz/ vt 1 opor-se a 2 (pessoa) enfrentar **opposed** adj contrário ▸ as opposed to: quality as ~ to quantity qualidade e não quantidade **opposing** adj contrário

opposite /'ɑpəzɪt/ adj 1 (GB) de frente: the house ~ a casa em frente/do outro lado da rua 2 contrário: the ~ sex o sexo oposto ● adv em frente ● prep (GB) ~ (to) sb/sth em frente de alguém/algo: ~ each other de frente um para o outro ● s o contrário

opposition /,ɑpə'zɪʃn/ s oposição

oppress /ə'pres/ vt 1 oprimir 2 angustiar **oppressed** adj oprimido **oppression** s opressão **oppressive** adj 1 opressivo 2 angustiante, sufocante

opt /ɑpt/ vi ~ to do sth optar por fazer algo ■ opt out (of sth) optar por não fazer algo, não participar (de algo)

optical /'ɑptɪkl/ adj óptico: ~ illusion ilusão de óptica

optician /ɑp'tɪʃn/ s oculista optician's (loja) óptica

optimism /'ɑptɪmɪzəm/ s otimismo **optimist** s otimista **optimistic** /,ɑptɪ'mɪstɪk/ adj otimista

optimum /'ɑptɪməm/ (tb optimal) adj ideal

option /'ɑpʃn/ s opção **optional** adj opcional

or /ɔːr/ conj 1 ou 2 senão 3 [depois de negativo] nem ▸ or so: an hour or so uma hora mais ou menos

oral /'ɔːrəl/ adj oral ● s (exame) oral

orange /'ɔːrɪndʒ; GB 'ɒr-/ s 1 (tb cor) laranja 2 (tb ~ tree) laranjeira ● adj (cor) laranja

orbit /'ɔːrbɪt/ s órbita ● vt, vi ~ (sth/around sth) descrever uma órbita, ficar em órbita (em torno de algo)

orchard /'ɔːrtʃərd/ s pomar

orchestra /'ɔːrkɪstrə/ s orquestra

orchid /'ɔːrkɪd/ s orquídea

ordeal /ɔːr'diːl/ s experiência penosa

order /'ɔːrdər/ s 1 ordem 2 (Com) pedido ▸ in order 1 em ordem 2 aceitável in order to/that... para/para que... in running/working order em perfeito estado de funcionamento out of order quebrado: It's out of ~. Não funciona. ● 1 vt ~ sb to do sth mandar alguém fazer algo: ~ sb around dar ordens a alguém 2 vt encomendar 3 vt, vi

~ (sth) (for sb) pedir (algo) (para alguém) **4** *vt* (*fml*) colocar em ordem, organizar

orderly /ˈɔːdərli/ *adj* **1** organizado **2** disciplinado

ordinance /ˈɔːdɪnəns/ *s* (*fml*) ordem, regulamento

ordinary /ˈɔːdəneri; GB ˈɔːdnri/ *adj* normal, comum ► **out of the ordinary** fora do comum

ore /ɔːr/ *s* minério

oregano /əˈreɡənoʊ; GB ˌɒrɪˈɡɑːnəʊ/ *s* orégano

organ /ˈɔːrɡən/ *s* (*Mús, Anat*) órgão

organic /ɔːrˈɡænɪk/ *adj* orgânico

organism /ˈɔːrɡənɪzəm/ *s* organismo

organization /ˌɔːrɡənɪˈzeɪʃn; GB -naɪˈz-/ *s* organização **organizational** *adj* organizacional

organize /ˈɔːrɡənaɪz/ **1** *vt, vi* organizar(-se) **2** *vt* (*pensamentos*) colocar em ordem **organizer** *s* organizador/a

orgy /ˈɔːrdʒi/ *s* (*pl* **-ies**) orgia

orient /ˈɔːriənt/ *vt* (*GB* **orientate**) /ˈɔːrienteɪt/ ~ **sb/sth (towards sb/sth)** orientar alguém/algo (para alguém/algo): ~ *yourself* orientar-se ● **the Orient** *s* o Oriente **oriental** /ˌɔːriˈentl/ *adj* oriental *s* **orientation** orientação

origin /ˈɔːrɪdʒɪn/ *s* origem

original /əˈrɪdʒənl/ *adj* **1** original **2** primeiro, primitivo ● *s* original ► **in the original** no original **originality** /əˌrɪdʒəˈnæləti/ *s* originalidade **originally** *adv* **1** originalmente **2** no princípio, antigamente

originate /əˈrɪdʒɪneɪt/ **1** *vi* originar-se, nascer **2** *vt* produzir

ornament /ˈɔːrnəmənt/ *s* adorno **ornamental** /ˌɔːrnəˈmentl/ *adj* decorativo

ornate /ɔːrˈneɪt/ *adj* **1** ornamentado **2** (*linguagem, etc.*) floreado

orphan /ˈɔːrfn/ *s* órfão ● *vt*: *be orphaned* ficar órfão **orphanage** *s* orfanato

orthodox /ˈɔːrθədɑːks/ *adj* ortodoxo

ostrich /ˈɑːstrɪtʃ/ *s* avestruz

other /ˈʌðər/ *adj* [com substantivos quando são precedidos de adjetivos possessivos ou demonstrativos] outro: *That ~ car was better.* Aquele outro carro era melhor. ► **sb/sth/somewhere or other** (*coloq*) alguém/algo/em algum lugar **the other day, week, etc.** outro dia, semana,

etc. ● *pron* **1** (*others*) outros/as: *Do you have any others?* Você tem mais? **2** (**the other**) o/a outro/a **3** (**the others**) [*pl*] os/as demais: *This shirt is too small and the others are too big.* Esta camisa é pequena demais e as outras são grandes demais. ● **other than** *prep* **1** exceto: *He never speaks to me ~ than to complain.* Ele não fala comigo a não ser para se queixar. **2** *He never behaves ~ than selfishly.* Ele nunca se comporta de uma maneira que não seja egoísta.

otherwise /ˈʌðərwaɪz/ *adv* **1** de outra maneira: *mulled wine, ~ known as Glühwein* vinho quente, também conhecido como Glühwein **2** sob outros aspectos ● *conj* senão, se não fosse assim ● *adj* diferente

otter /ˈɑːtər/ *s* lontra

ouch /aʊtʃ/ *interj* ai

ought /ɔːt/ *v modal* (*neg* **ought not** *ou* **oughtn't** /ˈɔːtnt/) NOTA **Ought** to é verbo modal, e as orações interrogativas e negativas são formadas sem o auxiliar *do*. **1** (*sugestões e conselhos*): *You ought to do it.* Você deveria fazê-lo. ◊ *I ought to have gone.* Eu deveria ter ido. **2** (*probabilidade*): *Five ought to be enough.* Cinco devem ser suficientes.

ounce /aʊns/ *s* (*abrev* **oz**) onça (*28,35 gramas*) ► Ver pág. 224

our /ɑr, ˈaʊər/ *adj poss* nosso

ours /ɑrz, ˈaʊərz/ *pron poss* nosso(s)/a(s): *a friend of ~* uma amiga nossa

ourselves /ɑrˈselvz, aʊərˈs-/ *pron* **1** [*uso reflexivo*] nós **2** [*uso enfático*] nós mesmos ► (**all) by ourselves** sozinhos

out /aʊt/ *adv* **1** fora: *be ~* não estar (em casa) **2** *The sun is ~.* O sol já saiu. **3** fora de moda **4** (*possibilidade, etc.*) descartado **5** (*luz, etc.*) apagado **6** *call ~* (*loud*) chamar em voz alta **7** (*cálculo*) errado **8** (*jogador*) eliminado **9** (*bola*) fora (*da quadra*) ► **be out to do sth** estar decidido a fazer algo NOTA Para o uso de **out** em PHRASAL VERBS ver o verbo, p. ex. **pick out** em PICK.

outbreak /ˈaʊtbreɪk/ *s* **1** surto **2** (*guerra*) deflagração

outburst /ˈaʊtbɜːrst/ *s* **1** explosão **2** (*emoção*) acesso

outcast /ˈaʊtkæst; GB -kɑːst/ *s* proscrito-a, pária

outcome /ˈaʊtkʌm/ *s* resultado

outcry /'aʊtkraɪ/ s (pl -ies) protesto

outdo /ˌaʊt'duː/ vt (3ª pess sing pres outdoes /-'dʌz/ pt outdid /-'dɪd/ pp outdone /-'dʌn/) superar

outdoor /'aʊtdɔːr/ adj ao ar livre

outdoors /ˌaʊt'dɔːrz/ adv ao ar livre, fora

outer /'aʊtər/ adj externo

outfit /'aʊtfɪt/ s 1 (roupa) conjunto 2 equipamento

outgoing /'aʊtgoʊɪŋ/ adj 1 para fora, de saída 2 (Pol) em fim de mandato 3 /aʊt'goʊɪŋ/ extrovertido

outgrow /ˌaʊt'groʊ/ vt (pt outgrew /-'gruː/ pp outgrown /-'groʊn/) 1 He's outgrown his shoes. Os sapatos dele ficaram pequenos. 2 (hábito, etc.) cansar-se de, abandonar

outing /'aʊtɪŋ/ s excursão (curta)

outlandish /aʊt'lændɪʃ/ adj esquisito

outlaw /'aʊtlɔː/ vt declarar ilegal ● s foragido/a

outlet /'aʊtlet/ s 1 escoadouro, saída 2 (fig) escape 3 (Com) ponto de venda 4 tomada

outline /'aʊtlaɪn/ s 1 contorno 2 linhas gerais, esboço ● vt 1 delinear 2 expor em linhas gerais

outlive /ˌaʊt'lɪv/ vt sobreviver a

outlook /'aʊtlʊk/ s 1 ~ (onto/over sth) perspectiva (de algo) 2 ponto de vista 3 prognóstico

outnumber /ˌaʊt'nʌmbər/ vt superar em número a

out of /'aʊt əv/ prep 1 fora de: jump out of bed pular da cama 2 (causa) de: eight out of every ten oito em cada dez 4 (material) de, com 5 out of work sem trabalho ▶ out of date 1 desatualizado 2 vencido

outpost /'aʊtpoʊst/ s posto avançado

output /'aʊtpʊt/ s 1 produção 2 (Fís) potência

outrage /'aʊtreɪdʒ/ s 1 atrocidade 2 escândalo 3 revolta ● /aʊt'reɪdʒ/ vt ultrajar outrageous /aʊt'reɪdʒəs/ adj 1 ultrajante 2 extravagante

outright /'aʊtraɪt/ adv 1 (sem rodeios) francamente 2 imediatamente 3 completamente 4 (vencer) indiscutivelmente ● adj 1 franco 2 (vencedor) indiscutível 3 (negativa) definitivo

outset /'aʊtset/ s ▶ at/from the outset (of sth) no/desde o princípio (de algo)

outside /ˌaʊt'saɪd/ s exterior: on/ from the ~ por/de fora ● prep (tb esp USA ~ of) fora (de): do lado de) fora, para fora ● /'aʊtsaɪd/ adj 1 externo, de fora 2 (chance) pequeno

outsider /ˌaʊt'saɪdər/ s 1 estranho/a 2 intruso/a 3 (competidor) azarão

outskirts /'aʊtskɜːrts/ s arredores

outspoken /aʊt'spoʊkən/ adj franco

outstanding /aʊt'stændɪŋ/ adj 1 excepcional 2 (visível) saliente 3 (pagamento, etc.) pendente

outstretched /ˌaʊt'stretʃt/ adj (braços) estendido

outward /'aʊtwərd/ adj 1 externo, superficial 2 (viagem) de ida outwardly adv por fora, aparentemente outwards adv para fora

outweigh /ˌaʊt'weɪ/ vt pesar/ importar mais que

oval /'oʊvl/ adj oval, ovalado

ovary /'oʊvəri/ s (pl -ies) ovário

oven /'ʌvn/ s forno

over /'oʊvər/ adv 1 knock sth ~ derrubar/entornar algo ◊ fall ~ cair 2 turn sth ~ virar algo 3 (lugar): ~ here/there (por/logo) aqui/ali/lá ◊ They came ~ to see us. Eles vieram para nos ver. 4 (left over) (sobrando): Is there any food left ~? Sobrou (alguma) comida? 5 (mais de): children of five and ~ crianças de cinco anos para cima 6 terminado: ~ and done with completamente terminado ▶ (all) over again (tudo) de novo over and over (again) repetidas vezes ● prep 1 sobre, por cima de 2 ~ the hill/ street do outro lado da colina/ rua 3 mais de 4 durante, enquanto: ~ lunch durante o almoço 5 por causa de: an argument ~ money uma discussão por questões de dinheiro 6 (via televisão, etc.) através: hear sth ~ the radio ouvir algo no rádio ▶ over and above além de NOTA Para o uso de over em PHRASAL VERBS, ver o verbo, p. ex. think over em THINK.

over- /'oʊvər/ pref 1 excessivamente 2 maior de: the ~60s os maiores de 60 anos

overall /ˌoʊvər'ɔːl/ adj 1 total 2 global 3 (vencedor) absoluto ● adv 1 no total 2 em geral ● /'oʊvərɔːl/ s 1 (GB) guarda-pó 2 (overalls) [pl] macacão

overbearing /ˌoʊvər'beərɪŋ/ adj dominador

overboard /'oʊvərbɔːrd/ adv pela borda: fall ~ cair ao mar

▶**go overboard** ficar extremamente entusiasmado

overcast /ˌouvərˈkæst; *GB* -ˈkɑːst/ *adj* nublado

overcharge /ˌouvərˈtʃɑrdʒ/ *vt, vi* ~ (**sb**) (**for sth**) cobrar a mais (de alguém) (por algo)

overcoat /ˈouvərkout/ *s* sobretudo

overcome /ˌouvərˈkʌm/ *vt* (*pt* **overcame** /-ˈkeɪm/ *pp* **overcome**) **1** superar, dominar **2** tomar, invadir

overcrowded /ˌouvərˈkraudɪd/ *adj* superlotado **overcrowding** *s* superlotação

overdo /ˌouvərˈduː/ *vt* (*pt* **overdid** /-ˈdɪd/ *pp* **overdone** /-ˈdʌn/) **1** exagerar, usar muito: ~ *it/things* passar das medidas **2** cozinhar demais

overdose /ˈouvərdous/ *s* overdose

overdraft /ˈouvərdræft; *GB* -drɑːft/ *s* saldo negativo

overdue /ˌouvərˈduː; *GB* -ˈdjuː/ *adj* **1** atrasado **2** (*Fin*) vencido (sem pagamento)

overestimate /ˌouvərˈestɪmeɪt/ *vt* superestimar

overflow /ˌouvərˈflou/ **1** *vt, vi* transbordar **2** *vi* extravasar ● /ˈouvərflou/ *s* **1** transbordamento **2** excesso **3** (*tb* ~ **pipe**) (cano) ladrão

overgrown /ˌouvərˈgroun/ *adj* **1** crescido/grande demais **2** ~ (**with sth**) coberto (de algo)

overhang /ˌouvərˈhæŋ/ *vt, vi, pp* **overhung** /-ˈhʌŋ/) projetar-se (sobre)

overhaul /ˌouvərˈhɔːl/ *vt* revisar ● /ˈouvərhɔːl/ *s* revisão

overhead /ˌouvərˈhed/ *adj* **1** elevado **2** (*cabos*) aéreo **3** (*luz*) de teto ● /ˈouvərhed/ *adv* por cima da cabeça, no alto

overhear /ˌouvərˈhɪər/ *vt* (*pt, pp* **overheard** /-ˈhɜːrd/) ouvir (por acaso)

overjoyed /ˌouvərˈdʒɔɪd/ *adj* ~ (**at sth**) eufórico (por/com algo) **2** contentíssimo

overland /ˈouvərlænd/ *adj* terrestre ● *adv* por terra

overlap /ˌouvərˈlæp/ *vt, vi* (**-pp-**) **1** sobrepor(-se) **2** coincidir em parte (com) ● /ˈouvərlæp/ *s* **1** sobreposição **2** coincidência

overleaf /ˌouvərˈliːf/ *adv* no verso (*de página*)

overload /ˌouvərˈloud/ *vt* sobrecarregar ● /ˈouvərloud/ *s* sobrecarga

overlook /ˌouvərˈlʊk/ *vt* **1** ter

vista para **2** passar por alto **3** não notar **4** (*perdoar*) deixar passar

overnight /ˌouvərˈnaɪt/ *adv* **1** durante a noite **2** da noite para o dia ● *adj* **1** durante/para a noite **2** (*sucesso*) repentino

overpass /ˈouvərpæs; *GB* -pɑːs/ *s* viaduto

overpower /ˌouvərˈpauər/ *vt* dominar, subjugar **overpowering** *adj* esmagador, insuportável

overrate /ˌouvərˈreɪt/ *vt* superestimar

override /ˌouvərˈraɪd/ *vt* (*pt* **overrode** /-ˈroud/ *pp* **overridden** /-ˈrɪdn/) **1** desprezar, ignorar **2** ter preferência/prioridade a **overriding** /ˌouvərˈraɪdɪŋ/ *adj* [*antes de substantivo*] prioritário

overrule /ˌouvərˈruːl/ *vt* **1** negar, anular **2** (*Jur*) revogar

overrun /ˌouvərˈrʌn/ (*pt* **-ran** /-ˈræn/ *pp* **-run**) **1** *vt* invadir **2** *vi* ultrapassar (o tempo)

overseas /ˌouvərˈsiːz/ *adj* exterior, estrangeiro ● *adv* no/do/ao estrangeiro

oversee /ˌouvərˈsiː/ *vt* (*pt* **oversaw** /-ˈsɔː/ *pp* **overseen** /-ˈsiːn/) supervisionar

overshadow /ˌouvərˈʃædou/ *vt* **1** ensombrecer **2** ofuscar

oversight /ˈouvərsaɪt/ *s* descuido

oversleep /ˌouvərˈsliːp/ *vi* (*pt, pp* **overslept** /-ˈslept/) perder a hora (*dormindo*)

overspend /ˌouvərˈspend/ (*pt, pp* **overspent** /-ˈspent/) **1** *vi* gastar em excesso **2** *vt* (*orçamento*) ultrapassar

overstate /ˌouvərˈsteɪt/ *vt* exagerar

overstep /ˌouvərˈstep/ *vt* (**-pp-**) ultrapassar: ~ *the mark* passar dos limites

overt /ouˈvɜːrt/ *adj* (*fml*) declarado

overtake /ˌouvərˈteɪk/ (*pt* **overtook** /-ˈtʊk/ *pp* **overtaken** /-ˈteɪkən/) **1** *vt, vi* (*GB*) (*carro*) ultrapassar **2** *vt* surpreender

overthrow /ˌouvərˈθrou/ *vt* (*pt* **overthrew** /-ˈθruː/ *pp* **overthrown** /-ˈθroun/) depor, derrubar ● *s* deposição

overtime /ˈouvərtaɪm/ *s, adv* hora(s) extra(s)

overtone /ˈouvərtoun/ *s* [*ger pl*] insinuação

overture /ˈouvərtʃər/ *s* **1** (*Mús*) abertura **2** proposta: *make overtures (to sb)* tentar uma aproximação (com alguém)

overturn /,ouvər'tɜːrn/ **1** vt, vi virar **2** vt, vi capotar **3** vt (decisão) anular

overview /'ouvərvjuː/ s panorama (geral)

overweight /,ouvər'weit/ adj com excesso de peso → FAT

overwhelm /,ouvər'welm/ vt **1** derrotar **2** desarmar **overwhelming** adj esmagador

overwork /,ouvər'wɜːrk/ vt, vi (fazer) trabalhar demais

owe /ou/ vt, vi dever, estar em dívida (com)

owing to /'ouɪŋ tuː/ prep devido a

owl /aul/ s coruja

own /oun/ adj, pron próprio: a house of your ~ uma casa própria ◊ It was my ~ idea. Foi idéia minha. ▶ (all) on your own **1** completamente **2** por si só, sem ajuda ● vt possuir, ter ■ **own up (to sth)** confessar(-se culpado) (de algo)

owner /'ounər/ s proprietário/a **ownership** s [U] propriedade

ox /ɑks/ s (pl **oxen** /'ɑksn/) boi

oxygen /'ɑksɪdʒən/ s oxigênio

oyster /'ɔɪstər/ s ostra

ozone /'ouzoun/ s ozônio

P p

P, p /piː/ s (pl **P's**, **p's** /piːz/) P, p

pace /peɪs/ s **1** passo **2** ritmo ▶ **keep pace (with sb/sth)** **1** acompanhar o ritmo (de alguém/algo) **2** manter-se atualizado (em relação a alguém/algo) ● vt, vi ~ **(up and down)** (a room, etc.) andar de lá para cá (em uma sala, etc.)

pacemaker /'peɪsmeɪkər/ s (Med) marca-passo

pacifier /'pæsɪfaɪər/ s chupeta

pacify /'pæsɪfaɪ/ vt (pt, pp **-ied**) apaziguar, pacificar

pack /pæk/ s **1** mochila **2** (GB) pacote → PACKAGE **3** (cigarros) maço **4** (animal) carga, matilha, alcatéia **5** (GB) (cartas) baralho ● **1** vt, vi fazer (as malas) **2** vt carregar **3** vt embalar **4** vt ~ **sth into sth** colocar algo em algo **5** vt ~ **sth in sth** envolver algo com algo **6** vt (caixa) encher **7** vt (comida) conservar em **8** vt (sala, etc.) lotar ▶ **pack your bags** (fazer as malas e) ir embora ■ **pack sth in** (coloq) deixar, abandonar algo **pack (sb/sth) into sth** espremer-se em algo,

colocar alguém/algo em algo (apertado) **pack up** (GB, coloq) deixar de funcionar **packed** /pækt/ adj **1** lotado **2** ~ **with sth** cheio de algo

package /'pækɪdʒ/ s pacote NOTA **Package** (GB **parcel**) é um pacote enviado pelo correio. **Pack** (GB **packet**) é o pacote ou saco que contém algum produto à venda numa loja: a pack of cigarettes/chips. Na Grã-Bretanha, **pack** (USA **set**) designa um conjunto de coisas diferentes que são vendidas juntas: The pack contains needles and thread.. ● vt empacotar **packaging** s embalagem

package tour (GB **package holiday**) s pacote turístico

packed lunch s (GB) almoço/ sanduíche que se leva de casa

packet /'pækɪt/ s (esp GB) pacote → PARCEL

packing /'pækɪŋ/ s **1** processo de embalar/fazer as malas **2** material para acondicionamento

pact /pækt/ s pacto

pad /pæd/ s **1** enchimento **2** (papel) bloco ● vt (-dd-) acolchoar ■ **pad about, along, etc.** andar (de pés) **pad sth out** encher lingüiça (livro, etc.) **padding** s enchimento **2** (fig) enchção de lingüiça

paddle /'pædl/ s remo de cabo curto▶ **have a paddle** andar com os pés na água ● **1** vt dirigir (remando) **2** vi remar **3** vi andar em lugar raso

paddock /'pædək/ s prado (onde pastam cavalos)

padlock /'pædlɑk/ s cadeado

paediatrician (GB) = PEDIATRICIAN

pagan /'peɪgən/ adj, s pagão

page /peɪdʒ/ s **1** página ● vt chamar por alto-falante

pager /'peɪdʒər/ s pager

paid /peɪd/ pret, pp de PAY ● adj **1** assalariado **2** remunerado ▶ **put paid to sth** acabar com algo

pain /peɪn/ s **1** dor **2** ~ **(in the neck)** (coloq) chato/a ▶ **be at pains to do sth** esforçar-se para fazer algo **take great pains with/over sth** esmerar-se muito em algo **pained** adj **1** aflito **2** ofendido **painful** adj **1** dolorido: be ~ doer **2** doloroso **3** (dever) penoso **4** (decisão) difícil **painfully** adv terrivelmente **painless**

adj **1** sem dor **2** sem dificuldades

painkiller /'pemkɪlə/ s
analgésico

painstaking /'pemzteɪkɪŋ/ adj **1**
laborioso **2** (pessoa) caprichoso

paint /pemt/ s tinta ● vt, vi pintar
painter s pintor/a **painting** s **1**
pintura **2** quadro

paintbrush /'pemtbrʌʃ/ pincel,
broxa

paintwork /'pemtwɜːrk/ s
pintura (superfície)

pair /peər/ s **1** par: a ~ of pants
umas calças/uma calça NOTA
As palavras que designam objetos compostos por dois elementos (pinça, tesoura, calça, etc.)
são seguidas de verbo no plural:
My pants are very tight. Minha
calça está muito apertada. Ao
nos referirmos a mais de um
objeto, utiliza-se a palavra **pair**:
I've got two pairs of pants.
Tenho duas calças. **2** casal: the
winning ~ o par vencedor ●
■**pair (sb) off/up (with sb)** formar par (com alguém)

pajamas /pə'dʒæməz; GB
-dʒɑːm-/ s [pl] pijama ● **pajama**
adj: ~ pants calça di pijama →
PAIR

pal /pæl/ s (coloq) **1** amigo/a **2**
colega

palace /'pæləs/ s palácio

palate /'pælət/ s **1** paladar **2**
palato

pale /peɪl/ adj (-er -est) **1** pálido:
go ~ empalidecer **2** (cor) claro **3**
(luz) tênue ● s ▶ **beyond the pale**
(conduta) inaceitável

pall /pɔːl/ vi (GB) ~ **(on sb)**
cansar, aborrecer (alguém) ● s
1 pano mortuário **2** (fig) nuvem

pallid /'pælɪd/ adj pálido

pallor /'pælər/ s palidez

palm /pɑːm/ s **1** (mão) palma **2** (tb
~ tree) palmeira ▶ **have sb in the
palm of your hand** ter alguém na
palma da mão ■**palm sb/sth off
(on sb)** (coloq) passar alguém/
algo (que não se quer) para
alguém

paltry /'pɔːltri/ adj (-ier, -iest)
insignificante

pamper /'pæmpər/ vt (freq pej)
mimar

pamphlet /'pæmflət/ s **1** folheto
2 panfleto

pan /pæn/ s panela

pancake /'pænkeɪk/ s panqueca
→ TERÇA(-FEIRA)

panda /'pændə/ s panda

pander /'pændər/ vi (pej) ~ **to sb/**
sth condescender com alguém/
algo

pane /peɪn/ s vidraça: ~ of glass
lâmina de vidro

panel /'pænl/ s **1** (TV, etc.) painel
2 júri **paneled** (GB **-ll-**) adj
revestido **paneling** (GB **-ll-**) s
revestimento

pang /pæŋ/ s pontada

panic /'pænɪk/ s pânico: panic-
stricken em pânico ● vt, vi (**-ck-**)
entrar em pânico, assustar(-se)

pant /pænt/ vi arfar

panther /'pænθər/ s **1** pantera **2**
(USA) puma

panties /'pæntiz/ s [pl] calcinha
→ PAIR

pantomime /'pæntəmaɪm/ s **1**
(GB) pantomima de Natal **2**
(fig) farsa

pantry /'pæntri/ s (pl -ies) despensa

pants /pænts/ s [pl] **1** (USA)
calça **2** (GB) cueca, calcinha
→ PAIR

paper /'peɪpər/ s **1** [U] papel
2 jornal **3** papel de parede
4 (papers) [pl] documentação
5 (papers) papéis **6** exame
(escrito) **7** (acadêmico) trabalho ▶ **on paper 1** por escrito **2**
em teoria ● vt revestir com
papel de parede

paperback /'peɪpərbæk/ s livro
tipo brochura

paperwork /'peɪpərwɜːrk/ s [U]
1 papelada **2** tarefas adminis-
trativas

par /pɑːr/ s ▶ **below par** abaixo do
esperado **on a par with sb/sth**
em pé de igualdade com
alguém/algo

parable /'pærəbl/ s parábola
(história)

parachute /'pærəʃuːt/ s pára-
quedas

parade /pə'reɪd/ s **1** desfile **2**
(Mil) parada **3** (tb ~ ground)
praça de armas ● **1** vi desfilar **2**
vi (Mil) passar em revista **3** vt
(conhecimentos) alardear **4** vt
exibir

paradise /'pærədaɪs/ s paraíso

paradox /'pærədɒks/ s paradoxo

paraffin /'pærəfɪn/ s querosene

paragraph /'pærəgræf; GB -grɑːf/
s parágrafo

parakeet /'pærəkiːt/ s periquito

parallel /'pærəlel/ adj (em) paralelo ● s **1** paralelo **2** paralela

paralysis /pə'ræləsɪs/ s **1** paralisia **2** paralisação

paralyze (GB **-lyse**) /'pærəlaɪz/ vt
paralisar

paramount /'pærəmaʊnt/ adj

primordial: *of ~ importance* de suma importância

paranoid /'pærənɔɪd/ *s, adj* paranóico/a

paraphrase /'pærəfreɪz/ *vt* parafrasear

parasite /'pærəsaɪt/ *s* parasita

parcel /'pɑːsl/ (GB) *s* pacote → PACKAGE

parched /pɑːtʃt/ *adj* 1 ressecado 2 sedento

parchment /'pɑːtʃmənt/ *s* pergaminho

pardon /'pɑːdn/ *s* 1 perdão 2 (Jur) indulto ● *vt* perdoar ► **pardon me?** (GB **pardon?**) como (disse)?, perdão, o que você disse?

parent /'peərənt/ *s* 1 mãe, pai 2 (parents) pais 3 ~ **company** (empresa) matriz parentage *s* 1 ascendência 2 pais parental /pə'rentl/ *adj* dos pais parenthood /'peərənhʊd/ *s* maternidade, paternidade

parenthesis /pə'renθəsɪs/ *s* (pl **-theses** /-θəsiːz/) parêntese, entre parênteses

parish /'pærɪʃ/ *s* paróquia: ~ **priest** pároco

park /pɑːk/ *s* parque: *parkland* zona verde 2 (esp USA) campo de esportes ● *vt, vi* estacionar

parking /'pɑːkɪŋ/ *s* estacionamento: ~ **meter** parquímetro

parking lot *s* estacionamento (local)

parliament /'pɑːləmənt/ *s* parlamento, congresso: *Member of Parliament* deputado parliamentary /ˌpɑːlə'mentəri/ *adj* parlamentar

parlor (GB **-our**) /'pɑːlər/ *s* salão

parody /'pærədi/ *s* (pl **-ies**) paródia

parole /pə'rəʊl/ *s* liberdade condicional

parrot /'pærət/ *s* papagaio

parsley /'pɑːsli/ *s* salsinha

parsnip /'pɑːsnɪp/ *s* chirívia

part /pɑːt/ *s* 1 parte 2 peça (máquina) 3 (TV) episódio 4 (teatro, etc.) papel 5 (USA) (cabelo) risca 6 (parts) [pl] região: *He's not from these parts.* Ela não é daqui. ► **do your part** (USA) fazer a sua parte **for my part** de minha parte **for the most part** no geral **on the part of sb/on sb's part:** *It was an error on my ~.* Foi um erro de minha parte. **take part (in sth)** tomar parte (em algo) **take sb's part** tomar partido de alguém **the best/better part of**

sth a maior parte de algo ● 1 *vt, vi separar(-se):* ~ *your hair* dividir o cabelo 2 *vt, vi* afastar (-se) ► **part company (with sb)** separar-se (de alguém), despedir-se (de alguém) ■ **part with sth** 1 renunciar a algo 2 (dinheiro) gastar algo

partial /'pɑːʃl/ *adj* ~ **(towards sb/ sth)** parcial (a favor de alguém/ algo): ~ *to sb/sth* apreciador de alguém/algo partially *adv* 1 parcialmente 2 de maneira parcial

participant /pɑː'tɪsɪpənt/ *s* participante

participate /pɑː'tɪsɪpeɪt/ *vi* participar participation *s* participação

particle /'pɑːtɪkl/ *s* partícula

particular /pə'tɪkjələr/ *adj* 1 em particular 2 especial 3 ~ **(about sth)** exigente (em relação a algo) ● **particulars** *s* dados particularly *adv* especialmente 2 em particular

parting /'pɑːtɪŋ/ *s* 1 despedida, separação 2 (GB) (cabelo) risca

partisan /ˌpɑːtɪ'zæn/ *adj* parcial ● *s* 1 partidário/a 2 (Mil) guerrilheiro/a

partition /pɑː'tɪʃn/ *s* 1 (Pol) divisão 2 divisória

partly /'pɑːtli/ *adv* em parte

partner /'pɑːtnər/ *s* 1 (Com) sócio/a 2 parceiro/a partnership *s* 1 parceria 2 (Com) sociedade

partridge /'pɑːtrɪdʒ/ *s* perdiz

part-time *adj, adv* (de) meio período

party /'pɑːti/ *s* (pl **-ies**) 1 (reunião) festa 2 (Pol) partido 3 grupo 4 (Jur) parte ► **be (a) party to sth** participar de algo

pass /pɑːs; GB pɑːs/ *s* 1 (exame) aprovação 2 (Esporte, ônibus) passe 3 (montanha) passo ► **make a pass at sb** (coloq) passar uma cantada em alguém ● 1 *vt, vi* passar: ~ *by sb/sth* passar ao lado de alguém/algo 2 *vt* (barreira) cruzar 3 *vt* (limite) superar 4 *vt* (exame, lei) aprovar 5 *vt* (carro) ultrapassar 6 *vi* acontecer ■ **pass as/for sb/ sth** passar, ser tomado por alguém/algo **pass sth around** circular algo **pass away** morrer **pass sb/sth by** 1 passar por cima de alguém/algo 2 passar despercebido a alguém/algo **pass sb/sth off as/sb/sth** fazer alguém/algo passar como alguém/algo **pass out** desmaiar **pass sth up** (coloq) deixar passar, não aproveitar algo

(oportunidade)

passable /'pæsəbl; GB 'pɑːs-/ *adj*
1 aceitável **2** transitável

passage /'pæsɪdʒ/ s **1** (*tb* **passageway**) passagem **2** (*livro, etc.*) passagem

passenger /'pæsɪndʒər/ s passageiro/a

passer-by /ˌpæsər 'baɪ; GB ˌpɑːsə-/ s (*pl* **-ers-by**) transeunte

passing /'pæsɪŋ; GB 'pɑːs-/ *adj* **1** passageiro **2** (*referência*) casual **3** (*tráfego*) que passa ● s **1** passagem **2** (*fml*) final ▸ **in passing** casualmente

passion /'pæʃn/ s paixão ▸ **passionate** *adj* ardente

passive /'pæsɪv/ *adj* passivo ● s (*tb ~* **voice**) (voz) passiva

passport /'pæspɔːrt; GB 'pɑːs-/ s passaporte

password /'pæswɜːrd; GB 'pɑːs-/ s senha

past /pæst; GB pɑːst/ *adj* **1** passado **2** *~* **students** antigos alunos **3** último **4** *The time is ~.* Acabou o tempo. ● s **1** passado **2** (*tb ~* **tense**) pretérito ● *prep* **1** *half ~ two* duas e meia ◇ *~ midnight* depois da meia-noite ◇ *It's ~ five o'clock.* Já passou das cinco. **2** (*com verbos de movimento*): *walk ~ sb/sth* passar por alguém/algo ◇ *go ~ sth* passar por, depois de: *It's ~ your bedtime.* Já passou sua hora de ir para a cama. ▸ **not put it past sb (to do sth)** crer que alguém seja capaz (de fazer algo) ● *adv* ao lado, pela frente

pasta /'pɑːstə; GB 'pæstə/ s massa(s) (*macarrão, etc.*)

paste /peɪst/ s **1** pasta **2** cola **3** patê

pastime /'pæstaɪm; GB 'pɑːs-/ s passatempo

pastor /'pæstər; GB 'pɑːs-/ s (*Relig*) pastor/a

pastoral /'pæstərəl; GB 'pɑːs-/ *adj* **1** bucólico **2** *~ care* aconselhamento de um pastor/educador

pastry /'peɪstri/ s (*pl* **-ies**) **1** massa (*torta, etc.*) **2** doce (*de massa*)

pasture /'pæstʃər; GB 'pɑːs-/ s pasto

pat /pæt/ *vt* (**-tt-**) **1** dar tapinhas em **2** acariciar ● s **1** tapinha **2** carícia **3** (*manteiga*) porção ▸ **give sb a pat on the back** dar tapinhas nas costas de alguém **2** felicitar alguém

patch /pætʃ/ s **1** remendo **2** (*cor*) mancha **3** (*neblina, etc.*) zona **4** pedaço de terra (*onde se culti-*

vam verduras, etc.) **5** (*GB, coloq*) (*área de trabalho*) zona ▸ **not be a patch on sb/sth** não ter nem comparação com alguém/algo ● *vt* remendar ▸ **patch sth up 1** remendar, consertar algo **2** (*disputa*) resolver ▸ **patchy** *adj* (**-ier, -iest**) **1** irregular: *~ rain/fog* áreas de chuva/neblina **2** desigual **3** (*conhecimento*) com lacunas

patchwork /'pætʃwɜːrk/ s **1** trabalho de retalhos: *~ quilt* colcha de retalhos **2** miscelânea

patent /'peɪtnt/ *adj* **1** patente **2** (*Com*) patenteado ● s patente ● *vt* patentear ▸ **patently** *adv* claramente

paternal /pə'tɜːrnl/ *adj* **1** paternal **2** paterno

path /pæθ; GB pɑːθ/ s **1** (*tb* **pathway**) trilha **2** passo **3** trajetória **4** caminho

pathetic /pə'θetɪk/ *adj* **1** patético **2** (*coloq*) lamentável

pathological /ˌpæθə'lɑdʒɪkl/ *adj* patológico ▸ **pathology** /pə'θɑlədʒi/ s patologia

pathos /'peɪθɑs/ s pathos

patience /'peɪʃns/ s (*tb* **cartas**) paciência

patient /'peɪʃnt/ s paciente ● *adj* paciente

patio /'pætioʊ/ s (*pl ~* **-oʊz/**) **1** terraço **2** pátio

patriarch /'peɪtriɑrk/ s patriarca

patriot /'peɪtriət; GB 'pæt-/ s patriota ▸ **patriotic** /ˌpeɪtri'ɑtɪk; GB ˌpæt-/ *adj* patriótico

patrol /pə'troʊl/ *vt* (**-ll-**) **1** patrulhar **2** (*guarda*) fazer a ronda ● s patrulha

patron /'peɪtrən/ s **1** patrocinador/a **2** mecenas **3** freguês ▸ **patronage** s **1** patrocínio **2** clientela **3** proteção

patronize /'peɪtrənaɪz; GB 'pæt-/ *vt* **1** tratar com condescendência **2** frequentar (*lugar*) ▸ **patronizing** *adj* condescendente

pattern /'pætərn/ s **1** estampa (*em tecido, etc.*) **2** (*costura, etc.*) modelo **3** padrão ▸ **patterned** *adj* estampado

pause /pɔːz/ s pausa ● *vi* fazer uma pausa

pave /peɪv/ *vt* pavimentar ▸ **pave the way (for sb/sth)** preparar o caminho (para alguém/algo)

pavement /'peɪvmənt/ s **1** (*USA*) pavimentação **2** (*GB*) calçada

pavilion /pə'vɪliən/ s pavilhão

paving /'peɪvɪŋ/ s pavimento: *~ stone* pedra de calçamento

paw /pɔː/ s **1** pata **2** (*coloq*) mão

● *vt* tocar com as mãos

pawn /pɔːn/ *s* (*xadrez*) peão ● *vt* penhorar

pawnbroker /'pɔːnbrəʊkər/ *s* agiota

pay /peɪ/ *s* [U] salário, pagamento: ~ *claim* pedido de aumento salarial ● (*pt, pp* **paid**) **1** *vt, vi* ~ (**for sth**) pagar (algo) **2** *vi* ser rentável **3** *vi* valer a pena **4** *vt, vi* compensar ▸ **pay attention (to sb/sth)** prestar atenção (em alguém/algo) **pay sb a compliment/pay a compliment to sb** elogiar alguém **pay sb/ sth a visit** visitar alguém/algo ■ **pay sb back (for sth)** vingar-se de alguém (por algo) **pay sb back sth; pay sth back** devolver dinheiro a alguém **pay sth in** depositar algo (*em banco*) **pay off** (*coloq*) dar resultado **pay sb off** pagar e despedir alguém, subornar alguém **pay sth off** acabar de pagar algo **pay up** pagar tudo payable *adj* pagável

payment /'peɪmənt/ *s* pagamento: *in/as* ~ *for sth* como recompensa por algo

pay-off *s* (*coloq*) **1** pagamento, suborno **2** recompensa

payroll /'peɪrəʊl/ *s* folha de pagamento

PC /ˌpiː 'siː/ *abrev* (*pl* **PCs**) **1** **p**ersonal **c**omputer microcomputador **2** (*GB*) **p**olice **c**onstable policial **3** **p**olitically **c**orrect politicamente correto

P.E. /ˌpiː 'iː/ *abrev* de **p**hysical **e**ducation educação física

pea /piː/ *s* ervilha

peace /piːs/ *s* **1** paz **2** tranqüilidade: ~ *of mind* paz de espírito ▸ **make (your) peace (with sb)** fazer as pazes (com alguém) peaceful *adj* **1** pacífico **2** tranqüilo

peach /piːtʃ/ *s* **1** pêssego **2** (*tb* ~ **tree**) pessegueiro **3** cor de pêssego

peacock /'piːkɒk/ *s* pavão

peak /piːk/ *s* **1** (*montanha*) cume **2** ponta **3** viseira (*boné, etc.*) **4** ponto máximo ● *adj* máximo: ~ *hours* horas de pico ◇ *in ~ condition* em ótima forma ● *vi* atingir o ponto máximo peaked *adj* **1** em ponta **2** com viseira

peal /piːl/ *s* **1** (*sinos*) repique **2** *peals of laughter* gargalhadas

peanut /'piːnʌt/ *s* **1** amendoim **2** (**peanuts**) [*pl*] (*coloq*) ninharia (*dinheiro*)

pear /peər/ *s* **1** pera **2** (*tb* ~ **tree**) pereira

pearl /pɜːrl/ *s* **1** pérola **2** (*fig*) jóia

peasant /'peznt/ *s* **1** camponês → **CAMPONÊS 2** (*coloq*) grosseirão

peat /piːt/ *s* turfa

pebble /'pebl/ *s* pedregulho

peck /pek/ **1** *vt, vi* bicar **2** *vt* dar beijinho em ▸ **pecking order** (*coloq*) ordem de importância ● *s* **1** bicada **2** beijinho

peckish /'pekɪʃ/ *adj* (*GB, coloq*) faminto: *feel* ~ ter vontade de comer algo

peculiar /pɪ'kjuːliər/ *adj* **1** excêntrico **2** especial **3** ~ (**to sb/ sth**) típico (de alguém/algo) peculiarity /pɪˌkjuːli'ærəti/ *s* (*pl* **-ies**) **1** peculiaridade **2** excentricidade peculiarly *adv* **1** particularmente **2** tipicamente **3** de maneira estranha

pedal /'pedl/ *s* pedal ● *vi* (*pt* **-l-**, *GB* **-ll-**) pedalar

pedantic /pɪ'dæntɪk/ *adj* pedante

pedestrian /pə'destriən/ *s* pedestre ● *adj* prosaico

pediatrician (*GB* **paedi-**) /ˌpiːdiə'trɪʃn/ *s* pediatra

pedigree /'pedɪɡriː/ *s* **1** pedigree **2** ascendência **3** passado ● *adj* **1** com pedigree **2** (*cavalo, etc.*) de raça

pee /piː/ *vi* (*coloq*) fazer xixi ● *s* (*coloq*) xixi

peek /piːk/ *vi* ~ **at sb/sth** dar uma espiada em alguém/algo

peel /piːl/ **1** *vt* ~ **sth** (**away/back/ off**) descascar, tirar algo **2** *vi* ~ (**away/off**) despregar(-se), descascar(-se) ● *s* [U] **1** pele (*de fruta*) **2** casca NOTA Para cascas duras, como a de noz ou ovo, usa-se **shell**. Para a casca do limão, **rind** ou **peel** (para a laranja, só se usa esta última). Para a casca da banana e a casca mais fina de outras frutas, como o pêssego, usa-se **skin**.

peep /piːp/ *vi* **1** ~ **at sth** dar uma olhada (*rápida ou cautelosa*) em alguém/algo **2** ~ **over, through, etc. sth** espiar por cima de, através de, etc. algo **3** ~ **out/through** (**sth**) surgir (em/através de) ● *s* **1** *have/ take a* ~ *at sb/sth* dar uma espiada em alguém/algo **2** pio (*de passarinho*)

peer /pɪər/ *vi* **1** ~ **at sb/sth** fitar alguém/algo NOTA Implica uma olhada prolongada que às vezes pressupõe esforço. **2** ~ **out** (**of sth**) olhar para fora (*de algo*) ● *s* **1** igual, par **2** contemporâneo/a **3** (*GB*) nobre the **peerage** *s* a nobreza

peeved /piːvd/ *adj* irritado

peg /peg/ s **1** (*GB*) (*tb clothes* ~) pregador (de roupa) **2** (*na parede*) gancho ▶**bring/take sb down a peg (or two)** abaixar a crista de alguém ● *vt* (-gg-) **1** (*preços, etc.*) fixar (o nível de) **2** prender

pejorative /prˈdʒɔːrətɪv; *GB* -ˈdʒɒr-/ *adj* (*fml*) pejorativo

pelican /ˈpelɪkən/ s pelicano

pellet /ˈpelɪt/ s **1** bola **2** chumbinho **3** grânulo

pelt /pelt/ s **1** pele (*animal*) ● **1** *vt* ~ **sb with sth** atirar algo em alguém **2** vi ~ (**down**) chover a cântaros ▪**pelt along, down, etc. (sth)** correr a toda velocidade: ~ **down the hill** descer o morro correndo

pelvis /ˈpelvɪs/ s pélvis **pelvic** *adj* pélvico

pen /pen/ s **1** caneta **2** cercado (*animais*) **3** (*bebê*) cercadinho

penalize /ˈpiːnəlaɪz/ *vt* **1** penalizar, punir **2** prejudicar

penalty /ˈpenlti/ s (*pl* -ies) **1** (*castigo*) pena **2** multa **3** desvantagem **4** (*Esporte*) penalidade, pênalti

pence /pens/ s (*abrev* p) pence (*centavos de libra*)

pencil /ˈpensl/ s lápis: ~ **sharpener** apontador

pendant /ˈpendənt/ s pingente

pending /ˈpendɪŋ/ *adj* (*fml*) pendente ● *prep* à espera de

pendulum /ˈpendʒələm; *GB* -djələm/ s pêndulo

penetrate /ˈpenɪtreɪt/ **1** *vt* penetrar **2** vi ~ **into/through sth** introduzir(-se) em, atravessar algo **3** *vt* infiltrar **penetrating** *adj* **1** perspicaz **2** penetrante

penguin /ˈpeŋgwɪn/ s pingüim

penicillin /ˌpenɪˈsɪlɪn/ s penicilina

peninsula /pəˈnɪnsələ; *GB* -nsjələ/ s península

penis /ˈpiːnɪs/ s pênis

penknife /ˈpennaɪf/ s (*pl* -knives /-naɪvz/) canivete

penny /ˈpeni/ s **1** (*pl* pence) (*GB*) pêni **2** (*pl* -ies) (*USA, coloq*) centavo: *It was worth every* ~. Valeu cada centavo que custou. **penniless** /ˈpeniləs/ *adj* sem dinheiro

pen pal s amigo/a por correspondência

pension /ˈpenʃn/ s pensão (*aposentadoria*) ▪**pension sb/ sth off** aposentar alguém, deixar de usar algo **pensioner** s aposentado/a

penthouse /ˈpenthaus/ s (apartamento de) cobertura

pent-up /ˌpent ʌp/ *adj* contido, reprimido

penultimate /penˈʌltɪmət/ *adj* penúltimo

people /ˈpiːpl/ s **1** [*pl*] gente: *People are saying that...* Estão dizendo que... **2** pessoas **3** (**the people**) [*pl*] o povo **4** (*nação*) povo (*apenas nesse sentido é contável*) ● *vt* povoar

pepper /ˈpepər/ s **1** pimenta **2** pimentão

peppermint /ˈpepərmɪnt/ s **1** hortelã-pimenta **2** bala de hortelã

per /pər/ *prep* por: ~ *annum* por/ ao ano

perceive /pərˈsiːv/ *vt* (*fml*) **1** perceber **2** interpretar

per cent /pər ˈsent/ *adj, adv* por cento **percentage** s porcentagem: ~ *increase* aumento percentual

perceptible /pərˈseptəbl/ *adj* **1** perceptível **2** (*melhora, etc.*) sensível

perception /pərˈsepʃn/ s (*fml*) **1** percepção **2** perspicácia **3** ponto de vista

perceptive /pərˈseptɪv/ *adj* perspicaz

perch /pɜːrtʃ/ s **1** (*para pássaros*) poleiro **2** posição elevada **3** (*peixe*) perca ● vi **1** empoleirar-se **2** colocar-se em lugar alto

percussion /pərˈkʌʃn/ s percussão

perennial /pəˈreniəl/ *adj* perene

perfect /pərˈfekt/ *vt* aperfeiçoar ● /ˈpɜːrfɪkt/ *adj* **1** perfeito **2** ideal **3** completo **perfection** /pərˈfekʃn/ s perfeição **perfectionist** s perfeccionista

perfectly /ˈpɜːrfɪktli/ *adv* **1** perfeitamente **2** completamente

perforate /ˈpɜːrfəreɪt/ *vt* perfurar **perforated** *adj* perfurado **perforation** s **1** perfuração **2** picote

perform /pərˈfɔːrm/ **1** *vt* (*função*) desempenhar ... **2** pessoas **3** (*operação*) realizar **3** *vt* (*compromisso*) cumprir **4** *vt, vi* (*teatro, etc.*) representar, atuar **5** *vt, vi* (*música*) interpretar

performance /pərˈfɔːrməns/ s **1** (*deveres*) cumprimento **2** (*pessoa*) desempenho **3** (*empresa*) resultados **4** (*Mús*) interpretação, apresentação **5** (*Teat*) representação: *the evening* ~ a sessão da noite

performer /pərˈfɔːrmər/ s **1**

(*Mús*) intérprete **2** (*Teat*) ator, atriz **3** (*variedades*) artista

perfume /pər'fjuːm/ *GB* pɜː'fjuːm/ *s* perfume

perhaps /pər'hæps; *GB* præps/ *adv* talvez

peril /'perəl/ *s* risco

perimeter /pə'rɪmɪtər/ *s* perímetro

period /'pɪəriəd/ *s* **1** período **2** época **3** (*Educ*) aula **4** (*Med*) menstruação, regras **5** ponto final

periodic /ˌpɪəri'ɒdɪk/ *adj* periódico (*tb* **periodical**)

periodical /ˌpɪəri'ɒdɪkl/ *s* periódico

perish /'perɪʃ/ *vi* (*fml*) perecer, falecer **perishable** *adj* perecível

perjury /'pɜːdʒəri/ *s* perjúrio

perk /pɜːk/ *s* mordomia ■ **perk up** (*coloq*) **1** sentir-se melhor **2** melhorar

perm /pɜːm/ *s* permanente (de cabelo) ● *vt*: *have your hair permed* fazer permanente no cabelo

permanent /'pɜːmənənt/ *adj* **1** permanente **2** (*dano*) irreparável **permanently** *adv* permanentemente

permissible /pər'mɪsəbl/ *adj* admissível

permission /pər'mɪʃn/ *s* permissão

permissive /pər'mɪsɪv/ *adj* permissivo

permit /pər'mɪt/ *vt, vi* (**-tt-**) (*fml*) permitir: *If time permits…* Se der tempo… → ALLOW ● /'pɜːmɪt/ *s* **1** permissão **2** passe

perpendicular /ˌpɜːrpən'dɪkjələr/ *adj* **1** perpendicular **2** (*rochedo a pique*) vertical

perpetrate /'pɜːpɪtreɪt/ *vt* (*fml*) perpetrar

perpetual /pər'petʃuəl/ *adj* **1** perpétuo **2** interminável

perpetuate /pər'petʃueɪt/ *vt* perpetuar

perplexed /pər'plekst/ *adj* perplexo

persecute /'pɜːrsɪkjuːt/ *vt* perseguir (*por raça, religião, etc.*) **persecution** *s* perseguição

persevere /ˌpɜːrsɪ'vɪər/ *vi* **1** perseverar **2** persistir **perseverance** *s* perseverança

persist /pər'sɪst/ *vi* **1** persistir **2** continuar **3** persistir **persistence** *s* **1** perseverança **2** persistência **persistent** *adj* **1** teimoso **2** persistente

person /'pɜːsn/ *s* pessoa NOTA Só se usa o plural *persons* em

linguagem formal.. ▶**in person** em pessoa **personal** *adj* pessoal, particular: *get* ~ passar a nível pessoal **personality** /ˌpɜːrsə'næləti/ *s* (*pl* **-ies**) personalidade **personalized** *adj* **1** personalizado **2** timbrado **personally** *adv* pessoalmente: *take sth* ~ ofender-se com algo

personify /pər'sɒnɪfaɪ/ *vt* (*pt, pp* **-ied**) personificar

personnel /ˌpɜːrsə'nel/ *s* (departamento de) pessoal

perspective /pər'spektɪv/ *s* perspectiva

perspire /pər'spaɪər/ *vi* (*fml*) transpirar **perspiration** *s* **1** suor **2** transpiração NOTA A palavra mais comum é **sweat**.

persuade /pər'sweɪd/ *vt* **1** persuadir **2** convencer **persuasion** *s* **1** persuasão **2** opinião **persuasive** *adj* persuasivo

pertinent /'pɜːrtɪnənt; *GB* -tɪnənt/ *adj* (*fml*) pertinente

perturb /pər'tɜːrb/ *vt* (*fml*) perturbar

pervade /pər'veɪd/ *vt* **1** (*odor*) espalhar-se **2** (*luz*) difundir-se **3** (*obra*) impregnar **pervasive** (*tb* **pervading**) *adj* difundido

perverse /pər'vɜːrs/ *adj* **1** (*pessoa*) obstinado, mal-intencionado **2** (*comportamento*) caprichoso **3** (*prazer, etc.*) perverso **perversion** *s* **1** perversão **2** deturpação

pervert /pər'vɜːrt/ *vt* **1** deturpar **2** corromper ● /'pɜːrvɜːrt/ *s* pervertido/a

pessimist /'pesɪmɪst/ *s* pessimista **pessimistic** /ˌpesɪ'mɪstɪk/ *adj* pessimista

pest /pest/ *s* **1** inseto/animal nocivo: ~ *control* dedetização/desratização **2** (*coloq*) peste

pester /'pestər/ *vt* incomodar

pet /pet/ *s* **1** animal de estimação **2** (*pej*) favorito/a ● *adj* **1** predileto **2** domesticado ● *vt* afagar, acariciar

petal /'petl/ *s* pétala

peter /'piːtər/ *v* ■ **peter out** extinguir-se pouco a pouco

petition /pə'tɪʃn/ *s* petição

petrol /'petrəl/ (*GB*) *s* gasolina: ~ *station* posto de gasolina

petroleum /pə'trəʊliəm/ *s* petróleo

petticoat /'petɪkoʊt/ *s* combinação, anágua

petty /'peti/ *adj* (**-ier**, **-iest**) **1** insignificante **2** (*delito, etc.*) pequeno: ~ *cash* fundo para pequenas despesas **3** (*conduta*) mesquinho

pew /pju:/ s banco de igreja

phantom /ˈfæntəm/ s fantasma ● adj imaginário

pharmaceutical /ˌfɑːməˈsuːtɪkl; GB -ˈsjuː-/ adj farmacêutico

pharmacy /ˈfɑːməsi/ s (pl -ies) farmácia NOTA Para "farmácia", diz-se **pharmacy** ou **drugstore** nos EUA e **chemist's** na GB. **pharmacist** s farmacêutico/a

phase /feɪz/ s fase ● vt escalonar ■ **phase sth in/out** introduzir/retirar algo por etapas

pheasant /ˈfeznt/ s faisão

phenomenon /fəˈnɒmɪnən; GB -nən/ s (pl -ena /-mə/) fenômeno **phenomenal** adj fenomenal

phew /fju:/ interj ufa

philanthropist /fɪˈlænθrəpɪst/ s filantropo/a

philosophy /fəˈlɒsəfi/ s (pl -ies) filosofia **philosopher** s filósofo/a **philosophic(al)** /ˌfɪləˈsɒfɪk(l)/ adj filosófico

phlegm /flem/ s 1 fleuma 2 (Med) catarro phlegmatic /flegˈmætɪk/ adj fleumático

phobia /ˈfoʊbiə/ s fobia

phone /foʊn/ Ver TELEPHONE

phone-in s programa de rádio ou televisão com participação do público por telefone

phon(e)y /ˈfoʊni/ adj (-ier. -iest) (coloq) falso

photocopy /ˈfoʊtoʊkɑpi/ vt (pt, pp -ied) fotocopiar ● s (pl -ies) fotocópia **photocopier** s fotocopiadora

photograph /ˈfoʊtəɡræf; GB -ɡrɑːf/ (tb photo /ˈfoʊtoʊ/) s (pl -s) fotografia ● 1 vt fotografar 2 vi: ~ well ser fotogênico **photographer** /fəˈtɒɡrəfə(r)/ s fotógrafo/a **photographic** /ˌfoʊtəˈɡræfɪk/ adj fotográfico **photography** /fəˈtɒɡrəfi/ s fotografia

phrase /freɪz/ s 1 expressão sem verbo principal, por exemplo: a bar of chocolate ◊ during the day 2 expressão: ~ book guia de conversação ● vt 1 expressar 2 (Mús) frasear

physical /ˈfɪzɪkl/ adj físico ● s exame médico **physically** adv fisicamente: ~ fit/handicapped em boa forma/deficiente físico

physician /fɪˈzɪʃn/ s médico/a

physics /ˈfɪzɪks/ s [sing] física **physicist** /ˈfɪzɪsɪst/ s físico/a

physiology /ˌfɪziˈɒlədʒi/ s fisiologia

physiotherapy /ˌfɪzioʊˈθerəpi/ s fisioterapia **physiotherapist** s fisioterapeuta

physique /fɪˈziːk/ s físico (aspecto)

piano /piˈænoʊ/ s (pl -s /-noʊz/) piano **pianist** /ˈpiənɪst/ s pianista

pick /pɪk/ 1 vt selecionar → CHOOSE 2 vt (fruta, etc.) colher 3 vt escarafunchar: ~ your teeth palitar os dentes ◊ ~ your nose botar o dedo no nariz ◊ ~ a hole (in sth) fazer um buraco (em algo) 4 vt ~ sth from/off sth tirar, remover algo de algo 5 vt (fechadura) forçar 6 vi ~ at sth lambiscar algo ▶ **pick a fight/quarrel (with sb)** comprar briga (com alguém) **pick and choose** ser exigente **pick holes in sth** achar defeito em algo **pick sb's brains** explorar os conhecimentos de alguém **pick sb's pocket** bater a carteira de alguém **pick up speed** ganhar velocidade ■ **pick on sb** 1 implicar com alguém 2 escolher alguém (para trabalho desagradável) **pick sth out** 1 identificar algo 2 destacar algo **pick sb/sth out** 1 escolher alguém/algo 2 (numa multidão, etc.) distinguir alguém/algo **pick up** 1 melhorar 2 (vento) soprar mais forte 3 continuar de onde se parou **pick sb up** 1 (esp com carro) buscar alguém 2 (coloq) conhecer alguém (em um bar, etc.) 3 prender alguém **pick sth up** 1 aprender algo 2 (doença, costume) pegar algo **pick sb/sth up** apanhar alguém/algo **pick yourself up** levantar-se ● s 1 seleção: Take your ~. Escolha o/a que quiser. 2 (the pick) (of sth) o melhor (de algo) 3 picareta

pickle /ˈpɪkl/ s picles ▶ **in a pickle** em apuros

pickpocket /ˈpɪkpɑkɪt/ s batedor/a de carteira

picnic /ˈpɪknɪk/ s piquenique

pictorial /pɪkˈtɔːriəl/ adj 1 ilustrado 2 (Arte) pictórico

picture /ˈpɪktʃə(r)/ s 1 quadro 2 ilustração 3 foto 4 retrato 5 (fig) beleza 6 (tb TV) imagem 7 (GB) filme 8 (the pictures) [pl] (GB) cinema ▶ **put sb in the picture** pôr alguém a par da situação ● vt 1 ~ yourself imaginar-se 2 fotografar

picturesque /ˌpɪktʃəˈresk/ adj pitoresco

pie /paɪ/ s 1 torta (com cobertura) 2 empadão

piece /piːs/ s 1 pedaço 2 peça 3

411

P

pit

parte **4** (*papel*) folha **5** a ~ *of
advice/news* um conselho/uma
notícia NOTA A piece of... e
pieces of... usam-se com substantivos não contáveis. **6** (*Mús*)
obra **7** (*Jornal*) artigo **8** moeda
▶ **a piece of cake** (*coloq*) uma
barbada **in one piece** ileso
to pieces: *pull/tear/smash sth to
pieces* desfazer algo em
pedaços/espatifar algo ◊ *take
sth to pieces* desmontar algo ◊
fall to pieces cair aos pedaços
■ **piece sth together 1** (*provas,
etc.*) juntar algo **2** (*passado*)
reconstituir algo

piecemeal /ˈpiːsmiːl/ *adv* pouco
a pouco ● *adj* gradual

pier /pɪər/ *s* molhe

pierce /pɪərs/ *vt* **1** (*faca, etc.*)
atravessar **2** perfurar: *have
your ears pierced* furar as orelhas **3** (*som, etc.*) penetrar em
piercing *adj* **1** (*grito*) agudo **2**
(*olhar*) penetrante

piety /ˈpaɪəti/ *s* devoção
(*religiosa*)

pig /pɪɡ/ *s* **1** porco → CARNE,
PORCO **2** (*tb greedy* ~) glutão

pigeon /ˈpɪdʒɪn/ *s* pombo

pigeon-hole *s* escaninho

piglet /ˈpɪɡlət/ *s* leitão, porqui-
nho/a → PORCO

pigment /ˈpɪɡmənt/ *s* pigmento

pigsty /ˈpɪɡstaɪ/ *s* (*pl* -ies)
chiqueiro

pigtail /ˈpɪɡteɪl/ *s* trança (*em
rabicho ou maria-chiquinha*)

pile /paɪl/ *s* **1** pilha **2** ~ (of sth)
(*coloq*) um monte de algo ● *vt*
empilhar ■ **pile in/out** entrar/
sair desordenadamente **pile up**
1 acumular **2** (*veículos*) chocar-
se uns nos outros **pile sth up**
acumular algo

pile-up *s* colisão em cadeia

pilgrim /ˈpɪlɡrɪm/ *s* peregrino/a
pilgrimage *s* peregrinação

pill /pɪl/ *s* (*tb anticoncepcional*)
pílula

pillar /ˈpɪlər/ *s* pilar

pillar box *s* (*GB*) caixa do
correio

pillow /ˈpɪloʊ/ *s* travesseiro

pillowcase /ˈpɪloʊkeɪs/ *s* fronha

pilot /ˈpaɪlət/ *s* **1** piloto **2** (*TV*)
programa piloto ● *adj* piloto
(*experimental*)

pimple /ˈpɪmpl/ *s* espinha (*na
pele*)

PIN /pɪn/ (*tb* ~ **number**) *s* personal identification number
senha (*cartão de crédito, etc.*)

pin /pɪn/ *s* **1** alfinete **2** broche **3**
cavilha ▶ **pins and needles**

formigamento ● *vt* (**-nn-**) **1** (*com
alfinete*) prender **2** (*pessoa,
braços*) segurar ■ **pin sb down 1**
fazer com que alguém se posi-
cione **2** imobilizar alguém (*no
chão*)

pincer /ˈpɪnsər/ *s* **1** (*Zool*) pinça **2**
(**pincers**) torquês → PAIR

pinch /pɪntʃ/ *s* **1** beliscar **2** *vt, vi*
(*sapatos, etc.*) apertar **3** *vt*
(*coloq*) surrupiar ● **1** beliscão
2 (*sal, etc.*) pitada ▶ **in a pinch**
em último caso

pine /paɪn/ *s* (*tb* ~ **tree**) pinho ● *vi*
1 ~ (**away**) definhar **2** ~ **for sb/
sth** sentir falta de, ansiar por
alguém/algo

pineapple /ˈpaɪnæpl/ *s* abacaxi

ping /pɪŋ/ *s* **1** tinido **2** (*bala*)
sibilo

ping-pong /ˈpɪŋ pɑŋ/ *s* (*coloq*)
pingue-pongue

pink /pɪŋk/ *adj* **1** cor-de-rosa,
rosado **2** (*de vergonha, etc.*)
corado ● *s* **1** (*cor*) rosa **2** (*Bot*)
cravina

pinnacle /ˈpɪnəkl/ *s* **1** auge **2**
(*Arquit*) pináculo **3** (*montanha*)
pico

pinpoint /ˈpɪnpɔɪnt/ *vt* localizar
com precisão

pint /paɪnt/ *s* **1** (*abrev* pt) quarti-
lho (*0,473 litros*) (*GB*) (*0,568
litros*) **2** (*GB*) *have a* ~ tomar
uma cerveja

pin-up *s* foto (*de pessoa atraente,
pregada na parede*)

pioneer /ˌpaɪəˈnɪər/ *s* pioneiro/a
● *vt* ser o pioneiro em **pioneering** *adj* pioneiro

pious /ˈpaɪəs/ *adj* **1** devoto **2** (*pej*)
beato

pip /pɪp/ *s* (*GB*) caroço, semente

pipe /paɪp/ *s* **1** tubo, cano
2 (**pipes**) [*pl*] encanamento
3 cachimbo **4** (*Mús*) flauta
5 (**pipes**) [*pl*] gaita de foles ●
vt canalizar ▶ **pipe down** (*coloq*)
calar a boca **piping** *adj* ▶ **piping
hot** fervendo

pipeline /ˈpaɪplaɪn/ *s* gasoduto,
oleoduto ▶ **in the pipeline 1**
(*pedido, etc.*) encaminhado **2**
prestes a ser implementado

piracy /ˈpaɪrəsi/ *s* pirataria

pirate /ˈpaɪrət/ *s* pirata ● *vt*
piratear

Pisces /ˈpaɪsiːz/ *s* Peixes

pistol /ˈpɪstl/ *s* pistola

piston /ˈpɪstən/ *s* pistão

pit /pɪt/ *s* **1** fossa **2** (*carvão*) mina
3 (**the pit**) (*Teat*) platéia **4** (**the
pits**) [*pl*] (*automobilismo*) box **5**
caroço (*fruta*) ▶ **be the pits**
(*coloq*) ser o fim da picada ■ **pit**

sb/sth against sb/sth opor alguém/algo a alguém/algo

pitch /pɪtʃ/ s **1** (GB) (Esporte) campo **2** (Mús) tom **3** (telhado) inclinação **4** (USA) ponto (em mercado, etc.) **5** piche: *pitch-black* preto como a asa da graúna ● **1** vt armar (barraca) **2** vt expressar **3** vt arremessar **4** vi cair **5** vi (barco) trepidar ■ **pitch in (with sth)** (coloq) **1** pôr mãos à obra **2** comer avidamente **3** colaborar (com algo) **pitched** adj (batalha) campal

pitcher /ˈpɪtʃər/ s **1** jarro **2** (GB) botija **3** (Esporte) arremessador

pitfall /ˈpɪtfɔːl/ s cilada

pith /pɪθ/ s cerne

pitiful /ˈpɪtɪfl/ adj **1** lamentável, comovente **2** desprezível

pitiless /ˈpɪtɪləs/ adj **1** impiedoso **2** implacável

pity /ˈpɪti/ s **1** compaixão: *take ~ on sb* ter compaixão de alguém **2** lástima ● vt (pt, pp -ied) compadecer-se de: *I ~ you.* Tenho pena de você.

pivot /ˈpɪvət/ s **1** eixo **2** pivô

placard /ˈplækɑːrd/ s cartaz

placate /ˈpleɪkeɪt; GB pləˈkeɪt/ vt aplacar

place /pleɪs/ s **1** lugar, vaga: *the exact ~ where I left it* o ponto exato onde o deixei **2** *It's not my ~ to...* Não me compete... **3** (coloq) casa ▶ **all over the place** (coloq) **1** por toda parte **2** desarrumado **in (the) first, second, etc. place** em primeiro, segundo, etc. lugar **out of place 1** desordenado, fora do lugar **2** descabido **take place** realizar-se ● vt **1** pôr, colocar **2** identificar **3** ~ **sth (with sb/sth):** *~ an order for sth with sb* encomendar algo a alguém ◊ *~ a bet on sth* apostar em algo **4** situar

plague /pleɪɡ/ s **1** peste **2** praga ● vt **1** importunar, atormentar **2** acossar

plaice /pleɪs/ s (pl plaice) solha

plaid /plæd/ s tecido xadrez de origem escocesa

plain /pleɪn/ s planície ● adj (~er, ~est) **1** evidente: *make sth ~* deixar algo claro **2** franco **3** simples: *yogurt* iorgurte natural ◊ *~ chocolate* chocolate amargo **4** liso, sem estampa: *~ paper* papel sem pauta **5** (físico) sem atrativos ● adv: *It's just ~ stupid.* É simplesmente uma estupidez. **plainly** adv **1** claramente **2** evidentemente

plain clothes adj à paisana

plaintiff /ˈpleɪntɪf/ s querelante

plait /plæt/ s (GB) trança

plan /plæn/ s **1** plano, programa **2** planta **3** projeto ● (-nn-) **1** vt planejar: *What do you ~ to do?* O que você pretende fazer? **2** vi fazer planos ■ **plan sth out** planejar algo

plane /pleɪn/ s **1** avião: *~ crash* acidente aéreo **2** plano **3** plaina

planet /ˈplænɪt/ s planeta

plank /plæŋk/ s **1** tábua **2** item de plataforma política

planner /ˈplænər/ s planejador/a

planning /ˈplænɪŋ/ s planejamento

plant /plænt; GB plɑːnt/ s **1** planta **2** (Mec) maquinaria **3** fábrica **4** (USA) power ~ central elétrica ● vt **1** plantar **2** semear **3** (coloq) colocar às escondidas (para incriminar) **4** (dúvidas, etc.) semear

plantation /plænˈteɪʃn; GB plɑːn-/ s **1** plantação **2** arvoredo

plaque /plæk; GB plɑːk/ s (tb dental) placa

plaster /ˈplæstər; GB ˈplɑːs-/ s **1** gesso: *put sth in ~* engessar algo **2** reboco **3** (GB) (tb sticking ~) band-aid ● vt **1** rebocar (parede) **2** emplastrar **3** cobrir

plastic /ˈplæstɪk/ s plástico ● adj (de) plástico

plasticine® /ˈplæstəsiːn/ s (GB) massa de moldar

plate /pleɪt/ s **1** prato **2** (metal, etc.) placa, chapa: *~ glass* vidro laminado **3** baixela (ouro/prata) **4** (imprensa) chapa

plateau /ˈplætəʊ; GB plæˈtəʊ/ s (pl ~s ou ~x /-təʊz/) platô

platform /ˈplætfɔːrm/ s **1** tribuna **2** plataforma **3** (Pol) programa

platinum /ˈplætɪnəm/ s platina

platoon /pləˈtuːn/ s (Mil) pelotão

plausible /ˈplɔːzəbl/ adj **1** plausível **2** (pessoa) convincente

play /pleɪ/ s **1** (Teat) peça **2** at ~ brincando ◊ *do sth in ~* fazer algo de brincadeira **3** folga (em engrenagem, etc.) **4** (de palavras) jogo **5** (de forças, etc.) interação ● vt, vi brincar **2** vt (Esporte, cartas) ~ (sb) jogar (com alguém) **3** vt, vi (música) tocar: *~ sth by ear* tocar algo de ouvido **4** vt (CD, etc.) pôr **5** vt (tacada) dar **6** vt (peça) pregar **7** vt (papel dramático) interpretar, fazer **8** vt: *~ the fool* fazer-se de bobo ▶ **play it by ear** (coloq) improvisar **play your cards well/right** saber aproveitar as

P

oportunidades ■ **play along
(with sb)** fazer o jogo (de
alguém) **play sth down** minimizar algo **play A off against B**
opor A a B **play (sb) up** (*coloq*)
dar trabalho (a alguém) **player** *s*
1 jogador/a **2** músico/a **playful**
adj **1** brincalhão **2** jocoso
playground /ˈpleɪɡraʊnd/ *s* pátio
de recreio
playgroup /ˈpleɪɡruːp/ *s* (*GB*)
jardim de infância
playing card *s* carta (*baralho*)
playing field *s* campo de
esportes
play-off *s* partida de desempate
playpen /ˈpleɪpen/ *s* (*bebê*) cercadinho
playtime /ˈpleɪtaɪm/ *s* recreio
playwright /ˈpleɪraɪt/ *s* dramaturgo/a
plea /pliː/ *s* **1** ~ **(for sth)** petição
(de algo) **2** súplica **make a ~ for
sth** suplicar algo **3** (*Jur*) declaração
plead /pliːd/ (*pt, pp* **pleaded,
pled**) **1** *vi* ~ **(with sb)** suplicar (a
alguém) **2** *vi* ~ **for sth** pedir algo
3 *vi* ~ **for sb** defender alguém **4**
vt (*defesa*) alegar ■ **plead guilty/
not guilty** declarar-se culpado/
inocente
pleasant /ˈpleznt/ *adj* (~**er**, ~**est**)
agradável **pleasantly** *adv* **1**
agradavelmente **2** amavelmente
please /pliːz/ **1** *vt, vi* agradar **2** *vt*
dar prazer a **3** *vi*: *for as long as
you* ~ o tempo que você quiser ◇
I'll do whatever I ~. Vou fazer o
que me der vontade. ■ **as you
please** como quiser **please
yourself** você é que sabe ■ *interj*
por favor: *Please do not smoke.*
Favor não fumar. ▶ **please do** por
claro **pleased** *adj* contente
→ GLAD **2** satisfeito ▶ **be pleased
to do sth** ter prazer em fazer
algo: *I'd be ~ to come.* Gostaria
muito de ir. **pleased to meet
you** prazer em conhecê-lo
pleasing *adj* agradável
pleasure /ˈpleʒər/ *s* prazer: *take
~ in sth* gostar de fazer algo
▶ **my pleasure** não há de quê
pleasurable *adj* prazeroso
pled /pled/ (*USA*) *pret, pp de*
PLEAD
pledge /pledʒ/ *s* **1** promessa
2 penhor ● **1** *vt, vi* (*fml*) comprometer-se **2** *vt* empenhar
plentiful /ˈplentɪfl/ *adj* abundante: *be in ~* supply abundar
plenty /ˈplenti/ *pron* **1** muito, de
sobra **2** bastante: *That's ~.*
Chega. ● *adv* **1** (*coloq*) o sufici-

ente: ~ *high enough* suficientemente alto **2** (*USA*) muito
▶ **plenty more 1** de sobra **2** outros tantos: *There's room for ~
more.* Há espaço para muitos
mais.
pliable /ˈplaɪəbl/ (*tb* **pliant**
/ˈplaɪənt/) *adj* **1** flexível **2** influenciável
pliers /ˈplaɪərz/ *s* [*pl*] alicate
→ PAIR
plight /plaɪt/ *s* situação difícil
plod /plɒd/ *vi* (**-dd-**) caminhar
com dificuldade ■ **plod away (at
sth)** executar algo a duras
penas
plonk /plɒŋk/ *v* ■ **plonk sth down**
deixar algo cair pesadamente
plot /plɒt/ *s* **1** lote **2** (*livro, etc.*)
trama **3** complô ● **1** *vt* (**-tt-**)
traçar **2** *vt* tramar **3** *vi* conspirar
plow (*GB* **plough**) /plaʊ/ *s* arado
● *vt, vi* arar ■ **plow (your way)
through sth** abrir caminho
através de algo ■ **plow sth back**
reinvestir em algo **plow into sb/
sth** chocar-se contra alguém/
algo
ploy /plɔɪ/ *s* estratagema
pluck /plʌk/ *vt* **1** colher **2** depenar **3** (*sobrancelhas*) tirar **4**
(*corda*) tanger ■ **pluck up
courage** criar coragem ● *s* coragem
plug /plʌɡ/ *s* **1** tampão **2** (*Elet*)
tomada (*aparelho elétrico*) **3**
vela (*ignição*) **4** (*coloq*) propaganda ● *vt* (**-gg-**) **1** tapar **2**
(*escape*) vedar **3** (*cavidade*)
encher **4** fazer propaganda de
■ **plug sth in(to sth)** ligar algo (a
algo)
plum /plʌm/ *s* **1** ameixa **2** (*tb* ~
tree) ameixeira
plumage /ˈpluːmɪdʒ/ *s*
plumagem
plumber /ˈplʌmər/ *s* bombeiro/a
(*hidráulico*) **plumbing** *s* encanamento
plummet /ˈplʌmɪt/ *vi* **1** despencar **2** despencar
plump /plʌmp/ *adj* roliço
■ **plump for sb/sth** optar por
alguém/algo
plunder /ˈplʌndər/ *vt* saquear
plunge /plʌndʒ/ **1** *vi* despencar **2**
vt afundar **3** *vi* mergulhar **4** *vt*
submerger **5** *vt* (*no bolso, etc.*)
meter ● *s* **1** mergulho **2** salto **3**
(*preços*) queda ▶ **take the
plunge** topar a parada
plural /ˈplʊərəl/ *adj, s* plural
plus /plʌs/ *prep* **1** (*Mat*) mais **2**
além de ● *conj* além ■ *adj* £500
~ no mínimo 500 libras ◇ *He's*

forty ~. Ele tem quarenta e muitos. **2** (*Elet, Mat*) positivo ● **s 1** (*tb* ~ **sign**) sinal de adição **2** (*coloq*) ponto a favor: *the pluses and minuses of sth* os prós e os contras de algo

plush /plʌʃ/ *adj* (*coloq*) luxuoso

Pluto /ˈpluːtəʊ/ *s* Plutão

plutonium /pluːˈtəʊniəm/ *s* plutônio

ply /plaɪ/ *s 1 Ver* PLYWOOD **2** (*papel*) espessura **3** (*lã*) fio ● *vt* (*pt, pp* **plied** /plaɪd/) **1** (*fml*) (*ofício*) exercer **2** (*rota*) trafegar ■ **ply sb with drink/questions** encher alguém de bebida/bombardear alguém de perguntas

plywood /ˈplaɪwʊd/ *s* madeira compensada

p.m. /ˌpiː ˈem/ *abrev* da tarde/noite NOTA Quando se usa **a.m.** ou **p.m.**, não se pode dizer **o'clock**: *at three o'clock/3 p.m.*

pneumatic /nuːˈmætɪk; *GB* njuː-/ *adj* pneumático

pneumonia /nuːˈməʊniə; *GB* njuː-/ *s* pneumonia

PO /ˌpiːˈəʊ/ *abrev de* **Post Office**

poach /pəʊtʃ/ **1** *vt* cozinhar **2** *vt* (*ovos*) fazer pochê **3** *vt, vi* (*caça*) pescar clandestinamente **4** *vt* (*idéia*) roubar **poacher** *s* caçador/a, pescador/a (*furtivo*)

pocket /ˈpɑkɪt/ *s* **1** bolso: ~ *money* mesada ◊ ~ *knife* canivete **2** núcleo ▶ **out of pocket** sem dinheiro ● *vt* **1** meter no bolso **2** embolsar

pod /pɑd/ *s* vagem (*feijão, etc.*)

podium /ˈpəʊdiəm/ *s* pódio

poem /ˈpəʊəm/ *s* poema

poet /ˈpəʊɪt/ *s* poeta **poetic** /pəʊˈetɪk/ *adj* poético: ~ *justice* justiça divina

poetry /ˈpəʊətri/ *s* poesia

poignant /ˈpɔɪnjənt/ *adj* comovente

poinsettia /ˌpɔɪnˈsetiə/ *s* bico-de-papagaio

point /pɔɪnt/ *s* **1** ponto: ~ *of view* ponto de vista **2** ponta **3** (*Mat*) vírgula **4** tomo: *The* ~ *is…* O fato é que… **5** sentido: *What's the* ~? Para quê? **6** (*GB*) (*tb* **power** ~) tomada **7** (**points**) (*GB*) (*ferrovia*) chaves ▶ **be beside the point** não ter nada a ver ■ **in point of fact** na verdade ■ **make a point of doing sth** fazer questão de fazer algo ■ **make your point** deixar claro o que se pensa ■ **take sb's point** levar em conta o que alguém tem a dizer ■ **to the point** a propósito, relevante ● *vt, vi* ~ (**sth at sb**); ~ (**at/to sth/sb**)

apontar (*algo para alguém*); (*para alguém/algo*) apontar para algo ■ **point sth out (to sb)** chamar a atenção (de alguém) para algo

point-blank *adj* **1** *at* ~ *range* à queima-roupa **2** categórico ● *adv* **1** à queima-roupa **2** de forma categórica

pointed /ˈpɔɪntɪd/ *adj* **1** pontudo **2** intencional

pointer /ˈpɔɪntər/ *s* **1** indicador **2** ponteiro **3** (*coloq*) dica **4** indicativo

pointless /ˈpɔɪntləs/ *adj* sem sentido

poise /pɔɪz/ *s* **1** porte **2** desenvoltura **poised** *adj* **1** suspenso **2** com desembaraço, seguro de si

poison /ˈpɔɪzn/ *s* veneno ● *vt* **1** envenenar **2** corromper **poisoning** *s* envenenamento **poisonous** *adj* venenoso

poke /pəʊk/ *vt* cutucar (*com o dedo, etc.*): ~ *your finger into sth* meter o dedo em algo ▶ **poke fun at sb/sth** zombar de alguém/algo ■ **poke about/around** (*coloq*) bisbilhotar **2** mexericar **poke out of sth** sair de algo

poker /ˈpəʊkər/ *s* **1** atiçador **2** pôquer

poker-faced *adj* de semblante impassível

poky /ˈpəʊki/ *adj* (**-ier, -iest**) (*coloq*) **1** (*USA*) lento **2** (*GB*) apertado

polar /ˈpəʊlər/ *adj* polar

pole /pəʊl/ *s* **1** (*Geog, Fís*) pólo **2** vara **3** (*telegráfico*) poste ▶ **be poles apart** divergir inteiramente

police /pəˈliːs/ *s* [*pl*] polícia: ~ *officer* policial ◊ ~ *force* polícia ◊ ~ *state* estado policial ● *vt* policiar

policeman /pəˈliːsmən/ *s* (*fem* **policewoman**) (*pl* **-men, -women**) policial

policy /ˈpɑləsi/ *s* (*pl* **-ies**) **1** política **2** apólice

polio /ˈpəʊliəʊ/ (*tb* **poliomyelitis** /ˌpəʊliəʊmaɪəˈlaɪtɪs/) *s* pólio(mielite)

polish /ˈpɑlɪʃ/ *vt* **1** dar brilho a, polir **2** (*sapatos*) engraxar **3** aperfeiçoar ■ **polish sb off** dar um fim em alguém **polish sth off** (*coloq*) **1** devorar algo **2** acabar algo de uma vez ● *s* **1** brilho **2** polimento **3** (*sapatos*) graxa **4** (*unhas*) esmalte **5** refinamento **polished** *adj* **1** lustroso **2** refinado **3** (*atuação*) impecável

polite /pəˈlaɪt/ *adj* cortês, educado

politics /ˈpɑlətɪks/ *s* **1** política **2** [*sing*] ciências políticas **3** [*pl*]

princípios políticos political
/pə'lıtıkl/ adj político/a
,pálə'tıʃn/ s político/a

polka dot /'pəʊkə dɒt/ s bolinha

poll /pəʊl/ s 1 eleição 2 votação 3
(the polls) as urnas 4 (tb opinion
~) sondagem

pollen /'pɒlən/ s pólen

pollute /pə'luːt/ vt 1 poluir 2 corromper pollution s 1 poluição 2
corrupção

polo /'pəʊləʊ/ s pólo

polo neck s (GB) gola rulê

polyester /,pɒli'estər/ s poliéster

polyethylene /,pɒli'eθəliːn/ s
polietileno

polystyrene /,pɒli'staıriːn/ s
isopor

pomp /pɒmp/ s 1 pompa 2 ostentação

pompous /'pɒmpəs/ adj 1 pomposo 2 pretensioso

pond /pɒnd/ s tanque, lago
pequeno

ponder /'pɒndər/ vt, vi refletir

pony /'pəʊni/ s (pl -ies) pônei

ponytail /'pəʊniteıl/ s rabo-de-
cavalo

poodle /'puːdl/ s poodle

pool /puːl/ s 1 poça 2 charco 3
piscina 4 (luz) facho 5 tanque 6
(dinheiro) fundo comum,
vaquinha 7 bilhar americano 8
(the football) pools) [pl] (GB)
loteria esportiva • vt (recursos,
idéias) reunir

poor /pɔːr/ adj (~er, ~est) 1 pobre
2 mau 3 (nível) baixo • the poor
s [pl] os pobres

poorly /'pɔːrli/ adv 1 mal 2 insu-
ficientemente • adj (GB)
doente

pop /pɒp/ s 1 estalo 2 estouro 3
(USA) papai 4 (música) pop •
adv: go ~ estourar • (-pp-) 1 vi
estalar 2 vi fazer bum 3 vt, vi
estourar 4 vt (rolha) fazer
saltar NOTA As expressões
seguintes indicam ação rápida
ou repentina. ■ pop down, out,
etc. (coloq) descer, sair, etc. pop
sth back, in, etc. (coloq) devolver, colocar, etc. algo pop in visitar pop out (of sth) sair (de
algo) pop up aparecer

popcorn /'pɒpkɔːrn/ s pipoca

pope /pəʊp/ s papa

poplar /'pɒplər/ s álamo, choupo

poppy /'pɒpi/ s (pl -ies) papoula

Popsicle® /'pɒpsıkl/ s (USA)
picolé

popular /'pɒpjələr/ adj 1 popular: be ~ with sb ser muito nas graças
de alguém 2 na moda 3 (corrente (crença) geral popular-

ize vt 1 popularizar 2 vulgarizar

population /,pɒpjʊ'leıʃn/ s
população: ~ explosion explosão demográfica

porcelain /'pɔːrsəlın/ s porcelana

porch /pɔːrtʃ/ s 1 alpendre 2
(USA) varanda

pore /pɔːr/ s poro ■ pore over sth
estudar algo detalhadamente

pork /pɔːrk/ s carne de porco
→ CARNE

pornography /pɔːr'nɑːgrəfi/
(coloq porn) s pornografia

porous /'pɔːrəs/ adj poroso

porpoise /'pɔːrpəs/ s peixe-boto

porridge /'pɔːrıdʒ/ GB /'pɒr-/ s
mingau (de aveia)

port /pɔːrt/ s 1 porto: ~ of call
porto de escala 2 (barco) bombordo 3 vinho do Porto

portable /'pɔːrtəbl/ adj portátil

porter /'pɔːrtər/ s 1 carregador 2
(GB) porteiro/a

porthole /'pɔːrthəʊl/ s vigia

portion /'pɔːrʃn/ s 1 porção 2
(comida) ração

portrait /'pɔːrtrət, -treıt/ s 1
retrato 2 descrição

portray /pɔːr'treı/ vt 1 retratar 2
representar portrayal s representação

pose /pəʊz/ 1 vi posar (para
retrato) 2 vi comportar-se de
forma afetada 3 vi ~ as sb/sth
fazer-se passar por alguém/
algo 4 vt (pergunta, etc.) colocar
• s 1 postura 2 pose

posh /pɒʃ/ adj (~er, ~est) 1 de
luxo 2 (zona) chique 3
(sotaque) requintado 4 metido
a besta

position /pə'zıʃn/ s 1 posição 2
situação: in a ~ to do sth em condição de fazer algo 3 ~ (on sth)
ponto de vista (com respeito a
algo) 4 (trabalho) cargo • vt
colocar, situar

positive /'pɑːzətıv/ adj 1 positivo
2 categórico 3 ~ (about sth)
certo (de algo) 4 total, verdadeiro positively adv 1 positiva-
mente 2 com otimismo 3 categoricamente 4 verdadeira-
mente

possess /pə'zes/ vt 1 possuir 2
apoderar-se de: What pos-
sessed you to do that? O que é
que te deu para fazer aquilo?
possession s 1 possessão 2:
be in ~ of sth ter posse de algo 2
(possessions) bens

possibility /,pɒsə'bıləti/ s (pl
-ies) 1 possibilidade: within/
beyond the bounds of ~ dentro/

além do possível **2** (**possibilities**) [pl] potencial

possible /'pɒsəbl/ *adj* possível: *make sth* ~ possibilitar algo ◇ *as quickly as* ~ o mais rápido possível **possibly** *adv* possivelmente: *You can't* ~ *go.* Você não pode ir de maneira alguma.

post /pəʊst/ *s* **1** poste, estaca **2** (*trabalho*) cargo **3** correio → MAIL ● *vt* **1** mandar pelo correio, pôr no correio **2** nomear (*para cargo, etc.*), enviar **3** postar (*soldados, etc.*) ► **keep sb posted** (**about sth**) manter alguém informado (sobre algo)

postage /'pəʊstɪdʒ/ *s* porte, franquia: ~ *stamp* selo postal

postal /'pəʊstl/ *adj* postal

postbox /'pəʊstbɒks; *GB* -bɒks/ *s* (*GB*) caixa do correio

postcard /'pəʊstkɑːd/ *s* cartão postal

postcode /'pəʊstkəʊd/ *s* (*GB*) código postal

poster /'pəʊstər/ *s* cartaz **2** pôster

posterity /pɒ'sterəti/ *s* posteridade

postgraduate /ˌpəʊst'grædʒuət/ *adj* de pós-graduado

posthumous /'pɒstjʊməs; *GB* 'pɒstʃəməs/ *adj* póstumo

postman /'pəʊstmən/ *s* (*fem* **postwoman**) *s* (*pl* **-men**, **-women**) (*GB*) carteiro/a

post-mortem /ˌpəʊst 'mɔːtəm/ *s* autópsia

post office *s* (agência do) correio

postpone /pəʊs'pəʊn/ *vt* adiar

postscript /'pəʊstskrɪpt/ *s* **1** pós-escrito **2** desfecho

posture /'pɒstʃər/ *s* **1** postura **2** atitude

post-war *adj* de após-guerra

pot /pɒt/ *s* **1** caçarola, panela: *pots and pans* bateria de cozinha (panelas, tigelas, etc.) **2** vasilhame **3** pote **4** (*planta*) vaso **5** (*coloq*) maconha ► **go to pot** (*coloq*) degringolar

potassium /pə'tæsiəm/ *s* potássio

potato /pə'teɪtəʊ/ *s* (*pl* **-es**) batata

potent /'pəʊtnt/ *adj* potente, poderoso **potency** *s* potência

potential /pə'tenʃl/ *adj* *s* potencial **potentially** *adv* potencialmente

pothole /'pɒthəʊl/ *s* **1** (*Geol*) cova **2** (*estrada*) buraco

potter /'pɒtər/ *s* ceramista

pottery /'pɒtəri/ *s* cerâmica

potty /'pɒti/ *adj* (**-ier**, **-iest**) (*GB*, *coloq*) ~ (**about sb/sth**) louco por alguém/algo ● *s* (*pl* **-ies**) (*coloq*) peniço (*de criança*)

pouch /paʊtʃ/ *s* **1** pochete **2** tabaqueira **3** (*Zool*) bolsa

poultry /'pəʊltri/ *s* [U] aves domésticas

pounce /paʊns/ *vi* **1** lançar-se **2** atacar

pound /paʊnd/ *s* **1** (*abrev* lb.) libra (*0,454 quilograma*) **2** (*dinheiro*) libra (£) → Ver pág. 224 ● *vt* **1** *vi* ~ (**at sth**) golpear (algo) **2** *vi* correr pesadamente **3** *vi* ~ (**with sth**) bater fortemente (de algo) (*medo, etc.*) **4** *vt* socar **5** *vt* esmurrar **pounding** *s* **1** surra **2** (*onda*) marulho

pour /pɔːr/ *vi* **1** fluir, correr: ~ *out* (*of sth*) sair em massa/verter (de algo) **2** *vi* (*tb* ~ **with rain**) chover a cântaros **3** *vt* (*bebida*) servir ■ **pour in 1** entrar de enxurrada **2** inundar **pour sth out 1** (*bebida*) servir algo **2** expressar algo

pout /paʊt/ *vi* **1** ficar de tromba **2** fazer beicinho

poverty /'pɒvəti/ *s* **1** pobreza **2** miséria **3** (*idéia*) falta **poverty-stricken** *adj* desprovido

powder /'paʊdər/ *s* pó ● *vt* pulverizar: ~ *your face* passar pó no rosto **powdered** *adj* em pó: ~ *sugar* açúcar para glacê

power /'paʊər/ *s* **1** poder **2** (**powers**) [pl] capacidade **3** força **4** potência **5** energia **6** eletricidade: ~ *outage* corte de energia ◇ ~ *plant* central elétrica ► **do sb a power of good** (*GB*, *coloq*) ser muito benéfico para alguém **the powers that be** os mandachuvas ● *vt* acionar **powerful** *adj* **1** poderoso **2** potente **3** forte **4** (*obra, etc.*) marcante **powerless** *adj* **1** ineficaz, impotente **2** ~ **to do sth** impossibilitado de fazer algo

practicable /'præktɪkəbl/ *adj* viável

practical /'præktɪkl/ *adj* prático: ~ *joke* brincadeira de mau gosto **practically** *adv* **1** praticamente **2** de forma prática

practice /'præktɪs/ *s* **1** prática **2** (*Esporte*) treinamento **3** (*Med*) consultório **4** (*profissão*) exercício ● *s* (*GB* **practise**) **1** *vt*, *vi* praticar **2** *vi* praticar-se **3** *vt*, *vi* ~ (**as sth**) (*profissão*) exercer (algo) **4** *vt* ter por costume **practiced** (*GB* **-tised**) *adj* ~ (**in sth**) experiente (em algo)

practitioner /præk'tɪʃənər/ *s* **1**

praticante **2** médico/a

pragmatic /præɡˈmætɪk/ *adj* pragmático

praise /preɪz/ *vt* **1** elogiar **2** (*Relig*) louvar • s [U] **1** elogio(s) **2** (*Relig*) louvor

praiseworthy /ˈpreɪzwɜːrði/ *adj* louvável

prawn /prɔːn/ *s* (*GB*) camarão

pray /preɪ/ *vi* rezar

prayer /preər/ *s* oração

preach /priːtʃ/ **1** *vt, vi* (*Relig*) pregar **2** *vi* (*pej*) fazer sermão **3** *vt* exortar **preacher** *s* pregador/a

precarious /prɪˈkeəriəs/ *adj* precário

precaution /prɪˈkɔːʃn/ *s* precaução **precautionary** /prɪˈkɔːʃneri/ *adj* de precaução

precede /prɪˈsiːd/ *vt* **1** preceder a **2** (*discurso*) introduzir

precedence /ˈpresɪdəns/ *s* precedência

precedent /ˈpresɪdənt/ *s* precedente

preceding /prɪˈsiːdɪŋ/ *adj* **1** precedente **2** anterior

precinct /ˈpriːsɪŋkt/ *s* **1** (*USA*) distrito policial **2** (*tb* precincts) recinto **3** (*GB*) zona

precious /ˈpreʃəs/ *adj* **1** precioso **2** ~ to sb de grande valor para alguém • *adv* ▸ precious little/few muito pouco/s

precipice /ˈpresəpɪs/ *s* precipício

precise /prɪˈsaɪs/ *adj* **1** preciso **2** (*explicação*) claro **3** meticuloso **precisely** *adv* **1** precisamente **2** (*hora*) em ponto **3** com precisão **precision** /prɪˈsɪʒn/ *s* exatidão

preclude /prɪˈkluːd/ *vt* (*fml*) excluir

precocious /prɪˈkoʊʃəs/ *adj* precoce

preconceived /ˌpriːkənˈsiːvd/ *adj* preconcebido **preconception** *s* idéia preconcebida

precondition /ˌpriːkənˈdɪʃn/ *s* pré-requisito

predator /ˈpredətər/ *s* predador **predatory** /ˈpredətɔːri/ *adj* **1** predatório **2** oportunista

predecessor /ˈpredɪsesər; *GB* ˈpriːdə-/ *s* predecessor/a

predicament /prɪˈdɪkəmənt/ *s* situação difícil

predict /prɪˈdɪkt/ *vt* **1** prever **2** prognosticar **predictable** *adj* previsível **prediction** *s* previsão

predominant /prɪˈdɒmɪnənt/ *adj* predominante **predominantly** *adv* predominantemente

pre-empt /ˌpri ˈempt/ *vt* antecipar-se a

preface /ˈprefəs/ *s* **1** prefácio **2** introdução

prefer /prɪˈfɜːr/ *vt* (**-rr-**) preferir → PREFERIR **preferable** /ˈprefrəbl/ *adj* preferível **preferably** /ˈprefrəbli/ *adv* preferivelmente **preference** /ˈprefrəns/ *s* preferência ▸ in preference to sb/sth em vez de alguém/algo **preferential** /ˌprefəˈrenʃl/ *adj* preferencial

prefix /ˈpriːfɪks/ *s* prefixo

pregnant /ˈpreɡnənt/ *adj* **1** grávida **2** prenhe **pregnancy** *s* (*pl* **-ies**) gravidez

prejudice /ˈpredʒudɪs/ *s* **1** [U] preconceito **2** prejuízo **3** parcialidade ▸ without prejudice to sb/sth (*Jur*) sem danos para alguém/algo • *vt* **1** (*pessoa*) predispor **2** influir em **3** prejudicar **prejudiced** *adj* **1** parcial **2** preconceituoso: *be ~ against sb/sth* ter preconceito contra alguém/algo

preliminary /prɪˈlɪmɪneri; *GB* -nəri/ *adj* **1** preliminar **2** (*Esporte*) eliminatório • **preliminaries** *s* preliminares

prelude /ˈpreljuːd/ *s* **1** (*Mús*) prelúdio **2** início

premature /ˌpriːməˈtʊər, -ˈtʃʊər; *GB* ˈpremətjuə(r)/ *adj* prematuro

premier /prɪˈmɪər; *GB* ˈpremiə(r)/ *s* primeiro-ministro, primeira-ministra • *adj* principal

première /prɪˈmɪər; *GB* ˈpremieə(r)/ *s* estréia

premises /ˈpremɪsɪz/ *s* [*pl*] **1** (*bar, etc.*) local **2** (*empresa*) escritório(s) **3** edifício

premium /ˈpriːmiəm/ *s* (*pagamento*) prêmio ▸ be at a premium custar mais (por ser difícil de obter)

preoccupation /priˌɒkjuˈpeɪʃn/ *s* preocupação **preoccupied** /priˈɒkjupaɪd/ *adj* **1** preocupado **2** absorto

preparation /ˌprepəˈreɪʃn/ *s* **1** preparação **2** (**preparations**) preparativos

preparatory /prɪˈpærətɔːri; *GB* -tri/ *adj* preparatório

prepare /prɪˈpeər/ *vt, vi* preparar(-se) ▸ be prepared to do sth estar disposto a fazer algo

preposterous /prɪˈpɒstərəs/ *adj* absurdo

prerequisite /ˌpriːˈrekwəzɪt/ *s* (*fml*) pré-requisito

prerogative /prɪˈrɒɡətɪv/ *s* prerrogativa

prescribe /prɪˈskraɪb/ *vt* **1** receitar **2** recomendar

prescription /prɪˈskrɪpʃn/ s **1** receita **2** prescrição

presence /ˈprezns/ s **1** presença **2** comparecimento **3** existência

present /ˈpreznt/ adj **1** presente **2** (tempo) atual: to the ~ day até hoje **3** (mês, ano) corrente ● s **1** (the present) (tempo) presente: for the ~ por enquanto **2** (lembrança) presente ▶ at present no momento ● /prɪˈzent/ vt **1** apresentar **2** entregar: ~ sb with a problem criar um problema a alguém **3** (argumento) expor **4** ~ itself (to sb) (oportunidade) apresentar-se (a alguém) **5** (Teat) representar **presentable** /prɪˈzentəbl/ adj **1** apresentável **2** de boa aparência

presentation /ˌprezɪnˈteɪʃn; GB ˌprezn-/ s **1** apresentação **2** (argumento) exposição **3** (Teat) representação **4** (prêmio) entrega

present-day adj atual

presenter /prɪˈzentər/ s apresentador/a

presently /ˈprezntli/ adv **1** (esp USA) no momento **2** (GB) [futuro: geralmente no final da frase] em breve: I will follow on ~. Vou em seguida. **3** (GB) [passado: geralmente no princípio da frase] logo em seguida **4** (GB) logo

preservation /ˌprezərˈveɪʃn/ s conservação, preservação

preservative /prɪˈzɜːrvətɪv/ adj, s conservante

preserve /prɪˈzɜːrv/ vt **1** conservar (comida, etc.) **2** preservar **3** proteger ● s **1** conserva (caça) reserva: the exclusive ~ of members o reduto exclusivo dos membros

preside /prɪˈzaɪd/ vi ~ (over/at sth) presidir (algo)

president /ˈprezɪdənt/ s **1** presidente/a **presidency** (pl -ies) presidência presidential /ˌprezɪˈdenʃl/ adj presidencial

press /pres/ s **1** (tb the Press) a imprensa: ~ conference entrevista coletiva ◇ ~ cutting recorte de jornal **2** prensa **3** (tb printing ~) prelo ● vt **1** vt, vi apertar **2** vt espremer **3** vi ~ (up) against sb apoiar-se em alguém **4** vt prensar **5** vt (uvas) pisar **6** vt passar (roupas) **7** vt, vi ~ (sb) (for sth) pressionar (alguém) (por algo) ▶ pressed for time com pouco tempo ■ press ahead/on (with sth) seguir em frente (com algo)

pressing /ˈpresɪŋ/ adj premente

press-up s flexão

pressure /ˈpreʃər/ s pressão: ~ gauge manômetro ◇ ~ cooker panela de pressão ▶ put pressure on sb (to do sth) pressionar alguém (a fazer algo) ● vt (tb pressurize /ˈpreʃəraɪz/) ~ sb into (doing) sth pressionar alguém a fazer algo

prestige /preˈstiːʒ/ s prestígio **prestigious** /preˈstɪdʒəs/ adj prestigioso

presumably /prɪˈzuːməbli; GB -ˈzjuːm-/ adv presumivelmente

presume /prɪˈzuːm; GB -ˈzjuːm/ vt, vi supor

presumption /prɪˈzʌmpʃn/ s **1** suposição **2** atrevimento

presumptuous /prɪˈzʌmptʃuəs/ adj presunçoso

presuppose /ˌpriːsəˈpəʊz/ vt pressupor

pretend /prɪˈtend/ vt, vi **1** fingir: They're pretending to be pirates. Eles estão fazendo de conta que são piratas. **2** ter pretensões a ● adj (coloq) **1** de brincadeira **2** falso

pretense (GB pretence) /prɪˈtens/ s **1** [U] fingimento **2** (fml) ostentação

pretentious /prɪˈtenʃəs/ adj pretensioso

pretext /ˈpriːtekst/ s pretexto

pretty /ˈprɪti/ adj (-ier, -iest) **1** bonito **2** (mulher) atraente ▶ not be a pretty sight não ser nada agradável (de se olhar) ● adv bastante ▶ FAIRLY, RATHER → pretty much/well praticamente, quase

prevail /prɪˈveɪl/ vi **1** (condições) imperar **2** triunfar **3** prevalecer ■ prevail (up)on sb to do sth (fml) convencer alguém a fazer algo prevailing adj **1** (fml) dominante **2** (vento) característico

prevalent /ˈprevələnt/ adj **1** difundido **2** predominante prevalence s **1** difusão **2** predomínio

prevent /prɪˈvent/ vt **1** impedir **2** evitar, prevenir prevention /prɪˈvenʃn/ s prevenção preventive adj preventivo

preview /ˈpriːvjuː/ s pré-estréia

previous /ˈpriːviəs/ adj anterior: ~ to doing sth antes de fazer algo previously adv anteriormente

pre-war /priː ˈwɔːr/ adj do pré-guerra

prey /preɪ/ s presa ● v ▶ prey on sb's mind atormentar alguém ■ prey on sb/sth **1** caçar alguém/algo **2** viver às custas de alguém/algo

price /praɪs/ s preço ▸ **not at any price** por nada no mundo ● *vt* **1** fixar o preço de **2** avaliar ▸ pôr preço em **priceless** *adj* inestimável

prick /prɪk/ s **1** picada **2** alfinetada ● *vt* **1** picar **2** atormentar (*a consciência*) ▸ **prick up your ears 1** empinar as orelhas **2** aguçar os ouvidos

prickly /'prɪkli/ *adj* (**-ier, -iest**) **1** espinhoso **2** que pica **3** (*coloq*) irritadiço

pride /praɪd/ s **1** ~ (**in sth**) orgulho (de algo) **2** soberba ▸ **sb's pride and joy** a menina dos olhos de alguém ▸ **take pride in (doing) sth** orgulhar-se de (fazer) algo ■ **pride yourself on sth** orgulhar-se de algo

priest /priːst/ s sacerdote, padre **priesthood** s **1** sacerdócio **2** clero **NOTA** A palavra **priest** usa-se em geral, para os padres católicos. Os párocos anglicanos chamam-se **clergyman/woman** ou **vicar**, e os das demais religiões protestantes, **minister**.

prig /prɪg/ s pessoa metida a besta **priggish** *adj* pedante

prim /prɪm/ *adj* (*pej*) (**primmer, primmest**) **1** pudico (*aspecto*) recatado

primaeval (GB) = PRIMEVAL

primarily /praɪ'merəli; GB 'praɪmərəli/ *adv* fundamentalmente

primary /'praɪmeri; GB -məri/ *adj* **1** primário **2** primordial **3** principal ● s (*pl* **-ies**) (*USA*) (*tb* ~ **election**) eleição primária

prime /praɪm/ *adj* **1** principal **2** de primeira: *a ~ example* um exemplo perfeito ● s ▸ **in your prime/in the prime of life** no auge (da vida) ● *vt* ~ **sb (for/with sth)** preparar alguém (para algo); instruir alguém (de algo)

prime minister s primeiro-ministro, primeira-ministra

primeval /praɪ'miːvl/ *adj* primevo

primitive /'prɪmətɪv/ *adj* primitivo

primrose /'prɪmrəʊz/ s **1** prímula **2** amarelo claro

prince /prɪns/ s príncipe

princess /,prɪn'ses/ s princesa

principal /'prɪnsəpl/ *adj* principal ● s (*Educ*) diretor/a, reitor/a

principle /'prɪnsəpl/ s princípio: ▸ **in/on principle** em/por princípio

print /prɪnt/ *vt* **1** *vt, vi* ~ (**sth**) (**out**)

imprimir (algo) **2** *vt* (*Jornal*) publicar **3** *vt* escrever em letra de imprensa **4** *vt* estampar ● s **1** (*tipografia*) letra **2** impressão **3** (*Arte*) gravura **4** (*Fot*) cópia **5** tecido estampado ▸ **in print** (*livro*) à venda ▸ publicado **out of print** fora do prelo **printer** s **1** tipógrafo/a **2** impressora **3** (**the printers**) [*pl*] (*oficina*) gráfica **printing** s **1** impressão (*técnica*): *a ~ error* um erro tipográfico ◇ ~ *press* prelo **2** (*livros*) impressão **printout** /'prɪntaʊt/ s cópia impressa

prior /'praɪər/ *adj* prévio ● **prior to** *adv* anterior a: ~ *to doing sth* antes de fazer algo

priority /praɪ'ɒrəti; GB -'ɒr-/ s (*pl* **-ies**) prioridade: *get your priorities right* saber estabelecer prioridades

prise (GB) = PRIZE v (2)

prison /'prɪzn/ s prisão: ~ *camp* campo de detenção **prisoner** s **1** presidiário/a **2** prisioneiro/a: *take/hold sb ~* capturar alguém/manter alguém em cativeiro **3** detido/a **4** (*em julgamento*) acusado/a, réu, ré

privacy /'praɪvəsi; GB 'prɪv-/ s privacidade

private /'praɪvət/ *adj* **1** privado: ~ *eye* detetive particular **2** (*do indivíduo*) particular **3** (*pessoa*) reservado **4** (*lugar*) tranqüilo ● s **1** (*Mil*) soldado raso **2** (**privates**) (*coloq*) partes (íntimas) ▸ **in private** em particular privately *adv* em particular privatize *vt* privatizar

privilege /'prɪvəlɪdʒ/ s **1** privilégio **2** (*Jur*) imunidade **privileged** *adj* **1** privilegiado **2** confidencial

privy /'prɪvi/ *adj* (*fml*) ~ **to sth** inteirado de algo

prize /praɪz/ s prêmio ● *adj* **1** premiado **2** de primeira: *a ~ idiot* um completo idiota ● *vt* **1** valorizar **2** ~ **sth apart, off, open etc.** separar, tirar, abrir etc. algo à força

pro /prəʊ/ *adj, s* (*coloq*) profissional ▸ **the pros and (the) cons** os prós e os contras

probable /'prɒbəbl/ *adj* provável **probability** /,prɒbə'bɪləti/ s (*pl* **-ies**) probabilidade ▸ **in all probability** com toda a probabilidade **probably** *adv* provavelmente **NOTA** Costuma-se usar o advérbio nos casos em que se usaria *é provável que* em português: *They will ~ go.* É provável que eles vão.

probation /prəʊˈbeɪʃn; *GB* prə-/ s **1** liberdade condicional **2** em (estágio de) experiência

probe /prəʊb/ s sonda ● **1** vt, vi (*Med*) sondar **2** vt interrogar **3** vi ~ (**into sth**) investigar (algo) **probing** adj (*pergunta*) inquisitivo

problem /ˈprɒbləm/ s problema **problematic(al)** adj **1** problemático **2** duvidoso

procedure /prəˈsiːdʒər/ s **1** procedimento **2** trâmite(s)

proceed /prəˈsiːd, prəʊ-/ vi **1** prosseguir **2** ~ **to (do) sth** passar a (fazer) algo **3** (*fml*) avançar, seguir **4** ~ (**with sth**) continuar, ir em frente (com algo) **proceedings** s [*pl*] **1** sessão **2** (*Jur*) processo **3** (*reunião*) ata

proceeds /ˈprəʊsiːdz/ s [*pl*] renda

process /ˈprəʊses; *GB* ˈprəʊsəs/ s processo: *be in the ~ of doing sth* estar fazendo algo ▶ **in the process** ao fazer (algo) ● vt **1** (*matéria-prima*) tratar **2** (*requisição*) dar andamento a **3** (*Fot*) revelar **4** (*Informát*) processar **processing** s **1** tratamento **2** (*Fot*) revelação **3** *word* ~ processamento de textos

procession /prəˈseʃn/ s desfile, procissão

processor /ˈprəʊsesər; *GB* ˈprəʊsesə(r)/ s processador *Ver* MICROPROCESSOR, FOOD PROCESSOR

proclaim /prəˈkleɪm/ vt proclamar **proclamation** s **1** pronunciamento **2** proclamação

prod /prɒd/ vt, vi (**-dd-**) **1** ~ (**at**) **sb/sth** cutucar alguém/algo ● s **1** empurrão **2** objeto pontudo

prodigy /ˈprɒdədʒi/ s (*pl* **-ies**) prodígio **prodigious** /prəˈdɪdʒəs/ adj prodigioso

produce /prəˈdjuːs; *GB* -ˈdjuːs/ vt **1** (*tb Cinema, TV*) produzir **2** (*cria*) dar **3** ~ **sth** (**from/out of sth**) sacar algo (de algo) **4** (*Teat*) pôr em cena ● /ˈprɒdjuːs; *GB* -duːs/ s [*U*] produtos (*agrícolas*): ~ *of France* produto da França → PRODUCT **producer** s **1** (*Cinema, TV*) produtor/a **2** (*Teat*) diretor/a

product /ˈprɒdʌkt/ s produto NOTA *Usa-se* **product** *para produtos industriais e* **produce** *para produtos agrícolas.*

production /prəˈdʌkʃn/ s produção: ~ *line* linha de montagem

productive /prəˈdʌktɪv/ adj produtivo **productivity** /ˌprɒdʌkˈtɪvəti, ˌprɒd-/ s produtividade

profess /prəˈfes/ (*fml*) **1** vi ~ **to be sth** pretender ser algo **2** vt ~ (**yourself**) **sth** declarar(-se) algo **3** vt (*Relig*) professar **professed** adj **1** suposto **2** declarado

profession /prəˈfeʃn/ s profissão → WORK **professional** adj profissional

professor /prəˈfesər/ s (*abrev* **Prof.**) **1** (*USA*) professor/a de ensino técnico ou universitário **2** (*GB*) catedrático/a

proficiency /prəˈfɪʃnsi/ s [*U*] competência **proficient** adj competente

profile /ˈprəʊfaɪl/ s perfil

profit /ˈprɒfɪt/ s **1** lucro, ganho: *do sth for ~* fazer algo com fins lucrativos ◊ *profit-making* lucrativo **2** vantagem, proveito ● vi ~ **from sth** beneficiar-se de algo **profitable** adj **1** rentável **2** proveitoso

profound /prəˈfaʊnd/ adj profundo **profoundly** adv profundamente

profuse /prəˈfjuːs/ adj profuso **profusely** adv profusamente

profusion /prəˈfjuːʒn/ s profusão: *in ~* em abundância

program (*GB* **programme**) /ˈprəʊɡræm, -ɡrəm/ s programa NOTA Em linguagem de computação escreve-se **program**, inclusive na Grã-Bretanha. ● vt, vi (**-mm-**) programar **programmer** (*tb* **computer ~**) s programador/a **programming** s programação

progress /ˈprɒɡres; *GB* ˈprəʊ-/ s [*U*] **1** progresso **2** avanço: *make ~* avançar ▶ **in progress** em curso ● /prəˈɡres/ vi progredir

progressive /prəˈɡresɪv/ adj **1** progressivo **2** (*Pol*) progressista

prohibit /prəʊˈhɪbɪt; *GB* prə-/ vt (*fml*) **1** proibir **2** impedir **prohibition** s proibição

project /ˈprɒdʒekt/ s projeto ● /prəˈdʒekt/ **1** vt projetar **2** vi sobressair **projection** s projeção **projector** s projetor (*cinema*): *overhead ~* retroprojetor

prolific /prəˈlɪfɪk/ adj prolífico

prologue (*USA tb* **prolog**) /ˈprəʊlɔːɡ; *GB* -lɒɡ/ s ~ (**to sth**) prólogo (de algo)

prolong /prəˈlɒŋ; *GB* -ˈlɒŋ/ vt prolongar

prom /prɒm/ s **1** (*USA*) baile de estudantes **2** (*GB, coloq*) (*tb* **promenade** /ˌpromaˈneɪd; *GB* -ˈnɑːd/) passeio (à beira-mar)

prominent /ˈprɒmɪnənt/ adj **1** proeminente **2** importante

promiscuous /prə'mɪskjuəs/ adj promíscuo

promise /'prɒmɪs/ s promessa: *show ~* ser promissor • vt, vi prometer **promising** adj promissor

promote /prə'məʊt/ vt 1 promover 2 estimular 3 (Com) fazer promoção de **promoter** s patrocinador/a **promotion** s promoção

prompt /prɒmpt/ adj 1 sem atraso 2 (serviço) rápido 3 pontual • adv pontualmente • 1 vt incitar 2 vt (reação) provocar 3 vt, vi (Teat) servir de ponto (a) **promptly** adv 1 com prontidão 2 pontualmente 3 em seguida

prone /prəʊn/ adj propenso

pronoun /'prəʊnaʊn/ s pronome

pronounce /prə'naʊns/ vt 1 pronunciar 2 declarar **pronounced** adj 1 (sotaque) forte 2 notável 3 (movimento) acentuado

pronunciation /prə,nʌnsi'eɪʃn/ s pronúncia

proof /pruːf/ s 1 [U] prova(s) 2 comprovação

prop /prɒp/ s 1 apoio 2 suporte • vt (-pp-) ~ sth (up) against sth apoiar algo contra algo ■ **prop sth up** 1 escorar algo 2 respaldar algo

propaganda /,prɒpə'gændə/ s propaganda

propel /prə'pel/ vt (-ll-) 1 impulsionar 2 propulsar **propellant** adj, s propulsor

propeller /prə'pelər/ s hélice

propensity /prə'pensəti/ s (fml) ~ (for/to sth) propensão (a algo)

proper /'prɒpər/ adj 1 apropriado 2 de verdade 3 conveniente 4 propriamente dito **properly** adv 1 bem 2 (comportar-se) direito 3 adequadamente

property /'prɒpərti/ s (pl -ies) 1 propriedade 2 [U] bens

prophecy /'prɒfəsi/ s (pl -ies) profecia

prophesy /'prɒfəsaɪ/ (pt, pp -ied) 1 vt predizer 2 vi profetizar

prophet /'prɒfɪt/ s profeta

proportion /prə'pɔːʃn/ s proporção ► **out of (all) proportion** 1 desproporcionadamente 2 desproporcional **proportional** adj proporcional

proposal /prə'pəʊzl/ s 1 proposta 2 (tb ~ of marriage) pedido de casamento

propose /prə'pəʊz/ 1 vt propor 2 vt ~ to do sth/doing sth propor-se a fazer algo 3 vi ~ (to sb) pedir a mão (de alguém)

proposition /,prɒpə'zɪʃn/ s 1 proposição 2 proposta

proprietor /prə'praɪətər/ s proprietário/a

prose /prəʊz/ s prosa

prosecute /'prɒsɪkjuːt/ vt processar: *prosecuting lawyer* promotor público **prosecution** s 1 (instauração de) processo 2 acusação **prosecutor** s promotor/a

prospect /'prɒspekt/ s 1 perspectiva 2 expectativa(s), possibilidade(s) 3 (antiq) vista **prospective** /prə'spektɪv/ adj 1 futuro 2 provável

prospectus /prə'spektəs/ s prospecto (brochura)

prosper /'prɒspər/ vi prosperar **prosperity** /prɒ'sperəti/ s prosperidade **prosperous** adj próspero

prostitute /'prɒstɪtjuːt; GB -tjuːt/ s 1 prostituta 2 (male ~) prostituto **prostitution** s prostituição

prostrate /'prɒstreɪt/ adj 1 prostrado 2 ~ (with sth) abatido (por algo)

protagonist /prə'tægənɪst/ s 1 protagonista 2 defensor/a

protect /prə'tekt/ vt proteger **protection** s proteção **protective** adj protetor

protein /'prəʊtiːn/ s proteína

protest /'prəʊtest/ s protesto • /prə'test/ 1 vi ~ (about/at/against sth) protestar (por/contra algo) 2 vt afirmar **protester** s manifestante

Protestant /'prɒtɪstənt/ adj, s protestante

prototype /'prəʊtətaɪp/ s protótipo

protrude /prəʊ'truːd; GB prə-/ vi sobressair: *protruding teeth* dentes salientes

proud /praʊd/ adj (~er, ~est) 1 orgulhoso 2 soberbo **proudly** adv orgulhosamente

prove /pruːv/ (pp **proven** /'pruːvn/, GB **proved**) 1 vt provar, demonstrar: ~ *your point* provar que se tem razão 2 vt, vi ~ (yourself) (to be) sth revelar-se (como sendo) algo: *The task proved very hard.* A tarefa acabou se revelando muito difícil.

proven /'pruːvn/ adj comprovado

proverb /'prɒvɜːrb/ s provérbio **proverbial** adj 1 proverbial 2 notório

provide /prə'vaɪd/ vt ~ sb (with sth); ~ sth (for sb) abastecer alguém (com algo); fornecer algo (a alguém) ∎ **provide for sb** prover alguém (de algo) **provide for sth 1** prevenir algo **2** precaver-se contra algo

provided /prə'vaɪdɪd/ (*tb* **providing**) *conj* com a condição de que, contanto que

province /'prɒvɪns/ *s* **1** província **2** (**the provinces**) [*pl*] o interior **3** alçada **provincial** /prə'vɪnʃl/ *adj* **1** provincial **2** (*pej*) provinciano

provision /prə'vɪʒn/ *s* **1** fornecimento **2** make ~ for sb assegurar o futuro de alguém ◊ make ~ for sth precaver-se contra algo **3** (**provisions**) provisões **4** (*Jur*) cláusula, estipulação

provisional /prə'vɪʒənl/ *adj* provisório

proviso /prə'vaɪzoʊ/ *s* (*pl* ~**s**) condição

provocation /ˌprɒvə'keɪʃn/ *s* provocação **provocative** /prə'vɒkətɪv/ *adj* provocante

provoke /prə'voʊk/ *vt* **1** provocar **2** ~ sb into doing sth/to do sth instigar alguém a fazer algo **3** causar

prow /praʊ/ *s* proa

prowess /'praʊəs/ *s* **1** proeza **2** destreza

prowl /praʊl/ *vt, vi* ~ (**about/around** (**sth**)) rondar algo, andar à espreita

proximity /prɒk'sɪməti/ *s* proximidade

proxy /'prɒksi/ *s* **1** procurador/a **2** procuração

prude /pruːd/ *s* (*pej*) pudico/a

prudent /'pruːdnt/ *adj* prudente

prune /pruːn/ *s* ameixa seca ● *vt* **1** podar **2** cortar **pruning** *s* poda

pry /praɪ/ (*pt, pp* **pried** /praɪd/) **1** *vi* ~ (**into sth**) intrometer-se (em algo); bisbilhotar **2** *vt* (*esp USA*) *Ver* PRIZE V (2)

P.S. /ˌpiː 'es/ *abrev de* **postscript** post-scriptum

psalm /sɑːm/ *s* salmo

pseudonym /'suːdənɪm; *GB* 'sjuːdənɪm/ *s* pseudônimo

psyche /'saɪki/ *s* psique, psiquismo

psychiatry /saɪ'kaɪətri/ *s* psiquiatria **psychiatric** /ˌsaɪkɪ'ætrɪk/ *adj* psiquiátrico **psychiatrist** /saɪ'kaɪətrɪst/ *s* psiquiatra

psychic /'saɪkɪk/ *adj* **1** (*tb* **psychical**) psíquico **2** (*pessoa*) paranormal

psychoanalysis /ˌsaɪkoʊə'næləsɪs/ *s* psicanálise

psychology /saɪ'kɒlədʒi/ *s* psicologia **psychological** /ˌsaɪkə'lɒdʒɪkl/ *adj* psicológico **psychologist** /saɪ'kɒlədʒɪst/ *s* psicólogo/a

pub /pʌb/ *s* (*GB*) bar

puberty /'pjuːbərti/ *s* puberdade

pubic /'pjuːbɪk/ *adj* púbico

public /'pʌblɪk/ *adj* público: ~ house (*GB*) bar ● **the public** *s* o público ▶ **in public** em público

publication /ˌpʌblɪ'keɪʃn/ *s* publicação

publicity /pʌb'lɪsəti/ *s* publicidade: ~ campaign campanha publicitária

publicize /'pʌblɪsaɪz/ *vt* **1** divulgar **2** promover

publicly /'pʌblɪkli/ *adv* publicamente

public school *s* **1** (*USA*) escola pública **2** (*GB*) escola particular → ESCOLA

publish /'pʌblɪʃ/ *vt* **1** publicar **2** tornar público **publisher** *s* **1** editor/a **2** editora **publishing** *s* mundo editorial: ~ house editora

pudding /'pʊdɪŋ/ *s* **1** (*GB*) sobremesa → NATAL **2** pudim **3** black ~ morcela

puddle /'pʌdl/ *s* poça

puff /pʌf/ *s* **1** sopro (*fumo*) baforada **3** (*vapor*) jato **4** tragada **5** (*coloq*) fôlego ● **1** *vi* arquejar **2** *vi* ~ (**away**) at/on sth dar tragadas em algo **3** *vt* lançar baforadas **4** *vt* (*cigarro, etc.*) tragar ▶ **puff sth out** inflar algo ∎ **puff up** inflar-se **be puffed** (*tb* ~ **out**) *adj* (*coloq*) sem fôlego **puffy** *adj* (**-ier, -iest**) inchado (*esp rosto*)

pull /pʊl/ *s* **1** puxão **2** the ~ of sth a atração de algo **3** It was a hard ~. Foi uma estirada e tanto. ● **1** *vt* puxar **2** *vt, vi* ~ (**at/on sth**) estirar algo **3** *vt* (*rolha, revólver*) sacar **4** *vt* (*dente*) extrair ▶ **pull sb's leg** (*coloq*) brincar com alguém **pull strings** (**for sb**) (*coloq*) mexer os pauzinhos (para alguém) **pull your socks up** (*GB, coloq*) tomar jeito **pull your weight** fazer a sua parte ∎ **pull sth apart** separar, romper algo **pull sth down 1** puxar algo para baixo **2** demolir algo **pull into sth; pull in (to sth) 1** (*trem*) chegar (a algo) **2** (*carro*) encostar em algo **pull sth off** (*coloq*) ser bem-sucedido em algo **pull out** (**of sth**) **1** (*negócio, etc.*) retirar-se (de algo) **2** (*veículo*) arrancar (de algo) **pull sb/sth out 1** retirar alguém/algo **2**

arrancar algo **pull over** (*carro, etc.*) encostar, chegar para o lado **pull yourself together** controlar-se **pull up** (*veículo*) parar **pull sth up 1** levantar algo **2** (*planta*) arrancar algo

pulley /'pʊli/ s roldana

pullover /'pʊləʊvər/ s pulôver

pulp /pʌlp/ s **1** polpa **2** (*madeira*) pasta

pulpit /'pʊlpɪt/ s púlpito

pulsate /pʌl'seɪt; GB pʌl'seɪt/ (*tb* **pulse**) vi palpitar

pulse /pʌls/ s **1** (*Med*) pulso **2** ritmo **3** pulsação **4** grãos (*feijão, etc.*)

pumice /'pʌmɪs/ (*tb* ~ **stone**) s pedra-pomes

pummel /'pʌml/ vt (**-l-**, GB **-ll-**) esmurrar

pump /pʌmp/ s **1** bomba **2** sapatilha ● **1** vt bombear **2** vt ~ **sth (up)** encher algo (*com bomba*) **3** vi (*coração*) bater **4** vt ~ **sb (for sth)** (*coloq*) sondar alguém; tirar informação de alguém

pumpkin /'pʌmpkɪn/ s abóbora

pun /pʌn/ s jogo de palavras

punch /pʌntʃ/ s **1** punção **2** (*para bilhetes*) furador **3** (*bebida*) ponche **4** soco ● vt **1** picotar: ~ *a hole* fazer um buraco **2** dar um soco em

punch-up s (GB, *coloq*) briga

punctual /'pʌŋktʃuəl/ adj pontual → **PONTUAL** **punctuality** /ˌpʌŋktʃu'æləti/ s pontualidade

punctuate /'pʌŋktʃueɪt/ vt **1** (*Gram*) pontuar **2** interromper

puncture /'pʌŋktʃər/ s furo ● **1** vt, vi furar **2** vt (*Med*) perfurar

pundit /'pʌndɪt/ s entendido/a (*conhecedor*)

pungent /'pʌndʒənt/ adj **1** acre **2** pungente **3** mordaz

punish /'pʌnɪʃ/ vt castigar **punishment** s **1** castigo **2** paulada

punitive /'pjuːnɪtɪv/ adj (*fml*) **1** punitivo **2** pesado

punk /pʌŋk/ s **1** (*tb* ~ **rock**) punk **2** (*pej, coloq, esp USA*) arruaceiro ● adj punk

punt /pʌnt/ s (*coloq*) chalana

punter /'pʌntər/ s (GB) **1** apostador/a **2** (*coloq*) cliente, freguês

pup /pʌp/ s **1** *Ver* **PUPPY 2** filhote

pupil /'pjuːpl/ s **1** aluno/a **2** discípulo/a **3** pupila (*olho*)

puppet /'pʌpɪt/ s fantoche

puppy /'pʌpi/ s (*pl* **-ies**) cachorrinho → **CÃO**

purchase /'pɜːrtʃəs/ s (*fml*) aquisição ● vt (*fml*) adquirir **purchaser** s (*fml*) comprador/a

pure /pjʊər/ adj (**-er, -est**) puro

purely adv simplesmente

purée /'pjʊəreɪ; GB 'pjʊəreɪ/ s purê

purge /pɜːrdʒ/ vt expurgar ● s **1** (*Pol*) expurgo **2** (*Med*) purgante

purify /'pjʊərɪfaɪ/ vt (*pt, pp* **-ied**) purificar

puritan /'pjʊərɪtən/ adj, s puritano/a **puritanical** /ˌpjʊərɪ'tænɪkl/ adj puritano

purity /'pjʊərəti/ s pureza

purple /'pɜːrpl/ adj, s roxo

purport /pər'pɔːrt/ vt (*fml*): *It purports to be...* Isso pretende ser...

purpose /'pɜːrpəs/ s **1** propósito: *for this* ~ para este fim ◊ *purpose-built* construído com um fim específico **2** determinação: *have no sense of* ~ não ter um objetivo na vida ▸ **for the purpose of** para efeito de **on purpose** de propósito **purposeful** adj decidido **purposely** adv intencionalmente

purr /pɜːr/ vi ronronar → **GATO**

purse /pɜːrs/ s **1** bolsa (*de mão*) **2** porta-moedas ● vt: ~ *your lips* franzir os lábios

pursue /pər'suː; GB 'sjuː/ vt (*fml*) **1** perseguir **NOTA** A palavra mais comum é **chase**. **2** dedicar-se a **3** (*conversa*) continuar (com)

pursuit /pər'suːt; GB 'sjuːt/ s (*fml*) **1** busca: *in* ~ *of sth* em busca de/ perseguindo algo **2** [*ger pl*] atividade

push /pʊʃ/ s ~ e empurrão ▸ **get the push/give sb the push** (GB, *coloq*) ser despedido/despedir alguém ● **1** vt, vi empurrar: ~ *past sb* passar por alguém empurrando **2** vt, vi ~ (**on/against**) **sth** (*botão*) apertar algo **3** vt (*coloq*) (*idéia*) promover ▸ **be pushed for sth** (*coloq*) ter pouco de algo ■ **push ahead/forward/on** (**with sth**) prosseguir (com algo) **push sb around** ser mandão com alguém **push in** furar fila **push off** (GB, *coloq*) ir embora

pushchair /'pʊʃtʃeər/ s carrinho de criança

push-up s flexão

pushy /'pʊʃi/ adj (**-ier, -iest**) (*coloq*) entrão

put /pʊt/ vt (**-tt-**) (*pt, pp* **put**) **1** pôr, colocar, meter: ~ *sb out of work* deixar alguém sem trabalho **2** dizer, expressar **3** (*pergunta, etc.*) fazer **4** (*tempo, etc.*) dedicar **NOTA** Para expressões com **put**, ver o substantivo, adjetivo, etc., p. ex. **put sth right**

em RIGHT. ■ **put sth across/over** comunicar algo **put yourself across/over** expressar-se **put sth aside 1** pôr, deixar algo de lado **2** (*dinheiro*) economizar **put sth away** guardar algo **put sth back 1** recolocar algo em seu lugar, guardar algo **2** (*relógio*) atrasar algo **3** adiar algo **put sth by 1** economizar algo **2** (*reservar*) guardar algo **put sth down** (*coloq*) depreciar alguém ■ **put sth down 1** pôr algo (no chão, etc.) **2** largar algo **3** anotar algo **4** (*rebelião*) sufocar **5** (*animal*) sacrificar algo **put sth down to sth** atribuir algo a algo **put sth forward 1** (*proposta*) apresentar algo **2** (*sugestão*) fazer algo **3** (*relógio*) adiantar algo **put sth into sth** dedicar algo a algo, investir algo para algo **put sth off 1** (*encontro/cancelar*) um encontro com alguém **2** perturbar alguém **put sb off ((doing) sth)** fazer alguém perder a vontade (de (fazer) algo) **put sth on 1** vestir, pôr algo (*luz, etc.*) acender algo **3** ~ on weight engordar **4** (*Teat*) apresentar algo **5** fingir algo **put sth out 1** aborrecer alguém **put sth out 1** tirar algo **2** apagar algo **3** (*mão*) estender algo **put yourself out (to do sth)** (*coloq*) dispor-se a (fazer algo) **put sb through (to sb)** pôr alguém em contato (com alguém) (*por telefone*) **put sb through** submeter alguém a algo **put sth through** concluir algo (*reforma, etc.*) **put sth to sb** propor algo a alguém **put sth together** preparar, montar algo (*aparelho*) **put sb up** alojar alguém **put sth up 1** (*mão*) levantar algo **2** (*edifício*) construir algo **3** (*cartaz, etc.*) pôr algo **4** (*preço*) aumentar algo **put up with sb/sth** agüentar alguém/algo

putrid /ˈpjuːtrɪd/ *adj* **1** podre **2** asqueroso

putter /ˈpʌtər/ s Ver CROSS-WORD, JIGSAW **2** mistério ● *vt* desconcertar ■ **puzzle sth out** resolver algo **puzzle over sth** dar tratos à imaginação acerca de algo

pygmy /ˈpɪgmi/ s (*pl* -ies) pigmeu ● *adj* anão

pyjamas (*GB*) = PAJAMAS

pylon /ˈpaɪlən/; *GB* -lɒn/ s torre de transmissão elétrica

pyramid /ˈpɪrəmɪd/ s pirâmide

python /ˈpaɪθən/; *GB* ˈpaɪθn/ s píton

Qq

Q, q /kjuː/ s (*pl* **Q's**, **q's** /kjuːz/) Q, q

quack /kwæk/ s **1** grasnido **2** (*coloq*) charlatão ● *vi* grasnar

quadruple /ˈkwɒdrʊpl; *GB* kwɒ-/ *adj* quádruplo ● / (*GB*) ˈkwɒ-/ *vt, vi* quadruplicar(-se)

quagmire /ˈkwæɡmaɪər, ˈkwɒɡ-/ s atoleiro

quail /kweɪl/ s (*pl* **quail** *ou* ~s) codorna ● *vi* ~ (at sb/sth) acovardar-se diante de alguém/algo

quaint /kweɪnt/ *adj* **1** curioso **2** (*lugar*) pitoresco

quake /kweɪk/ *vi* tremer ● s (*coloq*) terremoto

qualification /ˌkwɒlɪfɪˈkeɪʃn/ s **1** (*diploma, etc.*) título **2** requisito **3** modificação: without ~ sem restrição **4** qualificação

qualified /ˈkwɒlɪfaɪd/ *adj* **1** diplomado **2** qualificado **3** (*êxito, etc.*) limitado

qualify /ˈkwɒlɪfaɪ/ (*pt, pp* -ied) **1** *vt* ~ sb (for sth) capacitar alguém (a algo); dar direito a alguém (de algo) **2** *vi* ~ (for sth/ to do sth) ter direito (a algo/de fazer algo) **3** *vt* (*declaração*) modificar **4** *vi* ~ (as sth) obter o título (de algo): He doesn't exactly ~ as our best writer. Ele não é exatamente o nosso melhor escritor. **5** *vi* ~ (for sth) preencher os requisitos (para algo) **6** *vi* ~ (for sth) (*Esporte*) classificar-se (para algo) qualifying *adj* eliminatório

qualitative /ˈkwɒlɪtətɪv; *GB* -tət-/ *adj* qualitativo

quality /ˈkwɒləti/ s (*pl* -ies) **1** qualidade **2** classe **3** característica

qualm /kwɑːm/ s escrúpulo

quandary /ˈkwɒndəri/ s (*pl* -ies) dilema

quantify /ˈkwɒntɪfaɪ/ *vt* (*pt, pp* -ied) quantificar

quantitative /ˈkwɒntɪteɪtɪv; *GB* -tət-/ *adj* quantitativo

quantity /ˈkwɒntəti/ s (*pl* -ies) quantidade

quarantine /ˈkwɒrəntiːn; *GB* ˈkwɒr-/ s quarentena

quarrel /ˈkwɒrəl; *GB* ˈkwɒrəl/ s **1**

briga 2 queixa • *vi* (**-l-**, *GB* **-ll-**), **brigar** quarrelsome *adj* briguento

quarry /'kwɔːri; *GB* 'kwɒri/ *s* (*pl* **-ies**) **1** presa **2** pedreira

quart /kwɔːrt/ *s* (*abrev* **qt**) quarto de galão (*0,95 litro*)

quarter /'kwɔːrtər/ *s* **1** quarto: *It's (a) ~ to one.* Faltam quinze para a uma. ◊ *It's (a) ~ after one.* É uma e quinze. **2** trimestre **3** bairro **4** (*USA*) vinte e cinco centavos **5** (**quarters**) [*pl*] (*esp Mil*) alojamento ▶ **in/from all quarters** em/de toda parte

quarter-final *s* quarta-de-final

quarterly /'kwɔːrtərli/ *adj* trimestral • *adv* trimestralmente • *s* (*pl* **-ies**) revista trimestral

quartet /kwɔːr'tet/ *s* quarteto

quartz /kwɔːrts/ *s* quartzo

quash /kwɒʃ/ *vt* **1** anular **2** (*rebelião*) sufocar **3** (*boato, etc.*) pôr fim a

quay /kiː/ *s* (*tb* **quayside**) /'kiːsaɪd/ *s* cais

queen /kwiːn/ *s* **1** rainha **2** (*baralho*) dama → BARALHO

queer /kwɪər/ *adj* esquisito • *s* (*pej*) bicha

quell /kwel/ *vt* **1** (*revolta, etc.*) reprimir **2** (*dúvidas, etc.*) dissipar

quench /kwentʃ/ *vt* **1** (*sede*) saciar **2** (*fogo, paixão*) extinguir

query /'kwɪəri/ *s* (*pl* **-ies**) dúvida (*pergunta*) • (*pt, pp* **-ied**) *vt* **1** pôr em dúvida **2** *vi* perguntar

quest /kwest/ *s* (*fml*) busca

question /'kwestʃən/ *s* **1** pergunta **2** questão ▶ **out of the question** fora de questão **call sth into question** pôr algo em dúvida • *vt* **1** fazer perguntas a **2** duvidar de **questionable** *adj* questionável

questioning /'kwestʃənɪŋ/ *s* interrogatório • *adj* inquisitivo

question mark *s* ponto de interrogação

questionnaire /ˌkwestʃə'neər/ *s* questionário

queue /kjuː/ *s* (*GB*) fila • *vi* ~ (**up**) (*GB*) fazer fila

quick /kwɪk/ (**~er**, **~est**) *adj* rápido: *a ~ temper* um temperamento irritadiço • *adv* rapidamente

quicken /'kwɪkən/ *vt, vi* **1** acelerar(-se) **2** avivar(-se)

quickly /'kwɪkli/ *adv* depressa, rapidamente

quicksilver /'kwɪksɪlvər/ *s* mercúrio

quid /kwɪd/ *s* (*pl* **quid**) (*coloq, GB*) libra (£)

quiet /'kwaɪət/ *adj* (**~er**, **~est**) **1** tranquilo **2** calado: *Be ~!* Cale-se! **3** silencioso • *s* **1** silêncio **2** tranquilidade ▶ **on the quiet** em surdina • **1** (*GB* **quieten**) *vt* ~ (**sb/sth**) (**down**) acalmar (alguém/algo) **2** *vi* ~ (**down**) acalmar-se

quietly /'kwaɪətli/ *adv* **1** em silêncio **2** tranquilamente **3** em voz baixa

quietness /'kwaɪətnəs/ *s* tranquilidade, silêncio

quilt /kwɪlt/ *s* **1** colcha de retalhos **2** (*GB*) edredom

quintet /kwɪn'tet/ *s* quinteto

quirk /kwɜːrk/ *s* **1** singularidade (*de comportamento*) **2** capricho **quirky** *adj* esquisito

quit /kwɪt/ (**-tt-**) (*pt, pp* **quit**) **1** *vt, vi* deixar **2** *vt* (*coloq*) ~ (**doing**) **sth** parar (de fazer) algo **3** *vi* ir embora

quite /kwaɪt/ *adv* **1** bastante: ~ *well* bastante bem **2** (*GB*) totalmente → FAIRLY ▶ **quite a few/lot** um número considerável **quite a/some** um... e tanto: *She hasn't been seen for ~ some time.* Ela não é vista há um bom tempo.

quiver /'kwɪvər/ *vi* tremer • *s* estremecimento

quiz /kwɪz/ *s* (*pl* **quizzes**) competição (*de conhecimento*) • (**-zz-**) interrogar **quizzical** *adj* inquisitivo

quorum /'kwɔːrəm/ *s* quórum

quota /'kwoʊtə/ *s* quota

quotation /kwoʊ'teɪʃn/ *s* **1** (*livro, etc.*) citação **2** (*Fin*) cotação **3** orçamento

quote /kwoʊt/ **1** *vt, vi* citar **2** *vt* dar uma cotação **3** *vt* cotar • *s* **1** citação **2** orçamento **3** (**quotes**) (*tb* **quotation marks**) aspas

R r

R, r /ɑːr/ *s* (*pl* **R's**, **r's** /ɑːrz/) R, r

rabbit /'ræbɪt/ *s* coelho → COELHO

rabid /'ræbɪd/ *adj* raivoso

rabies /'reɪbiːz/ *s* raiva (*doença*)

raccoon /ræ'kuːn/ *s* guaxinim

race /reɪs/ *s* **1** raça: ~ *relations* relações raciais **2** corrida • **1** *vi* (*em corrida*) correr **2** *vi* correr a toda velocidade **3** *vi* competir **4** *vi* (*pulso*) bater muito rápido **5** *vt* ~ **sb** disputar uma corrida com alguém race car s carro de corrida

racehorse /'reɪshɔ:rs/ s cavalo de corrida

racetrack /'reɪstræk/ s 1 circuito (de automobilismo, etc.) 2 (*GB* racecourse /'reɪskɔ:rs/) hipódromo

racial /'reɪʃl/ adj racial

racing /'reɪsɪŋ/ s corrida: ~ bike bicicleta de corrida

racism /'reɪsɪzəm/ s racismo racist adj, s racista

rack /ræk/ s 1 suporte 2 bagageiro ● vt ▶ rack your brain(s) quebrar a cabeça

racket /'rækɪt/ s 1 (*tb* racquet) raquete 2 alvoroço 3 conto-do-vigário

racy /'reɪsi/ adj (-ier, -iest) 1 (estilo) animado 2 (piada) picante

radar /'reɪdɑr/ s radar

radiant /'reɪdiənt/ adj ~ (with sth) radiante (de algo) radiance s esplendor

radiate /'reɪdieɪt/ vt, vi irradiar

radiation /,reɪdi'eɪʃn/ s radiação: ~ sickness intoxicação radioativa

radiator /'reɪdieɪtər/ s radiador

radical /'rædɪkl/ adj, s radical

radio /'reɪdioʊ/ s (pl ~s) rádio

radioactive /,reɪdioʊˈæktɪv/ adj radioactive radioactivity /,reɪdioʊækˈtɪvəti/ s radioatividade

radish /'rædɪʃ/ s rabanete

radius /'reɪdiəs/ s (pl radii /-diaɪ/) raio

raffle /'ræfl/ s rifa

raft /ræft/ s jangada: life ~ bote salva-vidas

rafter /'ræftər/; *GB* /'rɑ:f-/ s viga (telhado)

rag /ræg/ s 1 trapo 2 (rags) farrapos 3 (coloq) jornaleco

rage /reɪdʒ/ s fúria: fly into a ~ enfurecer-se ▶ be all the rage estar na moda ● vi 1 enfurecer-se 2 (tempestade) estrondear 3 (batalha) seguir com ímpeto

ragged /'rægɪd/ adj 1 (roupa) esfarrapado 2 (pessoa) maltrapilho

raging /'reɪdʒɪŋ/ adj 1 (dor, sede) alucinante 2 (mar) revolto 3 (tempestade) violento

raid /reɪd/ s 1 ataque 2 (roubo) assalto 3 (polícia) batida ● vt 1 fazer uma batida em 2 saquear, assaltar raider s assaltante

rail /reɪl/ s 1 balaustrada 2 (Ferrovia, cortinas) trilho 3 by ~ de trem ◇ ~ strike greve de ferroviários

railing /'reɪlɪŋ/ s (*tb* railings) grade

railroad /'reɪlroʊd/ (*GB* railway) s 1 estrada de ferro: ~ station estação ferroviária 2 (*tb* ~ line/track) linha do trem

rain /reɪn/ s chuva: It's pouring with ~. Chove a cântaros. ● vi chover

rainbow /'reɪnboʊ/ s arco-íris

raincoat /'reɪnkoʊt/ s capa de chuva

rainfall /'reɪnfɔːl/ s [U] precipitação (atmosférica)

rainforest /'reɪnfɔːrɪst/ s floresta tropical

rainy /'reɪni/ adj (-ier, -iest) chuvoso

raise /reɪz/ s aumento (salário) ● vt 1 levantar 2 aumentar 3 (esperanças) dar 4 (nível) elevar 5 (alarme) soar 6 (assunto) pôr em discussão 7 (empréstimo) obter 8 (fundos) angariar 9 (filhos, animais) criar 10 (exército) recrutar ▶ raise your eyebrows (at sth) torcer o nariz (para algo) raise your glass (to sb) brindar à saúde (de alguém)

raisin /'reɪzn/ s passa

rake /reɪk/ s ancinho ● vt, vi revolver/limpar (algo) com ancinho ▶ rake it in fazer uma grana preta ■ rake sth up (coloq) desenterrar (passado, etc.)

rally /'ræli/ (pt, pp -ied) 1 vi ~ (around) unir-se 2 vt ~ sb (around sb) congregar alguém (em volta de alguém) 3 vi recuperar-se ● s (pl -ies) 1 comício 2 (tênis, etc.) rebatida 3 rali

ram /ræm/ s carneiro ● (-mm-) 1 vi ~ into sth bater contra/em algo 2 vt empurrar com força 3 vt ~ sth in, into, etc. sth meter algo em algo à força

ramble /'ræmbl/ vi ~ (on) divagar ● s excursão a pé rambling adj 1 labiríntico 2 (Bot) trepador 3 (discurso) desconexo

ramp /ræmp/ s 1 rampa 2 (estrada) lombada

rampage /ræmˈpeɪdʒ, ˈræmˈpeɪdʒ/ vi alvoroçar-se ● /ˈræmˈpeɪdʒ/ s alvoroço: go on the ~ causar tumulto

rampant /'ræmpənt/ adj 1 desenfreado 2 (plantas) exuberante

ramshackle /'ræmʃækl/ adj desconjuntado

ran /ræn/ pret de RUN

ranch /ræntʃ/; *GB* /rɑ:ntʃ/ s fazenda

rancid /'rænsɪd/ adj rançoso

random /'rændəm/ adj casual ● s ▶ **at random** ao acaso

rang /ræŋ/ pret de RING²

range /reɪndʒ/ s **1** (montanhas) cadeia **2** gama **3** (produtos) linha **4** escala **5** (visão, som) extensão **6** (armas) alcance ● **1** vi ~ **from sth to sth** estender-se, ir de algo até algo **2** vi ~ **between sth and sth**: ~ **between sth and sth** (cifra) oscilar entre algo e algo **3** vt ordenar **4** vi ~ **(over/through sth)** vaguear (por algo)

rank /ræŋk/ s **1** categoria **2** (Mil) posto ▶ **the rank and file** a massa (pessoas) ● **1** vt classificar **2** vi figurar: high-ranking de alto escalão

ransack /'rænsæk/ vt **1** ~ **sth (for sth)** revistar algo (em busca de algo) **2** pilhar

ransom /'rænsəm/ s resgate

rap /ræp/ s **1** pancada seca **2** (Mús) rap ● vt, vi (-pp-) dar uma pancada seca em

rape /reɪp/ vt violentar → VIO-LATE ● s estupro **rapist** s estuprador

rapid /'ræpɪd/ adj rápido **rapidity** /rə'pɪdəti/ s rapidez **rapidly** adv rapidamente

rapport /ræ'pɔːr/ s entrosamento

rapt /ræpt/ adj absorto

rapture /'ræptʃər/ s êxtase **rapturous** adj entusiástico

rare /reər/ adj (-er, -est) **1** raro **2** (carne) mal passado **rarely** adv raramente → ALWAYS **rarity** s (pl -ies) raridade

rash /ræʃ/ adj (~er, ~est) precipitado: In a ~ moment I told her... Num momento impensado eu disse a ela... ● s irritação na pele

raspberry /'ræzberi; GB 'rɑːzbəri/ s (pl -ies) framboesa

rat /ræt/ s rato ▶ **the rat race** (coloq) luta por um lugar ao sol

rate /reɪt/ s **1** razão (proporção) **2** tarifa: an hourly ~ of pay um pagamento por hora ◇ the exchange/interest ~ a taxa de câmbio/juros ▶ **at any rate** de qualquer modo **at this/that rate** (coloq) desse jeito

rather /'rɑːðər; GB 'rɑːðə/ adv (esp GB) um tanto, bastante: I ~ suspect... Acho... NOTA **Rather** seguido de palavra com sentido positivo indica surpresa por parte do falante: It was a ~ nice present. Foi um presente e tanto. Também é usado para cri-

ticar algo: This room looks ~ untidy. Este quarto está uma bela bagunça. ▶ **I'd, you'd, etc. rather...**: I'd ~ walk than drive. Prefiro ir a pé a ir de carro. **or rather** ou melhor **rather than** em vez de

rating /'reɪtɪŋ/ s **1** índice **2** (the ratings) (TV) os índices de audiência

ratio /'reɪʃiou/ s (pl ~s) proporção

ration /'ræʃn/ s ração ● vt **1** racionar **2** restringir **rationing** s racionamento

rational /'ræʃnəl/ adj racional **rationality** /ræʃə'næləti/ s racionalidade **rationalization** s racionalização **rationalize** vt racionalizar

rattle /'rætl/ **1** vt chocalhar **2** vi fazer retinir **3** vi ~ **along, off, past, etc.** mover-se fazendo muito barulho ▶ **rattle sth off** falar em disparada ● s **1** chocalhar **2** chocalho, guizo

rattlesnake /'rætlsneɪk/ s cascavel

ravage /'rævɪdʒ/ vt devastar

rave /reɪv/ vi **1** ~ **(at sb)** soltar os cachorros (em alguém) **2** ~ **(on) about sb/sth** vibrar com alguém/algo

raven /'reɪvn/ s corvo

raw /rɔː/ adj **1** cru **2** bruto: ~ material matéria-prima **3** (ferida) em carne viva

ray /reɪ/ s raio

razor /'reɪzər/ s navalha (de barba): ~ blade lâmina de barbear

reach /riːtʃ/ **1** vi ~ **(out) (to sb/for sth)** estender a mão (a alguém/para pegar algo) **2** vt alcançar **3** vt comunicar-se com **4** vt (acordo) chegar a ● s ▶ **beyond/out of/within (sb's) reach** fora do alcance/ao alcance (de alguém) **within (easy) reach (of sb/sth)** próximo (de alguém/algo)

react /ri'ækt/ vi **1** reagir **2** insurgir-se **reaction** s reação **reactionary** adj reacionário

reactor /ri'æktər/ s (tb nuclear ~) s reator (nuclear)

read /riːd/ (pt, pp read /red/) **1** vt, vi ler: ~ sth out ler algo em voz alta **2** vt ~ **sth (as sth)** interpretar algo (como algo) **3** vi (artigo) dizer **4** vt (marcador, etc.) marcar ▶ **read on** continuar a ler **read sth into sth** atribuir algo a algo **readable** adj agradável de ler **reading** s leitura: ~ glasses óculos (para ler)

reader /'ri:dər/ s 1 leitor/a 2 edição simplificada **readership** s [sing] (número de) leitores

ready /'redi/ adj (-ier, -iest) 1 pronto: get ~ preparar-se 2 disposto 3 ~ to do sth prestes a fazer algo 4 disponível **readily** adv 1 prontamente 2 facilmente **readiness** s prontidão: do sth in ~ for sth fazer algo em preparação a algo

ready-made adj 1 de confecção 2 (já) feito

real /'ri:əl/ adj 1 real, verdadeiro 2 autêntico: That's not his ~ name. Esse não é o nome dele de verdade.

real estate s (USA) [U] bens imobiliários: ~ agent corretor de imóveis

realism /'ri:əlɪzəm/ s realismo **realist** s realista **realistic** /,ri:ə-'lɪstɪk/ adj realista

reality /ri'ælətɪ/ s (pl -ies) realidade ▸ **in reality** na realidade

realize /'ri:əlaɪz/ vt 1 dar-se conta de 2 (plano, etc.) realizar **realization** s compreensão

really /'ri:əli, 'rɪli/ adv 1 de verdade: I ~ mean that. Estou falando sério. 2 muito, realmente 3 (surpresa, interesse, dúvida, etc.) é mesmo?: Really? É mesmo?

realm /relm/ s (fig) terreno

reap /ri:p/ vt ceifar

reappear /,ri:ə'pɪər/ vi reaparecer **reappearance** s reaparição

rear /rɪər/ 1 vt criar 2 vi ~ (up) (cavalo) empinar-se 3 vt erguer ● **the rear** s [sing] a parte traseira: a ~ window uma janela traseira

rearrange /,ri:ə'reɪndʒ/ vt 1 reorganizar 2 (planos) mudar

reason /'ri:zn/ s 1 ~ (for sth/why...) razão (de algo/pela qual...), motivo (para algo/pelo qual...) 2 razão, bom senso: make sb see ~ chamar alguém à razão ▸ **by reason of sth** (fml) em virtude de algo ▸ **in/within reason** nos limites do razoável ● vi raciocinar **reasonable** adj 1 razoável 2 tolerável **reasonably** adv 1 suficientemente 2 de forma sensata **reasoning** s argumentação

reassure /,ri:ə'ʃʊər/ vt tranqüilizar **reassurance** s 1 reconforto 2 palavras reconfortantes **reassuring** adj reconfortante

rebate /'ri:beɪt/ s desconto

rebel /'rebl/ s rebelde ● /rɪ'bel/ vi (-ll-) rebelar-se **rebellion** /rɪ'beljən/ s rebelião **rebellious** /rɪ'beljəs/ adj rebelde

rebirth /,ri:'bɜ:rθ/ s 1 renascimento 2 ressurgimento

reboot /ri:'bu:t/ vt, vi (Informát) reiniciar

rebound /rɪ'baʊnd/ vi 1 ricochetear 2 ~ (on sb) recair (sobre alguém) ● /'ri:baʊnd/ s ricochete ▸ **on the rebound** de ricochete

rebuff /rɪ'bʌf/ s (fml) 1 esnobada 2 recusa ● vt 1 esnobar 2 rechaçar

rebuild /,ri:'bɪld/ vt (pt, pp rebuilt /,ri:'bɪlt/) reconstruir

rebuke /rɪ'bju:k/ vt repreender ● s repreensão

recall /rɪ'kɔ:l/ vt 1 chamar de volta 2 pedir a devolução de (mercadoria defeituosa) 3 (parlamento) convocar 4 recordar

recapture /,ri:'kæptʃər/ vt 1 recapturar 2 (fig) recriar

recede /rɪ'si:d/ vi 1 retroceder: receding hairline entradas 2 (maré) baixar

receipt /rɪ'si:t/ s 1 ~ (for sth) recibo (de algo) 2 (fml) recebimento 3 (receipts) (Com) receitas

receive /rɪ'si:v/ vt 1 receber, acolher 2 (ferimento) sofrer

receiver /rɪ'si:vər/ s 1 (TV, etc.) receptor 2 fone 3 destinatário/a

recent /'ri:snt/ adj recente: in ~ years nos últimos anos **recently** adv 1 recentemente: until ~ até pouco tempo atrás 2 [antes de participio] recente

reception /rɪ'sepʃn/ s 1 recepção 2 acolhida **receptionist** s recepcionista

receptive /rɪ'septɪv/ adj receptivo

recess /rɪ'ses; GB rɪ'ses/ s 1 recesso 2 (USA) (escola) recreio 3 (nicho) vão 4 [ger pl] recôndito

recession /rɪ'seʃn/ s recessão

recharge /,ri:'tʃɑːrdʒ/ vt recarregar

recipe /'resəpi/ s ~ (for sth) receita (de algo)

recipient /rɪ'sɪpiənt/ s destinatário/a

reciprocal /rɪ'sɪprəkl/ adj recíproco

reciprocate /rɪ'sɪprəkeɪt/ vt, vi (fml) retribuir

recital /rɪ'saɪtl/ s recital

recite /rɪ'saɪt/ vt 1 recitar 2 enumerar

reckless /'rekləs/ adj imprudente

reckon /'rekən/ vt 1 considerar 2

crer 3 calcular ∎ **reckon on sth** contar com algo **reckon with sb/sth** contar com alguém, levar algo em conta: *You've got your father to ~ with.* Você tem que se haver com seu pai. **reckoning** *s* [*sing*] 1 cálculo 2 contas

reclaim /rɪ'kleɪm/ *vt* 1 recuperar 2 (*materiais, etc.*) reciclar reclamation *s* recuperação

recline /rɪ'klaɪn/ *vt, vi* reclinar(-se) **reclining** *adj* reclinável (*assento*)

recognition /ˌrekəg'nɪʃn/ *s* reconhecimento: *change beyond ~* estar irreconhecível

recognize /'rekəgnaɪz/ *vt* reconhecer **recognizable** *adj* reconhecível

recoil /rɪ'kɔɪl/ *vi* 1 recuar 2 retroceder

recollect /ˌrekə'lekt/ *vt* recordar **recollection** *s* lembrança

recommend /ˌrekə'mend/ *vt* recomendar

recompense /'rekəmpens/ *vt* (*fml*) recompensar ● *s* (*fml*) [*sing*] recompensa

reconcile /'rekənsaɪl/ *vt* 1 reconciliar 2 conciliar 3 ~ yourself to sth resignar-se a algo reconciliation *s* [*sing*] 1 conciliação 2 reconciliação

reconnaissance /rɪ'kɒnɪsns/ *s* (*Mil*) reconhecimento

reconsider /ˌriːkən'sɪdər/ *vt, vi* reavaliar

reconstruct /ˌriːkən'strʌkt/ *vt* reconstruir

record /'rekərd; *GB* 'rekɔːd/ *s* 1 registro: *keep a ~ of sth* anotar algo 2 antecedentes: *a criminal ~* uma ficha na polícia 3 disco: *a ~ company* uma gravadora ◇ *a ~ player* toca-discos 4 recorde ▶ **put/set the record straight** corrigir um equívoco ● /rɪ'kɔːd/ 1 *vt* registrar, anotar 2 *vt, vi* gravar 3 *vt* (*termômetro*) marcar **recording** *s* gravação

record-breaking *adj* sem precedentes

recorder /rɪ'kɔːrdər/ *s* 1 flauta doce 2 *Ver* TAPE RECORDER, VIDEO

recount /rɪ'kaʊnt/ *vt* relatar

recourse /rɪ'kɔːrs/ *s* (*fml*) recurso: *have ~ to sb/sth* recorrer a alguém/algo

recover /rɪ'kʌvər/ *vt* 1 recuperar 2 *vi* recuperar-se, refazer-se **recovery** /rɪ'kʌvəri/ *s* 1 (*pl* -ies) recuperação, resgate 2 restabelecimento

recreation /ˌrekri'eɪʃn/ *s* 1 recreação 2 recreio: *~ ground*

área de lazer

recruit /rɪ'kruːt/ *s* recruta ● *vt* recrutar **recruitment** *s* recrutamento

rectangle /'rektæŋgl/ *s* retângulo

rector /'rektər/ *s* (*GB*) pároco **rectory** *s* (*pl* -ies) presbitério

recuperate /rɪ'kuːpəreɪt/ 1 *vi* (*fml*) recuperar-se 2 *vt* recuperar

recur /rɪ'kɜːr/ *vi* (-rr-) repetir-se

recycle /ˌriː'saɪkl/ *vt* reciclar **recyclable** *adj* reciclável **recycling** *s* reciclagem

red /red/ *adj* (**redder, reddest**) 1 vermelho 2 (*rosto*) ruborizado 3 (*vinho*) tinto ▶ **a red herring** uma pista falsa ● *s* vermelho **reddish** *adj* avermelhado

redeem /rɪ'diːm/ *vt* 1 redimir 2 compensar 3 resgatar

redemption /rɪ'dempʃn/ *s* (*fml*) 1 salvação 2 resgate

redevelopment /ˌriːdɪ'veləpmənt/ *s* reedificação, reurbanização

redo /ˌriː'duː/ *vt* (*pt* **redid** /-'dɪd/ *pp* **redone** /-'dʌn/) refazer

red tape *s* [U] burocracia

reduce /rɪ'djuːs; *GB* rɪ'djuːs/ 1 *vt* reduzir 2 *vt* ~ **sth (by sth)** diminuir, baixar algo (em algo) 3 *vi* reduzir-se 4 *vt*: *The house was reduced to ashes.* A casa ficou reduzida a cinzas. ◇ ~ **sb to tears** levar alguém às lágrimas **reduced** *adj* reduzido

reduction /rɪ'dʌkʃn/ *s* 1 ~ **(in sth)** redução (de algo) 2 ~ **(of sth)** desconto (em algo)

redundancy /rɪ'dʌndənsi/ *s* (*pl* -ies) demissão (*por extinção de postos de trabalho*)

redundant /rɪ'dʌndənt/ *adj* 1 (*GB*) **be made** ~ ser demitido por motivo de extinção de postos de trabalho 2 supérfluo

reed /riːd/ *s* junco

reef /riːf/ *s* recife

reek /riːk/ *vi* feder

reel /riːl/ *s* 1 carretel 2 (*filme*) rolo ● *vi* 1 cambalear (*cabeça*) rodar ∎ **reel sth off** recitar algo (*de uma tirada só*)

re-enter /ˌriː'entər/ *vt* reingressar em **re-entry** *s* reingresso

refer /rɪ'fɜːr/ (-rr-) 1 *vi* referir-se 2 *vt, vi* recorrer

referee /ˌrefə'riː/ *s* 1 árbitro/a 2 mediador/a 3 (*GB*) (*para emprego*) referência (*pessoa*) ● *vt, vi* arbitrar

reference /'refərəns/ *s* referência ▶ **in/with reference to sb/sth**

com referência a alguém/algo

referendum /ˌrefəˈrendəm/ s plebiscito

refill /ˌriːˈfil/ vt reabastecer ● /ˈriːfil/ s refil

refine /rɪˈfaɪn/ vt 1 refinar 2 aprimorar refinement s 1 refinamento 2 (Mec) refinação 3 apuro refinery s (pl -ies) refinaria

reflect /rɪˈflekt/ vt, vi refletir ▸ reflect well, badly etc. on sb/sth ser favorável/desfavorável à imagem de alguém/algo reflection (GB tb reflexion) s 1 reflexo 2 reflexão: on ~ pensando bem ▸ be a reflection on sb/sth apontar a falha de alguém/algo

reflex /ˈriːfleks/ (tb ~ action) s reflexo

reform /rɪˈfɔːm/ vt, vi reformar(-se) ● s reforma reformation s 1 reforma 2 (the Reformation) a Reforma

refrain /rɪˈfreɪn/ vi (fml) abster-se ● s refrão

refresh /rɪˈfreʃ/ vt refrescar: ~ sb's memory refrescar a memória de alguém refreshing adj 1 refrescante 2 reconfortador

refreshments /rɪˈfreʃmənts/ s lanches NOTA Antes de substantivo, usa-se no singular: a refreshment stop.

refrigerate /rɪˈfrɪdʒəreɪt/ vt refrigerar refrigeration s refrigeração

refrigerator /rɪˈfrɪdʒəreɪtər/ s geladeira

refuge /ˈrefjuːdʒ/ s 1 refúgio: take ~ refugiar-se 2 (Pol) asilo

refugee /ˌrefjuˈdʒiː/ s refugiado/a

refund /rɪˈfʌnd/ vt reembolsar ● /ˈriːfʌnd/ s reembolso

refusal /rɪˈfjuːzl/ s 1 rejeição 2 ~ (to do sth) recusa (em fazer algo)

refuse¹ /rɪˈfjuːz/ 1 vt recusar, rejeitar: ~ sb entry proibir a entrada de alguém 2 vi negar-se

refuse² /ˈrefjuːs/ s [U] refugo

regain /rɪˈɡeɪn/ vt recuperar

regal /ˈriːɡl/ adj régio

regard /rɪˈɡɑːd/ vt 1 considerar 2 (fml) ~ sb/sth (with sth) olhar para alguém/algo (com algo) ▸ as regards sb/sth no que se refere a alguém/algo ● s 1 respeito: with no ~ for speed limits sem respeitar os limites de velocidade 2 (regards) [pl] (em correspondência) cordialmente ▸ in this/that regard a este/esse

respeito: in/with regard to sb/sth com respeito a alguém/algo

regarding prep com relação a

regardless adv apesar de tudo

regardless of prep independentemente de, sem levar em conta

regime /reɪˈʒiːm/ s regime (governo, etc.)

regiment /ˈredʒɪmənt/ s regimento regimented adj regrado

region /ˈriːdʒən/ s região ▸ in the region of sth por volta de algo

register /ˈredʒɪstər/ s 1 registro 2 (lista de) chamada ● 1 vt registrar 2 vi matricular-se 3 vt (surpresa, etc.) demonstrar

registered mail s porte registrado

registrar /ˌredʒɪˈstrɑː/ s 1 escrivão (registro civil, etc.) 2 (Educ) secretário/a (encarregado de matrículas, etc.)

registration /ˌredʒɪˈstreɪʃn/ s 1 registro 2 inscrição

registration number (GB) s número da placa

registry office /ˈredʒɪstri ɒfɪs/ (tb register office) s (GB) cartório

regret /rɪˈɡret/ s 1 ~ (at/about sth) lástima (por algo) 2 arrependimento ● vt (-tt-) 1 lamentar 2 arrepender-se de regretfully adv com pesar regrettable adj lamentável

regular /ˈreɡjələr/ adj 1 regular: get ~ exercise fazer exercício regularmente ◊ on a ~ basis com regularidade 2 habitual 3 normal: the ~ army o exército regular ● s cliente habitual regularity /ˌreɡjuˈlærəti/ s regularidade regularly adv 1 regularmente 2 com regularidade

regulate /ˈreɡjuleɪt/ vt regulamentar regulation s 1 regulamento 2 [ger pl] norma

rehabilitate /ˌriːəˈbɪlɪteɪt/ vt reabilitar rehabilitation s reabilitação

rehearse /rɪˈhɜːs/ vt, vi ensaiar rehearsal s ensaio

reign /reɪn/ s reinado ● vi reinar

reimburse /ˌriːɪmˈbɜːs/ vt reembolsar

rein /reɪn/ s rédea

reindeer /ˈreɪndɪər/ s (pl reindeer) rena

reinforce /ˌriːɪnˈfɔːs/ vt reforçar reinforcement s 1 consolidação 2 (reinforcements) (Mil) reforços

reinstate /ˌriːɪnˈsteɪt/ vt reintegrar

reject /rɪˈdʒekt/ vt rejeitar

● /'ri:dʒekt/ s **1** marginalizado/a **2** artigo defeituoso rejection s rejeição

rejoice /rɪ'dʒɔɪs/ vi (fml) ~ (at/in/over sth) regozijar-se (com/em algo)

rejoin /,ri:'dʒɔɪn/ vt **1** reincorporar-se a **2** voltar a unir-se a

relapse /rɪ'læps/ vi recair ● s recaída

relate /rɪ'leɪt/ **1** vt relatar **2** vt relacionar **3** vi ~ to sb/sth estar relacionado com alguém/algo **4** vi ~ to (sb/sth) identificar-se (com alguém/algo) related adj **1** relacionado **2** ~ (to sb/sth) aparentado (com alguém): ~ by marriage parente por afinidade

relation /rɪ'leɪʃn/ s **1** ~ (to sth) relação (a algo): in ~ to sth em relação a algo **2** parente/a **3** parentesco relationship s **1** relação **2** (relação de) parentesco

relative /'relətɪv/ s parente/a ● adj relativo

relax /rɪ'læks/ **1** vt, vi relaxar (-se) **2** vt descontrair(-se) relaxation s **1** relaxamento **2** descontração **3** passatempo relaxing adj relaxante

relay /'ri:leɪ/ s **1** turma (de trabalhadores), turno **2** (tb ~ race) corrida de revezamento ● /'ri:leɪ, rɪ'leɪ/ vt (pt, pp ~ed) **1** transmitir (TV, etc.) retransmitir

release /rɪ'li:s/ vt **1** libertar **2** soltar **3** (notícia) dar **4** (disco) lançar **5** (filme) estrear ● s **1** libertação **2** soltura **3** (disco) lançamento **4** (filme): The movie is on general ~. O filme entrou em cartaz em vários cinemas.

relegate /'relɪgeɪt/ vt **1** relegar **2** (esp GB) (Esporte) rebaixar relegation s **1** afastamento **2** (Esporte) rebaixamento

relent /rɪ'lent/ vi ceder relentless adj **1** implacável **2** contínuo

relevant /'reləvənt/ adj relevante relevance (tb relevancy) s relevância

reliable /rɪ'laɪəbl/ adj **1** (pessoa) de confiança **2** confiável **3** fidedigno **4** (método, aparelho) seguro reliability /rɪ,laɪə'bɪləti/ s confiabilidade

reliance /rɪ'laɪəns/ s ~ on sb/sth dependência de alguém/algo

relic /'relɪk/ s relíquia

relief /rɪ'li:f/ s **1** alívio **2** assistência **3** (pessoa) substituto/a **4** (Arte, Geog) relevo

relieve /rɪ'li:v/ vt **1** aliviar **2** ~ yourself fazer suas necessi-

dades **3** substituir ■ relieve sb of sth tirar algo de alguém

religion /rɪ'lɪdʒən/ s religião religious adj religioso

relinquish /rɪ'lɪŋkwɪʃ/ vt (fml) **1** renunciar a **2** abandonar NOTA A expressão mais comum é give sth up.

relish /'relɪʃ/ s gosto ● vt apreciar

reluctant /rɪ'lʌktənt/ adj ~ (to do sth) relutante (em fazer algo) reluctance s relutância reluctantly adv relutantemente

rely /rɪ'laɪ/ (pt, pp -ied) ■ rely on/upon sb/sth depender de, contar com alguém/algo

remain /rɪ'meɪn/ vi (fml) **1** ficar NOTA O verbo mais comum é stay. **2** permanecer remainder s [sing] restante, resto (tb Mat) remains s **1** restos **2** ruínas

remand /rɪ'mɑːnd/ vt: ~ sb on bail pôr alguém em liberdade sob fiança ● s custódia: on ~ sob prisão preventiva

remark /rɪ'mɑːk/ vt, vi comentar, observar: ~ on sth fazer um comentário sobre algo ● s comentário remarkable adj **1** extraordinário **2** notável

remedial /rɪ'miːdiəl/ adj **1** reparador, corretivo **2** (aulas) para crianças com dificuldade de aprendizado

remedy /'remədi/ s (pl -ies) remédio ● vt (pt, pp -ied) remediar

remember /rɪ'membər/ vt, vi lembrar-se (de): as far as I ~ pelo que me lembro NOTA Remember, seguido de infinitivo, faz referência a uma ação que ainda não se realizou: Remember to mail that letter. Lembre-se de pôr essa carta no correio. Quando é seguido de uma forma em -ing, refere-se a uma ação que já ocorreu: I ~ mailing that letter. Lembro que pus aquela carta no correio. ■ remember sb to sb dar lembranças de alguém a alguém remembrance s comemoração

remind /rɪ'maɪnd/ vt ~ sb (to do sth) lembrar alguém (de fazer algo) **2** ~ sb of sb/sth lembrar alguém de alguém/algo NOTA Usa-se a construção remind sb of sb/sth quando uma coisa ou pessoa faz lembrar algo ou alguém: Your brother reminds me of John. ◇ That song reminds me of you. reminder s **1** lembrete **2** aviso

reminisce /,remɪ'nɪs/ vi ~ (about

sth) relembrar (algo)
reminiscent /ˌremɪˈnɪsnt/ adj evocative reminiscence s reminiscência
remnant /ˈremnənt/ s 1 resto 2 vestígio 3 retalho (tecido)
remorse /rɪˈmɔːs/ s remorso remorseless adj 1 impiedoso 2 implacável
remote /rɪˈmoʊt/ adj (-er. -est) 1 afastado 2 (pessoa) distante 3 (possibilidade) remoto remotely adv remotamente: I'm not ~ interested. Não estou nem um pouco interessado.
remove /rɪˈmuːv/ vt 1 tirar NOTA A expressão mais comum é take sth off/out, etc. 2 eliminar 3 destituir removable adj removível removal s 1 eliminação 2 mudança
the Renaissance /ˈrenəsɑːns; GB rɪˈneɪsns/ s o Renascimento
render /ˈrendər/ vt (fml) 1 (serviço, etc.) prestar 2 She was rendered speechless. Ela ficou perplexa. 3 (Mús, Arte) interpretar
rendezvous /ˈrɒndɪvuː/ s (pl rendezvous /-zuː/) 1 encontro 2 local de encontro
renegade /ˈrenɪgeɪd/ s (fml) renegado/a, rebelde
renew /rɪˈnuː; GB -ˈnjuː/ vt 1 renovar 2 reatar 3 reafirmar renewable adj renovável renewal s renovação
renounce /rɪˈnaʊns/ vt (fml) renunciar a
renovate /ˈrenəveɪt/ vt restaurar
renowned /rɪˈnaʊnd/ adj famoso
rent /rent/ s aluguel: for ~ aluga(m)-se ● vt ~ sth (from/to sb) alugar algo (de/a alguém) rental s aluguel (carros, etc.)
reorganize /ˌriːˈɔːgənaɪz/ vt, vi reorganizar(-se)
rep /rep/ s (coloq) 1 representante 2 companhia de repertório
repair /rɪˈpeər/ vt 1 consertar 2 remediar ● s reparo: It's beyond ~. Não tem conserto. ▶ in (a good (state of) repair em bom estado de conservação
repay /rɪˈpeɪ/ vt (pt, pp repaid) 1 devolver 2 (pessoa) reembolsar 3 (dívida, etc.) pagar 4 (cortesia) retribuir repayment s 1 reembolso 2 prestação
repeat /rɪˈpiːt/ vt, vi repetir (-se) 2 vt (confidência) contar ● s repetição repeated adj 1 repetido 2 reiterado repeatedly adv repetidamente
repel /rɪˈpel/ vt (-ll-) 1 repelir 2

repugnar
repellent /rɪˈpelənt/ adj repelente ● s: insect ~ repelente
repent /rɪˈpent/ vt, vi ~ (of) sth arrepender-se de algo repentance s arrependimento
repercussion /ˌriːpərˈkʌʃn/ s [ger pl] repercussão
repertoire /ˈrepərtwɑːr/ s repertório (músico, ator, etc.)
repertory /ˈrepərtɔːri; GB -tri/ (tb ~ company/theater) s (pl -ies) companhia de repertório
repetition /ˌrepəˈtɪʃn/ s repetição repetitive /rɪˈpetətɪv/ adj repetitivo
replace /rɪˈpleɪs/ vt 1 repor 2 substituir 3 (algo quebrado) trocar replacement s 1 substituição, troca 2 (pessoa) substituto/a 3 (peça) reposição
replay /ˈriːpleɪ/ vi (pt, pp -ied) responder ● s (pl -ies) resposta
reply /rɪˈplaɪ/ vi (pt, pp -ied) responder ● s (pl -ies) resposta
report /rɪˈpɔːrt/ 1 vt informar de, comunicar 2 vt (crime, etc.) denunciar 3 vi ~ (on sth) informar (sobre algo) 4 vi ~ (to/for sth) apresentar-se em/para algo: ~ sick faltar por motivo de doença 5 vi ~ to sb prestar contas a alguém ● s 1 informação 2 notícia 3 (Jornal) reportagem 4 boletim escolar 5 (pistola) detonação reportedly adv segundo consta reporter s repórter
represent /ˌreprɪˈzent/ vt 1 representar 2 descrever representation s representação
representative /ˌreprɪˈzentətɪv/ adj representativo ● s 1 representante 2 (USA) (Pol) deputado/a
repress /rɪˈpres/ vt 1 reprimir 2 conter repression s repressão
reprieve /rɪˈpriːv/ s 1 suspensão temporária de uma pena 2 trégua
reprimand /ˈreprɪmænd; GB -mɑːnd/ vt repreender ● s repreensão
reprisal /rɪˈpraɪzl/ s represália
reproach /rɪˈproʊtʃ/ vt repreender ● s repreensão ▶ above/beyond reproach irrepreensível
reproduce /ˌriːprəˈduːs; GB ˈdjuːs/ vt, vi reproduzir(-se) reproduction s reprodução reproductive adj reprodutivo
reptile /ˈreptl; GB -taɪl/ s réptil
republic /rɪˈpʌblɪk/ s república republican adj, s (tb Republican) republicano/a

repugnant /rɪ'pʌgnənt/ *adj* repugnante

repulsive /rɪ'pʌlsɪv/ *adj* repulsivo

reputable /'repjətəbl/ *adj* **1** de boa reputação **2** (*empresa*) conceituado

reputation /ˌrepju'teɪʃn/ *s* reputação

repute /rɪ'pju:t/ *s* (*fml*) reputação **reputed** *adj* segundo consta: *He is ~ to be...* Ele é tido como... **reputedly** *adv* segundo consta

request /rɪ'kwest/ *s* ~ (**for sth**) solicitação (de algo): *make a ~ for sth* pedir algo ● *vt* solicitar NOTA O verbo mais comum é **ask**.

require /rɪ'kwaɪər/ *vt* (*fml*) **1** requerer **2** necessitar NOTA O verbo mais comum é **need**. **3** ~ **sb to do sth** exigir de alguém que faça algo **requirement** *s* **1** necessidade **2** requisito

rescue /'reskju:/ *vt* salvar ● *s* resgate: *come to sb's ~* socorrer alguém **rescuer** *s* salvador/a

research /rɪ'sɜːtʃ, 'riːsɜːtʃ/ *s* [*U*] pesquisa ● *vt, vi* pesquisar **researcher** *s* pesquisador/a

resemble /rɪ'zembl/ *vt* parecer(-se) com **resemblance** *s* semelhança

resent /rɪ'zent/ *vt* ressentir(-se) de/com **resentful** *adj* **1** (*olhar, etc.*) de ressentimento **2** ressentido **resentment** *s* ressentimento

reservation /ˌrezər'veɪʃn/ *s* reserva

reserve /rɪ'zɜːrv/ *vt* reservar(-se) ● *s* **1** reserva(s) **2** (**reserves**) (*Mil*) reservistas ▸ **in reserve** de reserva **reserved** *adj* reservado

reservoir /'rezərvwɑːr/ *s* **1** reservatório **2** acúmulo, grande quantidade

reshuffle /ˌriː'ʃʌfl/ *s* remanejamento (*governo*)

reside /rɪ'zaɪd/ *vi* (*fml*) residir

residence /'rezɪdəns/ *s* (*fml*) residência

resident /'rezɪdənt/ *s* **1** residente **2** (*hotel*) hóspede/a ● *adj* residente **residential** /ˌrezɪ'denʃl/ *adj* **1** residencial **2** (*curso*) com alojamento incluído

residue /'rezɪdu:; *GB* -'dju:/ *s* resíduo

resign /rɪ'zaɪn/ *vt, vi* demitir-se (de) ▪ **resign yourself to sth** resignar-se a algo **resignation** *s* **1** demissão **2** resignação

resilient /rɪ'zɪliənt/ *adj* **1** elástico

2 (*pessoa*) resistente **resilience** *s* **1** elasticidade **2** resistência, capacidade de recuperação

resist /rɪ'zɪst/ **1** *vt, vi* resistir (a) **2** *vt* opor-se a

resistance /rɪ'zɪstəns/ *s* resistência

resolute /'rezəluːt/ *adj* resoluto NOTA A palavra mais comum é **determined**. **resolutely** *adv* resolutamente

resolution /ˌrezə'luːʃn/ *s* **1** resolução **2** propósito

resolve /rɪ'zɑːlv/ (*fml*) **1** *vt, vi* resolver(-se) **2** *vi* decidir

resort /rɪ'zɔːrt/ *s*: *a holiday ~* um local de férias ◇ *a ski ~* uma estação de esqui ▪ **resort to sth** recorrer a algo

resounding /rɪ'zaʊndɪŋ/ *adj* ressoante: *a ~ success* um sucesso retumbante

resource /'riːsɔːrs/ *s* recurso **resourceful** *adj* desembaraçado

respect /rɪ'spekt/ *s* **1** respeito, consideração **2** sentido ▸ **with respect to sth** (*fml*) com respeito a algo ● *vt* respeitar **respectful** *adj* respeitoso

respectable /rɪ'spektəbl/ *adj* **1** respeitável **2** considerável

respective /rɪ'spektɪv/ *adj* respectivo

respite /'respɪt; *GB* -paɪt/ *s* **1** pausa **2** trégua

respond /rɪ'spɑːnd/ *vi* **1** reagir **2** responder NOTA **Answer** e **reply** são palavras mais comuns.

response /rɪ'spɑːns/ *s* **1** resposta **2** reação

responsibility /rɪˌspɑːnsə'bɪləti/ *s* (*pl* **-ies**) ~ (**for sb/sth**); ~ (**to sb/sth**) responsabilidade (por alguém/ algo); (perante alguém/algo)

responsible /rɪ'spɑːnsəbl/ *adj* ~ (**for sb/(doing) sth**); ~ (**to sb/sth**) responsável (por alguém/por (fazer) algo); (perante alguém/ algo)

responsive /rɪ'spɑːnsɪv/ *adj* **1** receptivo **2** sensível

rest /rest/ *vi* **1** descansar **2** *vt, vi* apoiar(-se) **3** *vi* (*fml*): *let the matter ~* encerrar o assunto ● *s* **1** the ~ (**of sth**) [*sing*] o resto (de algo) **2** [*pl*] os/as demais: *the ~ of the players* os outros jogadores **3** descanso: *get some ~* descansar ▸ **at rest** em repouso **come to rest** parar **restful** *adj* descansado

restaurant /'restərɑːnt; *GB* -trɒnt/ *s* restaurante

restless /'restləs/ *adj* **1** agitado **2** inquieto

restoration /ˌrestəˈreɪʃn/ s 1 devolução 2 restauração 3 restabelecimento

restore /rɪˈstɔːr/ vt 1 (fml) restituir 2 (ordem) restabelecer 3 (edifício, etc.) restaurar

restrain /rɪˈstreɪn/ vt 1 conter 2 ~ **yourself** controlar-se **restrained** adj moderado

restraint /rɪˈstreɪnt/ s 1 compostura 2 restrição 3 comedimento

restrict /rɪˈstrɪkt/ vt restringir **restricted** adj restrito **restriction** s restrição **restrictive** adj restritivo

restroom /ˈrestruːm/ s banheiro

result /rɪˈzʌlt/ s resultado ● vi 1 ~ **(from sth)** originar-se (de algo) 2 ~ **in sth** resultar em algo

resume /rɪˈzuːm/; GB rɪˈzjuːm/ (fml) vt, vi reatar 2 vt retomar **resumption** /rɪˈzʌmpʃn/ s (fml) retomada

resumé /ˈrezəmeɪ/ s curriculum vitae

resurgence /rɪˈsɜːrdʒəns/ s ressurgimento

resurrect /ˌrezəˈrekt/ vt ressuscitar: ~ old traditions reviver antigas tradições **resurrection** s ressurreição

resuscitate /rɪˈsʌsɪteɪt/ vt reanimar **resuscitation** s reanimação

retail /ˈriːteɪl/ s varejo: ~ price preço de venda ao público ● vt, vi vender(-se) a varejo **retailer** s varejista

retain /rɪˈteɪn/ vt (fml) 1 ficar com 2 conservar 3 reter

retaliate /rɪˈtælieɪt/ vi ~ **(against sb/sth)** vingar-se (de alguém/algo); retaliar (alguém/algo) **retaliation** s represália

retarded /rɪˈtɑːrdɪd/ adj retardado → RETARDADO

retch /retʃ/ vi estar em ânsias de vômito

retention /rɪˈtenʃn/ s (fml) retenção

rethink /ˌriːˈθɪŋk/ vt (pt, pp **rethought** /-ˈθɔːt/) reconsiderar

reticent /ˈretɪsnt/ adj reticente **reticence** s reticência

retire /rɪˈtaɪər/ 1 vt, vi aposentar(-se) 2 vi (fml) ir deitar-se 3 vi (fml) (Mil) retirar-se **retired** adj aposentado **retiring** adj 1 retraído 2 que se aposenta

retirement /rɪˈtaɪərmənt/ s aposentadoria

retort /rɪˈtɔːrt/ s réplica ● vt replicar

retrace /rɪˈtreɪs/ vt: ~ your steps refazer o mesmo caminho

retract ● vt, vi 1 (fml) (declaração) retratar-se (de) 2 (garra, etc.) retrair(-se)

retreat /rɪˈtriːt/ vi bater em retirada ● s 1 retirada (the retreat) (Mil) toque de retirada 3 retiro 4 refúgio

retrial /ˌriːˈtraɪəl/ s novo julgamento

retribution /ˌretrɪˈbjuːʃn/ s (fml) 1 castigo merecido 2 vingança

retrieval /rɪˈtriːvl/ s (fml) recuperação

retrieve /rɪˈtriːv/ vt 1 (fml) recobrar 2 (Informát) acessar **retriever** s perdigueiro

retrograde /ˈretrəɡreɪd/ adj (fml) retrógrado

retrospect /ˈretrəspekt/ s ▶ **in retrospect** em retrospectiva

retrospective /ˌretrəˈspektɪv/ adj 1 retrospectivo 2 retroativo ● s exposição retrospectiva

return /rɪˈtɜːrn/ 1 vi voltar, regressar 2 vt devolver 3 vt (Pol) eleger 4 vt: The jury returned a verdict of not guilty. O júri proferiu um veredicto de inocência. 5 vi reaparecer ● s 1 volta, retorno 2 reaparecimento 3 devolução 4 income tax ~ declaração de renda 5 ~ **(on sth)** rendimento (de algo) 6 (GB) [antes de substantivo] de volta: ~ ticket passagem de ida e volta ▶ **in return (for sth)** em troca (de algo)

returnable /rɪˈtɜːrnəbl/ adj 1 reembolsável 2 restituível

reunion /riːˈjuːniən/ s reunião

reunite /ˌriːjuˈnaɪt/ vt, vi 1 reunir(-se) 2 reconciliar(-se)

rev /rev/ s [ger pl] (coloq) rotação (motor) ● vt, vi (-vv-) ~ **(sth) (up)** acelerar (algo)

revalue /ˌriːˈvæljuː/ vt 1 reavaliar 2 revalorizar **revaluation** s reavaliação, revalorização

revamp /ˌriːˈvæmp/ vt modernizar

reveal /rɪˈviːl/ vt 1 revelar 2 mostrar, expor **revealing** adj 1 revelador 2 (roupa) ousado

revel /ˈrevl/ v (-l-, GB -ll-) ■ **revel in (doing)** sth deleitar-se com algo/em fazer algo

revelation /ˌrevəˈleɪʃn/ s revelação

revenge /rɪˈvendʒ/ s vingança: take ~ on sb vingar-se (de alguém) ● vt ~ **yourself/be revenged (on sb)** vingar-se (de alguém)

revenue /ˈrevənuː; GB -ənjuː/ s receita: government ~ rendimentos do governo

reverberate /rɪˈvɜːrbəreɪt/ vi **1** ecoar **2** ter repercussões reverberation s **1** reverberação **2 (reverberations)** repercussões

revere /rɪˈvɪər/ vt (fml) venerar

reverence /ˈrevərəns/ s **1** reverência (veneração) reverent adj reverente

reverend /ˈrevərənd/ (tb **the Reverend**) adj (abrev **Rev.**) reverendo

reversal /rɪˈvɜːrsl/ s **1** (opinião) mudança **2** (sorte) revés **3** (Jur) anulação **4** (papéis) inversão

reverse /rɪˈvɜːrs/ s **1 the ~ (of sth)** o contrário (de algo) **2** reverso **3** (papel) verso **4** (tb ~ **gear**) marcha a ré **1** vt inverter **2** vt, vi pôr em/ir em marcha a ré **3** vt (decisão) anular ► **reverse (the) charges** (GB) telefonar a cobrar

revert /rɪˈvɜːrt/ vi reverter

review /rɪˈvjuː/ s **1** exame, revisão **2** informe (Jornal) crítica **4** (Mil) revista ● **1** vt reconsiderar **2** vt examinar **3** vt (Jornal) fazer uma crítica de **4** vi revisar: ~ for a test estudar para uma prova **5** vt (Mil) passar em revista **reviewer** s crítico/a

revise /rɪˈvaɪz/ vt **1** rever **2** vt corrigir **3** vt, vi (GB) revisar (exame)

revision /rɪˈvɪʒn/ s **1** revisão **2** correção **3** (GB) estudo: do some ~ estudar

revival /rɪˈvaɪvl/ s **1** renascimento **2** (moda) ressurgimento **3** (Teat) reapresentação

revive /rɪˈvaɪv/ **1** vt, vi reanimar(-se) **2** vt reativar **3** vt, vi reativar **4** vt (Teat) reapresentar

revoke /rɪˈvoʊk/ vt (fml) revogar

revolt /rɪˈvoʊlt/ **1** vi revoltar-se **2** vt repugnar, dar nojo a ● s rebelião

revolting /rɪˈvoʊltɪŋ/ adj repugnante

revolution /ˌrevəˈluːʃn/ s revolução **revolutionary** adj, s (pl **-ies**) revolucionário/a

revolve /rɪˈvɑːlv/ vt, vi (fazer) girar: ~ around sb/sth girar ao redor de alguém/algo

revolver /rɪˈvɑːlvər/ s revólver

revulsion /rɪˈvʌlʃn/ s repugnância

reward /rɪˈwɔːrd/ s recompensa, prêmio ● vt recompensar **rewarding** adj gratificante

rewrite /ˌriːˈraɪt/ vt (pt **rewrote** /-ˈroʊt/ pp **rewritten** /-ˈrɪtn/) reescrever

rhetoric /ˈretərɪk/ s retórica

rhino /ˈraɪnoʊ/ (pl **~s**) (tb **rhinoceros** /raɪˈnɑːsərəs/) s rinoceronte

rhubarb /ˈruːbɑːrb/ s ruibarbo

rhyme /raɪm/ s **1** rima **2** (poema) verso ● vt, vi rimar

rhythm /ˈrɪðəm/ s ritmo

rib /rɪb/ s costela: ribcage caixa torácica

ribbon /ˈrɪbən/ s fita ► **tear, cut, etc. sth to ribbons** cortar algo em tiras

rice /raɪs/ s arroz: ~ field arrozal

rich /rɪtʃ/ adj (~**er**, ~**est**) **1** rico: get ~ enriquecer ◊ be ~ in sth ser rico em algo **2** suntuoso **3** (terra) fértil **4** (comida) pesado ● **the rich** s [pl] os ricos **riches** s riqueza(s) **richly** adv: ~ deserve sth merecer muito algo

rickety /ˈrɪkəti/ adj **1** desconjuntado **2** (móvel) bambo

rid /rɪd/ vt (-**dd**-) (pt, pp **rid**) **1** ~ **sb/sth of sb/sth** livrar alguém/ algo de alguém/algo; eliminar algo de algo **2 be/get ~ of sb/sth** livrar-se de alguém/algo

ridden /ˈrɪdn/ pp de RIDE ● adj: ~ **with/by sth** atormentado por algo

riddle /ˈrɪdl/ s **1** charada 2 enigma ● vt **1** crivar (balas) **2** (pej): riddled with sth cheio de algo

ride /raɪd/ vt (pt **rode** pp **ridden**) **1** vt (cavalo) montar a **2** vt (bicicleta, etc.) andar de **3** vi andar a cavalo **4** vi (veículo) viajar de, ir de ● s **1** (a cavalo) passeio **2** (de veículo) volta **3** carona ► **take sb for a ride** (coloq) levar alguém na conversa **rider** s **1** cavaleiro, amazona **2** ciclista **3** motociclista

ridge /rɪdʒ/ s **1** (montanha) cume **2** cumeeira

ridicule /ˈrɪdɪkjuːl/ s ridículo ● vt ridicularizar **ridiculous** /rɪˈdɪkjələs/ adj ridículo

riding /ˈraɪdɪŋ/ s (tb **horse ~**) equitação: I like ~. Gosto de andar a cavalo.

rife /raɪf/ adj: ~ **with sth** cheio de algo

rifle /ˈraɪfl/ s fuzil

rift /rɪft/ s **1** (Geog) fenda **2** divisão

rig /rɪg/ vt (-**gg**-) manipular ■ **rig sth up** armar, improvisar algo ● s **1** (tb **rigging**) aparelho (navio), enxárcia **2** apetrechos

right /raɪt/ adj **1** correto, certo: Is this the ~ color? Esta é a cor adequada? **2** oportuno: It wasn't the ~ time to say that. Não era o momento oportuno para dizer aquilo. **3** (*pé, mão, etc.*) direito **4** justo: *He was ~ to do that.* Ele agiu certo ao fazer isso. **5** (*GB, coloq*) completo: *a ~ fool* um perfeito idiota ▸ **get sth right 1** acertar/fazer algo bem **2** entender algo direito **put/set sb/sth right** corrigir alguém/algo, consertar algo ● *adv* **1** bem, direito **2** exatamente **3** completamente: *~ to the end* até o final **4** à direita **5** imediatamente: *I'll be ~ back.* Volto num instante. ▸ **right away** imediatamente **right now** agora mesmo ● *s* **1** certo **2** direito **3** (**the right**) (*Pol*) a direita: *on the ~* à direita ▸ **be in the right** ter razão   **by rights 1** de direito **2** em teoria   **in your own right** por direito próprio ● *vt* **1** endireitar(-se) **2** corrigir(-se)

right angle *s* ângulo reto

righteous /ˈraɪtʃəs/ *adj* **1** (*fml*) justo, honrado **2** (*indignação*) justificado

rightful /ˈraɪtfl/ *adj* legítimo

right-hand *adj*: *on the ~ side* do lado direito ▸ **right-hand man** braço direito **right-handed** *adj* destro

rightly /ˈraɪtli/ *adv* corretamente, justificadamente: *~ or wrongly* pelo certo ou pelo errado

right wing *s* direita ● **right-wing** *adj* direitista

rigid /ˈrɪdʒɪd/ *adj* **1** rígido **2** (*atitude*) inflexível

rigor (*GB* **-our**) /ˈrɪɡər/ *s* rigor **rigorous** *adj* rigoroso

rim /rɪm/ *s* **1** borda **2** (*óculos, roda, etc.*) aro

rind /raɪnd/ *s* **1** casca (*queijo, limão*) → PEEL **2** pele (*bacon*)

ring¹ /rɪŋ/ *s* **1** anel: *~ road* (*GB*) estrada periférica **2** aro **3** círculo **4** (*tb circus* ~) picadeiro (*circo*) **5** (*tb boxing* ~) ringue **6** (*tb bullring*) arena ● *vt* (*pt, pp* **ringed**) **1** ~ **sb/sth** (**with sth**) rodear alguém/algo (de algo) **2** (*pássaro*) pôr anel em

ring² /rɪŋ/ (*pt* **rang** *pp* **rung**) **1** *vi* soar **2** *vt* (*campainha*) tocar **3** *vi* ~ (**for sb/sth**) chamar (alguém/algo) **4** *vi* (*ouvidos*) zumbir **5** *vt, vi* (*GB*) ~ (**sb/sth**) (**up**) telefonar (para alguém/algo) ▸ *~ back* ligar de volta ◇ *~ off* desligar ● *s* **1** (*campainha*) toque **2** (*sino*) badalada **3** [*sing*] ressonância **4** (*GB, coloq*): *give sb a ~* dar uma ligada para alguém

ringleader /ˈrɪŋliːdər/ *s*

cabeça (*de gangue*)

rink /rɪŋk/ *s* pista (*patinação*)

rinse /rɪns/ *vt* ~ **sth** (**out**) enxaguar algo ● *s* **1** enxaguada **2** rinsagem

riot /ˈraɪət/ *s* motim ● *vi* causar distúrbios, amotinar-se **rioting** *s* desordem **riotous** *adj* **1** (*festa*) desenfreado **2** (*fml*) (*Jur*) desordeiro

rip /rɪp/ *vt* (**-pp-**) **1** *vi* rasgar-se **2** ~ **sth** (**up**) rasgar algo: *~ sth open* abrir algo rasgando ◇ *~ sth off/out* arrancar algo ▸ **rip sb off** (*coloq*) roubar alguém ● *s* rasgão

rip-off *s* (*coloq*) roubo

ripple /ˈrɪpl/ *s* **1** ondulação **2** murmúrio (*riso, interesse, etc.*) ● *vt, vi* ondular(-se)

rise /raɪz/ *vi* (*pt* **rose** *pp* **risen** /ˈrɪzn/) **1** subir **2** (*voz*) erguer **3** (*fml*) (*pessoa*) levantar-se **4** ~ (**up**) (*fml*) sublevar-se **5** (*sol, rio*) nascer **6** (*lua*) surgir **7** ascender (*em posição*) ● *s* **1** subida, ascensão **2** aumento **3** aclive **4** (*GB*) aumento (*salário*) ▸ **give rise to sth** (*fml*) ocasionar algo

rising /ˈraɪzɪŋ/ *s* **1** (*Pol*) insurreição **2** surgimento ● *adj* **1** crescente **2** (*sol*) nascente

risk /rɪsk/ *s* risco: *take ~s* arriscar-se ▸ **at risk** em perigo ● *vt* ~ (**doing sth**) arriscar(-se) a fazer algo ▸ **risk your neck** arriscar o pescoço **risky** *adj* (**-ier, -iest**) arriscado

rite /raɪt/ *s* rito

ritual /ˈrɪtʃuəl/ *s* ritual ● *adj* ritual

rival /ˈraɪvl/ *s* rival ● *adj* rival ● *vt* (**-l-, -ll-**) competir com **rivalry** *s* (*pl* **-ies**) rivalidade

river /ˈrɪvər/ *s* rio → RIO **riverside** /ˈrɪvərsaɪd/ *s* beira/orla do rio

rivet /ˈrɪvɪt/ *vt* **1** rebitar **2** (*olhos*) cravar **3** fascinar **riveting** *adj* fascinante

roach /rəʊtʃ/ *s* (*USA*) barata

road /rəʊd/ *s* **1** estrada: *~ sign* placa de sinalização ◇ *~ safety* segurança do trânsito ◇ *by ~* por terra **2** (**Road**) (*abrev* **Rd.**) rua: *Kings Road* Rua Kings → STREET ▸ **on the road to sth** a caminho de algo **roadside** *s* beira da estrada **roadway** *s* pista

roadblock /ˈrəʊdblɒk/ *s* barreira

roadworks /ˈrəʊdwɜːks/ *s* (*GB*) obras

roam /rəʊm/ *vt, vi* vagar (por)

roar /rɔːr/ *s* **1** rugido **2** estrondo ●

1 *vt, vi* berrar: ~ **with laughter** dar gargalhadas **2** *vi* rugir roaring *adj* ● **do a roaring trade** fazer um negócio da China

roast /roʊst/ **1** *vt, vi* assar **2** *vi* (*café, etc.*) torrar **3** *vi* (*pessoa*) tostar-se ● *adj, s* assado: ~ **rosbife**

rob /rɑb/ *vt* (**-bb-**) ~ **sb/sth** (**of sth**) roubar (algo) de alguém/algo NOTA **Rob** é usado com complementos de pessoa ou lugar: *He robbed me of all my money.* e **Steal** quando menciona-se o objeto roubado (de um lugar ou de uma pessoa): *He stole all my money (from me).* **Burglarize** refere-se a roubos a casas particulares ou lojas, normalmente quando os donos estão fora: *The house was burglarized.* **robber** *s* **1** ladrão/a **2** (*tb* **bank** ~) assaltante de banco → **THIEF robbery** *s* (*pl* **-ies**) **1** roubo **2** assalto

robe /roʊb/ *s* **1** roupão **2** manto, toga

robin /rɑbn/ *s* pintarroxo

robot /roʊbɑt/ *s* robô

robust /roʊbʌst/ *adj* robusto

rock /rɑk/ *s* **1** rocha: ~ **climbing** alpinismo **2** (EUA) pedra **3** (*tb* ~ **music**) (música) rock ● **on the rocks 1** em crise **2** (*bebida*) com gelo **rock bottom** nível mais baixo ● **1** *vt, vi* balançar(-se): *rocking chair* cadeira de balanço **2** *vt* (*criança*) embalar **3** *vt, vi* abalar

rocket /rɑkɪt/ *s* foguete ● *vi* disparar

rocky /rɑki/ *adj* (**-ier, -iest**) **1** rochoso **2** instável

rod /rɑd/ *s* **1** vareta **2** vara

rode /roʊd/ *pret de* **RIDE**

rodent /roʊdnt/ *s* roedor

rogue /roʊg/ *s* **1** (*antiq*) patife **2** brincalhão **3** [*função adjetiva*]: ~ **states** estados terroristas

role /roʊl/ *s* papel: ~ **model** modelo (a imitar)

roll /roʊl/ *s* **1** rolo **2** pãozinho **3** (*com recheio*) folheado **4** balanço **5** lista: *roll-call* ato de fazer a chamada **6** rufar (*dinheiro*) ● **1** *vt, vi* (fazer) rolar **2** *vi* ~ (**over**) dar voltas **3** *vt, vi* ~ (**sth**) (**up**) enrolar(-se) **4** *vt* aplainar com um rolo **5** *vt, vi* balançar(-se) ● **be rolling in it** (*coloq*) estar cheio da grana ■ **roll in** (*coloq*) chegar em grande quantidade **roll on** (*tempo*) passar **roll sth out** (*coloq*) estender algo **roll up** (*coloq*) chegar rolling *adj* ondulado

roller /roʊlər/ *s* **1** rolo **2** bob

(*para cabelo*)

Rollerblade /roʊlərbleɪd/ *s* patim (*em linha*) ● **rollerblade** *vi* patinar

roller coaster /roʊlər koʊstər/ *s* montanha russa

roller skate *s* patim (*de rodas*) ● *vi* patinar

rolling pin *s* rolo para massa

romance /roʊmæns/ *s* **1** romantismo **2** caso amoroso **3** história de amor

romantic /roʊmæntɪk/ *adj, s* romântico/a

romp /rɑmp/ *vi* ~ (**around/about**) brincar animadamente ● *s* **1** brincadeira animada **2** (*Teat*) obra divertida e despretensiosa

roof /ruːf/ *s* **1** telhado **2** (*carro*) teto **roofing** *s* [U] material para telhados

roof rack *s* bagageiro

rooftop /ruːftɑp/ *s* (cimo do) telhado

rook /rʊk/ *s* (*xadrez*) torre

room /ruːm/ *s* **1** aposento, sala **2** lugar: ~ **to breathe** espaço para respirar **3** *There's no* ~ *for doubt.* Não há a menor dúvida. ◇ *There's* ~ *for improvement.* Há como melhorar.

room-mate *s* companheiro/a de quarto

room service *s* serviço de quarto

room temperature *s* temperatura ambiente

roomy /ruːmi/ *adj* (**-ier, -iest**) espaçoso

roost /ruːst/ *s* poleiro ● *vi* empoleirar-se

rooster /ruːstər/ *s* galo

root /ruːt/ *s* raiz: *the* ~ *cause of sth* a verdadeira origem de algo ◇ *put down* ~*s* criar raízes ■ **root about/around** (**for sth**) vasculhar algo (em busca de algo) **root for sb/sth** (*coloq*) torcer por alguém/algo **root sth out 1** erradicar algo, arrancar algo pela raiz **2** encontrar algo

rope /roʊp/ *s* corda: ~ **ladder** escada de corda ● **show sb/ know/learn the ropes** colocar alguém/estar/ficar por dentro do assunto ■ **rope sb in** (**to do sth**) (*coloq*) persuadir alguém (a fazer algo) **rope sth off** isolar algo (*com cordas*)

rosary /roʊzəri/ *s* (*pl* **-ies**) rosário

rose /roʊz/ *pret de* **RISE** ● *s* rosa

rosé /roʊˈzeɪ/; GB /ˈrəʊzeɪ/ *s* (vinho) rosé

rosette /rouˈzet/ s roseta

rosy /ˈrouzi/ adj (-ier, -iest) 1 rosado 2 promissor

rot /rɒt/ vt, vi (-tt-) apodrecer

rota /ˈroutə/ s (pl -s) rodízio (tarefas)

rotate /ˈrouteɪt; GB rouˈteɪt/ 1 vt, vi (fazer) girar 2 vt, vi alternar (-se) rotation s 1 rotação 2 alternância ▶ in rotation por turnos

rotten /ˈrɒtn/ adj 1 podre 2 corrupto

rough /rʌf/ (~er, ~est) adj 1 áspero 2 (mar) agitado 3 (comportamento) violento 4 ~ (on sb) duro (com alguém) 5 aproximado 6 mal: I feel a little ~. Não estou me sentindo bem. ● adv duro ● s ▶ in rough (GB) em rascunho ● vt ▶ rough it (coloq) passar aperto roughly adv 1 asperamente 2 aproximadamente

roulette /ruːˈlet/ s roleta

round /raʊnd/ adj redondo ● adv (GB) 1 Ver AROUND 2 all year ~ o ano inteiro ◇ a shorter way ~ um caminho mais curto ◇ ~ the clock 24 horas ou dia ◇ ~ at Maria's na casa de Maria ▶ round na casa de Maria ▶ round the houses ~ about as casas da vizinhança ● prep (GB) 1 em volta (de): show sb ~ the house mostrar a casa a alguém 2 ao redor de: She wrapped a towel ~ her waist. Ela enrolou a toalha em volta da cintura. 3 em volta de: just ~ the corner virando a esquina ● s 1 ciclo 2 rodada (bebidas) 3 (Esporte) assalto, rodada 4 a ~ of applause uma salva de palmas 5 tiro ● vt (uma esquina) dobrar ▶ round sth off completar algo round sb/sth up reunir alguém, arrebanhar algo (gado) round sth up/down arredondar algo (cifra, etc.)

roundabout /ˈraʊndəbaʊt/ adj indireto ● s 1 carrossel 2 (GB) rotatória

round trip s viagem de ida e volta: round-trip ticket bilhete de ida e volta

rouse /raʊz/ vt 1 (fml) despertar 2 suscitar rousing adj 1 (discurso) inflamado 2 (aplauso) caloroso

rout /raʊt/ s derrota ● vt derrotar

route /ruːt; GB ruːt/ s rota

routine /ruːˈtiːn/ s rotina ● adj rotineiro routinely adv regularmente

row[1] /rou/ s 1 fila, fileira: ~ house casa geminada (dos dois lados)

2 go for a ~ ir remar ▶ in a row enfileirado: the third week in a ~ a terceira semana consecutiva ◇ four days in a ~ quatro dias seguidos ● vt, vi remar: Will you ~ me across the river? Pode me levar para o outro lado do rio?

row[2] /raʊ/ s (esp GB) (coloq) 1 briga NOTA Também se diz argument. 2 algazarra 3 barulho ● vi brigar

rowdy /ˈraʊdi/ adj (-ier, -iest) 1 barulhento, bagunceiro 2 tumultuado

royal /ˈrɔɪəl/ adj real

royalty /ˈrɔɪəlti/ s 1 realeza 2 (royalties) direitos autorais

rub /rʌb/ (-bb-) 1 vt esfregar, friccionar 2 vi roçar ▶ rub off (on/onto sb) passar (para alguém) rub sth out apagar algo (com borracha) ● s esfrega: give sth a ~ esfregar algo

rubber /ˈrʌbər/ s 1 borracha: ~ band elástico ◇ ~ stamp carimbo 2 (GB) borracha (de apagar) 3 (USA, coloq) camisinha

rubbish /ˈrʌbɪʃ/ (GB) s 1 lixo 2 asneiras

rubble /ˈrʌbl/ s entulho

ruby /ˈruːbi/ s (pl -ies) rubi

rucksack /ˈrʌksæk/ s mochila

rudder /ˈrʌdər/ s leme

rude /ruːd/ adj (-er, -est) 1 grosseiro, mal-educado: be ~ to do sth ser de má educação fazer algo 2 indecente 3 (piada, etc.) obsceno 4 rude

rudimentary /ˌruːdɪˈmentəri/ adj rudimentar

ruffle /ˈrʌfl/ vt 1 agitar 2 despentear 3 (plumas) encrespar 4 amarrotar 5 perturbar

rug /rʌg/ s 1 tapete 2 manta

rugby /ˈrʌgbi/ s rúgbi

rugged /ˈrʌgɪd/ adj 1 (terreno) acidentado 2 (feições) marcado

ruin /ˈruːɪn/ s ruína ● vt 1 arruinar 2 pôr a perder

rule /ruːl/ s 1 regra, norma 2 hábito 3 domínio 4 mandato 5 reinado ▶ as a (general) rule em geral ● vt, vi ~ (over) (sb/sth) (Pol) governar (alguém/algo) 2 vt, vi (Jur) decidir 3 vt (linha) traçar ▶ rule sb/sth out descartar alguém/algo

ruler /ˈruːlər/ s 1 governante 2 régua

ruling /ˈruːlɪŋ/ adj 1 dominante 2 no poder ● s (Jur) parecer

rum /rʌm/ s rum

rumble /ˈrʌmbl/ vi 1 retumbar 2 (estômago) roncar ● s estrondo

rummage /ˈrʌmɪdʒ/ vi ~ about/

around; ~ among/in/through sth (for sth) remexer, vasculhar algo (em busca de algo)

rumor (GB **-our**) /'ru:mər/ s rumor

rump /rʌmp/ s **1** garupa, anca **2** (tb ~ steak) (filé de) alcatra

run /rʌn/ s **1** corrida: go for a ~ ir correr **2** passeio (carro, etc.) **3** período **4** (Teat) temporada ▶ be on the run estar foragido make a run for it tentar escapar ● (-nn-) (pt ran pp run) **1** vt, vi correr: ~ around/about correr para todos os lados **2** vt, vi passar: ~ your eyes over sth dar uma olhada em algo ◊ A shiver ran down her spine. Ela teve um frio na espinha. **3** vt, vi (fazer) funcionar: Run the engine before you start off. Deixe o motor aquecer antes de arrancar. **4** vt estender-se: A fence runs around the field. Uma cerca circunda o campo. **5** vi (trem, etc.): The buses ~ every hour. Os ônibus saem de hora em hora. ◊ The train is running late. O trem está atrasado. **6** vt levar (de carro) **7** vi ~ (for...) (Teat) continuar em cartaz (por...) **8** vt: ~ a bath encher a banheira (para o banho) **9** vi: leave the faucet running deixar a torneira aberta **10** vi (nariz) escorrer **11** vi (tinta) soltar **12** vt (negócio, etc.) administrar, dirigir **13** vt (serviço, etc.) organizar, oferecer **14** vt (Informát) executar **15** vi ~ (for sth) (Pol) candidatar-se (a algo) **16** vt (Jornal) publicar ▶ run dry secar run for it dar no pé run in the family estar no sangue run out of steam (coloq) perder o ânimo run riot desenfrear-se run the risk (of doing sth) correr o risco (de fazer algo) ▶ run across sb/ sth topar com alguém/algo run after sb perseguir alguém run at sth: Inflation is running at 25%. A inflação está em 25%. run away/ off (with sb/sth) fugir (com alguém/algo) run (sb) into sb/ sth **1** topar com alguém/algo **2** bater (algo) em alguém/algo, atropelar alguém/algo run out **1** expirar **2** esgotar-se run out of sth ficar sem algo run sb over atropelar alguém

runaway /'rʌnəweɪ/ adj **1** fugitivo **2** fora de controle **3** galopante ● s fugitivo/a

run-down adj **1** (edifício) desmantelado **2** (pessoa) exaurido

rung /rʌŋ/ pp de RING² ● s degrau

runner /'rʌnər/ s corredor/a

runner-up s (pl **-ers-up**) segundo/a colocado/a

running /'rʌnɪŋ/ s **1** corrida **2** funcionamento **3** organização ▶ be in/out of the running (for sth) (coloq) ter/não ter chance (de conseguir algo) ● adj **1** contínuo **2** consecutivo: four days ~ quatro dias seguidos **3** (água) corrente

runny /'rʌni/ adj (-ier, -iest) **1** aguado **2** have a ~ nose estar com coriza

run-up s período anterior

runway /'rʌnweɪ/ s pista (aeroporto)

rupture /'rʌptʃər/ s ruptura ● vt, vi romper(-se)

rural /'rʊərəl/ adj rural

rush /rʌʃ/ **1** vi andar com pressa, apressar-se: They rushed out of school. Eles saíram correndo da escola. **2** vt agir precipitadamente **3** vt apressar **4** vt levar às pressas ● s **1** [sing] investida: There was a ~ to the exit. Houve uma debandada em direção à saída. **2** pressa: the ~ hour a hora do rush

rust /rʌst/ s ferrugem ● vt, vi. enferrujar

rustic /'rʌstɪk/ adj rústico

rustle /'rʌsl/ vt, vi (fazer) farfalhar ■ rustle sth up (coloq) preparar algo ● s farfalhada, sussurro

rusty /'rʌsti/ adj (-ier, -iest) **1** enferrujado **2** fora de prática

rut /rʌt/ s sulco ▶ be (stuck) in a rut estagnado

ruthless /'ru:θləs/ adj impiedoso, implacável ruthlessly adv impiedosamente ruthlessness s crueldade

rye /raɪ/ s centeio

Ss

S, s /es/ s (pl **S's, s's** /'esɪz/) S,s

the Sabbath /'sæbəθ/ s **1** (cristão) domingo **2** (judeu) sábado

sabotage /'sæbətɑːʒ/ s sabotagem ● vt sabotar

saccharin /'sækərɪn/ s sacarina

sack /sæk/ s **1** saca, saco **2** (the sack): give sb the ~ despedir alguém ◊ get the ~ ser despedido ● vt (GB, coloq) despedir

sacred /'seɪkrɪd/ adj sagrado, sacro

sacrifice /'sækrɪfaɪs/ s sacrifício ● vt sacrificar

sacrilege /'sækrɪlɪdʒ/ s sacrilégio

sad /sæd/ *adj* (**sadder, saddest**) **1** triste **2** lamentável **sadden** *vt* entristecer

saddle /'sædl/ *s* **1** (*cavalo*) sela **2** (*GB*) (*moto, etc.*) selim • *vt* **1** selar **2** ~ **sb with sth** sobrecarregar alguém com algo

sadism /'seɪdɪzəm/ *s* sadismo

sadly /'sædli/ *adv* **1** tristemente **2** infelizmente

sadness /'sædnəs/ *s* tristeza

safari /sə'fɑːri/ *s* (*pl* ~s) safári

safe /seɪf/ *s* cofre • *adj* (-er, -est) **1** a salvo **2** seguro **3** ileso **4** (*motorista*) prudente ▶ **be on the safe side** não correr risco **safe and sound** são e salvo **safely** *adv* **1** em segurança **2** sem perigo: ~ *locked away* guardado num lugar seguro

safeguard /'seɪfgɑːd/ *s* salvaguarda, proteção • *vt* ~ **sb/sth (against sb/sth)** proteger alguém/algo (de alguém/algo)

safety /'seɪfti/ *s* segurança: ~ *belt/pin/valve* cinto/alfinete/válvula de segurança

safety net *s* **1** rede de segurança **2** respaldo

sag /sæg/ *vi* (-gg-) **1** (*cama, etc.*) afundar **2** (*madeira*) vergar

Sagittarius /,sædʒɪ'teəriəs/ *s* Sagitário

said /sed/ *pret, pp de* SAY

sail /seɪl/ *s* vela ▶ **set sail (to/for)** zarpar (rumo a) • *vt, vi* navegar, velejar: ~ *around the world* dar a volta ao mundo de barco **2** *vi* zarpar: *The ship sails at noon.* O navio parte ao meio-dia. **3** *vt* (*objeto*) voar deslizando ■ **sail through (sth)** tirar (algo) de letra

sailboat /'seɪlbəʊt/ (*GB* **sailing boat**) *s* barco a vela

sailing /'seɪlɪŋ/ *s* **1** navegação **2** ~ *ir velejar* **2** *There are three sailings a day.* Há três saídas diárias.

sailor /'seɪlər/ *s* marinheiro

saint /seɪnt, snt/ *s* (*abrev* **St.**) santo/a: *Saint Bernard/Teresa* São Bernardo/Santa Teresa

sake /seɪk/ *s* ▶ **for God's, goodness', Heaven's, etc. sake** pelo amor de Deus **for sb's/sth's sake; for the sake of sb/sth** por alguém/algo

salad /'sæləd/ *s* salada

salary /'sæləri/ *s* (*pl* -ies) salário (*mensal*)

sale /seɪl/ *s* **1** venda: *sales department* departamento de vendas **2** liquidação ▶ **for sale** à venda: *For ~.* Vende-se. **on sale** em liquidação

salesperson /'seɪlzpɜːrsn/ *s* (*pl* -**people**) vendedor/a NOTA Esta é a forma preferida atualmente, embora também se usem **salesman** e **saleswoman**.

sales tax *s* (*USA*) imposto sobre circulação de mercadorias

saliva /sə'laɪvə/ *s* saliva

salmon /'sæmən/ *s* (*pl* **salmon**) salmão

salon /sə'lɒn; *GB* 'sælɒn/ *s* salão (*de beleza*)

saloon /sə'luːn/ *s* **1** salão (*navio, etc.*) **2** (*USA*) bar **3** (*GB*) (*tb* ~ *car*) sedã

salt /sɔːlt/ *s* sal **salted** *adj* salgado **salty** *adj* (-ier, -iest) salgado

salt shaker (*GB* **salt cellar**) *s* saleiro

saltwater /'sɔːltwɔːtər/ *adj* de água salgada

salutary /'sæljəteri; *GB* -tri/ *adj* salutar

salute /sə'luːt/ *vt, vi* **1** (*fml*) saudar **2** fazer continência (*a um militar*) • *s* **1** saudação **2** continência **3** salva

salvage /'sælvɪdʒ/ *s* salvamento • *vt* recuperar

salvation /sæl'veɪʃn/ *s* salvação

same /seɪm/ *adj* mesmo, igual: *the* ~ *thing* o mesmo NOTA Às vezes se usa para dar ênfase: *the very* ~ *man* o próprio. ▶ **at the same time** ao mesmo tempo **2** apesar disso **in the same boat** na mesma situação • *adv* **the same** da mesma forma, igualmente • *pron* **the same (as sb/sth)** o/a mesmo/a (que alguém/algo): *I think the* ~ *as you.* Penso como você. ▶ **all/just the same 1** mesmo assim **2** *It's all the* ~ *to me.* Para mim tanto faz. **same here** (*coloq*) eu também **(the) same to you** igualmente

sample /'sæmpl; *GB* 'sɑːmpl/ *s* amostra • *vt* provar

sanatorium /,sænə'tɔːriəm/ *s* sanatório

sanction /'sæŋkʃn/ *s* **1** aprovação **2** sanção: *lift sanctions* levantar as barreiras • *vt* autorizar

sanctuary /'sæŋktʃueri; *GB* -uəri/ *s* (*pl* -ies) **1** santuário **2** refúgio: *take* ~ refugiar-se

sand /sænd/ *s* **1** areia **2** (**the sands**) [*pl*] a praia

sandal /'sændl/ *s* sandália

sandcastle /'sændkæsl; *GB* -kɑːsl/ *s* castelo de areia

sandpaper /'sændpeɪpər/ *s* lixa

sandwich /'sænwɪtʃ; *GB* -wɪdʒ/

sanduíche ● *vt* inserir (*entre duas pessoas ou coisas*)

sandy /'sændi/ *adj* (**-ier, -iest**) arenoso

sane /sein/ *adj* (**-er, -est**) **1** são **2** sensato

sang /sæŋ/ *pret de* SING

sanitarium /ˌsænə'teəriəm/ (*USA*) = SANATORIUM

sanitary /'sænətri; *GB* -tri/ *adj* higiênico

sanitary pad (*GB* **sanitary towel**) *s* absorvente feminino

sanitation /ˌsænɪ'teɪʃn/ *s* saneamento

sanity /'sænəti/ *s* **1** sanidade **2** sensatez

sank /sæŋk/ *pret de* SINK

sap /sæp/ *s* seiva ● *vt* (**-pp-**) minar

sapphire /'sæfaɪər/ *adj, s* (cor de) safira

sappy /'sæpi/ *adj* (*coloq*) sentimental

sarcasm /'sɑːrkæzəm/ *s* sarcasmo **sarcastic** /sɑːr'kæstɪk/ *adj* sarcástico

sardine /sɑːr'diːn/ *s* sardinha

sash /sæʃ/ *s* faixa

sat /sæt/ *pret, pp de* SIT

satellite /'sætəlaɪt/ *s* satélite

satin /'sætɪn; *GB* 'sætɪn/ *s* cetim

satire /'sætaɪər/ *s* sátira **satirical** /sə'tɪrɪkl/ *adj* satírico

satisfaction /ˌsætɪs'fækʃn/ *s* satisfação

satisfactory /ˌsætɪs'fæktəri/ *adj* satisfatório

satisfy /'sætɪsfaɪ/ *vt* (*pt, pp* **-ied**) **1** satisfazer **2** (*requisitos, etc.*) preencher **3** ~ **sb (as to sth)** convencer alguém (de algo) **satisfied** *adj* satisfeito **satisfying** *adj* satisfatório: *a ~ meal* uma refeição que satisfaz

saturate /'sætʃəreɪt/ *vt* ~ **sth (with sth)** saturar algo (de algo) **saturation** *s* saturação

Saturday /'sætərdeɪ, -di/ *s* (*abrev* **Sat.**) sábado → MONDAY

Saturn /'sætərn/ *s* Saturno

sauce /sɔːs/ *s* molho

saucepan /'sɔːspæn; *GB* -pən/ *s* panela

saucer /'sɔːsər/ *s* pires

sauna /'sɔːnə, 'saʊnə/ *s* sauna

saunter /'sɔːntər/ *vi* caminhar vagarosamente: *He sauntered over to the bar.* Ele se dirigiu lentamente para o bar.

sausage /'sɔːsɪdʒ; *GB* 'sɒs-/ *s* salsicha, lingüiça: ~ *roll* (*GB*) folheado de salsicha

savage /'sævɪdʒ/ *adj* **1** selvagem

2 feroz **3** brutal: ~ *budget cuts* cortes drásticos no orçamento ● *s* selvagem ● *vt* atacar ferozmente **savagery** *s* selvageria

save /seɪv/ *vt* **1** salvar (*tb Informát*) **2** *vt, vi* ~ **(sth) (up)** (*dinheiro*) economizar (algo) **3** *vt* ~ **(sb) sth** poupar (alguém) de algo: *That will* ~ *us a lot of trouble.* Isso vai nos evitar muitos problemas. **4** *vt* (*Esporte*) defender ▸ **save face** salvar as aparências ● *s* defesa (*de bola*)

saving /'seɪvɪŋ/ *s* **1** economia **2** **savings** [*pl*] poupança

savior (*GB* **-our**) /'seɪvɪər/ *s* salvador/a

savory (*GB* **-oury**) /'seɪvəri/ *adj* **1** saboroso **2** (*GB*) salgado

saw /sɔː/ *pret de* SEE ● *vt* (*pt* **sawed** *pp* **sawed,** *GB* **sawn** /sɔːn/) serrar ■ **saw sth down** serrar algo ■ **saw sth off (sth)** cortar algo (de algo) com uma serra: *a sawed-off shotgun* uma espingarda de cano serrado ■ **saw sth up** serrar algo em pedaços ● *s* serra

sawdust /'sɔːdʌst/ *s* serragem

saxophone /'sæksəfoʊn/ (*coloq* **sax**) *s* saxofone

say /seɪ/ *vt* (3ª *pess sing pres* **says** /sez/ *pt, pp* **said**) **1** dizer **NOTA Say** costuma acompanhar palavras textuais ou introduzir uma oração em estilo indireto precedida por *that*: *"I'll leave at nine," he said.* ◊ *He said (that) he would leave at nine.* **Tell** introduz uma oração em estilo indireto e deve ser seguido de substantivo, pronome ou nome próprio: *He told me (that) he would leave at nine.* Com ordens ou conselhos costuma-se usar **tell**: *I told them to hurry up.* ◊ *She's always telling me what to do.* **2** *Take any writer, ~ Dickens...* Tomemos como exemplo um escritor qualquer, digamos Dickens... **3** *What time does it ~ on that clock?* Que horas são nesse relógio? ▸ **it goes without saying that...** é óbvio que... ■ **that is to say** ou seja ● *s* ▸ **have a/ some say (in sth)** ter poder de decisão (em algo) **have your say** expressar sua opinião

saying /'seɪɪŋ/ *s* provérbio

scab /skæb/ *s* casca (*ferida*)

scaffold /'skæfoʊld/ *s* cadafalso **scaffolding** /'skæfəldɪŋ/ *s* [*U*] andaime(s)

scald /skɔːld/ *vt* escaldar ● *s* escaldadura **scalding** *adj* escaldante

scale /skeɪl/ vt escalar, trepar em ● s 1 escala: *to ~ em escala* ◊ *a large-scale map* um mapa em grande escala 2 alcance, envergadura 3 escama

scalp /skælp/ s couro cabeludo

scalpel /'skælpəl/ s bisturi

scamper /'skæmpər/ vi correr aos pulos

scan /skæn/ vt (-nn-) 1 esquadrinhar 2 examinar com ultrassom 3 dar uma olhada em ● s ultra-sonografia

scandal /'skændl/ s 1 escândalo 2 fofoca **scandalize** vt escandalizar **scandalous** adj escandaloso

scanner /'skænər/ s scanner

scant /skænt/ adj (fml) escasso **scanty** adj (-ier, -iest) escasso **scantily** adv: *~ dressed* vestido sumariamente

scapegoat /'skeɪpɡoʊt/ s bode expiatório

scar /skɑr/ s cicatriz ● vt (-rr-) marcar (com uma cicatriz)

scarce /skeərs/ adj (-er, -est) escasso: *Food was ~.* Havia escassez de comida. **scarcity** /'skeərsəti/ s (pl -ies) escassez

scarcely /'skeərsli/ adv 1 mal: *There were ~ a hundred people present.* Mal havia cem pessoas presentes. 2 *You can ~ expect me to believe that.* Você não espera que eu acredite nisso.

scare /skeər/ vt assustar ■ **scare sb away/off** afugentar alguém ● s susto: *bomb ~* suspeita de bomba **scared** adj assustado: *be ~ of sth* ter medo de algo ◊ *be ~ stiff* morrendo de medo

scarecrow /'skeərkroʊ/ s espantalho

scarf /skɑrf/ s (pl **scarves**) 1 cachecol, echarpe 2 lenço de cabeça

scarlet /'skɑrlət/ adj, s escarlate

scary /'skeəri/ adj (-ier, -iest) (coloq) assustador

scathing /'skeɪðɪŋ/ adj mordaz

scatter /'skætər/ 1 vt, vi dispersar(-se) 2 vt espalhar **scattered** adj disperso: *~ showers* pancadas (de chuva) isoladas

scavenge /'skævɪndʒ/ vi 1 ir em busca de carniça 2 (pessoa) remexer (no lixo) **scavenger** s 1 animal/ave que se alimenta de carniça 2 pessoa que remexe no lixo

scenario /sə'nærioʊ; GB -'nɑːr-/ s (pl ~s) 1 (Teat) sinopse 2 hipótese

scene /siːn/ s 1 cena: *a change of ~* uma mudança de ares 2 cenário: *the ~ of the crime* o local do crime 3 escândalo 4 (**the scene**) (coloq) o panorama ▶ **set the scene (for sth)** 1 descrever o cenário (de algo) 2 desencadear (algo)

scenery /'siːnəri/ s [U] 1 paisagem NOTA **Scenery** tem forte conotação positiva, costuma ser acompanhado de adjetivos como *beautiful, spectacular*, etc., e refere-se, fundamentalmente, a paisagens naturais. **Landscape** costuma se referir a paisagens construídas pelo homem: *an urban landscape* ◊ *Trees and hedges are typical features of the British landscape.* 2 (Teat) cenário

scenic /'siːnɪk/ adj pitoresco, panorâmico

scent /sent/ s 1 aroma (agradável) 2 perfume 3 rastro **scented** adj perfumado

sceptic (GB) = SKEPTIC

schedule /'skedʒʊl; GB 'ʃedjuːl/ s 1 programa: *be a month ahead of/behind ~* estar um mês adiantado/atrasado (em relação ao prazo) ◊ *arrive on ~* chegar na hora prevista 2 horário ● vt programar: *scheduled flight* vôo regular

scheme /skiːm/ s 1 conspiração 2 (GB) plano, esquema: *training ~* programa de treinamento 3 *color ~* combinação de cores ● vi conspirar

schizophrenia /ˌskɪtsə'friːniə/ s esquizofrenia **schizophrenic** /ˌskɪtsə'frenɪk/ adj, s esquizofrênico/a

scholar /'skɑlər/ s 1 aluno/a 2 erudito/a **scholarship** s 1 bolsa de estudo 2 erudição

school /skuːl/ s 1 colégio, escola: *~ age/uniform* idade/uniforme escolar NOTA As palavras **school** e **church** são usadas sem artigo quando se vai ao colégio para estudar ou lecionar, ou à igreja para rezar: *I enjoyed being at ~.* ◊ *We go to church every Sunday.* Usa-se o artigo ao nos referirmos a esses lugares por outro motivo: *I have to go to the ~ to talk to John's teacher.* 2 (USA) universidade 3 *School begins at nine o'clock.* As aulas começam às nove. 4 faculdade: *law ~* faculdade de direito 5 (Arte) escola ▶ **school of thought** doutrina

schoolchild /'skuːltʃaɪld/ s (tb **schoolboy** /'skuːlbɔɪ/) (fem **schoolgirl** /'skuːlɡɜːrl/) aluno/a

schooling /'sku:lɪŋ/ s instrução

school-leaver s (GB) jovem recém-saído do ensino secundário

schoolteacher /'sku:lti:tʃər/ s (antiq **schoolmaster** /'sku:lmɑ:stər/; GB -mɑ:s/) (fem **schoolmistress** /'sku:lmɪstrəs/) professor/a

science /'saɪəns/ s ciência scientific /ˌsaɪən'tɪfɪk/ adj científico scientifically adv cientificamente scientist s cientista

sci-fi /ˌsaɪ faɪ/ s abrev **science fiction** (coloq) ficção científica

scissors /'sɪzərz/ s [pl] tesoura → PAIR

scoff /skɔ:f; GB skɒf/ vi ~ (at sb/sth) zombar (de alguém/algo)

scold /skoʊld/ vt ~ sb (for sth) ralhar com alguém (por algo)

scoop /sku:p/ s 1 pá: ice cream ~ colher de sorvete 2 colherada: a ~ of ice cream uma bola de sorvete 3 [Jornal] furo ● vt tirar (com pá): ~ sth out escavar algo (com mão, colher, etc.)

scooter /'sku:tər/ s 1 lambreta 2 patinete

scope /skoʊp/ s 1 oportunidade 2 âmbito

scorch /skɔ:rtʃ/ vt, vi chamuscar(-se) scorching adj escaldante

score /skɔ:r/ s 1 contagem: keep the ~ marcar os pontos ◊ The final ~ was 4-3. O placar foi 4 a 3. 2 (Educ) [U] pontos 3 (scores) muitos 4 (Mús) partitura 5 vintena ● on that score quanto a isso ● 1 vt, vi (Esporte) marcar 2 vt (Educ) tirar (nota) scoreboard s marcador

scorn /skɔ:rn/ s desdém ● vt desdenhar scornful adj desdenhoso

Scorpio /'skɔ:rpioʊ/ s (pl ~s) Escorpião

scorpion /'skɔ:rpiən/ s escorpião

Scotch /skɑtʃ/ s uísque escocês

Scotch tape® s durex® ● scotch tape vt colar com durex

scour /skaʊər/ vt 1 arear 2 ~ sth (for sb/sth) esquadrinhar algo (à procura de alguém/algo)

scourge /skɜ:rdʒ/ s açoite

scout /skaʊt/ s 1 (Mil) explorador 2 (tb (Boy) Scout) escoteiro 3 (tb (Girl) Scout) bandeirante

scowl /skaʊl/ s carranca ● vi olhar com um ar carrancudo

scrabble /'skræbl/ v ■ scrabble about (for sth) tatear (em busca de algo)

scramble /'skræmbl/ vi 1 trepar 2 ~ (for sth) lutar (por algo) 3 scrambled eggs ovos mexidos ● s [sing] luta

scrap /skræp/ s 1 fragmento: a ~ of paper um pedaço de papel ◊ scraps (of food) sobras 2 [U] refugo: ~ paper papel de rascunho 3 [sing] pingo 4 briga ● (-pp-) 1 vt jogar fora 2 vi brigar

scrapbook /'skræpbʊk/ s álbum de recortes

scrape /skreɪp/ 1 vt raspar 2 vt ~ sth off (sth) tirar (algo de) algo raspando 3 vi ~ (against sth) roçar (em algo) ■ scrape into/ sth conseguir algo com dificuldade: She just scraped into college. Ela entrou na universidade de raspão. scrape through (sth) passar (em algo) raspando scrape sth together/up conseguir juntar algo ● s arranhão

scratch /skrætʃ/ 1 vt, vi arranhar(-se) 2 vt, vi coçar(-se) 3 vt riscar ■ scratch sth away, off, etc. tirar algo raspando ● s 1 arranhão 2 [sing]: The dog gave itself a good ~. O cachorro se coçou para valer. ▶ from scratch do zero up to scratch à altura

scrawl /skrɔ:l/ 1 vt garatujar 2 vi fazer garranchos ● s [sing] garrancho

scream /skri:m/ 1 vt, vi gritar 2 vi esganiçar-se ● s 1 grito 2 [sing] (coloq) alguém/algo muito engraçado

screech /skri:tʃ/ vt, vi gritar de forma estridente ● s guincho

screen /skri:n/ s 1 tela 2 biombo

screw /skru:/ s parafuso ● vt aparafusar ■ screw sth up 1 (papel) amassar algo 2 (rosto) contrair algo 3 (coloq) (planos, etc.) estragar algo

screwdriver /'skru:draɪvər/ s chave de fenda

scribble /'skrɪbl/ 1 vt garatujar 2 vi rabiscar ● s rabisco

script /skrɪpt/ s 1 roteiro 2 letra 3 escrita ● vt escrever o roteiro para

scripture /'skrɪptʃər/ (tb Scripture/the Scriptures) s a Sagrada Escritura

scroll /skroʊl/ s rolo (pergaminho, papel)

scrub /skrʌb/ vt (-bb-) esfregar ● s 1 give sth a good ~ esfregar bem algo 2 [U] mato

scruff /skrʌf/ s ▶ by the scruff of the neck pelo cangote

scruffy /'skrʌfi/ adj (-ier, -iest) (coloq) desleixado

scrum /skrʌm/ s (rúgbi) luta

pelo posse da bola

scruples /'skru:plz/ s [pl] escrúpulo(s)

scrupulous /'skru:pjələs/ adj escrupuloso **scrupulously** adv escrupulosamente

scrutinize /'skru:tənaɪz/ vt examinar minuciosamente

scrutiny /'skru:təni/ s 1 exame minucioso 2 (tb Pol) escrutínio

scuba-diving /'sku:bə daɪvɪŋ/ s mergulho

scuff /skʌf/ vt esfolar

scuffle /'skʌfl/ s 1 tumulto 2 briga

sculpture /'skʌlptʃər/ s escultura **sculptor** /'skʌlptər/ s escultor/a

scum /skʌm/ s 1 espuma 2 escória

scurry /'skʌri/ vi (pt, pp -ied) correr a passos rápidos: ~ around correr de lá para cá

scuttle /'skʌtl/ vi: She scuttled back to her car. Ela correu de volta para seu carro. ◇ ~ away/ off escapulir-se

scythe /saɪð/ s foice grande

sea /si:/ s 1 mar: heavy/ heavy seas mar agitado ◇ ~ creatures/ air animais marinhos/brisa marinha ◇ ~ seaport porto marítimo → MAR 2 multidão ▸ **all at sea** desorientado **at sea** em alto mar

seafood /'si:fu:d/ s [U] frutos do mar

seagull /'si:gʌl/ Ver GULL

seal /si:l/ s 1 foca 2 selo ● vt 1 selar 2 lacrar 3 (envelope) fechar ▪ **seal sth off** isolar algo

seam /si:m/ s 1 costura 2 (Geol) filão

search /sɜ:rtʃ/ 1 vi ~ (for sth) buscar (algo) 2 vt ~ sb/sth (for sth) revistar alguém/algo (em busca de algo) ● s 1 ~ (for sb/ sth) busca (de alguém/algo) 2 (polícia) revista **searching** adj penetrante

searchlight /'sɜ:rtʃlaɪt/ s holofote

seashell /'si:ʃel/ s concha marinha

seasick /'si:sɪk/ adj enjoado

seaside /'si:saɪd/ adj da costa

season /'si:zn/ s 1 estação 2 temporada: ~ ticket passe (de trem, etc.) ▸ **in season** (que está) na estação **seasonal** adj de estação/temporada ● vt temperar, condimentar **seasoned** adj 1 condimentado 2 (pessoa) calejado **seasoning** s tempero

seat /si:t/ s 1 assento 2 (parque) banco 3 (teatro) lugar 4 (avião) poltrona 5 selim 6 (Pol) cadeira 7 (GB) (Pol) distrito eleitoral ● vt acomodar

seat belt s cinto de segurança

seating /'si:tɪŋ/ s [U] assentos

seaweed /'si:wi:d/ s alga marinha

secluded /sɪ'klu:dɪd/ adj 1 (lugar) retirado 2 (vida) isolado **seclusion** s 1 isolamento 2 privacidade

second /'sekənd/ (abrev 2nd) adj segundo ▸ **second thought(s): have ~ thoughts** reconsiderarse ◇ **On ~ thoughts...** Pensando bem... ● pron, adv o(s)/a(s) segundo/a(s)/a(s) ◇ ~ (the second) (o dia) dois 2 (tb ~ gear) s3gunda (marcha) 3 (tempo) segundo ● vt secundar

secondary /'sekənderi/ adj secundário

second best adj segunda opção

second-class adj 1 de segunda classe 2 (GB) (correio) de porte comum

second-hand adj, adv de segunda mão

secondly /'sekəndli/ adv em segundo lugar

second-rate cdj de segunda categoria

secret /'si:krət/ adj secreto ● s segredo **secrecy** s 1 sigilo 2 segredo

secretarial /ˌsekrə'teəriəl/ adj 1 (pessoal) administrativo 2 (trabalho) de secretário/a

secretary /'sekrəteri; GB -rətri/ s (pl -ies) secretário/a

Secretary of State s 1 (USA) Ministro das Relações Exteriores/a 2 (GB) Ministro/a

secrete /sɪ'kri:t/ vt (fml) 1 secretar 2 esconder **secretion** s secreção

secretive /'si:krətɪv/ adj reservado

secretly /'si:krətli/ adv secretamente

sect /sekt/ s seita

sectarian /sek'teəriən/ adj sectário

section /'sekʃn/ s 1 seção, parte 2 (estrada) faixa 3 setor 4 (lei) artigo

sector /'sektər/ s setor

secular /'sekjələr/ adj secular

secure /sɪ'kjʊər/ adj 1 seguro 2 (prisão) de alta segurança ● vt 1 prender 2 (acordo, etc.) conseguir 3 assegurar **securely** adv firmemente **security** s (pl -ies) 1 segurança: ~ guard (guarda de) segurança **2** (empréstimo) fiança

sedan /sɪ'dæn/ s sedã

sedate /sɪ'deɪt/ adj comedido ● vt sedar **sedation** s sedação: under ~ sob o efeito de sedativos **sedative** /'sedatɪv/ adj, s sedativo

sedentary /'sednteri; GB -tri/ adj sedentário

sediment /'sedimant/ s sedimento

sedition /sɪ'dɪʃn/ s sedição

seduce /sɪ'djuːs; GB sɪ'djuːs/ vt seduzir **seduction** s sedução **seductive** adj sedutor

see /siː/ vt, vi (pt saw pp seen) **1** ver: ~ a lot of sb ver alguém com freqüência ◊ She'll never ~ again. Ela nunca voltará a enxergar. ◊ I'm seeing Sue tonight. Vou encontrar com a Sue hoje à noite. **2** acompanhar **3** encarregar-se: ~ about (doing) sth encarregar-se de (fazer) algo ◊ I'll ~ that it's done. Tomarei providências para isso. **4** compreender ▶ **see you (around); (I'll be) seeing you** (coloq) até logo, a gente se vê ▶ **seeing that...** visto que... NOTA Para outras expressões com **see**, ver o substantivo, adjetivo, etc., p. ex. **make sb see reason** em REASON. ■ **see sb off 1** despedir-se de alguém **2** botar alguém para correr **see through sb/sth** não se deixar enganar por alguém/algo **see to sth** providenciar algo

seed /siːd/ s semente

seedy /'siːdi/ adj (-ier, -iest) sórdido

seek /siːk/ vt, vi (pt, pp sought) (fml) **1** ~ (after/for sth) procurar (algo) **2** ~ (to do sth) tentar (fazer) algo ■ **seek sb/sth out** ir ao encontro de alguém/algo

seem /siːm/ vi parecer NOTA Não é usado em tempos contínuos. **seemingly** adv aparentemente

seen /siːn/ pp de SEE

seep /siːp/ vi infiltrar-se

seething /'siːðɪŋ/ adj ~ with sth: ~ with rage fervendo de raiva ◊ ~ with people fervilhando de gente

see-through adj transparente

segment /'segmant/ s **1** segmento **2** (de laranja, etc.) gomo

segregate /'segrɪgeɪt/ vt segregar

seize /siːz/ vt **1** ~ (hold of) sth agarrar algo: We were seized by

panic. Fomos acometidos de pânico. **2** (drogas, etc.) apreender **3** capturar **4** confiscar **5** (controle) tomar **6** (oportunidade, etc.) aproveitar: ~ the initiative tomar a iniciativa ■ **seize on/upon sth** valer-se de algo **seize up** (motor) grimpar **seizure** /'siːʒər/ s **1** confisco, apreensão **2** (Med) ataque

seldom /'seldəm/ adv raramente → ALWAYS

select /sɪ'lekt/ vt escolher ● adj seleto **selection** s seleção **selective** adj seletivo

self /self/ s (pl selves) eu, ego: be your old ~ again voltar a ser o mesmo de sempre

self-centered (GB -centred) adj egocêntrico

self-confident adj seguro de si

self-conscious adj sem naturalidade

self-contained adj (apartamento) independente

self-control s autocontrole

self-defense s autodefesa

self-determination s autodeterminação

self-employed adj autônomo

self-interest s interesse próprio

selfish /'selfɪʃ/ adj egoísta

self-pity s autopiedade

self-portrait s auto-retrato

self-respect s amor-próprio

self-satisfied adj cheio de si

self-service adj de auto-serviço

sell /sel/ vt, vi (pp, pt sold) vender(-se) ▶ **sold out (of sth)** com o estoque (de algo) esgotado ■ **sell sth off** liquidar algo **sell out** (entradas) esgotar-se

sell-by date s (prazo de) validade

seller /'selər/ s vendedor/a

selling /'selɪŋ/ s venda

Sellotape® /'selateɪp/ s durex® ● **Sellotape** vt colar com durex

selves /selvz/ plural de SELF

semester /sə'mestər/ s semestre

semi /'semi/ s (pl ~s /'semiz/) (GB, coloq) casa geminada

semicircle /'semisɜːrkl/ s semicírculo

semicolon /'semikoulən; GB ,semi'k-/ s ponto-e-vírgula

semi-detached adj (GB) geminado

semi-final s semifinal

seminar /'semɪnɑːr/ s seminário (aula)

senate (tb **Senate**) /'senət/ s **1** (Pol) Senado **2** (Univ) junta administrativa **senator** (tb

Senator) /'senətər/ s (abrev **Sen.**) senador/a

send /send/ vt (pt, pp **sent**) 1 enviar, mandar ◇ fazer (com que): ~ sb to sleep (GB) dar sono a alguém ◇ *The story sent shivers down my spine.* A história me deu calafrios. ◇ ~ sb mad (GB) enlouquecer alguém ■ **send for sb** mandar buscar alguém **send (off) for sth** pedir algo pelo correio **send sb in** enviar alguém (esp tropas, polícia, etc.) **send sth in** enviar algo **send sth off 1** enviar algo pelo correio **2** despachar algo **send sth out 1** emitir algo **2** (convites, etc.) enviar algo **send sb/sth up** (GB, coloq) parodiar alguém/ algo sender s remetente

senile /'si:naɪl/ adj senil **senility** /sə'nɪləti/ s senilidade

senior /'si:niər/ adj **1** superior: ~ partner sócio principal **2** (abrev **Sr.**) sênior ● s mais velho **seniority** /ˌsiːni'ɒrəti/ GB ▪ /sə'nɒrəti; GB -'ɒr-/ s antiguidade (posição, anos, etc.)

senior citizen s idoso/a

senior high school s segundo grau

sensation /sen'seɪʃn/ s sensação **sensational** adj **1** sensacional **2** sensacionalista

sense /sens/ s **1** sentido: ~ of smell/touch/taste olfato/tato/paladar ◇ ~ of humor senso de humor ◇ *It gives him a ~ of security.* Isso o faz se sentir seguro. **2** bom senso: come to your senses recobrar o juízo ◇ make sb see ~ trazer alguém à razão ▶ **in a sense** de certo modo **make sense** fazer sentido **make sense of sth** decifrar algo **see sense** cair em si ● vt **1** perceber **2** detectar

senseless /'senslas/ adj **1** insensato **2** inconsciente

sensibility /ˌsensə'bɪləti/ s (pl **-ies**) sensibilidade

sensible /'sensəbl/ adj **1** sensato **2** (decisão) acertado **sensibly** adv **1** com prudência **2** (vestir-se) adequadamente

sensitive /'sensətɪv/ adj **1** sensível **2** (assunto, pele) delicado: ~ documents documentos confidenciais **sensitivity** /ˌsensə'tɪvəti/ s **1** sensibilidade **2** suscetibilidade **3** (assunto, pele) delicadeza

sensual /'senʃuəl/ adj sensual **sensuality** /ˌsenʃu'æləti/ s sensualidade

sensuous /'senʃuəs/ adj sensual

sent /sent/ pret, pp de SEND

sentence /'sentəns/ s **1** frase **2** sentença: a life ~ prisão perpétua ● vt condenar

sentiment /'sentɪmənt/ s **1** sentimentalismo **2** sentimento **sentimental** /ˌsentɪ'mentl/ adj **1** sentimental **2** melodramático **sentimentality** /ˌsentɪmen'tæləti/ s sentimentalismo

sentry /'sentri/ s (pl **-ies**) sentinela

separate /'seprət/ adj **1** separado **2** diferente ● /'sepəreɪt/ **1** vt, vi separar(-se) **2** vt dividir **separately** adv separadamente **separation** s separação

September /sep'tembər/ s (abrev **Sept.**) setembro → MAY

sequel /'si:kwəl/ s **1** resultado **2** (filme, etc.) continuação

sequence /'si:kwəns/ s seqüência

serene /sə'ri:n/ adj sereno

sergeant /'sɑːrdʒənt/ s sargento

serial /'sɪəriəl/ s seriado → SERIES

series /'sɪəri:z/ s (pl **series**) **1** série **2** sucessão **3** (TV, etc.) seriado NOTA **Series** é o seriado que conta uma história diferente a cada episódio e **serial** uma única história dividida em capítulos.

serious /'sɪəriəs/ adj **1** sério **2** grave **seriously** adv **1** a sério **2** gravemente **seriousness** s **1** seriedade **2** gravidade

sermon /'sɜːrmən/ s sermão

servant /'sɜːrvənt/ s empregado/a, serviçal

serve /sɜːrv/ **1** vt ~ sth (up) (to sb) servir algo (a alguém) **2** vi ~ (with sth) servir (em algo) **3** vt (cliente) atender **4** vt (pena) cumprir **5** vt, vi (tênis, etc.) sacar ▶ **serve sb right**: *It serves them right!* Bem feito pra eles. ■ **serve sth out 1** servir algo **2** distribuir algo ● s saque: *Whose ~ is it?* Quem é que saca?

server /'sɜːrvər/ s **1** (Informát) servidor **2** (Tênis) sacador/a **3** (Cozinha) [ger pl]: salad servers talheres de salada

service /'sɜːrvɪs/ s **1** serviço: on active ~ na ativa ◇ 10% extra for ~ 10% a mais pelo serviço **2** culto (religioso) **3** (carro) revisão **4** (tênis) saque ● vt fazer revisão

serviceman /'sɜːrvɪsmən/ s (fem **servicewoman**, **-women**) (pl **-men**, **-women**) militar

service station s posto de gasolina

session /'seʃn/ s sessão

set /set/ adj **1** situado **2** determinado **3** ~ (for sth)/(to do sth) preparado (para (fazer) algo) ● s **1** jogo, pacote **2** (pessoas) círculo **3** (Elet) aparelho **4** (ténis) set **5** (Teat) cenário **6** (Cinema) set **7** a shampoo and ~ lavagem e penteado ● (-tt-) (pt, pp set) **1** vt: The movie is ~ in Peru. O filme é ambientado no Peru. **2** vt colocar: Did you ~ the VCR to record the movie? Você programou o vídeo para gravar o filme? **3** vt estabelecer: They haven't ~ a date for their wedding yet. Eles ainda não marcaram a data do casamento. **4** vt (mudança de estado): They ~ the prisoners free. Libertaram os prisioneiros. ◊ It ~ me thinking. Isso me fez pensar. **5** vt (mandar) passar: She ~ them a difficult task. Ela deu uma tarefa difícil a eles. **6** vi (sol) pôr-se **7** vi solidificar-se, endurecer **8** vt (osso) engessar **9** vt (cabelo) fazer **10** vt (jóias) engastar NOTA Para expressões com set, ver o substantivo, adjetivo, etc., p. ex. set sail em SAIL. ■ set about (doing) sth pôr-se a fazer algo **set off** partir **set off** (**1**) detonar algo **2** ocasionar algo **set out** partir (viagem) **set out to do sth** propor-se a fazer algo **set up sth** montar algo

setback /ˈsetbæk/ s contratempo

setting /ˈsetɪŋ/ s **1** armação **2** ambientação, cenário **3** (sing) (do sol) ocaso

settle /ˈsetl/ **1** vi estabelecer-se, ficar para morar **2** vt/i (nervos, etc.) acalmar **4** vt (disputa) resolver **5** vt (conta) pagar **6** vi (sedimento) depositar(-se) ■ **settle down** acalmar-se: marry and ~ down casar-se e tomar juízo **settle for** aceitar algo **settle in/into sth** adaptar(-se) a algo **settle on sth** decidir-se por algo **settle up** acertar contas settled adj estável

settlement /ˈsetlmənt/ s **1** acordo **2** povoado **3** colonização

settler /ˈsetlər/ s colono/a, colonizador/a

seven /ˈsevn/ adj, pron, s sete **seventh 1** adj sétimo **2** pron, adv o(s)/a(s) sétimo(s)/a(s) **3** s sétima parte, sétimo

seventeen /ˌsevnˈtiːn/ adj, pron, s dezessete **seventeenth 1** adj décimo sétimo **2** pron, adv o(s) décimo(s) sétimo(s), a(s) décima(s) sétima(s) **3** s décima sétima parte, dezessete avos

seventy /ˈsevnti/ adj, pron, s setenta **seventieth 1** adj, pron septuagésimo **2** s septuagésima parte, setenta avos

sever /ˈsevər/ vt (fml) **1** cortar **2** (relações) romper

several /ˈsevrəl/ adj, pron vários

severe /sɪˈvɪər/ adj (-er, -est) **1** severo **2** (tempestade, etc.) forte **3** (dor) intenso

sew /soʊ/ vt, vi (pt sewed pp sewn /soʊn/ ou sewed) coser ■ **sew sth up** costurar algo: ~ up a hole cerzir um furo

sewage /ˈsuːɪdʒ; GB ˈsjuː-/ s [U] efluentes dos esgotos

sewer /ˈsuːər; GB ˈsjuː-/ s (cano de) esgoto

sewing /ˈsoʊɪŋ/ s costura

sex /seks/ s **1** sexo **2** relações sexuais

sexism /ˈseksɪzəm/ s sexismo **sexist** adj, s sexista

sexual /ˈsekʃuəl/ adj sexual **sexuality** /ˌsekʃuˈæləti/ s sexualidade

shabby /ˈʃæbi/ adj (-ier, -iest) **1** (roupa) surrado **2** (coisas) em mau estado **3** (pessoa) mal vestido **4** (comportamento) mesquinho

shack /ʃæk/ s cabana

shade /ʃeɪd/ s **1** sombra **2** abajur **3** persiana **4** (cor) tom **5** (significado) vestígio ● vt sombrear shady adj (-ier, -iest) sombreado

shadow /ˈʃædoʊ/ s **1** sombra **2** (shadows) trevas ● vt seguir e vigiar secretamente ● adj (Pol) da oposição shadowy adj **1** sombreado **2** indistinto

shaft /ʃæft; GB ʃɑːft/ s **1** dardo **2** haste **3** eixo **4** poço **5** (luz) raio

shaggy /ˈʃægi/ adj (-ier, -iest) peludo: ~ eyebrows sobrancelhas cerradas ◊ ~ hair cabelo desgrenhado

shake /ʃeɪk/ (pt shook pp shaken /ˈʃeɪkən/) **1** vt ~ sb/sth (about/around) sacudir alguém/algo **2** vi tremer **3** vt ~ sb (up) perturbar alguém ■ **shake sb's hand/shake hands (with sb)/shake sb by the hand** apertar a mão de alguém **shake your head** negar com a cabeça ■ **shake sb off** livrar-se de alguém **shake sb up** dar uma sacudida em alguém **shake sth up** agitar algo ● s (ger sing) sacudida: a ~ of the head uma negação com a cabeça shaky adj (-ier, -iest) **1** trêmulo **2** pouco firme

shall /ʃəl, ʃæl/ (contração 'll neg shall not ou shan't /ʃænt; GB ʃɑːnt/) *v aux* (*esp GB*) para formar o futuro: *I ~ tell her tomorrow.* Direi a ela amanhã. NOTA **Shall e will** formam o futuro em inglês. Usa-se **shall** com a primeira pessoa do singular e do plural, *I* e **we**, e **will** com as demais pessoas. Em inglês falado, tende-se a utilizar **will** (ou 'll) com todos os pronomes. • *v modal* NOTA **Shall** é um verbo modal, seguido de infinitivo sem *to*. As orações interrogativas e negativas são formadas sem o auxiliar *do*. **1** (*fml*) (*vontade*): *I shan't go.* Não irei. NOTA Neste sentido, **shall** é mais formal do que **will**, especialmente com pronomes que não sejam *I* e *we*. **2** (*oferta, sugestão*) (*GB*) *Shall we pick you up?* Vamos te buscar?

shallow /ˈʃæloʊ/ *adj* (~er ~est) **1** (*água*) raso **2** (*pessoa*) superficial

shambles /ˈʃæmblz/ *s* [*sing*] (*coloq*) confusão

shame /ʃeɪm/ *s* **1** vergonha **2** desonra **3** (*a shame*) (*coloq*) uma pena ▸ **put sb/sth to shame** deixar alguém/algo em situação constrangedora • *vt* **1** envergonhar **2** desonrar

shameful /ˈʃeɪmfl/ *adj* vergonhoso

shameless /ˈʃeɪmləs/ *adj* sem-vergonha

shampoo /ʃæmˈpuː/ *s* (*pl* ~s) xampu • *vt* (*pt, pp* ~ed *part pres* ~ing) lavar com xampu

shan't /ʃænt; *GB* ʃɑːnt/ = SHALL NOT *Ver* SHALL

shanty town /ˈʃænti taʊn/ *s* favela

shape /ʃeɪp/ *s* **1** forma: *take ~* concretizar-se **2** figura ▸ **give shape to sth** (*fig*) moldar algo **in any shape (or form)** (*coloq*) de qualquer tipo **in shape** em forma **out of shape 1** deformado **2** fora de forma • *vt* **1** ~ **sth (into sth)** dar forma (de algo) a algo **2** formar **shapeless** *adj* sem forma definida

share /ʃeər/ *s* **1** parte **2** (*Fin*) ação • **1** *vt* ~ **sth (out)** repartir algo **2** *vt, vi* compartilhar

shareholder /ˈʃeərhoʊldər/ *s* acionista

shark /ʃɑːrk/ *s* tubarão

sharp /ʃɑːrp/ *adj* (~er, ~est) **1** (*faca*) afiado **2** (*curva*) fechado **3** (*subida*) acentuado **4** nítido **5** (*som, dor*) agudo **6** (*sabor, etc.*) acre **7** (*vento*) cortante **8** (*pessoa*) pouco escrupuloso **9** (*Mús*)

sustenido • *s* sustenido • *adv* (*hora*) em ponto sharpen **1** *vt, vi* afiar(-se) **2** *vt* (*lápis*) apontar

shatter /ˈʃætər/ *vt, vi* **1** despedaçar(-se) **2** destruir shattering *adj* avassalador

shave /ʃeɪv/ **1** *vt, vi* barbear(-se) **2** *vt* (*corpo*) rapar

she /ʃiː/ *pron* ela (*também se usa para carros, barcos ou países*) ➔ YOU • *s*: *Is it a he or a ~?* É macho ou fêmea?

shear /ʃɪər/ *vt* (*pt* **sheared** *pp* **shorn** *ou* **sheared**) (*ovelha*) tosquiar **2** shears /ʃɪəz/ *s* [*pl*] tesoura de jardim ➔ PAIR

sheath /ʃiːθ/ *s* bainha

shed /ʃed/ *s* barracão • *vt* (-dd-) (*pt, pp* **shed**) **1** perder **2** (*a pele*) mudar **3** (*fml*) (*sangue, lágrimas*) derramar **4** (*luz*) lançar

she'd /ʃiːd/ **1** = SHE HAD *Ver* HAVE **2** = SHE WOULD *Ver* WOULD

sheep /ʃiːp/ *s* (*pl* **sheep**) ovelha ➔ CARNE sheepish *adj* encabulado

sheer /ʃɪər/ *adj* **1** (*absoluto*) puro **2** (*tecido*) transparente **3** íngreme

sheet /ʃiːt/ *s* **1** lençol **2** (*papel*) folha **3** (*vidro, metal*) chapa

sheikh /ʃeɪk/ *s* xeque

shelf /ʃelf/ *s* (*pl* **shelves**) prateleira

shell /ʃel/ *vt* bombardear • *s* **1** concha **2** (*ovo, noz*) casca ➔ PEEL **3** carapaça **4** (*barco*) casco **5** (*edifício*) estrutura **6** obus, granada

she'll /ʃiːl/ = SHE WILL *Ver* WILL

shellfish /ˈʃelfɪʃ/ *s* (*pl* **shellfish**) **1** (*Zool*) crustáceo **2** marisco

shelter /ˈʃeltər/ *s* **1** ~ **(from sth)** abrigo (contra algo): *take ~* refugiar-se **2** refúgio • **1** *vt* proteger, abrigar **2** *vi* refugiar-se, abrigar-se sheltered *adj* **1** abrigado **2** protegido

shelve /ʃelv/ *vt* engavetar

shelves /ʃelvz/ *plural de* SHELF

shelving /ˈʃelvɪŋ/ *s* prateleiras

shepherd /ˈʃepərd/ *s* pastor

sheriff /ˈʃerəf/ *s* xerife

sherry /ˈʃeri/ *s* (*pl* -**ies**) xerez

she's /ʃiːz/ **1** = SHE IS *Ver* BE **2** = SHE HAS *Ver* HAVE

shield /ʃiːld/ *s* escudo • *vt* proteger

shift /ʃɪft/ **1** *vi* mover-se, mudar de posição **2** *vt* mudar de lugar • *s* **1** mudança **2** (*trabalho*) turno

shifty /ˈʃɪfti/ *adj* (-**ier**, -**iest**) duvidoso

shilling /ˈʃɪlɪŋ/ *s* xelim

shimmer /'ʃɪmər/ *vi* **1** brilhar **2** bruxulear

shin /ʃɪn/ *s* **1** canela (*da perna*) **2** (*tb ~ bone*) tíbia

shine /ʃaɪn/ (*pt, pp* **shone**) **1** *vi ~ (at/in sth)* brilhar (em algo): *His face shone with excitement.* O rosto dele irradiava entusiasmo. ◇ *She's always shone at languages.* Ela sempre se destacou em idiomas. **2** *vt* iluminar com uma lanterna ● *s* brilho

shingle /'ʃɪŋgl/ *s* **1** telha de madeira **2** seixos

shiny /'ʃaɪni/ *adj* (**-ier, -iest**) brilhante

ship /ʃɪp/ *s* **1** barco, navio: *go on board ~* subir a bordo → BOAT ● *vt* (**-pp-**) enviar (por via marítima)

shipbuilding /'ʃɪpbɪldɪŋ/ *s* construção naval

shipment /'ʃɪpmənt/ *s* carregamento

shipping /'ʃɪpɪŋ/ *s* navegação, navios

shipwreck /'ʃɪprek/ *s* naufrágio ● *vt*: *be shipwrecked* naufragar

shirt /ʃɜːrt/ *s* camisa

shiver /'ʃɪvər/ *vi* **1** arrepiar-se **2** estremecer ● *s* calafrio

shoal /ʃoʊl/ *s* cardume

shock /ʃɑk/ *s* choque: *electric ~* choque elétrico ● **1** *vt* chocar **2** *vt, vi* escandalizar(-se) **shocking** *adj* **1** chocante **2** (*coloq*) horrível

shoddy /'ʃɑdi/ *adj* (**-ier, -iest**) de má qualidade

shoe /ʃuː/ *s* **1** sapato: *~ shop* sapataria ◇ *~ polish* graxa ◇ *What ~ size do you wear?* Que número você calça? → PAIR **2** ferradura ● *vt* (*pt, pp* **shod** /ʃɑd/) (*cavalo*) ferrar

shoestring /'ʃuːstrɪŋ/ (*GB* **shoelace** /'ʃuːleɪs/) *s* cadarço ● **on a shoestring** com muito pouco dinheiro

shone /ʃoʊn; *GB* ʃɒn/ *pret, pp* de SHINE

shook /ʃʊk/ *pret* de SHAKE

shoot /ʃuːt/ (*pt, pp* **shot**) **1** *vt* disparar: *~ rabbits* caçar coelhos ◇ *She was shot in the leg.* Ela levou um tiro na perna. ◇ *sb dead* matar alguém a tiros **2** *vi ~ at sb/sth* atirar em/contra alguém/algo **3** *vt* fuzilar **4** *vi* (*olhar*) lançar **5** *vt* filmar **6** *vi ~ along, past, out, etc.* ir, passar, sair, etc., disparado **7** *vi* (*Esporte*) chutar ■ **shoot sb/sth down** matar ou ferir/abater algo (a tiro) **shoot up 1** (*preços*) disparar **2** crescer rapidamente

● *s* (*Bot*) broto

shop /ʃɑp/ *s* **1** (*esp GB*) loja: *I'm going to the shops.* Vou fazer compras. **2** *Ver* WORKSHOP ● *vi* (**-pp-**) ir às compras, fazer compras: *~ for sth* procurar algo (*nas lojas*) ■ **shop around** ver o que há (*nas lojas*)

shop assistant *s* vendedor/a

shopkeeper /'ʃɑpkiːpər/ *s* lojista

shoplifting /'ʃɑplɪftɪŋ/ *s* furto (*em loja*) **shoplifter** *s* ladrão/ladra de lojas → THIEF

shopper /'ʃɑpər/ *s* comprador/a

shopping /'ʃɑpɪŋ/ *s* compra(s): *~ cart* carrinho de compras

shopping center (*tb* **shopping mall**) *s* centro comercial

shore /ʃɔːr/ *s* **1** costa: *go on ~* desembarcar **2** orla (*mar, lago*)

shorn /ʃɔːrn/ *pp* de SHEAR

short /ʃɔːrt/ *s* **1** *Ver* SHORT-CIRCUIT **2** (*Cinema*) curta-metragem ● *adj* (**~er, -est**) **1** curto **2** (*pessoa*) baixo **3** *I was only there for a ~ while.* Estive ali só um instante. ◇ *A ~ time ago* há pouco tempo **4** *~* (*of sth*): *Water is ~.* Está faltando água. ◇ *I'm a bit ~ of time just now.* Neste exato momento estou um pouco sem tempo. ◇ *I'm $5 ~.* Faltam-me cinco dólares. **5** *~ for sth*: *Ben is ~ for Benjamin.* Ben é o diminutivo de Benjamin. **for short** para abreviar **get short shrift** ser tratado com brusquidão **have a short temper** ser irritadiço **in short** em resumo

shortage /'ʃɔːrtɪdʒ/ *s* escassez

short circuit *s* curto-circuito **short-circuit 1** *vi* ter um curto-circuito **2** *vt* causar um curto-circuito

shortcoming /'ʃɔːrtkʌmɪŋ/ *s* deficiência, falha

short cut *s* atalho

shorten /'ʃɔːrtn/ *vt, vi* encurtar(-se)

shorthand /'ʃɔːrthænd/ *s* taquigrafia

shortlist /'ʃɔːrtlɪst/ *s* lista final de candidatos

short-lived *adj* de curta duração

shortly /'ʃɔːrtli/ *adv* **1** dentro em pouco **2** *~ afterwards* pouco depois

shorts /ʃɔːrts/ *s* [*pl*] **1** short **2** (*USA*) cuecas → PAIR

short-sighted *adj* **1** míope **2** imprudente

short-term *adj* a curto prazo

shot /ʃɑt/ *pret, pp* de SHOOT ● *s* **1** tiro **2** tentativa: *have a ~ at sth*

experimentar algo **3** (*Esporte*) tacada **4** (**the shot**) (*Esporte*) peso: *put the ~* lançar o peso **5** (*Fot*) foto **6** (*Eletr*) injeção, pico

shotgun /ˈʃɒtgʌn/ s espingarda

should /ʃəd, ʃʊd/ v modal (neg **should not** ou **shouldn't** /ˈʃʊdnt/) NOTA Should é um verbo modal, seguido de infinitivo sem to. As orações interrogativas e negativas são formadas sem o auxiliar do. **1** (*sugestões, conselhos*) dever: *You shouldn't drink and drive.* Você não deveria dirigir depois de beber. **2** (*probabilidade*) dever: *They ~ be there by now.* Eles já deveriam ter chegado. **3** *How ~ I know?* E como é que eu posso saber? **4** *Should we pick you up?* Vamos te buscar?

shoulder /ˈʃəʊldər/ s ombro • vt arcar com

shoulder blade s omoplata

shout /ʃaʊt/ s grito • vt, vi ~ (**sth**) (**out**) (**to sb**) gritar (algo) (para alguém) ■ **shout at sb** repreender alguém **shout sb down** fazer alguém calar com gritos

shove /ʃʌv/ **1** vt, vi empurrar **2** vt (*coloq*) meter • s empurrão

shovel /ˈʃʌvl/ s pá • vt (-l-, *GB* -ll-) (re)mover com pá

show /ʃəʊ/ s **1** espetáculo, função: *~ business* mundo do espetáculo **2** feira **3** demonstração: *make a ~ of sth* fazer alarde de algo ▶ **for show** para impressionar **on show** em exposição • (pt **showed** pp **shown** /ʃəʊn/) **1** vt mostrar **2** vt notar-se **3** vt demonstrar **4** vt (*filme*) passar **5** vt (*Arte*) expor ■ **show off** (to sb) (*coloq, pej*) exibir-se (para alguém) **show sb/sth off** (com orgulho) exibir alguém/algo **show up** (*coloq*) aparecer **show sb up** (*coloq*) envergonhar alguém

showdown /ˈʃəʊdaʊn/ s confrontação

shower /ˈʃaʊər/ s **1** aguaceiro **2** ~ (**of sth**) chuva (de algo) **3** ducha: *take a ~* tomar um banho de chuveiro • vt ~ **sb with sth** encher alguém de algo

showing /ˈʃəʊɪŋ/ s exibição

showroom /ˈʃəʊruːm/ s sala de exposição

shrank /ʃræŋk/ pret de SHRINK

shrapnel /ˈʃræpnəl/ s metralha

shred /ʃred/ s **1** (*verduras*) tira **2** (*tabaco*) filamento **3** (*tecido*) retalho **4** (*fig*) sombra • vt (-dd-) cortar em tiras

shrewd /ʃruːd/ adj (~er, ~est) **1** astuto **2** (*decisão*) inteligente

shriek /ʃriːk/ vt, vi ~ (**with sth**) guinchar (de algo): ~ *with laughter* rir às gargalhadas • s guincho

shrift /ʃrɪft/ s Ver SHORT

shrill /ʃrɪl/ adj (~er, ~est) **1** esganiçado **2** (*protesto*) estridente

shrimp /ʃrɪmp/ s camarão

shrine /ʃraɪn/ s **1** santuário **2** sepulcro

shrink /ʃrɪŋk/ vt, vi (pt **shrank** ou **shrunk** pp **shrunk**) encolher(-se), reduzir(-se) ■ **shrink from** (**doing**) **sth** esquivar-se de (fazer) algo

shrivel /ˈʃrɪvl/ vt, vi (-l-, *GB* -ll-) ~ (**sth**) (**up**) **1** secar, murchar (algo) **2** enrugar (algo), enrugar-se

shroud /ʃraʊd/ s **1** mortalha **2** manto • vt envolver: *shrouded in secrecy* rodeado do maior segredo

shrub /ʃrʌb/ s arbusto

shrug /ʃrʌɡ/ vt, vi (-gg-) ~ (**your shoulders**) encolher os ombros ■ **shrug sth off** não dar importância a algo • s encolher de ombros

shrunk /ʃrʌŋk/ pret, pp de SHRINK

shudder /ˈʃʌdər/ vi **1** estremecer **2** sacudir • s **1** arrepio **2** sacudida

shuffle /ˈʃʌfl/ **1** vt, vi (*baralho*) embaralhar → BARALHO **2** vt ~ **your feet** arrastar os pés **3** vi ~ (**along**) andar arrastando os pés

shun /ʃʌn/ vt (-nn-) evitar

shut /ʃʌt/ vt, vi (-tt-) (pt, pp **shut**) fechar(-se) ■ **shut sb/sth away** encerrar alguém/algo **shut sth down** fechar algo **shut sb/sth** (**up**) **in sth** trancar alguém/algo em algo **shut sth off** cortar algo (*fornecimento*) **shut sb/sth off** (**from sth**) isolar alguém/algo (de algo) **shut sb/sth out** (**of sth**) excluir alguém/algo (de algo) **shut up** (*coloq*) calar(-se) **shut sb up** (*coloq*) mandar alguém calar **shut sth up** fechar algo • adj [*depois do verbo*] fechado

shutter /ˈʃʌtər/ s **1** veneziana **2** (*Fot*) obturador

shuttle /ˈʃʌtl/ s **1** lançadeira **2** ~ *service* ponte (aérea, rodoviária) **3** (*tb* space ~) ônibus espacial

shy /ʃaɪ/ adj (~er, ~est) tímido: ~ *of sb/sth* acanhado com alguém/algo • vi (pt, pp **shied**) ~ (**at sth**) (*cavalo*) espantar-se (com algo) ■ **shy away from (doing) sth** evitar fazer algo por medo ou timidez shyness *s* timidez

sick /sɪk/ *adj* (~**er**, ~**est**) **1** doente: *be off* ~ faltar ao trabalho por motivo de doença **2** enjoado **3** (*coloq*) farto: *be* ~ *and tired of sth* estar (com algo) até a raiz dos cabelos **4** (*coloq*) mórbido ► **be sick** (*GB*) vomitar **make sb sick 1** fazer mal a alguém **2** (*fig*) dar nojo a alguém ● *s* (*GB, coloq*) vômito **sicken** *vt* enojar **sickening** *adj* repugnante

sickly /'sɪkli/ *adj* (-**ier**, -**iest**) **1** doentio **2** enjoativo

sickness /'sɪknəs/ *s* **1** doença **2** náusea

side /saɪd/ *s* **1** lado: *at /by sb's* ~ ao lado de alguém ◊ *be on our* ~ estar do nosso lado **2** fachada lateral: *a* ~ *door* uma porta lateral **3** (*montanha*) encosta **4** (*lago*) beira **5** (*Anat, pessoa*) flanco **6** (*animal*) ilharga **7** parte **8** (*GB*) (*Esporte*) equipe ► **get on the right/wrong side of sb** (não) conquistar a simpatia de alguém ● **on/from all sides/every side** por/de todos os lados/toda parte **put sth on/to one side** deixar algo de lado **side by side** lado a lado **take sides (with sb)** tomar o partido (de alguém) ■ **side with sb** ficar do lado de alguém

sideboard /'saɪdbɔːrd/ *s* aparador

side effect *s* efeito colateral

side street *s* rua transversal

sidetrack /'saɪdtræk/ *vt* desviar do assunto principal

sidewalk /'saɪdwɔːk/ *s* calçada

sideways /'saɪdweɪz/ *adv, adj* **1** de lado **2** (*olhar*) de soslaio

siege /siːdʒ/ *s* **1** sítio **2** cerco policial

sieve /sɪv/ *s* peneira ● *vt* peneirar

sift /sɪft/ **1** *vt* peneirar **2** *vt, vi* ~ **(through) sth** examinar algo minuciosamente

sigh /saɪ/ *vi* suspirar ● *s* suspiro

sight /saɪt/ *s* **1** vista: *in* ~ à vista **2** (**the sights**) os lugares de interesse ► **at/on sight** no ato **out of sight, out of mind** o que os olhos não veem, o coração não sente

sightseeing /'saɪtsiːɪŋ/ *s* turismo

sign /saɪn/ *vt, vi* assinar ■ **sign up for (for sth) 1** inscrever-se (em algo) **2**

associar-se (a algo) ● *s* **1** signo **2** sinal: ~ *language* linguagem de sinais ◊ *There are signs that...* Há indícios de que... **3** (*tráfego*) sinal de trânsito, placa **4** (*Med*) sintoma

signal /'sɪɡnəl/ *s* sinal ● *vt, vi* (-**l-**, *GB* -**ll-**) **1** ~ **(to sb to do sth)** fazer sinal (a alguém para que faça algo) **2** mostrar

signature /'sɪɡnətʃər/ *s* assinatura

significant /sɪɡ'nɪfɪkənt/ *adj* significativo **significance** *s* **1** significado **2** importância

signify /'sɪɡnɪfaɪ/ *vt* (*pt, pp* -**ied**) **1** significar **2** indicar

signpost /'saɪnpoʊst/ *s* poste de sinalização

silence /'saɪləns/ *s, interj* silêncio ● *vt* silenciar

silent /'saɪlənt/ *adj* **1** silencioso **2** calado **3** (*filme*) mudo

silhouette /ˌsɪlu'et/ *s* silhueta ● *vt*: *silhouetted against sth* em silhueta contra algo

silk /sɪlk/ *s* seda **silky** *adj* (-**ier**, -**iest**) sedoso

sill /sɪl/ *s* (*janela*) parapeito

silly /'sɪli/ *adj* (-**ier**, -**iest**) **1** tolo: *That was a very* ~ *thing to say.* Você disse uma bobagem muito grande. → TOLO **2** idiota

silver /'sɪlvər/ *s* **1** prata: ~ *paper* papel prateado **2** moedas (de prata) **3** prataria ● *adj* **1** de prata **2** (*cor*) prateado **silvery** *adj* prateado

similar /'sɪmələr/ *adj* semelhante **similarity** /ˌsɪmə'lærəti/ *s* (*pl* -**ies**) semelhança **similarly** *adv* **1** de maneira semelhante **2** igualmente

simile /'sɪməli/ *s* símile

simmer /'sɪmər/ *vt, vi* cozinhar em fogo brando

simple /'sɪmpl/ *adj* (-**er**, -**est**) **1** simples **2** (*pessoa*) simplório

simplicity /sɪm'plɪsəti/ *s* simplicidade

simplify /'sɪmplɪfaɪ/ *vt* (*pt, pp* -**ied**) simplificar

simplistic /sɪm'plɪstɪk/ *adj* simplista

simply /'sɪmpli/ *adv* **1** simplesmente **2** de maneira simples **3** meramente

simulate /'sɪmjuleɪt/ *vt* simular

simultaneous /ˌsaɪml'teɪniəs; *GB* ˌsɪm-/ *adj* ~ **(with sth)** simultâneo (a algo) **simultaneously** *adv* simultaneamente

sin /sɪn/ *s* pecado ● *vi* (-**nn-**) pecar

since /sɪns/ *conj* **1** desde que **2**

visto que ● prep desde: *It was the first time they'd won – 1974.* Foi a primeira vez que ganharam desde 1974. NOTA **Since** e **from** são traduzidos por "desde" e usados para especificar o ponto de partida da ação do verbo. Usa-se **since** quando a ação se estende até o momento presente: *She has been here – three.* Ela está aqui desde as três horas. Usa-se **from** quando a ação já terminou ou ainda não teve início: *I was there from three to four.* Estive lá desde as três até as quatro. ◇ *I'll be there from three.* Estarei lá a partir das três horas. → FOR ● adv desde então

sincere /sɪnˈsɪər/ *adj* sincero **sincerely** *adv* sinceramente **sincerity** /sɪnˈserəti/ *s* sinceridade

sinful /ˈsɪnfl/ *adj* pecaminoso

sing /sɪŋ/ *vt, vi* (*pt* **sang** *pp* **sung**) cantar **singer** *s* cantor/a **a singing** *s* canto, cântico

single /ˈsɪŋɡl/ *adj* 1 único: *every-day* todo dia 2 solteiro 3 (*cama*) de solteiro 4 (*GB*) (*passagem*) de ida ▶ **in single file** em fila indiana ● *s* 1 (*GB*) passagem de ida 2 (*disco*) compacto 3 (**singles**) (*Esporte*) individuais **single sb/sth out** escolher alguém/algo

single-handedly (*tb* **single-handed**) *adv* sem ajuda

single-minded *adj* decidido

singular /ˈsɪŋɡjələr/ *adj* 1 (*Gram*) singular 2 extraordinário ● *s* singular

sinister /ˈsɪnɪstər/ *adj* sinistro

sink /sɪŋk/ (*pt* **sank** *pp* **sunk**) 1 *vt, vi* afundar(-se) 2 *vi* baixar 3 *vi* (*sol*) ocultar-se 4 *vi* (*coloq*) (*planos*) arruinar **sink in** 1 absorver 2 *It still hasn't sunk in that...* Ainda não me entrou na cabeça que... **sink into sth** 1 (*líquido*) penetrar em algo 2 (*fig*) mergulhar em algo **sink sth into sth** cravar algo em algo ● *s* 1 (*USA*) lavabo 2 (*tb* **kitchen ~**) pia (de cozinha)

sinus /ˈsaɪnəs/ *s* seio (*de osso da cabeça*)

sip /sɪp/ *vt, vi* (**-pp-**) bebericar ● *s* gole

sir /sɜːr/ *s* 1 *Yes, ~.* Sim, senhor. 2 (**Sir**): *Dear Sir* Prezado Senhor 3 (**Sir**) /sər/: *Sir Paul McCartney*

siren /ˈsaɪrən/ *s* sirene (*polícia, etc.*)

sister /ˈsɪstər/ *s* 1 irmã 2 (*GB*) (*Med*) enfermeira-chefe 3 (**Sister**) (*Relig*) irmã 4 ~ **ship/organ-**ization navio gêmeo/organização congênere

sister-in-law *s* (*pl* **-ers-in-law**) cunhada

sit /sɪt/ (**-tt-**) 1 *vi* sentar(-se), estar sentado 2 *vt* ~ **sb/yourself (down)** sentar alguém; sentar-se 3 *vi* (*Arte*) posar 4 *vi* (*comitê, etc.*) reunir-se 5 *vi* (*objeto*) estar 6 *vt* (*GB*) (*exame*) fazer **sit down** ▶ ~ **around**: ~ *around doing nothing* passar o dia sentado, sem fazer nada **sit back** acomodar-se, relaxar **sit up** 1 endireitar-se na cadeira 2 passar a noite acordado

site /saɪt/ *s* 1 local: *construction ~* terreno de construção 2 (*de acontecimento*) lugar

sitting /ˈsɪtɪŋ/ *s* 1 sessão 2 (*para comer*) turno

sitting room (*GB*) *s* sala de estar

situated /ˈsɪtʃueɪtɪd/ *adj* situado

situation /ˌsɪtʃuˈeɪʃn/ *s* 1 situação 2 (*GB, fml*): ~*s vacant* vagas para emprego

six /sɪks/ *adj, pron, s* seis sixth 1 *adj* sexto 2 *pron, adv* o(s)/a(s) sexto(s)/a(s) 3 *s* sexta parte, sexto

sixteen /ˌsɪksˈtiːn/ *adj, pron, s* dezesseis **sixteenth** 1 *adj* décimo sexto 2 *pron, adv* o(s) décimo(s) sexto(s), a(s) décima(s) sexta(s) 3 *s* décima sexta parte, dezesseis avos

sixth form *s* (*GB*) os dois últimos anos do ensino secundário

sixty /ˈsɪksti/ *adj, pron, s* sessenta **sixtieth** 1 *adj* sexagésimo 2 *s* sexagésima parte, sessenta avos

size /saɪz/ *s* 1 tamanho 2 (*roupa, etc.*) número: *I wear ~ six.* Calço número 37. **size sb/sth up** (*coloq*) formar uma opinião sobre alguém/algo **siz(e)able** *adj* considerável

skate /skeɪt/ *s* patim (*roda, gelo*) ● *vi* patinar **skater** *s* patinador/a **skating** *s* patinação

skateboard /ˈskeɪtbɔːrd/ *s* skate

skeleton /ˈskelɪtn/ *s* esqueleto ● *adj* mínimo: ~ *staff/service* pessoal/serviço mínimo

skeptic /ˈskeptɪk/ *s* cético/a **skeptical** *adj* cético **skepticism** *s* ceticismo

sketch /sketʃ/ *s* 1 esboço 2 (*Teat*) esquete ● *vt, vi* esboçar **sketchy** *adj* (**-ier, -iest**) superficial, incompleto

ski /skiː/ *vi* (*pt, pp* **skied** *part pres* **skiing**) esquiar ● *s* esqui **skiing** *s* esqui

skid /skɪd/ *vi* (**-dd-**) 1 derrapar 2

(pessoa) escorregar ● **s** derrapagem

skies /skaɪz/ *plural de* SKY

skill /skɪl/ *s* **1** ~ (at/in (doing) sth) habilidade (para (fazer) algo) **2** destreza **skillful** (*GB* **skilful**) *adj* **1** ~ (at/in (doing) sth) hábil (para (fazer) algo) **2** habilidoso **skilled** *adj* ~ (at/in (doing) sth) habilitado (a (fazer) algo); especialista (em (fazer) algo): ~ **worker** trabalhador qualificado

skillet /ˈskɪlɪt/ *s* frigideira

skim /skɪm/ (**-mm-**) **1** *vt* desnatar, tirar a espuma de **2** *vt* roçar **3** *vi* ~ **(through/over)** sth ler algo por alto

skim milk (*GB* **skimmed milk**) *s* leite desnatado

skin /skɪn/ *s* **1** pele **2** (*fruta, etc.*) casca → PEEL **1** (*leite*) nata ▶ **by the skin of your teeth** (*coloq*) por um triz ● *vt* (**-nn-**) descascar, tirar a pele

skinhead /ˈskɪnhed/ *s* cabeça rapada

skinny /ˈskɪni/ *adj* (**-ier, -iest**) (*coloq*) magricela → MAGRO

skip /skɪp/ (**-pp-**) **1** *vt, vi* saltar **2** *vi* (*GB*) pular corda ● **s 1** salto **2** (*GB*) container (*para entulho*)

skipper /ˈskɪpər/ *s* capitão

skirmish /ˈskɜːrmɪʃ/ *s* escaramuça

skirt /skɜːrt/ *s* saia ● *vt* contornar ▪ **skirt around sth** *s* contornar algo **2** evitar algo

skirting board *s* rodapé

skull /skʌl/ *s* crânio

skunk /skʌŋk/ *s* gambá

sky /skaɪ/ *s* (*pl* **skies**) céu: *sky-high* elevadíssimo ◇ **skyline** linha do horizonte (numa cidade)

skylight /ˈskaɪlaɪt/ *s* clarabóia

skyscraper /ˈskaɪskreɪpər/ *s* arranha-céu

slab /slæb/ *s* **1** (*mármore*) placa **2** (*concreto*) laje **3** (*chocolate*) barra

slack /slæk/ *adj* (**~er, ~est**) **1** frouxo **2** (*pessoa*) descuidado

slacken /ˈslækən/ *vt, vi* ~ **(off/up)** afrouxar (algo)

slain /sleɪn/ *pp de* SLAY

slam /slæm/ (**-mm-**) **1** *vt, vi* ~ **(sth) (to/shut)** fechar (algo) batendo violentamente **2** lançar: ~ *on your brakes* frear de repente **3** *vt* (*coloq*) malhar (*alguém/algo*)

slander /ˈslændər; *GB* ˈslɑːn-/ *s* calúnia ● *vt* caluniar

slang /slæŋ/ *s* gíria

slant /slænt; *GB* slɑːnt/ **1** *vt, vi*

pender **2** *vt* apresentar de forma tendenciosa ● **s 1** inclinação **2** ~ **(on/to sth)** ângulo (de algo)

slap /slæp/ *vt* (**-pp-**) **1** esbofetear **2** (*ombro*) dar tapas em **3** atirar/deixar cair (com ruído) ● **s 1** (*ombro*) tapa **2** palmada **3** bofetada ● *adv* (*coloq*) em cheio: ~ *in the middle* bem no meio

slash /slæʃ/ *vt* **1** cortar **2** destruir a facadas **3** (*preços, etc.*) achatar ● **s 1** facada **2** corte **3** (*teclado*) barra

slate /sleɪt/ *s* **1** ardósia **2** telha (de ardósia)

slaughter /ˈslɔːtər/ *s* **1** (*animais*) abate **2** massacre ● *vt* **1** abater (*em matadouro*) **2** massacrar **3** (*Esporte*) dar uma surra em

slave /sleɪv/ *s* escravo/a ● *vi* ~ **(away) (at sth)** trabalhar como um escravo (em algo)

slavery /ˈsleɪvəri/ *s* escravidão

slay /sleɪ/ *vt* (*pt* **slew** *pp* **slain**) matar (*violentamente*)

sleazy /ˈsliːzi/ *adj* (**-ier, -iest**) (*coloq*) sórdido

sled /sled/ (*GB* **sledge** /sledʒ/) *s* trenó (*para neve*)

sleek /sliːk/ *adj* (**~er, ~est**) liso e lustroso

sleep /sliːp/ *s* sono: *go to* ~ adormecer/ir dormir ● (*pt, pp* **slept**) **1** *vi* dormir: ~ *through* sth não ser despertado por algo **2** *vt* acomodar, ter camas para ▪ **sleep in** ficar na cama até tarde **sleep on sth** consultar o travesseiro sobre algo **sleep off** dormir para recuperar-se de algo (*bebedeira*) **sleep with sb** dormir com alguém

sleeper /ˈsliːpər/ *s* **1** pessoa adormecida: *be a light* ~ ter sono leve **2** (*nos trilhos do trem*) dormente **3** vagão-leito

sleepless /ˈsliːpləs/ *adj* sem sono

sleepwalker /ˈsliːpwɔːkər/ *s* sonâmbulo/a

sleepy /ˈsliːpi/ *adj* (**-ier, -iest**) sonolento: *be* ~ estar com sono **2** (*lugar*) tranqüilo

sleet /sliːt/ *s* chuva com neve

sleeve /sliːv/ *s* manga (*roupa*) ▶ **(have sth) up your sleeve** (ter algo) escondido **sleeveless** *adj* sem mangas

sleigh /sleɪ/ *s* trenó

slender /ˈslendər/ *adj* (**~er, ~est**) **1** delgado **2** remoto

slept /slept/ *pret, pp de* SLEEP

slew /sluː/ *pret de* SLAY

slice /slaɪs/ s 1 fatia 2 (coloq) pedaço ● 1 vt ~ sth (up) cortar algo em fatias 2 vi ~ through/into sth cortar algo com facilidade

slick /slɪk/ adj (~er, ~est) 1 (apresentação) bem-sucedido 2 (vendedor) astuto ● s (tb oil ~) mancha de petróleo

slide /slaɪd/ s 1 escorregador 2 diapositivo: ~ projector projetor de slides 3 (microscópio) lâmina 4 deslizamento ● (pt, pp slid /slɪd/) 1 vi escorregar 2 vt deslizar

sliding door s porta corrediça

slight /slaɪt/ adj (~er, ~est) 1 quase imperceptível 2 mínimo, ligeiro: without the slightest difficulty sem a menor dificuldade 3 (pessoa) franzino ▶ not in the slightest em absoluto slightly adv ligeiramente: ~ better um pouco melhor

slim /slɪm/ adj (slimmer, slimmest) 1 magro → MAGRO 2 (oportunidade) escasso 3 (esperança) ligeiro ● vt, vi (-mm-) ~ (down) emagrecer

slime /slaɪm/ s 1 lodo 2 baba slimy adj lodoso, viscoso

sling /slɪŋ/ s tipóia ● vt (pt, pp slung) 1 (coloq) lançar (com força) 2 suspender

slink /slɪŋk/ vi (pt, pp slunk) mover-se (furtivamente): ~ away fugir furtivamente

slip /slɪp/ s 1 escorregão 2 lapso 3 (roupa) combinação 4 (papel) tira ▶ give sb the slip (coloq) escapar de alguém ● (-pp-) 1 vt, vi escorregar, deslizar 2 vi ~ from/out of/through sth escapar de/por entre algo 3 vt ~ sth (from/off sth) soltar algo (de algo) 4 vt ~ sth off/on tirar/vestir algo ▶ slip your mind: It slipped my mind. Fugiu-me da cabeça. ■ slip away escapulir slip out 1 dar uma fugida 2 escapulir 3 It just slipped out. Simplesmente me escapou. slip up (coloq) cometer uma gafe

slipper /'slɪpər/ s chinelo

slippery /'slɪpəri/ adj 1 escorregadio 2 inescrupuloso

slit /slɪt/ s 1 fenda 2 (num tecido) rasgão 3 corte 4 rachadura ● vt (-tt-) (pt, pp slit) cortar: ~ sb's throat degolar alguém ◇ ~ sth open abrir algo cortando

slither /'slɪðər/ vi 1 escorregar 2 resvalar

sliver /'slɪvər/ s 1 lasca 2 estilhaço 3 fatia fina

slob /slɒb/ s (coloq) 1 vadio 2 porcalhão

slog /slɒɡ/ vi (-gg-) (coloq) caminhar pesadamente ● slog (away) at sth suar sangue em algo

slogan /'sloʊɡən/ s slogan

slop /slɒp/ (-pp-) 1 vt fazer transbordar 2 vt, vi derramar(-se)

slope /sloʊp/ s 1 ladeira 2 (esqui) pista ● vi formar declive

sloppy /'slɒpi/ adj (-ier, -iest) 1 (trabalho) descuidado 2 desmazelado 3 (coloq) piegas

slot /slɒt/ s 1 ranhura 2 espaço ● (-tt-) 1 vi ~ in encaixar(-se) 2 vt ~ sth in meter algo

slot machine s caça-níqueis

slow /sloʊ/ (~er, ~est) adj 1 lento: make ~ progress avançar lentamente. 2 lerdo: He's a bit ~. Ele demora a entender as coisas. 3 (negócio) fraco 4 (relógio) atrasado ▶ be slow to do sth/in doing sth demorar em fazer algo ■ in slow motion em câmara lenta ● adv devagar ● vt, vi ~ (sth) (up/down) reduzir a velocidade (de algo): ~ up a process atrasar um processo ◇ Production has slowed. O ritmo da produção diminuiu. slowly adv devagar

sludge /slʌdʒ/ s 1 lodo 2 sedimento

slug /slʌɡ/ s lesma sluggish adj 1 lento 2 moroso 3 (Econ) fraco

slum /slʌm/ s 1 (tb ~ area) bairro pobre 2 favela

slump /slʌmp/ vi 1 ~ (down) despencar(-se) 2 (Com) sofrer uma queda ● s depressão (econômica)

slung /slʌŋ/ pret, pp de SLING

slunk /slʌŋk/ pret, pp de SLINK

slur /slɜːr/ vt (-rr-) pronunciar indistintamente ● s estigma

slush /slʌʃ/ s neve meio derretida e suja

sly /slaɪ/ adj (~er, ~est) 1 astuto 2 (olhar) furtivo

smack /smæk/ s palmada ● vt dar uma palmada ● ■ smack of sth cheirar a algo

small /smɔːl/ adj (~er, ~est) 1 pequeno: ~ change trocado ◇ in the ~ hours de madrugada ◇ ~ ads anúncios classificados ◇ make ~ talk bater papo 2 (letra) minúscula ▶ a small fortune um dinheirão it's a small world como o mundo é pequeno ■ the small print o texto em letra miúda (num contrato) NOTA Small costuma ser usado como antônimo de big ou large e pode ser modificado por advérbios:

Our house is smaller than yours.
◇ *I have a fairly ~ income.* **Little**
não costuma se acompanhado
por advérbios e com freqüência
segue outro adjetivo: *He's a hor-*
rid little man. ◇ *What a lovely*
little house!

smallpox /ˈsmɔːlpɒks/ s varíola

small-scale *adj* em pequena
escala

smart /smɑːt/ *adj* (~**er**, ~**est**) 1
esperto, vivo 2 (*esp GB*) ele-
gante • *vi* arder **smarten** *v* (*GB*)
■ **smarten (yourself) up** arrumar-se **smarten sth up** melhorar a aparência de algo

smash /smæʃ/ *vt* 1 despedaçar 2
vi fazer-se em pedaços ■ **smash**
against, into, through, etc. sth
espatifar-se contra algo **smash**
sth up destroçar algo • s 1
estrondo 2 (*tb* **smash-up**) acidente de trânsito 3 (*tb* ~ **hit**)
grande sucesso

smashing /ˈsmæʃɪŋ/ *adj* (*GB*)
estupendo

smear /smɪər/ *vt* 1 besuntar 2
untar 3 ~ **sth with sth** manchar
algo de algo

smell /smel/ s 1 cheiro → ODOR 2
(*tb* **sense of** ~) olfato • (*pt, pp*
smelled ou **smelt** /smelt/ (*GB*)
→ DREAM 1 *vt, vi* ~ **(of sth)**
cheirar (a algo): *What does it*
like? Cheira a quê? NOTA É
muito comum usar-se o verbo
smell com **can** ou **could**: *I can ~*
something burning. ◇ *I could ~*
gas. 2 *vi* farejar **smelly** *adj*
(**-ier, -iest**) (*coloq*) malcheiroso:
It's ~ in here. Cheira mal aqui.

smile /smaɪl/ s sorriso • *vi* sorrir

smirk /smɜːk/ s sorriso falso ou
presumido • *vi* sorrir com afe-
tação

smock /smɒk/ s 1 guarda-pó 2
túnica (*mulher*)

smog /smɒg, smɔːg/ s mistura de
nevoeiro e poluição

smoke /sməʊk/ 1 *vt, vi* fumar 2 *vi*
soltar fumaça 3 *vt* defumar • s 1
fumaça 2 (*coloq*): *have a ~*
fumar um cigarro **smoker** s
fumante **smoking** s fumar
smoky *adj* (**-ier, -iest**) 1 enfumaçado 2 (*sabor*) defumado 3
(*cor*) fumê

smolder (*GB* **smoulder**) /ˈsməʊl-
dər/ *vi* queimar (*sem chama*)

smooth /smuːð/ *adj* (~**er**, ~**est**) 1
liso (*pele, uísque, etc.*) suave 3
(*estrada*) plano 4 (*período, etc.*)
sem problemas 5 (*molho, etc.*)
uniforme 6 (*pej*) (*pessoa*) bajulador • *vt* alisar ■ **smooth sth**
over remover algo (*dificulda-*

des) smoothly *adv*: *go* ~ ir às mil
maravilhas

smother /ˈsmʌðər/ *vt* 1 asfixiar 2
~ **sb/sth with/in sth** cobrir
alguém/algo com algo 3
(*chamas*) abafar

smudge /smʌdʒ/ s mancha • *vt,*
vi sujar(-se)

smug /smʌg/ *adj* (**smugger**,
smuggest) presunçoso

smuggle /ˈsmʌgl/ *vt* contraban-
dear: ~ *sth in* fazer entrar algo
de contrabando **smuggler** s
contrabandista **smuggling** s
contrabando (*ato*)

snack /snæk/ s lanche: ~ *bar*
lanchonete • *vi* lambiscar

snag /snæg/ s obstáculo

snail /sneɪl/ s caracol

snake /sneɪk/ s cobra • *vi* serpentear (*estrada, etc.*)

snap /snæp/ (**-pp-**) 1 *vt, vi* estalar
2 *vt, vi* partir(-se) em dois com
um estalo ■ **snap at sb** falar/
responder a alguém bruscamente • s 1 estalo 2 (*GB* **snap-**
shot /ˈsnæpʃɒt/) (*Fot*) instantâneo • *adj* repentino (*decisão*)

snare /sneər/ s armadilha • *vt*
apanhar em armadilha

snarl /snɑːl/ s rosnado • *vi* rosnar

snatch /snætʃ/ 1 *vt* ~ **(at) sth**
(tentar) agarrar, arrancar algo
2 *vt* roubar com um puxão 3 *vt*
raptar 4 *vt, vi* ~ **(at) sth** (*oportu-*
nidade) aproveitar algo • s 1
(*conversa, etc.*) fragmento 2
roubo

sneak /sniːk/ 1 *vi* ~ **in, out, away,**
etc. entrar, sair, ir embora às
escondidas 2 *vt*: ~ *a look at sb/*
sth dar uma espiada em
alguém/algo • s (*coloq*) dedo-
duro

sneakers /ˈsniːkərz/ s [*pl*]
(*calçado*) tênis

sneer /snɪər/ s 1 expressão de
desdém 2 comentário desdenhoso • *vi* ~ **(at sb/sth)** sorrir
desdenhosamente (de alguém/
algo)

sneeze /sniːz/ s espirro • *vi*
espirrar

snicker /ˈsnɪkər/ (*GB* **snigger**)
/ˈsnɪgə(r)/ s riso contido • *vi* ~ **(at**
sb/sth) rir (com sarcasmo) (de
alguém/algo)

sniff /snɪf/ 1 *vi* fungar 2 *vi* farejar
3 *vt* cheirar 4 *vt* inalar 5 *vi* desdenhar • s fungada

snip /snɪp/ *vt* (**-pp-**) cortar (com
tesoura)

sniper /ˈsnaɪpər/ s franco-
atirador/a

snob /snɑb/ s esnobe **snobbery** s esnobismo **snobbish** adj esnobe

snoop /snuːp/ vi (coloq) ~ (about/around) bisbilhotar • s: have a ~ about/around sth bisbilhotar algo

snore /snɔːr/ vi roncar

snorkel /ˈsnɔːrkl/ s tubo para respirar

snort /snɔːrt/ vi bufar • s bufo

snout /snaut/ s focinho

snow /snoʊ/ s neve • vi nevar ▶ **snowed in/up** isolado pela neve **snowed under (with sth)**: I was snowed under with work. Eu estava sobrecarregado de trabalho.

snowball /ˈsnoʊbɔːl/ s bola de neve • vi aumentar (vertiginosamente)

snowdrift /ˈsnoʊdrɪft/ s monte de neve (acumulado pelo vento)

snowdrop /ˈsnoʊdrɑp/ s galanto (flor)

snowfall /ˈsnoʊfɔːl/ s nevada

snowflake /ˈsnoʊfleɪk/ s floco de neve

snowman /ˈsnoʊmæn/ s (pl -men) boneco de neve

snowy /ˈsnoʊi/ adj (-ier, -iest) 1 coberto de neve 2 de/com neve

snub /snʌb/ vt (-bb-) ignorar, desdenhar

snug /snʌg/ adj (snugger, snuggest) aconchegante

snuggle /ˈsnʌgl/ vi ~ (up to sb); ~ (down) aconchegar-se (a alguém)

so /soʊ/ adv, conj 1 tão: I'm so sorry! Sinto muito/tanto! 2 assim: The table is about so big. A mesa é mais ou menos deste tamanho. ◊ If so,... Se for esse o caso,... 3 I think/hope so. Acho/espero que sim. 4 (concordância): "I'm hungry." "So am I." —Estou com fome. —Eu também. NOTA Neste caso o pronome ou o substantivo vão após o verbo. 5 (surpresa): "Philip's gone home.""So he has." —O Philip foi para casa. —Ele foi mesmo. 6 [uso enfático]: He's as clever as his brother, maybe more so. Ele é tão esperto quanto o irmão, talvez até mais. ◊ She has complained, and rightly so. Ela reclamou, e com razão. 7 então ▶ and so on (and so forth) etcetera, etcetera is that so? não me diga! so?; so what? (coloq) e daí? so as to do sth para fazer algo so much/many tanto(s) so that para que

soak /soʊk/ 1 vt encharcar, colocar de molho: get soaked through encharcar-se 2 vi estar de molho ■ **soak into sth** ser absorvido por algo **soak through sth** passar por algo (líquido) **soak sth up** 1 absorver algo 2 embeber-se de algo **soaked** adj encharcado

soap /soʊp/ s [U] 1 sabão 2 sabonete

soap opera (tb soap) s novela (televisão)

soapy /ˈsoʊpi/ adj (-ier, -iest) com/como sabão

soar /sɔːr/ vi 1 (avião) subir 2 (preços) disparar 3 (ave) elevar-se

sob /sɑb/ vi (-bb-) (chorar) soluçar • s soluço sobbing s (choro) soluços

sober /ˈsoʊbər/ adj 1 sóbrio 2 sério

so-called adj chamado

soccer /ˈsɑkər/ s futebol → FUTEBOL

sociable /ˈsoʊʃəbl/ adj sociável

social /ˈsoʊʃl/ adj social

socialism /ˈsoʊʃəlɪzəm/ s socialismo **socialist** s socialista

socialize /ˈsoʊʃəlaɪz/ vi relacionar-se socialmente: He doesn't ~ much. Ele não sai muito.

social security s previdência social

social services s serviços de assistência social

social work s assistência social **social worker** s assistente social

society /səˈsaɪəti/ s (pl -ies) 1 sociedade 2 associação

sociologist /ˌsoʊsiˈɑlədʒɪst/ s sociólogo • **a sociology** s sociologia **sociological** /ˌsoʊsiəˈlɑdʒɪkl/ adj sociológico

sock /sɑk/ s meia (curta) → PAIR

socket /ˈsɑkɪt/ s 1 (olho) cavidade 2 tomada (elétrica) 3 (tb light ~) soquete de lâmpada

soda /ˈsoʊdə/ s 1 (Quím) soda 2 (tb ~ pop) (USA) refrigerante

sodden /ˈsɑdn/ adj encharcado

sodium /ˈsoʊdiəm/ s sódio

sofa /ˈsoʊfə/ s sofá

soft /sɔːft; GB sɒft/ adj (~er, ~est) 1 macio, mole: ~ option caminho mais fácil 2 suave ▶ **have a soft spot for sb/sth** (coloq) ter uma queda por alguém/algo **softly** adv suavemente

soft drink s bebida não alcoólica

soften /ˈsɔːfn; GB ˈsɒfn/ vt, vi 1 abrandar(-se), amolecer 2 suavizar(-se) **softener** s amaciante

soft-spoken adj de voz suave

software /'sɔːftweə; GB 'sɒft-/ s software

soggy /'sɑgi, 'sɔːgi/ adj (-ier, -iest) 1 encharcado 2 empapado

soil /sɔɪl/ s solo, terra ● vt (fml) 1 sujar 2 (reputação) manchar

solace /'sɑləs/ s (fml) consolo

solar /'soʊlə/ adj solar

sold /soʊld/ pret, pp de SELL

soldier /'soʊldʒər/ s soldado

sole /soʊl/ s 1 (do pé) planta 2 sola ● adj (antes de substantivo) 1 único 2 exclusivo

solemn /'sɑləm/ adj 1 sério 2 solene **solemnity** /sə'lemnəti/ s solenidade

solicitor /sə'lɪsɪtər/ s (GB) 1 advogado/a 2 procurador/a → ADVOGADO

solid /'sɑlɪd/ adj 1 sólido 2 compacto 3 contínuo: I slept for ten hours ~. Dormi por dez horas seguidas. ● s 1 (solids) alimentos sólidos 2 (Geom) sólido **solidly** adv 1 solidamente 2 sem parar

solidarity /ˌsɑlɪ'dærəti/ s solidariedade

solidify /sə'lɪdɪfaɪ/ vi (pt, pp -ied) solidificar(-se)

solidity /sə'lɪdəti/ s solidez

solitary /'sɑlətɛri; GB -tri/ adj 1 solitário: ~ confinement (prisão em) solitária 2 (lugar) afastado 3 (antes de substantivo) único

solitude /'sɑlɪtuːd; GB -tjuːd/ s solidão

solo /'soʊloʊ/ s (pl ~s) (Mús) solo ● adj, adv desacompanhado **soloist** s solista

soluble /'sɑljəbl/ adj solúvel

solution /sə'luːʃn/ s solução

solve /sɑlv/ vt resolver

solvent /'sɑlvənt/ s solvente

somber (GB **sombre**) /'sɑmbər/ adj 1 sombrio 2 (cor) escuro 3 melancólico

some /səm/ adj, pron 1 um pouco (de) 2 uns, alguns: Do you want ~ potato chips? Você quer batatas fritas? NOTA Some ou any? Ambos são usados com substantivos incontáveis ou no plural e, embora muitas vezes não sejam traduzidos, não podem ser omitidos em inglês. Geralmente, usa-se some nas orações afirmativas e any nas negativas e interrogativas: I've got ~ money. ◇ Do you have any children? ◇ I don't want any candy. Mas pode-se usar some quando em orações interrogativas se espera uma resposta afirmativa, por exemplo, quando se pede ou se oferece algo: Would you like ~ coffee? ◇ Can I have ~ bread, please? Quando any é usado em orações afirmativas, significa "qualquer": Any parent would have worried. Ver exemplos em ANY

somebody /'sʌmbədi/ (tb **someone** /'sʌmwʌn/) pron alguém: ~ else outra pessoa NOTA A diferença entre somebody e anybody, ou entre someone e anyone, é a mesma que há entre some e any. → SOME

somehow /'sʌmhaʊ/ adv 1 de alguma maneira 2 por alguma razão

someplace /'sʌmpleɪs/ Ver SOMEWHERE

somersault /'sʌmərsɔːlt/ s cambalhota: a forward/backward ~ uma pirueta para frente/trás ● vi (carro) capotar

something /'sʌmθɪŋ/ pron algo: ~ else (alguma) outra coisa NOTA A diferença entre something e anything é a mesma que existe entre some e any. → SOME

sometime /'sʌmtaɪm/ adv 1 (alg)um dia: ~ or other um dia destes 2 em algum momento

sometimes /'sʌmtaɪmz/ adv às vezes → ALWAYS

someway /'sʌmweɪ/ Ver SOMEHOW

somewhat /'sʌmwɑt/ adv [com adj ou adv] 1 algo, um tanto 2 bastante: We missed the bus, which was ~ unfortunate. Perdemos o ônibus, o que foi certa falta de sorte.

somewhere /'sʌmweər/ adv em algum lugar ● pron: have ~ to go ter para onde ir NOTA A diferença entre somewhere e anywhere é a mesma que há entre some e any. → SOME

son /sʌn/ s filho

song /sɔːŋ; GB sɒŋ/ s 1 canção 2 canto

son-in-law s (pl **sons-in-law**) genro

soon /suːn/ adv (~er, ~est) logo, dentro em pouco ▶ as soon as assim que: as ~ as possible o mais rápido possível (just) as soon do sth (as do sth): I'd (just) as ~ stay at home as go out. Para mim tanto faz ficar em casa ou sair. sooner or later (mais) cedo ou (mais) tarde the sooner the better quanto antes melhor

soot /sʊt/ s fuligem

soothe /suːð/ vt 1 acalmar 2 (dor,

etc.) aliviar

sophisticated /sə'fıstıkeıtıd/ adj
sofisticado **sophistication** s
sofisticação

sophomore /'sɒfməɔr/ s (USA)
estudante de segundo ano de
faculdade

soppy /'sɒpi/ (GB) = SAPPY

sordid /'sɔːrdıd/ adj sórdido

sore /sɔːr/ s machucado ● adj
dolorido: a ~ throat dor de garganta ◊ I have ~ eyes. Estou com
dor nos olhos. ▸ **a sore point** um
assunto delicado **sorely** adv:
She will be ~ missed. Ela fará
bastante falta. ◊ I was ~ tempt-
ed to do it. Eu fiquei bastante
tentado a fazê-lo.

sorrow /'sɒrəʊ/ s pesar

sorry /'sɒri/ interj 1 desculpe
(-me) → EXCUSE 2 (sorry?)
como? ● adj 1 I'm ~ I'm late.
Desculpe-me pelo atraso. ◊ say
you're ~ desculpar-se ◊ I'm so
~! Sinto muito! 2 arrependido! 3 (-ier, -iest) (estado)
lamentável

sort /sɔːrt/ s 1 tipo: It's a ~ of
autobiography. É uma espécie
de autobiografia. 2 (antiq,
coloq) pessoa ▸ **sort of** (coloq): I
feel ~ of uneasy. Eu me sinto um
pouco inquieto. ● vt organizar
▪ **sort sth out** separar algo 2
resolver algo **sort through sth**
classificar, organizar algo

so-so adj, adv (coloq) mais ou
menos

sought /sɔːt/ pret, pp de SEEK

sought after adj cobiçado

soul /səʊl/ s alma: There wasn't a
~ to be seen. Não se via vivalma.
◊ Poor ~! (Pobre) coitado!

sound /saʊnd/ s 1 som: ~ waves
ondas sonoras 2 ruído: without
a ~ sem fazer barulho 3 (the
sound) o volume ● 1 vi soar 2 vt
(instrumento) tocar 3 vt
(alarme) dar 4 vt pronunciar 5
vi parecer 6 vt (mar) sondar
▪ **sound sb out (about/on sth)**
sondar alguém (a respeito de
algo) ● adj (-er, -est) 1 são 2
(estrutura) sólido 3 (crença)
firme 4 (conselho) bom ▸ **of
sound mind** em pleno uso de
suas faculdades mentais ● adv
▸ **sound asleep** dormindo profundamente

soundproof /'saʊndpruːf/ adj à
prova de som ● vt tornar algo à
prova de som

soundtrack /'saʊndtræk/ s
trilha sonora

soup /suːp/ s sopa, caldo

sour /'saʊər/ adj 1 acre 2 (leite)
azedo: go/turn ~ azedar

source /sɔːrs/ s 1 (informação)
fonte 2 (rio) nascente

south /saʊθ/ s (tb the south, the
South) (abrev S.) sul: south-
bound em direção ao sul ● adj
(do) sul ● adv para o sul

south-east s (abrev SE) sudeste
● adj (do) sudeste ● adv para o
sudeste **south-eastern** adj (do)
sudeste

southern (tb **Southern**) /'sʌðərn/
adj do sul **southerner** s sulista

southward(s) /'saʊθwərdz/ adv
em direção ao sul

south-west s (abrev SW) sudoeste ● adj (do) sudoeste ● adv
para o sudoeste **south-western**
adj (do) sudoeste

souvenir /ˌsuːvəˈnɪr; GB ˌsuːvə-
ˈnɪə(r)/ s lembrança (objeto)

sovereign /'sɒvərın/ adj, s sobe-
rano/a **sovereignty** s soberania

sow[1] /saʊ/ s (Zool) porca
→ PORCO

sow[2] /səʊ/ vt (pt sowed pp sown
/səʊn/ ou sowed) semear

soy /sɔɪ/ (GB **soya** /sɔɪə/) s soja

spa /spɑː/ s estância hidro-
mineral

space /speıs/ s 1 [U] lugar 2 (tb
Aeronáut) espaço: a ~ flight um
vôo espacial ◊ stare into ~ ficar
olhando o vazio 3 (período)
intervalo ● vt ~ **sth (out)** espaçar
algo

spacecraft /'speıskræft; GB
-krɑːft/ s (pl spacecraft) (tb
spaceship /'speısʃıp/) nave
espacial

spacious /'speıʃəs/ adj espaçoso

spade /speıd/ s 1 pá 2 (spades)
(naipe) espadas → BARALHO

spaghetti /spə'geti/ s [U]
espaguete

span /spæn/ s 1 (ponte) vão 2
(tempo) período, duração: time
~ espaço de tempo ◊ life ~
expectativa de vida ● vt (-nn-) 1
(ponte) cruzar 2 abranger

spank /spæŋk/ vt dar uma surra/
palmadas em

spanner /'spænər/ (GB) s chave
inglesa

spare /speər/ adj 1 disponível,
de sobra: There are no ~ seats.
Não há mais lugares. ◊ the ~
room o quarto de hóspedes 2 de
reposição, de reserva 3 (tempo)
livre ● s peça de reposição,
estepe ● vt 1 (tempo, dinheiro,
etc.) dispensar, oferecer 2
poupar: No expense was spared.
Não se pouparam gastos. 3 eco-

nomizar ►**to spare** de sobra: *with two minutes to ~* faltando dois minutos **sparing** *adj* ~ **with sth** parco em algo; econômico com algo

spark /spɑːk/ *s* faísca ■ **spark sth (off)** provocar algo

sparkle /ˈspɑːkl/ *vi* cintilar ● *s* centelha **sparkling** *adj* **1** (*tb coloq* **sparkly**) brilhante **2** (*vinho*) espumante **3** (*água*) com gás **4** (*conversa*) animado

sparrow /ˈspærəʊ/ *s* pardal

sparse /spɑːs/ *adj* **1** escasso **2** (*população*) disperso **3** (*cabelo*) ralo

spartan /ˈspɑːtn/ *adj* espartano

spasm /ˈspæzəm/ *s* **1** espasmo **2** (*tosse, raiva, etc.*) acesso

spat /spæt/ *pret, pp* de SPIT

spate /speɪt/ *s* (*fig*) avalanche

spatial /ˈspeɪʃl/ *adj* (*fml*): ~ *awareness* noção de espaço

spatter /ˈspætər/ *vt* borrifar

speak /spiːk/ (*pt* **spoke** *pp* **spoken**) **1** *vt, vi* ~ **(to sb)** falar (com alguém); ~ **for sb** falar em favor de alguém ◊ ~ *the truth* dizer a verdade → FALAR **2** *vi* fazer um discurso → **generally, etc. speaking** em termos gerais **so to speak** por assim dizer **speak for itself**: *The statistics ~ for themselves.* As estatísticas falam por si mesmas. **speak your mind** falar sem rodeios ■ **speak up** falar mais alto

speaker /ˈspiːkər/ *s* **1** falante **2** orador/a, conferencista **3** alto-falante

spear /spɪər/ *s* **1** lança **2** (*pesca*) arpão

special /ˈspeʃl/ *adj* **1** especial **2** particular **3** (*reunião, etc.*) extraordinário ● *s* **1** (*edição, etc.*) especial **2** (*coloq*) oferta especial **specialist** *s* especialista

specialize /ˈspeʃəlaɪz/ *vi* especializar-se **specialization** *s* especialização **specialized** *adj* especializado

specially /ˈspeʃli/ *adv* **1** especialmente NOTA Ainda que tenham significados semelhantes, **specially** e **especially** são usados de maneiras diferentes. **Specially** usa-se basicamente com particípios e **especially** como conector entre frases: *~ designed for schools* ◊ *He likes dogs, especially poodles.* **2** (*tb* **especially**) particularmente, sobretudo

specialty /ˈspeʃəlti/ (*GB* **speciality** /ˌspeʃiˈæləti/) *s* (*pl* **-ies**) especialidade

species /ˈspiːʃiːz/ *s* (*pl* **species**) espécie

specific /spəˈsɪfɪk/ *adj* específico, preciso **specifically** *adv* especificamente, concretamente

specification /ˌspesɪfɪˈkeɪʃn/ *s* especificação

specify /ˈspesɪfaɪ/ *vt* (*pt, pp* **-ied**) especificar, precisar

specimen /ˈspesɪmən/ *s* espécime, amostra

speck /spek/ *s* **1** (*sujeira*) mancha **2** (*pó*) partícula **3** *a ~ on the horizon* um ponto no horizonte

spectacle /ˈspektəkl/ *s* espetáculo

spectacles /ˈspektəklz/ *s* (*abrev* **specs**) (*fml*) óculos NOTA A palavra mais comum é **glasses**. → PAIR

spectacular /spekˈtækjələr/ *adj* espetacular

spectator /ˈspekteɪtər; *GB* spek-ˈteɪtə(r)/ *s* espectador/a

specter (*GB* **spectre**) /ˈspektər/ *s* (*fml*) espectro: *the ~ of another war* a ameaça de uma nova guerra

spectrum /ˈspektrəm/ *s* (*pl* **-tra** /-trə/) **1** espectro (*cores*) **2** gama

speculate /ˈspekjuleɪt/ *vi* especular **speculation** *s* especulação

speculative /ˈspekjələtɪv/ *adj* especulativo

speculator /ˈspekjuleɪtər/ *s* especulador/a

speech /spiːtʃ/ *s* **1** (*tb Teat*) fala: *freedom of ~* liberdade de expressão ◊ ~ *therapy* fonoaudiologia **2** discurso

speechless /ˈspiːtʃləs/ *adj* sem fala, mudo

speed /spiːd/ *s* rapidez: *at ~* a toda velocidade ● *vt, vi* (*pt, pp* **speeded**) acelerar **2** *vi* (*pt, pp* **sped** /sped/) ir a toda velocidade: *I was fined for speeding.* Eu fui multado por excesso de velocidade. ■ **speed (sth) up** acelerar (algo)

speedometer /spiːˈdɒmɪtər/ *s* velocímetro

speedy /ˈspiːdi/ *adj* (**-ier, -iest**) rápido, pronto: *a ~ recovery* um pronto restabelecimento **speedily** *adv* rapidamente

spell /spel/ *s* **1** feitiço **2** período, acesso **3** ~ (*at/on sth*) turno (em algo) ● (*pt, pp* **spelled** *ou* **spelt** /spelt/ (*GB*)) → DREAM **1** *vt, vi* soletrar, escrever **2** *vt* resultar em ■ **spell sth out** explicar algo claramente

spelling /ˈspelɪŋ/ *s* ortografia

spend /spend/ vt (pt, pp **spent** /spent/) **1** gastar **2** (tempo livre) passar ▸ **~ sth on sth** dedicar algo a algo **spending** s gasto

sperm /spɜːm/ s (pl **sperm**) **1** espermatozóide **2** esperma

sphere /sfɪə(r)/ s esfera

sphinx /sfɪŋks/ (tb **the Sphinx**) s esfinge

spice /spaɪs/ s **1** tempero **2** interesse: add ~ to a situation tornar uma situação interessante ● vt temperar **spicy** adj (**-ier, -iest**) picante

spider /ˈspaɪdə(r)/ s aranha

spike /spaɪk/ s **1** ponta (ferro, etc.) **2** cravo (calçado esportivo) **spiky** adj (**-ier, -iest**) cheio de pontas, pontiagudo

spill /spɪl/ vt, vi (pt, pp **spilled** ou **spilt** /spɪlt/ (GB)) → DREAM derramar ■ **spill over** transbordar, vazar ● s **1** (tb **spillage**) **1** vazamento **2** o que foi derramado

spin /spɪn/ (**-nn-**) (pt, pp **spun**) **1** vt, vi ~ (**sth**) (**around**) girar (algo); dar voltas (em algo) **2** vt, vi centrifugar **3** vt fiar ■ **spin sth out** prolongar algo ● s **1** giro **2** (coloq) volta (passeio em carro/moto)

spinach /ˈspɪnɪtʃ; GB -ɪdʒ/ s [U] espinafre

spine /spaɪn/ s **1** (Anat) espinha **2** (Bot, Zool) espinho **3** (livro) lombada **spinal** adj da espinha: ~ column columna vertebral

spinster /ˈspɪnstə(r)/ s solteirona

spiral /ˈspaɪrəl/ s espiral ● adj (em) espiral

spire /ˈspaɪə(r)/ s (Arquit) agulha

spirit /ˈspɪrɪt/ s **1** espírito, alma **2** fantasma **3** coragem, ânimo **4** atitude **5** (**spirits**) (bebida) destilados **6** (**spirits**) [pl] estado de ânimo: in high spirits de muito bom humor **spirited** adj animado, vigoroso

spiritual /ˈspɪrɪtʃuəl/ adj espiritual

spit /spɪt/ (**-tt-**) (pt, pp **spat** /spæt/ ou esp USA **spit**) **1** vt, vi cuspir **2** vt (insulto, etc.) lançar **3** vi (fogo, etc.) crepitar ■ **spit sth out** colocar algo para fora ● s **1** saliva **2** ponta (de terra) **3** (metal) espeto

spite /spaɪt/ s despeito ▸ **in spite of** apesar de ● vt incomodar **spiteful** adj despeitado

splash /splæʃ/ s **1** chape **2** salpico **3** (cor) mancha ▸ **make a splash** (coloq) causar sensação ● **1** vi chapinhar **2** vt borrifar ■ **splash out (on sth)** (GB, coloq) queimar dinheiro (em algo),

dar-se ao luxo de comprar (algo)

splatter /ˈsplætə(r)/ vt borrifar

splendid /ˈsplendɪd/ adj esplêndido

splendor (GB **-our**) /ˈsplendə(r)/ s esplendor

splint /splɪnt/ s tala (para imobilizar membro)

splinter /ˈsplɪntə(r)/ s farpa ● vt, vi **1** estilhaçar(-se) **2** dividir(-se)

split /splɪt/ (**-tt-**) (pt, pp **split**) **1** vt, vi partir(-se) **2** vt, vi dividir(-se) **3** vt, vi repartir(-se) **4** vt fender(-se) ■ **split up (with sb)** separar-se (de alguém) ● s **1** divisão, ruptura **2** fenda ● adj partido

splutter /ˈsplʌtə(r)/ **1** vt, vi gaguejar, balbuciar **2** vi (fogo, etc.) crepitar ● s crepitar

spoil /spɔɪl/ (pt, pp **spoiled** ou **spoilt** (GB)) → DREAM **1** vt, vi estragar **2** vt (criança) mimar

spoils /spɔɪlz/ s [pl] espólio (de roubo, guerra)

spoilt /spɔɪlt/ pret, pp de SPOIL ● adj mimado

spoke /spəʊk/ pret de SPEAK ● s raio (roda)

spoken /ˈspəʊkən/ pp de SPEAK

spokesperson /ˈspəʊkspɜːrsn/ s (pl **~s** ou **-people**) porta-voz NOTA Esta é a forma preferida atualmente, embora também se usem **spokesman** e **spokeswoman**.

sponge /spʌndʒ/ s **1** esponja **2** (tb **~ cake**) pão-de-ló ■ **sponge on/off sb** (coloq) viver à custa de alguém

sponsor /ˈspɒnsə(r)/ s patrocinador/a ● vt patrocinar **sponsorship** s patrocínio

spontaneous /spɒnˈteɪniəs/ adj espontâneo **spontaneity** /ˌspɒntəˈneɪti/ s espontaneidade

spooky /ˈspuːki/ adj (**-ier, -iest**) (coloq) **1** de aspecto assustador **2** misterioso

spoon /spuːn/ s **1** colher **2** (tb **spoonful**) colherada ● vt: ~ the mixture out tirar a mistura com uma colher

sporadic /spəˈrædɪk/ adj esporádico

sport /spɔːrt/ s **1** esporte: sports center/facilities instalações esportivas **2** (coloq) cara legal: a good/bad ~ um bom/mau perdedor **sporting** adj esportivo

sports car s carro esporte

sportsman /ˈspɔːrtsmən/ s (fem **sportswoman** (pl **-men, -women**) esportista **sportsman-**

like *adj* esportivo (*justo*) sportsmanship *s* espírito esportivo

spot /spɒt/ *vt* (**-tt-**) encontrar, notar ● *s* **1** (*GB*) (*estampa*) bolinha **2** (*animais, etc.*) mancha **3** (*na pele*) espinha **4** lugar **5** ~ **of sth** (*GB, coloq*): *Would you like a* ~ *of lunch?* Quer comer uma coisinha? ◇ *have a* ~ *of bother* passar por um momento difícil

spotless /ˈspɒtləs/ *adj* imaculado

spotlight /ˈspɒtlaɪt/ (*tb* **spot**) *s* holofote ▸ **be in the** ~ ser o centro das atenções

spotted /ˈspɒtɪd/ *adj* **1** (*animal*) com manchas **2** (*tecido*) de bolinhas

spotty /ˈspɒti/ *adj* (*GB*) (**-ier**, **-iest**) **1** cheio de espinhas **2** (*tecido*) de bolinhas

spouse /spaʊs/ *s* (*Jur*) cônjuge

spout /spaʊt/ *s* **1** (*bule, etc.*) bico **2** calha ● *vt, vi* ~ (**sth**)(**out/up**) (fazer) jorrar (algo) **2** *vt, vi* (*coloq, freq pej*) declamar, dissertar

sprain /spreɪn/ *vt*: ~ *your ankle* torcer o tornozelo ● *s* entorse

sprang /spræŋ/ *pret de* SPRING

sprawl /sprɔːl/ *vi* **1** ~ (**out**) (**across/in/on sth**) escarrapachar-se (por/em algo) **2** (*cidade, etc.*) estender-se (*desordenadamente*)

spray /spreɪ/ *s* **1** borrifo **2** (*para cabelo, etc.*) spray ● *vt, vi* borrifar

spread /spred/ (*pt, pp* **spread**) **1** *vt* ~ **sth** (**out**) estender algo (em/sobre/por algo) **2** *vt* cobrir **3** *vt, vi* untar: *The cheese spreads well.* O queijo espalha bem. **4** *vt, vi* estender(-se), espalhar(-se) **5** *vt, vi* (*notícia*) espalhar(-se) **6** *vt* distribuir ● *s* **1** extensão **2** (*asas*) envergadura **3** propagação **4** pasta, patê, geléia para passar no pão

spree /spriː/ *s* farra: *go on a shopping/spending* ~ sair gastando dinheiro

spring /sprɪŋ/ *s* **1** (*tb* springtime /ˈsprɪŋtaɪm/) primavera: ~ *clean(ing)* faxina geral **2** salto **3** nascente **4** mola **5** elasticidade ● *vi* (*pt* **sprang** *pp* **sprung**) **1** saltar: ~ *into action* pôr-se em ação **2** brotar ▪ **spring back** pular/voltar para trás **spring from sth** originar-se de algo **spring sth on sb** (*coloq*) pegar alguém de surpresa com algo

springboard /ˈsprɪŋbɔːd/ *s* trampolim

sprinkle /ˈsprɪŋkl/ *vt* **1** borrifar **2** salpicar **sprinkling** *s* um pouquinho, uns poucos/umas poucas

sprint /sprɪnt/ *vi* **1** correr a toda (*pequena distância*) **2** (*Esporte*) disparar ● *s* corrida de velocidade

sprout /spraʊt/ **1** *vi* ~ (**out/up**) brotar **2** *vt* lançar (*brotos, etc.*) ● *s* **1** broto **2** couve-de-bruxelas

sprung /sprʌŋ/ *pp de* SPRING

spun /spʌn/ *pret, pp de* SPIN

spur /spɜː(r)/ *s* **1** espora **2** a ~ (**to sth**) um estímulo (para algo) ▸ **on the spur of the moment** impulsivamente ● *vt* (**-rr-**) ~ **sb/sth** (**on**) incitar alguém; estimular algo

spurn /spɜːn/ *vt* (*fml*) desprezar

spurt /spɜːt/ *vi* **1** ~ (**out**) jorrar (*carro*) arrancar ● *s* **1** jorro **2** arrancada

spy /spaɪ/ *s* (*pl* **spies**) espião: ~ *thriller* história de espionagem ● *vi* (*pt, pp* **spied**) **1** espionar **2** ~ (**on sb/sth**) espionar (alguém/algo)

squabble /ˈskwɒbl/ *vi* ~ (**about/over sth**) discutir (por algo) ● *s* bate-boca

squad /skwɒd/ *s* **1** (*Mil*) esquadrão **2** (*polícia*) brigada **3** (*Esporte*) seleção

squadron /ˈskwɒdrən/ *s* esquadrão

squalid /ˈskwɒlɪd/ *adj* sórdido

squalor /ˈskwɒlə(r)/ *s* miséria

squander /ˈskwɒndə(r)/ *vt* desperdiçar

square /skweə(r)/ *adj* quadrado ▸ **a square meal** uma refeição substancial (**all**) **square** empatado, quite ● *s* **1** (*Mat*) quadrado **2** esquadro **3** (*tabuleiro*) casa **4** (*abrev* **Sq.**) praça ▸ **back to square one** de volta ao ponto de partida ▪ **square up** (**with sb**) acertar (uma dívida) (com alguém)

squarely /ˈskweəli/ *adv* honestamente

square root *s* raiz quadrada

squash /skwɒʃ/ *vt* esmagar ● *s* **1** *What a* ~! Que aperto! **2** (*GB*) refresco (de frutas) **3** (*tb fml* ~ **rackets**) (*Esporte*) squash **4** (*Bot*) abóbora

squat /skwɒt/ *vi* (**-tt-**) ~ (**down**) **1** ficar de cócoras **2** agachar-se ● *adj* (**-tter**, **-ttest**) atarracado **squatter** *s* invasor/a de propriedade

squawk /skwɔːk/ *vi* guinchar ● *s*

guincho

squeak /skwi:k/ s 1 guincho 2 (*sapatos, etc.*) rangido ▸ *vt, vi* 1 guinchar 2 (*sapato*) ranger

squeaky *adj* (**-ier, -iest**) 1 (*voz*) esganiçado 2 (*sapatos*) rangente

squeal /skwi:l/ s grito, guincho ▸ *vt, vi* gritar, guinchar

squeamish /ˈskwi:mɪʃ/ *adj* melindroso

squeeze /skwi:z/ 1 *vt* apertar 2 *vt* espremer 3 *vt* torcer 4 *vt, vi* ~ (**sb/sth**) **into, past, through, etc.** (**sth**): Can you ~ *past/by?* Você consegue passar? ◊ *Can you* ~ *anything else into that case?* Você consegue colocar mais alguma coisa naquela maleta? ● *s* apertão: *a ~ of lemon* um pouquinho de limão 2 aperto 3 (*coloq*) aperto financeiro

squint /skwɪnt/ *vi* 1 ~ (**at/through sth**) olhar (*algo/através de algo*) com olhos semicerrados 2 ser estrábico ● *s* estrabismo

squirm /skwɜ:rm/ *vi* 1 contorcer-se 2 envergonhar-se

squirrel /ˈskwɜ:rəl/; *GB* /ˈskwɪrəl/ *s* esquilo

squirt /skwɜ:rt/ *vt, vi* ~ **sb/sth** (**with sth**) esguichar (*algo*) em alguém/algo: ~ *soda water into a glass* esguichar soda em um copo ● *s* esguicho

stab /stæb/ *vt* (**-bb-**) 1 apunhalar 2 cravar ● *s* facada ▸ **have a stab at** (**doing**) **sth** (*coloq*) tentar (fazer) algo **stabbing** *adj* pungente **stabbing** *s* esfaqueamento

stability /stəˈbɪləti/ *s* estabilidade

stabilize /ˈsteɪbəlaɪz/ *vt, vi* estabilizar(-se)

stable /ˈsteɪbl/ *adj* 1 estável 2 equilibrado ● *s* 1 cavalariça 2 haras

stack /stæk/ *s* 1 pilha (*livros, lenha, etc.*) 2 ~ **of sth** [*ger pl*] (*coloq*) monte de algo ▸ *vt* ~ **sth** (**up**) empilhar algo

stadium /ˈsteɪdiəm/ *s* (*pl* ~**s** ou **stadia** /-diə/) estádio

staff /stæf; *GB* stɑ:f/ *s* pessoal, empregados: *teaching* ~ corpo docente ▸ *vt* prover com pessoal: *The center is staffed by volunteers.* O centro é servido por voluntários.

stag /stæg/ *s* cervo → VEADO ● *adj*: ~ *night/party* despedida de solteiro

stage /steɪdʒ/ *s* 1 palco 2 (**the stage**) o teatro (*profissão*): *go*

on the ~ tornar-se ator 3 etapa: *by* ~ passo a passo ◊ *at this* ~ a esta altura ● *vt* 1 (*peça*) apresentar uma peça 2 (*evento*) organizar

stagger /ˈstægər/ 1 *vi*: *He staggered back home.* Ele voltou cambaleando para casa. ◊ *He staggered to his feet.* Ele se pôs em pé cambaleante. 2 *vt* deixar atônito 3 *vt* (*férias, etc.*) escalonar ● *s* cambaleio **staggering** *adj* assombroso

stagnant /ˈstægnənt/ *adj* estagnado

stagnate /ˈstægneɪt/; *GB* stægˈneɪt/ *vi* estagnar **stagnation** /stægˈneɪʃn/ *s* estagnação

stain /steɪn/ *s* 1 mancha 2 tinta (*para madeira*) ▸ 1 *vt, vi* manchar(-se) 2 *vt* tingir: *stained glass* vitral **stainless** *adj*: ~ *steel* aço inoxidável

stair /steər/ *s* 1 (**stairs**) [*pl*] escada 2 degrau

staircase /ˈsteərkeɪs/ (*tb* **stairway** /ˈsteərweɪ/) *s* escadaria

stake /steɪk/ *s* 1 estaca 2 (**the stake**) a fogueira 3 [*ger pl*] aposta 4 (*investimento*) participação ▸ **at stake** em jogo ▸ *vt* 1 apoiar com uma estaca 2 apostar ▸ **stake** (**out**) **a/your claim** (**to sb/sth**) mostrar interesse (por alguém/algo)

stale /steɪl/ *adj* 1 (*pão*) velho 2 (*alimento*) passado 3 (*ar*) viciado 4 (*idéias*) gasto

stalemate /ˈsteɪlmeɪt/ *s* 1 (*xadrez*) empate 2 impasse

stalk /stɔ:k/ *s* 1 haste 2 (*fruta*) cabo ● *vt* 1 (*caça*) aproximar-se (*sorrateiramente*) a 2 *vi* ~ (**along**) andar altivamente

stall /stɔ:l/ *s* 1 (*mercado, etc.*) banca 2 (*estábulo*) baia 3 (**stalls**) [*pl*] (*GB*) (*teatro*) platéia ● 1 *vt, vi* (*carro, etc.*) morrer (*por problema*) 2 *vi* ser evasivo

stallion /ˈstæliən/ *s* garanhão

stalwart /ˈstɔ:lwərt/ *s* partidário fiel ● *adj* leal

stamina /ˈstæmɪnə/ *s* resistência

stammer /ˈstæmər/ *vt, vi* ~ (**sth**) (**out**) gaguejar (*algo*) ● *s* gagueira

stamp /stæmp/ *s* 1 (*correio, fiscal*) selo: ~ *collecting* filatelia 2 carimbo 3 (*para metal*) cunho 4 (*com o pé*) batida ▸ 1 *vt, vi* bater (o pé), andar batendo o pé 2 *vt* (*carta*) selar 3 *vt* carimbar 4 *vt* carimbar ■ **stamp sth out** erradicar algo

stampede /stæmˈpi:d/ *s* debandada ▸ *vi* debandar

stance /stæns; *GB* stɑ:ns/ *s* ~ (**on**

sth) postura (em relação a algo)

stand /stænd/ s **1 ~ (on sth)** postura (em relação a algo): *take a ~ on sth* posicionar-se em relação a algo **2** (*geralmente em compostos*) suporte, apoio: *music ~* estante para partitura **3** estante para partitura **4** (*Esporte*) arquibancada **5** (*USA*) (*Jur*) banco das testemunhas ▸ **make a stand (against sb/sth)** opor resistência (a alguém/algo) ● (*pt, pp* stood) **1** *vi* estar de pé: *~ still* não mover-se **2** *vi ~ (up)* ficar de pé **3** *vt* pôr, colocar **4** *vi* medir **5** *vi* encontrar-se: *A house once stood here.* Antes havia uma casa aqui. **6** *vi* (*porta, etc.*) continuar em pé **7** *vi* estar: *as things ~* do modo como vão as coisas **8** *vt* suportar: *I can't ~ him.* Eu não o agüento. **9** *vi ~ (for sth)* (*GB, Pol*) candidatar-se (a algo) ▸ **it/that stands to reason** é lógico ▸ **stand a chance (of sth)** ter chance/possibilidade (de algo) ▸ **stand firm** manter-se firme ▪ **stand by sb** ficar do lado de alguém ▪ **stand for sth 1** significar, representar algo **2** ser a favor de algo **3** tolerar algo ▪ **stand in (for sb)** substituir (alguém) ▪ **stand out (ser melhor)** destacar-se ▪ **stand sb up** (*coloq*) deixar alguém esperando ▪ **stand up for sb/sth/yourself** defender alguém/algo, defender-se ▪ **stand up to sb** fazer frente a alguém

standard /ˈstændəd/ s padrão: *up to/below ~* acima/abaixo do padrão ● *adj* **1** padrão **2** oficial

standardize /ˈstændədaɪz/ vt padronizar

standard of living s padrão de vida

standby /ˈstændbaɪ/ s (*pl* -bys) **1** recurso **2** (*pessoa*) reserva ▸ **on standby 1** à disposição **2** em lista de espera

stand-in s substituto, dublê

standing /ˈstændɪŋ/ s **1** prestígio **2** *of long ~* de longa data ● *adj* permanente

standing order s (*GB*) débito automático

standpoint /ˈstændpɔɪnt/ s ponto de vista

standstill /ˈstændstɪl/ s: *be at a ~* estar parado ◇ *come to/bring sth to a ~* parar/paralisar algo

stank /stæŋk/ *pret de* STINK

staple /ˈsteɪpl/ *adj* principal ● s **1** grampo (*papel*) ● *vt* grampear **stapler** s grampeador

star /stɑr/ s estrela, astro ● *vi*

(-rr-) **~ (in sth)** protagonizar algo

starboard /ˈstɑrbərd/ s estibordo

starch /stɑrtʃ/ s **1** amido **2** goma (*para roupa*) **starched** *adj* engomado

stardom /ˈstɑrdəm/ s estrelato

stare /steər/ *vi* **~ (at sb/sth)** olhar fixamente (para alguém/algo)

stark /stɑrk/ *adj* (~er, ~est) **1** rígido **2** cru **3** (*contraste*) marcante

starry /ˈstɑri/ *adj* (-ier, -iest) estrelado

start /stɑrt/ s **1** princípio: *for a ~* para começar **2** (**the start**) (*Esporte*) a saída ▸ **get off to a good, bad, etc. start** começar bem, mal, etc. ● **1** *vt, vi* começar **2** *vi* (*carro, etc.*) dar partida **3** *vt* (*boato*) iniciar ▸ **start with** para começar ▪ **start off** partir ▪ **start out (on sth/to do sth)** começar (algo/a fazer algo) ▪ **start (sth) up 1** (*motor*) colocar em movimento **2** (*negócio*) começar

starter /ˈstɑrtər/ s (*GB*) (prato de) entrada

starting point s ponto de partida

startle /ˈstɑrtl/ vt sobressaltar **startling** *adj* assombroso

starve /stɑrv/ **1** *vi* passar fome: *~ to death* morrer de fome **2** *vt* matar de fome, fazer passar fome **3** *vt ~ sb/sth of sth* privar alguém/algo de algo **starving** *adj* morto de fome **starvation** s fome → FOME

state /steɪt/ *vt* **1** declarar **2** estabelecer ● s **1** estado: *~ of mind* estado de espírito ◇ *be in no ~ to drive* não estar em condições de dirigir **2** (**the States**) [*sing*] (*coloq*) os Estados Unidos ▸ **state of affairs** conjuntura ● *adj* (*tb* State) estatal: *a ~ visit* uma visita oficial ◇ *~ education* educação pública

stately /ˈsteɪtli/ *adj* (-ier, -iest) majestoso

statement /ˈsteɪtmənt/ s declaração: *bank ~* extrato bancário

statesman /ˈsteɪtsmən/ s (*pl* -men) estadista

static /ˈstætɪk/ *adj* estático ● s **1** (*rádio*) interferência **2** (*tb* ~ **electricity**) (eletricidade) estática

station /ˈsteɪʃn/ *vt* postar ● s **1** estação **2** *police ~* delegacia de polícia ◇ *nuclear power ~* (*GB*) usina nuclear ◇ *fire ~* corpo de bombeiros ◇ *gas ~* posto de gasolina **3** (*TV, etc.*) emissora

stationary /ˈsteɪʃənəri; GB -nri/ *adj* estacionário

stationery /ˈsteɪʃənəri; GB -nri/ *s* material de papelaria

station wagon *s* carro tipo perua

statistic /stəˈtɪstɪk/ *s* estatística statistics *s* [*sing*] (*Mat*) estatística

statue /ˈstætʃuː/ *s* estátua

stature /ˈstætʃər/ *s* 1 estatura 2 renome

status /ˈsteɪtəs/ *s* posição: *marital* ~ estado civil ◇ ~ *symbol* símbolo de status

statute /ˈstætʃuːt/ *s* estatuto: ~ *book* código (de leis) statutory /ˈstætʃətɔːri; GB -tri/ *adj* estatutário

staunch /stɔːntʃ/ *adj* (~er, ~est) incondicional

stave /steɪv/ *v* ■ stave sth off 1 (*crise*) evitar 2 (*ataque*) rechaçar

stay /steɪ/ *s* estadia ● *vi* ficar: *What hotel are you staying at?* Em que hotel você está? ◇ ~ *away from sth* ficar longe de algo ■ stay behind ficar (*depois que os outros foram embora*) stay in ficar em casa stay on (at...) ficar (em...) stay up ficar acordado

steady /ˈstedi/ *adj* (-ier, -iest) 1 firme 2 regular: *a ~ job* um emprego fixo ● (*pt, pp* -ied) 1 *vi* estabilizar(-se) 2 *vt* ~ yourself recuperar o equilíbrio

steak /steɪk/ *s* bife

steal /stiːl/ (*pt* stole *pp* stolen) 1 *vt, vi* roubar → ROB 2 *vi* ~ in, out, away, etc.: *They stole away.* Eles saíram às escondidas. ◇ ~ *up on sb* aproximar-se de alguém sem ser notado

stealth /stelθ/ *s* procedimento furtivo: *by* ~ às escondidas stealthy *adj* (-ier, -iest) sigiloso

steam /stiːm/ *s* vapor ● *vi* 1 soltar vapor: *steaming hot coffee* café fumegante 2 *vt* cozinhar no vapor ►get (all) steamed up (about/over sth) (*coloq*) ficar agitado (por algo) ■ steam up embaçar-se (*com vapor*)

steamer /ˈstiːmər/ *s* 1 navio a vapor 2 utensílio para cozinhar a vapor

steamroller /ˈstiːmroʊlər/ *s* rolo compressor

steel /stiːl/ *s* aço ● *vt* ~ yourself armar-se de coragem

steep /stiːp/ *adj* (~er, ~est) 1 íngreme: *a ~ mountain* uma montanha escarpada 2 (*coloq*)

excessivo steeply *adv* de maneira bastante inclinada: *The plane was climbing* ~. O avião estava subindo vertiginosamente. ◇ *Share prices fell* ~. As ações despencaram.

steer /stɪər/ *vt, vi* 1 guiar: *He steered the discussion away from the subject.* Ele levou a conversa para outro lado. 2 navegar steering *s* direção (*veículo*)

steering wheel *s* volante

stem /stem/ *s* haste ● (-mm-) 1 *vt* estancar 2 *vi* ~ from sth originar-se de algo

stench /stentʃ/ *s* fedor

step /step/ *vi* (-pp-) dar um passo: ~ *on sth* pisar (em) algo ◇ ~ *over sth* passar por cima de algo ■ step down deixar um cargo step in intervir step sth up aumentar algo ● *s* 1 passo 2 degrau 3 (*steps*) escada 4 medida: *take steps* tomar medidas ► be in step (with sb/sth) 1 estar no mesmo passo (que alguém) 2 estar de acordo (com alguém/algo) be out of step (with sb/sth) 1 estar fora do passo (com alguém) 2 estar em desacordo (com alguém/algo) step by step passo a passo

stepbrother /ˈstepbrʌðər/ *s* irmão de criação

stepchild /ˈsteptʃaɪld/ *s* (*pl* -children /-tʃɪldrən/) enteado/a

stepdaughter /ˈstepdɔːtər/ *s* enteada

stepfather /ˈstepfɑːðər/ *s* padrasto

stepladder /ˈsteplædər/ *s* escada (de mão)

stepmother /ˈstepmʌðər/ *s* madrasta

step-parent *s* padrasto, madrasta

stepsister /ˈstepsɪstər/ *s* irmã de criação

stepson /ˈstepsʌn/ *s* enteado

stereo /ˈsterioʊ/ *s* (*pl* ~s) estéreo

stereotype /ˈsteriətaɪp/ *s* estereótipo

sterile /ˈsteraɪl; GB ˈsteraɪl/ *adj* estéril sterility /stəˈrɪləti/ *s* esterilidade sterilize /ˈsteraɪlaɪz/ *vt* esterilizar

sterling /ˈstɜːrlɪŋ/ *adj* 1 (*prata*) de lei 2 excelente ● *s* (*tb* pound ~) libra esterlina

stern /stɜːrn/ *adj* (~er, ~est) severo ● *s* popa

stew /stuː; GB stjuː/ *vt, vi* guisar ● *s* guisado

steward /ˈstuːərd; GB ˈstjuːəd/ *s*

1 (*fem* **stewardess** /ˈstuːədəs; *GB* ˌstjuːəˈdes/) (*avião*) comissário/a de bordo: *air stewardess* aeromoça **2** (*barco*) camareiro/a

stick /stɪk/ s **1** pau **2** bastão **3** barra, talo: *a ~ of celery* um talo de salsão ◊ *a ~ of dynamite* um cartucho de dinamite ● (*pt, pp* **stuck**) **1** *vt* cravar: *~ a needle in your finger* espetar uma agulha no dedo **2** *vt, vi* grudar **3** *vt* (*coloq*) colocar **4** *vi* ficar preso **5** *vt* (*coloq*) agüentar: *I had to ~ it out.* Tive que agüentar. **6** *vi ~ at sth* persistir em algo **7** *~ by sb* continuar a apoiar alguém **8** *~ to sth* ater-se a algo ● **stick around** (*coloq*) ficar por perto **stick out/up** sobressair-se: *His ears ~ out.* As orelhas dele são muito salientes. **stick sth out** esticar algo: *~ your head out of the window* pôr a cabeça para fora da janela ◊ *~ your tongue out* mostrar a língua **stick together** manter-se unidos **stick up for yourself/sb/sth** defender-se, defender alguém/algo

sticker /ˈstɪkər/ s colante

sticky /ˈstɪki/ *adj* (**-ier, -iest**) **1** pegajoso **2** (*coloq*) (*situação*) difícil

stiff /stɪf/ *adj* (**~er, ~est**) **1** rígido, duro **2** (*articulação*) enrijecido: *~ neck* torcicolo **3** espesso **4** difícil **5** (*pessoa*) formal, frio **6** (*brisa, bebida alcoólica*) forte ● *adv* (*coloq*) extremamente: *bored/scared* ~ morto de tédio/medo

stiffen /ˈstɪfn/ **1** *vi* ficar tenso **2** *vi* (*articulação*) enrijecer-se **3** *vt* (*colarinho*) engomar

stifle /ˈstaɪfl/ **1** *vt, vi* sufocar(-se) **2** *vt* (*rebelião*) conter **3** *vt* (*bocejo*) segurar **stifling** *adj* sufocante

stigma /ˈstɪgmə/ s estigma

still /stɪl/ *adv* **1** ainda **NOTA** Usa-se em frases afirmativas e interrogativas, depois de verbos auxiliares e modais e diante dos demais verbos: *He ~ talks about me.* ◊ *Are you ~ here?* **Yet** é usado em frases negativas e sempre vem no final da oração: *Aren't they here yet?* ◊ *He hasn't done it yet.* No entanto, pode-se usar **still** em frases negativas para dar ênfase à idéia. Neste caso, vai sempre diante do verbo, mesmo que este seja um auxiliar ou um modal: *He ~ hasn't done it.* ◊ *He ~ can't do it.* **2** ainda assim, contudo ● *adj* **1** quieto: *~ life* natureza morta ◊ *Stand ~!* Não se

mova! **2** calmo **3** (*bebida*) sem gás **stillness** s quietude

stilt /stɪlt/ s **1** perna-de-pau **2** palafita

stilted /ˈstɪltɪd/ *adj* artificial

stimulant /ˈstɪmjələnt/ s estimulante

stimulate /ˈstɪmjuleɪt/ *vt* estimular **stimulating** *adj* **1** estimulante **2** interessante

stimulus /ˈstɪmjələs/ s (*pl* **-li** /-laɪ/) estímulo

sting /stɪŋ/ s **1** ferrão **2** (*ferida*) picada **3** dor aguda ● (*pt, pp* **stung**) **1** *vt, vi* picar **2** *vi* arder **3** *vt* atormentar

stingy /ˈstɪndʒi/ *adj* (*coloq*) avarento

stink /stɪŋk/ *vi* (*pt* **stank** *ou* **stunk** *pp* **stunk**) (*coloq*) **1** *~ (of sth)* feder (a algo) **2** (*fig*) ter cheiro ● **stink sth out** empestear algo ● s (*coloq*) mau cheiro **stinking** *adj* horrível

stint /stɪnt/ s período

stipulate /ˈstɪpjuleɪt/ *vt* (*fml*) estipular

stir /stɜːr/ (**-rr-**) **1** *vt* mexer (*mistura*) **2** *vt, vi* mover(-se) **3** *vt* (*imaginação, etc.*) despertar ● **stir sth up** provocar algo ● s **1** *give sth a ~* mexer algo **2** alvoroço **stirring** *adj* emocionante

stirrup /ˈstɪrəp/ s estribo

stitch /stɪtʃ/ s **1** (*costura, cirurgia*) ponto **2** *I got a ~.* Deu-me uma pontada. ▶ **in stitches** (*coloq*) morrendo de rir ● *vt, vi* costurar **stitching** s costura

stock /stɑk/ s **1** estoque: *out of/in ~* fora de/em estoque **2** reserva **3** gado **4** (*Fin*) [*ger pl*] ações **5** (*de empresa*) capital **6** (*Cozinha*) caldo ▶ **take stock (of sth)** fazer balanço (de algo) ● *adj* (*frase, etc.*) batido ● *vt* estocar ● **stock up (on/with sth)** abastecer-se (de algo)

stockbroker /ˈstɑkbroʊkər/ s corretor/a de bolsa de valores

stock exchange (*tb* **stock market**) s bolsa de valores

stocking /ˈstɑkɪŋ/ s meia (*seda, nylon*)

stocktaking /ˈstɑkteɪkɪŋ/ (*GB*) s balanço (*comercial*)

stocky /ˈstɑki/ *adj* (**-ier, -iest**) robusto

stodgy /ˈstɑdʒi/ *adj* (**-ier, -iest**) (*coloq*) (*comida, livro*) pesado

stoke /stoʊk/ *vt ~ sth (up)* alimentar algo

stole /stoʊl/ *pret de* STEAL

stolen /ˈstoʊlən/ *pp de* STEAL

stolid /ˈstɑlɪd/ *adj* impassível

stomach /'stʌmək/ s **1** estômago **2** abdome **3** ~ **for sth** vontade de algo • *vt* suportar

stone /stəʊn/ s **1** pedra **2** (*GB*) (*fruta*) caroço **3** (*GB*) (*pl* **stone**) 6,348 kg • *vt* apedrejar **stoned** *adj* (*coloq*) chapado (*com maconha*)

stony /'stəʊni/ *adj* (**-ier, -iest**) **1** pedregoso **2** (*olhar*) frio **3** (*silêncio*) sepulcral

stood /stʊd/ *pret, pp de* STAND

stool /stuːl/ s banquinho

stoop /stuːp/ *vi* ~ (**down**) curvar-se ▸ **stoop so low (as to do sth)** chegar tão baixo (a ponto de fazer algo) • s: *walk with a* ~ andar curvado

stop /stɒp/ (**-pp-**) **1** *vt, vi* parar, deter(-se): ~ *dead/short* parar de repente **2** *vt* (*processo*) interromper **3** *vt* acabar com **4** *vt* ~ **doing sth** deixar de fazer algo **5** *vt* ~ **sb/sth (from) doing sth** impedir que alguém/algo faça algo: ~ *yourself doing sth* esforçar-se para não fazer algo **6** *vt* cancelar **7** *vt* (*pagamento*) sustar **8** *vi* (*GB, coloq*) ficar (*por pouco tempo*) ▸ **stop short of (doing) sth** não fazer algo por pouco **stop off** dar uma parada • *s* **1** parada, pausa: *come to a* ~ *parar (trem, etc.)* **2** ponto **3** (*ortografia*) ponto **stoppage** *s* **1** paralisação **2** (**stoppages**) deduções (*de salário*)

stopgap /'stɒpgæp/ s **1** substituto **2** recurso provisório

stopover /'stɒpəʊvər/ s escala (*viagem*)

stopper /'stɒpər/ s tampão

stopwatch /'stɒpwɒtʃ/ s cronômetro

storage /'stɔːrɪdʒ/ s armazenagem

store /stɔːr/ s **1** provisão, reserva **2** (*esp USA*) loja ▸ **be/have sth in store for sb** ser/ter algo reservado para alguém (*surpresa, etc.*) • *vt* ~ **sth (up/away)** guardar algo

storekeeper /'stɔːrkiːpər/ s lojista

storeroom /'stɔːruːm/ s depósito

stork /stɔːrk/ s cegonha

storm /stɔːrm/ s **1** tempestade, temporal: *a* ~ *of criticism* uma enxurrada de críticas **2** ~ *in/ off/out* entrar/ir-se/sair furiosamente **2** *vt* assaltar **stormy** *adj* (**-ier, -iest**) **1** tempestuoso **2** (*debate*) inflamado **3** (*relação*) turbulento

story /'stɔːri/ s (*pl* **-ies**) **1** história **2** conto **3** (*Jornal*) notícia **4** (*GB* **storey**) andar

stout /staʊt/ *adj* **1** forte **2** corpulento

stove /stəʊv/ s **1** fogão **2** aquecedor

stow /stəʊ/ *vt* ~ **sth (away)** guardar algo

straddle /'strædl/ *vt* pôr-se a cavalo em

straggle /'strægl/ *vi* **1** (*planta*) esparramar-se **2** (*pessoa*) ficar para trás **straggler** s pessoa perdida **straggly** *adj* (**-ier, -iest**) desalinhado

straight /streɪt/ (~**er, ~est**) *adj* **1** reto: ~ *hair* cabelo liso **2** em ordem **3** direto **4** (*líquidos*) puro (*sem água*) ▸ **be straight (with sb)** ser franco (com alguém) **get sth straight** esclarecer as coisas **keep a straight face** manter uma cara séria • *adv* **1** em linha reta: *Look* ~ *ahead.* Olhe bem em frente. **2** (*sentar-se*) direito **3** (*pensar*) de maneira clara **4** (*ir*) diretamente ▸ **straight away** imediatamente **straight out** sem vacilar

straighten /'streɪtn/ **1** *vt, vi* tornar(-se) reto **2** *vt, vi* ~ (**sth**) (**up**) endireitar-se, endireitar (algo) **3** *vt* (*roupa*) arrumar ▪ **straighten sth out** acertar algo

straightforward /ˌstreɪtˈfɔːrwərd/ *adj* **1** (*pessoa*) honesto, franco **2** simples

strain /streɪn/ **1** *vi* esforçar-se **2** *vt* (*corda*) tensionar **3** *vt* (*ouvido, vista*) aguçar **4** *vt* (*músculo, etc.*) distender **5** *vt* (*voz, etc.*) forçar **6** *vt* (*relações*) tornar tenso **7** *vt* ~ **sth (off)** peneirar algo • s **1** tensão **2** distensão: *eye* ~ vista cansada **strained** *adj* **1** (*riso, etc.*) forçado **2** tenso

strainer /'streɪnər/ s coador

straitjacket /'streɪtdʒækɪt/ s camisa-de-força

straits /streɪts/ s [*pl*] estreito ▸ **in dire straits** em uma situação desesperadora

strand /strænd/ s **1** fio **2** mecha

stranded /'strændɪd/ *adj* abandonado

strange /streɪndʒ/ *adj* (**-er, -est**) **1** desconhecido **2** estranho **stranger** s **1** desconhecido/a **2** forasteiro/a

strangle /'stræŋgl/ *vt* estrangular

strap /stræp/ s **1** correia **2** (*vestido*) alça • *vt* **1** ~ **sth (up)** enfaixar algo **2** ~ **sth on** amarrar (*com correias*) **3** ~ **sb in** colocar cinto de segurança em alguém

strategy /'strætədʒi/ s (pl -ies) estratégia **strategic** /strə'ti:dʒɪk/ adj estratégico

straw /strɔ:/ s 1 palha 2 canudo (para beber) ▸ **the last straw** (para) a gota d'água

strawberry /'strɔ:bəri; GB -bəri/ s (pl -ies) morango

stray /streɪ/ vi 1 extraviar-se afastar-se ● adj 1 extraviado: a ~ dog um cão vadio 2 perdido

streak /stri:k/ s 1 risca 2 traço (de sorte) período: on a winning/losing ~ numa maré de sorte/azar ● vt 1 ~ sth (with sth) riscar algo (de algo) 2 vi correr/ passar como um raio

stream /stri:m/ s 1 riacho 2 (líquidos, palavras) torrente 3 (gente) fluxo 4 (carros) sucessão ● vi 1 escorrer (luz) jorrar 3 tremular (ao vento)

streamer /'stri:mər/ s serpentina

streamline /'stri:mlaɪn/ vt 1 tornar aerodinâmico 2 racionalizar

street /stri:t/ s (abrev St) rua NOTA Escreve-se **street** (o road) com maiúscula quando precedido pelo nome da rua. → **RUA** ▸ **(right) up your street:** This job is right up your ~. Este trabalho parece perfeito para você. **streets ahead (of sb/sth)** muito à frente (de alguém/algo)

streetcar /'stri:tkɑr/ s bonde

strength /streŋθ/ s 1 [U] força 2 resistência 3 (luz, emoção) intensidade 4 ponto forte ▸ **on the strength of sth** com base em algo, confiando em **strengthen** vt, vi fortalecer(-se)

strenuous /'strenjuəs/ adj 1 árduo 2 vigoroso

stress /stres/ s 1 tensão 2 (realce) ênfase 3 acento (tónico) ● vt 1 enfatizar, acentuar **stressful** adj estressante

stretch /stretʃ/ 1 vt, vi esticar (-se): ~ your legs esticar as pernas 2 vi espreguiçar-se 3 vi (área) estender-se 4 vt (pessoa) exigir o máximo de ■ **stretch (yourself) out** estirar-se ● s 1 have a ~ espreguiçar-se 2 elasticidade 3 (terreno) trecho 4 (tempo) período ▸ **at a stretch** sem interrupção

stretcher /'stretʃər/ s maca

strewn /stru:n/ adj 1 ~ (all) over sth esparramado por/sobre algo 2 ~ with sth coberto de algo

stricken /'strɪkən/ adj aflito: drought-stricken area área afetada pela seca

strict /strɪkt/ adj (~er, ~est) 1 severo 2 estrito: in strictest confidence com o maior sigilo **strictly** adv 1 severamente 2 estritamente: ~ prohibited terminantemente proibido ▸ **strictly speaking** a rigor

stride /straɪd/ vi (pt **strode**) 1 andar a passos largos 2 ~ up to sb/sth aproximar-se resolutamente de alguém/algo ● s 1 passada 2 (modo de andar) passo ▸ **take sth in your stride** enfrentar algo com calma

strident /'straɪdnt/ adj estridente

strife /straɪf/ s conflito

strike /straɪk/ s 1 greve 2 (Mil) ataque ● vt (pt, pp **struck**) 1 vt golpear, acertar 2 vt (raio) atingir 3 vt chocar(-se) contra 4 vi atacar 5 vt, vi (relógio) bater 6 vt (ouro, etc.) encontrar 7 vt (fósforo) acender 8 vt: It strikes me that... Ocorre-me que... 9 vt impressionar, chamar a atenção de ■ **strike back (at sb/sth)** revidar (a alguém/algo) **strike up (sth)** começar a tocar (algo) **strike up sth (with sb)** (conversa) entabular algo (com alguém) 2 (amizade) começar algo (com alguém)

striker /'straɪkər/ s 1 grevista 2 (Esporte) artilheiro/a

striking /'straɪkɪŋ/ adj chamativo, notável

string /strɪŋ/ s 1 barbante 2 (pérolas) cordão 3 (Mús) corda ▸ **(with) no strings attached/ without strings** sem restrições/ compromisso ● vt (pt, pp **strung**) ~ sth (up) pendurar algo (com cordão) ■ **string (sth) out** estender algo **string together** colocar algo em ordem (para formar frases)

stringent /'strɪndʒənt/ adj rigoroso

strip /strɪp/ s 1 (papel, metal, etc.) tira 2 (terra, etc.) faixa ● (-pp-) 1 vt (máquina) desmantelar 2 vt (papel, etc.) arrancar 3 vt ~ sb/ sth of sth despojar alguém/algo de algo 4 vt, vi ~ (off) despir(-se)

stripe /straɪp/ s listra **striped** adj listrado

strive /straɪv/ vi (pt **strove** pp **striven** /'strɪvn/ (fml) ~ (for/ after sth) esforçar-se (para obter algo)

strode /stroʊd/ pret de STRIDE

stroke /stroʊk/ s 1 vt afagar ● s 1 golpe: a ~ of luck um golpe de sorte 2 (natação) estilo 3 traço (caneta, etc.) 4 batida (sino, *relógio* **5** (*Med*) derrame ▶ **at a stroke** de um golpe   **not do a stroke (of work)** (*esp GB*) não trabalhar

stroll /strəʊl/ *s* passeio ● *vi* caminhar

stroller /ˈstrəʊlər/ *s* carrinho de criança

strong /strɒŋ; *GB* strɒŋ/ *adj* (~**er** /ˈstrɒŋgər/, ~**est** /ˈstrɒŋgəst/) forte ▶ **be going strong** (*coloq*) continuar firme **sb's strong point/suit** o forte de alguém **strongly** *adv* firmemente, bastante

strong-minded *adj* determinado

strove /strəʊv/ *pret* de STRIVE

struck /strʌk/ *pret, pp* de STRIKE

structure /ˈstrʌktʃər/ *s* **1** estrutura **2** construção ● *vt* estruturar

struggle /ˈstrʌgl/ *vi* esforçar-se **2** lutar ● *s* **1** luta **2** esforço

strung /strʌŋ/ *pret, pp* de STRING

strut /strʌt/ *s* escora ● *vi* (**-tt-**) ~ **(about/along)** pavonear-se

stub /stʌb/ *s* **1** (*cigarro, etc.*) toco **2** (*cheque*) canhoto

stubble /ˈstʌbl/ *s* **1** restolho **2** barba (por fazer)

stubborn /ˈstʌbərn/ *adj* **1** teimoso **2** (*mancha*) difícil (de remover)

stuck /stʌk/ *pret, pp* de STICK ● *adj* preso: **be ~ with sb/sth** ficar preso com alguém/algo

stuck-up *adj* (*coloq*) esnobe

stud /stʌd/ *s* **1** pino **2** (*em sapato*) cravo **3** garanhão **4** (*tb* ~ **farm**) haras

student /ˈstuːdnt; *GB* ˈstjuː-/ *s* estudante

studied /ˈstʌdid/ *adj* deliberado

studio /ˈstuːdiəʊ; *GB* ˈstjuː-/ *s* (*pl* ~**s**) estúdio

studious /ˈstuːdiəs; *GB* ˈstjuː-/ *adj* **1** estudioso **2** (*fml*) deliberado

study /ˈstʌdi/ *s* (*pl* -**ies**) **1** estudo **2** escritório (*em uma casa*) ● *vt, vi* (*pt, pp* -**ied**) estudar

stuff /stʌf/ *s* **1** material **2** [*U*] (*coloq*) coisas ● *vt* **1** encher, rechear **2** ~ **sth in; ~ sth into sth** meter algo (à força) (em algo) **3** ~ **yourself (with sth)** empanturrar-se (de algo) **4** (*animal*) empalhar ▶ **get stuffed** (*GB, coloq*) vai tomar banho **stuffing** *s* **1** recheio **2** (*estofado*) enchimento

stuffy /ˈstʌfi/ *adj* (-**ier**, -**iest**) **1** abafado **2** (*pessoa*) antiquado

stumble /ˈstʌmbl/ *vi* **1** tropeçar **2** ~ **(over sth)** equivocar-se (quan-

to a algo) **3** ~ **across/on sb/sth** topar com alguém/algo

stumbling block *s* obstáculo

stump /stʌmp/ *s* toco

stun /stʌn/ *vt* **1** (**-nn-**) assombrar **2** aturdir **stunning** *adj* impressionante

stung /stʌŋ/ *pret, pp* de STING

stunk /stʌŋk/ *pret, pp* de STINK

stunt /stʌnt/ *vt* atrofiar ● *s* **1** truque: *publicity* ~ golpe publicitário **2** acrobacia

stupendous /stuːˈpendəs; *GB* stjuː-/ *adj* estupendo

stupid /ˈstuːpɪd; *GB* ˈstjuː-/ *adj* (~**er**, ~**est**) tonto, estúpido → TOLO **stupidity** /stuːˈpɪdəti; *GB* stjuː-/ *s* burrice

stupor /ˈstuːpər; *GB* ˈstjuː-/ *s* estupor

sturdy /ˈstɜːrdi/ *adj* (-**ier**, -**iest**) **1** robusto **2** sólido **3** (*sapatos*) resistente

stutter /ˈstʌtər/ *vi* gaguejar ● *s* gagueira

sty /staɪ/ *s* (*pl* **sties**) **1** chiqueiro **2** (*tb* **stye**) terçol

style /staɪl/ *s* **1** estilo **2** maneira **3** modelo: *the latest* ~ a última moda **stylish** *adj* elegante

suave /swɑːv/ *adj* bem-educado (*às vezes excessivamente*)

subconscious /ˌsʌbˈkɑːnʃəs/ *adj, s* subconsciente

subdivide /ˌsʌbdɪˈvaɪd/ *vt, vi* subdividir(-se)

subdue /səbˈduː; *GB* -ˈdjuː/ *vt* subjugar **subdued** *adj* **1** (*voz*) baixo **2** (*luz, cor*) suave **3** (*pessoa*) abatido

subheading /ˈsʌbhedɪŋ/ *s* subtítulo

subject /ˈsʌbdʒɪkt/ *s* **1** assunto **2** matéria **3** (*Gram*) sujeito **4** súdito/a ● *adj* ~ **to sb/sth** sujeito a alguém/algo ● /səbˈdʒekt/ *vt* sujeitar **subjection** *s* sujeição

subjective /səbˈdʒektɪv/ *adj* subjetivo

subject matter /ˈsʌbdʒekt mætər/ *s* tema

subjunctive /səbˈdʒʌŋktɪv/ *s* subjuntivo

sublime /səˈblaɪm/ *adj* sublime

submarine /ˈsʌbməriːn; *GB* ˌsʌbməˈriːn/ *adj, s* submarino

submerge /səbˈmɜːrdʒ/ *vt, vi* submergir

submission /səbˈmɪʃn/ *s* **1** submissão **2** (*documento, etc.*) apresentação

submissive /səbˈmɪsɪv/ *adj* submisso

submit /səbˈmɪt/ (**-tt-**) **1** *vi* submeter-se **2** *vt* apresentar: *Appli-*

cations must be submitted today. As inscrições devem ser entregues hoje.

subordinate /sə'bɔːrdənət/ *GB* -dinət/ *adj, s* subordinado/a ● /sə'bɔːrdɪneɪt/ *GB* -dəneɪt/ *vt* subordinar

subscribe /səb'skraɪb/ *vi* ~ **to sth** 1 fazer a assinatura de algo 2 (*fml*) concordar com algo (*opinião*) **subscriber** *s* assinante **subscription** *s* 1 assinatura (*revista, etc.*) 2 cota (*clube*)

subsequent /'sʌbsɪkwənt/ *adj* posterior **subsequently** *adv* posteriormente **subsequent to** *prep* (*fml*) posterior a

subside /səb'saɪd/ *vi* 1 ceder 2 (*água*) baixar 3 (*vento, emoção*) acalmar(-se) **subsidence** /səb'saɪdns, 'sʌbsɪdns/ *s* afundamento (*muro, etc.*)

subsidiary /səb'sɪdieri/ *GB* -diəri/ *adj* subsidiário ● *s* (*pl* -**ies**) filial

subsidy /'sʌbsədi/ *s* (*pl* -**ies**) subvenção **subsidize** *vt* subvencionar

subsist /səb'sɪst/ *vi* ~ (**on sth**) subsistir (à base de algo) **subsistence** *s* subsistência

substance /'sʌbstəns/ *s* 1 substância 2 essência

substantial /səb'stænʃl/ *adj* 1 considerável 2 (*construção*) sólido **substantially** *adv* 1 consideravelmente 2 essencialmente

substitute /'sʌbstɪtuːt/ *GB* -tjuːt/ *s* 1 ~ (**for sb**) substituto/a (*de alguém*) 2 ~ (**for sth**) substitutivo (*para algo*) 3 (*Esporte*) reserva ● *vt* ~ **A for B/B with A** substituir B por A

subtitle /'sʌbtaɪtl/ *s* legenda

subtle /'sʌtl/ *adj* (-**er, -est**) 1 sutil 2 (*sabor*) delicado 3 (*pessoa*) perspicaz 4 (*odor, cor*) suave **subtlety** *s* (*pl* -**ies**) sutileza

subtract /səb'trækt/ *vt, vi* subtrair **subtraction** *s* subtração

suburb /'sʌbɜːrb/ *s* subúrbio **suburban** /sə'bɜːrbən/ *adj* suburbano

subversive /səb'vɜːrsɪv/ *adj* subversivo

subway /'sʌbweɪ/ *s* 1 metrô 2 (*GB*) passagem subterrânea

succeed /sək'siːd/ *vi* 1 ter sucesso, triunfar: ~ *in doing sth* conseguir fazer algo 2 *vt, vi* ~ (**sb**) suceder (a alguém) 3 *vi* ~ (**to sth**) herdar (algo): ~ *to the throne* subir ao trono

success /sək'ses/ *s* sucesso **successful** *adj* bem-sucedido: *the ~*

candidate o candidato vitorioso ◇ *be ~ in doing sth* ter sucesso em fazer algo

succession /sək'seʃn/ *s* 1 sucessão: *three times in quick ~* três vezes seguidas 2 série

successor /sək'sesər/ *s* sucessor/a

succumb /sə'kʌm/ *vi* sucumbir

such /sʌtʃ/ *adj, pron* 1 semelhante, tal: *in ~ a way that...* de tal maneira que... ◇ *I did no ~ thing!* Eu não fiz isso! ◇ *There's no ~ thing as ghosts.* Fantasmas não existem. 2 [*uso enfático*] tão, tanto: *I'm in ~ a hurry.* Estou com muita pressa. **NOTA** Usase **such** com adjetivos que acompanham um substantivo e **so** com adjetivos desacompanhados. Compare os exemplos: *The food was so good.* ◇ *We had such good food.* ◇ *You are so intelligent/such an intelligent person.* ▶ **as such** como tal: *It's not a promotion as ~.* Não é uma promoção propriamente dita. **such as** por exemplo

suck /sʌk/ *vt, vi* 1 chupar 2 (*bomba*) aspirar **sucker** *s* 1 ventosa 2 (*coloq*) otário/a

sudden /'sʌdn/ *adj* súbito, repentino ▶ **all of a sudden** de repente **suddenly** *adv* de repente

suds /sʌdz/ *s* [*pl*] espuma (*sabão*)

sue /suː/ *GB* sjuː/ *vt, vi* processar

suede /sweɪd/ *s* camurça

suffer /'sʌfər/ 1 *vt, vi* sofrer 2 *vi* ser prejudicado **suffering** *s* sofrimento

sufficient /sə'fɪʃnt/ *adj* suficiente

suffix /'sʌfɪks/ *s* sufixo

suffocate /'sʌfəkeɪt/ *vt, vi* sufocar(-se) **suffocating** *adj* sufocante **suffocation** *s* asfixia

sugar /'ʃʊɡər/ *s* açúcar: ~ *bowl/lump* açucareiro/torrão de açúcar

suggest /səɡ'dʒest/ *GB* sə'dʒ-/ *vt* 1 sugerir 2 indicar 3 insinuar **suggestion** *s* 1 sugestão 2 proposta 3 insinuação **suggestive** *adj* 1 ~ (**of sth**) indicativo (de algo) 2 insinuante

suicidal /ˌsuːɪ'saɪdl/ *adj* 1 suicida 2 a ponto de se suicidar

suicide /'suːɪsaɪd/ *s* 1 (*homem*) suicídio: *commit ~* suicidar-se 2 suicida

suit /suːt/ *GB* sjuːt/ *s* 1 (*homem*) terno 2 (*mulher*) tailleur 3 (*cartas*) naipe → BARALHO 4 (*Jur*) processo ● *vt* 1 cair bem: *Does the* skirt ~ me? A saia fica bem em mim? **2** convir a **3** fazer bem a

suitability /ˌsuːtəˈbɪləti; GB ˌsjuː-/ s conveniência

suitable /ˈsuːtəbl; GB ˌsjuː-/ adj **1** adequado **2** conveniente **suitably** adv devidamente

suitcase /ˈsuːtkeɪs; GB ˌsjuː-/ s mala

suite /swiːt/ s **1** (tb Mús) suíte **2** conjunto: a dining room ~ um jogo de sala de jantar

suited /ˈsuːtɪd; GB ˌsjuː-/ adj adequado: He and his wife are well ~ (to each other). Ele e a esposa são feitos um para o outro.

sulfur (GB **sulphur**) /ˈsʌlfər/ s enxofre

sulk /sʌlk/ vi emburrar **sulky** adj (-ier, -iest) emburrado

sullen /ˈsʌlən/ adj carrancudo

sultan /ˈsʌltən/ s sultão

sultana /sʌlˈtænə; GB -ɑːnə/ s uva passa (sem sementes)

sultry /ˈsʌltri/ adj (-ier, -iest) **1** úmido e quente **2** sensual

sum /sʌm/ s soma, total: good at sums bom em cálculo ■ **sum (sth) up** resumir (algo): to ~ up... em resumo... **sum sb/sth up** ter uma idéia de alguém/algo

summarize /ˈsʌməraɪz/ vt, vi resumir **summary** s (pl -ies) resumo

summer /ˈsʌmər/ (tb **summertime** /ˈsʌmərtaɪm/) s verão **summery** adj de verão

summit /ˈsʌmɪt/ s cume: ~ meeting reunião de cúpula

summon /ˈsʌmən/ vt **1** convocar, chamar: ~ help pedir ajuda **2** ~ sth (up) (coragem, etc.) armar-se de algo: I couldn't ~ up the energy. Eu não tive energia. ■ **summon sth up** evocar algo

summons /ˈsʌmənz/ s (pl -es) intimação (judicial)

sun /sʌn/ s sol: The ~ was shining. Estava ensolarado. ● vt (-nn-) ~ **yourself** tomar sol

sunbathe /ˈsʌnbeɪð/ vi tomar sol

sunbeam /ˈsʌnbiːm/ s raio de sol

sunburn /ˈsʌnbɜːrn/ s [U] queimadura de sol: get ~ queimar-se **sunburnt** adj queimado de sol

Sunday /ˈsʌndeɪ, -di/ s (abrev **Sun.**) domingo ► MONDAY

sundry /ˈsʌndri/ adj vários ► **all and sundry** (coloq) todo o mundo

sunflower /ˈsʌnflaʊər/ s girassol

sung /sʌŋ/ pp de SING

sunglasses /ˈsʌnɡlæsɪz; GB -ɡlɑːs-/ s óculos escuros ► PAIR

sunk /sʌŋk/ pp de SINK ► **sunk in**

sth mergulhado em algo

sunken /ˈsʌŋkən/ adj afundado

sunlight /ˈsʌnlaɪt/ s luz do sol

sunlit /ˈsʌnlɪt/ adj iluminado pelo sol

sunny /ˈsʌni/ adj (-ier, -iest) **1** ensolarado **2** (personalidade) alegre

sunrise /ˈsʌnraɪz/ s nascer do sol

sunset /ˈsʌnset/ s pôr-do-sol

sunshine /ˈsʌnʃaɪn/ s sol

sunstroke /ˈsʌnstroʊk/ s insolação

suntan /ˈsʌntæn/ s bronzeado: get a ~ bronzear-se **suntanned** adj bronzeado

super /ˈsuːpər/ adj estupendo

superb /suːˈpɜːrb/ adj magnífico **superbly** adv magnificamente

superficial /ˌsuːpərˈfɪʃl/ adj superficial **superficiality** /ˌsuːpərˌfɪʃiˈæləti/ s superficialidade **superficially** adv superficialmente

superfluous /suːˈpɜːrfluəs/ adj supérfluo

superhuman /ˌsuːpərˈhjuːmən/ adj sobre-humano

superimpose /ˌsuːpərɪmˈpoʊz/ vt ~ sth (on sth) sobrepor algo (a algo)

superintendent /ˌsuːpərɪnˈtendənt/ s **1** comissário/a (polícia) **2** superintendente

superior /suːˈpɪəriər/ adj **1** superior **2** (atitude) soberbo ● s superior/a **superiority** /suːˌpɪəriˈɒrəti/ s superioridade

superlative /suːˈpɜːrlətɪv/ adj, s superlativo

supermarket /ˈsuːpərmɑːrkɪt/ s supermercado

supernatural /ˌsuːpərˈnætʃərəl/ adj, s sobrenatural

superpower /ˈsuːpərpaʊər/ s superpotência

supersede /ˌsuːpərˈsiːd/ vt suplantar

supersonic /ˌsuːpərˈsɑːnɪk/ adj supersônico

superstition /ˌsuːpərˈstɪʃn/ s superstição **superstitious** adj supersticioso

superstore /ˈsuːpərstɔːr/ s hipermercado

supervise /ˈsuːpərvaɪz/ vt supervisionar **supervision** /ˌsuːpərˈvɪʒn/ s supervisão **supervisor** s supervisor/a

supper /ˈsʌpər/ s jantar, ceia: have ~ cear

supple /ˈsʌpl/ adj (-er, -est) flexível

supplement /ˈsʌplɪmənt/ s **1** suplemento **2** (livro) apêndice

● *vt* complementar

supplementary /ˌsʌplɪˈmentəri;
GB -tri/ *adj* adicional

supplier /səˈplaɪər/ *s* fornece-
dor/a

supply /səˈplaɪ/ *vt* (*pt, pp* -**ied**) **1** ~
sb (**with sth**) abastecer alguém
(com algo) **2** ~ **sth** (**to sb**) fornecer algo (a alguém) ● *s* (*pl* -**ies**) **1**
provisão **2** (**supplies**) [*pl*] (*Mil*)
suprimento ▶ **supply and
demand** oferta e procura

support /səˈpɔːrt/ *vt* **1** (*peso*)
suportar **2** apoiar: *a supporting
role* um papel secundário **3**
(*GB*) (*Esporte*) torcer para **4**
(*pessoa*) sustentar ● *s* **1** apoio **2**
suporte ▶ **supporter** *s* **1** (*Pol*) par-
tidário/a **2** (*GB*) (*Esporte*)
torcedor/a **3** seguidor/a ▶ **supportive** *adj* que ajuda: *be* ~ dar
apoio

suppose /səˈpoʊz/ *vt* **1** supor **2**
(*sugestão*): *Suppose we change
the subject?* Que tal mudarmos
de assunto? ▶ **be supposed to
do sth** dever fazer algo ▶ **supposed** *adj* suposto ▶ **supposedly**
adv supostamente ▶ **supposing**
(**that**) *conj* se, no caso de

suppress /səˈpres/ *vt* **1** reprimir
2 (*informação*) omitir

supremacy /suːˈpreməsi/ *s*
supremacia

supreme /suːˈpriːm/ *adj*
supremo

Supreme Court *s* (*USA*) o
Supremo Tribunal

surcharge /ˈsɜːrtʃɑːrdʒ/ *s* sobre-
taxa

sure /ʃʊər; *GB* ʃɔː/ *adj* (-**er**, -**est**) **1**
seguro: *He's* ~ *to be elected.* Ele
será eleito com certeza. **2** confiante, firme ▶ **be sure to do sth**:
Be ~ *to write to me.* Não deixe de
me escrever. **for sure** (*coloq*)
com certeza **make sure** (**of
sth**) assegurar-se (de algo):
Make ~ *you are home by nine.*
Esteja em casa às nove sem
falta. ● *adv* (*coloq*) claro ▶ **sure
enough** efetivamente

surely /ˈʃʊərli; *GB* ˈʃɔːli/ *adv* **1**
seguramente, com certeza:
Surely you can't agree? Certamente você não está de acordo!

surf /sɜːrf/ *s* espuma (*do mar*) ●
vi surfar

surface /ˈsɜːrfɪs/ *s* **1** superfície:
by ~ *mail* por via terrestre ou
marítima ◇ *a* ~ *wound* um ferimento superficial **2** face ● *vt* **1**
recobrir **2** *vi* subir à superfície

surge /sɜːrdʒ/ *vi*: *They surged
into the stadium.* Eles entraram
em tropel no estádio. ● *s* **1** onda

2 (*atividade*) surto

surgeon /ˈsɜːrdʒən/ *s* cirurgião

surgery /ˈsɜːrdʒəri/ *s* (*pl* -**ies**) **1**
cirurgia: *brain* ~ neurocirurgia **2**
(*GB*) consultório: ~ *hours* horas de
consulta surgical *adj* cirúrgico

surly /ˈsɜːrli/ *adj* (-**ier**, -**iest**) rude

surmount /sərˈmaʊnt/ *vt*
superar

surname /ˈsɜːrneɪm/ (*esp GB*) *s*
sobrenome

surpass /sərˈpæs; *GB* -ˈpɑːs/ *vt*
(*fml*) superar

surplus /ˈsɜːrpləs/ *adj, s* exce-
dente

surprise /sərˈpraɪz/ *s* surpresa:
take sb/sth by ~ tomar alguém/
algo de surpresa ◇ *to my* ~ para
minha surpresa ● *vt* surpreen-
der ▶ **surprised** *adj* ~ (**at sb/sth**)
surpreso (por alguém/algo) ▶
surprising *adj* surpreendente

surrender /səˈrendər/ **1** *vi* render-se **2** *vt* (*fml*) entregar ● *s*
rendição, entrega

surreptitious /ˌsʌrəpˈtɪʃəs/ *adj*
subreptício

surrogate /ˈsʌrəgət/ *s* (*fml*)
substituto: ~ *mother* mãe de
aluguel

surround /səˈraʊnd/ *vt* cercar ▶
surrounding *adj* circundante:
the ~ *countryside* o campo dos
arredores ▶ **surroundings** *s* arredores

surveillance /sɜːrˈveɪləns/ *s*
vigilância

survey /sərˈveɪ/ *vt* **1** observar **2**
(*Geog*) mapear **3** (*GB*) inspecionar (*um edifício*) **4** pesquisar
● /ˈsɜːrveɪ/ *s* **1** panorama **2** (*GB*)
inspeção (*casa, etc.*) **3** levantamento **surveying** /ˈsɜːrveɪɪŋ/ *s*
agrimensura **surveyor** /sər-
ˈveɪər/ *s* **1** (*GB*) inspetor/a (*de
imóveis*) **2** agrimensor/a

survive /sərˈvaɪv/ **1** *vt, vi* sobreviver (a) **2** *vi* ~ (**on sth**) subsistir
(à base de algo) **survival** *s*
sobrevivência **survivor** *s* sobrevivente

susceptible /səˈseptəbl/ *adj* **1**
suscetível **2** (*Med*) propenso

suspect /səˈspekt/ *vt* **1** ~ **sb** (**of
doing sth**) suspeitar de
alguém; suspeitar que alguém
tenha feito algo **2** (*motivo, etc.*)
duvidar de ● /ˈsʌspekt/ *adj, s*
suspeito/a

suspend /səˈspend/ *vt* **1** ~ **sth**
(**from sth**) pendurar algo (em
algo) → O verbo mais comum é
hang. **2** suspender: *suspended
sentence* suspensão da pena

suspender /səˈspendər/ *s* **1**
(**suspenders**) [*pl*] (*USA*) sus-

pensório(s) **2** (GB) liga (meia feminina)

suspense /səˈspens/ s suspense

suspension /səˈspenʃn/ s suspensão: ~ bridge ponte suspensa

suspicion /səˈspɪʃn/ s suspeita

suspicious /səˈspɪʃəs/ adj **1** receoso: They're ~ of foreigners. Eles desconfiam de estrangeiros. **2** suspeito

sustain /səˈsteɪn/ vt **1** manter **2** sustentar **3** (fml) (lesão, perda, etc.) sofrer

swagger /ˈswæɡər/ vi pavonear-se

swallow /ˈswɒləʊ/ s **1** andorinha **2** trago ● vt **1** engolir **2** ~ sb/sth (up) (fig) engolir alguém/algo; consumir algo

swam /swæm/ pret de SWIM

swamp /swɒmp/ s pântano ● vt **1** inundar **2** atolar

swan /swɒn/ s cisne

swap /swɒp/ vt, vi (-pp-) ~ (sth) (around) trocar (algo) (de lugar)

swarm /swɔːm/ s **1** enxame **2** (gente) multidão: swarms of people um mar de gente ■ swarm in/out estar em tropa swarm with sb/sth estar repleto de alguém/algo

swat /swɒt/ vt (-tt-) acertar com um tapa (inseto)

sway /sweɪ/ **1** vt, vi oscilar **2** vi rebolar **3** vt influenciar ● s **1** balanço **2** rebolado **3** domínio

swear /sweər/ (pt swore pp sworn) **1** vi dizer palavrões **2** vt, vi jurar: ~ sb in tomar juramento de alguém ■ swear by sb/sth confiar plenamente em alguém/algo

swear word s palavrão

sweat /swet/ s suor ● vi suar ▸ sweat it out (coloq) agüentar firme sweaty adj (-ier, -iest) **1** suado **2** que faz suar

sweater /ˈswetər/ s suéter

sweatshirt /ˈswetʃɜːrt/ s blusão de moletom

sweep /swiːp/ (pt, pp swept) **1** vt, vi varrer: ~ sth away/up limpar algo **2** vt arrastar **3** vi estender-se ● vi: ~ out of the room sair da sala majestosamente **5** vt, vi ~ (through, over, across, etc.) sth estender-se por algo ■ sweep sb off their feet arrebatar (o coração de) alguém ● s **1** varrida **2** gesto amplo **3** extensão **4** (de polícia) ronda

sweeping /ˈswiːpɪŋ/ adj **1** amplo, radical **2** (afirmação) taxativo

sweet /swiːt/ adj (~er, ~est) **1** doce **2** (odor) cheiroso **3** (som) melodioso **4** gracioso **5** (caráter) encantador ■ have a sweet tooth adorar doces ● s (GB) **1** doce **2** sobremesa sweetness s doçura

sweetcorn /ˈswiːtkɔːn/ s (GB) milho verde

sweeten /ˈswiːtn/ vt **1** adoçar **2** ~ sb (up) (coloq) abrandar alguém sweetener s adoçante

sweetheart /ˈswiːthɑːrt/ s **1** (antiq) namorado/a **2** (tratamento) benzinho

sweet pea s ervilha-de-cheiro

swell /swel/ vt, vi (pt swelled pp swollen ou swelled) inchar(-se) swelling s inchaço, protuberância

swept /swept/ pret, pp de SWEEP

swerve /swɜːrv/ vt, vi desviar (-se) bruscamente

swift /swɪft/ adj (~er, ~est) rápido: a ~ reaction uma reação imediata

swill /swɪl/ vt ~ sth (out/down) (esp GB) enxaguar algo

swim /swɪm/ (-mm-) (pt swam pp swum) **1** vi nadar **2** vt: ~ the English Channel atravessar o canal da Mancha a nado **3** vi (cabeça) rodar (por tontura) ● s nadada: go for a ~ (ir) nadar swimmer s nadador/a

swimming /ˈswɪmɪŋ/ s natação

swimming pool s piscina

swimming shorts (GB swimming trunks) s [pl] calção de banho ◆ PAIR

swimsuit /ˈswɪmsuːt/ (GB tb swimming costume) s maiô (mulher)

swindle /ˈswɪndl/ vt fraudar, trapacear ● s fraude, trapaça swindler s trapaceiro/a

swing /swɪŋ/ (pt, pp swung) **1** vt, vi balançar(-se) **2** vt, vi girar: ~ around dar meia-volta **3** vi [+ advérbio): The door swung open/shut. A porta se abriu/fechou. ● s **1** balanço **2** oscilação **3** mudança: mood swings alterações de humor

swirl /swɜːrl/ vt, vi rodopiar: Flakes of snow swirled in the cold wind. Flocos de neve faziam redemoinhos no vento frio.

switch /swɪtʃ/ s **1** interruptor **2** (tb switch-over) mudança ● vt **1** ~ (from sth) to sth mudar (de algo) para algo **2** vt trocar ■ switch (sth) off desligar (algo) switch (sth) on ligar (algo)

switchboard /ˈswɪtʃbɔːrd/ s (painel de) telefonista

swivel /'swɪvl/ (-l-, GB -ll-)
■ swivel (sth) (around) girar
(algo)

swollen /'swəʊlən/ pp de SWELL

swoop /swuːp/ vi ~ (down)
lançar-se ● s investida: Police
made a dawn ~. A polícia atacou
ao amanhecer.

swop = SWAP

sword /sɔːrd/ s espada

swore /swɔːr/ pret de SWEAR

sworn /swɔːrn/ pp de SWEAR

swum /swʌm/ pp de SWIM

swung /swʌŋ/ pret, pp de SWING

syllable /'sɪləbl/ s sílaba

syllabus /'sɪləbəs/ s currículo
escolar

symbol /'sɪmbl/ s símbolo symbolic /sɪm'bɑlɪk/ adj simbólico symbolism /'sɪmbəlɪzəm/ s simbolismo symbolize /'sɪmbəlaɪz/ vt simbolizar

symmetry /'sɪmətri/ s simetria symmetric(al) /sɪ'metrɪk(l)/ adj simétrico

sympathetic /ˌsɪmpə'θetɪk/ adj 1 ~ (to/towards/with sb) compreensivo, solidário (com alguém) → Para simpático, diz-se nice. 2 favorável: lawyers ~ to the peace movement advogados que apóiam o movimento pacifista

sympathize /'sɪmpəθaɪz/ vi ~ (with sb/sth) 1 compadecer-se (de alguém/algo) 2 ser favorável (a alguém/algo) sympathy s (pl -ies) ~ (for/towards sb) solidariedade (a alguém/algo)

symphony /'sɪmfəni/ s (pl -ies) sinfonia

symptom /'sɪmptəm/ s sintoma

synagogue /'sɪnəgɑg/ s sinagoga

synchronize /'sɪŋkrənaɪz/ vt, vi sincronizar

syndicate /'sɪndɪkət/ s sindicato

syndrome /'sɪndrəʊm/ s síndrome

synonym /'sɪnənɪm/ s sinônimo synonymous /sɪ'nɑnɪməs/ adj ~ (with sth) sinônimo (de algo)

syntax /'sɪntæks/ s sintaxe

synthetic /sɪn'θetɪk/ adj 1 sintético 2 artificial

syringe /sɪ'rɪndʒ/ s seringa

syrup /'sɪrəp/ s calda de açúcar

system /'sɪstəm/ s sistema ▸ get sth out of your system (coloq) colocar algo para fora (emoções) systematic /ˌsɪstə'mætɪk/ adj metódico

T t

T, t /tiː/ s (pl T's, t's /tiːz/) T, t

tab /tæb/ s 1 (lata de bebida) anel da tampa 2 etiqueta 3 (USA) conta

table /'teɪbl/ s 1 mesa: bedside ~ criado-mudo 2 tabela: ~ of contents índice

tablecloth /'teɪblklɔːθ/; GB -klɒθ/ s toalha de mesa

tablespoon /'teɪblspuːn/ s 1 colher de sopa 2 (tb tablespoonful) colherada (de sopa)

tablet /'tæblət/ s 1 comprimido 2 placa (comemorativa)

table tennis s tênis de mesa

tabloid /'tæblɔɪd/ s: the ~ press a imprensa sensacionalista

taboo /tə'buː; GB tæ-/ adj, s (pl ~s) tabu

tacit /'tæsɪt/ adj tácito

tack /tæk/ vt pregar (com tachinha) ■ tack sth on (to sth) (coloq) anexar algo (a algo) ● s 1 tachinha 2 política (de ação)

tackle /'tækl/ s 1 equipamento 2 (Esporte) entrada ● vt 1 enfrentar: ~ a problem colar de um problema 2 ~ sb about/on/over sth tratar com alguém sobre algo 3 (Esporte) dar uma entrada em

tacky /'tæki/ adj (-ier, -iest) 1 pegajoso 2 (coloq) brega

tact /tækt/ s tato tactful adj diplomático

tactic /'tæktɪk/ s tática tactical adj 1 tático 2 estratégico

tactless /'tæktləs/ adj sem tato: That was ~ of you. Foi falta de tato de sua parte.

tadpole /'tædpəʊl/ s girino

tag /tæg/ s 1 etiqueta 2 rótulo ● vt (-gg-) 1 etiquetar 2 rotular ■ tag along (behind/with sb) acompanhar alguém, seguir alguém de perto

tail /teɪl/ s 1 rabo 2 (tails) [pl] fraque 3 (tails) [pl] (moeda) coroa ● vt perseguir ■ tail away/off sumir

tailor /'teɪlər/ s alfaiate ● vt fazer algo sob medida

tailor-made adj (feito) sob medida/encomenda

taint /teɪnt/ vt 1 contaminar 2 (reputação) manchar

take /teɪk/ vt (pt took pp taken /'teɪkən/) 1 tomar 2 pegar 3 ~ sb/sth (with you) levar algo (com você): ~ sb out levar/convidar alguém para sair

4 ~ sb/sth (away) (from sb/sth) tirar alguém/algo (de alguém/ algo) **5** aceitar **6** receber (*notícia, etc.*) **7** (*tolerar*) suportar **8** (*tempo*) levar: *It won't ~ long.* Não vai demorar muito. **9** (*qualidade*) necessitar de: *It takes courage to speak out.* É preciso coragem para se falar o que se pensa. **10** (*tamanho*) (*esp GB*) usar: *What size shoes do you ~?* Que número você calça? **11** (*foto*) tirar **12** (*curso, exame*) fazer ▸ **take it (that...)** supor (que...) ▸ **take some/a lot of doing** (*coloq*) dar trabalho NOTA Para outras expressões com **take**, ver o substantivo, adjetivo, etc., p. ex. **take place** em PLACE. ▪ **take after sb** parecer-se com alguém (*mais velho da família*) **take sth apart** desmontar algo **take sth back 1** (*loja*) aceitar algo de volta **2** retirar algo (*que se disse*) **take sth down 1** trazer/levar algo para baixo **2** desmontar algo **3** tomar nota de algo **take sb in 1** acolher a alguém **2** enganar alguém **take sth in** entender algo **take off 1** (*roupa*) tirar algo **2 ~ the day off** tirar o dia de folga **take sb on** contratar alguém **take sth on** aceitar algo (*trabalho*) **take it/ sth out on sb** descontar algo em alguém **take sth out** tirar algo **take sth over** assumir o controle de algo (*empresa, situação, etc.*) **take over from sb** substituir alguém **take to sb/sth:** *I took to his parents immediately.* Gostei dos pais dele imediatamente. **take up sth** ocupar algo (*espaço, tempo*) **take sth up** começar algo (*hobby*) **take sb up on** (*coloq*) aceitar algo de alguém (*desafio, etc.*) **take sth up with sb** discutir algo com alguém

take-off *s* decolagem

takeout /ˈteɪkaʊt/ (GB **takeaway** /ˈteɪkəweɪ/) *s* **1** restaurante que vende comida para viagem **2** comida para viagem

takeover /ˈteɪkoʊvər/ *s* **1** (*empresa*) aquisição **2** (*Mil*) tomada de poder

takings /ˈteɪkɪŋz/ *s* [*pl*] arrecadação

talc /tælk/ (*tb* **talcum (powder)** /ˈtælkəm/) *s* talco

tale /teɪl/ *s* **1** conto **2** fofoca

talent /ˈtælənt/ *s* talento **talented** *adj* talentoso

talk /tɔːk/ *s* **1** conversa, papo **2** (**talks**) negociações **3** palestra ● **1** *vi* conversar → FALAR **2** *vt* falar

(de): *~ sense/business* falar algo sensato/de negócios **3** *vi* comentar ▸ **talk shop** (*pej*) falar de trabalho **talk your way out of (doing) sth** livrar-se de (fazer) algo com lábia ▪ **talk down to sb** falar com alguém como se este fosse estúpido **talk sb into/out of (doing) sth** persuadir alguém a (não) fazer algo **talkative** /ˈtɔːkətɪv/ *adj* tagarela

tall /tɔːl/ *adj* (**~er, ~est**) alto: *How ~ are you?* Quanto você tem de altura? → ALTO

tambourine /ˌtæmbəˈriːn/ *s* pandeiro

tame /teɪm/ *adj* (**~er, -est**) **1** domesticado **2** manso **3** (*festa, etc.*) sem graça ● *vt* domar

tamper /ˈtæmpər/ *v* ▪ **tamper with sth** mexer em algo

tampon /ˈtæmpɒn/ *s* tampão

tan /tæn/ *vt, vi* (**-nn-**) bronzear (-se) ● *s* bronzeado: *get a ~* bronzear-se ● *adj* (*cor*) castanho amarelado

tangent /ˈtændʒənt/ *s* tangente: *go/fly off at a ~* sair pela tangente

tangerine /ˈtændʒəriːn; GB ˌtændʒəˈriːn/ *s* tangerina ● *adj, s* (*cor*) laranja escuro

tangle /ˈtæŋɡl/ *s* **1** emaranhado **2** confusão: *get into a ~* entrar numa enrascada ● *vt, vi ~ (sth) (up)* emaranhar-se, emaranhar algo **tangled** *adj* emaranhado

tank /tæŋk/ *s* tanque

tanker /ˈtæŋkər/ *s* **1** petroleiro **2** carro-tanque

tantalize /ˈtæntəlaɪz/ *vt* atormentar **tantalizing** *adj* tentador

tantrum /ˈtæntrəm/ *s* acesso de raiva

tap /tæp/ *s* **1** (*GB*) torneira **2** pancadinha ● (**-pp-**) **1** *vt ~ sth (against/on sth)* bater levemente com algo (em algo) **2** *vt ~ sb/sth (on sth)* dar tapinhas em alguém/ algo **3** *vt, vi ~ (into) sth* explorar algo **4** *vt* (*telefone*) grampear

tape /teɪp/ *s* fita: *~ deck* toca-fitas ◇ *have sth on ~* ter algo gravado ● *vt* **1 ~ sth (up)** lacrar algo com fita adesiva **2** gravar

tape measure (*tb* **measuring tape**) *s* fita métrica

tape recorder *s* gravador

tapestry /ˈtæpəstri/ *s* (*pl* **-ies**) tapeçaria

tar /tɑr/ *s* alcatrão

target /ˈtɑrɡɪt/ *s* **1** alvo **2** meta ● *vt* **1** dirigir-se a: *We're targeting the young.* Temos como alvo os jovens. **2 ~ sth at/on sb/sth**

apontar algo na direção de alguém/algo

tariff /'tærɪf/ s **1** lista de preços **2** taxa de importação

Tarmac® /'tɑːmæk/ s **1** asfalto **2** pista (aeroporto)

tarnish /'tɑːnɪʃ/ **1** vt, vi embaçar **2** vt manchar (reputação, etc.)

tart /tɑːt/ s torta (doce, sem cobertura)

tartan /'tɑːtn/ s (tecido de) xadrez escocês

task /tæsk; GB tɑːsk/ s tarefa

taste /teɪst/ s **1** sabor **2** (bom) gosto **3** (comida) um pouco **4** amostra: her first ~ of city life sua primeira experiência da vida na cidade ● **1** vi sentir o gosto de **2** ti ter gosto de provar **4** vt (fig) experimentar

tasteful /'teɪstfl/ adj de bom gosto

tasteless /'teɪstləs/ adj **1** insípido **2** de mau gosto

tasty /'teɪsti/ adj (-ier, -iest) saboroso

tattered /'tætərd/ adj esfarrapado

tatters /'tætərz/ s ▸ **in tatters** em farrapos

tattoo /tæ'tuː; GB tə'tuː/ s (pl ~s) tatuagem ● vt tatuar

tatty /'tæti/ adj (-ier, -iest) (GB, coloq) em mau estado

taught /tɔːt/ pret, pp de TEACH

taunt /tɔːnt/ vt zombar de ● s zombaria

Taurus /'tɔːrəs/ s Touro

taut /tɔːt/ adj tenso

tavern /'tævərn/ s (antiq) taverna

tax /tæks/ s imposto: ~ return declaração de imposto de renda ● vt **1** taxar **2** (pessoas) cobrar imposto de **3** (recursos) exigir demais de **4** (paciência) esgotar, abusar de **taxable** adj tributável **taxation** s tributação **taxing** adj extenuante

tax-free adj livre de impostos

taxi /'tæksi/ s (tb **taxicab**) táxi: ~ driver taxista ● vi (pt, pp -ied part pres **taxiing**) (avião) taxiar

taxpayer /'tækspeɪər/ s contribuinte (do imposto de renda)

tea /tiː/ s **1** chá: ~ shop casa de chá **2** chá da tarde **3** (GB) jantar

tea kettle s chaleira

team /tiːm/ s **1** equipe, time ■ **team up (with sb)** trabalhar em equipe (com alguém)

teamwork /'tiːmwɜːrk/ s trabalho em equipe

teapot /'tiːpɒt/ s bule de chá

tear¹ /tɪər/ s lágrima: He was in tears. Ele estava chorando. **tearful** adj choroso

tear² /teər/ (pt **tore** pp **torn**) **1** vt, vi rasgar(-se): ~ sth up fazer algo em pedaços **2** vt ~ **sth out** arrancar algo **3** vi ~ **along/past** andar/passar a toda velocidade ■ **be torn between A and B** estar (dividido) entre A e B **tear sth down** derrubar algo ● s rasgo

tea room s casa de chá

tease /tiːz/ vt caçoar de

teaspoon /'tiːspuːn/ s **1** colher de chá **2** (tb **teaspoonful**) colherada de chá

teatime /'tiːtaɪm/ s (GB) hora do chá

technical /'teknɪkl/ adj técnico **technicality** /ˌteknɪ'kæləti/ s (pl -ies) **1** detalhes técnicos **2** (meros) detalhes técnicos **technically** adv **1** tecnicamente **2** estritamente

technical college s (GB) escola técnica superior

technician /tek'nɪʃn/ s técnico/a

technique /tek'niːk/ s técnica

technology /tek'nɒlədʒi/ s (pl -ies) tecnologia **technological** /ˌteknə'lɒdʒɪkl/ adj tecnológico

teddy bear /'tedi beər/ s ursinho de pelúcia

tedious /'tiːdiəs/ adj tedioso

tedium /'tiːdiəm/ s tédio

teem /tiːm/ v ■ **teem with sth** estar repleto de algo

teenage /'tiːneɪdʒ/ adj (de) adolescente **teenager** s adolescente

teens /tiːnz/ s [pl] adolescência

tee shirt s T-SHIRT

teeth /tiːθ/ plural de TOOTH

teethe /tiːð/ vi: The baby is teething. Os dentes do bebê estão nascendo. ▸ **teething problems/troubles** pequenas dificuldades do início de um negócio

telecommunications /ˌtelɪkəˌmjuːnɪ'keɪʃnz/ s telecomunicações

telegraph /'telɪgræf; GB -grɑːf/ s telégrafo

telephone /'telɪfoʊn/ s telefone: ~ call/box ligação/lista telefônica ▸ **on the telephone**: She's on the ~. Ela está (falando) ao telefone. ◇ We're not on the ~. Não temos telefone. ● vt, vi

~ (sb) telefonar (para alguém)
telephone booth (tb phone booth, GB (tele)phone box) s cabine telefônica

telescope /'teliskoup/ s telescópio

televise /'telivaiz/ vt televisionar

television /'telivi3n/ s (abrev TV) 1 televisão 2 (tb ~ set) televisor

tell /tel/ (pt, pp **told**) 1 vt dizer: I told you so. Eu lhe avisei. NOTA No discurso indireto tell é seguido de objeto direto: Tell him to wait. Diga a ele que espere. ◊ She told him to come. Ela disse a ele que viesse. → SAY 2 vt contar 3 vt, vi saber: you never can ~ nunca se sabe ◊ You can ~ she's French. Dá para notar que ela é francesa. 4 vt ~ A from B distinguir entre A e B ▶ **tell the time** (USA **tell time**) dizer as horas **there's no telling** é impossível saber/dizer **you're telling me** (coloq) e você acha que está me contando uma novidade ■ **tell sb off** (coloq) dar bronca em alguém **tell on sb** (coloq) delatar alguém

teller /'telər/ s caixa (banco)

telling /'teliŋ/ adj revelador, significativo

telling-off s bronca

telly /'teli/ s (pl -ies) (GB, coloq) TV

temp /temp/ s empregado/a temporário/a

temper /'tempər/ vt moderar • s humor, temperamento: in a bad ~ de mau humor ▶ **keep/lose your temper** manter/perder a calma

temperament /'tempremənt/ s temperamento temperamental adj temperamental

temperate /'tempərət/ adj 1 (clima) temperado 2 (caráter) moderado

temperature /'temprətʃuər/ s temperatura: have/run a ~ ter febre

template /'templit/ s molde

temple /'templ/ s 1 (Relig) templo 2 (Anat) têmpora

tempo /'tempou/ s 1 (pl tempi /'tempi:/) (Mús) andamento 2 (pl ~s) ritmo

temporary /'tempəreri; GB -prəri/ adj temporário temporarily adv temporariamente

tempt /tempt/ vt tentar ▶ **tempt fate** brincar com a sorte temptation s tentação tempting adj tentador

ten /ten/ adj, pron, s dez tenth 1 adj décimo 2 pron, adv o(s)/a(s) décimo(s)/a(s) 3 s décima parte, décimo

tenacious /tə'neiʃəs/ adj tenaz

tenacity /tə'næsəti/ s tenacidade

tenant /'tenənt/ s inquilino/a tenancy s (pl -ies) locação

tend /tend/ 1 vt cuidar de 2 vi tender, ter tendência **tendency** s (pl -ies) tendência

tender /'tendər/ adj 1 tenro 2 (ferida) dolorido 3 (olhar) carinhoso tenderly adv ternamente tenderness s ternura

tendon /'tendən/ s tendão

tenement /'tenəmənt/ s: a ~ block/house um cortiço

tenner /'tenər/ s (GB, coloq) (nota de) dez libras

tennis /'tenis/ s tênis

tenor /'tenər/ s tenor

tense /tens/ adj (-er **-est**) tenso • s tempo (verbal): in the past ~ no pretérito

tension /'tenʃn/ s tensão, ansiedade

tent /tent/ s 1 barraca (acampar) 2 (circo) toldo

tentacle /'tentəkl/ s tentáculo

tentative /'tentətiv/ adj 1 experimental 2 cauteloso

tenth Ver TEN

tenuous /'tenjuəs/ adj tênue

tenure /'tenjər; GB -juə(r)/ s 1 (de um cargo) mandato 2 (terra, etc.) posse

tepid /'tepid/ adj tépido

term /tɜ:rm/ s 1 período, prazo: ~ of office mandato (de um governo) ◊ in the long/short ~ a longo/curto prazo 2 período letivo (trimestre, na GB) 3 termo • vt (fml) considerar como

terminal /'tɜ:rminl/ adj, s terminal

terminate /'tɜ:rmineit/ 1 vt, vi terminar: This train terminates at Euston. O ponto final deste trem é Euston. 2 vt (contrato) rescindir

terminology /,tɜ:rmi'nɑlədʒi/ s (pl -ies) terminologia

terminus /'tɜ:rminəs/ s (pl termini /-nai/) (estação) terminal

termite /'tɜ:rmait/ s cupim

terms /tɜ:rmz/ s condições ▶ **be on good, bad, etc. terms (with sb)** manter boas, más, etc. relações (com alguém) **come to terms with sb/sth** aceitar alguém/algo

terrace /'terəs/ s 1 terraço 2 (the terraces) (GB) (Esporte) as arquibancadas **3** (GB) fileira de casas **4** (GB) (tb **terraced house**) casa geminada (dos dois lados)

terrain /təˈreɪn/ s terreno

terrible /ˈterəbl/ adj terrível **terribly** adv terrivelmente: *I'm ~ sorry.* Sinto muitíssimo.

terrific /təˈrɪfɪk/ adj (coloq) **1** tremendo **2** maravilhoso: *The food was ~ value.* A comida tinha um preço ótimo.

terrify /ˈterɪfaɪ/ vt (pt, pp -**ied**) aterrorizar **terrified** adj aterrorizado: *She's ~ of flying.* Ela morre de medo de voar. **terrifying** adj aterrorizante

territorial /ˌterəˈtɔːriəl/ adj territorial

territory /ˈterətəri; GB -tri/ s (pl -**ies**) território

terror /ˈterər/ s terror **terrorize** vt aterrorizar

terrorism /ˈterərɪzəm/ s terrorismo **terrorist** s terrorista

terse /tɜːrs/ adj lacônico: *a ~ reply* uma resposta seca

test /test/ s **1** teste: *blood ~* exame de sangue **2** (Educ) prova, exame ● vt **1** testar, pôr à prova **2** ~ **sb** (**on sth**) (Educ) examinar alguém (em algo)

testament /ˈtestəmənt/ s (fml) **1** ~ (**to sth**) prova (de algo) **2** testamento

testicle /ˈtestɪkl/ s testículo

testify /ˈtestɪfaɪ/ vt, vi (pt, pp -**ied**) testemunhar

testimony /ˈtestɪmoʊni; GB -məni/ s (pl -**ies**) testemunho

test tube s tubo de ensaio: *test-tube baby* bebê de proveta

tether /ˈteðər/ vt prender (com corda, etc.)

text /tekst/ s texto: *set ~* (GB) leitura obrigatória

textbook /ˈtekstbʊk/ s livro didático

textile /ˈtekstaɪl/ s [ger pl] tecido: *the ~ industry* a indústria têxtil

text message s mensagem de texto

texture /ˈtekstʃər/ s textura

ação de graças

that /ðæt/ adj, pron (pl those) isso, esse/a, esses, aquilo, aquele/a, aqueles/as ▶ **that is** (**to say**) ou seja **that's right/it é** isso ● adv tão: *It's ~ long.* É comprido assim. ◇ *~ much worse* tanto pior ● /ðət, ðæt/ conj, pron rel que: *I told him ~ he should wait.* Eu lhe disse que esperasse. ◇ *The horse ~ won is his.* O cavalo que ganhou é dele. ◇ *the job ~ I applied for* o emprego para o qual me candidatei ◇ *the year ~ he died* o ano em que ele morreu → QUE (2)

thatch /θætʃ/ vt cobrir com telhado de palha **thatched** adj com telhado de palha

thaw /θɔː/ vt, vi degelar ● s degelo

the /ðə/ → Pronuncia-se /ðɪ/ antes de vogal ou /ðiː/ quando se quer dar ênfase. art def o, a, os, as ▶ **the more/less… the more/less…** quanto mais/menos…, mais/menos… NOTA O artigo definido em inglês:
1 Não se usa com substantivos contáveis quando se fala em termos gerais: *Books are expensive.* ◇ *Children learn very fast.*
2 Omite-se com substantivos incontáveis quando se fala de uma substância ou idéia em geral: *I like cheese/pop music.*
3 Geralmente se omite antes de nomes próprios e substantivos que indicam relações familiares: *Mrs. Smith* ◇ *Ana's mother* ◇ *Grandma came yesterday.*
4 Com as partes do corpo e objetos pessoais, usa-se o possessivo, não o artigo: *Give me your hand.* ◇ *He put his tie on.*
5 School e **church** podem ser precedidos de artigo ou não, mas o significado difere. → SCHOOL

theater (GB **theatre**) /ˈθiːətər; GB ˈθɪətə(r)/ s **1** teatro **2** (USA) (tb **movie ~**) (sala de) cinema

theatrical /θiˈætrɪkl/ adj teatral

theft /θeft/ s roubo → THIEF, ROB

their /ðeər/ adj poss dele(s), dela(s)

theirs /ðeərz/ pron poss o(s)/a(s) deles/delas

them /ðəm, ðem/ pron **1** [objeto direto] os, as **2** [complemento/objeto indireto] lhes **3** [depois de prep e do verbo be] eles, elas: *They took it with ~.* Elas o levaram consigo.

theme /θiːm/ s tema

theme park s parque temático

themselves /ðəm'selvz/ pron 1 [uso reflexivo] se: They enjoyed ~. Eles se divertiram. 2 [com prep] si mesmos/as 3 [uso enfático] eles/as mesmos/as

then /ðen/ adv 1 então: from ~ on desde então 2 naquela época 3 logo, depois 4 nesse caso, então

theology /θi'ɒlədʒi/ s teologia
theological /ˌθiːə'lɒdʒɪkl/ adj teológico

theoretical /ˌθɪə'retɪkl/ adj teórico

theory /'θɪəri/ s (pl -ies) teoria

therapeutic /ˌθerə'pjuːtɪk/ adj terapêutico

therapy /'θerəpi/ s (pl -ies) terapia therapist s terapeuta

there /ðeər/ adv aí, ali, lá ▶ there and then no ato, ali mesmo ● pron ▶ there + to be: How many are ~? Quantos há? ◇ There has been very little rain recently. Tem chovido muito pouco ultimamente. → HAVER ▶ there + v modal + be: There might be rain later. Pode chover mais tarde. ◇ There shouldn't be any problems. Creio que não haverá problema algum. NOTA There também é usado com seem e appear: There seem/appear to be two possible approaches. Parece haver duas possibilidades de abordagem.

thereafter /ˌðeər'æftər; GB -'ɑːf-/ adv (fml) depois disso

thereby /ˌðeər'baɪ/ adv (fml) 1 por isso 2 desse modo

therefore /'ðeəfɔːr/ adv portanto

thermal /'θɜːrml/ adj 1 térmico 2 termal

thermometer /θər'mɒmɪtər/ s termômetro

thermostat /'θɜːrməstæt/ s termostato

these /ðiːz/ adj, pron pl de THIS

thesis /'θiːsɪs/ s (pl theses /'θiːsiːz/) tese

they /ðeɪ/ pron eles/as NOTA O pron pess não pode ser omitido em inglês.

they'd /ðeɪd/ 1 = THEY HAD Ver HAVE 2 = THEY WOULD Ver WOULD

they'll /ðeɪl/ = THEY WILL Ver WILL

they're /ðeər/ = THEY ARE Ver BE

they've /ðeɪv/ = THEY HAVE Ver HAVE

thick /θɪk/ (~er, ~est) adj 1 grosso: The ice was six inches ~. O gelo tinha seis polegadas de grossura. 2 espesso 3 (barba) cerrado 4 (sotaque) carregado 5 (coloq, esp GB) (pessoa) estúpido ● adv (tb thickly) espesso:

Don't spread the butter too ~. Não ponha uma camada muito grossa de manteiga. ● s ▶ in the thick of sth bastante envolvido em algo ▶ through thick and thin para o que der e vier thicken vt, vi engrossar thickly adv 1 espessamente 2 (povoado) densamente thickness s espessura, grossura

thief /θiːf/ s (pl thieves /θiːvz/) ladrão NOTA Thief é termo geral, é o ladrão que geralmente age sem ser visto e sem recorrer à violência; o robber rouba bancos, lojas, etc., geralmente com violência ou ameaças; burglar é o ladrão que rouba uma casa ou loja quando não há ninguém dentro; e shoplifter é a pessoa que leva coisas de uma loja sem pagar. → ROB

thigh /θaɪ/ s coxa

thimble /'θɪmbl/ s dedal

thin /θɪn/ (thinner, thinnest) adj 1 (pessoa) magro → MAGRO 2 fino, delgado 3 (sopa, cabelo) ralo ▶ thin on the ground (GB) escasso vanish, etc. into thin air desaparecer misteriosamente ● adv (tb thinly) fino ● vt, vi (-nn-) ~ (sth) (out) tornar algo/tornar-se menos espesso/volumoso

thing /θɪŋ/ s 1 coisa: Put your things there. Ponha as suas coisas ali. ◇ What's that ~ on the table? O que é isso sobre a mesa? ◇ I can't see a ~. Não consigo ver nada. ◇ the main ~ o mais importante ◇ Forget the whole ~. Esqueça todo o assunto. ◇ The way things are going... Do modo como está a situação... 2 Poor (little) ~! Coitadinho! 3 (the thing) Just the ~ business people need. Exatamente o que as pessoas de negócios precisam. ▶ first/last thing na primeira/última hora for one thing para começar get/keep things in proportion considerar/manter as coisas na devidas proporções it's a good thing (that)... ainda bem que... the thing is... a questão é...

think /θɪŋk/ (pt, pp thought) 1 vt, vi pensar: Just ~! Imagina! ◇ The job took longer than we thought. O trabalho levou mais tempo do que imaginávamos. 2 vi refletir 3 vt, vi crer: I ~ so. Acho que sim. ▶ I should think so eu espero que sim think the world of sb ter alguém em alta consideração ■ think about sb/sth 1 pensar em alguém/

algo **2** lembrar-se de alguém/ algo **3** levar alguém/algo em conta **think about (doing) sth** pensar em (fazer) algo **think of sth 1** pensar em algo **2** imaginar algo **3** lembrar-se de algo **think sth out**: *a well thought out plan* um plano bem pensado **think sth over** refletir sobre algo **think sth up** (*coloq*) inventar, pensar em algo

thinker /ˈθɪŋkər/ s pensador/a

thinking /ˈθɪŋkɪŋ/ s [U] modo de pensar: *What's your ~ on this?* O que você pensa disso? ◇ *Good ~!* Bem pensado! ● *adj* [*antes de substantivo*] racional, inteligente

third /θɜːrd/ (*abrev* **3rd**) *adj* terceiro ● *pron, adv* o(s)/a(s) terceiro(s)/a(s) ● *s* **1** terça parte, terço **2** (**the third**) o dia três **3** (*tb* ~ **gear**) terceira (*marcha*) **thirdly** *adv* em terceiro lugar (*em enumeração*)

third party *s* [*sing*] terceiros

Third World *s* (**the Third World**) o terceiro mundo

thirst /θɜːrst/ s ~ (**for sth**) sede de (algo) **thirsty** *adj* (**-ier**, **-iest**) sedento: *be ~* estar com sede

thirteen /ˌθɜːrˈtiːn/ *adj, pron, s* treze **thirteenth 1** *adj* décimo terceiro **2** *pron, adv* o(s)/a(s) décimo(s) terceiro(s), o(s)/a(s) décima(s) terceira(s) **3** *s* décima terceira parte, treze avos

thirty /ˈθɜːrti/ *adj, pron, s* trinta **thirtieth 1** *adj, pron* trigésimo **2** *s* trigésima parte, trinta avos

this /ðɪs/ (*pl* **these**) *adj, pron* isto, este/a ● *adv*: ~ *high/far* alto/ longe assim

thistle /ˈθɪsl/ *s* cardo

thorn /θɔːrn/ *s* espinho **thorny** *adj* (**-ier**, **-iest**) espinhoso

thorough /ˈθɜːroʊ/, *GB* /ˈθʌrə/ *adj* **1** profundo **2** (*pessoa*) meticuloso **thoroughly** *adv* **1** a fundo **2** completamente

those /ðoʊz/ *adj, pron pl de* THAT

though /ðoʊ/ *conj* embora, ainda que ● *adv* mesmo assim

thought /θɔːt/ *pret, pp de* THINK ● *s* **1** pensamento **2** idéia, intenção **thoughtful** *adj* **1** pensativo **2** atencioso: *It was very ~ of you.* Foi muito gentil da sua parte. **thoughtless** *adj* desatencioso, impensado, descuidado

thousand /ˈθaʊznd/ *adj, pron, s* mil: *thousands of people* milhares de pessoas **thousandth 1** *adj, pron* milésimo **2** *s* milésima parte

thrash /θræʃ/ *vt* dar uma surra

em **thrashing** *s* surra

thread /θred/ *s* fio: *needle and ~* agulha e linha ● *vt* **1** (*agulha*) colocar linha em **2** (*contas, etc.*) colocar em um fio **3** (*corda, etc.*) passar

threat /θret/ *s* ameaça **threaten** *vt* ameaçar **threatening** *adj* ameaçador

three /θriː/ *adj, pron, s* três

three-dimensional (*tb* **3-D** /ˌθriː ˈdiː/) *adj* tridimensional

threshold /ˈθreʃhoʊld/ *s* umbral, limiar

threw /θruː/ *pret de* THROW

thrill /θrɪl/ *s* **1** calafrio **2** emoção: *What a ~!* Que emocionante! **thrilled** *adj* entusiasmado **thriller** *s* obra de suspense (*filme, etc.*) **thrilling** *adj* emocionante

thrive /θraɪv/ *vi* ~ (**on sth**) desenvolver-se (em/com algo): *a thriving industry* uma indústria em pleno desenvolvimento

throat /θroʊt/ *s* garganta

throb /θrɑb/ *vi* (**-bb-**) vibrar, palpitar ● *s* vibração, latejamento

throne /θroʊn/ *s* trono

through (*tb USA, coloq* **thru**) /θruː/ *prep* **1** através de, por **2** durante, ao longo de: *I'm halfway ~ the book.* Eu estou na metade do livro. **3** por causa de: ~ *carelessness* por descuido **4** (*USA*) até... (inclusive): *Tuesday ~ Friday* de terça a sexta ● *adv* **1** de um lado para o outro: *Can you get ~?* Você consegue passar? **2** do princípio ao fim: *I've read the poem ~ once.* Eu li o poema inteiro uma vez. ◇ *all night ~* durante toda a noite NOTA Para o uso de **through** em PHRASAL VERBS, ver o verbo, p. ex. **break through** em BREAK. ● *adj* direto: *No ~ road* Rua sem saída

throughout /θruːˈaʊt/ *prep* por/ durante todo ● *adv* **1** por toda parte **2** todo o tempo

throw /θroʊ/ *s* **1** arremesso, lance: *It's your ~.* É sua vez (de jogar). ● *vt* (*pt* **threw** /θruː/ *pp* **thrown** /θroʊn/) **1** ~ **sth (to sb)**; ~ **sth (at sb/sth)** atirar, jogar algo (a/ para alguém/algo); algo (em alguém/algo) → **Throw sth at sb/sth** indica a intenção de acertar um objeto ou uma pessoa: *Don't ~ stones at the cat.* Não jogue pedras no gato. **2** [+ *adv*] jogar: ~ *back your head* jogar a cabeça para trás ◇ *She threw up her hands in horror.* Ela levantou as mãos horrorizada. **3** (*cavalo*) derrubar

4 (coloq) desconcertar **5** deixar (de determinada forma): We were thrown into confusion by the news. As notícias nos deixaram confusos. ◇ thrown out of work mandado embora do trabalho **6** (luz, etc.) projetar, fazer ■throw sth about/around esparramar algo ■throw sth away/out jogar algo fora (no lixo) throw sb out expulsar alguém throw sth out (proposta) recusar algo throw (sth) up vomitar (algo)

thrust /θrʌst/ (pt, pp thrust) **1** vt meter **2** vt, vi ~ at sb (with sth)/ sth at sb lançar-se sobre alguém (com algo) ■thrust sb/ sth on/upon sb impor alguém/ algo a alguém ● s **1** empurrão **2** (espada) estocada **3** ideia fundamental

thud /θʌd/ s baque surdo ● vi (-dd-) **1** fazer um ruído surdo, cair com um baque: ~ against/ into sth chocar-se contra algo (com um baque) **2** (coração) bater com força

thug /θʌg/ s criminoso/a, bandido/a

thumb /θʌm/ s polegar ● vi ~ through sth folhear algo ▶thumb a lift pedir carona

thump /θʌmp/ **1** vt golpear **2** vi (coração) bater com força ● s **1** golpe **2** baque

thunder /'θʌndər/ s [U] trovão: a clap of ~ uma trovoada ● vi **1** trovejar **2** estrondar

thunderstorm /'θʌndərstɔːm/ s tempestade com trovões

Thursday /'θɜːrzdeɪ, -di/ s (abrev **Thur.**, **Thurs.**) quinta(-feira) → MONDAY

thus /ðʌs/ adv (fml) **1** assim **2** portanto

thwart /θwɔːrt/ vt frustrar

tick /tɪk/ s **1** tique-taque **2** (GB) (marca) tique ● **1** vi fazer tique-taque **2** vt (GB) ~ sth (off) ticar algo (de uma lista) ■tick away/ by passar (tempo) tick over (GB) manter as coisas na rotina

ticket /'tɪkɪt/ s **1** (trem, etc.) passagem **2** (Teat., etc.) ingresso **3** (biblioteca) carteira **4** etiqueta

tickle /'tɪkl/ vt, vi fazer cócegas (em) ● s cócegas

ticklish /'tɪklɪʃ/ adj: be ~ ter cócegas

tidal /'taɪdl/ adj relativo à maré
tidal wave s maremoto

tide /taɪd/ s **1** maré **2** (fig) corrente

tidy /'taɪdi/ adj (-ier, -iest) **1** organizado **2** (aparência) arrumado ● vt (pt, pp -ied) ~ sth (up) arrumar, organizar algo: ~ sth away colocar algo no lugar

tie /taɪ/ **1** gravata **2** [ger pl] laço **3** (Esporte) empate ● (pt, pp tied part pres tying) **1** vt, vi ~ (sb/sth) (up) amarrar (alguém/algo): amarrar-se **2** vt (gravata) colocar **3** vt, vi (Esporte) empatar ■tie sb/yourself down comprometer alguém, comprometer-se: Having young children ties you down. Ter filhos pequenos prende a gente.

tier /tɪr/ s nível, camada

tiger /'taɪgər/ s tigre

tight /taɪt/ (~er, ~est) adj **1** apertado, justo **2** esticado **3** (controle) rigoroso ● adv com força: Hold ~! Agarre-se firme! tighten vt, vi ~ (sth) (up) apertar algo; apertar-se: ~ immigration controls tornar mais rigoroso o controle da imigração **tightly** adv com firmeza, rigorosamente

tightrope /'taɪtroʊp/ s corda bamba

tights /taɪts/ s [pl] **1** meia-calça **2** (para balé, etc.) malha → PAIR

tile /taɪl/ s **1** telha **2** azulejo, ladrilho **3** pedra (dominó) ● vt **1** cobrir com telha **2** ladrilhar **3** azulejar

till /tɪl/ **1** prep, conj Ver UNTIL ● s caixa (registradora)

tilt /tɪlt/ vt, vi inclinar(-se) ● s inclinação

timber /'tɪmbər/ s **1** madeira **2** [U] árvores (para corte) **3** madeiramento

time /taɪm/ s **1** tempo: all the ~ todo o tempo ◇ You've been gone a long ~! Você demorou muito! **2** hora: What ~ is it? Que horas são? ◇ It's ~ we were going/~ for us to go. Está na hora de irmos embora. ◇ by the ~ we reached home quando chegamos em casa ◇ (by) this ~ next year nesta data no ano que vem ◇ at the present ~ atualmente **3** vez: one at a ~ um de cada vez **4** época: at one ~ em certa época ▶ahead of time adiantado (and) about time (too) (coloq) já está/estava na hora at all times a qualquer hora at the time naquele momento/ tempo at times às vezes for a time durante algum tempo for the time being por enquanto from time to time de vez em quando have a good time/the time of your life divertir-se (muito) in good time cedo, com tempo in time com o

tempo in time (for sth/to do sth) a tempo (para algo/de fazer algo) on time na hora → PONTUAL take your time (over sth/doing sth) não se apressar (com algo/para fazer algo) time after time; time and (time) again repetidamente ● vt 1 programar, prever 2 ~ sth well/badly escolher o momento oportuno/errado (para fazer) algo 3 medir o tempo de, cronometrar timer s timer timing s 1 coordenação: the ~ of the election a data das eleições 2 cronometragem

timely /'taɪmli/ adj (-ier, -iest) oportuno

times /taɪmz/ prep multiplicado por: Three ~ four is twelve. Três vezes quatro é doze.

timetable /'taɪmteɪbl/ s horário

timid /'tɪmɪd/ adj tímido

tin /tɪn/ s 1 estanho: tinfoil papel-alumínio 2 (GB) lata: tin-opener abridor de latas

tinge /tɪndʒ/ vt tingir ● s tom

tingle /'tɪŋgl/ vi 1 formigar 2 tremer (emoção)

tinker /'tɪŋkər/ vi mexer

tinned /tɪnd/ adj em/de lata

tinsel /'tɪnsl/ s ouropel

tint /tɪnt/ s 1 tonalidade 2 (cabelo) tintura tinted adj 1 (cabelo) tingido 2 (vidro) escurecido

tiny /'taɪni/ adj (-ier, -iest) minúsculo

tip /tɪp/ s 1 ponta 2 (GB) depósito de lixo 3 gorjeta 4 dica ● vt, vi 1 ~ (sth) (up) inclinar (algo) 2 ~ (sth) (over) virar-se, derrubar (algo) 3 dar gorjeta (a) ■ tip sb off (coloq) dar uma dica a alguém

tiptoe /'tɪptoʊ/ s ▶ on tiptoe na ponta dos pés ● vi: ~ in/out entrar/sair na ponta dos pés

tire /'taɪər/ s pneu ● vt, vi cansar(-se) ■ tire sb/yourself out esgotar alguém/esgotar-se tired adj cansado ▶ (sick and) tired of sb/(doing) sth farto de alguém/de (fazer) algo tired out esgotado

tireless /'taɪərləs/ adj incansável

tiresome /'taɪərsəm/ adj 1 tedioso 2 (pessoa) chato

tiring /'taɪrɪŋ/ adj cansativo

tissue /'tɪʃuː/ s 1 (Biol, Bot) tecido 2 lenço de papel 3 (tb ~ paper) papel de seda

tit /tɪt/ s 1 (ave) chapim 2 (coloq) teta ▶ tit for tat olho por olho, dente por dente

title /'taɪtl/ s 1 título: ~ page pági-

na de rosto ◇ ~ role papel principal 2 título de nobreza 3 forma de tratamento 4 (Jur) direito: ~ deed título de propriedade

titter /'tɪtər/ s risada nervosa ● vi rir dissimuladamente

to /tə, tu:/ prep 1 (direção) para, a 2 [com complemento/objeto indireto] para, a 3 até 4 It lasts two to three hours. Dura de duas a três horas. 5 (hora): ten to one dez para a uma 6 de: the key to the door a chave da porta 7 (comparação) a: I prefer walking to climbing. Eu prefiro andar a escalar. 8 por: How many kilometers to the liter? Quantos quilômetros por litro? 9 (propósito): to go to sb's aid ir em ajuda de alguém 10 (opinião) a, para: It looks red to me. Parece vermelho para mim. ▶ to and fro de lá para cá NOTA To é utilizado para formar o infinitivo e tem vários usos: I came to see you. Eu vim para ver você. ◇ He didn't know what to do. Ele não sabia o que fazer. ◇ It's for you to decide. Você é que tem de decidir.

toad /toʊd/ s sapo

toast /toʊst/ s [U] 1 torrada: a slice/piece of ~ uma torrada 2 brinde ● vt 1 torrar 2 fazer um brinde a toaster s torradeira

tobacco /tə'bækoʊ/ s (pl ~s) tabaco tobacconist's s tabacaria → SELO

today /tə'deɪ/ adv, s 1 hoje 2 hoje em dia

toddler /'tɒdlər/ s criança (que começa a andar)

toe /toʊ/ s 1 dedo (do pé): big ~ dedão do pé 2 ponta (meia, etc.) ▶ on your toes alerta ● vt (pt, pp toed part pres toeing) ▶ toe the line seguir as regras

toenail /'toʊneɪl/ s unha do pé

toffee /'tɒfi; GB 'tɒfi/ s (bala) toffee

together /tə'geðər/ adv 1 juntos 2 ao mesmo tempo ▶ together with junto com, além de NOTA Para o uso de together em PHRASAL VERBS, ver o verbo, p. ex. pull yourself together em PULL. togetherness s unidade, harmonia

toil /tɔɪl/ vi (fml) trabalhar duramente ● s (fml) trabalho pesado

toilet /'tɔɪlət/ s 1 vaso sanitário: ~ paper papel higiênico 2 (em casa, público) banheiro NOTA No inglês britânico se diz toilet ou loo (coloq) para o banheiro de casa e the Gents, the Ladies, the toilets, the cloakroom ou public conveniences para banheiro público. No inglês americano se diz lavatory, toilet ou bathroom se é numa casa, e washroom ou restroom se é num edifício público. toiletries e artigos de higiene

token /'təʊkən/ s 1 sinal 2 ficha (máquina, etc.) 3 vale • adj (antes de substantivo) simbólico (pagamento, etc.)

told /təʊld/ pret, pp de TELL

tolerate /'tɒləreɪt/ vt tolerar tolerance s tolerância tolerant adj ~ (of/towards sb/sth) tolerante (com alguém/algo)

toll /təʊl/ s 1 pedágio 2 número de vítimas ▸ take its toll (of sth) provocar perda (de algo), causar dano (a algo)

tollbooth /'təʊlbuːθ/ s (barreira de) pedágio

toll road s auto-estrada com pedágio

tomato /tə'meɪtəʊ; GB tə'mɑːtəʊ/ s (pl -es) tomate

tomb /tuːm/ s tumba

tombstone /'tuːmstəʊn/ s lápide

tomcat /'tɒmkæt/ (tb tom) s gato macho → GATO

tomorrow /tə'mɒrəʊ/ adv, s amanhã: a week from ~ dentro de oito dias

ton /tʌn/ s 1 2.240 libras (1.016 kg) (GB) 2.000 libras (908 kg) (USA): metric ~ tonelada (métrica) 2 (tons) (coloq) toneladas

tone /təʊn/ s 1 tom 2 tonalidade ■ tone sth down suavizar (o tom de) algo

tongs /tɒŋz/ s [pl] tenaz ▸ PAIR

tongue /tʌŋ/ s 1 (Anat) língua: stick your ~ out mostrar a língua 2 (fml) idioma ▸ (with) tongue in cheek ironicamente

tonic /'tɒnɪk/ s 1 tônico (tb ~ water) (água) tônica

tonight /tə'naɪt/ adv, s esta noite: What's on TV ~? O que tem na TV hoje à noite?

tonne /tʌn/ s (GB) tonelada (métrica)

tonsil /'tɒnsl/ s amígdala tonsillitis /ˌtɒnsə'laɪtɪs/ s amigdalite

too /tuː/ adv 1 também → TAMBÉM 2 demais 3 bem, ainda por cima 4 muito: I'm not ~ sure. Não estou bem certo.

took /tʊk/ pret de TAKE

tool /tuːl/ s ferramenta

tooth /tuːθ/ s (pl teeth) dente: false teeth dentadura postiça

toothache /'tuːθeɪk/ s dor de dente

toothbrush /'tuːθbrʌʃ/ s escova de dentes

tooth decay s cárie

toothpaste /'tuːθpeɪst/ s pasta de dente

toothpick /'tuːθpɪk/ s palito de dente

top /tɒp/ s 1 a parte de cima, o alto: on ~ por cima 2 (montanha) cume 3 (de uma lista) topo 4 tampão 5 camiseta, blusa 6 pião ▸ at the top of your voice (gritar) o mais alto possível off the top of your head (coloq) de cabeça on top (of sth) no controle (de algo) on top of sth/sb 1 sobre alguém/algo 2 além de alguém/algo: And on ~ of all that… E além disso mais… • adj 1 superior: a top-floor apartment um apartamento no último andar ◇ ~ quality de alta qualidade ◇ the ~ jobs os melhores empregos ◇ a ~ Brazilian scientist um cientista brasileiro de primeira categoria 2 máximo • vt (-pp-) cobrir: ice cream topped with chocolate sauce sorvete com cobertura de chocolate ◇ and to ~ it all… e para finalizar… ■ top sth up : ~ up your glass completar o seu copo

top hat (GB tb topper /'tɒpər/) s cartola

topic /'tɒpɪk/ s tópico (tema) topical adj atual

topple /'tɒpl/ vt, vi ~ (sth) (over) (fazer) cair (algo)

top secret adj extremamente sigiloso

torch /tɔːtʃ/ s 1 lanterna 2 tocha

tore /tɔːr/ pret de TEAR²

torment /'tɔːment/ s tormento • /tɔː'ment/ vt atormentar 2 aborrecer

torn /tɔːn/ pp de TEAR²

tortoise /'tɔːtəs/ s tartaruga (terrestre)

torture /'tɔːtʃər/ s 1 tortura 2 (fig) tormento • vt 1 torturar 2 (fig) atormentar torturer s torturador/a

Tory /'tɔːri/ adj, s (pl -ies) (GB, Pol) conservador/a

toss /tɒs; GB tɒs/ 1 vt atirar (descuidadamente ou sem força) 2 vt (cabeça) sacudir 3 vi agitar-se: ~ and turn dar voltas (na cama) 4 vt, vi (moeda) tirar cara ou coroa: ~ sb for sth tirar cara ou coroa com alguém para decidir algo • s 1 (cabeça) sacudida 2 (moeda) tirada de sorte: win the ~ ganhar ao tirar cara ou coroa

total /'toʊtl/ *adj, s* total ● *vt* (**-l-**, *esp GB* **-ll-**) **1** somar **2** totalizar *totally adv* totalmente

totter /'tɑtər/ *vi* **1** cambalear **2** balançar

touch /tʌtʃ/ **1** *vt, vi* tocar(-se) **2** *vt* roçar **3** *vt* [*frases negativas*]: *You've hardly touched your steak.* Você mal tocou o bife. **4** *vt* comover **5** *vt* igualar ▸ **touch wood** (*GB*) isola **touch down** aterrissar **touch on/upon sth** mencionar algo ● *s* **1** toque: *at a ~ ao menor toque* ◊ *the finishing touches* os retoques finais **2** (*tb* *sense* *of* ~) tato **3** *a ~* (*of sth*) um pouco (de algo): *I've got a ~ of flu.* Estou um pouco gripada. **4** jeito ▸ **get/keep in touch (with sb)** entrar/manter-se em contato (com alguém) **in/out of touch** em/fora de contato **in/out of touch with sth** a par/desinformado sobre algo

touched /tʌtʃt/ *adj* comovido *touching adj* comovente

touchy /'tʌtʃi/ *adj* (**-ier, -iest**) **1** suscetível **2** (*tema, etc.*) delicado

tough /tʌf/ *adj* (**-er, -est**) **1** duro: *get ~ with sb* ser duro com alguém **2** forte, sólido **3** tenaz **4** (*medida*) rígido **5** (*decisão, etc.*) difícil **6** (*coloq*) *Tough luck!* Que azar! ▸ **(as) tough as nails/old boots** (*coloq*) duro na queda/como sola de sapato **toughen (-up)**, *vt, vi* tornar(-se) mais rígido/forte/difícil *toughness s* **1** dureza, resistência **2** firmeza

tour /tʊər/ *s* **1** excursão **2** visita **3** turnê → **VIAGEM** ● **1** *vt* visitar **2** *vi* viajar **3** *vt, vi* fazer turnê (por)

tourism /'tʊərɪzəm/ *s* turismo

tourist /'tʊərɪst/ *s* turista: *~ attraction* atração turística

tournament /'tɜːrnəmənt; *GB* 'tɔːn-/ *s* torneio

tow /toʊ/ *vt ~ sth (away)* rebocar algo ● *s* reboque ▸ **in tow** (*coloq*): *He had his family in ~.* Ele trazia a família toda a reboque.

towards /tə'rdz; *GB* tə'wɔːdz/ (*tb* **toward** /tɔːrd; *GB* tə'wɔːd/) *prep* **1** em direção a: *~ the end of the movie* quase no final do movie **2** (*para*) com: *be friendly ~ sb* ser amável com alguém **3** (*propósito*) para

towel /'taʊəl/ *s* toalha

tower /'taʊər/ *s* torre: *~ block* (*GB*) prédio alto ■ **tower above/over sb/sth** erguer-se acima de alguém/algo: *At six feet, he towers over his mother.* Com

1,80 m, ele passa a mãe.

town /taʊn/ *s* **1** cidade **2** centro (da cidade) ▸ **go to town (on sth)** (*coloq*) cair na farra **(out) on the town** de folga, divertindo-se na cidade

town hall *s* prefeitura (*edifício*)

toy /tɔɪ/ *s* brinquedo ■ **toy with sth** brincar com algo: *~ with the idea of doing sth* considerar a idéia de fazer algo

trace /treɪs/ *s* rastro: *He speaks without a ~ of an accent.* Ele fala sem o menor sotaque. ● *vt* **1** seguir a pista de **2** *~ sb/sth (to sth)* descobrir alguém/algo (em algo) **3** remontar(-se): *It can be traced back to the Middle Ages.* Isto remonta à Idade Média. **4** *~ sth (out)* traçar algo **5** fazer cópia (*decalcando*)

track /træk/ *vt* seguir a pista de ■ **track sb/sth down** localizar alguém/algo ● *s* **1** [*ger pl*] rastro (*animal, roda, etc.*) **2** trilha **3** (*Esporte*) pista **4** (*Ferrovia*) trilho **5** (*Mús*) faixa ▸ **keep/lose track of sb/sth** seguir/perder a pista de alguém/algo: *lose ~ of time* perder a noção do tempo **make tracks (for...)** (*coloq*) ir (para...) **off track** fora de rumo **on the right/wrong track** no caminho certo/errado

tracksuit /'træksuːt/ *s* (*GB*) training

tractor /'træktər/ *s* trator

trade /treɪd/ *s* **1** comércio **2** indústria **3** ofício: *He's a plumber by ~.* Ele é bombeiro por profissão. → **WORK** ● **1** *vi* negociar, comerciar **2** *vt ~* **sb/sth for sth** trocar algo por algo (com alguém) ■ **trade sth in (for sth)** dar algo como parte do pagamento (de algo)

trademark /'treɪdmɑrk/ *s* marca registrada

trader /'treɪdər/ *s* comerciante

tradesman /'treɪdzmən/ *s* (*esp GB*) (*pl* **-men**) **1** fornecedor: *tradesmen's entrance* entrada de serviço **2** comerciante

trade union *Ver* **UNION** (2)

trading /'treɪdɪŋ/ *s* comércio

tradition /trə'dɪʃn/ *s* tradição *traditional* /trə'dɪʃənl/ *adj* tradicional

traffic /'træfɪk/ *s* trânsito: *~ light* sinal de trânsito ◊ *~ jam* engarrafamento ◊ *~ circle* rotatória ● *vi* (**-ck-**) *~* (**in sth**) traficar (com algo) *trafficker s* traficante

tragedy /'trædʒədi/ *s* (*pl* **-ies**) tragédia

trail /treɪl/ *s* **1** esteira (*fumaça*)

2 vestígio (*sangue*) **3** trilha **4** rastro (*animal*): *on sb's ~* no encalço de alguém ● **1** *vi ~* **along behind (sb/sth)** seguir (alguém/algo) a passos lentos e cansados **2** *vi* perder

trailer /ˈtreɪlə(r)/ s trailer

train /treɪn/ s **1** trem **2** seqüência ▶ **train of thought** raciocínio ● **1** *vi* estudar, formar-se **2** *vt* adestrar **3** *vt, vi* (*Esporte*) treinar **4** *vt ~* **sth on sb/sth** (*câmera, etc.*) apontar algo para alguém/algo **trainee** /ˌtreɪˈniː/ s estagiário/a **trainer** s **1** (*atletas*) treinador/a **2** (*animais*) adestrador/a **3** (*GB*) (*calçado*) tênis **training** s **1** (*Esporte*) treinamento **2** formação

trait /treɪt/ s traço (*personalidade*)

traitor /ˈtreɪtə(r)/ s traidor/a

tram /træm/ s bonde

tramp /træmp/ **1** *vi* caminhar com passos pesados **2** *vt* percorrer a pé ● s vagabundo/a

trample /ˈtræmpl/ *vt, vi ~* **sb/sth (down)** ∼ **on sb/sth** pisar com força em alguém/algo

tranquilize /ˈtræŋkwəlaɪz/ *vt* tranqüilizar **tranquilizer** s tranqüilizante

transfer /trænsˈfɜː(r)/ (**-rr-**) **1** *vt, vi* transferir(-se) **2** *vt* transmitir **3** *vi* fazer baldeação ● /ˈtrænsfɜː(r)/ s **1** transferência **2** baldeação **3** (*GB*) decalcomania

transform /trænsˈfɔːm/ *vt* transformar **transformation** s transformação **transformer** s (*Elet*) transformador

translate /trænsˈleɪt/ *vt, vi* traduzir(-se) **translation** s tradução: *Camões* ∼ Camões traduzido **translator** s tradutor/a

transmit /trænsˈmɪt/ *vt, vi* (**-tt-**) transmitir **transmitter** s (*Elet*) transmissor

transparent /trænsˈpærənt/ *adj* **1** transparente **2** evidente

transplant /trænsˈplɑːnt/; *GB* -ˈplænt/ *vt* (*Bot, Med*) transplantar ● /ˈtrænsplɑːnt/; *GB* -plænt/ s transplante

transport /trænˈspɔːt/ *vt* transportar ● /ˈtrænspɔːt/ s (*USA tb* **transportation**) transporte

transvestite /trænzˈvestaɪt/ s travesti

trap /træp/ s armadilha: *lay/set a* ∼ armar uma cilada ● *vt* (**-pp-**) **1** prender, aprisionar **2** enredar

trapdoor /ˈtræpdɔː(r)/ s alçapão

trapeze /trəˈpiːz/; *GB* trə-/ s trapézio (*circo*)

trash /træʃ/ s (*USA*) **1** lixo: *It's* ∼. É uma porcaria. NOTA Em inglês britânico usa-se **rubbish** para *lixo* e **dustbin** para *lata de lixo*. **Trash** só é empregado em sentido figurado. **2** (*coloq*) ralé **trashy** *adj* que não vale nada

travel /ˈtrævl/ s **1** [*U*] viagem **2** (**travels**) [*pl*] (*esp GB*) *be on your travels* estar viajando ◊ *Did you see John on your travels?* Você viu John enquanto esteve fora? → VIAGEM ● (**-l-**, *GB* **-ll-**) **1** *vi* viajar **2** *vt* percorrer **traveler** (*GB* **-ll-**) s viajante

travel agency s agência de viagens

travel agent s agente de viagens

traveler's check (*GB* **traveller's cheque**) s cheque de viagem

tray /treɪ/ s bandeja

treacherous /ˈtretʃərəs/ *adj* traiçoeiro **treachery** s **1** traição **2** falsidade

tread /tred/ (*pt* **trod** *pp* **trodden** ou **trod**) **1** *vi* pisar **2** *vt ~* **sth (in/down/out)** pisotear algo **3** *vt* (*caminho*) marcar com passos ▶ **tread carefully** agir de forma cautelosa ● s [*sing*] passo

treason /ˈtriːzn/ s alta traição NOTA **Treason** é o ato de trair o próprio país.

treasure /ˈtreʒə(r)/ s tesouro ● *vt* dar grande valor a: *her most treasured possession* o seu bem mais precioso

treasurer /ˈtreʒərə(r)/ s tesoureiro/a

the Treasury /ˈtreʒəri/ s Ministério da Fazenda

treat /triːt/ *vt* **1** tratar: ∼ *sth as a joke* levar algo na piada **2** ∼ **sb (to sth)** convidar alguém (para algo): *Let me* ∼ *you.* Você é meu convidado. **3** ∼ **yourself (to sth)** dar-se ao luxo (de algo) ▶ **treat sb like dirt/a dog** (*coloq*) tratar alguém como lixo/como um cachorro ● s **1** prazer, regalo: *as a special* ∼ como um prêmio ◊ *give yourself a* ∼ presentear-se **2** *This is my* ∼. É por minha conta. ▶ **a treat** (*coloq*) às mil maravilhas

treatment /ˈtriːtmənt/ s tratamento

treaty /ˈtriːti/ s (*pl* **-ies**) tratado

treble /ˈtrebl/ *adj, s* **1** (*GB*) triplo **2** (*Mús*) (*do*) soprano: ∼ *clef* clave de sol ● *vt, vi* triplicar(-se)

tree /triː/ s árvore

trek /trek/ s caminhada ● *vi* (**-kk-**) **1** fazer trekking **2** caminhar (*penosamente*)

tremble /ˈtrembl/ *vi ~* **(with/at**

sth) tremer (de/por algo)

trembling /ˈtremblɪŋ/ *adj* trêmulo ● *s* tremor

tremendous /trəˈmendəs/ *adj* **1** enorme **2** fantástico tremendously *adv* muitíssimo

tremor /ˈtremər/ *s* tremor, estremecimento

trench /trentʃ/ *s* **1** (*Mil*) trincheira **2** vala

trend /trend/ *s* tendência ▸ **set a/the trend** lançar moda

trendy /ˈtrendi/ *adj* (**-ier, -iest**) (*coloq*) da moda

trespass /ˈtrespəs/ *vi* ~ (**on sth**) invadir (algo): *no trespassing* entrada proibida trespasser *s* intruso/a

trial /ˈtraɪəl/ *s* **1** julgamento: *stand* ~ ser julgado **2** prova: *a ~ period* um período de experiência ◊ *take sth on* ~ testar algo **3** (*Esporte*) teste ▸ **trial and error** (por) tentativa e erro: *learn sth by ~ and error* aprender algo por tentativas **trials and tribulations** percalços

triangle /ˈtraɪæŋgl/ *s* triângulo triangular /traɪˈæŋgjələr/ *adj* triangular

tribe /traɪb/ *s* tribo

tribute /ˈtrɪbjuːt/ *s* **1** homenagem **2 a ~ (to sth):** *That is a ~ to his skill.* Isso é prova da habilidade dele.

trick /trɪk/ *s* **1** truque, brincadeira: *play a ~ on sb* pregar uma peça em alguém ◊ *a dirty ~* uma ursada ◊ *a ~ question* uma pergunta capciosa **2** segredo **3** (*magia*): *conjuring tricks* mágicas ◊ *a ~ of the light* uma ilusão de óptica ▸ **every/any trick in the book** o possível e o impossível: *I tried every ~ in the book.* Tentei de tudo. **the tricks of the trade** as manhas do ofício ● *vt* enganar: ~ *sb into doing sth* induzir alguém a fazer algo ◊ *They tricked the old lady out of her savings.* Passaram a perna na velha e tomaram todas as economias dela. trickery *s* [*U*] trapaça, astúcia

trickle /ˈtrɪkl/ *vi* escorrer, gotejar ● *s* **1** fio **2** (*fig*) punhado

tricky /ˈtrɪki/ *adj* (**-ier, -iest**) complicado, difícil

trifle /ˈtraɪfl/ *s* **1** (*GB*) sobremesa com pão-de-ló, frutas e creme **2** ninharia ▸ **a trifle** um pouquinho ■ **trifle with sb/sth** fazer pouco de alguém/algo

trigger /ˈtrɪgər/ *s* gatilho ● *vt* ~ **sth (off) 1** desencadear algo **2** (*alarme, etc.*) acionar algo

trillion /ˈtrɪljən/ *adj, s* trilhão

trim /trɪm/ *adj* (**trimmer, trimmest**) **1** bem aparado **2** elegante ● *vt* (**-mm-**) **1** aparar **2** ~ **sth off (sth)** cortar algo (de algo) **3** (*vestido, etc.*) enfeitar ● *s* **1** aparada: *have a ~* aparar o cabelo **2** adorno trimming *s* **1** enfeite **2** (**trimmings**) [*pl*] (*comida*) acompanhamento

trip /trɪp/ (**-pp-**) **1** *vi* ~ (**over/up**) tropeçar **2** *vt* ~ **sb (up)** passar uma rasteira em alguém ■ **trip (sb) up** confundir-se/confundir alguém ● *s* viagem, excursão → VIAGEM

triple /ˈtrɪpl/ *adj, s* triplo: *at ~ the speed* três vezes mais rápido ● *vt, vi* triplicar(-se)

triplet /ˈtrɪplət/ *s* trigêmeo/a

triumph /ˈtraɪʌmf/ *s* triunfo: *return home in ~* regressar triunfante para casa ◊ *a shout of ~* um grito de vitória ● *vi* triunfar triumphal /traɪˈʌmfl/ *adj* triunfal triumphant *adj* **1** triunfante **2** exultante triumphantly *adv* triunfantemente

trivial /ˈtrɪviəl/ *adj* trivial triviality /ˌtrɪviˈæləti/ *s* (*pl* **-ies**) trivialidade

trod /trɒd/ *pret de* TREAD

trodden /ˈtrɒdən/ *pp de* TREAD

troop /truːp/ *s* **1** bando **2** (**troops**) soldados ■ **troop in(to), out (of), etc.** entrar, sair, etc. em bando

trophy /ˈtrəʊfi/ *s* (*pl* **-ies**) troféu

tropic /ˈtrɒpɪk/ *s* **1** trópico **2** (**the tropics**) os trópicos tropical *adj* tropical

trot /trɒt/ *vi* (**-tt-**) trotar ● *s* trote ▸ **on the trot** (*coloq*): *six days on the ~* seis dias seguidos

trouble /ˈtrʌbl/ *s* **1** [*U*] problema(s) **2** dificuldades **3** [*U*] incômodo, transtorno: *It's not worth the ~.* Não vale a pena. **4** distúrbios **5** (*Med*) doença ▸ **be in trouble** estar em apuros: *If I don't get home by ten, I'll be in ~.* Se eu não estiver em casa às dez, vai ter encrenca. **get into trouble** entrar numa fria **go to a lot of trouble (to do sth)** dar-se ao trabalho (de fazer algo) ● *vt* incomodar: *Don't ~ yourself.* Não se dê ao trabalho. **2** preocupar: *What's troubling you?* O que é que você tem? troubled *adj* **1** preocupado **2** (*período*) agitado **3** (*vida*) conturbado troublesome *adj* importuno

trouble-free *adj* **1** sem problemas **2** (*viagem*) sem acidentes

troublemaker /ˈtrʌblmeɪkər/ *s* encrenqueiro/a

trough /trɒf; GB trɒf/ s
1 bebedouro (animais) **2** come-
douro **3** canal

trousers /'traʊzərz/ s [pl] calça →
PAIR trouser adj: ~ leg/pocket
perna/bolso de calça

trout /traʊt/ s (pl trout) truta

truant /'truːənt/ s gazeteiro: play
~ matar aula

truce /truːs/ s trégua

truck /trʌk/ s **1** caminhão **2** (GB)
vagão

true /truː/ adj (truer, truest) **1**
certo, verdadeiro: It's too good
to be ~. É bom demais para ser
verdade. **2** (história) verídico **3**
real **4** fiel: be ~ to your word
cumprir o prometido ▶ **come true**
realizar-se **true to life** realista

truly /'truːli/ adv sinceramente,
realmente

trump /trʌmp/ s trunfo: Hearts
are trumps. Copas valem mais.

trumpet /'trʌmpɪt/ s trompete

trundle /'trʌndl/ **1** vi rodar lentamente **2** vt arrastar **3** vt empurrar

trunk /trʌŋk/ s **1** (Anat, Bot)
tronco **2** baú **3** (elefante) tromba **4** (trunks) [pl] calção de
banho → PAIR **5** porta-malas

trust /trʌst/ s **1** confiança **2** responsabilidade **3** fundação ● vt,
vi ~ **sb**; ~ **sb with sth** confiar em
alguém; algo a alguém: ~ **to sth**
confiar em algo trusting adj de
confiança trusting adj confiante

trustee /trʌ'stiː/ s **1** fideicomis-
sário/a **2** administrador/a

trustworthy /'trʌstwɜːrθi/ adj
digno de confiança

truth /truːθ/ s verdade truthful
adj sincero: be ~ dizer a verdade

try /traɪ/ (pt, pp tried) **1** vi tentar
NOTA Coloquialmente, try to o
infinitivo pode ser substituído
por try and + infinitivo: I'll ~ to/
and finish it. ● vt provar **2** vt (Jur,
caso) julgar ▶ **try sb's patience**
fazer alguém perder a paciência ■ **try sth on** experimentar
algo (roupa, etc.) ● s (pl tries)
1 tentativa **2** (rúgbi) ensaio trying adj difícil

T-shirt s camiseta

tub /tʌb/ s **1** tina **2** pote **3**
banheira

tube /tuːb; GB tjuːb/ s **1** tubo **2**
(the tube) (GB, coloq) metrô: by
~ de metrô

tuck /tʌk/ vt **1** ~ **sth (into sth)**
enfiar algo (em algo) **2** ~ **sth
around sb/sth** cobrir alguém/
algo com algo ■ **be tucked away**

1 (dinheiro) estar guardado **2**
(vilarejo, etc.) estar escondido
■ **tuck sb in/up** aconchegar
alguém (na cama)

Tuesday /'tuːzdeɪ, -di; GB 'tjuː-/ s
(abrev Tue., Tues.) terça(-feira)
→ MONDAY

tuft /tʌft/ s **1** (cabelo) mecha **2**
(plumas) penacho **3** (grama)
tufo

tug /tʌg/ (-gg-) **1** vi ~ **(at sth)**
puxar (algo) com força **2** vt
arrancar ● s **1** puxão **2** (tb
tugboat) rebocador

tuition /tu'ɪʃn; GB tjuː-/ s **1** (USA)
(taxa de) matrícula **2** (GB, fml)
ensino

tulip /'tuːlɪp; GB 'tjuː-/ s tulipa

tumble /'tʌmbl/ vi cair: ~ down
vir abaixo ● s tombo

tumble-dryer (tb tumble-drier) s
(GB) secadora (de roupa)

tumbler /'tʌmblər/ s copo (sem
pé)

tummy /'tʌmi/ s (pl -ies) (coloq)
barriga

tumor (GB -our) s /'tuːmər/ s
tumor

tuna /'tuːnə/ s atum

tune /tuːn/ s melodia ▶ **in/out of
tune** afinado/desafinado in/
out of tune with sb/sth em
harmonia/desarmonia com
alguém/algo ▶ **in** vt, vi (Mús)
~ **(sth) (up)** afinar (algo) **2** vt
(motor) regular ■ **tune in (to sth)**
sintonizar (algo) tuneful adj
melodioso

tunic /'tuːnɪk; GB 'tjuː-/ s túnica

tunnel /'tʌnl/ s túnel ● (-l-, GB
-ll-) **1** vi abrir um túnel **2** vt, vi
escavar

turban /'tɜːrbən/ s turbante

turbulence /'tɜːrbjələns/ s turbulência turbulent adj **1** turbulento **2** agitado

turf /tɜːrf/ s gramado ● vt relvar
■ **turf sb/sth out (of sth)** (GB,
coloq) colocar alguém/algo
para fora (de algo)

turkey /'tɜːrki/ s peru

turmoil /'tɜːrmɔɪl/ s tumulto

turn /tɜːrn/ **1** vi dar voltas **2** vt
fazer girar: ~ **sb around** girar
alguém **3** vt, vi ~ **(sth/-se)** ~
(around): ~ left virar à esquerda
◊ ~ your back on sb virar as
costas para alguém ◊ ~ back
virar-se para trás **4** vt ~ **(sth)**
dobrar **5** vi tornar-se: ~ white
ficar branco ▶ BECOME **6** vt, vi
transformar(-se) **7** vt: ~ 40 fazer
40 anos ▶ **turn a blind eye** (para algo)
fazer vista grossa (para algo)
turn back the clock voltar ao
passado **turn over a new leaf**

começar vida nova ∎ **turn away (from sb/sth)** afastar-se (de alguém/algo) **turn sb away (from sth)** negar-se a ajudar alguém, mandar alguém embora de algo **turn sb back** mandar alguém retornar **turn sb/sth down** rejeitar alguém/algo **turn sth down** abaixar algo (*volume*) **turn sth off** sair (*de um caminho*) **turn sb off** (*coloq*) tirar a vontade de alguém **turn sth off** 1 apagar algo (*luz*) 2 fechar algo (*torneira*) 3 desligar algo (*TV, motor*) **turn sb on** (*coloq*) excitar alguém **turn sth on** 1 acender algo (*luz*) 2 abrir algo (*torneira*) 3 ligar algo (*TV, motor*) **turn out** 1 comparecer 2 resultar **turn sb out** botar alguém para fora **turn sth out** apagar algo (*luz*) **turn over** manter as coisas na rotina **turn (sb/sth) over** virar (alguém/ algo) **turn to sb** recorrer a alguém **turn up** aparecer **turn sth up** aumentar algo (*volume*) ● **s** 1 volta 2 (*cabeça*) movimento 3 virada: *take a wrong* ~ dobrar no lugar errado 4 curva 5 (*circunstâncias*) mudança: *take a* ~ *for the worse* mudar para pior 6 vez 7 (*coloq*) mal-estar ▶ **a turn of phrase** um modo de se expressar **do sb a good/bad turn** fazer um favor/desfavor a alguém **in turn** por sua vez, um atrás do outro **take turns (at sth)** revezar-se (em algo)

turning /'tɜːnɪŋ/ *s* rua transversal

turning point *s* momento decisivo

turnip /'tɜːnɪp/ *s* nabo

turnout /'tɜːnaʊt/ *s* comparecimento

turnover /'tɜːnəʊvər/ *s* 1 (*negócio*) faturamento 2 (*mercadorias*) circulação 3 (*pessoal*) rotatividade

turnpike /'tɜːnpaɪk/ *s* autoestrada com pedágio

turns /tɜːrps/ *s* aguarrás

turntable /'tɜːnteɪbl/ *s* (*toca-discos*) prato

turpentine /'tɜːrpəntaɪn/ (*GB* **turps** /tɜːrps/) *s* aguarrás

turquoise /'tɜːrkwɔɪz/ *s* turquesa ● *adj* azul-turquesa

turret /'tɜːrət/ *s* torreão

turtle /'tɜːrtl/ *s* tartaruga (*marinha*)

turtleneck /'tɜːrtlnek/ *s* gola rulê

tusk /tʌsk/ *s* presa (*de elefante, etc.*)

tutor /'tuːtər; *GB* 'tjuː-/ *s* 1 professor/a particular 2 (*GB*) (*universidade*) professor/a

tutorial /tuː'tɔːriəl; *GB* tjuː-/ *adj* docente ● *s* seminário (*aula*)

tuxedo /tʌk'siːdəʊ/ (*USA*) (*pl* ~**s**) smoking

twang /twæŋ/ *s* 1 (*Mús*) dedilhado 2 (*voz*) nasalização

twelve /twelv/ *adj, pron, s* doze **twelfth** 1 *adj* décimo segundo 2 *pron, adv* o(s) décimo(s) segundo(s), a(s) décima(s) segunda(s) 3 *s* duodécima parte, doze avos

twenty /'twenti/ *adj, pron, s* vinte **twentieth** 1 *adj, pron* vigésimo 2 *s* vigésima parte, vinte avos

twice /twaɪs/ *adv* duas vezes: ~ *as much/many* o dobro

twiddle /'twɪdl/ *vt, vi* brincar com, girar ▶ **twiddle your thumbs** ficar à toa

twilight /'twaɪlaɪt/ *s* crepúsculo

twin /twɪn/ *s* 1 gêmeo/a 2 [*função adjetiva*] par: *a plane with* ~ *propellers* um avião com um par de hélices

twinge /twɪndʒ/ *s* pontada

twinkle /'twɪŋkl/ *vi* 1 brilhar 2 ~ **(with sth)** (*olhos*) reluzir (de algo)

twirl /twɜːrl/ *vt, vi* 1 fazer girar, dar voltas (em) 2 retorcer(-se)

twist /twɪst/ 1 *vt, vi* torcer(-se) 2 *vt, vi* enroscar(-se) 3 *vt, vi* (*rio, etc.*) serpentear 4 *vt* (*palavras, etc.*) deturpar ● *s* 1 torção 2 (*rio, etc.*) curva 3 (*limão, papel*) pedacinho 4 virada

twit /twɪt/ *s* (*coloq, esp GB*) idiota

twitch /twɪtʃ/ *s* 1 contração 2 tique (*nervoso*) 3 puxão ● *vt, vi* 1 contrair(-se) 2 ~ **(at) sth** dar um puxão em algo

twitter /'twɪtər/ *vi* gorjear

two /tuː/ *adj, pron, s* dois, duas ▶ **put two and two together** tirar conclusões

two-faced *adj* falso

two-way *adj* recíproco

tycoon /taɪ'kuːn/ *s* magnata

tying *Ver* TIE

type /taɪp/ *s* tipo: *She's not the artistic* ~. Ela não é chegada às artes. ● *vt, vi* ~ **(sth) (out/up)** datilografar (algo) **typing** *s* datilografia **typist** *s* datilógrafo/a

typescript /'taɪpskrɪpt/ *s* texto datilografado

typewriter /'taɪpraɪtər/ *s* máquina de escrever

typhoid (fever) /'taɪfɔɪd/ *s* febre tifóide

typical /'tɪpɪkl/ *adj* típico **typically** *adv* 1 tipicamente

2 como de costume

typify /'tɪpɪfaɪ/ vt (pt, pp -ied) ser o protótipo de

tyranny /'tɪrəni/ s tirania

tyrant /'taɪrənt/ s tirano/a

tyre (GB) = TIRE s

Uu

U, u /juː/ s (pl **U's, u's** /juːz/) U, u

ubiquitous /juːˈbɪkwɪtəs/ adj (fml) onipresente

UFO (tb **ufo**) /juː ef 'oʊ/ abrev (pl ~s) OVNI (= objeto voador não identificado)

ugh /ɜː, ʊ/ interj uf, puf

ugly /'ʌɡli/ adj (-ier, -iest) **1** feio **2** ameaçador

ulcer /'ʌlsər/ s úlcera

ultimate /'ʌltɪmət/ adj **1** último **2** supremo **3** fundamental **ultimately** adv **1** no final **2** fundamentalmente

umbrella /ʌmˈbrelə/ s guarda-chuva

umpire /'ʌmpaɪər/ s árbitro (tênis, críquete)

unable /ʌnˈeɪbl/ adj incapaz, impossibilitado

unacceptable /ˌʌnəkˈseptəbl/ adj inaceitável

unaccustomed /ˌʌnəˈkʌstəmd/ adj **1** be ~ to (doing) sth não estar acostumado a (fazer) algo **2** desacostumado

unambiguous /ˌʌnæmˈbɪɡjuəs/ adj inequívoco

unanimous /juːˈnænɪməs/ adj unânime

unarmed /ˌʌnˈɑːrmd/ adj **1** desarmado **2** indefeso

unattractive /ˌʌnəˈtræktɪv/ adj não atraente

unavailable /ˌʌnəˈveɪləbl/ adj indisponível

unavoidable /ˌʌnəˈvɔɪdəbl/ adj inevitável

unaware /ˌʌnəˈweər/ adj despercebido: be ~ of sth ignorar algo

unbearable /ʌnˈbeərəbl/ adj insuportável

unbeatable /ʌnˈbiːtəbl/ adj invencível

unbeaten /ʌnˈbiːtn/ adj (Esporte) invicto

unbelievable /ˌʌnbɪˈliːvəbl/ adj inacreditável

unbroken /ʌnˈbroʊkən/ adj **1** intato **2** ininterrupto **3** (recorde) mantido **4** (espírito) indômito

uncanny /ʌnˈkæni/ adj (-ier, -iest) misterioso

uncertain /ʌnˈsɜːrtn/ adj **1** inseguro, indeciso **2** incerto: It is ~ whether... Não se sabe se... **3** inconstante **uncertainty** s (pl -ies) incerteza

unchanged /ʌnˈtʃeɪndʒd/ adj inalterado

uncle /'ʌŋkl/ s tio

unclear /ʌnˈklɪər/ adj confuso

uncomfortable /ʌnˈkʌmfərtəbl; GB -ft-/ adj incômodo **uncomfortably** adv desconfortavelmente: The exams are getting ~ close. Os exames estão se aproximando de forma preocupante.

uncommon /ʌnˈkɑːmən/ adj incomum

uncompromising /ʌnˈkɑːmprəmaɪzɪŋ/ adj intransigente

unconcerned /ˌʌnkənˈsɜːrnd/ adj **1** ~ (about/by sth) indiferente (a algo) **2** despreocupado

unconditional /ˌʌnkənˈdɪʃənl/ adj incondicional

unconscious /ʌnˈkɑːnʃəs/ adj **1** inconsciente **2** be ~ of sth não se dar conta de algo • the unconscious s o inconsciente

unconventional /ˌʌnkənˈvenʃənl/ adj não convencional

unconvincing /ˌʌnkənˈvɪnsɪŋ/ adj inconvincente

uncouth /ʌnˈkuːθ/ adj grosseiro

uncover /ʌnˈkʌvər/ vt **1** destampar **2** (fig) desvendar

undecided /ˌʌndɪˈsaɪdɪd/ adj **1** pendente **2** indeciso

undeniable /ˌʌndɪˈnaɪəbl/ adj inegável **undeniably** adv indubitavelmente

under /'ʌndər/ prep **1** embaixo de **2** (idade) menor de **3** menos que **4** (governo, etc.) sob **5** (Jur) segundo (uma lei, etc.)

under- /'ʌndər/ pref **1** Women are under-represented in the group. Há menos mulheres no grupo do que o desejado. ◇ underused desperdiçado ◇ the under-fives os menores de cinco anos ◇ under-age drinking o consumo de bebidas alcoólicas por menores de idade

undercover /ˌʌndərˈkʌvər/ adj secreto

underestimate /ˌʌndərˈestɪmeɪt/ vt subestimar

undergo /ˌʌndərˈɡoʊ/ vt (pt underwent pp undergone /-ˈɡɔːn; GB -ˈɡɒn/) **1** experimentar, sofrer **2** (experimento) passar por **3** (série) realizar **4** (tratamento) submeter-se a

undergraduate /ˌʌndərˈɡrædʒuət/ s estudante universitário

underground /ˌʌndərˈɡraʊnd/ adv **1** debaixo da terra **2** clandestinamente ● adj **1** subterrâneo **2** clandestino ● s **1** (GB) metrô **2** organização clandestina

undergrowth /ˈʌndərɡroʊθ/ s vegetação rasteira

underlie /ˌʌndərˈlaɪ/ vt (pt **underlay** /-ˈleɪ/ pp **underlain** /-ˈleɪn/) formar a base de

underline /ˌʌndərˈlaɪn/ (tb **underscore** /ˌʌndərˈskɔːr/) vt sublinhar

undermine /ˌʌndərˈmaɪn/ vt minar

underneath /ˌʌndərˈniːθ/ prep embaixo de ● adv debaixo ● **the underneath** s [U] a parte inferior

underpants /ˈʌndərpænts/ s [pl] cueca(s) → PAIR

underprivileged /ˌʌndərˈprɪvəlɪdʒd/ adj desfavorecido

undershirt /ˈʌndərʃɜːrt/ s camiseta

underside /ˈʌndərsaɪd/ s parte inferior, base

understand /ˌʌndərˈstænd/ (pt, pp **understood** /-ˈstʊd/) **1** vt, vi entender (de) **2** vt compreender **3** vt ficar sabendo, concluir **understandable** adj compreensível **understandably** adv naturalmente

understanding /ˌʌndərˈstændɪŋ/ adj compreensivo ● s **1** compreensão **2** conhecimento **3** acordo (informal) **4** interpretação

understate /ˌʌndərˈsteɪt/ vt dizer que algo é menor ao menos importante do que é

understatement /ˈʌndərsteɪtmənt/ s eufemismo

undertake /ˌʌndərˈteɪk/ vt (pt **undertook** /-ˈtʊk/ pp **undertaken** /-ˈteɪkən/) (fml) **1** empreender **2** comprometer-se **undertaking** s **1** (fml) compromisso **2** (Com) empreendimento

undertaker /ˈʌndərteɪkər/ s (GB) agente funerário **the undertaker's** s (GB) casa funerária

underwater /ˌʌndərˈwɔːtər/ adj subaquático ● adv embaixo d'água

underwear /ˈʌndərwear/ s roupa de baixo

underwent /ˌʌndərˈwent/ pret de UNDERGO

the underworld /ˈʌndərwɜːrld/ s

1 o inferno **2** o submundo do crime

undesirable /ˌʌndɪˈzaɪərəbl/ adj, s indesejável

undisputed /ˌʌndɪˈspjuːtɪd/ adj inquestionável

undisturbed /ˌʌndɪˈstɜːrbd/ adj **1** (pessoa) tranqüilo **2** (coisa) intocado

undo /ʌnˈduː/ vt (pt **undid** /ʌnˈdɪd/ pp **undone** /ʌnˈdʌn/) **1** desfazer **2** desabotoar, desatar **4** (invólucro) tirar **5** anular: ~ the damage reparar o dano **undone** adj **1** come ~ desabotoar-se, desatar-se **2** inacabado

undoubtedly /ʌnˈdaʊtɪdli/ adv indubitavelmente

undress /ʌnˈdres/ vt, vi despir (-se) NOTA A expressão mais comum é **get undressed**. **undressed** adj nu

undue /ʌnˈduː; GB -ˈdjuː/ adj [antes de substantivo] (fml) excessivo **unduly** adv (fml) excessivamente

unearth /ʌnˈɜːrθ/ vt desenterrar, trazer a público

unease /ʌnˈiːz/ s mal-estar

uneasy /ʌnˈiːzi/ adj (-ier, -iest) **1** ~ (about/at sth) inquieto (por algo) **2** (silêncio) incômodo

uneducated /ʌnˈedʒukeɪtɪd/ adj inculto

unemployed /ˌʌnɪmˈplɔɪd/ adj desempregado ● **the unemployed** s [pl] os desempregados

unemployment /ˌʌnɪmˈplɔɪmənt/ s desemprego

unequal /ʌnˈiːkwəl/ adj **1** desigual **2** (fml): feel ~ to sth não se sentir à altura de algo

uneven /ʌnˈiːvn/ adj **1** desigual **2** irregular

uneventful /ˌʌnɪˈventfl/ adj sem incidentes

unexpected /ˌʌnɪkˈspektɪd/ adj inesperado

unfair /ˌʌnˈfeər/ adj **1** ~ (to/on sb) injusto (para com) alguém **2** (concorrência) desleal

unfaithful /ʌnˈfeɪθfl/ adj **1** infiel **2** (antig) desleal

unfamiliar /ˌʌnfəˈmɪliər/ adj **1** não familiar (cara, etc.) desconhecido **3** ~ with sth não familiarizado com algo

unfashionable /ʌnˈfæʃnəbl/ adj fora de moda

unfasten /ʌnˈfæsn; GB -ˈfɑːsn/ vt **1** desabotoar, desatar **2** abrir **3** soltar

unfavorable (GB -our-) /ʌnˈfeɪvərəbl/ adj desfavorável

unfinished /ʌnˈfɪnɪʃt/ adj

inacabado: ~ *business* assuntos pendentes

unfit /ʌnˈfɪt/ *adj* **1** inadequado, incapacitado **2** impróprio **3** fora de forma

unfold /ʌnˈfəʊld/ **1** *vt* estender, desdobrar **2** *vt, vi* revelar(-se)

unforeseen /ˌʌnfɔːˈsiːn/ *adj* imprevisto

unforgettable /ˌʌnfərˈgetəbl/ *adj* inesquecível

unforgivable /ˌʌnfərˈgɪvəbl/ *adj* imperdoável

unfortunate /ʌnˈfɔːrtʃənət/ *adj* **1** (*pessoa*) infeliz **2** lamentável: *It is ~ (that)...* É de lamentar que... **3** (*comentário*) inoportuno **unfortunately** *adv* infelizmente

unfriendly /ʌnˈfrendli/ *adj* (**-ier, -iest**) ~ (**to/towards sb**) antipático (com alguém)

ungrateful /ʌnˈgreɪtfl/ *adj* ~ (**to sb**) ingrato (com alguém)

unhappy /ʌnˈhæpi/ *adj* (**-ier, -iest**) **1** triste **2** ~ (**about/at sth**) preocupado, descontente (com algo) **unhappiness** *s* infelicidade

unharmed /ʌnˈhɑrmd/ *adj* ileso

unhealthy /ʌnˈhelθi/ *adj* (**-ier, -iest**) **1** doentio **2** insalubre **3** (*interesse*) mórbido

unhelpful /ʌnˈhelpfl/ *adj* que não ajuda

uniform /ˈjuːnɪfɔːrm/ *adj, s* uniforme: *in ~* de uniforme

unify /ˈjuːnɪfaɪ/ *vt* (*pt, pp* **-ied**) unificar

unimportant /ˌʌnɪmˈpɔːrt(ə)nt/ *adj* sem importância

uninhabited /ˌʌnɪnˈhæbɪtɪd/ *adj* desabitado

unintentionally /ˌʌnɪnˈtenʃənəli/ *adv* sem querer

uninterested /ʌnˈɪntrəstɪd/ *adj* ~ (**in sb/sth**) indiferente (a alguém/algo)

union /ˈjuːnɪən/ *s* **1** união **2** sindicato

unique /juˈniːk/ *adj* **1** único **2** ~ **to sb/sth** exclusivo de alguém/algo **3** extraordinário

unison /ˈjuːnɪsn/ *s* ▸ **in unison** em uníssono

unit /ˈjuːnɪt/ *s* **1** unidade **2** (*mobiliário*) módulo: *kitchen ~* (*GB*) móvel de cozinha

unite /juˈnaɪt/ *vt, vi* unir(-se)

unity /ˈjuːnəti/ *s* unidade

universal /ˌjuːnɪˈvɜːrsl/ *adj* universal, geral **universally** *adv* universalmente

universe /ˈjuːnɪvɜːrs/ *s* universo

university /ˌjuːnɪˈvɜːrsəti/ *s* (*pl* **-ies**) universidade → SCHOOL

unjust /ˌʌnˈdʒʌst/ *adj* injusto

unkempt /ˌʌnˈkempt/ *adj* **1** (*aparência*) descuidado **2** despenteado

unkind /ʌnˈkaɪnd/ *adj* cruel

unknown /ˌʌnˈnoʊn/ *adj* ~ (**to sb**) desconhecido (para alguém)

unlawful /ʌnˈlɔːfl/ *adj* ilegal

unleash /ʌnˈliːʃ/ *vt* **1** (*animal*) soltar **2** desencadear

unless /ənˈles/ *conj* a menos que

unlike /ʌnˈlaɪk/ *adj* **1** diferente **2** não típico de: *It's ~ him to be late.* É muito raro ele chegar tarde. ● *prep* ao contrário de

unlikely /ʌnˈlaɪkli/ *adj* (**-ier, -iest**) **1** improvável **2** (*história, etc.*) inverossímil

unlimited /ʌnˈlɪmɪtɪd/ *adj* ilimitado

unload /ˌʌnˈloʊd/ *vt, vi* descarregar

unlock /ˌʌnˈlɑk/ *vt, vi* abrir (*com chave*)

unlucky /ʌnˈlʌki/ *adj* (**-ier, -iest**) **1** infeliz, azarado: *be ~* ter azar **2** azarento

unmarried /ˌʌnˈmærid/ *adj* solteiro

unmistakable /ˌʌnmɪˈsteɪkəbl/ *adj* inconfundível

unmoved /ˌʌnˈmuːvd/ *adj* impassível

unnatural /ʌnˈnætʃərəl/ *adj* **1** não natural **2** antinatural **3** sem naturalidade

unnecessary /ʌnˈnesəsəri; *GB* -səri/ *adj* **1** desnecessário **2** (*comentário*) gratuito

unnoticed /ˌʌnˈnoʊtɪst/ *adj* despercebido

unobtrusive /ˌʌnəbˈtruːsɪv/ *adj* discreto

unofficial /ˌʌnəˈfɪʃl/ *adj* **1** extraoficial **2** (*fonte*) oficioso

unorthodox /ʌnˈɔːrθədɑks/ *adj* não ortodoxo

unpack /ˌʌnˈpæk/ **1** *vt, vi* desfazer (as malas) **2** *vt* desembrulhar

unpaid /ˌʌnˈpeɪd/ *adj* **1** não pago **2** não remunerado

unpleasant /ʌnˈpleznt/ *adj* **1** desagradável **2** (*pessoa*) antipático

unplug /ˌʌnˈplʌg/ *vt* desligar

unpopular /ˌʌnˈpɑpjələr/ *adj* impopular

unprecedented /ʌnˈpresɪdentɪd/ *adj* sem precedente

unpredictable /ˌʌnprɪˈdɪktəbl/ *adj* imprevisível

unqualified /ˌʌnˈkwɒlɪfaɪd/ *adj* **1** não habilitado **2** (*sucesso*) absoluto

unravel /ʌnˈrævl/ *vt, vi* (-l-, GB -ll-) desenredar(-se)

unreal /ʌnˈrɪəl/ *adj* irreal

unrealistic /ˌʌnrɪəˈlɪstɪk/ *adj* não realista

unreasonable /ʌnˈriːznəbl/ *adj* **1** insensato **2** excessivo

unreliable /ˌʌnrɪˈlaɪəbl/ *adj* inconfiável

unrest /ʌnˈrest/ *s* **1** agitação **2** (*Pol*) [U] distúrbios

unruly /ʌnˈruːli/ *adj* indisciplinado, rebelde

unsafe /ʌnˈseɪf/ *adj* inseguro

unsatisfactory /ˌʌnˌsætɪsˈfæktəri/ *adj* insatisfatório, inaceitável

unsavory (GB -oury) /ʌnˈseɪvəri/ *adj* desagradável

unscathed /ʌnˈskeɪðd/ *adj* **1** ileso **2** incólume

unscrew /ˌʌnˈskruː/ *vt, vi* desparafusar **2** desenroscar

unscrupulous /ʌnˈskruːpjələs/ *adj* inescrupuloso

unseen /ʌnˈsiːn/ *adj* despercebido

unsettle /ʌnˈsetl/ *vt* perturbar **unsettled** *adj* **1** (*pessoa*) inquieto **2** incerto, variável **3** (*assunto*) pendente **unsettling** *adj* inquietante

unshaven /ʌnˈʃeɪvn/ *adj* não barbeado

unsightly /ʌnˈsaɪtli/ *adj* feio

unskilled /ʌnˈskɪld/ *adj* **1** (*pessoa*) não qualificado **2** (*trabalho*) não especializado

unspoiled /ʌnˈspɔɪld/ (GB tb **unspoilt** /ʌnˈspɔɪlt/) *adj* intato

unspoken /ʌnˈspəʊkən/ *adj* tácito

unstable /ʌnˈsteɪbl/ *adj* instável

unsteady /ʌnˈstedi/ *adj* (-ier, -iest) **1** inseguro, vacilante **2** (*mão, voz*) trêmulo

unstuck /ʌnˈstʌk/ *adj* descolado ▶ **come unstuck 1** descolar(-se) **2** (*coloq*) fracassar

unsuccessful /ˌʌnsəkˈsesfl/ *adj* malsucedido: *be ~ in doing sth* não conseguir fazer algo *unsuccessfully adv* sem êxito

unsuitable /ʌnˈsuːtəbl/ *adj* **1** inadequado **2** (*momento*) inoportuno

unsure /ʌnˈʃʊər; GB -ˈʃɔː(r)/ *adj* **1** inseguro **2 be ~ (about/of sth)** não ter certeza (de algo)

unsuspecting /ˌʌnsəˈspektɪŋ/ *adj* que não desconfia de nada

unsympathetic /ˌʌnˌsɪmpəˈθetɪk/ *adj* **1** incompreensivo **2** antipático

unthinkable /ʌnˈθɪŋkəbl/ *adj* inconcebível

untidy /ʌnˈtaɪdi/ *adj* (-ier, -iest) **1** desarrumado **2** (*aparência*) desleixado **3** despenteado

untie /ʌnˈtaɪ/ *vt* (*pt, pp* **-ied** *part pres* **untying**) desamarrar

until /ənˈtɪl/ *prep, conj* até (que)

untouched /ʌnˈtʌtʃt/ *adj* **1** intato **2 ~ (by sth)** insensível (a algo) **3** não perturbado

untrue /ʌnˈtruː/ *adj* **1** falso **2 ~ (to sb/sth)** desleal (a/com alguém/algo)

unused *adj* **1** /ˌʌnˈjuːzd/ não usado **2** /ˌʌnˈjuːst/ não acostumado

unusual /ʌnˈjuːʒuəl/ *adj* incomum *unusually adv* excepcionalmente: ~ *talented* com um talento fora do comum

unveil /ʌnˈveɪl/ *vt* **1** (*monumento*) desvelar **2** (*fig*) revelar

unwanted /ˌʌnˈwɒntɪd/ *adj* **1** indesejado: *feel ~* sentir-se rejeitado **2** desnecessário

unwarranted /ʌnˈwɒrəntɪd; GB -ˈwɒr-/ *adj* injustificado

unwelcome /ʌnˈwelkəm/ *adj* inoportuno, desagradável: *feel ~* sentir-se indesejado

unwell /ʌnˈwel/ *adj* indisposto

unwilling /ʌnˈwɪlɪŋ/ *adj* relutante, não disposto *unwillingness s* falta de vontade

unwind /ˌʌnˈwaɪnd/ (*pt, pp* **unwound** /-ˈwaʊnd/) **1** *vt, vi* desenrolar(-se) **2** *vi* relaxar

unwise /ˌʌnˈwaɪz/ *adj* imprudente

unwittingly /ʌnˈwɪtɪŋli/ *adv* inconscientemente

up /ʌp/ *adv* **1** em pé: *Is he up yet?* Ele já levantou? **2** mais alto, mais acima: *Pull your socks up.* Puxe as meias para cima. **3 up (to sb/sth)**: *He came up (to me).* Ele se aproximou (de mim). **4** *tear/break sth up* fazer algo em pedaços ◊ *lock sth up* fechar algo à chave **5** *Your time is up.* O seu tempo terminou. **6** colocado: *Are the curtains up yet?* As cortinas já estão penduradas? ▶ **be up (with sb)**: *What's up with you?* O que é que está acontecendo com você? **be up to sb** ser decisão de alguém: *It's up to you.* Você que sabe. **not be up to much** não valer grande coisa **up and down 1** para cima e para baixo **2** *jump up and down* dar pulos **up to sth 1** (*tb* **until sth**): *up to now* até agora **2** à altura de algo: *I don't feel up to it*. Não me sinto capaz de fazê-lo. **3** (*coloq*): *What are you up to?* O que é que você está fazendo? ◇ *He's up to no good.* Ele está tramando alguma. NOTA Para os usos de **up** em PHRASAL VERBS, ver o verbo, p. ex. **go up** em GO. ● *prep* acima ▶ **up and down sth** de um lado para o outro em algo ● *s* ▶ **ups and downs** altos e baixos

upbringing /'ʌpbrɪŋɪŋ/ *s* criação (*em casa*)

update /ʌp'deɪt/ *vt* **1** atualizar **2** ~ **sb (on sth)** pôr alguém ao corrente (de algo) ● /ʌpdeɪt/ *s* **1** (*tb* **updating**) atualização **2** informação atualizada

upgrade /ʌp'greɪd/ *vt* **1** melhorar **2** (*pessoa*) promover

upheaval /ʌp'hiːvl/ *s* agitação

uphill /ʌp'hɪl/ *adj, adv* encosta acima: *an ~ struggle* uma luta difícil

uphold /ʌp'hoʊld/ *vt* (*pt, pp* **upheld** /ʌp'held/) **1** defender (*decisão, etc.*) **2** manter (*tradição, etc.*)

upholstered /ʌp'hoʊlstərd/ *adj* estofado **upholstery** *s* estofamento

upkeep /'ʌpkiːp/ *s* manutenção

uplifting /ʌp'lɪftɪŋ/ *adj* inspirador

upmarket /ʌp'mɑːrkɪt/ (*GB*) = UPSCALE

upon /ə'pɑn/ *prep* (*fml*) Ver ON

upper /'ʌpər/ *adj* **1** superior, de cima: ~ *case* letras maiúsculas ◇ ~ *limit* limite máximo **2** alto ▶ **gain, get, etc. the upper hand** ficar por cima

uppermost /'ʌpərmoʊst/ *adj* mais alto (*posição*): *be ~ in sb's mind* ser o que domina os pensamentos de alguém

upright /'ʌpraɪt/ *adj* **1** vertical **2** honesto ● *adv* em posição vertical

uprising /'ʌpraɪzɪŋ/ *s* insurreição

uproar /'ʌprɔːr/ *s* tumulto

uproot /ʌp'ruːt/ *vt* **1** arrancar (*com as raízes*) **2** ~ **sb/yourself** desenraizar-se / desenraizar alguém

upscale /ʌp'skeɪl/ *adj* de/para o cliente com dinheiro, caro

upset /ʌp'set/ *vt* (*pt, pp* **upset**) **1** transtornar, contrariar **2** (*recipiente*) entornar ● *adj* NOTA Diz-se /'ʌpset/ antes de substantivo. **1** contrariado **2** (*estômago*) embrulhado ● /'ʌpset/ *s* transtorno **2** (*Med*) indisposição

upshot /'ʌpʃɑt/ *s* consequência

upside down /ˌʌpsaɪd 'daʊn/ *adj, adv* **1** ao contrário, de cabeça para baixo **2** (*coloq*) (*fig*) de pernas para o ar

upstairs /ˌʌp'steərz/ *adv* (no andar) de cima ● *adj* do andar de cima ● *s* andar de cima

upstream /ˌʌp'striːm/ *adv* contra a corrente (*rio, etc.*)

upsurge /'ʌpsɜːrdʒ/ *s* ~ **(in/of sth)** aumento (de algo)

up to date *adj* **1** moderno **2** em dia

upturn /'ʌptɜːrn/ *s* melhora, aumento

upturned /ˌʌp'tɜːrnd/ *adj* **1** virado de cabeça para baixo **2** (*nariz*) arrebitado

upward /'ʌpwərd/ *adj* ascendente: *an ~ trend* uma tendência de alta ● *adv* (*tb* **upwards**) para cima **upwards of** *prep* mais de

uranium /ju'reɪniəm/ *s* urânio

Uranus /'jʊərənəs, ju'reɪnəs/ *s* Urano

urban /'ɜːrbən/ *adj* urbano

urge /ɜːrdʒ/ *vt* instar, tentar convencer ■ **urge sb on** incitar alguém ● *s* vontade, impulso

urgency /'ɜːrdʒənsi/ *s* urgência

urgent /'ɜːrdʒənt/ *adj* **1** urgente: *be in ~ need of sth* precisar de algo urgentemente **2** premente

urine /'jʊərɪn/ *s* urina

us /əs, ʌs/ *pron* **1** [*complemento*] nos ▶ LET¹ **2** [*depois de prep e do verbo be*] nós: *It's us.* Somos nós.

usage /'juːsɪdʒ/ *s* uso

use /juːz/ *vt* (*pt, pp* **used** /juːzd/) **1** utilizar **2** (*pessoa*) usar, aproveitar-se de **3** gastar ■ **use sth up** esgotar algo ● /juːs/ *s* **1** uso: *in ~* em uso ◇ *a machine with many ~s* uma máquina com muitas aplicações ◇ *find a ~ for sth* encontrar alguma utilidade para algo **2** *What's the ~ of crying?* De que serve chorar? ◇ *What's the ~?* Para quê? ▶ **be of use** ser útil ▶ **be no use** **1** não servir para nada **2** ser (um) inútil ▶ **have the use of sth** poder usar algo ▶ **make use of sth** aproveitar algo

used¹ /juːzd/ *adj* usado

used² /juːst/ *adj* acostumado: *get ~ to sth* acostumar-se a algo

used to /'juːst tə, 'juːst tu/ *v modal* NOTA Usa-se *used to + infinitivo* para descrever hábitos e situações que deixaram de

ocorrer: *I used to live in London.* Eu antes morava em Londres. As orações interrogativas ou negativas geralmente se formam com **did:** *He didn't use to be fat.* ◊ *You used to smoke, didn't you?*

useful /ˈjuːsfl/ *adj* útil **usefulness** *s* utilidade

useless /ˈjuːsləs/ *adj* **1** inútil, inutilizável **2** (*coloq*) incompetente

user /ˈjuːzər/ *s* usuário/a: *user-friendly* fácil de usar

usual /ˈjuːʒuəl/ *adj* usual, normal: *more than ~* mais que de costume ◊ *the ~* o de sempre ► **as usual** como de costume

usually /ˈjuːʒuəli/ *adv* normalmente → ALWAYS

utensil /juːˈtensl/ *s* utensílio

utility /juːˈtɪləti/ *s* (*pl* **-ies**) **1** utilidade **2** *public ~* empresa pública de fornecimento de água, luz, etc.

utmost /ˈʌtməʊst/ *adj* maior ● *s*: *do your ~* fazer todo o possível

utter /ˈʌtər/ *vt* pronunciar ● *adj* total **utterly** *adv* completamente

V v

V, v /viː/ *s* (*pl* **V's, v's** /viːz/) **1** V, v **2** *V-neck* (com) gola em V ◊ *V-shaped* em forma de V

vacant /ˈveɪkənt/ *adj* **1** vago **2** (*expressão*) distraído **vacancy** *s* (*pl* **-ies**) vaga **vacantly** *adv* distraidamente

vacate /ˈveɪkeɪt; *GB* vəˈkeɪt/ *vt* (*fml*) vagar

vacation /veɪˈkeɪʃn; *GB* və-/ *s* férias NOTA Na Grã-Bretanha, usa-se **vacation** sobretudo para as férias das universidades e dos tribunais de justiça. A palavra mais comum é **holiday**. Nos EUA, usa-se **vacation** de maneira mais generalizada.

vaccination /ˌvæksɪˈneɪʃn/ *s* **1** vacinação **2** vacina

vaccine /ˈvæksiːn; *GB* ˈvæksiːn/ *s* vacina

vacuum /ˈvækjuəm/ *s* **1** vácuo **2** (*tb ~ cleaner*) aspirador de pó ► **in a vacuum** isolado (*de pessoas, fatos, etc.*)

vagina /vəˈdʒaɪnə/ *s* vagina

vague /veɪɡ/ *adj* (**-er, -est**) **1** vago **2** (*pessoa*) indeciso **3** (*gesto*) distraído **vaguely** *adv* **1** vagamente **2** aproximadamente **3** distraidamente

vain /veɪn/ *adj* (**-er, -est**) **1** vaidoso **2** inútil ► **in vain** em vão

valiant /ˈvæliənt/ *adj* valente

valid /ˈvælɪd/ *adj* válido **validity** /vəˈlɪdəti/ *s* validade

valley /ˈvæli/ *s* vale

valuable /ˈvæljuəbl/ *adj* valioso **valuables** *s* objetos de valor

valuation /ˌvæljuˈeɪʃn/ *s* avaliação

value /ˈvæljuː/ *s* **1** valor **2** (**values**) (*moral*) valores ► **good value** muito barato ● *vt* **1 ~ sth (at sth)** avaliar algo (em algo) **2** valorizar

valve /vælv/ *s* válvula

vampire /ˈvæmpaɪər/ *s* vampiro

van /væn/ *s* furgão

vandal /ˈvændl/ *s* vândalo/a **vandalism** *s* vandalismo **vandalize** *vt* destruir (*intencionalmente*)

the vanguard /ˈvænɡɑːrd/ *s* a vanguarda

vanilla /vəˈnɪlə/ *s* baunilha

vanish /ˈvænɪʃ/ *vi* desaparecer

vanity /ˈvænəti/ *s* vaidade

vantage point /ˈvæntɪdʒ pɔɪnt; *GB* ˈvɑːn-/ *s* posição estratégica

vapor (*GB* **-our**) /ˈveɪpər/ *s* vapor

variable /ˈveəriəbl/ *adj, s* variável

variance /ˈveəriəns/ *s* discordância ► **be at variance (with sb/sth)** (*fml*) discordar (de alguém/algo)

variant /ˈveəriənt/ *s* variante

variation /ˌveəriˈeɪʃn/ *s* variação

varied /ˈveərid/ *adj* variado

variety /vəˈraɪəti/ *s* (*pl* **-ies**) variedade

various /ˈveəriəs/ *adj* vários

varnish /ˈvɑːrnɪʃ/ *s* verniz ● *vt* envernizar

vary /ˈveəri/ *vt, vi* (*pt, pp* **-ied**) variar **varying** *adj* variado: *in ~ amounts* em diversas quantidades

vase /veɪs, veɪz; *GB* vɑːz/ *s* vaso

vast /væst; *GB* vɑːst/ *adj* vasto: *the ~ majority* a grande maioria **vastly** *adv* imensamente

VAT /ˌviː eɪ ˈtiː; væt/ *abrev* (*GB*) **value added tax** Imposto sobre a Circulação de Mercadorias e Serviços (= ICMS)

vat /væt/ *s* tonel

vault /vɔːlt/ *s* **1** abóbada **2** cripta **3** (*tb bank ~*) caixa-forte **4** salto ● *vt, vi ~ (over) sth* saltar (algo) (*apoiando-se nas mãos ou com vara*)

VCR /ˌviː siː ˈɑːr/ *abrev* (*USA*) **video (cassette) recorder**

veal /viːl/ *s* vitela → CARNE

veer /vɪər/ vi **1** virar, desviar (-se): ~ off course sair do rumo **2** (vento) mudar (de direção)

vegetable /'vedʒtəbl/ s **1** legume **2** (pessoa) vegetal

vegetarian /ˌvedʒə'teəriən/ adj, s vegetariano/a

vegetation /ˌvedʒə'teɪʃn/ s vegetação

vehement /'vi:əmənt/ adj veemente

vehicle /'vi:əkl/ s **1** veículo **2** (for sth) meio (de algo)

veil /veɪl/ s **1** véu ● vt velar, encobrir veiled adj velado: veiled in secrecy rodeado de sigilo

vein /veɪn/ s **1** (tb fig) veia **2** (Geol) veio **3** tom, estilo

velocity /və'lɒsəti/ s (pl -ies) velocidade NOTA A palavra mais comum é speed

velvet /'velvɪt/ s veludo

vending machine /'vendɪŋ məʃi:n/ s máquina de vender

vendor /'vendər/ s (fml) vendedor/a

veneer /və'nɪər/ s **1** (madeira, etc.) folheado **2** (fig) verniz

vengeance /'vendʒəns/ s vingança: take ~ on sb vingar-se de alguém ▶ with a vengeance furiosamente, em excesso

venison /'venɪsn/ s (carne de) veado

venom /'venəm/ s veneno venomous adj venenoso

vent /vent/ s **1** orifício: air ~ respiradouro **2** (roupa) abertura ▶ give (full) vent to sth desabafar/dar vazão a algo ● vt descarregar

ventilator /'ventɪleɪtər/ s ventilador

venture /'ventʃər/ s projeto, empreendimento ● **1** vi aventurar-se **2** vt (fml) (opinião, etc.) aventurar

venue /'venju:/ s **1** lugar (de reunião) **2** (esp GB) local (para concerto) **3** campo (futebol, etc.)

Venus /'vi:nəs/ s Vênus

verb /vɜːrb/ s verbo

verbal /'vɜːrbl/ adj verbal

verdict /'vɜːrdɪkt/ s veredicto

verge /vɜːrdʒ/ s **1** (GB) borda de grama (em caminho, etc.) ▶ on the verge of (doing) sth prestes a (fazer) algo ▶ verge on sth aproximar-se de algo

verification /ˌverɪfɪ'keɪʃn/ s **1** verificação **2** ratificação

verify /'verɪfaɪ/ vt (pt, pp -ied) **1** verificar **2** (suspeita, etc.) confirmar

veritable /'verɪtəbl/ adj (fml) verdadeiro

versatile /'vɜːrsətl; GB -taɪl/ adj versátil

verse /vɜːrs/ s **1** poesia, verso **2** estrofe **3** versículo

versed /vɜːrst/ adj versado

version /'vɜːrʒn; GB -ʃn/ s versão

vertebra /'vɜːrtɪbrə/ s (pl -brae -ri:/) vértebra

vertical /'vɜːrtɪkl/ adj, s vertical

verve /vɜːrv/ s entusiasmo

very /'veri/ adv **1** muito **2** the ~ best o melhor possível ◊ at the ~ latest o mais tardar **3** versículo: the ~ next day logo no dia seguinte ◊ your ~ own pony um pônei só para você ● adj **1** at that ~ moment naquele mesmo momento ◊ You're the ~ man I need. Você é exatamente o homem de quem preciso. **2** at the ~ end bem no fim **3** the ~ idea/thought of... a mera idéia/ só de pensar em...

vessel /'vesl/ s **1** (fml) navio, barco **2** (fml) vasilha **3** vaso (sanguíneo, etc.)

vest /vest/ s **1** colete **2** (GB) camiseta

vested interest s: have a vested interest in sth ter interesse em algo (por esperar vantagens)

vestige /'vestɪdʒ/ s vestígio

vet /vet/ vt (-tt-) (GB) investigar

veteran /'vetərən/ adj, s veterano/a ● s (USA, coloq vet) veterano de guerra

veterinarian (GB vet) s veterinário/a

veto /'vi:tou/ s (pl -es) veto ● vt (part pres -ing) vetar

via /'vɪə, 'vaɪə/ prep por, via

viable /'vaɪəbl/ adj viável

vibrate /'vaɪbreɪt; GB vaɪ'breɪt/ vt, vi (fazer) vibrar vibration s vibração

vicar /'vɪkər/ s pastor (anglicano) ▶ PRIEST vicarage /'vɪkərɪdʒ/ s (GB) residência paroquial

vice /vaɪs/ s **1** vício **2** (GB) = VISE

vice- /vaɪs/ pref vice-

vice versa /ˌvaɪs 'vɜːrsə/ adv vice-versa

vicinity /və'sɪnəti/ s (fml): in the ~ (of sth) nas proximidades (de algo)

vicious /'vɪʃəs/ adj **1** cruel **2** (ataque) violento **3** (animal) feroz ▶ a vicious circle um círculo vicioso

victim /'vɪktɪm/ s vítima victimize vt tratar injustamente

victor /'vɪktər/ s (fml) vencedor/a victorious /vɪk'tɔːriəs/ adj **1** vitorioso: be ~ over sb triunfar sobre alguém **2** (*equipe*) vencedor

victory /'vɪktəri/ s (pl **-ies**) vitória

video /'vɪdiəʊ/ s (pl ~**s**) **1** vídeo **2** (GB) (tb ~ (**cassette**) **recorder**) (USA **VCR**) videocassete videotape /'vɪdiəʊteɪp/ s videoteipe

view /vju:/ s **1** vista **2** parecer: *in my ~* na minha opinião **3** conceito **4** (*imagem*) visão ▸ **in view of sth** (fml) em vista de algo **with a view to (doing) sth** (fml) com a intenção de fazer algo ● vt **1** ver, assistir a **2** considerar **viewer** s **1** telespectador/a **2** espectador/a **3** visor **viewing** s sessão

viewpoint /'vju:pɔɪnt/ s ponto de vista

vigil /'vɪdʒɪl/ s vigília

vigilant /'vɪdʒɪlənt/ adj vigilante

vigorous /'vɪgərəs/ adj vigoroso

vile /vaɪl/ adj (**-er, -est**) repugnante

village /'vɪlɪdʒ/ s povoado **villager** s habitante de aldeia

villain /'vɪlən/ s **1** (Teat., etc.) bandido **2** (GB, coloq) criminoso/a

vindicate /'vɪndɪkeɪt/ vt **1** vindicar **2** justificar

vine /vaɪn/ s **1** videira **2** trepadeira

vinegar /'vɪnɪgər/ s vinagre

vineyard /'vɪnjərd/ s vinha

vintage /'vɪntɪdʒ/ s safra ● adj **1** (*vinho*) de safra excepcional e de determinado ano **2** clássico **3** (GB) (*carro*) antigo

vinyl /'vaɪnl/ s vinil

violate /'vaɪəleɪt/ vt **1** violar (*leis, normas*) NOTA No sentido sexual, costuma-se usar rape. **2** (*confiança*) abusar de **3** (*intimidade*) invadir

violence /'vaɪələns/ s **1** violência **2** (*emoções*) intensidade

violent /'vaɪələnt/ adj **1** violento **2** (*emoções*) intenso

violet /'vaɪələt/ adj, s (tb Bot) violeta

violin /ˌvaɪə'lɪn/ s violino

virgin /'vɜ:rdʒɪn/ adj, s virgem

Virgo /'vɜ:rgoʊ/ s (pl ~**s**) Virgem

virile /'vɪraɪl/ adj viril

virtual /'vɜ:rtʃuəl/ adj virtual **virtually** adv praticamente

virtue /'vɜ:rtʃu:/ s **1** virtude **2** mérito ▸ **by virtue of sth** (fml) em virtude de algo **virtuous** /'vɜ:rtʃuəs/ adj virtuoso

virus /'vaɪrəs/ s vírus

visa /'vi:zə/ s visto

vis-à-vis /ˌvi:z ə 'vi:; GB ˌvi:z ɑ: 'vi:/ prep **1** com relação a **2** em

comparação com

vise /vaɪs/ s torninho (*carpinteiro*)

visible /'vɪzəbl/ adj **1** visível **2** patente **visibly** adv obviamente

vision /'vɪʒn/ s visão

visit /'vɪzɪt/ vt, vi visitar ● s visita: visiting a patient (*equipe, etc.*): ~ hours horário de visita **visitor** s **1** visitante, visita **2** turista

vista /'vɪstə/ s (fml) **1** vista **2** perspectiva

visual /'vɪʒuəl/ adj visual: ~ display unit monitor **visualize** vt **1** visualizar **2** prever

vital /'vaɪtl/ adj vitally adv: ~ important de importância vital

vitamin /'vaɪtəmɪn; GB 'vɪt-/ s vitamina

vivacious /vɪ'veɪʃəs/ adj vivaz

vivid /'vɪvɪd/ adj vivo (*cores, imaginação, etc.*) **vividly** adv vivamente

vocabulary /və'kæbjəleri; GB -ləri/ s (pl **-ies**) (tb coloq **vocab** /'vəʊkæb/) vocabulário

vocal /'vəʊkl/ adj **1** vocal **2** barulhento ● s [ger pl]: be on vocals ser o cantor/cantar

vocation /vəʊ'keɪʃn/ s vocação **vocational** adj: ~ training formação profissional

vociferous /vəʊ'sɪfərəs; GB və-/ adj vociferante

vogue /vəʊg/ s ~ (**for sth**) moda (de algo): in ~ em voga

voice /vɔɪs/ s voz: make your ~ heard fazer-se ouvir ● vt exprimir

void /vɔɪd/ s (fml) vazio ● adj (fml) nulo: make sth ~ anular algo

volatile /'vɒlətl; GB -taɪl/ adj **1** (*pessoa*) volúvel **2** instável

volcano /vɒl'keɪnəʊ/ s (pl ~**s** ou ~**es**) vulcão

volition /vəʊ'lɪʃn; GB və-/ s (fml): of your own ~ por sua própria vontade

volley /'vɒli/ s **1** (Esporte) voleio **2** (*balas, etc.*) saraivada **3** (fig) torrente

volleyball /'vɒlibɔ:l/ s voleibol

volt /vəʊlt/ s volt **voltage** /'vəʊltɪdʒ/ s voltagem: high ~ alta tensão

volume /'vɒlju:m; GB -jəm/ s volume

voluminous /və'lu:mɪnəs/ adj (fml) **1** amplo **2** (*texto*) extenso

voluntary /'vɒləntəri; GB -tri/ adj voluntário

volunteer /ˌvɒlən'tɪər/ s voluntário/a ● **1** vi oferecer-se (como voluntário) **2** vt oferecer (*informação*)

vomit /'vɒmɪt/ vt, vi vomitar NOTA É mais comum dizer-se **throw up**. • s vômito **vomiting** [U] s vômitos

voracious /və'reɪʃəs/ adj voraz

vote /vəʊt/ s **1** voto **2** votação **3** (**the vote**) direito de voto ▸ **vote of (no) confidence** voto de confiança/censura **vote of thanks** palavras de agradecimento • **1** vt, vi votar **2** vt (*dinheiro*) designar **3** vt propor voter s eleitor/a **voting** s votação

vouch /vaʊtʃ/ vi **1** ~ **for sb/sth** responder por alguém/algo **2** ~ **for sth** garantir algo

voucher /'vaʊtʃər/ s (GB) vale

vow /vaʊ/ s juramento • vt jurar

vowel /'vaʊəl/ s vogal

voyage /'vɔɪɪdʒ/ s viagem NOTA Geralmente se usa **voyage** para viagens espaciais, por mar e em sentido figurado. → VIAGEM

vulgar /'vʌlɡər/ adj **1** vulgar **2** grosseiro

vulnerable /'vʌlnərəbl/ adj vulnerável

vulture /'vʌltʃər/ s abutre

W w

W, w /'dʌbljuː/ s (pl **W's**, **w's** /'dʌbljuːz/) W, w

wade /weɪd/ **1** vi caminhar com dificuldade por água, lama, etc. **2** vt, vi vadear

wafer /'weɪfər/ s biscoito de baunilha

wag /wæɡ/ (**-gg-**) **1** vt sacudir **2** vt, vi (*rabo*) abanar(-se)

wage /weɪdʒ/ s [ger pl] ordenado (*semanal*) • vt: ~ **war on poverty** travar guerra contra a pobreza

wagon (GB tb **waggon**) /'wæɡən/ s **1** carroça **2** vagão

wail /weɪl/ **1** vi gemer **2** (*sirene*) apitar • s gemido

waist /weɪst/ s cintura

waistband /'weɪstbænd/ s cós

waistcoat /'weskət; GB 'weɪskəʊt/ (GB) s colete

wait /weɪt/ **1** vi ~ **for sb/sth** esperar (alguém/algo): *keep sb waiting* fazer alguém esperar ◊ *I can't* ~ *to...* Não vejo a hora de... → ESPERAR **2** vt (*vez*) esperar ▪ **wait on sb** servir alguém **wait up** esperar acordado • s espera: *We had a three-hour* ~ *for the bus.* Esperamos três horas pelo ônibus.

waiter /'weɪtər/ s (fem **waitress** /'weɪtrəs/) garçom, garçonete

waive /weɪv/ vt (fml) **1** (*pagamento*) renunciar a **2** (*norma*) não aplicar

wake /weɪk/ vt, vi (pt **woke** pp **woken**) ~ (**sb**) (**up**) acordar, despertar (alguém) ▪ **wake (sb) up** (fig) fazer alguém abrir os olhos **wake up to sth** dar-se conta de algo • s **1** velório **2** (*Náut*) esteira ▸ **in the wake of sth** em seguida a algo

walk /wɔːk/ **1** vi andar **2** vt passear: *I'll ~ you home.* Acompanho você até a sua casa. **3** vt percorrer (a pé) ▪ **walk away/off** ir-se embora **walk into sb/sth** chocar(-se) contra alguém/algo **walk out** (*coloq*) entrar em greve **walk out of sth** retirar-se de algo • s **1** passeio, caminhada **2** andar ▸ **a walk of life**: *people of all walks of life* pessoas de todas as classes e profissões walker s caminhante walking s andar: ~ *shoes* sapatos para caminhar ◊ ~ *stick* bengala walkout s greve

Walkman /'wɔːkmæn/ s (pl ~s) walkman

wall /wɔːl/ s **1** muro, parede **2** muralha walled adj murado

wallet /'wɒlɪt/ s carteira (*dinheiro*)

wallpaper /'wɔːlpeɪpər/ s papel de parede

walnut /'wɔːlnʌt/ s **1** noz **2** (tb ~ **tree**) nogueira

waltz /wɔːl(t)s/ s valsa • vi valsar

wand /wɒnd/ s varinha

wander /'wɒndər/ **1** vi andar ao acaso NOTA **Wander** pode ser seguido de **around**, **about** ou de outras preposições ou advérbios. Significa "andar à toa" e se traduz de diversas maneiras: *wander in* entrar distraidamente ◊ *wander across the road* atravessar a rua distraidamente ◊ *wander away/off* perder-se/afastar-se. **2** vi (*pensamentos*) devanear **3** vi (*olhar*) passear **4** vt vagar por

wane /weɪn/ (tb be on the ~) vi minguar

want /wɒnt/ **1** vt, vi querer NOTA **Like** também significa "querer", mas só se usa quando se oferece alguma coisa ou quando se convida alguém: *Would you like to come to dinner?* ◊ *Would you like something to eat?* **2** vt procurar: *You're wanted on the phone.* Querem falar com você ao telefone. • s **1** [ger pl] necessidade, vontade **2**

~ **of sth** falta de algo: *not for* ~ *of trying* não por não tentar 3 miséria *wanting adj* ~ **(in sth)** (fml) carente (de algo)

war /wɔːr/ s 1 guerra 2 conflito 3 luta

ward /wɔːrd/ s ala (hospital) ■ **ward sth off 1** (ataque) repelir algo **2** (perigo) afastar algo

warden /ˈwɔːrdn/ s guarda

wardrobe /ˈwɔːrdroʊb/ s guarda-roupa

warehouse /ˈweərhaʊs/ s armazém

wares /weərz/ s (antiq) mercadorias

warfare /ˈwɔːrfeər/ s guerra

warlike /ˈwɔːrlaɪk/ adj belicoso

warm /wɔːrm/ adj (~er, ~est) 1 (clima) temperado: be ~ fazer calor → FRIO **2** (coisa) quente **3** (pessoa): be/get ~ sentir calor/aquecer-se **4** (roupa) agasalho **5** cordial ● vt, vi ~ **(sth/yourself) (up)** esquentar algo; aquecer-se ■ **warm up 1** (Esporte) fazer o aquecimento **2** (motor) esquentar *warming s: global* ~ aquecimento global *warmly adv* 1 calorosamente **2** ~ *dressed* bem agasalhado *warmth s* 1 calor **2** simpatia, amabilidade

warn /wɔːrn/ vt 1 avisar, prevenir **2** ~ **sb (against doing sth)** advertir alguém (a não fazer algo) **3** ~ **sb (not) to do sth** ordenar a alguém que (não) faça algo (sob ameaça) *warning s* advertência

warp /wɔːrp/ vt, vi empenar *warped adj* pervertido: *a* ~ *sense of humor* um senso de humor deturpado

warrant /ˈwɔːrənt; GB ˈwɒr-/ s (Jur) autorização: *search* ~ mandado de busca ● vt (fml) justificar

warranty /ˈwɔːrənti; GB ˈwɒr-/ s (pl -ies) garantia

warren /ˈwɔːrən; GB ˈwɒrən/ s 1 coelheira **2** labirinto

warrior /ˈwɔːriər; GB ˈwɒr-/ s guerreiro/a

warship /ˈwɔːrʃɪp/ s navio de guerra

wart /wɔːrt/ s verruga

wartime /ˈwɔːrtaɪm/ s (tempo de) guerra

wary /ˈweəri/ adj (-ier, -iest) cauteloso: *be* ~ *of sb* desconfiar de alguém

was /wəz, wɑz, wɒz; GB wɒz/ pret de BE

wash /wɑʃ/ s 1 lavagem: *have a* ~ lavar-se **2 (the wash)** [sing]: *All my shirts are in the* ~. Todas as minhas camisas estão para

lavar. **3** (Náut) esteira ● 1 vt, vi lavar(-se) **2** vi ~ **over sth** cobrir algo **3** vi ~ **over sb** não atingir alguém **4** vt ~ **sb/sth (away)** arrastar alguém/algo: *be washed overboard* ser lançado ao mar pela correnteza ■ **wash off** sair ao lavar **wash sth off** tirar algo lavando **wash sth out** lavar algo **wash up 1** (USA) lavar-se (as mãos e o rosto) **2** (GB) lavar a louça **wash sth up 1** (GB) (pratos) lavar algo **2** (mar) arrastar algo até a praia *washable adj* lavável

washbasin /ˈwɑʃbeɪsn/ s (GB) pia (de banheiro)

washcloth /ˈwɑʃklɔːθ/ s toalhinha de rosto

washing /ˈwɑʃɪŋ/ s 1 lavagem: ~ *powder* (esp GB) sabão em pó **2** roupa para lavar **3** roupa lavada

washing machine s máquina de lavar roupa

washing-up s (GB) lavagem da louça: *do the* ~ lavar a louça ◇ ~ *liquid* detergente

washroom /ˈwɑʃruːm/ s (USA) banheiro → TOILET

wasn't /ˈwɑznt/ = WAS NOT Ver BE

wasp /wɑsp/ s vespa

waste /weɪst/ adj 1 ~ *material/products* resíduos **2** baldio (terreno) ● vt 1 esbanjar **2** (tempo, ocasião) perder **3** desperdiçar ▶ **waste your breath** perder seu tempo ■ **waste away** definhar ● s 1 perda, desperdício **2** esbanjamento **3** [U] resíduos, lixo ▶ **go to waste** desperdiçar-se *wasted adj* inútil (viagem, esforço) *wasteful adj* 1 esbanjador **2** anti-econômico

wastebasket /ˈweɪstbæskɪt/ (GB **waste-paper basket**) s cesta de papéis

wasteland /ˈweɪstlænd/ s terreno baldio

watch /wɑtʃ/ s 1 relógio (pulso) **2** quarto **3** sentinela: *keep* ~ **over sb** vigiar alguém ● 1 vt, vi observar, olhar **2** vt, vi vigiar **3** vt (TV, etc.) assistir **4** vt, vi ~ **(over) sb/sth** tomar conta de alguém/algo **5** vi ~ **for sth** estar atento a, esperar algo **6** vt ter cuidado com: *Watch your language*. Modere a linguagem. ▶ **watch your step** andar na linha ■ **watch out (for sb/sth)** ter cuidado (com alguém/algo): *Watch out!* Cuidado! *watchful adj* atento

watchdog /ˈwɑtʃdɔːɡ; GB -dɒɡ/ s órgão em defesa dos direitos do consumidor

watchword /'wɒtʃwɜːd/ s senha

water /'wɔːtər/ s água ▶ **under water** 1 embaixo d'água 2 inundado ● 1 vt regar 2 vi (olhos) lacrimejar 3 vi salivar ■ **water sth down** 1 diluir algo com água 2 amenizar algo

watercolor (GB **-our**) /'wɔːtərkʌlər/ s aquarela

watercress /'wɔːtərkres/ s agrião

waterfall /'wɔːtərfɔːl/ s cachoeira

watermelon /'wɔːtərmelən/ s melancia

waterproof /'wɔːtərpruːf/ adj, s impermeável

watershed /'wɔːtərʃed/ s momento decisivo

waterskiing /'wɔːtərskiːɪŋ/ s esqui aquático

watertight /'wɔːtərtaɪt/ adj 1 à prova d'água 2 (argumento) irrefutável

waterway /'wɔːtərweɪ/ s via navegável

watery /'wɔːtəri/ adj 1 aguado 2 (cor) pálido 3 (olhos) lacrimoso

watt /wɒt/ s watt

wave /weɪv/ 1 vt, vi ondular(-se) 2 vi ~ (at/to sb) acenar (para alguém) ■ **wave sth aside** ignorar algo (objeções) ● s 1 onda 2 enxurrada 3 aceno

wavelength /'weɪvleŋθ/ s comprimento de onda

waver /'weɪvər/ vi 1 vacilar 2 (voz) tremer

wavy /'weɪvi/ adj (-ier, -iest) 1 ondulado 2 ondulante

wax /wæks/ s cera

way /weɪ/ s 1 caminho: make ~ for sb abrir caminho para alguém ◇ a long ~ (away) muito longe ◇ ~ out saída 2 (Way) (em nomes) à rua: across/over the ~ em frente/do outro lado da rua ◇ Get out of my ~! Saia da minha frente! 4 direção: "Which ~?" "That ~." —Por onde? —Por ali. ◇ make your ~ towards sth ir-se em direção a algo 5 forma, maneira: Do it your own ~! Faça como quiser! 6 [ger pl] costume ▶ **by the way** a propósito **divide, split, etc. sth two, three, etc. ways** dividir algo em dois, três, etc. **get/have your own way** conseguir o que se quer **give way to sth** dar a preferência, ceder: give way to sth dar lugar a algo **go out of your way (to do sth)** dar-se ao trabalho (de fazer algo) **in a/one way; in some ways** de certo modo **no way** (coloq) nem pensar **one**

way or another de um jeito ou de outro ▶ **on your** ~ ir-se embora **the other way around** 1 às avessas 2 ao contrário **under way** em andamento **way of life** estilo de vida **ways and means** meios ● adv (coloq) muito ▶ **way back** muito tempo atrás: ~ back in the fifties lá pelos anos cinquenta

we /wiː/ pron nós → YOU

weak /wiːk/ adj (~er, ~est) 1 fraco 2 (Med) debilitado 3 (bebida) aguado 4 ~ (at/in/on sth) deficiente (em algo) **weaken** 1 vt, vi enfraquecer(-se) 2 vi ceder **weakness** s fraqueza

wealth /welθ/ s 1 [U] riqueza 2 abundância **wealthy** adj (-ier, -iest) rico

weapon /'wepən/ s arma

wear /wear/ (pt wore pp worn) 1 vt (roupa, etc.) usar 2 vt (expressão) ter 3 vt, vi ~ (sth) (down/out) gastar (algo) 4 vt (buraco, etc.) fazer 5 vi durar ■ **wear (sth) away** desgastar (algo)/desgastar-se ■ **wear sb down/out** esgotar alguém ■ **wear off** desaparecer (novidade, etc.) ● s 1 desgaste 2 uso 3 roupa: casual ~ roupa esportiva ▶ **wear and tear** desgaste

weary /'wɪəri/ adj (-ier, -iest) 1 exausto 2 cansado

weather /'weðər/ s tempo ▶ **under the weather** (coloq) indisposto ● vt superar (crise)

weave /wiːv/ (pt **wove** pp **woven**) 1 vt tecer 2 vt ~ sth into sth entrelaçar algo com algo 3 vi (pt, pp **weaved**) ziguezaguear

web /web/ s 1 teia (de aranha) 2 rede 3 (mentiras) emaranhado 4 (the Web) a Web

website /'websaɪt/ s site

we'd /wiːd/ 1 = WE HAD Ver HAVE 2 = WE WOULD Ver WOULD

wedding /'wedɪŋ/ s casamento: golden ~ bodas de ouro → CASAMENTO

wedge /wedʒ/ s 1 calço 2 (queijo, etc.) fatia 3 (limão) quarto ● vt 1 ~ sth open/shut manter algo aberto/fechado com calço 2 ~ itself/get wedged apertar-se (esp pessoas) entalar

Wednesday /'wenzdeɪ, -di/ s (abrev **Wed.**) quarta(-feira) → MONDAY

wee /wiː/ adj (esp Escócia) pequeno: in the ~ hours de madrugada

weed /wiːd/ s 1 erva daninha: weedkiller herbicida 2 [U] (na

água) alga **3** (GB, coloq) magricela ● vt capinar ■ **weed sb/sth out** livrar-se de alguém/algo

week /wiːk/ s semana: *a ~ from today* de hoje a oito dias ◊ *Monday ~* (GB) daqui a duas segundas **weekday** s dia de semana **weekend** /ˈwiːkend; GB ˌwiːkˈend/ s fim de semana

weekly /ˈwiːkli/ *adj* semanal ● *adv* semanalmente ● s (pl -ies) semanário

weep /wiːp/ vi (pt, pp wept) (fml) chorar **weeping** s choro

weigh /weɪ/ **1** vt, vi pesar **2** vt ~ **sth (up)** ponderar algo ▸ **weigh anchor** levantar âncora ■ **weigh sb/sth down** sobrecarregar alguém/algo: *weighed down with luggage* carregado de bagagem

weight /weɪt/ s peso: *lose/put on weight* emagrecer/engordar ● vt **1** pôr peso(s) em **2** ~ **sth (down)** sobrecarregar algo **weighting** s **1** (GB) London ~ suplemento salarial por trabalhar em Londres **2** importância **weightless** adj imponderável **weighty** adj (-ier, -iest) **1** pesado **2** importante

weir /wɪər/ s represa

weird /wɪərd/ adj (~er, ~est) **1** estranho **2** (coloq) esquisito

welcome /ˈwelkəm/ adj **1** bem-vindo **2** agradável **3** be ~ to (do) sth: *You're ~ to use my car/to stay.* Meu carro está à sua disposição./Você pode ficar, se quiser. ▸ **you're welcome** de nada ● s acolhida ● vt **1** receber **2** apreciar **3** acolher **welcoming** adj acolhedor

weld /weld/ vt, vi soldar

welfare /ˈwelfeər/ s **1** bem-estar **2** assistência: *the Welfare State* o Estado-Previdência **3** previdência social

well /wel/ s poço ● vi ~ (out/up) brotar ● adj, adv (comp better superl best) **1** bem: *get ~* ficar bom **2** (depois de can, could, may, might): *I can ~ believe it.* Não duvido. ◊ *I can't very ~ leave.* Não posso ir embora sem mais nem menos. ▸ **as well** também → **TAMBÉM as well as** assim como **do well 1** ser bem-sucedido **2** [só em tempos contínuos] recuperar-se **may/ might (just) as well** do sth: *We may as ~ go home.* O melhor a fazer é ir para casa. **well and truly** (GB, coloq) completamente ● interj **1** (surpresa) puxa **2** (resignação) paciência **3**

(interrogação) e então? **4** (dúvida) pois é

we'll /wiːl/ **1** = WE SHALL Ver SHALL **2** = WE WILL Ver WILL

well behaved adj bem-comportado: *be ~* portar-se bem NOTA Os adjetivos em que **well** é seguido de outra palavra geralmente são escritos como duas palavras depois de um verbo e com hífen antes de um substantivo: *She is always well behaved.* ◊ *well-behaved children.*

well-being s bem-estar

well earned adj merecido

wellington /ˈwelɪŋtən/ (tb ~ **boot**) s (esp GB) bota de borracha

well kept adj **1** bem conservado **2** (segredo) bem guardado

well known adj conhecido: *It's a well-known fact that...* É sabido que...

well meaning adj bem-intencionado

well-to-do (tb well off) adj rico

went /went/ pret de GO

wept /wept/ pret, pp de WEEP

were /wər, wɜːr/ pret de BE

we're /wɪər/ = WE ARE Ver BE

weren't /wɜːrnt/ = WERE NOT Ver BE

west /west/ s **1** (tb the west, the West) (abrev W.) (o) oeste: *westbound* em direção ao oeste **2** (the West) (o) Ocidente ● adj (do) oeste ● adv para o oeste

western /ˈwestərn/ adj (tb Western) do oeste, ocidental ● s livro/filme de cowboy **westerner** s ocidental

westward(s) /ˈwestwərd(z)/ adv em direção ao oeste

wet /wet/ adj (wetter, wettest) **1** molhado: *get ~* molhar-se **2** úmido **3** (tempo) chuvoso **4** (tinta, etc.) fresco **5** (GB, coloq) (pessoa) mole ● s **1** the wet (GB) a chuva **2** umidade ● (pt, pp wet ou wetted) vt umedecer: ~ *yourself/the bed* fazer xixi na calça/na cama

we've /wiːv/ = WE HAVE Ver HAVE

whack /wæk/ vt (coloq) bater em ● s pancada

whale /weɪl/ s baleia

wharf /wɔːrf/ s (pl wharves /wɔːrvz/) cais

what /wʌt, wɒt/ adj que: *What color is it?* (De) que cor é? ◊ *What a pity!* Que pena! ● pron interr o que: *What's your name?* Qual é o seu nome? ▸ **what about...? 1** que tal...? **2** o que é feito de...?

NOTA Which se refere a membros de um determinado grupo: *Which is your car, this one or that one?* **What** é usado quando há mais opções: *What are your favorite books?* **what if...?** e **se...?** ◆ *adj rel, pron rel* o/a que: *~ money I have* todo o dinheiro que eu tenho ◆ *interj* what? (coloq) (o) quê?, como?

whatever /wɒtˈevər/ *pron* **1** (tudo) o que: *Give ~ you can.* Dê o quanto você puder. **2** *~ happens* o que quer que aconteça ▶ **or whatever** (coloq) ou seja lá o que for ◆ *adj* qualquer: *~ time you come.* a qualquer hora em que você vier. ◆ *pron interr* que (diabo) ◆ *adv* (tb whatsoever) em absoluto: *nothing whatsoever* absolutamente nada

wheat /wiːt/ *s* trigo

wheel /wiːl/ *s* **1** roda **2** volante ● **1** *vt* (bicicleta, etc.) empurrar **2** *vt* (pessoa) levar **3** *vi* (pássaro) voar em círculo **4** *vi* **~ around** dar a volta

wheelbarrow /ˈwiːlbærəʊ/ *s* Ver BARROW

wheelchair /ˈwiːltʃeər/ *s* cadeira de rodas

wheeze /wiːz/ *vi* chiar, respirar ruidosamente

when /wen/ *adv interr, conj* quando ● *adv rel* em que

whenever /wenˈevər/ *conj* **1** quando (quer que): *Come ~ you like.* Venha quando quiser. **2** sempre que

where /weər/ *adv, conj* onde: *Where are you going?* Aonde você vai?

whereabouts /ˌweərəˈbaʊts/ *adv interr* onde ● /ˈweərəbaʊts/ *s* paradeiro

whereas /ˌweərˈæz/ *conj* (fml) enquanto

whereby /weərˈbaɪ/ *adv rel* (fml) pelo/pela qual

whereupon /ˌweərəˈpɒn/ *conj* após o que

wherever /weərˈevər/ *conj* onde (quer que): *~ you like* onde você quiser ● *adv interr* onde (diabo)

whet /wet/ *vt* (-tt-) ▶ **whet sb's appetite** pôr água na boca de alguém

whether /ˈweðər/ *conj* se: *It depends on ~ the letter arrives on time.* Depende de a carta chegar a tempo. ◇ *~ it rains or not* chova ou não chova

which /wɪtʃ/ *adj interr* que: *Do you know ~ one is yours?* Você sabe qual é o seu? → WHAT ● *pron interr* qual → WHAT ●

adj rel, pron rel **1** que: *the book ~ I have* o livro que eu tenho ◇ *the article ~ I read yesterday* o artigo que li ontem → QUE **2** [depois de prep] (fml) o/a qual: *in ~ case* caso em que ◇ *the bag in ~ I put it* a bolsa onde a coloquei **NOTA** Este uso é muito formal. É mais comum a preposição no final: *the bag ~ I put it in.*

whichever /wɪtʃˈevər/ *pron* o que (quer que): *~ you like* o que você quiser ● *adj* qualquer: *It's the same, ~ route you take.* Não importa o caminho que você vai tomar.

whiff /wɪf/ *s* baforada

while /waɪl/ *s* [sing] momento: *for a ~* durante algum tempo ● *conj* (GB tb whilst /waɪlst/) **1** enquanto: *~ you're at it* aproveitando já que está **2** *I drink coffee ~ she prefers tea.* Eu bebo café, ela no entanto prefere chá. **3** (fml) embora ■ **while sth away**: *~ the morning away* passar a manhã de maneira agradável

whim /wɪm/ *s* capricho

whimper /ˈwɪmpər/ *vi* choramingar ● *s* lamúria

whip /wɪp/ *s* **1** chicote **2** (Pol) líder da bancada parlamentar ● (-pp-) *vt* **1** chicotear **2** *~ sth (up) (into sth)* (Cozinha) bater algo (até obter algo): *whipped cream* creme chantilly ■ **whip sth up 1** preparar algo rapidamente **2** atiçar algo

whir (GB whirr) Ver WHIZ

whirl /wɜːl/ **1** *vt, vi* (fazer) rodar **2** *vi* (folhas) redemoinhar ● *s* [sing] **1** giro **2** rodopio: *a ~ of dust* um redemoinho de pó **3** turbilhão: *My head is in a ~.* Minha cabeça está dando voltas.

whirlpool /ˈwɜːlpuːl/ *s* redemoinho

whirlwind /ˈwɜːlwɪnd/ *s* redemoinho de vento ● *adj* (fig) furacão

whisk /wɪsk/ *s* batedeira (elétrica) ● *vt* (Cozinha) bater ■ **whisk sb/sth away/off** levar alguém/algo rapidamente

whiskers /ˈwɪskəz/ *s* [pl] **1** (animal) bigode **2** (homem) suíças

whiskey /ˈwɪski/ *s* (GB whisky, (pl -ies)) uísque

whisper /ˈwɪspər/ **1** *vi* sussurrar **2** *vi* cochichar **3** *vt* falar em voz baixa ● *s* **1** cochicho **2** sussurro

whistle /ˈwɪsl/ *s* **1** assobio **2** apito

● *vt, vi* assobiar, apitar

white /waɪt/ *adj* (**-er, -est**) **1** branco **2** ~ (**with sth**) pálido (de algo) ● s **1** branco **2** clara (ovo)

white-collar *adj:* ~ *workers* funcionários de escritório

whiteness /'waɪtnəs/ s brancura

White Paper s (GB) relatório oficial (governo)

whitewash /'waɪtwɒʃ/ s cal ● *vt* **1** caiar **2** (fig) encobrir

who /huː/ *pron interr* quem: *Who is it?* Quem é? ● *pron rel* que: *people* ~ *eat garlic* gente que come alho ◊ *the man* ~ *I had spoken to* o homem com o qual eu havia falado → QUE

whoever /huː'evər/ *pron* **1** qualquer um que **2** quem quer que: *Whoever calls, I'm not in.* Não importa quem telefone, eu não estou.

whole /hoʊl/ *adj* **1** inteiro **2** todo: *forget the* ~ *thing* esquecer tudo ● s todo: *the* ~ *of August* o mês de agosto inteiro ► **on the whole** de um modo geral

wholehearted /ˌhoʊl'hɑrtɪd/ *adj* irrestrito **wholeheartedly** *adv* sem reservas

wholesale /'hoʊlseɪl/ *adj, adv* **1** (Com) por atacado **2** em grande escala

wholesome /'hoʊlsəm/ *adj* saudável

wholewheat /'hoʊlwiːt/ *adj* integral

wholly /'hoʊlli/ *adv* totalmente

whom /huːm/ *pron* (fml) quem: *the investors, some of* ~ *bought shares* os investidores, alguns dos quais compraram ações ◊ *To* ~ *did you give the money?* Para quem você deu o dinheiro? ◊ *the person to* ~ *this letter was addressed* a pessoa a quem esta carta foi endereçada NOTA É mais natural dizer *Who did you give the money to?* ou *the person this letter was addressed to.*

whose /huːz/ *pron interr, adj interr* de quem ● *adj rel* cujo(s)/a(s): *the people* ~ *house we stayed in* as pessoas na casa de quem ficamos

why /waɪ/ *adv interr, adv rel* por que: *Why not go to the cinema?* Por que não vamos ao cinema?

wicked /'wɪkɪd/ *adj* (**-er, -est**) **1** malvado **2** travesso **3** (coloq) ótimo **wickedness** s maldade

wicker /'wɪkər/ s vime

wide /waɪd/ *adj* (**-er, -est**) **1** amplo, extenso **2** largo: *How* ~ *is it?* Quanto tem de largura?

→ BROAD ● *adv* completamente: ~ *awake* bem acordado ► **wide open** (competição) sem favoritos **widely** *adv* muito **widen** *vt, vi* ampliar(-se)

wide-ranging *adj* de grande alcance (investigação, etc.)

widespread /'waɪdspred/ *adj* difundido

widow /'wɪdoʊ/ s viúva **widowed** *adj* viúvo **widower** s viúvo

width /wɪdθ, wɪtθ/ s largura

wield /wiːld/ *vt* **1** empunhar **2** (poder) exercer

wife /waɪf/ s (pl **wives**) mulher, esposa

wig /wɪg/ s peruca

wiggle /'wɪgl/ *vt, vi* (coloq) menear(-se)

wild /waɪld/ *adj* (**~er, ~est**) **1** selvagem **2** (planta) silvestre **3** (tempo) tempestuoso **4** desenfreado **5** furioso **6** (coloq) ~ **about sb/sth** louco por alguém/ algo ● s **1** (**the wild**) a selva: *in the* ~ em estado selvagem **2** (**the wilds**) [pl] (o) mato

wilderness /'wɪldərnəs/ s **1** terra inculta **2** selva

wildlife /'waɪldlaɪf/ s fauna

wildly /'waɪldli/ *adv* **1** loucamente **2** violentamente

will /wɪl/ (contração 'll *neg* **will not** ou **won't** /woʊnt/) *v aux* [futuro]: *I hope it won't rain.* Espero que não chova. ◊ *That'll be the postman.* Deve ser o carteiro. → SHALL ● *v modal* NOTA Will é um verbo modal seguido de infinitivo sem *to*. As orações interrogativas e negativas são formadas sem o auxiliar *do*. **1** (vontade): *She won't go.* Ela não quer ir. ◊ *Will the car start?* Esse carro vai pegar ou não? → SHALL **2** (oferta, pedido): *Will you help me?* Você pode me ajudar? ◊ *Will you stay for tea?* Você fica para o chá? ◊ *Won't you sit down?* Sente-se, por favor. **3** (regra geral): *Oil* ~ *float on water.* O óleo flutua na água. ● s **1** vontade **2** desejo **3** testamento ► **at will** à vontade

willful (esp GB **wilful**) /'wɪlfl/ *adj* **1** (pej) intencional **2** (delito) premeditado **3** (pessoa) voluntarioso **willfully** *adv* deliberadamente

willing /'wɪlɪŋ/ *adj* **1** prestativo **2** disposto **3** (apoio, etc.) espontâneo **willingly** *adv* de boa vontade **willingness** s **1** disposição **2** ~ (**to do sth**) vontade (de fazer algo)

willow /'wɪloʊ/ s salgueiro

willpower /'wɪlpaʊər/ s força de vontade

wilt /wɪlt/ vi 1 murchar 2 esmorecer

win /wɪn/ (-nn-) (pt, pp **won**) 1 vi ganhar 2 vt vencer 3 vt (vitória) obter 4 vt (apoio, amigos) conquistar ■ **win sb/sth back** reconquistar alguém/algo **win sb over/around (to sth)** convencer alguém (de algo) ♦ s vitória

wince /wɪns/ vi 1 contrair-se 2 estremecer

wind¹ /wɪnd/ s 1 vento 2 fôlego, resistência 3 (GB) [U] (Med) gases ▸ **get wind of sth** tomar conhecimento de algo

wind² /waɪnd/ (pt, pp **wound**) 1 vi serpentear 2 vt enrolar 3 vt ~ **sth (up)** dar corda em algo ■ **wind down 1** relaxar (atividade) **2** findar ■ **wind sb up** (coloq) **1** irritar alguém **2** provocar alguém **wind (sth) up** terminar, liquidar algo (negócio) **♦** adj **1** sinuoso **2** (escada) de caracol

windfall /'wɪndfɔːl/ s **1** fruta caída (da árvore) **2** sorte grande

windmill /'wɪndmɪl/ s moinho de vento

window /'wɪndoʊ/ s **1** janela: ~ sill/ledge peitoril **2** guichê **3** (tb **windowpane** /'wɪndoʊpeɪn/) vidraça **4** vitrine: go window-shopping ir ver vitrines

windshield /'wɪndʃiːld/ (GB **windscreen** /'wɪndskriːn/) s pára-brisa

windsurfing /'wɪndsɜːrfɪŋ/ s prancha a vela

windy /'wɪndi/ adj (-ier -iest) **1** ventoso **2** exposto ao vento

wine /waɪn/ s vinho

wing /wɪŋ/ s **1** asa: the right ~ of the party a facção de direita do partido **2** (GB) pára-lama **3** (the **wings**) bastidores

wink /wɪŋk/ **1** vt, vi ~ (at sb) piscar (o olho) (para alguém) **2** vi (luz) piscar ♦ s piscadela

winner /'wɪnər/ s vencedor

winning /'wɪnɪŋ/ adj **1** vencedor **2** premiado **3** atraente **winnings** s ganhos

winter /'wɪntər/ (tb **wintertime** /'wɪntərtaɪm/) s inverno ● vi hibernar, passar o inverno **wintry** adj de inverno

wipe /waɪp/ vt **1** ~ **sth (away/off/up)**; ~ **sth (from/off sth)** limpar, enxugar algo (de algo) **2** ~ **sth (from/off sth)** apagar algo (de algo) **3** ~ **sth across, onto, over, etc. sth** limpar passando algo

por algo ■ **wipe sb/sth out 1** aniquilar alguém/algo **2** erradicar algo

wire /'waɪər/ s **1** arame **2** (Elet) fio **3** alambrado **4** (USA) telegrama ● vt **1** ~ **sth (up)** fazer a instalação elétrica de algo **2** ~ **sth (up) to sth** ligar algo a algo **3** (USA) mandar um telegrama a **wiring** s [U] **1** instalação elétrica **2** fiação

wireless /'waɪərləs/ s (antiq) rádio

wisdom /'wɪzdəm/ s **1** sabedoria: ~ tooth dente do siso **2** bom senso

wise /waɪz/ adj (-er, -est) **1** sensato **2** sábio ▸ **be no wiser/none the wiser; not be any the wiser** continuar sem entender nada

wish /wɪʃ/ **1** vt, vi ~ **for sth**; ~ **sb sth** desejar algo (a alguém) **2** vt (fml) querer **3** vt (que não pode se realizar): I ~ he'd go away. Eu gostaria de que ele fosse embora. ◊ She wished she had gone. Ela se arrependeu de não ter ido. NOTA O uso de **were**, e não **was**, com **I**, **he** ou **she** depois de **wish** é considerado mais correto: I ~ I were rich! Quem me dera ser rico! **4** vi expressar um desejo ● s **1** ~ **(for sth/to do sth)** vontade (de fazer algo) **2** (wishes): (with) best wishes, Mary (com) saudações cordiais, Mary **wishful** adj ▸ **wishful thinking**: It's ~ thinking on my part. Estou sonhando acordado.

wistful /'wɪstfl/ adj melancólico

wit /wɪt/ s **1** humor, presença de espírito **2** (pessoa) espirituoso/a **3** (wits) [pl] inteligência ▸ **be at your wits' end** não saber o que fazer (por preocupação ou desespero) **be frightened/scared out of your wits** morto de medo

witch /wɪtʃ/ s bruxa

witchcraft /'wɪtʃkræft; GB -krɑːft/ s [U] bruxaria

witch-hunt s caça às bruxas

with /wɪð, wɪθ/ prep **1** com: He's ~ ICI. Ele trabalha na ICI. ◊ be: Fill the glass ~ water. Encha o copo de água. ◊ tremble ~ fear tremer de medo **3** (apoio e conformidade) (de agosto) com ▸ **be with sb** (coloq): I'm not ~ you. Não estou te entendendo. **with it** (coloq) **1** em dia **2** da moda **3** He's not ~ it today. Ele não está muito ligado hoje. NOTA Para o uso de **with** em PHRASAL VERBS, ver o verbo, p. ex. **bear with** em BEAR.

withdraw /wɪð'drɔː, wɪθ'd-/ *(pt* **withdrew** /-'druː/ *pp* **withdrawn** /-'drɔːn/) **1** *vt, vi* retirar(-se) **2** *vt (dinheiro)* sacar **3** *vt (fml) (palavras)* retratar **withdrawal** /-'drɔːəl/ *s* **1** retirada, retratação **2** ~ **symptoms** síndrome de abstinência **withdrawn** *adj* retraído

wither /'wɪðə(r)/ *vt, vi* ~ **(sth) (away/up)** murchar (algo), secar (algo)

withhold /wɪð'hoʊld/ *vt (pt, pp* **withheld** /-'held/) *(fml)* **1** reter **2** *(informação)* ocultar **3** *(consentimento)* negar

within /wɪˈðɪn/ *prep* **1** *(tempo)* no prazo de: ~ *a month* dentro de um mês **2** *(distância)* a menos de **3** *(espaço)* ao alcance de: *It's* ~ *walking distance*. Dá para ir a pé. ● *adv (fml)* dentro

without /wɪˈðaʊt, -əʊt/ *prep* sem

withstand /wɪðˈstænd/ *vt (pt, pp* **withstood** /-ˈstʊd/) *(fml)* resistir a

witness /'wɪtnəs/ *s* ~ **(to sth)** testemunha *(de algo)* ● *vt* **1** presenciar **2** ser testemunha de

witness stand *(GB* **witness box)** *s* banco dos testemunhas

witty /'wɪti/ *adj (-ier, -iest)* espirituoso

wives /waɪvz/ *plural de* WIFE

wizard /'wɪzəd/ *s* mago

wobble /'wɒbl/ **1** *vi* cambalear **2** *vi (cadeira)* balançar **3** *vi (gelatina)* tremer **4** *vt* mover **wobbly** *adj (coloq)* **1** cambaleante **2** pouco firme **3** bambo

woe /wəʊ/ *s* desgraça ▸ **woe betide (sb)** coitado *(de alguém)*

wok /wɒk/ *s* frigideira chinesa

woke /wəʊk/ *pret de* WAKE

woken /ˈwəʊkən/ *pp de* WAKE

wolf /wʊlf/ *s (pl* **wolves** /wʊlvz/) lobo

woman /'wʊmən/ *s (pl* **women** /'wɪmɪn/) mulher

womb /wuːm/ *s* útero

won /wʌn/ *pret, pp de* WIN

wonder /'wʌndə(r)/ **1** *vi (fml)* ~ **(at sth)** admirar-se *(de/com algo)* **2** *vt, vi* perguntar-se: *It makes you* ~. Faz a gente pensar. ◇ *I* ~ *if/ whether he's coming.* Será que ele vem? ● *s* **1** assombro **2** maravilha ▸ **do/work wonders** *(coloq)* fazer milagres **it's a wonder (that...)** é um milagre que... **no wonder (that...)** não admira que...

wonderful /'wʌndəfl/ *adj* maravilhoso

won't /wəʊnt/ = WILL NOT *Ver* WILL

wood /wʊd/ *s* **1** madeira **2** lenha **3** *[freq pl]* bosque **wooded** *adj* arborizado **wooden** *adj* **1** de madeira **2** *(perna)* de pau

woodland /'wʊdlənd/ *s* bosque

woodwind /'wʊdwɪnd/ *s* instrumentos de sopro

woodwork /'wʊdwɜːk/ *s* **1** madeiramento **2** carpintaria

wool /wʊl/ *s* lã **woolen** *(GB* **-ll-)** *(tb* **wooly,** *GB* **-ll-)** *adj* de lã

word /wɜːd/ *s* palavra ▸ **have a word (with sb)** falar *(com alguém)* **in other words** em outras palavras, isto é **keep/break your word** cumprir/faltar com a palavra **put in/say a (good) word for sb** recomendar alguém, interceder por alguém **take sb's word for it (that...)** acreditar em alguém *(quando diz que...)* **words to that effect:** *He told me to get out, or words to that effect.* Ele me mandou sair, ou coisa parecida. ● *vt* redigir **wording** *s* redação

word processor *s* processador de textos **word processing** *s* processamento de textos

wore /wɔː(r)/ *pret de* WEAR

work /wɜːk/ *s* **1** *[U]* trabalho: *a piece of* ~ um trabalho ◇ ~ *experience* experiência profissional **2** obra: *Is this your own* ~? Foi você mesmo que fez isso? **3** *(works)* obras NOTA A palavra mais comum é *roadworks.* ▸ **get (down)/set to work (on sth)** pôr-se a trabalhar *(em algo)* NOTA A diferença entre **work** e **job** é que **work** é incontável e **job** é contável: *I've found work/a new job at the hospital.* **Employment,** mais formal que **work** e **job,** é usado para nos referirmos a quem tem emprego: *Many women are in part-time employment.* **Occupation** é o termo que se utiliza nos impressos oficiais: *Occupation: student.* **Profession** usa-se para trabalhos que requerem curso universitário: *the medical profession.* **Trade** é usado para designar os ofícios que requerem uma formação especial: *He's a carpenter by trade.* ● **1** *vi* trabalhar: ~ *on the assumption that...* basear-se na hipótese de que... **2** *vi* ~ **for sth** esforçar-se por *(fazer)* algo **3** *vi (Mec)* funcionar **4** *vi* surtir efeito: *It will never* ~. Não vai dar certo nunca. **5** *vt (máquina)* operar **6** *vt (pessoa)* fazer trabalhar **7** *vt (mina)* explorar **8** *vt (terra)* cultivar ▸ **work free/loose** soltar (-se), afrouxar(-se) **work like**

a **charm** ter um efeito mágico
work your fingers to the bone
matar-se de trabalhar ■ **work
out 1** resultar, dar certo **2**
resolver-se **3** fazer ginástica
work sth out 1 calcular algo **2**
solucionar algo **3** planejar, elaborar algo **work sb up (into sth)**
incitar alguém (a algo): *get
worked up* enervar-se **work sth
up** desenvolver algo: ~ *up an
appetite* abrir o apetite work-
able *adj* praticável

workaholic /ˌwɜːrkəˈhɒlɪk/ s
(*coloq*) pessoa obcecada com
trabalho **NOTA Workaholic** é
um derivado bem-humorado de
work, em combinação com
-holic, que é o sufixo de alco-
holic. Inventaram-se outras
palavras com esse sufixo, como
chocaholic (viciado em chocolate) e **shopaholic** (viciado em
fazer compras).

worker /ˈwɜːrkər/ s **1** trabalha-
dor/a **2** operário/a

workforce /ˈwɜːrkfɔːrs/ s mão-
de-obra

working /ˈwɜːrkɪŋ/ *adj* **1** ativo **2**
de trabalho **3** ~ *day* dia útil **4**
que funciona **5** (*conhecimento*)
básico ● s **workings** [*pl*] funcionamento

working class s (*tb* **working
classes**) classe operária ● *adj*
de classe operária

workload /ˈwɜːrkloʊd/ s carga de
trabalho

workman /ˈwɜːrkmən/ s (*pl*
-men) operário **workmanship**
s **1** (*pessoa*) arte **2** (*produto*)
fabricação

workmate /ˈwɜːrkmeɪt/ (*GB*) s
colega de trabalho

workplace /ˈwɜːrkpleɪs/ s local
de trabalho

workshop /ˈwɜːrkʃɒp/ s oficina

worktop /ˈwɜːrktɒp/ s (*GB*) (*cozinha*) superfície de trabalho

world /wɜːrld/ s **1** mundo: *world-
famous* famoso no mundo
inteiro **2** mundial worldly *adj*
(**-ier, -iest**) **1** mundano **2** (*bens*)
~ *goods* bens materiais **3**
conhecedor do mundo

worldwide /ˈwɜːrldwaɪd/ *adj*
mundial ● *adv* /ˌwɜːrldˈwaɪd/ *adv* por
todo o mundo

worm /wɜːrm/ s **1** verme
2 minhoca

worn /wɔːrn/ *pp de* WEAR

worn out *adj* **1** gasto **2** (*pessoa*)
esgotado

worry /ˈwʌri/ (*pt, pp* **-ied**) **1** *vt, vi*
~ (**yourself**) (**about sb/sth**) preocupar-se (com alguém/algo) **2**

vt preocupar: *be worried by sth*
estar preocupado com algo ● s
(*pl* **-ies**) **1** [*U*] preocupação **2**
problema worried *adj* **1** ~ (**about
sb/sth**) preocupado (com
alguém/algo) **2** be ~ that…: *I'm
~ (that) he might get lost.* Pre-
ocupa-me que ele possa se
perder. worrying *adj* inquietante

worse /wɜːrs/ *adj, adv* (*comp de*
bad, badly) pior: *get* ~ piorar
▶ **make matters/things worse**
para piorar as coisas ● s o *pior*:
take a turn for the ~ piorar wors-
en *vt, vi* piorar, agravar(-se)

worship /ˈwɜːrʃɪp/ s **1** veneração
2 ~ (**of sb/sth**) (*Relig*) culto (a
alguém/algo) ● v (**-p-,** *GB* **-pp-**) **1**
vt adorar **2** *vt, vi* render culto (a)
worshipper s devoto/a

worst /wɜːrst/ *adj* (*superl de* **bad,
badly**) pior: *My* ~ *fears were
confirmed.* Aconteceu o que eu
mais temia. ◇ *the* ~ *hit areas* as
áreas mais atingidas ● **the worst**
s o *pior* ▶ **at (the) worst; if the
worst comes to the worst** na pior
das hipóteses

worth /wɜːrθ/ *adj* **1** com um valor
de: *be* ~ *$5* valer cinco dólares **2**
be ~ **doing sth**: *It's* ~ *reading.*
Vale a pena ler. ▶ **be worth sb's
while (to do sth)** valer a pena
(fazer algo) ● s **1** valor **2** (*em
dinheiro*): *$10* ~ *of gas* dez dóla-
res de gasolina **3** (*tempo*): *two
weeks'* ~ *of supplies* provisões
para duas semanas worthless
adj **1** sem valor **2** (*pessoa*) desprezível

worthwhile /ˌwɜːrθˈwaɪl/ *adj* que
vale a pena: *be* ~ *doing/to do sth*
valer a pena fazer algo

worthy /ˈwɜːrði/ *adj* (**-ier, -iest**) **1**
merecedor: ~ *of sth* digno de
algo **2** (*causa*) nobre **3** (*pessoa*)
respeitável

would /wəd, wʊd/ (*contração* **'d**
neg **would not** *ou* **wouldn't**
/ˈwʊdnt/) *v aux* (*condicional*):
Would you do it if I paid you?
Você o faria se eu lhe pagasse?
◇ *He said he* ~ *come.* Ele disse
que viria. ● *v modal* **NOTA
Would** é um verbo modal,
seguido de infinitivo sem *to*. As
orações interrogativas e negativas são formadas sem o auxiliar
do. **1** (*oferecimento, pedido*):
Would you like a drink? Quer
tomar alguma coisa? ◇ *Would
you come this way?* Quer vir por
aqui? **2** (*propósito*): *I left a note
so (that) they'd call us.* Deixei
recado para nos ligarem. **3**
(*vontade*): *He wouldn't shake my*

hand. Ele não queria apertar a minha mão.

wouldn't = WOULD NOT *Ver* WOULD

wound[1] /wu:nd/ s ferimento • *vt* ferir the wounded s [*pl*] os feridos → FERIMENTO

wound[2] /waʊnd/ *pret, pp de* WIND[2]

wove /woʊv/ *pret de* WEAVE

woven /woʊvn/ *pp de* WEAVE

wow /waʊ/ *interj* (*coloq*) uau

wrangle /'ræŋgl/ s disputa • *vi* discutir

wrap /ræp/ *vt* (-pp-) **1** ~ **sb/sth** (**up**) envolver alguém/algo **2** ~ **sth around sb/sth** enrolar algo ao redor de alguém/algo ▶**wrapped up in sb/sth** absorto em alguém/algo ∎**wrap (sb/ yourself) up** (*GB*) agasalhar alguém, agasalhar-se **wrap sth up** (*coloq*) concluir algo • s **xale** wrapper s invólucro wrapping s embalagem: ~ *paper* papel de embrulho

wrath /ræθ; *GB* rɒθ/ s (*fml*) ira

wreath /ri:θ/ s (*pl* ~s /'ri:ðz/) coroa (*funerária*)

wreck /rek/ s **1** navio naufragado **2** (*coloq*) ruína **3** veículo, avião, etc. destroçado • *vt* destruir, afundar wreckage /'rekɪdʒ/ s destroços (*acidente, etc.*)

wrench /rentʃ/ *vt* ~ **sth off** (**sth**); ~ **sth out of sth** arrancar algo (de algo); tirar algo de algo (*com puxão*) • s **1** puxão **2** (*fig*) golpe **3** chave inglesa

wrestle /'resl/ *vi* lutar wrestler s lutador/a wrestling s luta livre

wretch /retʃ/ s desgraçado/a

wretched /'retʃɪd/ *adj* **1** infeliz, desconsolado **2** maldito

wriggle /'rɪgl/ *vt, vi* ~ (**about**) contorcer(-se): ~ *free* conseguir soltar-se

wring /rɪŋ/ *vt* (*pt, pp* wrung) **1** ~ **sth (out)** espremer algo: ~ *sb's neck* torcer o pescoço de alguém **2** ~ **sth out of/from sb** arrancar algo de alguém

wrinkle /'rɪŋkl/ s ruga • *vt, vi* enrugar(-se) **2** *vt* (*cenho, etc.*) franzir

wrist /rɪst/ s pulso

write /raɪt/ *vt, vi* (*pt* wrote *pp* written) escrever: ~ *off for sth* escrever pedindo algo **write back** responder **write sth down** anotar algo **write sth off 1** cancelar algo (*dívida*) **2** destruir algo **write sb/sth off** (as sth) excluir alguém/algo (por algo) **write sth out 1** escrever algo (por extenso ou a limpo) **2** copiar

write-off s (*veículo*): *The car was a* ~. O carro ficou um estrago só.

writer /'raɪtər/ s escritor/a

writhe /raɪð/ *vi* contorcer(-se)

writing /'raɪtɪŋ/ s **1** escrita **2** escrito **3** estilo de redação **4** letra **5** (**writings**) obras ▶**in writing** por escrito

written /'rɪtn/ *pp de* WRITE • *adj* por escrito

wrong /rɔ:ŋ; *GB* rɒŋ/ *adj* **1** mau, injusto: *He was* ~ *to say that.* Ele errou em dizer aquilo. **2** errado: *be* ~ estar enganado **3** inoportuno, equivocado: *the* ~ *way up/ around* de cabeça para baixo/ao contrário **4** *What's* ~? Qual é o problema? • *adv* mal, equivocadamente, incorretamente ▶**get sb wrong** (*coloq*) interpretar mal alguém **get sth wrong** enganar-se em algo **go wrong 1** enganar-se **2** (*máquina*) quebrar **3** dar-se mal ∎ s mal **2** (*fml*) injustiça ▶**be in the wrong** não ter razão wrongful *adj* injusto wrongly *adv* mal, incorretamente

wrote /roʊt/ *pret de* WRITE

wrought iron /ˌrɔ:t 'aɪən/ s ferro forjado

wrung /rʌŋ/ *pret, pp de* WRING

X x

X, x /eks/ s (*pl* X's, x's /'eksɪz/) X, x

Xmas /'krɪsməs, 'eksməs/ s (*coloq*) Natal

X-ray s radiografia: *X-rays* raios X

xylophone /'zaɪləfoʊn/ s xilofone

Y y

Y, y /waɪ/ s (*pl* Y's, y's /waɪz/) Y, y

yacht /jɑt/ s iate yachting s iatismo

yank /jæŋk/ *vt, vi* (*coloq*) ~ (**sth**) (**off/out**) puxar (algo) bruscamente

Yankee /'jæŋki/ (*tb* Yank) s (*coloq*) ianque

yard /jɑrd/ s **1** jardim **2** (*GB*) pátio **3** (*abrev* **yd.**) jarda (*0,9144 m*) → Ver pág. 224

yardstick /'jɑrdstɪk/ s padrão

yarn /jɑrn/ s **1** fio **2** longa história

yawn /jɔːn/ vi bocejar • s bocejo
yawning adj enorme

yeah /jeə/ interj (coloq) sim

year /jɪər/ s 1 ano 2 (GB) (escola) série 3 a two-year-old (child) uma criança de dois anos ◇ I am ten (years old). Tenho dez anos. NOTA Ao se dizer a idade, pode-se omitir years old. → OLD

yearly /ˈjɪərli/ adj anual • adv anualmente

yearn /jɜːrn/ vi 1 suspirar 2 ~ (to do sth) ansiar (por fazer algo) yearning s 1 ~ (for sb/sth) desejo (de alguém/algo); anseio (por algo) 2 ~ (to do sth) ânsia (por/de fazer algo)

yeast /jiːst/ s fermento

yell /jel/ vi, vt 1 (sth) (out) (at sb/ sth); ~ (in/with sth) gritar (algo) (para alguém/algo); gritar (de algo) • s grito

yellow /ˈjeloʊ/ adj, s amarelo

yelp /jelp/ vi 1 ganir 2 (pessoa) gritar

yes /jes/ interj, s sim

yesterday /ˈjestərdeɪ, -di/ adv, s ontem

yet /jet/ adv 1 [frases negativas] ainda → STILL 2 [frases interrogativas] já NOTA Yet ou already? Só se usa yet em frases interrogativas e negativas, e sempre no final da oração: Have you finished it yet? Already é usado em frases afirmativas e interrogativas; normalmente vai depois dos verbos auxiliares ou modais e na frente dos demais verbos: He already knew her. Quando already indica surpresa com o fato de uma ação se haver realizado antes do esperado, pode ser usado no final da frase: He has found a job already? ◇ Is it there already? That was quick! Ver exemplos em ALREADY 3 [depois de superlativo]: his best film — seu melhor filme até hoje 4 [antes de comparativo] ainda: ~ more work mais trabalho ainda ▶ yet again outra vez • conj contudo: It's amazing — true. É assombroso, mas é verdade.

yew /juː/ (tb ~ tree) s teixo

yield /jiːld/ vt 1 produzir, dar 2 vt (Fin) render 3 vi render-se, ceder NOTA O verbo mais comum é give in. • s 1 produção 2 colheita 3 (Fin) rendimento yielding adj 1 flexível 2 submisso

yogurt (tb **yoghurt**, GB tb **yoghourt**) /ˈjoʊɡərt/ GB /ˈjɒɡət/ s iogurte

yoke /joʊk/ s jugo

yolk /joʊk/ s gema (ovo)

you /juː/ pron 1 [sujeito] tu, você(s), o(s) senhor(es), a(s) senhora(s) 2 [frases impessoais]: You can't smoke in here. Não se pode fumar aqui. NOTA Nas frases impessoais pode-se usar one com o mesmo significado que you, mas é mais formal. 3 [objeto direto] te, o(s), a(s), você(s), o(s) senhor(es), a(s) senhora(s) 4 [objeto indireto] te, lhe(s), a você(s), ao(s) senhor(es), à(s) senhora(s) 5 [depois de prep] ti, você(s), o(s) senhor(es), a(s) senhora(s) NOTA Não se pode omitir o pron pess em inglês.

you'd /juːd/ 1 = YOU HAD Ver HAVE 2 = YOU WOULD Ver WOULD

you'll /juːl/ = YOU WILL Ver WILL

young /jʌŋ/ adj (~er /ˈjʌŋɡər/, ~est /ˈjʌŋɡest/) jovem: ~ people jovens ◇ He's a year younger than me. Ele é um ano mais novo do que eu. • s [pl] 1 (animais) filhotes 2 (the young) os jovens

youngster /ˈjʌŋstər/ s jovem

your /jʊər/ GB jɔːr/ adj poss teu(s), tua(s), seu(s), sua(s), de você(s), do(s) senhor(es), da(s) senhora(s): break ~ arm quebrar o braço

you're /jɔːr/ = YOU ARE Ver BE

yours /jʊərz/ GB jɔːrz/ pron poss o(s) teu(s), a(s) tua(s), o(s) seu(s), a(s) sua(s), o de você(s), o do(s) senhor(es), o(s) da(s) senhora(s): a friend of ~ uma amiga sua/de vocês/dos senhores ▶ Yours faithfully/ sincerely Atenciosamente

yourself /jʊərˈself/ GB jɔːrˈself/ pron (pl -selves /-ˈselvz/) 1 [uso reflexivo] te, se, o(s), a(s): Enjoy yourselves! Divirtam-se! 2 [uso enfático] você(s) mesmo(s)/ a(s) 3 [depois de prep] ti, si mesmo(s) ▶ (all) by yourself/ yourselves sozinho(s) be yourself/yourselves ser natural: Just be ~. Simplesmente seja você mesma.

youth /juːθ/ s 1 [U] juventude: In my youth... Quando eu era jovem... ◇ ~ club/hostel clube/ albergue para jovens 2 (freq pej) jovem youthful adj juvenil

you've /juːv/ = YOU HAVE Ver HAVE